D1538157

the
AMERICANA ANNUAL

1979

AN ENCYCLOPEDIA OF THE EVENTS OF 1978

YEARBOOK OF THE ENCYCLOPEDIA AMERICANA

This annual has been prepared as a yearbook for general encyclopedias. It is also published as *Encyclopedia Year Book.*

© GROLIER INCORPORATED 1979

Copyright in Canada © by Grolier Limited

Library of Congress Catalog Card Number: 23-10041

Standard Book Number: ISBN 0-7172-0210-0

Printed in the United States of America
Lithography by Rand McNally & Company

Copyright protected by Universal Copyright Convention
and Pan American Copyright Conventions

All rights reserved under Inter-American
Copyright Union (1910) by Grolier Incorporated

| Editor in Chief | EDWARD HUMPHREY |
| Executive Editor | JAMES E. CHURCHILL, JR. |

Art Directors

ERIC E. AKERMAN   FRANKLIN N. SAYLES

Assistant Editors

JEFF HACKER

SAUNDRA FRANCE   EDWARD M. KURDYLA, JR.

Special Editor, Mexico
and Latin America   PEDRO LÓPEZ CORTEZO

Indexers

JILL SCHULER   SUSAN DEROMEDI

Proofreading   SUZANNE SCHUTZ

Editorial Assistants

DORIS LECHNER   NANCY GEPFER

Layout Artist   PATRICIA E. BYERS

Photo Research

DIANE T. GRACE   PAT ZIMMERMAN

MANUFACTURING DEPARTMENT

Director	DALE E. BOWMAN
General Manager, Production	LUIS GONZALEZ
Manager, Pre-Press Services	ELIZABETH CHASE
Assistant, Pre-Press Services	ALAN PHELPS

• • • • • • • • •

GROLIER INCORPORATED

| Senior Vice-President, Publishing | HOWARD B. GRAHAM |
| Vice-President and Editorial Director | WALLACE S. MURRAY |

CONTENTS

THE ALPHABETICAL SECTION

Separate entries on the continents, the major nations of the world, U. S. states, Canadian provinces, and chief cities will be found under their own alphabetically arranged headings.

CONTRIBUTORS

ADAMS, LEON D., Author, *The Wines of America* and *Commonsense Book of Wine:* INDUSTRIAL REVIEW—*American Wine Industry*

ADRIAN, CHARLES R., Professor of Political Science, University of California, Riverside; Coauthor, *Governing Urban America:* BIOGRAPHY—*Howard Arnold Jarvis;* CALIFORNIA; LOS ANGELES

AHERN, TOM, Public Affairs Editor, *The News-Times,* Danbury, Conn.: CONNECTICUT

ALEXANDER, ROBERT J., Professor of Economics and Political Science, Rutgers University: ECUADOR; GUYANA; URUGUAY

ALLER, LAWRENCE H., Professor of Astronomy, University of California; Author, *Atoms, Stars, and Nebulae* and *Astrophysics, I and II:* ASTRONOMY

ALLSEN, PHILIP E., Department of Physical Education, Brigham Young University; Author, *Racquetball—Paddleball: GETTING AND KEEPING FIT—Racquetball, Paddleball, and Platform Tennis*

AMBRE, AGO, Economist, Bureau of Economic Analysis, U. S. Department of Commerce: INDUSTRIAL REVIEW

ANABLE, DAVID, Overseas News Editor, *The Christian Science Monitor:* THE POWER OF THE MEDIA—*The Changing Face of the American Newspaper*

BALLINGER, RONALD B., Professor of History, Rhode Island College: RHODESIA; SOUTH AFRICA

BANKS, RONALD F., Department of History, University of Maine: MAINE

BARMASH, ISADORE, Assistant to the Financial Editor, *The New York Times:* RETAILING; RETAILING—*Shopping Malls*

BECK, KAY, School of Urban Life, Georgia State University: GEORGIA

BERGEN, DAN, Professor, Graduate Library School, University of Rhode Island: LIBRARIES

BERLIN, MICHAEL, Reporter, *New York Post:* UNITED NATIONS

BEST, JOHN, Chief, *Canada World News,* Ottawa: NEW BRUNSWICK; PRINCE EDWARD ISLAND

BIDDLE, JAMES, President, National Trust for Historic Preservation: CONSERVATION—*The Nation's Landmarks*

BISSELL, RICHARD E., Research Associate, Foreign Policy Research Institute; Author, *Apartheid and International Organizations:* AFRICA

BÖDVARSSON, HAUKUR, Coeditor, *News From Iceland:* ICELAND

BOLUS, JIM, Sportswriter, *The Louisville Times;* Author, *Run for the Roses:* BIOGRAPHY—*Steve Cauthen;* SPORTS—*Horse Racing*

BOND, DONOVAN H., Professor of Journalism, West Virginia University: WEST VIRGINIA

BOREN, CHARLES WILLIAM, Associate Director of Psychiatric Education, Institute of Living, Hartford, Conn.: MEDICINE AND HEALTH—*Mental Health*

BOTSIA, ELMER E., President, The American Institute of Architects: ARCHITECTURE

BOULAY, HARVEY, Assistant Professor of Political Science, Boston University: BOSTON; MASSACHUSETTS

BOVEY, JOHN A., Provincial Archivist of Manitoba: MANITOBA

BOWERS, Q. DAVID, President, Professional Numismatists Guild; Columnist, *Coin World;* Author, *Collecting Rare Coins for Profit:* COINS AND COIN COLLECTING

BRADDOCK, WILLIAM, formerly Sportswriter, *The New York Times:* SPORTS—*Miscellaneous Summary*

BRAMMER, DANA B., Director, Bureau of Governmental Research, University of Mississippi: MISSISSIPPI

BRANDHORST, L. CARL, Associate Professor of Geography, Oregon College of Education: OREGON

BRODIN, PIERRE E., Director of Studies, Lycée Français de New York: LITERATURE—*French*

BROEG, ROBERT W., Sports Editor, *St. Louis Post-Dispatch:* SPORTS—*Baseball*

BROWNING, JIM, Paris-based Journalist: BIOGRAPHY—*Mobutu Sese Seko;* ZAIRE

BURKS, ARDATH W., Professor of Asian Studies, Rutgers University; Author, *China, Korea and Japan:* JAPAN

BURNHAM, BONNIE, Executive Director, International Foundation for Art Research, New York City; Author, *The Art Crisis; Art Theft: Its Scope, Its Impact and Its Control:* ART—*Art Theft and Vandalism*

BUSH, G. W. A., Senior Lecturer in Political Studies, University of Auckland, New Zealand: NEW ZEALAND

BUTWELL, RICHARD, Vice President for Academic Program and Professor of Political Science, Murray State University, Murray, Ky.; Author, *Southeast Asia Today and Tomorrow:* ASIA; BURMA; CAMBODIA; LAOS; PHILIPPINES; VIETNAM

CAIRNS, JOHN C., Professor of History, University of Toronto: FRANCE

CALABRESE, MICHAEL, National Aeronautics and Space Administration: SPACE EXPLORATION (article written independent of NASA)

CAMMACK, PAUL, St. Antony's College, Oxford: BOLIVIA

CANN, STANLEY, Consultant, *The Forum,* Fargo: NORTH DAKOTA

CAREY, WILLIAM D., Executive Officer, American Association for the Advancement of Science: INDUSTRIAL REVIEW—*Industrial Research and Development*

CHALMERS, JOHN W., Faculty of Education, University of Alberta: ALBERTA

COCKRUM, E. LENDELL, Professor and Head, Department of Ecology and Evolutionary Biology, University of Arizona: ZOOLOGY

COHEN, SIDNEY, Clinical Professor of Psychiatry, Neuropsychiatric Institute, University of California, Los Angeles; Author, *The Beyond Within: The LSD Story* and *The Drug Dilemma:* DRUG ADDICTION AND ABUSE

COLLINS, BOB, Sports Editor, *The Indianapolis Star;* Author, *The Best of Bob Collins;* Coauthor, *What's It Like Out There?:* SPORTS—*Auto Racing*

COMMANDAY, ROBERT, Music and Dance Critic, *San Francisco Chronicle:* BIOGRAPHY—*Luciano Pavarotti;* MUSIC

CONRAD, ED, Sports Department, *Sunday Express,* Montreal; Author, *Humor in Hockey:* BIOGRAPHY—*Guy Lafleur;* SPORTS—*Hockey*

COPPAGE, NOEL, Contributing Editor, *Stereo Review:* MUSIC, POPULAR

CORLEW, ROBERT E., Department of History, Middle Tennessee State University: TENNESSEE

CORNWELL, ELMER E., JR., Professor of Political Science, Brown University: RHODE ISLAND

CUNNIFF, JOHN, Business Analyst, The Associated Press: INFLATION

CUNNINGHAM, PEGGY, Staff Reporter, *Baltimore News-American:* MARYLAND

CURRIER, CHET, Writer on Investing and the Stock Market, The Associated Press: STOCKS AND BONDS

CURTIS, L. PERRY, JR., Professor of History, Brown University: IRELAND

DANIELS, ROBERT V., Professor of History, University of Vermont: VERMONT

DARBY, JOSEPH W. III, Reporter, *The Times-Picayune,* New Orleans: LOUISIANA

DAVIS, WILLIAM A., Travel Editor, *The Boston Globe:* TRAVEL

DE GREGORIO, GEORGE, Sports Department, *The New York Times:* SPORTS—*Introduction, Boxing, Skiing, Swimming, Track*

DELZELL, CHARLES F., Professor of History, Vanderbilt University; Editor, *The Future of History:* ITALY

DENNIS, LARRY, Associate Editor, *Golf Digest;* Coauthor, *How to Become a Complete Golfer:* BIOGRAPHY—*Nancy Lopez;* SPORTS—*Golf*

DILLIN, JOHN, Staff Correspondent, Washington Bureau, *The Christian Science Monitor:* BIOGRAPHY—*William Webster;* UNITED STATES—*The FBI*

DIONNE, E. J., Reporter, *The New York Times:* NEW YORK CITY—*Radio City Music Hall*

DOBLER, CLIFFORD, Professor Emeritus of Business Law, University of Idaho: IDAHO

DOLAN, PAUL, Professor of Political Science, University of Delaware; Coauthor, *Government of Delaware:* DELAWARE

DORPALEN, ANDREAS, Professor of History, The Ohio State University; 1978 recipient of the Distinguished Service Award of the Ohio Academy of History: GERMANY

DRACHKOVITCH, MILORAD M., Senior Fellow, The Hoover Institution, Stanford University; Author, *U. S. Aid to Yugoslavia and Poland:* YUGOSLAVIA

DRAKE, FRANK D., Director, National Astronomy and Ionosphere Center, Goldwin Smith Professor of Astronomy, Cornell University: SPACE EXPLORATION—*Life On Other Planets?*

DRIGGS, DON W., Professor and Chairman of Political Science Department, University of Nevada: NEVADA

DUFF, ERNEST A., Professor of Political Science, Randolph-Macon Woman's College; Author, *Agrarian Reform in Colombia:* COLOMBIA

DULLEA, GERARD J., Assistant Staff Director, U. S. Chess Federation: CHESS

DUROSKA, LUD, Sports Department, *The New York Times;* Author, *Football Rules in Pictures* and *Great Pro Quarterbacks:* SPORTS—*Football*

DURRENCE, J. LARRY, Department of History, Florida Southern College: FLORIDA

ELAZAR, DANIEL J., Professor of Political Studies, Chairman, Center for Jewish Community Studies, Bar Ilan University, Israel: RELIGION—*The American Jew: Is There a Dilemma?*

ELGIN, RICHARD, State Desk, *The Patriot-News,* Harrisburg: PENNSYLVANIA

ENSTAD, ROBERT H., Reporter, *Chicago Tribune:* CHICAGO; ILLINOIS

ETCHESON, WARREN W., Graduate School of Business Administration, University of Washington: WASHINGTON

EWEGEN, BOB, Editorial Writer, *The Denver Post:* COLORADO

FAIRHALL, JOHN H., Reporter, *Times-Union,* Albany, N.Y.: NEW YORK

FISHER, PAUL, Director, Freedom of Information Center, University of Missouri: CENSORSHIP

FOLEJEWSKI, ZBIGNIEW, Professor and Chairman, Department of Slavic Studies and Modern Languages, University of Ottawa: LITERATURE—*Soviet*

FRIIS, ERIK J., Editor-Publisher, *The Scandinavian-American Bulletin;* Author, *The American-Scandinavian Foundation, 1910–1960: A Brief History:* DENMARK; FINLAND

GAILEY, HARRY A., Professor of History and Coordinator of African Studies, San Jose State University, California: GHANA; NIGERIA

GARFIELD, ROBERT, Associate Professor of History, Co-Director, Afro-American Studies Program, DePaul University, Chicago: KENYA; OBITUARIES—*Jomo Kenyatta;* TANZANIA; UGANDA

GEIS, GILBERT, Professor, Program in Social Ecology, University of California, Irvine; Author, *Man, Crime, and Society:* CRIME

GJESTER, THOR, Editor, *Okonomisk Revy,* Oslo: NORWAY

GOODMAN, DONALD, Associate Professor of Sociology, John Jay College of Criminal Justice: PRISONS

GORDON, MAYNARD M., Editor, *Motor News Analysis* and *The Imported Car Reports:* AUTOMOBILES

GOUGH, BARRY, Associate Professor of History, Wilfrid Laurier University; Author, *To the Arctic and Pacific with Beechey* and *Canada:* CANADA—*Political and International Affairs, The Canadian West*

GRAYSON, GEORGE W., Professor of Government, College of William and Mary; Author, *El Partido Demócrata Cristiano Chileno:* PORTUGAL; SPAIN

GROTH, ALEXANDER J., Professor of Political Science, University of California, Davis; Author, *People's Poland:* POLAND

GRUBERG, MARTIN, Professor of Political Science, University of Wisconsin, Oshkosh: CIVIL LIBERTIES AND CIVIL RIGHTS; LAW—*International*

GUNN, JOHN M., Former Professor of Radio-TV-Film, State University of New York, Albany: TELEVISION AND RADIO; TELEVISION AND RADIO—*Public Television*

HALLMUNDSSON, HALLBERG, Author and editor: STATISTICAL AND TABULAR DATA—*Nations of the World*

HALLMUNDSSON, MAY NEWMAN, Adjunct Associate Professor of English, Pace University: WOMEN

HAND, SAMUEL, Professor of History, University of Vermont: VERMONT

HARVEY, ROSS M., Assistant Director of Information, Government of the Northwest Territories: NORTHWEST TERRITORIES

HAYDEN, DOROTHY, Head, Prairie History Room, Regina Public Library: SASKATCHEWAN

HAYES, KIRBY M., Professor of Food Science and Nutrition, University of Massachusetts: FOOD

HECHINGER, FRED, President, New York Times Company Foundation; Adjunct Professor, City University of New York; Special Lecturer, New School for Social Research: YOUTH

HELMREICH, E. C., Thomas B. Reed Professor of History and Political Science, Bowdoin College, Bowdoin, Me.: AUSTRIA

HELMREICH, J. E., Professor of History and Dean of Instruction, Allegheny College, Meadville, Pa.; Author, *A Study in Small Power Diplomacy:* LUXEMBOURG

HELMREICH, PAUL C., Professor of History, Wheaton College: SWITZERLAND

HELMS, ANDREA R. C., Associate Professor of Political Science, University of Alaska: ALASKA

HENDERSON, JIM, Soccer Writer, *The Tampa Tribune, The Sporting News;* Author, *Annual Soccer Guide:* SPORTS—*Soccer, The Rising Popularity of American Soccer*

HENRIKSEN, THOMAS H., Associate Professor of History, State University College, Plattsburgh, N. Y.; Author, *Mozambique: A History:* ANGOLA; MOZAMBIQUE

HERBERT, WALTER B., Consultant on Canadian Cultural Matters; Fellow of the Royal Society of Arts: CANADA—*Cultural Affairs*

HOGGART, SIMON, Political Correspondent, *The Guardian,* London; Author, *The Pact:* BIOGRAPHY—*Peter Jay;* GREAT BRITAIN; LONDON

HOOVER, HERBERT T., Professor of History, The University of South Dakota; Author, *To Be An Indian; The Chitimacha People:* SOUTH DAKOTA

HOPKO, THOMAS, REV. Assistant Professor, St. Vladimir's Orthodox Theological Seminary: RELIGION—*Orthodox Eastern*

HOWARD, HARRY N., Board of Governors, Middle East Institute, Washington, D. C.; Author, *Turkey, the Straits and U. S. Policy:* TURKEY

HUME, ANDREW, Former Reporter, *The Whitehorse* (Yukon) *Star:* YUKON TERRITORY

HUTH, JOHN F., JR., Reporter-Columnist, *The Plain Dealer,* Cleveland: OHIO

JACKSON, LIVIA E. BITTON, Associate Professor, Department of Classical and Oriental Languages, Herbert H. Lehman College, City University of New York: OBITUARIES—*Golda Meir;* RELIGION—*Judaism*

JAFFE, HERMAN J., Department of Anthropology, Brooklyn College, City University of New York: ANTHROPOLOGY; OBITUARIES—*Margaret Mead*

JARVIS, ERIC, Department of History, University of Western Ontario: TORONTO

JAVITS, JACOB K., United States Senator from New York: THE PANAMA CANAL TREATIES

JENKINS, BRIAN M., Associate Head, Social Science Department, Director of Research on Guerrilla Warfare and International Terrorism, The Rand Corporation; Author, *International Terrorism: A New Mode of Conflict:* INTERNATIONAL TERRORISM

JEWELL, MALCOLM E., Professor of Political Science, University of Kentucky; Author, *Legislature Representation in the Contemporary South;* Coauthor, *Kentucky Politics:* KENTUCKY

JOHNSTON, ROBERT L., Editor, *The Catholic Review,* newsweekly of the Baltimore Archdiocese: BIOGRAPHY—*Pope John Paul II;* OBITUARIES—*Pope Paul VI, Pope John Paul I;* RELIGION—*Roman Catholicism*

JOHNSTONE, JOHN K., Professor of English, University of Saskatchewan; Fellow of the Royal Society of Literature; Author, *The Bloomsbury Group, A Study of E. M. Forster, Lytton Strachey, Virginia Woolf, and Their Circle:* LITERATURE—*English*

JONES, H. G., Curator, North Carolina Collection, University of North Carolina Library; Author, *For History's Sake* and *The Records of a Nation:* NORTH CAROLINA

KARNES, THOMAS L., Professor of History, Arizona State University; Author, *Failure of Union: Central America, 1824–1960:* CENTRAL AMERICA

KARSKI, JAN, Professor of Government, Georgetown University; Author, *Story of a Secret State:* BULGARIA; HUNGARY; RUMANIA

KASH, DON E., Professor, University of Oklahoma; Author, *Our Energy Future: The Role of Research, Development, and Demonstration in Reaching a National Consensus on Energy Supply:* ENERGY

KEHR, ERNEST A., Stamp News Bureau; Author, *The Romance of Stamp Collecting:* STAMP COLLECTING

KELLER, EUGENIA, Formerly Managing Editor, *Chemistry* magazine: CHEMISTRY

KIMBALL, LORENZO K., Professor of Political Science, University of Utah: UTAH

KIMBALL, THOMAS, Executive Vice President, National Wildlife Federation: ZOOLOGY—*A New Look at the Endangered Species*

KIMBELL, CHARLES L., Supervisory Physical Scientist, United States Bureau of Mines: MINING; STATISTICAL AND TABULAR DATA—*World Mineral Production*

KING, PETER J., Associate Professor of History, Carleton University: ONTARIO; OTTAWA

RICHARD, JOHN B., Department of Political Science, University of Wyoming; Author, *Government and Politics of Wyoming:* WYOMING

RICHMOND, ROBERT W., Assistant Director, Kansas State Historical Society; Author, *Kansas: A Land of Contrasts:* KANSAS

RODRIGUEZ, ALFRED, Professor, Department of Modern and Classical Languages, University of New Mexico: LITERATURE—*Spanish and Spanish-American*

ROEDER, RICHARD B., Professor of History, Montana State University: MONTANA

ROSE, ERNST, Professor Emeritus, New York University; Author, *A History of German Literature:* LITERATURE—*German*

ROSS, RUSSELL M., Professor of Political Science, University of Iowa; Author, *Government and Administration of Iowa; State and Local Government and Administration:* IOWA

ROTH, MARTHA, Former Managing Editor, *Modern Medicine:* MEDICINE AND HEALTH

ROTHSTEIN, MORTON, Professor of History, University of Wisconsin, Madison: SOCIAL WELFARE

ROWLETT, RALPH M., Professor of Anthropology, University of Missouri: ARCHAEOLOGY

RUFF, NORMAN J., Assistant Professor, University of Victoria, B. C.: BRITISH COLUMBIA

RYCROFT, ROBERT W., Assistant Professor, Graduate School of International Studies, University of Denver; Coauthor, *Our Energy Future: The Role of Research, Development, and Demonstration in Reaching a National Consensus on Energy Supply:* ENERGY—*Oil—Friend and Foe*

SAKURAI, EMIKO, Professor, Department of East Asian Languages, University of Hawaii: LITERATURE—*Japanese*

SALSINI, PAUL, State Editor, *The Milwaukee Journal:* WISCONSIN

SAVAGE, DAVID, Lecturer, Department of English, Simon Fraser University: LITERATURE—*Canadian: English*

SCHWAB, PETER, Associate Professor of Political Science, State University of New York at Purchase; Author, *Decision-Making in Ethiopia:* AFRICA—*The Horn;* ETHIOPIA

SCOTT, EUGENE L., Publisher, *Tennis Week;* Author, *Tennis: Game of Motion* and *Racquetball: A Cult:* SPORTS—*Tennis*

SETH, R. P., Associate Professor of Economics, Mount Saint Vincent University, Halifax: NOVA SCOTIA

SHAPIRO, STANLEY, Assistant Professor of History, Wayne State University: LABOR—*A Review of the Taft-Hartley Act*

SHINN, RINN-SUP, Senior Research Scientist, Foreign Area Studies, The American University, Washington, D. C.; Coauthor, *Area Handbook for North Korea; Area Handbook for South Korea:* KOREA

SHOGAN, ROBERT, National Political Correspondent, Washington Bureau, *Los Angeles Times;* Author, *A Question of Judgment* and *Promises to Keep:* UNITED STATES—*Domestic Affairs, Elections*

SIEGEL, STANLEY E., Professor of History, University of Houston; Author, *A Political History of the Texas Republic, 1836–1845:* HOUSTON; TEXAS

SIMMONS, MARC, Author, *New Mexico, A Bicentennial History:* NEW MEXICO

SLOAN, HENRY S., Associate Editor, *Current Biography:* BIOGRAPHY—*Woody Allen, Diane Keaton, Jack Lemmon, John Travolta, Rosalyn S. Yalow*

SMERK, GEORGE M., Professor of Transportation, School of Business, Indiana University; Coauthor, *Urban Mass Transportation: A Dozen Years of Federal Policy; Mass Transit Management: A Handbook for Small Cities:* TRANSPORTATION

SPERA, DOMINIC, Associate Professor of Music, Indiana University; Author, *The Prestige Series—16 Original Compositions for Jazz Band; Jazz Improvisation Series—Book I "Blues and the Basics," Book II "Making the Changes":* MUSIC—*The Jazz Revival*

STAHL, WILLIAM W., JR., Director, American Decorative Arts, Sotheby Parke Bernet, Inc.: ART—*The American Antique Market*

STERN, JEROME H., Associate Professor of English, Florida State University: LITERATURE—*American*

STOKES, WILLIAM LEE, Professor, Department of Geology and Geophysics, University of Utah; Author, *Essentials of Earth History* and *Introduction to Geology:* GEOLOGY

STOUDEMIRE, ROBERT H., Senior Research Consultant, Bureau of Government Research and Professor of Government, University of South Carolina: SOUTH CAROLINA

SYLVESTER, LORNA LUTES, Associate Editor, *Indiana Magazine of History,* Indiana University: INDIANA

TABORSKY, EDWARD, Professor of Government, University of Texas, Austin; Author, *Communism in Czechoslovakia, 1948–1960;* and *Communist Penetration of the Third World:* CZECHOSLOVAKIA

TAFT, WILLIAM H., Professor of Journalism and Director of Graduate Studies, University of Missouri; Author, *American Journalism History:* PUBLISHING

TAN, CHESTER C., Professor of History, New York University; Author, *The Boxer Catastrophe* and *Chinese Political Thought in the 20th Century:* CHINA

TAYLOR, WILLIAM L., Associate Professor of History, Plymouth State College; Author, *A Productive Monopoly: The Effect of Railroad Control on the New England Coastal Steamship Lines:* NEW HAMPSHIRE

THEISEN, CHARLES W., Staff Writer, *The Detroit News:* MICHIGAN

THOMAS, JAMES D., Professor, Department of Political Science and Bureau of Public Administration, The University of Alabama: ALABAMA

TOBIN, MARY, Business Writer, United Press International: INTERNATIONAL TRADE AND FINANCE

TOWNE, RUTH W., Professor of History, Northeast Missouri State University: MISSOURI

TURNER, ARTHUR CAMPBELL, Professor of Political Science, University of California, Riverside: IRAN; IRAQ; ISRAEL; MIDDLE EAST

VALESIO, PAOLO, Professor of Italian, Yale University; Author, *Between Italian and French: The Fine Semantics of Active Versus Passive:* LITERATURE—*Italian*

VAN RIPER, PAUL P., Professor and Head, Department of Political Science, Texas A&M University; Author, *History of the United States Civil Service* and *The American Federal Executive* and *Handbook of Practical Politics:* POSTAL SERVICE; UNITED STATES—*Civil Service Reform*

VLIET, GARY C., Associate Professor, Mechanical Engineering, University of Texas, Austin: ENERGY—*Solar Energy*

VOGT, BILL, SR., Editor, *National Wildlife* and *International Wildlife* magazines; Author, *How to Build a Better Outdoors:* ENVIRONMENT

VOLSKY, GEORGE, Center for Advanced International Studies, University of Miami: CUBA

WALL, JAMES M., Editor, *The Christian Century;* Author, *Church and Cinema:* RELIGION—*Protestantism*

WALLOT, JEAN-PIERRE, Professor, Department of History, University of Montreal; Author, *Un Québec qui bougeait:* MONTREAL; QUEBEC

WALTON, JOHN, University of California, Davis; Coauthor, *Cities in Change: Studies on the Urban Condition;* Coeditor, *The City in Comparative Perspective:* CITIES AND URBAN AFFAIRS

WATTERS, ELSIE M., Director of Research, The Tax Foundation: TAXATION

WEEKS, JEANNE G., Member, American Society of Interior Designers; Coauthor, *Fabrics for Interiors:* INTERIOR DESIGN

WEISMAN, CELIA B., Professor, Wurzweiler School of Social Work, Yeshiva University; Director, Yeshiva University Gerontological Institute; Author, *The Future Is Now:* OLDER POPULATION

WEISS, JONATHAN M., Department of Modern Languages, Colby College, Waterville, Me.: LITERATURE—*Canadian: Quebec*

WEISS, PAULETTE, Popular Music Editor, *Stereo Review:* RECORDINGS

WENTZ, RICHARD E., Chairman, Religious Studies Department, Arizona State University; Author, *Saga of the American Soul:* RELIGION—*Survey, Far Eastern Religions*

WILLARD, F. NICHOLAS: JORDAN; LEBANON; SYRIA

WILLIAMS, DENNIS A., Associate Editor, *Newsweek:* ETHNIC GROUPS

WILLIS, F. ROY, Professor of History, University of California, Davis; Author, *Italy Chooses Europe* and *France, Germany, and the New Europe:* EUROPE

WOLF, BOB, Sports Columnist, *Milwaukee Journal;* Author, *Batboy of the Braves:* SPORTS—*Basketball*

WOLF, WILLIAM, Film Critic, *Cue* Magazine; Lecturer, New York University, St. John's University; Author, *The Landmark Films* and *The Marx Brothers:* MOTION PICTURES

WOLINETZ, STEVEN B., Associate Professor, Department of Political Science, Memorial University of Newfoundland; Author, *Party Realignment in the Netherlands:* NETHERLANDS

WOOD, JOHN W., Professor of Political Science, University of Oklahoma: OKLAHOMA

WOODS, GEORGE A., Children's Books Editor, *The New York Times;* Author, *Vibrations* and *Catch a Killer:* LITERATURE—*Children's*

YOSHIZAKI, HIROTAKA, Staff Reporter, Tokyo Bureau, *The New York Times:* TOKYO

YOUNGER, R. M., Author, *Australia and the Australians* and *Australia's Great River* and *Australia! Australia! March to Nationhood:* AUSTRALIA; OBITUARIES—*Sir Robert Menzies;* OCEANIA; SOLOMON ISLANDS

ZABEL, ORVILLE H., Professor of History, Creighton University, Omaha: NEBRASKA

The Economy's Number One Problem

UPI

INFLATION

The Consumer's Number One Complaint

By John Cunniff, *Business Analyst, The Associated Press*

Like a consuming disease, inflation continued to ravage the U. S. economy in 1978, eroding a fragile confidence built by four years of expansion and threatening an eventual financial collapse.

Extent. In the first ten months of the year, prices rose more than 7.2%, an annual rate of 9.6%, paring the dollar's buying power to just one-half its 1967 strength. Stated another way, the U. S. Labor Department's consumer price index, which averaged 100 during 1967, rose to 200.09 by the end of October 1978. This meant that the consumer paid $200.09 for what cost $100 in 1967. The inflation trend compelled President Jimmy Carter to impose strict but voluntary wage-price standards and, as interest rates reached double digit levels, forced the Federal Reserve Board into a severely restrictive policy.

Inflation's impact was pervasive. By the end of the year, those who once borrowed rarely, and only for big ticket items, sometimes found their borrowings paying for necessities instead. Food costs alone rose more than 10%, the price of the typical single-family home even more. The cost of a college education, cars, medical care, clothing, and vacations soared. Inflation changed attitudes and lifestyles. Women took jobs outside the home in record numbers. Big-spending politicians lost their jobs. Parents decided a community college would suffice in place of a big name school. Eating patterns changed as the "all-cut beef" price, a term that includes the worst as well as the best of beef, reached a record $1.95 a pound in June, before falling slightly as consumers resisted. Depending upon circumstances, people might have felt inflation's fever in various ways, but the common symptom was a chronic irritability that accompanied them everywhere. The American dream, people said, had become a nightmare.

"IT FINALLY ARRIVED BUT IT'S NOT ASSEMBLED"

COPYRIGHT 1978 BY HERBLOCK IN THE WASHINGTON POST

Alfred E. Kahn, Chairman, Council on Wages and Price Stability

Causes and Effects. While the economy actually expanded throughout the year, as it had since early 1975, few Americans felt it in their hearts or pocketbooks. One poll after another showed that inflation was the number one concern of the people, but the polls only documented the obvious. As the year closed, more and more economists were forecasting a recession for 1979, and fears grew that it could be more extensive and prolonged than in 1973–1975. "Depression" reentered the vocabulary. Nevertheless, President Carter and his advisers, who had so often underestimated the pervasiveness of the disease, continued to forecast continued growth in 1979. People wondered, though: Did he believe it?

The causes were no mystery: unparalleled federal budget deficits, easy credit, high material expectations by both public and private sectors, costly oil imports, falling productivity, and restrictive regulations. And there were many more reasons, too. The most ironic of them was the growing practice of buying in anticipation of even higher prices later, a sure sign that the administration had lost a degree of believability.

The administration had lost credibility abroad also, and the relative price of the dollar, symbolic of what was considered to be the precarious state of the American economy, fell precipitously throughout the year. Too many dollars were floating around the world, currency traders said, a consequence of the mammoth imbalance—averaging for most of the year about $2.5 billion a month—in the U. S. foreign payments account. Such persistent imbalances indicated to money traders—not solely speculators, but governments and businesses, too—that it was safer to hold Japanese yen or German marks, or simply gold—at prices like $238 an ounce. (*See* International Trade and Finance.)

The Carter Programs and Reactions. At first President Carter resorted to the remedies of jawboning, cajoling, imploring, advising, even
threatening. But the unrelenting economics of the problem could not be
talked away. They spread. On October 24, for the third time in two years
and the second time in 1978, the president announced an anti-inflation
program, setting voluntary guidelines that roughly limited company wage
increases to an average of 7% and price increases to 5.75%.

"We are going to hold down government spending, reduce the budget
deficit, and eliminate government waste," the president pledged in a television address to the American people. "We will slash federal hiring and
cut the federal work force," he said. "We will eliminate needless regulations. We will bring more competition back to our economy." His
promises, he said, were not simply rhetorical or political. He indicated
he had no other choice.

The next day he named as his chief inflation fighter Alfred E. Kahn,
an economist who had won renown as a deregulator while serving as Carter's chairman of the Civil Aeronautics Board. Kahn outlined the challenges. He would monitor bureaucrats to discourage the mindless enforcement of regulations. He would discourage the passing of costly new
laws. Above all Kahn would seek to have the voluntary guidelines widely

With food prices increasing
at an annual rate exceed-
ing 10%, many shoppers
purchased "no frills"
brands, which carry very
plain labels indicating the
type of product and sell
at a lower cost than
standard brands.

UPI

UPI

The price tags at a local vegetable stand are an obvious indicator of the high cost of food. In fact, some fruits and vegetables were so expensive that consumers simply did not buy.

accepted and to penalize companies that ignored them. His main weapon would be the threat of withholding government business from violators.

Despite Kahn's reputation as a man of action, the initial response to the guidelines was not entirely favorable. Those who grudgingly supported them managed to insert their fears, too. The measures could fail; they might lead us down the road to controls; they were inherently unfair. Even prior to Carter's announcement, *The Wall Street Journal* published a classic of brevity, a four-deck, front-page headline that crammed all the criticisms into just 28 words: "Carter's Guideline Plan Is Given a Slim Chance of Reducing Inflation. Glum View Is Held by Labor, Business, His Own Aides; Teamster Talks Crucial. Do Mandatory Curbs Loom?"

Carter denounced the pessimistic views and pleaded for the public to give his guidelines a chance. Many large concerns pledged support, but, ominously and as expected, George Meany, AFL-CIO president, declined. Although an opponent of mandatory controls, Meany said they would be fairer than the administration's plan.

Despite Carter's promises to cut the 1979 budget deficit to $39 billion from earlier estimates that were $20 billion higher, and the anticipated 1980 budget deficit to $30 billion, the dollar continued to sink. By October 30, the decline had brought it all the way from a value of 2.31 German marks in the fall of 1977 to just 1.73. Now the dollar was falling even against weaker currencies, such as the Italian lira. The stock market, worried about inflation and budget deficits, also was in trouble, suggesting Carter's anti-inflation program was unconvincing. More would have to be done, and quickly, to avert the growing crisis.

Action came with astonishing suddenness on the morning of Wednesday, November 1, when administration officials called reporters to the

White House for a 9 o'clock announcement. What they heard from the president, Treasury Secretary W. Michael Blumenthal, and G. William Miller, chairman of the Federal Reserve Board, was an elaborate international plan to save the dollar and crack down harder on inflation. The continuing decline in the exchange value of the dollar "threatens economic progress at home and abroad, and the success of our anti-inflation program," said Carter. "It is now necessary to act."

That final sentence in particular was noted by those who felt the president, for political or other reasons, had been reluctant to commit the country to a harsh anti-inflation program. The details now convinced them. The federal discount rate—the interest rate charged to banks that borrow from the Federal Reserve—was raised a full point to a record 9.5% and, through regulatory changes, $3 billion was shaved from the funds banks could lend. Through cooperation with its trading partners, the United States amassed $30 billion in foreign currencies to buy dollars on foreign exchanges, thus supporting the price and foiling speculators. Simultaneously, the government would greatly increase its sale of gold, a move aimed at lowering the price of that metal and encouraging those who had sought security therein to invest in dollars instead.

The reaction was as sudden as the announcement. On the very same day, the dollar rose 5% against the yen, 7% against the mark, and 7.5% against the Swiss franc. Gold plunged $23 by Friday, November 3. Brokers were ankle-deep in buy orders on the New York Stock Exchange, where prices had fallen sharply after announcement of wage and price guidelines just a week before. The Dow Jones index of 30 industrial stocks topped 800 points again after a surge of 35 points.

A new mood was created, but it was far from euphoric, notwithstanding the initial response to the new measures. As with experimental therapy for a dangerously ill patient, the remedy could be dangerous, too. Recession, technically a downturn in output for at least two months in a row, now became in the mind of some more a probability than a possibility. The unmentionable word "depression" was being spoken.

Kahn was the first in the administration to use it. "Let's use the impolite word rather than the polite one," he said in an address to retailers on November 16. And he did. He chose "depression" over "recession." "So far as I can see," he said, departing from his prepared text, "if the inflation accelerates, is permitted to accelerate, sooner or later, we will have such a tightening, such a total breakdown of the organization and morale of our economy that we will have a deep, deep depression."

The audience was chilled. The Dow Jones average resumed its fall. And after a few days, a somewhat irritated Miller asked government spokesmen and others to refrain from using the word, which he indicated could spread a negative philosophy and induce the condition feared.

Public and Economists' Views. Weary of the scourge that had already weakened them, Americans were fearful that another attack, this time from a severe economic downturn, would disable them. Kahn's warning was not likely to be forgotten, despite a subsequent, almost apologetic, reminder that he did not expect a depression or even a recession. Many private-sector economists lent support to this view, foreseeing some expansion in 1979, but the number clearly was diminishing. Henry Kaufman, partner in the brokerage firm of Salomon Brothers and highly respected as a student of monetary and economic matters, said in effect that the possibility of avoiding a recession hardly existed.

"Because we expect it (inflation) to happen, it does happen, and once it starts, wages and prices chase each other up and up."
PRESIDENT
JIMMY CARTER

"Unfortunately there is no quick fix to the problem of inflation."
G. WILLIAM MILLER
Federal Reserve Board

Still, the administration held to the official view that in 1979 it could attain growth of about 3%, sufficient to keep the jobless rate under 7% while reducing inflation to 6%. Understandably, Americans were dubious. The dollar was a fragment of its old self. About the only thing unchanged about it was George Washington's appearance, and some said that were he aware of the problems the country was having, he, too, would look weary and bowed. Increasingly, the public wrath was vented against federal budget overspending. Privately, businessmen were enraged by admonitions and exhortations from Washington, where, in their view, the problem began.

Small savers were equally angry at the personal consequences, for example, in buying a U. S. Savings Bond, which Uncle Sam promoted as the easy way to pay college tuitions and later for retirement. No matter what the promises, they learned, such notions were absurd so long as inflation persisted. A $75 bond that paid 6% interest for five years did indeed grow to $100 face value. But at the 1978 rate of inflation, its buying power in five years would be nearer to $65. The same erosion occurred to life insurance policies and bank accounts. But perhaps even worse than the financial loss was the cynicism inflation engendered, including a loss of faith in government. It was, commentators said, a moral issue. The thrifty who saved for tomorrow's rainy day lost their buying power, while those who borrowed as if there were no tomorrow were able to pay back in cheaper dollars.

And how Americans borrowed! In September 1978, the Federal Reserve reported personal borrowing at a rate equal to $18.40 of each $100 of after-tax income. And to pay off old loans, they spent $15.80 of each $100. Even the normally conservative Edith Bunker, Archie's wife, ex-

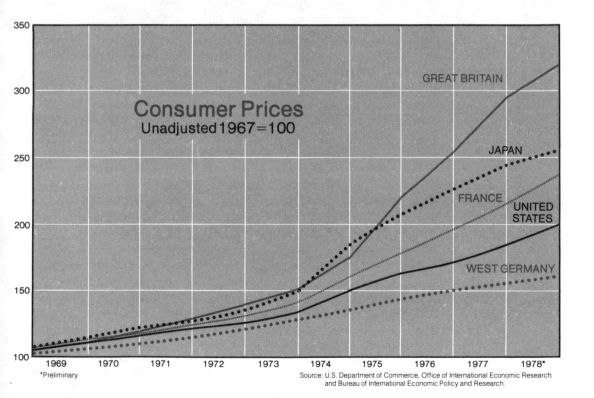

Consumer Prices
Unadjusted 1967=100

GREAT BRITAIN
JAPAN
FRANCE
UNITED STATES
WEST GERMANY

*Preliminary

Source: U.S. Department of Commerce, Office of International Economic Research and Bureau of International Economic Policy and Research.

claimed about the delights of credit. "With credit you can buy anything you can't afford," she explained in a November program. But people were frightened, too. A Louis Harris poll found that 58% of Americans surveyed were extremely worried about their growing debt load. They said they were forced to borrow because prices kept rising.

Overall Outlook. Business joined the stampede. Although industry was built largely by equity rather than debt capital, *Business Week* magazine estimated that in just three years corporate debt grew 36% to $1 trillion. In 1947, the total was about $100 billion.

Figures from the Office of Management and Budget showed that in fiscal 1975, as the country emerged from the worst recession since the 1930's, the federal deficit was $45.1 billion. Despite steady economic expansion since then, the longest such period in the 20th century, deficits ranging from $39 billion to $66.4 billion a year prevailed. By past criteria, the deficits should have shrunk and even disappeared.

Debt-induced inflation had at least one ameliorative effect for millions of Americans. Owners of collectibles profited. Collectibles—objects of inherent beauty, value, and rarity, such as gold, diamonds, antiques, paintings, limited edition books, signed and numbered lithographs, and the like—generally rose in price. During the inflation of 1978 the term and the concept were expanded to include anything of real rather than paper substance. Real estate, including single-family houses, became a collectible. The two- and three-home family became common. Investment advisers urged them on, and easy credit paved the way.

As a consequence, new homes in some areas of southern California were rationed by builders, because potential buyers, already well-housed, sought to buy and quickly resell at a profit. Late in the year, new homes averaged close to $100,000. Existing homes, a record 3.9 million of which were sold during the year, participated in the inflation. The National Association of Realtors reported a median price of $50,000 in September. This was 14.6% higher than a year earlier, about 5% greater than the inflation rate. Said the realtors: "It now appears certain that the inflation in home prices in 1978 will be the worst in the 12 years since statistics have been kept on this market." Obviously, existing homeowners did not join the realtors in using the term "worst."

"... dreading that climax of all human ills, the inflamation of his weekly bills."
LORD BYRON
1788–1824

As the year ended, families were receiving lessons in inflation almost every day. The Thanksgiving turkey joined in the rise, costing 90 cents a pound. And a Michigan State University professor estimated that Christmas tree prices rose $1.50 a foot retail, a 10% to 15% increase in one year. Reports abounded that Americans were now aware there was no easy way out of their problems and that they were ready to take the medicine, even if it meant a period of restricted incomes and rising joblessness.

Albert Sindlinger, a well-known market researcher, said people were even eager to take their dose and get it over with. Listening at his Media, Pa., home to their telephone responses to questions, he said people were tired of inflation's buffetings and longed for a return to stability. Overseas, the dollar continued to gain strength, and monetary and financial analysts generally issued reassuring messages. In Washington, Carter and Miller vowed there would be no recession.

Perhaps it all was true, but ordinary Americans, wise to the necessity of optimism in public statements, wary of promises, and weary of economic mismanagement, were not necessarily happier to see 1979 come than they were to bid good-bye to 1978.

The instruments of ratification of the new Panama Canal treaties are exchanged.

UPI

THE PANAMA CANAL TREATIES
The Basis of a New Era

By JACOB K. JAVITS, *U. S. Senator*
Member, Senate Foreign Relations Committee

On Friday, June 16, 1978, President Jimmy Carter and Brig.-Gen. Omar Torrijos stepped out on a balcony overlooking the Fifth of May Plaza in Panama City. They waved to the crowd. The leaders of one of the largest and of one of the smallest American nations had just exchanged the ratifications for new treaties governing the future of the international waterway that bisects the isthmus of Central America—the Panama Canal.

A new chapter in the relations of North and South America was being written with this major artery of world trade as the central point. Built by the United States and U. S.-run for nearly three quarters of a century, the Panama Canal was passing into the jurisdiction of the Republic of Panama.

The United States had for some years been running against the course of history. But the ceremony in Panama City marked the beginning of a new era. After long years of deliberations the Panama Canal issue was resolved. From the U. S. perspective the new treaty was a major revision of foreign policy and a vindication of the efforts of four administrations, Republican and Democrat, to place U. S.-Panama relations on a new foot-

A CROWN HE IS ENTITLED TO WEAR.

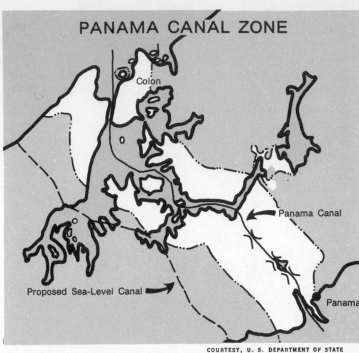

COURTESY, U. S. DEPARTMENT OF STATE

A contemporary cartoonist approved of President Theodore Roosevelt's role as U. S. negotiator of the 1903 Panama Canal treaty. At right, a map of the Panama Canal Zone showing a proposed route for a new sea-level canal.

ing. For the Panamanians, the agreement meant a move toward greater national integrity, an exciting episode in the history of a young country.

The instruments of ratification exchanged on June 17 in Panama related to treaties signed by Carter and Torrijos in September 1977. According to the U. S. Constitution, the pacts had to be submitted to the Senate for its "advice and consent"—a process that resulted in the addition of several important amendments and reservations. The treaties were the culmination of negotiations between the United States and Panama, begun during the Johnson, Nixon, and Ford years, to put the U. S. presence in the isthmus on a new legal basis for a fixed term of years. New arrangements were considered necessary to end Panamanian dissatisfaction and what appeared to many in the international community as a colonial anachronism.

Historical Background. The circumstances in which the United States built the canal and occupied a zone of land around it resulted from a treaty concluded in 1903 granting the United States rights "as though sovereign" that would last "in perpetuity." Negotiations conducted during the administrations of Presidents Franklin Roosevelt and Dwight Eisenhower changed the treaty in some respects, but basic Panamanian grievances remained. These included U. S. control of the area's major resource, the canal; the presence of a very friendly but nonetheless foreign country considered in fact the sovereign owner of the Panama Canal Zone; and the alleged inadequacy of the Panamanian share of the tolls.

Much of the Panamanian ill-feeling was grounded in the 1903 treaty, the celebrated Hay-Bunau-Varilla Treaty, that had been concluded when Panama was weak and vulnerable. Panama had declared its independence from Colombia two weeks earlier when the Colombian government rejected a similar pact with the United States. A French adventurer, Philippe Bunau-Varilla, had maneuvered himself into a position of representing the fledgling Panamanian government in Washington, D. C. He emerged from negotiations with President Theodore Roosevelt and Secretary of State

John Hay with a treaty, subsequently endorsed by the Panamanians, and with a fat commission.

In the succeeding years, the relationship established in 1903 remained largely unchanged, although Panamanian restlessness was growing. But in 1964 a dispute over the flying of the U. S. and Panamanian flags in the Canal Zone led to riots in which many were killed or wounded. The fear that such turmoil could erupt again provided impetus to open negotiations to replace the 1903 treaty. These talks dragged on through the 1960's and 1970's, punctuated by anti-U. S. demonstrations in Panama and some embarrassment for the United States in such international forums as the United Nations Security Council and the Organization of American States. However, a joint agreement on principles, signed in February 1974 by Secretary of State Henry Kissinger and Panamanian Foreign Minister Juan Tack, provided a genuine basis for the compromise eventually devised by the special negotiating teams appointed by President Carter and General Torrijos.

The Canal's Significance. For all the controversy surrounding the treaties and the role of the United States in Panama, no one disputes that the canal itself was a tremendous achievement which will stand as an historic tribute to U. S. engineering, technology, and determination. With steam shovels, dynamite, and dredges, the United States built a waterway equal in volume to a channel dug 10 feet (3 m) deep and 55 feet (16.8 m) wide from Maine to Oregon. A "miracle" by the U. S. Army Medical Corps lifted the scourges of malaria and yellow fever from a whole country. The completed canal allowed a ship in eight hours to pass from the Atlantic Ocean to the Pacific Ocean, and complete in 51 miles (82 km) a journey that had until then been thousands of miles long and taken many weeks.

The Panama Canal was, and is, an achievement of U. S. ingenuity on behalf of the international trading community. The principal users of the canal, apart from the United States and the many vessels sailing under the Panamanian flag, are the world's leading maritime powers—Greece, Japan, the United Kingdom, and Norway. On the canal depends the foreign trade of Ecuador, Peru, Chile, and other South American countries; it has become a vital link in Pacific commerce bringing the produce of Australasia and East Asia to the eastern seaboard of the United States and to Europe.

In 1967–77, more than 12,000 vessels made the passage through the canal between the Panamanian cities of Colón and Balboa. These ships carried one eighth of the total American waterborne exports and imports. Beyond its commercial importance, the canal was considered vital to the U. S. Navy until the end of World War II. Since then, the size of many modern ships, military and commercial, has exceeded the capacity of the locks.

The Canal Zone extends for five miles (8 km) on either side of the canal. Governed by a Commission of the United States, the zone has been home to some 30,000 Americans, 10,000 of whom are military personnel entrusted with the canal's defense. About 4,000 civilians work in the zone. Included are 200 men with incomparable skills—the pilots who navigate ships with only a few feet of clearance through the locks and channels. The prospect of training Panamanians for this task, from which they have felt excluded, was a big point in treaty negotiations.

Panamanian attitudes toward the United States in the twentieth century have veered between resentment and admiration. The countries are tied by tight economic links: direct U. S. investment in Panama approaches

$1.8 billion compared with a total Panamanian gross national product of about $2 billion in 1976. Generations of Panamanian politicians and military leaders have been schooled in the United States and in the various military training facilities established in the zone.

Some resentment stemmed from the Panamanian belief that the country did not get its fair share of benefit from the canal. Panamanians felt excluded from top positions in the zone. Annual payments to Panama out of canal tolls—totaling approximately $2 million—were deemed insufficient. When President Eisenhower sent his brother Milton on a fact-finding tour to Panama in the 1950's, a Panamanian official told him: "You in the United States inherited mineral wealth. Africa was given gold and diamonds. The Middle East is rich in oil. God gave Panama nothing but a waterway. We must make our living, as others have."

The New Treaties. The Carter-Torrijos accords, as signed in September 1977, proposed replacing the 1903 treaty with two new treaties: the Panama Canal Treaty, regulating the U. S. presence in Panama until the year 2000, and the Treaty Concerning the Permanent Neutrality and Operation of the Panama Canal (the Neutrality Treaty), providing for the defense of the canal for the years after 2000.

Key provisions of the Panama Canal Treaty are:

1. A new U. S. government commission will administer the canal until the last day of 1999. Five Americans and four Panamanians will compose its board. A U. S. national will serve as administrator of the commission until 1990 when a Panamanian will assume the position.

2. The Panamanian share of canal revenues will be increased to an estimated $40 million a year (based on Panama receiving 30 cents a ton for a laden vessel passing through the canal) plus an annuity of $10 million a year.

3. Until 2000, the United States will have primary responsibility for the defense of the canal, with the right to station, train, and move its military forces within Panama.

4. The Canal Zone will be abolished. Lands unnecessary for the canal operation will be returned to Panama. The law of Panama will be governing, although some types of crimes committed on Panamanian territory by U. S. soldiers and canal employees will continue to be tried under U. S. law, at least during an interim period.

5. Panama and the United States agree to study the feasibility of building a new, sea-level canal and reserve the exclusivity of this right.

The Neutrality agreement contains the following points:

1. The Panama Canal will be designated an international waterway which will be neutral in times of peace and war and will remain secure and open to peaceful passage by the ships of every country equally.

2. In times of war or emergency, U. S. naval vessels and Panamanian warships will enjoy the right of "expeditious passage."

3. Both the United States and Panama will have the right, permanently, to act in defense of the canal's neutrality.

4. Following the termination of the Panama Canal Treaty in 2000, only the Republic of Panama will operate and maintain defense sites and military installations within its territory.

Both treaties were to become operative no later than Oct. 1, 1979.

Debate. The debate about the treaties during the fall of 1977 and the spring of 1978 was not confined to issues of commerce and defense. As Secretary of State Cyrus Vance put it: "the Panama Canal has always had

RAY HALIN, RAPHO

Some 4,000 civilians work in the Canal Zone. Overall canal operations are handled at the Control Center (above). A group of some 200 well-trained pilots navigate ships through the canal's locks and channels. It takes a ship eight hours to pass through the canal.

COURTESY, U. S. DEPARTMENT OF STATE

an extra dimension for us beyond its basic military and commercial importance. . . . The canal came to represent perseverance and ingenuity."

The intensity of the lobbying and debate on the canal treaties is explained by the deep attachment of the people of the United States to the canal as a symbol of U. S. strength and achievement. It has often been associated with President Theodore Roosevelt, a dashing and inspiring figure of an exciting age in U. S. history, who secured the 1903 treaty. Inevitably the issue quickly became one of whether, in a mood of post-Vietnam pessimism, the United States was abdicating its world responsibilities and "giving away" the canal; or whether, on the contrary, the treaties represented a new and principled basis for a strong foreign policy in Latin America.

I took the view that the treaties were needed to put the United States in accord with the logic of modern historical development. When the Suez Canal was nationalized by Egypt in 1956, the United States opposed the armed intervention of France, Britain, and Israel and in doing so made a final decision that there must be an end to the kind of presence in a sovereign country that could be considered colonialism. And by colonialism I mean extraterritorial rights and extraterritorial laws—vestiges of which were perceived in the relationship between the United States and Panama and could no longer be sustained.

In January 1978, against a background of heavy constituent mail and strenuous campaigning, a number of senators, myself among them, traveled to Panama to talk with General Torrijos and to see the situation first hand. Some of my colleagues were concerned about Panamanian violations of human rights under General Torrijos, who had come to power in 1968.

In the unstable political conditions of Panama during the twentieth century—oscillation between ineffective democracy and half-hearted dictatorship—the charges against the Torrijos regime could not be considered new. But that aside, a majority of senators came to see that the treaties had to be considered on their merits. At the end of January, the Senate Foreign Relations Committee recommended ratification of the treaties— subject to important clarifications of U. S. defense rights.

The full Senate debate on the Neutrality Treaty commenced on February 8 at a time when public opinion polls showed a big majority of the American public opposed to ratification. Since the Neutrality Treaty involved the difficult question of ensuring the security of the canal, even after U. S. forces had left Panama under the terms of the Canal Treaty, it preoccupied the Senate longer.

In a February 1 television broadcast, President Carter admitted there was much popular opposition to the treaties but blamed much of it on "misunderstanding and misinformation." "The most important reason— the only reason—to ratify the treaties is that they are in the highest national interest of the United States and will strengthen our position in the world. Our security interests will be stronger. Our trade opportunities will be improved. We will demonstrate that as a large and powerful country we are able to deal fairly and honorably with a proud but smaller sovereign nation." The president put the weight of the administration's considerable lobbying effort behind this view.

Senators required explicit assurances on defense rights, however. These had come in the form of a Statement of Understanding issued by President Carter and General Torrijos on Oct. 14, 1977. It said the United States had no right of intervention in the internal affairs of Panama, but equally had the right to act against any aggression or threat directed against the canal; and that this could include action against Panamanian elements in Panama posing such threat of aggression.

When debate got under way, it was clear that to ensure the two-thirds vote required for acceptance, two key amendments, embodying the Statement of Understanding, were necessary. In addition, the leadership amendments spelled out that the expeditious passage of U. S. warships in times of emergency meant they could "go to the head of the line of vessels" which might be waiting to transit the canal.

Later in the debate, language alleged to be clarifying was offered in a reservation by Sen. Dennis DeConcini of Arizona. I considered the proposal controversial and opposed it. As passed by the Senate on March 16, the DeConcini reservation stated that if the canal were closed or its operations interfered with, the United States and Panama each had the right independently to take any steps, including the use of force, to reopen it.

Official Panamanian response to the leadership amendments was guarded; but to the DeConcini reservation it was vehement. General Torrijos, holding in check extreme nationalists who believed the amendments embodied substantial alterations, stated that Panama would find "unacceptable any reservation that dishonors the national dignity or is intended to impede the exercise of Panama's sovereignty."

He determined, however, that the October 1977 plebiscite of the Panamanian people, a 2–1 vote in favor of the treaties, was still valid and that the Senate leadership amendments represented understandings already in the treaties. As to the DeConcini reservations, more needed to be done. Accordingly, when consideration of the Panama Canal Treaty began in April, the U. S. Senate leadership suggested a further amendment. Intended in part to calm Panamanian criticism, it also spelled out an essential element in the treaty—that it would not be interpreted as giving the United States the right to intervene in or to impugn the political independence of Panama. Shortly after the Senate vote on the Panama Canal Treaty, on April 18, one month after the Neutrality Treaty was ratified, General Torrijos indicated that all the amendments and reservations were acceptable.

As debate ranged across the Senate floor, open for the first time to live

FRANÇOIS BOTA, LIAISON

Panamanian soldiers take a break during training exercises. The new Neutrality Treaty provides for the defense of the canal after the year 2000.

FRANÇOIS BOTA, LIAISON

A group of Americans in the Canal Zone vehemently express their opposition to the new agreements.

radio coverage for all Americans to hear, disagreement had crystallized around a number of themes.

One was the issue of sovereignty and the interpretation of the treaty of 1903. As determined by Sen. Jesse Helms of North Carolina, the late Sen. James Allen of Alabama, and others who figured prominently in opposition to the treaties, the United States possessed sovereignty. In their view, the United States built, paid for, and operated the canal and no changes were needed.

Another issue that worried many more senators was the security of the canal in the years to come. The question—what if Panama went Communist or allied itself with hostile powers?—persisted. This uncertainty was caused by suspicion of the regime of General Torrijos and was based on the allegation that Torrijos was Marxist and sympathetic to Cuba. The issue was complicated further by suggestions that General Torrijos' family and entourage were implicated in narcotics smuggling into the United States. However, it is the view of many that General Torrijos is in the tradition of the Hispanic caudillo, the Latin American ruler who, far from being bound to left-wing ideology, often creates pragmatic and authoritarian regimes with which the United States needs to work for its own interest.

On the practical question of the security of the canal, proponents of the treaties argued that the self interest of the Panamanians was the major factor. Under the treaties, said Cyrus Vance, "more ships will mean more money for Panama. For Panama to cut off access to any country, let alone to close the canal, would be for it to inflict a terrible wound on itself." The point was taken up during the Congressional testimony of the Joint Chiefs of Staff. It was their view that the canal is easier to defend in the midst of a friendly environment. A lock canal such as this one is vulnerable to sabo-

COURTESY, U. S. DEPARTMENT OF STATE

Panamanians hold a massive rally, demonstrating their support of their leader, Omar Torrijos.

tage. Such sabotage is more likely if Panamanian nationalism is frustrated. Passage of the treaties would contribute to an atmosphere in which anti-American sentiment would be defused.

A third point of disagreement—did the treaties illustrate some weakness in U. S. foreign policy?—was the hardest to assess. As the former diplomat John Davis Lodge put it: "We got tired of the Vietnam War, we refused to help in Angola, and so now it is proposed that 217 million Americans should cave in and run away before the ominous threat of 1.5 million people in Panama." Against this view was the attitude that it was an index of U. S. strength that the nation could peacefully transfer control of the canal to the country where it is situated. The treaty supporters noted the strong views of friendly countries such as Venezuela, whose President Carlos Andres Pérez asked, "How can the United States, which is a leader of democracy in the world, take a colonial's stance?"

It is the hope of President Carter and many of us in Congress that the ratification of the treaties will raise materially the confidence in the United States of Latin American leaders, including President José López Portillo of Mexico, and of the Latin American peoples.

The new treaties do not resolve all issues, but they provide a transition period of 23 years in which to work out many of the problems of the operation and defense of the canal, and they end any colonialist implications. U. S. relations with Panama will be radically changed, but so also will U. S. relations with all of Latin America. Whatever happens, the ratification of the treaties establishes one important principle for U. S. diplomacy. It establishes, as long as the canal is useful at all, a special relationship, based on equality, between the most powerful country in the Americas and one of the weakest. The relationship could be a model for the years ahead.

JOHN NEUBAUER

GETTING AND KEEPING FIT

By Capt. James A. Lovell, USN (Ret.),
Chairman, President's Council on Physical Fitness and Sports

The American people are engaging in physical exercise in larger numbers and with greater enthusiasm than ever before. Getting and keeping fit has become a priority in the lives of millions, not only for health purposes, but for fun, relaxation, and general well being. The young and the old, alone or with family and friends, have taken to gyms, health spas, tennis and racquet courts, fields, parks, and even their own basements to run, swim, or stretch themselves into shape.

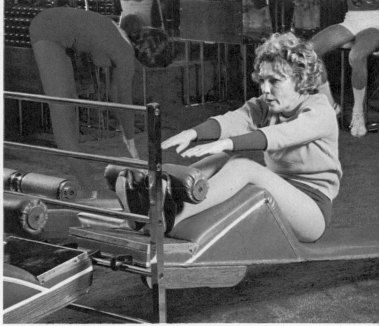

DIANE M. SPECHT   JOHN NEUBAUER

"Exercise and temperance
can preserve something of
our early vigor even in
our old age."
Cicero, 44 B.C.

Between 1961 and 1978, the percentage of adults (18 years old and over) who said they exercise "daily, or almost daily" nearly doubled, from 24 to 47 percent. At the same time, participation in some activities, notably running and the racquet sports, grew even faster. For example:

- In 1973 there were 20 million tennis players in America. In 1978 there were nearly 30 million.
- In 1970 racquetball was an obscure sport that claimed only 50,000 adherents. In 1978 the game was played by an estimated three million Americans.

It is the runners, though, who constitute the most pervasive sign of the physical fitness explosion. A species that scarcely existed in America before 1962, they now swarm the streets and parks of every city and town in increasing numbers.

In 1972, a national survey counted six million runners. By 1975 that number had grown to more than eight million. Since that time, the number of runners has doubled, reaching nearly 17 million. One of every nine adult Americans is a runner.

ARTHUR SHAY

An annual marathon race is a major event in many large U.S. cities.

The current physical fitness revival is much more sweeping than any that has occurred in the past. The fact is evident from some of the more striking features of the movement:

- Women and girls are involved on an unprecedented scale. In three activities—bicycling, swimming, and tennis—the number of female participants rivals or exceeds the number of participating men.
- Interest in athletic activities cuts across all age levels. Participation is highest in the younger age groups, but 38% of Americans aged 50 and over say they exercise "daily, or almost daily."
- The intensity and frequency of participation are growing. One of every four runners runs at least two miles (3.2 km) per day.
- Employers are investing millions of dollars in employee fitness programs. Facilities range from spartan shower-and-changing-room combinations in basement garages to elaborate layouts with swimming pools, gymnasiums, and running tracks.
- Physical fitness testing is becoming institutionalized. Nearly 20 million boys and girls between the ages 10 and 17 took part in school testing programs in 1977–78, and more than 700,000 of them earned the Presidential Physical Fitness Award.

Evidence of the vigor of the fitness movement is pervasive. Books on running and exercise appear routinely at the top of the best-seller lists.

DIANE M. SPECHT

It has been estimated that one of every nine Americans is a runner.

Sports shoes have become a billion dollar business with three great industrial powers, the United States, Japan, and West Germany, contesting for market dominance. Bicycle sales in the United States have topped $700 million a year.

There are many forces behind these dramatic changes. The growth in popularity of sports and fitness activities coincides closely with the life of the President's Council on Physical Fitness and Sports. The movement received its greatest impetus from President John Kennedy's advocacy of exercise and sports participation.

To some extent, the popularity of fitness activities can be attributed to the increased mobility of the American people and to the greater amount of leisure time they enjoy. Most adult fitness enthusiasts, however, are driven by the conviction that exercise is healthful and may prolong their lives.

When persons who exercise regularly were questioned during a recent national survey, nearly half of them said they exercise for health reasons, or "because it's good for you." An additional 13% said they exercise to lose weight, or to keep their weight down.

Medical evidence is solidly on the side of the exercisers. Research shows that regular physical activity helps reduce both weight and blood pressure. Since obesity and hypertension are among the leading risk factors for heart attack and stroke, it is apparent that exercise provides a measure of protection against two of our leading killers.

The results of a 22-year study of 3,600 longshoremen were presented at the 1978 convention of the American Heart Association. The results suggested that the risk of fatal heart attack is cut nearly in half by a pattern of hard physical work. Looked at another way, the evidence indicated that habitual physical inactivity constitutes a risk of heart attack equal to cigarette smoking or high blood pressure.

Regular exercise also enhances physical performance and appearance, and there is some evidence that it precipitates desirable changes in lifestyle. For instance, persons involved in endurance exercise programs apparently find it easier to give up smoking or modify their diets.

The phenomenal growth of exercise and sports participation has been accompanied by a similarly rapid advance in knowledge. More and more people are following exercise programs based on scientific principles. The positive implications for the health and fitness of the American people are highly encouraging.

There are three basic components of physical fitness: muscular strength, flexibility, and cardiovascular endurance. The latter quality is crucial to good health and is developed by sustained, rhythmical activities—such as

Senior citizens participate in a well-regimented exercise program.

ARTHUR SHAY

EUROPEAN HEALTH SPAS

A well-equipped exercise room at one of the 3,000 health spas across the United States.

brisk walking, running, swimming, bicycling, or cross-country skiing—which accelerate breathing and pulse rate. Most research indicates that approximately 20 minutes of such activity are necessary to produce the desired "training effect."

Muscular strength is promoted by such exercises as pushups and situps, or by working with weights. Flexibility is fostered by stretching, bending, and twisting movements.

The President's Council recommends daily workouts with an appropriate mix of endurance, strength, and flexibility exercises. A rule of thumb is that three workouts a week are required for a "maintenance" program and that at least five workouts a week are necessary for rapid progress.

Approximately one out of every two Americans is attempting to improve his or her fitness by following an exercise regime. As it becomes increasingly apparent that many of our health problems are the consequence of inactivity, or the result of behavioral aberrations, the President's Council remains convinced that ever larger numbers of people will turn to such measures.

DIANE M. SPECHT

Platform tennis (above and figure 1) is expanding at an annual rate of 25% and is one of the fastest growing sports in the United States. The popular game was developed during the 1920's.

Racquetball (below and figure 2) combines the basics of regular tennis and handball and is played with a string racquet.

ARTHUR SHAY

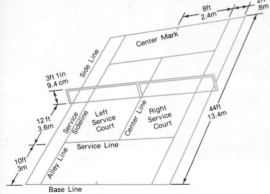

FIGURE 1

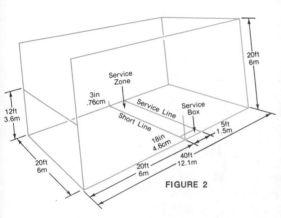

FIGURE 2

The Racquet Sports

By Philip E. Allsen
Professor, Physical Education, Brigham Young University
Coauthor, *Racquetball-Paddleball*

A major facet of the recent fitness craze is a tremendous rise in popularity of the racquet sports, especially racquetball, paddleball, and platform tennis. It is probably true that many present-day players of the racquet sports knew little or nothing about the games a few years ago. The relative inexpensiveness of the equipment, the ease with which one can learn the games, and the excellent physical activity offered are basic reasons for the new popularity. Because of the similarities among the racquet sports, an analysis of each follows.

PADDLEBALL AND RACQUETBALL

Paddleball is a combination of handball and tennis. Earl Riskey of the University of Michigan is credited with developing the concepts of the game during the 1930's. The first equipment consisted of tennis balls and wooden paddle tennis racquets. The rules for paddleball were adapted from handball, and the game is played on a handball court.

In 1949, in the Greenwich (Conn.) YMCA, Joe Sobek of Bridgeport began using a string racquet rather than the solid wooden type. Sobek felt that the string racquet would afford better control and impart greater speed to the ball. Initially, only tennis balls were available for play. Today, pressurized balls, making for an active and speedy game, are used.

Since the introduction of the game, there has been some controversy regarding the best type of racquet. Those associations that utilize the solid wooden racquet refer to their game as "paddleball," while those that use the string racquet call their game "racquetball."

Basic Rules. A short-handled racquet is used to hit a pressurized rubber ball. It is recommended that the racquet be approximately 8 inches (2 cm) wide and 17 inches (4.3 cm) in length. A thong is attached to the handle and placed over the wrist during play to keep the racquet from slipping from the hand.

The game may be played by two (singles), three (cutthroat—in which the server is playing against two receivers), or four players (doubles). It can be played on a one-, three-, or four-walled court (see figure 2).

To start the game, the server stands within the service zone and, after letting the ball bounce once, strikes it, causing it to rebound off the front wall. For it to be in play, the ball must then land behind the short line. If the first serve is not legal, then another is allowed. The opponent must then return the ball in such a manner that it will hit the front wall before it strikes the floor, and play continues until either the serving or receiving side is unable to return the ball legally. A point is won by the serving side if the receiver returns the ball illegally. If the server fails to return the ball, he loses his serve. His opponent now becomes the server and the former server now becomes the receiver. A complete game ends when one side gains 21 points. A match consists of two out of three games.

PLATFORM TENNIS

Platform tennis was developed by James Cogswell and Fessenden Blanchard in the 1920's as an alternative to tennis. Originally, the game was known as paddle tennis. Cogswell and Fessenden reduced the dimensions of the tennis court and enclosed it with wire. Since shots can be hit off the wire, the enclosure is an important part of the game's strategy.

Basic Rules. The ball is made of a solid sponge rubber. The paddle, which is wood, metal, or plastic, is approximately 8 inches wide (2 cm) and 17 inches (4.3 cm) in length. To reduce the air resistance the paddle head is perforated with small holes.

Platform tennis may be played by two (singles) or four players (doubles). In tournament competition, the doubles variety is usually played. Figure 1 contains the dimensions of the court.

To put the ball in play, the serving player is allowed only one service. The server stands behind his own baseline to one side of the center mark and tosses the ball into the air and must hit it before it strikes the court. The serve must then land on the fly in the opposing team's service court. The players then hit the ball back and forth over the net until one team is unable to return it; that team loses the point. If the ball hits the wire screen after bouncing off the court, it is still in play and can be hit back over the net. It is this aspect of platform tennis that makes it so exciting.

A game is won by the first team to score four points, unless the game reaches a score of 3–3. In that case, a team must gain two consecutive points to win. The service is changed after each game. The first team to win six games wins the set. If each team has won five games, play continues until one side goes ahead by two games. A match is normally the best of three sets; the best of five sets is sometimes played in men's tournaments.

JONESTOWN, GUYANA

Paradise Lost

*San Francisco
Bureau Chief,
"Newsweek" Magazine*

Late on Sunday, Nov. 19, 1978, radio and television audiences began to receive disquieting news about the deaths of scores, or possibly hundreds, of Americans in an unknown place called Jonestown, Guyana. The world was soon to learn the appalling details of a community of some thousand souls, extinguished in a mass suicide in obedience to the command of their leader.

It began as a fundamentalist Christian pursuit of racial harmony and social justice and ended in a paroxysm of madness. Along the way, the Rev. Jim Jones, the self-proclaimed messiah of the Peoples Temple, led his devoted followers on a spiritual and geographic odyssey from the heartland of America to the heart of darkness in the South American jungles of Guyana. Jones created a utopian façade on an infrastructure of deceit and manipulation, a false-front Christian commune with a foundation of Socialist atheism. In the end, the façade collapsed, killing U. S. Rep. Leo Ryan (D-Calif.) and 917 others in an elaborately rehearsed act of murder and suicide.

Jones began battling the reality of racism in Indianapolis, Ind., in the 1950's, when segregation was a way of life. His integrated congregation was a constant target for local bigots. The substance of his social gospel and the activist stance of his church were established early. He exhorted his followers to hark back to the days of Christianity, when Jesus' followers lived by their commitment to universal equality and social justice. He set up a soup kitchen for the hungry, clothed the poor, found jobs for the unemployed, and eventually was named director of the city's human rights commission.

At about the same time, a split began to develop between his public self, a socially conscious, caring disciple of Christ, and his private lust for power and ego gratification. He dabbled in questionable real estate deals, practiced faith healing, and became fascinated by Father Divine, a black cult figure who demanded total devotion from his followers.

After a visit with Father Divine, Jones' demands for the personal loyalty of his modest flock began to increase. His sermons focused less and less on the traditional Christian gospel of love and developed into hours-long harangues, exaggerating the bitter plight of his largely black following and the bleak future that lay before them. Their only salvation lay in following Jones, the Lord's chosen shepherd, to a promised land of their own creation.

His Christian faith dwindled as his megalomania grew. The threat of outside enemies became a keystone of his theology. He established an interrogation committee, the forerunner of a much more elaborate temple hierarchy, to question and intimidate anyone who threatened his authority. He proclaimed an apocalyptic vision in which the world would be destroyed and only those who followed him unflinchingly would survive.

The Rev. Jim Jones, leader, Peoples Temple.

In 1962 he went to Bel Horizonte, Brazil, to do missionary work. When he returned in 1964 his own renunciation of faith was complete and his determination to move his flock was set. He laid plans to move his congregation to Redwood Valley, a tiny hamlet in northern California, which he divined would be safe from the nuclear holocaust he foresaw. And he began to tell his followers that he himself was Jesus Christ.

By the time Jones moved to California, his lust for control over his flock was insatiable. They were taught to call him "father" and "prophet," believe in his healing powers, and implicitly trust his judgment in all matters. "You go out and preach me," Jones told black Assistant Minister Archie Ijames, "and I'll back it up with miracles." The miracles were pure carnival hokum, carefully contrived to convince the credulous who flocked in ever increasing numbers from San Francisco and Oakland to the remote valley 100 miles (160 km) south. Fake cancers were plucked from startled old women. Accomplices rose from wheelchairs and walked on purportedly crippled legs. In one memorable "miracle" staged shortly after the assassination of Martin Luther King in 1968, Jones stuffed a plastic bag filled with blood under his shirt. When an accomplice "shot" him with blanks, Jones burst the bag and fell to the floor as if dead before his stunned congregation. A short time later he reappeared, brandishing the bullet plucked from his wound and claiming that he had raised himself from the dead. The bloodstained shirt was installed in a glass case as a temple icon.

Suddenly there were no limits to what Jones could do. He spoke with spirits of the departed—aides hidden in crawl spaces in the ceiling. He struck people dead and raised them up, read people's minds, and foresaw the future, all according to carefully worked out scripts that involved his most loyal followers. "He didn't conduct services," says one former

PHOTOS UPI

Rep. Leo Ryan (D-Calif.) was killed in Guyana.

assistant minister. "They were performances planned in advance and designed to deceive."

To make sure his secrets were safe, Jones instituted a two-tiered hierarchy. There was a band of angels, 12 or 15 of his closest advisers, who handled the temple's increasingly lucrative financial affairs, helped devise strategy, and kept up the hothouse atmosphere in which Jones' mad vision flowered. While the bulk of the membership was elderly or black, the leadership was largely white, drawn increasingly from the disaffected youth of the late 1960's, who saw interracial, collective socialism as the answer to the racist, capitalist materialism they had rejected.

By the time the temple moved to San Francisco in the early 1970's, it had become a smoothly-functioning organism, totally dependent on Jones. There were good projects, to be sure, calculated to swell the membership, fill the coffers, and advance the cause. Old people, ignored by society, were taken in and given care and a communal home. In return, they signed over their social security checks to the temple. Foster children were given a "Christian" home, paid for by welfare, and turned back on the streets to beg money for the temple.

Meanwhile, Jones was adapting the techniques of the human potential movement, using encounter sessions to break down individual members and make them totally reliant on him. He wanted to create a new social order based on racial equality, revolutionary communalism, and sexual liberation. While he had sexual relations with every member of his inner circle, male and female, he forced husbands and wives to sleep with other partners, arguing that monogamous relationships and affection were ugly vestiges of the system they sought to destroy.

UPI

The headquarters of the Peoples Temple was in San Francisco.

His own paranoia heightened by heavy use of amphetamines, Jones made spying a permanent part of the church structure, convincing his closest followers they could trust no one and must report everything to him. Constantly testing their loyalty, Jones forced his followers to sign confessions that they had plotted to kill the president or had sexually abused their children. Their minds were dulled by the seemingly endless, all-night harangues. Physical abuse also was common, as members were slowly reshaped in Jones' own insane image. The only reality they knew and trusted was inside the locked and guarded doors of the temple.

Slavishly loyal, Jones' followers were the perfect political pawns. Never numbering more than a few thousand, they exerted influence far beyond their numbers by their fanatic devotion to Jones. For example, they wrote thousands of letters to oppose the nomination of G. Harrold Carswell to the Supreme Court in 1970. At the same time, they were constantly pressured to produce income for the church. New members were required to tithe 10% of their income, and the truly devoted were expected to turn over all their money. Members who lived in the church's communal housing gave all their property and possessions to the church. Marathon weekend revivals in Los Angeles and other west coast cities might generate $25,000. Aides spent every Monday taking the weekend's proceeds to several different banks so as not to attract attention. By the mid-1970's, the accumulated wealth of the Peoples Temple was running into the millions.

In 1974, his vision of a nuclear holocaust fading, Jones negotiated a lease with the Guyanese government for 27,000 acres (10,800 ha) of jungle. Here, Jones and his followers would build their utopia. Work was proceeding on this so-called agricultural mission when the tight veil of secrecy around the temple's activities in San Francisco began to slip. News stories in 1977 revealed the bizarre practices within the temple. After failing in a fierce battle to block their publication, Jones himself fled to Guyana and began laying plans to have his flock join him.

By this time, Jones' vision of a conspiracy was in possession of him. The conspirators changed daily as his mind became increasingly erratic. But he convinced his followers that they also were targets, through their involvement with him. If black members didn't flee to Guyana, he claimed, they would be put into concentration camps and killed. Whites were told that their names appeared on secret CIA lists and that they would be murdered if they didn't follow him to Jonestown.

Through the autumn of 1977, the bulk of his followers made their way to Jonestown, and the buff-colored church headquarters in San Francisco became little more than a supply depot for Jones' Guyana paradise. But the crude facilities of that paradise were sorely strained by the migration. Rice and beans became the staples, and people were jammed into narrow wooden barracks. Meat was scarce, the workday grew intolerably long, and the commune's security forces imposed increasingly harsh discipline. Jones himself began to deteriorate physically. He relied on drugs more heavily, his rantings became more deranged, and Jonestown became a virtual concentration camp.

Fearing for their relatives in Jonestown, temple defectors sought help from the U. S. State Department and from Congressman Leo Ryan, a liberal Democrat with a penchant for personal involvement. In November 1978, Ryan set out on a fatal journey to Jonestown, accompanied by a party of defectors and press representatives. During their brief visit, Jones fought to maintain the façade of harmony, but several residents asked to leave with Ryan. Their defection confirmed Jones' worst paranoid fears.

He sent a crew of avenging angels to the airport at Port Kaituma in pursuit of the defectors. In a hail of gunfire, Ryan and four members of his party were murdered. Then came the final act of Jones' mad charade. He declared a "white night," a carefully rehearsed mass suicide in which all his followers would drink Flavour-Aide laced with cyanide. They had gone through the ritual on numerous occasions, but this would be real, the final sacrament. Summoning his followers to a "revolutionary suicide council" Jones told them of the deaths at Port Kaituma. "We are sitting on a powder keg," he said. "If we can't live in peace, let's die in peace."

He instructed the mothers with young babies to come forward. Although there were some protests, most of the women voluntarily shot the death-dealing liquid into the mouths of their offspring. Surrounded by guards armed with rifles and crossbows, the rest of the flock lined up quietly to carry out their mad messiah's final bidding. "Dad has brought us this far," shouted one follower. "My vote is to go with Dad." And in the end, nearly one thousand members of the Peoples Temple followed their leader to extinction.

An overall view of the village of Jonestown, Guyana, where nearly 1,000 members of the Peoples Temple died in November 1978.

UPI

Shaping World Opinion

THE POWER OF THE MEDIA

By Edwin Newman
Correspondent
NBC News

There are few words more annoying, to me at any rate, than media. Media should be used only as the plural of medium, and when referring to the news business it conceals and misleads. Some people in news use it to make what they are doing sound more scientific and technical and so more important.

A sometimes quoted authority (me) has had this to say: "I entered the news business 35 years ago, and at the proper time I would like to leave it. I do not want to make my exit from the media. Others may. I do not."

But I have been asked to write about "the power of the media in shaping world opinion," so I will, this once, put aside my objections to the word and get on. It is clear that newspapers, television, radio, magazines, along with films and books, in large part supply us with the elements we use to make up our minds, to form opinions, to take or forsake a course of action.

Of course we talk to each other, to our neighbors, and we learn some valuable things at first hand. Such information, however, is limited, frequently less than balanced or conclusive. One learns little about the value of the dollar in Tokyo at any given moment by talking to a passerby.

Public opinion surveys, which are increasingly used by news organizations, are generally boring and sometimes of questionable validity. They are to be cited with skepticism, if at all. I think it would be possible to lead a reasonably happy existence without ever coming into contact with one. Certainly, no survey is needed for us to know that television has altered what we know, how we know, and how fast we know; along with the way we talk, what we say, what we eat, what we buy, whether we stay up late or get up early, whether we stay at home and what we do there, and even when we go to the bathroom, when we eat, whether we believe it is going to rain or shine, and who we expect our next president to be.

Television has also changed the other parts of the news business. It has overwhelmed some of our largest weekly magazines, and helped to cause the deaths of *Life, Look, Colliers,* and *The Saturday Evening Post,* while at the same time spawning the most widely circulated weekly publication in the United States, *TV Guide.*

One of the big stories of 1978 was the uncovering of some evidence that television viewing in the United States had peaked, that the average amount of time the set was on (not necessarily with anyone watching)

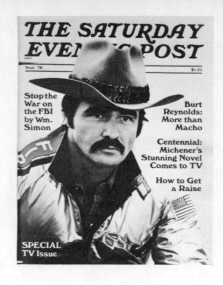

REPRINTED FROM "THE SATURDAY EVENING POST"
© 1945 & 1978 THE CURTIS PUBLISHING COMPANY

Covers designed by artist Norman Rockwell were a trademark of the old *Saturday Evening Post.* The famous weekly ceased publication in 1969 following a long career. A monthly edition of the magazine (*right*) was later introduced.

had gone down slightly, although no one ventured to say what people were doing instead.

Another indication that television viewing may have peaked was the fact that *Life* went back on the newsstands in October 1978 in a somewhat altered form. Moreover, *Look* may follow and *The Saturday Evening Post* was there already, although it is a much smaller operation than before.

The effect of television and television news can be gauged by more than the numbers of people watching or the draw of a particular commercial in bringing customers to the market. Television has an effect on the nation that is comparable to the way the railroads and later the automobile shaped the United States and its people. It can be stated simply: In 1946 there were 8,000 television sets in America. Thirty-two years later, there were nearly 120 million. One way to know the effect of television on its audience would be to conduct a controlled experiment by withdrawing it from use. The idea of New York or some other city without television for a year is almost unthinkable. However, if it were done and then the sets were turned on again, it would be as though that city were rejoining the rest of America. Television provides a common bond; it is our most persistent, persuasive national institution. Jeff Greenfield, in his book, *Television, The First Fifty Years,* writes: "Television had come to stand alone in the range and reach of its influence. It *IS* our society as is no other institution."

The press operates independently of television as well as with and for it. On its own, the U. S. press has established a domination of news distribution that is worldwide. The Associated Press says its dispatches reach a billion people every day. United Press International news is translated into 48 languages. Exports of American films now produce 49 percent of the industry's total revenue, estimated at $600 million in 1977 in overseas rentals. *Time* magazine's international editions are sold in 145 countries. For that matter, a quarter of the American television revenue is said to come from overseas.

Americans may be pleased with this, but others are not. Third World nations are often sharply critical of Western news coverage, complaining that it dwells on disaster, crisis, and confrontation and reports on developing nations in East-West terms rather than in African, Asian, or Latin American.

At least two international conferences have considered a proposal by Roger Tatarian, a former director of United Press International, that West-

U. S. HOUSEHOLDS WITH TV SETS

	No Set	One Set	Two or More Sets
1955	33%	65%	2%
1960	12	77	11
1965	8	73	19
1970	4	67	29
1975	3	52	45

Source: U. S. Bureau of the Census

RCA

Since the introduction of the first commercially built black and white television in the 1940's, the instrument has become so popular that by the mid-1970's 97% of U. S. households had at least one set.

ern and Third World journalists pool resources by forming a multinational news organization to fill the gap in reporting by Western news agencies. So far it is only a proposal and, at a guess, it will never get off the ground. There is too much suspicion on the Third World side. However, approximately 50 Third World nations have plans to "pool" the output of their own news services. Yugoslavia's Tanjug agency is directing the project.

News is a business, relentlessly so. The power of news organizations to help shape our lives is unquestioned, but there is much questioning of the press, and there is a dwindling faith in the news business among some of its most respected practitioners. One speaks of a news business in which organizations compete with each other. Unfortunately, competition is decreasing. *Editor & Publisher* reports that competition among newspaper owners has disappeared in 97 percent of American cities. A. J. Liebling in "The Wayward Press: Do You Belong In Journalism?" observed, in 1960, "What you have in a one-paper town is a privately owned public utility that is constitutionally exempt from regulation, which would be a violation of freedom of the press." Liebling also observed, "Freedom of the press is guaranteed only to those who own one."

Another journalist, John B. Oakes, former senior editor of *The New York Times,* said: "The development of the American press today is in the direction either of quasi-monopoly, remote control under chain ownership, or multimedia conglomerates with their built-in conflicts of interest, or not infrequently, all three."

Donald McDonald, editor of *The Center Magazine,* a publication of the Fund for the Republic's Center for the Study of Democratic Institutions, caused a stir with his attack on the big business nature of the press and the increasing concentration of ownership in fewer hands. It is McDonald's belief that today the "threat to consistently responsible journalism comes not so much from the government as from the mass media themselves." Some news organizations have assigned their legal staffs to marshall replies to McDonald.

Another complaint by John Oakes is that television supplies viewers with what he described as "chewing gum for the eyes" and newspapers are trying to capture the attention of readers by supplying "chewing gum for the brain."

While it is true that the reader and viewer are farther than ever from the owner or managers of the news organizations and have little if any contact with them or their stockholders, there are some advantages in bigness.

We live at a time when it is virtually impossible to say anything of importance without offending someone. With big business, big labor, big government, and big movements such as the women's movement and the environmental movement, a news organization must be on something like an equal footing if it is to be as independent and enterprising as news organizations ought to be. A willingness to do battle with the president of the United States on issues such as Vietnam or impeachment has to be backed by sizable resources. Equally, of course, the resources have to be backed by the willingness.

There is no pleasure to be had in writing that bigness may, at times, be necessary. The quirky small-town editor is a folk hero. But few parts of our society can resist technological change and its consequences. The news business certainly cannot.

I have long been among those who believe that the news business has not been sufficiently criticized, from without and within. This was remedied, almost single-handed, by Aleksandr Solzhenitsyn, when he spoke at the Harvard commencement exercises in June. He charged the American press with inaccuracy, guesswork, rumors, suppositions, hastiness, immaturity, superficiality, sensationalism, and misleading judgments. Others had, of course, made the same charges in the past. Most people in the news business would accept the charges, in some degree, at some times. Solzhenitsyn's indictment was too broad, and too unspecific, to have much effect.

A more useful contribution came from Thomas Griffith of *Time,* who found the American press and people "overdosed on excitement," and from Stephen Hess, a senior fellow at the Brookings Institution, who thought that a basic reason for poor relations between the Carter administration and the press was the simple fact that Carter and those around him "bore the Washington press corps."

Boredom is a problem, built into a business in which papers have to be sold and television programs watched. If the subject is boring to the reporter, or the reporter thinks it boring to his audience, it may be neglected and much of what on other counts could be called news may go unreported.

The first victim of boredom in the American press is foreign news. *Time* says "The most scandalous neglect occurs in newspaper chains. The wealthy Newhouse chain, with 29 metropolitan papers (circ. about 3.5 million), has no foreign staff. Neither has the Knight-Ridder chain, with important papers in Detroit, Philadelphia, and Miami. The Gannett papers (circ. 3 million), which proudly report increased earnings for 42 quarters in a row, now have 77 papers—and not one foreign correspondent.

In an article in *The New York Times,* "Where Are The Media?," Harold Willens, an adviser to the U. S. delegation at the United Nations disarmament session, said that although it was the first international gathering of world leaders on disarmament since 1932, "the treatment by the press, radio, and television has been abysmal." At the same time, he said: "We were all barraged by the news-media blitz that preceded and accompanied the opening of legalized gambling in Atlantic City, N. J."

Willens did not mention, but perhaps should have, the case of a New York dentist accused of fondling a female patient while she was under an anesthetic. It took one day short of three weeks for the trial to be ended, and

"THE SUPREME COURT MEDIA STYLE BOOK PREFERS A SEMI-COLON TO A COMMA AFTER THE USE OF THE PAST PLUPERFECT SUBJUNCTIVE!"

some New York papers and television found space for detailed and smirking coverage every day. It was an unpleasant incident of the tiniest significance covered as though it were of surpassing importance. The gap between news value and titillation value was tremendous—and all too typical.

Welcoming criticism, whether informed or uninformed, is very different from welcoming an intrusion into the area of the press by the courts. Unfortunately, the courts did enter that area in a significant way in 1978. There was an increase in gag rules, in subpoenas, in efforts to force revelation of confidential information.

In June 1978, the Supreme Court handed down a 5-to-3 decision that reversed earlier rulings and startled editors across the nation. The court ruled that if a judge has issued a warrant, the police seeking evidence have the right to enter a newsroom unannounced even if the occupant is not suspected of involvement in the crime. "The right to rummage" by the police, in this case, was in the newsroom of the *Stanford University Daily*. The danger arises because the police can often find a judge willing to issue a search warrant with slight justification. Some newsmen believe that if the ruling had been in effect at the time, it could have prevented the publication of the Pentagon Papers by *The New York Times,* and the pursuit of Watergate by *The Washington Post.*

Others believe that this is an alarmist view, and that in practice, the ruling will have few, if any, drastic effects. Whichever side is right, the ruling may in the long run be helpful to the practice of journalism. We who are journalists tend to become stodgy, to become creatures of habit, to take things for granted. A decision on such a subject wakes us up, and makes us think about what our function is, and what we ought to be doing. It makes other people think about our function and what we ought to be doing. That will almost certainly be helpful, for although higher standards may come from inside the business, they are more likely to come if an informed public demands them.

The Changing Face of the American Newspaper

By David Anable
Overseas News Editor
The Christian Science Monitor

There are revolutionary changes going on under the familiar, inky face of the American newspaper. Perhaps the three most crucial areas of change are the rapid concentration of ownership and control, a subtle shift in emphasis from hard news to special features and similar "soft" news, and the adoption of radical new technologies.

Where once the family-owned newspaper was a basic staple of small town and big city America, today these sturdy independents are fading away. For better or for worse, and often a bit of both, they are being gobbled up by a small number of powerful newspaper chains. Some chains, in turn, are merging into or being consumed by mighty, multi-interest conglomerates.

Where once the great majority of Americans obtained much of their worldwide information from the daily newspaper, today less than half the people say they get most of their news from that source. Television has become the major source of news for most Americans. So, many newspapers are now counterattacking with a flood of local editions, "soft" news features, and leisure supplements. Critics say this is groveling to people's wants rather than fulfilling their (and democracy's) needs.

Where once Americans perused, often with blackened fingers, a product that had been thrown together via molten lead and pounding rotary presses, the time is approaching when they will be able to select their news from pocket computers and read it on a screen at home.

It is the trend toward concentration of news control that most worries many Americans inside and outside the news business. One of them is U. S. Representative Morris Udall (D-Ariz.). He describes the trend as something which goes to the "heart of what the country is all about."

"What I fear," he says, "is that, the way this spiral of acquisitions and mergers is going, in 15 years or so from now we'll end up with three or six, or eight or nine, very large communications conglomerates that are feeding you your newspaper news, that are owning your television stations, giving you your books and news magazines, and hit you from clear across the spectrum of communications."

By 1978, the ten largest chains controlled 36% of U. S. daily newspaper circulation. Conversely, the number of independent dailies dropped from 1,376 at the end of World War II to 715. All across the country, daily newspapers had been succumbing to rising costs and fierce competition for advertising dollars; by 1978, only some 37 U. S. cities and towns retained genuinely competing dailies.

Chain ownership can result in greater access to national news bureaus, increased funding for plant modernization, better staffs, and, in general, a welcome freedom from family overlordship. The risks, however, are a greater concern for conglomerate profits than for journalistic integrity and a reduction in the exhilarating variety and gruff independence of U. S. newspapers.

The trend toward "soft" news—leisure columns and news interpretation instead of hard facts—appears to be a belated reaction to the rapid growth of television. There has been a visible proliferation of new special sections, including *The New York Times*' "Home," "Weekend," "Living," and "Sports Monday" sections, the *Los Angeles Times*' weekly fashion section, Long Island *Newsday*'s special section for children, and others.

The big question is whether these changes jeopardize the dissemination of the hard news needed to maintain an informed electorate. *The New York Times*' publisher, Arthur Ochs Sulzberger, says that his new ventures are all supplementary and in no way diminish hard news coverage. Some critics, however, worry that many American newspapers are becoming, in Professor Ben Bagdikian's words, "entertainment, cultural and leisure-time consultants for affluent middle class households."

As for the technological revolution, this tends to take two forms: one, the modernization of the newspaper in its present form—producing newsprint more efficiently and tailoring it to each reader's particular preferences; and two, developing "electronic newspapers"—push-button information displayed in digital letters on television screens that are available in the home.

Both aspects depend heavily on computers. "Tailor-made" newspapers need powerful computers to keep track of subscriber preferences and to control the delivery of particular editions and selections to the proper address. A new invention, the computer-controlled ink-jet press, may someday permit completely "personalized" newspapers to be published.

Meanwhile, mammoth computer "brains" already are becoming the central information storehouses from which "readers" will be able to choose a particular type of news and then watch the print displayed on TV screens at home or in the office. Simpler versions of such systems, including the BBC's "Ceefax," the British Post Office's "Viewdata," and Reuter's cable television business news service, already exist. These are the embryos of tomorrow's electronic newspapers.

Munich, 1972 Olympic Games: demonstrators demand a halt to Arab terrorism.

INTERNATIONAL TERRORISM

The Extremists' Newest Tool

By Brian M. Jenkins

Director of Research on Guerrilla Warfare and International Terrorism

The Rand Corporation

Unless some world war or other cataclysmic event occurs, future historians will almost certainly describe the 1970's as the decade of the terrorist. Terrorism has become part of our daily news diet. Hardly a day goes by without news of an assassination, political kidnapping, hijacking, or bombing somewhere in the world.

Repeatedly, during the last decade, small groups of political extremists have demonstrated that by using terrorist tactics they can achieve disproportionate effects. They attract worldwide attention to themselves and their causes; they arouse worldwide alarm, and can create international incidents that national governments are compelled to deal with, often before a worldwide audience.

Terrorism has become of increasing concern to governments and of increasing interest to scholars. Terrorism has occasioned scientific inquiry; it has also inspired novelists, script writers, and even designers of women's clothes, who in 1977 made it fashionable in Europe to wear a new look which the French called "terrorist chic."

Definition and Background. The term "terrorism" has no precise or universally accepted definition. It has become a fad word used promiscuously and is often applied to a variety of acts of violence which are not, strictly speaking, terrorist in nature. Terrorism can be described as the use of actual or threatened violence to create fear and alarm, which in turn will cause people to exaggerate the strength of the terrorists and the importance of their cause. Terrorist tactics can be used to publicize, frighten, disrupt, or coerce.

International or "transnational" terrorism, as some scholars prefer, comprises those incidents of terrorism that have clear international consequences: incidents in which terrorists go abroad to strike their targets, select victims or targets because of their connections to a foreign state (diplomats, executives of foreign corporations), attack airliners on international flights, or force airlines to fly to a country of the terrorists' choosing. International terrorism excludes the considerable amount of violence carried out by terrorists operating within their own country against their fellow citizens. For example, the 1978 kidnapping and murder of Aldo Moro, a former premier of Italy, by Italian terrorists in Rome, would not be counted as an incident of international terrorism (unless, of course, subsequent investigations revealed the participation of foreign terrorists). Such incidents of domestic terrorism are nonetheless of importance, for they both inspire and are inspired by incidents of international terrorism, and add to the overall volume of political violence.

Terrorism itself is not new, but the kind of international terrorism seen in the past decade is a relatively recent activity that has both political and technological origins. The Israeli defeat of Arab armies in the Six Day War of 1967 caused the Palestinians to abandon their total dependence on Arab military power and to turn to terrorism. The failure of the rural guerrilla movements in Latin America led to increasing emphasis on urban guerrilla warfare and the use of terrorist tactics. And the student-led anti-Vietnam war and antigovernment demonstrations in Western Europe, Japan, and the United States ultimately spawned terrorist groups such as the Baader-Meinhof Gang and the Japanese Red Army.

UPI

In March 1978, Arab guerrillas hijacked an Arab bus near Haifa, Israel. During an exchange of gunfire between the terrorists and Arabs, the bus burst into flames and 37 civilians were killed.

UPI

As violence mounts in Italy, private citizens pay as much as $230 for bulletproof vests.

Capabilities and Incidents. Contemporary technology also provided terrorists with new targets and new capabilities. Jet air travel gave them both dramatic targets and the mobility to strike anywhere in the world. Television, radio, and the press afford terrorists almost instantaneous access to a worldwide audience. The increasing availability of explosives and weapons, some quite sophisticated, also increases the terrorists' capacity for violence. At the same time, new vulnerabilities, arising from modern society's increasing dependence on technology, afford terrorists opportunities to create greater disruption.

Bombings, the most common terrorist tactic, account for more than half of all incidents of international terrorism. Explosives can easily be purchased, stolen, or manufactured from commercially available materials. Knowledge of at least primitive explosives is widespread. A bombing requires little organization; it can easily be a one-man operation. The targets are often embassies and consulates, national tourist agencies, offices of foreign corporations, ticket offices and terminals of national carriers, and sometimes even the planes themselves. Although most of the bombings are symbolic and not intended to cause any casualties, there have been deadly exceptions: 73 persons were killed in the 1976 crash of a Cuban Airlines jet, sabotaged by anti-Castro emigrés; 88 persons were killed in the 1974 crash of a TWA airliner for which Palestinian terrorists claimed responsibility; 121 persons died in the 1978 bombing of an apartment building in Beirut, Lebanon, which housed the headquarters of one of the Palestinian groups; the bombing was attributed to a rival Palestinian faction.

Many incidents of international terrorism involve the taking of hostages. Terrorists seize hostages—diplomats, corporate executives, tourists, sometimes just anybody handy—deliberately to heighten the drama of the episode, guarantee widespread publicity, and increase their leverage by placing human life in the balance. Although kidnapping for political reasons is an ancient practice, the current wave of political kidnappings by guerrilla groups began during the Cuban revolution when Castro's guerrillas kidnapped a world-famous Argentine race car driver as a publicity stunt. The tactic was copied by leftist guerrillas in Latin America and soon spread throughout the world. In subsequent incidents, however, terrorists often demanded the release of prisoners, publication of political manifestos, and other political concessions. In Argentina, urban guerrillas concentrated on kidnapping the executives of large foreign corporations, extracting multimillion dollar ransoms for their safe release. Some hostages spent months in captivity. Geoffrey Jackson, the British ambassador to Uruguay, kidnapped by the Tupamoros, remained locked in a tiny cell in an underground "people's prison" for more than nine months. Françoise Claustre, a French archaeologist, spent nearly three years as a prisoner of Muslim rebels in Chad.

Terrorists also take hostages by seizing embassies or other public buildings, creating what police commonly refer to as barricade-and-hostage situations, since the terrorists are barricaded with their hostages and must bargain for their escape as well as for their other demands. There have been a number of spectacular international hostage incidents in the 1970's. In September 1972, eight members of Black September, a Palestinian group,

SIPA PRESS FROM BLACK STAR

In May 1972, members of the Japanese Red Army, hired by Palestinian terrorists, killed 25 persons at Lod Airport, near Tel Aviv.

broke into the Israeli quarters at the Olympic games in Munich and seized nine athletes as hostages, all of whom were subsequently killed during a gun battle with police. Arab terrorists were also responsible for the seizure of the Israeli embassy in Bangkok in 1972, in 1973 the Saudi Arabian embassies in Paris and in Khartoum (where one Belgian and two American diplomats were murdered), the Japanese embassy in Kuwait in 1974, the Egyptian embassy in Madrid in 1975, the Syrian embassy in Rome in 1976, and the Iraqi embassy in Paris in 1978. Japanese terrorists seized the French embassy in The Hague in 1974 and the American consular offices in Kuala Lumpur, Malaysia, in 1975. In 1975, a group of Palestinian and West German terrorists led by one Venezuelan seized 60 people, including several important oil ministers, at the Organization of Petroleum Exporting Countries (OPEC) headquarters in Vienna. To press their demands on the Dutch and Indonesian governments for the creation of an independent South Molucca, Moluccan extremists in Holland have hijacked trains, seized hostages at government buildings, the Indonesian consulate, and, on one occasion, 100 children in a schoolhouse.

Airline hijackings are a third common form of taking hostages. Most of the early hijackings were carried out by individuals fleeing from Communist countries in Europe or wanting to return to Havana from the United States, but terrorist groups adopted the tactic in the late 1960's. In 1970, members of the Popular Front for the Liberation of Palestine, in a well-coordinated plan, hijacked four airliners (a fifth hijacking attempt failed). One of the planes was flown to Cairo where it was blown up shortly after the passengers were evacuated. The other three were flown to a desert landing strip in Jordan. All of the passengers were eventually released after three European governments acceded to the hijackers' demands, but the three planes were blown up. Hijackings declined after this episode, but they seem to have risen again in the last few years. In 1977, Japanese Red Army members hijacked a Japan Airlines jet and

WIDE WORLD

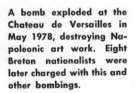

A bomb exploded at the Chateau de Versailles in May 1978, destroying Napoleonic art work. Eight Breton nationalists were later charged with this and other bombings.

flew it to Dacca, Pakistan, where it was held until the Japanese government yielded to their demands for the release of prisoners.

Governments have grown generally more resistant to the demands of terrorists holding hostages. In barricade-and-hostage and hijacking incidents government officials are more likely to order an armed assault by commando units that have been created and specially trained to respond to terrorism. In 1976, Israeli commandos successfully rescued hostages held by Palestinian hijackers at Entebbe Airport in Uganda. In 1977, West German commandos rescued the passengers of a hijacked Lufthansa airliner at Mogadishu, Somalia. All such operations have not been successful. In 1978, Egyptian commandos sent to rescue passengers held by Palestinian hijackers in Cyprus found themselves fighting against Cypriot soldiers.

Still other terrorist incidents consist mainly of assassinations and armed assaults. Croatian terrorists assassinated the Yugoslav ambassador to Sweden in 1971, the same year Palestinian terrorists assassinated the Jordanian prime minister in Cairo. In 1973, a number of Palestinian representatives in Europe were assassinated by Israeli agents. Armenian extremists avenging the death of over one million Armenians during World War I assassinated four Turkish diplomats between 1975 and 1978. Internal battles within the ranks of the Palestinian organizations resulted in the deaths of several Palestinian and Arab government officials in 1978. The bloodiest armed assaults by terrorists include the 1972 Lod Airport massacre where three Japanese terrorists, operating on behalf of a Palestinian group, attacked passengers with machine guns and hand grenades, killing 25 people and wounding 76, and the 1973 attack on an airliner at the Rome airport by Arab terrorists who killed 32 people and wounded 18.

Incidents of this scale have tended to occur very infrequently. The actual amount of terrorist violence has been exaggerated—evidence of its success in gaining worldwide attention. Measured against the world volume of violence, the amount of terrorist violence is minuscule. Since 1968, fewer than 2,000 persons have died in international terrorist incidents— upward of 10,000 if the casualties of domestic political violence, as in Belfast or Buenos Aires, are included. By contrast, in the United States alone, approximately 20,000 persons are murdered every year. More than six million persons have died in wars since 1968.

But terrorism is more appropriately measured by the amount of attention it receives, by its ability to create national and international crises, by the enormous costs of protecting against attacks, by the alarm it creates, and by the consequences for society.

Effect and International Reaction. In response to the threat posed by terrorists, governments and corporations have been compelled to divert increasing manpower and money to the protection of political leaders and diplomats, airports, portions of the energy system, and other potential terrorist targets. A second effect of terrorism has been a growing corpus of law to deal with politically motivated crime, specifically acts of terrorism. In many cases, terrorism has been identified as a crime different from and in most cases more serious than the traditional crimes that terrorists commit—murder, kidnapping, arson. New criminal offenses, such as air piracy, have been identified. Legislation has also broadened police powers. Several nations have created groups at the national level to coordinate national efforts against terrorists. New special antiterrorist organizations have been created with police departments and military establishments. Private security services also have grown tremendously.

FRANÇOIS LOCHON, GAMMA

In October 1977, four Arabs, claiming solidarity with the kidnappers of West German industrialist Hans-Martin Schleyer, hijacked a Lufthansa airliner. German troops later stormed the plane and freed the hostages unharmed.

International cooperation has been limited. Most nations are now parties to the Tokyo (1963), Hague (1970), and Montreal (1971) conventions to cooperate against airline hijackings. In 1978, the heads of seven nations, meeting in Bonn, agreed to cut off air services to and from any country that fails to prosecute or extradite hijackers. There is less consensus in other areas. Few nations can agree on what "international terrorism" is, and, for reasons of ideology or politics, not all nations are threatened equally. Defining terrorism, outlawing it, and carrying out measures against terrorists therefore tend to be matters of politics rather than matters of international law. Moreover, it is difficult to enforce any sanctions against terrorist groups operating abroad and headquartered in foreign territory without violating sovereignty and risking war. Hence, international cooperation beyond the problem of airline hijacking has been limited to governments of like mind in Western Europe, Japan, Israel, and North America. The recent invention of the term "Euroterrorism" suggests recognition by European governments that the problem of terrorism is a mutual one that merits the increased cooperation seen, for example, in the apprehension of West German terrorists in the Netherlands, Switzerland, the United Kingdom, Yugoslavia, and Bulgaria.

Although no terrorists have achieved their stated long-range goals, the use of terrorist tactics probably will persist as a mode of political expression, of gaining international attention, and of achieving limited political goals. Terrorists will remain mobile, able to strike targets throughout the world. And they appear to be getting more sophisticated. Some of the new weapons being developed for military arsenals, such as shoulder-fired, surface-to-air missiles, are finding their way into terrorists' hands. Terrorist groups appear to be strengthening their links. From these links, multinational terrorist teams have emerged. There also is the potential for nations to employ terrorist groups to wage surrogate warfare against their opponents. Finally, there is the possibility that terrorists may resort to weapons of mass destruction.

Because of the vulnerabilities of modern industrialized society, the increasing capacities for violence afforded by new developments in weaponry, and the demonstrated use of terrorist tactics for achieving limited goals, the power to publicize, to disrupt, to alarm, and to coerce is descending to smaller and smaller groups. Bands of irreconcilables and fanatics, which have always existed, are emerging as an increasingly potent force.

PHOTOS UPI

ALDO MORO
(1916–1978)

Aldo Moro was found dead in a car trunk in Via Michaelangelo, Rome, May 9. The former prime minister of Italy had been kidnapped by terrorists, March 16. Italian police, searching for Moro and later for his murderers, set up roadblocks throughout the nation. Italians, shocked by Moro's death, signed official books of mourning. Although, as Brian Jenkins of the Rand Corporation points out, the crime cannot be classified as an incident of international terrorism, it added "to the overall volume of political violence" so prevalent today.

STATE FAIR OF TEXAS

The State Fair of Texas, held annually in Dallas, drew some 3.1 million visitors in 1978.

STATE AND COUNTY FAIRS

The Revival of an Old American Institution

By Lila Perl
Author,
*America Goes
to the Fair*

State and county fairs are among America's best-loved institutions. A blend of nostalgic lure and modern entertainment, they appeal to people of all ages. After a leveling-off in attendance during the mid-1970's, over 150 million men, women, and children visited major fairs in the United States and Canada in 1978, according to the International Association of Fairs and Expositions.

The rising attendance figures since 1976 are indeed a tribute to the intrinsic value of the fair itself and to the responsiveness of administrators in modernizing and streamlining this old American institution. Personal appearances by performers widely known through television and recordings have unquestionably been the top drawing cards. In 1978, entertainers such as Frank Sinatra, Bob Hope, Bill Cosby, Roy Clark, Dolly Parton, and Charley Pride played to capacity crowds at major fairs.

WESTERN WASHINGTON FAIR

Agricultural events, including cattle judging, remain particularly popular at fairs across the United States.

INDIANA STATE FAIR PHOTO

Horse pulling contests are a regular attraction at many state fairs, including Indiana's (left). A young boy participates in the sheep shearing event at the Big "E," West Springfield, Mass.

EASTERN STATES EXPOSITION

FLORIDA STATE FAIR

A large crowd enjoys an antique auto show at the Florida State Fair, Tampa.

Other magnetizing entertainment events included a wide variety of breath-stopping amusement rides and a broad range of spectator thrills, such as rodeos, horse races, demolition derbies, stunt driving, stock car races, motorcycle feats, and aerial acrobatic acts. Improvements in parking and camping facilities, restrooms, fairground transportation, and food and beverage quality also helped draw more visitors.

Traditional fair activities that remained popular in 1978 were such agricultural events as livestock-judging, ox and tractor pulls, farm product and machinery displays; arts, crafts, and homemaking competitions; youth, vocational, and community-interest features; midway games of chance and sideshow attractions; and special exhibits dealing with such timely subjects as drug abuse, energy conservation, and preservation of the environment.

The American past was vividly recalled through reconstructed villages and farmhouses, with working craftsmen and displays of memorabilia. The heritage of American Indian groups was portrayed through ceremonial dances, arts, and implements. Many larger fairs featured international bazaars and exhibits. Among the exhibits celebrating America's varied ethnics groups, the Puerto Rican pavilion at the Eastern States Exposition

PHOTOS NORTH CAROLINA STATE FAIR

**NORTH CAROLINA
STATE FAIR**

1st prize culinary division

1st prize home furnishings
division

Native Indian dancing is a
special treat at the New
Mexico State Fair, Albu-
querque.

NEW MEXICO STATE FAIR

in West Springfield, Mass., was a first for 1978. Presented by the Commonwealth of Puerto Rico, this pavilion featured folkloric music and dance, and the display and sale of island crafts, exotic plants, and food products.

National farm and youth organizations are enthusiastic participants at state and county fairs. The oldest of these is the Grange, a fraternal order founded in 1867 to provide educational, recreational, and legislative services for farm families. Chapters of the 4-H Club and Future Farmers of America sponsored hobby- and career-oriented programs for young people attending the fairs. And to keep the interest of the young at a high pitch, the fairs scheduled bubblegum, baton-twirling, gymnastics, and skateboarding contests, as well as circus acts, marionette shows, and, for the youngest fairgoers, petting zoos.

In 1978 there were 38 state fairs and 2,350 county fairs in the United States. Most fairs were held in August, September, and October, with the major ones lasting an average of ten days. The largest, with about 3.1 million visitors, was the 17-day State Fair of Texas at Dallas. The largest fair in North America, however, was the Canadian National Exhibition at Toronto, which attracted over 3.5 million visitors. The Ohio State Fair at Columbus boasted more than 2.6 million, and four other fairs recorded gates of roughly 1.3 million: the Indiana State Fair at Indianapolis, the Tulsa State Fair, the State Fair of Oklahoma at Oklahoma City, and the Minnesota State Fair at St. Paul. The largest county fair was the Los Angeles County Fair at Pomona, with well over 1.2 million visitors.

State and county fairs originated in the first half of the 19th century as an outgrowth of the European-style market fairs of the pre-revolutionary United States. Elkanah Watson, a gentleman farmer from Pittsfield, Mass., is credited with running the first agricultural-display fair in the United States. In 1807 he exhibited prize Merino sheep to the neighboring farmers of Berkshire County. Within a few years, the Berkshire County Fair was featuring livestock, produce, cookery, and needlework competitions, and offering prize money to the winners. The market or trade fair of the past, a buying and selling event, had been transformed into an annual exhibition and competition designed to improve, expand, and glorify American farming. The first statewide fair, patterned after the Berkshire event, was the New York State Fair held at Syracuse in 1841.

Despite a predominantly urban population in the United States today, fairgoers are about evenly divided between city and rural residents. The fairs are well publicized in large population centers, and they present a variety of attractions to young people, families, and senior citizens. In addition, they provide a generally wholesome atmosphere at prices that are relatively low compared to other leisure-time offerings.

The enduring and increasing popularity of state, county, and local fairs in the United States and Canada in the late 1970's is undeniably linked to the opportunity they offer for participatory experiences. As opposed to movies, television, radio, and recordings, fairs offer live action and first-hand thrills. The joy of seeing a chick hatched or a cow milked, the excitement of a ride on the Twister or the Cyclone, or the warm satisfaction of winning first prize for a pet animal or a patchwork quilt—these are the principal attractions of the American fair. Good fairs go beyond entertainment and diversion; they also inform and often inspire. In their broadest sense, the state and county fairs of today are communication centers, preserving the best of the American past, yet flexible and responsive in reflecting the changing world around us.

UPI

The United States Liaison Office in Peking is carefully guarded. Following a United States-Chinese agreement establishing diplomatic relations, announced in mid-December 1978, a full-scale U. S. embassy was to open in Peking on March 1, 1979.

CHRONOLOGY 1978

PHOTOS UPI

U. S. President Jimmy Carter delivers his first State of the Union Message to Congress, as Vice President Walter Mondale, *left*, and Speaker of the House Thomas O'Neill look on. Budget Director James McIntyre (right) displays documents from the $500.2 billion U. S. budget for fiscal 1979.

JANUARY

1 Chile's President Augusto Pinochet wins an overwhelming vote of confidence in the nation's first popular elections in nearly five years.

6 With a feeling of pride in "the friendship we received and the friendship we left behind," U. S. President Jimmy Carter returns to Washington from a nine-day trip to Europe, India, and the Middle East.
The crown of St. Stephen is officially returned to Hungary by U. S. Secretary of State Cyrus Vance.

11 The United States announces a 6.4% unemployment rate for December 1977, the lowest in three years.
India's former Prime Minister Indira Gandhi is ordered to stand trial for contempt, after refusing to testify before a judicial commission investigating her government's rule.
Two Soviet cosmonauts dock their Soyuz 27 spacecraft with an orbiting space station and join two comrades who entered Salyut 6 on Dec. 11, 1977.
Rioting erupts in Nicaragua following the murder of a prominent newspaper editor and antigovernment leader.

12 British firemen vote to end their two-month strike.

13 The United States and Japan reach a trade agreement intended to "achieve basic equity" in trade relations between the two nations.

15 The body of Sen. Hubert H. Humphrey, who died of cancer January 13, lies in state in the Capitol Rotunda.
The Dallas Cowboys defeat the Denver Broncos, 27–10, to win the National Football League Super Bowl game.

16 The National Aeronautics and Space Administration selects 35 new astronauts for the space shuttle program; the group includes six women, three blacks, and one person of Oriental descent.

17 The Turkish government of Prime Minister Bulent Ecevit wins a vote of confidence in the National Assembly.

18 Egyptian President Anwar el-Sadat abruptly recalls his peace delegation from negotiations with Israel in Jerusalem.

19 U. S. President Carter delivers his first State of the Union Message.

20 David Marston (R), U. S. attorney in Philadelphia who is credited with successful prosecutions of Democratic politicians, is dismissed by U. S. Attorney General Griffin Bell.
President Carter delivers to Congress the U. S. budget for fiscal 1979. Receipts and outlays are estimated at $440 billion and $500 billion, respectively.

24 Soviet reconnaissance satellite with a nuclear reactor aboard breaks up over Canada's Northwest Territories; the search for radioactive debris begins.

30 The largest trade deficit in the history of the United States, $26.7 billion, is reported for 1977.
Francis Fox, solicitor-general of Canada, resigns after it is disclosed that he illegally obtained an abortion for a woman with whom he had a "brief liaison."

PHOTOS UPI

The northeastern states were brought to a stand-still for more than three days in early February by up to 50 inches (127 cm) of snow. An estimated 5,000 cars were abandoned by drivers in the Providence, R. I., area (above).

3 Following the resignation of West German Defense Minister Georg Leber, Chancellor Helmut Schmidt reshuffles his cabinet.
The government of Sri Lanka shifts to a presidential system; Prime Minister Junius Richard Jayewardene is inaugurated as the first president.
Vietnam's ambassador to the United Nations, Dinh Ba Thi, is ordered to leave the United States because of his alleged complicity in an espionage case.

5 Rodrigo Carazo Odio, the leader of a four-party coalition, is elected president of Costa Rica.

6 The New England area of the United States is paralyzed by the worst snowstorm in its history.

8 Austria's Chancellor Bruno Kreisky and Soviet officials conclude two days of trade talks in Moscow.

9 William H. Webster, a 53-year-old U. S. Appeals Court judge from St. Louis, is confirmed by voice vote of the U. S. Senate for a ten-year term as director of the Federal Bureau of Investigation.
Canada accuses 13 Soviet diplomats of trying to infiltrate the security system of the Royal Canadian Mounted Police.

12 South Africa breaks the color line by naming a tennis player of mixed race, Peter Lamb, to its Davis Cup team.
Alfredo Stroessner, president of Paraguay since 1954, wins a landslide election victory for another five-year term.

15 Muhammad Ali loses a split decision to Leon Spinks and is dethroned as the world heavyweight boxing champion.
A bomb explodes in the Alaskan oil pipeline, and thousands of barrels of oil spill across the tundra.
Canada's Prime Minister Pierre Elliott Trudeau and the premiers of the nation's ten provinces conclude an economic conference in Ottawa

16 After almost a year of negotiations, China and a group of private Japanese industrialists sign an eight-year, $20-billion trade agreement.
The leaders of 12 Asian and Pacific Commonwealth nations conclude a four-day meeting in Sydney, Australia, during which "regional questions and wider international issues" were discussed.

18 Six persons are killed and 125 injured in antigovernment riots in Tabriz, Iran.

19 Egyptian commandos land at Larnaca Airport in Cyprus in an attempt to rescue a Cypriot jetliner hijacked by Palestinian terrorists who had murdered the editor of an influential Egyptian newspaper. Cypriot National Guardsmen intercept the Egyptians, killing 15 commandos. After a one-hour battle, the Palestinian hijackers free their captives and surrender.

23 The U. S. dollar reaches a record low against the Swiss franc and West German mark; sharp declines against the British pound, French franc, and Japanese yen continue.

25 Legislative elections are held in five southern states of India; the Congress Party of former Prime Minister Indira Gandhi wins control of two of the states.

FEBRUARY

PHOTOS UPI

Palestinian guerrillas (left) in Tyre, Lebanon, stand guard as French units of the United Nations peace-keeping force move into position in the southern, coastal region of the country. (Right): Israeli Defense Minister Ezer Weizman, *extreme right*, briefs Prime Minister Menahem Begin, March 15, on Israel's reprisal campaign against Palestinian guerrillas in southern Lebanon.

MARCH

3 Prime Minister Ian Smith and three black nationalist leaders sign an agreement providing for black-majority rule in Rhodesia by the end of the year.
The U. S. Senate confirms the appointment of G. William Miller as chairman of the Federal Reserve Board.

5 After reappointing Hua Kuo-feng as premier, adopting a new constitution, and establishing a ten-year economic plan, the fifth session of China's National People's Congress concludes.

9 After eight months of fighting, Somalia agrees to withdraw its forces from the Ogaden region of Ethiopia.

11 Palestinian terrorists seize an Israeli bus near Haifa and race toward Tel Aviv. During an exchange of gunfire with police, the bus bursts into flames and 37 civilians are killed.
In Italy, Giulio Andreotti forms a new coalition with parliamentary support from the Communist Party.

13 The Guatemalan Congress declares Romeo Lucas Garcia president-elect, after it is realized that no candidate received more than 50% of the vote in the presidential election held on March 5.

14 Israel launches a major invasion of southern Lebanon to wipe out Palestinian terrorist bases.
A special team of 60 Dutch marines storms a local government building in Assen, the Netherlands, and frees 70 hostages held by South Moluccan terrorists.

16 The U. S. Senate ratifies the Treaty Concerning the Permanent Neutrality and Operation of the Panama Canal.
Aldo Moro, former prime minister of Italy, is kidnapped in Rome.

17 The Amoco Cadiz, an American-owned supertanker, runs aground and breaks up near Brest, France, spilling a record amount of oil along the shoreline.
Soyuz 27, with cosmonauts Lt. Col. Yuri Romanenko and Georgi Grechko aboard, returns to earth following a record 96 days in space.

19 In France, pro-government parties win 291 seats and the left-wing opposition gains 200 seats in the final round of legislative elections.

22 A 4,000-man UN peacekeeping force enters southern Lebanon.

24 Rank and file members of the United Mine Workers ratify the third contract offer by the Bituminous Coal Operators Association, bringing to an end the longest miners' strike in U. S. history.

26 Baron Edouard-Jean Empain, the Belgian industrialist who was kidnapped on Jan. 23, 1978, is released outside Paris.

27 Chief Clemens Kapuuo, a principal black nationalist leader in South-West Africa, is killed.

28 The Japanese government postpones the opening of Tokyo's new international airport, following demonstrations against the facility.

PHOTOS UPI

(Right): Senators Dennis DeConcini (D-Ariz.), *left*, and Frank Church (D-Idaho) confer at the Capitol during Senate debate on the second Panama Canal treaty. (Left): Panama's Chief of Government Gen. Omar Torrijos holds a press conference April 18 after learning of the treaty's ratification by the U. S. Senate.

3 President Carter concludes a tour of four African and Latin American nations—Venezuela, Brazil, Nigeria, and Liberia.

Tongsun Park, a Korean businessman and a principal figure in a U. S. Congressional scandal, begins public testimony before the U. S. House of Representatives' Committee on Standards of Official Conduct.

China and the European Community sign a five-year trade agreement.

5 President Carter names U. S. Air Force Gen. David C. Jones to succeed Gen. George S. Brown as chairman of the Joint Chiefs of Staff.

6 President Carter signs into law a bill raising the legal mandatory retirement age for most employees to 70.

8 Heads of state of the European Community conclude their annual meeting in Copenhagen, Denmark.

9 Antigovernment demonstrations occur in Manila following the first parliamentary elections in the Philippines since martial law was imposed in 1972.

A coup attempt by Army officers in Somalia is put down by loyalist forces.

Gary Player wins the Masters Golf Tournament in Augusta, Ga.

10 L. Patrick Gray, former acting director of the Federal Bureau of Investigation, and two former FBI officials are indicted by a federal grand jury on charges of approving a plan involving illegal break-ins and searches.

Canada's Finance Minister Jean Chrétien introduces the federal budget for fiscal 1979, projecting a C$11.5 billion deficit.

14 A total of 52.58 million shares of stock is sold as the New York Stock Exchange records the heaviest day of trading in its history.

17 Bill Rogers, a 30-year-old runner from Melrose, Mass., wins the 82d Boston Marathon.

18 The U. S. Senate ratifies a second Panama Canal treaty, which will turn the waterway over to Panama on Dec. 31, 1999.

Rumania's President Nicolae Ceauşescu concludes a seven-day state visit to the United States.

20 A South Korean airliner en route from Paris to Seoul crosses into Soviet territory. A Soviet jet fires on the plane, causing it to crash on a frozen lake. Two of the 110 passengers are killed and 13 are injured.

France's National Assembly gives the cabinet of Premier Raymond Barre, named on April 5, a vote of confidence.

21 Paintings valued at more than $1 million, including the Rubens masterpiece, "The Three Graces," are stolen from the Pitti Palace museum in Florence, Italy.

26 Arkady Shevchenko, 47-year-old Soviet diplomat, announces that he has resigned as UN undersecretary general for political and Security Council affairs and has asked for asylum in the United States.

30 Afghanistan's Armed Forces Revolutionary Council names Nur Mohammed Taraki prime minister. (President Mohammed Daud Khan was overthrown by insurgents during heavy fighting on April 27.)

APRIL

Tourists relax in a Rome café May 10, a day after former Prime Minister Aldo Moro is found slain. Posters behind them read: "Aldo Moro has been assassinated. His faith in liberty lives in our hearts."

MAY

1 Sun Day is observed across the United States in support of the use of solar energy.

4 In a speech before the Los Angeles County Bar Association, President Carter asserts that the American people are "overlawyered and under-represented."
South African troops enter Angola and attack bases on the South-West Africa People's Organization, the guerrilla force fighting for control of Namibia (South-West Africa).

9 Former Italian Prime Minister Aldo Moro is found murdered in the center of Rome.

10 China's Premier Hua Kuo-feng ends a five-day visit to North Korea.

11 Secessionist guerrillas invade Zaire's southern Shaba Province.
China accuses Soviet forces of crossing the Sino-Soviet border and shooting several Chinese citizens on May 9.

15 The U. S. Senate approves the Carter administration's plan to sell fighter aircraft to Saudi Arabia, Egypt, and Israel.

16 The government of Ethiopia launches a major attack against secessionist guerrillas in Eritrea Province.

17 The body of Charlie Chaplin, stolen March 2 from its grave in Corsier-sur-Vevey, Switzerland, is recovered.

18 Belgian and French troops are flown to Zaire to help rescue more than 2,500 Europeans trapped in that country by recent fighting.
Yuri F. Orlov, a Russian physicist, is sentenced to 5 years in prison and 7 years in exile for "anti-Soviet agitation."
The Italian Parliament gives final approval to a bill permitting abortion on demand for any woman over the age of 18.

19 The seventh session of the UN Law of the Sea Conference ends in Geneva.
The U. S. Postal Service Board of Governors approves a new rate package, including an increase in the cost of first-class mail.

20 In Peru, a wave of looting and rioting provoked by a series of price increases leads President Francisco Morales Bermudez to declare a state of emergency.
Chiang Ching-kuo is sworn in as president of Nationalist China.

21 Egyptian voters approve President Anwar el-Sadat's plan to curb government opposition.

25 The Montréal Canadiens capture the National Hockey League Stanley Cup for the third consecutive year.

26 In the Dominican Republic, Antonio Guzmán of the opposition Dominican Revolutionary Party is declared the winner of the presidential election. (Vote counting had been interrupted May 16 by army forces who feared that the incumbent, Joaquín Balaguer, would lose.)
Legalized casino gambling officially begins in Atlantic City, N. J.

31 Representatives of the 15-member North Atlantic Treaty Organization adopt a mutual long-term defense program, bringing to a close a two-day summit conference in Washington, D. C.

PHOTOS UPI

Allan P. Bakke (left) takes a break from his engineering job June 28 after hearing of the Supreme Court ruling that he must be admitted to the University of California Medical College at Davis. Despite a concurrent ruling that race may be considered in the selection process, a group of San Franciscans lodged an emotional demonstration against the decision.

1 A U. S. official reveals that electronic monitoring devices have been discovered in the U. S. Embassy building in Moscow.

4 In Bangladesh, Maj. Gen. Ziaur Rahman wins the first presidential election since he took over the government in November 1975.

5 It is reported in Hong Kong that China has released 110,000 political prisoners held since an "anti-rightist" campaign in 1957.
Julio César Turbay Ayala is declared the winner of Colombia's June 4 presidential election.

6 In California, Proposition 13, a voter initiative which would cut property taxes by 57%, is approved by the electorate by a 65–35% margin.

7 The Washington Bullets defeat the Seattle Supersonics four games to three to win the National Basketball Association championship.

10 Affirmed, with Steve Cauthen up, wins the Belmont Stakes and horse racing's Triple Crown.

11 Joseph Freeman, Jr., becomes the first black priest in the Church of Jesus Christ of Latter-day Saints, two days after Mormon church officials struck down their 148-year-old policy of excluding blacks from the priesthood.

JUNE

12 Prime Minister Pierre Trudeau introduces to the Canadian Parliament his proposal for a new constitution.

13 Israel withdraws the last of its invasion forces from southern Lebanon, turning over the 6-mile (9-km) deep strip along the border to Lebanese Christian militia units.

15 King Hussein of Jordan marries Elizabeth Halaby, a 26-year-old American, and proclaims her queen.

18 A new Constituent Assembly is elected in Peru as voters go to the polls for the first time since military rule was established in October 1968.

23 The United States recalls its ambassador to Chile in a dispute over the investigation of the 1976 murders of Orlando Letelier, former Chilean foreign minister, and his colleague, Ronnie Moffitt, in Washington, D. C.

25 Argentina, the host country, wins soccer's World Cup.

26 A bomb explodes in the Palace of Versailles outside Paris, France; three ground-floor rooms, containing valuable Napoleonic art work, are destroyed.
South Yemen's President Salem Rubaya Ali is deposed and executed following several hours of heavy fighting. (The unrest occurred following the June 24 assassination of Yemen's President Ahmed Hussein al-Ghashmi.)

28 The U. S. Supreme Court upholds a lower court order requiring the University of California Medical School to admit Allan P. Bakke, a 38-year-old white engineer who charged that the school's minority-admission program had made him a victim of "reverse discrimination." At the same time, the court rules that race may be a factor in selecting college applicants for admission.

Jewish protesters, *right*, march to the Soviet Union's Embassy in London July 9 to protest the impending trial of Anatoly Shcharansky and other Soviet human rights activists. Mrs. Natalya Shcharansky, wife of the dissident mathematician, holds her head at a press conference July 14 after learning that her husband had been sentenced to 13 years in prison.

JULY

1 Fighting erupts in and around Beirut, Lebanon, between Arab peace-keeping forces and Christian militia groups; at least 200 persons are killed and 500 wounded.

3 China announces the end of all economic aid to Vietnam, reportedly in response to Vietnam's June 29 admission into Comecon, the Soviet-bloc economic alliance.

5 Gen. Ignatius Kutu Acheampong resigns as Ghana's head of state and is succeeded by his deputy on the ruling military council, Lt. Gen. Fred W. K. Akuffo.

7 The Solomon Islands gain independence from Britain.

8 Björn Borg wins his third consecutive men's singles tennis title at Wimbledon. Earlier Martina Navratilova had captured the women's crown.

9 The Israeli Cabinet officially rejects an Egyptian peace proposal calling for Israel's withdrawal from the Gaza Strip and the West Bank.
Sandro Petrini, an 81-year-old Socialist, is inaugurated as the president of Italy.
Some 100,000 demonstrators march on Washington, D. C., to support a deadline extension for ratification of the Equal Rights Amendment (ERA).

10 President Moktar Ould Daddah of Mauritania is arrested in a bloodless coup led by the army chief of staff Col. Mustapha Ould Salek.

13 In Geneva, Switzerland, U. S. Secretary of State Cyrus Vance and Soviet Foreign Minister Andrei Gromyko fail to resolve differences over a new strategic arms limitation treaty.

14 Anatoly B. Shcharansky, a leader of the Jewish emigration movement in the Soviet Union and an alleged spy for the U. S. Central Intelligence Agency, is sentenced to 13 years in Soviet prison and labor camps. (Alexsandr Ginzburg, a Jewish human rights activist, was sentenced by a Soviet court to eight years' imprisonment July 13.)

17 At their fourth annual economic summit conference in Bonn, West Germany, the leaders of the seven largest industrial democracies agree on measures to minimize world unemployment "without rekindling inflation."

18 Two American correspondents in Moscow, Craig R. Whitney of *The New York Times* and Harold D. Piper of *The Baltimore Sun,* are found guilty of libel by a Soviet Court.

21 President Hugo Banzer Suárez of Bolivia resigns in the face of a rebellion led by Gen. Juan Pereda Asbún, whose election as president July 9 was annulled.

24 For the first time since World War II, the exchange rate for the U. S. dollar falls below the 200 yen level in Japan.

25 A 5 lb.-12 oz. (2.64 kilo.) baby girl, grown from an egg fertilized in a laboratory, is born in Lancashire, England. It is the first authenticated case of a "test tube baby."

27 Portuguese Prime Minister Mário Soares is dismissed by President António Ramalho Eanes, dissolving a six-month-old Socialist government.

31 An Arab gunman storms the Iraqi Embassy in Paris, France, and takes several hostages. After his surrender, Iraqi security officials open fire on him, but also kill a French police inspector.

PHOTOS UPI

In the wake of a press-men's strike that shut down New York City's three major daily news-papers—*The New York Times, New York Daily News,* and *New York Post* —a host of interim papers appeared on city stands. The pressmen's walkout began August 9.

1 In his first nationwide address in two years, Canadian Prime Minister Pierre Elliott Trudeau announces new, immediate government measures to stimulate the economy. Baseball's Pete Rose goes hitless in a game against the Atlanta Braves, bringing to an end his 44-consecutive-game hitting streak.

3 Terrorists believed to be linked to Iraq invade the Paris, France, office of the Palestine Liberation Organization and kill a chief PLO representative and an aide.

4 Representatives of the five-member Association of Southeast Asian Nations (ASEAN) and U. S. officials conclude two days of economic talks in Washington, D. C.

7 In a bloodless military coup d'etat, President Juan Alberto Melgar Castro of Honduras is overthrown.

8 President Carter signs into law a bill giving (U. S.) $1.65 billion in federal long-term loan guarantees to New York City.

10 The 10 provincial premiers of Canada unanimously reject Prime Minister Trudeau's proposal for a new national constitution.

12 The foreign ministers of China and Japan sign a 10-year treaty of peace and friendship in Peking.

15 Australia's Treasurer John Howard introduces to Parliament an (A.) $28.87 billion (U. S. $33.49 billion) budget for 1978–79.

16 Communist China's Chairman Hua Kuo-feng begins official visit to Rumania.

17 Three American businessmen complete the first transatlantic crossing in a balloon, as they land in Miserey, France.

20 As antigovernment riots erupt throughout Iran, a fire in a movie theater in Abadan, allegedly started by Muslim extremists, kills 430 people.
An El Al Israel Airlines crew bus is attacked by Palestinian terrorists in London, killing a stewardess and wounding nine others.

22 President Jomo Kenyatta, the leader of Kenya's struggle for independence, dies in Mombasa at the age of 83.
Antigovernment rioting sweeps Nicaragua, as 25 guerrillas of the Sandinista Liberation Front invade the National Palace in Managua. Threatening to execute hundreds of hostages, the guerrillas secure a cash ransom, the release of 59 political prisoners, and safe passage to Panama.
The U. S. Congress completes action on a constitutional amendment granting the District of Columbia full voting representation in Congress. The amendment now goes to the states for ratification.

26 During its first day of balloting, the Sacred College of Cardinals in the Vatican elects Albino Luciani, 65, the 263d Pope of the Roman Catholic Church; Luciani selects the papal name of John Paul I. (Pope Paul VI had died of a heart attack on August 6.)

28 Alfredo Nobre da Costa, a politically independent technocrat chosen by President Antonio Ramalho Eanes, is sworn in as the premier of Portugal after the major political parties failed to agree on a governing coalition.

AUGUST

UPI

Egypt's President Anwar el-Sadat, U.S. President Carter, and Israel's Prime Minister Menahem Begin sign Middle East peace accords at the White House.

SEPTEMBER

5 Joshua Nkomo, a leader of the black nationalist Patriotic Front in Rhodesia, announces that his guerrilla forces were responsible for shooting down a civilian passenger plane with 56 persons aboard.

U. S. Rep. Daniel J. Flood (D-Pa.) is indicted by a federal grand jury in Los Angeles on charges of lying about political payoffs he allegedly received.

7 British Prime Minister James Callaghan announces that the general elections expected for the fall will be postponed.

A Moscow city court convicts American businessman Francis J. Crawford of black market dealings and gives him a suspended 5-year sentence.

8 Iranian Army troops fire submachine guns into crowds of political and religious demonstrators in Tehran. Hours earlier, Shah Mohammed Reza Pahlavi declared martial law in the capital and 11 other cities to control growing civil disorders.

10 Prime Minister Ian Smith imposes martial law in parts of Rhodesia and announces a crackdown on black nationalist guerrilla groups.

At the new National Tennis Center in Flushing, N. Y., Chris Evert wins her fourth consecutive U. S. Open women's championship by defeating 16-year-old Pam Shriver. Jimmy Connors defeats Björn Borg for the men's title.

11 The value of the Canadian dollar falls to 85.94 U. S. cents, the lowest in 45 years.

15 Nicaraguan troops begin heavy rocket and strafing attacks on the rebel-occupied city of León. Leftist guerrillas of the Sandinista Liberation Front had stepped up attacks on Sept. 9.

Muhammad Ali wins a unanimous decision over World Boxing Association heavyweight champion Leon Spinks in New Orleans, La.

17 Egyptian President Anwar el-Sadat, Israeli Premier Menahem Begin, and U. S. President Jimmy Carter sign the "Framework of Peace in the Middle East" and the "Framework for the Conclusion of a Peace Treaty Between Egypt and Israel." The agreements climax 11 days of secluded, U. S.-sponsored talks at Camp David, Md., and set in motion negotiations between Egypt and Israel for a formal peace treaty by the end of 1978.

19 The 33rd session of the UN General Assembly convenes.

20 South Africa rejects a UN plan for establishing an independent Namibia.

25 At least 150 persons are killed as a Pacific Southwest Airlines jetliner collides with a small, single-engine plane above San Diego, Calif.

26 China breaks off talks with Vietnam a day after Hanoi charged Peking with deploying masses of heavily armed troops near its border.

28 South Africa's ruling National party elects Pieter Willem Botha to succeed John Vorster as prime minister. Vorster had resigned for reasons of health.

29 Pope John Paul I dies of a heart attack after only 33 days as pontiff.

Complying with a federal court order and President Carter's back-to-work directive, striking railway clerks end their 4-day walkout against 43 railroad lines across the United States.

UPI

6 The U. S. Senate approves a three-year extension of the ratification deadline for the Equal Rights Amendment (ERA).

7 Syria declares a unilateral cease-fire in and around Beirut, Lebanon, after a week of fierce fighting with Christian militia forces. The decision comes a day after the UN Security Council endorsed a call for peace by the United States.

U. S. Rep. Charles C. Diggs, Jr. (D-Mich.), the senior black member of Congress, is convicted of mail fraud and of illegally directing employee funds to his own use.

10 Belgian Prime Minister Leo Tindemans and his coalition government resign in a dispute over the proposed transformation of Belgium into a federated state.

The White House announces the resignation of Paul C. Warnke as director of the Arms Control and Disarmament Agency.

11 Aristides Royo is elected and inaugurated as the president of Panama, although Brig. Gen. Omar Torrijos, as commander of the army, retains control of the government.

13 President Carter signs into law the Civil Service Reform Bill, the first major revision of the U. S. Civil Service system since its establishment in 1883.

Ola Ullsten, the leader of Sweden's minority Liberal party, becomes prime minister, eight days after Thorbjörn Fälldin submitted his resignation in a dispute over nuclear power policy.

14 Daniel arap Moi, who served as Jomo Kenyatta's vice president for 11 years, is sworn in as the president of Kenya four days after his election.

After completing action on energy and tax-cut legislation, the 95th Congress adjourns.

15 Gen. João Baptista da Oliveira Figueiredo is elected president of Brazil. He is to take office March 15, 1979.

16 Karol Cardinal Wojtyla, the 58-year-old archbishop of Krakow, Poland, is elected the first non-Italian Pope of the Roman Catholic Church in 456 years. He takes the name of John Paul II.

Canada's majority Liberal party suffers a severe setback in parliamentary by-elections, losing 13 of 15 vacated seats.

17 The New York Yankees capture their second consecutive world championship of baseball by defeating the Los Angeles Dodgers in the sixth game of the 75th World Series.

World chess champion Anatoly Karpov of the Soviet Union retains his title as challenger Viktor Korchnoi resigns in the 32nd game of their championship match at Baguio, The Philippines.

24 Contempt of court citations against *The New York Times* and reporter Myron Farber for withholding evidence in the Bergen County, N. J., murder trial of Dr. Mario E. Jascalevich are suspended when Jascalevich is acquitted.

25 President Carter appoints Alfred Kahn, chairman of the U. S. Civil Aeronautics Board (CAB), to replace Robert Strauss as the leader of the administration's anti-inflation effort. The selection comes a day after Carter announced to the nation voluntary wage and price guidelines to reduce U. S. inflation to 6–6.5% in 1979.

Carlos Alberto Mota Pinto is appointed prime minister of Portugal by President Antonio Ramalho Eanes.

A walkout by Canada's 23,000 indoor postal workers ends on its tenth day.

For the second time in a little more than a month cardinals of the Roman Catholic Church prepare to elect a new pontiff.

OCTOBER

UPI

KEN HEYMAN

The United States suffered the loss of a favorite artist and a famed cultural anthropologist in November. Artist Norman Rockwell and anthropologist Margaret Mead died November 8 and 15 respectively.

NOVEMBER

1 President Carter announces a series of emergency measures to bolster the U. S. dollar. The announcement has an immediate positive effect, as the dollar rises sharply on world money markets and the Dow Jones Industrial Average records the biggest one-day gain in its history.

Uganda announces that it has occupied and annexed 700 square miles (1,820 km²) of Tanzanian territory, following a series of border clashes.

2 The Caribbean island of Dominica gains full independence from Great Britain.

Soviet cosmonauts Vladimir Kovalenok and Alexander Ivanchekov return safely to earth after establishing a new space endurance record of 139 days and 15 hours.

3 Vietnam and the Soviet Union sign a 25-year treaty of friendship and cooperation.

5 The Arab League concludes a four-day summit conference in Baghdad, Iraq, with a communiqué calling for Egypt not to sign a separate peace treaty with Israel.

Former Prime Minister Indira Gandhi makes a political comeback as she wins election to India's lower house of parliament.

6 Shah Mohammed Reza Pahlavi puts Iran under military rule one day after the resignation of Premier Jaffa Shafir Emami and his civilian cabinet. In making the announcement, the shah also promises "to make up for past mistakes, to fight corruption and injustice, and to form a national government to carry out free elections."

The New York Times and the *New York Daily News* return to the stands, following an 88-day shutdown by striking unions.

7 In U. S. midterm elections, the Republican Party makes solid gains, but the Democrats retain strong majorities in Congress and among state governors.

13 The government of Mexico announces the discovery of a new oil basin with possible reserves of 100 million barrels.

17 The Danish parliament ratifies legislation which would grant home rule to Greenland, pending a local referendum.

18 U. S. Rep. Leo J. Ryan (D-Calif.) and four members of his party are shot to death at an airport near Jonestown, Guyana, by members of the Peoples Temple, a California-based religious cult led by the Rev. Jim Jones. Shortly thereafter, more than 900 members of the jungle colony commit suicide at Jones' summoning.

20 Wall posters critical of the late Communist party chairman Mao Tse-tung and current Premier Hua Kuo-feng appear in Peking and other Chinese cities. The poster campaign apparently had the approval of Deputy Premier Teng Shiao-ping.

23 UNESCO approves a declaration on freedom of the worldwide press.

24 After only four months in office, Bolivian President Juan Pereda Asbun is ousted in a bloodless coup led by army commander Gen. David Padilla Arancibia.

27 Premier Takeo Fukuda of Japan loses the first round of elections for the presidency of his ruling Liberal Democratic party. He withdraws his candidacy, assuring LDP Secretary General Masayoshi Ohira of becoming the nation's next premier.

George Moscone, the mayor of San Francisco, and Harvey Milk, a city supervisor, are assassinated inside City Hall.

UPI

Tokyo, December 7: Members of Japan's lower house of Parliament applaud the nation's new prime minister, Masayoshi Ohira.

3 Luis Herrera Campíns is elected president of Venezuela.

4 At least 600 Vietnamese "boat people" are permitted to land in Malaysia as the government lifts its ban on admitting the refugees.
France and China conclude an agreement to increase trade and economic cooperation.

5 Afghanistan and the USSR sign a 20-year treaty of friendship and cooperation.
Leaders of the European Community approve plans for a new European monetary system.

6 Spanish voters overwhelmingly approve a new constitution establishing a parliamentary monarchy and full individual liberties.

7 Edward Schreyer is appointed the 22nd governor general of Canada.

8 Golda Meir, former prime minister of Israel, dies in Jerusalem at age 80.

9 Four probes of the Pioneer Venus II satellite enter the Venusian atmosphere and radio back to earth a wealth of photographs and scientific data.

15 President Carter announces that China and the United States have agreed to establish formal diplomatic relations on January 1. The United States will end diplomatic relations with Nationalist China and terminate its 1954 defense treaty.
Cleveland fails to repay $15.5 million in loans and becomes the first major U.S. city since the depression to default.

17 The 13-member Organization of Petroleum Exporting Countries (OPEC) announces a 14.5% increase in the price of crude oil by October 1, 1979.
Egypt and Israel fail to reach a peace agreement by the deadline specified in the Camp David accords. The two sides have not met since November 16.

19 The lower house of the Indian parliament expels former Prime Minister Indira Gandhi and orders her to prison on charges of contempt and breach of privilege.

23 U. S. Secretary of State Cyrus Vance and Soviet Foreign Minister Andrei Gromyko conclude three days of talks in Geneva on strategic arms limitation. Although no formal treaty is concluded, the two sides announce that they have reached agreement on "most" issues.

26 The Turkish government declares martial law in Istanbul and 12 other cities following three days of street fighting over political and religious issues.

27 Algerian President Houari Boumedienne dies in Algiers. Rabah Bitat, speaker of the National Popular Assembly, is proclaimed interim president.

29 After ongoing strikes virtually paralyze the Iranian economy, Shah Mohammed Reza Pahlavi names opposition leader Shahpur Bakhtiar to head a new, civilian government.
Spanish Prime Minister Adolfo Suárez dissolves parliament and calls for general elections on March 1.

30 At the end of its two-year inquiry, the House Select Committee on Assassinations reports that the murders of former President John F. Kennedy and Dr. Martin Luther King were likely the result of conspiracies.

DECEMBER

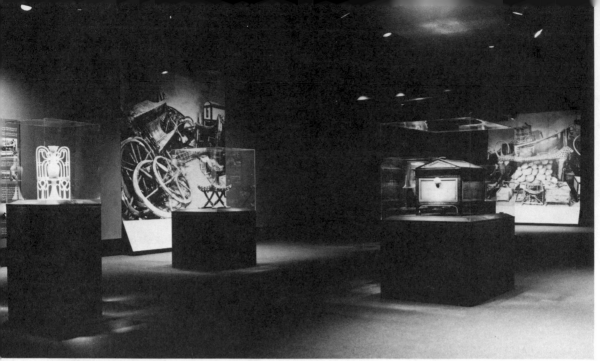

COURTESY, FIELD MUSEUM OF NATURAL HISTORY, CHICAGO

The "Treasures of Tutankhamen" drew record crowds. The magnetic exhibit of ancient Egyptian artifacts was ending a two-year tour of the United States with a December opening at the Metropolitan Museum of Art.

Australia's tallest building, featuring two revolving restaurants, convention facilities, and observation towers, was completed in Sydney.

Mickey Mouse of Walt Disney fame turned 50 in 1978. A television special and a White House party helped to mark the event.

PETER KELLY, AUSTRALIAN INFORMATION SERVICE

UPI

The board of directors of the New York Stock Exchange approved a mockup of a new, all-inclusive design for the stock trading floor. Large, easily visible video screens are featured.

UPI

REVIEW OF THE YEAR

UPI

The present and two former occupants of the Oval Office met briefly at a memorial service for Sen. Hubert Humphrey.

UPI

Vietnamese refugees prepare to go ashore to the Pulau Bidong Refugee Camp in Malaysia. It was a difficult year for those who sought escape from Indochina. Many drowned in tragic accidents at sea.

ACCIDENTS AND DISASTERS

AVIATION

Jan. 1—Minutes following takeoff from Bombay, an Air India Boeing 747 explodes in midair and crashes into the Arabian sea, killing 213 persons.

Jan. 24—Soviet reconnaisance satellite falls into earth's atmosphere and disintegrates in the Northwest Territories of Canada; radiation is detected from the debris.

Feb. 10—Thirty-one persons are killed on a commercial flight of a Uruguayan Air Force transport as it attempts an emergency landing at Artigas.

Feb. 11—A Pacific Western Airline jet overshoots the runway while attempting to land during a snowstorm at Cranbrook, British Columbia, Canada, killing 41 passengers.

March 3—A government-owned Venezuelan airliner crashes into the Caribbean shortly after takeoff from the Caracas airport, killing 47 persons.

March 16—A Bulgarian airliner on a flight from Sofia to Warsaw crashes shortly after takeoff, killing 66 passengers and 7 crew members.

March 25—Forty-eight persons are killed as a Burmese airliner explodes shortly after takeoff from Rangoon.

June 26—An Air Canada jet with 107 persons aboard goes off the end of the runway in Toronto and breaks into three sections, resulting in the death of three persons and the injury of 79.

Sept. 4—In Derry, Pa., a helicopter dropping prize numbers at a Labor Day St. Joseph's Catholic Church festival picnic crashes into the crowd, killing at least six persons.

Sept. 25—At least 150 persons are killed when a Pacific Southwest Airlines jetliner preparing to land at San Diego's Lindbergh Field collides with a Cessna plane.

Nov. 15—A chartered DC-8 owned by Icelandic Airlines and leased with a 13 man crew to Garuda Indonesian Airlines crashes outside the airport of Colombo, Sri Lanka; 202 of the 262 persons aboard are killed.

Nov. 19—An Indian air force transport plane crashes while landing at Leh airport in the northern state of Kashmir, killing 77 persons.

Dec. 23—An Alitalia jetliner lands in the Tyrrhenian Sea just short of its destination of Palermo, Sicily; at least 108 persons are believed dead.

Dec. 28—A United Airlines DC-8 airliner carrying 172 persons crash-lands near Portland (Ore.) International Airport, killing eight passengers and two crewmen.

EARTHQUAKES

Jan. 13—An earthquake registering 7 on the Richter scale hits the Izu peninsula, 80 miles (128 km) southwest of Tokyo; the death toll is 23.

June 12—An earthquake hits Japan's Honshu Island killing at least 21 persons and injuring 350.

June 20—An earthquake strikes Salonika, Greece, killing at least 47 persons and injuring 150.

Aug. 13—An earthquake hits Santa Barbara, Calif., and five coast counties causing widespread damage.

Sept. 16—An earthquake hits the community of Tabas in northeastern Iran, leveling the town and killing at least 15,000 persons. Another 10,000 lives are lost in 100 smaller villages in a radius of 60 miles (96 km).

FIRES AND EXPLOSIONS

Jan. 13—Severe drought in eastern Australia brings on brush fires which kill three persons and cause millions of dollars worth of damage.

Jan. 28—Sixteen persons die as Coates House hotel in Kansas City, Mo., is destroyed by fire.

June 10—Twenty people are killed and more than 55 are injured as a fire of unknown origin sweeps through a five-story hotel in Boras, Sweden.

July 8—Fire rages through Rio de Janeiro's Museum of Modern Art and destroys nearly a thousand paintings, including works by Picasso, Dali, Matisse, Miró, Klee, and the bulk of the work of Joaquin Torres Garcia.

July 11—A 38-ton tank truck, carrying liquid industrial gas, overturns, explodes, and tumbles into a Mediterranean campsite near Tarragona, Spain; at least 170 persons are killed by the explosion, and hundreds more are seriously injured.

Aug. 20—Four hundred and thirty people die as a fire set by arsonists consumes a movie theater in Abadan, Iran.

LAND AND SEA TRANSPORTATION

Feb. 9—A bus is reported to have plunged into a river 65 miles (104 km) from Allahabad, India, killing 53 Hindu pilgrims and injuring 12 others.

Feb. 15—A school bus falls into a ravine off a narrow mountain road 13 miles (24 km) south of San Juan, P. R., killing 11 students and injuring 30 more.

Feb. 25—Eleven cars of an express train heading south from Tucuman to Buenos Aires, Argentina, derail as the train hits a heavy truck at a railway crossing 42 miles (67 km) north of Santa Fe, Argentina; the collision kills 37 persons and injures 120.

Feb. 26—Near Youngstown, Fla., 8 persons are killed and 67 injured as chlorine gas spills out onto a highway, after the sabotage derailment of a tank car.

March 9—The collision of a bus with a heavy truck in São Paulo, Brazil, kills 19 people and injures 5.

April 15—Two trains collide in the mountains outside of Bologna, Italy, killing at least 43 persons.

July 17—In Cairo, Egypt, a bus breaks through a retaining wall and falls into the Nile River, killing at least 56 passengers.

July 26—Two hundred Vietnamese refugees are reported to have drowned when their boat capsized in the South China Sea.

Aug. 4—A bus carrying mentally and physically handicapped people plunges into Lac D'Argent 50 miles (80 km) southeast of Montréal, Quebec, drowning 40 persons.

Oct. 5—Algerian merchant ship *Colo* sinks after colliding with an Italian vessel in the Mediterranean off the coast of southern Spain; 26 seamen are missing.

Nov. 22—Approximately 200 Vietnam refugees drown when the fishing boat on which they had escaped capsizes after being towed by police from the coast of Malaysia.

Dec. 21—In Salamanca, Spain, a school bus and a locomotive collide at a railroad crossing, killing 27 children and one adult.

STORMS AND FLOODS

Jan. 25–26—A "killer blizzard" 1,000 miles (1,600 km) wide and with winds of up to 100 mph drops 31 inches (79 cm) of snow over several Midwestern states, killing more than 100 persons and disrupting the economy.

Jan. 28 through 30—Blizzards strike Scotland's northern Highlands, killing five and stranding hundreds.

Feb. 5 through 7—Nearly 60 storm-related deaths occur and vast economic losses are reported as a blizzard paralyzes the Northeast.

Feb. 10—Nearly 20 persons are dead in Los Angeles as heavy rains and winds cause flooding and mud slides.

March 17—A tornado, rare to India, hits the northern outskirts of New Delhi, killing 22 and injuring 700 persons.

April 8—Approximatey 1,000 people are believed drowned as a result of a storm which sank 100 cargo boats in the Bay of Bengal in Bangladesh.

April 16—Two tornados hit eastern India, killing 600 people and injuring hundreds more.

July 10—Floods are reported to have taken at least 122 lives in Afghanistan and northern Pakistan.

July 24—About 100 persons are reported to have been killed due to flooding in the state of Uttar Pradesh in northeastern India.

Aug. 6—Twenty-five thousand people are marooned following heavy rains and flooding in at least 92 villages in the states of Uttar Pradesh and Punjab in northern India.

Aug. 8—The death toll reaches 26 as a week of flash flooding in north central and west central Texas begins to recede.

Aug. 8—At least 23 persons are killed as floods hit the Swiss and Italian Alps.

Sept. 8—Severe floods are reported to have taken nearly 1,000 lives in northern India.

Oct. 13—Indochina peninsula monsoon floods leave thousands facing starvation and millions in need of emergency relief as the rice crop in Thailand and Cambodia is seriously damaged; 20% of the cattle in Vietnam are destroyed; and 500,000 Laotians are threatened with starvation.

MISCELLANEOUS

April 28—At St. Marys, W. Va., inside the cooling tower of an unfinished power plant for Monongahela Power Company scaffolding rips loose from a 200-foot (61-m) concrete cone and plunges 51 men 170 feet (52 m) to their deaths.

May 21—In Garland, Tex., a church roof collapses, killing a nine-year-old girl and injuring 57 other people.

ADVERTISING

Advertising continues to be one of America's fastest growing industries. Increasing at a rate of 12.5% in 1978, advertising outgrew the gross national product for the third consecutive year. Due to the aggressively competitive marketing environment, the heavy use of advertising and promotion is no longer viewed as a temporary phenomenon. However, advertisers continued to reel from ever mounting media costs, with no relief in sight. To avoid further government intervention, the industry was in the process of reducing television "clutter"—the amount of commercial and promotional time on any given program.

Laws and Regulations. There was considerable debate in 1978 over an inquiry and formal hearing by the Federal Trade Commission (FTC) concerning advertising aimed at children. A ban or restriction of such advertising would have a significant impact on both the television industry and advertisers. At stake are some half billion (U. S.) dollars spent annually by supporters of children's television programs.

In 1978 the FTC was also busy redefining its celebrity endorsement standards. In a bench mark decision, the agency charged the manufacturer of an acne medication with false and deceptive claims and held singer Pat Boone, who endorsed the product, financially liable. While the FTC decision has not scared off the stars, it has caused some of them to demand protective clauses in their contracts.

Media. The television rating race continued at a frenzied pace, as did the escalating cost of advertising time. The result of these pressures has been what the media call "the living schedule," where networks change, shift, or preempt programs to outpull the competition. Despite continued network dominance, cable television and satellite broadcast stations are steadily gaining ground and will eventually offer important new vehicles to television advertisers. Because of the soaring cost of television time, advertisers continue to turn to the magazine industry as an alternative. The reappearance of *Life* and *Look* magazines supplies two examples of the resurging prosperity of magazines. The merger of the nation's only major magazine research firms, Simmons and TGI, caused concern among publishers whose reputations often depend on the findings of such firms. To fill the vacancy, other research firms are gearing up to enter the magazine field.

Volume. Advertisers spent $42.8 billion in 1978, up by 12.5% from $38 billion in 1977. The biggest increase in outlay was in local television advertising, which climbed 25%, to $2.4 billion. Local television advertising was still running third after network spending of $3.9 billion (up by 12%) and spot spending of $2.6 billion (up by 16%). The largest outlays were for the print media, with newspapers first at $12.5 billion (up by 12%); magazines matched 1977 gains, with a total of $2.6 billion (up by 20%). All other gains were below 10%: direct mail and radio increased by 9.5% to $5.8 billion and $2.8 billion, respectively; outdoor advertising was up by 9% to $454 million; and farm publications rose by 5.5% to $95 million. All other media—from bus shelters to skywriting—totaled $8.3 billion, an increase of 11%.

Canada. Although the government lifted wage and price controls, the Canadian economy remained sluggish. Double digit inflation, increased unemployment, strikes, a weakened dollar, and increased government regulations plagued Canadian advertisers throughout the year. In its continuing program to gallicize the province, the Quebec government passed a new consumer protection bill requiring that the French language be used for all transit and outdoor advertising. Measured media spending increased by 13% in 1978, pushing total spending over $800 million. Television advertising increased by 14% to $431 million. Magazines continued to exhibit tremendous growth in advertising, showing an increase of 21% to $73 million. Newspaper ads were up by 9% to $156 million, not including local retail advertising. Radio advertising made an impressive turnaround, increasing by 12% to $65 million.

EDWARD H. MEYER
Grey Advertising Inc.

AFGHANISTAN

Major and historic changes took place in Afghanistan during 1978.

Politics. On April 27–30 a bloody coup overthrew the regime of President Mohammed Daud. Daud, his family, and key ministers, were slaughtered in the presidential palace. Fighting between rebel and loyal troops resulted in hundreds of deaths. The coup was led by Soviet-trained military officers headed by Deputy Chief of the Air Force Colonel Abdul Qadir. The military rebels first organized a Revolutionary Military Council (RMC) but soon turned power over to a leftist civilian group led by Nur Mohammed Taraki, the leader of the *Khalq* (Masses) party.

Although political parties were not officially recognized in Afghanistan, *Khalq* had been operating underground for several years. Publicly its platform was socialist and nationalist but most Afghans considered the party to be communist. In July 1977 *Khalq* merged with the *Parcham* (Banner) party, another leftist group of strong and dogmatic Marxist-Leninist persuasion. The two parties formed the new *Peoples Democratic Party* (PDP). As leader of this united PDP, Taraki took over as president of Afghanistan.

The leftist coup has had repercussions far beyond the boundaries of Afghanistan. Many observers suspect that the coup was masterminded by the USSR. So far there is no hard evidence of Soviet involvement. Taraki denies

Nur Mohammed Taraki took over the government of Afghanistan following a bloody coup in late April.

UPI

that the new Afghan government is communist and has reasserted the traditional Afghan position of nonalignment. He asserts that the coup was aimed simply at removing the 140-year dictatorial rule of the Mohamadzai clan of the Durrani tribe, of which both Daud and the former king (overthrown by Daud) were members. Taraki admits, however, that he anticipates very close relations with the USSR. Following the coup Afghanistan signed many new aid agreements with the USSR, and a flood of new Soviet advisers arrived in Kabul. In addition in December, Afghanistan and the Soviet Union signed a 20-year treaty of friendship and cooperation, pledging mutual economic, military, and technical assistance. The agreement followed two days of discussions between Taraki and Soviet President Leonid Brezhnev in Moscow. At international meetings Afghan representatives adopted and advocated strong pro-Soviet and anti-Western positions.

Domestic Affairs. The Taraki regime has purged or imprisoned most officials of the former regime and replaced them with PDP members or sympathizers. Taraki has tried to reassure the people and the religious leaders by proclaiming respect and support for the Islamic nature of the country. Nevertheless the new regime faces strong internal opposition from several quarters. The vast majority of Afghans are strong anti-communists and devout Muslims. The coup had the support of only a small politicized portion of the armed forces. The former regime still has many sympathizers. The commercial classes are alarmed by the reputed communist ideology of the new regime. The PDP itself seems to be breaking up into its original factions. In an internal purge in the summer of 1978 Taraki dismissed the leaders of *Parcham* from their ministerial posts and exiled them to diplomatic positions abroad. He also arrested Defense Minister General Qadir, the leader of the military coup.

Foreign Relations. The coup has upset the delicate balance of forces in South and West Asia. Both Iran and Pakistan fear a strongly pro-Soviet neighbor on their flanks. Both countries have dangerous separatist tribal movements (Pushtun and Baluch) in provinces bordering on Afghanistan. They fear the increased potential of a Soviet-dominated Afghanistan to foment conflicts.

The thrust of increased Soviet influence in Afghanistan alarms some observers as an attempt to outflank the Middle East (particularly Iran) with its vital oil supplies, and as an attempt to destabilize the entire area, thus diverting Western attention and resources from other theaters of Soviet activity, such as Africa. Afghanistan thus emerges as a new focus for possible superpower confrontation.

Economics. Economic activity was heavily depressed by the prevailing political instability. Lack of confidence among the commercial classes resulted in a flight of capital and the cessation of internal investment. Internationally, trade activity was nearly normal.

LEON B. POULLADA
Northern Arizona University

―――― **AFGHANISTAN • Information Highlights** ――――

Official Name: Democratic Republic of Afghanistan.
Location: Central Asia.
Area: 250,000 square miles (647,497 km²).
Population (1978 est.): 17,800,000.
Chief Cities (1975 est.): Kabul, the capital, 749,000 (met. area); Kandahar, 209,000; Herat, 157,000.
Government: *Head of state and government,* Nur Mohammed Taraki, president and premier. *Policymaking body*—35 member Revolutionary Council.
Monetary Unit: Afghani (45 afghanis equal U. S.$1, Sept. 1978).
Manufactures (major products): Textiles, cement, carpets, furniture, soap, shoes, fertilizer.
Agriculture (major products): Wheat, cotton, fruit and nuts, karakul pelts, wool, mutton.

AFRICA

Africa in 1978 became a continent with two distinct trends. In the troubled areas of East and Southern Africa violence spread, with warfare breaking out on several fronts. In West and Central Africa, by way of contrast, a number of disputes cooled off, and several sources of conflict appeared to be dissipating. Any semblance of continental unity was thereby disspelled, particularly when viewed against the backdrop of the complete impotence of the Organization of African Unity (OAU), a shadow of its former self as it struggled to survive in war-torn Addis Ababa. The divergent trends were far more pronounced at the end of the year than at the beginning, with few prospects for Africa returning to a coherent whole.

AMERICAN-SOVIET INFLUENCE

The superpowers once again dominated the international transactions of the African continent, with each power attempting to establish differing ground rules. The Soviet influence was felt through arms transfers and the presence of Cuban and Soviet forces, while the United States continued to press for nonviolent solutions to regional conflicts. It appeared that African leaders were better understanding the nature of both presences by year-end, with Africans able to a large degree to manipulate the pace of diplomatic cooperation and conflict.

The American Approach. For much of 1978, U. S. policy followed the guidelines established at the beginning of the Carter administration, with strategy clearly guided by UN Ambassador Andrew Young and his assistants. The high point of this approach came in April, with the trip of President Jimmy Carter to Nigeria and Liberia, where he received warm official welcomes. April was also the season for the final agreement between South Africa and the five Western nations over the future of Namibia (South West Africa), where negotiations were led by Young's deputy, Ambassador Donald McHenry. The agreement, covering the administration of elections in the former League of Nations mandate by the United Nations, came unraveled. In December, South Africa held unilateral elections in the area. As expected, the government-favored Democratic Turnhalle Alliance (DTA) won, and the future of Namibia remained in doubt as the year ended.

The U. S. policy, which had begun to be battered, by the end of the year had undergone a serious transformation. In May, the invasion of Zaire's Shaba province by exiles from Angola occurred, in a replay of the March 1977 disorders. In this case, it was clear that the government of Mobutu Sese Seko in Zaire might not survive, and the Carter administration, already sensitive to the emerging role of Cuban- and Soviet-supported governments in Africa, chose

UPI

Nigeria's leader, Lt. Gen. Olusegun Obasanjo, warmly welcomed President Carter to Lagos in April.

to give its full support to the intervention in Shaba by Belgian and French paratroopers. Before the disorders were controlled, the U. S. administration and public received an economic scare in the cutoff of cobalt and copper production from the Shaba mines. The strategic significance of Southern African minerals was conveyed through the marketplace at the time of the invasion.

The second force beyond the administration's control was the drive in the United States for economic sanctions against the repressive regime of Idi Amin of Uganda. With the movement coordinated by Rep. Donald Pease (D-Ohio) in the House of Representatives, Congress passed a bill in September to end imports of Ugandan coffee. President Carter signed the bill, just as he had responded to pressure in late 1977 to end helicopter training for Ugandan pilots.

An intensive debate also emerged in the United States with regard to continuing American investments in South Africa. Repeated disorders occurred on American campuses, beginning in the spring, with demands for university trustees to divest their endowment portfolios of

Zambia's President Kenneth Kaunda reviewed the south Africa situation with President Carter in May.

company stocks that profited from South African operations. By the summer of 1978, the American black organizations were taking stands as well, with the NAACP calling for "disinvestment." Most universities argued that their adherence to the provisions of the "Sullivan principles," developed by Reverend Leon Sullivan and endorsed by more than 100 major U. S. firms operating in South Africa, would result in greater progress and equality for South African blacks. Sullivan's six-point program included the integration of all company facilities; development of equal and fair employment practices; equal pay for equal or comparable work; the addition of more blacks in managerial positions; establishment of training programs for nonwhites; and an improvement in housing, transportation, education, and health facilities for employees. The argument was not settled, but it did result in greater awareness of and involvement in African problems by the U. S. public.

American policy made a fundamental shift in late October, with the visit of Secretary of State Cyrus Vance to South Africa in an effort to keep alive the decolonization process in South West Africa. Vance and Carter decided to offer the new South African Prime Minister, P. W. Botha, carrots instead of sticks to urge along the diplomatic process. Vance conveyed to Botha the possibility that, if the Namibia peace process went forward, the United States would invite Botha for a state visit, and that the United States would settle for a more gradual process of change in South Africa to end apartheid. The new approach provoked some resentment among American advocates of radical change in southern Africa, and the effectiveness of the approach would not really be tested until 1979.

The Soviet Approach. The year presented the Soviet Union with no watersheds—only a continuation of the progress it had been making since 1974 in increasing its influence over the African diplomatic scene. It had its usual mix of successes and failures, but clearly the overall trend was toward a substantial increase in leverage over events of the region.

In the Horn of Africa, the Soviet Union clearly achieved predominance in influencing the drift of events. The massive airlift near the beginning of the year set the stage for the Ethiopian rollback of the Somali invaders. (*See* Special Report page 80.)

The Soviet Union also entrenched itself further in the conflicts of southern Africa. The escalation of the Rhodesian war gave the Soviets an opportunity to become further involved, particularly in cultivating more cordial relations with Robert Mugabe, leader of the Patriotic Front forces in Mozambique. Where the Soviet Union had previously shipped only to Joshua Nkomo's forces in Zambia, they now supplied Mugabe as well, and broadcast continual moral support to those carrying on the war through guerrilla fighting. The Chinese, formerly close to Mugabe, appeared to be edged out of any influence, not only in relation to Mugabe, but also in Mozambique itself. The use of East Europeans as advisers to the Mozambique government grew, and the Chinese found themselves largely without influence in southern Africa.

Soviet policy found itself restricted in one sphere, namely West Africa. In late May, word leaked out that the Guinean government had withdrawn the right of Soviet reconnaissance planes to use Guinean bases for flights over the South Atlantic. The Soviet Navy also suffered some withdrawal of privileges at Guinean naval bases.

The U. S. reaction to Soviet policy in Africa never appeared to have coherence. A major policy review occurred in April and May, after the establishment of Soviet primacy in the Horn, but the results of that review were never publicized. Verbal warnings were made by President Carter and National Security Adviser Zbigniew Brzezinski, to the effect that Cuban military influence in Africa needed to be contained, but those warnings came under attack by other administration officials as well as by a number of African leaders.

EAST AFRICA IN DISORDER

Conflicts of both major and minor dimensions flared up in East Africa during 1978. The most dramatic conflict was the war in the Horn, a situation that all parties hoped to contain in the Somali-Ethiopian context. Historical tensions between Somalia and Kenya did not prove to be so dangerous, since Kenya stayed out of the war, as did the threat represented by small, coveted Djibouti.

The end of the Somali-Ethiopian war allowed the Ethiopians to turn their forces against the Eritrean secession movement in the north. The reported reluctance of the Cubans to become involved on the ground in that civil war caused the Ethiopian forces to be far less effective, and the war dragged on inconclusively throughout the year. Ethiopia ended the year with its borders formally intact, but securely controlling an indeterminate portion of the country. Clearly, the continuing Eritrean rebellion, as well as uncontrollable royalist remnants in the country, made governing a difficult task.

The end of the war also left the Somali government isolated regionally and internationally. The Somali initiation of war caused nearly all states to shy away from supplying arms. Somalia was able to rely only on intermittent trickles of aid from friends in the various states of the Arab world.

A major opportunity for disruption occurred in Kenya with the death in August of Jomo Kenyatta, founder and president of that country. Speculation had been rampant that Kenya would collapse without Kenyatta. Instead, a very peaceful transition occurred, with Vice President Daniel Arap Moi becoming the new leader. As Kenya settled into its usual routine under the new leadership, the region gave out an audible sigh of relief.

However, the other two partners of the defunct East African Community, Uganda and Tanzania, were not enjoying such tranquillity. In late October a mutiny broke out among some Ugandan Army units in the southern part of the

Sam Nujoma hopes to become head of Namibia (South West Africa), once an independence pact is concluded.

country. Amin moved to quell the disturbance, and the fighting spilled over into Tanzania. Within a few days, Amin announced that Tanzania had invaded his country, and moved to occupy a section of territory north of the Tagera River near Lake Victoria. This initiation of warfare by President Amin drove Tanzania's President Julius Nyerere to mobilize his forces, and dispatch them to the border to evict the Ugandan forces from his territory.

Robert Mugabe (left) and Joshua Nkomo urge the UN Security Council to condemn the Rhodesian settlement.

PHOTOS UPI

Zaire's President Mobutu is briefed during the invasion of Shaba Province by exiles from Angola.

UNEASY SOUTHERN AFRICA

The countries of southern Africa were clearly in transition, but it never became clear whether the situation was improving or disintegrating. Diplomatic contacts and armed conflicts were occurring between various parties and at various levels, but with no concrete results.

The members of the Salisbury government engaged in extensive diplomacy during the year, first soliciting contacts with Joshua Nkomo in Zambia—with secret meetings arranged with Ian Smith in Lusaka. The Salisbury group also attempted to sell their program abroad, visiting the United States in October amid great controversy over the granting of a visa to the "rebel leaders." The two leaders of the Patriotic Front, Nkomo and Mugabe, also conferred and then split in disagreement during the year, as each maneuvered for maximum political advantage in the anticipated settlement for Rhodesia. The settlement, however, appeared further away at the end of the year, as Rhodesian security forces expanded the war, carrying out a series of raids against Nkomo's forces in Zambia in October and November, killing an estimated 1,000 to 2,000 soldiers. Earlier, Rhodesian forces engaged in small-scale raids into Botswana, as the number of guerrilla bases outside Rhodesia escalated.

Change was even occurring inside South Africa, as Prime Minister B. J. Vorster suffered ill health during the summer, and finally resigned, to be replaced by Defense Minister P. W. Botha. Prime Minister Botha was welcomed by hardliners for his sterling record in building up an effective South African Defense Force during the last decade, and he was welcomed by liberals for his enlightened views in dealing with nonwhites in the defense force and in his native Cape Province.

The most dramatic international event, however, occurred in October when President Kenneth Kaunda of Zambia decided to reopen the railway through Rhodesia and South Africa. The tie-up of the Tazara Railroad that carried goods to the port of Dar es Salaam in Tanzania forced President Kaunda to reverse his decision on the closure of the Rhodesian frontier. President Kaunda cited the desperate need to get Zambian copper to market, as well as the import of essential fertilizer for the Zambian maize crop, due for planting in November. The only ports and transportation links with adequate capacity, apparently, were those in South Africa and Rhodesia. While embarrassing politically, the decision also pleased much of the Zambian public, who felt that they were paying economically for a Rhodesian boycott that would gain them little in the long run.

Bophuthatswana, South Africa's second black homeland (after Transkei), which had declared its independence on Dec. 6, 1977, following agreement between South Africa and Chief Lucas M. Mangope of the homeland, did not receive general diplomatic recognition in 1978. The UN and the international community generally considered the state "a manifest injustice toward the black population of South Africa."

CENTRAL AFRICA IN TRANSITION

The countries of Central Africa passed through another war, and into a period of reconciliation. The war, called Shaba II, involved another invasion by Zairian exiles from Angola into the mineral-rich province of Shaba in Zaire. Many lives were lost, both Zairian and those of expatriate technicians in the local copper mines, and the situation restabilized only when Western forces intervened. The government of President Mobutu apparently recognized the need for greater regional stability, and negotiations were undertaken with President Agostinho Neto of Angola. An agreement to suppress dissident movements in Angola and Zaire emerged. Angola agreed to move the Shaban refugees further away from the border, and Zaire cut off supplies to the FNLA and UNITA, Angolan movements opposed to Neto.

The economic instability of the region also improved during the year, as the threatened bankruptcy of the government in Zaire was prevented by a massive loan organized by Citibank of New York. At the same time, the World Bank was brought in to manage the economy of Zaire, with some hope of avoiding payments shortfalls that had plagued the government in recent years. The Angolan economy also appeared to stabilize, particularly as internal civil war subsided. The project most important to both countries, however, the reopening of the Banguela railroad, awaited 1979.

WEST AFRICA: PROBLEM-SOLVING

Economic developments and changes of government provided evidence that West Africa was indeed the region of growth and reasonable stability in Africa during 1978.

The most important political conflict of the region, that which has pitted Guinea's Sékou Touré against the rest of the leaders, appeared ready for reconciliation. Touré, relatively isolated since his "independent" decision in 1958 to seek autonomy from France, took several steps to regain respectability. He reduced the Soviet military presence in Guinea. He attended a meeting in Monrovia, Liberia, in March with the leaders of Senegal and Ivory Coast. The latter two governments had long suffered from subversive incursions from Guinea, and President Touré attempted to heal the international wounds. Guinea also declared its intention of obtaining full membership in ECOWAS (Economic Community of West Africa), launched by Nigeria in 1977.

Ghana had a change of government in July, as Gen. Ignatius Acheampong was forced to step aside in favor of his deputy, Gen. Fred Akuffo. While the fundamental problems of Ghana remained, certain hopeful signs followed the discovery of oil in commercial quantities off the coast.

Mauritania's President Moktar Ould Daddah was overthrown in July. The leaders of the coup indicated a dissatisfaction with the continuing war against the Polisario over the Western Saharan region that was consuming 50% of the Mauritanian government budget. The attempts of the new leaders to obtain a peace did not succeed, but there was a determined lowering of the war effort to keep the cost of the war within reasonable bounds.

The Nigerian presence in West Africa continued to be overwhelming, and indeed, the Nigerians deliberately established a diplomatic presence to keep the region reasonably stable. A number of conflicts over refugees in the region clearly had the potential for war, but they were suppressed through mediation. The Nigerians, however, faced problems of their own: production of petroleum dropped from 1977's level of two million barrels per day to about 1.5 million barrels per day. The loss of revenue, caused primarily by a temporary glut of oil on the international market, necessitated a cutback in government plans for spending. The Nigerian government weathered the problems, however, and went ahead with plans for return to civilian rule in 1979.

AFRICA: A REGION WITHOUT COHERENCE

The annual meeting of the Organization of African Unity was held in Khartoum, Sudan, in September, where only one substantive action was taken. The OAU voted to refuse recognition to the new government of the Comoro Islands— a government established by mercenary forces led by Col. Bob Denard in May. The government remained in power, even though it did not attend OAU meetings, due to the vote. On all other decisions, the OAU could not arrive at a consensus. As observers dryly noted, the OAU summit was notable: the organization survived.

See also articles on the major independent nations of Africa; the nations of the world listing, pages 566–569.

RICHARD E. BISSELL
Foreign Policy Research Center

WILLIAM CAMPBELL, SYGMA

Uganda's President Idi Amin attends OAU meeting in Khartoum, the Sudan. Experts pointed out that the meeting accomplished little.

The Horn

The Horn of Africa, an area incorporating Ethiopia, Somalia, and Djibouti, is a part of the world whose strategic location has thrust it into the international arena as a potential crisis zone. Overlapping the Indian Ocean and the Middle East, it flanks the oil-rich states of Arabia; controls the Bab el Mandeb Straits, which is one of the narrow arteries through which oil passes to Israel, Western Europe, and the United States; dominates a part of the Gulf of Aden and Indian Ocean through which oil tankers are constantly moving; and overlooks the passages where the Red Sea, the Gulf of Aden, and the Indian Ocean converge. Rivalry in the Horn of Africa between the United States and the Soviet Union is in large part due to the strategic location of the Horn and has been exacerbated recently because of changing domestic conditions in the area.

Ethiopia and Somalia. Since independence on July 1, 1960, Somalia has evidenced its desire to obtain control over the northeastern province of Kenya, Djibouti, and the Ogaden region of Ethiopia. Somalia maintains that its concept of "Greater Somalia"—the incorporation of territories whose population is made up of Somali-speaking ethnic groups—is nothing more than the regaining of "lost territories." Somalia took the first step toward achieving its goal in mid-July 1977. At that time it invaded the Ogaden region in support of the indigenous Western Somali Liberation Front (WSLF), in an attempt to wrest control of the Ogaden from Ethiopia.

There appeared to be two reasons for Somalia's decision to storm the Ogaden in July. First, Ethiopia, which was taken over by a Marxist military junta on Sept. 12, 1974, when Emperor Haile Selassie was toppled from power, was in the midst of a raging civil war in Eritrea province, and its military junta (Dergue) was battling ideological opponents throughout the country. About half of the regular Ethiopian armed forces, 20,000 troops, were in Eritrea, fighting the secessionist insurgents. The Dergue was also combating the Ethiopian People's Revolutionary Party (EPRP), a Marxist organization founded in 1975 by students and intellectuals. The EPRP maintains that Marxism must be organized from the grass roots, via the peasantry, and cannot be imposed from above by the military. Forced underground by the Dergue, the EPRP began in 1977 to initiate a reign of violence utilizing execution squads to assassinate members of the Dergue. The violence was met by counterviolence from the Dergue. To fight the EPRP, "flame squads" were organized in 1977 by the Ethiopian junta to root out and execute EPRP leaders. In 1978 the Red Terror campaign was begun by the junta to destroy the EPRP. In addition, the Dergue in 1977 was

under attack by the Ethiopian Democratic Union (EDU), an organization made up of former aristocrats demanding democratically elected civilian rule. Its fighters engaged in guerrilla attacks around the towns of Gondar and Dessie, and the Ethiopian army in 1977 was engaged in full scale battles with the EDU. War with secessionists in Tigre province was also raging.

Second, Somalia was heavily supported by the Soviet Union. In April 1977 the United States halted its extensive military aid program to Ethiopia because of the regime's ideology and its use of violence to eliminate opponents. Since 1963 the USSR had granted to Somalia more than U.S.$200 million in military aid and stationed some 300 advisers in the country. And since 1969 the USSR had installed advanced naval and communications facilities in Berbera, Somalia's port on the Gulf of Aden. The tie between Russia and Somalia seemed to be strong.

Somalia apparently believed that Ethiopia was in such political turmoil and so weak militarily that it would not be able to withstand a Somali move into the Ogaden. Between July and December 1977, Somalia and the WSLF occupied 90% of the region and Somalia had every reason to believe that the Ogaden would soon be under its sovereign control.

In May 1977, however, the Soviet Union signed a Treaty of Friendship and Cooperation with Ethiopia, believing it could maintain relations with Marxist Ethiopia and socialist Somalia, despite their enmity, through the common factor of ideology. As part of the treaty, Ethiopia, in July, began receiving more than $875 million in Soviet weapons. The Soviet aid to Ethiopia had an immediate impact on the war. The tide began to turn in November 1977, and one month later Ethiopian forces held firm against attacking Somalis in Harar and Diredawa, the two major cities in the Ogaden. On Nov. 13, 1977, Somalia, in reaction to the Soviet policy in Ethiopia, expelled all Soviet personnel and closed the Soviet naval facilities at Berbera. The Soviets moved to support Ethiopia fully.

Between January and March 1978, more than 16,000 Cuban troops, 1,500 Soviet advisers, East German technicians, and a handful of South Yemen troops arrived in Ethiopia. All were used in the Ogaden to stem the Somali onslaught. In January and February, Ethiopia drove Somali troops back from Harar and Diredawa and by March Somali forces were in disarray. On March 9, Somalia withdrew from the Ogaden in defeat. The WSLF continued small scale guerrilla tactics but with little impact.

Ethiopia and Eritrea. On Nov. 14, 1962, Eritrea had become the 14th province of Ethiopia. With half its population Muslim, many in the

Young Somalis who volunteered for military service are trained in the use of an anti-aircraft gun. Somalia's attempt to gain control of the Ogaden region in the Horn of Africa ended unsuccessfully in 1978.

UPI

province resented control by Christian Ethiopia. In 1962, the Eritrean Liberation Front (ELF) was organized and began its secessionist drive. In 1966, the Eritrean People's Liberation Front (EPLF), a Marxist organization, initiated its own drive for the secession of Eritrea. Between 1962 and April 1978, the Eritrean liberation forces obtained control of some 95% of the province and seemed to be on the verge of secession.

Ethiopia has consistently maintained that it would never allow Eritrea to be independent, as Ethiopia would then be landlocked. Djibouti, which received its independence from France on June 27, 1977, offers another avenue to the sea. A railroad line between Addis Ababa and the port at Djibouti has existed since 1917. Since Somalia claims Djibouti under its "Greater Somalia" concept Ethiopia has maintained that it cannot allow itself to be dependent upon Djibouti and thus must maintain its control over Eritrea.

In April 1978, one month after Somalia was defeated in the Ogaden, Cuban troops and Soviet advisers moved into Asmara, the provincial capital of Eritrea, to aid Ethiopia in its counteroffensive against the secessionists. In January, Ethiopia had broken through secessionist lines to reopen the road from Asmara to Massawa, the site of Ethiopia's naval base, and had strengthened its control of Asmara. In July and August, Ethiopia retook a number of towns from rebel forces, although it was rebuffed at Keren. Ethiopia's counteroffensive continued through the fall of 1978.

The international situation in Eritrea is unclear. Fidel Castro maintained that Cuban troops were not doing any fighting and that he was pushing for a political settlement of the war. Ethiopia's head of state, Mengistu Haile Mariam,

and the ELF both maintained in 1978 that Cuban and South Yemen troops were fighting alongside Ethiopian troops in Eritrea. The Soviet Union refused to comment on the role of its advisers. In July, South Yemen stated it would continue to aid Ethiopia in Eritrea while Egypt, Syria, Iraq, and Saudi Arabia maintained their support of the Eritrean rebels. In the autumn the ELF/EPLF still maintained control of most of Eritrea while Assab, Massawa, Asmara, and some smaller towns were dominated by Ethiopia. The civil war continued unabated.

The United States and the Soviet Union. The USSR entrenched itself in Ethiopia in 1978 by its act of giving aid to Ethiopia in the war against Somalia. U. S. Secretary of State Cyrus R. Vance maintained that the United States was "seriously concerned" that the Soviet Union would attempt to position itself via a naval facility in Massawa or Assab so as to be threatening to the United States. The USSR has naval facilities in Aden, South Yemen, and on South Yemen's Indian Ocean island of Socotra. With a naval presence in Eritrea its position around the Horn of Africa would be formidable. To counter Soviet moves, the United States moved to speed up the construction of its naval facilities on the Indian Ocean island of Diego Garcia. Scheduled for completion in 1980 the base, costing $175 million, will consist of three communication sites, a 12,000-foot (3,650-m) runway, a refueling capacity for ships and aircraft, and a fuel storage dump.

The United States has also moved to preempt Soviet moves on the Horn of Africa by militarily aiding pro-Western regimes in Kenya, the Sudan, Egypt, North Yemen, Iran, and Saudi Arabia.

PETER SCHWAB

A tractor assembly plant in Shantung Province, China. According to an official source, the nation is making "big efforts to develop industry which promotes farm mechanization."

UPI

AGRICULTURE

Abundant summer rains brightened prospects for large cereal crops in 1978, promising the world high food carry-over stocks, shrinking trade in 1978–79, and a leveling off in price of key food commodities, according to the UN Food and Agriculture Organization (FAO) and the U. S. Department of Agriculture (USDA). But weather was only one of several critical factors in influencing output and agricultural policy during 1978. Direct government intervention increased throughout the industrialized, non-Communist countries in an effort to enhance long-established price/income farm support programs and to stabilize sagging world prices of wheat, sugar, and other commodities.

Throughout the world, politics dominated much of the agricultural picture. The People's Republic of China appeared destined for a greatly-expanded role as a food importer as its leadership moved to keep up with population growth and to modernize its farm economy. In Geneva, more than 90 countries participating in the multilateral trade negotiations (Tokyo Round) tried to resolve conflicts stemming from attempts to liberalize trade in farm and industrial products. During the course of the talks, disagreements threatening to the negotiations erupted over differing farm policies in the United States, Japan, and the European Community (EC).

Production and Prices. In the United States, the Carter administration, Congress, farmers, and consumer groups became embroiled over such issues as increased foreign investment in American farmland, shrinking number and size of farms, environmental regulations, and anti-inflation measures affecting the output of beef and sugar.

But no single development tinged the U. S. agricultural sector so much, especially during the first few months of 1978, as the unsuccessful effort by the American Agriculture Movement to launch a nationwide strike by refusing to plant crops. (*See* Special Report, page 85.)

As a result of actions taken by the administration, Congress, and farmers themselves, U. S. wheat production decreased 12% from the previous year's level. Nevertheless, wheat and feed grain stocks reached their highest levels in a decade: 72 million metric tons, according to the USDA.

Around the world the picture was similar. Governments and consumers were encouraged, but producers were often frustrated. FAO put the world's cereal crop (wheat, coarse grains, and rice) output at (U. S.) 1.4 billion tons, up 4% from 1977. The UN agency revised its forecast upward during the early autumn, despite uncertainties over the impact of monsoons in Asia and Africa and other occurrences likely to affect the end of the growing season in the Northern Hemisphere. Better prospects for coarse grain crops, mainly in the United States, and for wheat in China, more than offset reduced gains in wheat output in Europe and the Near East, the FAO reported.

FAO predicted that 1978 wheat production worldwide would increase 5.7% to 408 million tons, below the 1976 record of 418 million tons. Coarse grains production of a record 721 million tons represented a 2.3% growth over the year before. Rice production topped 375 million tons, slightly above the 1977 record of 372 million tons.

The rise in world grain output was larger than world consumption, which resulted in the build-up of substantial stocks, mainly in the United States. But as early as midsummer, the FAO was warning that the concentration of stocks in the United States and Canada could provoke serious logistical problems if a major food emergency required the quick movement of additional supplies—a fear minimized by U. S. officials.

Cereal prices in world trade leveled or began dropping during the first half of the year in anticipation of ample supplies, especially from the Soviet Union. USDA estimated that its 1978 harvest would top 230 million tons, 50 million tons higher than the average of the last five-year plan which ended in 1975. A major factor was generally favorable weather in the high-risk area extending from the Volga River eastward.

By early September, worldwide coarse grain export prices had dropped by 20%, reflecting ample export supplies and slackening import prospects. Worldwide wheat prices, however, remained relatively stable due to a self-imposed U. S. withdrawal of some 10.5 million tons from the market, an amount equal to 13% of the nation's wheat supplies.

World sugar output for 1978–79 was between 87 and 91 million metric tons, slightly above the level of the previous year. As in the case of grains, however, world output exceeded consumption, which totaled 88 million tons. A slight addition to the world's sugar stocks was thereby assured.

Consequently, downward pressures on sugar also continued. Although world sugar prices strengthened slightly in August, they remained slightly below the August 1977 average of 7.61 cents per pound. USDA analysts reported that there was little likelihood of prices stabilizing so long as carry-over stocks remained at high levels.

The Carter administration continued pursuing stabilization agreements by which buffer stocks would be used to limit abrupt changes in price and supply by providing international floors and ceilings. Negotiations of wheat and sugar agreements advanced significantly during 1978, while progress was also made in talks, all held under UN auspices, concerning such other commodities as rubber, cocoa, and tin.

International Negotiations and Agreements. Wheat negotiations drew representatives of a dozen major importing and producing countries, including the United States, Japan, and the EC, who met alternatively in London and Geneva. Their goal was to present a draft agreement to the 50-nation International Wheat Council, which hopes to reach sweeping trade liberalization agreements by 1980. But crucial differences emerged over such questions as the size of the proposed international wheat reserve—the EC favoring 15 million tons and the United States 30 million tons. Most of the participating countries disagreed on the range of floor and ceiling prices for wheat and coarse grains.

Opposition in the U. S. Congress began to materialize early in the summer, as key farm-state senators warned of possible export-restrictive provisions in a future cereals agreement. Acting independently of the wheat talks, a group of U. S. and Canadian legislators established a task force aimed at guaranteeing a $4-per-bushel international selling price for wheat. However, U. S. and other officials rejected this as unrealistic. Export analysts noted that the 1978–79 price for U. S. wheat averaged about $2.75 per bushel and that it would be difficult to push the price up.

A similar effort revolved around the International Sugar Agreement (ISA) signed by the United States and 50 other nations in December 1977. ISA's aim was to boost world market prices to between 11 cents and 21 cents per pound and to maintain that level through export quotas and buffer stocks. Major snags developed, however, as U. S. domestic sugar programs, aimed at increasing sugar prices beyond the ISA levels, were launched in Congress. U. S. ratification of the pact therefore was delayed.

Another complication was that the EC hesitated to join, largely because of its potentially large excess supply of sugar. But USDA analysts warned that if the EC did not join its exports might be curtailed by a provision in the ISA limiting imports from nonsignatories.

In 1978 the American sugar industry began facing up to what many analysts said would prove even more damaging in the long run: the emergence of high fructose corn syrup (HFCS) as a major competitor of sugar. In the United States, the food and soft drink industry, which consumes approximately 75% of all sugar sold, gradually began switching to HFCS. Analysts predicted that the newly developed product would take away up to one half of sugar's industrial market within a few years.

Another major impasse developed in the Tokyo Round trade talks, this one stemming from the Carter administration's insistence that major concessions for U. S. farm exports be made by the EC and Japan. By early autumn, U. S. officials warned that the longer the impasse lasted over such farm products as American beef, oranges, and tobacco, the greater the danger that agreements on other trade issues would unravel.

U. S. Scene. Domestic politics dominated most agricultural questions and were considered in light of a greatly-improved outlook for the U. S. farm community in general. Net income for the nation's 2.7 million farmers in 1978 was estimated at roughly $6 billion above the $20 billion of 1977, the highest level reached since 1975. Exports rose 19%, to a record $27.3 billion. Lending by the cooperative Farm Credit System reached record levels in loan volume of $39.6 billion and in loans outstanding of $44.9 billion, up respectively by 8% and 11% from the 1977 levels. Farmland prices continued rising, although at somewhat reduced rates.

A major stir was created over widespread concern in Congress and among farm groups that an increasing number of foreigners had purchased American farmland, to the value of nearly $1 billion in 1977. Although acreage held by foreigners was judged insignificant in absolute terms, Congress passed a law in October requiring non-Americans and corporations owning land to register it with USDA, specifying the amount of land bought, the price paid, and its intended use.

In June the White House decided it was time to dampen rising beef prices by increasing beef imports. The National Cattlemen's Association, representing 280,000 cattle producers and feeders, strongly countered that it would have only minimal impact on food-price inflation and that it would threaten the industry's recovery following several price-depressed years. Although the administration got its way, beef production continued its decline, boosting cattle prices substantially.

The World Scene. The EC finished the year with a bumper grain crop as wheat production rose 20% over 1977 levels, although coarse grain output fell 3% as the result of a smaller barley crop. Total meat production in Western Europe rose moderately—about 2.5%—as supplies of pork continued abundant and were expected to increase by about 3% during the 12 month period ending March 1979.

The Soviet Union's agricultural prospects also were favorable. Taking into account a possible 224-million-ton record grain crop, 1978–79 grain utilization was forecast at 234 million tons, including 125 million tons for livestock feed, a key priority. Total grain areas planted came to within a million hectares of equaling the 130.4 million of 1977. The overall wheat area planted was the largest since 1973, with winter wheat at a record 23.1 million hectares.

Livestock numbers on state and collective farms throughout the Soviet Union as of August 1 also showed gains compared with 1977. Poultry and hog numbers made the largest gains—up 8% and 7%, respectively. Meat output was up 7% and whole milk and dairy products up 3% with the exception of butter, which declined 2% from the 1977 record.

In the People's Republic of China, overall agricultural production rose in 1978, but increases for a number of crops were below planned levels, according to USDA. Nevertheless, total wheat production reached 44 million tons, only slightly less than the record 45 million tons of 1976. China's agricultural imports, particularly grains, cotton, and vegetable oil, were sharply above normal levels during 1978, stemming from chronic, sluggish performance on the farms, plus an improved foreign exchange position.

China's grain imports in 1977–78, nearly all wheat, reached a record 8.6 million tons. Cotton imports soared to an estimated 2 million bales, triple the 1976–77 level. Imports from the United States, paced by wheat, cotton, soybean oil, and some tallow, topped $500 million, more than half the total two-way U. S.-PRC trade.

India's total food grain output during 1978–79 aggregated over 130 million tons, up from 125.5 million tons in the previous year.

In Africa, Morocco had an excellent wheat harvest, but the grain entered markets only slowly, with the result that imports ran to over 1.3 million tons, roughly comparable to the level of the 1977 drought period. A similar situation developed in Algeria, whose imports were even higher. Egypt's agricultural production increased slightly over 1977 levels, but imports of food reached record levels—$2 billion, consisting mainly of wheat, flour, and corn. At the same time, production of cotton, Egypt's main cash crop, declined.

Locusts proved a major threat to crops in East Africa. Although damage early in the year was limited mainly to Ethiopia and Somalia, the danger was expected to spread. Moisture conditions in the Sudan, Kenya, and Tanzania were reported to be particularly favorable to locust breeding in 1978–79.

The Sahel countries were in general adequately supplied with rainfall during the year; the exceptions were Senegal and most of Mauritania. The drought zone shifted several hundred miles south to the cocoa-producing areas of West Africa, USDA reported in October.

Throughout Latin America, agricultural production exceeded the 1977 record by more than 4%. Significant reductions in harvests of early crops in Brazil, Chile, Paraguay, and Peru were more than offset by expansion in such countries or areas as Argentina, Mexico, Central America, the Caribbean, Colombia, and Venezuela.

Further gains were projected in Latin American output of coffee, sugar, bananas, sorghum, and livestock products. But because of drought losses in Brazil, the area's production of soybeans and corn fell sharply.

AXEL KRAUSE
McGraw-Hill Publications

UPI

U. S. trade negotiator Robert Strauss and Japan's Minister of Agriculture and Forestry Ichiro Nakagawa prepare for farm-trade discussions.

Farmers' Strike

On Nov. 25, 1977, several hundred farmers marched through Plains, Ga., protesting low crop prices and urging support for a nationwide "farm strike," planned for December 14. It was the first major public demonstration of the American Agriculture Movement (AAM), a loosely-organized effort by U.S. farmers to force crop price increases through political action. The movement peaked during dramatic meetings with government officials in Washington early in 1978, then lost momentum and collapsed.

Although similar movements have appeared previously, including the Farm Holiday Movement of the 1930's, none proved so significant or focused so much attention on the U.S. farm economy as the AAM. Its goal was stated simply: obtain 100% of parity for all products grown and consumed in the United States. (The parity price of a commodity is the price that would give a unit of the commodity—a bushel of wheat, for example—the same purchasing power that it had in a 1910–1914 base period.) If that demand was refused by the nation, the AAM planned to halt all food production and distribution, starting December 14, and continuing until the demand was met.

Demanding higher crop prices, farmers from across the United States gather on the steps of the Capitol.

UPI

From November 1977 through March 1978, the AAM captured the attention of the news media, Congress, and the Carter administration, largely through disquieting actions—blocking mail delivery in Colorado; halting distribution of an antistrike newspaper in Texas; and blocking cattle trucks entering the United States from Canada. But the focus of action was Washington. Wearing baseball caps, several thousand farmers drove tractors through the nation's capital on December 10 and January 18 in two "tractorcade" demonstrations. As a result, farmbloc congressmen began urging emergency legislation to boost crop prices.

But the Carter administration resisted. In January, administration officials began stressing the benefits of existing government price/income support programs, while warning that 100% parity would lead to extremely high costs to consumers and taxpayers, as well as a drop in per capita food consumption.

On January 25, AAM leaders announced they were no longer urging a total strike, but a 50% cutback in 1978 crop plantings. Many observers viewed this as the beginning of the movement's demise. It soon became apparent that the AAM lacked the support of most U.S. farmers and reflected primarily the economic hardships of grain farmers in the South and Southwest. Also, lack of cohesion and pure economic necessity precluded implementation of the farmers' threats.

On February 14, President Carter met with AAM leader Lawrence L. Bitner, who, upon leaving the White House, told reporters that the president was not moved by his threats. Meanwhile, growing demand improved crop prices.

Turning to Congress, hundreds of farmers lobbied for new price support schemes. Several key lawmakers, including members of the House and Senate agriculture committees, introduced bills that attempted to boost prices. But others in Congress questioned the high costs involved.

The movement took a dramatic turn on March 16 when some 50 farmers broke into the locked administration building of the Department of Agriculture, forcing the evacuation of Secretary Bob Bergland. Earlier that day, farmers released dozens of goats and chickens on the lawns of Capitol Hill, protesting the government's inaction. Shortly thereafter, farmers began to return home for spring planting, marking the collapse of the movement.

But just prior to Easter recess, Congress passed legislation granting U.S. farmers $744 million in additional government supports.

A permanent liaison office was opened near the Congressional offices.

AXEL KRAUSE

Vice President Walter Mondale administers the oath of office to Alabama's new senator, Maryon P. Allen, who was appointed to the seat upon the death of her husband. Senate Majority Leader Robert Byrd was at the ceremony.

UPI

ALABAMA

Popular interest in politics was unusually high in Alabama during 1978. Gov. George Wallace, who had dominated politics for years, was constitutionally prohibited from succeeding himself in office. Sen. John Sparkman's retirement from Congress and the death of Sen. James B. Allen on June 1 created an exceptional situation in which both seats in the U. S. Senate had to be filled at the same election. It was first thought that Governor Wallace would seek one of these seats, but he decided not to participate actively in the 1978 elections.

Elections. The primary election held on September 5, and the runoff primary held on September 26, focused mainly on the Democratic party's contests for the gubernatorial and senatorial nominations. Forrest (Fob) James, an Opelika businessman with little previous political experience, received the nomination for governor. Howell Heflin, a former chief justice of the state Supreme Court, received the nomination for the Senate seat vacated by Sparkman. Mrs. Maryon Pittman Allen, who was appointed to fill her late husband's seat until a successor could be elected for the unexpired term, sought election to the position, but was defeated in the Democratic primaries by State Senator Donald Stewart. Republican James D. Martin, a former Congressman, originally Heflin's opponent in the general election, switched positions and ran as Stewart's Republican opponent. In the general election held on November 7, James defeated the Republican nominee for governor, Guy Hunt; Heflin was elected to the Senate without Republican opposition; and Stewart was elected for the two-year remainder of Senator Allen's term. Republicans continued to hold three of Alabama's seven seats in the U. S. House of Representatives.

Legislative Sessions. Governor Wallace called the first of two special sessions for January 3 to adjust Alabama's unemployment compensation law. Having enacted the necessary legislation, the legislature adjourned on January 9. The regular session, which convened on January 10 and adjourned on April 24, was most notable for its failure to pass the education appropriation. That situation necessitated a second special session, extending from July 31 to August 4, during which a set of property-tax relief measures supported by Governor Wallace, as well as the education appropriation, were approved.

These relief measures, one of which was a proposed constitutional amendment, were designed to offset the increase in property taxes expected to result from the revaluation program previously ordered by a federal court to equalize property tax burdens in the state. Submitted to the voters at a referendum held in conjunction with the general election, the amendment was adopted by a substantial margin.

Significant Trials. State Treasurer Melba Till Allen was relieved of office on June 8, following her conviction in state court on conflict-of-interest charges. Governor Wallace appointed Mrs. Annie Laurie Gunter, director of the Office of Consumer Protection, to the vacancy. In November she was elected state treasurer.

On October 13, Tommy Lee Hines, Jr., a mentally retarded black man, was convicted and sentenced to 30 years' imprisonment on rape charges in a setting of racial demonstrations reminiscent of the 1960's. Hine's attorney immediately announced his intention to appeal the decision.

JAMES D. THOMAS
The University of Alabama

─────── **ALABAMA • Information Highlights** ───────

Area: 51,609 square miles (133,667 km²).
Population (1977 est.): 3,690,000.
Chief Cities (1970 census): Montgomery, the capital, 133,386; Birmingham, 300,910; Mobile, 190,026.
Government (1978): *Chief Officers*—governor, George C. Wallace (D); lt. gov., Jere L. Beasley (D). *Legislature*—Senate, 35 members; House of Representatives, 105 members.
Education (1977–78): *Enrollment*—public elementary schools, 395,116 pupils; public secondary, 366,764; colleges and universities, 162,308. *Public school expenditures,* $1,016,152,000 ($1,259 per pupil).
State Finances (fiscal year 1977): *Revenues,* $3,124,-417,000; *expenditures,* $2,966,281,000.
Personal Income (1977): $20,745,000,000; per capita, $5,622.
Labor Force (July 1978): *Nonagricultural wage and salary earners,* 1,307,500; *unemployed,* 103,500 (6.1% of total force).

ALASKA

Alaska's battle with the federal government over control of the state's land and election results were the headline events of 1978.

Elections. Alaska's open primary system created an unprecedented challenge. Jay Hammond (R), the incumbent governor and a moderate on development, was strongly opposed in his bid for another term. However, a great number of independents and Democrats joined liberal Republicans to give Hammond a slim 98-vote lead over Walter J. Hickel, former governor and Secretary of Interior under President Nixon. Democrat Chancy Croft, Anchorage attorney and state senator, beat off a challenge from Fairbanks attorney Ed Merdes, an agricultural developer and former legislator. The margin of defeat in each case was so narrow that Hickel and Merdes went to court to argue that a series of mishandled election events had irremediably prejudiced the election outcome. Superior Court judge Ralph Moody ordered a new primary election, but was overruled by the Alaska Supreme Court. In spite of a remarkable write-in campaign by Hickel supporters, Governor Hammond was reelected.

In other elections, Ted Stevens, incumbent Republican U. S. senator was reelected by 75% of the vote, and Don Young (R), Alaska's only Congressman, narrowly defeated a surprisingly strong challenge from Pat Rodey (D) of Anchorage.

Voters rejected a plan permitting the state to borrow $966 million to move the state capital from Juneau to Willow and approved bond issues totaling $240 million for various facilities.

In December 1978, Senator Ted Stevens was injured and his wife, Ann, was killed when the executive jet in which they were traveling crashed in an attempt to land at the Anchorage International Airport. Four other persons were killed and another was injured in the accident.

Land. Alaska's Democratic Senator, Mike Gravel, took credit for "killing" a D-2 bill at the end of the legislative session. D-2 refers to section 17(d)(2) of the Alaska Native Land Claims Act, which authorizes the federal government to withdraw Alaska lands for public interest purposes. The bill would have authorized 180 million acres (73 million ha) of Alaskan land withdrawals into wilderness, parks and recreation areas, and preserves. Secretary of Interior Cecil Andrus in November ordered a freeze on 110 million acres (45 million ha) of federal land under authority of the Bureau of Land Management Organic Act. The act requires preservation of roadless areas that are under consideration for wilderness areas. The state charged that Andrus' action was illegal and promptly filed a lawsuit in federal district court. On December 1 President Carter designated as National Monuments 17 of Alaska's most critical areas, approximately 56 million acres (23 million ha). These areas of valuable resources will re-

main permanent monuments until Congress agrees to act.

On election day Alaskans also approved an initiative calling for as many as 30 million acres (12 million ha) of free land to be distributed to residents of the state who pay surveying costs. Three-year residents are entitled to have up to 40 acres (16 ha) and ten-year residents can receive up to 160 acres (65 ha).

In September the state assumed responsibility for the North Slope Haul Road and planned to construct more than $9 millions' worth of maintenance camps and other facilities. The road remains closed to use by the general public.

Economy. Oil production continued to increase. By July 1978 it had reached a total of 39,910,516 barrels. Gas production was 170,-430,545,000 cubic feet for the same period.

On February 15 a bomb exploded 6 miles (10 km) east of Fairbanks, damaging the Alaska oil pipeline. Thousands of barrels of oil were lost.

The route for the natural gas pipeline will be from the North Slope to Fairbanks, then south and east through Canada. Construction of the gasline will start no earlier than 1981.

Exploration of a major mineral find in the Tongass National Forest was delayed due to difficulty in obtaining permits to construct an access road into the area.

The year saw a huge harvest of salmon in the major state fisheries. It was expected that more than 70 million salmon would be taken by the end of the season, making it the best harvest since 1949, when 78.2 million were caught. The improved harvest was attributed to warmer waters, enforcement of the 200-nautical mile (370-km) limit North Pacific Fishing Treaty, and recent restrictions on commercial taking of salmon.

The Indians. The Indian Claims Commission awarded $11.2 million to Pribilof Island Aleuts in a 27-year-old claim against the government. The award was given as compensation for mistreatment of the Indians by the government and its lease holders during the seal monopoly of 1870–1946.

ANDREA R. C. HELMS
University of Alaska

——— **ALASKA · Information Highlights** ———

Area: 586,412 square miles (1,518,807 km²).
Population (Jan. 1978 est.): 406,000.
Chief Cities (1970 census): Juneau, the capital, 6,050; Anchorage, 48,081; Fairbanks, 14,771.
Government (1978): *Chief Officers*—governor, Jay S. Hammond (R); lt. gov., Lowell Thomas, Jr. (R). *Legislature*—Senate, 20 members; House of Representatives, 40 members.
Education (1977–78): *Enrollment*—public elementary schools, 50,398 pupils; public secondary, 39,946; colleges and universities, 21,522. *Public school expenditures*, $338,525,000 ($3,123 per pupil).
State Finances (fiscal year 1977): *Revenues*, $1,391,-605,000; *expenditures*, $1,147,589,000.
Personal Income (1977): $4,311,000,000; per capita, $10,586.
Labor Force (July 1978): *Nonagricultural wage and salary earners*, 168,400; *unemployed*, 18,800 (10.9% of total force).

ALBANIA

China's decision in early July to halt economic and military assistance to Albania marked the formal end of the Sino-Albanian alliance.

Foreign Relations. Chinese-Albanian relations, which had been rapidly deteriorating since the death of Mao Tse-tung in September 1976, took a new turn for the worse during the first half of 1978. Tiranë and Peking became embroiled in a bitter dispute over various aspects of China's aid programs in Albania. Albania also criticized the Chinese for taking sides in the Vietnam-Cambodia conflict and accused Peking of using "blackmail" and "pressure" in its quarrel with Vietnam. It was against this background that China terminated its Albanian assistance programs.

Tiranë responded to the Chinese action by recalling the Albanians studying in China and by ending its participation in the Joint Sino-Albanian Shipping Company, which handled the bulk of trade between the two countries. Albania further escalated its ideological polemics by branding its former allies "revisionists" and "social-imperialists," designations previously reserved for the Soviet Union. Tiranë also attacked Chinese Chairman Hua Kuo-feng, especially after his visits to Yugoslavia, Rumania, and Iran.

Despite their economic and ideological break, China and Albania indicated a desire to maintain diplomatic relations, at least for the time being. Although the Soviet Union expressed its willingness to assume China's economic commitments in Albania, Tiranë rejected rapprochement with Moscow.

Politics. Enver Hoxha, the first secretary of the ruling Albanian Party of Labor (APL) since its establishment in 1941 and the country's dominant political personality, observed his 70th birthday in October. Although Hoxha continued to maintain an active schedule, there was concern about his health.

Economy. For the second consecutive year, Albania's economy failed to realize the major goals of the current (1976–80) five-year plan. Industrial production was scheduled to increase by 8.5% and agricultural output by 28% in 1978.

NICHOLAS C. PANO
Western Illinois University

──────── ALBANIA • Information Highlights ────────
Official Name: People's Socialist Republic of Albania.
Location: Southern Europe, Balkan peninsula.
Area: 11,100 square miles (28,748 km²).
Population (1978 est.): 2,600,000.
Chief Cities (1975): Tiranë, the capital, 192,000; Shkodër, 62,400; Dürres, 60,000.
Government: *Head of state,* Haxhi Lleshi, president of the Presidium (took office 1953). *Head of government,* Maj. Gen. Mehmet Shehu, premier (took office 1954). *First secretary of the Albanian Party of Labor,* Enver Hoxha (took office 1941). *Legislature* (unicameral)—People's Assembly.
Monetary Unit: Lek (4.1 lekë equal U. S.$1, July 1978).
Manufactures (major products): Textiles, timber, construction materials, fuels, semiprocessed minerals.
Agriculture (major products): Corn, sugar beets, wheat, cotton, tobacco, potatoes.

UPI

In Alberta for the Commonwealth Games, Queen Elizabeth tours the Indian village at Lac Cardinal Park.

ALBERTA

While Alberta, like the rest of Canada, suffered from high inflation, the province's unemployment remained under 5%. With removal of wage and price controls, however, labor unrest reached high levels in both public and private sectors. It was especially prevalent in the construction industry, which, nevertheless, established new records, particularly in such cities as Edmonton and Calgary.

Agriculture. Favorable summer weather produced excellent field crops, but heavy rain in September delayed harvest and affected grades. Improving prices provided badly needed succor for the livestock producers.

Industry. Energy resources and prospects again dominated industry. These included discovery of a major oil field and natural gas potentials, completion of a second oil sands plant on the Athabasca, approval of a pipeline to carry gas from Alaska to the lower 48 states, and maturing plans for the exploitation of heavy crude in eastern Alberta.

Commonwealth Games. Forty-six Commonwealth countries competed in Edmonton during

──────── ALBERTA • Information Highlights ────────
Area: 255,285 square miles (661,189 km²).
Population (1978 est.): 1,948,000.
Chief Cities (1976 census): Edmonton, the capital, 461,361; Calgary, 469,917.
Government (1978): *Chief Officers*—lt. gov., Ralph Steinhauer; premier, Peter Lougheed (Progressive Conservative); atty. gen., James L. Foster; chief justice, Supreme Court, Appellate Div., William A. McGillivray; Trial Div., James V. H. Milvain. *Legislature*—Legislative Assembly, 75 members.
Education (1976–77): *Enrollment:* public elementary and secondary schools, 445,300 pupils; private, 5,-620; Indian (federal) schools, 3,920; post-secondary, 48,890. *Total expenditures,* $1,254,265,000.
Public Finance (1977): *Revenues,* $3,577,000,000; *expenditures,* $3,329,000,000.
Personal Income (average weekly salary, May 1978): $272.81.
Unemployment Rate (July 1978, seasonally adjusted): 4.8%.
(All monetary figures are in Canadian dollars.)

August in the Friendly Games, with Canadians emerging as top contenders for the first time. Opened by Queen Elizabeth, the Games were produced without construction or financial problems.

Government. In the absence of elections, the political scene was dominated by federal-provincial confrontations, mainly respecting control of natural resources. Several cabinet ministers and other members indicated their intention not to seek reelection at forthcoming provincial elections.

Recreation. The provincial government completed work on two large parks in Edmonton and Calgary, and continued development of wilderness facilities.

Education. Continuing financial restrictions and falling enrollments in elementary and postsecondary levels have created employment problems for teachers and difficulties for educational institutions.

JOHN W. CHALMERS, *University of Alberta*

ALGERIA

Algeria's crash development of its natural gas reserves, which are meant to finance ambitious industrial expansion plans, paid off in 1978 with the first deliveries of liquefied natural gas (LNG). But domestic criticism continued of heavy reliance on foreign financing and technology and of failure to implement promised land and social reforms. President Houari Boumedienne died in December.

Economy. Algeria showed it could deliver on its promise of fast production of natural gas by opening in February, four months ahead of schedule, its first LNG plant at Arzew. Creating the new and very expensive machinery of gas liquefaction—supercooling gas into liquid at 1/600 of its former volume—as well as the pipelines (including one begun under the Mediterranean to Italy) and the tankers needed for delivery has been a multi-billion dollar bonanza for U. S. and West European companies, working in cooperation with the state energy agency.

In March, the first LNG tanker docked at a Maryland terminal with gas for one of Algeria's biggest American customers. The speedy delivery was intended to prove Algeria could meet

UPI

Liquefied natural gas is unloaded for the first time from Algeria's LNG tanker at Cove Point, Md.

production schedules, to reassure Western banks about financing of the costly programs, and to bring pressure to bear on the Carter administration, which was still mulling over approval of more long-term LNG deals with U. S. companies. The long delays irritated Algeria because its industrialization programs depend on anticipated revenues from gas exports. Even without the new contracts, the United States was still the largest single importer of Algerian gas in 1978.

A massive effort to develop infrastructure, particularly in the south, was symbolized by stepped-up construction of a modern tarmac road, begun in 1971, across the Sahara Desert. Some (U. S.) $8 billion has been pledged for development of the south, which has deposits of uranium, cobalt, gold, manganese, and iron.

Government attempts to bring inefficient agricultural production under control by means

--- **ALGERIA · Information Highlights** ---

Official Name: Democratic and Popular Republic of Algeria.
Location: North Africa.
Area: 919,595 square miles (2,381,741 km²).
Population: (1978 est.): 18,400,000.
Chief Cities (1974): Algiers, the capital, 1,000,000; Oran, 330,000; Constantine, 254,000.
Government: *Head of state and government*, Rabah Bitat, interim president (December 1978).
Monetary Unit: Dinar (3.89 dinars equal U. S.$1, Sept. 1978).
Manufactures (major products): Petroleum, gas, petrochemicals, fertilizers, iron and steel, textiles, transportation equipment.
Agriculture (major products): Wheat, barley, oats, wine, fruits, olives, vegetables, livestock.

of cooperatives were not successful. Three quarters of the small farmers still remained outside the state system. In 1978, the country had to import most of its sugar and butter, a fifth of its cereals and a third of its milk. Inflation was running at 20% annually.

Politics and Government. On December 27 President Houari Boumedienne, who ruled Algeria for 13 of its 16 years of independence and was regarded as a shrewd and powerful ruler, died in Algiers after almost six weeks in a coma. Boumedienne, who was believed to have had Waldenstrom's disease (a rare blood and bone marrow disease), was considered a major force in the Arab community and the Third World. Speaker of the National Popular Assembly Rabah Bitat was named interim president in accordance with the two year old constitution.

Foreign Relations. The always fragile and highly charged relations with France, which deteriorated in 1977 and early 1978 over France's military role on the side of Morocco and Mauritania in the Western Sahara war against separatists backed by Algeria, took a turn for the better in August. The catalyst for Algerian-French détente was the July ouster of the Mauritanian leader by the army, which believed the war had all but ruined Mauritania's economy. The new regime made peace overtures to Algeria and the Polisario Front, which quickly declared a truce with Mauritania. Algeria and France then tried to work out a settlement, but, even with mediation efforts by other interested parties, including Libya and Spain, the diplomacy collapsed.

JOSEPH MARGOLIS
"African Update" African-American Institute

ANGOLA

The year 1978 witnessed efforts by the government to consolidate its power and develop the economy against persistent rebellion in the countryside and economic dislocation inherited from the process of decolonization.

Politics. The ruling *Movimemto Popular de Libertação de Angola* (MPLA) held its first congress in December 1977 at which it was reconstructed as a Marxist-Leninist Vanguard Party. Now it is called MPLA-Party of Labor. The new statutes mandate that a majority of the membership must be of working class origin. All former members of the Central Committee were reelected to the eleven-position political bureau. The seven-day congress represented the most ambitious gathering since the founding of the MPLA in 1956. Thirteen years of guerrilla war (1961–74) with Portugal, and two with rival nationalist movements, precluded large conferences. A lingering bush war is a legacy of the three-party nationalist civil war. In the southeast, the *União Nacional para Independência Total de Angola* (UNITA), under the leadership of Jonas Savimbi, dominated a vast rural area despite the efforts of MPLA forces and their Cuban, East German, and Soviet allies. Up north, the *Frente Nacional de Libertação de Angola* (FNLA) reduced its raids from Zaire. In the tiny, oil-rich Cabinda enclave fighting appeared ended as the Front for the Liberation of the Enclave of Cabinda called for peace talks with the MPLA.

Shock waves from the abortive coup of May 1977 were still felt. Nito Alves' message of black power raised up many opponents to the racially mixed MPLA leadership. During the ensuing purge which went into 1978, eight of the sixteen provincial commissioners were removed. Thousands of "nitists" were detained as the purge swept through the army, trade unions, women's organizations, and university.

Foreign Affairs. Relations with neighboring states directly influenced internal events. Zaire's and South Africa's support for FNLA and UNITA, for example, created problems for the MPLA in the countryside. In retaliation, Angola allowed Katanga rebels to launch a raid into Zaire in May. After that relations improved between the two countries.

The United States dispatched a representative to Luanda to discuss the future of Namibia which borders Angola. Washington does not recognize the MPLA because of the presence of 23,000 Cuban troops. Luanda established diplomatic relations with Portugal and opened talks with the European Community. Angola exchanged eight South African prisoners for three Cubans captured in the civil war when South Africa invaded on the side of UNITA.

Economy. Economic imperatives have spurred a foreign policy of nonalignment in order to achieve wider foreign aid. Foremost prewar exports of diamonds, coffee, and maize have not reached the targeted 1973 levels. Staples were imported for consumption. Only Gulf Oil's operations in Cabinda have attained the 1973 output, earning indispensable foreign currency. To rejuvenate production, DIAMANG, the diamond consortium, was nationalized and President Agostinho Neto designated 1978 as a year of agriculture. Food and cash crops occupy 85% of the population. The army was used in planting and harvesting sugar, cotton, and coffee.

THOMAS H. HENRIKSEN
State University of New York, Plattsburgh

ANGOLA · Information Highlights ————

Official Name: People's Republic of Angola.
Location: Southwestern Africa.
Area: 481,351 square miles (1,246,700 km²).
Population (1978 est.): 6,400,000.
Chief Cities (1973): Luanda, the capital, 540,000; Huambo, 89,000; Lobito, 74,000.
Government: *Head of state,* Agostinho Neto, President (took office Nov. 1975). *Head of government,* Lopo do Nascimento, prime minister (took office Nov. 1975).
Monetary Unit: Kwanza (38.71 kwanzas equal U. S.$1, April 1977).
Manufactures (major products): Various light industries, cement, fishing.
Agriculture (major products): Coffee, cotton, sisal, tobacco.

ANTHROPOLOGY

Important developments in the field of anthropology during 1978 included an analysis of aggression in chimpanzees, fossil discoveries, and a heated debate over the tenets of sociobiology (the theory that animal behavior evolves biologically and is genetically transmitted).

Dr. Jane Goodall, who studied a group of chimpanzees living in the Gombe Stream National Park in Tanzania, described how the group split into two factions and how the larger band systematically killed the members of the smaller band. While no definite explanations could be given, Dr. Goodall suggested that the split occurred because there were too many male chimps and an excess of tension in the group. In this regard, Goodall noted, the chimpanzee behavior was similar to that of human beings.

Fossil bones of the elbow and upper arm of *Aegyptopithecus,* approximately 30 million years old, were found in Egypt's Fayum Depression by Duke University primatologist Dr. Elwyn L. Simons. Simons pointed out that the bones have both human and ape characteristics and show that *Aegyptopithecus* was an evolutionary link between more primitive primates and later apes.

Human teeth found in China in 1965 were dated by a new method and found to be 1.7 million years old. The teeth are said to come from a very early form of *Homo erectus,* an extinct species that included Peking Man. This early form of *Homo erectus* was named Yuanmou Man, after the town near which the tooth specimens were discovered. The new dating of the Chinese specimens supported the view that *Homo erectus,* after developing in Africa between 1.7 and 1.8 million years ago, spread rapidly to other parts of the world. The new dating technique is based on the reversals of the earth's magnetic field, which have taken place at irregular intervals throughout history, and on the layers of sediment, glacial deposits, and other geologic residues in the earth's crust.

In February 1978, Dr. Mary D. Leakey announced the discovery of humanlike footprints about 3.59 million years old. They were found at Laetolil, Tanzania, where many other hominid fossils have been discovered, on the bottom of what once had been a watering hole. The footprints were covered by a layer of volcanic ash which had protected them from erosion. They are about 6 inches (15.2 cm) long and 4.5 inches (11.4 cm) wide and very close together. The creature who made the prints was estimated to be about 4 feet (1.22 m) tall and thought to have a rolling, slow-moving gait.

A major debate erupted in 1978 between anthropologists and proponents of sociobiological theory. The controversy actually began in 1975 with the publication of *Sociobiology: The New Synthesis,* by Edward O. Wilson, a Harvard sociobiologist. The book presents evidence showing that social behavior has developed similar patterns in a number of animal species. It is suggested that since human beings evolved from earlier animal forms, they still have genes that influence, perhaps even direct, social behavior. Sociobiologists claim that their theory adequately explains many aspects of human behavior, including homosexuality, male dominance, parent-offspring conflict, sibling rivalry, ethnocentrism and racial prejudice, and sex role differences. At the annual meeting of the American Association for the Advancement of Science, held in February 1978 in Washington, D. C., a symposium entitled "Sociobiology: Beyond Nature-Nurture" outlined the dimensions of the debate. Claims made by some sociobiologists seemed to go far beyond what even Wilson claimed. "Sociobiology is not a theory that human behavior has a genetic base," Dr Wilson explained, but a scientific discipline exploring the roots of social behavior in all animals. Dr. Jerome H. Barkow, an anthropologist at Dalhousie University, claimed that sociobiological concepts have been misapplied to human social behavior, since relations among men are culturally, as well as biologically, derived. Sociobiological theory, Dr. Barkow maintains, is more applicable to the evolution of culture than to specific human behaviors.

HERMAN J. JAFFE
Brooklyn College
City University of New York

Humanlike footprints, lower center and bottom right, over 3.5 million years old were discovered on hardened volcanic ash in the Laetolil region of Tanzania. Above are small antelope tracks and large elephant footprints.

UPI

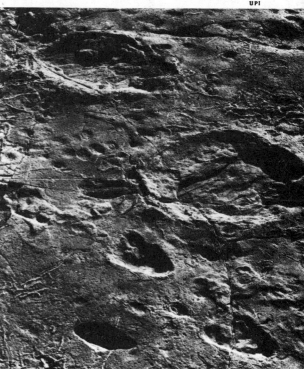

ARCHAEOLOGY

Royal burial grounds highlighted the archaeological discoveries of 1978 in the eastern hemisphere, while research in the western hemisphere focused on early cultures.

EASTERN HEMISPHERE

Paleolithic. In Tanzania, human footprints were found in a stratum 3.5 million years old. The prints belonged to an australopithecine animal who did not yet make stone tools.

The encampment of early Aurignacian hunters (32,000 B. C.) was excavated at Lommersum, West Germany. The camp ground was occupied at least three times, apparently by the same community of hunters. Most of the stone tools found were skin and meat processing implements, and most of the animal bones were from reindeer.

Pacific Stone Age. Evidence of human occupation of the Bismarck Archipelago, northeast of New Guinea, now goes back to c. 4,500 B. C. The earliest occupants lived in rock shelters, made stone chipping tools (including some of imported obsidian), and presumably were not agricultural like the later Lapitans.

During the excavation of a stone burial platform on Easter Island, lithic eyes for the great stone statues were discovered. The whites of the eyes were represented by white coral ellipses and the irises by red lava. This lava was also used for the top knots, or hats, originally worn by the great stone heads (A. D. 500 and 1200).

Bronze Age. A Danish expedition on Bahrain found a harbor of the Dilmun culture cut into the bedrock of the island. The harbor dates from the third millennium B. C., like the ancient Indus civilization harbors of Ur and Lothal. The quay measures 40 meters (131 ft) in length. Distinctive Dilmun seals of the Persian Gulf were found in both Mesopotamia and the Indus sites, confirming trade between these regions. Fragmentary and intact ceramic boat models corroborate the Dilmun interest in shipping.

Beneath an artificial mound at Dendra, Greece, archaeologists uncovered a series of Early Bronze Age graves older than the famous shaft graves of Mycenae. These burial grounds, dated c. 2,500 B. C., include the graves of two horses and may mark the arrival in Greece of horse prizing Indo-Europeans, the direct forerunners of later Greeks.

The tops of the Stonehenge lintel stones were finally examined in 1978. On the outer ring of Sarsen stones two holes marking a sunrise alignment were found. Other holes in the lintels mark significant positions of the moon.

The mummy of Queen Tiye, grandmother of Pharaoh Tutankhamen, was at last identified. It was excavated in 1912. X rays of her skull matched closely those of her mother, Thuya. Moreover, electron microprobe analysis of hair from her scalp matched precisely that of hair in a hieroglyphically labeled golden chest in the tomb of Tutankhamen. Tiye was the daughter of two blond foreigners who had been brought to Egypt to teach horsemanship.

The tomb of Horemheb, Tutankhamen's adviser and later king in his own right, was also located. The 48 x 17 meters (157 x 56 ft), mud brick structure contains two courtyards. The

UPI

A sculpture of Cihuacoatl, sometimes called Serpent Woman, a manifestation of the Aztec earth goddess who ruled childbirth and death, was found in Mexico City early in 1978.

walls are decorated with reliefs showing Tutankh-amen, Asiatic and Nubian captives, and a seated Horemheb receiving tribute from the Egyptians. Most of the grave's treasures were taken by ancient plunderers, but a golden earring and imported Mycenean pottery were found.

A wind-swept hill north of Thisted, Denmark, holds an earth tumulus set about with stones. A 20-gram (0.7-ounce) gold armlet identified the grave as that of a chieftain from the Middle Bronze Age.

A grave containing a variety of feminine articles—a bronze mirror, cosmetics box, perfume flask, and household articles—was found in the village of Gvardeitsj, the Soviet Union. More surprising, however, were the short sword and quiver of arrows found buried with this Iron Age woman! This discovery supports Herodotus' accounts of female warriors in this European-Asian frontier zone.

American and Saudi Arabian geologists believe they have found the fabled King Solomon's mine. The ancient mine, which produced the gold that adorned the great temple in Jerusalem, lies halfway between Mecca and Medina at a place called Mahd Adh Dhahab (Gold Pits). There is evidence that the mine was worked in the first millennium B. C.

Pompeii produced 25 remarkable finds on the eve of the 1,900th anniversary of its destruction. These bronze objects—lamps, a decorated bowl, and ornamental fibulae—came from a restaurant for the well-to-do. A nearly life-size bronze statue was also found.

The high chief of the Coskei tribe in South Africa sponsored the excavation of the grave of his great-great-grandfather, a resister of colonialism. According to official British records, he had drowned in 1852 while attempting to escape from confinement. The recovered skeleton, however, shows a neat bullet hole in the left shoulder blade.

Vikings. The final graves and bodies of Gorm the Old, first king of Denmark, and his wife Thyra, were found beneath the remains of a stave church built at Jelling, Denmark, by their son Harold Bluetooth, the first Christian king of Denmark. The original grave mounds of Harold's parents were excavated in 1822, but the tombs were empty. Apparently, so as to Christianize his beloved parents, Harold moved them from their pagan tombs to graves under the church. Artifacts include openwork crosses, a silver dragon ornament, and an ornamental dove.

WESTERN HEMISPHERE

Amid the debris of a Viking Age settlement at Godthaab, Greenland, an Iron Age axe modeled after an Eskimo form by early Norsemen, was found. Also unearthed, at a level dated A. D. 1300, was a small silver shield bearing the coat-of-arms of Clan Campbell of Highland Scotland.

Paleo-Indians and Before. At the Shriver Site in northwest Missouri, a flake-tool assemblage was recovered from loess *beneath* a fluted point Paleo-Indian assemblage dated c. 10,000 B. C. The heavily worn tools were first produced by a prepared core technique somewhat like the Levalloisian method used in the Old World. Some of the most common tools were scrapers, burins, and enigmatic bifaces broken crossways. Such tools had been found before, but never in a clear context. This tool industry is dated by thermoluminescence to earlier than 13,000 B. C.

At Taima-Taima, Venezuela, projectile points of the El Jobo complex were found at a swamp kill site. One of the points still lay in the pubis area of a juvenile mastodon. Wooden stakes were preserved in the wet soil. The origin of these objects, according to radiocarbon dating, is c. 12,000 B. C.

Mastodon remains and human tools are rarely found in the same North American kill site. At the Manis site in the state of Washington, however, a bone projectile was found stuck in the skeleton of a mastodon. An ovate stone scraper provided further evidence of human presence at this Ice Age site.

South American Stone Age Farmers. A food gathering and perhaps primitive agricultural people (c. 5,000 B. C.) periodically camped at La Paloma, Peru. The dead were buried beneath and inside their houses, along with such artifacts as preserved textiles and shellfish.

The Valdivia Culture of Ecuador is marked by the close similarity of its earliest pottery (c. 2,500 B. C.) to that of the Jomon Culture of Japan. The Valdivian site of Real Alto is remarkable in a different regard, however. Examination of phytoliths, small siliceous bodies found in grassy stems, shows that corn (native to Meso-America) was grown there by 3,000 B. C. The skeleton of a woman from about the same time was found buried beneath the entrance to a templelike structure. The temple appeared to have been rebuilt at least eight times. The bottom of the grave held the remains of a powerfully built young man whose legs had been severed at the knees and whose arms and legs were staked to the grave's floor. Seven stone knives were buried along with him. A short distance away lay the burial ground of seven other men.

Remains of the Bahia Culture (c. 500 B. C.) in Ecuador include gold decorations for the nose, lips, and ears; figurines of bearded men, some in a squatting position; and pottery depicting houses with peaked roofs.

North American Farmers. The concurrent recovery of carbonized squash seeds from Phillips Spring in Missouri and three other Archaic sites on the Green River in Kentucky provided the oldest evidence of agriculture in North America (c. 2,500 B. C.). Like corn, the squash originally came from Meso-America. Corn was grown nearly, but not quite, as long ago on the eastern seaboard of North America.

RALPH M. ROWLETT, *University of Missouri*

ARCHITECTURE

The single most important development in architecture in 1978 was a growing public awareness of architecture's effect on our lives. This emerging awareness is still too new to have achieved any formal articulations, but the breadth of the interest aroused is notable. There are many clear indications that people are yearning and searching for a better quality of life. While different individuals or groups offer different definitions of what a good life is, all seem deeply committed to finding a more satisfying quality of life.

In this new climate, it is not surprising that architecture is receiving a great deal of attention. As the world becomes increasingly shaped into urban patterns, its architecture has more and more impact on life. In an urban society, architecture is without question the major physical element affecting men's lives. In fact, architecture has such a pervasive influence that until recently most people have been oblivious to it.

One result of current society's concern for values is that architecture is receiving wider and more intensive examination than ever before. As a result, the public is witnessing greater experimentation by the architectural profession than ever before.

Architects share the concerns of the general public. Society is beginning to recognize that the resources of the United States and of the world are limited. Architects know that the public cannot afford to squander its resources in the construction of meaningless buildings or structures that demean the quality of life. The result of this recognition can be seen in discernible changes in attitude toward the environment. Two of the more obvious trends in this direction are:

1. A dramatic increase in the "recycling" or extended use of existing buildings. This phenomenon is developing across the United States, in hamlets as well as in cities of all sizes. The general public, government officials, developers, owners, and money lenders recognize that much of the existing building stock is entirely too valuable to destroy in favor of new buildings. It has now been amply demonstrated that many existing buildings can be retrofitted to meet the most demanding criteria for current usage. Furthermore, these older buildings can generally be upgraded at a lower unit cost than that of replacement. Architects and the public are also finding that these retrofitted buildings often bring a warmth and style to the cities that newer construction has not been able to achieve.

2. The creation of a second generation of energy-conscious design. When energy shortages began to affect the United States, the first approach to solving building problems was the hardware approach. This basically consisted of installing more insulation, refining mechanical systems, and improving maintenance and operational procedures. These actions, while beneficial and necessary, did not generate the energy savings necessary to meet U. S. needs. As a result, there was, and still is, much talk of lowering the standards of comfort and returning to a "simpler life style." This will not be a satisfactory solution for many. Instead, a second generation of energy conscious design involves greater reliance on architectural solutions. Such architectural solutions include proper orientation of buildings to reduce or increase the solar load; selected mass location design; natural daylighting and glare control to reduce artificial lighting requirements; natural ventilation and greater use of outside air to condition interior spaces; and similar considerations such as proper location of openings and reflective surfaces. Architects are even experimenting in buildings located wholly or partially underground. Such construction takes advantage of constant temperature conditions below grades. In addition to the pure conservation approach, extensive work is going on in the alternative energy field. Some of this includes research of on-site solar design. The two major thrusts in this area are solar heating and cooling and waste products utilization. Of the two, solar heating and cooling is the most widespread and shows great potential in residential design. Solar heating of domestic hot water is now readily obtainable, and solar-assisted heating systems are becoming increasingly available. In their most advanced use, these systems are so thoroughly integrated into the overall building design that they actually enhance the building's visual delight.

This concern for conservation is accompanied by a growing respect for the architecture of the past. While the public's regard may be partially founded in nostalgia for a simpler life of the past, it is not nostalgia alone which brings about this concern for man's historical heritage. Society is beginning to recognize the true value of older buildings. Their delightful play of forms and materials inspires the public, and this important link with man's heritage will help to meet future emotional needs. This respect for the past marks a maturing of architecture and heralds the advent of a more unified urban scene, one that better responds to the public's emotional needs. It is a recognition of the architectural profession's responsibility. It transcends the simple, single design statement of a single building or even a complex of buildings. Architects and the public must endeavor to create the new elements of urban buildings that will enhance their older existing neighbors.

In their constant search for new spaces for people, architects are beginning to go beyond the established design styles that were once determined by a few highly gifted professional leaders. Architects are deliberately attempting to create spaces and forms that offer wider vari-

UPI

Architects, generally, are searching for more energy-conscious designs. A mirrowed glass wall of the new engineering center of the Southern California division of Fluor Engineers and Constructors, Inc., reflects the image of a free-standing tower that directs climate-controlled air into the building. The facility provides engineering and construction services to its world-wide clients.

ety than in the recent past. There is a greater sense of whimsy in many of these attempts, most notably experiments in color and texture. While some of this new work is forced, and therefore ill at ease, both the public and the architectural profession are becoming more sure in their search and thus in their directions, and these minor faults will soon disappear. In all probability, an emerging new style of architecture is being sensed.

It is doubtful that, even at this new level of awareness, the first style direction taken will satisfy the real needs of the public. Perhaps that is the true joy of the creation of new architecture. There can never be a perfect building. For, as the architectural profession develops new skills and expertise, the public becomes more sophisticated and more demanding. Where these new directions will lead is not known, but all the evidence points to the creation of buildings with a greater sense of visual delight and human scale.

Finally, there is increasing involvement by citizens in the decision-making process of architectural development. In the past, public involvement has all too often been a counterproductive, negative action, wasteful of time and money. Frequently, outstanding projects were delayed until they withered or were killed off outright, often leaving scars of demolition and a wasteland of parking lots and rubble.

Confrontation is slowly giving way to co-operation. As this happens, progress is speeded up and, more importantly, people experience a heightened sense of pride and glory in the end product. The architectural profession becomes more sure of itself with each new project. As the public places greater trust in the architectural guild, substantial strides will be made in the creation of architecture that truly enhances the quality of life. The future of architecture is remarkably bright. For, as people comprehend the total impact architecture has on living, they will seek further understanding of the architectural elements which shape their living spaces.

As the search grows for architecture that will bring a greater sense of contentment to the user, there will be greater demands for general public education about architecture. This education should not dwell on what is good architecture or bad architecture, for those decisions are transitory at best. It should instead teach the public about the fundamentals of architecture, and show them what criteria to use to evaluate the options offered at all levels of the architectural design and building process. In time, the public may recognize that the definition of architecture is not "the building of structures," but rather "the creation of spaces, both positive and negative, that people live in, work in, play in, and move through, to get from one activity to another." When that understanding occurs, architects and the public will truly be able to create cities that are a delight to the senses.

See also ENERGY; HOUSING.

ELMER E. BOTSAI
President
The American Institute of Architects

95

AMERICAN INSTITUTE OF ARCHITECTS' 1978 AWARD WINNERS

Buildings cited included: the Art Institute of Chicago (*above*, *left*), "as a significant work of urban sculpture in a major open space;" the Charles Eames House, Pacific Palisades, Calif., "a prototype of modern style;" and the Robert Elliott House (*below*), Chevy Chase, Md., a "Gothic Revival cottage" expanded into a "modern house with an addition that is original and reflective."

PHOTOS, COURTESY AIA

President Jorge Videla welcomes Chile's Orrego Vicuna to a ceremony commemorating Argentina's independence.

UPI

ARGENTINA

Argentina hosted the world soccer championship play-offs in June and went on to win the World Cup for the first time.

Government and Human Rights. After his retirement from the army on July 31, Jorge Videla remained as president of Argentina; his tenure was extended for a three year period. The plan was announced in March, on the second anniversary of the 1976 coup against Isabel Perón. Under the new formula, the president would be a retired military officer, with vastly increased presidential powers. The plan called for the appointment of new commanders of the armed services, who would form the ruling junta. Accordingly, Gen. Roberto Viola replaced Videla, Vice Admiral Armando Lambruschini assumed the post held by Adm. Emilio Massera, and the air force would replace Gen. Orlando Agosti in 1979. The decision to elevate Videla was opposed by Admiral Massera, who had presidential ambitions of his own. Videla promised an eventual return to a constitutional democracy in which the armed forces would be assured of an active role.

Meanwhile, five charges were being pressed in the courts against deposed President Perón. In the cases charging her with embezzlement, detention was ordered. She has been held on her late husband's estate near Buenos Aires, since August.

Government officials admitted that the army and police had been excessive, at times, in the suppression of left-wing terrorism. Human rights

organizations, while praising the Videla regime for publishing a list of 3,600 people jailed for security reasons, urged the junta to crack down on right-wing terrorist groups. Rights organizations divulged the names of 2,542 persons whose abduction by armed groups had been reported, but who were not included in the government list. Rights groups revealed also that an average of 75 missing-person reports were being filed each month. A report by the U. S. State Department, that appeared in Buenos Aires in February, maintained that there were between 12,000 and 17,000 political prisoners in Argentina, of whom only 5,000 to 7,500 were being held in official jails. The remainder were in secret military camps and police detention centers.

As the government attributed the suppression of human rights to persistent left-wing terrorism, leftist remnants continued to attack po-

---

ARGENTINA · Information Highlights

Official Name: Republic of Argentina.
Location: Southern South America.
Area: 1,072,158 square miles (2,776,889 km²).
Population (1978 est.): 26,400,000.
Chief Cities (1975 est.): Buenos Aires, the capital, 2,972,453; Cordoba, 781,565; Rosario, 750,455.
Government: *Head of state and government,* Jorge Videla, president (assumed office March 1976). *Legislature*—Congress (dissolved March 24, 1976); Legislative Advisory Commission established.
Monetary Unit: Peso (981.5 new pesos equal U. S.$1, Dec. 28, 1978).
Manufactures (major products): Processed foods, motor vehicles, consumer durables, textiles, chemicals, printing, metallurgy.
Agriculture (major products): Grains, oilseeds, livestock products.

lice facilities and government officials. In April, a key labor specialist in the ministry of economy was assassinated and attempts were made on the life of President Videla's top civilian adviser. Vice Admiral Lambruschini narrowly escaped death in August in a bomb blast that killed his 15-year-old daughter. Targets of state terrorism have been professionals and religious groups, including Jews.

Foreign Affairs. Relations with Chile deteriorated after Argentina rejected arbitration awarding Chile three disputed islands in the Beagle Channel. When it appeared that talks were not going to produce an acceptable solution, Argentine cities began preparations for air raids, land and maritime forces were mobilized, and the naval commander was sent into the disputed territory. Some Chileans in Argentina were deported. Pleas for a peaceful resolution of the border conflict came from the Vatican as well as from intellectuals and churchmen in both countries.

President Videla traveled to the Bolivian oil fields at Yacuiba on October 25, for talks with his Bolivian counterpart, President Juan Pereda. An international bridge over the Pilcomayo was dedicated by the two heads of government, and the extension of an Argentine railway into Bolivia was discussed.

Joint planning with Paraguay of a (U. S.) $4 billion hydroelectric dam on the Paraná River at Yaciretá advanced, but the Paraguayan and Argentine Corpus dam on the same river remained under discussion. In September, another round of talks was held in Brazil, without a decision on the height of the Corpus project. The Brazilian-Paraguayan Itaipú dam project would be affected by the height of the downstream Corpus dam.

In September, foreign minister Oscar Montes met with U. S. Secretary of State Cyrus Vance to revive relations between the two countries following a bitter note from General Videla to his counterpart, President Jimmy Carter. The strong statement coincided with testimony before the U. S. House of Representatives by Patricia Derian, a top human rights official in the U. S. State Department.

Economy. In spite of a rigorous application of anti-inflationary policies, inflation reached an annual rate of 150% in September. The 1978 budget was balanced at 8,000 billion pesos. Monetary reserves at the Central Bank rose to (U. S.) $6 billion in July, leading Argentina to repay some foreign loans ahead of schedule. Exports of meat, maize, cotton, and soybeans increased.

The first offshore oil discovery was announced in March. Petroleum was located at 10,169 feet (3,100 m) in the South Atlantic, at the Gulf of San Jorge. Despite the prospect of greater quantities of available petroleum, production of cars and motorized vehicles plunged; tractor production fell by 76% over 1977. General Motors and Citroën have announced their withdrawal from car and truck production in Argentina.

An improved economic situation has made additional credit available. The Inter-American Development Bank lent $105 million in December 1977 for the construction of a petrochemical complex in Bahía Blanca. A World Bank loan of $105 million was arranged to finance the installation of 20 grain elevators. A requested $270 million loan for the purchase of 20 turbines for the Yaciretá hydroelectric project, rejected in August by the U. S. Export-Import Bank because of a failure to respect human rights in Argentina, was approved in November.

Labor. Labor seriously had challenged the military government in October 1977, when railroad and subway workers, as well as employees of some other state enterprises, walked off their jobs. After an immediate offer by the government of wage increases of up to 40% was rejected, the workers were forced back to their jobs. Peace was partially restored and Argentina was represented in June 1978 at the annual meeting of the International Labor Organization (ILO), in Geneva, Switzerland, by spokesmen for 25 unions that have remained independent of government control, and represent about 30% of the labor force.

LARRY L. PIPPIN, *Elbert Covell College*
University of the Pacific

ARIZONA

After only four months in office, Arizona Gov. Wesley Bolin died in March of a heart attack. His unexpected death put State Attorney General Bruce Babbitt, also a Democrat, into the governor's office. The popular and youthful governor then went on to defeat his Republican opponent, Evan Mecham, in the November gubernatorial elections.

Elections. Governor Babbitt's popularity with Arizona voters did not extend to all of his fellow Democratic hopefuls. The November election returns showed Arizonans evenly dividing up the various state and national offices, with Republicans winning the attorney general's,

---
ARIZONA • Information Highlights

Area: 113,909 square miles (295,024 km²).

Population (Jan. 1978 est.) 2,321,000.

Chief Cities (1970 census): Phoenix, the capital, 581,-562; Tucson, 262,933; Scottsdale, 67,823.

Government (1978): *Chief Officers*—governor, Bruce Babbitt (D). *Legislature*—Senate, 30 members; House of Representatives, 60 members.

Education (1977–78): *Enrollment*—public elementary schools, 358,889 pupils; public secondary, 154,928; colleges and universities, 181,503 students. *Public school expenditures,* $780,874,000 ($1,349 per pupil).

State Finances (fiscal year 1977): *Revenues,* $2,107,-037,000; *expenditures,* $1,865,661,000.

Personal Income (1977): $14,943,000,000; per capita, $6,509.

Labor Force (July 1978): *Nonagricultural wage and salary earners,* 831,500; *unemployed,* 61,400 (6.1% of total force).

treasurer's, and state mine inspector's offices. Democrats were elected to the offices of secretary of state and superintendent of public instruction. In the four Congressional races, all four incumbents were reelected: John Rhodes (R), Morris Udall (D), Robert Stump (D), and Eldon Rudd (R).

Also of interest in this election was the passage of a proposition limiting legislative expenditures to 7% of the total personal income in the state. This proposition reflected the national trend to limit government spending, and thus provide relief for the taxpayer.

Republicans captured control of both houses of the state legislature in 1978, marking a shift away from Democratic leadership in the state senate.

The Economy. The economic picture in Arizona was clouded by the troubled copper industry. Arizona produces in excess of 60% of the nation's copper, but a steep rise in imports, coupled with expensive pollution control outlays, resulted in a slump in the state's copper industry. Some 5,000 jobs were eliminated in 1978, and efforts were made to seek federal action to limit copper imports to the United States.

Legislation. The governor and legislature gave top priority to prison reform. The poor condition of the state's correction system was dramatized when two convicts escaped from the Florence State Prison in July, wielding guns that were smuggled in by the sons of one of the escapees. The two, together with three other persons, then went on a ten-day shooting spree throughout Arizona, Utah, and Colorado, which resulted in the murder of four innocent victims and the disappearance of a couple, presumed murdered, in Colorado. The "Tison gang" was finally captured near Casa Grande, Ariz. in a shoot-out which left two of the suspects dead. It was one of the most violent crimes in the state's history.

The legislature attempted to remedy the severe problems of overcrowding and low employee morale in the prison system with a $34 million appropriation, which includes plans for the construction of two new prisons. The state's criminal code was completely revised, abolishing obsolete laws and requiring mandatory sentencing for certain crimes.

The Milk Scandal. The state's dairy industry was involved in two public controversies in 1978. Four Arizona dairy companies were named in a federal lawsuit which charged them with price-fixing. Three of the four pleaded no-contest and agreed to repay consumers $4 million. Later in the year, excessive levels of aflatoxin, a chemical added to livestock feed, were found in the state's milk supplies. Charges in the scandal included a cover-up on the part of state officials whose job it is to monitor the dairy industry throughout the state.

JEANNE NIENABER
University of Arizona

ARKANSAS

While elections, the impact of inflation, and tax issues dominated the Arkansas political scene, the unexpected also attracted public attention. The University of Arkansas Razorback's 1978 Orange Bowl gridiron upset victory over the University of Oklahoma thrilled the state. A record 12-inch (31-cm) rain storm in Pulaski County caused loss of life and multimillion dollar flood damage to property. Health and environmental hazards caused by derailment of tank cars filled with toxic materials and by exposure of employees to industrial chemicals horrified the public.

Elections. The death of six-term U. S. Sen. John L. McClellan in 1977 created an exciting, wide-open Democratic primary as office-holding incumbents vacated positions to compete for the Senate seat. In a hotly contested primary and runoff primary, Governor David Pryor defeated two outstanding, popular U. S. Representatives—Jim Guy Tucker of Little Rock and Ray Thornton of Fordyce—for the senatorial nomination. Youthful Bill Clinton, state Attorney General and consumer interest advocate, overwhelmed four other candidates for the gubernatorial nomination. Following a lackluster general election campaign, Democrats defeated most Republican challengers except in northwestern Arkansas, where John Paul Hammerschmidt was reelected to a seventh term in the U. S. House of Representatives, and in the metropolitan Little Rock area where Ed Bethune, in a surprise victory, won a second House seat for the Republicans. Nonpartisan contests for the 100 delegate seats to the 1979 constitutional convention were spirited.

Inflation. The public clamored for limits on governmental expenditures while teachers and public employees pressed for needed salary increases. A consumer-initiated amendment to exempt food and drugs from the 3% state sales tax was decisively defeated. North Little Rock residents by referendum rejected a rate increase for the city electric utility.

Taxes. School districts and cities criticized

———— ARKANSAS • Information Highlights ————

Area: 53,104 square miles (137,539 km²).
Population (Jan. 1978 est.): 2,159,000.
Chief Cities (1970 census): Little Rock, the capital, 132,483; Fort Smith, 62,802.
Government (1978): *Chief Officers*—governor, David Pryor (D); lt. gov., Joe Purcell (D). *General Assembly*—Senate, 35 members; House of Representatives, 100 members.
Education (1977–78): *Enrollment*—public elementary schools, 240,447 pupils; public secondary, 218,331; colleges and universities, 71,255 students. *Public school expenditures,* $591,983,000 ($1,134 per pupil).
State Finances (fiscal year 1977): *Revenues,* $1,568,-624,000; *expenditures,* $1,521,155,000.
Personal Income (1977): $11,878,000,000; per capita, $5,540.
Labor Force (July 1978): *Nonagricultural wage and salary earners,* 726,000; *unemployed,* 57,300 (5.6% of total force).

administration of the property tax. Locally elected county tax assessors had assessed property at 3% to 14% of market value instead of the recommended 20%. Metropolitan counties lost substantial amounts of state aid to public schools because the state Assessment Coordination Division falsely certified for these counties lower than actual tax assessments ratios, upon which state aid was based. A circuit court judge ruled the property tax assessments unconstitutional and ordered property to be reassessed at 20% of its market value—a program which could increase tax bills in some counties by as much as 600%.

Administration. A 10-year controversy over the constitutionality of the treatment of state prisoners ended when a federal judge approved a consent decree governing future practices. State officials began withholding funds from nursing homes that provide inadequate care to Medicaid patients. A legislative consultant report concluded that Arkansas made a weaker financial commitment to an inadequate public school system than any other state. Despite a record $2 billion state revenue collection, the state's financial future was not rosy. State agencies searched for funds to maintain services and also requested big budget increases for the next biennium.

WILLIAM C. NOLAN
Southern Arkansas University

ARMS CONTROL AND DISARMAMENT

In May, representatives of 149 countries, all members of the United Nations, met in New York for the General Assembly Special Session on Disarmament. The session resulted from the initiative taken by the nonaligned nations, and its purposes were to emphasize the importance of making progress in arms control and to support future arms control negotiations. In 1978 the major arms control effort was the attempt by the United States and the Soviet Union to negotiate a SALT II treaty to replace the SALT I agreement which limited intercontinental ballistic missiles (ICBM's) and submarine launched ballistic missiles (SLBM's). The SALT I accord had expired in 1977 but the two nations agreed to abide by its terms while the new arrangement was being worked out.

SALT II. The basic outline of the proposed SALT II treaty reflects agreement between Moscow and Washington on the principle of "equal aggregates." This means that both nations will have equal numbers of strategic nuclear delivery systems, i.e., of ICBM's, SLBM's, and long range bombers, but that the apportionment of the total weapons among the systems will be left up to the individual nation. The aggregate figure generally referred to is 2,400 weapons. It is expected that the United States and the USSR will agree that no more than 1,320 missiles, either ICBM's or SLBM's, may be equipped with multiple individually-targeted re-entry vehicles (MIRV's).

Although the general parameters of the SALT II agreement appeared clear, and seemingly acceptable to both nations, several areas of needed agreement eluded the negotiators. One of these concerned the American cruise missile. A Pentagon report released in November indicated the U. S. cruise missile could penetrate Soviet air defenses, and could continue to do so even after the expenditure by the Soviets of the equivalent of (U. S.) $50 billion. Consequently, the Soviet negotiators were insistent upon constraints being placed upon the American weapon.

Intense negotiations also concerned whether to limit the Soviet Backfire bomber. According to some Americans, this craft could reach the United States under certain conditions. Hence, it was argued that it should be counted against the 2,400 aggregate. The Soviets insisted the Backfire is not a strategic bomber designed to hit the United States and therefore should not be counted against the numerical ceiling.

In late December, U. S. Secretary of State Cyrus Vance held prolonged talks with Soviet Foreign Minister Andrei A. Gromyko regarding a SALT II treaty. Although the year ended without a new pact, a SALT II treaty was said to be near.

Near the end of the year several events beclouded the fate of the possible SALT II treaty ratification in the Senate. The man primarily responsible for arms control negotiations in the Carter administration, Paul C. Warnke, director of the Arms Control and Disarmament Agency, resigned. The president nominated George M. Seignious, a retired Army lieutenant general and president of The Citadel, as his successor.

The November elections which resulted in several new senators of hardline reputation going to Washington altered the makeup of the Senate, where 34 negative votes could defeat a treaty. This produced speculation that President Carter might appeal to former public officials, including former Secretary of State Henry Kissinger, to assist in providing bipartisan support for the agreement.

Civil Defense. Late in November the president asked that new funds be added to the 1979 budget for civil defense activity, and that work be expanded on the development of the MX ICBM and the Trident II SLBM. Some observers suggested these requests were actually designed to strengthen the president's hand when it came time for him to argue that it was safe for the United States to sign a new arms accord with the Soviet Union.

Other Matters. While the attention of much of the world was focused on the SALT II efforts, the United States and the USSR also conducted arms control negotiations regarding other matters. These included talks about the possibility of banning hunter-killer satellites in space, and the limitation of the naval rivalry in the Indian Ocean.

ROBERT M. LAWRENCE
Colorado State University

ART

A 12th century Mosan plaque from the Robert von Hirsch collection sold for more than $2 million.

UPI

The year's highlights in the art world included the auction of the collection of Robert von Hirsch; the continued success of the Tutankhamen exhibition; and the opening of a new wing at the National Gallery.

The "Auction of the Century." The fabulous art collection of Robert von Hirsch, who died in 1977 in Basel, Switzerland, at the age of 94, was auctioned in June by Sotheby Parke Bernet in London for a record breaking total of $34.1 million. The Frankfurt-born leather manufacturer had been permitted to emigrate to Switzerland in 1933, taking his already famous collection with him, in return for leaving behind a Cranach painting. He had bought his first picture, a Toulouse-Lautrec, in 1907 and since then had added to his collection, which dated to the Middle Ages and Renaissance. Works in a variety of media were included. The period after World War I saw the dispersal of many historic private collections in Austria, Germany, and the USSR. This offered a collector like Hirsch an opportunity that will probably never be repeated. At his death he owned more than 700 works of the highest quality, including painting, sculpture, drawings, enamels, ivories, furniture, porcelain, and carpets. It was a collection reflecting Hirsch's own taste, not acquired for investment purposes, as is often the case now, but out of love, and it was a part of his everyday life. The collection was so remarkable that before its dispersal, it was shown in museums in Frankfurt, Zurich, and London. Unlike many modern patrons, Hirsch did not bequeath his treasures to a museum with his name attached, but directed that the works be sold in order to give other collectors the chance to enjoy acquisition and ownership. However, very few objects went to private owners.

The museums of West Germany acquired the bulk of the Hirsch collection for a price of almost $20 million. Following a secret plan coordinated by German government officials and financed by a combination of federal, state, and museum funds, art dealers of different nationalities bid successfully against other collectors and dealers and won for a number of German museums every desired object. They were all works with German associations, either by German artists or of historical importance. Thus, for example, the enamel plaque worn by Frederick Barbarossa as part of his imperial regalia went to the Nuremberg Museum ($2,024,000); a twelfth century candlestick, attributed to a Cologne artist and part of the Guelph collection, returned to Hannover ($312,800); a Mosan plaque from the Stavelot retable went to the Staatliche Museum in Berlin ($2,208,000); an eighteenth century dressing table, by Abraham Roentgen for the Elector of Saxony ($369,000), and a Dürer watercolor landscape ($1,177,600), the last remaining in private hands and the only one ever to have been auctioned, were acquired for Germany. Of objects bought by others, the most significant were a twelfth century candlestick believed to have been made in Gloucester which was purchased as an investment by the pension fund of the British Rail Workers ($1,012,000) and a painting by the Sienese, Giovanni di Paolo, which went to the American collector Norton Simon ($1 million). Although the pension fund had to outbid the British Museum for the candlestick, the museum was given the privilege of exhibiting it.

Other auction records were also set in 1978, continuing a recent trend. Again, London-based houses led all others. Sotheby's increased its

UPI

Three Gutenberg Bibles, the first books printed by movable type, were sold within a six-month period.

sales over 1977 by 42% and Christie's by 45%. Sales of the former totaled $302,250,000 and the latter equaled $164,846,100. Generally, painting led all other categories, jewelry, surging well forward, reached second place, while furniture fell to third place. House sales were of increasing importance, and new categories like dolls and photographs became news.

Considering the rarity of the Gutenberg Bibles, it was quite an event that three of them were sold in New York within a six-month period of 1978. One was sold by Christie's for $2.2 million to a dealer acting for the Stuttgart Library. The other two were sold through dealers, one going to the Gutenberg Museum in Mainz and the other to the University of Texas.

Ancient Art. There has been an unusual interest in ancient art recently. "The Treasures of Tutankhamen," a record-topping show, ended a two-year tour of the United States in New York in December. Not only were the crowds of visitors everywhere phenomenal, but the theme of the show and the items in it inspired exploitation to an unprecedented degree. This went far beyond the traditional selling of books, photographs, and museum reproductions, and the usual lectures and guided tours. "Tutomania" swept the country, and Egyptian motifs decorated everything from bed linen to T-shirts. Some museums were accused of merchandising objects in very poor taste, but the public was happy, and so were the museums, with high profits assured, including the $5 million or so that was scheduled to go to the Cairo Museum.

It was the promise of this much-needed sum for restoration and new installations in Cairo that had enabled the Metropolitan Museum to negotiate the art loan.

A similar traveling exhibition came from the Naples Museum, "Pompeii 79 A. D." It opened its U. S. tour in Boston after very successful runs in London and Copenhagen and was to go to Chicago, Dallas, and New York. This exhibition was also showing objects never before removed from their place of origin; in this case the principal treasures were wall frescoes from Pompeii and Herculaneum.

Expansion of the National Gallery. On June 1, 1978, President Jimmy Carter inaugurated the new East Wing of the National Gallery (*see* page 105). A gift from members of the Mellon family, who were responsible for the original 1941 structure and also donated many of their treasures, it was designed by I. M. Pei at a cost of $94.4 million. In strong contrast to the academic, neoclassical style of the earlier building, the new one presents a thoroughly contemporary appearance with dramatic geometric forms and sharp angles, both inside and out. However, there is a certain harmony of character in the similar air of monumentality and grandeur, underscored by the use of the same Vermont marble veneer.

The wing consists of two parts, a larger one for exhibition space and a smaller one to house a Center for Advanced Study in the Visual Arts, with a library and study rooms for scholars, to be opened in 1979. There is a large court between the two sections covered by an 80-foot (24.4-m) high glass ceiling that provides space for several huge works of art specially commissioned for it, including a Calder mobile and a 30-foot (9-m) high Miró tapestry. The interior of the gallery building was left to the museum staff to design to suit the exhibitions, and it reveals an amazing variety of spaces.

As the National Gallery has changed its style of architecture, so also has it changed its collecting policy. Originally the National Gallery attempted to amass established Old Masters and famous names. Now it collects modern works and commissions contemporary artists.

It has been accused of using its position as a national museum to influence donors who might otherwise give to local museums. And by insisting on being the first to inaugurate foreign loan exhibitions, the National Gallery has particularly irked the Metropolitan Museum of New York, hitherto the undisputed leading American museum. Thus the National Gallery receives most of the publicity and the credit for exhibitions that have been jointly arranged with other museums, even when the other institutions have done most of the work. This was the case with "The Treasures of Tutankhamen." The Metropolitan did most of the planning and the negotiating with the Egyptian government for the exhibit but was the last to receive the show.

Theft and Vandalism

Cultural institutions and law enforcement officials throughout the world have been joining forces to solve a disturbing and rapidly growing problem: the theft and defacement of valuable works of art.

In France and Italy, police statistics indicate that between 1970 and 1975 art theft increased by 400%, a rate far exceeding that of other crimes. In 1977, in Italy, more than 800 incidents of art theft were recorded, and more than 16,500 objects disappeared. A 1978 study released by the New York-based International Foundation for Art Research indicated that theft has become a chronic problem for art owners. An estimated 73% of all art dealers in the United States and 72% of all U. S. museums have experienced at least one theft in the last five years. In 1978, multiple thefts were reported in Europe and the United States. Among the most noteworthy were three small bronze statues by the French sculptor Auguste Rodin, stolen February 20 from the St. Louis (Mo.) Art Museum; the *Three Graces,* a masterpiece by the Flemish painter Peter Paul Rubens, and nine other paintings stolen from the Pitti Palace museum in Florence, Italy on April 21; the *Manneken Pis,* Belgium's most famous statue, stolen from a square in downtown Brussels, April 26; and Rembrandt's *Portrait of a Rabbi,* valued at more than $1 million, taken from San Francisco's DeYoung Memorial Museum in December.

Art vandalism, although rarer in occurrence, poses a more serious threat. Generally unknown before the 1970's, this form of violence seems to represent a disturbed retaliation against society and its aesthetic heritage. The most outstanding incidents of art vandalism in 1978 were the slashings of Vincent Van Gogh's *La Berceuse* in the Municipal Museum at Amsterdam and his *Self-Portrait in Gray Hat* in Amsterdam's Van Gogh Museum; the acid attack on three Rembrandt paintings in Kassel, Germany; and the slashing of the 17th-century masterpiece by Nicholas Poussin, *Adoration of the Golden Calf,* at the National Gallery in London.

The 1973 hammer attack on Michelangelo's *Pietà,* the spray painting of Pablo Picasso's *Guernica* that same year, and the 1974 slashing of Rembrandt's *Night Watch* also received wide publicity in the media, which may have contributed to the spread of the problem. Today, every museum must take extreme security precautions to guard against such acts. These measures reduce the pleasure of visiting a museum and impair one's ability to appreciate works of art.

Art theft and vandalism can be attributed to several causes. One is the sharp increase in the last 20 years in the market value of paintings, sculptures, and other works of art. In response to intense competition among museums, collectors, and investors, art prices have skyrocketed. The sale of artistic masterpieces for millions of dollars has become a common affair. In addition, art is becoming increasingly popular. Museum education programs and exhibitions continuously promote and expand the public appreciation of art. In 1979, some 1.3 million people are expected to attend the traveling Tutankhamen exhibition during its stay in New York. The combination of increased publicity and increased prices has made art objects more conspicuous and more desirable than ever before.

Their uniqueness, fragility, and great public appeal have made works of art vulnerable targets for ransom thefts, commonly referred to as "artnapping." For example, in 1972, a young radical cut Jan Vermeer's celebrated *Love Letter* from its frame and demanded a ransom of 20 million French francs on behalf of Bengali refugees. In 1974, Irish radicals "artnapped" a valuable collection from the home of British industrialist Sir Albert Beit and demanded a huge ransom. Although such extortion attempts are rarely successful, they do provide wide exposure for the thieves and their cause.

While "artnappings" have accounted for the most notorious cases of the last decade, they represent only a small portion of all the art thefts that occur. In some cases, thefts are commissioned by private collectors for their own personal pleasure. In 1977, a Viennese millionaire, Gerhard Berger, was convicted of commissioning art thefts for a clandestine private collection.

Most common, however, is the art thief who robs a small museum, a local church, or a private collection. The objects are sold in areas remote from the place of theft and eventually find their way into the collections of innocent buyers or into the open market. Art thieves often benefit from differences in national laws pertaining to theft. In some countries, such as France and Belgium, a statute of limitations requires prosecution for art theft within three years.

The search for famous lost works is led by Interpol, the international police agency, which circulates information on stolen items and annually publishes a list of the *12 Most Wanted Works of Art.* Also, several European governments maintain sophisticated records on art theft; art dealer associations circulate notices of suspicious objects; and the Art Theft Archive, established by the International Foundation for Art Research, annually publishes an Index of Stolen Art. The many objects recovered through the efforts of these agencies suggest the continuing need for a worldwide network of cooperation and information exchange to combat art theft.

BONNIE BURNHAM

As Washington is the nation's capital, some foreign governments choose it in preference to other cities, as happened in the case of the exhibition from mainland China, "The Archeological Finds of the People's Republic of China," which was not shown in New York at all. The major new international loan exhibition, "The Splendor of Dresden: 500 Years of Collecting," opened in Washington with the inauguration of the East Wing and went to New York at the end of the year. The Dresden show is memorable for its reconstruction of the "Kunstkammer" (art room) begun in 1560 by the Elector of Saxony. It is full of exotic objects, natural and man-made, artistic and scientific. In addition there is a selection of choice pieces of jewelry, armor, silver, and porcelain, as well as paintings, prints, and bronzes.

The Metropolitan Museum of Art. Thomas Hoving's era as director of the Metropolitan Museum of Art came to an end officially, and a new policy was instituted to separate the financial and artistic responsibilities. The museum's chief executive (whose title is president) is now an administrator with no previous experience in the field of art, William Macomber, a retired diplomat. The former acting director, Philip de Montebello, was promoted to director, but in a position subordinate to the president. He will supervise exhibitions, acquisitions, publications, etc. Most other American museum directors criticized the Met's decision to separate the artistic and administrative functions of the head, but the Metropolitan has grown into such a large and complex organization that this may well be the only solution. It is an admission of the fact, already often noted, that the museum has become a big business and must be run like one. In 1977 the Metropolitan's operating budget was $32.7 million, up from $9.2 million in 1968. In order to augment funds from endowment and because of increased costs and expanded programs, it became the policy to move aggressively into such business enterprises as restaurants, garages, publishing, and merchandising. In 1977 sales totaled $14.1 million, 45% of the total revenue, although profit was only $1.5 million, due to the large expenses of the merchandising operations. Criticism is often expressed of the propriety of engaging in business on such a large scale and of the poor taste of some of the ventures, but the policy continues. The new director has forecast some restrictions in spending which will probably entail fewer loan exhibitions and million-dollar purchases.

Meanwhile the Met continues to expand, rivaling the National Gallery. A highlight was the opening of the Sackler Wing which houses the only complete Egyptian temple in America. Under a giant skylight and with one 200-foot (60-m) wall entirely of glass to let in the light and the view of Central Park, and with a reflecting pool to simulate the Nile, the small temple, constructed in traditional Egyptian style by Augustus between 23 and 10 B. C., has been rebuilt. It was a gift from Egypt in gratitude for American aid in saving Nubian monuments from flooding.

The Met's exhibition, "Monet's Years at Giverny," showed how the painter moved beyond Impressionism, as traceable in 50 years of painting the same theme: his garden in the village on the Seine where he lived from 1883 to 1926. Photographs of the garden were an interesting supplement to the paintings.

Other Exhibitions. The Boston Museum of Fine Arts also featured Monet, "Monet Unveiled," a new look at the museum's Monet holdings which are the largest outside the Louvre. Another nineteenth century giant, Courbet, was rediscovered with a large show at the Grand Palais in Paris on the occasion of the centenary of his death, Dec. 31, 1877. And also in Paris, the sculptor Auguste Rodin was honored with an exhibition devoted entirely to his "Burghers of Calais," with a comprehensive view of his preparatory studies and models of this one piece.

Some established contemporary artists had important shows. Frank Stella was featured: "Stella since 1970" at the Fort Worth Museum. It was the first large Stella show since the Museum of Modern Art retrospective eight years earlier. The sculptor Isamu Noguchi was represented with a large stone carving commissioned for the East Wing of the National Gallery. His smaller sculptures were exhibited in Minneapolis at the Walker Art Center, "Noguchi's Imaginary Landscapes." The year also saw the unveiling of his 36-foot (10.8-m) high portal in the plaza of the Justice Center in Cleveland and the completion of the Civic Center Plaza, in downtown Detroit, occupying several acres and including a huge fountain.

Rockefeller's Enterprise. The John D. Rockefeller family has a long history of interest in art, both in terms of private collections and museum donations. In fact, for years the New York City apartment of Nelson A. Rockefeller contained several originals by well-known artists, including a Matisse mural, a Picasso, an African bronze, Meissen china. Now it contains reproductions of the works. Since leaving the vice presidency Rockefeller has turned his attention to his art collection and has invested about $4 million in a new mail-order business, the Nelson Rockefeller Collection, Inc. The new enterprise is a plan to market high quality reproductions of 118 objects from the Rockefeller collection. The market for the reproductions is the upper-middle class who enjoy art but cannot afford the best. The former vice president also planned to publish books on his collection to supplement the new reproductions. The unorthodox venture was received with misgivings by many art enthusiasts.

See also PHOTOGRAPHY.

ISA RAGUSA
Department of Art and Archaeology
Princeton University

PHOTOS © 1978 DENNIS BRACK, BLACK STAR

The East Building, National Gallery of Art

The new East Building of Washington's National Gallery of Art was opened to the public in June 1978. Designed by I. M. Pei, the showcase was completed at an estimated cost of $95 million. Alexander Calder's 980-pound (445 kg) aluminum mobile hangs in the inner court.

The American Antique Market

American antiques—the furniture, folk art, books, pottery, pewter, silver, and other items produced mainly along the eastern seaboard of the United States prior to the Industrial Revolution—have been fetching increasingly high prices and attracting greater numbers of amateur and professional collectors for almost 30 years. The trend reached unprecedented proportions in 1977 and 1978, as antique shows, auctions, flea markets, and shops were flooded with determined buyers. Record prices were paid for objects ranging from rare books to Chippendale furniture.

There has been much speculation about the reasons for this intense new interest in collecting American antiques. A frequently heard explanation is that Americans are becoming increasingly aware of the richness of their heritage. The desire to own part of that heritage, be it a piece of 18th century furniture or a 19th century quilt, makes furnishing a house or apartment an enjoyable and enriching experience. Another reason for the new popularity of antiques is, no doubt, their value as investments. Many Americans have turned to antiques as a way to hedge against rampant inflation.

Today's collectors are inclined to be middle-aged, and discriminating. While they may not be the ones to pay top dollar for the most sought-after pieces, they are the ones furnishing new homes in the now popular Americana style. Dealers consider them well schooled in virtually every aspect of the American antique field and fully aware of the kinds of objects they would most like to own.

With respect to furniture, there are five generally recognized American periods, each with distinct features of style and construction: Pilgrim Century (c. 1650–1690), William and Mary (c. 1690–1720), Queen Anne (c. 1720–1750), Chippendale (c. 1750–1780), and Federal (c. 1790–1820). The Empire and Victorian periods continue through the third quarter of the 19th century. The value of a particular item depends largely on when it was made. While traditional Queen Anne and Chippendale forms have steadily and substantially increased in value during the 20th century, case and seat pieces produced during the Pilgrim Century and Federal periods have tended to fall in and out of favor over the years. In recent years, interest in Pilgrim furniture has been rekindled among serious private collectors. A carved and painted oak blanket chest, attributed to the 17th century Massachusetts carver, William Searle, recently was sold for (U. S.) $50,000. The same piece had been purchased some 20 years previously for under $1,000.

On the basis of more detailed features, it is also possible to identify the geographical location in which a particular piece was made. The shape of a chair's legs or the type of surface and under-surface wood in a table, for example, might indicate a Philadelphia or Massachusetts origin. The regional characteristics of a piece of furniture can also have an enormous effect on its value. Although thousands of chests of drawers were produced in several regions during the Chippendale period, one rare bombé chest, made in Boston between 1755 and 1785, was sold for a record $135,000 in 1977.

In the area of American works of art, a dramatic example of how the antique market has boomed in the past three decades is the history of a Pennsylvania-German birth record written in Fraktur type by an unknown artist in 1766. This item, from the collection of George Horace Lorimer, was first sold in 1944 for the highly respectable sum of $55. The new owner, Arthur J. Sussel, sold the document in 1958 for the unheard of price of $900. In January 1974, the piece was auctioned with other items of the Garbisch Collection; it took in a record $6,500, an overall increase of nearly 1,200% since the original sale.

Part of the explanation for the 30-year-old trend is that virtually all the serious scholarship relating to 19th century folk art has occurred in the past three decades. As scholars began to take the field more seriously, prices for naive paintings, pottery, quilts, scrimshaw, weather-vanes, and other objects created by self-taught artisans of the 1800's began to increase significantly.

The American decorative arts have shown a similar correspondence between the rise of serious scholarship and the enormous increase in money paid for antiques. In the early 1950's, the Henry Francis du Pont Winterthur Museum, near Wilmington, Dela., in conjunction with the University of Delaware, was the first institution to grant an advanced degree in this field. Yale University initiated a similar program some years later.

American pewter, which was recognized as a legitimate art form by only a few people during the early 20th century, has also become popular among antique collectors in recent years. Eighteenth century pewter, by such craftsmen as Colonel William Will and Samuel Hamlin, has always been costly. Flatware (including plates) and holloware, however, were produced in such large quantities during much of the 19th century that they are still quite affordable. One of the attractions of American antique collecting, and of pewter in particular, is that one can begin a collection for a modest amount of money.

WILLIAM STAHL

PHOTOS © SOTHEBY PARKE BERNET, INC., NEW YORK

The antique business booms. Above: a packed-house attends an auction at New York City's Sotheby Parke Bernet. Tiffany lamps are a big favorite. The Lotus lamp, far left, sold for an unprecedented $60,000. Below: a young couple peruse the catalog and the offerings at an auction in a Dodge-family home in Madison, N. J.

"ANTIQUES MONTHLY," TUSCALOOSA, ALA.

PAT ZIMMERMAN

A dealer's booth at a typical antique show. Many dealers specialize in a particular type of antique or in a special period.

The Flea and Antique Market, held annually in Litchfield, Conn., attracts the collectors and the curious from all parts of the New England-New York area. A great variety of items, with a wide price range, is sold.

ASIA

The year 1978 was a watershed one in the post World War II history of Asia. Sino-American, Sino-Japanese, Sino-Indian, and Vietnamese-Southeast Asian relations underwent major changes in the pursuit of greater stability and influence by the major governments of the hemisphere and interested external powers. The influence of China increased, while the United States restated its interest in Asia more pointedly than at any time since the Vietnam war. The influence of the Soviet Union declined.

The Sino-Japanese Treaty. Following six years of negotiation, China and Japan signed a peace and friendship treaty that included a controversial "anti-hegemony" clause strongly opposed by the USSR. The Japanese asserted that the "anti-hegemony" reference was not directed at any particular nation, but the Soviets knew that the word "hegemony" was Peking's favorite one for identifying Moscow's alleged desire for domination of the continent.

The significance of the pact was the opportunity it provided for increased economic and political cooperation between Peking and Tokyo. The hitherto elusive peace agreement was a major setback for the USSR. It signaled Tokyo's clear preference for doing economic and political business with Peking (as contrasted with Moscow) in the years ahead. The Soviets, however, may have had only themselves to blame, having refused for 30 years to return four former Japanese islands in the northwestern Pacific seized in the wake of World War II.

Moscow-Peking Rivalry. Not only did the Soviet Union lose ground in northeast Asia (where China's leader Hua Kuo-feng visited and wooed Kim Il Sung of North Korea in April), but the USSR also had to deal with growing Chinese activity in south and southeast Asia. China sought to improve relations with India and to contain Moscow's influence in Vietnam by cautiously siding with Cambodia in its escalating war with neighboring pro-Soviet Vietnam. The USSR, which reportedly sought use of the former U. S. naval facility at Cam Rahn Bay, mounted a major airlift to Vietnam in August, flying in war supplies and other aid to replace halted Chinese assistance. Three months later, Moscow and Hanoi signed a 25-year defense treaty.

According to China, Moscow also established a guided missile base in Vietnam. The latter action, otherwise unconfirmed, paralleled a build-up of both Soviet and Chinese forces along their long and tense common border.

Sino-Vietnamese Tension. Vietnamese efforts to eradicate private business mainly hurt resident ethnic Chinese, large numbers of whom sought to flee to China, causing a new major crisis between Hanoi and Peking. The crisis came to a head in July with the abrupt termination of all Chinese aid to Vietnam. Such assistance was estimated to total between (U. S.) $10 billion and $18 billion over the previous 20 years.

A factor contributing to the growing tension was undoubtedly Chinese support of Cambodia in its war with Vietnam. However, Vietnam's willingness, strongly encouraged by Moscow, to join the Soviet-controlled (and largely European Communist) Council of Mutual Economic Assistance may have been more important.

China's Asian Peace Offensive. In addition to successfully negotiating a peace treaty with Japan, China sought to woo various of its southern neighbors. Deputy Premier Teng Tsiao-ping visited Burma and Nepal in January. And China subsequently told India that it was willing to participate in friendly negotiations over the 14,000 square miles (35,160 km²) of territory it seized in the 1962 war. That dispute resulted in more than fifteen years of strained relations between Peking and New Delhi.

Even in the escalating Vietnamese-Cambodian border conflict in which China aided Phnom Penh with military supplies, Peking sought to restrain the Cambodians from widening the war (and perhaps alienating possible Chinese friends in Southeast Asia who might perceive Peking as a proxy participant in the struggle).

A Third Indochina War? The non-Communist nations of Southeast Asia had feared a united and aggressive Indochina following the fall of Vietnam and Cambodia in 1975. By 1978, however, animosity between Hanoi and Phnom Penh had reached such a point that the two Communist countries were fighting one another in what could become the "third Indochina war" since World War II. Cambodia, with Chinese-furnished arms and ammunition, battled numerically superior Vietnamese troops supplied by the USSR.

Chief root of the conflict was Cambodian fear of revived Vietnamese imperialism, which had been interrupted by nearly a century of French colonial rule. Vietnam, seeking to avoid the image of aggressor (present or potential), endeavored to improve relations with all of Southeast Asia's non-Communist governments. The move was intended to balance Chinese diplomatic gains in the region and undercut possible identification with Cambodia's fears.

Increased American Interest. Fifteen months after the inauguration of the Carter administration, Vice President Walter Mondale and Presidential Adviser for National Security Affairs Zbigniew Brzezinski made the first visits by ranking officials of the Carter administration to Asian capitals. Mondale traveled to the Philippines, Thailand, Indonesia, Australia, and New Zealand in early May. He was followed by a Brzezinski trip to China, Japan, and South Korea.

Mondale pledged a continuing U. S. commitment to non-Communist Asian states, while President Carter himself subsequently was host to the foreign ministers of the ASEAN (Association of Southeast Asian Nations) countries—Indonesia, *(Continued on page 112.)*

CHINA: 1978

China's Premier and Communist Party leader Hua Kuo-feng leads party leaders in applause for workers in the city of Tangshan.

The fifth session of the National People's Congress met in Peking, February 26—March 5.   During the meeting, Hua was reappointed; a new Constitution was adopted; and a new ten-year economic plan was accepted.

Women workers inspect the fabrics at the Tung-feng Printing and Dyeing Mill in Changchow. China has long been known for its beautiful floral prints.

Commune members examine a hybridized semi-late rice plant (*above*). Its threshed yield is sun-drying (*left*). According to the nation's economic goals, grain output should increase by some 60% from 1977 to 1985.

Children practice their figure skating in preparation for winter sports competition in Sinkiang-Uighur Autonomous Region.

China and Iran signed a cultural cooperation agreement, following formal talks between Chairman Hua Kuofeng and the shah in Teheran in August.

UPI

the Philippines, Thailand, Malaysia, and Singapore—in Washington.

U. S.-Chinese Relations. China, concerned over possible Soviet "encirclement" (as reflected in Moscow's dominant influence in Vietnam), continued to seek an "opening to the West" through improved relations with the United States and other nations suspicious of Soviet intentions. U. S.-Chinese trade doubled in the first half of 1978, as Peking continued its drive to modernize and improve its defenses with technology and weapons from the West.

Late in the year, China and the United States announced that they had agreed to establish diplomatic relations. Embassies were to open in the two capitals on March 1, 1979. In establishing relations, the United States cut ties with the regime on Taiwan and China agreed that the U. S.-Taiwan defense treaty would not have to be abrogated until one year after normalization. Washington also announced that it would continue to sell defensive arms to Taiwan.

The anti-Soviet character of Chinese foreign policy was also reflected in state visits by Chairman Hua Kuo-feng to Yugoslavia, Rumania, and Iran. Peking's endorsement of ASEAN was also motivated by an anti-Soviet attitude.

Other States. Japan experienced new strains in its complicated economic-defense relationship with the United States. The weak American dollar and huge Japanese export surplus were the major problem areas. India drew direct Soviet criticism as it sought to improve relations with Peking after 17 years of impasse over border and related problems. Public support for the Morarji Desai regime declined, however.

Thailand improved relations with Vietnam and Cambodia. South Korea's President Park Chung Hee was "reelected," and the United States continued its troop reduction in that nation. Hundreds of thousands of Cambodians lost their lives in the most brutal consolidation of power in decades.

Nepal's former Premier B. P. Koirala returned from medical treatment in the United States in September to agitate for greater democracy, while Communist Naxalite terrorism reappeared in the country. Outer Mongolia instituted internal travel restrictions to curb an increasing flow of peasants to the cities, an Asiawide social problem. And an older Asian problem, cholera, killed 203 people in the Maldives through September.

RICHARD BUTWELL, *Murray State University*

UPI

Yugoslavia's President Tito and a guard of honor welcome Hua Kuo-feng to Belgrade. Throughout 1978, the Chinese chairman sought to increase his nation's influence in international affairs.

ASTRONOMY

Among the major astronomical advances of 1978 were the discovery of the duplicity of the outermost planet, Pluto; the launching of the International Ultraviolet Explorer satellite; and the amassing of new evidence for the existence of black holes, especially at centers of galaxies.

Instrumentation. The 2.3-meter infrared telescope at the University of Wyoming was operational by the end of 1977. At an excellent site atop Mauna Kea, Hawaii, important progress was made on two high-resolution infrared telescopes, the National Aeronautics and Space Administration's 3-meter and Britain's 3.8-meter instruments.

The Very Large Array (VLA), near Socorro, N. Mex., became operational on February 20. When completed in 1981, it will consist of 27 movable dishes, each of 25-meter diameter, placed along the 3 arms of a Y-shaped configuration. Two arms have lengths of 21 kilometers and the third is 19 kilometers long.

The International Ultraviolet Explorer satellite, a combined effort of NASA, the European Space Agency, and the British Research Council, was launched on January 26. It is a 45-centimeter-aperture, focal-ratio-15 system covering the spectral range 115–320 nanometers. Among observations obtained with this instrument were those showing high-excitation gaseous envelopes (akin to the solar chromosphere) in certain cool binary star systems. A second high energy astronomical observatory satellite (HEAO) was also launched.

Solar System. Continuing studies of lunar rocks gave an even clearer picture of the early history of the lunar and solar systems. Seismographs showed 1,700 meteorite impacts, evidence for moonquakes triggered by tidal stresses, and one seismic quake sufficiently severe to define a lunar core about 300 kilometers (186 mi) in diameter.

Two new asteroids whose orbits are close to that of the earth were discovered. The Apollo type object, 1978CA, which passes within the earth's orbit, has a diameter of about 2 kilometers (1.24 mi) and a 6% reflectivity; it rotates in 3 hours, 44 minutes. The yet smaller 1978DA moves from just outside the earth's orbit to the distance of Jupiter. The diameter (243 kilometers, or 150 mi) and approximate shape of 532 Herculina, one of the largest of stony surface asteroids, were found from stellar occulations. Kowal's object, Chiron, found in 1977, has a period of 50.7 years and moves outside the orbits of Jupiter and Saturn. It may be a cometary nucleus.

A rare gas, germanium hydride, presumably dredged up by rising currents in a violently convective atmosphere, has been detected on Jupiter.

A total of 9 rings has now been deduced for Uranus; five were found in 1977 and four were discovered from new observations and rediscussions of 1977 data. By observing Uranus with a narrow spectral band pass at the center of one of the methane bands (where the planet's reflectivity is about 1%) it has been possible to detect the rings which shine by reflected sunlight.

Elongated images of Pluto obtained on Naval Observatory (Flagstaff) plates indicate that the planet has a satellite 2–3 magnitudes fainter than Pluto itself. The satellite moves in an orbit with a radius of about 20,000 kilometers (12,427 mi) and a period of 3.39 days. The mass of Pluto is found to be 0.0017 that of the earth (or about a seventh that of the moon). Hence, Pluto can hardly qualify as a planet. It would appear to be an escaped satellite with a companion.

Stars. Searches continued for planetlike companions of nearby stars. The visual binary 61 Cygni (period-720 yrs) involves 2 stars, each of 0.6 solar masses. Each may have one (or possibly 2) companions of about 5 Jovian masses. AN Ursae Majoris (which is similar to AM Herculis, HZ Herculis, Cygnus X2, and ScoX1) was discovered to consist of a red star (about ¼ solar mass) and a white dwarf which emits X rays.

Black Holes. Arguments for the presence of black holes in the centers of certain active galaxies, still inconclusive, have become more persuasive. Two possible candidates are the radio galaxy NGC 6251 and the giant elliptical M87 in the Virgo cluster. NGC 6251 is an optical galaxy with two large radio-frequency-emitting lobes on either side. Outside its visible nebula a jet pointing in the direction of the lobes is observed. Presumably, material is being ejected with very high energy from the nucleus, suggesting a black hole with a mass of perhaps 100 million suns.

The M87 galaxy has a very bright nucleus and a fragmented bluish jet about 6,000 light years long that emits synchrotron radiation. Both the brightness of the nucleus and the broadening of spectral lines indicate that there is a mass equal to 5,000 million suns near the center. Much of this mass may be concentrated in a black hole; the jet is associated with energetic particles accelerated in its neighborhood.

Although in our galaxy and neighboring Andromeda galaxy, M31, radio and optical emissions from the central regions are relatively weak, some galaxies, like the N and radio galaxies, have very bright nuclei.

It is theorized that rapid light fluctuations in the nuclei of active galaxies show that the emitting region must be millions of times smaller than the galaxies that contain them. While no particles or radiation can escape from them, black holes can convert up to 10% of the in-falling mass to observable energy. Because black holes must rotate, in-falling matter is spread out in a radiant disk. Matter may also be ejected at high velocity along the spin axis of the black hole, thereby producing the double lobes seen in radio galaxies. A rigorous demonstration of the theory is still wanted.

LAWRENCE H. ALLER, *University of California*

A state funeral was held for Sir Robert Menzies in Melbourne, May 19. Sir Robert, who served as Australia's prime minister (1939–41, 1949–66), died May 15.

PATRICK MCARDELL, AUSTRALIAN INFORMATION SERVICE

AUSTRALIA

A lackluster mood prevailed throughout Australia in 1978 as Prime Minister Malcolm Fraser's coalition continued to bear down on inflation.

Economy. With a 48-seat parliamentary majority, Fraser was able to hold inflation below 8%. Other features of the year were the fifth consecutive annual rise in unemployment (to over 6%), a slowing of wage increases (to 9%), and sluggish business activity. The national budget reversed the recent easing of personal income tax and increased taxes on gasoline, beer, and cigarettes. The trade situation worsened, leading to a balance of payments shortfall requiring heavy foreign borrowing. Farm incomes rose.

Treasurer John Howard's budget estimate of total spending, (U. S.) $33,200,000,000, was up by 11%. The estimated revenue of $29,950,000,-000 left a deficit of $3,250,000,000, about $600 million less than the actual deficit in fiscal 1978. The main thrust of the budget was to encourage an inflow of investment capital. The policy of trimming the deficit with a check on government spending was backed by lower business taxes so that an investment-led recovery might develop.

Fraser admitted that employment did not improve so much as the government had hoped, mainly because of slow growth in the world economy. He reiterated his view that strike-backed demands for wage increases in excess of officially sanctioned guidelines were "part of a selfish campaign by unions" to frustrate efforts to restore the economy.

Politics. What one observer called "political anguish, anger, and absurdity" followed Fraser's dismissal of his Senate leader, Sen. Reginald Withers, when an administrative impropriety was adjudged against him. However, Withers accepted the move without rancor, leaving Fraser's leadership unimpaired.

There were also changes in the leadership of the Australian Labor Party (ALP). With the resignation of Edward Gough Whitlam, the mantle of parliamentary leadership went to 45-year-old Bill Hayden. Hayden quickly became embroiled in a factional argument within the party branch in his home state of Queensland.

Robert Hawke did not seek reelection to the presidency of the ALP but remained head of the Australian Council of Trade Unions.

Discussions of constitutional change died when a 120-man convention, meeting in Perth, failed to reach agreement on any issues.

The Northern Territory moved closer to statehood at midyear when a full parliamentary-backed administration was installed.

Foreign Relations. The year 1978 was one of intense efforts in bilateral and multilateral consultations and negotiations. Two immediate issues were seen as especially important: sluggish growth in the economies of developed countries and the need to accommodate the interests of developing countries. Fraser urged an end to "unreasonable protectionism" in world trade and continued his criticism of EEC trade policies. In May, Foreign Affairs Minister Andrew Peacock emphasized "the necessity of a new and imaginative approach and of more practical recognition of the problems of interdependence."

As a first step to broaden Australia's links with the Third World, a task force including experts from nongovernment sectors was set up to review Australia's relations with developing countries.

Aboriginal Affairs. The National Aboriginal Council (NAC), a 35-member body elected every three years by Aboriginal voters, was established in 1978. Five NAC members also were voted to the ten-member Council on Aboriginal Development, the federal government's formal advisory body. Fraser assured the NAC that its creation represented a "real turning point" in the quest for equal opportunity in Australia.

—— AUSTRALIA · Information Highlights ——
Official Name: Commonwealth of Australia.
Location: Southwestern Pacific Ocean.
Area: 2,967,900 square miles (7,686,861 km²).
Population (1978 est.): 14,300,000.
Chief Cities (1976 census, met. areas): Canberra, the capital, 215,414; Sydney, 3,021,299; Melbourne, 2,603,578.
Government: *Head of state,* Elizabeth II, queen; represented by Sir Zelman Cowen, governor general (took office December 1977). *Head of government,* Malcolm Fraser, prime minister (took office December 1975). *Legislature*—Parliament: Senate and House of Representatives.
Monetary Unit: Australian dollar (0.87 A. dollar equals U. S.$1, Dec. 1978).
Manufactures (major products): Motor vehicles, iron and steel, textiles, chemicals.
Agriculture (major products): Cereals, sugarcane, fruits, wine grapes, sheep, cattle, dairy products.

Large areas of land in the Northern Territory were handed over for permanent occupation by traditional Aboriginal owners. However, self-management of Aboriginal communities reached the headlines after the state government of Queensland refused to meet the demands of some local groups seeking autonomy in local affairs.

Other Developments. The federal government had difficulty in reaching an agreement with various groups on the mining and export of uranium. Most of the contention revolved around uranium deposits in Northern Territory land already granted to the Aboriginal Northern Land Council. During the discussions, the council was divided on the issue but finally agreed to make a firm commitment.

Australia's tallest building rose in downtown Sydney. The 940-foot (287-m) Centrepoint Tower will have two revolving restaurants and two observation levels in a bulbous turret topped by a telecommunications antenna system. The building's lower section will contain convention and exhibition facilities.

Interscan, a microwave aircraft landing system designed by Australian scientists, was adopted by the International Civil Aviation Organization (ICAO) for use at all world airports.

The state funeral of Sir Robert Menzies in Melbourne in May was attended by royalty, heads of state, and political leaders from all over the world. (*See* Obituary, page 376.)

R. M. YOUNGER
Australian Author

AUSTRIA

The "Schubert Year of 1978" was marked by festivals and concerts commemorating the 150th anniversary of Franz Schubert's death. As in many other industrial countries, economic activity in Austria was slow.

Politics. On November 5, the socialist government of Chancellor Bruno Kreisky was shaken by the results of the first national referendum on the use of nuclear energy. By a slim majority, the Austrian people voted to scrap a $530 million nuclear power station. The next day, Kreisky abandoned his threat to resign.

Economic Developments. In 1977 the Austrian trade deficit increased by 15% over the 1976 amount, to a record 4.7 billion (U. S.) schillings. This was the main topic of discussion when Chancellor Bruno Kreisky visited Moscow in February 1978. In a joint statement, Austria and the USSR announced efforts to balance their trade. As one measure to cut imports, Austria raised the value-added tax on luxuries from 18% to 30% on Jan. 1, 1978. In comparison with 1977, the trade deficit was reduced by 15% during the first four months of 1978. While the real gross national product increased by 3.5% in 1977, the estimated increase for 1978 was from 1.5 to 2.5%. The unemployment rate (1.3% in June 1978) and the annual rate of inflation (3.2%) were among the lowest in Europe.

Foreign Affairs. The Permanent Council of the Organization of American States (OAS) agreed on April 5 to grant observer status to Austria. On April 8–9, the Austrian minister of interior met in Bern with his counterparts from Switzerland, Italy, and West Germany. The ministers agreed to establish a "hot line" communication system to facilitate antiterrorist procedures. In late April, the first meeting of the European Democratic Union (EDU) was held in Klesheim, Austria. Representatives of center and conservative parties in Europe sought to lay a basis for combating Marxism and to establish cooperation in the first direct election of the European Community (EC) parliament.

When, at the end of March, the UN was establishing a peacekeeping force in southern Lebanon, Austria refused to shift any of its forces from the Golan Heights so long as the shooting continued. However, during the year Austria continued its efforts to further peace in the Middle East. On February 11, in a meeting in Salzburg arranged by Chancellor Kreisky, President Sadat of Egypt conferred with Shimon Peres, leader of Israel's opposition Labor party. Sadat also conferred with Kreisky himself at that time. In July, Sadat returned to Austria where he met with Nahum Goldman, former president of the World Jewish Congress. He met again with Shimon Peres on July 9 and then with Israel's defense minister, Ezer Weizman.

ERNST C. HELMREICH
Bowdoin College

——— AUSTRIA · Information Highlights ———
Official Name: Republic of Austria.
Location: Central Europe.
Area: 32,376 square miles (83,853 km²).
Population (1978 est.): 7,500,000.
Chief Cities (1975 est.): Vienna, the capital, 1,650,000; Graz, 253,000; Linz, 207,000; Salzburg, 132,000.
Government: *Head of state,* Rudolf Kirchschläger, president (took office July 1974). *Head of government,* Bruno Kreisky, chancellor (took office April 1970). *Legislature*—Federal Assembly: Federal Council and National Council.
Monetary Unit: Schilling (14.04 schillings equal U. S.$1, Sept. 1978).
Manufactures (major products): Iron and steel, chemicals, capital equipment, consumer goods.
Agriculture (major products): Livestock, dairy products, grains, barley, oats, corn, sugar beets, potatoes.

The first American VW plant opened in New Stanton, Pa., in April 1978.

UPI

AUTOMOBILES

U. S. manufacturers produced more than 8.9 million cars and 4 million trucks in the 1978-model run. Truck output set a new record, and car production was third only to the 9,915,802 units assembled as '73 models, and the '77-model total of 9,104,994 units. GM model-run output fell by approximately 100,000 cars to 5,288,360; Ford Motors showed a gain of 200,000 cars to 2,480,293; Chrysler Corp. declined 220,000 units to 1,133,996, and American Motors dropped nearly 45,000 to 137,860.

Chevrolet, the leading builder of small cars, led the industry in '78-model production gains. Output rose more than 10% in the first eight months of 1978 to 1,552,805, with its restyled midsize Malibu series up 40%. Addition of a four-door sedan to the Chevette line for 1978 raised its January–August production to more than 215,000 from 101,000 for 1977.

Buick and Pontiac divisions of GM increased production for the '78-model run, while Oldsmobile held its position as third-highest domestic producer. Models that sparked the Pontiac surge included the sporty Firebird and Sunbird subcompacts, while Buick's Regal, with a new turbocharger engine, was its standout model. The calendar-year production totals were as follows: Olds, 582,000; Pontiac, 576,000, and Buick, 548,000.

Ford assembled nearly 300,000 of the new Fairmont and Zephyr compacts in the first eight months of 1978, a first-year record. Nearly 190,-000 Omni and Horizon sub-compacts were assembled by Chrysler Corp. in the '78-model year, offsetting declines for the company's larger compacts, intermediates and standards. Production rose by two thirds from 1977 for American Motors' top line for 1978, the Concord compact. AMC discontinued its Matador series at the end of the '78 season.

1979 Models. Fuel-economy requirements and new-car prices both advanced with the start of the '79-model year. Domestic and imported cars were expected to meet a corporate average fuel economy standard of 19 miles per gallon—a demand which brought on another round of decreasing size and introduction of new "fuel-efficient" engines. U. S. producers boosted '79-model prices by only 3%–4% on the average, after a series of 1% midyear increases which kept the '78 models in line with rising labor and materials costs.

WORLD MOTOR VEHICLE DATA 1977

Country	Passenger Car Production	Truck And Bus Production	Motor Vehicle Registrations
Argentina.................	168,126	67,230	3,487,822
Australia..................	368,807	83,785	6,343,200
Austria...................	...	8,177	1,987,183
Belgium..................	300,659	35,813	3,031,565
Brazil....................	463,897	455,345	7,173,978
Canada..................	1,162,519	612,926	11,713,700
Czechoslovakia...........	158,987	39,584	1,978,132
France...................	3,092,429	415,442	18,660,000
Germany, East...........	170,000	39,000	2,600,345
Germany, West..........	3,790,544*	313,672	20,501,743
Hungary.................	...	13,313	870,348
India....................	47,443	41,702	1,791,422
Italy....................	1,440,470	143,477	17,174,263
Japan...................	5,431,045	3,083,477	30,069,280
Mexico..................	187,637	93,176	3,673,564
Netherlands..............	53,368	13,060	4,132,782
Poland..................	294,300	79,700	1,814,300
Portugal.................	...	1,202	993,000
Rumania.................	70,000	36,000	300,000
Spain...................	988,964	140,736	6,458,000
Sweden.................	235,383	51,518	3,059,703
Switzerland..............	...	985	2,044,372
United Kingdom.........	1,327,820	386,420	16,265,380
United States............	9,213,654	3,489,128	138,549,263**
USSR...................	1,280,000	800,000	7,500,000
Yugoslavia..............	231,117	26,645	2,005,207
Total...............	30,477,089#	10,471,483#	341,710,845***

* Includes 223,354 micro-buses.
** U.S. total includes 110,351,327 cars and 28,197,936 trucks, excluding Puerto Rico (663,794 and 146,654 respectively); Canal Zone (17,356 and 461); and Virgin Islands (33,000 and 6,300).
*** World registration total includes all countries, of which nonproducing countries exceeding 1 million registrations were: Venezuela, 1,324,500; South Africa, 3,063,800; New Zealand, 1,527,204; Denmark, 1,594,764; Finland, 1,181,473; and Norway, 1,170,842.
\# Excludes car, truck, and bus assemblies, principally in Belgium, South Africa, Iran, Venezuela, and Taiwan.

Source: Motor Vehicle Manufacturers Association of the United States, Inc.

New '79 entries included "personal luxury" coupes from three GM divisions—the Buick Riviera, Olds Toronado and Cadillac Eldorado— all with front-wheel drive and lowered in weight more than 900 pounds from their predecessors. Ford restyled its Mustang and Capri sporty coupes, as well as its now smaller-sized Ford LTD and Mercury Marquis cars. Chrysler followed suit with a major length and weight reduction for its top-of-the-line "full-size" series—the Chrysler Newport and New Yorker and a new Dodge St. Regis. Two-door coupes also were unveiled by Chrysler for its subcompact Omni and Horizon. AMC redesigned its Gremlin subcompact series, adding a liftback model and re-naming the line the Spirit.

To meet fuel average requirements U. S. automakers offered more four-cylinder and six-cylinder options throughout '78 and '79 lines. Chrysler equipped its Omni and Horizon with four-cylinder engines purchased from Volkswagen. A turbocharged four-cylinder engine was introduced for the '79 Mustang and Capri by Ford, and GM expanded production of its most economical engine, the diesel V-8. Diesel engines were available to new car purchasers in the United States from Oldsmobile, Cadillac, VW, Peugeot, and Mercedes-Benz.

Imported Cars. Despite 1978-model price increases due to foreign currency fluctuations against the dollar, 1,418,000 imported new cars were sold in the United States during the January– August period, 30,000 fewer than the previous year. Toyota, Datsun, and VW declined in sales, while Honda, Subaru and Mazda posted sharp rises.

At a new plant in New Stanton, Pa., VW became the first import to begin domestic assembly. Ford retailed more than 60,000 of its new front-drive Fiesta imports and Chrysler added two front-drive subcompacts, the Plymouth Champ and Colt Hatchback, to its import list in 1978. Renault and American Motors announced plans for a distribution and manufacturing agreement.

Maynard M. Gordon, *"Motor News Analysis"*

BANGLADESH

The major events in Bangladesh in 1978 were the June presidential election won overwhelmingly by the incumbent, Maj. Gen. Ziaur Rahman, and the promise of parliamentary elections in December.

Politics and Government. General Zia, who rose to power in a coup in late 1975 and assumed the presidency in 1977, scheduled a presidential election for June and parliamentary elections for December. Zia was one of 10 candidates in the presidential election, the first to be decided by adult suffrage. Former army general Ataul Ghany Osmany, leader of the Bangladesh army during the 1971 war of independence against Pakistan, presented the only real challenge to Zia. The primary issue in the campaign was the form of government Bangladesh would adopt. Zia favored retention of the presidential system, and Osmany supported the establishment of a parliamentary system. On May 7, Zia assured the nation that the Parliament would be a sovereign body, have the power to amend the constitution, enact laws, and remove the president. A threatened boycott by the opposition caused the parliamentary elections to be postponed until February 1979.

Zia was elected president incontrovertibly on June 3, receiving more than 15 million of the 20 million votes cast. Osmany amassed close to 4.5 million votes, while the remaining candidates, led by country doctor Hakim Ahmed, received negligible totals. Ahmed, who claimed during the campaign to have the ability to restore sexual virility to the aged, received 77,000 votes.

President Zia was sworn in on June 12; he appointed a 28-member Council of Ministers (cabinet) on June 29 to replace the Council of Advisers to the President created by his predecessor. The Council of Ministers was comprised of 11 members of the coalition parties that supported Zia's election, 16 members of the former Council of Advisers, and a business executive.

Foreign Relations. Bangladesh's relations with other nations were generally good in 1978 when, as in the past, it was the recipient of considerable aid from abroad, often in the form of foodstuffs. Other aid came in the form of the cancellation of debts by the Dutch, July 10, and by the British, July 31. British Prime Minister James Callaghan had visited Bangladesh in January during a tour of southern Asia.

Refugees. After three days of discussion and negotiation between Bangladesh and Burma, a tentative agreement was reached concerning the disposition of some 200,000 Burmese refugees in Bangladesh. The July 9 accord called for the return of all refugees to Burma.

Political Prisoners. On Feb. 27, 1978, Amnesty International, winner of the Nobel Peace Prize in 1977, issued a report estimating the number of political prisoners in Bangladesh to be 10,000 to 15,000 persons. The report also stated that the total prison population in Bangladesh was 36,685, although the prisons had been built to hold only 14,000 persons.

Carl Leiden
Professor of Government
The University of Texas at Austin

—— **BANGLADESH · Information Highlights** ——

Official Name: People's Republic of Bangladesh.
Location: South Asia.
Area: 55,126 square miles (142,776 km²).
Population (1978 est.): 85,000,000.
Chief Cities (1974 census): Dacca, the capital, 1,310,-972; Khulna, 436,000; Chittagong, 416,733.
Government: *Head of state,* Ziaur Rahman, president (took office April 1977).
Monetary Unit: Taka (14.67 takas equal U. S.$1, Aug. 1978).
Manufacturing (major products): Jute products, cotton textiles, processed foods, wood products.
Major Agricultural Products: Rice, jute, sugarcane, tea, oilseeds, pulses, forest products.

BANKING

The most important features of banking in the United States and elsewhere in 1978 were the continued efforts at diversification by all types of financial institutions.

Commercial banks and thrift institutions alike continued to strive for more powers in an effort to provide fuller service for the business and individual customer. And the regulatory changes effected and planned during the year largely involved adjusting government's regulatory role to these new powers.

In the United States the most significant development of long-run impact was the authorization of Automatic Transfer Service for banks and thrift institutions on a nationwide basis. In its simplest term, Automatic Transfer Service (ATS) is permission for a bank, savings bank, or other institution that offers the public both checking accounts and savings accounts to link these deposits together. Thus, if a customer does not have enough money in a checking account to cover the checks written, the institution can automatically move money from the savings account to cover the difference.

In the United States, commercial banks have been prohibited from offering interest on checking accounts since the early 1930's. By authorizing this linkage, the banks can in effect provide such interest on checking again. For the depositor's money can now stay in an interest bearing savings account until the moment it is needed to cover checks that have been written and can then be moved automatically. To the public, this is the same as getting interest on checking again after all these years.

As banks developed their ATS programs, however, another trend became clear. The banking industry is turning back from being all things to all people. Whereas in the past banks tried to cater to the holder of small amounts of money and offer him considerable service at low cost, now the industry is recognizing how expensive the provision of this service is. Thus as ATS is offered, the banks are establishing minimum balance requirements for those who want the service free and are charging those without enough funds to meet the minimum balance a price that may deter many from wanting the service.

American banking is thus becoming more selective in what it will offer the public. It is evidently becoming willing to accept a decline in the number of people using its most advanced services if there is no profit in them for the bank. This is a decided reversal from the marketing efforts of the recent past.

Commercial banks also devoted considerable effort to examining lending policies to make sure that they were consistent with the new Community Reinvestment Act. In the past banks had complete freedom to lend and invest as they wished, provided they met sound standards that protected depositors' funds. Now this new act has reduced that freedom. For the law of the land now states that if banks are not servicing all the needs of their communities, they will be subject to regulatory pressures that could take the form of denial of many requests for new branches or changes in structure, and of other petitions to the regulatory authorities. The beneficiaries of the new legislation will be the areas of the economy that have suffered decay—both urban and rural—where bank funds could help with renewal.

Thrift institutions have changed in similar manner in 1978. They too have continued their efforts at diversification into more and more of the services formerly the exclusive province of the commercial bank. Through development of the service of electronic funds transfer they have solicited more and more of the payments function business of the United States, while credit unions have continued to develop their share drafts, which are really interest bearing checking accounts.

The thrift institutions have also continued to develop mortgage pass-through securities. These enable the savings institutions, and banks, too, to make mortgage loans, package them into blocks, and sell them to investors who normally would buy corporate and government bonds.

Through this procedure the United States is altering the flow of capital market funds, with the result that the percentage of available investment money going into home loans is continuing to grow at the expense of plant and equipment investment and other fund uses. To some observers, this skewing of funds flow to housing is hurting the economy, as it is concentrating too much of our capital into consumption goods—the new home and its fixtures—and not enough into new plant and equipment that could increase efficiency and help cut inflation.

Internationally, the trends in banking are similar. In both England and Canada, the governments are reexamining the regulatory structure of banks and thrift institutions so that the laws and regulations under which the industries operate can adjust to the changing powers of the various institutions. In other nations as well there has been the trend to "scrambled finance," with each type of financial institution trying to broaden its role in the economy.

In 1978 there were also announcements that foreign banks have made bids to buy major U. S. banking organizations in an effort to develop their role in the U. S. banking market. Little American objection to these foreign inroads is likely. American bankers recognize that this "foreign invasion" of U. S. banking just parallels what American banks have been doing overseas for years.

See also Feature article on inflation, pages 10–16; UNITED STATES: ECONOMY.

PAUL S. NADLER
Professor of Business Administration
Rutgers—The State University of New Jersey

BELGIUM

The proposed devolution of the Belgian state, its military and financial support for the government of Zaire, and a shaky economy were the focuses of attention in 1978.

Politics. The continuing clash between Belgium's French- and Dutch-speaking communities not only toppled another ministerial coalition but also halted the government's construction and debate of the controversial devolution bill.

On October 10, Prime Minister Leo Tindemans submitted the resignation of his four-party coalition government after internal disagreements over a plan to create separate assemblies and executive agencies for Dutch-speaking Flanders, French-speaking Wallonia, and bilingual Brussels. The crisis was provoked by the Flemish wing of Tindemans' own Social Christian party (PSC/CVP), which claimed that some of the measures were unconstitutional. It was the second time during the year that Tindemans resigned. His first resignation, over disagreements in economic policy with the Socialist party, was delivered June 15 but rejected by King Baudouin.

When the 18-month-old government fell in October, it was deeply involved in a "compromise of the communities," aimed at creating the administrative machinery to deal with a wide range of policies in the projected three-part division of Belgium. There had been a clear sense of optimism until the talks broke down.

On October 20, Defense Minister Paul Vanden Boeynants, also a Social Christian, was sworn in as prime minister of the caretaker government. No other changes were made in the Tindemans cabinet. The Boeynants government called a general election for December 17. A reconstructed coalition and a strong leader were seen as crucial if the strife were to end.

But the voting produced a near duplication of the existing party distribution in parliament. The Liberal party gained four seats, for a total of 37; the Social Christians gained two, for a total of 82; and the Socialists lost four, leaving them with 58. A day later, Boeynants resigned, saying that the elections had resolved nothing. At year's end, it was still unclear who would lead the government and what would be the fate of the devolution project.

Involvement in Zaire. For the second time in two years, Belgium became involved in the turmoil in Zaire, a former colony. The Shaba region, with its rich copper, cobalt, and uranium mines, was invaded in May by Katangese rebels in Angola, and President Mobutu Sese Seko's shaky regime again was threatened. To protect the huge economic interests of Belgian banks and mining companies in Zaire, and to save the many Belgian citizens working in that country, the Tindemans government joined a military effort by France and the United States to drive out the rebels. It also contributed to a (U. S.) $1 billion Western fund to shore up Zaire's econ-

UPI

Belgium's Foreign Minister Henri Simonet addresses the UN General Assembly's conference on world disarmament.

omy. However, Belgium's support caused friction with France, which was seen as a new competitor in the area. It also had severe domestic repercussions, as Tindemans and Foreign Minister Henri Simonet were widely criticized and argument raged within Belgium's major political parties (*see* ZAIRE).

The Economy. Government measures to control inflation were only partly successful. Although the franc remained strong and prices increased more slowly than in other European states, the growth of the Belgian economy lagged behind that of its neighbors and competitors. Unemployment increased by less than 1%, to 7%.

PIERRE-HENRI LAURENT, *Tufts University*

——— **BELGIUM · Information Highlights** ———

Official Name: Kingdom of Belgium.
Location: Northwestern Europe.
Area: 11,781 square miles (30,513 km²).
Population (1978 est.): 9,900,000.
Chief Cities (1976): Brussels, the capital, 1,042,052; Antwerp, 206,786; Liège, 135,347.
Government: *Head of state,* Baudouin I, king (acceded 1951). *Head of government,* undetermined at year's end. *Legislature*—Parliament: Senate and Chamber of Representatives.
Monetary Unit: Franc (29.47 francs equal U. S.$1, Dec. 28, 1978).
Manufactures (major products): Fabricated metal, iron and steel, coal, textiles, chemicals.
Agriculture (major products): Sugar beets, potatoes, grain, tobacco, vegetables, fruits, livestock, poultry.

BIOCHEMISTRY

Genetic Manipulation. In September 1978 California scientists announced that they had made human insulin, which may be useful in treating diabetics, from subunits produced by bacteria. Genes directing bacterial insulin production had been chemically synthesized, nucleotide-by-nucleotide, in the laboratory. Earlier in the year, Harvard University researchers reported production of a form of rat insulin by bacteria using a gene copied from the rat gene.

Stanford biochemists announced the first transplant of a functioning gene between mammalian species. African green monkey cells growing in laboratory culture used a rabbit gene attached to a virus to produce a rabbit blood protein, hemoglobin. In addition, Belgian researchers moved a selected gene into plant cells. To do so, they exploited a natural gene transfer system: microorganisms called agrobacteria inject deoxyribonucleic acid (DNA) into plant cells to force them to produce a nutrient on which only agrobacteria thrive. The investigators used a bacterial gene for drug resistance as their experimental implant, but they are optimistic that they will soon be able to insert plant genes that increase resistance to insects and rotting or that improve protein production.

Attempts to legislate safety regulations stalled in the U. S. Congress, as many scientists expressed growing doubt that recombinant DNA research was likely to produce any public health hazard. The National Institutes of Health revised their 1976 guidelines to ease restrictions on experiments they now view as safe.

Chromosome Analysis. Recombinant DNA techniques were used to provide raw material for analyses of genes and of the DNA that links them. More evidence was accumulated to support the theory that the genes of higher plants and animals and their viruses contain "intervening sequences," segments that are snipped out of the intermediary between DNA and protein synthesis and thus are not represented in any protein product.

While scientists have long known the code that relates DNA and protein, they cannot yet decipher DNA's regulatory actions. Biochemists have begun examining the sequences of specific regulatory regions of different organisms in the hope of finding an answer.

Individual genes on a chromosome can be detected by probing with small pieces of radioactively labeled DNA. In 1978, Stuart H. Orkin of Children's Hospital in Boston put that technique to practical use to identify a prenatal gene. Orkin used DNA from cells of amniotic fluid taken from around the fetus. He demonstrated that one fetus, suspected of having blood abnormality delta beta-thalassemia, had a copy of the normal gene. Thus the baby would be normal but a carrier of the trait. With increased knowledge of genetic diseases, it should become possible to construct DNA probes to examine other crucial genes prenatally.

Brain Chemicals. More details were uncovered in 1978 of the enigmatic, natural brain chemicals. The opiatelike molecules, endorphins, were implicated in pain relief following placebo treatment. Those experiments were the first to identify a biochemical basis for placebo effects.

Studies on rats indicated that the brain chemicals, enkephalins, not only relieve pain, but also induce pleasure and can initiate epileptic-like seizures. A Dutch researcher reported that enkephalins reduce memory loss, and a related substance, beta-endorphin, appears to play a role in body temperature regulation.

New roles were also suggested for the more traditional brain chemicals, which carry signals between nerve cells. Acetylcholine was proposed as a future treatment for senility. In animal experiments, chemicals that raise acetylcholine levels in the brain increased long-term memory and improved learning ability. Norepinephrine, another transmitter chemical, was required in animal experiments for experience-dependent, long-term brain changes. And norepinephrine was the first brain chemical reported to be distributed differently in the right and left halves of the brain. That result suggests neurotransmitter distribution may reflect varying brain activities.

Carbohydrates. New analytical techniques promise to speed progress in determining the sequences, syntheses, and functions of carbohydrates and related compounds. Molecules made partly of sugars and partly of protein appear important in "social functions" of cell surfaces —intercellular communication, regulation of growth, immunity, and even malignancy.

Purification of enzymes that make specific cuts in sugar structures portends an explosion of information about the structure of the sugar portions of molecules. In an early application of the enzyme technique, Akir Kobata of Kobe University in Japan reported two different sugar arrangements in the carbohydrate portion of ovalbumin, a major component of egg white. Other researchers characterized a set of enzymes that should also be useful in structural analyses —enzymes that add specific sugar molecules to carbohydrate chains.

Knowledge of carbohydrate chemistry led to a new approach to fighting bacterial infections. Nathon Sharon of the Weizmann Institute in Israel discovered that a surface protein on the bacteria that cause urinary tract infections is capable of attaching to the sugar mannose of human cell membranes. Sharon and his colleagues reported that flooding the cell surface with mannose can prevent bacterial binding and release bacteria already attached. Different sugars appear to participate in the binding of other disease agents, so the biochemists predict simple sugars will be useful in stopping various infections before they get a firm grip.

JULIE ANN MILLER, *"Science News"*

BIOGRAPHY

A selection of profiles of persons prominent in the news during 1978 appears on pages 121–131. The affiliation of the contributor is listed on pages 6–9. Included are sketches of:

ALLEN, Woody

One of the great comic geniuses of his time, Woody Allen scored a major triumph at the 50th Academy Awards presentations on April 3, 1978, when his romantic comedy film *Annie Hall* won four Oscar awards —best director, best actress, best picture, and best original screenplay. Replete with zany humor as well as poignant socio-sexual insights, *Annie Hall* is based in part on Allen's own romance with Diane Keaton, his co-star in the film.

Typecast as a "vulnerable schlemiel doing constant battle against a mad, surrealistic universe" (*Esquire*, May 1977), Woody Allen has been trying to transcend that image. *Interiors,* a serious family drama which he wrote and directed, was released in August 1978. In midsummer 1978, Allen began filming another romantic comedy.

Woody Allen was born Allen Stewart Konigsberg in Brooklyn, N.Y., on Dec. 1, 1935 into a middle-class Jewish family. An indifferent student, he had the distinction, at 18, of being expelled from both New York University and City College. While still in high school he began to write jokes, and eventually he wrote comedy material on a regular basis for celebrities and television shows. In 1957 he received a Sylvania award for a script he wrote for Sid Caesar.

After several years of success as a nightclub comedian, Allen wrote his first film scenario, *What's New, Pussycat?* (1965), in which he had a supporting role. His first play, the comedy *Don't Drink the Water* (1966), had a successful Broadway run, as did his *Play It Again, Sam* (1969), which he made into a movie in 1972.

Other films with Allen as writer, director, and star include *Take the Money and Run* (1969), *Bananas* (1971), *Everything You Always Wanted to Know About Sex But Were Afraid to Ask* (1972), *Sleeper* (1973), and *Love and Death* (1975).

Allen, who has also made several LP recordings of comic monologues, plays the clarinet with a jazz band and has published two books, *Getting Even* (1971) and *Without Feathers* (1975).

Admittedly a loner and something of a cynic, Allen, who has been divorced twice, lives in New York City.
HENRY S. SLOAN

UPI

Woody Allen did not attend the Academy Award ceremonies so that he could follow his usual routine and play the clarinet in a New York City pub. His film, *Annie Hall*, won several Oscars.

As expected, former basketball star and Rhodes scholar Bill Bradley ran for a U. S. Senate seat in 1978.

UPI

BOTHA, Pieter Willem

Following the resignation of John Vorster as prime minister of South Africa, Pieter Botha, the nation's defense minister since 1966, was chosen by the ruling Nationalist Party for the post. Immediately following the election, Botha promised "to carry out the [racial] policy of my party with all its consequences." He also said that South Africa would maintain its "strategic position on the Cape sea route, which with our mineral resources puts us in a position where we are coveted by others."

As leader of South Africa, Botha faces not only increasing international tensions caused by the nation's apartheid policies, but also such domestic problems as growing unrest by the nation's blacks, a dwindling economy, and a considerably greater number of emigrating whites. During his tenure as defense minister, a position he announced that he would continue to hold, Botha was responsible for the invasion of Angola in 1975.

In spite of Botha's reputation as a hard-liner, he has supported improved living conditions for the nation's blacks. In fact in reshuffling his Cabinet, he named Pieter G. Koornhof, a recognized reformer, as minister of plural relations and development.

Pieter Willem Botha was born Jan. 12, 1916, in the Paul Roux district of the Orange Free State. Following graduation with a law degree from the University of Orange Free State, he took a seat in Parliament. He has also served as the chief secretary of the Cape Nationalist Party (1948–58), deputy minister of the interior (1958–61), and minister of community development, public works, and coloured affairs (1961–66).

South Africa's eighth prime minister is married to Elize Rossouw. They are the parents of five children. Botha's favorite leisure-time activities include shooting and game hunting.

JAMES E. CHURCHILL, JR.

BRADLEY, Bill

On November 7, 1978, the political aspirations of Bill Bradley were realized. The 35-year-old former basketball star outpolled Jeffery Bell to become a U. S. senator from New Jersey. Bradley had received the Democratic nomination June 8 when he defeated State Treasurer Richard C. Leone in the party primary.

Bradley had been a resident of New Jersey for only a few years before entering politics. He was known primarily as an athlete, being a member of the New York Knicks basketball team from 1967 to 1977. His reputation as an athlete, however, tended to obscure his accomplishments in other areas.

William Warren Bradley was born July 28, 1943, in Crystal City, Mo., the only son of a bank president and a former school teacher. While attending Princeton University in the early 1960's, he became known as one of the greatest collegiate basketball players in history. After graduating in 1965, he was a Rhodes Scholar at Oxford for two years, studying philosophy, politics, and economics. During that time he was also an overseas correspondent for CBS radio. In 1976 he published *Life on the Run*, a highly acclaimed autobiography and reflection on the life of an athlete in contemporary American Society.

Prior to running for the Senate, Bradley had had no experience in elective politics. Yet campaign literature accurately described him as having "long been active in social and political causes." After teaching basic education skills at an Urban League street academy in 1968, he served as an assistant to the director of the federal Office of Economic Opportunity. In the senatorial campaign he pursued a moderate liberal course, relying heavily on a high recognition factor and extensive travel.

His wife, Ernestine, whom he married in 1974, is a professor of comparative literature at Montclair State College. The Bradleys live with their young daughter in Denville, N. J.

HERMANN K. PLATT

BRZEZINSKI, Zbigniew

Known as "Zbig" to his friends, Zbigniew Brzezinski serves as Assistant to the President for National Security Affairs in the Carter administration. In this capacity he is the president's closest foreign relations adviser, exercises major influence on policy developments, and plays a central role in managing the National Security Council system.

Brzezinski espouses foreign policy change, but through gradualism, avoiding identification with the status quo and conveying a sense of progress and improvement. He participated in developing most foreign relations themes of President Carter: increased emphasis on human rights, bilateralism, openness, and Third World interests. Two policy areas are especially identified with him—a harder line toward the USSR and a new global order. He holds that the Soviet Union

UPI

Former Columbia University professor Zbigniew Brzezinski serves as President Carter's top foreign affairs adviser.

is less central to U. S. foreign relations strategy than was previously the case, and that the United States needs to avoid the appearance of participating in a Soviet-American condominium. Convinced of widespread transition from nationalism to globalism, he argues for courting the developing nations.

Born in Warsaw in 1928, the son of a Polish diplomat, he was educated at McGill and Harvard universities. Rising rapidly through the academic ranks, he paralleled his teaching with research and administrative assignments, first at Harvard and, beginning in 1960, at Columbia University. He has published widely on foreign policy and world politics, and is the recipient of honorary degrees and a substantial number of foundation and other awards. He served on the Policy Planning Staff of the Department of State and as a consultant to the Rand Corporation.

Much of Brzezinski's innovation is reducible to matters of style rather than policy substance. He is acknowledged to be hardworking, intelligent, highly energetic in both thought and action, and a sharp-tongued debater. A team worker, he possesses a gift for synthesis as well as a probing mind, and does not suffer from a sense of either inferiority or insecurity.

Disdaining the overuse of personal diplomacy, he usually remains in the background. Criticizing the "Lone Ranger" and "acrobatic" methods of dealing with foreign affairs, he prefers what he calls the "architectural approach." This does not mean that he has not propounded his own brand of overall foreign relations strategy, but he has not promulgated a grand design for the United States in world affairs.

ELMER PLISCHKE

CAUTHEN, Steve

In 1978, at the age of 18, Steve Cauthen achieved a feat that only nine other jockeys have attained in the history of thoroughbred racing. He won the Triple Crown. Riding flawlessly in his first appearance in each of these three races, Cauthen triumphed aboard Harbor View Farm's Affirmed by one-and-a-half lengths in the Kentucky Derby, by a neck in the Preakness, and by a head in the Belmont.

In 1976, his first year of professional riding, Cauthen demonstrated his immense talents by ranking as the country's leading apprentice jockey in races won (240) and money earned by mounts ($1,244,423). Cauthen followed up with a sensational year in 1977, earning a world record $6,151,750 in purses. The old record was $4,709,500. In addition, Cauthen rode 487 winners in 1977, tops in the country.

Variously nicknamed "Stevie Wonder," "The Walton Wizard," "The Kentucky Kid," and "The Kid," Cauthen has impressed racing followers with his riding form, his patience and composure, his judgment of pace, and his ability to get the most out of his mounts.

One of Cauthen's finest rides came aboard Johnny D. in the 1977 Washington, D. C., International. Recognizing a slow pace, Cauthen seized the initiative with slightly more than half a mile to go, opened up an insurmountable lead of eight lengths, and won by 2½ lengths.

Cauthen was born May 1, 1960, in Covington, Ky. His family lives in Walton, Ky. His father, Tex, is a blacksmith, and his mother, Myra, has trained racehorses.

Howard Jarvis, the sponsor of a taxpayers' revolt, became a U.S. folk hero.

UPI

Already a celebrity, the young jockey has been pictured on the cover of national magazines, and his life has been told in the book *The Kid,* by Pete Axthelm. Cauthen is being hailed as the finest rider to come along in decades. As Harbor View Farm owner Louis Wolfson put it, "We may not ever see anything like this youngster in our lifetime."

JIM BOLUS

CHURCH, Frank

Member of the Senate for more than 20 years and of its Foreign Relations Committee since 1959, Frank Church (D-Idaho) became chairman of the Senate Foreign Relations Committee in January 1979. As such, he is expected to invigorate the committee's role in shaping American foreign policy in the 1980's.

Born on July 24, 1924, in Boise, Idaho, he served in the Army as an intelligence officer in the China-Burma-India theater during World War II. He was educated at Stanford University—B. A. (Phi Beta Kappa, 1947) and LL. B. (1950). He practiced law in Boise until his election to the Senate in 1956, then its youngest member.

Now in his fourth term, he has mastered Senate politics. In addition to serving on the Foreign Relations Committee and several of its subcommittees, he has been a member of the Democratic Steering and the Energy and National Resources committees, and chairman of a Special Committee on Aging. He also co-chaired the special committee established to curtail executive emergency authority and chaired a special Committee on Intelligence. In 1966 he was a member of the U. S. delegation to the UN General Assembly, and during 1969 he led the American delegations to several U. S.-Canadian Interparliamentary Conferences.

Respected by his congressional colleagues for his intelligence, diligence, and legislative skills, he approaches his new task with distinct advantages as well as predispositions. A champion of the powers of Congress in its relations with the executive, he is not afraid to disagree with the president. He was one of the first senators to oppose the Vietnam war, and frequently attacked the foreign aid program, especially military assistance to dictators. He has favored a curb on breeder reactors and the new Panama Canal treaties, but has opposed the B-1 bomber and SST landings. He has also proven himself by leading the 16-month Senate investigation of the intelligence community. The investigation produced a nearly unanimous, fair-minded report and led to the establishment of a permanent Senate Intelligence Committee to oversee legislated reforms.

As Foreign Relations chairman, Senator Church possesses the advantages of long committee service, friendly working relations with minority leadership, and a core of committee associates who generally share his philosophical views. The test of his success will be the degree to which he is able to establish control over the full committee without alienating the chairmen of his subcommittees. At the same time, he must maintain productive relations with the executive branch without becoming a White House proconsul.

ELMER PLISCHKE

JARVIS, Howard A.

Howard Arnold Jarvis, at the age of 75, suddenly became a national folk hero, as he began the so-called U. S. taxpayers revolt of 1978. Together with the less colorful Paul Gann, a Sacramento, Ca., realtor, he organized a petition drive to put what became Proposition 13 on the June 6 California ballot.

Jarvis was born in 1902 in Magda, Utah, of Mormon parents. His father was a lawyer and a Utah state judge. Young Jarvis earned a law degree from the University of Utah in the 1920's, but never practiced. Instead, he bought and published a string of weekly small-town newspapers. In 1932, he served as a press aide in Herbert Hoover's presidential campaign and met Earl Warren, with whom he became friends. Jarvis moved to California shortly thereafter, having sold his weeklies at a profit. He bought and developed a small multiproducts firm, Femco Corp., which prospered. In 1962, at the age of 59, Jarvis retired.

It was not long, however, before he became active in politics, with tax cutting as his theme. Beginning in 1962, cantankerous Jarvis ran for the U. S. Senate, the California State Board of Equalization, and mayor of

Los Angeles. He lost each time and remained unknown to most voters. Other than serving part-time as director of the Apartment Association of Los Angeles, Jarvis and his wife lived quietly and unostentatiously in Los Angeles.

The rapid rise of California property values after 1975 finally gave Jarvis his chance. He ran a colorful campaign that attracted much media attention. After Proposition 13 won by a margin of almost 2 to 1, Jarvis enjoyed his long-delayed public attention. He appeared on numerous television talk shows and at political conferences. He confidently agreed to help secure tax limitations in the federal government and in other states. It was not immediately clear, however, just how large a movement Howard Jarvis had in fact begun.

CHARLES R. ADRIAN

JAY, Peter

Peter Jay, 41, Britain's ambassador to Washington, was once described by the *Sunday Times* as "the cleverest young man in England." Even if he is not the most brilliant, he is somewhere in the top 40, and his performance as ambassador is not likely to lead the experts to dispute his placing.

Jay, the son of a former British cabinet minister, was born on Feb. 7, 1937, and was educated at Oxford. He is the brother of the "Jay twins," two delightful young women who were fashion trend-setters in the Britain of the 1960's, and is married to Margaret Callaghan, the daughter of Britain's prime minister. After a period as an expert in the Treasury, Britain's department of finance, he became economics editor of the *London Times*. His writing was uncompromisingly for the specialists, with few if any concessions made to the general reader. In spite of this, he later became presenter of the country's most prestigious television news program, *Weekend World*. As such, he became famous for skillful interviewing and impenetrably long questions.

His appointment as British ambassador to the most important world capital was announced to universal mirth in May 1977. Not only was he the prime minister's son-in-law, but the man who made the appointment, Foreign Secretary David Owen, was a close friend. The apparently nepotistic appointment caused deep anxiety and offense to admirers of Callaghan, yet even the severest critics have since admitted that the choice was first-rate.

Doubts have persisted, however, about Jay's view of Britain's economy. Jay has always been deeply pessimistic about his country's prospects and his seemingly miraculous conversion to the government team has been cynically received. Nevertheless, his energy and enthusiasm for his Washington job have won friends even among his critics. Jay has attempted to trim Britain's large Washington diplomatic staff, arousing admiration among the general public if annoyance among professional diplomats.

A former member of the Royal Navy, the economist-diplomat is a keen sailor. He has taken part in several demanding yacht races.

SIMON HOGGART

JOHN PAUL II, POPE

Known widely by Polish Catholics as the "worker cardinal" because of his early years as a laborer and his deep concern for the working classes, Pope John Paul II, the former Karol Cardinal Wojtyla of Cracow, is at once a pastor, scholar-theologian, administrator, and church leader devoted to renewal of Catholicism.

John Paul II is the first non-Italian pope in 455 years and the first from a Communist nation. Although he was mentioned among the possible candidates for the papacy, the 58-year-old churchman's election by the College of Cardinals was so totally unexpected it shocked the world. Nevertheless, the choice was viewed generally as symbolizing the universal nature of the church.

As Archbishop of Cracow in southern Poland since 1964, Cardinal Wojtyla had been a strong but subtle critic of the Polish government, especially for what he saw as a denial of basic human and religious rights. At the same time, he maintained an effective liaison with the government which had led to the continuation of a vigorous church life among Cracow's Catholics and the ongoing implementation of Vatican II reforms among his people.

A tall, heavyset man described as "compassionate but firm," "sensitive but a realist," the new pope visited the United States in 1969 and 1976, on the latter occasion leading a delegation of Polish bishops to the International Eucharistic Congress in Philadelphia. He subsequently toured many American cities with large Polish populations.

In his first major message as pope, John Paul II pledged to carry on the work of his predecessors, citing the importance of fidelity to Church teaching, particularly in doctrine and liturgy, and indicating a move toward decentralization and internationalization of the Church's administrative body, the Roman Curia.

Born in Wadowice, Poland, May 18, 1920, he studied philology at the Jagiellonian University, Cracow. His studies were interrupted by World War II, but in 1942 he began preparing secretly for the priesthood despite the Nazi occupation. Ordained in 1946, he later earned a doctorate in theology and held the chair of ethics at the Catholic University of Lublin. Named a bishop in 1958 at age 38, he was active in the deliberations of Vatican II. He was appointed Archbishop of Cracow in 1964, and made a cardinal by Pope Paul VI in 1967. In 1972, he published a book, *Foundations of Renewal*, aimed at implementation of Vatican II reforms. That same year he launched a seven-year pastoral synod aimed at deepening the religious life of members of the Cracow archdiocese. He was a member of three Vatican congregations.

ROBERT L. JOHNSTON

KAHN, Alfred E.

As the new "inflation czar" of the Carter administration, Alfred Kahn hopes to repeat the success he enjoyed on the U. S. Civil Aeronautics Board (CAB) which, under his chairmanship, deregulated the airline industry, precipitating reductions of air fares by as much as 50% and boosting the airlines' business.

On Oct. 25, 1978, Kahn was named chairman of the Council on Wage and Price Stability, and a member of the Economic Policy Group, giving him a range of economic influence extending beyond inflation problems. One of his primary concerns is to reduce government waste and bureaucratic inefficiency, as he did at the Civil Aeronautics Board, and, before that, as chairman of the New York Service Commission, 1974–77.

Kahn is famous for his quips. He has campaigned against official government "gobbledygook" and "bafflegab," noting that "If you can't explain what you're doing in simple English, you are probably doing something wrong." When asked why he had accepted the thankless job of inflation adviser, he responded: "I'm 61 years old. What am I saving it for?" And after being chastised by the administration for referring to "a possible depression," Kahn began using the expression the "worst banana in years."

Background. Born in Paterson, N. J., on Oct. 17, 1917, Kahn earned his A. B. and A. M. degrees from New York University in 1936 and 1937, respectively, and a Ph. D. in economics from Yale in 1942. After serving as an economist for the departments of commerce and justice, Kahn chaired the economics department at Ripon College (1945–47). In 1947 he began his long association with Cornell University, where he served as professor, chairman of the economics department, and dean of the College of Arts and Sci-

UPI

Diane Keaton was named the year's best actress for her performance in the title role of *Annie Hall*.

ences, and where he continues to be the Robert Julius Thorne Professor of Economics. When he is at Cornell, Kahn likes to indulge in his favorite avocation: singing baritone roles in amateur productions of Gilbert and Sullivan operettas.

Kahn is the author of several books, including *Integration and Competition in the Petroleum Industry* (1959), and *The Economics of Regulation* (1971). He and his wife, the former Mary Simmons, have three children.

EDWARD M. KURDYLA, JR.

KEATON, Diane

For her sparkling performance in the title role of Woody Allen's romantic comedy film *Annie Hall*, actress-comedienne Diane Keaton was honored as best actress at the 50th annual Academy Award ceremonies on April 3, 1978. Praised by critics for her wholesome charm, acting skill, and flair for comedy, Diane Keaton also received a 1977 Golden Globe award and a National Society of Film Critics award, among other honors. Woody Allen has said of her, "I'd rather work with Diane Keaton than anyone. She's ... a natural."

Miss Keaton also won plaudits as a serious dramatic actress for her performance as Theresa in the chilling *Looking for Mr. Goodbar* (1977), Richard Brooks' film adaptation of Judith Rossner's best-selling novel about a schizoid personality who was a dedicated teacher of deaf children by day, but who cruised singles bars at night. In *Interiors,* released in August 1978, Diane Keaton played one of three daughters in a troubled family.

Diane Keaton, whose surname was originally Hall, was born in Los Angeles, Calif., on Jan. 5, 1946, the oldest of four children. As a child she sang in a church choir and performed in school talent shows. At 19, after briefly attending Santa Ana College and Orange Coast College, she went to New York to study acting with Sanford Meisner. In 1968 she appeared on Broadway in the rock musical *Hair,* and in 1969 she co-starred with Woody Allen in his Broadway comedy *Play It Again, Sam;* she repeated her role in its 1972 film version. She also co-starred with Allen in his films *Sleeper* (1973) and *Love and Death* (1975). Other films in which she appeared include *Lovers and Other Strangers* (1970), *The Godfather* (1972), *The Godfather, Part II* (1974), *I Will, I Will ... For Now* (1976), and *Harry and Walter Go to New York* (1976). In 1976 she starred in the Off Broadway comedy *The Primary English Class.* Keaton has also had success as a nightclub singer.

Diane Keaton is unmarried and makes her home in New York City.

HENRY S. SLOAN

LAFLEUR, Guy Damien

Back home in Quebec, Canada's only predominantly French province, his name translates into "The Flower." Since the 1975–76 season, Guy Lafleur has indeed supplied the fragrance to the Montreal Canadiens' clear-cut superiority in the National Hockey League (NHL). During three consecutive Stanley Cup championship seasons, Lafleur has been his team's top scorer, most prolific playmaker, and most valuable player. He is also Canada's most popular athlete.

Blessed with exceptional speed and mobility, Lafleur has been the offensive sparkplug of a Montreal Canadiens team that compiled a 177–29–34 regular season record and a 36–6 play-off record in three seasons. In those 282 games, Lafleur, who plays right wing, scored a phenomenal 446 points—210 goals and 236 assists. He captured the Art Ross Trophy as the NHL's top scorer in 1975–76 (125 points), 1976–77 (136 points), and 1977–78 (121 points). He was also the recipient of the Hart Trophy as the league's most valuable player in 1976–77 and 1977–78. This made him only the third player in NHL history to win both the Art Ross and Hart trophies in consecutive seasons.

Background. Guy Damien Lafleur was born on Sept. 20, 1951, in Thurso, Que., a village of 1,400 residents near Montreal. He began playing hockey as a young boy and excelled in the local juvenile leagues. Lafleur was eventually given the opportunity to play for the Quebec Ramparts, an amateur "junior" team in Quebec City, and he performed brilliantly.

In June 1971, Guy Lafleur became the Montreal Canadiens' first selection—and the premier choice of all eligible players—in the NHL's amateur draft. He was signed to a professional contract and participated in 73 games with the Canadiens as a rookie; he scored 29 goals and 64 total points that year. The first real recognition of Guy Lafleur by his peers came during the 1974–75 season when he was named to the first all-star team.

Lafleur, who is 6 feet (1.83 m) tall and weighs 180 pounds (81.6 kg), actually had had his heart set on becoming a member of the Royal Canadian Mounted Police while still in his youth. The rewards of a major league professional hockey career, however, and an annual salary estimated at (U. S.) $148,500 in 1978 (not including bonuses) have made him very content.

ED CONRAD

MARTHA SWOPE

Jack Lemmon returned to the Broadway stage in 1978. A new play, *Tribute*, was written for him.

LEMMON, Jack

Veteran actor Jack Lemmon returned to the Broadway stage for the first time in 18 years when he opened on June 1, 1978, in *Tribute*, a new play written for him by Bernard Slade. Although the play received mixed reviews, Lemmon won critical acclaim for his portrayal of Scotty Templeton, a lovable but irresponsible middle-aged publicity agent who, after learning that he is dying of leukemia, sets out to put his affairs in order and to effect a reconciliation with his estranged son. Critic Rex Reed called his performance "just plain fabulous," and Lemmon himself found *Tribute* to be "the greatest single professional experience" of his long-established career.

Described as "likable and respectable and civilized," Lemmon is perhaps best known for his light comedy film performances, often as an amiable "fall guy" caught in the middle. But he has proved himself equally adept in such serious dramatic roles as that of a harassed businessman driven to corruption in *Save the Tiger* (1973), which earned him an Academy Award as best actor. Earlier he had won an Oscar as best supporting actor for his portrayal of the frolicsome Ensign Pulver in *Mister Roberts* (1955). He received Academy Award nominations for *Some Like It Hot* (1959), *The Apartment* (1960), and *Days of Wine and Roses* (1962).

Background. John Uhler Lemmon 3d, the son of a corporation executive, was born in Boston, Mass., on Feb. 8, 1925. He was educated in private schools and at Harvard, where he was president of the Hasty Pudding Club and, after service as an ensign in the U.S. Navy, obtained his B. A. and B. S. degrees in 1947. Over the next few years he acted in hundreds of radio and television dramas and in summer stock. Lemmon made his Broadway debut in a revival of *Room Service* (1953) and later appeared on Broadway in *Face of a Hero* (1960). His first film, *It Should Happen to You* (1954) co-starred Judy Holliday; subsequently, he has appeared in more than 35 motion pictures. He made his debut as a film director in *Kotch* (1971). His television credits include an Emmy-Award-winning George Gershwin special (1972) and a dramatic special, *The Entertainer* (1976). An accomplished musician, he composed the score for the film *Fire Down Below.*

Lemmon and his wife, actress Felicia Farr, have a daughter; he also has a son from his previous marriage.

HENRY S. SLOAN

LOPEZ, Nancy

"I'm enjoying it now, because it will never be like this again," said Nancy Lopez, midway through the 1978 golf season. She may be right. No rookie in golf—or possibly any other sport—has matched the impact that this smiling Mexican-American made on her game and the nation in her first full season on the Ladies Professional Golf Association (LPGA) tour. And no woman golfer has equaled her one-year accomplishments.

Nancy Marie Lopez and her parents moved to Roswell, N. M., shortly following her birth in Torrance, Calif., on Jan. 6, 1957. When she was eight her father, Domingo, the operator of an auto body shop, began teaching her the game of golf. Miss Lopez performed brilliantly in amateur and collegiate competition on her way to the top of the professional heap. She captured the national girls' junior championships in 1972 and 1974 and later won the women's intercollegiate crown.

Named *Golf Digest's* Rookie of the Year for 1977 after just half a professional season, Nancy really turned it on in 1978. She won nine tournaments. Five of these were in a row, including the LPGA championship, eclipsing Mickey Wright's record of four straight wins. During her official rookie season, from mid-1977 to mid-1978, she won $161,235 to break Jerry Pate's first-year record, and during the 1978 calendar season she banked an LPGA record $189,814. She became the first to win simultaneous LPGA Rookie of the Year and Player of the Year honors.

Miss Lopez does it with a powerful, slightly unorthodox swing that is made effective by superb, deliberate tempo. She is also, according to rival JoAnne Carner, "the best putter ever on tour."

While she is making all those low scores (her average of 71.76 was the lowest on tour and earned her the Vare Trophy), Nancy flashes a dazzling smile and a personable warmth that captivates the fans. Her friendly cooperation and remarkable poise also make her a favorite with the press. Virtually every national magazine did a feature profile on her during the year.

As the LPGA continues its rush toward dizzying success, Nancy Lopez has become its new image, an Arnold Palmer with skirts and laughing eyes.

LARRY DENNIS

Businessman G. William Miller became chairman of the Federal Reserve System.

UPI

MILLER, George William

Few jobs in Washington are as demanding as the chairmanship of the Federal Reserve, and few men would be as hard to follow in that role as Arthur Burns. As 1978 ended, G. William Miller, however, seemed to be measuring up to both.

Appointed to succeed Burns on Dec. 28, 1977, Miller managed in 1978 to tighten the inflation-generating growth of the money supply without choking off the nation's fragile recovery. Although interest rates were pushed up substantially, no credit crunch developed.

Nor did Miller prove willing to sacrifice the reserve's traditional independence. In frequent appearances before Congressional committees, he repeatedly refused to bow to pressures from liberal legislators to expand the credit supply. And he did not hesitate to speak out on economic issues, usually in support of business.

A lawyer by trade, Miller has nonetheless, by all accounts, mastered the complexities of his job. In a number of technical areas, he moved to correct outmoded practices. He also strove to reverse the historic decline of Federal Reserve bank membership.

Background. George William Miller was born March 9, 1925, in Sapulpa, Okla. He attended the Coast Guard Academy, serving after graduation in the Far East where he met and married his wife, Ariadna. Although originally interested in engineering, he shifted to law and attended the University of California at Berkeley Law School.

After four years with Cravath, Swaine & Moore, a top New York firm, he was hired in 1956 by Textron, Inc., a conglomerate based in Providence, R. I. He rose quickly, becoming president in 1960, at the age of 35, and chairman in 1974. He acquired a reputation as a hard-working, demanding manager with great intellectual depth, and helped build Textron into one of the nation's largest companies.

Meanwhile, Miller found time to become involved in public service, working for three Democratic presidents on unemployment and minority problems. Just six months before his appointment to the Federal Reserve, he became chairman of a major effort to find jobs for Vietnam veterans.

Miller's only previous contact with monetary policy was several years of service as a director of the Federal Reserve Bank of Boston.

STEVEN RATTNER

MOBUTU Sese Seko

In 1978, for the second year in a row, an invasion of southern Zaire by Angola-based rebels threatened to topple Zaire's President Mobutu Sese Seko, the former army chief of staff who took power in a 1965 military coup. As in the past, however, Mobutu adroitly defended himself against both the rebellion and the pressures for political and economic change which came from his Western allies. He won the military support of France in driving out the rebels, and the continued financial support of the International Monetary Fund (IMF) member nations, to which Zaire owes more than (U. S.) $2 billion.

In the process, Mobutu, known in Zaire as The Guide, was obliged to sacrifice extensive financial authority by placing an IMF-appointed official in effective control of the national bank. The president resisted Western pressure to share power with the diverse tribal and regional interests in Zaire, however, and retained almost total political control. In a Western-supported effort to reduce regional tensions, Mobutu also established diplomatic relations with Socialist Angola, and

UPI

Zaire's President Mobutu Sese Seko successfully defended himself against a rebel invasion in 1978.

tacitly agreed to drop his support of antigovernment guerrillas there. His biggest challenge remained Zaire's nearly bankrupt economy.

Mobutu Sese Seko, formerly known as Joseph Mobutu, has been president of Zaire for thirteen of the eighteen years since independence from Belgium in 1960. To avoid challenges to his authority, he has intentionally kept the army weak, and has occasionally jailed political rivals for treason. He was reelected without opposition to a third seven-year term in late 1977, despite a constitutional limitation of two terms per president.

Born in Lisala, Équateur Province in the Belgian Congo, Mobutu was educated in Christian missionary schools and at the Institute of Social Studies in Belgium. He rose through the ranks to become an officer in the preindependence paramilitary force of the Belgian Congo. He also spent time as a journalist, supporting an independence movement among Congolese students in Belgium. He was named army chief shortly after independence, and his 1965 coup ended a long period of political instability. Although he cut back on his personal flamboyance in 1978 and attempted to spend money less ostentatiously, Mobutu nevertheless chose to arrive at an African summit meeting in Paris during Zaire's military crisis wearing a set of camouflage-colored jungle fatigues.

JIM BROWNING

MURDOCH, Rupert

In less than 25 years, Rupert Murdoch has built a newspaper and magazine empire in Australia, Great Britain, and the United States that would be the envy of William Randolph Hearst, Lord Beaverbrook, and Citizen Kane. Yet the competitive and resourceful Australian has been widely criticized for promoting sensationalist journalism. His papers are assailed for their gaudy photographs, huge headlines, and steady diet of crime, sex, and sports. One of his dailies in Australia once carried the headline, presumably written by Murdoch himself, "Leper Rapes Virgin, Gives Birth to Monster Baby."

Murdoch created a storm of controversy in 1976 when he purchased the *New York Post,* a major daily, and the New York Magazine Company. The latter publishes *New York* and *New West* magazines, as well as the *Village Voice,* a weekly New York newspaper. In 1978 Murdoch was again the center of attention as he negotiated with striking pressmen, who halted publication of the *Post, New York Times,* and *Daily News.* The shrewd owner of the *Post* reached a settlement weeks before the other publishers and dominated the market for the interim.

Background. Keith Rupert Murdoch was born March 11, 1931 in Melbourne, Australia. He was educated at Geelong Grammar School (the Australian counterpart of Eton) and Oxford University. After receiving his Master's degree in economics and political science, he became a junior editor for Lord Beaverbrook's London *Daily Express.* In 1954 he returned to Australia to manage the Adelaide *News,* a small daily inherited from his father. The *News* became enormously successful, and Murdoch began building his empire. In 1964 he launched Australia's first national newspaper, the *Australian,* a serious and highbrow journal. By 1968 his holdings in newspapers, magazines, and broadcasting were worth some $50 million. Setting his sights on Great Britain, Murdoch first acquired London's *News of the World.* He then purchased the *Sun,* which became one of London's widest-circulation dailies. His first venture in the United States was to annex the San Antonio (Tex.) *Express* and *News.* After launching the *National Star,* a weekly supermarket tabloid, the apparently insatiable Murdoch sought a major city daily in the United States. His ambition was realized in November 1976 with the purchase of the *New York Post.*

JEFF HACKER

WNET

Luciano Pavarotti is the first artist to give a televised recital from the stage of the Metropolitan Opera House.

PAVAROTTI, Luciano

The operatic era of the 1970's can be called a golden age of the lyric tenor, and one of the reasons is Luciano Pavarotti. He is possessed of a finely focused voice with a ringing top register and undaunted high C's, and the musical intelligence and sensibility to go with this extraordinary instrument.

Pavarotti was born in Modena, Italy, Oct. 12, 1935, the son of a baker and professional tenor who started him singing at age four. In 1961, as a reward for winning the Concorso Internazionale, Pavarotti made his historic debut as Rodolfo in "La Bohème" at the Teatro Municipale in Reggio Emilia, Italy. The Mimi opposite him was another debutante and native of Modena, the lyric soprano Mirella Freni, his friend since infancy. Rodolfo was again his debut role at Covent Garden, 1963, San Francisco, 1967, and the Metropolitan Opera, 1968.

Pavarotti quickly made his way to the world's other principal opera houses and won seven major awards. For London Records, he recorded the principal tenor roles in 18 operas, ten of these opposite Joan Sutherland. His bel canto opera recordings include Bellini's "Beatrice di Tenda" and "I Puritani," Donizetti's "La Fille du Regiment" and "La Favorita." In recent years, Pavarotti has been slowly acquiring heavier lyric roles, first as Manrico in Verdi's "Il Trovatore" (the San Francisco Opera, 1975, and on a recording), then as Cavaradossi in Puccini's "Tosca" (Chicago Lyric Opera, 1976) and Calaf in "Turandot" (San Francisco Opera, 1977, also recorded).

Pavarotti and his wife, Adua Veroni, wed in 1961, have three daughters. He is an excellent cook and ardent tennis player, his great girth reflecting the first hobby more than the second. As a world-renowned tenor, he travels constantly. In 1978 his scheduled appearances included Munich, New York, Verona, San Francisco, and Milan. A highlight of his career occurred in February 1978 with his recital at the Metropolitan Opera, the first to be televised from that stage, and nationwide in coverage.

ROBERT COMMANDAY

UPI

Cincinnati's Pete Rose hit safely in 44 straight games.

ROSE, Peter Edward

The 1978 baseball season was highlighted by two remarkable achievements—both by Pete Rose, the indefatigable 16-year veteran of the Cincinnati Reds. With a solid single to left field on May 5 against the Montreal Expos, Rose became only the 13th player in baseball history to get 3,000 career base hits. An accomplishment of even greater moment, however, came on July 25 when the switch-hitting third baseman hit in his 38th consecutive game, bettering the modern National League record previously held by Tommy Holmes of the old Brooklyn Dodgers. The streak did not end until the 37-year-old Rose had hit safely in 44 straight games, just 12 shy of Joe Dimaggio's "untouchable" major league record set in 1946.

Talking to reporters after base-hit 3,000, Rose said of himself, "There are a lot of players better than me, but I do the same thing day in and day out, year in and year out." Rose is the acknowledged "spark plug" of Cincinnati's "Big Red Machine," perhaps the most successful baseball team of the decade. The type of player who runs full-speed to first base on a walk, dives into the stands for a foul ball, and slides head-first into any base, Rose has become known in baseball circles as "Charlie Hustle."

Background. Peter Edward Rose was born in Cincinnati, Ohio, on April 14, 1942. He was reared in a comfortable middle-class home, with a brother and two sisters. His father, a semi-professional football player, introduced Peter to sports at an early age. In high school, Pete excelled in football and baseball, but opted for a career in the latter and signed with the Reds after graduation. After three successful years in the minor leagues, Rose became a starting player for the Reds in 1963 and was named the National League Rookie of the Year.

Rose is the only active player to hit over .300 for nine consecutive seasons. He has led the National League in hits four times and tied for the lead twice. He has also led the league in hitting three times: .335 in 1968, .348 in 1969, and .338 in 1973. He was named the league's Most Valuable Player in 1973 and the MVP of the 1975 World Series, as his team defeated the Boston Red Sox in seven games. In 1978, Pete Rose played in the 11th All-Star game of his career.

At the end of the 1978 season, the star became a free agent and signed a large contract with Philadelphia.

JEFF HACKER

SINGER, Isaac Bashevis

Upon hearing that he was the recipient of the 1978 Nobel Prize for Literature, I. B. Singer at first expressed disbelief; then with customary self-effacement he observed that the greatest writers of all time never received it. He said that "the prize, while it's pleasant ... doesn't prove really so much. ..." His modesty was typical of a writer who has long considered his function to be that of entertainment. He calls himself only a storyteller.

Isaac Bashevis Singer was born on July 14, 1904, in Radzymin, Poland. He was the second of three sons and one daughter born to Rabbi Pinchas Menachem Singer and Bathsheba (Zylberman) Singer, and was early encouraged to become a rabbi. He was given a traditional Hebrew education. For a time he studied at the Tachkemoni Rabbinical Seminary in Warsaw, but the influence of his older brother, a noted Yiddish writer, proved too strong, and he began secular writing. In the early 1920's he took a job as a proofreader and by 1926 had begun to publish. In 1932 he became co-editor of the Yiddish literary magazine *Globus* which serialized his first novel, *Satan in Goray.*

In 1935 he migrated to New York City. Shortly thereafter he began contributing work to a Yiddish newspaper, *Jewish Daily Forward.* He became a regular contributor in 1943, and most of his novels and short stories originally appeared there.

In 1950 he achieved his first success in the English speaking world with publication in English of *The Family Moskat.* Since that time he has written eight novels, ten children's books, four memoirs, and scores of short stories. His work has been translated into many languages.

Singer's literary inspirations come from the folklore and mysticism of the culture of the Jews of Eastern Europe. His works include most of the major themes of fiction.

He has a son Israel from a failed first marriage and is presently married to the former Alma Haimann.

SAUNDRA FRANCE

STRAUSS, Robert Schwarz

During most of 1978, U. S. economic news was dominated by one man—Robert Strauss—whose influence within the Carter administration reached a pervasiveness achieved by very few in modern times.

Appointed special counselor on inflation in April 1978, Strauss launched a major campaign to win commitments from business to moderate price increases and from labor to moderate its wage demands. Although tangible results were not immediately apparent, Strauss' efforts served to focus national attention on the inflation problem.

Strauss also serves as special trade representative, a Cabinet-level post which he has held since early 1977. In that role, he has devoted his political and organizational skills to achieving a new international agreement to lower trade barriers, a requisite for future world economic growth.

Following a major presidential address in late October, Alfred Kahn succeeded Strauss as the president's inflation adviser.

Strauss also used his own formidable reputation and wide acquaintance to bolster the administration's faltering credibility. Drawing on his charm and persuasiveness, the grey-haired, distinguished-looking politician injected himself successfully into a wide variety of issues. He was, for example, instrumental in winning Senate approval for the Panama Canal treaties and in settling the coal strike in early 1978.

Robert Strauss was born Oct. 19, 1918, in the small town of Lockhart, Tex. His parents, who ran a dry goods store, sent him to the University of Texas, where he formed a lasting acquaintance with John B. Connally, later secretary of the treasury.

After graduation from law school in 1941 and a stint with the FBI during World War II, Strauss founded his own law firm in Dallas and made a small fortune in real estate, banking, and radio stations. On the side he became involved in state Democratic politics, working in the successful gubernatorial campaign of his friend Connally in 1962.

As chairman of the 1968 Humphrey-Muskie campaign in Texas, Strauss demonstrated his now legendary talents for money raising and reconciliation. Those abilities proved even more useful beginning in 1970 when he served as treasurer and later chairman of the Democratic party. His principal achievement was reuniting the party after the 1972 McGovern debacle.

Along the way, Strauss made the contacts and did the favors that are now paying off in his work as President Carter's troubleshooter. Throughout 1978, Strauss commuted with his wife Helen between Washington and Dallas.

STEVEN RATTNER

TRAVOLTA, John

Hollywood's latest superstar, John Travolta, won unanimous acclaim for his brilliant disco dancing performance in the film *Saturday Night Fever*. His portrayal of Tony Manero, the "king" of a Brooklyn discotheque, earned him an Academy Award nomination for best actor of 1977 and a citation from the National Board of Review. Travolta further demonstrated his acting and dancing talents in *Grease* (1978), the film adaptation of the long-running Broadway musical about youth in the 1950's.

Previously, Travolta had been known primarily to teenagers for his portrayal of Vinnie Barbarino, leader of a youth gang called the Sweathogs, in the popular ABC television comedy series *Welcome Back, Kotter*. His success in the film medium, however, seemed further assured by his performance in *Moment to Moment* (1978).

John Travolta was born on Feb. 18, 1954, in Englewood, N. J., the youngest of six children of an Irish-Italian family. Encouraged by his parents, he acted in local theatrical productions as a boy. After dropping out of school at 16 he moved to New York, where he acted in television commercials and on the Off Broadway stage. Travolta made his Broadway debut in the musical *Over Here!* (1974). He also appeared in a minor role with the national touring company of *Grease* (1972–73).

On the West Coast he appeared in such television shows as *The Rookies* and *Medical Center* and acted in minor parts in the films *The Devil's Rain* (1975) and *Carrie* (1976). He won plaudits for the television film *The Boy in the Plastic Bubble*, in which he portrayed an ailing teenager.

As a pop singer, Travolta has two LP albums and several single recordings to his credit.

Travolta, whose main hobby is flying, makes his home in West Hollywood and practices scientology. His brief love affair with actress Diana Hyland, 18 years his senior, ended with her death from cancer in 1977.

HENRY S. SLOAN

WEBSTER, William H.

Following a Feb. 23, 1978, swearing in ceremony, Judge William H. Webster became only the third permanent director in the 54-year history of the nation's premier law enforcement agency, the Federal Bureau of Investigation. As he moved into the fortress-like FBI headquarters on Pennsylvania Avenue, Webster had three primary goals: to restore public confidence in the bureau; to boost the sagging morale of the agency's 19,500 employees; and to prove that someone besides the late J. Edgar Hoover could control the bureau's far-flung operations.

In order to succeed, the judge, who has never carried a gun or made an arrest, will have to prove himself tough. Clarence M. Kelley, the previous director, had been unable to take charge the way he wished, partly because he remained surrounded by aides loyal to Hoover's memory and partly because of revelations of illegal FBI practices. Webster's success or failure in the job could hinge on his administrative abilities, which are largely untested.

Background. William Hedgcock Webster was born on March 6, 1924, in St. Louis, Mo. He was educated in Webster Groves, near St. Louis, and at Amherst College, where he met Stansfield Turner, now the director of the Central Intelligence Agency. Webster earned his law degree at Washington University in St. Louis in 1949. He has spent most of his career as an attorney in a St. Louis law firm, though he served as a U. S. attorney in 1960 and 1961. His first judgeship came in 1970, when President Nixon appointed him to the United States District Court for Eastern Missouri. In 1973 he was elevated to the U. S. Court of Appeals for the Eighth District. The decision to accept the FBI post was a difficult one for Webster, who was comfortable in his role as judge. Moving to Washington also meant being farther away from the family farm in Callaway County, Mo. Webster is married to his childhood sweetheart, Drusilla Lane, and they have three children.

JOHN DILLIN

YALOW, Rosalyn Sussman

On Dec. 10, 1977, Dr. Rosalyn S. Yalow of the Bronx Veterans Administration Hospital in New York became the second woman to be awarded a Nobel Prize in medicine or physiology. She received the award for her development, in collaboration with the late Dr. Solomon A. Berson, of analytic radioimmunoassay (RIA), a laboratory technique that through the use of radioisotopes and immunologic procedures measures with a high degree of accuracy the presence of such biological substances as hormones, enzymes, and proteins in the blood or other body fluids. Of the Berson-Yalow partnership, it has been said that "he provided the biological brilliance, and she the mathematical muscle. Berson was something of a romantic. Dr. Yalow was keen and scientific, and certainly a steadying influence."

Sympathetic with the goals of the professional working woman, Dr. Yalow declared at the Nobel ceremonies at Stockholm: "The world cannot afford the loss of the talents of half of its people [women] if we are to solve the many problems that beset us." A sign in her office declares: "Whatever women do, they must do twice as well as men to be thought half as good. Luckily this is not hard." A dynamo in a field long dominated by men, Dr. Yalow was the first woman to be awarded the Albert Lasker Basic Medical Research Award (1976). In the fall of 1978, she acted as hostess of a public television series on the life of Madame Curie.

Background. Dr. Yalow was born Rosalyn Sussman in the Bronx, N. Y., on July 19, 1921. She was graduated *magna cum laude* from Hunter College in 1941 and received a Ph. D. in physics from the University of Illinois in 1945. In 1950, after a stint as a physics lecturer at Hunter, Dr. Yalow joined the Bronx Veterans Administration Hospital. There she worked on the development of RIA and other projects. Dr. Yalow was appointed senior medical investigator at the VA hospital in 1972 and became director of the new Solomon A. Berson Research laboratory there the following year. In 1974 she was named distinguished service professor at Mt. Sinai School of Medicine.

A very colorful personality, Dr. Yalow has won a reputation as a superscientist, superwife, and supermother. She is married to Dr. A. Aaron Yalow, a physics professor at Cooper Union. They are the parents of a grown son and daughter. The Nobelist frequently works 60–80 hours per week, and still contrives to do much of her own cooking.

HENRY S. SLOAN

BOLIVIA

In November 1977, President Hugo Banzer Suárez announced that the elections scheduled for 1980 would be moved up to July 1978. Evidently he was hoping that a restricted amnesty and the short notice would hamper the organization of an opposition capable of defeating him. By manipulating the electoral process and the massive peasant vote, he would be able to satisfy U. S. pressure for a return to democratic rule and resume negotiations with Chile over a route to the sea with a popular mandate and an elected Congress behind him.

With Banzer's position weakened by Bolivia's economic difficulties, particularly in the petroleum sector, and by nationalist opposition both within and outside the armed forces, the calling of the elections was a calculated risk. When Banzer announced his own candidacy, stating that he would hand over power at year's end to Interior Minister Gen. Juan Pereda Asbún, opposition within the armed forces was such that he withdrew his name. But he remained in office and assumed the created position of commander in chief of the armed forces, while continuing to orchestrate support for himself in the hope of imposing his candidacy at a later time.

While peasant organizations showed little sympathy with Banzer's aspirations, organized labor and urban civilian groups took advantage of division in the armed forces and rejected Banzer's appointed "labor coordinators" and political allies, in favor of their own banned and exiled leaders. They mounted protests and hunger strikes against a pre-Christmas amnesty that excluded hundreds of leading exiles and detainees. Without an effective means of resistance, Banzer was forced to declare a full amnesty and lift all restriction on trade union activity.

In April 1978, President Banzer failed to persuade armed forces chiefs to call off the elections. Meanwhile, former presidents Hernán Siles Suaso and Victor Paz Estenssoro and miners' leader Juan Lechín failed to unite behind a single candidate. Nine different groups thus contested in the July 9 elections. With the peasant vote cast overwhelmingly against the official candidate, only massive fraud was able to ensure

victory for Pereda. With the results still coming in, however, the electoral tribunal declared the elections null and void. In the ensuing confusion, Pereda led a military uprising from Santa Cruz, deposed Banzer, and assumed the presidency.

But on November 24, an army faction led by Gen. David Padilla Arancibia toppled Pereda's government in a bloodless coup. Padillo quickly swore in a cabinet that included moderate and progressive military men. The new regime promised that free elections would be held on July 1, 1979, and that power would be turned over to the elected president on August 6.

PAUL CAMMACK
St. Anthony's College, Oxford

BOSTON

Schools. For the first time since federal court-ordered desegregation began in the Boston public schools in 1974, the opening of school in September 1978 was quiet and orderly throughout the city. In a move of major symbolic significance, Federal Judge W. Arthur Garrity, Jr. ended direct federal control over South Boston High, one of the city's most troubled schools. In an effort to provide additional stability, the Boston School Committee appointed Dr. Robert C. Wood, former president of the University of Massachusetts, the Superintendent of Schools.

Taxes. Two issues involving property taxes proved controversial in 1978, Mayor Kevin H. White announced in September that the property tax rate would remain unchanged. (It was last increased in 1976.) Since Boston had received a record amount of state aid for 1978, many Bostonians felt that a reduction in the tax rate was in order. The dispute over taxes highlighted a continuing controversy over assessing practices in the city. The city was under court order to reassess all real property at 100% of its fair market value. Massachusetts state courts also demanded that property tax valuations be equalized in all sections of the city. In response, the White administration sponsored an amendment to the state constitution that would permit business and residential property to be taxed at different rates. In the statewide vote in November the measure was approved by an overwhelming margin.

Other Developments. The final portion of the Quincy Market, a complex of stores and offices in the downtown area behind historic Faneuil Hall, was opened in early summer. With the completion of the "north market" section, the city Visitors Bureau estimated that almost 40,000 people per day visited the area during the summer. (*See also* RETAILING.)

The major crime rate in Boston has been slowly declining in recent years and so Bostonians were shocked when five persons, including a television investigative reporter, were slain in a downtown bar on June 28. Two men were later arrested and charged with the murders.

HARVEY BOULAY, *Boston University*

——— **BOLIVIA · Information Highlights** ———

Official Name: Republic of Bolivia.
Location: West-central South America.
Area: 424,164 square miles (1,098,581 km²).
Population (1978 est.): 4,900,000.
Chief Cities (1976 census): Sucre, the legal capital, 63,259; La Paz, the actual capital, 654,713; Santa Cruz de la Sierra, 255,568; Cochabamba, 204,414.
Government: *Head of state and government,* David Padilla Arancibia (took office Nov. 1978). *Legislature*—Congress (suspended Sept. 1969): Senate and Chamber of Deputies.
Monetary Unit: Peso (20 pesos equal U. S.$1, Sept. 1978).
Manufactures (major products): Textiles, cottage industries, processed goods, vegetables.
Agriculture (major products): Potatoes, corn, sugarcane, cassava, cotton, barley, rice, wheat, coffee, bananas.
Major Export Commodities: Tin, petroleum.

BOTANY

In 1978, the field of botany was highlighted by the isolation of a promising growth-inducing substance and by new studies concerning the behavior and evolution of plants.

Wonder Chemical. Plant scientists were excited over a new growth substance, 1-triacontanol, isolated from the alfalfa plant by Dr. Stanley K. Reis and his associates at Michigan State University. Triacontanol is non-nitrogenous and increases plant growth, in the greenhouse at least, by 10 to 40 percent. It is a long-chain alcohol and, unlike most chemicals, occurs naturally in beeswax and the waxy coating on leaves.

Dr. Reis is cautious about the benefits of triacontanol, however, since the substance has not yet proved so effective under field conditions as in the greenhouse.

Plants at War. The dominance of green plants in the earth's ecosystem, according to botanist June Moffat, is no accident. "Although plants are considered to be purely passive organisms," she states, "their survival is actually due in large part to their own defensive strategies." Plants contain a veritable arsenal of toxic chemicals and various physical defenses such as hairs, thorns, and spines.

Recent studies on the defense mechanisms of plants have led to the discovery of clues to the patterns of their evolution. When a plant develops a defense mechanism against a certain pest, the pest develops counterdefenses. For example, a plant may develop a mechanism for resistance to a specific disease. The disease organism then develops, by mutation, a race or strain to which the plant is not resistant. The battle then begins again.

The most successful "tactic" of plants in their war against insects and other pests is to become inedible. This is accomplished by the endogenous production of chemicals that are either toxic or repugnant to predators. Many plants have developed substances that are highly toxic, thus making them inedible. Proteins, alkaloids, and various other types of toxic chemicals are produced in plants. Some varieties of potato, for example, produce a sufficiently high level of alkaloid in the tuber so that they are unsafe to eat unless the tuber is cooked. However, the plants have not been completely successful in developing defense mechanisms for all pests, and synthetic pesticides must therefore often be used in crop production.

Another interesting defense mechanism is demonstrated by the oak tree. Tannins in oak leaves form complexes with protein, thereby reducing the food value of the leaves and resisting digestion. This mechanism results in a reduction in growth rate or fertility of predators that feed on oak leaves.

DONALD W. NEWSOM
Department of Horticulture
Louisiana State University

BRAZIL

Politics dominated events in Brazil in 1978, the year of the first contested presidential election since the military coup of 1964. However, a spirited campaign by the opposition, fully utilizing recently restored freedom of the press, was not enough to prevent the government-dominated electoral college from casting a substantial majority of votes for the official candidate, Gen. João Batista Figueiredo.

Presidential Campaign. In January, President Ernesto Geisel formally announced that Figueiredo, a three-star general and chief of Brazil's intelligence service, was his choice as successor. Although Geisel's declaration for Figueiredo was expected, it was not welcome in some military circles and among certain civilian members of the National Renovation Alliance (ARENA), the government political party. While many anti-Figueiredo military men rallied around Euler Bentes Monteiro, a retired general, disgruntled ARENA politicians tended to favor Sen. José de Magalhães Pinto, a key civilian figure in the 1964 coup.

The power of the incumbent president, however, prevailed with both the military and ARENA. In March the high military command approved Figueiredo's promotion to four-star general and endorsed his presidential candidacy. At ARENA's convention in April, Figueiredo received 775 of 802 votes cast, to win the party's nomination for the six-year presidential term scheduled to begin in March 1979.

In May supporters of Magalhães Pinto and Bentes Monteiro joined with Brazil's only legal opposition party, the Brazilian Democratic Movement (MDB), to form the National Front for Redemocratization. Magalhães Pinto's hopes for becoming the Front's presidential candidate were dashed in August, when the MDB gave its nomination to Bentes Monteiro, who endorsed the party's call for a constitutional convention. If elected, the MDB nominee was to serve as provisional president for three years, after which direct elections for president were to be held.

Since ARENA would have a large majority in the electoral college (composed of Congressmen and state legislators), the task of the MDB was to convince a substantial number of ARENA politicians, many already chafing under military rule, that they would fare better under the regime of full democratic freedom proposed by the opposition. President Geisel and his candidate, Figueiredo, insisted that they too favored democratization. In May the government ended all political censorship of the print media (but not of radio and television), which largely favored the opposition. Despite difficulties with the press, Figueiredo pledged that liberalization would continue under his administration. "I will impose democracy," he declared, "whatever the cost." In October the electoral college elected him president by a vote of 355 to 226.

President Ernesto Geisel welcomes U. S. President and Mrs. Carter to Brazil.

UPI

Proposed Reforms. Geisel assisted Figueiredo's campaign with a government-sponsored reform program. In August, Geisel submitted to Congress a set of proposed constitutional amendments that would abolish the death penalty, restore habeas corpus for political detainees, provide for the organization of new political parties, and revoke the president's powers to close Congress and suspend the political rights of individuals. Opposition Congressmen resisted the president's reform package, charging that it did not go far enough, that it would not end broadcast censorship, or restore direct elections of the president, senators, and state governors. Outside Congress, clergymen and journalists continued to denounce the government for violations of human rights and "assaults on liberty."

Foreign Affairs. President Geisel was busy on the diplomatic front during his last full year in office. In February the Brazilian president flew to West Germany where he was warmly received by government and business leaders. Geisel and Chancellor Helmut Schmidt reaffirmed the 1975 pact whereby West Germany agreed to sell Brazil eight complete nuclear power plants and a uranium reprocessing facility. The U. S. administration of President Jimmy Carter tried to thwart the sale, fearing that the Brazilian-German agreement did not provide sufficient safeguards to prevent the diversion of materials into the production of nuclear weapons. Indignantly denying any Brazilian intention to enter the nuclear arms race, Geisel charged that the United States was trying to obstruct

Brazil's economic development. Relations between Brazil and the United States were at a low point when President Carter landed at Brasília in March for a long-awaited state visit.

Carter's airport reception was chilly, as the U. S. president restated his intention to "speak frankly" with the Brazilians about nuclear policy and human rights. During the visit U. S.-Brazilian relations warmed somewhat, as Carter reportedly convinced Geisel that despite their disagreements the United States wanted strong ties with Brazil. But prior to his departure, Carter met with several prominent opposition figures and human rights activists—which did not please the host government. It countered by revealing that since 1975 Brazil had steadfastly refused to collaborate with the United States in anti-Marxist activities in Africa.

Such demonstrations of independence from Washington tended to allay the fears of some of Brazil's neighbors, who had long regarded the Brazilians as agents of "Yankee imperialism." Brazil's improved relations with other South American countries were evidenced in July as foreign ministers from several nations—including staunchly anti-imperialist Venezuela and Guyana —journeyed to Brasília to sign the Amazon pact. The signatories pledged mutual cooperation in scientific research and data gathering for regional development of the Amazon Basin.

Economy. Brazilian industrial and agricultural production and exports all rose modestly in 1978. But imports (mainly capital goods and petroleum) were also up, thereby increasing the pressure of inflation. The rate of inflation climbed to about 40% for the year.

A persistent rise in the cost of living, coupled with continued low wages, produced the most serious labor unrest in Brazil in ten years. Large gatherings of trade unionists on May 1 signaled a new militancy on the part of the Brazilian labor force. A few days later, 10,000 automobile workers walked off their jobs in Brazil's first major strike in a decade. Startled by the size of this illegal strike movement, but reassured by its nonpolitical nature, the government pressured management to make concessions to the workers. By the end of May most workers had returned to their jobs with guarantees of a 15% wage increase. Presidential candidate Figueiredo declared himself in favor of changing the law to allow collective bargaining and the right to strike.

New State. In 1978 the southern region of Mato Grosso was organized as a new state— Mato Grosso do Sul, with its capital in Campo Grande. This brought the number of states in the Brazilian federal union to 22.

NEILL MACAULAY
University of Florida

———— **BRAZIL • Information Highlights** ————

Official Name: Federative Republic of Brazil.
Location: Eastern South America.
Area: 3,286,478 square miles (8,511,965 km²).
Population (1978 est.): 115,400,000.
Chief Cities (1975 est.): Brasília, the capital, 241,543; São Paulo, 7,200,000; Rio de Janeiro, 4,860,000; Belo Horizonte, 1,560,000.
Government: *Head of state and government,* Ernesto Geisel, president (took office March 1974); João Batista Figueiredo, president (to be inaugurated March 1979). *Legislature*—National Congress: Federal Senate and Chamber of Deputies.
Monetary Unit: Cruzeiro (18.9 cruzeiros equal U. S.$1, Aug. 1978).
Manufactures (major products): Steel, chemicals, petrochemicals, machinery, consumer goods, motor vehicles.
Agriculture (major products): Coffee, rice, beef, corn, milk, sugarcane, soybeans, cacao.

BRITISH COLUMBIA

A 64-day session of the legislature in late spring saw the passage of 39 bills. The interim report of the Royal Commission on Electoral Reform, calling for the redefinition of electoral districts, was immediately implemented. The legislature was thereby increased from 55 to 57 seats. Major forestry legislation included a new Range Act, changes in forest tenures, logging taxation, and incentives for effective forest management. Provision was also made for an Urban Transit Authority, a new Family Relations Act, and a controversial program for the compulsory treatment of heroin addicts. The provincial government announced its intention to proceed with the Fort Nelson extension of the British Columbia Railway despite recommendations for its abandonment by the Royal Commission of Inquiry. The declining value of the Canadian dollar afforded a further stimulus to the continuing economic recovery of the province both in export trade and tourism. The latter was given extra attention in 1978 with the promotion of the Captain Cook bicentennial celebration.

Economy. In line with a commitment to maintain public expenditures at a level 1% below the growth rate of the provincial economy, a balanced budget was proposed for 1978–79, with an expenditure of (C.) $4,280,000,000. Measures to stimulate the economy included a 2% reduction of the sales tax, a reduction of the parimutuel betting tax, and changes in exemptions to sales and corporation capital taxes. These measures were in part offset by an increase in the cigarette and tobacco tax and in the price of liquor and licensing fees. New expenditures included $120 million for a long-term health care program, an increase in the home owner grant to senior citizens, increased assistance for medical service premiums, and additional aid to first-time home purchasers. The 1976–77 surplus of $76 million was allocated to 11 accelerated job development programs. In September, a surplus of $140 million was reported for the fiscal year 1977–78, on a total general fund expenditure of $3,999,000,000. Spending cuts and funding reallocations announced by the federal government during 1978 were expected to result in a loss of between $76 and $81 million to the province. The federal government also reimbursed the province for the cost of the first six months of the sales tax reduction under a general federal-provincial agreement. In British Columbia, however, this reduction was maintained as a permanent tax cut.

Government and Politics. A new provincial Conservative Party leader, Vic Stephens, successfully contested a by-election for the seat vacated by the former leader, Scott Wallace. An investigation into travel expense reporting by Minister of Transport Jack Davis resulted in his resignation from the cabinet. Upon his conviction for fraud, he was also forced to resign his seat in the legislature. A change also occurred in the office of Lieutenant Governor, as Walter Owen retired and was replaced by Henry Bell-Irving.

NORMAN J. RUFF
University of Victoria

— **BRITISH COLUMBIA • Information Highlights** —

Area: 366,255 square miles (948,600 km²).
Population (1978 est.): 2,530,100.
Chief Cities (1976 census): Victoria, the capital, 62,551; Vancouver, 410,188.
Government (1978): *Chief Officers*—lt. gov., Henry Bell-Irving; premier, William R. Bennett (Social Credit party); chief justice, Court of Appeal, John L. Farris; Supreme Court, Nathaniel T. Nemetz. *Legislature*— Legislative Assembly, 55 members.
Education (1976–77): *Enrollment*—public elementary and secondary schools, 540,790 pupils; private schools, 20,450; Indian (federal) schools, 2,790; post-secondary, 50,620 students.
Personal Income (average weekly salary, May 1978): $300.06.
Unemployment Rate (July 1978, seasonally adjusted): 7.7%.

(All monetary figures are in Canadian dollars.)

BULGARIA

On March 3, 1978, Bulgaria celebrated the 100th anniversary of the San Stefano treaty, which ended the Russo-Turkish War of 1877–78 and made Bulgaria an autonomous state. The centennial was marked by nationwide festivities.

Domestic Affairs. The general standard of living in Bulgaria continued to be low in 1978, and the economy was marked by inefficiency. In his report to the National Assembly in March, Todor Zhivkov, first secretary of the Communist party and Bulgarian head of state, blamed "cold spells, drought, early frost, and two earthquakes," as well as the "international economic situation" for the lack of growth in industrial and agricultural production. He also criticized managerial ineptitude and lack of initiative. In April and July there were sweeping personnel changes in the government and Communist party.

In August, the Politburo discussed the problem of increasing agricultural labor shortages. While in 1976 there were some 3,325,000 farm workers in Bulgaria, the estimated number for 1980 was less than 1,140,000. A series of remedial measures, including economic incentives, eventually was agreed upon.

The tourism industry in Bulgaria continued to grow. In 1977 some 4,600,000 foreign visitors entered the country; the target for 1978 was 5,000,000. To promote the industry, tourists were accorded a premium of 50% over the official foreign currency exchange rate.

Foreign Affairs. The shah of Iran, the president of Mexico, and the premiers of Turkey and Greece all paid official state visits in 1978. Foreign Minister Petar Mladenov and Zhivkov visited West Germany and Austria respectively. On the eve of the August 16 visit by Chinese Premier Hua kuo-feng to Rumania, Zhivkov held a conference with Soviet President Brezhnev in the Crimea. The resulting joint communiqué referred to "intrigues and machinations by forces hostile to détente" and explicitly condemned "China's hegemonism." Relations with Yugoslavia deteriorated, with the denial of national identity to the Macedonian minority in Bulgaria being a main bone of contention.

JAN KARSKI
Georgetown University

BURMA

Burma was troubled in 1978—unable to solve persisting problems of internal disunity and economic stagnation and facing deteriorating relations with big neighbor China.

Politics. The reelection by the 464-member People's Congress in March of President Ne Win to a second four-year term suggested stability in Burmese politics that was not there. The Congress also elected a 26-member Council of State (chaired by Ne Win).

Mahn Ngwe Aung, an official of the ruling Burma Socialist Program Party, and two others were sentenced to death in February for plotting in 1977 to assassinate government leaders. Congress member U Htien Lin was also sentenced in February to die for planning to make Arakan in western Burma an independent state. Arakan was the site of major discontent in April–May. Some 200,000 Muslims, charging atrocities by the Burmese army, fled into Bangladesh.

Internal Security. China-aided Communists and some members of all of the country's chief minorities continued in arms against the government. The Communists, numbering an estimated 10,000 insurgents in the northeast, were engaged in their most vigorous offensive against the Ne Win regime since 1973.

Economy. Agricultural output, principally rice, barely met growing domestic demand. Mineral and timber exploitation continued to be limited by insurgent activity. Domestic private investment and foreign investment were practically nonexistent. Only in offshore fishing and processing was there new activity, and this was in terms of announced plans.

Foreign Relations. Scrupulous neutrality remained Burma's foreign policy. Peking's Vice Premier Teng Hsiao-ping visited Rangoon in January. Teng sought to counter the influence of the Soviet Union in Vietnam and Laos and to urge Ne Win to criticize any country seeking to establish "hegemony" in Asia. Partly because of Chinese aid to Burma's Communist rebels, Ne Win refused, and relations between the two governments subsequently became more strained.

RICHARD BUTWELL
Murray State University

———— BULGARIA · Information Highlights ————

Official Name: People's Republic of Bulgaria.
Location: Southeastern Europe.
Area: 42,758 square miles (110,743 km²).
Population (1978 est.): 8,800,000.
Chief City (1975): Sofia, the capital, 965,728.
Government: *Head of State,* Todor Zhivkov, president of the State Council and first secretary of the Communist party (took office July 1971). *Head of government,* Stanko Todorov, chairman of the Council of Ministers (took office July 1971).
Monetary Unit: Lev (0.94 lev equals U. S.$1, 1978).
Manufactures (major products): Processed agricultural products, machinery.
Agriculture (major products): Grain, tobacco, fruits, vegetables.

———— BURMA · Information Highlights ————

Official Name: Socialist Republic of the Union of Burma.
Location: Southeast Asia.
Area: 261,218 square miles (676,555 km²).
Population (1978 est.): 32,200,000.
Chief Cities (1975 est.): Rangoon, the capital, 2,100,-000; Mandalay, 417,000; Moulmein, 202,000.
Government: *Head of state,* U Ne Win, president (took office March 1974). *Head of government,* U Maung Maung Kha, prime minister (took office March 1977). *Legislature* (unicameral)—People's Assembly.
Monetary Unit: Kyat (6.7 kyats equal U. S.$1, Sept. 1978).
Manufactures (major products): Agricultural processing, textiles, wood and its products, petroleum refining, construction materials.
Agriculture (major products): Rice, jute, sesame, ground nuts, tobacco, cotton, pulses, sugarcane, corn.

CALIFORNIA

A sharp cutback in the general property tax, elections, the weather, and natural disasters were the major news in California during 1978.

Proposition 13. In the June primary election, 65% of the state's voters endorsed Proposition 13, the so-called Jarvis-Gann initiative. This amendment to the California constitution limits the general property tax to 1% of the property's true market value as of 1976 (or, if sold later, its value at the date of sale) and provides an average statewide tax cut of about 57%. It allows property valuations to be raised to the market value when the property is sold, or by no more than 2% annually. It also requires a two-thirds majority in a popular vote to impose any new local nonproperty taxes.

Although local governments depended heavily on general property taxes, the immediate effect of the amendment was not so great as expected. Gov. Edmund G. Brown, Jr., who had opposed Proposition 13, immediately secured from the legislature a "bailout" bill which used up almost all of the state's $5.8 billion surplus but held program reductions to about 10% of local budgets. Even so, local governments laid off some 24,200 persons as of July 1, and the future financing of local services was expected to be a problem for the legislature. The "bailout" bill provided that local employees could receive cost-of-living increases no larger than those of state employees, but Brown then vetoed *any* increases for state employees. The governor also proposed an amendment that would allow government spending to increase at a rate no greater than the increase rate of personal income.

Election. The general election produced few surprises. The Republicans gained a few seats in each house of the state legislature, but the Democrats retained large majorities. Rose E. Bird, Brown's appointee as chief justice of the Supreme Court, won a narrow victory under an unusual California law requiring voter confirmation of justices on the state's highest court. It was the closest vote on this question in the state's history.

UPI

The 1978 concerns of Gov. Edmund G. Brown, Jr., included California's finances and a reelection campaign.

Governor Brown easily won reelection, getting 56% of the vote. Ironically, the last poll before the election showed that only 25% of Californians thought he was doing a "good job." The easy win could be attributed to the fact that his opponent, Att. Gen. Evelle J. Younger, did not excite the state's large body of independent voters, failed to exploit Brown's opposition to Proposition 13, and ran a particularly inept campaign.

The Republicans gained three seats in California's 43-member Congressional delegation. This left the membership favoring the Democrats, 26 seats to 17.

A proposition requiring the dismissal of any public school employee who was an avowed homosexual or who advocated a homosexual lifestyle was defeated. Another proposed amendment, severely restricting smoking in public places, also was defeated. Opponents of the anti-smoking measure spent more money than had ever been spent on a propositional campaign; most of it came from cigarette manufacturers.

Budget. The state's budget totaled $14.73 billion after the governor vetoed $388.5 million in pay raises for state employees, increases in welfare grants, and other items. The total budget was slightly less than in the previous year and represented the first decrease in 17 years. However, it did not include the $5 billion in "bailout" funds to local governments.

The legislature prohibited most publicly funded abortions, refused to vote money for new prison construction, rejected most of the proposed mental health programs, and sharply cut funds for the state Conservation Corps. But it did increase appropriations for child care and drug abuse treatment programs.

Weather and Natural Disasters. Heavy rains between December and April produced the state's largest annual rainfall in the 20th century,

---

CALIFORNIA • Information Highlights

Area: 158,693 square miles (411,015 km²).
Population (Jan. 1978 est.): 22,083,000.
Chief Cities (1970 census): Sacramento, the capital, 257,105; Los Angeles, 2,809,596; San Francisco, 715,674.
Government (1978): *Chief Officer*—governor, Edmund G. Brown, Jr. (D); lt. gov., Mervyn M. Dymally (D). *Legislature*—Senate, 40 members; Assembly, 80 members.
Education (1977–78): *Enrollment*—public elementary schools, 2,540,582 pupils; public secondary, 1,748,588; colleges and universities, 1,743,243 students. *Public school expenditures,* $8,478,454,000 ($1,649 per pupil).
State Finances (fiscal year 1977): *Revenues,* $26,108,228,000; *expenditures,* $22,439,586,000.
Personal Income (1977): $173,214,000,000; per capita, $7,911.
Labor Force (July 1978): *Nonagricultural wage and salary earners,* 9,015,100; *unemployed,* 868,300 (8.1% of total force).

bringing to an end a severe two-year drought. On August 13, an earthquake measuring 5.1 on the Richter scale struck the Santa Barbara area. There were no deaths and property damage was not great, but more than 100 persons were injured. The extensive growth of underbrush following the rains brought fires in the autumn. The worst, in October, destroyed more than 200 homes in the Malibu area of southern California.

See also LOS ANGELES.

CHARLES R. ADRIAN
University of California, Riverside

CAMBODIA

Cambodia, now officially known as Kampuchea, fought two escalating wars in 1978 and witnessed the restructuring of its society.

Politics. Cambodia continued to resemble a huge national prison work-camp, portions of its population literally being worked to death in pursuit of the goal of self-reliance. Political control was in the hands of no more than 10 men, of whom 53-year old Pol Pot, premier and Communist party secretary, was the most important and most powerful.

Insurrectionary activity, led by Vietnamese-aided former members of the Communist "Khmer Rouge" rebels, who battled the previous Lon Nol regime, expanded in the Krau region in the northeastern part of the country. Vietnam's purpose in backing the insurgents appeared to be the toppling of Pol Pot's government and its replacement by one sympathetic to Hanoi.

The estimates of Cambodian dead in the three and one half years since Cambodia fell to Communist rule (in April 1975) ranged from 500,000 to two million, in a population of seven million persons. The deaths resulted from executions, starvation, overwork, or disease. The total compared with 600,000 indigenous Cambodian deaths in the Cambodian war of 1970–75.

Society. The Pol Pot Communist revolution seemed to be remaking the basic fabric of Cambodian society. Practice of Buddhism was made punishable by death. The family unit was largely broken up. Society appeared to be organized into distinct and largely segregated groups of adult males, adult females, elderly men and women, young children (6–15), and teenage youth.

Economy. The chief economic activity of most of the Cambodian population was the reconstruction of dikes and irrigation canals destroyed during the 1970–75 war. Work brigades, composed mainly of youth, were engaged on the water projects, while rice and other farming was carried on in agricultural cooperatives. All nationals 6 years old and above worked full days all but three days a month. Food rations were extremely limited, and there was literally no money in circulation.

War With Vietnam. The incursion into Vietnam by Cambodian forces in mid-1977 apparently led to larger Vietnamese thrusts into Cambodia in December 1977 and May–June 1978. By late 1978, the conflict had escalated into a veritable third Indochina war. Vietnamese insurgents joined with Cambodian rebels and moved steadily across Cambodia during December. On Jan. 7, 1979, Phnom Penh fell and the Pol Pot regime collapsed. The Hanoi-backed Cambodian "liberation movement" installed a new government the next day, with Heng Samin as president of the People's Revolutionary Council of Cambodia.

Other Foreign Relations. China sided with Cambodia in its war with Vietnam (allied with the Soviet Union) but did not dramatically increase its military aid to the Pol Pot government. Cambodia also partly normalized its relations with neighboring non-Communist Thailand, Indonesia, Malaysia, and Singapore in Southeast Asia and sought Japanese economic assistance.

RICHARD BUTWELL, *Murray State University*

CAMBODIA · Information Highlights

Official Name: Democratic Kampuchea.
Location: Southeast Asia.
Area: 69,898 square miles (181,035 km²).
Population (1978 est.): 8,200,000.
Chief City (1976 est.): Phnom Penh, the capital, 100,000.
Government: *Head of state,* Khieu Samphan, president (took office April 1976). *Head of government and secretary of the Communist party,* Pol Pot, prime minister. *Legislature* (unicameral)—People's Representative Assembly.
Monetary Unit: Riel (1,111.11 riels equal U. S.$1, Dec. 1976).
Manufactures (major products): Textiles, cement, paper products.
Agriculture (major products): Rice, rubber.

UPI

Cambodian boys attend the school of a commune south of Phnom Penh. Under a restructuring of Cambodian society, children (6–15) are organized into a distinct group. Work, not education, receives prime emphasis.

CANADA

More than ever before in history, Canadians, in 1978, questioned the viability of their nation. Tensions between English-speaking and French-speaking Canadians continued. The tensions tended to accentuate the difficulties of the national economy, which continued to experience minor fluctuations. Canada's performance in world trade continued to show strong signs. Decline in the value of the Canadian dollar in relation to its United States counterpart and particularly such other currencies as the Japanese yen and the West German mark, was related to international uncertainty about Canada. On the other hand, the lower dollar encouraged Canadians to export more. Lumber exports from British Columbia and processed food exports from New Brunswick showed sharp increases. Higher bank loan rates, introduced in October and November, indicated the determination of the Bank of Canada to strengthen the nation's economic position. The percentage of Canadians unemployed was down in November to 8.2, the lowest in many years. Moreover, Canada continued to lead western nations in the creation of new jobs on a per capita basis. Monthly reports from the national capital in Ottawa show Canada experiencing about 8% inflation, lower than the double digit inflation in the United States.

In 1978 the economy moved forward in a relatively stable pattern, with government continuing to put increased restraints on spending. On September 8, for instance, Ottawa unveiled proposals for cuts of (C) $2.5 billion in spending and for a new $300 million incentive program for industry. Despite the planned cuts, federal spending will experience an 8.9% rise, from $48 billion in 1978 to $53 billion in 1979. Provincial financing reflects these same trends.

In December, Edward Schreyer, 42-year-old leader of Manitoba's New Democratic party, was named Canada's 22d governor general. He was scheduled to take office in January 1979.

DOMESTIC AND INTERNATIONAL AFFAIRS

Trudeau in Trouble. The national government led by Pierre Elliott Trudeau of the Liberal Party experienced one of its rockiest years. Trudeau, age 59, celebrated his tenth year as prime minister on April 20. The national mood, however, did not reflect the "Trudeaumania" that had swept him into power a decade before. Heavily criticized by the media, Trudeau's popularity fell to an all-time low in December's Gallup poll. This showed Joe Clark's Progressive Conservatives as clear leaders in national popularity. Leaders of the Western world regard Trudeau as a fine statesman. U. S. Vice President Walter Mondale, for instance, called him "a priceless asset to the Western world." Yet at home Trudeau has found difficult the harmonizing of the disparate views and diverse needs of the nation.

UPI

Prime Minister Trudeau was criticized in Canada but was praised as a statesman by Western leaders.

Provincial premiers, especially Parti Québécois leader René Lévesque in Quebec and Progressive Conservative head Peter Lougheed in Alberta, have been championing provincial rights at the expense of centralized power. Lévesque's government, for instance, is dedicated to separatism or to its most immediate alternative, sovereignty association, a form of quasi-independence that would give Quebec full control over foreign and cultural affairs. Lougheed's Alberta government wants more provincial power over the affairs of the nation affecting Alberta. The "blue-eyed Arabs of the West," as they have been called by suspicious outsiders, are regarded by many Canadians as a more dangerous threat to the nation than Lévesque's Parti Québécois, whose power waned somewhat after the provincial Liberal party elected Claude Ryan, former publisher of the Montreal newspaper *Le Devoir,* as its leader on April 15. Ryan, a distinguished federalist, has promised to make the unity of the country his primary task.

Canadian unity was the subject of a special conference held at Banff, Alberta, in late March.

At this Premier Lougheed called for more provincial representation on federal regulatory boards. He also argued that no province, meaning Quebec, could have special status in the nation. Saskatchewan's government, led by Premier Allan Blakeney of the New Democratic Party, argued that English-speaking provinces may have to provide more in the way of French-language services. In return he said, "we can expect to demand equal treatment for anglophones in Quebec." The question of national unity is ongoing. Clark has said that if the Parti Québécois receives support for independence in a provincial referendum he, as prime minister, would negotiate Quebec's secession. The British North America Act, Canada's Constitution, does not contain any legal mechanism for such secession. Trudeau has categorically stated that he will not negotiate with Quebec, or for that matter, any province on the dismemberment of the country.

Constitution. To strengthen Canada against internal threats to national unity, Prime Minister Trudeau announced, on June 12, a new constitution. Entitled "A Time for Action," the blueprint included a means whereby provinces would have a say in appointments to the Senate and the Supreme Court of Canada. The restructured Senate would be renamed the House of the Federation. The Supreme Court would be given constitutional status for the first time in Canada's

111-year history. The monarchy would be retained, with written descriptions of the crown's role included in the constitution. These functions would reflect the present day practice of viceregal authority in Canada. Trudeau's plan also called for an updated Bill of Rights to be enshrined in the constitution. Finally, it proposed establishing an amending formula whereby the British North America Act of 1867 and its several amendments could be patriated, that is, brought home. In the future, the constitution could be modified by appropriate federal and provincial consent.

Twice previously, in 1971 and 1977, proposed amending formulas have failed to win unanimous provincial support. Lévesque remains adamant that Quebec has no interest in constitutional reform until results of the proposed Quebec independence referendum (now scheduled for 1979) are known. On NBC-TV's show *Today*, May 18, Lévesque emphasized that self-government and association were the main points of the referendum question. Trudeau has set 1981 as the target date for the adoption of his new constitution. He has set only two conditions for constitutional reform. These are, first, that Canada would continue as a genuine federation with a federal parliament retaining "real powers which apply to all parts of the country, and provincial legislatures with 'equally real powers' within their respective territories," and second, that a "charter of basic rights and freedoms" would be included in any new constitution. In the latter instance this charter would apply equally within both provincial and federal governments.

Prime Minister Trudeau's proposals were tested at the First Ministers' Conference in Ottawa in early November. Lévesque remained adamant against patriation; Lougheed championed Alberta's financial rights; and Blakeney proved to be a useful negotiator for facilitating arrangements that may lead in the next meeting, scheduled for February 1979, to some political compromise.

Meanwhile, on October 16, Trudeau's Liberals suffered a setback in federal by-elections. Only three Liberals were returned in fifteen ridings. The vote which returned nine Progressive Conservatives revealed Canadian frustrations with uncertain economic performance, regional disparities and, as some have said, uncertain leadership. These have been orchestrated by the media in strong attacks on Trudeau. Rumors that Trudeau would step down before the next federal election, scheduled for 1979, were not substantiated.

Alberta-born Joe Clark, dubbed "Joe Who" by the media when he was chosen as Progressive Conservative leader Feb. 22, 1976, emerged as a potential successor to Trudeau. At 39 he stands for greater provincial rights, a view reflecting the support increasingly given by provinces to his party. He is prepared to let Quebec secede from

THE CANADIAN MINISTRY

(According to precedence, November 1978)

Pierre Elliott Trudeau, Prime Minister
Allan Joseph MacEachen, Deputy Prime Minister and President of the Queen's Privy Council for Canada
Jean Chrétien, Minister of Finance
Donald Campbell Jamieson, Secretary of State for External Affairs
Robert Knight Andras, Minister of State and President of the Board of Economic Development Ministers
Otto Emil Lang, Minister of Transport
Alastair William Gillespie, Minister of Energy, Mines and Resources and Minister of State for Science and Technology
Martin Patrick O'Connell, Minister of Labour
Eugene Francis Whelan, Minister of Agriculture
W. Warren Allmand, Minister of Consumer and Corporate Affairs
James Hugh Faulkner, Minister of Indian Affairs and Northern Development
André Ouellet, Minister of Public Works and Minister of State for Urban Affairs
Daniel Joseph MacDonald, Minister of Veterans Affairs
Marc Lalonde, Minister of Justice and Attorney General of Canada
Jeanne Sauvé, Minister of Communications
Raymond Joseph Perrault, Leader of the Government in the Senate
Barnett Jerome Danson, Minister of National Defence
J. Judd Buchanan, President of the Treasury Board
Roméo LeBlanc, Minister of Fisheries and the Environment
Marcel Lessard, Minister of Regional Economic Expansion
Jack Sydney Cullen, Minister of Employment and Immigration
Leonard S. Marchand, Minister of State (Environment)
John Roberts, Secretary of State of Canada
Monique Bégin, Minister of National Health and Welfare
Jean-Jacques Blais, Solicitor General of Canada
Anthony C. Abbott, Minister of National Revenue and Minister of State (Small Businesses)
Iona Campagnolo, Minister of State (Fitness and Amateur Sport)
Jack H. Horner, Minister of Industry, Trade and Commerce
Norman Cafik, Minister of State (Multiculturalism)
Gilles LaMontagne, Postmaster General
John M. Reid, Minister of State (Federal-Provincial Relations)
Pierre De Bane, Minister of Supply and Services

Canada. In October, Nova Scotia elected a Provincial Conservative government, defeating Gerald Regan's longstanding Liberals; in April Alex Campbell's Liberal strength in Prince Edward Island was greatly reduced in a provincial election there. These indicators of a swing away from Liberalism show why Trudeau's constitutional review has been difficult to implement.

Pipelines. In 1978 Canada adopted important legislation for the building of a gas pipeline linking Alaskan natural gas reserves to the lower 48 states. The biggest capital project of modern times in Canada, the undertaking has economic benefits but threatens the northern environment and native land rights. In January, Chief Justice Thomas Berger of the British Columbia Supreme Court released his second report, asking that the settlement of native claims in the Yukon and Northwest Territories should be of prime importance in government decision-making. If a pipeline had to be built, he suggested that the Alaska Highway route is preferable to the Mackenzie Valley proposal. In the Mackenzie Valley, he said, environmental damage would take place, leading to wildlife loss and natives' economic hardships. He called for government policies that would encourage renewable resource economics and reduce the boom-and-bust cycle characteristic of past northern development.

Long-term gas needs in the United States resulted in an initiative by Vice President Mondale in January. He visited Alberta and Ottawa to push for closer trade relations in energy. He promised that the Carter administration would move to change a convention tax that had cost the Canadian tourist industry $35 million in 1977 and increase U. S. residents' duty free allowances from $100 to $250 on consumer purchases outside the country. Mondale also discussed with Canadian officials a gas-swapping proposal. Under this, Alberta would ship additional gas to the United States now in exchange for Alaskan gas when the highway pipeline is completed in the early 1980's.

Canada's parliament ratified the 5,000-mile (8,000-km), $10 billion pipeline on April 4 by a vote of 139 to 11. Construction will start in 1981. A connecting link from the Mackenzie

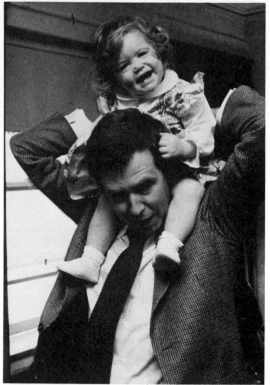

TED GRANT, CANADA WIDE

Opposition leader Joe Clark enjoys some time with his daughter. The Progressive Conservatives hope to unseat Prime Minister Trudeau's Liberals in 1979.

Delta to the mainline at Whitehorse in the Yukon is planned. Canadian and United States governments approved a 56-inch (142-cm) low pressure pipeline. Canadian manufacturing interests took an active role in the political process. They are anxious that mills in Regina, Sask., and Hamilton, Ont., be able to compete with American, Japanese, and German pipe producers. In fact, Canadian politicians believe that 56-inch pipe laid in Canada will be mainly Canadian made. Parliament also passed legislation setting up a northern pipeline agency that would oversee construction of the pipeline and monitor environmental changes. In May, Mitchell Sharp, longtime Toronto member of Parliament and Liberal cabinet minister, became commissioner of the new agency.

International Affairs. In 1978 Canada undertook to maintain a strong interest in the North Atlantic Treaty Organization (NATO) and the UN and increase growing trade with the European Community, with which Canada has a contractual link. Canada's main foreign area of interest remained the United States. Relations between the two countries continued to be cordial, with both nations cooperating on key areas of joint interest, including trade, finance, and energy policy.

BARRY M. GOUGH, *Wilfrid Laurier University*

--- **CANADA • Information Highlights** ---

Official Name: Canada.
Location: Northern North America.
Area: 3,851,809 square miles (9,976,185 km²).
Population (1978 est.): 23,600,000.
Chief Cities (1976 met. census): Ottawa, the capital, 693,288; Montreal, 2,802,485; Toronto, 2,803,101.
Government: *Head of state,* Elizabeth II, queen; represented by Jules Léger, governor general (took office Jan. 1974). *Head of government,* Pierre Elliott Trudeau, prime minister (took office April 1968). *Legislature*—Parliament: Senate and House of Commons.
Monetary Unit: Canadian dollar (1.1831 dollars equal U. S.$1, Sept. 1978).
Manufactures (major products): Motor vehicles and parts, fish and forest products, petroleum and natural gas, processed and unprocessed minerals.
Agriculture (major products): Wheat, livestock and meat, feedgrains, oilseeds, dairy products, tobacco, fruits, and vegetables.

THE ECONOMY

Recovery from the 1975–76 economic slump remained slow, with real gross national product rising at about 2.5%, inflation running at 9%, and unemployment exceeding 8%. Despite a recovery in commodity exports, which were about (C) $3 billion in excess of imports, the balance of payments remained in deficit due to travel, service payments, debt charges, and a capital outflow. The result was devaluation of the Canadian dollar to 85% of the U. S. dollar and an unprecedentedly rapid rise in the prime lending rate of the Bank of Canada, to 10.5%. The latter move was to prevent higher interest rates in the United States from further strengthening the capital outflow. The Canadian dilemma became evident when devaluation added to inflationary pressures.

With the exception of metals, the resource sector fared better than manufacturing, which continued to decline as a source of employment in the economy. Business investment advanced at 1.5%, indicating that the slump of 1976 had bottomed out, although not in a strong recovery. Bankruptcies, particularly among importers and construction contractors, rose to 75% of the U. S. total. High import prices and a 20% decline in housing starts were the main causes. The general decline of manufacturing was associated with severe competition in textiles from low wage countries and a general decline in the production of automobile parts as the major manufacturers imported from the United States. The 1977 resource sectors, particularly fishing and forest products, enjoyed good markets in the United States and which took 72% of all Canadian exports, up more than 9%. Oil and natural gas also enjoyed an investment boom. The result was markedly higher rates of growth in the Maritime Provinces and Alberta, an average rate of growth in British Columbia, and low rates of growth in Ontario and Quebec.

The continuing high rate of inflation, despite generally depressed conditions, derived in part from the strength of the resource sector, which in the case of export-oriented fish and forest products gained a 16% windfall from devaluation and in the case of oil and gas received substantial government support. Increases in the supply of money (more than 10%) and in personal disposable income also contributed to the inflation. Despite average weekly earnings, rising at 3% below the rate of inflation, personal disposable income increased at about 4% above the rate of inflation.

In the face of these difficulties federal policies became increasingly uncertain. Severe cutbacks in services and the bureaucracy were paired off with an increasing deficit. Oil and gas policy remained uncertain. The producing provinces argued for less federal interference and more exports to the United States to cure the balance of payments problem. The federal government initially sought subsidized piping of gas to Quebec and the Maritime Provinces to replace imported oil. Two fundamental problems underlay these uncertainties: constitutional quarrels over control of natural resources, marked by a Supreme Court decision denying Saskatchewan the right to regulate trade in potash; and the continued internal problems of the ruling Liberal Party. The two could not be separated. The future constitution of the nation was at stake.

R. F. NEILL

Department of Economics, Carleton University

THE CANADIAN ECONOMY

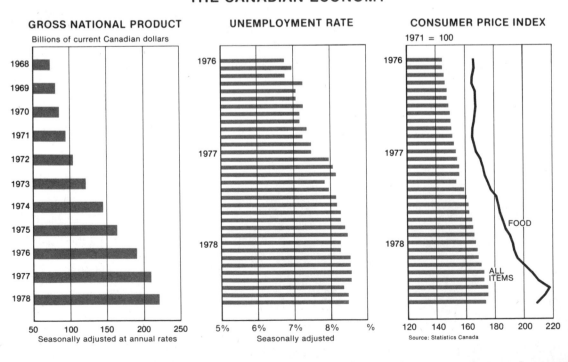

COURTESY, THE STRATFORD SHAKESPEAREAN FESTIVAL FOUNDATION OF CANADA

As part of its 1978 program, the Stratford Shakespearean Festival presented *The Winter's Tale*, directed by Robin Phillips and Peter Moss.

CULTURE

Throughout Canada in 1978, cultural politics gained more public attention than did any of the elements of the arts scene. Most of it was related to two factors: widespread antigovernment sentiment and a new, powerful lobby of cultural activities executives. In recent years Canadian governments have been the financial mainstay of the arts, subsidizing groups and individuals, underwriting travel programs, and providing scholarships and work-grants. The federal government's arts agency, the Canada Council, normally budgets for about $50 million in grants annually, and several federal ministries vote generously for capital projects and exceptional cultural activities. The provincial governments also have important cultural-support programs and provide large subsidies for local development of the arts. (Most of the latter funds are raised by official lotteries.) An inevitable result of this generous official support has been an ill-founded expectation by arts organizations of increased government grants as a matter of right. In 1977 the governments, acutely aware of mounting fiscal problems, announced clearly that financial support for the arts would be an area of restraint and cutbacks. Few executives in the arts world paid heed to the warning. When hopes for funding increases did not materialize, theaters, orchestras, dance groups, film societies, and individuals assailed the "hold the line" policy. Statements by arts promoters concerning the reductions were headlined as "discrimination," "disaster," "catastrophe," and "bad faith." But the governments held firm and limited fiscal support for the arts to 1976–77 levels. The cultural establishment executives expressed rage and frustration and, by employing skillful public relations techniques, achieved notable press, radio, and television exposure of their views. However despite disappointment and anger, most organizations and individuals involved with the arts in Canada managed to survive their involuntary belt-tightening.

Music. On the music scene, the winter visit of the Toronto Symphony Orchestra to mainland China must be seen as a notable event of 1978. Participating in an official Canada-China cultural exchange program, the orchestra, with Maureen Forrester as soloist, was well received by Chinese officials, musicians, and citizens. In addition to being an artistic success, the tour was regarded as an important diplomatic achievement. In March the T. S. O. played a successful one-night stand at Carnegie Hall in New York City, and the Vancouver Symphony did well in its initial tour of seven American cities. Arthur Fiedler directed the Boston Pops Orchestra before a crowd of 45,000 enchanted Canadians at Brantford, Ont., in August.

Management officials of all major Canadian orchestras were worried by new immigration regulations which tended to restrict the employment of non-Canadian musicians. The aim of the new regulations is, of course, to increase job opportunities for graduates of Canadian music schools, but a consequent lowering of artistic standards is involved when the law bars many gifted American youths from employment with Canadian orchestras.

The Toronto-based Canadian Opera Company had to use the "sold out" sign repeatedly during its September–November season. Works featured included *Joan of Arc, Der Rosenkavalier, Rigoletto,* and *Don Giovanni.* The International Clarinet Congress, which usually convenes in Denver, was held at the University of Toronto in August and attracted instrumentalists from many countries. On October 1 a Canadian Broadcasting Corporation concert, featuring Maureen Forrester and the National Arts Centre Orchestra (Ottawa), was broadcast live to an estimated 250 million listeners.

Theater. After ten years of talk and indecision, the dream of a "national Canadian theater" became a reality with the launching of twin English and French companies based at the National Arts Centre in Ottawa. A special inauguration grant of $1 million by the hard-pressed federal treasury sparked a major political dispute. Feelings ran high in view of the fact that earlier in the year the lack of a $75,000 federal grant had caused the demise of THEATRE CANADA, an organization that was chartered in 1932 (as the Dominion Drama Festival) and was widely regarded as the only effective friend of theater in Canada.

The Stratford Festival continued its success story. At season's end the enterprise announced that it had fallen short of an operating profit. Box-office receipts totaled $4.1 million for 16 productions. A surprise was the notably favorable reception the critics gave the company's first performance of Shakespeare's *Titus Andronicus.* Trade union disputes with actors, musicians, and the new Playwrights Guild were a serious worry for management.

A 1978 national survey, conducted by Statistics Canada, revealed some encouraging information about public interest in the arts in general and theater in particular. The indication was that 25% of the adult population were attending the theater.

Dance. Competition between the big dance companies and the little ones for the box-office

---

CANADA—SPECIAL REPORT:

The Great West

The great Canadian West comprises four provinces, each with its own identity. In fact, there is not one Canadian West but many Wests. A look at a map showing provincial boundaries, topography, and road and rail transportation links will show how this is the case. Manitoba ("place of sun"), the most easterly province, has its capital in Winnipeg, a regional distributing center. Divided from Ontario by the Canadian shield, Manitoba's historic links with Europe are by Hudson Bay and with the United States by the Red River Valley. Farther west, Saskatchewan (from the Cree for "swift-flowing," after the great river of the same name) is a generally flat area of rich agricultural lands covering a great reserve of potash and sulfur and, farther north, uranium. Farther west again and stretching to the continental divide is Alberta, named for the wife of Governor General Lord Lorne. It is the home of cattle barons, farmers, and oilmen. And west to the Pacific Ocean lies British Columbia, a "sea of mountains," where relatively mild climate and rich resources are geographical features of a society centered in the port city of Vancouver.

Although the Western provinces possess their own individual characteristics, they also share a larger identity. Citizens of the four boast a heady pride and a fierce identity different from that of central Canada. They share complaints against big eastern business interests, federally controlled railways and freight rates, and national tariff structures.

Canadian Westerners also point with pride to their peculiar political culture, a culture of pro-test. During the great depression of the 1930's the Canadian West gave birth to political parties that are still in existence in some provincial and federal governments. The first of these is the Cooperative Commonwealth Federation, now the New Democratic Party (NDP), a brand of Christian democratic socialism that had its origins in Protestant ideology, labor discontent, and university liberalism. Another is Social Credit, born in Alberta under the auspices of William ("Bible Bill") Aberhart of the Prophetic Bible Institute of Calgary. Originally a collectivist-oriented party designed to stimulate consumer spending to fight depression, it has held power for long periods in British Columbia and Alberta. All of the Western provinces, except Alberta, have had at some time New Democratic Party governments. Canada's first hospitalization plan was introduced in Saskatchewan by Thomas Douglas' NDP government in 1946. The plan became the model for other provincial and federal medicare schemes.

The West has given rise to other political agencies or groups, including the grain growers' associations, the United Farmers movement, and the Progressive Party (now part of the federal Progressive Conservative Party). It has also contributed heavily to the Social Gospel, a church-based, socially aware, activist ideology that permeated Protestant churches, in particular the United Church of Canada, throughout the 20th century.

(Continued on page 146.)

Photo: Banff National Park, Alberta.

dollars developed into an interesting situation. For the three major companies (Toronto's National Ballet, Montréal's Grands Ballets Canadiens, and the Royal Winnipeg Ballet), the enormous costs of just maintaining the status quo in a time of recession created massive problems. Meanwhile the smaller contemporary groups, which have gained much popularity in recent years, pressed hard for public support. With more flexible financing and less rigid programming, the small companies were better able to face up to so-called hard times in Canada. The Canada Council's grants to dance companies in 1978 totaled $3.6 million.

Aside from the financial woes, however, there were good-news events to record. A ten-day dance festival in Montréal in October saw enthusiastic audiences greeting performances by 23 groups from various parts of Canada. The Royal Winnipeg Ballet, which had performed in 375 cities in 23 countries, made its New York debut in March, and Toronto's National Ballet was warmly welcomed in July to its sixth appearance at New York's Lincoln Center.

Filmmaking, Sculpture, Miscellaneous. With a Commonwealth Festival in Edmonton, a World Festival in Montréal, an Animation Festival in Ottawa, and a Festival of Festivals in Toronto, filmmaking was the newsworthy element of the visual arts. There was a lot of excitement and squabbling related to each, but the film buffs and producers made the most of it, and the mass media loved it.

For the first time in 20 years, the International Sculpture Congress was held in Canada, at York University in Toronto. More than a thousand sculptors, critics, curators, and educators attended. A notable collection of contemporary North American works was displayed by a number of local art galleries.

WALTER B. HERBERT
Consultant on Canadian Cultural Affairs

RIC ERGENBRIGHT-LENSTOUR

Of all the parts of Canada, the West is the most identifiable ethnically. The four provinces are home for persons of Icelandic and Dutch, Ukrainian and German, Russian and Polish, English and Scottish, and other backgrounds. They are also home of some of the largest populations of native Indians. The mixed-blood (French, Scots, and Indian) Métis have called the Prairie West their home since fur-trading days. The West has also been home for religious refugees, including Mennonites, Hutterites, and Doukhobors, who homesteaded there in the late 19th and early 20th centuries. British Columbia is home for Chinese, Japanese, and East Indian communities. With these various peoples, the Canadian West contributes heavily to the national ethnic mosaic. At the same time, the West is firmly Canadian, with a strong identification with the monarchy, a respect for law and order, and a firm commitment to commercial development. The West is the home of the new Canadians who may be, as historian Arthur Lower observed, the real Canadians.

In the late 1970's Westerners are reflecting an effervescent sense of pride and place. They confidently point to their natural resources as keys to their future. In Alberta, for instance, where Premier Peter Lougheed's 1971 Conservative electoral victory ended a Social Credit dynasty dating from 1935, a boom in oil and natural gas production has made Albertans the wealthiest Canadians on a per capita income basis. Lougheed and the oil barons on which his government's power is based have been called "the blue-eyed Arabs." Rising oil and gas exports to Eastern Canada and the United States have greatly stimulated the economy. Oil accounted for more than 50% of the new jobs created in Alberta during the 1960's. Between 1941 and 1976, the province's population grew from 800,000 to 1.8 million. By the 1970's Alberta's population was highly urbanized, and farm incomes were no longer the basis of the province's wealth. Alberta Gas Truck Line, the Mannix-Loran group, ATCO Industries, and the Alberta Energy Corporation are the new commercial giants of the West. Together, they exert an increasing influence on the nation. At Fort McMurray, Alberta, the Athabasca tar sands are being exploited for oil in one of the largest capital-intensive projects in Canadian history. Construction of the projected Alaska gas line from Prudhoe Bay to markets in the continental United States is already further stimulating the Alberta economy. Taxation revenue from energy profits has been converted into a mammoth Heritage Fund, the interest from which provides Albertans with a fine education system and a cultural identity.

In Saskatchewan, NDP Premier Alan Blakeney's government is also profiting from oil and natural gas. But if nature did not endow Saskatchewan with so bountiful a supply of oil and natural gas as Alberta, it gave Saskatchewan sulfur, potash, and uranium. In 1977 Blakeney's governor expropriated American-controlled potash industries. Meanwhile, Saskatchewan's rich farmers produced bumper crops of wheat, rapeseed, and other grains and transported them to Canada's ocean and Great Lakes ports for sale to the USSR, Poland, China, and elsewhere.

In 1977 Manitobans elected a Conservative government under Sterling Lyon. The government is dedicated to cutting taxation and government spending, and stimulating the economy. Like Alberta and Saskatchewan, Manitoba grows in confidence. In 1970 the Hudson's Bay Company transferred its headquarters from London to Winnipeg. This giant of Canadian department store merchandizing also maintains stores in the North, where its economic hold over native peoples has invited criticism from Indian, Métis, and Inuit groups.

The most westerly province, British Columbia, enjoys strong trade links with Japan, China, Hong Kong, and Singapore. Investment capital from Asia contributes greatly to the rise of urban apartment and commercial buildings. Pulp and paper and lumber exports to the United States are keys to forest development. Canada's new 200-nautical-mile (370-km) fishing limits provide protection against Russian and Japanese encroachment. Copper, molybdenum, zinc, lead, gold, and silver production continue at an accelerated pace. Coal from the Kootenay Mountains, natural gas from Peace River, and hydroelectric power from dams of the Columbia River system add to the earning power of British Columbians who in 1972 replaced David Barrett's NDP government with a right-wing Social Credit government under William R. Bennett, son of W. A. C. Bennett whose individualistic political style reflected a growing British Columbian sense of assurance about its role in Confederation. The most populous of the western provinces, British Columbia has nearly 3 million persons, half of whom live in the metropolitan service and transportation core.

Citizens of the Canadian West are generally acquiring a new prosperity. Their growing populations now collectively give them as much voting power in the federal House of Commons as Quebec. Angered by Ottawa's policies that seem to favor industrial central Canada at the expense of the West, Westerners are expressing a tendency toward separatism perhaps as serious as that of Quebec. In 1978 Prime Minister Pierre Elliott Trudeau, a Liberal, challenged the West to take over Canada if it so wished. But over the past 50 years the West's anti-Ottawa stance has been translated into a steady support for the Progressive Conservative party which has been chronically in opposition in Ottawa and only in power eleven years since 1921. But one thing is certain: Westerners face the future with confidence. And many of them hope that their future will be with Canada.

BARRY M. GOUGH

CARIBBEAN

A presidential election in the Dominican Republic and a major move toward independence by the area's dependent states highlighted 1978 events in the Caribbean.

Dominican Republic. History was made in May 1978 with the election of a new president in the Dominican Republic and the subsequent peaceful change of government. Joaquín Balaguer, 70 years old and in poor health, failed in his effort to secure a fourth term as president. The winner was a wealthy cattle rancher, Antonio Guzmán, candidate of the left-leaning Dominican Revolutionary Party. Guzmán, whose candidacy was opposed by the armed forces, was inaugurated in August. His peaceful installation as president was made possible largely by the peace-making efforts of Balaguer and the expressions of confidence by representatives of the United States government. Once in power, Guzmán tapped leading industrialists and businessmen to form his cabinet and moved quickly to assign officials from the armed forces to Dominican embassy posts overseas. At the same time, the new president pardoned and released all political prisoners in the country.

Independence Movement. In the field of politics, elections and movements toward independence marked the year's activity. On Jan. 2, 1978, cancer took the life of the reform governor of the Virgin Islands, Cyril King. Several months later, cancer also took the life of his good friend, Robert Bradshaw, premier of St. Kitts and Nevis. Bradshaw was 60 years old when he died and had governed the islands for about 30 years. He was replaced by a member of his own party, Deputy Premier Paul Southwell, a native of Dominica who rose to political prominence in St. Kitts through the labor union movement.

St. Kitts and Nevis were scheduled to become independent from Great Britain in 1978, but an unauthorized referendum on the island of Nevis indicated that 99% of the island's population wished to follow the example of Anguilla, which broke away from St. Kitts-Nevis-Anguilla in 1967. The lack of unity displayed by this referendum, the adverse economic climate, and the prolonged illness of the late premier combined to postpone indefinitely independence for the Associated State of St. Kitts and Nevis. Lack of unity and virtual economic bankruptcy also postponed indefinitely plans for the independence of the Associated State of Antigua and Barbuda.

In November, the Associated State of Dominica, located between the two French islands of Guadeloupe and Martinique, became independent from Great Britain. Although independence was welcomed by most Dominicans, the opposition Dominica Freedom party criticized the action claiming that the island was not prepared for the responsibilities of independence. The Soviet Union immediately recognized Dominica upon its independence because of the socialist orientation of Dominican Prime Minister Patrick John. The scheduled December 13 independence of St. Lucia from Great Britain was postponed until 1979. (*See also* DOMINICA.)

St. Vincent was expected to gain independence in January 1979. This and St. Lucia would be the third and fourth Associated State to move into independence since the states were created in 1968. Grenada, Dominica, and St. Vincent will have become independent, while St. Kitts-Nevis and Antigua-Barbuda will remain associated with Great Britain, at least temporarily.

Presidential election in the Dominican Republic: Soldiers deliver the ballot boxes to election headquarters for tabulating. Antonio Guzmán (*right*), a wealthy rancher, won the contest.

PHOTOS UPI

Haiti. Amnesty for political prisoners was under discussion in Haiti, where the Inter-American Human Rights Commission spent ten days in August hearing complaints against the government for violations of the civil rights of persons opposing Jean-Claude Duvalier, the Haitian president.

Economic Developments. The two largest English speaking islands in the Caribbean, Trinidad and Jamaica, continued to experience the extremes of poverty and prosperity in 1978. Oil flowed in increasing abundance out of deposits in and around Trinidad. The island, which is the base of one of the largest air carriers of the Caribbean, felt the impact of a six-month pilot strike.

In the western Caribbean, Jamaica continued to be caught up in serious economic difficulties. With the fifth devaluation of the Jamaican dollar since Prime Minister Michael Manley began his second term in 1976, the currency fell to 48% of its original value. The devaluation and a domestic consumption tax, intended to produce $130 million in revenue, were required before Jamaica could receive a $250 million loan from the International Monetary Fund.

The drought that had plagued the Caribbean since 1973 was finally broken in 1978. A slightly above-average rainfall was noted for the entire region, perhaps due to the ten tropical storms that formed in and around the Caribbean during the hurricane season. It was too early to discern any marked improvement in agriculture in 1978, but should the rains continue, 1979 may see a reverse in the declining sugar and fruit production of the islands.

The Caribbean began to receive a flow of badly needed funds in 1978. The Special Fund for the Financing of the Caribbean Group was created within the World Bank to raise the (U. S.) $1.95 billion needed by the countries in the region. An emergency grant of $122 million from the World Bank was made to the Caribbean Development Bank in 1978. On its own initiative, the government of Venezuela gave impetus to economic support for various national and regional entities in the Caribbean. Barbados, Jamaica, Guyana, Surinam, St. Lucia, St. Vincent, and the Association of Caribbean Universities were some of the entities favored by substantial grants or loans from Venezuela.

THOMAS MATHEWS
Institute of Caribbean Studies
University of Puerto Rico

CENSORSHIP

For the first time in recent years, the world-wide trend toward censorship appeared to abate. Freedom House, in its annual Comparative Survey of Freedom, reported improvement in political and civil freedom in 26 nations. Surveys by the Associated Press and the Inter-American Press Association echoed these findings.

However, the Freedom House report was tempered by the realization that "Despite strides made . . . two thirds of all people suffer political repression, cannot expect relief from courts, and are denied free speech and access to free news media." Foreign correspondents testified to such conditions in many Third World countries, where the threat of physical violence must now be added to explicit and implicit censorship.

There was concern in the free world over a draft declaration by UNESCO that, if adopted, would declare governments to be responsible in the international sphere for all mass media under their jurisdiction. Free world spokesmen view the draft as a mandate for censorship, while defenders argue that it is needed to control the media and ensure balance in news reporting.

U. S. Developments. The courts continued their strong reluctance to allow prior government restraint of communications. In cases involving the American Nazi Party, they ruled unconstitutional village ordinances that required permits for public assemblies and prohibited dissemination of materials likely to incite hatred.

Disclosures by former employees of the Central Intelligence Agency (CIA) brought before the courts the question—seemingly destined for Supreme Court review—of whether oaths sworn at the time of employment are binding contracts not to be breached on a plea of First Amendment rights. In the latest action, a federal court impounded profits gained by the author of a book about CIA activities in Vietnam. The same author was ordered to submit two proposed magazine articles to the CIA for review.

Censorship and Community Standards. Although the Federal Communications Commission (FCC) is expressly forbidden by statute to exercise censorship, the Supreme Court ruled that the commission has authority to impose sanctions on broadcast licensees if they broadcast "obscene, indecent, or profane language" (*FCC* v. *Pacifica Foundation*).

In its unending quest for a definition of obscenity, the Supreme Court ruled that adults, "sensitive and insensitive"—but not children—are to be considered in a jury's determination of the standards of morality of the "average person" in a particular community (*Pinkus* v. *U. S.*).

Censorship at the Source. News-media concern over the withholding of information by state or federal government focused on such court practices as the issuance of "gag" or restrictive orders that silence all participants in a trial once they are outside the courtroom. An equally troublesome development found some courts closing pretrial hearings to the public. Arguing that such closures are in reality prior restraints on publication of the news, one newspaper chain is seeking Supreme Court review of their constitutionality.

PAUL FISHER
Director, Freedom of Information Center
University of Missouri, Columbia

CENTRAL AMERICA

For most of the people of Central America the year 1978 began with feelings of joy and ended with feelings of considerable apprehension. The high point was achieved with the ratification by the United States and Panama of the treaties turning the Panama Canal over to Panama at the end of the century, for most Central Americans shared with Panamanians their satisfaction at this symbol of increased sovereignty (*see* pages 17–25). But the region continued to suffer from poverty and its partners, violence and repression. This was expressed most clearly in Nicaragua where civil war broke out in a major attempt to overthrow the Somoza regime. Central American states have regularly exported their troubles to one another as easily as exiles cross the borders, and even normally calm Costa Ricans could fear inadvertent involvement in Nicaragua's crisis. This was publicly expressed by Costa Rica's vice president, who declared that he found people everywhere discontented, and that none of the other five states could consider itself safe from explosion.

Generally the economies bore him out; although the gross national product of each of the states showed moderate growth, none of them had eliminated inflation, substantial underemployment, or the heavy dependency upon the export of vulnerable agricultural products.

COSTA RICA

In its traditional fashion Costa Rica quietly held a presidential election in 1978, and a coalition of Christian Democrats, Calderonists, and Unión Popular members carried the day for Rodrigo Carazo Odio, who was also aided by a splintering of the leadership in the once-powerful National Liberation Party. Carazo was inaugurated in May before some 20,000 people; the United States was represented by Rosalyn Carter. Carazo's chief administrative danger lay in the small plurality that his National Unification Party held in the legislature.

The new government seems to have rid itself of the Vesco albatross. Robert Vesco, wanted in the United States for embezzling more than $200 million, fled to Costa Rica in 1973, where, it was reported, he received protection from extradition by his close ties with Costa Rican government officials. At his inauguration President Carazo announced that he would not harbor "international delinquents," and after Vesco left

Costa Rica on business, refused to permit his return.

Perhaps Carazo's most serious domestic problem was a strike in August by thousands of hospital workers at more than one hundred medical centers. The strike, which paralyzed medical services for ten days, was finally suspended when the government promised to negotiate the matter of wage increases. In other respects, the economy looked better; per capita income remained the best in Central America, industrial production rose about 11%, and inflation moderated. Boding favorably for the future was a vast hydroelectric and irrigation project commenced in Guanacaste province that will nearly double electric potential by 1983.

EL SALVADOR

There was little improvement in the lives of Salvadoreans. The government of President Carlos Humberto Romero was still haunted by charges of a completely fraudulent election in 1977 and remained trapped between forces of left- and right-wing extremists determined to make his administration powerless. The main target of right-wing terrorists seemed to be certain members of the clergy and principally Archbishop Oscar Arnulfo Romero (no relation), who openly denounced the government for its repression of the peasants. He alleged that several dozen political fugitives were missing, and that a number of clergymen had been tortured by the government. The rightists, calling themselves "Orden," were opposed by several bands of terrorists of the left, called the "Popular Revolutionary Bloc," and claiming a membership of thousands of peasants, students, and urban workers. Their major weapon was kidnapping, and some wealthy industrialists paid millions of dollars to be released. In addition, the dean of a college and a former president of congress were assassinated.

At the heart of the troubles were heavy population pressure on scarce resources and a maldistribution of wealth that gave 90% of the people less than 50% of the nation's income. Nevertheless on two fronts some progress occurred. The government declared itself closer to resuming full relations with Honduras, still strained from the "Soccer War" of 1969. And it appeared possible that the nation's substantial sources of geothermal energy might in the next decade significantly reduce the need for importing expensive petroleum.

CENTRAL AMERICA • Information Highlights

Nation	Population (in millions)	Area In sq mi (km²)	Capital	Head of State and Government
Costa Rica	2.1	19,575 (50,700)	San José	Rodrigo Carazo Odio, president
El Salvador	4.4	8,260 (21,392)	San Salvador	Carlos Humberto Romero, president
Guatemala	6.6	42,042 (108,890)	Guatemala City	Romeo Lucas Garciá, president
Honduras	3.0	43,277 (112,087)	Tegucigalpa	Policarpo Paz García, leader, ruling junta
Nicaragua	2.4	50,193 (130,000)	Managua	Anastasio Somoza, president
Panama	1.8	29,209 (75,650)	Panama City	Omar Torrijos Herrera, commander, National Guard Aristides Royo, president

PHOTOS UPI

Civil war broke out in Nicaragua. The Sandinista National Liberation Front, led by Zero, *above*, sought to overthrow President Somoza, *below*.

GUATEMALA

Guatemala held its presidential election in 1978, and while there were the usual charges of fraud, apathy marked the attitude of most of the public. Scarcely 20% of the electorate went to the polls or cast countable ballots. Romeo Lucas García had only a plurality and was chosen president by the congress. The new administration brought little change in the nation's affairs or policies. Amnesty International claimed that "death squads" roamed the land with "total impunity," accounting for the assassination of more than 20,000 persons in recent years. As in El Salvador, terrorists of the left and right engaged in kidnapping public officials or wealthy industrialists, regardless of nationality.

Some of Guatemala's long-standing class conflict revealed itself in May when a number of Indians were killed by the army in a land dispute at Panzós. The Indians had long grown corn on the land, but when roads opened the region, large landowners interested in nickel or perhaps petroleum tried to force them off the communal holdings. Urban strife occurred, too, and the nation was paralyzed for several weeks by strikes of public employees and, later, transportation workers, all seeking wage increases.

Nevertheless, the nation's economy expanded. Over the past few years Guatemala has been the only Central American state to show a trade balance within the Central American Common Market, most of this surplus being composed of manufactured articles and chemical products. Coffee prices remained high, enabling the nation to maintain a growth in per capita gross domestic product.

HONDURAS

In an August coup that was as surprising as it was quiet, the Honduran administration of Gen. Juan Alberto Melgar Castro was replaced by a triumvirate of generals, led by Policarpo Paz García. Melgar Castro, who had taken the presidency in a 1975 coup following charges of bribery in the United Brands case, presumably lost his office because of differences within the armed forces.

The Hondurans have been under military rule since 1972 and took this latest change in stride. The most clearly expressed opposition came from a national association of farm workers, which has little political strength. Honduras' human rights position ranked better in Washington than did those of its neighbors, and as a result Honduras received rewards from the Carter government in the form of economic assistance. Nevertheless, the Catholic Church protested that the lives of some of the clergy had been threatened by the military government for agitating the peasants.

Discussions continued with El Salvador concerning the location of their common border, a dispute contributing to the 1969 war. Like all of

Central America, the nation faced occasional strikes in 1978, one serious crisis affecting the ministry of public health. The government boasted of an agrarian reform program but the farmers' associations minimized the accomplishments. The gross domestic product expanded at about the same rate as inflation, about 9%.

NICARAGUA

The most important development in Central America in many years reached its climax in 1978 with an all-out assault on the regime of Anastasio Somoza Debayle. The Somoza family, which has ruled Nicaragua since 1937, had created many enemies through its oppressive and venal policies. Many Nicaraguans were especially incensed at the opportunism their government exhibited during the tragic days of the 1972 earthquake. The opposition Sandinistas, named for César Sandino, a folk-hero of the 1930's, burst into action with successful kidnappings for ransom in 1974. The National Guard kept the lid on conditions until late 1977, when a new offensive began. By then the Sandinistas were receiving support from a wide variety of Somoza opponents, from Marxists to conservative businessmen. The archbishop's New Year's message condemned the government for murder and corruption, and in January 1978, the government's most outspoken opponent, newspaper editor Pedro Joaquín Chamorro, was assassinated in downtown Managua. It mattered little who committed the act; the nation condemned Somoza. The struggle now moved from crisis to civil war.

Conservatives demanded Somoza's resignation, but he repeatedly declared that he would remain president until 1981 and then permit a free election. From time to time strikes nearly paralyzed the land, and the guard had its hands full with uprisings in every corner of Nicaragua. The National University closed in response to an invasion of the campus by the guard, and in one village some 2,000 Indians fought off the troops with sticks and rocks.

In August the guerrillas seized the national palace in a gun battle and took scores of hostages, including relatives of the president. The government surrendered more than 80 political prisoners and gave up a large amount of ransom as the guerrillas took their prizes off to Panama. A few days later another general strike began as the Sandinistas succeeded in capturing several major towns. In heavy fighting with hundreds of casualties, the guard gradually recaptured all of the towns and the guerrillas fled to the backlands or into exile.

Several nations offered to mediate the struggle, and in October the Somoza regime accepted the efforts of the Organization of American States. However, the civil struggle was continuing as the year ended.

THOMAS L. KARNES
Arizona State University

CHEMISTRY

In 1978 two important changes were noticeable in the field of chemistry. One was a more serious attitude toward conservation of resources and the search for renewable sources of energy. The other was some relaxation of job discrimination against women chemists.

Energy. RCA was issued a patent for cells to collect solar energy. The key material is hydrogenated noncrystalline silicon produced from silane gas (SiH_4) and diborane (B_2H_6) or phosphine (PH_3) as a dopant. These materials, when subjected to a low temperature process, deposit an extremely thin film of hydrogenated silicon on either glass or metal. This product, actually a semiconductor, can be made into 1-foot (0.3-m) squares, in contrast to the 3-inch (7.6-cm) wafers for crystalline silicon semiconductors. Solar cells made in this way were said to be inexpensive and efficient—6% of the solar energy reaching the cells is collected. With further research, the scientists hope to approach the theoretical limit of 15%.

In addition to the collecting of solar energy, considerable attention was given to storage. One method is based on the principle that a solid, when liquefying, absorbs heat which it gives off when resolidifying. A promising material is Glauber's salt (sodium decahydrate). The substance is inexpensive and melts at the convenient temperature of 32.2° C (89.9° F). But crystals tend to build up on the container walls, thus forming an insulation that inhibits the escape of heat as the salt resolidifies. To prevent this, General Electric devised a horizontal tank that rotates three times a minute, just enough to prevent buildup of an insulating layer of crystals. Such a tank, 22 feet (6.7 m) long and 2 feet (0.6 m) wide is said to be able to heat an average house for 24 hours when the temperature outside is −17.7° C (14° F).

By 1978, enthusiasm for using hydrogen as a fuel had waned, although the gas is ideal for reducing air pollution since its sole combustion product is water. It was felt that significant use would not be achieved until the cost of fossil fuels is three or four times present levels. Derek P. Gregory, a vice president of the Institute of Gas Technology, long a proponent of hydrogen fuel, foresaw only specialized use, such as in fleet vehicles, by the late 1980's. By the late 1990's, some experimental aircraft may be powered by hydrogen, and such installations as military bases or national laboratories may use hydrogen fuels on a trial basis.

Waste Disposal. Urban garbage, paper, and such agricultural wastes as wheat straw and peanut hulls, when treated with the enzyme cellulase, can be converted into simple sugars. These sugars can in turn be fermented into alcohol and used as motor fuel. There are, however, two main problems: the reactions are slow and the cost of the alcohol cannot compete with that of petroleum fuels. A different cellulase, produced by the fungus *Thielatin terrestris,* found in rotting logs by scientists at the Stanford Research Institute, may help solve these problems. This enzyme works at a fairly high temperature (60°–70° C, 140°–158° F), which means that the reaction can proceed faster. The reaction itself produces enough heat to maintain the needed temperature without the cost of additional heating.

Air Pollution. General Motors claimed to have produced an improved catalytic converter that, by increasing decomposition of nitrogen oxides in the exhaust, will eliminate automobiles as a major source of air pollution. It uses an electronic system that controls precisely the air-to-fuel ratio at 14.6 parts air to 1 part fuel. Three car models equipped with the new converter were sold in California, and installation in all new car models is planned by 1981.

Women Chemists. Marie Curie, doing research on radioactivity early this century in France, was the first scientist to win two Nobel prizes. But her achievements did little to enhance career opportunities for women chemists. In 1978, 35 major universities employed 1,182 chemistry faculty members, of whom only 34 were women. Only eight women had tenure. However, in 1978 three notable events suggested some improvement in this area. Anna J. Harrison became president of the prestigious American Chemical Society, and Mary L. Good became chairman of the board of directors. Also, Shannon Wells Lucid became the first chemist to be selected as an astronaut candidate. After successful completion of training she will become eligible to be mission specialist on a space shuttle flight. Many women chemists, however, attribute this progress to fear of litigation rather than to a genuine change in attitude. They fear that the trend will not continue.

Forensic Science. In August 1978, the Law Enforcement Assistance Administration of the U. S. Department of Justice reported a three-year study of 250 police laboratories in the United States and Canada. The object of the study was to determine how accurately the laboratories could analyze clues found on the scene of a crime. In such work, blood stain analysis is of prime importance. Yet 71% of the laboratories reported unacceptable results when presented with samples, the origins of which were known only to persons conducting the study. The laboratories scored best in identifying drugs —only 2% gave wrong answers. The lowest scores were made in distinguishing hair, such as from dogs, cats, cows, mink, and deer.

However, crime analysts questioned the real significance of these findings. They pointed out that simple yes and no answers are rarely used in court testimony. Rather, chemical and physical evidence is presented as found and weighed by judges and juries in conjunction with other testimony.

EUGENIA KELLER
*Formerly, Managing Editor
"Chemistry"*

CHESS

World champion Anatoly Karpov defended his title for the first time in 1978. Karpov, a 27-year-old Russian, beat back a strong challenge from Viktor Korchnoi, 47, a defector from the Soviet Union. Their match in Baguio City, the Philippines, was won by Karpov, 6–5; there were 21 draws. The players shared a record purse of $700,000.

After the quarrels and confusion that have become almost traditional for championship matches, the grandmasters got off to an even start, working the score to 1–1 amid several draws. Karpov then gained an apparently insurmountable lead of 4–1 after 17 games, and 5–2 after 27.

UPI

Anatoly Karpov defeated Viktor Korchnoi to retain his world chess title.

In Chicago's high crime areas, police canine units began in 1978 to patrol the city's rapid transit units.

UPI

Korchnoi, who had defeated former world champions Tigran Petrosian and Boris Spassky on the way to the Karpov match, then reeled off an unprecedented three victories in the next four games, tying the score at 5–5. In the very next game, virtually a sudden-death playoff, Karpov engineered a crushing victory to retain the title he had won by default in 1975.

Karpov was considered a sure bet to win the 1978 chess "Oscar." Besides defending his title, he tied for first place at Bugojno, Yugoslavia, in one of the strongest tournaments in history. Sharing first place there was former World Champion Boris Spassky.

Perennial women's World Champion Nona Gaprindashvili was not so fortunate in her title defense. She lost to Maia Chiburdanidze by a score of 8½–6½. At 17, Chiburdanidze is the youngest world champion in history, and her performance in this match suggests she will be a dominant force in women's chess, as well as a threat to the best male players. Both Gaprindashvili and Chiburdanidze are from the USSR.

Computer chess also had a big year in 1978. In 1968, International Master David Levy of Scotland made a wager that in ten years no computer could beat him in a match. *Chess 4.7*, the World Champion computer program, proved a worthy opponent. It had already defeated two grandmasters in relatively casual games, but Levy won the match with three victories, one loss, and one draw.

The 1978 United States Closed and Zonal Championship was won by Lubomir Kavalek, a native of Czechoslovakia and now a resident of Washington, D. C. Edmar Mednis and Leonid Shamkovich will play a match to determine the third American player in the 1979 Interzonal Tournaments. Three-time champion Walter Browne left the 1978 event after a dispute about playing conditions. Joseph Bradford was the surprise winner of the 1978 U. S. Open.

The 1978 World Open in Philadelphia set a new record for attendance with 1,063 players competing for the $40,000 prize fund. Seven players shared first place.

Gerard J. Dullea, *U. S. Chess Federation*

CHICAGO

Chicago started the year in a winter that broke one foul-weather record after another. A record winter snowfall of 82.2 inches (209 cm) left the city streets and cars buried for weeks. The frigid temperatures were only slightly higher than the record cold of the 1977 winter. Destructive potholes plagued motorists well into the summer.

The performing arts generated great interest in Chicago during 1978. Theatergoers enjoyed Jackie Gleason in *Sly Fox* and Sammy Davis, Jr., in *Stop the World—I Want to Get Off*.

Well over 100,000 persons crowded around the new Grant Park band shell for a Fourth of July concert capped by cannon fire and fireworks for the grand finale of Tchaikovsky's "1812 Overture." City Hall sponsored the most successful musical event in the city's history, the ChicagoFest. The rock, pop, and country music festival, held at the rejuvenated Navy Pier on the lakefront, attracted 350,000 spectators.

ChicagoFest was a real political plus for Michael Bilandic who, during his second year as mayor, built his own political power base, despite periodic charges of favoritism and questionable activity in City Hall.

Bilandic named new police and fire chiefs during the year. The scandal-ridden police department was reorganized by the new chief, and Bilandic pushed the first home mortgage plan through the City Council. The $100 million plan, backed by municipal bonds, granted home buyers mortgages of 7.99% instead of the 9.75% interest rate charged in the private sector.

Renewal of parts of the city was accelerated. Construction continued on the project to turn State Street into a pedestrian mall in an effort to revitalize sagging retail trade in the Loop. The city was granted $114.3 million in federal funds to rehabilitate deteriorating neighborhoods, and another $7 million to develop two new industrial parks. Plans were announced, but not made final, for the complete renovation of seven downtown blocks at a cost of approximately (U. S.) $1 billion.

The project is a joint venture of the city, the state of Illinois, and private business interests.

Demonstrations were in the news again in Chicago. The National Socialist Party of America (NSPA), or Nazi Party, created a furor with its announcement that it would hold a march through Skokie, Chicago's most heavily Jewish suburb. Court battles and public pressure forced the demonstration to Chicago's Marquette Park.

On March 4, the *Chicago Daily News* ceased publication, 102 years after its first edition. The *Daily News,* Chicago's last afternoon newspaper, had a reputation for hard-nosed and flamboyant reporting.

ROBERT ENSTAD, *Chicago Tribune*

CHILE

In late 1978, Chile appeared to be emerging from a long period of repression and austerity. However, the political atmosphere was clouded by the indictment of the former head of the secret police in connection with the 1976 assassination of Orlando Letelier in Washington, D. C.

Plebiscite Backs Pinochet. President Augusto Pinochet Ugarte interpreted a January 4 plebiscite as meaning he did not have to call elections before 1986 and that he could issue a new constitution for an "authoritarian democracy" without a ratification vote. He had called the plebiscite after the United Nations General Assembly criticized human rights violations in Chile. Part of the statement to be approved or rejected by six million voters read: "In the face of the international aggression unleashed against the government of the homeland, I support President Pinochet in his defense of the dignity of Chile." Of 5,350,000 voting, 75% approved, 20.4% voted no, and 4.6% cast blank or null votes; another 700,000 abstained.

Two junta members, Air Force Gen. Gustavo Leigh Guzman and Adm. José Toríbio Merino Castro, opposed the plebiscite, as did the Roman Catholic bishops and the outlawed Christian Democratic Party.

Pinochet Reduces Tensions. On March 27, Carlos Lazo, a prominent Socialist, was released from jail. As part of a new program of amnesty for civilian prisoners who would be pardoned or allowed to go into exile, he went to France on April 1.

On March 31, the Santiago curfew was lifted, although restaurants and nightclubs were to close at 1:00 A. M. in order "to save fuel and energy."

On April 12, President Pinochet appointed Sergio Fernández, a long-time associate, as the first civilian minister of the interior since the military coup of September 1973 which ousted President Salvador Allende Gossens. Subsequently, 3 more civilians were appointed to the cabinet, which was composed of 11 civilians and 5 military officers late in 1978.

Air Force Officers Ousted. On July 24, General Leigh was dismissed from the junta and his Air Force position. Once considered the most conservative junta member, Leigh became increasingly disenchanted with Pinochet's growing personal power and determination not to allow civilian rule until the late 1980's. Leigh was replaced by 53-year-old Gen. Fernando Matthei. Eight other Air Force generals who outranked Matthei were automatically retired while ten other Air Force generals resigned in support of Leigh.

U. S. Indicts Seven. On August 1, a Washington, D. C. grand jury indicted Gen. Manuel Contreras Sepulveda, former head of the now dissolved DINA or secret police, two other Chilean officers, and four Cuban exiles in connection with the 1976 assassination of Orlando Letelier in Washington, D. C. In September, the United States requested extradition of the three Chileans.

On August 11, Michael Vernon Townley, a 35-year old American who lived in Chile during most of the past 20 years, admitted he made and planted the bomb which killed Letelier, a former Chilean foreign minister, and a U. S. colleague. The United States withdrew Ambassador George Landau for ten days as a sign of its displeasure with Chilean reluctance to cooperate with the investigation.

Economy. Copper prices, which had fallen to 51 cents a pound in August 1977, rose to 56 cents in January and 68 cents in September, with world consumption expected to rise.

Inflation was reduced to 7.8% for the first three months of 1978, compared with 18.9% for the same period in 1977. Overall inflation in 1977 was 63.5%, compared with 174.3% in 1976. Minimum wages remained low at $2.10 per day. The agricultural planning office also estimated a 27% drop in 1978 production of 14 important crops including wheat and corn; food imports were expected to increase $500 million.

Foreign Relations. Negotiations continued with Argentina over disputed ownership of three small islands in the Beagle Channel near Cape Horn. Military maneuvers and air raid alerts marked increased tensions. In late December, Pope John Paul II appointed a special envoy to help mediate the dispute.

NEALE J. PEARSON
Texas Tech University

--------- **CHILE · Information Highlights** ---------

Official Name: Republic of Chile.
Location: Southwestern coast of South America.
Area: 292,257 square miles (742,330 km²).
Population (1978 est.): 10,800,000.
Chief Cities (1975 met. est.): Santiago, the capital, 3,186,000; Valparaiso, 248,972
Government: Head of state and government, Gen. Augusto Pinochet Ugarte, president (took power Sept. 1973). Legislature—Congress (dissolved Sept. 1973).
Monetary Unit: Peso (33.21 pesos equal U. S.$1, Sept. 1978).
Manufactures (major products): Small manufacturing, refining.
Agriculture (major products): Wheat, rice, oats, barley, fruits, vegetables, corn, sugar beets, beans, wine, livestock.

UPI

Chinese Vice-Premier Teng Hsiao-ping, *right*, meets with U. S. Sen. Edward Kennedy on Jan. 4, 1978, in Peking.

CHINA

The year 1978 was an eventful one for both the People's Republic of China (Communist China) and the Republic of China (Nationalist China). The announcement on December 15 that Communist China and the United States had agreed to establish formal diplomatic relations and that the United States would terminate its defense treaty with Taiwan was the most important event in decades. The new president of Nationalist China, Chiang Ching-kuo, was determined to continue the struggle against Peking, while the primary goals of Communist China were to modernize its industries and armed forces and to curb Soviet influence in the world.

PEOPLE'S REPUBLIC OF CHINA

A new, pragmatic approach to domestic affairs, characterized by the modernization of education, science, and technology, was a drastic departure from Maoist doctrine, which stressed revolutionary ideology rather than professionalism.

The People's Congress. The fifth People's Congress, China's nominal legislature, was convened on February 26 to act on the proposals of the Chinese Communist party. It reappointed Premier Hua Kuo-feng and First Deputy Premier Teng Hsiao-ping. It did not fill the position of state president, which was left vacant when Liu Shao-ch'i was purged during the 1966 Cultural Revolution. Yeh Chien-ying, the aging marshal, was elected chairman of the Standing Committee of the People's Congress to carry out the ceremonial functions of the head of state. Hsu Hsiang-ch'ien, who had stressed professionalism and discipline in the army, replaced Yeh as minister of defense.

Power Structure. The People's Congress reconfirmed China's political structure without clarifying the power relationship among the top leaders. Hua Kuo-feng remained the highest ranking official, but Teng Hsiao-ping seemed to hold more executive power. Teng had deeply rooted relations with the military and bureaucrats, while Hua clearly lacked a power base in the army. After his appointment as deputy premier and vice chairman of the party in 1977, Teng steadily consolidated his power and took steps to remove his adversaries, especially those who had played an important role in the Cultural Revolution. In 1978, it was the more pragmatic Teng who appeared to formulate and administer basic policy. Hua, recognizing the need for unity, seemed to step back.

Flexible Ideology. The new pragmatic leadership took immediate steps to reshape the party line. In subtle ways they promoted a flexible interpretation of the thought of Mao Tse-tung. The basic principles of Mao, said Teng Hsiao-ping, must be integrated with reality. "If we just copied past documents word for word, we wouldn't be solving any problem, let alone solving any problem correctly." Peking did not reject the whole of Mao's teachings, but it did deny any religious reverence for his ideology.

In late November, wall posters indirectly critical of Mao and Hua began to appear in Peking and other cities. The posters, which were part of a public campaign for democracy and civil liberties, were given qualified approval by Teng.

Civil Rights. The new Chinese Constitution, approved by the People's Congress in March, restored to the people the right to a trial defense and to lodge complaints against government officials. It also provided that ethnic minorities have the right to preserve or reform their customs.

In June, Peking reportedly set free 110,-000 political prisoners detained since the "anti-rightist" campaign in the 1950's. In addition, thousands of Communist cadres and intellectuals purged during and after the Cultural Revolution were put in rehabilitation programs.

A newly built greenhouse of Yuyuantan Commune in a Peking suburb provides fruits and vegetables for market.

Education, Science and Technology. In education the Communist leadership made broad changes that reversed the policy of Mao Tse-tung. Speaking at a national conference on education in April, Teng Hsiao-ping declared that examinations were imperative to schools. High standards and rigid discipline must be enforced if China is to become a modern industrial power by the end of the century, he said.

A far-reaching program of scientific and technological advancement was launched in 1978. A conference held in Peking March 18–31 was attended by 6,000 delegates to discuss their role in modernization. Two programs were revealed: a three-year plan to speed up research and development in such technical fields as genetic engineering, laser technology, and computer technology; and an eight-year plan to lay the foundation for overtaking more advanced western countries in a broad stratum of science and technology by the year 2000. Peking planned to send thousands of students to study in foreign countries, including the United States.

Military Modernization. Because of the Maoist doctrine that the decisive factor in war is man-power and not weapons, the Chinese army had made do with old and obsolete weapons. By 1978, the need for military modernization was recognized. "It is foolish to think," declared the Commission on Science and Technology for National Defense, "that it would be possible to use old weapons to fight an enemy equipped with missiles and nuclear weapons."

Peking therefore decided to improve its weapons to whatever extent possible, given its financial means. Chinese representatives were sent to France and West Germany to examine advanced weapons for possible purchase. In May, a Chinese military delegation visited France to discuss purchase of long-range, wire-guided antitank missiles. In November, Britain reportedly sold to China diesel engines for use in naval vessels.

Economic Development. Comprehensive economic growth, with a rapid modernization of the industrial sector, was a goal set in 1978. Toward that end, Peking ended its economic isolation and broadened its dealings with foreign capitalist countries. For the first time in its history, the Communist regime made policy changes that would allow foreign loans and joint ventures. Chinese banks were to receive deposits from foreign traders and international loans could be arranged.

Peking expressed interest in setting up joint manufacturing facilities with foreign firms in China, Hong Kong, and Macao. Five American oil companies—Union, Exxon, Pennzoil, Gulf, and Phillips—sent delegations to China to discuss offshore oil exploration. (In late November, the Coastal States Gas Corporation announced an agreement to import 3.6 million barrels of crude oil from Communist China; it will be the first U. S. company to do so since the Communists came to power.) On November 4, U. S. Energy Secretary James Schlesinger announced in Peking that the Chinese had agreed on a tentative list of cooperative energy development projects.

China's foreign trade rose sharply in the first half of 1978. Exports increased by 29% and imports by 60%, compared with the same period in 1977. Total 1978 trade was expected to exceed (U. S.) $20 billion.

Foreign Relations—United States. Six years after the 1972 Shanghai communiqué calling for normalization of relations between China and the United States, that goal finally was reached. On Jan. 1, 1979, the two nations officially established diplomatic relations. As announced simultaneously in Washington and Peking, December 15, Teng was to visit the United States on January 29 and embassies were to be established on March 1. The agreement was the result of months of secret negotiations in which the United States finally agreed to sever ties with

Taiwan. The Chinese Communists had insisted that this was the prerequisite of normalization with Washington.

For most of the year, the Carter administration sought to improve relations with the People's Republic without granting full recognition. By expanding trade, exchanging technology, and approving allied arms shipments, Carter hoped to induce Peking to soften its stand on Taiwan.

That was the thinking that Zbigniew Brzezinski, President Carter's national security adviser, took to Peking on May 20. Brzezinski and Chinese leaders discussed global strategy, emphasizing their mutual concern over Soviet domination in various parts of the world. Peking was pleased by Brzezinski's emphasis on the "congruence of fundamental interests" between China and the United States. It was receptive to signs that Washington was moving away from détente with the Soviet Union in favor of closer Sino-American relations.

Although no agreement was reached on Taiwan, the two countries did agree to step up trade and continue to share technological capabilities. In a reversal of policy, Washington agreed to sell China an airborne geological exploration system with an infrared scanning system. That device, used primarily for oil exploration, also has potential military uses.

In July, a delegation of U. S. scientists headed by Frank Press, President Carter's science adviser, visited China. Peking, interested in promoting basic and applied science, suggested cooperation in the form of student exchanges, seminars, and joint research projects.

Peking bought 3.9 million metric tons of wheat from the United States in 1978, its first purchases in four years. This augured well for the expansion of grain trade and perhaps the sale of other farm products to China.

In November, China signed a $500-million contract with Pan American World Airways to build and operate a chain of hotels in Peking, Shanghai, and other cities. In late December, the Coca-Cola Company announced that it would begin sales in China in January. Coke would become the first U. S. consumer product to be sold in China since the Communist takeover.

Soviet Union. The antagonism between China and the USSR turned into an intensive diplomatic war. Containing Soviet influence was the overriding idea in Chinese foreign policy. When Moscow offered to hold talks to improve relations, China dismissed the gesture as propaganda.

Sino-Soviet relations were exacerbated by a border incident on May 9. Peking charged that 30 Soviet troops, supported by a helicopter and navy boats, crossed the Ussuri River into the Hulin area of Heilungkiang Province. The troops allegedly shot at Chinese inhabitants, wounding a number of them. The Soviet Union expressed regret over the incident, but denied that its troops had shot or beaten Chinese citizens.

On May 29, at the UN General Assembly special session on disarmament, Chinese Foreign Minister Huang Hua called the Soviet Union "the most dangerous source of a new world war." Huang added that Moscow was "increasing its military threat to western Europe, striving to expand its influence in the Middle East, and carrying out a series of military adventures in Africa."

On September 6, China announced that by April 29 it would terminate the 1950 Sino-Soviet treaty of mutual defense. The pact was intended as a defense measure against Japan and its allies, including the United States.

Europe. On April 3, China signed its first trade agreement with the European Community (EC), not only to bring itself closer to the industrial strength of western Europe, but also, in the words of Peking, "to support its struggle against hegemony (Soviet domination)."

During the year, Europeans flocked to Peking to arrange business deals. West German firms signed a (U. S.) $4 billion contract to build and equip seven coal mines. Danish and Dutch concerns concluded agreements to expand harbors. British and West German companies submitted bids for the building of a $14 billion integrated steel mill in Hopei Province, while the French were negotiating a $12 billion loan for the purchase of French power-generating equipment.

It was in eastern Europe, the backyard of the Soviet Union, that the Chinese launched the boldest assault on the Soviet diplomatic frontier. On August 16, Chairman Hua Kuo-feng arrived in Rumania for a five-day visit. The first ruler in China's history to visit an eastern European nation, he was given a boisterous reception, with half a million Rumanians thronging the streets of Bucharest to cheer him. Hua toured major industrial plants and held lengthy talks with President Nicolae Ceauşescu. At a state dinner, Hua took the opportunity to declare that those who sought to rule the world would eventually be crushed under the iron blows of the people. It was plain that the remark was directed against the Kremlin.

Hua left Bucharest for Yugoslavia on August 21. He was warmly welcomed in Belgrade. In a statement referring to possible Soviet interven-

---

— COMMUNIST CHINA · Information Highlights —

Official Name: People's Republic of China.
Location: Central part of eastern Asia.
Area: 3,705,396 square miles (9,596,976 km²).
Population (1978 est.): 930,000,000.
Chief Cities (1974 est.): Peking, the capital, 7,600,000; Shanghai, 10,800,000; Tientsin, 4,000,000.
Government: *Chairman of the Chinese Communist Party:* Hua Kuo-feng (took office Oct. 1976). *Head of government,* Hua Kuo-feng, premier (took office April 1976). *Legislature* (unicameral)—National People's Congress.
Monetary Unit: Yüan (1.73 yüan equal U. S.$1, 1978—noncommercial rate).
Manufacturing (major products): Iron and steel, coal, machinery, cotton textiles, light industrial products.
Major Agricultural Products: Rice, wheat, corn, millet, cotton, sweet potatoes.

tion, he observed that "Yugoslavia is ready at all times to repel the enemy."

China's friendship with Yugoslavia and rapprochement with capitalist nations led to a rift with Albania, once an ideological ally.

East Asia. It was Japan also, a great economic power, that Peking was particularly eager to align with in its scheme against the Soviet Union. A significant step toward that end was the signing of a peace and friendship treaty between the two countries on August 12. Negotiations for the treaty had been suspended in 1975 because Japan was unwilling to accept the Chinese proposal that the treaty should provide against "hegemony" by a third country. Moscow raised strong objections to the hegemony clause, maintaining that it was aimed at the Soviet Union. Apparently encouraged by the United States, Japan brushed aside fears of Soviet retaliation and dispatched Foreign Minister Sunao Sonoda to Peking to sign the treaty. Under it, Japan agreed to oppose efforts by any country to establish hegemony in the Asia-Pacific region or anywhere else.

Another step taken toward closer Sino-Japanese relations was the signing of a $20 billion eight-year agreement between Peking and a Japanese trade group on February 16. China undertook to export oil and coal to Japan in exchange for Japanese plants and technology.

On May 4, Chairman Hua Kuo-feng visited North Korea. He appeared successful in drawing Pyongyang away from the USSR.

Southeast Asia. China's relations with Vietnam, once a close ally, had badly deteriorated since the end of the Vietnam War in 1975. Vietnam's war with Cambodia gave rise to the Chinese apprehension that Hanoi, backed by Moscow, was aiming to dominate Indochina.

In March, Hanoi ordered a crackdown on private commerce. Ethnic Chinese in southern Vietnam in particular were given harsh treatment. Their stores were closed, their property confiscated, and many of them forced to move to uninhabited forests. By the middle of July, 140,-000 ethnic Chinese had fled into China. Peking demanded that Vietnam immediately stop its policy of persecuting the Chinese.

On July 3, China announced the termination of all economic aid to Vietnam. Border clashes took place on August 25 and November 1. In the latter, six Chinese were killed. Peking lodged a protest with Vietnam, warning that the Vietnamese must bear responsibility if they continued their armed intrusions at the Chinese border.

The Soviet Union and Vietnam signed a friendship treaty on November 2. The parties agreed to consult each other with a view toward eliminating attacks or threats of attack to either country. The Chinese denounced the treaty as a "military pact" that threatened world peace.

China and India, hostile to each other since their border war in 1962, showed signs of reconciliation in 1978.

REPUBLIC OF CHINA

The election of Premier Chiang Ching-kuo as president of Nationalist China added strength to the administration and its policies. The new leadership called for continued economic growth and increased military capability. Foreign trade and the gross national product were expected to rise in 1978.

The normalization of relations between Washington and Peking caused Taiwan acute anxiety. The result was further isolation for the Republic of China. Nevertheless, the Nationalists were determined to continue their struggle against the Peking regime.

The New Administration. Premier Chiang Ching-kuo was elected to a six-year term as president of the Republic of China on March 21, 1978. Chiang, elder son of the late President Chiang kai-shek, received 1,184 votes out of the 1,204 cast by the Assembly.

Chiang Ching-kuo had been premier of the Nationalist Government since 1972 and chairman of the ruling Kuomintang party since 1975. Under his premiership, Taiwan had achieved its primary objective of political stability and economic prosperity. He was largely responsible for the vast construction which took place under the Ten Major Projects plan. The successful launching of that program contributed greatly to the modernization of Taiwan's economy. A capable administrator, Chiang is noted for his integrity and determination.

In his inauguration speech on May 20, the new president reaffirmed the Nationalist determination to oppose Communism. Referring to Washington's approach to normalization with Peking, he warned against any illusion that Communist China could be recruited as a balancing force against the Soviet Union. In domestic policy, he emphasized increasing national strength and improvement of the livelihood of the people.

Hsieh Tung-min, governor of Taiwan Province, was elected vice president by the National Assembly on March 22. Born in Taiwan, he had long worked in the Nationalist government and was known for his loyalty to the Kuomintang. His elevation to the vice presidency was expected further to reduce the resentment of some native Taiwanese against the political dominance of the mainlanders.

Sun Yun-suan, formerly minister of economic affairs, was nominated to be premier by President Chiang. The nomination was approved by the Legislative Yüan (parliament) on May 26, in accordance with constitutional provisions. A practical, modest man, Sun was expected to carry out the new president's policy of speeding up economic reconstruction.

The Economy. Taiwan's domestic policy was directed toward continuing economic growth, raising the standard of living, and integrating economic development with defense capabilities.

UPI

Technicians work in the control room of Nationalist China's first nuclear power plant in northern Taiwan.

Efforts were made to stabilize commodity prices and diversify foreign markets. To strengthen its trade competitiveness, Taiwan planned to move away from labor-intensive industries in favor of more sophisticated industries. The government promoted research into applied technology and the private sector assisted by putting new technology into production.

Taiwan's economy made significant progress in 1978. It was expected to achieve a 12% economic growth by year's end. Private consumer expenditures were expected to reach $11,692,-000,000, an increase of 7.9% over 1977. The number of employed persons was expected to reach 6,134,000, up by 3.1%, with an unemployment rate of about 2%.

Taiwan's two-way foreign trade in the first nine months of 1978 totaled $16,984,400,000, an increase of 32.5% over the same period a year earlier. Exports increased by 37.6% to $9,132,100,000 and imports by 27% to $7,852,-300,000, leaving a surplus of $1,279,800,000. Industrial products led the list of exports, constituting 88.8% of the total, while raw materials accounted for 68.3% of imports. The two-way foreign trade was expected to exceed $20.3 billion for the entire year.

Foreign Affairs. With most countries moving toward formal recognition of the Peking regime, Taiwan made strenuous efforts to break out of its diplomatic isolation. Although it maintained formal relations with only 23 nations, it had substantial ties with more than 140. It increased its participation in international conferences, encouraged exchange visits, and held a variety of exhibitions at home and abroad.

In its struggle with the Communists, Taiwan had depended greatly on the support and assistance of the United States, its historic ally. Gravely concerned about the U. S. inclination to normalize relations with Peking, Taiwan had made every effort to dissuade Washington from that course. The American attempt to check the Soviet Union by moving closer to Communist China was impractical, said President Chiang. Peking only wanted to "embroil the United States and the Soviet Union in a conflict which would cripple both."

Even before Washington decided to end (on Dec. 31, 1979) its defense treaty with Taiwan, its rapprochement with Peking had direct effects on Taiwan's military system. On November 6, Washington rejected Taipei's request for long-range jet fighters capable of striking the Chinese mainland. Instead it offered F-5E fighters, good for defensive purposes only.

Taiwan's relations with Saudi Arabia were further strengthened by several cooperative projects. Saudi Arabia granted loans totaling $110 million for the Taiwan Area Freeway and the island's western railway electrification project. In return, Taiwan sent experts to assist with construction projects in Saudi Arabia.

See also ASIA.

CHESTER C. TAN, *New York University*

—NATIONAL CHINA · Information Highlights—

Official Name: Republic of China.
Location: Taiwan, island off the southeastern coast of mainland China.
Area: 13,885 square miles (35,961 km²).
Population (1978 est.): 16,900,000.
Chief Cities (1977): Taipei, the capital, 2,125,046; Kaohsiung, 1,037,230; Taichung, 569,411.
Government: *Head of state,* Chiang Ching-kuo, president (installed May 1978). *Head of government,* Sun Yun-suan, premier (took office May 1978). *Legislature* (unicameral)—Legislative Yüan.
Monetary Unit: New Taiwan dollar (37 NT dollars equal U. S.$1, Jan. 1979).
Manufacturing (major products): Textiles, electronics, light manufactures, cement.
Major Agricultural Products: Sugarcane, sweet potatoes, rice, vegetables, asparagus, mushrooms.

CITIES AND URBAN AFFAIRS

The U. S. urban crisis, so prominent an issue just ten years ago, seems to have faded in the political landscape and yielded its priority to a new set of national concerns. Some might see this as a sign of the gradual amelioration of the urban problem, but as the events of 1978 again demonstrated, that interpretation would be grossly mistaken.

Fiscal Crises. Perhaps the most serious urban problem has been the fiscal crunch. New York City clearly represents the archetypal urban fiscal crisis, but the malady is found all across the United States. It is particularly acute in the older cities, such as Detroit, Philadelphia, Cleveland, St. Louis, San Francisco, and others. The steady declines in urban population (particularly the affluent population), businesses and industrial enterprises, and commercial sales, have brought with them a decline in municipal income and tax revenues. On the other hand, the cost of municipal services has risen because of inflation, the need for extended services, reasonable wage increases to public employees, the maturation of pension benefits, and a host of other reasons. The resulting crunch forced cities such as New York to extend their indebtedness to the point that they were unable to make good on municipal bonds.

In the case of New York City, the U. S. Congress agreed to an historic measure to keep the city afloat. On Aug. 8, 1978, President Carter signed into law a bill giving New York City (U. S.) $1.65 billion in federal long-term loan guarantees.

But in New York and many other cities throughout the United States, the fiscal crisis continued to cause a cutback of municipal employees and a sharp reduction in public services. These often included such "essential" services as police and fire departments, but also such services to individuals as education, health, welfare, and special programs for the disadvantaged. In short, the urban poor and the cities themselves (governments and public employees) paid the costs of an urban problem whose origins likely lie far beyond local confines.

Other Problems. It was officially estimated that by the end of 1978 the U. S. national unemployment rate would be just below 6%, a decrease of about 2.5% from 1975. While unemployment varies by region, the official rate in older urban areas tends to be in excess of 8%. Independent, nongovernmental surveys, however, place it between 11 and 15%. More dramatically, among large segments of the urban population, such as black and Hispanic youth, unemployment may be as high as 40%. This "hard core" jobless category appears the least affected by economic stimulus and training programs.

Though inadequately explored, there is doubtless a connection between unemployment and crime rates. Property crimes, which have risen faster than most other categories, seem to be particularly associated with unemployment. With unemployment and crime rates exceeding national averages, cities are burdened with the costs of welfare and law enforcement.

In the area of education, the most celebrated of current urban problems is school busing. The irony of the busing controversy is that it merely reflects the deeper and politically less manageable problem of residential segregation. Nevertheless, each September brings the outbreak of new resistance to plans for school busing. Having been upheld regularly by the courts, these plans are carried through and usually, save for more acrimonious situations, such as that in Boston, one year's controversy tends to fade into the next. However, one of the most common solutions to the problem has been "white flight," or the creation of new, private, effectively segregated schools. The real problem has not been addressed and probably will not be until the issue of residential segregation is confronted. The

Following a face-lifting, Chicago's old Water Tower was due to open as a visitors' information center.

UPI

City Hall steps, New York, August 8: Flanked by Mayor Edward Koch (*left*), Mrs. Carter, and N. Y. Gov. Hugh Carey, President Carter exhibits the just-signed New York City Loan Guarantee Act.

UPI

U. S. Supreme Court contributed to this standoff by ruling against any requirement for metropolitan area-wide school district integration. In effect, urban minorities and the less affluent white ethnic populations of the inner cities have been left to fight it out among themselves, while suburban schools maintain the homogeneity of the neighborhoods.

Curiously, the elderly living in cities share many of the problems that plague school age youth and the unemployed. Living on meager or fixed incomes, and often requiring such urban services as transportation and health care to be close at hand, many elderly persons are unable to escape the cities to retire. Sadly, many are also unable to maintain their homes in the city as rents and property taxes rise. Forced to sell their homes, their last retreat is to retirement or nursing homes, themselves the subject of debate.

There is a tendency to regard many of these problems as the natural outcome of changing tastes and market forces which a nominally free society cannot prevent. In fact, quite the opposite is true. The federal government has intervened on a massive scale to subsidize the construction and purchase of single family suburban housing, as well as to make these areas convenient to downtown employment and commerce on federally funded expressways. The private sector has contributed to this deliberately constructed urban form through practices of "disinvestment," whereby the funds raised by urban banks and profits accruing to urban mortgage lenders are used to finance suburban development. The much deplored practice of "redlining" —denying mortgage and home improvement loans to "blighted" or (racially) "transitional" zones within the central city—is but one of the cruder forms of urban disinvestment which, through a variety of political and economic stratagems, has helped to create inequality.

Policies and Prospects. In 1978, the United States still had nothing that could be properly termed a national urban policy. The programs of the 1960's—including model cities, urban renewal, manpower training, and community development—have, for the most part, fallen into disuse. The urban policy of the 1970's—revenue sharing—has proven to be ineffectual with respect to the urban poor and the fundamental problems of the cities. General revenue sharing returns to the states and cities an amount in federal dollars determined by a formula based on population size, per capita income, and tax effort. Under this system, cities and states able to tax themselves more heavily will receive a larger federal allocation. Moreover, localities are not constrained in how to spend the subsidies, and this has resulted in lack of funding for services to individuals and programs to assist the urban poor.

The most far reaching plan for a national urban policy was contained in a document issued by President Carter in March 1978, the "New Partnership to Conserve America's Communities." The omnibus plan called for cooperation among various levels of government, the private sector, and citizen groups. It called for a National Development Bank; tax credits for urban investors and employers; aggressive action against redlining; supplementary fiscal assistance to protect cities from the type of crisis that hit New York; the location of new federal facilities in inner cities; and programs to revitalize urban neighborhoods.

Despite the impressive diversity of Carter's overall plan, Congress rejected most of the individual proposals. Perhaps one reason was that such well-intentioned measures place unrealistically high hopes on capital investment strategies. Some of the more persistent and fundamental urban problems may require more aggressive and redistributive action from government. In the meantime, U. S. cities can be expected to continue to languish in muted crisis, their most serious ills scarcely touched by current versions of decentralization and economic liberalism.

JOHN WALTON, *University of California, Davis*

CIVIL LIBERTIES AND CIVIL RIGHTS

In 1978, the people and courts of the United States were faced with a series of delicate issues pertaining to civil liberties and civil rights. All in all, it was a year of shifting alliances, lack of cohesion, and uncertain directions.

Affirmative Action. In a 5–4 vote, the Supreme Court decided that Allan Bakke, a Caucasian, was illegally discriminated against in being denied admission to a California medical school. In a 154-page decision, expressing six different opinions, the court also held that race can nevertheless be taken into account by college admissions officers. As in the areas of reapportionment, capital punishment, and obscenity, the court appeared to be zigzagging into a judicial quagmire. Were all quotas dead or only those for which previous discrimination had been proven? Did the decision apply only to educational affirmative action or to industrial employment policies as well?

On the final day of its 1977–78 term, the Supreme Court let stand a 1973 decree requiring AT&T to hire and promote more women and minorities and to pay $42 million in back wages to its discrimination victims. The position of the court was still in doubt, however, as the plan was due to expire in a short time anyway.

Women's Rights. With time running out on the seven year ratification period for the Equal Rights Amendment (ERA) and with little progress in the unratifying states, proponents sought from Congress legislation to extend the life of the proposed amendment. In the absence of ERA, however, supporters of women's rights had an uphill battle trying to convince the (predominantly male) legislative and judicial branches of their claim to equity.

One area of success for feminists was a Supreme Court ruling that unequal contributions by men and women to employer-operated pension plans discriminate unlawfully against women under the 1964 Civil Rights Act. What effect the court's decision will have on pension and insurance plans in which the contributions of men and women are equal but the payout is different, is not clear. Most private pension plans will not be affected because they are noncontributory and are based on earnings and years of service rather than the sex of the employee. Also, insurance companies may still be able to use male-female actuarial tables for policies they sell directly to customers, since that practice is not barred under the Civil Rights Act.

Rights of Other Minorities. For almost one year, a small group of Chicago Nazis sought permits to stage a march, first in Chicago's Marquette Park and then in the predominantly Jewish suburb of Skokie. Opponents tried to bar the demonstrations because of the prospect of physical or psychological damage. The American Civil Liberties Union, at the cost of membership and funds, maintained that the right of peaceful demonstration took priority over maintenance of the public peace. Eventually, all policies and ordinances designed to thwart the Nazi march were invalidated by the courts.

For the nation's homosexuals, 1978 was a year on the defensive. After the repeal of a gay rights ordinance in Miami, Fla., in 1977, foes put similar propositions on the ballot in Eugene, Ore.; Wichita, Kans.; and St. Paul, Minn. The results were the same. Though New York City's mayor, Edward Koch, announced support for employment rights for gays, opponents in California sought a statewide referendum on that issue.

Freedom of the Press. The attitude of the Burger court seemed to be that the press has no more right to information than the general public. In one case, the Supreme Court ruled that the press has no special access to prisons for the purposes of interviewing inmates or bringing in cameras and sound equipment. In another case, however, it ruled that the press cannot be prevented from reporting information that is already in their possession.

Probably the most heated reaction from the press came in the wake of a Supreme Court decision that the police may obtain a warrant and conduct an unannounced search of newspaper offices for evidence of a crime, even if the paper and its employees are not suspected of any criminal activity. The only requirement is that the police have probable cause for believing that the paper has such evidence. Opponents of the decision feared intimidation of the press and the loss of its vital confidential sources, while law enforcers shopped around for compliant judges who would issue the warrant. Bills were introduced to require a subpoena (to be granted after an adversary court proceeding) instead of a search warrant.

The Supreme Court's 1972 denial of a reporter's right to withhold information from confidential sources was reflected in the case of a *New York Times* reporter who was sent to jail for contempt of court in a murder trial. The *Times* itself was also heavily fined, as the reporter refused to turn over his files pertaining to several mysterious deaths in a New Jersey hospital.

The often divided Supreme Court, in another 5–4 decision, upheld the power of the Federal Communications Commission to restrict radio broadcasts that are "offensive," even if not "obscene."

Defendant's Rights. In cases pertaining to law enforcement, the Supreme Court came out in favor of the defendant more than 50% of the time. (In its previous five terms it did so only one third of the time.) The court again grappled with the death penalty, striking down the Ohio statute for not allowing consideration of all possible mitigating factors.

MARTIN GRUBERG
University of Wisconsin, Oshkosh

COINS AND COIN COLLECTING

Rarities made news in 1978. Two specimens of the 1913 United States Liberty Head Nickel, a coin of which just five are known, changed hands. One was sold for $200,000, and in Washington, D. C., the Smithsonian Institution announced the receipt of another specimen, the gift of Hon. and Mrs. R. Henry Norweb of Cleveland, Ohio.

The American Numismatic Society of New York received as a gift an 1804 dollar, called "the King of American coins," a piece valued at several hundred thousand dollars, and other properties from the Chase Manhattan Bank Collection.

The N. M. Kaufman Collection was auctioned by Rarcoa and realized more than $2.25 million, including $140,000 paid for a rare variety of an 1825 U. S. $5 gold piece. In August, Bowers & Ruddy Galleries of Los Angeles sold at auction the Robert E. Branigan Estate Collection for more than $2 million. A 1915 commemorative coin set issued at the Panama Pacific International Exposition sold for $70,000.

Elsewhere, a Civil War token issued privately in 1863 sold for $1,840, a record price for an item of this nature.

In June the Memphis Coin Club hosted the second International Paper Money show, with hundreds of enthusiasts attending. The Smithsonian Institution received a collection of 800 pieces of U. S. currency which have a face value of more than $500,000 and a substantially higher numismatic value. These notes were saved by U. S. Treasury officials years ago when late 19th century bank notes were being redeemed. Included were many one-of-a-kind items.

Breaking precedent, the Philadelphia Mint offered to the public for $20 each Assay Commission medals of the previous year, 1977. In earlier years, medals of this type had been distributed only to people participating in the event.

Toward year's end the U. S. Treasury announced the adoption of a new small-size dollar coin, midway in diameter between the present quarter and half dollar pieces. Production was expected to begin in 1979. Featuring the portrait of Susan B. Anthony, the piece is intended to facilitate transactions in vending machines and other coin-operated devices and to lessen the public need for $1 notes. The larger Eisenhower dollar, minted since 1971, will be discontinued.

The Soviet Union unveiled an elaborate coinage program for the 1980 Olympic Games.

The new "Official ANA Grading Guide," released by the American Numismatic Association, received wide acceptance.

Toward year's end the rise in the price of gold spurred additional interest, particularly from those who purchase coins of gold and silver metal as a hedge against inflation. Throughout the year, collecting activity continued at a brisk pace.

Q. DAVID BOWERS
Bowers & Ruddy Galleries, Inc.

COLOMBIA

The last vestiges of the National Front, under which the Liberal and Conservative parties shared political power for 20 years, came to an end in 1978. The year also saw the election of a new Congress and a new president. Both were immediately faced with a near breakdown of social institutions, brought about by escalating terrorism and increased drug traffic.

Politics. The Congressional elections held in March also served as an indirect means of choosing the Liberal party candidate for the July 4 presidential election. The two leading Liberals, former president Carlos Lleras Restrepo and Gabriel Turbay Ayala, each submitted complete slates of 311 candidates. Although barely 30% of the electorate voted, Turbay won handily. Meanwhile, the Conservative party rallied behind the candidacy of Belisario Betancur.

The presidential election, marked by 60% voter abstention, resulted in a narrow victory for Turbay and the Liberals. Sworn in as president on August 7, Turbay became the first president in 20 years not bound by the National Front agreement to appoint equal numbers of Conservatives and Liberals to the cabinet. Because of his narrow victory, however, the new president appointed ministers from both parties and the military.

Economy. The Colombian economy returned to an annual growth rate of between 6 and 7%. Inflation also eased during the year. Estimates of the annual rate of inflation at year's end were about 20%. Tax revenues were up by 25.7% during the first six months of 1978. Coffee, despite a bumper crop, produced 24% less in foreign exchange earnings during the first six months because of lower world prices. The exchange rate for the peso remained fairly firm at 38.95 per U. S. dollar.

Narcotics. The production and export of illegal narcotics—mainly marijuana and cocaine—were probably Colombia's major industries and major problems in 1978. One estimate placed the annual trade in these commodities at over (U. S.) $2 billion.

ERNEST A. DUFF
Randolph-Macon Woman's College

————COLOMBIA • Information Highlights————

Official Name: Republic of Colombia.
Location: Northwest South America.
Area: 439,737 square miles (1,138,914 km²).
Population (1978 est.): 25,800,000.
Chief Cities (1976 est.): Bogotá, the capital, 3,102,000; Medellin, 1,195,000; Cali, 1,003,000.
Government: *Head of state and government,* Gabriel Turbay Ayala, president (took office Aug. 1978). *Legislature*—Congress: Senate and Chamber of Representatives.
Monetary Unit: Peso (38.95 pesos equal U. S.$1, Oct. 1978).
Manufactures (major products): Textiles, beverages, processed food, clothing and footwear, chemicals, metal products, cement.
Agriculture (major products): Coffee, bananas, rice, cotton, sugarcane, tobacco, corn, plantains, flowers.

Richard D. Lamm (D) was elected to a second term as governor, of Colorado. He defeated state Sen. Ted Strickland.

© 1978 "THE DENVER POST"

COLORADO

A continued economic boom fueled by the development of natural resources brought expanded economic opportunity to Colorado in 1978. A rash of problems was also connected with the swift growth. Uranium and coal development paced extractive industries increasing their Colorado operations. But the greatest impact continued to be in the Denver metropolitan area, as resource-related industries expanded their corporate, research, and support facilities to underpin mounting operations throughout the Western states.

Water has always been a concern in this semiarid state, and many farmers began to fear they would lose agricultural water to industrial or municipal interests as the boom continued.

Gov. Richard D. Lamm, though a Democrat, criticized the Carter administration's veto of a number of Western water projects, including three in Colorado. Lamm's independent stance kept him from being tarred by President Jimmy Carter's low standing in the West.

In the fall, Lamm effected a remarkable political comeback from his poor showing in 1975–76, winning a crushing 3–2 reelection victory over his Republican challenger, state Sen. Ted Strickland. Strickland's campaign was plagued by a series of public gaffes. The governor's landslide, however, did not help Democrats in the legislature. The Republican party kept control over both houses, boosting its Senate edge to 22–13 and its House margin to 38–27.

U. S. Rep. Bill Armstrong, a popular conservative Republican, moved to the U. S. Senate with a nearly 3–2 victory over one-term incumbent Democrat Floyd Haskell, a liberal. Three Democrats and two Republicans were elected to the U. S. House of Representatives.

Drought continued to hurt much of the southern and eastern parts of the state, though it eased elsewhere. Water rationing continued in most of the Denver metropolitan area, not because of a shortage of raw water but because proposed new treatment plants have been held up by environmental controversies.

The American Agricultural Movement, originally organized in Springfield, Colo., led demonstrations throughout the state and nation to dramatize the plight of U. S. farmers caught between soaring costs and dwindling prices. But after much talk of a "farm strike," virtually all returned to their fields when the spring weather permitted. In contrast to embattled grain farmers, cattlemen prospered as prices rose after years of poor returns.

The Denver Center for the Performing Arts opened the new 2,700 seat Boettcher Concert Hall. The asymmetrical "surround" design won plaudits of the visiting critics as one of the nation's finest. The hall is the centerpiece of a complex that will include three theaters and a cinema. (See also Music.)

Construction was well advanced on the federal Solar Energy Research Institute near Golden, Colo., which President Carter visited on "Sun Day."

There was widespread concern over air pollution in the Denver area but the legislature and governor could not agree on a proposed program to deal with it. Governor Lamm vetoed a Strickland-proposed bill as too weak.

"Broncomania" was dampened but not extinguished when the Denver Broncos were defeated, 27–10, by the Dallas Cowboys in the 1978 Super Bowl.

BOB EWEGEN
Editorial Writer, The Denver Post

─────── **COLORADO · Information Highlights** ───────

Area: 104,247 square miles (270,000 km²).
Population (Jan. 1978 est.): 2,643,000.
Chief Cities (1970 census): Denver, the capital, 514,678; Colorado Springs, 135,060; Pueblo, 97,453.
Government (1978): *Chief Officers*—governor, Richard D. Lamm (D); lt. gov., George L. Brown (D). *General Assembly*—Senate, 35 members; House of Representatives, 65 members.
Education (1977–78): *Enrollment*—public elementary schools, 287,613 pupils; public secondary, 274,194; colleges and universities, 153,967 students. *Public school expenditures,* $1,186,681,000 ($1,552 per pupil).
State Finances (fiscal year 1977): *Revenues,* $2,394,-258,000; *expenditures,* $2,151,503,000.
Personal Income (1977): $18,752,000,000; per capita, $7,160.
Labor Force (July 1978): *Nonagricultural wage and salary earners,* 1,034,800; *unemployed,* 72,800 (5.5% of total force).

The roof of the sports arena of the Hartford Civic Center collapsed under the pressure of heavy snow and ice. A redesigned structure is scheduled for completion in January 1980.

UPI

CONNECTICUT

The elections, new legislation, a near tragedy in the state capital, and a crippling snowstorm were the major news developments in Connecticut in 1978.

Politics. Gov. Ella T. Grasso, who four years earlier was the first woman to be elected without prior appointment, became the first woman governor to be reelected in her own right. Grasso defeated the Republican candidate, U. S. Rep. Ronald Sarasin, by almost 200,000 votes. Her victory capped a successful year for her party. The Democrats won five of the state's six congressional seats and increased their control of the state legislature.

Legislature. Education remained the key problem facing the Connecticut General Assembly. The state Supreme Court ordered Connecticut to revamp its funding of public education so as to equalize educational opportunities and offerings among the communities. Some $20 million was appropriated from the state treasury to meet this obligation. A school finance advisory panel was scheduled to report in early 1979 on ways to satisfy permanently the court's dictates.

In 1978, Connecticut became the fifth state in the country to pass a "bottle bill." To encourage recycling, state lawmakers placed a 5¢ deposit on beverage containers. The law will not take effect until 1980.

A controversial new law banning Sunday shopping, except between Thanksgiving and Christmas, and amended to exclude those who worship on Saturday, took effect on October 1. For the third time in two years, however, state courts struck down the "blue laws." The act was expected to be rewritten in 1979.

Other major accomplishments of the legislature were a $5 million pilot program to purchase developmental rights of state farmland and an annual automobile inspection program to begin in 1980. The latter was designed to curb air pollution in Connecticut, the worst in the country except for Los Angeles.

Economy. Under the stewardship of Governor Grasso and the General Assembly, the state experienced another good fiscal year. The budget surplus, $73.4 million in 1977, increased to an estimated $86.3 million in 1978. Unemployment, 6.7% in August 1977, dipped to 4.3% in September 1978. The 1977 state per capita income climbed to $8,061, second highest in the country. A $2,135,000,000 budget, the largest in Connecticut history, was passed by the assembly and signed by the governor.

Coliseum Roof Collapse. A near tragedy occurred on January 18, when the 1,400-ton steel and concrete roof of the Hartford Civic Center Coliseum collapsed under the weight of built up ice and snow. The coliseum was empty and no one was injured, although some 4,700 spectators had attended a University of Connecticut basketball game several hours earlier.

Blizzard. On February 6 and 7, less than three weeks after the civic center roof fell in, up to 25 inches (64 cm) of snow fell on Connecticut in less than 30 hours. Governor Grasso ordered all roads and highways closed, and National Guardsmen were airlifted in to help with the cleanup. Nine persons died.

Other Developments. A teachers' strike in Bridgeport kept schools closed for 19 days, and 260 faculty members were jailed for ignoring a judge's back-to-work order.

"Yankee Doodle" was named the state song.

TOM AHERN, *"Danbury News-Times"*

CONNECTICUT · Information Highlights

Area: 5,009 square miles (12,973 km²).
Population (Jan. 1978 est.): 3,111,000.
Chief Cities (1970 census): Hartford, the capital, 158,-017; Bridgeport, 156,542; New Haven, 137,707.
Government (1978): *Chief Officers*—governor, Ella T. Grasso (D); lt. gov., Robert K. Killian (D). *General Assembly*—Senate, 36 members; House of Representatives, 151 members.
Education (1977–78): *Enrollment*—public elementary schools, 416,769 pupils; public secondary, 199,620; colleges and universities, 149,660 students. *Public school expenditures,* $1,650,000,000 ($1,780 per pupil).
State Finances (fiscal year 1977): *Revenues,* $2,857,-967,000; *expenditures,* $2,656,060,000.
Personal Income (1977) $25,055,000,000; per capita, $8,061.
Labor Force (July 1978): *Nonagricultural wage and salary earners,* 1,326,200; *unemployed,* 67,900 (4.4% of total force).

165

Landmarks of the United States

As the American people were celebrating the 200th anniversary of the Declaration of Independence, it became increasingly clear that they were embarked upon a new revolution—this one a quiet, grassroots revolution in values. The ethic of conservation was being applied to the built environment. Historic preservation had come of age.

All across the country today, individuals, businesses, and preservation organizations are rehabilitating and restoring residential and commercial structures, adapting sound old buildings to new and profitable uses, establishing officially-designated historic districts to protect the character of neighborhoods, saving and restoring old ships, training young people in such old skills as cabinetmaking and rigging sailboats, and operating historic museum properties. The National Trust for Historic Preservation estimates that in 1978 there were at least two million Americans engaged in some aspect of historic preservation.

An early preservation effort in the private sector was undertaken by the Mount Vernon Ladies' Association of the Union, which was chartered in 1856 and raised some (U. S.) $200,-000 to buy and endow George Washington's home and plantation and to open an historic museum. Individual historic properties were the focus of private efforts for almost a century. These were obtained by nonprofit organizations for patriotic, cultural, and environmental reasons. The National Trust estimates that there are some 4,000 historic structures open to the public today.

Involvement by the federal government began in 1889 when Congress authorized the president to protect the Casa Grande ruins in Arizona by removing the land from public settlement or sale. The Antiquities Act of 1906 was the first major preservation legislation, and in the Historic Sites Act of 1935, Congress declared that "it is a national policy to preserve for public use historic sites, buildings, and objects of national significance for the inspiration and benefit of the people of the United States." In 1949, Congress chartered the National Trust for Historic Preservation as a private organization to encourage and assist the private sector in its preservation efforts. In 1966, Congress authorized matching grants to help states survey and inventory their historic resources, to help with acquisition and restoration of officially-designated historic structures, and to help the National Trust in its efforts. The endeavor is administrated by historic preservation officers in each state and territory and the District of Columbia.

Since 1966, the historic preservation movement has exploded. At that time there were only some 100 communities in the United States that had commissions empowered to oversee and protect landmarks and historic districts. Today the number approaches 600, and 22 of the nation's 25 largest cities have such commissions. Examples of historic districts are the Vieux Carré in New Orleans, with its 18th and 19th century buildings; the Pioneer Square-Skid Road District, a late 19th century commercial center in Seattle; and the Frank Lloyd Wright-Prairie School of Architecture District in Oak Park, Ill.

Landmarks may be designated by federal, state, or local governments. There are some 1,500 National Historic Landmarks designated by the U. S. secretary of the interior. Among these are the Alaska Native Brotherhood Hall in Sitka; the Scott Joplin Residence at 2658-A Morgan Street in St. Louis, Mo.; the Martin Luther King, Jr., Historic District in Atlanta, Ga., which includes the birthplace and gravesite of the noted civil rights leader; and the Ford (Motor Company) River Rouge Complex in Dearborn, Mich.

Perhaps the most widely-known structure designated by a city as a landmark is Grand Central Terminal in New York. In 1978, its owners argued in the U. S. Supreme Court that the designation, which prohibited them from altering the station's appearance without permission from the New York City Landmark Commission, unconstitutionally deprived them of their property. In an opinion of vast significance to the preservation movement, the court held that the New York City law was not unconstitutional.

In addition to officially-designated landmarks, many lesser structures of local importance are being saved and put to new use. Among the most famous are Ghiradelli Square, a former chocolate factory in San Francisco; Trolley Square, a shopping and entertainment complex in Salt Lake City's old trolley barns; and the Faneuil Hall-Quincy Market in Boston, now a thriving downtown shopping and restaurant complex. Old train stations have been converted into offices, schools, and, in Richmond, Va., even a science museum. Old schools are being used for housing, as are old wharf buildings, a piano factory in Boston, and a high-rise office building in Los Angeles.

The demolition of old urban buildings has not yet been halted, but it has been slowed. The high costs of new construction, the impossibility of duplicating the craftsmanship of earlier years, the sterility of much contemporary urban architecture, tax benefits, and, most of all, a new-found respect and affection for older buildings, have contributed to the current boom in the historic preservation movement in the United States.

JAMES BIDDLE

COURTESY, LOUISIANA OFFICE OF TOURISM

In recent years, historic preservation has come of age in the United States. The Vieux Carré, New Orleans' old French Quarter, *top*, has been designated as an historic district; the old railroad station in Richmond, Va., has been turned into a science museum; and Ford Motor Company's River Rouge Complex, a very large, concentrated industrial area in Dearborn, Mich., has been classified as an historic landmark.

COURTESY, THE SCIENCE MUSEUM OF VIRGINIA

COURTESY, FORD MOTOR COMPANY

CONSUMERISM

The major problem confronting American consumers in 1978 was also the number one economic problem, inflation (*see* feature article, pages 10–16). Even though consumers were gloomy about inflation and the chances of curbing it, they were not gloomy enough to stop buying.

The public reaction against inflation was also spreading into a reaction against what was believed to be excessive government regulatory control that was pushing prices up. A broad spectrum of government regulations was coming under question: were they accomplishing their purpose, or simply feeding inflation? There is heated debate over the cost to consumers of much government regulation. One must be objective in measuring the cost/benefit aspects of such regulation. Business cannot afford to be over-regulated, and consumers cannot risk being exposed to an economy that is devoid of adequate regulation, either of the safety of the products they buy, or of a marketplace that permits deceptive practices and price fixing.

The White House. On Feb. 8, 1978, the House of Representatives, by a vote of 227 to 188, defeated a bill to establish an office of consumer representation. This bill was basically a watered-down consumer agency bill. President Carter's failure to get some form of a consumer protection bill through Congress forced him to redirect his efforts in the area of consumers affairs. On Aug. 12, 1978, the president named his Special Assistant for Consumer Affairs, Esther Peterson, to serve also as the Director of the Office of Consumer Affairs. In addition, the president asked his special assistant to prepare recommendations for strengthening the consumer representation functions of the various federal agencies and for streamlining and improving the consumer functions of the federal bureaucracy.

Consumer Laws. Consumer legislation passed during 1978 included a bill to create a consumer cooperative bank which will use federal funds of up to $300 million to get started. The proponents of this bill believe the project will broaden competition, lower prices, and improve the quality of goods and services. In addition, an electronic funds transfer (EFT) bill was passed. This legislation would protect a consumer from losing more than $50 if his or her EFT card is stolen or improperly used. It would also require that a receipt be given to the user at the time of an EFT transaction, and it would require that a detailed monthly statement be provided.

Consumer Citizen Participation. Certain federal agencies and offices are increasingly trying to subsidize consumer participation in government proceedings. The Federal Trade Commission (FTC) has an on-going program funded for the purpose of consumer participation. In addition, the Consumer Product Safety Commission, the Community Services Administration, the Department of State, and the National Highway Traffic Safety Administration have started funding such participation in regulatory hearings and proceedings. It is hoped that these programs will generate valuable contributions and give the consumer a better chance to be heard.

Generic Products. During 1978 supermarkets across the United States were moving toward buying and selling of more products by their generic names instead of their brand names. Generic products have very plain labels indicating the type of product inside, carry no brand name, and sell for considerably less than brand name products. For example, while a "no-name" brand or generic can of cream style golden corn was priced at 19¢ a can, the brand name products were selling at 34¢ and 39¢. The generic product label stated, "This corn may vary in color and consistency. It is suitable for regular home meals." The products were comparable in nutrition. Cost-conscious consumers were buying generic products at such a pace that supermarkets were having difficulty in keeping them in stock.

Advertising by Professionals. Historically, professionals, such as medical doctors, dentists, ophthalmologists, optometrists, opticians, lawyers, and certified public accountants, have been prohibited, by state laws or professional codes of ethics, from advertising. In 1978 the U. S. Supreme Court and the FTC stipulated that such prohibitions are an infringement of freedom of speech, and that such prohibitions are anticompetitive and not in the best interests of consumers. There has been no great rush by professionals to advertise their services and fees, but some have begun to advertise and are giving consumers information about the services they offer and the fees they charge.

Deceptive Advertising. An FTC rule, upheld by the Supreme Court, stipulated that Warner-Lambert Company, the manufacturer of Listerine, must spend $10 million to advertise that their mouthwash "will not help prevent colds or sore throats or lessen their severity," as it had claimed, or else stop advertising altogether. Warner-Lambert chose to include the FTC statement in future Listerine ads.

Canada. The Canadian Parliament passed amendments to its medical device regulations requiring manufacturers of such medical devices to submit data to the government on the safety and effectiveness of the devices. In addition, the manufacturers must receive notice from the government that they are in compliance with the law *prior* to marketing the product. Parliament also sought to control product size proliferation by enacting a packaging law, limiting the packaging of peanut butter to just seven sizes, ranging from 250 grams (.5 lb) to two kilograms (4.4 lbs). Previously there were 20 different packaging sizes for the product.

STEWART M. LEE
Chairman, Department of Economics and Business Administration, Geneva College

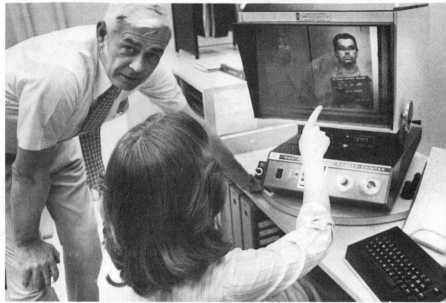

UPI

Law enforcement employees in St. Louis make use of up-to-date computer equipment. A description of a suspect is typed on a keyboard; the computer responds with color photos suggesting 29 possibles from its memory system of more than 12,000 persons previously arrested in St. Louis County.

CRIME

"Apprehension in America over crime appears to be on the decline for the first time in a decade," Louis Harris reported to the Joint Economic Committee of Congress in 1978. The assumption was based on Harris public opinion polls. Harris found that in smaller towns and in the U. S. South and West generally there was a slight increase in citizen fear of crime, but that nationally the downward trend was pronounced. A Gallup poll survey found the same condition, noting that there was a "significant decrease" in 1978, as compared with earlier periods, in the number of people who believe that there is more crime in the neighborhood in which they live. Crime issues also virtually disappeared from the 1978 political campaigns, reversing a trend that began in the 1966 elections.

Various interpretations are offered to account for these developments. "People in the big cities have gotten used to crime," one public opinion pollster believes. Another thinks that concern with inflation now overshadows fear of crime. As for political campaigns, opposing candidates often neutralized crime as an issue, with all adopting a similar position, favoring more law enforcement officers, tougher judges, and longer and mandatory prison sentences. At the same time, the public appears to be more sophisticated in its understanding that control of crime will not yield to simple solutions, and that changes in public policy will make only a very small dent in national crime rates.

Career Criminals. Efforts to determine where resources might best be used have been combined with the tendency to "get tough" with apprehended criminals. To this end, researchers at the Rand Corporation in Santa Monica, Calif.,

have been studying "career criminals," persons with long criminal records. The researchers found that the 49 prisoners serving time for robbery in one state institution who also had a previous prison record had been responsible during the past 20 years for a total of 10,000 serious crimes, or an average of about 200 offenses each. The offenders did not show a pattern of crime specialization, but rather moved from one type of offense to another. The researchers discovered that seriousness and frequency of juvenile delinquency were strongly related to the likelihood that a person would have a high rate of adult criminal behavior.

Interviews by the Rand group with 624 persistent criminal offenders housed in five state institutions found them listing economic factors—unemployment, debts, and the need for a regular income—as the primary motivation for their crimes. Second on the list were things such as "excitement" and "kicks," including a desire for money which could be used for high living and the purchase of drugs/alcohol. Fits of temper and passion were placed lowest on the list of reported motives for criminal behavior.

The social stability of a person was found to relate directly to the likelihood that he would violate the law. Steady employment, a tranquil marriage, and continuing residence in the same place correlated highly with lesser amounts of crime. Most inmates interviewed by the Rand team verbally supported the value of criminal laws, which they agreed were necessary for public safety. But they were critical of the courts, saying that judicial procedures did not adequately protect the rights of defendants. The study found that for the 624 persons the chance of arrest for any single criminal offense ran from 21% for armed robbery, to 10% for assault or rape, to 7% for burglary, to 6% for forgery, and to only .02% for sale of drugs.

The Rand group, which will continue its work until 1981, does not believe that "career criminals" can be identified prior to their violation of the law. The best predictor of their behavior proved to be their own descriptions of themselves. Demographic information—age, amount of education, and marital status—was much less valuable for foretelling which persons would engage in criminal acts. The researchers reached only 40% accuracy in forecasting who might commit future crimes within the inmate group.

Battered Women. The feminist movement, which several years ago helped focus public attention on the crime of rape, today is concentrating reformist energy upon the plight of women who are victims of intrafamily violence. Feminists insist that the laws do not adequately protect women from assaults within the home, and that the police avoid interfering in family disputes, often leaving wives at the mercy of drunk and abusive husbands. Women who do not have independent funds to support themselves may feel that they have no choice but to remain in a house or an apartment with a violent husband. The feminist groups are calling for more effective injunctive laws to force abusive husbands to abandon the family house. They are also demanding more criminal prosecutions of husbands and other abusive men who do not obey court orders to leave victimized women alone.

Several court cases arose during the year in which women who had killed their husbands claimed that their actions were a legitimate response to long-standing and insufferable abuse. The Center for Women Policy Studies in Washington, D. C., suggested that self-defense might be a reasonable plea for battered women who retaliate lethally against their husbands. The law indicates that for self-defense "deadly force" may be met with equivalent deadly force. A Fort Lauderdale, Fla., case was typical of those involving such circumstances. The defendant testified that she had emptied a gun into her husband's body while he lay injured on the front lawn because he had come after her with a kitchen knife. Her husband's two former wives testified on her behalf as to his violent nature, and she was acquitted. The developing legal theory is that a woman with a weapon, because of her size and her attitudes toward violence and aggression, is only evenly matched with a man less well armed or not at all armed.

Arson. The fastest growing crime in the United States is said to be arson. Authorities employ the term "epidemic" to describe the spread of fires that are set intentionally, either to harm people and property or to defraud insurance companies. It is estimated that arson accounts for between 500 and 1,000 deaths and for $2.5 to $4.5 billion (U. S.) in property damage each year. A *modus operandi* of "torches," persons who engage in arson for profit, is to locate businessmen in financial trouble and suggest that they can save themselves by collecting insurance for a fire and the "loss" of merchandise. Techniques of professional firebugs include drilling holes in the rafters of a building and filling them with magnesium, which explodes or burns readily on contact with water. A fire is then started in the usual way. When the firemen arrive, the water from the hoses causes the magnesium to blow up and destroy the building.

Some police departments have formed special arson patrols to keep an eye on the headquarters and supply warehouses of companies that are known to be in financial straits. Arson is also common in decaying inner cities where homeowners find that their property has depreciated below the price for which it is insured. In the Bronx, N. Y., more than 30,000 buildings have been abandoned and burned during the past decade. Of all fires believed to be incendiary or of a suspicious nature, only 1% result in criminal convictions. Efforts have been made in the U. S. Congress to define arson as a major crime in order to focus greater attention on it and secure more resources for combating it.

White-Collar Crime. There was stepped-up attention during the year to white-collar crime, offenses such as corruption, bribery, overbilling to government programs, and antitrust violations. In a June speech, President Carter noted that "powerful white-collar criminals cheat consumers of millions of dollars. Public officials who abuse their high rank damage the integrity of our nation in profound and long-lasting ways."

Barbara Williams, mother of four, was charged with filing welfare claims for 34 children at 8 different welfare offices in a swindle of about $250,000.

UPI

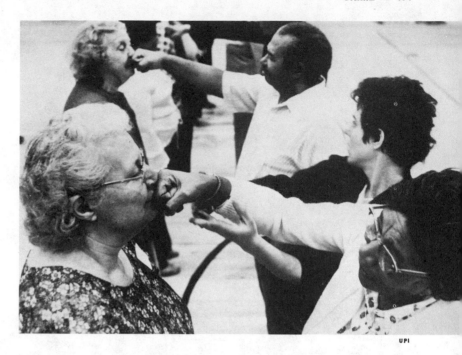

A "self defense for the elderly" class is held at a recreational center in Detroit. Crime against the elderly remained a serious U. S. problem.

The president also noted that such "big-shot crooks" often manage to escape the consequences of their acts. He called for a program concerned with the enforcement of laws regulating professional and political behavior.

A Treasury Department statement underlined the financial costs of one type of white-collar crime. It indicated that $16.3 billion more was paid out by banks in interest and $2.9 billion more in dividends than was reported by U. S. taxpayers to the Internal Revenue Service. The resulting loss in federal tax revenue was estimated to be almost the same as the amount involved in so-called "street" crimes, such as robbery. But the government said that it would not beef up enforcement efforts because this might "generate taxpayer resentment so great as to jeopardize the very foundation of our entire system of voluntary compliance." Testifying before the Subcommittee on Crime of the House Committee on the Judiciary in June, one witness labeled the Treasury Department statement "doublespeak" and observed that its moral seemed to be that if enough powerful people are crooks their potential unhappiness at being found out will guarantee them immunity from government prosecution.

LEAA Work. A 15-month grant from the Law Enforcement Assistance Administration (LEAA) was given to Albert J. Reiss, Jr., and Albert D. Biderman, both of the Bureau of Social Science Research in Washington, D. C., to explore methods for establishing a national statistical reporting system on the extent and nature of white-collar crime. The two researchers plan to examine reporting procedures for 35 federal agencies to determine criteria for calculating rates of white-collar crime.

A reorganization of LEAA, target of numerous attacks by President Carter during his presidential campaign, was proposed by the president in July. The proposed legislation would "streamline and redirect the LEAA program by simplifying the grant process and eliminating unnecessary paperwork; by targeting funds to areas of greatest need; by eliminating wasteful uses of LEAA funds; by strengthening the role of local governments; and by increasing community and neighborhood participation in program decisions." Under the proposals, the civil and criminal research efforts of the Department of Justice would be consolidated in a new national institute of justice and a bureau of justice statistics would oversee civil and criminal statistical programs. Congress adjourned without final action on the proposals.

Prisons. A major difficulty with the "get tough" philosophy that now pervades crime control efforts has been a lack of facilities to house convicted criminals. There are 300,000 prison inmates in the United States, with 300 to 400 more persons entering correctional institutions each week than are discharged. The shortage of prison cells is so severe that authorities use tents, airport hangars, old warships, and warehouses to supplement space in the country's 200 long-term institutions and the 1,000 or so places to house persons with shorter terms. Community opposition generally forces officials to build prisons in rural areas, where inmates, who most often come from the cities, are far removed from the possibility of regular family visits.

See also PRISONS; UNITED STATES—SPECIAL REPORT: THE FBI; WOMEN.

GILBERT GEIS
University of California, Irvine

Some construction, an important economic index, is evident in this May 1978 photo of Havana, Cuba's capital.

CUBA

Late in 1978 the Cuban Government began what appeared to be a reevaluation of its foreign and domestic policies. Without deviating basically from its Marxist-Leninist ideology, Cuba seemed to be taking a new look at the wisdom of its foreign initiatives. On the domestic front, the Castro Government started tentative liberalizing steps, releasing some political prisoners and relaxing state controls over some means of production.

Domestic Affairs. At the end of the year, the Cuban Revolution celebrated its 20th anniversary. Its introspective mood was understandable even in purely personal terms: the Cuban leadership has remained virtually the same since Jan. 1, 1959, when Fidel Castro, then the victorious guerrilla leader, became the de facto ruler of the small Caribbean island country.

Late in October 1978, Castro, the First Secretary of the ruling Communist Party of Cuba, Cuba's commander in chief and president of the Council of State and of the government, made a statement that could signal a new course for the Cuban Revolution. "We are not only Marxists-Leninists," he said, "we are also nationalists and patriots." This political definition has not been heard in Cuba since 1959, when the Cuban Revolution, strongly nationalistic and leftist, was not yet Marxist.

Castro's statement underlined his growing contacts with the generally anti-Communist exile community in the United States and other countries, something that was unthinkable only a year earlier. The exiles had been described by Havana as an undesirable social element of which Socialist Cuba was well rid. On October 21, however, Castro spoke of the exiles in highly laudatory terms: "I'm glad, indeed I feel proud, that Cubans who live abroad, even those who have been our adversaries, are trying to preserve their language, their culture, and their integrity. We are satisfied and glad because we are nationalists and patriots." Castro explained that one of the reasons for his new posture vis-à-vis the exiles was that the Cuban Revolution has become an "irreversible" fact which, he said, even his bitter enemies have come to accept.

Foreign Relations. At the beginning of 1978, however, nothing in Cuba's actions indicated anything but a continuation of aggressive, often defiant policies of growing foreign involvement in close collaboration with the Soviet Union. According to Castro, beginning in mid-December 1977 and early January 1978, Cuban army "specialists" started arriving in Ethiopia, whose forces were then retreating in the Ogaden desert before a combined onslaught of Somali guerrillas and regular army units. Within weeks, Cuban tank, artillery, and aviation specialists took over the training of Ethiopian forces and, as Castro said, the actual fighting, "since the Ethiopians didn't have the time to learn how to handle the weaponry." Those weapons were being sent to Ethiopia at the same time by the Soviet Union. In February and March, during the Ethiopian counter-offensive, "medium-sized units" of Cuban regulars fought alongside the Ethiopian troops. Cuban infantry units participated in the final stages of the Ogaden campaign, which came to an end when the Somali army, beaten by the Cuban troops, withdrew from Ethiopian territory.

Despite this victory, numerous Cuban military contingents remained in Ethiopia. It seemed that the Havana government might be directly involved in Ethiopia's protracted fighting against Eritrean guerrillas. In April 1978, Lt. Col. Mengistu Haile Mariam, Ethiopia's strongman, declared in Havana that the Eritreans were "agents of imperialism and of Arab reaction." But Castro pointedly avoided the issue and only stated that Cuban troops would stay in Ethiopia for the time agreed by both governments. In September, Fidel Castro visited Addis Ababa and again failed to mention the Eritrean conflict. On September 15, in a major address in the Ethiopian capital, he asserted that Cuba would not bow to Western pressure and withdraw its troops from Africa. Castro described the presence of Cuban troops in Africa as an "act of international solidarity."

Earlier in the year, the U. S. State Department estimated that in 14 African countries Cuba maintained more than 45,000 men, of whom 39,000 were soldiers. In Angola there were about 20,000 troops, and some 16,000 in Ethiopia. Western intelligence officers estimated that in the three years of operations about 1,500 Cubans were killed and 4,500 wounded in African combat. In Angola, where the losses were estimated at about 1,000 in 1978, the Cubans continued to wage offensive and defensive operations against pro-Western guerrillas. Ironically, at the same time, Cuban troops were protecting Western oil fields in Angola's Cabinga Province and guarding Western specialists repairing Angolan airports. Elsewhere in Africa, the Cubans were training the Rhodesian Patriotic Front guerrillas of black nationalist leaders Joshua Nkomo and Robert Mugabe, who traveled to Ethiopia to meet Castro in September.

At the end of the year, however, Havana gave the impression of wanting to underplay its role in Africa, and the number of troops had not increased. Both Havana and Moscow appeared to be realizing that there was a limit to the military and political expansion in Africa, a continent that historically has not been too kind to foreign invaders and occupiers, or even self-proclaimed friends. Many African governments, which previously had looked with sympathy at Havana's actions, were becoming wary of Cuba's "internationalism." At various international conferences, Third World countries accused the Havana Government of being an agent of Soviet imperialism. The Eritreans were particularly bitter, charging that Soviet napalm dropped by Cuban pilots was no different from the napalm used by Americans in Vietnam several years earlier.

Cuba's involvement, or near-involvement, in the March 1978 invasion of Shaba Province of Zaire by Angola-based Katangan rebels deepened the uneasiness of many African countries about the size and activities of the Cuban "Afrika Korps." At the July Belgrade meeting of 86 non-aligned nations, some 30 delegations, among them a number from Africa and China, indicated they might boycott the non-aligned summit conference scheduled for Havana in September 1979. There were similar, though more limited, calls for Cuban disengagement from the continent of Africa at the 11th World Festival of Youth and Students held in Havana in August and attended by more than 18,500 persons from 145 countries.

Although Cuban-American relations appeared very strained at the beginning of the year, the tension eased somewhat at the end of 1978. Some observers have speculated that Washington, for years concerned over the long shadow cast by Cuba in Africa, has concluded that the African involvement might actually have weakened the Castro regime at home and abroad, particularly in the Third World.

Economy. Apparently, Cuba was well compensated economically by the Soviet Union for engaging a large number of Cubans in activities thousands of miles away. The Cuban economy was also doing better. The 1978 sugar harvest, the country's economic mainstay, aggregated 7,300,000 tons, the second largest in the country's history. Cuba's economy continued to be tied increasingly to the economics of the Soviet European bloc, resulting in growing trade exchanges with East European nations. In 1978, Soviet aid to Cuba was larger than in the previous year. Western specialists estimated that Cuba received from Moscow about $6 million a day in direct and indirect economic support. The Soviet Union supplied Cuba 200,000 barrels of oil per day at half the world price, and bought close to 4 million tons of sugar at four times the world price, paying partly with hard currency. Soviet experts continued to be involved in every sector of the Cuban economy, in addition to the military and internal security force.

See also AFRICA.

GEORGE VOLSKY
Center for Advanced International Studies
University of Miami

─────── **CUBA · Information Highlights** ───────

Official Name: Republic of Cuba.
Location: Caribbean Sea.
Area: 42,823 square miles (110,922 km²).
Population (1978 est.): 9,700,000.
Chief Cities (1970 census): Havana, the capital, 1,755,-400; Santiago de Cuba, 276,000; Camaguey, 196,900.
Government: *Head of state and government,* Fidel Castro Ruz, president (took office under a new constitution, Dec. 1976). *Legislature* (unicameral)—National Assembly of People's Power.
Monetary Unit: Peso (0.74 peso equals U. S.$1, Dec. 1978).
Manufactures (major products): Refined sugar, metals.
Agriculture (major products): Sugar, tobacco, rice, coffee, beans, meat, vegetables, tropical fruits.

UPI

Early in 1978, Spyros Kyprianou was elected, unopposed, to his own five-year term as president of Cyprus.

CYPRUS

Throughout 1978, northern Cyprus remained occupied by Turkish troops, while the rest of the island was controlled by the Greek Cypriot government. Spyros Kyprianou, who succeeded the late Archbishop Makarios as president in 1977, began his own five-year term on March 1, after presidential elections were cancelled because of the lack of an opposition candidate.

Turkish Occupation. Kyprianou's major problems were the same ones that had faced Makarios: how to end the Turkish occupation, reconcile Greek and Turkish Cypriots, and provide for some 200,000 Greek Cypriots displaced from their homes during the 1974 Turkish invasion. Kyprianou and his government refused to recognize the Turkish Federated State in the north or its self-proclaimed president, Rauf Denktash.

In April, a Turkish Cypriot plan prepared under the aegis of the Turkish government was submitted to UN Secretary General Kurt Waldheim. The proposal called for a bizonal federation which would leave Turkish Cypriots (who make up 18% of the population) with one third of the island. Although he was prepared to accept the idea of a federal union, Kyprianou described this particular plan as totally inadequate.

Kyprianou also opposed President Carter's efforts to persuade Congress to lift their arms embargo on Turkey. In June, the Cypriot president appeared before the U. S. Senate Foreign Relations Committee and the House International Relations Committee to urge the continuation of the ban. Congress lifted the embargo, but explicitly stated that Turkey had to show good faith in seeking a Cyprus settlement. Kyprianou reaffirmed his dissatisfaction.

President Kyprianou continued Makarios' precedent of using the UN as a forum for reciting grievances against Turkey. He called for demilitarization of the island with provision for a Greek Cypriot and Turkish Cypriot police force under the UN. In November, the UN General Assembly urged the Security Council to implement an earlier resolution calling for the removal of foreign troops from the island.

The Larnaca Incident. On February 18, Youssef el-Sebai, editor of Cairo's *Al Ahram* newspaper, was assassinated at a conference in Nicosia by two Arab gunmen. The two gunmen took 30 hostages and forced the government to turn over a Cyprus Airways DC-8. The hijackers were denied permission to land in several countries and returned to Larnaca airport, Cyprus, the next day. While the Cypriot government was negotiating with the gunmen, Egyptian commandos landed at the airport and attacked the plane. Cypriot National Guardsmen opened fire on the Egyptians, killing 15. After a one-hour battle, the gunmen freed their captives and surrendered. Relations between Egypt and Cyprus suffered. Cairo formally severed diplomatic ties on February 22.

Politics. Although Kyprianou was unopposed for the presidency (this was intended by all Greek Cypriot parties as a sign of unity against the Turkish occupation), he was not without critics. Tassos Papadopoulos, Greek Cypriot negotiator for intercommunal talks with the Turkish Cypriots, was dismissed from his post in July after publicly criticizing the president. Glafkos Clerides, former acting president, was alienated by President Kyprianou's cabinet changes in March; Clerides became the leader of an important right-wing party, the Democratic Rally. However, Communists and Socialists gave Kyprianou their support, especially in foreign affairs.

GEORGE J. MARCOPOULOS
Department of History
Tufts University

─────── **CYPRUS • Information Highlights** ───────

Official Name: Republic of Cyprus.
Location: Eastern Mediterranean.
Area: 3,572 square miles (9,251 km²).
Population (1978 est.): 600,000.
Chief Cities (1974 est.): Nicosia, the capital, 117,100; Limassol, 80,600.
Government: *Head of state and government,* Spyros Kyprianou, president (took office Aug. 1977). *Legislature*—House of Representatives.
Monetary Unit: Pound (0.3626 pound equals U. S.$1, Sept. 1978).
Manufactures (major products): Food and beverage processing, nonmetallic mineral products.
Agriculture (major products): Potatoes, grapes, citrus fruits, wheat, barley, carobs, sheep, goats, pigs.

CZECHOSLOVAKIA

The year 1978 was marked by the anniversaries of four major events in the history of Czechoslovakia: the 60th anniversary of the birth of modern Czechoslovakia; the 40th anniversary of the Munich Agreement, which led to Czechoslovakia's dismemberment; the 30th anniversary of the Communist take-over; and the 10th anniversary of the emergence of Alexander Dubček's "socialism with a human face" and its suppression by the Soviet invasion.

Dissidents. It was the anniversary of the Soviet invasion that caused the regime of Gustav Husák the most concern. It was feared that demonstrations against the continuation of the "temporary" presence of Soviet troops might undermine the carefully cultivated image of "normalcy" and satisfaction with the status quo. Czechoslovak communications media mounted an intensive campaign expressing gratitude for the Soviet Union's "fraternal aid" in quashing the "counterrevolution" of 1968. Dissidents at home, as well as those who had found refuge in the West, were denounced as traitors. Despite increased harassment, representatives of the Charter 77 movement managed to hold a secret meeting with members of the Polish Committee for Social Self-Defense. The two dissident groups issued a joint statement deploring the continued violations of human rights in their countries.

Economy. Midway through the Sixth Five-Year Plan (1976 to 1980) Czechoslovakia registered increases in the main sectors of the economy. Those increases were: industrial production, 5.5%; construction, 5.2%; labor productivity in industry, 4.8%, and in construction, 4.5%; freight transportation, 2.6%; retail trade, 6%; foreign trade, 9%; average wage in centrally planned industry, 4.1%; and average income, 3.7%. While most of the goals were attained or exceeded, several objectives were not met. These included output of lignite (brown coal); construction, both commercial and residential; exports to nonsocialist countries; and the reduction of production costs.

Foreign Affairs. A visit by Gustav Husák to West Germany in April was the first ever by a Czechoslovak head of state. Husák and West German Chancellor Helmut Schmidt signed a document calling for stronger relations between the two nations. A cultural agreement, designed to promote scientific, cultural, and educational cooperation was signed by the foreign ministers of the two countries.

In May–June, a delegation from the Soviet Union, headed by President Leonid Brezhnev, visited Czechoslovakia. The occasion was marked by the signing of the Joint Declaration on the Further Development of Fraternal Friendship and All-Around Cooperation of Czechoslovakia and the Soviet Union.

As a reward for Czechoslovakia's contribution to *Intercosmos*, the joint space program of the USSR and the Communist countries of Central and Eastern Europe, Capt. Vladimír Remek was chosen as the first foreign cosmonaut for a Soviet space flight.

EDWARD TABORSKY
University of Texas at Austin

— CZECHOSLOVAKIA • Information Highlights —

Official Name: Czechoslovak Socialist Republic.
Location: East-central Europe.
Area: 49,374 square miles (127,877 km²).
Population (1978 est.): 15,200,000.
Chief Cities (Dec. 1976): Prague, the capital, 1,175,522; Brno, 363,179; Bratislava, 350,025.
Government: *Head of state,* Gustav Husák, president (took office 1975). *Head of government,* Lubomír Štrougal, premier (took office 1970). *Communist party secretary general,* Gustáv Husák (took office 1969). *Legislature*—Federal Assembly: Chamber of Nations and Chamber of the People.
Monetary Unit: Koruna (5.97 koruny equal U. S.$1, 1977).
Manufactures (major products): Machinery and equipment, chemicals, petroleum products, sheet glass, textiles, iron and steel products, cement, motor vehicles, arms and armaments, footwear, glassware.
Agriculture (major products): Sugar beets, wheat, potatoes, rye, oats, corn, barley, hogs, cattle, horses.

DANCE

For dance in the United States, 1978 was a year of increased national recognition. The U. S. Postal Service issued four stamps commemorating American dance. The first National Dance Week was celebrated throughout the country with proclamations at the state and city level. President Jimmy Carter attended the openings of several dance companies, and Rosalynn Carter was honorary patron of the Alvin Ailey American Dance Theater's 20th-anniversary gala.

Baryshnikov. At the same time, it was a season dominated by a single personality, the former Russian ballet star, Mikhail Baryshnikov. The dancer's announcement that he was leaving American Ballet Theater to join the New York City Ballet rocked the dance world. Baryshnikov was ballet's top superstar. Now, he said, he preferred to work in a company with a no-star policy but molded by the creative genius of its founder-choreographer, George Balanchine.

It was Balanchine who choreographed one of the year's most brilliant ballets. His "Kammermusik No. 2," to Paul Hindemith's concerto, was dazzling in its complexity—a study in counterpoint for a male ensemble and four soloists, Karin von Aroldingen, Colleen Neary, Sean Lavery and Adam Luders. By contrast, his other premiere for the City Ballet was a light, airy ballet, "Ballo della Regina," to Verdi and centered on Merrill Ashley and Robert Weiss. Another company success was Peter Martins' first ballet, a duet for Heather Watts and Daniel Duell. Martins named the work after the music, Charles Ives' "Calcium Light Night." After Balanchine fell momentarily ill, he delegated the choreography of his projected ballet, "Tricolore" to Martins, Jean-Pierre Bonnefous and Jerome Robbins. All found the commissioned score by Georges Auric unsuitable, and the ballet was not well received. "A Sketchbook" fared better. This makeshift premiere consisted of several works-in-progress by Robbins and Martins.

Meanwhile, the initial ovations surrounding Baryshnikov's first performances in July with the City Ballet in Saratoga, N. Y., suggested that his superstar aura would follow him into the company. Yet when he made his New York debut with the troupe in November, he experienced the same problems encountered by all newcomers to the City Ballet. Balanchine's concealed virtuosity required adjustment to a new style that played up speed and pure movement, rather than dramatic characterization.

Before leaving Ballet Theater, Baryshnikov staged his own version of the 19th-century "Don Quixote" and danced outstandingly in it with Gelsey Kirkland. He also appeared as guest artist with the Eliot Feld Ballet, cast as a cowboy in Feld's solo, "Santa Fe Saga." At Chicago's International Dance Festival, he balanced an excerpt from the classic "Giselle" with his American debuts in Balanchine's "Apollo" and Robbins' "Afternoon of a Faun." Until his move, one month later, to the City Ballet, Baryshnikov had been seen mainly in the 19th-century classics.

It was these ballets that became the staple of American Ballet Theater's repertory in 1978. Except for Baryshnikov's "Don Quixote" and Glen Tetley's "Sphinx," the year offered no new ballets. The company's dancers were in fine form, however. Fernando Bujones was especially praised for a major breakthrough in both his artistry and dancing.

New Works. New works were offered by the Eliot Feld Ballet and the Joffrey Ballet. Feld turned to Latin themes, inspired by Aaron Copland's music, in "La Vida" and "Danzon Cubano." His "Half-Time" satirized the cheerleader mystique. The Joffrey Ballet offered a wider range. It became the first American company to stage the witty Frederick Ashton–Gertrude Stein ballet, "A Wedding Bouquet." Anthony Dowell, who took leave from Britain's Royal Ballet to dance with Ballet Theater, served as narrator as the Joffrey dancers caught the ballet's comic spirit. Gerald Arpino choreographed "Suite Saint-Saëns" and two ballets in honor of Russian ballerinas, "Choura" and "L'Air d'Esprit." Oscar Araiz' "Heptagon" was a powerful all-male piece in the José Limon style but his "Chopin Préludes," with its Gothic characters, left the audience unsure whether it should laugh with the ballet or at it. In "A Bridegroom Called Death," Agnes de Mille created a moving ballet in a folk ritual style.

The Season. The ballet season was unusually full. Visitors from abroad included Belgium's Royal Ballet of Flanders, Canada's Royal Winnipeg Ballet and National Ballet of Canada, as well as the Dutch National Ballet with Rudolf Nureyev (who appeared in the same engagement with the Murray Louis Dance Company).

The Berlin Opera Ballet made its American debut with Valery and Galina Panov, the former Russian ballet stars, as guest artists. Panov's versions of "Cinderella" and "The Rite of Spring" shared the season with classics such as "Giselle," in which Eva Evdokimova was highly praised.

Miss Evdokimova was seen again with Ballet Theater and the London Festival Ballet, which was dominated by Nureyev's presence in nearly all the ballets. These included "Le Spectre de la Rose," "Scheherazade," and his flamboyant theatrical version of "Romeo and Juliet." His other ballerinas, who made a fine impression, were Elisabetta Terabust and Patricia Ruanne.

Another company at the Metropolitan Opera and the Kennedy Center was the National Ballet of Cuba, directed by its prima ballerina, Alicia Alonso. The troupe's American debut was a personal triumph for the American-trained ballerina, who starred in her acclaimed staging of "Giselle," "Carmen," and shorter ballets. The corps was praised for its discipline, and the Cuban style was considered close to the Ballet Theater style of Miss Alonso's past. Among the well-received premieres were Antonio Gades' "Blood Wedding" and Alberto Mendez' "Tarde en la Siesta."

By contrast, no superstar was singled out within the Performing Arts Ensemble of China, which appeared at the Met shortly after the Cubans. Americans had their first glimpse of a live "revolutionary ballet" in an excerpt from "The Red Detachment of Women." The theatricalized folk dances on this debut program looked sentimental, but the musical sequences were greeted with interest and the dance passages from the Peking Opera were brilliantly performed.

Modern Dance. The two major modern dance events were the Martha Graham Dance Company's debut at the Metropolitan (the first modern-dance company to appear there) and Merce Cunningham's two weeks at the City Center. Miss Graham's new interest in small-scaled works produced two stunning premieres, "Ecuatorial" and "The Owl and the Pussy Cat," with Liza Minnelli as narrator. "Flute of Pan," another premiere, rounded out a season with outstanding performances of such Graham classics as "Night Journey" and "Clytemnestra."

Cunningham, the avant-garde dancer-choreographer who had rebelled against Miss Graham, offered a rare repertory season. In his new "Inlets," with decor by Morris Graves, he suggested a symbolic cyclical mood, of time passing. "Fractions" was another outstanding premiere. Other new works were "Exchange" and "Tango."

Alwin Nikolais' "Castings" and "Gallery," Paul Taylor's "Airs," and Erik Bruhn's appearance with the José Limon company also highlighted the season.

In the summer, Gov. James B. Hunt, Jr., of North Carolina welcomed the American Dance Festival to its new home at Duke University.

ANNA KISSELGOFF, *"The New York Times"*

MARTHA SWOPE

"Dancin'," choreographed and directed by Bob Fosse, was a Broadway hit in 1978.

MIMI COTTER

Martine van Hamel and John Meehan perform in the American Ballet Theater production of "Don Quixote," with Mikhail Baryshnikov.

Rudolf Nureyev and Margot Fonteyn display their artistry in the choreographed version of "Romeo and Juliet."

The Dance Explosion

When Isadora Duncan proclaimed, "I see America dancing," she was not merely paraphrasing Walt Whitman. More than 50 years later, her vision has come true. The United States is in the midst of a new cultural development, the dance explosion.

At no other time in the country's history has dance—notably ballet and modern dance—been so popular. Nor has an art form flourished in such concentrated creativity and diversity of styles. Within the last decade, the United States has been recognized as the dance capital of the world.

While Americans interested in the art form once had to visit Europe to keep abreast of its development, today every major dance troupe, from Russia's famed Bolshoi Ballet to the relatively young National Ballet of Canada, feels its reputation has no international seal unless it performs in New York City. Since 1969, the dance season there has run nonstop from September to the following August.

This vitality is echoed on a national scale. Companies have proliferated. A total of 121 regional troupes, both professional and "civic," are members of the National Association for Regional Ballet while modern dance companies bring the total of American dance groups to 850. Attendance has soared spectacularly. Nancy Hanks, former chairman of the National Endowment for the Arts, the federal arts agency, once told Congress, "Dance is the fastest growing live performing art in the nation."

This was hardly the case in 1965, when a Rockefeller Brothers Fund panel report, supervised by Miss Hanks, surveyed the arts. Expressing grave doubt about American dance's viability, the report noted that annual dance attendance in the United States was at the low figure of one million. Today it is 20 million.

Statistics are not needed to measure the success of dance-oriented films such as *Saturday Night Fever* and *The Turning Point,* featuring the Russian ballet superstar, Mikhail Baryshnikov. Much of the current dance boom has been hastened by the drawing power of charismatic virtuoso dancers such as Baryshnikov and Rudolf Nureyev, both of whom defected from Leningrad's Kirov Ballet. Nureyev, who arrived in the West in 1961, has played a large role in attracting a new audience to dance. With his partner, Margot Fonteyn of Britain's Royal Ballet, he helped usher in the new glamour that is one aspect of dance activity.

Historically, dance as an art form was held in low esteem by most Americans. Theatrical dance in the United States did not have the state-supported opera-house tradition of Europe or the

MARTHA SWOPE

The supported *arabesque en pointe*, executed *above* by Patricia McBride in the New York City Ballet production of "Raymonda," is one of ballet's most beautiful poses. *Right:* Gelsey Kirkland and Ivan Nagy dance in the American Ballet Theater's "Giselle."

MIMI COTTER

Patricia McBride is captured *sur la pointe* in "Coppelia."

MARTHA SWOPE

royal patronage of Asia. On the local level, dance never had the institutional backing of prominent citizens who preferred, for reasons of social prestige, to establish symphonies and opera companies. Today, there has been a dramatic shift. The Houston Ballet, for instance, was formed just over a decade ago by some of the city's wealthiest citizens and is controlled by a board headed by an executive of Shell Oil. This development is in marked contrast to the pattern whereby a creative artist forms a dance company and then tries to survive through grueling schedules of one-night stands.

American dance as it exists today can be traced to the pioneering modern dance and ballet movements of the 1930's. Faced with the lack of a native dance tradition, choreographers such as Martha Graham, George Balanchine, and Ruth Page found a holdover from another tradition: an American puritanism that was suspicious of the physicality of dance and which frowned upon men who considered dance as a career. Dance's backwater status was also related to the bias of the American intellectual community against an art form that seemingly appealed to the senses over the mind.

But in the 1960's, dance became respectable. The critic and novelist, Susan Sontag, in an anti-elitist stance, embraced dance because she felt it had a direct, democratic appeal to the senses.

There is no doubt that the crucial decade in the growth of American dance was the 1960's. To many observers, there was a link between the rise in dance popularity and the breaking of sexual taboos in the counterculture. A generation that dressed in miniskirts and tight pants and gyrated in discotheques did not snicker at male dancers in tights.

More important, it was a generation raised on television. "Dance and movies are the thing for young people," a dance observer told *The New York Times* in 1969. "It's the age of McLuhan. They are trained to look at visual images." This new young audience came to dance without the preconceptions of its elders. It was at ease with the visual and physical aspects of dance. It could appreciate dance for its own sake, and it was in the 1960's that pure-movement works by George Balanchine of the New York City Ballet and Merce Cunningham, the leading avant-garde modern dancer, gained the widest acceptance. While dance works with stories were once preferred by the older audience, the new plotless style actually made dance more accessible. There was no need to search for symbols or ask, "What does it mean?" Instead, choreographers asked the public merely to look at dancing and enjoy it. At a time when abstraction was familiar in all of the arts, a nonverbal art such as dance had a special appeal.

In the same period, technique in dance made extraordinary progress. Unprecedented virtuosity was revealed by dancers like Nureyev and Baryshnikov, who became models to other male dancers. Natalia Makarova, who left the Kirov Ballet in 1970, served as a different model, an example of pure classical style. All three Russian dancers have appeared with the American Ballet Theater, a company that had huge box office success with foreign guest stars who satisfied a star-hungry public.

Other major American ballet companies pursued a deliberate no-star policy, in which the ballet itself was considered more important than who was dancing its main roles. The leader here was Balanchine's New York City Ballet. The Joffrey Ballet rose in popularity with a similar policy, as did the Dance Theater of Harlem, the Pennsylvania Ballet, and the San Francisco Ballet.

It was clear that ballet offered an ideal vision of human perfection. People simply enjoyed watching what the body could do at its extreme limit. Dance had a powerful athleticism within an artistic context.

Statistics from the National Endowment measured dance growth very clearly. In 1966, the allocation for the Endowment's Dance Program was $605,250. In 1978, it was $6,938,270. In 1966, the Endowment began a touring program that exposed more Americans to dance. Under the program, a local sponsor (usually a college) paid only one third of a visiting dance company's fee. The Endowment and the state arts council shared the rest. In 1966–67, the program had four companies performing for a total of eight weeks in two states. In 1977–78, 160 companies were eligible: 117 were sponsored in 49 states for 439 "residency" weeks.

The most significant shift was geographical. In 1964–65, 68% of dance performances took place in New York City with 32% elsewhere. By 1975, 80% were outside New York. This growth was encouraged by government agencies and private foundations—especially the Ford Foundation, followed by the Rockefeller and Mellon foundations. Business support for dance has also increased. The National Corporate Fund for Dance received annual gifts from 125 corporations in 1978 as opposed to 14 corporation gifts in 1972–73.

Yet the chief factor in the dance explosion has been creativity. Unlike theatrical dance in many parts of the world, American dance stresses *new* work. Martha Graham in modern dance and Balanchine and Jerome Robbins in ballet are recognized as the world's greatest choreographers. Companies like the Eliot Feld Ballet are built around the esthetic of their choreographer-directors. In modern dance, leading choreographers are Paul Taylor, Merce Cunningham, Alwin Nikolais, Alvin Ailey, Erick Hawkins, Murray Louis, Twyla Tharp, followed by others—including the experimental group known as New Dance.

As the monthly, *Dance News,* wrote in a 1978 editorial, "dance is here to stay."

ANNA KISSELGOFF

DELAWARE

Delaware continued to be confronted with school problems during 1978. In addition, the state went through a lacklustre political campaign.

Schools. Under a desegregation order of the U. S. District Court eleven school districts of northern New Castle County, including the city of Wilmington, were merged into one comprehensive district, divided into four administrative areas. Busing was ordered between outlying suburban areas and Wilmington, and teachers were shifted within the four areas. The shift resulted in some teachers receiving higher pay than others teaching at the same grade levels, because of variation in pay scales among the former districts. Prolonged negotiations to arrive at a new teachers' contract in the newly formed district broke down in late September, and a strike ensued. Although it is illegal in Delaware for public employees to strike, no legal action was taken against individual teachers directly, and the strike continued into late autumn, severely disrupting the school programs and incurring the ire of parents. Public school population continued to fall. Private schools in the state showed a slight increase.

Elections. Election day in Delaware found the electorate splitting its ballots extensively. Joseph R. Biden (D) won reelection to the U. S. Senate, and Thomas B. Evans (R) was returned to U. S. House of Representatives. Richard R. Wier (D) was defeated for attorney general by Richard Gebelein (R). Thomas C. Carper (D) was reelected state treasurer, and Richard Collins (R) was reelected auditor. Democrats retained control of the state House of Representatives, 21–20, and the Senate, 13–8. Approximately 58% of eligible voters voted.

Economy. Unemployment in Delaware fluctuated between 9.5% and 6.5% during the year, with the low point reached in late October. No major industrial unrest occurred. Agricultural production was up, with corn, soybeans, and broilers the leading products. Due to severe February ice conditions in the Delaware estuary shipping was slightly impaired. Total net tonnage at the Port of Wilmington was approximately 3,000,000 tons, an increase of close to 10%. New housing starts declined slightly in 1978.

Legislation. Legislation to permit jai alai frontons in Wilmington was declared unconstitutional by the state supreme court, whereupon an unsuccessful attempt to amend the constitution was initiated. The General Assembly increased the membership of the state supreme court from three to five. Former Chancellor of the Court of Chancery W. T. Quillen and attorney H. R. Horsey were named to the high bench. The legislature was met by serious citizen protest respecting the relatively high state income tax. The state budget increased approximately 12%. Demands for passing a state sales tax eased somewhat.

PAUL DOLAN, *University of Delaware*

DENMARK

In late August 1978 Prime Minister Anker Jørgensen restructured his Social Democratic minority government by entering into a working relationship with the Liberal Party and by including seven members of that party in his cabinet. It was the first time that the Social Democrats had sought a coalition with a party to the right. Henning Christophersen, who succeeded Poul Hartling as the leader of the Liberal Party, became foreign minister, while other Liberals headed the ministries of justice, economic affairs, agriculture, commerce, interior, and public works. By keeping no less than 13 ministries for his own party, Prime Minister Jørgensen retained a Social Democratic stamp on the nation's ruling body. The new coalition, however, controlled only 88 votes in Parliament and was two votes short of a majority. Among the most challenging problems facing the new cabinet were widespread unemployment, inflation, an ever increasing balance of payments deficit, and lagging production.

One of Denmark's senior statesmen, Karl Skytte, resigned from his post as Presiding Officer of the Folketing (Parliament) in October. He had been a member of Parliament since 1947 and a former minister of agriculture. He was succeeded as the head of the legislature by K. B. Andersen, formerly minister of foreign affairs.

DELAWARE • Information Highlights

Area: 2,057 square miles (5,328 km²).
Population (Jan. 1978 est.): 582,000.
Chief Cities (1970 census): Dover, the capital, 17,488; Wilmington, 80,386; Newark, 21,078.
Government (1978): *Chief Officers*—governor, Pierre S. duPont IV (R); lt. gov., James D. McGinnis (D). *General Assembly*—Senate, 21; House of Representatives, 41 members.
Education (1977–78): *Enrollment*—public elementary schools, 57,967; public secondary, 60,033; colleges and universities, 30,960 students. *Public school expenditures,* $247,000,000 ($1,979 per pupil).
State Finances (fiscal year 1977): *Revenues,* $712,204,000; *expenditures,* $696,692,000.
Personal Income (1977): $4,477,000,000; per capita, $7,697.
Labor Force (July 1978): *Nonagricultural wage and salary earners,* 243,400; *unemployed,* 23,500 (8.4% of total force).

DENMARK • Information Highlights

Official Name: Kingdom of Denmark.
Location: Northwest Europe.
Area: 16,631 square miles (43,074 km²).
Population (1978 est.): 5,100,000.
Chief Cities (Jan. 1, 1977): Copenhagen, the capital, 1,251,226; Aarhus, 245,866; Odense, 167,616.
Government: *Head of state,* Margrethe II, queen (acceded Jan. 1972). *Head of government,* Anker Jørgensen, prime minister (took office Feb. 1975). *Legislature* (unicameral)—Folketing.
Monetary Unit: Krone (5.362 kroner equal U. S.$1, Sept. 1978).
Manufactures (major products): Industrial and construction equipment, electronics, furniture, textiles.
Agriculture (major products): Dairy products, meat, fish, fur.

UPI

Denmark's Social Democratic minority government of Anker Jørgensen underwent restructuring in 1978.

Local elections were held throughout Denmark on March 7 and showed that the Social Democrats were able not only to retain but also to strengthen their position as the nation's leading party. The Liberals and the Conservatives each gained less than half the number of votes cast in favor of Social Democratic representatives but were far ahead of Denmark's other ten political parties. A noteworthy aspect of the elections was the fact that about 13,000 Finnish, Icelandic, Norwegian, and Swedish citizens, who are permanent residents of Denmark, were allowed to vote for the first time.

The squatters who live in the former Copenhagen military barracks, now called Christiania, were allowed by the Danish Parliament to continue to live in the area, which comprises no less than 175 buildings on an 18-acre (7.2-ha) site. The permission was granted in spite of a Supreme Court decision to clear the area without delay.

On November 17 the Danish Parliament approved legislation granting home rule to Greenland. A referendum was scheduled for early 1979 to give the islanders an opportunity to accept or reject the home rule offer. If accepted, the islanders would elect their first Parliament in April 1979.

ERIK J. FRIIS
Editor, "The Scandinavian-American Bulletin"

DOMINICA

On Nov. 3, 1978, the 289 square mile (749 km²), English speaking, West Indian island of Dominica was granted independence from Great Britain. Governing authority was officially turned over by Princess Margaret, representing Queen Elizabeth. Since the breakup of the West Indian Federation in 1967, Dominica had been one of the Associated States of the Caribbean, dependent upon Great Britain for its defense and foreign affairs. With independence came a British

───── DOMINICA · Information Highlights ─────

Official Name: Commonwealth of Dominica.
Location: West Indies—Windward Island chain.
Area: 289 square miles (749 km²).
Population (1978 est.): 80,000.
Chief City: Roseau, the capital.
Government: *Head of state,* Elizabeth II; represented by Sir Louis Cools-Lartigue, governor general. *Head of government,* Patrick John, prime minister.
Monetary Unit: East Caribbean dollar.
Manufactures (major products): Soap, coconut oil.
Agriculture (major products): Bananas.

grant of about $19 million to be dispersed over three years. Dominica also joined the UN.

Although independence was not marked by the violence seen in nearby Grenada in 1974, the population of about 80,000 did not move smoothly to end colonial ties. Strikes among civil servants and dockworkers, wrangling among the various political parties, and a shakeup in the cabinet of Prime Minister Patrick John all occurred in the months prior to independence. Eventually the striking workers were promised salary adjustments, the various political groups agreed on independence, and the majority party weathered the dismissal of two cabinet members charged with sympathy toward Cuba.

THOMAS G. MATHEWS, *University of Puerto Rico*

DRUG ADDICTION AND ABUSE

Since the upsurge in drug abuse, which began in the mid-1960's, shifts in usage level have taken place. Although the sharp increases in the extent of drug abuse, prevalent during the 1960's, have leveled off, a substantial problem regarding excessive drug-use remains.

Marijuana use continues to increase, especially in the 18 to 25 age group. An estimated 16 million people were smoking marijuana at least once monthly in 1978. Ten percent of high school seniors were daily users according to a U. S. survey.

The number of people addicted to heroin has stabilized during the past few years at about 500,000. From 1960 to 1970 heroin addiction had increased from 60,000 to 600,000 persons. During the early 1970's there was a gradual decline to the present level. This partial success in combating heroin addiction in the United States was accomplished by a two-headed effort: to reduce supplies by supporting other governments in crop substitution and eradication programs, and to reduce demand by providing treatment opportunities.

Sedative dependence (sleeping pills and tranquilizers) remains at high levels, with all age groups contributing to their misuse. Prescriptions for barbiturates have gradually declined since 1970 as a result of the availability of safer agents to counter insomnia and a greater awareness by physicians of the dangers of barbiturates.

The abuse of amphetamines and related stimulants has either leveled off or decreased. Certainly the "speed freak" phenomenon—the use of enormous amounts of amphetamines intravenously—has almost disappeared. Tighter controls on prescriptions may be a factor, although illicit supplies persist.

Cocaine, a stimulant seemingly destined for greater popularity, is increasing in use. An estimated 1.5 million people take the drug each month. Only unavailability and cost limit its further growth.

The use of LSD and other hallucinogens, prominent among youth in the mid-1960's, has declined. While they have not disappeared, their adverse reactions are encountered much less frequently. One exception is PCP, phencyclidine (Angel Dust) whose popularity was on the rise during 1978. It is readily available and relatively inexpensive. Unfortunately, its use has produced an array of complications, including deaths due to overdose, prolonged psychosis resembling schizophrenia, severe depressions, and brain hemorrhages. In addition, unpredictable violence and bizarre behavior can result from the taking of PCP, causing major social and law enforcement problems. The long term use of phencyclidine may also be associated with possibly irreversible brain impairment.

The sniffing of commercial products containing volatile solvents or the contents of some aerosol sprays is essentially a juvenile practice. This practice, particularly by high school students, appears to be increasing. Both acute lethality (sudden sniffing death) and chronic damage to certain body organs have been documented. This practice, too, over a long term may produce irreversible mental impairment.

Dependency on the socially acceptable drugs, alcohol and tobacco, was on the increase among some groups in 1978. Over 9 million people were having problems with their drinking, with the alcoholism rate for women rising faster than for men. Young people were also drinking more, and more often. Fifty-five million Americans smoke cigarettes daily, and an estimated 300,000 people die prematurely each year from illnesses related to smoking. While the smoking trend has remained fairly stable over the past few years, young females show an increased rate of smoking.

SIDNEY COHEN, M. D.
UCLA School of Medicine

ECUADOR

The plan for a return to constitutional government announced in 1977 by the military regime headed by Adm. Alfredo Poveda Burbano was put into action during 1978.

The first step was a referendum on January 15 to choose between two constitutions, one entirely new, the other a revision of the 1945 document. The new constitution, supported by most political parties and labor groups, received 43% of the vote. The revised version received 32%; 23% of the voters spoiled their ballots; and 2% voted in blank.

On February 20, the military junta issued a new election law forbidding former presidents and native Ecuadoreans whose parents were not born in the country to run for president. This disqualified former presidents Carlos Arosemena and José María Velasco Ibarra, as well as Assad Bucaram, the charismatic leader of the Concentracion de Fuerzas Populares (CFP), whose parents were born in Lebanon. As a result of the new law, most members of the Tribunal Supremo del Referendum, who had presided over the constitutional vote, resigned in protest.

When the election was finally held on July 16, Jaime Roldos, the son-in-law of Bucaram and the substitute CPF candidate, won 31% of votes. He was followed by Sixto Duran, the principal right-wing candidate, with 23%. Slightly behind Duran was the Liberal Party's Raul Clemente Huerta. Rodrigo Borja of the socialist Partido Izquierda Democratica, got 11%; independent rightist Abdon Calderon Muñoz, 9%; and René Mauge, of a pro-Moscow leftist coalition, 5%.

A runoff election was scheduled for three months later, but the government announced in early October that it would not be held until April 1979. The government also decreed that the congressional elections originally scheduled after the installation of a new president would be held simultaneously with the runoff presidential poll. By the end of 1978 there was still wide doubt as to whether the return to a constitutional regime would be realized.

Economy. In February, government officials announced a 1977 trade deficit of $89 million, largely because of a decline in oil exports. The oil industry continued to have difficulties throughout 1978. A promising development in the banana trade, Ecuador's second largest source of exports, was the signing of a long-term contract with Del Monte, a U. S. company, guaranteeing the purchase of between 70,000 and 100,000 boxes of bananas per week.

Foreign Affairs. Major events during the year were the hijacking of a Saeta Airline plane to Cuba on January 18 and a border clash with Peru late in the same month. Also significant was the February visit of Gen. Cesar Mendoza of the Chilean military junta.

ROBERT J. ALEXANDER, *Rutgers University*

——— **ECUADOR • Information Highlights** ———

Official Name: Republic of Ecuador.
Location: Northwest South America.
Area: 104,506 square miles (270,669 km²).
Population (1978 est.): 7,800,000.
Chief Cities (1974): Quito, the capital, 557,113; Guayaquil, 814,064.
Government: *Head of state and government,* Alfredo Poveda Burbano, president of military junta (took office Jan. 1976). *Legislature*—Congress (dissolved Feb. 1972).
Monetary Unit: Sucre (25 sucres equal U. S.$1, Sept. 1978).
Manufactures (major products): Food products, textiles, light consumer goods, light industrial goods.
Agriculture (major products): Bananas, coffee, cacao, rice, corn, sugar, livestock.

UPI

In California, teachers, parents, and students demonstrate against possible cuts resulting from Proposition 13.

EDUCATION

U. S. education in 1978 was affected by continuation of the minimum competency test movement; back-to-basics reached up to university level; Congress rejected college tuition tax credit and hesitated over a cabinet-level Education Department; and in a compromise Bakke decision, the U. S. Supreme Court struck down rigid admission quotas while allowing affirmative action for redress. Abroad, post-Mao China favored academic excellence over doctrinal purity, vowing to make China a modern nation; and Britain laid plans to raise educational quality while meeting declining school enrollment problems.

UNITED STATES

Teachers' Strikes. Some 75 teachers' strikes delayed fall school openings in 15 states involving more than 35,000 teachers and affecting more than 625,000 students. Cities involved included Seattle and Tacoma, Wash.; New Orleans, La.; and Cleveland, Ohio. Striking teachers who opposed court-ordered return to work were jailed in Dayton, Ohio, and Bridgeport, Conn. Hardest hit states included Illinois, Indiana, Massachusetts, Maine, Pennsylvania, Minnesota, New York, New Jersey, and California. Higher education faculty members also were on strike in

Chicago teachers' colleges and several Michigan universities. The number of strikes was double that of September 1977, allegedly because of inflation, classroom violence, falling student test scores, public criticism, and antitax mentality following California's Proposition 13 vote. The federally estimated average teacher's salary of $15,250 is below the median national income for a family of four. Between 1975–78, teachers' salaries rose an average of 5.9% per year while inflation averaged over 7.1% per year.

Minimum Educational Competency Laws. The number of states requiring school subject mastery tests at various stages increased to 34 in 1978, 20 of which require a test for high school graduation. Critics say that the social promotion concept caused many high school graduates to be deficient in fundamental educational skills, some of them being functionally illiterate. Between 1975 and 1978, the number of Americans who rated public schools as good or excellent dropped 25%. A 1977 Gallup poll showed 83% of those polled favored the back-to-basics movement.

In Florida, 91% of 11th graders passed a new English test but only 64% passed a new math test, with most failures being minority members. A National Education Association (NEA) investigating team criticized the Florida program for over-emphasizing reading and math and neglecting other subjects. The NEA charged that millions were being spent to prove problems already known and that minimum competency narrowed the curriculum. Advocates say the tests make students work harder and teachers more thorough. Opponents say that the tests fail to reflect students' abilities and subvert community control, that teachers are blamed for poor student performance, and that when enough students, minorities or otherwise, fail the tests, the minimum competency movement will collapse. A federal education official said that competency testing is beneficial only if used to diagnose difficulties.

Harvard's New Core Curriculum. On May 2, Harvard University's Faculty of Arts and Sciences voted 182 to 65 for a more structured undergraduate curriculum. Beginning in 1983, students will select 25% of their program from 80 to 100 core courses in 5 areas: literature and the arts, history, social and philosophical analysis, science and math, and foreign languages and culture. This first major curriculum change since Harvard ushered in General Education in 1945 (a more flexible revamping of the Liberal Arts) marked a swing away from the free-choice, student-dominated curricula of the 1960's, when student activists demanded more relevance and more options. The University of California at Berkeley and a few other colleges joined Harvard in tightening course requirements.

Tuition Tax Credit. Rival tuition tax credit bills went to Congress in wake of California's Proposition 13 antitax sentiment and the rise of tuition costs to $2,210 at public colleges and $5,231 at private colleges. President Carter and education leaders opposed the Moynihan-Packwood bill that would allow parents up to $500 income tax credit per student in college or in nonpublic elementary and secondary schools. President Carter vowed to veto this bill as excessive and its aid to parochial and private students as unconstitutional. Despite his veto threat, the House passed in June a tuition tax credit bill for both college and nonpublic elementary and secondary students. A Roper poll in May showed that 64% of those polled rejected tuition credit for nonpublic elementary and secondary students but that an overwhelming majority wanted tax relief for college tuition. In August the Senate struck down the nonpublic elementary and secondary aid provision and passed a college tuition tax credit bill (the Pell bill, which President Carter supported) that would grant up to $250 a year tax credit per college student. Before adjourning in mid-October, the Senate defeated the House-Senate conference proposal that families paying high school and college tuition get tax relief. The action averted a presidential veto.

Carter's Education Budget. President Carter on February 28 asked Congress for a (U. S.) $12.9 billion fiscal 1979 education budget, a 24% increase over the fiscal 1978 federal education budget, the largest such increase requested since the Johnson years. Besides giving his education budget a back-to-basics label, the president indicated that the budget increase would go to underprivileged children, the handicapped, and college student aid. The new budget increased only slightly the federal share of total U. S. spending on education, with states and local districts spending about 91%. Reflecting pressures to reduce taxes, the House adopted a 2% cut in appropriations for most Health, Education, and Welfare (HEW) programs.

Cabinet-Level Education Department. In his January 19 State of the Union Address President Carter asked for a cabinet-level department of education. Advocates said that it would give education more prestige and more budget control; that it would allow a clear federal education policy by pulling together education programs from various federal agencies; and that it would stand visibly apart from the unwieldy HEW, whose major concerns are welfare and health.

Opponents argued that uncoordinated education programs are caused not by faulty administrative structure but by too many Congressional committees; that, constitutionally, education is a state and local responsibility; that a separate department would be an unacceptable European-type ministry of education controlling what is taught; that an independent education secretary would have less influence than an HEW secretary, and that a separate department would isolate education from the labor, civil rights, and welfare coalition which had restored Nixon-Ford education budget cuts.

President Carter's NEA-backed plan requested a department administering 164 existing programs, with a budget of $17.5 billion and a staff of 23,325. But strong opposition influenced the elimination from the proposed Senate bill of Project Head Start for disadvantaged preschoolers on the ground that its success depended on local parents, community, and social agency involvement; the national school lunch program, on the ground that the food and nutrition involved are best administered by the Department of Agriculture; Indian education, because tribal leaders feared that their benefits would fare worse under an education department than under the Bureau of Indian Affairs and that their schools would disappear into the public school system; and civil rights, whose advocates prefer an independent Office of Civil Rights under HEW. Congressional committees backed away from the education department idea. Critics said that it would break the tradition of limiting federal involvement in education to general welfare, such as the post-World War II GI Bill as an educational alternative to millions of jobless returned service men and women, post-Sputnik education programs to aid U. S. Cold War defense, and Great Society education programs to promote civil rights and income redistribution. The stripped-down education department proposal died in committee.

Bakke Decision. On June 28 the U. S. Supreme Court voted 5–4 that Allan P. Bakke, a white engineer, must be admitted to the University of California, Davis, Medical School that twice had rejected him over 16 less qualified minority students. The court found that fixed racial quotas were unconstitutional. Justices Stevens, Stewart, Rehnquist, and Burger said the Davis special admission plan violated Title VI of the Civil Rights Act. Justices Brennan, White, Marshall, and Blackmun said the Davis special admission plan was constitutional according to the 14th Amendment. Justice Lewis F. Powell, Jr., cast the deciding vote, saying that while race alone cannot be the deciding factor, it can be one among several admissions criteria, such as ethnic, geographic, and economic considerations. The court's compromise vote boiled down to rigid quotas, no, affirmative action for redress, yes, reflecting the American public's ambivalence. A poll on the question of the Bakke implications found that 75% of respondents believed schools should admit the best candidates even if fewer minorities are accepted; 62% said schools should give special consideration to helping more minorities be admitted. Extremists were unhappy. Minority advocates were glad that affirmative action programs would continue. Whites who feared reverse discrimination felt that, in getting Bakke accepted, their voice had been heard.

White Flight. University of Chicago sociologist James S. Coleman, whose 1966 school report supported court-ordered desegregation, repeated his belief, first stated in 1975, that court-ordered desegregation and forced busing have caused white flight to the suburbs and thus resulted in urban resegregation. He added that residential patterns, which cannot be ended by court orders, caused school segregation.

Desegregation advocates were further disturbed by Rand Corporation sociologist David Armor's 1978 study which supports Coleman. Armor found that up to 60% of the large white flight resulted from forced busing. He said that whites keep moving farther out or enroll their children in private schools. His partial remedy is more "magnet" schools which draw qualified white and black students from neighborhoods by their superior academic facilities.

School Finance. Passage of California's Proposition 13 to cut property taxes affected school financing, 60% of which comes from property tax. Summer school programs were suspended, despite the state's $5 billion surplus, half of which was to be used to aid schools. Another effect was to equalize state spending between rich and poor school districts, as required by a 1971 state Supreme Court ruling.

Following precedents in several states, the New York State Supreme Court on June 23 ordered a revamping of the financing of the state's 700-plus school districts. Winners will be the big cities which complained that, because of the many services they had to offer and because of

UPI

Some U. S. teachers went to jail in 1978 as strikes delayed the fall opening of schools in 15 states.

their increasingly poor populations, their proportion of state school aid was too small.

U. S. Enrollments, Costs, Graduates. HEW and the Bureau of the Census issued the following 1978–79 education estimates (1977–78 comparisons in parentheses):

Enrollments, kindergarten through grade 8: 32,600,000 pupils, —2% (33,231,000); high school: 15,600,000, —1% (15,800,000); colleges and universities, 11,600,000, +3% (11,286,000), and will rise until 1982; total: 59,800,000, —1% (60,317,000), representing the third annual decline from a 1975 record of 61,300,000.

Percentage of age group enrolled: 92% of 5-year-olds (kindergarten); 99% of 6 to 13-year-olds (grades 1–8); 94% of 14 to 17-year-olds (grades 9–12); and 30% of 18 to 24-year-olds (college).

Number of teachers, elementary and secondary, 2,400,000 (same); colleges and universities, 830,000, +1% (700,000).

Graduates, high school, 3,150,000 (same); bachelor's degrees, 1,000,000 (969,000); first professional degrees, 67,000 (64,000); master's degrees, 347,000 (356,000); doctorates, 37,000 (35,000).

Education directly involves 63,400,000 people (63,700,000), or 3 out of every 10 Americans; at an expenditure for public schools and colleges of about (U. S.) $127 billion ($117 billion), plus $28 billion ($27 billion) for private institutions; or a grand total expenditure of $155 billion

($144 billion), with the $11 billion increase mainly for keeping pace with inflation and especially for raising salaries (in some districts half the budget is for salaries); divided among state governments, $57.1 billion, or 36.8% ($50.8 billion, 35.3%); local, $43.3 billion, 27.9% ($41.2 billion, 28.6%); Federal, $16.5 billion, 10.6% ($15.2 billion, 10.5%); and all other sources, including endowments, gifts, tuition, and student fees, $38.3 billion, 24.7% ($36.8 billion, 25.6%).

INTERNATIONAL

People's Republic of China. To make China a modern nation by the year 2000, China's post-Mao leaders announced the following new policies in 1978: the school entry age will be lowered from 7 to 6; by 1985 all rural youths will have 8 years of education, ages 6–14; all urban youths will have 10 years, ages 6–16. The school ladder will include 5-year primary school, ages 6–11; 3-year junior middle school, ages 11–14; 2-year senior middle school, ages 14–16; followed by work or higher education. National exams for university entrance have been reinstated. The 80 most important universities will choose the best of the top 30% middle school graduates. The other 400 universities will choose from the remainder of this top 30%. Most youths (70%) will go to work in rural communes and factories, but an increasing variety of farm and factory-based adult education programs and post-middle school institutes is planned.

Britain. Recent educational surveys and reports reflect Britain's adjustment from past school growth to a current decline caused by a falling birth rate. Also, the prospect that North Sea oil income will help refurbish old industrial plants and so improve Britain's manufacturing and economic position depends on trained manpower, especially technologists.

The government's late 1978 *Progress in Education* report indicated these plans: to offset a 25% decline in enrollment by 1989, the government will retrain the fewer teachers needed, with a greater proportion slated to serve handicapped and disadvantaged children and with retraining to fill long-standing shortages in secondary math, science, and technology. Some surplus schools will be closed and others remodeled for adult education and youth recreation needs. For pre-schoolers, plans are to enroll by the mid-1980's 90% of all 4-year-olds (53% enrolled, 1978) and 50% of all 3-year-olds (15% enrolled, 1978). While the comprehensive secondary school movement, begun in 1965, has gone well (83% now enrolled in comprehensives), back-to-basics curriculum upgrading is planned in English, math, modern languages, science, and career guidance toward technology, with national assessment tests already in progress and expected to be ongoing. National exam changes which are intended to cater to a wider range of student abilities include: one exam at age 16+ to replace the General Certificate of Education Ordinary Level and the

UPI

On July 1, 1978, Hanna Holborn Gray became president of the University of Chicago. Dr. Gray, 48, had taught history at the university and had served as acting president of Yale (1977–78).

Certificate of Secondary Education; a pre-university entrance certificate exam after the first year of Sixth Form at age 17+; and 2 complementary exams for the university entrance General Certificate of Education Advanced Level Exam at age 18+. After 1980 all teachers must have a degree (marking the end of the 3-year teacher certificate) and will be more carefully selected and prepared, with older teachers financially aided to retire or to be retrained. Still being pondered is how to cope when, by the mid-1990's, university enrollments will likely be only 75% of their 1978 size.

USSR. Soviet authorities are experimenting in selected Moscow schools with a sex education program for students aged 15–17. Some teachers initially resisted the program, parents were uneasy, but students responded enthusiastically. Said a teacher in the experimental program: "We are trying to educate children in such a way that they have no strivings to have intimate relations without love. We want sex instincts to come as late as possible."

Behind the sex education experiment may be these USSR statistics: the divorce rate has risen from 1 in 9 marriages in 1960 to 1 in 3 in 1978. One sixth of divorces occur within 90 days of the wedding. Adultery is blamed for most divorces. One tenth of children are born out of wedlock. The program will be tried and evaluated for up to 5 years before its approval for use throughout the Soviet Union.

FRANKLIN PARKER
West Virginia University

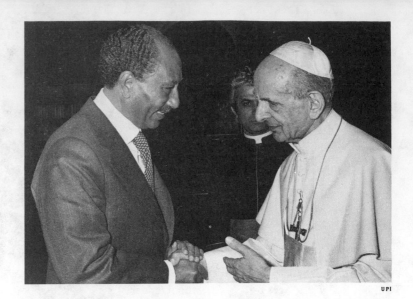

Egypt's President Anwar el-Sadat and Pope Paul VI discussed the Middle East situation at the Vatican early in the year.

UPI

EGYPT

The year 1978 was filled with the aftermath of President Anwar el-Sadat's historic visit to Jerusalem in November 1977, negotiations between Egypt and Israel at Camp David, and the final preparations for a peace treaty between Israel and Egypt.

Relations with Israel. President Sadat made an unprecedented visit to Jerusalem, Israel, Nov. 19, 1977. Prime Minister Menahem Begin in turn visited Egypt at year-end. The beginning of 1978 was also then the beginning of detailed negotiations between Israel and Egypt over ending their 30-year history of belligerency.

At stake were things that were strictly between Egypt and Israel, but there were also issues involving the wider Arab world. The fate of the Palestinians was one of these; another major issue was the future status of the old city of Jerusalem itself, which is a holy city to Jews, Christians, and Muslims.

The return of Sinai did not seem to involve any real complication, but there were already Israeli settlements in Sinai. The Egyptians naturally demanded their dismantling; the Israelis were reluctant to do so. The problem for Egypt was how to negotiate a separate peace with Israel and at the same time salvage some of the requirements of other Arabs, notably Palestinians. Sadat, by his trip to Jerusalem, was already isolated to some degree in the Arab world; he did not seem to want to risk more. In any event the negotiations in Egypt and in Israel had broken down by the early spring; each side complained about the other. The United States continued to urge an accommodation, and high American officials continued to travel to the Middle East to reestablish effective communication between Israel and Egypt.

In May the United States agreed to sell jet fighters, although different kinds, to Egypt, Israel, and Saudi Arabia. Arabs in general considered this an important "watershed" decision;

Sadat said that it had "reopened" the way to peace negotiations. Nevertheless, as spring ripened into summer, nothing much seemed to be accomplished. By July, however, the Israeli and Egyptian foreign ministers were to meet in London to exchange views, and Sadat himself had traveled to Vienna to talk to Shimon Peres, Israeli opposition leader, and Ezer Weizman, defense minister. None of this came to much. By August all seemed bogged down again. But by then both Israel and Egypt were on the road to the summit at Camp David, Md.

In early September, Sadat, Begin, and Carter met in a variety of talks, consultations, and mutual bargaining that resulted, after 13 days, in Sadat-Begin accords that pointed directly to a peace agreement that would be signed, it was announced, within three months. Much publicity was generated by the Carter administration in announcing the accords to the world; there was an impressive ceremony in the presence of Congress that gave Carter an opportunity to extol the American role. Not long after this it was announced that the Nobel Peace prize was to be awarded jointly to Sadat and Begin.

The months of September through December were spent in negotiating the final treaty or agreement between the two belligerents. Some difficulty arose at this stage, and the December 17 treaty deadline passed without a formal agreement. (Sadat even refused to attend the Nobel ceremony.) The document was to specify the return of Sinai to the Egyptians, the freeing of international waterways (including the Suez Canal) for the Israelis, and the normalization of relations, including exchange of ambassadors, between the two nations.

It was in fact a separate peace agreement between Egypt and Israel and was in Arab terms something of a sellout by Egypt of general Arab interests and particularly those of the Palestinians. Sadat, of course, was well aware of this; perhaps this motivated his final reluctance to sign the document and his effort to link the agreement to some timetable for Palestinian "independence" in Gaza and the West Bank. Nevertheless, 1978 witnessed an enormous move by Israel and Egypt to end their years of warring with one another.

Other Foreign Relations. Naturally the rapprochement between Israel and Egypt colored much of Egypt's other foreign relations. Sadat traveled extensively during the year, several times to the United States and to Europe, in order to build support for his stand with Israel. Among the Arabs, he received some support from Morocco, Tunisia, and Sudan. Saudi Arabia, although not happy with Sadat's relations with the Israelis, continued to support Egypt financially. An Arab summit meeting in Baghdad in November was generally considered to have failed in mobilizing real support against him. Strong anti-Sadat sentiments were expressed, however.

Egypt announced on July 24 that it would not permit its athletes to participate in sporting events in such hardline Arab nations as Algeria, Iraq, Libya, Syria, and Southern Yemen. Earlier, Egyptian athletes had been attacked by Libyan athletes and fans at the African games in Algiers.

In February the editor of *Al-Ahram,* Youssef el-Sebai, was assassinated in Nicosia, Cyprus, by Palestinian gunmen, who also seized a number of hostages. A subsequent raid by the Egyptians failed to capture the terrorists involved; the result was a break in diplomatic relations with Cyprus. Sadat accused Cyprus of harboring Egypt's enemies. Another retaliation in terms of constraints was applied to Palestinians within Egypt.

In early 1978 Pope Paul VI praised Sadat for his peace efforts. In February Egypt got into a brief tiff with Kenya over Egyptian planes (carrying munitions to Somalia) being seized by Kenya. In March Egypt strongly protested Israel's attack on southern Lebanon. And in December Egypt broke relations with Bulgaria following a quarrel over Egyptian rental rights in a building purchased by Bulgarians in Cairo. Also in late 1978 the Arab League announced that it would hold no more meetings in Egypt.

Domestic Affairs. Sadat apparently had the support of the Egyptian people in his various pourparlers with the Israelis, even if he lost two Egyptian foreign ministers as a result. However,

he faced considerable dissent from some Egyptians in Egypt and abroad. In June, former Lt. Gen. Saad Eddin el-Shazli, in exile and speaking from Portugal, called Sadat a dictator and spoke approvingly of a possible coup against him. In May, Sadat banned travel abroad for some of his critics, including the well-known editor and writer Muhammad Hassanien Heykal. Sadat legitimized some of his crackdown on critics by announcing a national referendum to show support for his policies; on May 22, it was announced that 98.29% of the 85% of 11 million eligible voters approved of Sadat's political activity. Throughout the year there were "shakeups" in the government and in the military.

According to Sadat's new terminology, Egypt is an "ethical democracy"; his critics still seem suspicious about what the term really means. At year's end Sadat seemed firmly in control at home, and in control as well of his foreign policy.

CARL LEIDEN
University of Texas at Austin

In Cairo, a woman carries an empty oil drum past a billboard advertising the latest movie attractions.

UPI

EGYPT · Information Highlights

Official Name: Arab Republic of Egypt.
Location: Northeastern Africa.
Area: 386,660 square miles (1,001,449 km²).
Population (1978 est.): 39,600,000.
Chief Cities (1975 est.): Cairo, the capital, 8,400,000; Alexandria, 2,500,000.
Government: *Head of state,* Anwar el-Sadat, president (reelected for a second six-year term, Sept. 1976). *Head of government,* Mamdouh Muhammad Salem, prime minister (took office April 1975). *Legislature* (unicameral)—People's Assembly.
Monetary Unit: Pound (0.39 pound equals U. S.$1, Nov. 1978).
Manufactures (major products): Textiles, processed foods, tobacco manufactures, chemicals, fertilizer, petroleum and petroleum products.
Agriculture (major products): Cotton, rice, wheat, corn.

Miners in Asbury, Mo., dig for bituminous coal. Experts emphasize that future U. S. energy needs require a greater dependence on the nation's coal resources.

UPI

ENERGY

The winter of 1977–78 was abnormally cold, but despite the fact that the United Mine Workers carried out the longest coal strike in U. S. history, the United States did not experience a repeat of the factory and school closings and associated economic and social disruptions of the previous winter. The worst consequences of an energy shortage were escaped by a number of short-term modifications taken as a direct result of problems that had developed during the winter of 1976–77. Specifically, many factories and other large energy users increased the quantity of their local energy storage and installed systems for switching to alternative fuels. The pipeline industry used the year to develop better contingency plans and greater flexibility for transferring gas among pipelines. Anticipating the coal strike, both electric utilities and industry increased their stockpiles of coal. Some coal users were able to switch to Western mines for short-term coal supplies, since most of the Western mines continued to operate during the United Mine Workers prolonged strike.

By the summer of 1978 there was a world surplus of oil. Because of limited economic growth in Europe, world demand for oil had grown slowly and that in combination with new production from the North Sea and Alaska contributed to the surplus. For many Americans the experience of the winter of 1977–78 followed by an oil glut in the summer only confirmed their belief that the energy situation was not critical. In fact, there were some reasons for real optimism, in that energy consumption did not grow so rapidly as expected with a growing domestic economy. Most energy experts, however, believe nothing occurred which changed the basic facts that led to the energy crisis of 1973, and that the public drew incorrect conclusions, therefore, from the experience of 1978.

Upon close review, 1978 provided an impressive accumulation of evidence concerning the complexity and seeming intractability of the nation's and the world's energy situation. Nationally, the immediate energy problem is economic and results from a heavy dependence on high-cost imported oil. Due to the delivery of approximately 1 million barrels of oil a day through the Alaska pipeline system, imports declined slightly from the 1977 rate, but imported oil still supplied approximately 25% of the nation's energy, or 50% of the total amount of oil consumed.

Assuming it is possible to increase Alaskan pipeline delivery to its full projected capacity of 2 million barrels per day, Alaskan production should hold imports steady through 1979. At that point, unless other factors change, imports and the associated drain on the American dollar must increase. Oil imports, which cost the nation approximately (U. S.) $45 billion in 1978, were a major contributor to an undesired balance of payments deficit estimated at between $25 and $30 billion.

Most energy experts believe that, given continued economic growth, world oil supplies will cease being able to meet world demand sometime in the 1980's. The only issue being debated is precisely when that will happen. Some studies suggest that the timing question will depend on whether Soviet oil production declines to a point where the Soviets become net oil importers and therefore competitors for Middle Eastern oil.

International Developments. Although the lack of economic and social disruption resulting from the severe winter and coal strike of 1977–78 reduced domestic pressure for Congressional passage of a comprehensive energy program, international pressure for such legislation increased. Central to much of the international concern was the precipitous drop in the value of the dollar against such strong currencies as the German mark, the Japanese yen, and the Swiss franc. Foreign leaders, particularly German Chancellor Helmut Schmidt, publicly criticized the United States for not protecting the value of the dollar and attributed its decline to what they saw as the balance of payments deficit produced by large oil imports. The principal demand articulated by European and Japanese leaders was for a clear U. S. energy policy that would reduce oil imports by the United States.

The declining value of the dollar also created pressure for price increases among the members of the Organization of Petroleum Exporting Countries (OPEC). During the year some members of OPEC argued for a higher cartel price to compensate for the loss in the dollar's buying power. At its annual meeting in Abu Dhabi in December, OPEC decided to increase world oil prices by 14.5%. The increase was to occur in quarterly stages during 1979 and that meant an average increase of 10% for the year. The increase was slightly higher than expected and caused the dollar to fall even more and Wall Street stocks to drop, too. As a result of the move, the U. S. bill for imported oil was expected to rise by $6 billion in 1979, and the cost of gasoline and home heating oil would also increase for the American consumer. Following the announcement, W. Michael Blumenthal, U. S. secretary of the treasury, upped his 1979 inflation forecast by a point, to "between 7 and 7.5%."

The United States was disappointed that Saudi Arabia could not or did not exert greater pressure in urging OPEC to hold the price line. Prior to the meeting, the Saudi position appeared to reflect a sensitivity to the adverse world economic consequences of a price rise, a recognition of the world oil surplus, and a desire to support U. S. policy. However, with Iran's oil production severely reduced due to a domestic crisis, Saudi Arabia was forced to pump oil at full capacity during the last weeks of the year. This reduced the Saudi's influence at the OPEC meeting. In fact, the Saudis were said to have fully supported the OPEC action.

A new and unpredictable factor in the international energy picture during 1978 was the reported discovery of major new oil and gas reserves in Mexico. Development of these reserves to a point where Mexican production will have a major impact on world supplies will doubtless require 8 to 10 years. Although Mexican oil could reduce U. S. dependence on the Middle East, it will likely be as expensive as Middle Eastern oil and will do nothing to reduce the drain of American dollars to pay for oil imports.

An even more unpredictable development on the international scene was the sudden indication by the Chinese that they would be willing to let foreign oil companies develop their offshore oil resources. Estimates of Chinese oil resources vary greatly, but it is generally believed that Chinese resources are large. If the Chinese develop and export those resources to pay for desired imports of technology, the impact on the world energy system could be significant.

Some energy and economic experts clearly stated that they saw such new oil producers as Mexico and China as the only way to end OPEC's stranglehold on world oil prices.

In the latter days of 1978, political unrest in Iran produced another unknown in the world's energy supply assessment. Iran produces between 5 and 6 million barrels of oil a day and exports a major portion of it. Should political changes in that country disrupt that source of supply, the world's surplus would immediately disappear. Iranian oil is particularly sensitive since it is the source of a major portion of the energy used in Israel. Should Iranian oil be denied to Israel, the United States would doubtless be under great pressure to help find alternative sources for its ally.

U. S. Legislation. Toward the end of the 1978 Congressional session, President Jimmy Carter was able to win support for the passage of his long-stalled energy program. It was widely reported that the sudden turnaround of the Congress on energy legislation resulted from international developments and particularly the growing concern about the impact of oil imports on the value of the dollar. Using the fear of the declining dollar as the key instrument in its legislative efforts, the administration was able to muster the support of a coalition of Democrats and Republicans to pass a natural gas bill.

The controversy over natural gas had been the major barrier to passage of energy legislation. The Congressional stalemate over the legislation revolved around the issue of whether natural gas prices would be regulated. In the end, a compromise evolved which would move the nation toward full deregulation of gas prices by the mid 1980's. Between 1979 and the mid 1980's, a complex set of government-regulated prices will be applied to gas. This complex pricing system will pose a major administrative challenge for the Department of Energy.

The new natural gas legislation will incrementally increase gas prices. The administration hopes that increased natural gas prices will have two beneficial effects. One is that higher prices will result in more efficient use and therefore less gas consumption. The other is that higher prices will stimulate the search for, discovery of, and production of more gas.

In the short term, the natural gas legislation seems certain to increase the availability of gas for most Americans. Increased availability will result from the elimination of the distinction between intrastate and interstate gas. Before the passage of the natural gas legislation of 1978, gas used within the producing state (intrastate) was not regulated. The result was a much higher price for intrastate gas than for interstate gas and, therefore, a gas surplus in producing states. The new legislation regulates all gas production and should increase supplies available to the interstate market. In addition, Congress enacted measures allowing tax cuts for home insulation and penalties for gas-guzzling autos, and requiring new industrial and utility plants to use coal or a fuel other than oil or gas.

Earlier, Congress passed another important piece of energy legislation, the "Outer Continental Shelf Lands Act Amendments of 1978." This legislation, the result of several years of Congressional activity, has several objectives: to provide greater protection of the environment, to give adjoining coastal states greater access to information regarding oil and gas development and other activities, and to increase the opportunity for smaller companies to participate in offshore operations. Like the natural gas legislation, the Outer Continental Shelf Lands Act is very complex and will pose an administrative challenge to those government agencies which must implement it.

Original Carter proposals calling for a tax rebate to buyers of gas-saving cars, a tax on crude oil, and a tax on utility and industrial use of oil and natural gas were not enacted. The rebate proposal was rejected by the House Ways and Means Committee and the tax bills were killed in conference.

Other Energy Technologies. Little apparent progress was made during 1978 in deciding on the future energy replacements for oil and gas. By general agreement, coal will be the major near-term substitute, but its many environmental problems require development of new technologies to make it clean and efficient to use. In an effort to find more acceptable technologies for the use of coal, as well as other energy sources, the Department of Energy carried out an intensive review of 17 new technologies during the year. The purpose of that review was to identify any technologies ready for commercialization. The findings of the review had not been released at year-end. In sum, the United States had yet to decide on its future energy technologies, and that means that most new technologies are at least a decade away from being of any general commercial use.

For nuclear energy 1978 was a year of indecision in which the scientific community raised as many new questions as it provided answers.

In general, construction continued on previously ordered conventional nuclear electric plants. There were, however, few orders for new plants. The controversy over nuclear power was repeatedly brought to public attention by demonstrations at nuclear construction sites such as Seabrook, N. H.

Perhaps the greatest uncertainty over the future of nuclear power concerns the disposal of used fuel from reactors. Primary attention has been focused on finding and demonstrating a safe burial site for the used fuel.

The Carter administration continued to limit development of the next generation of nuclear technology, the Liquid Metal Fast Breeder Reactor. The administration opposes rapid development of this technology because this reactor produces plutonium, which can be used for making nuclear weapons.

Solar energy technologies received increased attention. Federal support for the development and commercialization of solar technologies grew by roughly 25%, to $511 million. The Solar Energy Research Institute established by the Department of Energy in 1977 continued its rapid development. The question of when solar energy will become economically competitive with other energy sources, however, seemed no closer to an answer at the end of 1978 than it was at the beginning. (*See* Special Report page 194.)

DON E. KASH
Science and Public Policy Program
University of Oklahoma

COPYRIGHT 1978 BY HERBLOCK IN "THE WASHINGTON POST"

TROPHY ROOM

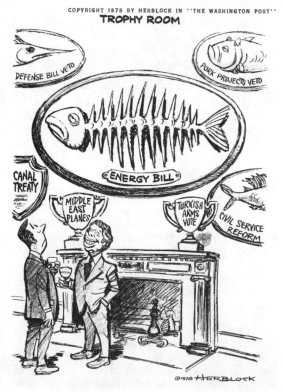

Oil — Friend and Foe

Five years after the 1973 oil embargo, there is an ever-growing gap between the production and consumption of energy in the United States. In 1978, domestic energy production continued its steady post-embargo decline, while consumption rose to levels characteristic of the pre-embargo period. As a consequence, demand greatly outstripped supply, and America found itself relying on foreign sources of energy more than ever before. A series of widely heralded federal programs has had little effect.

The energy crunch of the 1970's can be traced in large part to America's dependence on crude oil and its products. The shortfall is a direct result of the disparity in the supply of and demand for that most preferred fuel, petroleum. The energy problem, therefore, may be resolved by public policies that promote trade-offs between the societal costs and benefits of oil use. For while oil helps provide Americans with one of the highest standards of living in the world, their complete dependence on it as an energy resource also poses significant dangers for the entire society. Quite simply, oil is at once the energy consumer's best friend and worst foe.

The benefits of oil consumption are found in each energy demand sector of society—transportation, industry, residential and commercial interests, and the production of electricity. Transportation uses, which account for more than half of all the petroleum demand in the United States, represent by far the greatest oil-consuming activities. In fact, it is passenger transportation in general, and gasoline consump-

tion in particular, that sets the U. S. energy-use pattern apart from those of other advanced industrial countries. The largest single petroleum consumer in the transportation sector is the passenger car. The luxurious style of American automobile transportation, featuring the individualized, highly flexible use of the private vehicle, has become the standard for the entire world. Over the last three decades, the automobile has become very much a part of the American life-style, reflecting the nation's increased affluence and altering housing and employment patterns in ways that increase the individual's mobility and independence. All this has come about through the use of oil. And although the price of gasoline has nearly doubled in the period since the oil embargo, the American consumer still enjoys relatively cheap retail prices. Other transportation, particularly trucking and air transport, has also benefited from low fuel prices. As a result, the consumption of petroleum for transportation continues to rise. The most recent data suggest that motor gasoline demand in 1978 increased about 2% over the previous year, while aviation fuel consumption rose at a slightly lower rate. Americans continue to give high priority to fast and convenient transportation.

In industry, the benefits of petroleum consumption are greatest for the most energy-intensive manufacturing and agricultural activities. Of the major manufacturing concerns, the petrochemical and oil refining industries are among the heaviest users of oil. And in agriculture, the production of fertilizers is heavily dependent on the consumption of oil and its products. In

UPI

Record amounts of oil gush from the grounded supertanker Amoco Cadiz off the coast of Brittany, France, in March 1978, dramatizing one disadvantage of world reliance on petroleum—environmental pollution.

most instances, the oil demand in the industrial sector is relatively inflexible because there are simply no known substitutes in many industrial processes. Thus, despite the rising costs and occasional shortages of petroleum as a feedstock, American industry's demand for oil contributed to the more than 3% increase in the use of residual fuel oil and middle distillates in 1978.

The major contribution of oil to the residential-commercial demand sector is in the use of distillate fuel for residential space heating and the use of residual fuel for commercial space heating. The generation of electricity is another benefit of oil to consumers. Although coal and nuclear power plants are replacing many existing oil-fired facilities, oil is the source of about one sixth of the electricity generated in the United States. Petroleum is a major contributor not only to such residential and commercial energy uses as air conditioning, water heating, refrigeration, and cooking, but also to many industrial processes as well.

Taken together, these benefits of oil help explain why the United States continues to rely on petroleum for approximately half its total energy needs long after a world oil shortage has become a real possibility. But petroleum has its dangerous aspects in addition to the risk of interrupted supply. These dangers have become increasingly apparent in recent years. Dependence on oil has three major disadvantages for American society: the environmental costs of pollution, the political threat of monopolistic behavior by a powerful oil industry, and the economic burden of high fuel prices.

Oil consumption leads to environmental pollution in two ways. First, the growing demand for petroleum has induced the oil industry into exploration and production activities in environ-

ENERGY—SPECIAL REPORT:

The Solar Energy Alternative

As evidenced by Sun Day celebrations on May 3, 1978, solar energy is becoming a popular alternative in the United States today. Increasing numbers of individuals and businesses are installing solar heating and cooling systems in their homes and offices, and many other solar power systems have become operational. There has been considerable growth and maturing in the technological and institutional areas of the industry.

Water heating remains the primary area of application because of a good, year-round matching of energy supply and load. In addition to the federally funded projects under the Residential Solar Heating and Cooling Demonstration Program and the Florida and Northeastern States Solar Hot Water Initiatives programs, solar water heating is gaining wider acceptance in the private sector.

Unlike water heating systems, solar space heating is economically viable only in certain regions, with local fuel costs and duration of the heating season being the determining factors. Because of their high cost, solar cooling systems are relatively rare. This is an area, however, where major research and development continues. Under the Department of Energy's Solar Heating and Cooling Program, 7,157 residential and 253 commercial solar demonstration units have been funded.

While most of the publicity and funding for solar heating and cooling have gone to "active" systems, there has also been a significant grass roots interest in "passive" systems. Active systems employ collectors, pumps, heat exchanges, storage, and controls. The passive approach, on the other hand, is dependent upon the judicious design, orientation, and location of buildings for temperature control. In many regions of the United States passive design is more attractive.

The development of low cost photovoltaic cells and solar thermal power systems is a prime area of solar electric research and development. A goal in the development of photovoltaic cells is the reduction in manufacturing cost from the current $14 per peak watt to $0.50 by the late 1980's. Research is being pursued in developing both crystalline and amorphous photovoltaic materials. Recent sales of photovoltaic cells are about $25 million annually. Major demonstration projects are under way in solar thermal power systems, including the presently operational 5 MW (thermal) test facility at Sandia Laboratories and a 10 MWe facility scheduled for completion at Barstow, Ca. in 1981–82. Two solar water pumping demonstration projects are under way at Phoenix, Ariz. and Willard, N. M.

Extensive research and development is also being carried out in other solar technologies. Both biochemical and thermochemical conversion of biomass resources (wood and plants grown specifically for energy and available agricultural and forest residues) are being investigated. Projects include a 10 MWe wood burning plant in Vermont and facility in Oklahoma to make synthetic gas from manure. Ocean thermal conversion (OTEC) uses the ocean thermal gradients, and a 10 MWe demonstration project is planned for 1982–83.

Institutional factors that affect the implementation of solar energy include tax incentives, government loans, insurance company and bank

mentally marginal areas. The pristine nature of frontier regions such as Alaska or the outer continental shelf makes these locations extremely vulnerable to oil spills. Equally hazardous are the long transportation linkages from these remote regions to the major demand centers. The trans-Alaskan pipeline is perhaps the best example of a vulnerable oil transport system. Second, the extensive use of oil for passenger transportation has led to major air pollution problems in most American urban centers. The automobile is a significant contributor to levels of carbon monoxide, unburned hydrocarbons, nitrogen oxides, and other pollutants in the atmosphere. Some studies have estimated that, in urban centers, motor cars may emit as much as 90% of these pollutants.

The threat of anticompetitive behavior by the oil industry has been a political concern in the United States for most of this century. Two aspects of the industry's structure have been particularly threatening to the public: vertical and horizontal integration. Vertical integration is the involvement by oil companies in all stages of petroleum development, from the well to the pump; horizontal expansion is the tendency of oil firms to become involved in the development of resources other than oil, such as coal and uranium.

Finally, oil use today poses substantial economic costs as a result of price increases by the Organization of Petroleum Exporting Countries (OPEC). The shock waves of OPEC pricing decisions have affected the entire American economy, severely damaging the U. S. balance of payments situation, and placing a particularly heavy burden on low income families who must spend a greater portion of their income on energy.

ROBERT W. RYCROFT

policies, building codes, and labor practices. Several states presently provide tax credits, the most progressive being California's 55% income tax credit (up to $3,000 per home). A federal income tax credit (graduated and up to $2200 per home) was passed by Congress in October 1978. Low interest government loan legislation has been proposed, and lending institutions are also becoming more receptive to the idea of loans for new solar construction. Little progress has been made regarding the legal aspects of solar power, and more effort is needed in adapting building codes to solar installations. The growth of the solar energy industry will be greatly affected by institutional factors.

GARY C. VLIET

The "Solarmobile," *left*, Europe's first solar-powered vehicle, makes a test run in Sasbach, West Germany. *Right*, two technicians are mirrored in a 400-sq.-ft. (37 m²) heliostat (sun-tracking mirror) in Huntington Beach, Ca.

PHOTOS UPI

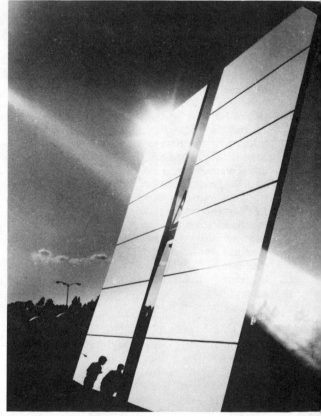

ENGINEERING, CIVIL

A variety of construction projects, including cable-stayed bridges, canals for low cost water transport, dams for storing water for hydroelectric power, and subway tunnels for mass transit were planned, under construction, or completed in 1978.

BRIDGES

United States. When completed in 1981, the 2.1-mile (3.4-km) bridge across the Mississippi River near New Orleans, La., will have a 1,235-foot (376-m) cable-stayed main span, the longest of its type in the western hemisphere. The $135 million structure will carry the four-lane Interstate 310, clearing the navigation channel by 133 feet (41 m). Its superstructure will include twin steel box girders, 14 feet (4.3 m) deep, extending 2,745 feet (837 m) over five river spans. From two A-shaped steel box towers, 12 cables will support the superstructure and orthotropic deck.

England. Some 20 miles (32 km) west of London, British Railways strung Europe's first cable-stayed mainline railroad bridge. Completed in late 1978, the two continuous-span, 360-foot (110-m) crossings carry two freight line tracks over an eight-lane expressway. The 37.5-foot (11.4-m) wide prestressed concrete spans are supported by two pairs of steel cables, 4-inch (10-cm) in diameter, that extend from each side of twin 85-foot (26-m) high reinforced concrete towers.

Spain. In 1978, Vigo Bay was spanned by the world's second longest cable-stayed bridge. The Puente de Strande is on the Atlantic coast, 20 miles (32 km) north of the Portuguese border. Its main span of 1,313 feet (400 m) is exceeded in length only by the cable-stayed Pont de Saint-Nazaire (1,325 ft; 404 m) over the Loire River in France.

Turkey. Though the Bosporus Strait was bridged at Istanbul in 1973, heavy truck traffic has already raised the need for a second span to link European and Asian Turkey. A new, six-lane suspension bridge, located north of the existing structure, is expected to get under way in 1979 and to open in 1982. Its 3,825-foot (1 166-m) main span will be 302 feet (92 m) longer than the first Bosporus bridge, making it the fourth longest in the world. It is expected to cost $85-million, compared with $35 million for the initial structure. Vertical clearance will be around 210 feet (64 m).

CANALS

United States. A flood control channel is being constructed to divert water flow at the Tulsa County, Okla., project of the U. S. Corps of Engineers. Scheduled for completion in 1981, the $6.5 million job will include widening and installing concrete lining along 8,800 feet (2 682 m) of a flood control channel 17 feet (5.2 m)

deep. Top channel width will vary from 40 to 200 feet (12 to 61 m), while the bottom width will range from 40 to 107 feet (12 to 33 m).

West Germany. The upper 45-mile (72-km) section of the 106-mile (171-km) Europa Canal was completed in 1978 at a cost of $400 million. Started in 1963, the waterway extends from the Main River south to Nuremberg. The lower remaining section, reaching to the Danube River, is being dug from both ends. Scheduled to open by 1985, it is expected to cost $750 million. To the south, the canal cuts through mountain ridges requiring a series of locks; each lock, 623 by 39 feet (190 by 12 m), will handle self-powered tandem barges. Also known as the Rhine-Main-Danube Canal, the 180-foot (55-m) wide, 13-foot (4-m) deep waterway will eventually connect the North Sea and the Black Sea.

DAMS

United States. The highest earthfill dam in the United States is proposed for Alaska. An 810-foot (247-m) high embankment would be located on the Sustina River about 150 miles (241 km) north of Anchorage and some 75 miles (121 km) from Willow. The state capital will be moved from Juneau to Willow beginning in 1980. Watana Dam will form a lake 54 miles (87 km) long. Downstream from Watana, another barrier, Devil Canyon Dam, is proposed for 1986. This 610-foot (186-m) high thin arch concrete structure would back up water 28 miles (45 km). The two hydroelectric dams together would generate 6,100 Mw, supplying energy for the new state capital and industrial development. The project is expected to cost more than (U. S.) $2 billion.

Canada. Hydro-Quebec is building one of the world's greatest electric energy complexes on La Grande River in the James Bay area of Canada. Four major dams and powerhouses will use a 1,200-foot (366-m) drop in the river to produce 10,000 Mw of power. The (U. S.)$16 billion project will include 150 earth dams and embankments totaling 59 miles (95 km) in length to store water in six reservoirs. Largest of the dams is LG 2, scheduled for completion in 1980. It will be 525 feet (160 m) high, 1,804 feet (550 m) across its base, and will have a crest length of 9,300 feet (2 835 m). It will contain 29,-000,000 cubic yards (22 172 000 m³) of material. The entire complex is expected to be completed in 1985.

Nigeria. The most populous country in Africa is building Bakolori Dam on the Sokoto River at a cost of $350 million. Begun in 1975, the dam is scheduled for completion in 1981. Its primary purpose is to reclaim land through irrigation, with auxiliary benefits of flood control, power generation, and water supply. Agricultural production in northwest Nigeria is expected to increase by from 200 to 300%. The 3.4-mile (5.5-km) long concrete/earth structure will have a

Controlled blasting is used to drive through hard rock on the Mondawmin tunnels of the Baltimore Region Rapid Transit Project. The 8-mile (13-km), 9-station system is scheduled for revenue operation in late 1982.

COURTESY, MARYLAND MASS TRANSIT ADMINISTRATION

1,181-foot (360-m) gravity spillway section, be 161 feet (49 m) high, and contain 222,352 cubic yards (170 000 m⁰) of concrete. Flanking rockfill embankments will total 3.2 miles (5.1 km) in length. The storage reservoir created by the dam will measure 9 by 19 miles (15 by 30 km).

USSR. When completed in 1979, Nurek Dam on the Vakhsh River will be the world's highest rockfill dam. Located 1,900 miles (3 058 km) southeast of Moscow, it will be 984 feet (300 m) high, 3,280 feet (1 000 m) long, and will contain 75,900,000 cubic yards (58 000 000 m³) of material. Its nine turbine generators will produce 2,700 Mw of electric energy. Cost of the project is estimated to be $933 million.

TUNNELS

United States. A 61-mile (98-km) rapid transit system, of which 10 miles (16 km) are tunnel, is being constructed in Atlanta, Ga. The first phase is a 13.7 mile (22-km) section with 4.5 miles (7.2 km) underground, 5.6 miles (9 km) at grade, and 3.6 miles (5.8 km) elevated. The depth of the tunnel will range from 25 to 45 feet (8 to 14 m). Started in 1975, the first phase is scheduled for completion by 1981. The cost of the entire system is estimated to be (U. S.) $2.1 billion.

The city of Baltimore, Md., is spending some $721 million to build an 8-mile (13-km) transit system to be completed in 1982. This nine-station line will have 4.5 miles (7.3 km) of tunnel, 1 mile (1.6 km) at grade, and 2.5 miles (4 km) elevated.

A water diversion tunnel is being bored under the streets of Hartford, Conn. A $23 million

Corps of Engineers contract calls for a 9,100-foot (2 774 m) tunnel, 22 feet (6.7 m) in diameter, varying in depth from 150 to 200 feet (46 to 61 m). This section is part of an overall project to divert flood waters from Park River, flowing through the western part of the city, to the Connecticut River, Hartford's eastern boundary.

Mexico. Two hard rock tunnels, 4.2 and 2.3 miles (6.7 and 3.7 km) long, are part of a 72-mile (116-km) aqueduct under construction to bring water from the Colorado River to Tijuana in Baja California. The $120 million project is expected to be operating in 1979. Hard rock encountered in driving the 10-foot (3-m) diameter tunnels, increased the construction time.

Venezuela. Started in 1976, the Caracas Metro mass transit system will total 31 miles (50 km) in length upon its completion in 1982. The project is expected to have cost about (U. S.) $2 billion. The Caracas Metro, it is hoped, will solve the rapidly growing transportation problems in one of the world's most densely populated cities.

Iran. A four-line, 68-station mass transit system, that will cost about (U. S.) $2.2 billion, was begun in Tehran in 1977. Almost half of the 39-mile (63 km) length will be a bored tunnel with an average depth of 66 feet (20 km). The initial 1.7-mile (2.7 km) segment of the system has three stations and is expected to be in operation during 1980. The entire system should be functioning by 1988.

See also TRANSPORTATION.

WILLIAM H. QUIRK
"Construction Industry International" Magazine

UPI

High school students in California, concerned about the staggering decline in the state's anchovy population, solicit signatures on a petition calling public attention to the problem.

ENVIRONMENT

The year 1978 brought some promising signs of global awareness of environment. It also brought spectacular outbreaks of insect pests and some grim new warnings—timber famine, extinction of plant and animal species, and dramatic changes in the earth's climate. In the United States, the federal bureaucracy took some significant steps toward interpreting and enforcing recently enacted environmental laws.

WORLD DEVELOPMENTS

In most countries, burgeoning populations and stark economic necessities continued to outweigh long-term environmental concerns. There was hope, however, that the economic incentives for sound environmental planning would outweigh the costs. Mostafa Kamal Tolba, who heads the United Nations Environmental Program (UNEP), said in his 1978 State of the World Environment message that many global environmental ills could be remedied by better utilization of natural resources. Although the world grows enough food to feed twice its present population, 500 million people are malnourished because of waste and inadequate distribution of resources.

Toxic Substances. There are some 30,000 chemicals loose in the environment today, according to the UNEP report, and several hundred others going into commercial production every year. World health officials said that concentrations of the pesticide DDT in mothers' milk in areas of intensive spraying often exceed safe levels by several hundred times. Tests were especially discouraging in Guatemala and Iran.

In April 1978, representatives of 16 countries met in Stockholm to discuss international control of toxic substances. The delegates identified research and action priorities, and the United States pressed for a formal international convention on toxic and hazardous chemicals. Most Western industrialized countries have enacted, or are considering, laws for toxic substance control.

Insect Pests. Dozens of malarial mosquito species have built up an immunity to the insecticides DDT and Dieldrin, and the disease is coming back. The UNEP reported in 1978 that malaria is killing a million children every year, and that in Africa, one fourth of all adults are stricken. Conservationists are encouraging natural controls, such as the release of sterile male mosquitoes into infested areas and the introduction of insectivorous fish.

Outbreaks of another insect pest, the locust, destroyed crops in parts of Ethiopia, Somalia, and Sudan. Control of the swarming pests was hampered by war and political unrest. The result was more toxic insecticides being released into the environment and less food for hungry nations.

Deforestation. The year brought warnings that the world's tropical moist forests are being seriously depleted. At the current rate of agricultural settlement, they could all disappear within 60 years. Experts made conflicting projections as to how many years the forests might last, but all agreed that the situation is reaching crisis proportions. If the depletion rate is not checked through reforestation and sound timber harvesting methods, the world stands to lose about 90% of its plant and animal species. Moreover, carbon dioxide escaping from cutover soils, added to the amount already in the atmosphere from the burning of fossil fuels, could warm the earth's climate.

Wildlife. An International Whaling Commission (IWC) meeting in London produced mixed results. A proposed 10-year moratorium on commercial whaling was scrapped, but a moratorium on the taking of sei whales in the southern hemisphere was adopted, along with an increased bowhead whale quota for Alaska Eskimos (18 landed or 27 struck, whichever occurs first). U. S. Eskimos left the meeting in protest and threatened not to comply.

The United States lifted most of its export restrictions on wild ginseng plants and the pelts of bobcat, lynx, and river otter. These species are protected under the Convention on International Trade in Endangered Species and Fauna, and the United States submitted new data showing that these exports would not be detrimental to the species' survival.

Rays of Hope. In 1978, international efforts of environmentalists focused on regional agreements, pooled technology, and education. Eight South American countries—Bolivia, Brazil, Colombia, Ecuador, Guyana, Peru, Surinam, and Venezuela—agreed to include extensive environmental studies in their plans for the 2 million-square mile (5.18 million-m²) Amazon Basin. By September, a number of nations began implementing training programs for environmental planners, administrators, and educators. In Nairobi, Kenya, the UN Environment Program began setting up a Regional Seas Center to assist governments in formulating regional plans of action.

U. S. DEVELOPMENTS

The nation's energy woes were in the public spotlight during much of 1978. Congress wrestled with President Carter's proposed deregulation of natural gas and some new incentives to conserve fuel. On May 3, the country turned out for Sun Day to celebrate solar power as a potential energy alternative. At Seabrook, N. H., environmentalists protested the construction of a nuclear power plant. There was some good news about the nation's waterways and some frightening news about environmental pollution.

Pollution and Health. In 1978, there was new evidence of how hazardous the American environment has become. The U. S. Environmental Protection Agency (EPA) released a study of the air quality in 105 urban areas and a sampling of U. S. counties. Of the nation's 105 largest population centers, only Honolulu had air clean enough to meet federal standards.

In Niagara Falls, N. Y., abnormally high incidences of miscarriages and birth defects prompted state health officials to advise residents that the area was unsafe for pregnant women and children under the age of two. Investigators found the community heavily contaminated with toxic chemicals that had been washed out of an old industrial dump by heavy rains.

Researchers noted that many lakes in the Adirondack Mountains of New York are devoid of fish because of rain made acid by atmospheric discharges as far away as the upper Midwest.

Water. The President's Council on Environmental Quality (CEQ) labeled 1978 as "the beginning of a new phase for the control of water pollution." There were encouraging reports that all but 400 of the country's major industrial polluters are showing "satisfactory" progress in meeting their legal deadlines for reducing water pollution. However, the CEQ noted also that pollution from "nonpoint" sources—surface runoff from farms, cities, and highways—"remained widespread, and control measures are still rudimentary."

Toxic chemicals, such as a group of industrial wastes called PCBs (polychlorinated biphenyls), still persist in the bottom of many waterways and make their way up the food chain to fish and higher mammals. The year brought new reports of high concentrations of PCBs in Puget Sound seals. In New York, where the Hudson River has been closed to fishing because of buildups of the substances in fish, the state announced a $25 million cleanup plan.

Land Use. Heavy rains—too heavy in parts of Texas and the Southwest—brought relief from a nationwide drought. Still, it was apparent that supplies of underground and surface water would not be sufficient to meet the demands of agriculture, industry, and some municipalities. Interior Secretary Cecil Andrus grimly predicted water shortages that will rival the energy crunch. The result could be water rationing, higher use fees, and conservation measures as stringent as those proposed for gasoline.

The national forests became a center of controversy as the U. S. Forest Service completed its survey of roadless areas (RARE II) and presented more than 60 million acres (24 million ha) to be considered for wilderness set-asides. Timber interests contended that since 51% of the nation's softwood sawtimber is in western national forests, set-asides of this magnitude would depress the forest industry.

Wildlife. Endangered species laws were the year's major wildlife issue. The U. S. Supreme Court stopped construction of the Tellico Dam on the Little Tennessee River because the structure would threaten the survival of the snail darter, a fish about 3 inches (7.6 cm) long. The decision led to Congressional revision of the Endangered Species Act of 1973.

See also CONSERVATION; ZOOLOGY—SPECIAL REPORT (page 558).

WILLIAM M. VOGT, *"National Wildlife" and "International Wildlife" Magazines*

UPI

In 1978, the U. S. Supreme Court held that the Tennessee Valley Authority (TVA) had acted illegally in constructing its $116 million Tellico Dam project on the Little Tennessee River by not considering the possible extinction of the 3-inch (7.6-cm) snail darter.

As Ethiopia prepares for war with Somalia early in the year, young Ethiopian boys undergo military training with make-believe rifles.

UPI

ETHIOPIA

Domestic and external conflicts continued to rack Ethiopia's Marxist military government in 1978. A counteroffensive against Eritrean secessionists was organized in April, one month after Somalia withdrew its invading troops from Ethiopia's contested Ogaden region. Ethiopia's relationship with the Soviet Union was strengthened. Executions of political opponents of the regime went on throughout the year.

Civil War. On March 9, Somalia's President Mohammed Siad Barre ordered the withdrawal of Somali troops from Ethiopia's Ogaden. Since July 1977, the troops had been supporting the Western Somali Liberation Front (WSLF) in its attempt to wrest control of the Ogaden from Ethiopia and to integrate it with Somalia. The overwhelming support given Ethiopia by more than 16,000 Cuban troops, 1,500 Soviet military advisers, 200 troops from South Yemen, and logistical technicians from East Germany was said to have turned the tide of the war in Ethiopia's favor. Some $875 million in Soviet military weaponry was reported to have been shipped to Ethiopia under the terms of the Treaty of Friendship and Cooperation signed by both nations in 1977.

In April 1978, three months after Ethiopian troops had reopened the road from Eritrea's capital, Asmara, to the port at Massawa, some 3,000 additional Cuban troops and many Russian advisers arrived in Eritrea to aid Ethiopia in combating the insurgent movements attempting secession. Cuban President Fidel Castro maintained that Cuba was pushing for a political settlement in Eritrea and denied that Cubans had helped Ethiopia retake a number of towns. In late April, the Eritrean Liberation Front and the Eritrean People's Liberation Front agreed to unite their combat units under joint military command in the face of the Cuban-Soviet involvement.

Domestic Strife. In November 1977 Maj. Atnafu Abate, the vice-chairman of the Dergue (military committee), was executed for "counter-revolutionary activity." Five leaders of the opposition Ethiopian People's Revolutionary Party (EPRP), an underground Marxist group opposed to the military junta, were "liquidated" in January 1978, while 300 EPRP proponents were arrested. The attack on the EPRP was the start of a government campaign known as the Red Terror. The campaign lasted for six months during which time thousands of opponents of the Dergue were reported executed and thousands more were arrested and sent to "re-education camps." Head of State Mengistu Haile Mariam's authority was strengthened by the action.

Human Rights. The Human Rights Division of the U. S. State Department released its report on the status of human rights on February 9. In relation to Ethiopia, the report stated "respect for human rights ... has deteriorated since the assumption of power by the ... military. The use of arbitrary arrest and lengthy imprisonment of opponents of the government has been common. We have received a few allegations of torture which appear to be valid."

Natural Disaster. In June 1978, 600,000 to 1.5 million Ethiopians were reported starving in the worst famine to hit Ethiopia since 1973. The famine was the result of a major drought, which was severest in the north around Wello province. Also, in June swarms of invading locusts ravaged the drought-stricken area.

Bibliography. New books dealing with Ethiopia included: Colin Legum & Bill Lee, *Conflict in the Horn of Africa* (1977); David Ottaway & Marina Ottaway, *Revolution in Ethiopia* (1978); John Markakis, *Class and Revolution in Ethiopia* (1978).

PETER SCHWAB
State University of New York at Purchase

─── **ETHIOPIA · Information Highlights** ───

Official Name: Ethiopia.
Location: Eastern Africa.
Area: 471,778 square miles (1,198,316 km²).
Population (1978 est.): 30,200,000.
Chief Cities (1976 est.): Addis Ababa, the capital, 1,-242,555; Asmara, 340,206.
Government: *Head of state and government,* Mengistu Haile Mariam, chairman of the Provisional Military Administra'ive Committee (took office Feb. 1977).
Monetary Unit: Birr (2.07 birrs equal U. S.$1, Sept. 1978).
Manufactures (major products): Processed foods, textiles, cement, building materials, hydroelectric power.
Agriculture (major products): Cereals, coffee, pulses, oilseeds, hides, skins, meat.

ETHNIC GROUPS

In many ways, 1978 was a year marked by conservatism, and for America's racial minorities that can often mean trouble. California's Proposition 13, designed to lower property taxes, helped to trigger a movement for tax cuts and limited government spending that dominated political campaigns across the United States. Although passage of Proposition 13 did not immediately endanger government services or social welfare programs in California, there was some concern that it might stall initiatives on behalf of minorities. In fact, Vernon Jordan of the National Urban League labeled the attitude "the new minimalism."

The Bakke Case. The U. S. Supreme Court's decision in the case of *The Regents of the University of California* v. *Allan Bakke* was anxiously awaited as a test for affirmative action programs intended to give special consideration to minorities and women, who had previously been discriminated against. In the Bakke case, a white applicant had been denied admission to the University of California at Davis Medical School, even though he claimed that less qualified minority candidates had been accepted under a special admissions program that reserved 16 places for nonwhite applicants. Bakke sued, saying that he had been denied equal protection under the law because of his race. His case became the best-known example of what some called "reverse discrimination."

But, not surprisingly, the court's decision was not so clear-cut as many had hoped. On the one hand, Bakke won a personal victory when the court ruled 5–4 that he had been discriminated against and must be admitted to medical school. That same 5–4 majority also held that the special admissions program at Davis, based on a strict numerical quota, was not permissible. On the other hand, the court held, again 5–4, that race is a valid criterion for university admissions—meaning that affirmative action programs could legally continue if they are not based on rigid quotas. It was a confusing decision and a delicate balance: Justice Lewis Powell provided the majority vote in each instance.

Thurgood Marshall, the only black Supreme Court justice, recorded a harsh dissent to the opinion that the Davis program was unconstitutional, and the Rev. Jesse Jackson called the decision "devastating." But most other black leaders were confident that the decision would allow affirmative action to continue.

Economics. If the year's big civil-rights news was ambiguous, the economic picture for black Americans was not. The Urban League issued a report, "The State of Black America 1978," with largely negative findings. The annual median income for blacks, according to the report, remained constant at $9,242—only 59% of the white median income, which rose to $15,537. The percentage of black families headed by a

UPI.
Vice President Mondale, Los Angeles Mayor Bradley (*center*), and National Urban League President Vernon Jordan attend the league's annual convention.

woman went up to 36%; 38% of black children were on welfare—and for the first time more than half were born out of wedlock. Unemployment for blacks stood at 13%, about double the national rate, and unemployment for black teenagers was near a staggering 40%.

Humphrey-Hawkins. Because the job shortage was so severe, one of the major priorities for many black advocates was the Humphrey-Hawkins Full Employment Bill. Named for the late Sen. Hubert Humphrey and Black Caucus member Rep. Augustus Hawkins of California, the bill was meant to commit the government to bringing the unemployment rate down to 4% and to require the government itself to provide jobs as a last resort. But the bill was thought by many, including President Carter, to be inflationary because of the high cost of jobs programs. A compromise was reached that authorized no federal spending at all, but merely set the 4% figure as a target.

Even the compromise bill was slow in attracting support, however, and there was some question of whether the bill would ever pass. At a meeting between the Black Caucus and Carter, Rep. John Conyers of Michigan angrily walked out after accusing the president of not fully supporting the bill. Finally, in the closing days of the Congressional session, yet another compromise was reached: a provision setting a target of a zero inflation rate by 1983 was attached to the bill. That was enough to get Humphrey-Hawkins passed, but the new act was a mere shadow of the original proposal.

Hispanics. For a number of reasons, Hispanic-Americans came into prominence in 1978 as "the new minority." It was widely noted that Hispanics, with an average age of 16 (ten years younger than the national average) and a high birth rate, will surpass blacks as the largest nonwhite population in the United States by the 1990's. A highly successful West Coast play, Luis Valdez' *Zoot Suit* based on 1943 Los Angeles race riots, helped focus the attention.

According to census figures, there are over

UPI

On the grounds of the Washington Monument, Sen. Edward M. Kennedy addresses a group of native American activists. The Indians were in Washington to demand support for their rights.

7 million Hispanics in the United States, including Mexican-Americans in the Southwest, Puerto Ricans concentrated in New York and the Northeast, Cubans who live mainly in Florida, and others from various Latin American countries. Like blacks, they are at an economic and social disadvantage: 27% of Hispanic families earn less than $7,000 a year; unemployment in the second quarter of 1978 was at 8.9%; only 40% are high school graduates; and the urban school dropout rate sometimes reaches as high as 85%.

Mexican-Americans, already by far the largest minority in the largest state, California, make up 60% of Hispanic-Americans, and their concerns reflect some of the high-priority problems of Latinos throughout the country: bilingual education to give their children a fair chance at educational parity; organized political activity so they can exert influence equal to their numbers; and equal justice, as related to the emotional issue of police brutality. In the spring of 1978, for example, Mexican-American advocates won a victory of sorts when the federal government, under pressure, agreed to prosecute Houston policemen in the death of José Campos Torres, a Chicano who had mysteriously drowned while in police custody. Three police officers were convicted of violating Torres' civil rights, but to the dismay of the Chicano community, the federal judge in the case gave the policemen only one-year sentences.

Illegal Aliens. In 1977, President Carter sought to tackle the perplexing problem of illegal aliens in the country. Such aliens number from 4 to 12 million, more than half of them Mexicans. Carter proposed an amnesty for illegal residents who had been in the country since before 1970, making them eligible for "permanent resident" status. Aliens who had entered since then would be able to stay and work for a specified number of years. The proposals remained controversial and were defeated in the hectic final days of the 1977 Congressional session.

But the issue did not go away. Subsequently, the Immigration and Naturalization Service announced that it would spend $4.4 million to construct 3 fences, 6 miles (9.6 km) long and 10 feet (3 m) high, along the Mexican border in California, Arizona, and Texas. Chicano groups quickly condemned the idea.

Indian Rights. Over the 1978 summer, a group of native American activists mounted one of the largest Indian-rights demonstrations in years. Starting from Alcatraz Island in San Francisco Bay, Indians conducted a five-month march across the country, billed as "The longest walk." They arrived in Washington, pitched tepees on the Mall, and spent several days holding rallies and lobbying against several proposed pieces of legislation that would curtail water, fishing, and hunting rights for Indians. One proposed bill, called the Native American Equal Opportunity Act, would simply cancel all the government's treaties with the Indians.

None of the bills was likely to pass anytime soon, but the protesters felt that the proposals symbolized a backlash against Indian rights. The march gave visibility to the Indian cause, and also gave Indians a chance to mend some internal rifts among militants like the American Indian Movement, traditional Indian religious leaders, and tribal government officials.

Apparently, part of the reason for the perceived increase in white resentment was the progress Indians had made recently in court cases to win back land they once held. In the spring of 1978, the Justice Department agreed to take the state of Maine to court on behalf of the Penobscot and Passamaquoddy Indians, who sought $300 million and 350,000 acres (141,639 ha) of land in compensation for 12.5 acres (5 ha) of Maine land they said was taken from them in violation of a 1790 treaty. In October, Maine political leaders approved an out-of-court settlement that would give the Indians $27 million in cash and $10 million with which to buy 100,000 acres (40,468 ha) of timberland from the state's large paper companies. There was a good chance the tribes would approve the deal.

DENNIS A. WILLIAMS, *"Newsweek"*

EUROPE

In 1978, the long-expected recovery from the economic depression precipitated by the quadrupling of oil prices in 1973–74 was again delayed, in part because of the growing weakness of the U. S. dollar. Unemployment and inflation continued to rise in many countries, magnifying the division between the few economically strong states and the many weak. Political discontent followed these economic difficulties, shaking the socialized economies of Scandinavia, compounding the problems of the southern tier of states from Portugal to Turkey, and causing unrest in parts of Communist Eastern Europe. Nevertheless, at the international level, certain encouraging signs were seen. Détente was pursued through the Strategic Arms Limitation Treaty (SALT) talks and the reexamination of the Helsinki agreements of 1975. The European Community (EC) prepared for the major constitutional change of direct election of the European Parliament by universal suffrage. Regional minority problems provoked less violence, but no solutions to the problems in Ireland and Cyprus were in sight.

Recovery Delayed. At midyear, the Organization for Economic Cooperation and Development (OECD) predicted that its 24 member nations would achieve a growth rate of only 3.5% in 1978, with the growth of the West European members being much lower. The nine-member European Community was expected to achieve only 2.7% growth in real GNP, thus causing unemployment to rise. Countries like West Germany and Switzerland, with the lowest inflation rates and the strongest currencies, would pay for their stability by lack of growth. In West Germany, for example, where inflation had been reduced to less than 3%, the growth rate fell to 2% and unemployment rose to one million. An intermediate group of states, including Britain, France, and the Scandinavian countries, showed moderate progress in growth and disturbing rates of inflation. The increasing flow of North Sea oil into Britain, however, began to aid the balance of payments, and Prime Minister James Callaghan, clinging to power with the shaky support of minority parties, felt sufficiently strong to postpone general elections until 1979. Economic conditions were most difficult in the southern European states and posed enormous problems for the newly democratized governments of Portugal, Spain, and Greece. Portugal, dependent upon loans of more than (U. S.) $2 billion from the United States and other Western countries, suffered from an inflation rate of 33%. Its Socialist premier, Mário Soares, was compelled to resign in December 1977, resumed office with a new coalition in January 1978, but was replaced by a technocrat in August. The largely hidden discontent in Eastern Europe became visible in the coal mining region of Rumania, where troops were needed to keep order following violent strikes in 1977.

The causes of the bleak economic outlook were numerous. The decline of the U. S. dollar disrupted European currency markets. West German and Swiss exports were threatened by the overvaluation of their currencies. Protectionist measures were invoked in such industries as steel and textiles. Austerity programs, which the International Monetary Fund (IMF) had required Portugal and other countries to adopt, dampened internal demand. No solution seemed to have been found for "stagflation," the combination of inflation and stagnancy of growth. Worse, some economists were even predicting that the capitalist world was entering a new "Kondratieff cycle," a half-century of economic decline that would follow the boom of the post-World War II years.

Monetary Coordination. As a result of the weakness of the dollar, the EC turned again to the problem of creating a common European currency. At a two-day meeting in Brussels in December, leaders of the European Community nations approved plans for a new European Monetary System (EMS). The plan was scheduled to take effect Jan. 1, 1979. The new system featured a "parity grid" that would establish the value of the currency of each member country against the currencies of the other members. A 2.25% fluctuation in the value of the currency against a determined figure would be allowed. A reserve facility (the European currency unit) is to support EMS. Britain decided against joining the system.

Politically, the EC's main preoccupation was preparing for the direct election of the European Parliament which, the heads of government decided at their Copenhagen summit meeting in April, should be held in June 1979. Many leading political figures announced their attention of running for election to the 410-member parliament, which was expected to renew pressure within the EC for greater political integration. Negotiations with Greece, Portugal, and Spain over their applications for EC membership continued, until late in the year; Greece was admitted to the union.

Continuing Détente. Relations between East and West Europe improved slightly. Soviet President Leonid Brezhnev visited West Germany in May and signed a long-term cooperation agreement. EC authorities agreed to open negotiations with the East European Council for Mutual Economic Aid (Comecon) on possible formal relations. There was renewed hope for an agreement in the Mutual and Balanced Force Reduction talks in Vienna between NATO and Warsaw Pact representatives, when, after five years of stasis, the Soivet Union agreed to limit the land and air troops of each alliance in Europe to 900,000. At the time, NATO authorities believed that Warsaw Pact troops outnumbered NATO troops in Europe by 150,000. Some progress was made in the SALT talks between the Soviet Union and the United States despite Soviet demands for limitation of the American cruise missile and American insistence that the Soviet Union cut production of its Backfire bombers. West Europeans worried, however, that the American government had weakened NATO by deferring production of the neutron bomb.

Continuing evidence of suppression of political dissent in Eastern Europe disturbed relations with the West, even though the Belgrade Conference on Security and Cooperation held in October 1977, which reviewed implementation of the Helsinki agreements of 1975, glossed over disagreements on human rights. In 1978, the condemnation in Soviet courts of physicist Yuri Orlov and political dissident Anatoly Shcharansky raised doubts in Western Europe about the reality of détente between the two blocs.

Roads to Communism. Independence from Soviet leadership was expressed by the national Communist leaders of several other European countries. The enthusiastic welcome extended to Chinese Party Chairman Hua Kuo-feng on his tour of Rumania and Yugoslavia during the summer was proof of their refusal to side with the USSR in its ongoing feud with China. In Western Europe, the three so-called "Eurocommunist" parties—in Spain, France, and Italy—continued to proclaim their faith in the democratic process, with its plurality of parties and periodic changes in power. Although some polls indicated that this attitude of the French Communists might help bring them to power with the Socialists in the March elections, disagreements between the two parties, at a time when the anti-inflation program of Premier Raymond Barre was showing success, led to their defeat. Although the Communists retained 21% of the vote, the Communist-Socialist alliance received only 200 seats, in comparison to the government coalition's 290. The Italian Communist party's popularity was damaged by widespread ultraleftist terrorism, which culminated in the murder of former Premier Aldo Moro, even though the Communists condemned such actions.

Terrorism. Moro's murder was perhaps the most dramatic of the growing number of acts of terrorism in Western Europe. Many kidnappings, especially in Italy, were for financial extortion only. Other actions, especially by the Red Army faction in West Germany and the Red Brigades in Italy, were directed against government leaders and industrialists held to be class enemies. A third type of terrorist action was carried out by national minorities, such as the Basques in Spain and the Bretons in France, who were demanding greater autonomy for their regions. The Bretons even claimed responsibility for the bombing of one wing of the Palace of Versailles outside Paris in June. Leftist political terrorists obtained money and arms from countries outside Europe, such as Libya and South Yemen, while relying on a network of several thousand supporters inside Europe. In response, most European governments increased surveillance, coordinated information exchange, and trained antiterrorist forces. Yet terrorism continued to magnify the sense of worry over the future of European society, a worry that the continuing economic problems had created. *See also* INTERNATIONAL TERRORISM (page 44).

F. ROY WILLIS
University of California, Davis

UPI

In European social circles, the event of the year was the June marriage of Monaco's Princess Caroline, daughter of Prince Ranier and Princess Grace (Kelly) to Philippe Junot, a French financial counselor.

FASHION

For the world of fashion, 1978 was a case of giving a few, taking a few. With the women borrowing this and that from masculine wardrobe, men picked up a change or two from women's fashions.

The U. S. Scene. Shoulders were broader. Skirt and pant lines slimmed down. The overblown Big Look, with its yards of fullness that many women found too much of a muchness, was replaced by a new shape. It was not, we hasten to say, the only shape around. It was simply the latest.

In its most extreme European form, the new shape could be likened to an inverted wedge. Its American interpretations sidestepped the quarterback effect that U. S. merchants and journalists took to calling "the Joe Namath" as they viewed the huge shoulders lumbering down the runways at advance fall-winter showings in Milan and Paris.

Searching for points of reference among all the padded and puffed sleeves that mark the 1978 season's hyper-chic fashions meant delving into the past. Comparisons with Joan Crawford's Adrian styles and Schiaparelli's wide-at-the-top whimsicalities became commonplace. Theirs was the era of knock-'em-out glamour, as those who lived through it the first time around will remember. Dressing up was the rule.

By 1978 the young women who spent their adolescence and early 20's living in scruffy blue jeans had grown up, mellowed, discovered the charm and the worth of antique clothes, discovered the allure and the fun of fashion, and they were ready to dress up—ready, the fashion moguls hoped, for glamour. Older women, weary of overcasual looks, were thought to be ready for it too.

So glamour obliged. It came back. Mostly, it was true, for the evening. But big bogus jewels were not out of place on gray flannel. Shetland jackets had leather gloves tucked in the pocket. Fewer heads were hatless, either during the day or at night. Sinuous satins— black satins—that have been out of circulation for years were suddenly in. Heels were higher, skirts were longer—for the moment. The high-fashion hemline was creeping up in Paris, where tight slit skirts of dresses were at the knee.

But American designers paid little mind to what the French were doing to skirt lengths.

Adapted from various articles written by Phyllis Feldkamp, Margaret de Miraval, and Margaret Ness for *The Christian Science Monitor*. Reprinted by permission from *The Christian Science Monitor* © 1978 The Christian Science Publishing Society, all rights reserved.

UPI

Comparisons with Joan Crawford fashion styles were common in 1978. Indeed it was the year for elegance and dressing up. Knock-'em-out glamour returned.

U. S. fashion demonstrated a new assurance. It was no longer totally dependent in imported ideas. When key directions like the season's military or leather-shock-troop trends were picked up, the translation was loose and easy, modified, pitched to American living—not line-for-line literal as it once was.

The Bill Blass brand of fall-winter "retro" elegance owed more to Carole Lombard (his neighbor down the street in the small Indiana town where he grew up) than high jinks at Maxim's or a gala night at La Scala. Ralph Lauren turned his back completely on the whole of "abroad," except for the British Isles, the source for his tweed and menswear looks. His Annie Hall outfits were undeniably home-grown. His

COURTESY, RAFAEL FASHIONS LTD.

Hats were "in" and the big word was small. Hair styles were geared to accommodate the new millinery.

Dressing up was the new rule. Heels were higher; black satin, out of circulation for years, was featured.

GINFRAY-MOUTIN, GAMMA

rip-roaring new Western clothes were as American as all get-out and responsible for an entirely fresh crop of prairie dresses and frontier jackets currently in the junior miss departments throughout the nation's stores.

Many others—among them timeless Bonnie Cashin, Vera Maxwell (celebrating her 30th year in business), young Stephen Burrows and Willi Smith—were indigenous talents. Burrows' love of dancing spilled over into his high-spirited clothes which, along with Danskin and Capezio, joined forces in style with a dance craze that swept the country.

John Travolta, Diane Keaton, "Star Wars," the active sports boom, camping out, and survival gear were all native products and major fashion influences on both sides of the Atlantic. The U. S. teenage girl was buying circular felt poodle skirts, shades of the 1950's; she and her elders and their counterparts in Europe were fascinated by vintage clothes.

Mention the American contribution in the past and the serious student of fashion might have guffawed of chortled. Today the United States is on an equal footing in the give and take of international style.

The Canadian View. "The message for the fall silhouette for most of the Canadian designers who design for manufacturing firms narrowed down from a real width at the top," said Mary Stephenson, director of the Fashion Designers Association of Canada. "But," according to Joyce Carter, fashion editor of the *Toronto Globe and Mail*, "we've been so comfortable in loose clothes that retailers were scared to buy the new skimpy skirts in depth."

As for the coat, shoulders were broad; the double-breasted style was common. Gloves were the rule.

The feminine look: the dress is a two-piece silk print. The accessories demand both a hat and high heels.

UPI

GARY SETTLE, THE NEW YORK TIMES

Canadian manufacturers and retailers have always been on the cautious side, so there's usually a time lag from the beginning of a drastically new trend. "Paris exaggerates to make a point," continued Joyce Carter. The fashion editor of the *Toronto Star,* Stasia Evasuk, concurs: "Coats and dresses in the early fall were still full but watch for the new slimness to make its appearance in a few months." The Canadian name designers such as Leo Chevalier, Michel Robichaud, John Warden, and Hugh Garber slanted their fall collections in the direction of this new pared-down look, complete with more structure and more shape.

Quilted coats were also on the market. One parka firm in Winnipeg was producing a down or fiber-filled quilted style with real or fake fur-trimmed parka hoods.

The craze for quilting also carried over into leather. In fact, soft leather was one of the biggest fall items. Leather trenchcoats with the widened shoulders were expected to be very popular, fitting with the military theme.

Colors dominant in Canadian fashion fell into the neutral category—running from winter white to beige, brown, gray, and black. Silver gray and the earth tones including sand and faded brick were also key.

Belts played the starring role in accessories, and usually in leathers featuring military inspiration and bandolier effects. Worn with everything, styles included silver-tipped cowboy, punched leather, polo, and various Sam Browne versions.

In other accessories Beth Hammond reported that in leather boots there was a new shorter

GINFRAY-MOUTIN, GAMMA

The layered look in menswear included thinned-down lapels, shorter shirt collars, narrower ties. In general, tweeds and textured materials were popular.

length, lower than midcalf but above the ankle. It was an important new trend. There was also a riding boot influence on lower heels with neater toes.

Paris and Other Fashion Capitals. Rarely have the "ins" and "outs" been so clearly defined and a lot of little things, usually relatively inexpensive, added up to a very satisfactory whole. The power of the accessory could not be overestimated.

Starting with the "ins," hats headed the list, with gloves coming in for a photofinish. Millinery accompanied everything from streetwear to dinner and theater ensembles, not to mention an occasional ultraformal gown.

Many women under the age of 30 had never worn hats or gloves except in a strictly functional manner when the snow was deep and midwinter gales were howling. A new generation of young women is going to discover the fun and morale-boosting effects of wearing something flirtatious, utterly frivolous, and often bordering on the downright ridiculous.

The big word was small. Even long-haired fur toques (with matching muffs) fitted close to the head. There were snug little helmets and profile cloches, tiny pillboxes, miniature bowlers, beanies and calottes, tambourines, clown and dunce caps with peaked crowns, stylized

versions of an American sailor's hat, and Saint Laurent's interpretation of the Nehru cap. The common denominator, apart from the small scaling, was that all hats were worn straight and tipped slightly forward over the brow.

Trimmings were as fanciful as the shapes. Naughty wisps of black veiling accentuated the eyes; quills were speared through narrow upturned brims, and pillboxes were anchored with jeweled hat pins. The new coiffures were modified to accommodate the millinery.

If one was not wearing an honest-to-goodness hat, there were all sorts of exotic trims and ornaments to crown the complicated hairstyles: wispy ostrich feathers, combs studded with glittering stones, a galaxy of baroque jewels, or flowers nestled into French rolls and buns.

Makeup was bold and vibrant. Gloves often stepped out in assorted fabrics and colors. Dimestore jewelry and ultrasheer stockings were also among the "ins."

The Men's Turn. The changes, need we say, were nondrastic. Seasonal differences in menswear move inch by inch, the majority of men being the relatively conservative creatures they are about dress. (Their slow acceptance of new styling pays off for them. On a price-for-price ratio, the quality of men's clothing is higher than women's because cut and workmanship—fabric, too—are meant to make men's apparel last longer, which it does.)

The changes—fall menswear's thinned-down lapels, smaller shirt collars, narrower (even skinny) ties, and layered sportswear, which all bespeak of sartorial barter between the sexes—may sound minor.

But the shirt with the higher, smaller collar, the business suit with less rigid construction, roomier armholes, less indentation at the waist, and perhaps pleats at the trouser top were heralded by the Men's Fashion Association (MFA) of America's Chip Tolbert as "the first major innovation in silhouette and detailing in a decade."

Men who jettisoned their narrow ties, little-collared shirts, and wide-bodied suits with thin lapels long before their wives tossed out their miniskirts, could shake their heads.

Shoulders for the males were trimmer—not broader—and had less, rather than more, padding.

Other news notes from MFA's Tolbert point to "country look" tweeds and textured materials, shadow plaids and checks, elbow patches and other leather trims, and straighter trousers, pants having been influenced by the formfit jeans of the moment.

Single-breasted two-button suits and double-breasted four-button suits almost invariably came with vests.

As to topcoats; they were generally of two types: the double-breasted town topper, so-called, in a dressy fabric with perhaps a shawl collar, and the country look.

PHOTOS, COURTESY, FINNISH TOURIST BOARD

The Savonlinna Opera Festival at Olavinlinna Castle attracts many tourists. A medieval castle tower is part of the setting for a production of *Il Trovatore*.

FINLAND

President Urho K. Kekkonen was reelected early in the year for a fifth term as Finnish head of state. His current term will expire in 1984 at which time he will be 84 years of age. The unique manner in which Finns elect their president includes the election of an Electoral College of 300 representatives bound by the selections made by their parties. In the Electoral College 260 electors represented the six major parties, all of which had called for the reelection of Kekkonen. The Electoral College voted by secret ballot on February 25; incumbent received 259 votes. The other candidates trailed far behind: Raino Westerholm (25 votes), Veikko Vennamo (10 votes), and Ahti M. Salonen (6 votes). A fifth candidate, Eino Haikala, of the Unity Party, did not gain a single electoral vote in the Electoral College.

According to Finnish traditions, the prime minister and his cabinet resign at the time of an election or reelection of a president. However, Prime Minister Kalevi Sorsa's five-party coalition cabinet tendered its resignation earlier than expected due to divided opinions within the cabinet

FINLAND · Information Highlights

Official Name: Republic of Finland.
Location: Northern Europe.
Area: 130,129 square miles (337,032 km²).
Population (1978 est.) 4,800,000.
Chief Cities (1976): Helsinki, the capital, 491,516; Tampere, 165,769; Turku, 164,380.
Government: *Head of state,* Urho Kaleva Kekkonen, president (elected February 1978 for 5th term). *Head of government,* Kalevi Sorsa, prime minister (took office May 1977). *Legislature* (unicameral)—Eduskunta.
Monetary Unit: Markka, or Finnish mark (3.97 markkaa equal U.S.$1, Dec. 28, 1978).
Manufactures (major products): Timber and forest products, machinery, ships, clothing, transportation equipment, food products, electrical equipment, appliances.
Agriculture (major products): Dairy, wheat and other grains, livestock, furs, berries.

regarding the necessity of devaluing the Finnish mark by 8% in order to promote the sales of Finnish products abroad. At the request of Kekkonan, Sorsa formed a new cabinet, representing a majority coalition of four parties, the Center Agrarians, the Social Democrats, the Liberal Party, and the Communists. The Swedish Party decided to stay out of the new government. The new government controls 136 votes in the 200-member Parliament.

The thirtieth anniversary of the signing of the Finnish-Soviet Treaty of Friendship, Cooperation, and Mutual Assistance was marked on April 5 with ceremonies in Helsinki's Finlandia Hall, at which President Kekkonen and Soviet Foreign Minister Andrei Gromyko spoke.

In 1978 the economic situation continued to be problematic at best. The improvement in the foreign trade balance noted in 1977 was accompanied by persistently high inflation and increasing unemployment. During the first half of the year, export volume was some 9% above the corresponding period of the previous year. Private investment remained sluggish, largely due to low capacity utilization. Imports continued to decline due to weak domestic demand and the improved price competitiveness of Finnish goods. The modest growth of total output, which started toward the end of 1977, continued in 1978. The pace of inflation was reduced in spite of the 8% devaluation of the Finnish mark in the spring. This devaluation of the Finnish mark was the third within a year. In September there was a 4% general wage increase.

Also in September, an extensive Consumer Protection Act came into force. It deals with the relationship between traders and consumers, and includes regulations for marketing, contract terms, the purchase of consumer goods, and home and mail order sales. The act also authorized the appointment of a consumer ombudsman, a market court, and a consumer complaint board.

In May President Kekkonen recommended that the Nordic countries enter into arms control negotiations among themselves as well as with the great powers. The aim would be a nuclear-free Scandinavia and a guarantee by the great powers not to use nuclear weapons against the Nordic nations under any circumstances. The reaction to his proposal was rather favorable in Sweden, was somewhat less favorable in Denmark, and was very negative in Norway.

ERIK J. FRIIS
Editor, "The Scandinavian-American Bulletin"

FLORIDA

An exciting governor's election, constitutional revision, functional literacy tests, and casino gambling preoccupied Floridians and attracted attention throughout the United States during 1978.

Gubernatorial Election. With Reubin Askew being ineligible under Florida law for a third term, more than a half-dozen Democrats tossed their hats into the ring. Millionaire dairyman-developer Bob Graham, a state legislator, forced front running Attorney General Robert Shevin into a run-off election. Although Shevin had won great respect and popularity during his eight years as attorney general, especially for his favorable stand on environmental issues and capital punishment, he suffered a shocking upset. The Harvard-educated Graham won a narrow victory by his promise to impose a two-year freeze on property taxes and by his strategy of working 100 days on 100 different jobs.

Although Florida's registered Democrats outnumber Republicans two to one, the Republican gubernatorial candidate, drugstore magnate Jack Eckerd, waged a strong challenge. The largest number of voters ever in a gubernatorial election went to the polls. Fifty-six percent of the vote went to Graham and 44% to Eckerd..

Constitutional Revision. Approximately 60% of Florida's registered voters cast ballots to vote against nine constitutional amendments. As required by the 1968 constitution, a citizens' Constitutional Revision Commission was appointed to review the state's constitution to determine if alterations were necessary. Most Floridians apparently believed that few changes should be made, but the Commission recommended 88 changes, grouped into eight amendments. The most radical changes would have eliminated the election of state cabinet officers and would have created single-member legislative districts. Revision Two was a state version of the national Equal Rights Amendment. This latter amendment received far more debate and lobbying than any of the others; however, 58% of the voters rejected the "little-ERA," along with the other seven.

The casino gambling issue arose when a group in Dade County successfully petitioned to add Revision Nine—legal casino gambling—to the ballot. Pro-casino forces in Miami organized a media-blitz which was more than equaled by the anti-casino forces led by Governor Askew. Seventy-one percent of the voters rejected casino gambling.

Education. Bitter debate continued on the functional literacy tests given to high school juniors in November 1977. The tests were adopted in an attempt to assess and improve the quality of education; however, controversy erupted when more than one third of the students in some counties failed the exams. Charges of racial discrimination forced some changes in the test and scoring procedures, but they were to be administered in 1978 under a new name, the student assessment test. A court challenge is still pending.

Environment. The state Supreme Court in November struck down the landmark Environmental Land and Water Management Act of 1972, the law enabling the state to limit development of these areas which supply water to the underground aquifer, the source of the watersupply.

J. LAWRENCE DURRENCE
Florida Southern University

FLORIDA • Information Highlights

Area: 58,560 square miles (151,670 km²).
Population (Jan. 1978 est.): 8,506,000.
Chief Cities (1970 census): Tallahassee, the capital, 72,586; Jacksonville, 528,865; Miami, 334,859.
Government (1978): *Chief Officers*—governor, Reubin O'D. Askew (D); lt. gov., J. H. Williams (D). *Legislature*—Senate, 40 members; House of Representatives, 120.
Education (1977–78): *Enrollment*—public elementary schools, 776,714; public secondary, 758,856; colleges and universities, 364,509 students. *Public school expenditures*, $2,677,901,000 ($1,466 per pupil).
State Finances (fiscal year 1977): *Revenues,* $5,707,077,000; *expenditures,* $5,391,507,000.
Personal Income (1977): $56,496,000,000; per capita, $6,684.
Labor Force (July 1978): *Nonagricultural wage and salary earners,* 2,970,300; *unemployed,* 260,900 (6.8% of total force).

FOOD

The supply of food for the world is subject to many factors. Of these, weather vagaries play the most important role, since dry spells, droughts, or prolonged rains can create shortages in regional areas while normal crops are being harvested in other regions. However, under the existing world food distribution system, such food shortages are not easily overcome. In 1978, several weak spots in overall crop production developed in China and Southeast Asia, due to severe floods and other natural causes. This production loss was the first lowering of record or near-record crop yields in several years.

WORLD SUPPLY

In 1975 the world food supply began to rise as crop production reacted to lessening drought and ample rain fall. This increase continued in 1976, and generally maintained the same level in 1977. However, in 1978 changes in weather patterns, crop diseases, and floods apparently affected the continued rise in overall production. In China, a slightly below-average harvest led to a purchase of United States wheat. The sale was estimated to be in the vicinity of 2.5 million metric tons of wheat having a total value of $340 million. Other agricultural imports were expected to have an added value of approximately $160 million. The People's Republic of China has a population growth of 1.7% per year, or approximately 17 million more people to feed each year. This population rise requires more than 4 million tons of food grains annually to maintain supplies. In 1978, demand outstripped domestic needs as food grain production remained essentially level (270 million tons) for the third year.

In the United States, total crop output in 1978 was expected to be only a little below the record high of 1977. While the wheat crop was estimated to be 10–12% below 1977's large harvest, corn and other coarse grains appeared to be higher.

In other areas, output was up. The European Community, India, and the Soviet Union were expected to equal or slightly exceed previous record crops. In Argentina and Australia, the 1978 crop was expected to be much higher than the drought-affected production of 1977. Overall world grain production (wheat, coarse grain, milled rice) was expected to be 4% higher than 1977.

However, in several areas of the world, trouble spots existed. Southeast Asia was hard hit by monsoon floods and rains that resulted in extensive damage to the vital rice crop. Particularly affected were Laos, Vietnam, Thailand, and Cambodia. Other parts of Asia, including the Philippines, Hong Kong, and India, were also affected.

An outbreak of the desert locust in Ethiopia and Somalia reached dangerous levels. If the outbreak reaches plague level, it is feared that migrating swarms could possibly consume crops in other countries of Africa, the Arabian Peninsula, and some Asian countries. Also in Africa, both Cape Verde and Madagascar have been severely hurt by prolonged drought.

Worldwide, food prices continued to advance. Of 16 countries regularly surveyed, only West Germany, the Netherlands, and Belgium had lower prices than the United States. However, during 1978 the rate of increase in food prices was higher in the United States than in 7 of the other 15 countries. Such food price increases in all countries can reflect in lessened consumer buying power and a resultant effect on the nutritional level of the population of the entire world.

In a totally different development that relates directly to the amount of food available in the world, a sizable and generally unexpected drop in fertility has occurred in the less developed countries. The birth rates in the less developed world fell from 42 to about 37 per thousand in the period 1970–77. While this process is uneven geographically throughout the world, it is taking place where diets appear to be slowly improving and health services are available to more people. In Thailand the birth rate in the 1950's was approximately 47 per thousand, and today is in the low 30's, yet Syria with the same original figure has not changed appreciably. In Africa, no fertility decline has apparently taken place, thus making any explanation difficult. While the drop may be dramatic, the birth rate is still more than double the 17 per thousand rate of developed countries. However, should this drop in birth rate continue, it is possible that future population estimates may be down by 200–400 million in the year 2000. A population drop of this magnitude could, if maintained, have an upward effect on food supply in the future.

Related to population and to food supply, a survey of world food conditions by the UN Food and Agriculture Organization (FAO) pointed up considerable differences between the nutrition of rich and poor nations as well as within individual nations. The survey points out that "preschool children, younger women, and school-age children suffer most often and most severely from poor nutrition." The FAO survey stated that the daily calorie supply in developed countries rose 7% to 2,360 in 1972–74, yet in "most seriously affected (MSA)" countries it dropped from its early 1960's level to 2,030 calories in 1972–74. The figures relate to 1.4% increase in food production per person in developed countries, while in MSA countries food production declined by 0.4% per year in 1970–76.

U. S. SUPPLY

In the United States estimates of crop prices are for prices below the spring's peak prices, although the forecast is open to debate. While farm exports were expected to be above 1977, and with the storage of 552 million bushels of corn, wheat, oats, barley, and sorghum in a national grain reserve, plus government idling of grain acreage, food prices were expected to continue to rise at the consumer level. Overall, the consumer's food bill was expected to be higher in 1978 than in 1977, even though supplies of all foods appeared to be adequate, or more than adequate. As prices rise, new trends in the marketing of food have shown up. In an effort to lower consumer prices and increase returns to the growers, direct marketing of food to consumers via food cooperatives, roadside stands, and farmers' markets was on the upswing.

FOOD AND NUTRITION

America's population and its overall profile are changing. The population growth rate of 0.8% has remained steady for seven years; the total population is about 217.8 million. Of the total, a majority (51.2%) is female, with the median age of the population rising to 29.4 years in 1977. While the number of married persons has dropped, other changes, such as increased incomes and larger numbers of employed persons, indicate future changes in food, nutrition, and the food supply.

Currently, the field of nutrition is receiving a great deal of attention. Over 50 million Americans are recipients of food assistance programs provided by the federal government. The programs, at a cost of over $8 billion, are: food stamps for low-income households; milk for needy children; child nutrition (pre-school-high school); special supplemental food for women, infants, and children (WIC); food distribution; and feeding the elderly. While these programs, administered by the U. S. Department of Agriculture (USDA), have been criticized for being nutritionally inadequate, failing to reach eligible persons, and being poorly operated, the programs provide food to many people who otherwise might have to do without. As a result, many changes are being made to upgrade the programs. In late 1977 President Carter signed legislation that significantly changed the child nutrition programs. It included a provision for a new program of nutrition education and training.

Congress' Office of Technology Assessment issued a statement that U. S. federal research on nutrition has failed to keep up with the times. It said the research has emphasized undernutrition and paid too little attention to evidence linking modern eating habits with fatal diseases. The report stated that continued studies into human nutrition would produce little of practical value for the United States, and that more emphasis should be placed on biochemical functions of nutrients, and on undernutrition in developing countries.

In response to much criticism, the Senate Select Committee on Nutrition issued a modified "Dietary Goals." The modifications relate to the reduction of cholesterol consumption; they endorse eggs as a good source of protein, and lessen the stigma attached to meat and egg consumption. In yet another related area, USDA is tentatively testing full substitution of plant protein sources as alternates for meat, fish, and poultry in School Lunch Programs. In the saccharin controversy, Congress in 1977 enacted legislation to permit an 18-month moratorium on the FDA ban. A provision of the law requires that warning labels appear on all products shipped in interstate commerce. The warning reads "Use of this product may be hazardous to your health. This product contains saccharin, which has been determined to cause cancer in laboratory animals." Other warning notices must be located in stores selling products containing saccharin and on vending machines. The Food and Drug Administration (FDA) is to develop and distribute information on saccharin, and further studies are to be conducted by the National Academy of Science.

A controversy developed over the use of nitrites in processed and cured meat products. On Aug. 11, 1978, USDA and FDA regulations warned that sodium nitrite may cause cancer and should be phased out. The warning was based on an extensive study done at MIT that showed an increase of lymphatic cancer in rats fed daily doses of nitrite. The controversy has been debated ever since it was shown that nitrosamines (formed in the stomach or during cooking) caused cancer in laboratory animals. The MIT study was the first to indict nitrite alone as a carcinogen. Even though regulations issued earlier by USDA reduced levels of nitrite, and included the addition of ascorbate to block formation of nitrosamine, the issue is such that Congress may enter the debate. Further complicating the situation are the facts that nitrite inhibits botulinum food poisoning, and gives the product its characteristic flavor and coloring. In Canada, government officials believe that nitrite is safe when used under controlled conditions, and plan no phase-out until safe and effective substitutes are available. Overall, the problem comes down to recognition of the risk from botulism if nitrite is banned.

Other food developments, regulatory actions, and marketing actions included label warnings for protein supplements used in low-calorie diets, proposed label declarations for drained weight or solid content weight (fill weight) for canned fruits and vegetables, and combined (FDA, USDA, and FTC) hearings on food labeling in five U. S. cities. These hearings will focus on ingredient labeling, nutrition and other dietary labeling, open dating, food fortification, and other topical subjects. They will be of interest to the consumer, the food industry, and the various government agencies.

See also INFLATION (pages 10–16); AGRICULTURE.

KIRBY M. HAYES
University of Massachusetts

UPI

The presidents of France and the United States at Omaha Beach, Normandy, France.

FRANCE

The crisis of the regime, expected by many, did not occur. The public institutions of France again escaped the fundamental test of a clash of policy and will between a center-right president and a left-wing prime minister and cabinet. After the spring elections of 1978, everything was anti-climax.

DOMESTIC AFFAIRS

The build-up toward the elections for the 491 National Assembly seats had been extraordinary. An incessant torrent of talk flowed in the press, on the radio and television. The real war was less between government and opposition than between the rival clans in each camp.

President Valéry Giscard d'Estaing, leader of the Independent Republicans, remained locked

213

UPI

in combat with former prime minister Jacques Chirac, leader of the Gaullist Rassemblement pour la République. Posing as the presidential arbiter above the battle, Giscard was in fact the leader of the ruling coalition, with prime minister Raymond Barre his standard-bearer. At Blois, January 7, Barre revealed the program: a two-year freeze on personal and corporate taxes, larger pensions and family allowances, an overall 5-year blueprint said to cost less than half that of the Socialists, packaged under the label, "reform, not upheaval; evolution, not revolution." The enraged Gaullists denounced this as smug stand-patism, denied it suited them, and demanded measures to encourage reflation, to reduce unemployment, and to increase consumption. The air was heavy with talk of the Independent Republicans and their Radical and Reformist allies (grouped as the Union pour la Démocratie Française) and the RPR running rival candidates in the first round of balloting, with agreement jointly to support the front-runner only in the second. Giscard appealed for unity and campaigned for Barre. With the polls showing the left likely to win by a slim majority, he attacked their collectivist program, warned the nation that as President he could not prevent a leftist government from executing it, and called for "the right choice." Chirac declared himself satisfied. François Mitterrand, leader of the Socialists, denounced this presidential descent into the market-place. Giscard's retort was that the President "cannot remain indifferent to the fate of France. . . . His electoral district is France." Thus the ambiguity of the presidential role continued to fire controversy. Because they needed each other, Giscard and Chirac muted their quar-

rel, but at the mass meeting he staged in Paris on February 11 it was clear that Chirac intended to displace Giscard in the 1981 presidential election.

The left alliance had been in ruins since September 1977; the "common program" of 1972 had vanished. Bent on as much warfare against the Socialists as the party faithful would stand, the Communists immediately denounced the Socialists' program. Their leader, Georges Marchais, berated Mitterrand for his interview with President Jimmy Carter, accusing him of treachery in league with "forces beyond our frontier." Trailing the Socialists in recent elections, the Communists were ready to throw the national elections rather than play second fiddle. Therefore, Marchais announced he would break the electoral agreement in the first round, but might support front-running Socialist candidates in the second if the Communists got at least 21% of the vote. Otherwise, he would prefer to remain in opposition. In February, after he veered sharply to say he had been promised six or seven seats in a Mitterrand cabinet, and Mitterrand denied the possibility of any such deal with Marchais between rounds, l'Humanité called the Socialist leader a liar. The paradox was that while polls gave the left a slight edge, most Socialists did not want Communists in the government.

The level of the campaign was low. Giscard's pose as guardian of all French interests was an unconvincing mimicry of General de Gaulle's act. When Barre's austerity measures did not infuriate the nation, they put it to sleep. Chirac, the darling of the wealthy, barely curbed his bitter ambition. Marchais, at once brutal and bantering, transparently communicated his conviction that the left should not win. Mitterrand labori-

UPI

French voters elected a new National Assembly in March 1978 (page 214). The Communist Party, under the leadership of Georges Marchais, and the Gaullists, led by Jacques Chirac, obtained 86 and 148 seats respectively, as the ruling government coalition emerged the winner.

UPI

ously plowed on to assure hesitant moderates that he could control the Communists. The press revealed gross meddling by diplomats with the overseas vote, government stonewalling, and eventual disqualification of certain ballots.

Nearly 34 millions were eligible to vote, including 6 million new voters aged 18 to 21. In the first round, March 12, the opposition drew 48.4%, the ruling coalition 46.5%. Giscard's UDF took 21.5%, Chirac's RPR 22.6%, Mitterrand's Socialists 22.5%, Marchais' Communists 20.5% (their worst showing in a decade). Marchais made a chilling election night television appearance in which, in tough-guy stance, he confirmed the fears of many would-be supporters of political change. This cold spectacle ended illusions that Eurocommunism had come to France, as it ended Mitterrand's quest to become prime minister. If it was not recklessly intended, it was marvelously stupid. In response to Mitterrand's call for a patched-up truce, Marchais bargained for half the ministries in a left cabinet. By acquiescing, Mitterrand reneged

on his previous assurances and was seen not to be able to control the Communists. Taking no chances, Giscard weighed in, on the eve of the second ballot, with a powerful but constitutionally irregular television address.

On March 19, 85% of the voters turned out. The government triumphed with a slim 50.49% to the left's 49.5%. Translated into seats, as a consequence of what the left has always considered electoral rigging, this gave the Barre government 291 seats, the opposition 200. Slipping slightly, the RPR took 148 seats, the UDF 137 seats. Both the Socialists with 103 seats and the Communists with 86 seats slightly increased their strength over 1973. The small Left Radicals and the extreme left lost seats. Momentarily, Chirac was checked and Giscard the principal winner, but their struggle went on. Chirac's appeal was to the right; Giscard hoped to free himself from the RPR grip.

Post-election recriminations were bitter on the left. Marchais blamed the Socialists for refusing to update the 1972 program as the Communists wished. Mitterrand accused him of wrecking the alliance. Robert Fabre took his small Left Radical party out of the alliance, then abandoned its presidency. The political disarray was total. Yet the grass-roots strength was impressive, almost half the electorate. Hence Giscard's invitation to consult the leaders of the opposition, and the unfamiliar spectacle of Mitterrand, Marchais, Fabre, and the trade union leaders, Georges Séguy (CGT), André Bergeron (Force Ouvrière), and Edmond Maire (CFDT) entering the Elysée. It was window-dressing, nothing came of it, probably nothing was expected of it.

Barre formed his third government on April 3. Most ministers were carried over and approved by the Assembly. Clearly, Giscard had done nothing to accommodate the other half of the nation. Riding his success, he challenged Chirac by backing the candidacy for Assembly president of former prime minister Jacques Chaban-Delmas, a once-popular Gaullist, in retirement after exposure of his 4-year (legal) evasion of income tax. The RPR candidate, incumbent Edgar Faure, who might normally have expected reconfirmation, was beaten in a stand-up fight, April 3, marked by defection of 20 RPR deputies who switched to Chaban. In this and in a hundred other, minor struggles, from appropriations to protocol, the president and the mayor of Paris battled toward 1981. It seemed unlikely either one would have to confront Mitterrand. Within the Socialist party his authority was being challenged by the young, tough, and able Michel Rocard.

Marchais suffered no such personal challenge, but there was grumbling in the party. At the central committee meeting, April 27, he attacked Socialist "obstinacy" and demands for freer party debate. Having closed *l'Humanité* to his critics, Marchais saw the debate spill over into scandal when six party intellectuals criticized him in *le Monde*. Unable to silence them, Marchais bided his time. By summer's end he referred to them as loyal comrades who were "obvious proof of the democracy that reigns within the party's breast." The storm seemed to be over.

Strikes and Protest. The country had been braced for strikes, whatever the election results,

but the failure of the left occasioned no upheaval. The strikes which did follow in the spring—at Renault, in textiles, in the new Lyon subway system, among dockworkers, air traffic-controllers, truck drivers and railwaymen, even a slowdown by the Paris police—were not extraordinary.

More troublesome was continued Breton and Corsican separatism. In Brittany bombs went off against army and electricity board installations, a Rennes radio station and the Dinard townhall, at various police stations and law courts. Following the immense, 200,000-ton oil-spill from the supertanker *Amoco Cadiz* which, grounded on a reef fouled more than 100 miles (160 km) of beach, destroying fishing grounds, oyster beds, seaweed crops and tourist facilities, the Shell Oil headquarters in Nantes were bombed several times. On June 26 Breton Republican Army bombs wrecked three rooms of the Palace of Versailles. Quickly arrested and tried, the perpetrators variously received 2 to 8 year prison sentences, suspended sentences and one acquittal for lack of evidence. The court recognized the sincerity of their convictions.

In Corsica bombs exploded all year, directed against radar units, a Belgian army resort, businesses and the sugar magnate Ferdinand Beghin's chateau. Despite the fact that all Corsican parties favored a regional assembly, Giscard, on a visit, June 7–9, promised reform but no autonomy. "Our struggle," promised Corsican National Liberation Front leaflets, "is one of self defense and we will conduct it to the end."

Activist groups were tiny, but sentiments of regionalist yearnings were much more widely felt. But, "The French urbanization of the 1960's," Michel Crozier has said, "has left a mass of frustrated people who feel they can no longer influence their own lives." Philippe de Commines (alias André Bercoff) published a best-selling novel that featured the government of 1980 being held to ransom by regionalists.

Economy. Like all governments facing elections, the French government announced a smaller trade deficit for late 1977. Before mid-March, nevertheless, money left the country, and the franc fell. Confidence returned after the election, and both the currency and the stock market moved up. Taking advantage of victory, Barre immediately put through price increases for transport, fuel, electricity and gas, among other things, while rejecting labor's demands and raising the minimum wage gradually in three small hikes. Inflation continued high (14% in April). Holding to his free-market philosophy, the prime minister began in June to dismantle the 30,000 price control decrees accumulated since 1945. Business was warned to be responsible, foreign competition was welcomed. The government refused to bail out the collapsing Boussac textile conglomerate. The 1979 budget deficit, it was hoped, would be reduced by higher alcohol, gasoline, and tobacco taxes. How to reduce

---

FRANCE • Information Highlights

Official Name: French Republic.
Location: Western Europe.
Area: 211,207 square miles (547,026 km²).
Population (1978 est.): 53,400,000.
Chief Cities (1975 census): Paris, the capital, 2,299,830; Marseille, 908,600; Lyon, 456,716; Toulouse, 373,796.
Government: *Head of state,* Valery Giscard d'Estaing, president (took office May 1974). *Chief minister,* Raymond Barre, prime minister (took office Aug. 1976). Legislature—Parliament: Senate and National Assembly.
Monetary Unit: Franc (4.83 francs equal U. S.$1, Nov. 1978).
Manufactures (major products): chemicals, automobiles, processed foods, iron and steel, aircraft, textiles, clothing.
Agriculture (major products): cereals, feed grains, livestock and dairy products, wine, fruits, vegetables.

the number (1.2 million) of unemployed was a thornier issue.

Defense. A powerful (2 to 3 megaton) underground explosion was reported at the Mururoa Atoll site in July, but the defense ministry did not confirm it. It did deny exploding a neutron bomb. Emphasis this year was on disarmament proposals revealed on January 25 and presented by Giscard to the UN General Assembly special session on May 25. They provided for a satellite monitoring agency, taxation of "overarmed" countries, the convening of a Helsinki powers conference to examine the problem "from the Atlantic to the Urals." This call, with its neo-Gaullist ring, electrified no one, although the Russians claimed to be examining it.

FOREIGN POLICY

Relations with Spain, though troubled by economic conflicts, were affirmative. Giscard's visit, June 28–July 1, was the first by a French chief of state in 72 years. He supported Spain's application to enter the Common Market, but warned the Cortes, July 29, that France would protect her wine-growers. "Our attitude is clear: France believes that Spain's place is in Europe." Besides conferring with King Juan Carlos and his government, Giscard met the Socialist and Communist leaders. Dodging the Basque separatist issue (much more violent on the Spanish side of the frontier) he was not spared hostile demonstrations; on July 30 firebombs were thrown at the French consulate and Renault's offices in Valencia. French opposition critics insisted that Spain's order for 48 Mirage F-1 fighters (only 20% of the construction would be done by Spaniards) was the price of France's support.

In Portugal, Giscard promised that France would support Portugal's application to the Market, protect the 750,000 Portuguese working in France and help Portugal's trade deficit with a $100 million loan.

Relations with Great Britain were much as usual—cordial, with a dash of ill-will, not least because of the insistent British desire to modify the Market accords on fishing and agriculture (believed to benefit French farmers at the expense of British consumers), but also because Britain seemed to waver before entering a French-German-British consortium to produce the Airbus A-310.

The regular meetings with Chancellor Helmut Schmidt of West Germany took place, in Paris, February 6–7, and Bremen, July 6–7. The two states agreed on joint action against the rising tide of terrorism.

A brief contretemps developed with Denmark when prime minister Anken Jorgensen was reported to have said Mitterrand would win the elections. Jorgensen claimed to have said only that Mitterrand would make a good partner and not change French policy. If only to appease Chirac and the fanatic gaullists, Giscard staged an absurdly shrill protest that momentarily troubled the April 7–8 Copenhagen meeting of the EEC Council of Ministers. The election results deflated this mini-crisis.

With the Soviet Union, relations were normal, despite expulsion of a Soviet assistant military attaché for espionage.

President Anwar el-Sadat of Egypt visited Paris in February and continued to purchase Mirage F-1 fighters. But France played no significant role in the Middle East.

Africa was another story. Relations with former colonies continued to be close, and involvement in Zaire and Chad was direct. France has been supporting the bankrupt, corrupt and crumbling regime of President Mobutu Sese Seko, who visited Paris once in January and twice in May. Thousands of Congolese National Liberation Front guerillas from Angola invaded wealthy Shaba in May. Previously, in 1977, France had merely airlifted Moroccan troops to assist Mobutu's army. This time, May 19–20, France and Belgium sent in their own forces, airlifted by U. S. transports. Too late to prevent the massacre of some 600 Africans and 130 Europeans in Kolwezi, they were able to expel the invaders and prevent some of Mobutu's own ragtag soldiers pillaging, if not murdering, in turn. Brussels was furious that Giscard had acted without first seeking Belgium's accord. Mobutu charged Belgium with moving too late. The fifth annual 21-nation African summit, held in Paris, May 22–23, endorsed the intervention. By mid-June the 700 French Legionnaires were withdrawn. A series of meetings in Paris, June 5 and 13–14, effected a compromise between Mobutu's demand for $1 billion in aid and more modest sums offered by an international consortium. Great Britain and the United States rejected a French proposal to establish a pan-African peacekeeping force. They preferred ad hoc action in cooperation with the Organization of African Unity.

In Chad French military advisers and Legionnaires were active in support of the government. In Mauritania French jets struck Polisario bases during May. "Africa for the Africans," Giscard told the Paris summit. But as self-appointed leader of the West in this area, France had definite ideas about which Africans.

Relations with China were good. Barre, visiting Peking in January, signed scientific and technical accords, called for détente in South-East Asia, and prepared the way for a $700 million antitank and antiaircraft missile sale which was concluded in October. The Chinese were not, however, permitted to purchase the 50 Mirage F-1 fighters they wanted.

Franco-American relations were normal. President Carter visited Paris, Jan. 4–6, and received Giscard in Washington, May 26. Franco-Canadian relations remained unchanged, diffident and awaiting events in Québec.

JOHN C. CAIRNS, *University of Toronto*

GARDENING AND HORTICULTURE

An estimated 32 million Americans now have kitchen gardens, and this number will almost certainly increase with a projected rise in food costs of six to eight percent in 1979. The question of how much money can be saved with a home garden has therefore become important. According to the National Association for Gardening, an average home gardener can save more than $350 a year in vegetable costs. According to its 1977 study, an initial investment of about $20 for seed, plants, and fertilizer, and a garden plot of 20 by 30 feet (6 by 9 m), will yield about 500 lbs. (227 kg) of the most typically-grown vegetables—tomatoes, green beans, onions, cucumbers, peppers, radishes, lettuce, carrots, squash, beets, cabbage, and mixed greens. The smaller the garden, of course, the smaller the savings.

Many gardeners, however, are less concerned with saving money than with the recreational and therapeutic value of home gardening.

All-America Selections. Two hybrid tea roses and a grandiflora won All-America Awards for 1979. These flowers are characterized by their bright and interesting colors. Friendship is a clear, bright pink hybrid tea; Paradise is an amazing combination of lavender and bright pink, also a hybrid tea; and Sundowner is a very intense orange grandiflora.

Sundowner has medium to large gleaming-orange blossoms borne on very long stems.

Friendship, a clear, bright pink hybrid tea rose, was selected as an All-America winner for 1979.

COURTESY OF ALL-AMERICA ROSE SELECTIONS

When first opening, this rose has such intense coloring that it gives the appearance of being fluorescent. The 40-petal flowers are slightly ruffled, with excellent form and substance. As the bloom approaches maturity, salmon tints appear on the outer edges of the petals, giving the flower an apricot cast, gradually fading to a soft pink as the petals drop. The brilliant blooms exude a delightful, spicy fragrance. Early in the season the roses are borne singly on long, strong stems, with the typical floribunda blossom cluster appearing late in the summer. Sundowner is a very tall-growing rose; to keep the cultivar at a lower height the flower should be cut frequently.

The Sundowner's foliage is large, lustrous moss green, with interesting coppery tints which make the plant attractive even without the blossoms. This rose has shown considerable resistance to disease and appears to be at least as hardy as most tea and grandiflora roses.

Sundowner is the first grandiflora to be introduced in the United States by Mr. Sam McGredy IV, the scion of a U. S. rose breeding family. It is the third All-America honor for McGredy, the other winners being Cathedral and Electron.

Paradise is one of the most distinctive and novel hybrid tea roses ever produced. While its color combination is most unusual, it remains a rose of striking beauty. From the long, pointed, deep ruby buds to the double, four-inch (10.2-cm) open blooms, many shades of lavender, purple, bright pink, and rich ruby come and go during the various stages of opening. The blooms hold their color through maturity, and as the petals fall there are bursts of new ruby buds ready to take their place. The flowers have a truly classical tea rose shape, are distinctly fragrant, and are produced on fairly long, strong canes in great abundance. The plant is vigorous and bushy and well covered with large, deep glossy green foilage.

For the first time in the 38-year history of the All-America Awards, Paradise was selected as a winner by acclamation, without a formal vote being taken. The flower was developed by Ollie Weeks, who also produced Gypsy, Arizona, and Perfume Delight.

Friendship is a rugged, strong-growing, bushy hybrid tea rose. It makes a tall bush, producing a profusion of very large blooms throughout the season. This is somewhat surprising, as most roses that produce large flowers usually bloom sparingly. The blossoms are borne on long stems suitable for cutting. Color descriptions of this clear, bright tea rose vary from pink to coral to flesh color.

Friendship was developed by Robert V. Lindquist, Sr., who also developed the All-America winners Granada, Tiffany, and Command Performance.

DONALD W. NEWSOM
Department of Horticulture
Louisiana State University

GENETICS

The year 1978 saw remarkable advances in the basic understanding of the organization and expression of genes and in the application of genetic theory to medical needs.

Major areas of research were spurred by the recognition and use of a new class of enzymes, "restriction enzymes," which are capable of highly specific cleavage of DNA (deoxyribonucleic acid). Cleavage by the enzyme Eco RI is restricted to sites comprising the nucleotide base sequence 5'-GAATTC-3'. When applied to the alpha and beta globin genes, which code for the α and β polypeptide chains of hemoglobin, Eco RI does not cleave the α sequence, but does cleave the β globin sequence at one specific site, producing two large fragments. Combined with techniques to separate, characterize, and identify the fragments of DNA, various restriction enzymes permit detailed analyses of gene structure and gene splicing or recombination experiments.

Until recently, 35 years of biochemical research seemed to establish that the sequence of nucleotides in DNA was transcribed into a complementary sequence of nucleotides in messenger RNA (mRNA), and that the mRNA code was then translated into a co-linear sequence of amino acids (three nucleotides per amino acid) in the polypeptide chains of proteins. The DNA, RNA, and protein sequences, however, may not line up so neatly. Molecular cloning in the bacterium E. coli and analysis with restriction enzymes have shown "spacer sequences" in an impressive series of genes.

For more than a decade, analyses of mutation in bacteria and viruses had provided evidence that certain kinds of signals must be coded for in the DNA, outside the sequence that codes for the structure of the protein product. These signal sequences determine the start, rate, and termination of the transcription of the mRNA copy and nontranslated sequences in the mRNA which are essential for the binding of the mRNA to cytoplasmic ribosomes where protein synthesis occurs. The situation is far more complex in yeasts, plants, animals, and animal viruses. In these, the initial RNA copied from long stretches of DNA in the cell nucleus is modified extensively to generate smaller functional mRNAs which direct protein synthesis. These results are significant for recombinant DNA studies.

Recombinant DNA experiments involve the insertion of DNA fragments or specific gene sequences into the DNA of other species through restriction enzymes. These experiments have captured the public imagination because genes from human or other higher organisms may be inserted into bacteria to grow large amounts of the bacteria as a cellular factory for the gene products—hormones, viral antigens for vaccines, or enzymes for biological nitrogen fixation in plants. Scientists in the forefront of this work pointed out as early as 1974 the danger that unforeseen transformations of the bacteria might occur from such gene insertions, with possible ecological or public health hazards. As a result, the scientific work has been carried forward with caution, employing special physical containment facilities and certain multiple-mutant strains of E. coli as host organisms incapable of escaping from the laboratory. Ingenious protocols have been developed, for example, to generate bacterial lines capable of producing insulin, the hormone needed in the treatment of diabetic patients. A team of scientists at Harvard University has obtained mRNA for the precursor of insulin from a rat tumor that produced large amounts of insulin. They enzymatically synthesized a double-stranded DNA copy of the mRNA and spliced the synthesized DNA into a ring of DNA (plasmid) from the E. coli host in a way that fused the proinsulin gene with a gene for the bacterial enzyme penicillinase, which E. coli secretes. Human insulin may, in the future, be produced similarly by starting with human insulin-producing tumors.

A quite different approach was employed by a team of researchers in California. With knowledge of the mRNA sequences for the A and B polypeptide chains of insulin, they chemically (rather than enzymatically) synthesized double-stranded DNA corresponding to these mRNAs. They connected each DNA sequence separately to the genes controlling production of the enzyme β-galactosidase, inserted these into an appropriate plasmid, put the plasmid into the E. coli host, induced production of the insulin by turning on the β-galactosidase complex, and then purified the A and B chains and combined them into active insulin. The differences between bacterial and mammalian gene organization and nucleic acid processing outlined above make selective insertions essential for successful production of mammalian proteins in bacterial cells. At the same time, these differences provide potent barriers to unintended side effects of these experiments.

Restriction enzymes have also opened the way to more direct studies of human gene variation at the DNA level, complementing methods already employed to detect variants and defects in proteins. A particularly interesting application is in prenatal diagnosis. Prenatal diagnosis has revolutionized genetic counseling for testable disorders, such as Down syndrome (mongolism) and neural tube closure defects (spina bifida). Prenatal diagnosis of sickle cell anemia and thalassemias has required analysis of fetal blood cells in order to study the hemoglobin. The way is now being opened to use amniotic fluid cells, which can be obtained much more simply and safely, and to test for deletions or mutations in key sites of the appropriate genes by use of particular restriction enzymes.

GILBERT S. OMENN
University of Washington

GEOLOGY

Geology and its related sciences prospered in both their pure and applied aspects during 1978. Important advances were made in fitting together ancient land masses; great new sections of the continental shelves were opened to exploration; geologic hazards were identified; and the job market for graduates was the best in years.

Global Tectonics. Opposition to the theory of sea-floor spreading has declined with discoveries of confirming evidence on all fronts. A time table of movements for the major land masses and coincident opening and closing of water bodies is becoming stabilized. Chief efforts are now being directed at filling in the details. During 1978 evidence for truly radical displacements of continental material was announced. Most of the evidence has to do with piecemeal crossings of the Pacific Ocean. Geologist Amos Nur presented evidence that a large continental mass that he calls Pacifica moved from a position adjacent to Antarctica and Australia, broke up, and scattered, to implant fragments in South America, North America, Alaska, Japan, and East Asia. A far-traveled fragment, not necessarily part of Nur's Pacifica, is thought to have collided with western North America, leaving exotic fragments in parts of Alaska, Canada, and perhaps the Pacific Northwest of the United States. It has been named Wrangellia because the largest piece is incorporated in the Wrangell Mountains of southeastern Alaska.

Perhaps the ultimate in continental drifting, called the Siberian Connection by J. W. Sears and R. A. Price who noted the possibility, is the detachment of a large chunk of western North America and its ultimate lodgement in northeast Asia. The separation took place about 1.5 billion years ago before the appearance of abundant fossils. The composition, structure, and age of rifted edges of North America and the Siberian mass are strikingly similar, and Sears and Price have made a good case for their theory.

Solution to a long standing puzzle was achieved with the predrift placement of Madagascar adjacent to Somalia, Kenya, and Tanzania rather than next to Mozambique. Evidence for this reconstruction was mainly the magnetic record of sedimentary rocks laid down when Madagascar was attached to the mainland.

Geologic Hazards—The Palmdale Bulge. The problems of earthquake prediction continue to plague geologists. With a U. S. Congressional appropriation of over $30 million, funds for earthquake-related research doubled during the 1979 fiscal year. Geologists view with apprehension the so-called Palmdale bulge in south central California, a mysterious uplift affecting 32,400 square miles (83,916 km²) centering in the western Mojave Desert, southern California, between the intersection of the Garlock and San Andreas faults. The feature as such was first detected in 1976 but uplift had been in progress since about 1959. About mid-1961 the central area rose abruptly about 10 inches (25 cm). Greatest uplift has been 18 inches (45 cm) at a spot between Blythe and Palmdale. Unexpectedly, certain parts have subsided as much as 4 inches (10 cm). A precise releveling program is underway involving more than 300 specialists and a cost of $1.4 million. Experts say that release of energy stored in this uplift could produce an earthquake equal to that of 1857, magnitude 8 Richter. On the other hand the energy might dissipate through a series of small quakes or no quakes at all.

The USGS. Secretary of the Interior Cecil D. Andrus accepted the resignation of U. S. Geological Survey (USGS) Director V. E. McKelvey, effective Jan. 1, 1978. There had been friction between the director and the Carter administration as McKelvey defended USGS estimates of oil and gas resources, which were higher than those of other experts. Geologists generally were dismayed by the action. Under its new director, Henry William Menard, Jr., a marine geologist and oceanographer, the USGS was expected to have expanded responsibilities as the search for new resources shifts to submarine realms.

Offshore Exploration. Geology faces one of its greatest challenges in exploring for offshore oil and gas. The United States is bordered by about 1.3 million square miles (about 3.4 million km²) of continental shelf and slope equal in area to one third of its land area. The mineral and energy resources of offshore areas are undoubtedly immense but are expensive to discover and extract. In addition to natural obstacles, artificial obstacles exist in regulations that prohibit drilling for environmental reasons.

Offshore drilling will require a degree of cooperation unheard of in onshore exploration. The USGS is responsible for approving all leasing and drilling and at the same time is providing information too expensive for oil companies to obtain individually. The survey is supervising the drilling of a number of strategically placed stratigraphic test wells to obtain information, not to discover oil or gas. For example, Ocean Production Company, working under a USGS permit, has drilled an information well on a cost-sharing basis for 25 oil companies interested in the petroleum potential of the Southeast Georgia Embayment. The 13,254-foot (4,040-m) well revealed potentially good source and reservoir rocks, and the individual companies will have some degree of guidance in leasing and exploring the area. Similar projects are scattered along all favorable U. S. coasts. Test wells have been drilled off south Texas, southern California, the Atlantic coast, and Alaska.

Employment. The widening search for energy and mineral resources has created a golden age for geoscientists. Good students with master's degrees are likely to receive a number of job offers, with excellent starting salaries.

WILLIAM LEE STOKES, *University of Utah*

GEORGIA

Foreign investment, mergers, crime and politics dominated Georgia news in 1978.

Foreign Investment. Gov. George Busbee's efforts to attract foreign companies to Georgia began to pay off. His flights to Japan, Western Europe, and Latin America have resulted in the opening of foreign trade offices in Atlanta, and several foreign companies have opened plants in south Georgia. The establishment of direct transatlantic air service between Atlanta and London, and Atlanta and Brussels in 1978 may spur more foreign investment in Georgia.

Mergers. Subject to final negotiations and approval by private and government entities, General Electric, the giant Connecticut-based manufacturing company, will merge with Atlanta-based Cox Broadcasting Corporation, one of the nation's largest independent non-network group broadcasters. The New Jersey-based Grand Union food company completed arrangements to take over Atlanta-based Colonial Stores, the nation's fifteenth largest supermarket chain. California's American Jet Industries bought Grumman American Aviation, a Georgia aircraft manufacturer. Neptune Industries, an Atlanta company and one of the largest U. S. suppliers of water pollution-control equipment, agreed to merge with New Hampshire-based Wheelbrator, Inc.

Crime. Two national figures involved in the publishing of pornographic materials made news in Georgia. Larry Flynt, owner of *Hustler* magazine and his Georgia attorney were shot and wounded as they entered a county courthouse where Flynt was being tried for distributing obscene materials.

Atlantan Mike Thevis, known as the "king of pornography" was arrested in Connecticut. On the FBI Ten Most Wanted list after he escaped from an Indiana jail in 1978, Thevis was later charged with the recent ambush killing of Roger Dean Underhill, a key witness against Thevis in another Atlanta murder case.

Reidsville Prison, near Atlanta, was the scene of racially-motivated violence and murder. Five

UPI

Betty Talmadge, former wife of the Georgia senator, ran unsuccessfully for a seat in Congress.

inmates and one guard were killed in 1978 in a series of brawls. Prison workers were charged with allowing some inmates to keep weapons and with selling contraband.

Politics. In the November election, Governor George Busbee overwhelmed his Republican opponent to become the first governor in Georgia's history to serve a second four-year term.

Georgia's junior senator, Sam Nunn was reelected by a substantial margin. The senior senator, Herman Talmadge, was investigated by the Senate ethics committee for disputed reimbursements of campaign expense claims. Talmadge's former wife, Betty, lost her bid for Congress from the sixth district. In congressional races four incumbent Democrats were easily reelected.

Voters rejected a proposed constitutional amendment that would have doubled the terms of state legislators and approved a uniform statewide recall law.

Other Events. It is estimated that the boycott of Georgia by proponents of ERA has cost Atlanta $15 million in potential convention expenditures.

President Carter signed legislation which creates a national recreation area along a 48-mile (77-km) segment of the Chattahoochee River near Atlanta.

Loew's Grand Theatre, where the world premiere of the famous movie *Gone With the Wind* was held, burned to the ground.

KAY BECK, *Georgia State University*

GEORGIA • Information Highlights

Area: 58,876 square miles (152,489 km²).

Population (Jan. 1978 est.): 5,083,000.

Chief Cities (1970 census): Atlanta, the capital, 497,421; Columbus, 155,028; Macon, 122,423.

Government (1978): *Chief Officers*—governor, George D. Busbee (D); lt. gov., Zell Miller (D). *General Assembly*—Senate, 56 members; House of Representatives, 180 members.

Education (1977–78): *Enrollment*—public elementary schools, 663,110 pupils; public secondary, 426,515; colleges and universities, 173,708 students. *Public school expenditures,* $1,336,190,000 ($1,111 per pupil).

State Finances (fiscal year 1977): *Revenues,* $3,579,-450,000; *expenditures,* $3,440,030,000.

Personal Income (1977): $30,358,000,000; per capita, $6,014.

Labor Force (July 1978): *Nonagricultural wage and salary earners,* 1,935,800; (July 1977) *unemployed,* 148,700 (6.7% of total force).

UPI

The leaders of the major industrial powers in the non-Communist world meet at the Bonn Economic Summit July 16–17 to discuss noninflationary ways to spur world economic growth.

GERMANY

Despite occasional heated exchanges, relations between the Federal Republic of Germany (West Germany) and the German Democratic Republic (East Germany or DDR) were not seriously troubled in 1978. Bonn did not play up or encourage internal dissension in the DDR, feeling that its impact would be limited and that further normalization of relations would yield more constructive results. East Berlin, in turn, wished to improve relations with Bonn in the hope of increasing the influx of West German goods and currency.

Owing to these policies, travel to and from the DDR increased. East Germans with families in the West also found it a little easier to reunite. Bonn and East Berlin agreed to build jointly a four-lane highway across East German territory, linking West Berlin and Hamburg. At the Leipzig Fair, the party chief of East Germany's ruling Socialist Unity Party (SED), Erich Honecker, singled out West German products for special praise. There was even talk of an exchange of visits between Honecker and West German Chancellor Helmut Schmidt. As Schmidt revealed, the two leaders occasionally spoke with each other on the telephone.

But there also was friction. In the spring, two reporters of the West German weekly *Der Spiegel* were expelled from East Berlin on charges of slandering the DDR. Disagreements over the extent of ties between West Berlin and West Germany also continued. At times during these disputes, the East German authorities hampered highway traffic between West Berlin and West Germany. However, since both governments were anxious to avoid serious crises, overall relations between the two states remained unaffected.

FEDERAL REPUBLIC OF GERMANY
(West Germany)

The government of Chancellor Helmut Schmidt, a coalition of Social Democrats and right-of-center Free Democrats, held a precarious 10-vote majority in the *Bundestag*. The coalition owed its survival partly to the impressive personal performance of Schmidt and partly to the inability of the opposition parties, the Christian Democratic Union (CDU) and its Bavarian offshoot, the Christian Social Union (CSU), to present a credible leader and an alternative program to deal with the country's problems.

Nonetheless the Schmidt government faced difficulties. The Free Democrats suffered new setbacks in two state elections. There also was the danger that Schmidt's legislative program might be blocked in the *Bundesrat,* the upper house of the parliament, in which the CDU and CSU held a majority.

A major political scandal erupted in the spring when it was revealed that Hans Karl Filbinger, the minister-president of Baden-Wuerttemberg and a former navy judge, had passed several death sentences for rather minor offenses during World War II. He had also allowed an execution to be carried out *after* the end of the war. What aroused public indignation most, however, was Filbinger's failure to show any sign of regret. His own party, the CDU, forced him to resign his government post. Yet to the dismay of many, the party retained him as its deputy leader in deference to its conservative wing.

Economy. The economy was sluggish throughout 1978. Output increased by only 2.8% in the first six months, largely due to productivity gains. Even though manufacturers continued to build plants abroad to avoid West Germany's high production costs, exports continued to grow. The rising value of the Deutsche Mark was offset by rising prices in other countries. West Germany's own inflation rate dropped to 2.2%; and unemployment in October was only 3.8%.

To stimulate growth, the government proposed some tax cuts in the 1979 budget. Given the nation's high rate of saving, however, it was uncertain whether the tax reductions would increase consumer demand. One important feature of the new budget was its emphasis on research and development. As Finance Minister Hans Matthofer explained, German industry, in order to remain competitive, would have to continue to improve its technology and remain innovative and creative. Help was to be given to small and medium-sized enterprises in particular.

Social Conditions. West Germany's birth rate continued to decline. From 1,000,000 births in 1965, the number dropped to 500,000 in 1977 and is now one of the lowest in the world. The government is considering financial and other measures to encourage childbearing.

The number of foreign workers in West Germany decreased from 2.6 to 1.9 million, but most of those will stay on because Germans refuse to do the "dirty" work of street cleaning, garbage removal, mining, and hotel and restaurant work. Yet foreign laborers continue to face a distinctly hostile environment; they live in ghettos and receive no adequate language instruction or social counseling. Their children are largely unprepared for German schools. Informed observers are greatly concerned that this "subproletariat" will cause grave problems unless remedial measures are taken soon.

Terrorism. In 1978, the West German government was more successful in bringing terrorism under control than ever before. Except for one attempted murder in West Berlin, no serious terrorist acts were committed. Several terrorists were killed by the police and many others arrested. Yet intercepted letters and the discovery of arms caches confirmed that terrorist plotting continued.

New antiterrorist laws authorized the minister of interior to order telephone taps and mail openings where there are "factual grounds" for suspicion of high treason or danger to national or foreign security. Road checks and house searches were permitted without judicial warrant

West German Chancellor Helmut Schmidt, in a television interview, urges a stronger U.S. role in world affairs.

in emergency cases. These have also been police checks of car rental contracts (since terrorists often use rented cars) and checks of the circulation of "radical" books in public libraries.

This last measure, never legally authorized, as well as certain unauthorized practices at border checkpoints, raised constitutional questions. There also were renewed objections to the ever more exacting "loyalty" screenings of applicants for government jobs. As a result, some of these measures were discontinued or modified. (*See* feature article pages 44–51.)

Neo-Nazism. Anti-Jewish activities by various neo-Nazi groups also caused some concern. Though small in membership, these groups have become more aggressive—disrupting meetings, desecrating Jewish cemeteries, staging anti-Jewish demonstrations, and harassing individual Jews. According to one official report, the number of incidents attributed to right-wing extremists increased from 319 in 1976 to 616 in 1977. Most of the neo-Nazis are young people, rather than veterans of the Nazi era. While anxious not to exaggerate the significance of these activities but wary of their proliferation, the government warned in its annual report that "right-wing extremism continues to be a source of danger to public security."

Foreign Affairs. Relations with the United States were made tense by differences on several issues. Washington urged Bonn to speed up its economic growth so that West Germany would import more goods from other countries and thereby help shield them from another recession. However, the Schmidt government would not take any major new steps lest its own inflation increase. It insisted that a comprehensive energy

Chancellor Schmidt welcomes Chinese Vice Premier Ku Mu (*left*) and Energy Minister Tsien Cheng-ying to Bonn, June 6.

UPI

program and reduced oil imports in the United States, as well as a stable dollar, would be more effective remedies for the West's troubles.

President Carter's decision to defer production of the neutron bomb also elicited criticism, since Chancellor Schmidt had worked hard to overcome strong domestic opposition to the deployment of the bomb on West German soil. Carter's human rights campaign likewise met with objection; the policy was viewed as unproductive and incompatible with détente.

A visit from Soviet President Leonid Brezhnev to Bonn produced new agreements for economic, industrial, and technical cooperation. Both governments pledged also to avoid confrontations over the status of West Berlin.

In June, Chancellor Schmidt visited Nigeria and Zambia to promote the expansion of economic relations between West Germany and those countries. Much to the disappointment of his hosts, however, Chancellor Schmidt was less willing to take sides in Africa's black-white confrontation.

In Zaire, a West German rocket company acquired the right to test and set up a launching system for commercial satellites. The arrangement aroused considerable concern among Zaire's neighbors who feared, despite official denials, that the satellite program might serve military purposes.

— WEST GERMANY • Information Highlights —

Official Name: Federal Republic of Germany.
Location: North-central Europe.
Area: 97,883 square miles (253,517 km²). West Berlin, 186 square miles (481 km²).
Population (1978 est.): 61,300,000.
Chief Cities (Dec. 1976): Bonn, the capital, 285,000; Hamburg, 1,698,600; Munich, 1,314,600.
Government: *Head of state,* Walter Scheel, president (took office July 1974). *Head of government,* Helmut Schmidt, federal chancellor (took office May 1974). *Legislature*—Parliament: Bundesrat and Bundestag.
Monetary Unit: Deutsche Mark (1.8595 D. Marks equal U. S.$1, Dec. 28, 1978).
Manufactures (major products): Iron, steel, coal, cement, chemicals, machinery, ships, vehicles.
Agriculture (major products): Grains, potatoes, sugar beets.

GERMAN DEMOCRATIC REPUBLIC
(East Germany)

In 1978 there were indications of continuing dissatisfaction in the DDR. The government responded by exiling or imprisoning critics. An anti-Leninist manifesto published in *Der Spiegel* suggested strong discontent even within the SED. But since the author of the manifesto was unknown, the truth of its account could not be established.

Economy. To improve living conditions, the government increased old age pensions, reduced working hours for mothers, and extended paid vacations and maternity leaves. However, production could not keep up with the increase in purchasing power, and new shortages developed.

In a further effort to improve living conditions and to bring in West German currency, the government continued to let its citizens accept Deutsche Marks from West German relatives and spend them in so-called Inter-Shops, in which Western goods were sold against foreign exchange. To allay the resentment of citizens with no West German ties, special "Exquisit" and delicatessen stores sold Western goods (at high prices) for East German marks. In addition, 10,000 Volkswagen automobiles were imported in exchange for East German products. To make these high-priced cars available to less affluent buyers, an installment plan, with an interest rate of 1%, was offered. Ideological and economic objections remained to this type of "consumer socialism."

Social Conditions. In 1977 births exceeded deaths for the first time in 8 years. Figures for the first half of 1978 indicated a continuation of this trend. It was attributed to the generous financial aid and the preferential treatment accorded to working mothers. These privileges, however, intensified the labor shortage and thereby reduced production. Mothers were urged to work additional hours.

There was considerable teenage vandalism and other misconduct, culminating in repeated clashes with the police. The causes of this unrest appeared to be boredom and resentment of the existing regimentation. Perhaps in order to instill greater discipline, "military education" courses were introduced in the schools. Officially, this instruction was justified on the grounds that the DDR was being threatened by "unmitigated imperialist aggressors." The measure caused widespread concern.

The Protestant Church. Relations between state and church improved noticeably after a meeting in March between Bishop Albrecht Schönherr and SED party chief Erich Honecker. A church congress at Leipzig, organized in May with official help, was attended by 50,000 people. Attendance at church services also increased. Yet the church was among the outspoken critics of the new military education, warning that it might accustom the young to rely on force as the best way to solve conflicts. Protestant clergymen called attention to the persistence of Nazi-like attitudes in the DDR—anti-Semitism and contempt for Poles and other non-Germans. These

latter feelings, it was hinted, were being encouraged by continual official announcements about East Germany's outstanding achievements. Church leaders insisted, however, that their warnings were intended merely to help implement the government's own objectives.

Foreign Relations. Party and government leaders traveled outside the socialist bloc more often than ever before. Honecker visited Vietnam, North Korea, and the Philippines; Foreign Minister Oskar Fischer went to Japan; and other officials traveled to a host of African states. The DDR provides military instruction and other aid to several African states. However, reports that East German soldiers took part in some of the fighting on African soil were denied.

WEST BERLIN

The year passed without any serious incidents along the Berlin Wall. The city's most intractable problems continued to be economic. In June, the chairmen of all parties represented in the *Bundestag* pledged further financial aid for the continued development of scientific and technical resources in West Berlin.

New difficulties arose over the growing influx of foreigners, especially Pakistanis, who asked for asylum as alleged political refugees. These foreigners are lured to West Berlin by unscrupulous organizers who promise them jobs but demand as much as $3,000 for getting them there. These would-be immigrants are flown to East Berlin and then cross into West Berlin, which has no border controls. While many of them eventually are sent back to their homeland, such forcible return involves a long, costly process at the city's expense.

ANDREAS DORPALEN
The Ohio State University

—— EAST GERMANY · Information Highlights ——

Official Name: German Democratic Republic.
Location: North-central Europe.
Area: 41,768 square miles (108,179 km²).
Population (1978 est.): 16,700,000.
Chief Cities (1975 est.): East Berlin, the capital, 1,106,-267; Leipzig, 564,596; Dresden, 510,408.
Government: *Head of state,* Erich Honecker, chairman of the Council of State. *Head of government,* Willi Stoph, Chairman, Council of Ministers Presidium. *First secretary of the Socialist Unity* (Communist) party, Erich Honecker (took office 1971). *Legislature* (unicameral)—Volkskammer (People's Chamber).
Monetary Unit: DDR mark (2.05 DDR marks equal U.S.$1, 1978).
Manufactures (major products): Electrical and precision engineering products, fishing vessels, steel, machinery, chemicals.
Agriculture (major products): Potatoes, grains, sugar beets, meat and dairy products.

Nazi signs reappear on the Berlin Wall at Potsdam Square. Message at right reads: "Halt—freedom ends here."

UPI

GHANA

The economic and political problems which have plagued Ghana for a decade combined to end Gen. Ignatius Acheampong's control of the government.

Economics. Ghana was in deep financial trouble even before a coup led by Gen. Acheampong overthrew the civil government of Dr. Kofi Busia in January 1972. Bad weather resulted in a succession of poor harvests of cocoa, Ghana's major export, and high market prices for cocoa could not make up for the low production levels. Poor harvests also forced the military government to import such staple items as rice and maize. Ghana's foreign exchange situation, unhealthy since the rise in petroleum prices in 1974, grew steadily worse. The Ghanaian government and private firms could therefore not import many of the materials necessary to keep the economy functioning. By midyear it was almost impossible to find most standard consumer products, and those available were overpriced. In June there was an acute oil shortage which brought commercial activity to a standstill. Government attempts at monetary regulation failed. In June the official exchange rate was 1.15 cedis to the U. S. dollar. But the black market rate, which approximated the true worth of the cedi, stood at c10 to the dollar. This encouraged producers to smuggle cocoa into neighboring states. Ghana's inflation rate by midyear was estimated at 145%, the highest in West Africa. Even the discovery of petroleum offshore at Saltpond did little to relieve widespread demands for dramatic economic and commercial changes.

Politics. In 1977 General Acheampong announced that the Supreme Military Council (SMC) would turn over control to a civilian regime by July 1, 1979. The government opened the question of the future type of government to nationwide debate. Acheampong favored a union government system, with no political parties and with the army having a specified role. A large number of influential men in Ghana opposed the plan, and it received only hesitant approval (56%) in a March 30 referendum. Following the referendum, Acheampong's government further undermined its position by arresting and holding without trial a number of important Ghanaians who had opposed union government. As criticism mounted, the senior officers of the SMC decided to act and on July 5 they forced Acheampong to resign; he was placed under detention. Lt. Gen. F. W. K. Akuffo became the new head of state and acted immediately to gain the people's confidence. Some of Acheampong's closest supporters were dismissed, most of the people held in detention were released, and the SMC reiterated its commitment to a return to civilian rule in July 1979. Akuffo's tentative economic policy had some success. The cedi was allowed to float, a £10 million line of credit was obtained from Britain, and a relatively good cocoa crop and high prices temporarily eased the foreign exchange imbalance.

HARRY A. GAILEY
San Jose State University

GHANA • Information Highlights

Official Name: Republic of Ghana.
Location: West Africa.
Area: 92,100 square miles (238,538 km²).
Population (1978 est.): 10,900,000.
Chief Cities (1973 est.): Accra, the capital, 848,800; Kumasi, 249,000.
Government: *Head of state and government,* Gen. F. W. K. Akuffo (took office July 1978). *Legislature* —National Assembly (dissolved Jan. 1972).
Monetary Unit: New cedi (2.75 new cedis equal U. S.$1, Sept. 1978).
Manufactures (major products): Minerals, lumber, fish, aluminum.
Agriculture (major products): Cocoa, timber, coconuts, coffee, subsistence crops, rubber.

GREAT BRITAIN

In another year of greatly mixed fortunes for Britain, the most surprising political event was the sudden and utterly unexpected decision of the prime minister, James Callaghan, not to call a general election. In Britain an election must be held no more than five years after the previous one, though with the task of choosing the date in the hands of the prime minister, it is rare indeed for the full five years to elapse. Generally a prime minister will carefully study the opinion polls, make his own assessment of the nation's mood, and then choose the date he believes will give his own particular political party the best chance of victory.

Politics. By September 1978, everything pointed in the direction of Callaghan calling an election the following month. His governing Labour party was in a minority in the House of Commons, his party's standing in the polls appeared to be rising, and recent by-elections indicated an upsurge in his own popularity. Even Labour headquarters in London had made all their preparations. Then, as the nation waited, Callaghan calmly announced that he would continue in office without a vote. He argued that there was no need for an election, and that he could continue to govern the country successfully for another year. A more convincing explanation was fear. Some of the senior ministers closest to Callaghan had apparently convinced him that the opposition Conservative party would snatch victory unless the vote was delayed.

The background to his decision included the ending of the "Lib-Lab Pact," a unique constitutional arrangement in Britain by which the tiny Liberal party, with 13 parliamentary seats, had agreed to bolster the much larger Labour party through crucial House of Commons votes. In exchange, the Liberals were consulted about all government plans, and were able to exercise a power of veto over legislation they did not like. The pact was the particular pride of the Liberals'

James Callaghan and his wife, Audrey, celebrated their 40th wedding anniversary in July. The British prime minister surprised everyone by not calling an election in 1978.

young leader, David Steel, who saw it as the first stage in his party's plans to regain major status in British affairs. But through the months the Liberals had suffered badly in both opinion polls and by-elections, and their own grass roots membership was beginning to rebel against the pact. They argued that it benefited only the ruling Labourites who won all the prestige to be gained from the country's increased economic stability. Steel used his own popularity to keep the pact going, but in summer had to admit defeat. The pact ended formally in the fall, after parliament resumed business.

At this point, politicians and commentators alike assumed that Callaghan would have to seek a renewed mandate from the people. Instead he decided to rely on his own good luck and judgment, both of which appeared well vindicated at the beginning of the new parliamentary session. Instead of the long-predicted defeat, he won the first important vote of the new session—on his government's legislative plans—by a majority of 12.

Inflation. Meanwhile, there were unhappy omens for the future of the country's fight against inflation. After three years of voluntary pay restraint, based on cooperation among labor unions, workers, government, and employers, Britain's inflation rate had fallen from a disastrous 27% to a poor but less appalling figure

PHOTOS UPI

In honor of her birthday, Margaret Thatcher was presented with a large key marked No. 10. The Conservative party leader would like to move into 10 Downing St. in 1979.

UPI

Following a long strike, employees of the Ford Motor Company received wage increases averaging 17%.

of about 8%. The government hoped to bring it down still further by pegging wage increases to 5% in 1978–79. It soon became clear that there was little chance of this occurring. After a strike lasting nearly two months, the huge Ford Motor Company gave its employees raises averaging 17%, and the important British Oxygen Company awarded 10%. After three years of meager returns and frequent (if small) lowerings in the standard of living, workers were anxious to recover lost ground, and it was clear that only those with the least industrial power would settle for a raise as poor as 5%. The government insisted that its goal was not hopelessly lost, and it embarked on a policy of so-called sanctions against firms that broke the limit. Such companies were to be refused government grants, assistance, and contracts. This scheme, which could only work when breaches of the guidelines were infrequent, was condemned by employers and the opposition Conservatives as unjust, unfair, and arbitrary. It did in many ways have the appearance of a last-ditch stand by a government petrified of losing all the advantages it had won in its fight against inflation and the policy was defeated in a Commons vote in December.

Even so, the government made some special wage awards. Faced with a massive drop in police manpower, the pay of policemen was increased by 45% in stages spread over two years. The armed forces were given 14%, with a considerable increase to follow 12 months later. Firemen, who had been on strike earlier in the year, and whose work was done by inexperienced soldiers, also won a two-stage increase designed to minimize the inflationary effect.

Chancellor of the Exchequer Denis Healey tried to buy some support for his policy of wage restraint by reducing taxes. In his April budget he distributed some £2,500 million in tax concessions, and was later obliged through parliamentary votes to give away more. The working people of the country clearly did not respond with the gratitude Chancellor Healey had indeed expected.

The Conservatives. Politically, one of the most fascinating battles was between the leader of the Conservative party, Mrs. Margaret Thatcher, who would become prime minister if her party won an election, and her predecessor, former Prime Minister Edward Heath. For three years, since his displacement in 1975, Heath had made little secret of his dislike of and near contempt for Mrs. Thatcher. He was antipathetic to her personally and thought her policies dangerous and unworkable. Throughout the year he made thinly veiled references to her and her policies. In July, however, after months of persuasion by his friends, Heath made a speech supporting the Conservative party generally and Mrs. Thatcher's leadership. It was not an especially generous speech, but was received with near ecstasy by the anxious Conservatives.

Three months later came the retraction. Heath himself has always been a strong believer in a firm wages policy as the only means of both combating inflation and distributing wealth fairly. Mrs. Thatcher, however, inclines to the view that only the free play of market forces will lead to prosperity and fairness. Heath took the opportunity of the Conservative party's annual conference to make a series of broadcasts disagreeing strongly with the Thatcher policy, thus again blowing wide the gap in Conservative thinking. He committed the heresy of supporting the policy of the Labour prime minister, Callaghan. Most galling of all for Mrs. Thatcher, polls showed that a far higher proportion of the population agreed with him, and indicated that, if he were still party leader, the Conservatives would stand a far better chance of winning a general election.

Immigration. Another issue on which Heath disagreed with Thatcher was race and immigration, long a sore topic in Britain. Until recently both main parties have been anxious to hold roughly the same policy for fear of exacerbating racial tensions and to avoid the accusation of touting irresponsibly for votes. But at the end of January Mrs. Thatcher appeared on television and called for stricter immigration controls. Many British people felt, the conservative leader said, that they were being "swamped" by colored immigrants.

The use of that particular emotional word touched off a storm of controversy, not least in the Conservative party. Mrs. Thatcher had not previously sought the advice of her closest supporters, who were left with the job of producing a policy and a plan of action to match her words. This proved no easy task, since immigration into Britain had been cut down by successive governments until it consisted almost entirely of the dependents of those already in the country. After some months of confusion, the Conservatives came up with a "quota" system. This meant that dependents and the handful of others who had the full right to enter the country would be allowed to do so, but at a rate determined by the annual quota which could be adjusted by government as it pleased. Not surprisingly the plan was fiercely attacked.

Meanwhile, the only overtly racist political party in Great Britain, the National Front, appeared to suffer a moderate but steady decline in its standing. One cause of this might have been the formation of a huge and popular movement known as the Anti-Nazi League, which organized many marches and demonstrations across the country designed to rally antiracist opinion, chiefly among young people. Some tens of thousands attended their biggest meetings, which usually featured top rock bands as well as political speeches.

Mideast, Northern Ireland. London continued, unhappily, to be one of the stages on which the conflicts of the Middle East are fought. In January, a leader of the Palestine Liberation Organization, Said Hammami, was shot dead in his office by an unknown gunman. In July a former prime minister of Iraq, Abdul Razak al-Naif, was shot dead in Hyde Park. Two people were killed when Arab terrorists ambushed an Israeli airline bus on its way to Heathrow Airport.

Britain's native civil war, in Northern Ireland, was at its quietest for many years, though inevitably attended by some appalling incidents. In February some dozen people died when a popular and crowded restaurant near Belfast was deliberately bombed without warning. Two people died when the Provisional IRA bombed a railway train on its way to Belfast, at a time when the train would normally be standing in a crowded station. IRA prisoners in the Maze prison demonstrated for their right to "political" status and privileges by refusing to clean out their cells, and so existed in a state of filth. The British government determined not to give way to their demands.

Although there were desultory talks aimed at setting up some form of local government, little changed politically in the province. Various attempts within Britain to win a withdrawal of the army from patrol duties in the province of Northern Ireland were feebly received and got nowhere.

Queen Elizabeth welcomes President Nicolae Ceauşescu of Rumania to London.

UPI

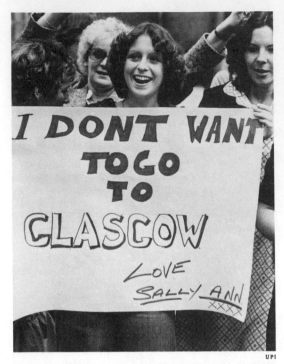

In July, some 300 Britons demonstrated against a plan to disperse civil-service jobs to Scotland.

Scandals. It was another year, inevitably, for the traditional British political scandal. The Thorpe case came to trial. This related to Jeremy Thorpe, a former leader of the small Liberal party, who was accused of conspiring to murder Norman Scott, a male model. Scott had alleged for years that he and Thorpe had had a homosexual love affair long before Thorpe's marriage, and that Thorpe had endeavored to kill him to keep him quiet. Little notice would have been paid to this allegation but for the fact that in 1975 a gunman did kidnap Scott briefly, shot his dog, and apparently attempted to kill him.

Over the years Thorpe denied the allegations, but after painstaking police investigations, he and three other men were charged in August. In spite of this and pleas from his colleagues, he insisted on attending the Liberal party conference and contrived to appear strikingly confident. The committal hearings, by which magistrates decide whether the accused person has a case to answer, opened amid a blaze of international publicity at a tiny court in the quiet vacation village of Minehead in November.

A less spicy but probably more significant scandal involved the discovery that in spite of legal sanctions against the sale or supply of goods to the illegal regime in Rhodesia, two British oil companies had been supplying petroleum to that country. Not only had they done this, by means of an elaborate "swap" arrangement with a French company, but the Harold Wilson government of the day had known and had declined to do anything about it. In the uproar that followed, Wilson denied all knowledge of any such undercover deal. Yet his ministers insisted that they had informed him steadily. They had, they said, decided not to take action against the oil companies for fear of retaliation by South Africa. At year-end, members of parliament from all parties were insisting on and won a full inquiry.

Royal Family. It was a mixed year for the Royal Family. Princess Margaret, the only sister of the Queen, divorced her husband, Lord Snowdon, after 18 years of marriage and two children. In June, another close relative of the Queen, Prince Michael of Kent, married a Roman Catholic, Baroness Marie-Christine von Reibnitz. The Queen has to grant her permission for royal marriages and this she willingly did, in spite of centuries of anti-Catholic feeling. But Pope Paul VI refused to allow the couple to marry in a Catholic church.

Crime. In March, sentences totaling 120 years were given to 17 people who had been involved in the manufacture of the drug LSD on a massive, worldwide scale. The ringleader of the operation was jailed for 13 years, and police costs in breaking this vast syndicate were estimated at some £500,000. A more grotesque crime was the murder of Georgi Markov, a dissident Bulgarian writer who had fled to London and worked for the British Broadcasting Corporation. Markov died a few days after complaining of having been stabbed in the leg by someone wielding an umbrella in a bus queue.

Other Headline Events. In October, public opinion forced the cancellation of a "seal cull" by which thousands of young and mother seals were to have been shot off the northern islands of Scotland in order to preserve fish stocks. In June, a 12-year-old girl won permission to play for her local boys' soccer team. Theresa Bennett had to use the recently passed Sex Discrimination Act to win her case.

The birth, in August, of the world's first test-tube baby pleased the nation. (*See also* MEDICINE AND HEALTH.)

SIMON HOGGART
Political Correspondent, *The Guardian*, London

GREAT BRITAIN · Information Highlights

Official Name: United Kingdom of Great Britain and Northern Ireland.
Area: 94,250 square miles (244,108 km²).
Population (1978 est.): 56,000,000.
Chief Cities (1974 est.): London, the capital, 7,173,900; Birmingham, 1,003,500; Glasgow, 816,265; Liverpool, 561,100.
Government: *Head of state,* Elizabeth II, queen (acceded Feb. 1952). *Head of government,* James Callaghan, prime minister (took office April 1976). *Legislature*—Parliament: House of Lords and House of Commons.
Monetary Unit: Pound (0.5083 pound equals U. S.$1, Nov. 1978).
Manufactures (major products): Heavy engineering and metal manufactures, textiles, motor vehicles and aircraft, electronics, chemicals.
Agriculture (major products): Cereals, livestock, livestock products.

Scotland and the Issue of Home Rule

A major constitutional change took place in Great Britain during 1978. On July 31, Queen Elizabeth gave her Royal Assent to acts granting devolution—limited self-government—to Scotland and Wales.

For Scotland, whose proposed Assembly will receive more power than that of Wales, the consequences are momentous. Devolution could satisfy the growing urge of the Scottish people for more control over their own affairs. This is what the Labour government led by Prime Minister James Callaghan devoutly hopes.

Devolution could, however, be the first step toward dissolving the union of Scotland and England and establishing independence and sovereignty for a Scotland conscious that North Sea oil could be the basis of a new prosperity.

Independence is the goal of the Scottish National Party. The rapid growth of the Scottish Nationalists since the late 1960's caused alarm in Britain's major parties—the Labourites and the Conservatives. Both parties espoused devolution as a compromise that would preserve the integrity of the United Kingdom and meet the reasonable aspirations of the Scottish people.

Successive public opinion polls taken in Scotland show that support for devolution has never fallen lower than 60%. The proportion of those supporting total independence, however, was only about 20% in 1978. Since the Labour government's commitment to devolution became clear after introduction of the Scotland bill during the 1977–78 session of Parliament, Labour has kept two Scottish seats it was expected to lose to Scottish Nationalists.

But devolution is not yet a *fait accompli*. Early in 1978, an amendment tacked onto the Scotland Act specified that Parliament could repeal the act if less than 40% of Scotland's eligible voters said "Yes" in a referendum. If, for example, 77.4% of the electorate go to the polls (and this is the average of the past nine general elections), 51.7% would have to vote "Yes." The fewer the voters, the higher the majority will have to be.

The referendum was expected in early 1979. The Labour government, which is a minority in the House of Commons, needed the support of the 11 Scottish Nationalists and three Welsh Nationalists to survive a vote of confidence, and an early referendum was seen as one means of ensuring this support.

Once the Scotland Act surmounts this hurdle, the way will be cleared for the election of the first Scottish Assembly, probably in the autumn of 1979. The Assembly will have about 150 seats, two or three from each of Scotland's present 71 House of Commons constituencies. The legislative body will have a four-year term.

The powers of the prospective Assembly are carefully limited. It would have control over health, except for abortion; schools and higher education, except for universities; the environment; transportation; local government; and criminal law, except for treason and certain other cases. It would have jurisdiction over the arts, freshwater fisheries, crofting (small scale farming), tourism, licensing laws, and, for the most part, the courts.

Administering these services would cost an estimated 2,000 million British pounds (about U. S.$4 billion) per year. But the Assembly has been given no power to tax. It will receive a block grant from the central government, negotiated every three years.

This is the provision of the Scotland Act most fiercely attacked by the Scottish Nationalists, who regard it as "representation without taxation." Many observers believe that the Assembly would be engaged in a constant battle with the central government to gain more power, most notably the power to tax.

Among other powers reserved to the central government are foreign affairs, defense policies, international trade, energy, North Sea oil economic policy, labor-management relations, industrial policy, forestry, abortion law, betting, and gaming.

The Scottish Assembly will elect one of its members to be First Secretary—in effect, the prime minister of Scotland. The First Secretary will head the Scottish Executive, also drawn from the Assembly, to run government affairs. Members of the executive will be known as Scottish Secretaries and will be appointed by the Secretary of State for Scotland on the advice of the First Secretary. There will be no change in the Scottish secretary of state's position as a member of the British cabinet.

If, in the general election which Mr. Callaghan must hold by October 1979, the opposition Conservatives come to power, there will be a further complication. Mrs. Margaret Thatcher, the leader of the Conservative Party, is passionately dedicated to maintaining the integrity of the United Kingdom. Under her leadership, the Conservatives want to reconsider the whole question of devolution. The installation of a Conservative government in London could lead to serious conflicts between the Scottish Assembly and the central government, or even to Conservative efforts to delay Assembly elections. Observers of the present British scene believe that such efforts could cause a backlash that would revive the fortunes of the Scottish Nationalists and give new élan to their demand for total independence.

TAKASHI OKA

Greek Prime Minister Constantine Caramanlis, *right*, chats informally with his Turkish counterpart, Bülent Ecevit, during a NATO summit meeting in Washington in May.

UPI

GREECE

During 1978 the government of Premier Constantine Caramanlis faced challenges from leftist opposition, while the still unresolved Cyprus dispute and a quarrel over rights in the Aegean Sea continued to embitter Greek-Turkish relations.

Parliamentary Opposition. After the parliamentary elections in November 1977, Andreas Papandreou and his Panhellenic Socialist Movement (PASOK) emerged as the leading opposition to Caramanlis' New Democracy party. Anti-American and anti-NATO, Papandreou criticized Caramanlis' domestic and foreign policies during 1978. In October he accused the government of failing to present Greek viewpoints to the world as successfully as Turkey presents its views.

The Turkish Arms Embargo. President Carter's support for the lifting of an American arms embargo, imposed after Turkey had invaded and occupied a part of Cyprus in 1974, caused consternation in Greece. When the U. S. Congress enacted legislation in the summer of 1978 allowing the president to lift the embargo—which he did on September 26—the Caramanlis government responded negatively.

Municipal Elections. Municipal elections held on October 15, followed by runoff elections in some localities on October 22, resulted in a general strengthening of leftist representation. While the government tried to downplay the results, Papandreou called them a victory for democratic forces and the people of Greece. Outside observers wondered whether the attitude of the American government toward the Cyprus issue had deflected the Greek public from a pro-Western orientation.

State Visits. A few days before the municipal runoff elections, Warren Christopher, U. S. deputy secretary of state, paid a short visit to Greece. Although he publicly stated that the United States wanted Greece to be a strong, democratic state, no tangible results of his visit were immediately announced. The most pressing issue was Greek-Turkish relations, concerning not only Cyprus but also air space and continental shelf rights in the Aegean Sea.

Premier Caramanlis took several trips outside Greece in 1978. Among these were a journey to Switzerland in March to meet with Premier Bülent Ecevit of Turkey, and a visit to the United States for a NATO conference May 30–31, where he met Ecevit again. On June 5 he addressed the UN special session on disarmament. While in the United States he saw President Carter and Secretary of State Cyrus Vance. In July, Caramanlis made a two-day trip to Bulgaria, where he was warmly received by Chairman Todor Zhivkov. Visits to Italy, France, Great Britain, and Denmark were intended to promote Greece's entry into the European Community, a goal which Caramanlis repeatedly emphasized. In late December it was announced that Greece would join the Common Market by 1981.

Foreign Minister George Rallis visited Moscow in early September to improve Greek-Soviet relations. His visit was the first journey of a Greek foreign minister to the USSR since Greece recognized the Communist regime in 1924. Later that month, Caramanlis and Rallis received the foreign minister of China, Huang Hua.

Earthquakes. A series of tremors hit the northern city of Thessaloniki, beginning in the last week of May. The most devastating was the temblor that shook the city on June 20, causing widespread destruction, the loss of about 50 lives, and countless injuries.

GEORGE J. MARCOPOULOS, *Tufts University*

─────── **GREECE · Information Highlights** ───────

Official Name: Hellenic Republic.
Location: Southeastern Europe.
Area: 50,961 square miles (131,990 km²).
Population (1978 est.): 9,300,000.
Chief Cities (1971 census): Athens, the capital, 867,023; Salonika, 345,799; Piraeus, 187,458.
Government: *Head of state,* Constantine Tsatsos, president (took office June 1975). *Head of government,* Constantine Caramanlis, prime minister (took office July 1974). *Legislature*—Parliament.
Monetary Unit: Drachma (36.45 drachmas equal U. S.$1, Nov. 1978).
Manufactures (major products): Food products, textiles, metals, chemicals, electrical goods, cement, glass.
Agriculture (major products): Grains (dried fruit, citrus, deciduous), vegetables, olives and olive oil, tobacco, cotton, livestock, and dairy products.

——— GUYANA · Information Highlights ———

Official Name: Cooperative Republic of Guyana.
Location: Northeast coast of South America.
Area: 83,000 square miles (214,969 km²).
Population (1978 est.): 800,000.
Chief City (1976 est.): Georgetown, the capital, 205,-000 (met. area).
Government: *Head of state*, Arthur Chung, president (took office March 1970). *Head of government*, Forbes Burnham, prime minister (took office Dec. 1964). *Legislature* (unicameral)—National Assembly.
Monetary Unit: Guyana dollar (2.55 G. dollars equal U. S.$1, Sept. 1978).
Agriculture (major products): Sugar, rice.

GUYANA

The tiny republic of Guyana was the focus of a horrified world in late 1978 after the assassination of U. S. Rep. Leo J. Ryan (D-Calif.) and the cult murders and suicides of over 900 members of the Rev. Jim Jones' Peoples Temple (*see* Feature Article, page 34). The government of Guyana sought to absolve itself of any responsibility for both events. On November 20, it emphasized that no Guyanese were involved in the incidents and that Jones had presented excellent references from high ranking U. S. officials upon entering the country.

Politics. Activity centered on a move by the People's National Congress (PNC) government of Prime Minister Forbes Burnham to rewrite the Guyanese constitution. The proposal called for a presidential form of government, giving the chief executive power to appoint vice presidents (one of whom would be prime minister) and to veto any law passed by parliament. In April, the PNC government pushed through parliament a measure which postponed parliamentary elections, scheduled for October, until the new constitution had been adopted. A referendum in July resulted in ostensible support of 97.4% for the government's proposal. However, the opposition People's Progressive Party (PPP) had called for a boycott of the referendum and its leader, Cheddi Jagan, claimed that "the results are obviously faked." Soon after the referendum, parliament began to write the new constitution, a process which was expected to take one year to 18 months.

Economy. Harvesting of Guyana's major foreign exchange commodity was reduced by a 135-day strike of sugar workers. The union protest caused the sugar crop to drop from 330,000 tons in 1976–77 to 241,527 tons in 1977–78.

In March, the government introduced its new budget. A total expenditure of $252 million was projected, with $71 million allotted to the government's eight-year development plan.

ROBERT J. ALEXANDER, *Rutgers University*

HAWAII

Hawaii had an important and busy political year in 1978. On election day, Hawaiians not only chose their major state officers but also voted on a host of constitutional amendments.

——— HAWAII · Information Highlights ———

Area: 6,450 square miles (16,706 km²).
Population (Jan. 1978 est.): 901,000.
Chief Cities (1970 census): Honolulu, the capital, 324,-871; Kailua, 33,783; Kaneohe, 29,903; Hilo, 26,353; Waipahu, 22,798.
Government (1978): *Chief Officers*—governor, George R. Ariyoshi (D); lt. gov., Nelson K. Doi (D). *Legislature*—Senate, 25 members; House of Representatives, 51 members.
Education (1977–78): *Enrollment*—public elementary schools, 90,299; public secondary, 82,057; colleges and universities, 47,038 students. *Public school expenditures*, $358,904,000 ($1,806 per pupil).
State Finances (fiscal year 1977): *Revenues*, $1,456,-564,000; *expenditures*, $1,502,093,000.
Personal Income (1977): $6,773,000,000; per capita, $7,677.
Labor Force (July 1978): *Nonagricultural wage and salary earners*, 370,800; *unemployed*, 30,800 (7.5% of total force).

Elections. Democrats continued their dominance of Hawaiian politics. Having survived a spirited challenge by Mayor Frank Fasi of Honolulu in the Democratic primary, incumbent Gov. George Ariyoshi coasted to an easy win in the general election. Chosen as lieutenant governor was Jean King (D), the first woman to hold that position. The Democratic plurality in the legislature remained intact: 17 to 8 in the Senate, and 42 to 9 in the House of Representatives.

The city and county councils were even more heavily Democratic. Hawaii's two incumbent U. S. Congressmen, Cecil Heftel (D) and Daniel Akaka (D) were reelected.

Constitutional Convention. In 1978, the state of Hawaii held its third constitutional convention since 1950. Unlike previous convention delegations, the 1978 contingent (102 delegates) was younger, had more women, and included only six members who previously had held elected political office. Despite reports that the public favored the use of initiative and referendum, the majority held firm in its opposition to such measures. The convention adopted more than 100 amendments to the constitution, which were grouped in 34 categories for ratification by the electorate. To the surprise of many, all of the amendments were approved. Among the major changes adopted were: a return to open primary elections; spending limits for state government; the creation of an intermediate court of appeals; more environmental protection controls; and a series of measures to assist persons of Hawaiian ancestry.

Energy. With an island economy almost totally dependent on imported oil for its energy needs, Hawaii continued its search for alternative power sources. While solar energy seemed to be gaining popularity among individual homeowners, the state, with federal assistance, continued its research into harnessing the geothermal force of Hawaii's volcanoes. Of particular significance were plans for three ocean thermal energy conversion (OTEC) projects at Keahole, on the island of Hawaii.

RICHARD H. KOSAKI
University of Hawaii

COPYRIGHT US POSTAL SERVICE 1978

HAWAII—SPECIAL REPORT:

The 200th Anniversary of Capt. Cook's Arrival

On Jan. 18, 1778, on his third voyage through the Pacific Ocean in search of a navigable northern route to the Atlantic, Capt. James Cook first sighted the islands of Oahu, Kauai, and Niihau at the western end of the Hawaiian chain. The discovery of the Sandwich Islands, as Cook called them, seemed to him "to be the most important that had hitherto been made by Europeans throughout the extent of the Pacific Ocean."

Captain Cook's arrival in Hawaii coincided with a period of special religious observances, and the Hawaiians regarded him as the god Lono. Ironically, upon his return to the islands for rest and provisions after a voyage to the Arctic, on Feb. 14, 1779, Cook was killed in a skirmish with native Hawaiians.

The 200 years since Captain Cook's discovery have seen momentous changes in Hawaii. Seldom has a society moved so rapidly from relative isolation into the midst of modern civilization. In 1900 Hawaii became a territory of the United States and in 1959 the 50th state of the Union. The Hawaiian economy, once supported by pineapple and sugar production, is now dominated by tourism. In 1977, 3.2 million tourists visited Hawaii and spent an estimated (U. S.) \$1.4 billion.

The bicentennial of Captain Cook's landing was marked by celebrations honoring not only the English explorer but also the islands themselves. It was a time to rediscover the Hawaiian heritage.

This spirit was exemplified in the outstanding exhibit assembled at the Bishop Museum in Honolulu called "Artificial Curiosities," an exposition of native wares collected on the three Pacific voyages of Captain Cook. Adrienne Kaeppler, who was largely responsible for this remarkable collection, explained that it was "not an exhibition in honor of Captain Cook the explorer-navigator, but rather, an exhibition that acknowledges and honors the achievements of Pacific peoples as they were before the impact of Cook and others of the Western world irrevocably changed their lives."

Gov. George R. Ariyoshi, in proclaiming the period from Jan. 18, 1978 to Feb. 14, 1979 as the Captain Cook Hawaii Bicentennial Year, spoke of the "tragedy and the benefits" of Captain Cook's "discovery." The proclamation called for a rekindling of the Hawaiian spirit—"a

COURTESY, THE HAWAII BICENTENNIAL COMMITTEE

COURTESY, UNITED AIRLINES

COURTESY, HAWAII BICENTENNIAL COMMITTEE

A commemorative stamp, parades, dance pageants, and other festivities marked the bicentennial of Captain Cook's landing in Hawaii. Contemporary island explorers enjoy the luxury hotels that border the palm-studded beaches.

priceless human warmth which today we call the 'aloha spirit'."

The observance in Hawaii began with a festive celebration at Waimea, Kauai, where Captain Cook first landed on Hawaiian soil on Jan. 20, 1778. Two 13¢ U. S. commemorative stamps, one picturing Captain Cook's ships anchored in Hawaiian waters, were issued in Honolulu on Jan. 20, 1978. On February 14, *The Honolulu Advertiser* issued a special edition in honor of the English explorer. The museums in Hilo and on Kauai also had special Captain Cook exhibits. The University of Hawaii summer theater staged a new monodrama, *Captain Cook,* by local playwright Aldyth Morris. In June, an Hawaiian outrigger canoe was taken to Europe, paddled across the English Channel, and donated to the town of Middlesborough, England, not far from the birthplace of Captain Cook.

There are few memorials to Captain Cook in Hawaii today. A monument and a plaque in a rather inaccessible area at Kealakekua Bay mark the spot where Cook was killed. The village above the bay is called Captain Cook, and there is a street named after him in Honolulu. There is little else, except for a stone monument in Cook's honor in front of the Public Archives in Honolulu. That monument, erected during the Captain Cook sesquicentennial in 1928, simply reads: "Captain James Cook, Forerunner of modern civilization in the Pacific Ocean."

RICHARD H. KOSAKI

RAY MANLEY, SHOSTAL

VAN BUCHER, PHOTO RESEARCHERS

A pointed peak, *above,* rises on the northern coast of Kauai, the Garden Isle, near the village of Haena. *Left:* In an aerial view of Honolulu, Waikiki Beach is seen in the center and Diamond Head in the background.

HONG KONG

The financial status of Hong Kong in 1978 was very good. The major events of the year included the extension of Gov. Murray Mac-Lehose's term of office to September 1979; the lifting of water restrictions in April; and the election of five prominent left-wing leaders to the Chinese People's Consultative Conference, two of them to the Presidium.

Economy. In the first half of 1978, total exports increased by 10.7%, re-exports by 28.6%, and imports by 20.5%, compared with the same period in 1977. The Hong Kong Commodity Exchange began to deal in raw sugar futures in 1978, and a silver bullion market was also opened. On August 4, a site next to the Mass Transit Railway's Admiralty Station in Central District was sold at (U. S.) $2,940 per square foot, a record high price that caused active trading in property shares that month. The Hong Kong and Shanghai Bank planned to merge with the Marine Midland Bank of New York State by acquiring 51% ownership of the bank for an outlay of about $260 million. The United States remained important to Hong Kong's economy, accounting for half of its overseas investments and one quarter of its foreign-owned companies.

Immigration. The number of legal immigrants from China rose from 26,449 in all of 1977 to 23,378 in the first half of 1978 and continued to rise because of China's newly relaxed emigration policy. The Hong Kong government expressed to Peking its concern over the influx of immigrants and sent back to China more than 1,600 illegal aliens. Many more remained.

Transportation. The Tuen Mun-Tsuen Wan highway, which was opened to traffic in 1978, will be extended to Kowloon by 1980. Helicopter passenger service between Hong Kong and Macao would begin after China allowed the helicopters to fly over its airspace.

Police Corruption. After a mob of policemen stormed the headquarters of the Independent Commission Against Corruption (ICAC), the governor tried to appease the discontented officers in November 1977 by granting partial amnesty for offenses committed before that year. The trial of 35 alleged conspirators in the Mongkok police corruption case began in April 1978 and ended in August. Two were convicted.

Education. The public Secondary School Entrance Examination was abolished in 1978, and the allocation of Primary Six pupils into secondary school now depends upon their marks on a public Academic Aptitude Test and three tests taken at school. In September 1978, free education was extended to Form 1 and Form 3 in government schools. The only television station that allotted time to educational programming, CTV, ceased operation in August.

CHUEN-YAN DAVID LAI
University of Victoria, British Columbia

HOUSING

U. S. Housing production remained strong throughout 1978. Internationally, the gap between the housing standards of the developed and undeveloped nations continued to widen.

THE UNITED STATES

The number of new housing units started in the United States was down sharply at the beginning of 1978. The decline reflected a well-earned winter breathing spell after the dramatic rebound in housing starts during 1977. As the spring weather improved building conditions, starts recovered and almost reached the record levels of 1977. Starts leveled off in April and began declining slightly in the summer. The average rate for 1978 was about 2 million units. Single-family home construction remained a strong sector of the housing market and condominium construction and conversion (changing rental units to owned units) also appeared strong. Apartment construction declined late in the year, primarily because of high interest rates.

The Outlook. Total housing production for 1979 should be in the range of 1.7 to 1.9 million units. Demand for housing should be good, but a tightening money supply may make interest rates high (10% or above) and funds for new construction should become more scarce.

Inflation and High Interest Rates. The average price for new and used homes in 1978 was between $54,000 and $58,000, with prices expected to continue rising at a 10% annual rate. Higher labor costs, land costs, and more stringent environmental protection measures were cited as reasons for the higher costs.

The most apparent reason for the high price of housing is the high demand for housing. Families are viewing the home as one of the best hedges against inflation. Most homeowners are seeing the equity in their home (price-mortgage) increase at an even greater rate than the value of the home. Families still view the traditional home as the "best" way to live. They are willing to sacrifice to purchase their first home and then ride the inflation bandwagon.

A key factor in the demand for housing may be the number of people reaching the age of 30. Thirty-year-olds represent the "first time" homebuyers entering the market. Because of the World War II baby boom, the number of people reaching the age of 30 between 1975 and 1980 will be 50% greater than between 1965 and 1970. Despite talk of a lower birth rate, the number of persons reaching 30 will remain at very high levels until the year 2000. These new entrants into the housing market are expected to keep demand high for years to come.

Interest rates for typical single-family home mortgages ranged between 9% and 10¼%. Usually, demand for single-family mortgages slackens when interest rates reach high levels and certainly 1978 rates were the highest buyers have ever seen. However, unlike previous periods of high interest rates, single-family mortgage demand remained strong. Apparently, buyers did not believe interest rates would fall, did not wish to wait for rates to fall, or were so sure that a home is a good investment that they were willing to buy in spite of high interest rates.

High interest rates have affected multifamily housing construction. The vacancy rates in multifamily housing were at very low levels (around 5%) late in 1978, and usually low vacancy is the signal for new construction. However, unless rental rates increase dramatically, new construction was just not feasible with the high interest rates for mortgage money.

Alternative Mortgage Instruments. High interest rates and the needs of the elderly have caused lenders to develop mortgages other than the standard mortgage with which most homeowners are familiar. The standard or "level payment" mortgage has a life of 25 to 30 years, a fixed rate of interest, and equal monthly payments. Some of the new alternative mortgage instruments are:

1. The graduated payment mortgage (GPM). The GPM uses lower payments in the early years of the mortgage and higher payments in the later years. This mortgage instrument is designed to help the young family with a rising income by "matching" the rising mortgage payment to the rising income.

2. The variable rate mortgage (VRM). Unlike the conventional mortgage or the GPM, the interest rate on the VRM would change with interest rates in the money market. A person who obtains a mortgage when interest rates are high would benefit from this feature. As interest rates decline, the interest rate on the mortgage would decline. Of course, the lender would benefit if the borrower obtained a variable rate mortgage when interest rates were relatively low.

3. The reverse annuity mortgage (RAM). The RAM is designed to help the elderly who have a great deal of equity in their homes. The homeowner could borrow against the equity in the home, obtaining those borrowed funds in whatever amounts and whenever the homeowner chooses (rather than a single lump sum as with a conventional mortgage). The lender would charge interest only on the amount actually borrowed. One possible use of the borrowed money would be to pay the property taxes on the home. Rising property taxes have placed a real burden on many elderly homeowners with fixed income.

All of these new types of financing are attempts by lenders to meet the needs of society and soften the affects of today's high interest rates and high housing costs. New types of financing may enable some buyers to enter the housing market who could not do so with conventional mortgages. Unfortunately, many Americans still cannot afford the costs of a single-family home.

Proposition 13. The most significant step to reduce housing costs was taken not by government but by the people, as California voters overwhelmingly approved the Jarvis-Gann amendment, Proposition 13. California property taxes are now limited to 1% of assessed value and, unless a sale occurs, increases in the property owner's tax bill are limited to 2%. The popularity and notoriety of Proposition 13 caused other states and other politicians to look seriously at the mood of America's taxpayer.

Single-family houses especially, and real estate in general, in California have appreciated rapidly in value. California has a very efficient system of assessing property for tax purposes, so the property owner's tax bill immediately reflects the increase in value. Each property tax bill is determined by a tax rate and the value of the property. Logically, one would expect that if property values are increasing the tax rate should be decreasing and the amount of revenue collected would remain unchanged. However, the temptation to spend was too great and local government found new ways to spend these vastly greater property tax revenues. Many taxpayers feel the new programs on which this money was spent are programs they can easily do without.

THE WORLD SITUATION

The developing countries continued to struggle with the migration of the rural population to urban areas; in the developed countries, the emphasis was on housing rehabilitation.

South America. Most of the Latin American countries were still experiencing a tremendous rural-urban migration. The rural poor were reaching the city with no job, no money, and no place to live. Overcrowding was widespread and caused more rapid deterioration of the existing housing.

Europe. Much of the European housing stock is fairly old. Realizing that this housing stock can be a great asset, governments are concentrating efforts on renovation and rehabilitation. France and Great Britain have established nonprofit, quasipublic housing organizations special-

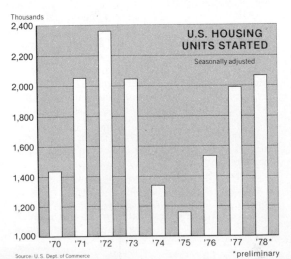

Thousands

U.S. HOUSING UNITS STARTED

Seasonally adjusted

2,400
2,200
2,000
1,800
1,600
1,400
1,200
1,000

'70 '71 '72 '73 '74 '75 '76 '77 '78*

Source: U.S. Dept. of Commerce

*preliminary

izing in rehabilitation. Their experience is that a high degree of competency and efficiency can be achieved.

Soviet Union. Soviet cities continued to experience severe housing shortages. Most young married couples must spend several years living with their parents while waiting for an apartment. When apartments do become available, they are usually the one-room, efficiency type which makes raising a family difficult. Soviet officials continue to emphasize increased industrial production. Although housing is a critically important consumer good, it does not attract the resources to produce what most Americans would think of as "adequate housing."

Canada. Housing production continued to be moderate to weak through 1978. Total starts were approximately 235,000 units. Most authorities cited lack of strong growth in terms of real gross national product and tightening monetary policy in the United States as important reasons for a sluggish housing market.

EDGAR J. MCDOUGALL, JR.
University of Connecticut

HOUSTON

The tremendous growth that has characterized the city of Houston since World War II continued in 1978. Attracted by seemingly unlimited employment prospects and a booming housing market, more than 1,000 families per month swelled the South's largest city.

Urban Problems. A decisive step was taken to ensure the city's continued expansion when voters approved a mass transportation plan. Calling for vastly increased bus service and, eventually, elevated rail facilities, the plan is expected to help Houston ease its clogged traffic arteries. However, many smaller suburban communities in the Houston area refused to endorse the plan because of the burdensome tax features that accompanied it.

State and federal agencies continued to work with the city in the fight against pollution, a major problem in the nation's largest petrochemical center.

Political Issues. Minority civil rights and demands for tax reduction were the principal issues that faced Jim McConn in his first year as mayor. The Mexican-American community was insistent in its demands that a civilian review board be created to investigate charges of police brutality, but no action was taken. However, in an effort to alleviate a potentially explosive situation, police chief Harry Caldwell announced a drive to recruit more police officers from among the black and Mexican communities.

Various citizen groups appeared before the mayor and city council urging a tax rollback or, at least, a pledge not to raise property taxes in the future. City officials announced that they were in sympathy with some form of tax relief, but they refrained from making commitments to any specific proposal.

UPI

Linda Williams of Houston obtained a federal court order allowing her to play on her high school baseball team.

Education. A federal district court denied the right of the proposed Westheimer School District, an all white area, to break away from the Houston Independent School District. Opposition to moderate court-ordered integration was at the root of the Westheimer action. Further controversy was spawned within the school system when a teacher's union and a principal's association passed resolutions condemning school board policies and expressing a lack of confidence in Superintendent Billy Ragan. In the midst of this turmoil, Deputy Supt. Linus Wright accepted an offer to head the Dallas public school system.

The Arts. Lawrence Foster resigned as director of the Houston Symphony after a distinguished career. Beverly Sills, singing the lead in the *Merry Widow,* was the hit of the local season. The Museum of Fine Arts garnered much attention with a memorable showing of French impressionist paintings, and the Alley Theater maintained its reputation as one of the leading theaters in the nation.

STANLEY E. SIEGEL
University of Houston

HUNGARY

Domestic Affairs. The Central Committee of the Hungarian Social Workers' Party (HSWP) passed several resolutions praising Hungary's growing cooperation with the West, especially the United States, but condemning the revival of the "petit bourgeois way of thinking" among the Hungarian people. The committee also called for the elimination of the critical housing shortage. In order to improve the competitiveness of Hungarian products abroad, the 23–25% increase in real wages allowed under the current five-year plan was to be reduced to 18–20%. Béla Biszku, secretary of the Central Committee, was removed and replaced by Károly Németh.

In July, Premier György Lázár, in his report to the National Assembly, pledged support for the Helsinki Final Act and criticized Communist China for its "anti-détente policies" in Vietnam.

In May, the National Organization of Retail Dealers, representing some 11,000 private businessmen, held its meeting under government sponsorship.

Organized dissident groups reappeared in 1978. Thirty-four intellectuals signed a public letter supporting Charter 77, and three *samizdat* (underground) collections of writings—*Marx in the Fourth Decade; Profile;* and *One Tenth of One Percent*—reached the public.

Alcoholism continued to be a serious problem, as the number of alcoholics in Hungary reached 1,000,000. In the previous seven years, per capita consumption increased by 70%. In July 1978, the government countered by raising the price of alcohol by 25%.

Foreign Relations and Trade. There were a great many official diplomatic visits made in 1978, and Hungary's contribution to world trade grew dramatically. Hungary participated in 102 multilateral and 165 bilateral specialization and cooperation agreements, mostly with the COMECON (Council for Mutual Economic Assistance) countries. In 1977, exports increased by 18.5% and imports by 13.3% over the previous year. Exports to the United States amounted to $60,000,000, while imports reached $135,000,000.

In March, the United States accorded Hungary most favored nation (MFN) status, by which some products could enter the U. S. market with import duties reduced by as much as 50%. Soon after, 18 leading U. S. businessmen of Hungarian origin visited Budapest.

On January 6, the Crown of St. Stephen was returned to the Hungarian people after 33 years of U. S. custody.

JAN KARSKI, *Georgetown University*

ICELAND

Politics. There were dramatic upsets in the local and state elections held in the spring of 1978. The Independence and Progressive parties, in power since 1974, each lost five seats in the Althing (legislature). The Independence party, while remaining the largest party, lost municipal control of Reykjavik, a stronghold for decades. The Progressive party became the smallest delegation in the Althing, after being the second largest. The winners in the election were two left-of-center opposition parties; the Social Democrats won nine new seats and the People's Alliance won an additional three seats in the 60-member Althing. After a series of canvasses, a new government emerged by September 1. It was led by Ólaful Jóhannesson of the Progressive party and had the support of the former opposition parties. Interestingly, the People's Alliance was for the first time participating in a government not calling for the phasing out of the U. S.-manned Iceland Defense Force.

Economy. With inflation exceeding 50% for the 12-month period ending in August, the new Cabinet's first task was to stave off wholesale shutdowns of Iceland's fish plants, while maintaining a truce with the labor front. Measures by the new government included a currency devaluation (the second of the year), a ceiling on wage increases, the elimination of sales tax on food products, and retroactive supplementary taxes.

Fisheries and Maritime Jurisdiction. Although the take of bottom fish declined in 1978, reflecting the efforts of conservationists, the total catch was expected to exceed that of 1977. As the local herring stock recovered, a larger catch of that fish was authorized. The world demand

─────── HUNGARY · Information Highlights ───────

Official Name: Hungarian People's Republic.
Location: East-central Europe.
Area: 35,920 square miles (93,031 km²).
Population (1978 est.): 10,700,000.
Chief Cities (Jan. 1977): Budapest, the capital, 2,081,-696; Miskolc, 203,393; Debrecen, 191,918.
Government: *Head of state,* Pál Losonczi, chairman of the presidential council (took office April 1967). *Head of government,* György Lázár, premier (took office 1975). *First secretary of the Hungarian Socialist Workers' party,* János Kádár (took office 1956). *Legislature* (unicameral)—National Assembly.
Monetary Unit: Forint (19.48 forints equal U. S.$1, 1978, noncommercial rate).
Manufactures (major products): Precision and measuring equipment, pharmaceuticals, textiles, transportation equipment.
Agriculture (major products): Corn, wheat, potatoes, sugar beets, vegetables, fruits.

─────── ICELAND · Information Highlights ───────

Official Name: Republic of Iceland.
Location: North Atlantic Ocean.
Area: 39,709 square miles (102,846 km²).
Population (1978 est.): 225,000.
Chief City (1977 est.): Reykjavik, the capital, 85,000.
Government: *Head of state,* Kristján Eldjárn, president (took office for 3d 4-year term Aug. 1976). *Head of government,* Ólafur Jóhannesson, prime minister (took office Sept. 1978). *Legislature*—Althing: Upper House and Lower House.
Monetary Unit: Króna (307.5 krónur equal U. S.$1, Sept. 1978).
Manufactures (major products): Fish products, aluminum.
Agriculture (major products): Hay, cheese, fodder, livestock.

for fish remained strong, but this contributed to inflationary pressures.

After the departure of a fleet of West German trawlers in late 1977, the only foreign fishing in Icelandic waters was done by a small number of Norwegian, Faroese, and Belgian vessels. The new government sought to extend territorial limits (distinct from the fishery jurisdiction) from 4 to 12 nautical miles (6.6 to 22.2 km). There was talk of obtaining fishing rights off the island of Jan Mayen (claimed by Norway) and in the area of Rockall (claimed by Great Britain).

Other Developments. The Krafla geothermal power project remained a disappointment, and fears of a volcanic outbreak in the vicinity were unabated. The Sigalda hydro station was operating smoothly, and work on another such facility was begun.

HAUKUR BODVARSSON
Coeditor, "News From Iceland"

IDAHO

Elections. Idaho elected its first Mormon governor and passed a tax cutting "Proposition 13." John Evans (D) soundly defeated Allan Larsen (R) for the governorship. Sen. James McClure (R), Rep. Steve Symms (R) and Rep. George Hansen retained their congressional seats. In the state legislature the Republicans increased their majority to 50–20 in the House but lost one seat in the Senate, to retain a 19–16 margin. Republicans were also elected lieutenant governor, attorney general, superintendent of public instruction, and secretary of state.

Legislature. The Legislature increased general fund appropriations from $282 million to $319 million. It gave $22 million tax relief but made little progress in much needed tax reform. It increased from $200 to $400 the maximum "circuit breaker" tax relief for the elderly and gave an additional $10 a year grocery tax credit for those over 65. The Legislature passed the state's first water plan to map development of the state's water resource, upgraded state officials' salaries, raising them as one writer said "from the level of embarrassment to mediocrity," allowed resort cities to enact hotel-motel taxes, and set up legislative review of administrative rules. It also passed a bill purporting to legalize laetrile, the controversial drug used to treat cancer.

It killed bills which provided for no-fault insurance, mandatory teacher negotiations, local option taxes for cities, health insurance for alcoholics and drug addicts, banning the use of radar to catch speeders, repeal of the 1975 land use planning act, and changing primary elections from August to May.

Controversy. Controversies still existed over implementation of RARE II (Roadless area review and evaluation) which decides how much land will go into wilderness classification, alloca-

WIDE WORLD

Sen. Frank Church (D-Idaho), *left,* shares a laugh with members of the Senate Foreign Relations Committee. Church prepared to become chairman of the committee in 1979.

tion of cedar timber to keep small logging operations in existence, division of salmon runs on the Snake River between Indians and non-Indians, use of abandoned missile silos in the southwestern desert to store atomic wastes, and guarantee of equal rights for women in athletics under Title IX.

Disputes between loggers and environmentalists over the amount of land to be withdrawn from logging in the Gospel Hump and St. Joe River areas were settled by a compromise method suggested by Sen. Frank Church and written into federal law under his guidance.

Other Events. The drought of 1977 was followed by heavy precipitation, especially during harvest, causing damage to wheat and pea crops.

CLIFFORD DOBLER, *University of Idaho*

--- **IDAHO • Information Highlights** ---

Area: 83,557 square miles (216,413 km²).
Population (Jan. 1978 est.): 870,000.
Chief Cities (1970 census): Boise, the capital, 74,990; Pocatello, 40,036; Idaho Falls, 35,776.
Government (1978): *Chief Officers*—governor, John V. Evans (D); lt. gov., William J. Murphy (D). *Legislature*—Senate, 35 members; House of Representatives, 70 members.
Education (1977–78): *Enrollment*—public elementary schools, 105,591; public secondary, 95,842; colleges and universities, 40,200 students. *Public school expenditures,* $260,146,000.
State Finances (fiscal year 1977): *Revenues,* $785,989,000; *expenditures* $772,627,000.
Personal Income (1977): $5,128,000,000; per capita, $5,980.
Labor Force (July 1978): *Nonagricultural wage and salary earners,* 321,500; *unemployed* 20,400 (4.8% of total force).

UPI

Charles Percy acknowledges applause following his re-election. The Illinois senator fought a difficult campaign.

ILLINOIS

Politics, a prison riot, the Equal Rights Amendment, and a march of neo-Nazis in the Jewish community of Skokie were prominent Illinois headlines in 1978.

Politics. Republican Gov. James R. Thompson won reelection with a 600,000-vote margin over his Democratic opponent, State Comptroller Michael Bakalis. After two years in office Thompson continued to win strong voter approval by balancing the state budget—the first time in four years—and by vowing to reduce taxes and government waste. Political pundits were quick to project the 40-year-old governor into the 1980 Presidential sweepstakes. Thompson did little to discourage the talk.

Reelection was more difficult for Illinois' senior United States senator, Republican Charles Percy. In a hard-fought campaign Percy came from behind to defeat Democrat Alex Seith, a political unknown who few thought would give Percy much of a race. Percy was elected to his third term.

Illinois voters elected the first black to statewide office when Roland Burris, a Democrat, was elected state comptroller. They also gave an 82% "yes" vote to a proposition sponsored by Thompson that urges the General Assembly to limit state spending and taxes.

Prison Riot. In July a bloody prison riot left three guards dead and $2.5 million in damages at the Pontiac Corrections Center, an antiquated state prison built in the late 1870's. Summer heat and overcrowding, as well as tension between the guards and the inmates, were said to be the principal causes of the outbreak. Pontiac had an authorized capacity of 1,277 prisoners, but at the time of the riot had close to 2,000.

The state has announced plans to build two new prisons but as yet no funding has been approved for the facilities. "We should have been building prisons five years ago," Governor Thompson said after the riot. "Illinois waited too long."

ERA. Efforts to win ratification of the Equal Rights Amendment (ERA) focused on Illinois when the Illinois House for the 13th and 14th time rejected the ERA. On the 14th vote it fell just two votes short of ratification, leaving Illinois the only northern state that has not approved it.

Skokie. The Chicago suburb of Skokie, which has a 40% Jewish population, received world attention during the year. In 1977 a small group of neo-Nazis from Chicago announced plans to march in Skokie. Skokie Jews and political leaders were incensed. Three local ordinances were quickly passed that were designed to prevent the march to the village hall.

The American Civil Liberties Union, seeing a First Amendment violation in the ordinances, quickly brought suit against the village. Ultimately the United States Supreme Court refused to review a lower court ruling that the ordinances were a clear infringement of First Amendment rights. But two justices dissented. One, Justice Harry Blackmun, said a Nazi march in Skokie "just might fall into the same category as one's right to cry 'fire' in a crowded theater." After the Nazis won their court fight they decided to stay away from Skokie and held their march in a Chicago park instead.

Economy. Illinois' economy remained strong during 1978. A record 5,060,000 persons employed during the month of September caused unemployment to fall to 5.5%, the lowest level in Illinois in four years.

See also CHICAGO.

ROBERT ENSTAD
Chicago Tribune

ILLINOIS • Information Highlights

Area: 56,400 square miles (146,076 km²).
Population (Jan. 1978 est.): 11,273,000.
Chief Cities (1970 census): Springfield, the capital, 91,753; Chicago, 3,369,359; Rockford, 147,370.
Government (1978): *Chief Officers*—governor, James R. Thompson (R); lt. gov., Dave O'Neal (R). *General Assembly*—Senate, 59 members; House of Representatives, 177 members.
Education (1977–78): *Enrollment*—public elementary schools, 1,450,086 pupils; public secondary, 730,238; colleges and universities, 616,209 students. *Public school expenditures*, $4,909,637,000 ($1,910 per pupil).
State Finances (fiscal year 1977): *Revenues*, $9,852,-612,000; *expenditures* $9,939,241,000.
Personal Income (1977): $87,436,000,000; per capita, $7,768.
Labor Force (July 1978): *Nonagricultural wage and salary earners*, 4,748,500; *unemployed* (Sept. 1978), 344,900 (5.5% of total force).

INDIA

The year 1978 was a difficult one for the new Janata government. The party suffered from internal dissension and a considerable loss of popular support and seemed unable to deal effectively with the basic problems of the country. Mrs. Indira Gandhi, however, staged a remarkable political comeback despite charges of past misconduct by a special one-man commission. The economic situation was mixed, but the draft of the Sixth Five-Year Plan (1978–83) called for a new development strategy. It was also an active year in foreign affairs, with important developments in India's relations with the United States and China.

Elections and Mrs. Gandhi's Recovery. The political landscape in India was again transformed in 1978. This was mainly the result of the increasing difficulties of the ruling Janata party and the political comeback of Mrs. Gandhi. In a few states, notably West Bengal and Tamil Nadu, neither the Janata nor Mrs. Gandhi's Congress party had much strength.

Mrs. Gandhi's remarkable comeback was dramatized in late February by the results of legislative assembly elections in several states. Having split her own party a few weeks before, Mrs. Gandhi's wing—Congress (I)—seemed unprepared for an election campaign. But to everyone's surprise, it won a substantial majority in the assemblies of two major southern states, Karnataka and Andhra Pradesh. And while it placed third in the state of Maharashtra to the Janata party and "regular" Congress party —Congress (R)—it formed a coalition and kept the Janata out of power.

In indirect elections for approximately one third of the Rajya Sabha (the upper house of parliament) in late March and early April, the Congress (I) did not fare so well. It lost 12 seats. The Janata party gained 27 seats, making it the largest party in the Rajya Sabha, but still far short of a majority.

With victories in a number of crucial by-elections, Mrs. Gandhi was able to make some inroads in the northern states, including her home state of Uttar Pradesh, where her party had not been able to win a single seat in the sixth general elections a year before. After her defeat in 1977, Mrs. Gandhi insisted that she had no desire to reenter parliament, but she was persuaded to contest a by-election in the Chikmagalur Lok Sabha constituency of Karnataka in early November. In the most highly publicized by-election of the year, Gandhi won decisively over a field of 28 candidates, including the Janata candidate, Verendra Patil, a former chief minister of the state. As a result of her victory, Mrs. Gandhi became the recognized opposition leader in the Lok Sabha (lower house of parliament). This gave her a powerful forum for promoting her political recovery and for defending herself against charges of abuse

UPI

President Carter walks Indian Prime Minister Morarji R. Desai to the White House gate after a meeting, June 14.

of authority during the state of emergency in 1975–77.

Despite insistent demands from influential leaders that Mrs. Gandhi and her chief lieutenants be brought to trial for their "excesses" during the emergency, the Janata government seemed unable to decide what steps to take. In March, in its first interim report, the one-man Shah Commission, appointed in 1977, concluded that the imposition of the emergency "was not warranted by the circumstances then prevailing in the country." It found Mrs. Gandhi guilty of "gross misuse of power and authority" in several cases. In late July, a special judge ordered Mrs. Gandhi and five others to appear before him to answer charges of criminal conspiracy and abuse of official authority relating to campaign practices in 1977.

On December 19, the Lok Sabha voted to expel Mrs. Gandhi and send her to jail for contempt and breach of privilege over an incident in 1975. The move sparked protest demonstrations in many parts of the country. Gandhi was not released until December 26, when parliament officially adjourned.

UPI

Mrs. Indira Gandhi, 61, returned to the political arena and won election to the Indian Parliament in November.

Janata's Mixed Record. Differences over the way to treat Mrs. Gandhi were among the many causes for a growing dissension in the top ranks of the Janata government. Prime Minister Morarji Desai favored a more cautious approach than did the number two man in the cabinet, Charan Singh. Singh was also dissatisfied with the slow progress in implementing the party's pledges to work for decentralization. Singh's power base in the north, especially in Bihar, Uttar Pradesh, and Haryana, was eroded by inept and allegedly corrupt leadership in these key states. On April 29, he resigned from the Janata party's working committee and central parliamentary board. On July 30, at the request of the prime minister, he submitted his resignation as home minister. Also asked to resign was Minister of Health and Family Welfare Raj Narain, who had become increasingly vociferous in his criticisms of top Janata party leaders. Desai's firm actions in dealing with challenges to his authority seemed to strengthen his position in the party. But there was an undercurrent of opinion that the future of the Janata party should rest with a younger group of leaders, including External Affairs Minister Atal Behari Vajpayee and the party's president, Chandra Shekhar.

Although there were some complaints of restrictions of freedom, especially from academic circles and the press, the Janata government generally maintained its record of restoring the freedoms that had been curtailed during the emergency. In April, Samachar, the news agency set up during the emergency, was abolished. It was succeeded by four independent news agencies. Two important amendments to the Indian Constitution were designed to provide further safeguards. One provision, calling for a referendum whenever a constitutional amendment is proposed that would affect the "basic features" of the constitution, received wide criticism.

Social Problems. A disturbing feature of the social scene was an increase in crime, violence, and communal and caste conflicts. Attacks on members of scheduled castes became alarmingly common in several states. In Bihar, communal and caste violence was triggered by a bill providing that 26% of the state's civil service jobs should be reserved for members of backward castes. (Another 24% were already reserved for members of scheduled castes.)

The reaction against Mrs. Gandhi's forced sterilization program during the emergency resulted in a massive setback for the family planning campaign. During the Janata government's first year in office, the rate of sterilization fell to only about 10% of that achieved during the last year of Mrs. Gandhi's rule.

The Economy. While the Janata government was widely criticized for its vagueness in economic planning and for its failure to devote sufficient attention to basic economic problems, the general economic picture was unclear. Food grain production reached a record level of 125 million tons, bringing the country close to self-sufficiency. The balance of payments continued to be unfavorable, and the rate of growth of exports declined. Export earnings in 1977–78 were (U.S.) $5.8 billion, but the cost of imports was about $6.5 billion. Repayment of $600 million in foreign debt was somewhat offset by an increase in foreign aid. The Aid-India Consortium pledged $2.3 billion, and the United States resumed its development assistance program for the first time since Mrs. Gandhi had declined such assistance in 1971. The United States and India reached three agreements in August for a total of $60 million in U.S. aid. India's foreign exchange reserves rose sharply, reaching more than $5 billion. The government also liberalized its import-export policy.

───── **INDIA · Information Highlights** ─────

Official Name: Republic of India.
Location: South Asia.
Area: 1,269,346 square miles (3,287,590 km²).
Population (1978 est.): 634,700,000.
Chief Cities (1973 est.): New Delhi, the capital, 3,600,-000; Bombay, 6,000,000; Madras, 2,500,000.
Government: *Head of state,* Neelam Sanjiva Reddy, president (took office July 1977). *Head of government,* Morarji R. Desai, prime minister (took office March 1977). *Legislature*—Parliament: Rajya Sabha (Council of States) and Lok Sabha (House of the People).
Monetary Unit: Rupee (7.7519 rupees equal U.S.$1, Nov. 1978).
Manufactures (major products): Textiles, processed food, steel, machinery, transport equipment, cement, jute.
Agriculture (major products): Rice, pulses, oilseeds, cotton, jute, tea, wheat.

The overall growth rate reached a relatively satisfactory level of approximately 6% in 1977–78. A substantial increase in agricultural growth and a small increase in industrial growth were largely offset by slowdowns in such key industries as steel, coal, textiles, and cement. Domestic and foreign investments continued to decline. Wholesale prices were stabilized, but retail prices increased by more than 10%.

The economies of West Bengal and large parts of northern India were severely affected by some of the worst monsoon floods in recent years. In West Bengal, Bihar, eastern Uttar Pradesh, New Delhi, and parts of Rajasthan, thousands of people perished, millions were left homeless, and property damage was staggering.

The Budget and the Sixth Plan. The annual budget for 1978–79, presented to parliament by the finance minister on February 28, provided for significant increases in expenditures for agriculture, defense, programs for scheduled and backward castes, and annual plan outlays by the central government and states (estimated at $6.3 billion and $6.65 billion, respectively). The budget envisioned a deficit of about $1.1 billion, compared with $93.3 million in the 1977–78 budget.

In 1978, the Fifth Five-Year Plan (1974–79) was terminated one year ahead of schedule. The Sixth Plan (1978–83), based on "a new strategy of development," was announced. The new plan will give greater impetus to the long-standing goals of "full employment, the eradication of poverty, and the creation of a more equal society." It envisioned a total expenditure of about $77.1 billion (almost double the expenditure of the Fifth Plan), an annual growth rate of 4.4%, and substantial increases in outlays for agriculture and irrigation, small industry, energy, and the Minimum Needs Program. In concluding their review of the last 25 years of planning, the drafters of the Sixth Plan admitted that "the most important objectives of planning have not been achieved, the most cherished goals seem to be almost as distant today as when we set out on the road to planned development."

State Visits. In 1978, an unusually large number of foreign political leaders made official visits to India. These included President Carter, British Prime Minister James Callaghan, the Shah of Iran, Prime Minister Pham Van Dong of Vietnam, the president of Ireland, and the king of Bhutan. Prime Minister Desai went to Sydney, Australia, in February for the first Asian and Pacific Regional Meeting of Commonwealth Heads of Government. In June, he made an official visit to the United States and addressed the Special Session of the UN General Assembly on Disarmament. Minister for External Affairs Atal Behari Vajpayee also spent a great deal of time on the international circuit. In September he visited the Soviet Union and in October the United States. A visit to China scheduled for November was postponed for health reasons. Vajpayee also went to Japan, Pakistan, Bangladesh, Sri Lanka, and South Korea, among others. He made brief appearances at the Special UN General Assembly Session on Disarmament in June; the ministerial conference of nonaligned nations in Belgrade, Yugoslavia, in August; and the regular session of the UN General Assembly in October.

Relations with the USSR and China. In keeping with its desire for a "more genuine" nonalignment, the Janata government sought to maintain good relations with the Soviet Union and to improve relations with China and the United States. During a September visit to the Soviet Union, External Affairs Minister Vajpayee assured his hosts that India would make no deals with China at the expense of the USSR. In March, a Chinese trade delegation—the first Chinese delegation to visit India since the border war of 1962—was warmly welcomed. The following month, an official Chinese goodwill delegation was given the same reception. In early March, Vajpayee told the Lok Sabha that he had accepted "in principle" an invitation to visit China.

Relations with the United States. President Carter's visit to India in January and Prime Minister Desai's visit to the United States in June highlighted the significant improvement in U. S.-Indian relations. In New Delhi, President Carter addressed a special meeting of the Indian Parliament. The "Delhi Declaration," issued at the end of his visit, was heralded as "an historic document," but it attracted little attention in either India or the United States. In his June visit, Prime Minister Desai addressed large audiences in New York, California, Nebraska, and Washington, D. C. He also met with members of the U. S. Congress and President Carter. In private conversations between the two leaders "a few" differences remained unresolved. These differences revolved around nuclear energy, in particular the policies of the superpowers, adherence to the nuclear nonproliferation treaty, and the resumption of shipments of enriched uranium to India. The latter issue was a particularly sensitive one in Indo-U. S. relations. However, President Carter agreed to resume shipments of enriched uranium, despite considerable opposition in the United States and despite his failure to get assurances from Mr. Desai regarding nuclear safeguards. This and the resumption of U. S. economic assistance to India did much to improve the climate of Indo-American relations. In all of his public statements in the United States, Desai staunchly defended India's position on nuclear matters. But as he told members of the National Press Club in Washington, "Indo-U. S. friendship is something bigger and of greater moment to the world and its problems."

Norman D. Palmer
Department of Political Science
University of Pennsylvania

INDIANA

Legislation enacted by the 1978 Indiana General Assembly made for perhaps the most significant, if not the most interesting, "short session" since the alternate-year, 30-day sessions began in 1972. In addition, weather and the energy crisis headlined events in the state during the year.

Legislation. Bills passed by the legislature dealt with child abuse, a new juvenile code, and private financing of public housing. Legislators established a fourth Indiana court of appeals district with three new judges; made it a felony to produce, distribute, or sell child pornography; and enacted a victims' aid bill making up to $10,000 available to victims of violent crimes and guaranteeing rape victims emergency hospital treatment. Measures granting collective bargaining rights to policemen and firemen and establishing statewide standards of relief for the poor and providing state aid to townships unable to meet poor relief expenses were not enacted during the 1978 legislative session.

Budget. Urged by Gov. Otis R. Bowen, the General Assembly increased the state gross income tax reduction for the elderly, increased the income qualifications for people claiming old-age property deductions, and provided a $25 tax credit for taxpayers over 65 earning less than $15,000 annually as relief for sales tax paid on utility bills. The formula for financing public schools included a 1% hike in the local property tax levy, thus adding an annual $34.5 million in extra money for public education. As an aid to motorists the General Assembly also eliminated the 4% state sales tax on state and federal motor fuel taxes and required that the total price of gasoline be registered on the pump.

The $40.2 million operating budget included funds for developing energy technology, community health and disability centers, and crippled children programs. The State Highway Commission received $34 million from the $78 million highway budget, while $44 million went directly to counties and municipalities. Funds for community mental retardation centers at Columbus

and New Albany and for a state police post at Indianapolis were included in the $43.7 million construction budget.

Elections. Republicans made significant gains in Indiana's elections. For the first time since 1970 all state officers will be Republican, and the GOP also gained control of both houses of the state legislature, the Senate by a 28–22 majority, the House by 54–46. Both victories will aid Governor Bowen in his effort to continue property tax controls beyond 1980 and will give the Republicans an advantage in redistricting state and national legislative districts. Democrats won victories in 7 of 11 congressional districts, only one fewer than in 1976. Voters defeated a proposed constitutional amendment allowing sheriffs unlimited terms, and approved another constitutional amendment that clarifies the question of gubernatorial succession.

Weather. A blizzard on January 25–26 almost immobilized the Hoosier State. Governor Bowen declared a four-day state of emergency and restricted travel to emergency vehicles. The lowest temperatures and heaviest snowfall on record occurred during February. Since 96% of Indiana's electrical energy is produced by coal, a lengthy coal strike compounded the problems created by the inclement weather and resulted in power brownouts and blackouts throughout the state.

LORNA LUTES SYLVESTER
Indiana University

─────── INDIANA • Information Highlights ───────

Area: 36,291 square miles (93,994 km²).
Population (Jan. 1978 est.): 5,339,000.
Chief Cities (1970 census): Indianapolis, the capital, 744,743; Fort Wayne, 178,021; Gary, 175,415; Evansville, 138,764.
Government (1978): *Chief Officers*—governor, Otis R. Bowen (R); lt. gov., Robert D. Orr (R). *General Assembly*—Senate, 50 members; House of Representatives, 100 members.
Education (1977–78): *Enrollment*—public elementary schools, 585,346 pupils; public secondary, 558,376; colleges and universities, 224,992 students. *Public school expenditures,* $1,846,570,000 ($1,371 per pupil).
State Finances (fiscal year 1977): *Revenues,* $3,763,796,000; *expenditures,* $3,456,564,000.
Personal Income (1977): $36,890,000,000; per capita, $6,921.
Labor Force (July 1978): *Nonagricultural wage and salary earners,* 2,195,400; *unemployed,* 145,000 (5.6% of total force).

INDONESIA

Politics. The major event of the year was the reelection of President Suharto by the Supreme Consultative Assembly.

Because he controlled appointments to the assembly and had the support of the major political party, Golkar, the president was expected to win with little difficulty. Between October 1977 and the end of the assembly session in March 1978, however, university students and devout Muslims mounted an intense and sustained campaign against him. Students were most concerned with corruption in high government officials, including Suharto and his family, and they resented government efforts to promote an officially-sponsored youth organization at their expense. Muslims in the largest opposition party, Partai Persatuan Pembangunan, were concerned about the government's economic development policies, which appeared to be increasing the gap between rich and poor. They were also incensed by presidential support for the claims of Javanese mystical groups to have their beliefs and practices given equal status with Islam, Hinduism, and Christianity.

Oppositional activity reached a peak in midJanuary. Amid signs that one or more army generals might be maneuvering to replace him should the disruptions persist, Suharto banned Jakarta's leading newspapers, arrested many student activ-

FRANÇOIS LOCHON, GAMMA-LIAISON

Indonesia's President Suharto greets the crowds during one of his trips to the east of Java.

ists, and stationed troops on the most volatile campuses. Muslims at first held firm in their rejection of the president's pro-mystical proposals but finally joined with Golkar, the Indonesian Democracy Party, and other pro-government groups in a unanimous vote for a third five-year term for Suharto. Vice President Sultan Hamengku stepped down, citing ill health, and was replaced by Adam Malik, the longtime foreign minister and most recently the chairman of the assembly and parliament.

The Third Development Cabinet, appointed after the presidential election, affirmed the strong position of the technocrats under Professor Widjojo Nitisastro, director of the National Planning Council and coordinating minister for economics, finance, and industry. A new faction of intellectuals, under the wing of Lt. Gen. Ali Moertopo, gained several key positions. The new minister of defense was Mohammed Jusuf, a friend of Suharto and former minister of industries.

Economy. Toward the end of the year, Indonesia's economic planners began to formulate Repelita III, the Third Five-Year Development Plan. Three main objectives—equality, growth, and stability—were announced. With the end of the 1974–77 oil boom, however, revenues available to the government for either growth or redistribution were expected to be considerably reduced. Rice purchases on the international market, though down according to early 1978 estimates, were also a major drain on the budget

and on foreign exchange reserves. Domestic inflation was held to 12%, and Indonesia's exports in several categories rose substantially. New studies indicated that the rate of population growth is perhaps as low as 2%.

Foreign Affairs. In response to criticism from Amnesty International and other foreign groups, Indonesia released a large number (10,000, according to the government) of political prisoners in 1978. Increased military purchases and assistance were also sought from the United States. A major reason for seeking military aid was to end guerrilla resistance to the 1976 takeover of the former Portuguese colony of East Timor.

R. WILLIAM LIDDLE
Department of Political Science
Ohio State University

——— **INDONESIA • Information Highlights** ———

Official Name: Republic of Indonesia.
Location: Southeast Asia.
Area: 735,432 square miles (1,904,769 km²).
Population (1978 est.): 140,200,000.
Chief Cities (1974 est.): Jakarta, the capital, 5,000,000; Surabaja, 2,000,000; Bandung, 2,000,000; Medan, 1,000,000.
Government: *Head of state and government,* Suharto, president (took office for third 5-year term March 1978). *Legislature* (unicameral)—People's Consultative Assembly (inaugurated most recently Oct. 1977).
Monetary Unit: Rupiah (415 rupiahs equal U. S.$1, Sept. 1978).
Manufactures (major products): Textiles, food and beverages, light manufacturing, cement, fertilizer.
Agriculture (major products): Rice, rubber, cassava, copra, coffee, soybeans, palm oil, tea.

COURTESY, GENERAL ELECTRIC

A flat-screened color television set with a picture tube three times the size of the standard 25-inch (64-cm) screen was introduced during 1978.

INDUSTRIAL REVIEW

Industrial production in 1978 grew faster in the United States than in the other major Western industrial countries combined. Textiles, steel, aluminum, shipbuilding, and petrochemicals were the sore spots in industrial production, as countries struggled with insufficient domestic demand and global competition.

THE UNITED STATES

The U. S. industrial output increased 5.8% in 1978, according to preliminary estimates. The Federal Reserve Board's index of industrial production topped 144, which means that the U. S. industry produced 44% more goods in 1978 than in 1967, the base year of the index. The dollar value of industrial output in 1978 was nearly $900 billion, accounting for about 40% of the gross national product (GNP).

Among broad categories, business equipment registered the highest output gain, 8%. Defense equipment gained more than 5%, and consumer goods output increased less than 3%. The output of intermediate products increased some 6%.

Among industries, manufacturing output grew 6.1%, mining gained 5.3%, and utilities increased their production by 2.5%.

Production of durable goods was up 7.4%. Leading the gains in durables manufacturing was railroad equipment, up nearly 28%; aircraft and parts, up 17%; construction equipment, up 10%; hardware, plumbing, and struc-

tural materials, up nearly 10%; industrial instruments, up 10%; basic steel and steel mill products, up 10%; electronic components, up 10%; furniture and fixtures, up 9%; office equipment, up 9%; and engines, up 7%.

Manufacturers of nondurable goods increased their production 4.5% in 1978. Output gains were highest for plastic products, up 15%; synthetic materials, up 9%; paper and paper products, up nearly 5%; tobacco products and food products, both up about 4%; drugs and medicines, soaps and toiletries, also up nearly 4%.

Production declines were noted for tires, down almost 2%, and for leather and leather products, down nearly 2%. Marginal gains, about 1%, were registered for apparel, agricultural chemicals, and petroleum products.

The steel industry in the United States poured 136 million tons of raw steel, 9.5% more than in 1977. The industry increased its rate of capacity utilization, from 78% in 1977 to 86% in 1978. Steel imports rose to another record in 1978, some 15% ahead of the 19.3 million-ton high reached in 1977. Imports from Japan dropped almost 16%, while imports from the European Community countries increased well over 20%. Third World countries stepped up their steel flow to the United States by 90%.

Passenger car production in the United States reached 9.2 million in 1978, just about .5% less than in 1977. Truck builders rolled out a record

3.6 million units, topping the previous high of 3.4 million units produced in 1977. Full-size autos lost popularity in 1978, dropping both in the number produced and in market penetration. Subcompacts accounted for about 13% of the U. S. auto demand, a 2 percentage point increase from 1977. The demand for luxury cars, at 6% of the market, and for compacts, at about 24%, remained unchanged.

Light trucks continued to be substituted for passenger cars. Light conventional truck output increased 10% in 1978, sport-utility vehicles output grew by 44%, and the production of vans was stepped up by 25%. More and more light trucks were fitted out with options that once were associated with passenger cars. Two out of five light trucks produced in 1978 came equipped with air-conditioning, almost 25% came with an adjustable steering wheel; power steering and power front disc brakes were included on nine out of ten, automatic transmissions came with three out of four, and almost 50% of the light trucks had tinted glass. The 25 to 44 age group accounted for about half of the van and pickup sales.

The production of heavy trucks was the highest since 1974. Output of trucks with a gross vehicle weight of over 19,500 pounds (8,833 kg) rose nearly 8% in 1978, to about 360,000.

Appliance manufacturers continued to court consumers with undiminished zeal. Their efforts were reflected in the 7% gain in the output of household appliances and in the 6.5% gain in the production of television and radio sets. Among old standbys, blenders improved further on their 1977 sales of more than 5 million units, and food processor sales doubled in 1978 to 1.5 million units. Camera producers established production records, profiting from the quantum jump in amateur photography in the past couple of years. Some 20 million still cameras were sold in 1977.

Television manufacturers had both good and bad news: the demand for color television sets reached a record 10 million, but profit margins were squeezed thin by hefty discounts. Although the Japanese had agreed to limit their exports to the United States for a three-year period, other countries stepped up their exports and the U. S. manufacturers produced and competed more aggressively. The average color television set was priced about $350 at the factory in 1978, compared with about $360 in 1967. Being aware of the doubling of retail prices in general over the past decade, consumers have responded with alacrity to the bargain that color sets offered.

Encouraged by a 50% increase in the demand in 1977, manufacturers of snow blowers raised production to 400,000 units. Equipment makers doubled blower output in 1978 and were pleasantly surprised by the continuing strength of consumer demand. Plans built on snow can melt quickly, however, as snowmobile manufacturers have found out. Back in 1971, snow-

mobile makers numbered 100 and sold some 400,000 units. The 7 U. S. manufacturers still in the business shared in the 200,000 unit sale in 1977 and were braced for even a lower total in 1978. Looking for substitutes that would duplicate the initial success of the snowmobile, manufacturers turned to making vehicles that would pretty much do the same thing on water that the snowmobiles do on the snow. Advertised as Wetbikes and Jet Skis, these new water vehicles met with enthusiastic demand.

Individual cutting of firewood increased in popularity in 1978, and fueled the demand for chain saws. Manufacturers of such saws claimed a 25% gain in production, and saw the market expand to over $500 million.

Pleasure boat manufacturers shipped 3% fewer units in 1978 than in 1977, but the dollar value of shipments increased nearly 14%. That reflected strong demand for boats and inflation.

Consumers interest in electronics continued. Microprocessor technology enabled one firm to introduce a hand-held calculator-like device that can help with translation in 13 languages. The manufacturer sold some 15,000 of the $225 device soon after announcing its availability for Christmas season. Also meeting with brisk demand are small computers for home use.

Production of primary energy materials increased about 4% in 1978, as crude oil output increased and coal production declined.

The increased flow from Alaska helped boost the U. S. crude petroleum output. Drilling activity also increased substantially, more than 10% in both number of wells and footage drilled.

Coal production slipped 6% in 1978, to 650 million tons, mainly because of the 110-day strike that began late in 1977 and ended in March 1978. The effect of the strike was substantially lessened by the operation of new mines in the West, where coal is produced by strip mining and by non-union labor. About 55% of the nation's coal reserves are in the West. Some 27% of the nation's coal came in 1978 from the states west of the Mississippi, compared with 20% in 1977. Productivity in Western strip mines is far higher than in deep mines in the East. It took 700 workers to produce 26 million tons of coal in Montana in 1977 but 54,000 workers were required to produce 110 million tons in West Virginia.

Business spending on plant and equipment amounted to $153 billion in 1978, according to preliminary estimates by the Bureau of Economic Analysis. That was a 13% gain over 1977. Biggest investment increases were recorded by aircraft producers, 37%; stone, clay, and glass producers, about 25%; and electrical machinery producers, 20%. Durables manufacturers as a group increased their investment by 14%, compared with 12% for the nondurables manufacturers. Among the latter, rubber, food, textiles, and petroleum led the capital outlays, with increases ranging from 13 to 20%. Among nonmanufacturing industries, capital outlays were boosted by 45% by air transport firms and by 15% by the railroads.

The attraction of the United States as a base for manufacturing operations became stronger for foreign firms. Japan's Toshiba Corporation became the sixth Japanese television producer to open a U. S. plant. Four Japanese motorcycle manufacturers have plants underway or are manufacturing vehicles in the United States. The first foreign car to be produced in the United States was Volkswagen: about 200,000 gasoline-powered Rabbits were rolled out of the Stanton, Pa., plant in 1978. Substantial investments in U. S. manufacturing plants have been reported by Canadian and West European firms.

INTERNATIONAL

Industrial production grew sluggishly in the highly developed countries. The big six foreign countries—Canada, France, West Germany, Italy, and the United Kingdom—registered a combined advance of 3% in 1978.

Japan and Britain, with industrial production increases well over 5%, led the developed countries. Canada posted a nearly 4% gain, but West Germany, Italy, and France produced gains in the range from less than 1% up to 2%. The steel, shipbuilding, and textile industries represented the most difficult overcapacity problems for the highly industrialized world. Britain benefited substantially from the expansion in oil production in the North Sea. Japan's industrial production reflected gains in automobiles, chemicals, and cement. France and Italy could point to production advances in autos, chemicals, and metal processing. Germany had a notable increase in the output of capital goods.

Industrial production in developing countries varied widely in 1978, from a growth rate of just .5% in Nigeria to well over 30% in Taiwan. Most developing countries are tardy in issuing economic reports, but available information pointed to notable production increases also in South Korea, over 20%, and Mexico, nearly 9%. India raised production by more than 5%.

South Korea and Taiwan stepped up their output of consumer electronics. Korea became a major producer of citizens' band radios, and Taiwan increased substantially its output of television sets. Both developments had a special impact on Japanese producers of like products. South Korea was poised to become a factor in the worldwide automotive market: its 1978 production of 220,000 units was slated for a 300% increase by 1980. India advanced its oil production to 12.7 million tons, an increase of about 25% from 1977. India is well on the way to self-sufficiency in oil. In 1978 production accounted for 50% of the domestic oil consumption, and the development of new fields was being given the highest priority.

Oil was also fueling Mexico's industrial production growth. As recently as 1972, proved and probable reserves were estimated at 2.6 billion barrels. At the end of 1978 they were put at 40 billion barrels, with broad hints of substantially higher potential. Production, now well above one million barrels a day, is scheduled for doubling by 1982. Mexico revamped its steel industry, and posted a 17% production increase, to 6.6 million tons in 1978. That will just about take care of the domestic demand. Mexico's steel industry, constructed with equipment from half a dozen countries, has been wrestling with enormous problems caused by the lack of uniformity in spare parts. The industry is in a favorable position in terms of fuel availability: huge reserves of natural gas have been discovered fairly close to major plants.

China has embarked on an ambitious program of industrialization, having mapped out an eight-year plan that calls for more than doubling its steel production, to 60 million tons by 1985. Also planned were 10 new oil and gas fields, 30 electric power plants, and dozens of new plants to manufacture agricultural equipment. To finance the imports of Western technology that will enable China to reach its goals, it has launched an aggressive export drive that is giving a foretaste of things to come. For instance, China has already become the largest single supplier of cotton textiles to the United States, much to the consternation of U. S. growers and manufacturers alike. China is planning to push its oil exports to 42 million tons by 1985. It will use the earnings to finance its new leap forward that will require sophisticated equipment for coal mines, rail and highway transportation, and petrochemical industries.

The Soviet Union reported its industrial production up nearly 5% in 1978, better than the 4.5% called for by the five-year plan. Heavy industry production led with a 5.3% increase, while the output of consumer goods grew 4%. Soviet industrial growth depends more and more on increasing work productivity, as the limits of quick and easy expansion have been reached. The labor productivity gain was 3.6% in 1978, a little short of the planned 3.8%.

The 1976–80 five-year plan projected average annual industrial production increases of 6.5%, considerably less than the increases called for in the two preceding five-year plans. The difficulties in meeting the production levels planned for 1978 were attributed to bottlenecks, poor quality of goods, bad management, poor utilization of materials, and low productivity.

Coal production eked out a 1% gain over 1977, reaching 729 million tons in 1978. Soviet oil production was reported to have reached 4.2 billion barrels, just about what was planned. With daily production a little over 11 billion barrels, the Soviet Union was the world's largest oil producer in 1978. But the Soviet oil industry is seriously handicapped by a lack of advanced equipment and technology.

AGO AMBRE, *U. S. Department of Commerce*

U.S. Research and Development

For the first time since the end of World War II, there are signs that U. S. industrial research and development may be in trouble. Since the national economy is largely driven by industrial vitality, any significant leveling off or decline in the rate of technological innovation is cause for concern.

Research and development (R&D) serve to create and replenish the stock of knowledge needed for innovation. While they may represent significant investments in themselves, they are dwarfed by the cost of translating new knowledge into full-scale innovation and marketing. The decision to proceed with technological innovation is a difficult and often risky one. The greater the uncertainty, however, the greater the risk to technological innovation. In 1978, the climate for industrial research appeared to be clouded by such uncertainty.

In terms of funds committed to research and development, the picture is not bad. In current (inflationary) dollars, industry's investment in R&D has been growing steeply during the past two decades, from (U. S.) $5 billion in 1960 to about $18 billion in 1977. In dollars adjusted for inflation, the "real" level of investment growth is only about one-half of this, or about $7 billion. On the other hand, these figures reflect industry's use of its own money.

Since most of the federal government's expenditures for R&D are turned over to industrial performers through contracts, the combined expenditures on R&D in industry (industry funds plus government funds) approaches $30 billion in current dollars and $20 billion in constant dollars. The latter figure works out to roughly the same as the 1968 amount, indicating no real increase in the level of effort over the last decade.

The mix of industrial investment in R&D has also changed over the last two decades, partly as a reaction to patterns of government spending. This is most apparent in the case of basic scientific research. Basic research, by definition, is extremely long-range and speculative, although it constitutes the creative force upon which technological innovation firmly depends. At present, the federal government supports almost 70 percent of all basic research, while the industry share has declined precipitously from 28 percent in 1960 to less than 15 percent by the late 1970's. These data suggest strongly that industry is underinvesting in fundamental research, with conceivably serious negative consequences a decade hence.

Federally-funded R&D accounts for more than half of the total U. S. outlay for R&D and is growing at a modest rate in constant dollars. While federally-sponsored research yields some benefits to industrial knowledge, there is little evidence that it translates into economic gains on anything resembling the returns from industrial R&D. Thus, massive federal spending for R&D is not a substitute for equivalent industry investment, and sound national policy must take this into account.

Government-funded research is dedicated chiefly to special missions rather than to stocking industry's knowledge. Basic research in industry itself has fallen off sharply, and the rate of formation of additional innovative companies is reported to be very low. Industry spokesmen allude increasingly to the rising costs and risks of breakaway R&D and to the deferment of long-term research and innovation. If between one half and one third of all promising research proposals cannot be financed either by government or by industry, the R&D system will run well below its capacity. To the degree that these indications dampen confidence in investment, the technology base is arrested and will gradually diminish.

U. S. industry, in the 1970's, experienced intense competition in research, development, and innovation from other developed economies whose institutional arrangements encourage close cooperation between industry and government. One effect is to shorten the period of comparative U. S. technological advantage and to lower the economic returns from innovation. In the United States, relations between industry and government are conducted at arm's length and border on the adversarious. Much of industry's present discontent arises from concern over strict government regulation and uncertainty as to policy. Without a reasonably stable downstream outlook regarding the cost of borrowing, the course of inflation, tax policies, and regulatory zeal, decision-makers in industry are strongly motivated to hedge on both R&D and commitments to innovation. They turn instead to short-range research and "defensive" work aimed at adapting products and processes to the requirements of environmental and health and safety regulations. Risk-taking is constrained, and innovation as a response to market forces is inhibited.

In his 1978 State of the Union Message, President Carter called for "a strong new surge of technological innovation." A few months later, the White House established a 14-member Cabinet committee to develop a set of policy options regarding the issues and problems of industrial innovation. The study is to be completed by late summer 1979, but the effects of possible changes in policy are unlikely to take hold on industrial R&D until the mid-1980's.

WILLIAM D. CAREY

The American Wine Industry

The dramatic expansion of the U. S. wine industry, which began in the second and third decades after World War II, was accompanied by an equally significant increase in the quality and consumption of American wines. No winegrowing area in the world experienced so rapid a development, nor so radical an improvement in the quality of its product as the United States between 1965 and 1977.

In 1978, production and consumption continued to increase dramatically, and the quality of American sparkling and light table wines rivaled that of their European competitors. On the basis of average annual increases since 1976, the Bank of America estimated a 637,000,000-gallon (2,411,045,000 L) wine market for the United States in 1978; this represented a 59 percent increase over the 1977 total. By the beginning of 1978, consumption of light wines (less than 14% alcohol, by volume) had more than trebled in comparison with the 1965 amount.

During the 1970's a fourth of the nation's vineyards were replanted, with wine grapes replacing the less desirable grape varieties grown since the beginning of Prohibition for grape juice, raisins, or for fresh shipment. The new plantings expanded the national total from an estimated 700,000 acres (283,500 ha) to more than 800,000 acres (324,000 ha).

Wine is produced commercially in 32 of the 50 states. Between 1968 and 1978, 17 states changed their laws to encourage the establishment of "farm wineries"—small cellars operated in conjunction with vineyards, with wine available on the premises for consumption. Eleven new wineries opened in states that had produced little or no wine in this century, and the number of bonded wine premises increased from 435 in 1965 to more than 700 in 1978. More than 200 new wineries were established during the 1970's in 23 states. Vineyardists have planned additional wineries in virtually every state except those with growing seasons of less than 120 days between the killing spring and autumn frosts.

The "wine revolution," as it has been called by the print and broadcast media, not only brought about an increase in the volume of wine produced in the United States, but radical changes as well in the type of wine consumed. The former pattern, in which appetizer and dessert wines (those above 14% in alcoholic content) had constituted half to three fourths of production and shipments since the repeal of national Prohibition in 1933, was reversed. Consumption of light wines more than trebled, from the equivalent of .423 gallons (1.6 L) per capita in 1965 to 1.486 gallons (5.625 L) in 1977. Total wine movement, including imports, rose from 180,677,000 gallons (683,862,440 L) in 1965, equivalent to .980 gallons (3.709 L) per capita, to 400,348,000 gallons (1,515,317,100 L) or 1.851 gallons (7.006 L) per capita in 1977, of which the appetizer and dessert types represented less than one fifth. The revolutionary character of these changes is evident in the fact that the 1977 per capita wine consumption rate was more than three times the .568 gallon (2.150 L) record in 1914, the highest in the pre-Prohibition era.

By 1965, everyday American table wines, sold in jugs and plastic pouches, were already the best of the inexpensive wines in the world. By the 1970's, the finer American bottled wines were equaling or excelling the classic wines of France and Germany in most of the "blind tastings" (with hidden labels) held by connoisseurs, and were winning high awards in international competitions. During the 1970's, for the first time in history, some California Chardonnays and Cabernet Sauvignons and New York State White Rieslings were bringing higher prices in leading American stores and restaurants than were paid for some world-famous French and German wines of the same ages and types.

New types of American wines appeared during the 1970's. White wines made fragrantly sweet by *Botrytis cinerea,* the "noble mold" on grapes called *pourriture noble* in France and *Edelfäule* in Germany, were introduced by several California and New York State vineyards and were found to equal the more famous white wines of Germany. *Vins nouveaux,* red table wines mostly produced by the *macération carbonique* method as in France, appeared for the first time in 1972 in California, reaching the Christmas market before the Beaujolais *primeurs* imported from France. A wide assortment of fruit-flavored, lightly-carbonated, low-alcohol sweet "pop" wines reached the market in the late 1960's and early 1970's, bridging the gap between the cola-tastes of American youth and the traditional dry mealtime wines. By the mid-1970's, the popularity of the "pop" wines had begun to decline. In 1974 and 1977 wineries in Maryland and California introduced the first American *eisweins,* the German rarities.

A notable development of the 1970's was a white wine boom, in which American consumers for the first time in history began purchasing as much or more white table wine than red. Before and after Prohibition, red table wine consumption had exceeded that of whites by as much as two or three to one. The white wine boom resulted from a trend among consumers to choose white table wine as a pre-meal apéritif in place of spirituous cocktails. California wineries, experiencing a shortage of white table wines, began producing an unusual proportion of *blancs*

PHOTOS WINE INSTITUTE

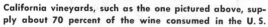

California vineyards, such as the one pictured above, supply about 70 percent of the wine consumed in the U. S.

The aging process is explained to visitors of a California winery. The grape juice is stored in wooden barrels.

de noirs, white wines fermented from the juice of black grapes.

The predominant production of American wines is in California, which, with a long growing season, mild winters, and long, rainless summers, grows most of the *Vitis vinifera* (winebearing) grapes of Old World origin produced in the United States. The Golden State has 80 percent of the nation's vineyards, produces 86 percent of the nation's grapes, and supplies 70 percent of the wine consumed in the United States. Other states historically have supplied a seventh of the wine consumed, while the rest has come from foreign countries, led by Italy, France, Spain, and Portugal. California's 646,-000 acres (261,630 ha) of vines in 1977 were almost four times the acreage of the other states combined.

The states east of the Rockies have shorter growing seasons, colder winters, and summer rains. Four fifths of eastern and midwestern vineyards grow the Concord and other native varieties, which are principally of *Vitis labrusca* parentage and have the foxy flavor of methyl anthranilate, a Labrusca characteristic pleasing in grape juice but not in dry table wines. The northeastern and midwestern states have produced increasing quantities of dry table wines from French-American hybrid grapes, such as Seyval Blanc, Aurore or Aurora, and Rayon d'Or among the whites and Baco Noir, Chelois, and De Chaunac among the reds. The northeastern states also have some notably fine but small plantings of Vinifera, mainly of white varieties such as Riesling and Chardonnay.

New York State is second in vineyard acreage to California, with 43,000 acres (17,415 ha) mainly in the Finger Lakes, Chautauqua Grape Belt, and Niagara districts. Following the repeal of Prohibition, New York State produced more champagne than any other state, but it has since been succeeded in this respect by California.

Since the 1960's, third place among the grape-growing states has been taken by Washington, which grows both Vinifera and Labrusca varieties. Vinifera plantings in the Yakima Valley and the Columbia Basin have raised Washington state above Michigan in total vineyard acreage.

In the southeastern states, from the Carolinas to Florida, the principal grapes grown are the native Muscadines, *Vitis rotundifolia,* of which the best known is the Scuppernong. New breeding techniques give winegrowing a promising future in Alabama, the Carolinas, Georgia, Mississippi, Florida, and Tennessee.

LEON D. ADAMS

ALEXANDER GEORGES

The interior design of the First National Bank of Amarillo, Tex., emphasizes a great deal of light.

INTERIOR DESIGN

But soft! What light through yonder window breaks?

William Shakespeare, *Romeo and Juliet*

Light control, energy conservation, and cost are important considerations in designing window treatments. These fundamentals apply equally to the city high-rise and to the rural one-story structure.

According to a study entitled "Window Design Strategies to Conserve Energy," by Robert Hastings and Richard W. Crenshaw of the National Bureau of Standards Center for Building Technology, "poorly designed window treatments can be an energy burden."

To be more specific, a seven by eight-foot (2.1 by 2.4 m) window can absorb enough heat in summer to require almost one ton (906 kg) of air conditioning. Proper window covering can reject up to 75% of the heat.

As important as these considerations have become, other factors also have caused the design community to rethink the problem of window treatments. Maintenance and aesthetics are two primary concerns.

For the contract designer, maintenance is of utmost importance. Today's typical structure requires heating and air conditioning vents under windows, at baseline level. Few weaves or fibers can withstand the extremes in heat and cold

—sometimes as much as 70° F. (21° C.)—in a given day. Fibers relax with the moisture of air conditioning and contract with dry heat. This constant rising and sagging (also known as yo-yoing) soon takes its toll in unsightly, uneven hemlines.

The life of many fibers is shortened by chemicals in the urban air. Fabric replacement becomes a costly affair, as it often entails thousands of yards every two years.

Offices. It is interesting to note that in the Pennzoil towers in Houston, Tex. (architect, Philip Johnson; interior designers, Gensler & Associates), not one curtain or casement enshrouds the vast expanse of glass curtainwall. Horizontal, narrow-slat blinds are used to deflect the shimmer of the Texas sun.

Jeanne Hartnett & Associates framed horizontal thin-slat blinds with fabric-covered lambrequins to soften the harshness of the metal in the law offices of Charfoos and Charfoos in Detroit, Mich.

In the Seventh Avenue (New York City) offices of Charlotte Ford, a space in grey monotones, interior designer Sheldon Littels devised custom louver blinds in a matching grey, aesthetically unifying the architectural lines of the space.

Banks. In Boston, Mass., where the climate needs warming, Sasaki Associates left the large plate glass windows of the Union Warren Savings Bank absolutely bare. At night, the bank comes alive for pedestrians with its brightly lit, cheerful, and colorful interiors.

The architecture division of 3D International shielded the First National Bank of Amarillo (Tex.) with tall, narrow-slat metal blinds.

Restaurants. The sight of people masticating is best hidden behind curtains. Curtains, long known for their acoustical qualities, also lend warmth and intimacy to the restaurant atmosphere. Rita St. Clair, of the American Society of Interior Designers (ASID), however, came up with an alternative. She hung baskets of verdant plants in the otherwise undressed windows of the Chopstick Restaurant in Baltimore, Md.

Dale Keller Associates framed the windows of the Manila (Philippines) Hotel coffee shop with ornate Victorian lattice work.

The colonial setting for Gadsby's Tavern near Washington, D. C., has uncurtained venetian blinds softened only by intricately draped valances and jabots. The restaurant was restored by the Potomac, Md., chapter of the ASID.

Residences. "The fantastic escalation in construction costs has cut down the size of interior space. These new constraints are forcing designers to virtually expand interiors into the greater outdoors. Miles and miles of fabric on windows is like having an unnecessary blanket." (*Residential Interiors,* July/August 1978).

With minimal design and the "natural" look being currently in fashion, shutters, blinds, roll-up fabric shades, and sliding screens made a

IDAKA

Jeanne Hartnett & Associates skillfully subdued the harshness of the metal in a Detroit law office.

return in 1978 as alternatives to the fabric-swathed window.

Old fashion louvered shutters protect the windows of the Simon Swan home on Long Island, N. Y., designed by Charles Moore.

At a residence in New York City, fashioned by Valerian Rybar, shining vertical stripes of silver Mylar shade the rooms, protect the interior from outside view, and reflect the interior lights. Designer John Dickinson stretched panels of neutral color fabric over window frames in the Neal Fox residence in San Francisco, Ca.

Robert Lewis, an interior designer, created roll-up fabric shades in a showcase house for the North Shore Science Museum at Roslyn, N. Y.

The green fabric was intended to pick up the color of the trees outside.

In a renovated New York office building and apartment house, Robert Perkins, an architect, created curved-roof greenhouses to replace windows in otherwise unusable structural setbacks.

At the residence of Martin Greenburg, architect Edward Hicks used patterned stained glass to highlight the windows.

Sliding shoji screens of heavy translucent paper protect the occupants of a Malibu, Ca., beach house, designed by Ray Gray, from sunlight and the view of passersby.

JEANNE WEEKS
American Society of Interior Designers

© GEORGE CSERNA 1978

Hanging baskets of verdant plants are used to add warmth to the windows of a Baltimore restaurant.

OLIPHANT, THE WASHINGTON STAR AND LOS ANGELES TIMES SYNDICATE

INTERNATIONAL TRADE AND FINANCE

The world economic picture was slightly improved toward the end of 1978, with major industrial nations sustaining moderate growth and with the United States and its major trading partners taking steps to narrow massive trade imbalances.

During the first half of the year, world trade grew by some 6%, compared with an increase of 4% in 1977 as a whole. The growth of world trade for all of 1978 was also expected to be somewhat higher than in 1977.

Although several nations made progress in lowering inflation, it continued to trouble some of the major industrialized countries—notably the United States—and the General Agreement on Tariffs and Trade (GATT) warned these countries that they can only move toward increased growth and employment and more stable exchange rates if they reduce inflation levels to the rates experienced through the mid-1960's.

Tokyo Round. The hoped-for conclusion of the five-year-old Tokyo Round of trade liberalization talks in Geneva looked doubtful as the year closed. If successful, the negotiations, begun in 1973 under the auspices of GATT, will, over a seven-year period, greatly liberalize the world's $1.15 trillion annual trade. The 97 non-Communist nations involved in the Tokyo Round account for 90% of world trade.

The main areas of disagreement remained between the United States and European Community (EC) nations over adjustments the United States made in November in its offers concerning tariffs on steel, textile, and chemical products. The Common Market ministers were also disgruntled by failure of the Congress to extend the U. S. waiver of countervailing, or penalty, import duties on foreign goods which are subsidized. Involved are $700 million worth of EC exports to the United States. EC negotiators said that the Tokyo Round could not be concluded until Congress acted. President Jimmy Carter assured EC ministers that he would ask the new Congress to reintroduce the waiver in January, but community negotiators, especially the French, seemed ready to wait until all areas of disagreement are worked out.

Although there were still some unresolved issues between the United States and Japan, including free entry of U. S. beef and citrus products into Japan and Japanese exports of textiles to the United States, negotiators said there were no longer any "political problems" to settle between the two countries. The U. S. waiver issue did not affect Japan because that country's exports are not subsidized.

The aim of the Tokyo Round is to have major industrial countries lower tariffs on imports to an average of 3–4% over a seven-year period. More importantly, since tariffs—or customs duties—represent only 20% of current barriers to free trade, there would be significant reductions in non-tariff barriers such as quota restrictions, subsidies, temporary import restrictions to protect domestic industries, government procurement, and health standards.

U. S. Trade Deficit. Despite progress made in increasing exports and in cutting oil imports, the United States trade deficit was projected at a record (U. S.) $34 billion for 1978. This higher deficit was due almost entirely to the growth in imports on non-petroleum products. U. S. imports of petroleum declined substantially in 1978.

At the end of November, the West German Parliament approved a $7.8 billion program to cut taxes and encourage Germans to buy U. S. products. The German proposals included tax cuts and pump priming measures and were said to be in response to Chancellor Helmut Schmidt's promise at the July Bonn summit meeting that he would work to increase the growth of the West German gross national product, from the projected 3% to 4%.

Japan's economic growth showed slight acceleration, with a further decline in domestic inflation. The sharp appreciation of the yen, along with additional export self-restraint to which the Japanese government has agreed, may exert an adverse effect on GNP growth.

The trade surplus of the Organization of Petroleum Exporting Countries (OPEC) was expected to show an even sharper decline in 1978 than it did in 1977. At the same time the deficit of developing countries that import oil was expected to increase by 33%, which could cause them problems in financing.

The end of 1978 presented an uncertain picture, and it was made more worrisome by the continued weakness of investment. Gross fixed investment everywhere, except in the United States and West Germany, was increasing at much lower rates and less rapidly than consumption. The level of new real investment in plant and equipment remained below the 1973 level in almost every industrial country.

The Declining Dollar. The 1978 international financial picture was heavily colored by the decline in value of the U. S. dollar relative to the currencies of the other major industrial nations. The decline not only threatened the economies of those nations but caused great losses to oil exporting nations that take payment in dollars, and to developing nations that keep their reserves in dollars. By October 1978, the dollar's sharp decline, which began in mid-1977, threatened to disrupt world trade and push the industrialized world into another sharp recession. Since World War II, the dollar had been the world's key trade currency and as such helped finance the recovery from the war and the expansion of world trade.

Between September 1977 and the end of October 1978 the dollar declined by 12% against other currencies on a trade-weighted basis. The trade-weighted basis measures the dollar against a basket of 15 currencies of major U. S. trading partners, with each currency weighted according to the amount of trade the United States does with that country. For example, if the United States does twice as much trade with Canada as with West Germany (which it does), the changes

in parity with the Canadian dollar would be given twice as much weight as changes against the West German mark. Since Canada has its own problems with inflation, unemployment, and political unrest, which in part are a result of the U. S. economic imbalance, the U. S. dollar has appreciated against the Canadian dollar, thereby distorting the huge losses against the so-called "hard currencies."

Over the same period, the dollar depreciated by 32% against the Japanese yen, by 23% against the West German mark, and by 35% against the Swiss franc. Since the underlying economies of these three countries and of other European countries, against the currencies of which the dollar has depreciated to a lesser extent, are much smaller than the U. S. economy, the flow of international money into their currencies threatens to overwhelm the economies of the countries involved.

There are several "fundamental" reasons for the dollar's decline in value over the last several years. The United States has been running a huge balance of payments deficit, particularly in the merchandise trade account. The U. S. trade deficit was $31 billion on a balance of payments basis in 1977 and was expected to run $34 to $35 billion in 1978. At the same time West Germany and Japan continued to report huge surpluses. Part of the reason for this imbalance is that the U. S. recovery from the 1973–74 worldwide recession was sharper and faster than that of its allies, and the United States continues to be less dependent on trade than they are. Foreign trade accounts for 17% of the gross national product in the United States while in West Germany it accounts for 53% of GNP and in Japan 26% of GNP.

However, as previously noted, the U. S. inflation rate continued to soar, while West Germany and Japan either slowed or halted inflationary growth. U. S. consumer prices climbed at an annual rate of 8%, while Japan and Germany held their inflation within a 2 to 4% rate, and Switzerland held its inflation rate to zero. The productivity growth rate declined in the United States to 1.4%, while it rose 4.5% in Germany and more than 8% in Japan.

But the chief villain in the dollar's sharp decline, and the reason the U. S. partners were so concerned, was the $500 billion to $800 billion floating outside the United States in the Eurodollar market. This "excess" of dollars in large part represented holdings of multinational U. S. firms and was used in the conduct of business. But many millions represent so-called "hot" money, or uncommitted dollars that float on foreign exchange markets to either the stronger currencies or to the currencies of countries that offer the highest interest rates. It is this speculative element that countries with strong currencies fear. Should even a portion of this huge amount be traded, for example, for the West German mark, it would drive the value

American tourists were generally alarmed when they personally experienced the declining value of the U. S. dollar.

UPI

of that currency to a value unbearably high for West Germany.

The dollar's position as the international "reserve" currency has derived from the economic strength of the United States—which strength is also a major weakness. The huge demand for dollars abroad has enabled the government to expand the money supply with impunity. While this expansion (which began while rates were relatively stable under the Bretton Woods Agreement of 1944), helped the world recover from World War II, it came to haunt the United States under the "floating" exchange rate system.

Another cause of the dollar's decline was that in late 1977 and early 1978 U. S. government officials seemed to be deliberately talking the dollar down. It was noted to the satisfaction of some and the worry of others that the huge amounts of dollars being bought by foreign central banks to keep their currencies from rising too far against the dollar were helping to finance the ever-ballooning U. S. budget deficit. In 1977 foreigners (largely central banks) used their excess dollars to buy approximately $31 billion of the $52 billion in new treasury paper that was sold to finance the U. S. deficit. While this enabled the United States to expand its deficit without increasing taxes, it also threatened to enlarge future balance of payments deficits. The $31 billion in treasury paper sold to foreigners cost $2 billion a year in interest.

The meeting of leaders of the world's industrial nations in Bonn in July did not substantially help the dollar. The United States periodically announced measures to support the dollar, such as increasing gold sales during the summer, but did little to follow through on these measures. By the end of October 1978, the dollar's decline was beginning to have serious repercussions at home. It was estimated that the dollar depreciation added at least 1% to the U. S. inflation rate, not only because imported automobiles, cameras and television, textiles and shoes cost more, but because each time importers were forced to raise prices as a result of the appreciation of their currencies, U. S. manufacturers raised prices of domestically-produced goods. Despite a steady tightening of credit the Federal Reserve Board had little success in reducing the expansion of monetary aggregates and in dampening consumer demand. Americans were spending in anticipation of still higher prices, impelling a spiral that further threatened confidence in the dollar.

In a stunning step on November 1, just after the dollar had reached historic lows against all major trading currencies, President Carter announced a series of moves to aid it. These included a 1 percentage point increase in the Federal Reserve's discount rate; supplementary reserve requirements for banks; doubling of gold sales by the U. S. Treasury; expansion of "swap" agreements with the Bundesbank and the Swiss Central Bank and activation of the swap agreement with the Bank of Japan, to make a total of $30 billion available to support the dollar; and issuance of foreign-currency-denominated securities. These actions were followed by a forceful intervention by central banks and by a strong follow-through by administration officials. The dollar rose sharply and most monetary experts saw a stabilization at least through the first quarter of 1979. The measures were admittedly short-term.

OPEC's Price Increase. A great threat to the U. S. economy and the economies of all industrialized and developing countries was the OPEC decision in mid-December to increase the price of oil by 14.5% in 1979. The increase was to be a four-step process beginning with a 5% rise on Jan. 1, 1979. Although some increase had been deemed inevitable, U. S., European, and Japanese leaders were shocked at its size. Following the initial 5% increase, OPEC plans called for 3.809% on April 1, 2.294% on July 1, and 2.691% on October 1. Because the increase will be applied in stages, it worked out to a 10% hike for the year, but the brunt will hit in the fall of 1979, when consumption is heaviest. The Arab oil embargo of 1973, followed by sharp increases in the price of OPEC crude, threw much of the non-Communist world into recession from which it was just beginning to recover. Saudi Arabia, the world's biggest producer, had opted for a much smaller hike, and the decision was called a compromise between the Saudi position and that of the more militant states, which wanted an across-the-board 15% increase.

Iran, which is normally OPEC's second-largest producer, suffered an 80% cutback in production because of civil unrest and this was thought to be a factor in determining the size of the increase. The oil-cartel leaders also cited the drop in the value of the dollar, in which they take payment for oil, and inflation that has raised the cost of goods they import. The increases were expected to add approximately $4.5 billion to the U. S. oil bill—and to its trade deficit—in 1979 and $5 billion to that of the EC nations.

However, the increase stands to hit hardest at developing nations, most of which have serious payments problems. Industrial nations succeeded in avoiding any increase in overall petroleum consumption during 1978; through the first half of the year oil consumption fell in the United States. In the developing countries, by contrast, petroleum consumption continued to expand strongly. At current rates of production, the price hikes were expected to boost oil income of OPEC member nations from $142 billion in 1978 to $156 billion in 1979.

Unified European Currency. A unified European currency seemed a step closer to realization as the nine-nation European Community (Common Market) set up the European Monetary System (EMS) to go into effect Jan. 1, 1979. But problems developed from the beginning, and the system threatened to widen differences it was meant to narrow. Britain, Italy, and Ireland did not join the EMS initially, but Italy and Ireland joined a week later. Switzerland and other non-EC member countries expressed interest in joining the float. The push for unity took a further blow when Norway and Sweden, members of the expiring European monetary agreement known as the "snake," and which regulated exchange rates by intervention, announced that they were pulling out and would not join the EMS at present. The EMS aims to isolate European currencies from the turmoil of fluctuations in the U. S. dollar. The Common Market, however, assured the United States that the system "is in no way harmful" to the dollar.

West Germany and France were the most staunch advocates of EMS, while Britain voiced the loudest objections. Britain felt that countries with weaker currencies—such as Britain's pound—would face lower industrial output and higher unemployment and inflation if they were forced to maintain their currencies at artificially high levels to stay in line with the West German mark and other strong currencies.

Countries joining the system are to agree to keep their currencies within close tolerances of one another. This is intended to ease internal trade and present a joint front against speculators. The EMS is to be backed by a reserve facility to be known as the European currency unit. Participating countries are to pool part of their foreign and national currency reserves into a fund that can be used to prop up the agreed exchange limits. The system is to work in much the same way as the International Monetary Fund (IMF) operates on a world level.

The advocates of the EMS said that lack of monetary union puts the EC at a disadvantage against its two major trade rivals, the United States and Japan, both of which enjoy stable internal currencies. Critics claimed that it is impossible in the long run to tie together currencies of countries having widely differing rates of growth and inflation.

The EMS was introduced in the wake of an announced increase in oil prices of almost 15%. France and West Germany promised that countries with weaker currencies will be allowed to enter the EMS on easier terms. But Britain could not gain the concessions it sought as the price for its membership. Britain sought a reform of the EC's agricultural support system and reform of the EC budget.

Gold. The market price of gold rose steadily through the end of September as demand continued to exceed supply, even allowing for the IMF gold sales and the sales by the U. S. Treasury. By the end of the third quarter gold had risen to $190 an ounce from $170 an ounce at the beginning of the year. The continuing weakness of the dollar drew investment buyers into the gold market. Confidence was increased by the IMF decision to reduce from 16.3 to 14.6 tons the amount of gold offered at its monthly auctions. By the end of September the price had risen to around $219 an ounce. Some of this increase was justified by the fact that gold mining costs rose dramatically. In South Africa, the world's largest producer, it cost $72 to mine an ounce of gold in March 1976. At the end of March 1978 the cost had exceeded $104 an ounce and it was expected that inflation alone would make that figure much higher.

Although supply and demand—and inflation—would probably have pushed the price of gold over $200 an ounce, the weakness of the dollar drew speculators into the market in unprecedented numbers; by the end of October gold had risen to an historic high of $245 an ounce. With the announcement November 1 that beginning in December the United States would increase

For the first time in post World War II history, the U. S. dollar crashed below the 180 yen mark October 26.

its monthly gold sales to at least 1.5 million ounces from 750,000 ounces, the price of gold plunged in two weeks to $198 an ounce and by the end of the year was approximately $215 an ounce. The sharpness of the drop was attributed in part to the forced liquidation of gold contracts by the general public, who had entered the market in droves when gold hit $215 an ounce. Also, while the previous IMF and U. S. Treasury gold sales had actually helped stabilize the market by keeping supply and demand about even, the doubled amount of U. S. gold entering the market would not be easily absorbed.

Newly mined gold amounted to approximately 1,366 tons, down from 1,429 tons during 1977. Between 200–250 tons came into the market from official sources (excluding the increased U. S. sales), for a total of between 1,566 tons and 1,616 tons. From this total, it was expected that if the price of gold remained in the $170–$190 an ounce range, carat jewelry consumption should remain at about 979 tons; other industrial and commercial uses, including electronic, decorative plating, dental and medical and medals, should remain at about 272 tons. Strong demand for gold coins, especially the South African kruger rand, which reached record sales, was expected to absorb at least 150 tons. This would leave between 50 and 250 tons available for private sector bullion investment, representing between $300 million and $1.5 billion at an average price of $180 an ounce.

World output has been steadily declining since 1970, when it reached a peak of 1,639 tons. In 1970 the free world contribution to that total was 78%, or 1,274 tons. In 1977, the free world contribution to the total 1,429 tons was 965 tons, or 68%. In the absence of major new discoveries, Consolidated Gold Fields, Ltd. estimates that South African production will stay at about the 700-ton level through the mid-1980's, when it will fall.

The Communist bloc nations remain an unknown factor. The Soviet Union is the second largest gold-producing country in the world, and Consolidated estimates on the basis of an extensive study that current levels of production run between 330 and 450 tons a year. Of this, COMECON nations absorb between 50 and 100 tons, giving the USSR a surplus capacity of between 300 and 400 tons. Soviet sales during 1976 and 1977 were roughly 350 tons. Whether the Soviets will increase that amount will depend on hard currency requirements, future economic performance, and political attitudes. China, also an unknown factor, was seen during 1978 as a net purchaser of gold.

IMF. IMF powers were greatly expanded with approval of the Second Amendment of the Articles agreement, which went into effect April 1. The new rules gave the IMF the ability to lend countries far more money than they would have been entitled to under the old system; the right to investigate whether individual countries are manipulating their currency-exchange rates to gain an unfair competitive advantage; and an additional $16 to $22 billion on top of the $6 to $7 billion it had to lend to financially-troubled members.

The world's economic watchdog also got a new managing director, Jacques de Larosière, who took over in June with the retirement of Johannes Witteveen. Under the new rules, the managing director was given the specific responsibility of "firm surveillance" over the disorganized exchange rates.

One of the most important effects of the revised articles was the scrapping of the official gold price of $42.22 an ounce. As a result, central banks will be subject to no gold policy and will be able to buy and sell on the market on equal terms with market operators. At the same time, the articles took steps to expand and enhance the value of the IMF's special drawing rights, which are no longer expressed in gold. Beginning July 1, 1979, the value of the SDR's will be determined by a basket of currencies of the 16 IMF member countries with the largest exports of goods and services for the period 1972–76. In the new list the currencies of Saudi Arabia and Iran replace those of South Africa and Denmark. The currencies used to determine the value of the SDR will be reviewed every five years. Given the hostility of most governments toward outside interference with the way they manage their currencies, de Larosière's job was not expected to be easy.

See also feature article on Inflation, pages 10–16.

MARY TOBIN
United Press International

IOWA

An upset in the general election in November, a busy state legislature, and a generally healthy economy marked Iowa in 1978.

Elections. In the 1978 general elections incumbent Democratic U. S. Sen. Dick Clark was defeated by Republican Roger Jepsen. Gov. Robert Ray was reelected for the fifth time. His tenure when the term is completed will total 14 years. Terry Branstad (R) was elected lieutenant governor, Melvin Synhorst (R), secretary of state, Lloyd Smith (R), state auditor, Maurice Barringer (R), state treasurer, and Robert Lounsberry (R), secretary of agriculture. Republicans gained control of both the Iowa House and Senate for the first time in four years. The 1979 legislature, according to official totals, has 28 Republicans and 22 Democrats in the Senate, while the House has 56 Republicans and 44 Democrats.

Government. The 67th Iowa General Assembly meeting in the second half of the biennial session was unusual in that the legislature recessed for nearly six weeks from the second week of May until July to allow a special study committee to examine the necessity for a change in the State usury statute.

Gasoline taxes were increased by three cents per gallon, with one and one half cent of the increase going into effect July 1, 1978, and the remainder on July 1, 1979. The diesel fuel tax also rose by three and one half cents per gallon.

Among the more controversial bills enacted into law was the "ban the can" law which will require Iowans to pay at least a five cent deposit on liquor bottles, effective May 1, 1979, and on beer and soft drink containers, effective July 1, 1979.

The first optional tax for cities and counties was authorized with a hotel-motel tax approved. Any city or county that desired to impose the tax must have it approved by a majority of those voting on the issue and must spend at least fifty percent of the revenue for recreation or convention type services. The maximum rate permitted may be 7% of the hotel-motel bill and the minimum 1% service charge.

IOWA · Information Highlights

Area: 56,290 square miles (145,791 km²).
Population (Jan. 1978 est.): 2,883,000.
Chief Cities (1970 census): Des Moines, the capital, 201,404; Cedar Rapids, 110,642; Davenport, 98,469.
Government (1978): *Chief Officers*—governor, Robert D. Ray (R); lt. gov., Arthur A. Neu (R). *General Assembly*—senate, 50 members; House of Representatives, 100 members.
Education (1977–78): *Enrollment*—public elementary schools, 306,345 pupils; public secondary, 282,415; colleges and universities, 125,744 students. *Public school expenditures,* $1,245,125,000 ($1,899 per pupil).
State Finances (fiscal year 1977): *Revenues,* $2,542,726,000; *expenditures,* $2,552,312,000.
Personal Income (1977): $19,802,000,000; per capita, $6,878.
Labor Force (July 1978): *Nonagricultural wage and salary earners,* 1,079,500; *unemployed,* 53,400 (3.7% of total force).

Low-income and elderly as well as handicapped Iowans will get larger property tax rebates in 1979, while all persons installing solar heating systems will receive a property tax break for a five year period.

The legal drinking age was increased from eighteen to nineteen by the General Assembly and was signed by Governor Ray.

A major piece of legislation approved by both the legislature and the governor after more than four years of study was a total overhaul of the Iowa Juvenile Code.

In November 1978 the electorate of Iowa approved a state constitutional amendment giving constitutional home rule to counties, similar to an amendment passed ten years ago for Iowa cities.

Other Events. On September 16th a "killer" tornado struck south of Grinnell, Iowa, killing seven persons and causing an estimated $7 million in property damage.

A flash fire in a department store in the oldest and largest shopping center in Iowa, Merle Hay Plaza in Des Moines, killed ten employees and caused an estimated $20 million loss.

Iowa farmers planted 12.5 million acres (5 million ha) of corn and 7.5 million acres (3 million ha) of soybeans in 1978, which produced a nation-leading 1,318,900 bushels of corn and 270,000,000 bushels of soybeans.

RUSSELL M. ROSS
University of Iowa

IRAN

At the beginning of the year Iran was a prosperous country with a rapidly growing economy, functioning public services, and a high level of public order. It was the most important state in the Persian Gulf region, a pillar of stability and free enterprise.

By the end of the year it was a scene of political and economic disintegration. In the capital city of Tehran, the public order had deteriorated into chaos and public services had come to a standstill. Neither taxes nor garbage were being collected. Many buildings had been burned and most businesses were shut down. Tehran airport was closed intermittently. Shah Mohammed Reza Pahlavi was still on his throne, but the government had become largely ineffective. The army alone stood between government and anarchy. The oil industry, which had been second only to that of Saudi Arabia, was crippled by strikes; Iran was *importing* oil for its essential needs.

The Opposition. The crisis resulted from a convergence of two movements which had only one thing in common—opposition to the shah. On one hand, there was a radical movement composed of a wide spectrum of leftist groups. These groups were organized in December 1977 into the "Union of National Front Forces," a coalition that included the Iran party and the Society of Iranian Socialists. Directly opposed in ideology,

From exile in Iraq and France, religious leader Ayatollah Ruholla Khomeini sought the downfall of the shah of Iran.

but perhaps even more vociferous, were the Muslim critics. In their view, the shah (himself a Shi'ite Muslim) was too liberal. They called for strict adherence to Koranic law; the return of mosque territory appropriated since 1962 in the shah's land reform program; the closing of liquor stores and cinemas; and a reversal of the improvement in the status of women that had permitted them to attend colleges, abandon the veil, and wear Western clothes.

It was the belief of the shah that such policies were calculated to set the nation of Iran back 1,500 to 2,000 years.

An Oppressive Regime? The easy cliché was that Iran's troubles were due to the oppressive policies of the shah. But Iran had been undergoing a progressive liberalization since 1976, and it was in those years that the dissent had grown unruly. In 1978, as the pace of reform quickened, and as a great number of specific grievances were in fact remedied, the violence and disorder grew even worse. Although there were corruption and inefficiency in the shah's government, the reform policies of Prime Minister Jamshid Amouzegar were never given a chance. The real cause of the uprising was the disruption of traditional Muslim society by rapid economic development and hasty modernization.

The Silent Center. One of the more mysterious features of the Iranian situation was the political ineffectiveness of the large and growing middle class, who had profited greatly from the boom conditions of the previous 15 years. There were many who wanted neither a socialist state nor Islamic atavism, but their timidity and political incompetence kept them from enunciating their point of view. There were two very large pro-shah demonstrations in Qom in January and others later in the year, but these were overshadowed by hostile demonstrations against the shah.

Riots and Demonstrations. On January 9, demonstrations in the "holy city" of Qom against the shah's land reform program and for the wearing of the veil by women led to between 5 and 20 deaths. (Opposition leaders routinely claimed a much higher number of deaths than did government sources. The total number of riot-related deaths during the year was between 500 and 1,000.) The next great outbursts occurred in Tabriz between February 18 and 23 and in several other cities from March 26 to April 2. Things assumed a more serious aspect in May, when Tehran was torn by violence for the first time. On May 9, mobs ran through the streets of Qom for ten hours, burning shops, fighting police, and stopping trains. The May riots caused the shah to cancel a diplomatic trip to Europe. About 40 persons were killed in anti-government riots in Meshed, July 23–25; six Muslim extremists in Isfahan, August 10; and several others in Shiraz, August 12. The August 20 fire in a cinema at Abadan, in which 430 perished, was attributed by the government to "Islamic Marxists" and further inflamed passions.

Intermittent disorder persisted for the remainder of the year. The worst riots occurred in the capital on November 5, when the mob burned, looted, and destroyed downtown Tehran without interference from the police or military. The government vacillated between firmness and conciliation. National Front leader Karim Sanjaby was imprisoned, then released; press censorship was imposed, then abandoned.

The campaign against the government was orchestrated largely by the exiled religious leader Ayatollah Ruholla Khomeini. Khomeini, who had lived in Iraq since the 1960's, was expelled from Iraq on October 6 and moved to France. His calls for a one-day general strike on October 1 and for an oil strike in November were both

---

IRAN • Information Highlights

Official Name: Empire of Iran.
Location: Southwest Asia.
Area: 636,300 square miles (1,648,000 km²).
Population (1978 est.): 35,500,000.
Chief Cities (1976 census): Tehran, the capital, 4,496,-159 (met. area); Isfahan, 671,825; Meshed, 670,180.
Government: *Head of state,* Mohammed Reza Pahlavi, shah (acceded Sept. 1941; crowned Oct. 1967). *Head of government,* Shahpur Bakhtiar, prime minister designate (appointed Dec. 29, 1978). *Legislature—*Parliament: Senate and Majlis (Lower House).
Monetary Unit: Rial (74 rials equal U.S.$1, Dec. 28, 1978).
Manufactures (major products): Petrochemicals, textiles, cement, processed foods, steel, aluminum.
Agriculture (major products): Wheat, rice, barley.

heeded. The oil workers' strike, which lasted almost the entire month of November and was resumed during the third week in December, had a devastating effect on the economy.

Government Changes. Several unavailing attempts to meet grievances and allay discontent were made during the course of the year. Jamshid Amouzegar, prime minister since August 1977, was replaced on Aug. 27, 1978, by former Premier Jaffar Shafir Emami, who immediately imposed martial law. The ancient Muslim calendar was restored; the post of minister for women's affairs was abolished; and all gambling places were closed. On June 6, the shah dismissed the head of *Savak,* the secret police. On September 26 he issued a decree severely restricting the financial activities of his family.

The great Tehran outbreak of November 5 led to the ouster of Emami and the appointment of a military government under Gen. Gholam Reza Azhari. But in the desperate weeks at the end of the year, the shah sought to find a new civilian premier. Continuing strikes and violence forced him to yield some of his power, but he would not give up his throne completely. On December 29, he named opposition leader Shahpur Bakhtiar to head the new, civilian government. Some measure of order was restored, as many oil workers returned to the fields and the presses began operating. But Khomeini called the government "illegal," and the monarchy remained in peril. At year's end it was difficult to envisage what alternative consensus could be put together from the utterly disparate elements of the opposition.

ARTHUR CAMPBELL TURNER
University of California, Riverside

IRAQ

The Ba'ath party administration, under the leadership of President Ahmed Hassan al-Bakr, continued to pursue its idiosyncratic but rather successful course of "Arab socialism." Saddam Hussein Takriti, vice chairman of the Revolutionary Command Council and reputed strongman of the Iraqi regime, played an increasingly prominent role. Domestic order was maintained by the rigidly authoritarian government, while increased oil production and revenue permitted ambitious social and educational programs. In foreign affairs, it was a year of surprises and policy reversals.

Domestic Affairs. Although there were no changes at the highest level of government, there were several changes in the cabinet. Three ministers lost their posts in a reshuffling announced February 18. One of those posts, that of the minister for higher education and scientific research, was at first filled on an interim basis only. But a permanent appointment was made on April 2, when the president of Mosul University, Issam Abed Ali, was named. The appointment reflected the government's increasing emphasis on higher education, especially in the fields of science and technology. On February 26, it was announced that a Japanese consortium had won a $182 million contract to build a new science and engineering university in each of Iraq's six major cities.

President Bakr's government also continued its long-term policy of investing the country's oil revenues in large-scale industrial and agricultural development programs. A series of projects costing $500 million was launched in April.

At the end of April there was a major reorganization of administrative and diplomatic personnel. Forty-one ambassadors and more than 1,000 civil servants were either reassigned or dismissed. There was no punishment, however, suggesting a softening of the harsh climate of Iraqi politics. At a cabinet meeting April 17, Bakr urged his ministers to exercise tight supervision over their departments.

The 1978 budget, introduced at the beginning of January, was a record—17% higher than in 1977. Public health costs were to increase by 32% and the cost of higher education by 30%. Compulsory primary education was scheduled to begin in academic year 1978–79.

Foreign Affairs. In 1978, Iraq's foreign policy was a tangled skein with many paradoxical elements. Good relations with the USSR did not inhibit and apparently were not affected by the execution in April of 21 members of the pro-Soviet Iraqi Communist Party. Relations with Iran, formerly regarded as an enemy, continued to improve. Diplomatic ties with Egypt, broken off in December 1977, were restored the following month.

The "Tripoli Front," opposed to the peace initiative of Egyptian President Anwar el-Sadat, tried to woo Iraq into its ranks, and for several months Syria blockaded Iraq's trade routes to Turkey. The campaign at first had little effect, but in a surprising change of policy, the Iraqi government "came in from the cold" and gave up its role as erratic loner of the Arab world. It hosted a summit conference, November 2–5 in Baghdad, of 21 Arab states. Plans were announced for a "joint command" with Syria. At a time when Egypt was a pariah and Iran was spiraling down toward chaos, Iraq suddenly emerged in a position of regional leadership.

See also MIDDLE EAST.

ARTHUR CAMPBELL TURNER
University of California, Riverside

——— **IRAQ · Information Highlights** ———

Official Name: Republic of Iraq.
Location: Southwest Asia.
Area: 169,284 square miles (438,446 km²).
Population (1978 est.): 12,200,000.
Chief Cities (1970 est.): Baghdad, the capital, 2,183,-800 (met. area); Basra, 370,900; Mosul, 293,100.
Government: Head of state and government, Ahmed Hassan al-Bakr, president (took office July 1968).
Monetary Unit: Dinar (0.2953 dinar equals U. S.$1, Sept. 1978).
Manufactures (major products): Petroleum, cement.
Agriculture (major products): Barley, wheat, dates.

UPI

Prime Minister Jack Lynch announced in 1978 that the ruling Fianna Fail party sought to reunite Ireland by abolishing the north-south border.

IRELAND

Economy. Labor disputes slowed the rate of economic growth in Ireland during 1978. Clerical workers for Aer Lingus went on strike for seven weeks and shut down the airline until May 5, when they agreed to settle for a 5% wage increase. The economy suffered even more from a strike by post office engineers, which disrupted telephone and telex services from February 7 to May 4; business firms lost an estimated $5 million a day during this three month period. These losses in production and earnings were made all the more serious by Ireland's high inflation rate.

On February 1, Minister for Finance George Colley introduced a budget which included tax cuts for single and married persons in lower income groups and the abolition of the three-year-old wealth tax. The government hoped to stimulate the economy by encouraging spending. The budget also increased social welfare benefits and withdrew income tax exemptions from some 7,000 farmers. These changes raised the national debt to 13% of the Gross National Product (compared with 10% in 1977). Colley's desire to achieve a 7% growth rate in 1978 hinged upon the cooperation of organized labor.

On March 22 the Irish Congress of Trade Unions agreed to limit wage increases to 8%. Although the vote of the delegates was close, the agreement was a victory for Prime Minister Jack Lynch's plan to curb inflationary trends. Many workers remained dissatisfied, however, as the cost of living crept steadily higher.

Politics. The level of political violence over the partition of Ireland fell off markedly during the year. Early in January, Premier Lynch angered both Ulster Unionists and many British politicians when he declared that the aim of the ruling Fianna Fail party was to reunite the country by abolishing the border between north and south. He called on Britain's leaders to withdraw all troops from the six northeast counties and to grant "some form of amnesty" to members of the Irish Republican Army once the hostilities ceased. These disclosures caused an uproar, and Lynch was forced to qualify his remarks by saying that the proposed amnesty did not apply to anyone convicted of a violent crime. On a visit to the United States, May 23–27, he promoted peaceful solutions to the Northern Ireland problem.

As part of his government reorganization, Lynch appointed Dr. Martin O'Donoghue Minister for Economic Planning and Development. The prime minister also named seven parliamentary secretaries and three backbench members of the ruling Fianna Fail party to become ministers of state.

On January 19, Chief Commissioner of Police Edmund Garvey resigned under pressure. Although no explanation was given, newspapers speculated that several scandals in the police department were the cause. Leaders of the Fine Gael opposition protested this ouster, but Lynch stood firm and appointed Patrick MacLaughlin as the new commissioner.

On August 1, Archbishop Tomás Ó Fiaich, the Roman Catholic Primate of Ireland, issued a strong statement denouncing the squalid and "inhuman conditions" in the prison camp at Long Kesh, west of Belfast. He asked the British Government to grant special status to all political prisoners there. But Roy Mason, the British Minister for Northern Ireland, made clear his opposition to any privileges for imprisoned terrorists.

L. PERRY CURTIS, JR.
Department of History
Brown University

──────── IRELAND · Information Highlights ────────

Official Name: Ireland.
Location: Island in the eastern North Atlantic Ocean.
Area: 27,136 square miles (70,282 km²).
Population (1978 est.): 3,200,000.
Chief Cities (1973 est.): Dublin, the capital, 680,000; Cork, 224,000; Limerick, 140,000.
Government: *Head of state,* Patrick J. Hillery, president (took office Nov. 1976). *Head of government,* Jack Lynch, prime minister (taoiseach, took office June 1977). *Legislature*—Parliament; House of Representatives (Dáil Éireann) and Senate (Seanad Éireann).
Monetary Unit: Pound (0.5071 pound equals U.S.$1, Sept. 1978).
Manufactures (major products): Food processing, textiles, electronics equipment, machinery, chemicals, brewing.
Agriculture (major products): Cattle and dairy products, wheat, potatoes, barley, sugar beets, turnips, hay.

ISRAEL

Menahem Begin, prime minister of Israel since June 1977, remained in power throughout the year, and despite repeated bouts with heart trouble and exhaustion, proved himself a strong and able politician. He did not win on every issue, even within his own cabinet, but he far outdistanced all political rivals in skill and determination. In every critical vote in the Knesset (parliament), his coalition government secured overwhelming support for its policies. Toward the end of the year, increased support for Begin came as a national response to U. S. criticism of Israel for not reaching a final peace agreement with Egypt.

Negotiations with Egypt. The most important events of the year were the intermittent negotiations with Egypt, upon which Israel's whole future depended. The talks all took place as a consequence of Egyptian President Anwar el-Sadat's epic visit to Jerusalem, Nov. 19–21, 1977, and Begin's to Cairo, Dec. 25–26, 1977. A third party to all negotiations was Israel's essential backer and ally, the United States. Despite the promise of Sadat's visit and the Camp David summit in September, the long negotiations did not achieve any definitive success during 1978. The major stumbling block was the future of the West Bank territories conquered from Jordan in 1967 and administered by Israel ever since. Israel's attitude was based on a reluctance to see the West Bank in the hostile hands of the Palestinian Liberation Organization (PLO). The Arabs objected to the expansion of Israeli settlements in the area, a practice which was abandoned after Camp David.

Reactions Inside Israel. The Labor opposition naturally blamed Begin for the ultimate lack of success in the negotiations with Egypt. The premier also had to contend on the one hand with the nationalist Gush Emunim (Bloc of the Faithful), who favored the expansion of Jewish settlements on the West Bank, and on the other hand with the small but vociferous "Peace Now" movement, which demanded whatever concessions were conducive to peace. The deadlocked negotiations indeed contrasted sharply with the euphoria of the Sadat visit and Camp David, but Begin was hardly to blame for the stalemate and suffered surprisingly little from it.

The Israeli-Egyptian Political Committee began talks on January 17 in Jerusalem, but these were suspended the next day when Sadat abruptly recalled the Egyptian delegation. The Israeli cabinet called Sadat's action "extreme" and said that Egyptian demands "would have removed every prospect of peace and endangered the very existence of the Jewish state."

The establishment of four new Israeli settlements on the West Bank was reported January 29 and 31. The United States warned that this might further imperil diplomacy with Egypt, but Israel's Foreign Minister Moshe Dayan denied that he had ever pledged that there would be no new settlements in the area. All that he had promised, he said, was that any new settlements would be in the framework of existing military camps. The Israeli cabinet was divided on the issue, but decided February 26 on a policy of establishing limited settlements in the Sinai Peninsula and West Bank. Defense Minister Ezer Weizman favored a halt to the expansion during peace negotiations with Egypt and on March 6 threatened to resign over the issue. This maneuver helped stall the founding of any new settlements for about two months.

In a debate in the Knesset on March 9, Labor Party leaders Yitzhak Rabin, Golda Meir, and Yigael Allon asserted that Begin's hard-line position was threatening the achievement of peace with Egypt. These criticisms were sharpened after Begin's unproductive visit to Washington, March 21–22. On March 24, Weizman called for a national coalition government to speak for Israel with a united voice. But on March 26, the cabinet unanimously endorsed Begin's peace proposals: self-rule for the Arabs in the West Bank

ALAIN MINGAM, GAMMA-LIAISON

Israel's Prime Minister Menahem Begin accepts the Nobel Peace Prize. He and Egypt's President Anwar el-Sadat shared the award "not only to honor actions already performed in the services of (Mideast) peace but also to encourage further efforts to work out practical solutions. . . ."

ALAIN MINGAM, GAMMA-LIAISON

Golda Meir, the "grandmother of Israel," died in December. She was buried in Mount Herzl Cemetery, near Jerusalem.

and Gaza Strip, with Israel maintaining military forces in both areas. Three days later, the Knesset approved this plan. On April 16, the cabinet formally restated its acceptance of UN Security Council Resolution 242 as a "basis for negotiation." Their interpretation, however, was that the resolution does not necessarily call for *complete* withdrawal from occupied territories. A "Peace Now" rally brought 25,000 to Tel Aviv on April 1, and a much smaller rally was held April 26. Begin met again with President Carter in Washington on May 1.

Disagreements within the cabinet and Knesset persisted throughout the summer. Weizman, whose notions of cabinet solidarity took second place to his desire for peace, differed violently with Begin and Dayan at a cabinet meeting June 25 but retained his post. Weizman and Labor Party leader Shimon Peres met with Sadat at Salzburg, Austria, July 13, evoking a disclaimer from the cabinet: "The exclusive authority of conducting negotiations with Egypt or any state in a state of war with Israel is given to the government and its authorized representatives." Dayan had little success in talks with Egyptian Foreign Minister Mohammed Kamel and U. S. Secretary of State Cyrus Vance at Leeds Castle, England, July 18–19. On July 26, the Knesset defeated by a vote of 70–16 a Labor motion of no confidence in Begin's handling of foreign policy.

After Camp David. The Israeli reaction to the Camp David summit meeting (September 6–17) and the resulting accords was generally positive, with strong dissent coming from right-wing groups only. On September 24 the cabinet voted to approve the accords, with one member resigning. On September 28 the Knesset gave formal approval by a vote of 84 to 19, with 17

abstentions. The most controversial item in the accords was the requirement that Jewish settlements be removed from the Sinai.

In protest, some 150 members of the Gush Emunim attempted to stake out new settlements near Nablus, September 19, and Hebron, September 21, but they were forcibly evicted by Israeli soldiers. In a parallel incident on December 27, some 65 Gush Emunim families were evicted from the unauthorized settlement of Nebi Samuel, north of Jerusalem.

The draft peace treaty achieved in Washington October 12–22 left many points unsettled. In the last two months of the year, Sadat introduced new amendments and interpretations totally unacceptable to Israel. Subsequent U. S. pressure on Israel had a unifying effect on national opinion. When Vance visited Israel just before Christmas he ran into a storm of resentment and protest. The Labor Party swung solidly behind Begin, and on December 23 the Knesset agreed almost unanimously that U. S. criticism of Israel was "one-sided, unjust, and does not contribute to the advancement of peace."

Lebanon. On March 12, PLO terrorists based in Lebanon attacked two public buses on the road between Tel Aviv and Haifa, killing 33 Israelis. Three days later Israeli forces moved into southern Lebanon to eliminate PLO encampments along the border. By March 21, Israeli troops had set up a "security belt" 15 miles (24 km) into Lebanon. A UN peacekeeping force arrived March 22, and Israel began its pullout April 11.

Other Events. The 1978–79 budget, proposed in the Knesset January 9, envisaged expenditures of about $13 billion and an inflation rate of 30%. In 1978, the rate of inflation was nearly 33%. The 30th anniversary of the founding of the State of Israel was celebrated May 11. Yitzhak Navon, 57, was sworn in as the fifth president of Israel on May 29, succeeding Ephraim Katzir. Begin's candidate, Yitzhak Chavet, withdrew from the race in March. Death claimed two eminent Israelis in 1978: former Prime Minister Golda Meir, "grandmother of the nation"; and Pinhas Rosen, justice minister from 1948 to 1961. *See also* MIDDLE EAST; OBITUARIES—Golda Meir.

ARTHUR CAMPBELL TURNER
University of California, Riverside

─────── **ISRAEL · Information Highlights** ───────

Official Name: State of Israel.
Location: Southwest Asia.
Area: 7,848 square miles (20,325 km²).
Population (1978 est.): 3,700,000.
Chief Cities (1977): Jerusalem, the capital, 366,000; Tel Aviv-Jaffa, 348,600; Haifa, 228,100.
Government: *Head of state,* Yitzhak Navon, president (took office May 1978). *Head of government,* Menahem Begin, premier (took office June 1977). *Legislature* (unicameral)—Knesset.
Monetary Unit: Pound (18.62 pounds equal U. S.$1, Dec. 28, 1978).
Manufactures (major products): Processed foods, textiles, metal products, electronics.
Agriculture (major products): Citrus, other fruits, cotton, wheat, grains, vegetables, dairy.

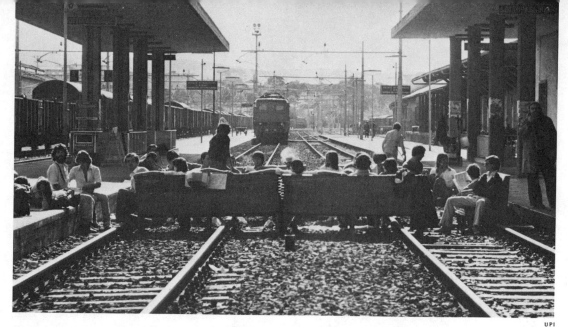

Left stranded by a three-day strike on ferry lines to Sardinia, disappointed travelers strike back by blocking railroad traffic at Civitavecchia, September 22.

UPI

ITALY

In 1978 Italy reeled under a series of shocks —mounting terrorism, the kidnapping and murder of a former premier, the resignation in disgrace of the head of state, and the deaths of two popes—but managed to survive the year with most institutions intact.

POLITICS

Catholic-Communist "Competitive Cooperation." Italy's continuing political crisis stemmed from a deadlock in the May 1976 parliamentary elections. At that time the Christian Democrats, with 38.8% of the vote, won enough of a majority to remain in power, but not enough to govern without at least the consent of the Communists, who had polled 34.5% of the vote. In August 1976, a bargain was worked out whereby the Communists agreed to support Giulio Andreotti's new Christian Democratic government in exchange for an informal say in shaping government policy.

Andreotti's government stayed in office for 17 months under this arrangement. Then, on Jan. 16, 1978, it was forced to resign when the Communists, with encouragement from Socialists and Republicans, made it clear that they must henceforth be formally included in an "emergency government." An eight-week crisis ensued. Staying on as "caretaker" premier, Andreotti resisted pressure from Enrico Berlinguer's Communist Party to give it a part in the government. U. S. officials made it clear they would be very unhappy if Communists were allowed in. An agreement finally was reached among five parties (Christian Democrats, Communists, Socialists, Democratic Socialists, and Republicans) that fell short of Berlinguer's proposal. The Communists

would not hold seats in the cabinet but would vote with the government majority in parliament and have a voice in policymaking. On the basis of this "competitive cooperation," Andreotti announced on March 11 the formation of a new government composed solely of Christian Democrats.

Berlinguer indicated that his Communists would back efforts by the new government to moderate wage demands by workers but wanted in return a crackdown on big tax evaders. A further agreement permitted reorganization of the police force. Except for a few elite units, the police would be "demilitarized" and shifted to civilian status, making them eligible to form a union.

Early in the year there was also an understanding that after the expiration of the term of President Giovanni Leone, the Communists would support the election of Aldo Moro. Moro, a former premier, was president of the Christian Democratic Party at that time.

Kidnapping and Murder of Aldo Moro. On March 16, Italy was suddenly thrown into turmoil by the kidnapping of Moro and the brutal murder of five of his bodyguards by terrorists of the Red Brigades. The kidnappers demanded that 15 Red Brigade leaders on trial in Turin be freed within 48 hours. The Andreotti government, with firm backing from the Communists, took an uncompromising position against the terrorists. The trial in Turin continued under intensified security measures. Acts of terrorism also continued, especially in the northern industrial cities, where firebombings, kidnappings, "kneecappings," and murders became a weekly pattern.

In mid-April, the Red Brigades informed the government that their "trial" of Moro was finished and that he was sentenced to die. The captive politician wrote letters, probably under duress, in which he pleaded with Christian Democratic leaders to make a deal. His wife made similar appeals, but to no avail. On May 9, Moro's bullet-riddled body was found in a parked car in downtown Rome, a short distance from the headquarters of both the Christian Democratic and Communist parties.

At the behest of Moro's embittered widow, a private funeral was held in the village of Torrita Tiberina. But the government insisted on supplementing this with a state memorial service, without the body, in the Basilica of St. John Lateran on May 13. Pope Paul VI, a longtime friend of Moro, celebrated the mass, but Moro's widow refused to attend.

Political Repercussions of the Moro Affair. In local elections the next day (May 14), the Christian Democrats made substantial gains. The Communists lost votes to the Socialists but remained the second largest party. The Christian Democrats captured 42.6% of the vote, compared with only 26.2% for the Communists and 13.1% for the Socialists. On the extreme right, the Italian Social Movement-National Right and National Democracy parties together polled 5% of the vote. Many voters apparently believed that despite the Communist Party's denunciation of Moro's kidnapping and murder, it was at least indirectly responsible for the climate of violence; the Red Brigades were seen as an offshoot of the party. Despite their election setback, the Com-

munists continued to support the Andreotti government.

A national referendum on June 11 strongly endorsed a joint call by the Communists and Christian Democrats for the retention of tough law-and-order legislation that gave the police almost unlimited right to use firearms.

In Turin, the 15-week trial of Red Brigade leaders ended on June 23, with 29 of the accused sentenced to up to 15 years in prison; 16 were acquitted. Renato Curcio and Pietro Bassi each received 15-year sentences. By autumn, the police had succeeded in finding several Red Brigade hideouts in Rome and Milan and had arrested a number of suspects in the Moro case.

New President of the Republic. On June 15, six months before the expiration of his seven-year term as head of state, the Christian Democratic president of Italy, Giovanni Leone, unexpectedly announced his resignation. Facing tax fraud charges, he was under pressure from Socialist and Communist forces in parliament to step down. Judiciary authorities were launching an inquiry to determine whether there were grounds for prosecuting him. Leone was reportedly involved in a partnership with two key defendants in the much publicized Lockheed payoff scandals that were being exposed in Italy's highest court.

The selection of a successor to Leone was the responsibility of the Electoral Assembly, composed of members of parliament and 58 representatives of Italy's regional governments. For several days, the Christian Democrats, Socialists, and Communists remained deadlocked. Finally, on July 8, Sandro Pertini, an 81-year-old Socialist, was chosen as Italy's seventh president. On the decisive 16th ballot he received 832 votes out of 995 cast. A hero of the anti-Fascist resistance during World War II, Pertini had spent many years in jail or exile under the Mussolini dictatorship. The first official act of the new head of state was to reinstate the government of Premier Andreotti, which had tendered its resignation as a pro forma gesture.

New Christian Democratic Party Leadership. The Christian Democratic Party's highest decision-making body, the 170-member National Council, met in August. After endorsing the "hang tough" handling of the Moro case by Premier Andreotti and party secretary Benigno Zaccagnini, the council elected a new party president to replace Moro. He was Flaminio Piccoli, 62, head of the party's parliamentary group. His only serious rival was former premier Amintore Fanfani, a vociferous foe of any tie with the Communists. Piccoli was not expected to make the presidential office as important as it was under Moro, who possessed a unique grasp of political strategy and an almost inexhaustible patience.

In the autumn, the party was greatly embarrassed by revelations that Moro, while in captivity, had made bitter denunciations of Andre-

COPYRIGHT 1978 BY HERBLOCK IN "THE WASHINGTON POST"

SHADOW GOVERNMENT

TERRORISM

ITALY

©1978 HERBLOCK

Tourists from Australia and South Africa save on travel expenses by picnicking in Rome's Piazza del Popolo.

UPI

otti, Zaccagnini, and several other Christian Democratic leaders.

An additional cause for sadness was the death on October 17 of 91-year-old Giovanni Gronchi, former president of the republic (1955–62). Gronchi was one of the early proponents of the opening up of Italian politics to leftist influences.

Legalized Abortion. In April, a bill to legalize abortion was introduced in the Italian parliament for the third time. It was approved in the Chamber of Deputies by a vote of 308 to 275 and in the Senate by 160 to 148. Opposition came from the Christian Democrats and neo-Fascists. The new law provides for abortion on demand during the first 90 days of pregnancy for any woman over the age of 18 whose physical or mental health would be endangered by childbearing. Physicians who declared their opposition to performing abortions were exempted from doing so. Cardinal Poletti, the vicar of Rome, called on doctors to refuse to carry out abortions —a position that was quickly endorsed by Pope Paul VI. By midsummer, many Catholic doctors and nurses had taken advantage of this provision in the law.

Changes in the Papacy. In Italy, the death of Pope Paul VI on August 6 produced not only religious shockwaves but political repercussions as well. The pontiff had been a close friend of Moro and had endorsed the trade-offs with the Italian Communist Party that had enabled Christian Democrats to retain nominal control of the government since 1976. Upon Paul's death, many observers thought that "hard-liners" in the curia would persuade the next pontiff to reverse this policy. These fears were allayed, however, by the election in September of a compromise candidate, Albino Cardinal Luciani of Venice, who took the name of John Paul I as a sign of his intention to continue the policies of John XXIII and Paul VI.

The sudden death of John Paul I one month later came as an even greater shock. Because of a split among the Italian cardinals, the first non-Italian in 455 years was elected pope: Karol Cardinal Wojtyla of Poland, who adopted the title John Paul II. Most political analysts predicted that the election of the 58-year-old Pole would probably remove much of the Vatican's influence over Italian politics. The "orphaned" Christian Democratic Party would now have to act for itself. Italian Communists adopted a wait-and-see attitude.

One of the major problems facing the new pope was the revision of the Lateran Concordat signed with the Mussolini government in 1929. After prolonged secret negotiations between Italy and the Vatican, a draft for a new concordat was presented to parliament in 1976. John Paul II must decide whether to keep the same negotiating committee and endorse the proposed revisions. The new concordat would end the constitutional enshrinement of Roman Catholicism as Italy's state religion, terminate compulsory religious teaching in the schools, and give equal weight to civil and church marriages.

Faltering Catholic-Communist Partnership. By autumn it was clear that Italy's precarious Catholic-Communist partnership might have trouble surviving the winter. The small but pivotal Republican Party was threatening to pull out of the government coalition. The Socialist Party was doing its best to chase out the Communists, while steadily increasing the need for its own participation. Half of the Christian Democratic leadership encouraged the Socialists, while the other half urged the Communists to hold fast.

The Communists no longer seemed sure that holding fast was a good idea; many felt they had come out as losers in the deal. Taunted by the Socialists for their orthodox Leninism and by ultra-leftists for their "revisionism," the Communists had reason to fear the success of both these parties. Communist losses in the May 1978 local elections ran from 5% to 12%, their biggest loss in any election since the war. The Socialist Party captured many of the defectors, increasing its share of the vote from 9.5% to 13.1%. Heartened further by their election of Pertini to the presidency of the republic, the Italian Socialist Party sought to recreate the situation in France, where the Socialists have replaced the Communists as the strongest party on the left.

After several years of promoting a "soft line" Eurocommunism designed to attract middle-class support, the Italian Communist Party appeared in the autumn to be switching to a tougher policy in order to strengthen its declining influence on the left. Berlinguer signaled such a change in a speech in Genoa in September; he declared that the party must remain loyal to Marxist principles by pursuing a revolutionary course aimed at defeating capitalism.

ECONOMICS

Italy's economy in 1978 was somewhat better than the year before. In 1977 the gross national product (GNP), adjusted for inflation, had grown by only 1.7%. The new Andreotti government hoped to increase this to 4% in 1978. Italy's rate of inflation was whittled down from 18.3% in 1977 to about 13% in November 1978. In July, the Bank of Italy repaid in advance about (U. S.) $1 billion of the $2 billion loan made by West Germany in December 1976.

Laws were tightened to catch the thousands of tax evaders, but much cheating continued, especially in the area of disability pensions.

Unemployment remained at 7.5% (1.5 million). About half of the unemployed were under the age of 28, and many were university graduates.

In December 1978, despite protests by the Communist party, the government approved Italy's entry into the new European Monetary system with special concessions.

CHARLES F. DELZELL, *Vanderbilt University*

--------- ITALY · Information Highlights ---------

Official Name: Italian Republic.
Location: Southern Europe.
Area: 116,318 square miles (301,264 km²).
Population (1978 est.): 56,700,000.
Chief Cities (1976): Rome, the capital, 2,883,996; Milan, 1,705,086; Naples, 1,223,927; Turin, 1,190,621.
Government: *Head of state,* Sandro Pertini, president (took office July 1978). *Head of government,* Giulio Andreotti, prime minister (took office July 1976). *Legislature*—Parliament: Senate and Chamber of Deputies.
Monetary Unit: Lira (838.50 lire equal U. S.$1, Nov. 1978).
Manufactures (major products): Automobiles, machinery, chemicals, textiles, shoes.
Agriculture (major products): Wheat, grapes, citrus fruits, rice, olives.

JAPAN

Thirty-three years after the end of World War II, Japan had clearly entered the elite circle of leading industrial democracies. Although suffering from a stubborn domestic recession, the nation's aggressive export program produced a record semiannual trade surplus of (U. S.) $10 billion in the first half of fiscal 1978 (April–September). The resulting monetary disequilibrium, particularly the sharp rise of the yen in relation to the dollar, placed severe strains on Japan's economic relations with its allies. Meanwhile, on May 30 at a UN special session on disarmament, Foreign Minister Sunao Sonoda, speaking for the only nation in the world bearing atomic wounds, urged the 149 member-nations to conclude a comprehensive test ban and to halt the nuclear arms race. He argued for the peaceful use of nuclear energy under strict international surveillance.

INTERNATIONAL AFFAIRS

Japan's major contribution to peace and stability in Asia, according to Premier Takeo Fukuda, was the ratification of the long-delayed Japan-China peace treaty in October. The reaction in Washington was positive, but the USSR, with which Japan has yet to conclude a peace treaty, reacted negatively.

Relations with China. In historic ceremonies on October 23 at the prime minister's official residence in Tokyo, Foreign Minister Sonoda and his Chinese counterpart, Huang Hua, exchanged instruments of ratification of a peace and friendship treaty. The exchange was witnessed by Premier Fukuda and Deputy Premier Teng Hsiao-ping, the highest-ranking Chinese official to visit Japan. Teng explicitly expressed to Fukuda China's support for the Japan-U. S. security arrangement, but he denounced as "deceptive" the U. S.-USSR efforts toward détente and criticized Soviet "escalation" of the nuclear arms race. Later, in an audience with Emperor Hirohito, Teng stated that China was "letting bygones be bygones" and would endeavor to expand peaceful relations with Japan. The Emperor admitted that there were "unhappy events" in the long relationship, thereby expressing regret over Japan's invasion of China forty years before.

Indeed, there had been tension between the two powers right up to the eve of signing the treaty on August 12 in Peking. Three years before, negotiations toward a treaty had halted because Japan objected to China's inclusion in the draft of an "anti-hegemony" clause. The wording was obviously aimed at the USSR. Also at issue was the 1950 Sino-Soviet treaty, which openly identified Japan as a potential common enemy. In an accommodation worked out by Sonoda and Huang, Japan indicated that the "anti-hegemony" clause was not directed at any specific third party. In return, China indicated

Japanese Premier Takeo Fukuda, *right*, and Chinese Deputy Premier Teng Hsiao-ping make a toast in honor of the new Japanese-Chinese peace treaty.

UPI

that the 1950 Soviet treaty would be allowed to lapse.

Earlier, on February 16 in Peking, Japan and China concluded an eight-year private trade agreement, under which each country set an export target of (U. S.) $10 billion. Japan is to import crude oil and coal, and China is to receive industrial plants, construction equipment, and patent royalties and licensing fees.

Relations with the USSR. On June 12, Soviet Ambassador Dmitri Polyansky conveyed a formal protest to the Japanese foreign ministry over the proposed treaty with China. Moscow warned Tokyo that the conclusion of an amity treaty was part of China's anti-Soviet strategy. On February 23 Moscow had unilaterally unveiled a draft proposal for a USSR-Japan cooperation treaty. The next day, Tokyo rejected the draft, explaining that a peace treaty could come only after settlement of Japan's claims to the southern Kuril Islands, off Hokkaido. Late in May, Moscow notified Tokyo that the Soviet-occupied islands would be used for military maneuvers June 6–12.

Relations with the United States. Japan's relations with the United States were given top priority in Premier Fukuda's basic foreign policy. Since Japan's defense capability is constitutionally limited, he said, the nation must rely on the U. S. security treaty. Washington generally supported the Japan-China peace treaty and informed Japan one hour in advance of the announcement of its decision to recognize Peking. The Japanese government expressed the hope that it would contribute to peace throughout Asia.

On May 24, U. S. presidential security adviser Zbigniew Brzezinski told Premier Fukuda that Washington would continue to strive for a SALT II agreement with Moscow, regardless of other differences.

The greatest source of tension between Washington and Tokyo was, of course, economic. In September, the Japanese trade balance with the United States (based on customs clearance) showed a surplus of $1,035,000,000, the third largest on record. Late in October, just before President Carter announced his anti-inflation and dollar-support schemes, the U. S. dollar sank to a post-World War II low of 176.08 yen on the Tokyo market. In February, the Bank of Japan had purchased U. S. dollars in an attempt to stave off further declines. As a result of such purchases, Japan's gold and foreign currency reserves reached an all-time high of $24.2 billion by March 1.

In January, U. S. trade representative Robert Strauss visited Tokyo to secure trade agreements which would reestablish import-export equilibrium. But, he warned, tentative settlement would not ease the pressure on Washington to enact protectionist measures. On May 3 in Washington, President Carter assured Premier Fukuda of continued American security support, despite the trade problems. Fukuda admitted at a press conference that his government might have considerable difficulty in attaining its goals of 7% economic growth for fiscal 1978 and reducing the current accounts surplus to $6 billion by March 31, 1979.

In October, Michiya Matsukawa, adviser to the finance ministry, warned against expecting an excessively high rate of growth or an increase in imports. With increased prices, a result of the appreciation of the yen, exports would soon display a 4% drop in volume, he warned. This slowdown would inevitably and adversely affect Japan's economic growth, a key to the recovery of world economy. Such delicate balances were also the subject of consultations with other industrial powers.

UPI

Foreign Minister Sunao Sonoda answers questions after addressing the UN General Assembly on disarmament.

Relations with Other Industrial Nations. At a conference in Bonn, West Germany, July 16–17, Japan and six other industrial democracies reached agreement on a coordinated program for international economic recovery. Premier Fukuda repeated his government's promise to take any necessary action to keep Japan from falling short of its projected 7% growth rate. On October 13, West German Chancellor Helmut Schmidt concluded a four-day visit to Tokyo, joining Premier Fukuda in urging stabilization of the international monetary situation. At about the same time, officials from Japan and the European Community (EC) completed a meeting in Brussels in a cordial mood, heartened by a moderation of Japan's trade surplus with the EC. In October, Japan announced plans to sound out the United States and other Western industrial nations on a proposal to hold the next summit in Tokyo, June 1979.

Relations with the Middle East. On September 18, officials of the Japanese foreign ministry cautiously praised the Camp David summit accord. Japan stood prepared to provide economic assistance to countries in the region. Between September 5 and 13, Premier Fukuda toured the Middle East and expressed Japanese concern for stability and peace in the area. He was the first Japanese leader ever to visit the region. His tour included stops in Iran, Qatar, the United Arab Emirates, and Saudi Arabia.

DOMESTIC AFFAIRS

As a result of general elections for the (lower) House of Representatives in December 1976 and for the (upper) House of Councillors in July 1977, the Liberal-Democratic party (LDP) clung to a bare majority. Late in December 1976, the Diet had selected LDP President Takeo Fukuda to be prime minister. But in late November 1978, the LDP seemed to withdraw its support of Fukuda in favor of party Secretary General Masayoshi Ohira.

Party Politics and Elections. Even before the official start of the LDP presidential campaign on November 1, the party already had four strong contenders. Fukuda was determined to retain the premiership, but he refrained from campaigning until after the visits of Teng Hsiao-ping and Mexican President José Lopez Portillo. Masayoshi Ohira and Executive Council Chairman Yasuhiro Nakasone also announced their candidacies at that time. International Trade and Industry Minister Toshio Komoto, businessman turned LDP politician, announced his intention to run at a meeting of a party faction led by former Premier Takeo Miki.

It was Miki who earlier proposed a preliminary vote similar to the U. S. party primary. On November 27, members and associates of the LDP gave Masayoshi Ohira a surprising victory over Fukuda, 748 points to 638 (one point equals 1,000 votes). Although a run-off election, in which only members of the LDP Diet would vote, was scheduled for December 1, Fukuda withdrew in favor of Ohira. On December 7, Masayoshi Ohira was installed as the new prime minister.

The LDP was encouraged by the results of two local elections. Early in April, the LDP-backed Yukio Hayashida ended some three decades of leftist rule in Kyoto by winning the governorship. Shortly thereafter, a former LDP vice minister, Michikazo Saigo, was elected mayor of Yokohama. He replaced the popular Ichio Yasukata, who also left to fill the chairmanship of the chief opposition party, the Japan Socialists (JSP).

Japan's political parties were puzzled over two contradictory rulings made by different benches of the Tokyo High Court. On September 11, the court held that unevenness in popular representation between underpopulated (rural) and overpopulated (urban) districts was not unconstitutional. Urban areas, the court said, enjoyed certain "cultural and economic advantages." On September 13, another bench ruled that the December 1976 general election was unconstitutional because Diet seats were not evenly allotted to electoral districts. Although the LDP, whose majority traditionally comes from rural districts, had the most to lose by this decision, the presiding judge refused to overturn the results of the 1976 general election.

Economy. In statements both abroad and before the Diet on October 1, Premier Fukuda committed his government to an economic growth rate of 7% in fiscal 1978. However, by year's end this goal was proving difficult to attain

A shipment of Japanese automobiles, still a popular commodity in the United States, is unloaded at Jacksonville, Fla.

UPI

because of a slowdown in exports. Affected by the sharp appreciation of the yen, the value of certified exports declined for the third quarter in a row. Although the volume of exports rose by 16.4% in the July–September quarter, their value dropped by 12.4%. According to the Research Institute on the National Economy, Japan was expected to attain a 5.3% net economic growth in 1978, 5.9% in 1979, and an annual average of 6% for the four-year period 1978–81. According to the institute, Japan would successfully shift from its present export-oriented economy to a domestic demand-oriented economy.

The Japanese economy nonetheless proved formidable. At the end of fiscal 1977 (March 31) the nation's gross national product (GNP) was running at an inflation-adjusted total of $448 billion. Japanese per capita income in nominal terms stood at $7,167 (compared with $9,150 in the United States). As in all industrial democracies, however, inflation sliced into economic gains. In September, the consumer price index (CPI) in Tokyo's 23 wards rose by 1.3% over the previous month (125.9 against 1975 = 100). The nationwide CPI increased by only 0.1% (August over July; 123.1 against 1975 = 100), for an annual rate of 4.2%.

Although the economy showed signs of structural adjustment and business recovery, the unemployment rate remained stubbornly high. Total unemployment in March stood at 1,410,-000 (well over 2% of the labor force), the third highest figure since 1956.

On March 15, the fiscal 1978 national budget was passed by the lower house. It provided for a total expenditure of 34.3 trillion yen, an increase of some 20% over the previous year. Even so, the government found it necessary to pass a supplementary expenditure measure in September; it included a $4 billion emergency import plan for fiscal 1978.

Narita Airport. In 1971–72, plans were made to expand the overused, but still convenient, Haneda international airport. Instead, the government decided to relegate Haneda to domestic flights only and to build a new airport. The New Tokyo International Airport was planned for Narita, some 40 miles (64 km) from downtown Tokyo. Seven years later, after expenditures of $600 billion, the loss of four lives, over 4,000 injuries, and 1,700 arrests, Narita was still not completed. One of two runways was expected to be opened on April 2, 1978, but huge throngs of displaced farmers, supported by bands of radical students, were determined to interrupt the formal opening. Facing them, behind barbed wire to protect the facility, were some 13,000 trained riot police.

On March 26, the police were diverted by an assault on one of Narita's gates, and a small band of protesters entered the control tower. They proceeded to wreck the sensitive directional equipment required for safe landings and takeoffs. Amid embarrassment to the government and a growing concern for security among the international airlines, it was announced that the

——— JAPAN · Information Highlights ———

Official Name: Japan.
Location: East Asia.
Area: 147,470 square miles (381,947 km²).
Population (1978 est.): 114,400,000.
Chief Cities (1975 census): Tokyo, the capital, 11,540,-283; Osaka, 2,778,987; Yokohama, 2,621,771; Nagoya, 2,079,740.
Government: *Head of state,* Hirohito, emperor (acceded Dec. 1926). *Head of government,* Masayoshi Ohira, prime minister (took office Dec. 1978). *Legislature—* Diet: House of Councillors and House of Representatives.
Monetary Unit: Yen (188.40 yen equal U. S.$1, Nov. 1978).
Manufactures (major products): Machinery and equipment, metals and metal products, textiles, automobiles, chemicals, electrical and electronic equipment.
Agriculture (major products): Rice, vegetables, fruits, milk, meat, natural silk.

UPI

Despite the steady appreciation of the yen on the foreign exchange, imported goods remain expensive in Japan.

vice chairman of Lockheed, and John W. Clutter, former head of the company's Tokyo office, were received under a U. S.-Japan mutual judicial agreement. In return for their testimony, the Lockheed officials were promised immunity from prosecution by the Japanese Supreme Court.

The testimony, accepted on September 21, alleged that Yoshio Kodama, a shadowy power broker, and Kenji Osano, a transport tycoon, were deeply involved in Lockheed's Japanese sales drive. Kodama and Osana were named as defendants in trials involving this affair. On April 3, a Marubeni official had implicated the former prime minister, Kakuei Tanaka. Both Kodama and Osano were friends of Tanaka.

Natural and Man-Made Disasters. On June 12, an earthquake, registering 5 on the Japanese scale of 7, shook several prefectures in the northern section of the island of Honshu. The largest city in the path of the quake was Sendai, which reported 21 deaths and 350 injuries.

Japan continued to set legal precedents by holding corporate bodies responsible for chemical damage to citizens. On August 3, the Tokyo District Court ordered the state and three pharmaceutical companies to pay 3.3 billion yen in compensation to 133 victims of a nervous disease. The disorder was caused by a medication for intestinal disorder which contained quinoform and its drug relatives. On October 15, prosecutors in a Kumamoto court demanded a three-year sentence for two former executives of the Chisso corporation. The two were charged with involuntary manslaughter in connection with an outbreak of mercury poisoning called "Minamata disease." Former Chisso president Kiichi Yoshioka and Eiichi Nishida, manager of that company's Minamata plant, were the first corporate officers to be charged with criminal responsibility for pollution damage. The Kumamoto District Court was expected to hand down a ruling in the spring of 1979.

ARDATH W. BURKS
Rutgers University

formal opening would be postponed until May 20. Meanwhile, the Diet passed stringent security measures to protect the airport.

On May 22, two days after a subdued ceremony to dedicate the facility, the new airport went into operation. Despite continued demonstrations and threats, Narita was operating at full force by the end of the year. The airport handles some 356 arrivals and departures per day, or 10 million travelers per year.

Lockheed Scandal. A different sort of aircraft problem continued to make headlines in 1978, as the so-called Lockheed affair plodded through the courts. Marubeni officials, representing Lockheed in Japan, testified that undue influence had been brought to bear on the purchase of L-1011 (TriStar) aircraft. The court then sought evidence from a court in Los Angeles, Calif. Depositions taken from A. C. Kotchian, former

UPI

Leftist radicals protest the opening of the new Tokyo International Airport near Narita in May.

JORDAN

From the outset of the dramatic Egyptian peace initiative to the aftermath of the signing of the Camp David agreements between Israel and Egypt, Jordan's King Hussein was forced to walk a tightrope between opposing forces in what he called the most serious crisis of his 26-year reign. Pursuing a middle course in the complicated world of Arab politics, Hussein sought to minimize the criticism of Egyptian President Anwar el-Sadat while preserving Arab unity and maximizing his personal options.

Middle East Diplomacy. On Jan. 1, 1978, King Hussein concluded talks with U. S. President Jimmy Carter in which Carter tried to persuade him to join Israeli-Egyptian negotiations on the future status of the occupied Arab territories and east Jerusalem.

Two days later, Hussein articulated the concerns which formed the basis of his yearlong refusal to participate in the negotiations. He declared that as long as the Israelis refused to make a commitment to total withdrawal from the occupied territories, a negotiated peace in the Middle East was impossible. In muting his initial criticism of Sadat's move, Hussein also said that peace could not be achieved unless the Palestinians were given the right to exercise self-determination "under conditions of total freedom."

Although Hussein hedged his opposition and at times appeared willing to join the talks, his main concern was keeping communications open with the United States, Saudi Arabia, and Syria. Some 40% of Hussein's (U. S.) $1.1 billion budget is financed from abroad: the United States provides the bulk of his military aid and the Saudis provide more than $300 million a year. With Syria's President Hafez al-Assad at odds with Sadat, Hussein's middle course was tailored to prevent a misunderstanding which could threaten Jordan's borders with Palestinian infiltration.

While resisting constant U. S. pressure to join the talks, Hussein sought to convene a "reconciliation" summit to keep Sadat in the Arab fold. These efforts were intensified, with little success, after the Camp David accords

UPI

King Hussein married Lisa Halaby, an American, in Amman in June. She became Queen Noor al-Hussein.

were announced.

Impact of Camp David. On September 26, Assad met with Hussein in Amman to discuss the specifics of the Camp David "framework" for Middle East peace. While agreeing that the accords needed reexamination, it was clear that Hussein would favor joining the talks if the United States made public commitments to Israel's total withdrawal from the West Bank and east Jerusalem.

However, in response to Assad's charge that Sadat had "stabbed the Arabs in the back," the Jordanian monarch spent October working with other moderate Arab leaders to prevent the ostracism of Sadat at the Arab summit held the first week of November in Baghdad. Sadat rejected economic aid, offered if he would not sign a separate treaty with Israel. Hussein was able to strengthen his own position by obtaining a $1.3 billion Arab grant over the next decade.

Domestic Affairs. On April 17, Hussein's request for the formation of a National Consultative Assembly to replace the suspended Jordanian Parliament was ratified. The 60-member assembly will serve as an advisory board until the problem of representation for Jordan's Palestinian population is solved.

On June 15, Hussein married his fourth wife, an American, and named her Queen Noor al-Hussein.

F. Nicholas Willard

--- JORDAN · Information Highlights ---

Official Name: Hashemite Kingdom of Jordan.
Location: Southwest Asia.
Area: 37,738 square miles (97,740 km²).
Population (1978 est.): 2,900,000.
Chief Cities (1976): Amman, the capital, 691,120; (1976 est.): Zarqa, 235,000; Irbid, 120,000.
Government: Head of state, Hussein ibn Talal, king (acceded Aug. 1952). Head of government, Mudar Badran, prime minister (took office July 1976). Legislature—National Consultative Assembly, ratified April 1978, displaces National Assembly (dissolved Nov. 1974).
Monetary Unit: Dinar (0.2932 dinar equals U. S.$1, Nov. 1978).
Manufactures (major products): Cement, phosphate, petroleum refining.
Agriculture (major products): Wheat, fruits, olive oil, vegetables.

UPI

Supporters of a homosexual rights ordinance in Wichita, Kans., celebrate in spite of the fact that the law was repealed by a wide margin.

KANSAS

The Kansas economy remained strong in 1978 despite the vagaries of agricultural prices. Per capita income stayed above the national average and unemployment was still among the nation's lowest. Industrial development continued at a strong pace, as did the development of energy resources.

Agriculture. Wheat production for 1978 stood at 309 million bushels, the smallest crop in eight years. The corn crop, estimated at 147 million bushels, and sorghum grain harvest, estimated at 196 million, were down from 1977. Soybean production was on a par with 1977 at 25.74 million bushels. Cattle, sheep, and hog production was up slightly, with the figures at 6.5 million, 195,000, and 1.9 million head, respectively. The cattle market turned up in the last half of the year, the soybean market was down but still strong, and wheat prices were up slightly over 1977.

However, the future of farm profits remains uncertain, and Kansas farmers were among those participating in the American Agriculture Movement and its various protest demonstrations as the year began. Despite strike threats, Kansas farmers generally followed their usual production patterns and no further organized protest came until October, during a presidential visit to the state. AAM leaders indicated that the winter of 1978–79 would bring additional complaints. (*See also* AGRICULTURE.)

Weather. There were extended periods of drought in some portions of the state, accompanied by invasions of grasshoppers and chinch bugs. There was little severe weather in the form of flood or tornadic activity.

Legislation. Democrats continued to control the State House in the 1978 session, while the Republicans maintained a narrow margin in the Senate. The legislature provided for a pilot program in competency-based education, for a transfer of funds to assist local units of government in street repair, and for a community corrections program for nonviolent offenders. More money was appropriated for school finance, and the regulation of nursing homes was strengthened.

In a surprise, last minute move, a bill allowing restaurants to serve liquor by the drink was approved for inclusion on the 1978 general election ballot. (Fifteen counties approved the measure in November, but following the election the state Supreme Court ruled the measure unconstitutional.) Bills pertaining to energy and water resources were passed, as was a provision for a presidential primary.

Election. Two major candidates picked to lose by pollsters won in November. John Carlin, Democratic speaker of the Kansas House, defeated incumbent Republican Gov. Robert Bennett, and Nancy Landon Kassebaum, in her first political race, won over Democrat Bill Roy, a former congressman. Mrs. Kassebaum, the daughter of the 1936 Republican presidential nominee and former Kansas governor, Alf Landon, is the first woman to be elected to the U. S. Senate in her own right. Incumbent Republican congressmen Keith Sebelius and Larry Winn won, as did Democrat Dan Glickman, but two-term Democrat Martha Keys lost to Jim Jeffries. Retiring GOP congressman Joe Skubitz was succeeded by Robert Whittaker (R). State Treasurer Joan Finney (D), Insurance Commissioner Fletcher Bell (R), and Secretary of State Jack Brier (R) were reelected. Attorney General Curt Schneider (D) was defeated by Robert Stephan.

ROBERT W. RICHMOND
Kansas State Historical Society

--------- KANSAS · Information Highlights ---------

Area: 82,264 square miles (213,064 km²).
Population (Jan. 1978 est.): 2,340,000.
Chief Cities (1978 est.): Topeka, the capital, 144,221; Wichita, 261,862; Kansas City, 170,708; Overland Park, 82,400.
Government (1978): *Chief Officers*—governor, Robert F. Bennett (R); lt. gov., Shelby Smith (R). *Legislature*—Senate, 40 members; House of Representatives, 125 members.
Education (1977–78): *Enrollment*—public elementary schools, 266,232 pupils; public secondary, 179,893; colleges and universities, 127,447 students. *Public school expenditures,* $823,940,000 ($1,590 per pupil).
State Finances (fiscal year 1977): *Revenues,* $1,766,-107,000; *expenditures* $1,718,799,000.
Personal Income (1977): $16,594,000,000; per capita, $7,134.
Labor Force (July 1978): *Nonagricultural wage and salary earners,* 891,700; *unemployed,* 36,800 (3.2% of total force).

KENTUCKY

The year began with the state's coal fields paralyzed by a strike and most of the state suffering from cold weather and a series of snow storms virtually unprecedented in their severity and duration. Both men and nature contributed to energy shortages and power cutbacks during the winter. By the end of the year the state was enjoying economic prosperity and high employment that extended generally to business and industry, coal mining, and agriculture.

Coal Strike. The nationwide, 109-day strike of the United Mine Workers, which ended in late March, had serious effects in Kentucky. It slowed down the economy in the eastern part of the state, precipitated tension and some violence involving nonunion mines, and created coal and power shortages that came close to forcing serious industrial and business curtailments throughout the state. In the longer run, the strike may have damaged the state's economy by accelerating national trends toward more reliance on coal production in the western part of the country rather than in Kentucky.

Economy. Kentucky continued to enjoy economic growth during the year. Employment increased more rapidly than in most recent years and faster than the national average. One notable trend of recent years that continued in 1978 was the increase of population and jobs in the rural parts of the state, not just in the larger cities. It was also a good year for agriculture in most parts of the state, though sections of western Kentucky suffered from prolonged dry spells.

Nixon Visit. In early July former President Richard Nixon chose the small, eastern Kentucky town of Hyden to make his first public appearance since his resignation. His visit, to dedicate the new Richard Nixon Recreation Center, attracted national press coverage and temporarily put Hyden, Kentucky, on the map.

Legislative Session. The most important action of the 1978 session was the adoption of Gov. Julian Carroll's (U.S.) $7.5 billion two-year budget. The budget was highlighted by a large increase in funding for elementary and secondary education, and included significant increases in funds for strip-mine regulation and fire-and-safety-code regulation. There was no general increase in taxes, although the coal severance tax was expanded. The Appropriations and Revenue Committee reviewed the budget more carefully than in some past years and persuaded the governor to make some budgetary changes, an unusual practice in Kentucky.

The most publicized and dramatic action of the General Assembly was its decision, after prolonged and emotional debate, to rescind the state's ratification of the Equal Rights Amendment to the U. S. Constitution. In the governor's absence from the state, Lt. Gov. Thelma Stovall

Service stopped on the Chesapeake RR system following the dynamiting of a bridge in Walbridge, Ky.

UPI

vetoed the rescission, setting off controversy about the legal effect of her action.

For the first time, the Kentucky Educational Television network provided daily coverage of the session. The legislature, which is constitutionally limited to a 60-day session, proposed a constitutional amendment to permit more flexible scheduling of interim committees and legislative sessions.

Elections. Democratic Senator Walter Huddleston was reelected. Republicans gained one congressional seat following the defeat of a Democratic incumbent in a primary. Voter turnout was low.

MALCOLM E. JEWELL, *University of Kentucky*

KENTUCKY · Information Highlights

Area: 40,395 square miles (104,623 km²).

Population (Jan. 1978 est.): 3,473,000.

Chief Cities (1970 census): Frankfort, the capital, 21,-902; Louisville, 361,958; Lexington, 108,137; Covington, 52,535.

Government (1978): *Chief Officers*—governor, Julian M. Carroll (D); lt. gov., Thelma Stovall (D). *General Assembly*—Senate, 38 members; House of Representatives, 100 members.

Education (1977–78): *Enrollment*—public elementary schools, 441,632 pupils; public secondary, 255,368; colleges and universities, 131,515 students. *Public school expenditures*, $900,000,000 ($1,202 per pupil).

State Finances (fiscal year 1976): *Revenues*, $2,746,-691,000; *expenditures*, $2,641,107,000.

Personal Income (1977): $20,561,000,000; per capita, $5,945.

Labor Force (July 1978): *Nonagricultural wage and salary earners* 1,220,900; *unemployed*, 84,100 (5.3% of total force).

Oct. 14, 1978, Kenya's new President Daniel arap Moi enjoys inauguration day.

UPI

KENYA

The year witnessed the death of President Jomo Kenyatta and subsequently the securing of a smooth succession to the presidency.

Kenyatta. Jomo Kenyatta, founding father of Kenyan nationalism and the only president of his country from the time of its independence, died on Aug. 22, 1978 in Mombasa. Fear of this moment had haunted Kenyan life for a decade, but a transition was made smoothly. Every faction of the ruling Kenya African National Union (KANU) and every tribal and pressure group seemed resolved not to cause a crisis that would fracture the nation's unity or violate the nation's Constitution.

Presidential Succession. On October 14, Daniel arap Moi, Kenyatta's vice president since 1967 and a member of Parliament since 1957, was sworn in as the nation's second president. The 54-year old Moi had been seen as Kenyatta's political heir ever since the murder of Labor Minister Tom Mboya in 1969, and the ruling party had moved quickly to ensure his leadership. Constitutional provisions had already eliminated most challengers, and internal opposition within KANU ebbed quickly after Moi won the backing of the powerful Kenyatta family and the Kikuyu tribe which dominates the political life of the party and country. Coming from the small Tugena tribe, and originally a teacher, Moi was seen as an assurance that the moderate social and economic policies of Kenyatta would be continued, and that no one tribal group would gain exclusive control. In addition, as a sign of stability, Moi retained almost all of Kenyatta's cabinet ministers.

Economy. The world boom in coffee prices buoyed the Kenyan economy in 1978, earning the country over $350 million. The huge increase, however, also led to smuggling and theft of coffee, with persons high in the government possibly involved. Despite the general prosperity, unemployment remained high. Over 13% of the work force was idle, and the average high school graduate was waiting an average of three years for a job. The government tried to help by banning all importation of textiles, and increasing investment in the industry to provide employment.

To slow further the decrease of the country's vast game herds, the foundation for its lucrative tourism industry, Kenya forbade the sale of any animal skins or trophies and ordered shops with such goods to sell off all their stock and close by March 13, 1978. Hunting had been banned in 1977, but the trophy stores had been seen as an encouragement to poaching.

Writer's Arrest. Leading Kenyan novelist and playwright Ngugi wa Thiong'o was arrested in January 1978, and his books and papers seized, even though no formal charges had been placed. It was suggested that Thiong'o, who wrote in Kikuyu and was thus more widely read than English-language authors, was arrested because of his plays' veiled assertions that those who rule Kenya had been collaborators with the British during the Mau Mau uprising, and that Kenya was being exploited and divided into classes by the liberal capitalism encouraged by the leaders, who profited enormously thereby.

Foreign Affairs. Kenya kept a low profile in foreign affairs in 1978. Kenya's closeness to the United States was underscored by a U. S. promise of arms, including F-5 jets, and a commitment to Kenya's "defensive capabilities." Kenyan fears of a Somali move against its North-East District, whose population is 60% ethnic Somali, prompted the arrangement.

ROBERT GARFIELD
DePaul University

--------- **KENYA · Information Highlights** ---------

Official Name: Republic of Kenya.
Location: East coast of Africa.
Area: 224,961 square miles (582,649 km²).
Population (1978 est.): 14,800,000.
Chief Cities (1977 est.): Nairobi, the capital, 776,000; Mombasa, 371,000.
Government: *Head of state and government,* Daniel arap Moi, president (took office Oct. 1978). *Legislature* (unicameral)—National Assembly.
Monetary Unit: Kenya shilling (7.544 shillings equal U. S.$1, Sept. 1978).
Manufactures (major products): Petroleum products, cement, beer.
Agriculture (major products): Corn, wheat, rice, sugarcane, coffee, tea, sisal, pyrethrum, meat and its products.

In May, the Korean Military Armistice Commission discusses the reported infiltration of South Korea by a North Korean spyboat.

UPI

KOREA

As the year drew to a close, the two Koreas were pondering the uncertain implications of the Sino-American diplomatic rapprochement for their respective domains. On balance, the external milieu tended to reinforce the impetus toward a stable if uneasy status quo in Korea. South Korea's self-confidence was measurable as a result of its successful "export-first-ism" policy; in December, President Park Chung Hee went so far as to predict that by 1986 South Korea (Republic of Korea—ROK) would join the ranks of the top ten advanced nations in terms of steel production, shipbuilding, petrochemicals, automobiles, and cement. In contrast, President Kim Il Sung appeared more self-conscious of constraints on North Korea (Democratic People's Republic of Korea—DPRK); a sense of urgency was pervasive in his efforts to compete with the more resourceful South on the economic and defense fronts.

SOUTH KOREA

Economy. South Korea's real growth rate was 13%, and the per capita GNP rose to $1,225. The export goal of $12.5 billion was met, although barely, in the face of protectionist pressures abroad; imports exceeded $15 billion. The continued high growth policies fueled inflation, estimated at 15 to 25%. Foreign debts reached $8.5 billion but there was no default on payments due by the government.

Living conditions improved unevenly. Distributive injustice remained the foremost concern of those subsisting on wages, which were kept low by the regime to ensure its export competitiveness and to lure foreign capital. The average factory wage per hour was 62 cents (against the hourly minimum of U. S.$1 for urban families). In November this situation prompted an opposition lawmaker to decry: "Seoul is a paradise for the affluent but a hell for the have-nots." Yet Seoul's population grew by

4% in 1978, attesting to unchecked migration from rural areas. Infrastructural stresses in Seoul posed potential sociopolitical problems.

Politics. Apart from corruption, the year was marked by renewed festering of labor unrest, of restiveness on college campuses, and of activism among Christian social workers. On December 22 the government announced an amnesty for some 4,000 prisoners and more than 100 other political prisoners, including the opposition leader Kim Dae Jung.

In May, the 2,538-member presidential electoral college, the National Conference for Unification, was popularly chosen, with the opposition parties boycotting it. The conference, in turn, predictably renewed President Park's tenure from 1978 to 1984. Park's name was the only one on the ballot.

Park's prestige suffered an indirect setback in the parliamentary elections of December, held under the muzzle of an emergency decree banning any criticism of him and his 1972 constitution. His ruling party returned 68 of the 154 elective seats against the opposition New Democrats' 61; a splinter group took 3 and independents, 22. Park's control of the 231-member National Assembly was assured, however, under the constitution that empowers him to appoint 77 deputies. The returns were unprecedented if only because the listless, factious opposition outpolled the

---

SOUTH KOREA · Information Highlights

Official Name: Republic of Korea.
Location: Northeastern Asia.
Area: 38,022 square miles (98,477 km²).
Population (1978 est.): 37,100,000.
Chief Cities: (Oct. 1978) Seoul, the capital, 7,823,195; (1978 est.) Pusan, 2,678,000.
Government: *Head of state,* Park Chung Hee, president (took office Dec. 1963). *Head of government,* Choi Kyu Hah, prime minister (took office Dec. 1975). *Legislature* (unicameral)—National Assembly.
Monetary Unit: Won (485 won equal U. S.$1, Dec. 1978).
Manufactures (major products): Textiles, clothing, electronic equipment, petrochemicals, ships, plywood, hair products, processed foods, metal products.
Agriculture (major products): Rice, barley, wheat, soybeans, sweet potatoes, fish.

UPI

A huge effigy of North Korea's President Kim Il Sung burns during a rally in Seoul.

ruling Democratic Republicans, 34% to 32%. The antiregime trend was strongest in the cities of Seoul, Pusan, and Kwangju.

Foreign Policy and Defense. Several developments proved reassuring to ROK. In March, an "Operation Team Spirit '78" was staged jointly by the ROK and the United States and was premised on a hypothetical North Korean attack. In April, the United States revised the timetable for withdrawing its ground troops from Korea so that only 3,400 men would be pulled out in 1978, with 2,600 men scheduled to depart in 1979; by 1981 or 1982, 7,000 Army noncombatants and 9,000 Air Force personnel would remain in Korea. In July the security commitment to Seoul was reaffirmed by the United States, and ROK's spokesman expressed optimism that the removal of United States ground forces would not adversely affect its security as long as the United States stands ready to provide air and naval support when needed. In September the U. S. Congress endorsed a measure transferring $800 million worth of military equipment cost-free to ROK no later than 1982. South Korea successfully tested a surface-to-surface missile with a range of up to 100 miles (160 km). In November a Combined Forces Command was inaugurated in Seoul to replace the existing U. S. command structures and give Korean commanders a more responsible role in the planning and operations of the joint ROK-U. S. forces. By October the Congressional probe of Seoul's lobbying scandals had ended on a low-key note, with minimal damages to the future of ROK-U. S. relations. A Congressional delegation resumed junketing to Seoul in November amid indications pointing to a Park-Carter summit in June 1979.

NORTH KOREA

Economy. Kim Il Sung's pressing concern was economic as underlined in his New Year message and again in November. Extractive industries, especially coal production (defined as "an acute" problem), were given top priority to lessen dependence on foreign oil, to raise exports, and to satisfy domestic needs. North Korea's two-way trade was estimated at $1.6 billion in 1978. Grain production in 1977 was said to be 8.5 million tons. The problem of overdue payments on external debts (between U. S. $1.5 and $2.0 billion) remained unrelieved. But in October an interest-free loan of $50 million was secured from Iraq for unspecified purposes.

Preoccupation with economic performance was underscored by the ascendancy of technocrats to top government posts; and two-thirds of all cabinet-level bodies were assigned to economic functions. Labor shortage was evident; women accounted for 48% of the labor force.

In November the ruling party adopted a policy guideline aimed at energizing the economy and making it more "self-reliant, modernized, and scientific." It called for reliance, in 1979, on "domestic technology and resources" and for advance in the utilization of modern science and technology in industries, especially in "the conservation of fuel and energy." On a cautionary note, the party stated: "We should not worship modernization and scientification nor try to realize them at once."

Politics. President Kim, evidently healthy, was firmly in command. The "succession" issue was still unclear. His 38-year-old son, Chong Il, was reportedly well, contrary to the story that he had become a "vegetable man," a victim of a rumored assassination attempt. The speculation that the term "party center" as used in the North was a discreet reference to Chong Il gained some credence; whether this practice was designed to prime the public for his succession was open to question.

More conspicuous in 1978 than ever was the intensity with which the regime tried to heighten

Union members, protesting alleged U. S. bugging of President Park's residence, clash with police.

UPI

the level of "revolutionary zeal and creativity." This drive was intended to motivate the masses toward greater economic achievements. All functionaries were exhorted to renew their ideological faith, to be more responsive in working with the grass roots, and to abide by the tenets of "socialist life and law." In November the party stated that "a firm prospect has been opened for completing this year's (1978) quota ahead of schedule and attaining higher goals." The party statement was coupled with a reminder that the people's economic task for 1979 would be "indeed heavy and enormous" and that "they should not tremble or waver before difficulties."

Foreign Policy and Defense. As often has been the case, DPRK's policies and actions were clouded by ambiguity, lending themselves to conflicting interpretations among observers. An effort by Yugoslavia's Marshal Tito, in early 1978, to interest President Carter in tripartite talks involving the United States and both North and South Korea proved unacceptable to DPRK; and Rumanian President Nicolae Ceauşescu's attempt as an intermediary between the DPRK and the United States was equally fruitless—in this case, because of coolness in Washington. In June DPRK rejected ROK's overture for "unconditional" resumption of dialogue and for economic cooperation, denouncing it as a crafty smokescreen to cover up its policy of confrontation and division. On December 4 North Korea repeated the position that its door was open for talks with the United States and "even with South Korea's puppet clique and political parties." Two days later, the United States reemphasized its readiness to discuss with both Koreas "ways to reduce the level of tension on the Korean Peninsula."

Among the foreign leaders visiting DPRK were: the Chinese Premier Hua Kuo-feng and Rumania's Ceauşescu—both in May; and the Chinese Vice Premier Teng Hsiao-ping, in Sep-

tember. Speculations about DPRK's "pro-Chinese tilt" were more apparent than real; the North retained its independent stance regarding Peking and Moscow, both of which supported Kim's policy of peaceful reunification. In September, coinciding with Teng's presence in Pyongyang, DPRK emphasized that "the most realistic method" for unification "at present" was to establish a "North-South confederal system" as a practical, intermediate step. On October 25, while visiting Japan, Teng said that as far as he knew, North Korea would not resort to force, "unless the South moves first." His reassurance sounded hollow two days later when the United Nations Command accused the North of digging yet another tunnel beneath the demilitarized zone and into South Korean territory—an accusation dismissed as a "fabrication."

Sixteen percent of North Korea's 1978 budget was earmarked for defense spending as the regime intensified the charges that the United States and South Korea were preparing for war against North Korea.

RINN-SUPP SHINN
Foreign Area Studies
The American University

—— **NORTH KOREA • Information Highlights** ——

Official Name: Democratic People's Republic of Korea.
Location: Northeastern Asia.
Area: 46,540 square miles (120,533 km²).
Population (1978 est.): 17,100,000.
Chief Cities (1978 est.): Pyongyang, the capital, 1,379,-170; Chongjin, 343,140.
Government: *Head of state,* Kim Il Sung, president (nominally since Dec. 1972; actually in power since May 1948). *Head of government,* Li Jong-ok, premier (took office Dec. 1977). *Legislature* (unicameral)—Supreme People's Assembly. The Korean Workers (Communist) Party: General Secretary—Kim Il Sung.
Monetary Unit: Won (2.15 won equal U. S.$1, Dec. 1978).
Manufactures (major products): Cement, metallurgicals, coke, pig iron, ferroalloys, textiles.
Agriculture (major products): Rice, corn, sweet potatoes, barley, soybeans, livestock, apples, fish.

LABOR

Problems of inflation and unemployment continued in 1978 to beset the U. S. and other industrialized nations.

UNITED STATES

In the United States, with an assist from public jobs programs, the official unemployment rate was reduced to less than 6%, more than 1% below a year earlier. Inflation proved less manageable, rising above a 9% annual rate.

Toward year's end, the Carter administration addressed the inflation problem with a program of "voluntary" wage-price guidelines, the main aim of which was to keep increases in wages and fringe benefits in the private sector to 7% and to hold price increases to .05% less than the average increases for the past two years—roughly to between 6 and 6.5%. Included in the program is an "insurance" provision whereby workers would get a tax rebate if living costs exceed the 7% guidepost. This provision is subject to Congressional enactment. Also, exceptions to the ceiling were established for those earning less than $4 an hour or in situations where a greater increase is offset by cost-saving changes in work rules and "demonstrable" improvements in productivity.

In the case of business, President Carter cited pressures and incentives that could be used to promote compliance, such as withholding government contracts from violators. The AFL-CIO Executive Council, representing most of organized labor, rejected the voluntary program "with reluctance." Instead, the council proposed mandatory controls across the board for wages, prices, profits, dividends, interest rates, executive compensation and other sources of income. The administration rejected the council proposal, calling instead for a "fair test" of the voluntary program.

Strikes. Work stoppages declined to 3,975 in the first 9 months of 1978 from 4,895 in the same 1977 period, but idleness due to stoppages reached 32.6 million worker-days, or 0.2% of total working time put in, the highest since 1974. That was due largely to four main strikes—a 110-day strike by 160,000 bituminous coal miners, which lasted to late March 1978; a strike by Railway Clerks on the Norfolk & Western, which lasted from July 10 to late September and which in the final week was extended to nearly all the railroads; a 109-day strike by pilots of Northwest Orient Airlines, ending in mid-August, and an 89-day strike against New York City newspapers, which ended November 5. The rail strike was halted by court order and the submission of the dispute, involving mainly job security, to a Presidential Emergency Board. The other big strikes concluded after settlements were reached and ratified.

Strikes in the public sector were also major factors in the idleness toll, and they were considerably more extensive than in 1977. They involved policemen, firefighters, teachers, and other local public workers, and they occurred despite laws forbidding such strikes in most states. These disputes caused extended shutdowns of schools in many cities, reduced public security, and paralyzed some public services. In a few communities, fires went unfought because of firefighter stoppages. Financial stringency in numerous communities, linked to public pressures to hold the line on taxes, precipitated many of the strikes, as public officials stood firm against demands for wage increases and other improved benefits. Most of the public-sector strikes ended with compromise settlements, but a few were broken, leaving a bitter aftermath.

Wage Trends. For workers as a whole, "real" earnings in terms of buying power declined 3% from 1977. Settlements in major negotiated agreements during the first nine months of 1978 —prior to imposition of the administration's voluntary controls—yielded average wage increases of 7.8% in the first contract year, the same as in 1977. Over the life of multi-year agreements, the increases averaged 6.5%, up from 5.8% in 1977.

Agreements in the coal industry, reached after a lengthy strike, sharply exceeded the average, aggregating 39% in wages and fringes over three years. Also, agreements entered into by most rail unions, produced wage and benefit increases averaging more than 36% over 39 months. As an offset, the railroads won some cost-reducing rules changes. Manning disputes also caused the strike against New York City newspapers.

In addition, the United Transportation Union signed agreements with CONRAIL and the Milwaukee Road, permitting train crew reductions, with a major portion of the savings going to higher compensation for retained employees. These accords were expected to set patterns for agreements on other railroads.

Federal civil service workers fared less well than private sector workers. By executive order they were held down to 5.5% pay increases in 1978. Postal unions, negotiating separately with the autonomous Postal Service, did somewhat better after threatening to strike.

Wage pacts in the building field lagged, as they did in 1977. Construction unions, striving to stem inroads by nonunion contractors and to recover lost jobs, settled for average 6% pay increases, agreed to curbs on strikes, and gave up or modified some long-standing work rules which, employers charged, impaired productivity and ran up costs.

Work Changes. Increases were reported in use of part-time workers. Also, "flex-time" plans, allowing for flexible reporting and quitting hours, became more prevalent, with about 6% of the U. S. work force on flextime. The U. S. Labor Department estimated that not over 2% of American workers are on compressed workweek schedules (generally, four days, 40 hours).

Union Strength. The AFL-CIO reported that membership of its affiliates is rising, after a three-year decline. In the first half of 1978, AFL-CIO membership rose by 382,000, or nearly 3%, to 13,662,660. The independent Auto Workers reported a 5% gain, and the Teamsters, also independent, a 1.25% gain.

INTERNATIONAL

Canada. Strikes spurted in the spring after the phase out of mandatory wage-price controls imposed by the government in 1975. In terms of strikes, unions sought to recover ground lost during the controls era when wage increases, which had been rising by up to 20%, were limited to 8% in the first two years, and 6% in the third. Prices were also controlled, but the annual inflation rate kept rising.

By the end of August, worker-days lost in strikes totaled 4.7 million, more than the 3.3 million figure for all of 1977. The strikes affected varied industries, but the most dramatic occurred in the postal service. The union representing 19,000 letter carriers settled in September after brief strikes in nine cities. However, the Canadian Union of Postal Workers, representing 23,000 employees who work inside post offices, staged a series of rotating strikes starting in mid-October, after negotiations with postal officials, which had been going on for 18 months, broke down.

Wage settlements, after exceeding the U. S. rate for several years, slid back to an average of 6.4% in the second quarter of 1978.

Unemployment stood at 8.2% during October. Union membership in Canada reached 3,300,000 in 1978, up 4% from 1977. Over 31% of the total labor force in Canada is now organized.

Japan. A continued mild recession in Japan had a sharp effect on wages. In the spring "shunto," or annual wage offensive, the customary strikes and demonstrations yielded pay increases averaging only 5.9%, far below the 9% settlements in 1977. Unemployment rose to a new high for Japan—over 1.4 million, or 2.4% of the labor force, the highest since 1959. True joblessness, taking into account excess labor in many plants, is estimated to be much higher.

So-called "lifetime employment" has eroded in Japan, as more and more companies provide bonuses and other incentives to induce older workers to retire early. An opposite trend is growing. A Ministry of Labor survey showed that the average mandatory retirement age in the private sector has risen to 57.6 years, and that in one third of the firms the compulsory retirement age is now 60 years.

Still another trend shows that many firms now stop automatic yearly raises at ages as low as 35 or 40, instead of maintaining the pay escalator to 55. Others shift high-paid older workers to subsidiaries which have lower pay rates.

Great Britain. The British government sought to persuade the labor movement to accept a 5% lid on wage increases, 50% of the 1977 ceiling, in an effort to pare the nation's 8% inflation rate (down from 15% in 1977). However, the British Trades Union Congress rejected the 5% formula, though its leaders promised "restraint" in collective bargaining. In major industries, unions were offered more at key companies. Meantime, unemployment passed the 6% mark, up substantially from the previous year.

West Germany. Although it edged up, the West German unemployment rate held below 4%, lower than in most of Western Europe. Industrial production, after slumping in the first half, went up in the second to 3% above a year ago. Living costs rose at an annual rate of 3%. Seeking a 35-hour week, steelworkers staged the first strike in West Germany in 50 years.

France. Turmoil marked the industrial front as the government pressed an austerity program, including an easing of price controls. Strikes hit the railroads, a slowdown was instituted by traffic controllers, a dockers' strike hampered shipping, and stoppages occurred in other private and public operations. The unemployment rate rose above 6%, up from 4%-plus in 1977. Wage increases kept slightly ahead of the inflation rate.

Elsewhere in Europe. Strikes were widespread in Italy. Some were called to protest unemployment, though the jobless rate was estimated at less than 4%. Norway imposed a freeze on prices and income in an effort to lower the nation's 8%-plus inflation rate. In Sweden, moderate wage increases, currency devaluation, and fiscal restraint reduced the inflation rate to below 5%, while unemployment exceeded 7%.

Latin America. Labor was squeezed by inflation and military rule in most of Latin America during 1978. The unions in Argentina were hamstrung by the military regime from bargaining over wages and working conditions, and were barred from striking. In Brazil, some strikes were tolerated by the military-run government, notably in the auto industry, where unions won an extra 20% pay increase above government-set ceilings.

In Chile, unions were taken over by the military junta, which prohibited collective bargaining and strikes. However, in late October the junta authorized elections for union leadership, but outlawed seven unions. Also, despite a strike ban, many copper miners struck for higher wages. The government response was to arrest strike leaders.

In Mexico, the government's austerity program led to strikes by independent unions not affiliated with the semi-official Confederation of Mexican workers, which had agreed to hold wage increases to under 12%, less than the inflation rate. The government used troops and police to break some of the strikes. Meantime, half of Mexico's labor force was estimated to be unemployed or under-employed.

RUBEN LEVIN, *Editor and Manager, "Labor"*

A Review of the Taft-Hartley Act

In what proved to be the longest coal miners' strike in U. S. history, 165,000 members of the United Mine Workers (UMW) left their jobs in December 1977. At issue were wages, medical benefits, and the firing of wildcat strikers. On March 6, 1978, President Carter invoked the Taft-Hartley Act and ordered the miners back to work. Accordingly, the Federal District Court in Washington, D. C., issued a 10-day temporary restraining order against the UMW. As had happened several times in the history of the union, however, rank and file members defied the president and ignored the back-to-work order. Moreover, the court then refused to extend the injunction because the government failed to show that the strike would cause "irreparable harm to the national health and safety." A final settlement was eventually worked out by representatives of the UMW and the Bituminous Coal Operators Association, without federal interference. The whole episode seemed to confirm that Taft-Hartley is indeed ineffectual and that there is reason for a reappraisal of the act.

The Labor Management Relations Act, known as the Taft-Hartley Act, originally was intended to create a balance between labor and management in collective bargaining. The popular feeling after World War II was that New Deal legislation had tipped the balance in favor of the unions. The Wagner Act (1935) had specified the unfair labor practices for which management could be liable. As a result, conservatives argued, the unions had become arrogant, selfish monopolies who abused their members and threatened the economy. The ability of unions to win favorable strike settlements led to a demand for amendment of the Wagner Act.

When a Republican Congress was elected in November 1946, Sen. Robert Taft of Ohio and Rep. Fred Hartley of New Jersey sponsored a bill to provide reciprocal curbs on unfair union practices. Taft-Hartley was passed in 1947 over the adamant opposition of organized labor and a veto by President Truman.

The most controversial features of Taft-Hartley dealt with union security and federal intervention in strikes imperiling "national health and safety." Section 14(b) of the statute allowed the states to outlaw "closed" or "union shops" (through right-to-work laws). In "national emergency" disputes the president could, after inquiry by a special board, apply to the federal courts for an 80-day injunction against the strike action. These two provisions prompted organized labor to label Taft-Hartley a "slave labor" law. In 1951 Congress relaxed the procedure for installing the union shop, but the Landrum-Griffin Act of 1959 tightened the prohibitions on secondary boycotts and organizational picketing.

While the most outstanding features of Taft-Hartley were the sections outlining the executive power of intervention and the bar against closed shops, the act covered a wide range of issues. The theme throughout was pro-management. Employers were guaranteed full freedom of expression, short of threat or bribery, during organizational campaigns by prospective unions. They could call for elections to determine the bargaining agent in wage negotiations. In addition to the affirmation of these management rights, restrictions were put on union activities. Unions could not coerce employers; they could not engage in secondary boycotts, jurisdictional strikes, strikes to enforce featherbedding, nor refuse to bargain collectively. In the event of termination or modification of any agreement, unions had to give 60-day notice and were suable for breach of contract. They were also forbidden to make contributions to political campaigns. Internal union affairs were also regulated. Union officers were required to file non-Communist affidavits. Annual reports on administrative organization and finances were to be submitted to the government, and initiation fees regulated. A more neutral aspect of Taft-Hartley involved administrative reform. A general counsel was added to the National Labor Relations Board, and the Federal Mediation and Conciliation Service was created to step into disputes threatening interstate commerce.

Pro-labor lobbyists and President Truman's Democratic constituency argued that the law would make the federal government a permanent third force in industrial relations. In practice, the law has turned out to be less important and less anti-labor than originally expected. Right-to-work legislation was passed in 21 states, but after defeat in some of the heavily industrial states, the movement lost its momentum and eventually foundered in the 1960's. Union membership, both absolute numbers and share of the total labor force, continued to grow. The act's widely debated provisions for settling strikes have been invoked only 34 times, and only once between 1971 and 1977. As it became clear that the 80-day "cooling off" period had no appreciable effect on negotiations, the federal government resorted increasingly to special boards, presidential influence, and the Federal Mediation and Conciliation Service.

If anything, the long-term effects of Taft-Hartley on organized labor have been positive. Over the years, the public image of unions has been enhanced, while unions themselves have been stimulated to increase their political and social influence to fend off the enactment of similar legislation in the future.

STANLEY SHAPIRO

The long-running campaign against J. P. Stevens & Co. was stepped up as labor sought more success in organizing the textile industry.

MARTIN ADLER LEVICK, BLACK STAR

SPECIAL REPORT:

The Changing Tactics of Organized Labor

For the U. S. labor movement, 1978 was a very trying year. In attempting to adapt itself to changes in the work force and to the rise of new political strengths, labor suffered a series of bitter defeats. With George Meany, 84, nearing the end of his 23-year reign as head of the AFL-CIO, the year should have been a time of preparation for the future. It was, instead, a time of retrenchment. There were further declines in union membership, crushing legislative defeats in Congress, and a break between labor and President Jimmy Carter, labor's candidate in 1976.

Membership declines continued a trend that has been in evidence since 1945. At that point 36 percent of the American work force belonged to unions. By the middle of 1978, the figure had fallen to less than 24 percent. In the long run, membership declines represent the most serious challenge to a union movement which is failing to reach new young workers.

The AFL-CIO has seen the need to reverse the declines. It has chosen the South, the least organized area of the country, as the logical target for gains. Attempts to organize the South had failed before. But starting in 1977 labor hoped to find new success in organizing the textile industry, the South's largest employer. The prime target was J. P. Stevens & Co., which labor spokesmen call the most anti-union company in the nation. The Amalgamated Clothing and Textile Workers stepped up a long-running campaign against Stevens, feeling that if it could crack that tough company, others would follow.

That campaign had mixed results during the year. In the courts and in the media, labor made telling points. U. S. courts consistently ruled against Stevens for using tactics such as wiretapping the telephones of organizers and firing union workers. The unions organized a boycott of Stevens' products and devised a clever pressure tactic to harm the company's relations with the rest of the business community. The union threatened to withdraw pension fund deposits from Manufacturers Hanover Trust and forced Stevens' chairman to resign from the bank's board of directors.

In terms of tangible results, 1978 found no more Stevens' plants under contract than there were 10 years earlier. The problem, the unions said, was a lack of enforcement mechanisms in the 1935 National Labor Relations Act that governs how unions and businesses deal with each other. The unions argued that recalcitrant employers are free to flout the law, with only modest penalties. Their solution was a series of amendments to the law, which became known as "the labor law reform bill." Basically, the bill would increase the penalties for labor law violations, quicken the procedure for settling unfair labor practices, and give more power to unions during organizing campaigns. The bill had passed the House of Representatives in 1977.

The bill became the target of a massive lobbying campaign in the Senate. While labor was able to muster a clear Senate majority, it was unable to come up with 60 votes to break a conservative filibuster. The bill was sent back to Senate committee to die.

The fragile relationship between Meany and President Carter fractured on the failure of labor law reform. Labor lobbyists had privately criticized the president's lack of zeal during Senate maneuverings. In addition, administration talk about holding down wage increases to fight inflation angered labor. Meany hit out at Carter for not doing enough on the reform bill and he attacked a postal pay agreement the administration had negotiated. Carter was reported to be furious, but Meany gave no evidence that he would change his views.

George Meany wants to leave labor's house in order when he departs from active leadership. Labor changed some of its tactics in 1978 to begin the effort to shape the future. Those changing tactics were largely failures.

KENNEDY P. MAIZE

The Labor Year

PHOTOS UPI

A strike by 160,000 U. S. coal miners ended in its 110th day, March 25, 1978, with the signing of a new three-year agreement. During the strike, the miners received various relief aid, including food (*left*).

PHOTOS KEN HAWKINS, SYGMA

The city of Memphis, Tenn., was particularly hard hit by labor unrest. The city's firemen staged a brief walkout in July and joined a wildcat police strike in August.

UPI

In July, postal workers demonstrated outside New York City's main Post Office. A new contract, agreed to at the last minute, averted a threatened U. S. postal strike.

The U.S. Job Outlook

Occupation	Estimated Employment, 1976	Average Annual Openings, 1976–1985	Expected Growth in Employment to 1985
Accountants	865,000	51,500	Average
Architects	49,000	3,100	Average
Artists, commercial	67,000	3,600	Average
Bank clerks	456,000	36,000	Good
Bank officers and managers	319,000	28,000	Good
Bookkeepers	1,700,000	95,000	Poor, but many openings
Carpenters	1,010,000	67,000	Average, but many openings
Chemists	148,000	6,300	Average, but many openings
Computer operating personnel	565,000	8,500	Good, except keypunchers
Computer programmers	230,000	9,700	Good
Computer systems analysts	160,000	7,600	Good
Construction workers	715,000	40,000	Average
Cooks and chefs	1,065,000	79,000	Good
Cosmetologists	534,000	30,000	Average, but many openings
Dental assistants	135,000	13,500	Excellent
Dentists	112,000	4,800	Average, but many openings
Economists	115,000	6,400	Generally good
Electricians	560,000	29,600	Average—good
Engineers, aerospace	50,000	1,500	Poor
Engineers, civil	155,000	8,900	Average
Engineers, electrical	300,000	12,800	Average
Engineers, industrial	200,000	10,500	Good
Engineers, mechanical	200,000	9,300	Average
Firefighters	210,000	8,300	Average
Health care administrators	160,000	16,000	Excellent
Hotel managers	137,000	7,000	Poor
Inspectors, manufacturing	692,000	52,000	Good
Insurance underwriters, agents, and brokers	490,000	27,500	Average
Lawyers	396,000	23,400	Good, but competitive
Librarians	128,000	8,000	Good, but competitive
Machinists (all-around)	405,000	20,000	Average
Mail carriers	250,000	5,300	Poor
Mathematicians	38,000	1,000	Poor; competitive
Mechanics, airplane	110,000	5,200	Good
Mechanics, automobile	790,000	32,000	Average, but many openings
Medical laboratory workers	240,000	20,000	Good
Medical technicians, emergency	287,000	37,000	Excellent
Musicians	127,000	7,200	Average; competitive
Newspaper reporters	40,500	2,100	Poor; competitive
Nurses, licensed practical	460,000	53,000	Excellent
Nurses, registered	960,000	83,000	Good
Oceanographers	2,700	150	Average; competitive
Personnel and labor relations workers	335,000	23,000	Good
Pharmacists	120,000	8,900	Average
Photographers	85,000	3,700	Poor
Physicians	375,000	21,800	Excellent
Physicists	48,000	1,100	Poor
Pilots, airplane	83,000	4,100	Good, but competitive
Plumbers and pipefitters	385,000	30,000	Good
Police officers	500,000	32,500	Good
Printing press operators	145,000	5,100	Poor, due to new technology
Public relations workers	115,000	8,300	Good, but competitive
Radio and T.V. announcers	26,000	1,300	Good, but competitive
Real estate agents and brokers	450,000	45,500	Good, but competitive
Receptionists	500,000	38,000	Good
Retail trade workers	2,725,000	155,000	Poor, but heavy turnover
Secretaries and stenographers	3,500,000	295,000	Generally good
Security guards	500,000	63,000	Average
Social workers	330,000	25,000	Good
Teachers, college and university	593,000	17,000	Openings, but competitive
Teachers, primary	1,364,000	70,000	Openings, but competitive
Teachers, secondary	1,111,000	13,000	Openings, but competitive
Telephone operators	340,000	11,600	Declining rate
Typists	1,000,000	63,000	Average, but many openings
Urban planners	16,000	1,000	Good
Waiters and waitresses	1,260,000	71,000	Average, but many openings
Wholesale trade workers	808,000	41,000	Average

Source: *Occupational Outlook Quarterly*, spring 1978

LAOS

Laos was only modestly troubled internally and internationally, in comparison with its Indochinese neighbors, Vietnam and Cambodia (Kampuchea), but there were signs of increasing difficulties at home and abroad.

Politics. Premier Kaysone Phomvihane seemed secure as Laos' political leader, although there continued to be some popular resentment of his partial Vietnamese ancestry and his obvious dependence on adjacent Vietnam, which had helped his Pathet Lao gain control of the country in the early 1970's.

Discontent was reflected in the continued outpouring of refugees, totaling 130,000 since the end of the Indochina war in 1975. Some 40,000 political prisoners were detained in "political re-education" camps—the worst of which were in the north near the Chinese border.

Assorted rebels, including onetime CIA-financed Meo hill-tribesmen, former anti-Communist government soldiers, and disaffected former Communist Pathet Lao insurgents, fought against the government. Poor leadership and insufficient arms limited their threat to the regime, but they did pose problems for travel and other activity in some parts of the country. Eight persons were sentenced to death in May for trying to overthrow the government in what apparently was not a serious threat to the regime.

Economy. The 1977–78 rice crop was 40% less than usual as a result of 1977 rainfall 75% below normal. This was followed by a dramatic reversal of the weather as disastrous monsoon rains in 1978 destroyed 43% of the anticipated 1978–79 crop of the grain. The government declared in October that one sixth of the country's 3 million inhabitants faced famine if the country did not obtain 180,000 tons of relief rice.

Prices, which had been escalating since the Indochina war's end, rose sharply, partly in response to the grain shortage. Urban government workers, who do not grow their own food, earned only $15 a month (condensed milk cost $2 a can). Goods, except locally grown food, were plentiful but very expensive. The historically unstable Laotian kip fluctuated considerably on an officially tolerated currency black market. All of the people in the areas actively ruled by the Kaysone regime were required to work one day a week for the government at no pay.

Foreign Relations. Laos did not initially take sides in neighboring Vietnam's quarrels with China and Cambodia. But in July, probably pressed by Hanoi and the Soviet Union, the Vientiane government openly attacked China's "big power chauvinism" and Cambodia's "narrow nationalism." An estimated 40,000 Vietnamese troops remained in the country, mainly to help maintain order, although some of them were relocated near the Laotian-Cambodian border. Several hundred Soviet political advisers and technicians also were in the country.

WIDE WORLD

Laotian refugees arrive at a Bangkok transit center for processing before departure for France.

Most of the Chinese troops which had been building roads in northern Laos—at the invitation of an earlier Laotian government—withdrew during the year. Vientiane, like Hanoi, cracked down on ethnic Chinese private businessmen in midyear.

In June the United States gave Laos $5 million in food assistance. Laos reciprocated in August by offering to return the remains of four American Indochina war MIA's (servicemen missing in action). Laotian authorities turned over the bodies to a U. S. congressional delegation that was visiting Vientiane.

In August the French government severed diplomatic relations with Laos. The Laotian government had demanded the withdrawal of France's only remaining diplomat in Vientiane.

RICHARD BUTWELL
Murray State University

——— LAOS · Information Highlights ———

Official Name: Lao People's Democratic Republic.
Location: Southeast Asia.
Area: 91,429 square miles (236,800 km²).
Population (1978 est.): 3,600,000.
Chief Cities (1973 census): Vientiane, the capital, 176,-637; Savannakhet, 50,690.
Government: *Head of state,* Prince Souphanouvong, president. *Head of government,* Kaysone Phomvihane, prime minister. *Legislature* (unicameral)—National Congress of People's Representatives.
Monetary Unit: New Kip (200 new kips equal U. S.$1, Dec. 1977).
Manufactures (major products): Tin, lumber.
Agriculture (major products): Rice, corn, coffee, cotton, tobacco.

LASERS

Laser research and development continued at an accelerating pace in 1978. Applications of lasers ranged from improved surgical techniques to laser gyroscopes for guidance systems, and from proposed use in a border surveillance system to the creation of power through controlled nuclear fusion.

Remote Sensing. Although laser applications in the area of remote sensing were initially military, applications are now possible to the measurement of atmospheric pollutants and to weather research and forecasting. Tracing the global flow of pollutants and water vapors provides valuable information. Careful measurement of ozone and carbon dioxide concentrations in the atmosphere is crucial in determining any long term changes in the amount of these key gases. A decline in ozone would lead to increased ultraviolet radiation at the earth's surface, while increased CO_2 concentration could lead to worldwide temperature changes. Satellite-based laser measurements of cloud-top winds would also aid in weather forecasting; they would, for example, facilitate the monitoring of potential hurricane systems.

Isotope Separation. Lasers now can be used for isotope enrichment of material for nuclear fuel. At present, the enrichment process (gaseous diffusion or centrifuge) uses natural uranium with 99.3% U-238 (non-fissionable) and 0.7% U-235 (fissionable). The output is divided into enriched material with 3.2% U-235 and depleted material with 0.25% U-235. Present plans call for laser enrichment (to the naturally occurring 0.7% value) of the depleted uranium. This enriched material could then be processed in the usual way. This approach could significantly extend the uranium fuel supply for conventional nuclear reactors. Plans call for thorough tests by the year 1980, followed by a pilot plant by 1985.

Communications. The combination of laser and high quality optical fibers has led to a rapid expansion and improvement of the technology of communications. Indeed, the largest potential market for lasers appears to be telecommunications. Test systems are operating in a number of locations. Telephone signals are converted into light pulses by a laser and transmitted through the fiber. At the other end of the fiber the signal is reconverted. With such a system, smaller cables can carry much more information. Tests by the Bell System on voice and video communication also indicate a reduction in outage time and a major increase in the accuracy of digital signal transmission. In Europe, prototype systems are operational or under construction in London, West Berlin, and Turin. The financial stakes are enormous, since the potential telecommunications market is in the multibillion dollar range.

Laser Annealing. A promising application of lasers to the preparation of semiconductors has been developed. In the microelectronics industry, ion implantation is the method widely used to add to pure semiconductor material the proper amount of impurities in the appropriate location. These added elements give the device its special characteristics. Unfortunately the energetic ions tend to destroy the crystalline order of the semiconductor. To put the atoms back in their crystal sites, the semiconductor (with implanted impurities) is annealed at high temperatures. The laser light is absorbed near the surface, where the damage has been done, and the process is so fast and so narrowly confined that hazardous side effects are avoided. Work with pulsed ruby lasers and with pulsed neodymium YAG (yttrium-aluminum-garnet) lasers shows very positive results, with the semiconductor apparently returning to its crystalline form after laser heating.

GARY MITCHELL
Department of Physics
North Carolina State University

COURTESY OF THE LAWRENCE LIVERMORE LABORATORY

The Shiva laser system at the Lawrence Livermore Laboratory, University of California, will deliver more than (U. S.) 30 trillion watts of optical power in less than one billionth of a second.

June 21, 1978, President Carter assures the OAS that common U. S.-Latin American goals, including "a more just economic system, enhanced human rights and dignity, and permanent peace for us all," can be achieved.

UPI

LATIN AMERICA

Ratification of the Panama Canal treaties by the United States, a bloody civil war in Nicaragua, military coups in Bolivia and Honduras, and hotly contested presidential elections in several republics highlighted Latin American events in 1978. Despite some obvious setbacks, the region as a whole seemed to move away from military domination and toward representative democracy and respect for human rights. No democratic governments fell to military coups, while several dictatorships loosened their grips during the year.

Free Elections. Three countries distinguished for their long adherence to democratic processes —Costa Rica, Colombia, and Venezuela—elected new presidents in 1978. In Costa Rica, the opposition candidate, Rodrigo Carazo, a moderate conservative, won the election by a clear majority in February and took office in May. His party also won a slim plurality of the seats in Congress.

Colombia's ruling Liberal party retained control of both the congress and the presidency, ending 20 years of coalition government under which Liberals and Conservatives alternated as president. Although the coalition agreement formally expired with his inauguration in August, the new chief executive, Julio César Turbay Ayala, pledged to continue to share power with the Conservatives and appointed five to his 12-man cabinet. A low voter turnout, 20% of eligible voters, boded ill for a country already beset by social unrest stemming from rising rates of inflation and crime.

In the Venezuelan presidential elections on December 3, Luis Herrera Campins of the opposition Social Christian party (Copei) defeated Luis Pinerua Ordaz of the ruling Democratic Action Party (AD) and eight other candidates.

Military Threats. Elsewhere in Latin America national armed forces intervened, to varying degrees, in the electoral process. In the Dominican Republic, when the military-backed incumbent, President Joaquín Balaguer, fell behind in the vote count following the May election, troops stopped the counting and seized the ballot boxes. This move provoked demonstrations in the Dominican Republic and stern protests from the governments of the United States, Costa Rica, Colombia, Venezuela, and Panama. Bowing to foreign and domestic pressure, the military released the ballot boxes, and President Balaguer conceded to opposition candidate Antonio Guzmán, who took office in August. Guzmán's center-left Dominican Revolutionary Party apparently won a majority in both houses of Congress, but the armed forces insisted that Balaguer's conservative Reformist Party retain control of the Senate.

In Guatemala, two generals and a colonel fought it out in elections in March to determine who would succeed Gen. Kjell Laugerud as president. After numerous charges of fraud and a temporary halt in the vote count, it was announced that no candidate had obtained the required majority, and the decision was left to Congress. The winner in Congress was Gen. Romeo Lucas García, a centrist and the choice of the army high command. Inaugurated in July, Lucas García appealed to the moderate left for their support.

In military-ruled Ecuador, an inconclusive presidential election was held in July. Jaime Roldós of the center-left Concentration of Popular Forces clearly outpolled candidates of the traditional Conservative and Liberal parties, but apparently failed to win a majority. The official vote count proceeded slowly amid charges of fraud and the resignations of two chief election supervisors. In August it was announced that the official results would not be available until November. Despite military misgivings about Roldós' strong showing, Admiral Alfredo Poveda, Ecuador's head of government, promised that a runoff between the two top candidates would be held after the official results were in. Congressional elections, Poveda announced in September, would be held concurrently with the runoff, thus setting the stage for the transfer of power from the armed forces to an elected government in 1979.

Brazil experienced its first contested presidential election since the military seized power in 1964. The opposition candidate, Euler Bentes Monteiro, a retired general, waged a spirited campaign but had little chance under Brazil's system of indirect presidential elections. The electoral college in October voted overwhelmingly for the candidate of outgoing President Ernesto Geisel and the army high command, Gen. João Batista Figueiredo. Nevertheless, the fact that the government permitted the issues to be debated in an atmosphere of nearly complete freedom of the press indicated that Brazil was making progress toward democracy.

Military Coups. Bolivian troops seized ballot boxes at gunpoint when the vote count after the July presidential election indicated that the candidate backed by the military government was losing. Gen. Juan Pereda, the official candidate, at first called for annulment of the election on grounds of fraud. Then, apparently fearing that incumbent President Hugo Banzer would take advantage of the crisis to perpetuate himself in power, Pereda declared himself president and ousted Banzer in a military coup. Banzer did not resist.

In Honduras, Gen. Juan Alberto Melgar Castro was deposed as president in August by a military faction that accused him of flirting with leftists. A three-man junta, headed by right-wing Gen. Policarpo Paz García, was installed following a bloodless coup.

Peruvian Assembly. Peru's military regime, which has moved from left to right in recent years, convoked a constituent assembly in 1978 amid considerable social and political unrest. In the June elections for assembly delegates, the American Popular Revolutionary Alliance (APRA), led by the venerable Víctor Raúl Haya de la Torre, won 35% of the vote, the largest share. When the assembly convened in July, Haya was elected its presiding officer. While the centrist APRA seemed to have the upper hand, the assembly included communists and other leftists who proved to be popular. President Francisco Morales Bermúdez insisted that the reforms of the military regime be incorporated in the constitution that the assembly was to draw up. The consensus among the delegates, however, was that they comprised a sovereign body and would take orders from no one.

Latin America and the U. S. The ratification of the Panama Canal treaties by the U. S. Senate in April (*see* feature article, page 17) was widely acclaimed in Latin America. It was a major victory for Panama's Gen. Omar Torrijos, who in October stepped down as chief of state—while keeping command of Panama's armed forces. A new president, Aristedes Royo, was elected by the National Assembly on Torrijos' advice.

U. S. President Jimmy Carter briefly visited Panama in June to exchange treaty ratification documents with Torrijos. Earlier, in March, Carter paid longer visits to Venezuela and Brazil. While stressing that the United States valued the friendship of both countries, Carter acknowledged U. S. differences with Venezuela on aid to developing nations and with Brazil on human rights. Brazil, however, moved closer to the U. S. position on human rights during the year.

The Carter administration was pleased by a slight easing of repression in Chile and by the military regime's cooperation in the investigation of the murder in Washington of former Chilean Foreign Minister Orlando Letelier. Continued transgressions against human rights by the Argentine military regime led to the denial of a $270 million development loan to Argentina by the U. S. Export-Import Bank in July. In October, however, the U. S. government reversed itself and approved the loan.

War in Nicaragua. The assassination in January of opposition newspaper publisher Pedro Joaquín Chamorro set off a general strike aimed at toppling Nicaragua's military strongman, President Anastasio Somoza Debayle. Although the strike had widespread support from Nicaraguans of all classes, Somoza retained the backing of the armed forces and survived this and other strike efforts. He also weathered guerrilla attacks and foreign pressure—from the United States and various Latin American governments—to resign. In August, Marxist-led Sandinista guerrillas seized the National Palace and successfully held some 70 high government officials for ransom. After their comrades had flown to safety in Panama, the Sandinistas in Nicaragua went on the offensive throughout the country. The people rallied to their cause. Two weeks of full-scale civil war followed, as Somoza's troops blasted the rebels out of Nicaragua's major cities, killing some 1,500 persons, many of them noncombatants.

In October, Somoza welcomed a team of mediators from Guatemala, the Dominican Republic, and the United States and entered into indirect negotiations with non-Marxist opposition leaders.

NEILL MACAULAY
University of Florida

LAW

Legal developments in the United States during 1978 were highlighted by final adjudication of the controversial Allan Bakke reverse discrimination case. Rulings by the Supreme Court in the areas of freedom of the press, equal protection, criminal punishment, and others, further demonstrated the court's moderate position. Meanwhile, lawyers and the legal profession came under widespread attack. (The issues are examined in a special report on page 297.) At the international level, the law of the sea, human rights, arms control, space, and antiterrorist measures were the focuses of attention.

U. S. Supreme Court

The most important action taken by the Supreme Court during its 1977–78 term was to order the admission of Allan P. Bakke to the University of California at Davis School of Medicine. Bakke, a 38-year-old white engineer, had twice been denied admission, while minority applicants with lower grades and test scores had been accepted under a program that reserved 16 places each year for members of minority groups. Comparable affirmative action programs, some required by legislation or court order, were in effect throughout the country in educational institutions, business, and industry.

The Bakke case (*Regents of the University of California* v. *Bakke*) presented the court with a dilemma. The Davis quota involved classification by race, an apparent violation of the 14th Amendment "equal protection" clause. But a ruling that all remedial programs undertaken to compensate minorities for past racial discrimination would challenge the great progress made in race relations since the 1954 *Brown* v. *Board of Education* decision.

The court avoided both horns of the dilemma. Justices Stevens, Stewart, Rehnquist, and Chief Justice Burger held that the Davis quota was in flat violation of the 1964 Civil Rights Act. But Justices Brennan, White, Marshall, and Blackmun held that racial classification is unconstitutional when its result is to stigmatize, demean, or insult, but not when it is used to remedy past injustices.

Justice Powell took a middle position and wrote the court's opinion: racial quotas are indeed unconstitutional and Bakke must be admitted. But the court also ruled that educational institutions could consider race along with other factors for the purpose of securing a diverse student body. This compromise ruling was generally regarded as permitting many affirmative action programs to continue.

The Bakke decision was evidence of the moderate position taken by the court during the term. Rulings were dominated by a centrist group composed of Powell, Stewart, White, Blackmun, and Stevens. Brennan and Marshall, the only surviving Warren Court liberals, cast 40 and 41 dissents, respectively, while Rehnquist on the right dissented 42 times, and Burger 30 times. The court handed down 129 signed opinions, of which only 36 (28%) were unanimous. This compared with 32% unanimity in the previous term. The court issued 15 per curiam opinions.

The Press and the First Amendment. It was a bad year for the press. The court upheld (4–3) an action of the Palo Alto, Calif., police who, with a warrant, searched the files and premises of the Stanford student newspaper for photographs that might help identify participants in a campus riot (*Zurcher* v. *Stanford Daily*). Under this ruling, any person, even if not suspected of involvement in criminal activity, can have his or her premises searched for evidence of crimes committed by others.

A second blow was *Houchins* v. *KQED*, in which the court held that journalists have no more right to visit prisons than do other members of the public. Burger wrote that the First Amendment "mandates [no] right of access to government information."

By declining to review several lower court decisions, the Supreme Court denied a reporter's right to maintain the confidentiality of his sources, even in civil cases. It also refused to interfere with a judge's gag order on lawyers and other participants in a criminal trial.

The court did agree that a reporter who accurately quotes charges against a public figure is protected from damages for libel (*Edwards* v. *New York Times*). However, it left open the question of whether a public figure who contends that he has been libeled has a right to examine the state of mind of the reporters and editors who prepared the account (*Herbert* v. *Lando*). The court struck down a law imposing criminal penalties for publishing accounts of confidential proceedings before a state judicial review commission (*Landmark Communications* v. *Virginia*).

Adhering to the "community standards" test for obscenity, the court held that the possible reactions of children should be excluded from any definition, but that the view of "sensitive adults" and "deviant sexual groups" could be weighed (*Pinkus* v. *U. S.*). The court ruled that the Federal Communications Commission (FCC) has authority to order "indecent" language off the air (*FCC* v. *Pacifica*). It permitted civil litigation against a television network on charges that a rape scene in one of its telecasts led to a real-life criminal reenactment (*NBC* v. *Niemi*). In the subsequent trial, however, the suit was terminated when the judge ruled that the plaintiff had to prove that the network intended viewers to imitate the violent scene.

Common ownership of a newspaper and broadcasting station in the same community was held properly forbidden by FCC rules, although existing cross-ownerships could continue (*FCC* v. *National Citizens Committee*).

Reporter Myron A. Farber went to jail rather than surrender his notes used for articles involving three New Jersey murders. The Supreme Court ruled that Farber was required to surrender the files.

UPI

Religion. A provision in the Tennessee constitution banning priests and ministers from running for public office was held unconstitutional (*McDaniel* v. *Paty*), as was a New York law reimbursing religious schools for state-mandated record-keeping and testing services (*N. Y.* v. *Cathedral Academy*). The court barred the governor of New Hampshire from ordering flags lowered on state buildings on Good Friday (*Brown* v. *Thomson*). It left standing a lower court order upholding a search warrant under which the FBI had broken into a church building and seized documents of a controversial sect (*Founding Church of Scientology* v. *U. S.*).

Equal Protection. In the area of sex discrimination, the court held that women may not be forced to make higher pension contributions than men even though they tend to live longer and collect more benefits (*Los Angeles* v. *Manhart*). Employers may not take away seniority rights from women on pregnancy leave, but they need not grant them sick pay (*Nashville Gas Co.* v. *Satty*).

The court left standing a lower court decision approving sexually separate public high schools for academically superior students (*Vorchheimer* v. *Philadelphia*). It also let stand a decision declaring that punishment of males, but not of females, for the crime of statutory rape is a form of sex discrimination (*Helgemoe* v. *Meloon*).

The court upheld South Carolina's use of teacher tests that disqualified 83% of black applicants and only 17.5% of white applicants (*NEA* v. *South Carolina*).

Under the 1977 Age Discrimination in Employment Act, a 59-year-old test pilot was returned to his job with back pay (*McDonnell Douglas* v. *Houghton*); however, the ruling does

not apply to employees in pension plans existing before passage of the act (*United Air Lines* v. *McCann*).

Privacy. The court continued to avoid the homosexuality issue, refusing to review the dismissal of a Washington school teacher on those grounds (*Gaylord* v. *Tacoma*). It also let stand a decision permitting North Carolina to prosecute consenting adults for private homosexual acts (*Enslin* v. *Bean*). The Supreme Court struck down a Wisconsin law requiring a man with a legal obligation of child support to get a judge's approval before remarrying (*Zablocki* v. *Radhail*).

Criminal Punishment. The court's position on capital punishment is that every person subject to the death penalty must be permitted to offer mitigating evidence tending to forestall such a sentence. It therefore invalidated an Ohio law which defined mitigating considerations too narrowly (*Lockett* v. *Ohio*). It also declined to review rulings from New York and Pennsylvania that invalidated state capital punishment laws.

The court ruled that the police can compel a driver to get out of his car when stopped for a minor traffic violation (*Pennsylvania* v. *Mimms*).

Arson investigators must obtain a search warrant before entering a building, except during and immediately after a fire (*Michigan* v. *Tyler*). The same rule applies to police making a nonemergency search at the scene of a murder (*Mincey* v. *Arizona*). Likewise, warrants must be obtained by inspectors from the Occupational Safety and Health Administration (OSHA) before making spot searches of employers' premises (*Marshall* v. *Barlow's*). For the first time, the court held that a person charged with a crime has the right to challenge evidence against him on the ground that the prosecutor obtained a search warrant by making false statements to the issuing judge (*Franks* v. *Delaware*).

Two decisions upheld wiretapping practices. Law enforcement agents need not make an effort to minimize the interception of private conversations when conducting court-authorized wiretaps (*Scott* v. *U. S.*), and a telephone company can be ordered to assist covertly federal investigators installing a device for recording numbers dialed (*U. S.* v. *New York Telephone Co.*).

The plea bargaining power of prosecutors was enhanced by a ruling that they may threaten a defendant with a second, more serious indictment if he refuses to plead guilty to the initial charge (*Bordenkircher* v. *Hayes*). The court declared unconstitutional a five-member jury, holding that criminal juries must have at least six members (*Ballew* v. *Georgia*).

Prison officials cannot be sued for negligently failing to mail a prisoner's letters, if they have not acted maliciously (*Procunier* v. *Navarette*). The court upheld a federal judge's ruling that conditions in Arkansas prisons constituted "cruel and unusual punishment" (*Hutto* v. *Finney*).

Federalism. The court held that a Washington state law barring oil supertankers from its territorial waters and imposing design standards more stringent than federal requirements was an unconstitutional burden on interstate commerce (*Ray* v. *Atlantic Richfield*). Likewise, New Jersey could not forbid neighboring states from dumping wastes within its borders (*Philadelphia* v. *New Jersey*). An Alaska law requiring employers to give state residents preference in hiring violates the "privileges and immunities" clause of the Constitution (*Hicklin* v. *Orbeck*). However, reducing the benefits of welfare recipients who move from the United States to Puerto Rico is not a violation of their right to travel (*Califano* v. *Torres*); and Montana was upheld in charging out-of-state elk hunters a $225 fee and state residents only $30 (*Baldwin* v. *Montana Fish and Game Commission*).

Immunity. Applying the doctrine of judicial immunity, the court held that a judge could not be sued for ordering the sterilization of a 15-year-old girl without her knowledge (*Stump* v. *Sparkman*). But federal prosecutors have only a limited immunity from suit if they are charged with violating the civil rights of citizens during an investigation (*Goodwin* v. *Briggs*). Federal officials, including cabinet members, can also be sued if they deliberately violate an individual's constitutional rights (*Butz* v. *Economou*). The court limited congressional immunity by permitting a civil suit against Sen. John McClellan (D-Ark.) and three aides for seizing and copying private papers (*McAdams* v. *McSurely*).

Cities may be sued for damages under federal antitrust laws when operating such businesses as utilities, hospitals, and transit systems (*Lafayette* v. *Louisiana Light & Power Co.*). Cities and municipal agencies may also be sued for federal civil rights violations (*Mondell* v. *Department of Social Services*).

Other Rulings. In two rulings on bar ethics, the court upheld the traditional ban on "ambulance chasing," but forbade disciplinary action against an attorney who offered free legal aid to a potential client on behalf of a nonprofit organization (*Ohralik* v. *Ohio State Bar, In re Primus*).

The Endangered Species Act was held to protect a small fish in the Little Tennessee River, the snail darter, even if it required halting a major Tennessee Valley Authority (TVA) dam project (*TVA* v. *Hill*). The court upheld a statute limiting the liability of a nuclear power company to $560 million for any single nuclear accident (*Duke Power Co.* v. *Carolina Environmental Group*). It also upheld New York's designation of Grand Central Terminal as an historic landmark, prohibiting construction of a 53-story office building above it (*Penn Central* v. *New York City*).

Reversing a recent pattern of decisions barring discrimination against aliens, the court upheld the right of New York and 32 other states to restrict membership in state police forces to citizens (*Foley* v. *Connelie*). Finally, the court ruled that White House tape recordings played at the 1974 Watergate trial may not be released for public broadcast or commercial reproduction (*Nixon* v. *Warner Communications*).

C. HERMAN PRITCHETT
University of California, Santa Barbara

International Law

From the international legal conferences, resolutions, and communiqués, there emerged some useful proposals and valuable agreements.

Law of the Seas. The seventh session of the Third United Nations Conference on the Law of the Seas (UNCLOS) met in Geneva, Switzerland, April–May, 1978. Five of the scheduled eight weeks were spent on procedural matters, but the participating nations did agree to hold another four-week session beginning in late August in New York.

The UNCLOS meetings have bogged down in recent years over the issue of deep seabed mining. The Third World countries would like to see a "new international economic order," whereby the seabeds would be the "common heritage of mankind" and would be administered by a strong international authority. The industrial nations, which alone have the technological capacity to mine the deep sea, prefer more limited funding and jurisdiction for the controlling authority. If the stalemate persists, countries such as the United States are threatening to take unilateral action to begin commercial exploitation.

Yet this largest, longest, and most complex international conference in recent history has come to the verge of general agreement on a considerable number of issues, including the limits of the territorial sea, navigation in straits and territorial waters, exercise of national jurisdiction beyond the territorial sea, and protection of the marine environment.

In the absence of a UNCLOS agreement, many nations have declared 200-mile (370-km) offshore fishing jurisdictions and have embarked on bilateral diplomatic negotiations over access to these new national zones. The United States and Canada, for example, discussed reciprocal fishing rights in their coastal waters.

After the Amoco Cadiz disaster off the coast of Brittany, France, in March 1978, French President Giscard d'Estaing called for a new international agreement prohibiting oil tankers from coming within 12 nautical miles (22 km) of any coast. France unilaterally announced measures requiring tankers entering the English Channel to remain 7 nautical miles (13 km) off the coast and to notify the authorities of their position, intended route, and difficulties encountered. The United States, while urging UNCLOS to draft regulations to bolster the rights of coastal countries to prevent offshore pollution, has not yet ratified a 1973 international convention which would stiffen safety standards for oil tankers and establish a (U. S.) $200 million compensation fund for oil spill damage.

Space. The disintegration over northwestern Canada of Cosmos 954, a Soviet satellite carrying radioactive nuclear power sources, led

Experts check for radioactivity in debris from a Soviet satellite that disintegrated over Canada. The incident led to a call for new safeguards.

UPI

to a dispute between the two countries and to a call for new international safeguards. A 1972 United Nations treaty entitled Canada to compensation for property damage and obligated it to return any parts of the satellite that were recovered. Canada also asked the USSR to pay the costs of the investigation, but the UN treaty is vague on this point and the Soviets declined. The USSR also took the position that additional regulations were not necessary. U. S. President Carter urged the Soviets to sign a pact which would bar earth satellites from carrying radioactive materials. An analysis by the Los Alamos Scientific Laboratory, however, concluded that banning nuclear reactors from space satellites would deny to supersatellites economical sources of power.

Human Rights. In 1978, there again were conflicting perceptions of which countries were guilty of abusing the rights of their citizens. The 35-nation Belgrade Conference on Security and Cooperation in Europe, which concluded in March 1978, heard an exchange of accusations between East and West.

The UN, which in November 1977 approved a mandatory arms embargo against South Africa (the first time such action was ever taken against a member nation) was conspicuously silent about the reigns of terror in Cambodia and Ethiopia, while condemning rights violations in Chile and Palestine.

The Organization of American States called on Chile, Paraguay, and Uruguay to eliminate abuses. The European Court of Human Rights censured the United Kingdom for its treatment of political prisoners in Northern Ireland.

Terrorism. There was some progress in developing transnational means for dealing with a common enemy, terrorism. The Moro kidnapping spotlighted the importance of police liaison across national boundaries. Bulgaria's return of terrorists to West Germany and Yugoslavia's arrest of several German incendiaries were other indications of the recognition of a common foe. At their Bonn summit conference, July 16–17, the major Western industrial nations agreed to cut off commercial air service to any country that harbored airline hijackers.

Arms Control. For the first time since the 1932 Disarmament Conference in Geneva, representatives of the entire international community gathered in May 1978 for a five-week UN General Assembly Special Session on Disarmament. This meeting, called largely at the initiative of the nonaligned nations, was not, however, a negotiating session. Proposals were made for the reduction of military stockpiles and for the transfer of technology and personnel from war preparation to peace efforts. Although the appearance of President d'Estaing broke a 16-year French boycott of disarmament talks, the superpowers gave the deliberations only perfunctory recognition.

MARTIN GRUBERG
University of Wisconsin, Oshkosh

The Legal Profession

There are approximately 500,000 lawyers in the United States today, making them the largest professional group in that or any other nation; the American Bar Association, with 230,000 members is the largest professional organization in the world. While the day of the single practitioner is by no means gone, the trend is markedly toward the concentration of lawyers in ever larger firms. One such firm has nearly 500 lawyers in nineteen locations, ten others have more than 200 lawyers, and dozens have more than 100.

The increasing complexity of American law has stimulated growth in other areas of the profession. Corporations have vastly expanded their in-house legal departments, often rivaling in size the large private firms. Government lawyers also have increased at the national, state, and local levels. Similarly, the number of lawyers who serve the needs of the poor in criminal and civil matters has been greatly enlarged because of two developments: (1) beginning in 1963 the Supreme Court required that all persons charged with a crime be provided with competent counsel, at the government's expense in the case of indigents; and (2) concern for the civil legal needs of the poor prompted the federal government to provide legal service lawyers to meet at least part of those needs. The public interest lawyer is another relative newcomer to the legal arena. Although the number of these self-appointed guardians of the public interest is still small, they have had a significant impact on matters of great importance, both private and public. Finally, to meet these growing needs, the law faculties of U. S. universities have expanded their teaching staffs more than threefold in less than 25 years.

Meanwhile, the number of judges in federal, state, and local courts has risen more slowly, indeed less rapidly than the case load, which has all but overwhelmed many courts. The fact is that Americans are a litigious people, who apparently believe that nearly all disputes, public and private, large and small, can be resolved by the courts.

The role of lawyers in the United States has always been significant. More than half the signers of the Declaration of Independence and U. S. Constitution were lawyers, and today more than half the members of Congress are lawyers. In public and private affairs, lawyers are called upon to deal with nearly every problem of contemporary society.

Despite, or perhaps because of, this level of dependence on legal skills, the profession is attacked. That is nothing new; lawyers have always been under attack—by Plato, Jesus, Shakespeare, and, most recently, by President Jimmy Carter, among others. Curiously, individuals tend to be satisfied with their own lawyers while critical of the profession as a whole. In fact, a 1978 Harris Poll rated public confidence in lawyers at the same low level as confidence in Congress, organized labor, and the advertising profession. Why is this? Do lawyers induce unnecessary litigation; or do individual citizens believe that better and quicker solutions can be found in courts than elsewhere?

This much at least can be said. While the delays in securing answers in court are greater than desirable, courts are likely to give more definite answers than the other branches of government, and usually more quickly. Moreover, the courts are generally perceived as fair and uninfluenced by political considerations.

The legal profession is, for the most part, free of external regulation. Lawyers are less regulated by government than any other profession despite the fact that they are entrusted with the delivery of justice. Qualifications for admission into the nearly 200 law schools are fixed by the law faculties, with only loose supervision by the American Bar Association. Standards for admission to the bar are fixed by bar examiners in each state working under the direction of their respective high courts. Discipline of lawyers is done by lawyers themselves, usually as a function of a state bar association and pursuant to the terms of the Code of Professional Responsibility.

The only recent limitations on this closed circle of regulation have been decisions by the U. S. Supreme Court to strike down minimum fee schedules, to permit lawyer advertising, and to open the way for prepaid legal services plans.

The legal profession remains a preferred career choice for many more college graduates than the law schools can accommodate. The number of law students more than tripled in the 25 years between 1953 and 1978; and each year more than 30,000 new lawyers are admitted to the bar.

The issue that most visibly stirs lawyers and nonlawyers alike is the question of lawyer competency. Chief Justice Warren E. Burger has alleged that a substantial proportion of litigators are not competent advocates. The bar has responded with proposals to improve the level of competency, beginning with law school training, more rigorous bar examinations, and emphasis on continuing legal education.

The ultimate goals of the legal profession are three: (1) assurance of access to justice for all; (2) effective delivery of justice; and (3) improvement in the administration of justice. If these objectives are kept in focus, the profession will deserve its free rein in serving the American public.

ROBERT B. MCKAY

In spite of the efforts of UN peacekeeping troops, *left*, outbreaks of heavy fighting continued in Lebanon in 1978.

UPI

LEBANON

Outbreaks of severe fighting between right-wing Christian militia and Syrian peacekeeping forces in February, July, and October hamstrung attempts by Lebanese President Elias Sarkis to restore stability to his war-ravaged country in 1978. Sarkis' attention to domestic security was diverted by Arab factionalism over the Egyptian peace initiative and Israel's massive invasion and 91-day occupation of southern Lebanon after a terrorist attack in March.

Domestic Instability. Although the 30,000-member Arab League peacekeeping force had managed to return Beirut to an acceptable state of security, January and February were marked by a continuation of the fighting between Christian rightists and Palestinian guerrillas. Supported by Israel, Pierre Gemayel's Christian Phalangist Party and Camille Chamoun's National Liberal Party sought to drive the Palestinians out of the territory between the Litani River and the Israeli border. Because of the threat of provoking Israel, Syrian troops of the Arab Deterrent Force (ADF) have not interfered with Christian offensives since 1977.

Palestinian resilience in the south and a reconciliation between the Palestine Liberation Organization (PLO) and Syria after Egyptian President Anwar el-Sadat's visit to Jerusalem, induced the Christians to upset the status quo in the capital. A Christian attack on the Syrians led to four days of bloody fighting before a cease-fire was achieved. On February 19, Chamoun declared that the ADF's mandate should be terminated, but that until it was ADF forces should stay out of Christian east Beirut. Chamoun's statement indicated that his party had no intention of cooperating with Sarkis' plan to disarm the militia and reassert the central government's power.

Israeli Intervention. Christian losses in the south during the first week of March and a murderous terrorist outbreak on March 12 provided a pretext for Israel's March 14–15 invasion of Lebanon. Although officially a reprisal, it appeared that the object of the Israelis was to accomplish what their Christian allies could not: the destruction of Palestinian resistance in the south. To this end, all of Lebanon south of the Litani was occupied.

Lebanon's request for UN Security Council support brought about a March 21 cease-fire and the arrival of the first units of a 4,500-man UN interim force. The UN's role was to supervise the Israeli withdrawal—which took until June 13—while keeping Christian and Palestinian forces separated, the latter goal made difficult by Israeli determination to leave the area in the hands of the Christians.

Aftermath of the Invasion. The Israeli action, creating 250,000 refugees in a week, had a pro-

UPI

Lebanese refugees gather their possessions in the Karantina section of Beirut, scene of heavy fighting.

found polarizing effect on Lebanon's disintegrating domestic stability. Seeking a political solution, both Sarkis and Syrian President Hafez al-Assad agreed that a strong central government and more equitable sharing of power between Christians and Muslims were needed. However, the Christians were badly split on how to deal with the future. Gemayel's and Chamoun's groups refused either to disarm or to permit deployment of ADF troops in Christian enclaves, because to do so would be to abandon hope of restoring their former privileges. The other major faction, led by former President Suleiman Franjieh, advocated a policy of cooperating with the government.

The response by Christian factions to Sarkis' attempts to reassert power in April and May was bitter infighting, culminating in a June 13 Phalangist assault on Franjieh's Ehden villa and the killing of his son, daughter-in-law, and grandchild.

Beirut Under Siege. In July and October, Beirut residents suffered the worst rocket and artillery barrages in Lebanon's history, as the 28,000-man Syrian ADF contingent tried to batter the Christians into submission. Assad received permission from Sarkis to resort to overwhelming force when the Christians again refused to disarm. However, suffering in the Beirut suburb of Ain al-Rummaneh reached such proportions by July 8 that Sarkis threatened to resign unless the fighting stopped. A cease-fire was not arranged until Foreign Minister Fuad Butros met with Assad in Damascus.

Although the cease-fire held, despite constant violations, even worse fighting broke out on September 28 and lasted one week. By the time another UN cease-fire resolution was accepted on October 7, 700 more Lebanese had died (bringing the three-year death toll to at least 100,000), and the northeast suburb of Hadath had been devastated.

Most observers believed the fighting was provoked by Syria to lure Israel into intervention and thereby scuttle the results of the Egyptian-Israeli Camp David accords. However, the attempt to destroy the accords was unsuccessful, although the Israelis did shell Palestinian and Syrian positions in west Beirut on October 5.

Following acceptance of the cease-fire, Sarkis called on the delegates of the six ADF contributors to seek a formula for reducing tensions. Despite initial Syrian opposition, the negotiations led to a redeployment of Syrian troops and their replacement by Saudi and Sudanese units on October 19. The plan was apparently a success, as it gave time for developing the capacity of the Lebanese Army to replace ADF forces. Even the Christian leadership expressed a willingness to seek a political solution at year's end.

F. NICHOLAS WILLARD

LIBRARIES

An earthquake was felt in the American library community during 1978. By year-end, however, the significance of that tremor remained obscure. On June 6, California voters endorsed Proposition 13, a measure that reduced property taxes by about 57% and imposed a limit on future levels of such taxation. The amendment led to a general "tax revolt" across the nation. However, the total effect on libraries, particularly public, school, and community college libraries, which are dependent on property taxation, was unclear. Staff reductions, cuts in services, and reduced hours were threatened, but did not become reality.

Librarians in California who lobbied against the proposition had to ponder whether the welfare of their institutions was more important than their historic interest in keeping libraries as neutral as possible on public issues. Moreover, Robert Alvarez, a librarian who edits *Administrator's Digest,* reminded his colleagues that the controversy forced "librarians to think about their staffs and services and facilities in a way they never had to before."

Library of Congress. An administrative reorganization of the Library of Congress was approved by Congress in late 1977 and in 1978. Only a proposal to merge the independent Law Library with the Research Services Division was defeated. Of special interest were the creation in the Office of the Librarian of a Council of Scholars and a Center for the Book and in the Research Services Division of a Motion Picture, Broadcasting, and Recorded Sound Division.

The Council of Scholars will consist of individuals representing American history and civilization, European history and civilization, Asian history and civilization, African and Middle Eastern history and civilization, Hispanic history and civilization, as well as science and technology, the social sciences, the humanities, and books, bibliography, and librarianship. Coming to the library on a rotating basis for one-year terms, the members of the council will assess the collections and make recommendations for their improvement.

The privately-supported Center for the Book will study and promote the role of the book in U. S. society. Authorized by legislation enacted

——— **LEBANON** · Information Highlights ———

Official Name: Republic of Lebanon.
Location: Southwest Asia.
Area: 4,000 square miles (10,350 km²).
Population (1978 est.): 2,900,000.
Chief Cities (1974 est.): Beirut, the capital, 1,000,000; Tripoli, 128,000.
Government: *Head of state,* Elias Sarkis, president (took office Sept. 1976). *Head of government,* Selim al-Hoss, prime minister (took office Dec. 1976). *Legislature* (unicameral)—Chamber of Deputies.
Monetary Unit: Lebanese pound (2.965 pounds equal U. S.$1, Nov. 1978).
Manufactures (major products): Service industries, food processing, textiles, cement, oil refining, chemicals, some metal fabricating.
Agriculture (major products): Fruits, tobacco, wheat, corn, barley, potatoes, olives, onions.

in 1977, the center will have a National Advisory Board chaired by George C. McGhee, former chairman of the board of *The Saturday Review*. On February 23, the center sponsored a seminar with the Association of American Publishers on improving the international flow of books and book programs; on April 13 and 14, the center held a planning meeting at which its possible role in encouraging the study of books and printing was discussed; and on April 26 and 27, the center cosponsored with the U. S. Office of Education a seminar on "Television, the Book, and the Classroom."

On July 31, a prominent historian of broadcasting, Erik Barnouw, became chief of the new Motion Picture, Broadcasting, and Recorded Sound Division. This exciting new enterprise will unite the Motion Picture Section, the Recorded Sound Section, and the American Television and Radio Archive, mandated by the Copyright Revision Act of 1976. This division will share a user facility with the Music Division in the $150 million James Madison Memorial Building which the Library of Congress intends to occupy in 1980–81. All of these changes are intended to make the Library of Congress a stronger center of scholarship.

National Commission on Libraries and Information Science. Frederick Burkhardt, chairman of the National Commission on Libraries and Information Science since its inception, resigned in July. In May, President Carter had nominated five new appointees to the commission. They were Robert W. Burns, Jr., assistant director of libraries for research service at the Colorado State University Libraries; Joan H. Gross, an advertising copywriter from New York City; Clara S. Jones, director of the Detroit Public Library; Frances H. Naftalin, president of the Minneapolis Public Library Board; and Horace E. Tate, executive secretary of the Georgia Association of Educators and associate professor of education at Fort Valley (Georgia) State College. Later, Charles W. Benton of Britannica Films was also named to the commission. Since three of the appointees have direct connections with librarianship, it was expected that library influence on the commission would increase. In a related development, the commission had announced on April 18 that 47 of the 50 states and all of the territories had set dates for conferences that will precede the next White House Conference on Libraries and Information Services.

Personnel Changes and New Facilities. Women appeared to be advancing within the administrative ranks in librarianship. During 1978, Joan Collett became city librarian in St. Louis; Jane Hale Morgan was named director of the Detroit Public Library; Linda M. Bretz was appointed director of the Rochester (N. Y.) Public Library; and Patricia Meyer Battin was selected as university librarian at Columbia University.

In Chicago, the Central Library Building, the second oldest building on Michigan Avenue, was renovated and was rededicated in late 1977 as the Chicago Public Library Cultural Center. The new Central Library of the Chicago Public Library, books for which are now shelved in the Mandel Building on Michigan Avenue, will be located in the North Loop Area, about four blocks from the Cultural Center. The $80 million Central Library will be completed in the late 1980's. The Columbia Broadcasting System gave $2 million to strengthen the cultural life of New York City, including $330,000 to the financially-troubled New York Public Library.

American Library Association. The 97th annual conference of the American Library Association was held in Chicago, June 24–30, 1978. Russell Shank, university librarian at the University of California at Los Angeles, became president of the association and Thomas J. Galvin, dean of the Graduate School of Library and Information Sciences at the University of Pittsburgh, was elected vice president and president-elect. Important topics of discussion at the conference were the Equal Rights Amendment and the implications for libraries of the "tax revolt." The association again sponsored National Library Week, April 2–8. Its theme was "Info to Go."

International Library Activities. The World Congress of the International Federation of Library Associations and Institutions was held at Strbake Pleso, Czechoslovakia, August 28–September 3. Employing as its theme, "New Trends in Documentation and Information," the 39th Congress of the International Federation for Documentation met in Edinburgh, Scotland, September 25–28. The Canadian Library Association held its annual meeting in Edmonton, Alta.

DAN BERGEN, *Graduate Library School*
University of Rhode Island, Kingston

Major Library Awards of 1978

Beta Phi Mu Award for distinguished service to education for librarianship: Frances E. Henne, retired professor, School of Library Service, Columbia University

Randolph J. Caldecott Medal for distinction in picture book illustration: Peter Spier, *Noah's Ark*

Melvil Dewey Medal for creative professional achievement of a high order: Frederick G. Kilgour, director, Ohio College Library Center

Grolier Foundation Award for stimulating the reading interests of young people: Dorothy C. McKenzie, Pasadena, Calif.

Joseph W. Lippincott Award for distinguished service in the library profession: Henry T. Drennan, Office of Libraries and Learning Resources, U. S. Office of Education

John Newbery Medal for the most distinguished contribution to children's literature: Katherine Paterson, *Bridge to Terabithia*

Ralph R. Shaw Award for library literature: Frederick Wilfrid Lancaster, Graduate School of Library Science, University of Illinois, for *The Measurement and Evaluation of Library Services*

H. W. Wilson Library Periodical Award: *Documentation et Bibliothèques,* Hubert Perron, editor

In Libya, an elaborate military parade and ceremony marked the ninth anniversary of the rule of Muammar el-Qaddafi.

ZOUHAIR SAADEH, GAMMA-LIAISON

LIBYA

Libya's major political preoccupation in 1978 was its alliance with other radical Arab states in a "steadfast front" opposed to any accommodation with Israel.

Foreign Relations. Egyptian President Anwar el-Sadat's November 1977 trip to Jerusalem and the signing of the Camp David accords in September 1978 brought bitter criticism from government officials, culminating in a decision to sever relations with Egypt. Libya vowed to thwart improved Egyptian-Israeli relations by actively working for Sadat's overthrow, seeking increased cooperation between the Soviet Union and Arab states, and forming joint political and military agencies with other regional governments opposed to the settlement. Libyan economic aid to Syria and Jordan increased markedly in 1978, and at least some of the funds were intended for the purchase of military materiel.

On the African front, Libya supported the efforts of the Polisario movement in former Spanish Sahara to gain independence from Morocco and Mauritania. Early in the year it appeared that Libya and Chad would resolve their long-standing disputes over borders and alleged Libyan support of rebel groups in northern Chad. Although a cease-fire was negotiated and peace talks did begin, the two sides could not agree on key issues and the talks collapsed. One positive result of the negotiations, however, was the improvement of Libya's relations with the Sudan and Niger, both of which Libya had feuded with in the past. The Sudan and Niger agreed to help police an anticipated Libyan-Chad cease-fire, and this led Libya to normalize relations with them.

The United States expressed its dissatisfaction with Libya's overall foreign policy by refusing to permit American firms to export such equipment as transport planes and heavy trucks. These items, it was feared, might be used to support terrorist activities or to oppose governments friendly with the United States.

Domestic Affairs. The government increased its original 1978 budget by almost 20%, emphasizing defense, health, and education. Agricul-

tural development, however, received the largest single allocation; several European and American consultants were employed to bolster Libya's land utilization programs. Unpopular government innovations, such as conscription and limits on privately owned property, lent credence to occasional reports of antiregime sentiment. However, President Muammar el-Qaddafi seemed in control.

Oil resources continued to supply the overwhelming bulk of Libya's financial revenue. Although oil production in 1977 had reached its highest point in several years, the demand for low-sulfur crude oil began to decline, especially as its price rose in comparison with Mid-East oil. As a result, production was cut at the beginning of 1978. Output did rise gradually and steadily as the year progressed, but by midyear production lagged some 10% behind the 1977 level. Prices were lowered in an effort to attract customers, but exports to the extremely important European market fell by 13%. This loss was offset by an increase of more than 50% in exports to North America. The United States accounted for more than one third of Libya's total exports; nearly 10% of the total amount of oil imported by the United States came from Libyan fields. Libyan oil production averaged about 2 million barrels a day.

KENNETH J. PERKINS
University of South Carolina

——————— LIBYA · Information Highlights ———————

Official Name: Socialist People's Libyan Arab *Jamahiriya* ("state of the masses").
Location: North Africa.
Area: 679,360 square miles (1,759,540 km²).
Population (1978 est.): 2,800,000.
Chief Cities (1975 est.): Tripoli, the capital, 295,000; Benghazi, 190,000.
Government: *Head of state,* Muammar el-Qaddafi, secretary general of the General People's Congress (took office 1969). *Head of government,* Abdullah Obeidi, chairman of the General Popular Committee. *Legislature*—General People's Congress (met initially Nov. 1976).
Monetary Unit: Dinar (0.296 dinar equals U. S.$1, Sept. 1978).
Manufactures (major products): Crude petroleum, processed foods, textiles, paper products, soap.
Agriculture (major products): Wheat, barley, dates, olives, peanuts, cereals, citrus fruits, livestock.

LITERATURE

American Literature

Although the publishing industry continued to thrive, 1978 was a subdued year for American letters. Media attention focused on such matters as the high fees for paperback rights, a spirited "Don't buy books from crooks" campaign directed against Richard Nixon's *RN,* and a book which claimed that a successful human cloning had been performed.

The 89-day New York City newspaper strike made it difficult for many books to gain recognition. Publishers seemed to be preoccupied with promoting books with movie or bestseller potential and less inclined to support more serious literary efforts.

Awards. One bright spot was the awarding of the 1978 Nobel Prize in literature to Isaac Bashevis Singer. An émigré from Poland in the 1930's, Singer's unabashed use of supernatural phenomena, psychological grotesquerie, and pessimism interwoven with a celebration of life has influenced many contemporary writers. Although he writes in Yiddish, he supervises all English translations of his work.

The National Book Critics Circle announced its third annual awards in January 1978. Their four prizes were: Fiction—Toni Morrison's *Song of Solomon;* Poetry—Robert Lowell's *Day by Day;* Nonfiction—Walter Jackson Bate's *Samuel Johnson;* and Criticism—Susan Sontag's *On Photography.*

National Book Award winners were: History—David McCullough's *The Path Between the Seas: The Creation of the Panama Canal, 1870–1914;* Fiction—Mary Lee Settle's *Blood Tie;* Biography—Walter Jackson Bate's *Samuel Johnson;* Poetry—Howard Nemerov's *Collected Poems;* Contemporary Thought—Gloria Emerson's *Winners & Losers;* Translation—Uwe George's *In the Deserts of This Earth,* translated by Richard and Clara Winston; and Children's Literature—Judith and Herbert Kohl's *The View From the Oak: The Private Worlds of Other Creatures.*

In April, the Pulitzer Prize in Biography was awarded to Walter Jackson Bate for *Samuel Johnson,* giving the book triple recognition; it was the second Pulitzer Prize for Bate. Other awards went to: Alfred D. Chandler, Jr.'s *The Visible Hand: The Managerial Revolution in American Business* (History); James Alan McPherson's collection of short stories, *Elbow Room* (Fiction); Howard Nemerov's *Collected Poems* (Poetry); Carl Sagan's *The Dragons of Eden* (General Nonfiction); and Donald L. Coburn's *The Gin Game* (Drama). A special citation was given to the late humorist, essayist, and author of *Charlotte's Web,* E. B. White.

Novels. Isaac Bashevis Singer's eighth novel, *Shosha,* convincingly recreates the life of a young man growing up in pre-World War II Poland. A struggling Jewish artist surrounded by commercial exploitation and extravagant self-indulgence, he finds his salvation as a man and as an artist in his intense feelings for a childhood sweetheart.

In contrast to Singer's straightforward use of his own past is John Irving's *The World According to Garp.* Here the autobiographical elements are blended with wild fantasy and macabre inventions. The result is an intense and tender book in which reality and imagination stand in rich counterpoint.

When he died in 1977, James Jones had almost completed *Whistle,* the last work of his World War II trilogy, begun by *From Here to Eternity* and carried on in *The Thin Red Line.* In the naturalistic tradition of the first two works, *Whistle* concentrates on the destruction of soldiers' minds and bodies after the war. Anton Myrer's *The Last Convertible* deals with a group of 1938 Harvard College graduates who find themselves plunged into war. Herman Wouk again demonstrates his considerable ability as a storyteller in *War and Remembrance,* a continuation of his *Winds of War.* Stefan Kanfer's *The Eighth Sin* tells the horrendous story of the Nazis' treatment of Gypsies.

The war in Vietnam presents special difficulties for the novelist. Ordinary war themes—the testing of courage, the implacable evil of the enemy, the dawning of purpose—all seem irrelevant. Tim O'Brien successfully uses the Vietnam experience in his surrealistic *Going After Cacciato,* a soldier's elaborate fantasies about revenge, escape, and peace.

A civil rights crusade is the setting for Ernest J. Gaines' *In My Father's House,* the story of a black minister confronted by the son he abandoned 20 years before. Raymond Andrews' *Appalachee Red,* winner of the first James Baldwin Prize for Fiction, describes life in a small Georgia town.

The new visibility of "born again" Christianity perhaps inspired Joyce Carol Oates' *Son of the Morning,* the story of a God-struck evangelist. Dotson Rader's *Miracle* makes use of the author's childhood experiences with born-again preachers, actors, and businessmen. Religious enthusiasm is also at the heart of Gore Vidal's *Kalki,* a social satire based on a Vietnam veteran who predicts the end of the world.

Although Paul Theroux has only lately gotten the attention he deserves, *Picture Palace,* his story of an elderly woman photographer looking over her life, is perhaps one of his least successful works. Thomas Berger's retelling of the Arthurian legends, *Arthur Rex,* seems to fall somewhere between tribute and parody.

Some promising first novels also appeared in 1978. Mary Gordon's *Final Payments* is a well written account of a Catholic woman whose father's death frees her to experience the complex pains of the world and to discover her own peculiar answers. Michael Brodsky's brilliant but difficult *Detours* is an almost plotless first person narrative whose texture is formed by literary references, cinematic allusions, and minute analyses of small but significant actions. Ellen Schwamm's *Adjacent Lives* deals perceptively with two people who are surprised to find themselves in a love affair.

Don De Lillo's interest in conspiracy is again seen in *Running Dog,* the story of a woman reporter who stumbles into a plot involving gangsters, spies, politicians, and art dealers. Richard Price's third novel, *Ladies' Man,* recounts one week in the life of a wandering New Yorker. Hubert Selby proves he has lost none of his interest in depravity and violence in *Requiem for a Dream.* William Kotzwinkle produced another curiosity, *Herr Nightingale and the Satin Woman,* and Charles Simmons, whose *Powdered Eggs* was acclaimed as an extremely promising first novel, brought out *Wrinkles.* A surprising novel from John Updike is *The Coup,* in which an African dictator tells his own story.

Short Stories. *The Stories of John Cheever* brings together 61 tales which have appeared since the 1940's. Cheever's perceptive and meticulously crafted chronicles of the disappointments and sadness of middle class life have made him one of the great American short story writers. Other important retrospective collections are Irwin Shaw's *Short Stories: Five Decades,* and Conrad Richter's *The Rawhide Knot.* Barry Hannah's *Airships* are alternately humorous, menacing, touching, and violent stories of dislocated southerners. Her previous works were the novels *Geronimo Rex* and *Nightwatchmen.* Eight stories by Susan Sontag are collected for the first time in *I, Etcetera.*

Poetry. The American poetic sensibility was plunged into the 20th century largely at the urgings of Harriet Monroe's *Poetry* magazine. *Poetry* published the early works of T. S. Eliot,

Wallace Stevens, and Ezra Pound and continued to recognize the important poets of succeeding generations. The *"Poetry" Anthology,* collected by Daryl Hine and Joseph Parisi from 65 years of *Poetry* magazine, is an important chapter in American literary history.

Karl Shapiro, onetime editor of *Poetry,* brings his life's work together in *Collected Poems 1940– 1977.* Shapiro's poems about war, love, and religion speak with an urgency and clarity that transcend poetic schools or fashions.

The title poem of John Hollander's new collection, *Spectral Emanations,* is a complex allegory with prose poem commentary on the return of the golden lamp to Jerusalem. Also ambitious and praiseworthy is Daniel Mark Epstein's *Young Men's Gold,* a long dramatic monologue by a Civil War veteran whose grandson is about to enter World War I.

Adrienne Rich writes with intimacy and strength about the possibility of communicating in *The Dream of A Common Language.* The need to be in touch with nature is reaffirmed in William Stafford's *Stories that Could Be True.* Anthony Hecht creates beauty from chaos in his treatment of death and destruction in *Millions of Strange Shadows.* In *Mind Breaths* Allen Ginsberg demonstrates his continued growth as a serious poet.

Joyce Carol Oates' *Women Whose Lives are Food, Men Whose Lives are Money* is her fifth major volume of poetry since 1969. An interesting experiment is Robert Coles' *A Festering Sweetness,* in which he sets to poetry the language of people he interviewed during his research on Americans under stress. Witter Bynner (1881–1968) is rediscovered in *Selected Poems,* edited by Richard Wilbur, and in *Light Verses and Satires,* edited by William Jay Smith.

Literary History and Criticism. Autobiography, literary reminiscences, and criticism are brought together in three interesting books. Malcolm Cowley's—*And I Worked at the Writers Trade*

© TESSA J. DALTON/COURTESY OF RANDOM HOUSE

© 1978 RANDOM HOUSE

James Michener's historical novel, *Chesapeake,* covers four centuries of life on Maryland's eastern shore.

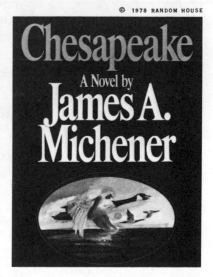

Chesapeake

A Novel by

James A. Michener

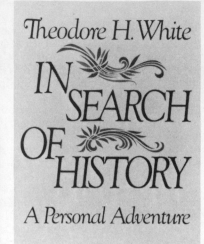

Theodore H. White, *right*, won acclaim for his autobiographical *In Search of History*. Arthur Schlesinger's *Robert Kennedy and His Times* was praised for its insight into national politics.

CARL MYDANS, COURTESY OF
HARPER & ROW

© 1978 HARPER & ROW

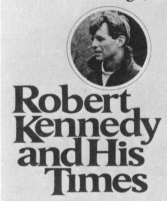

REPRINTED BY PERMISSION OF HOUGHTON MIFFLIN
COMPANY, PHOTOGRAPH BY PAUL SLADE © 1978

deals with the many authors Cowley encountered during his years of expatriation after World War I. Alfred Kazin's *New York Jew* discusses the authors of the 1940's and 50's. Tillie Olsen's *Silences* discusses her own problems as a writer, as well as the difficulties encountered by other literary figures.

In *On Moral Fiction,* the novelist John Gardner offers a spirited attack on modern fiction for its pessimism and absence of heroes. More sympathetic is Josephine Hendin's review of American fiction since 1945, *Vulnerable People.* The shallowness of Gardner's polemic is implicitly demonstrated by Lawrence Langer's *The Age of Atrocity: Death in Modern Literature* and Robert Alter's *Defenses of the Imagination: Jewish Writers and the Modern Historical Crisis.*

Cleanth Brooks, who has already written so well on Faulkner's major novels, turns to his poetry, early prose, and late novels in *William Faulkner: Toward Yoknapatawpha and Beyond.* M. L. Rosenthal deals with the classic modernist poets—Yeats, Pound, and Eliot—in *Sailing into the Unknown.* Louis Simpson discusses the next generation of 20th century poets—Thomas, Ginsberg, Plath, and Lowell—in *A Revolution in Taste.*

In *The Criminal as Victim and Artist,* H. Bruce Franklin argues that the literature created in America's prisons forms a significant body of work which should be studied on its own terms. Walter Blair's and Hamlin Hill's *American Humor: From Poor Richard to Doonesbury* adds to the remarkably few serious works on that subject.

Collections of essays are particularly important in that they preserve pieces which would otherwise remain unavailable. Eudora Welty's *The Eye of the Story* offers insightful reflections on the writing of fiction. Other novelists who have collected their critical writings are Ishmael Reed (*Shrovetide in Old New Orleans*), William H. Gass (*The World Within the Word*), and Wilfred Sheed (*The Good Word*). Howard Nemerov, the prize-winning poet, speculates on the place of the artist in a scientific age in *Figures of Thought.* Stimulating essays are brought together in Stanley Edgar Hyman's posthumous *The Critic's Credentials,* edited by Phoebe Pettingell. Irving Howe's *Celebrations and Attacks* is gleaned from 30 years of cultural commentary. Diana Trilling's *Nation* pieces are assembled in *Reviewing the Forties,* and the reviews of Nona Balakian are collected in *Critical Encounters.*

Joseph Killarin's *Selected Letters of Conrad Aiken,* Matthew Bruccoli's *Selected Letters of Frank O'Hara,* and Bruccoli's *Notebooks of F. Scott Fitzgerald* are significant contributions to the U. S. literary heritage. The journal letters between the critic F. O. Matthiessen and his friend, Russell Cheney, are brought together by Louis Hyde in *Rat & the Devil. Henry Miller: Years of Trial and Triumph 1962–1964* contains Miller's correspondences with Elmer Gertz, the lawyer who defended *Tropic of Cancer* against obscenity charges.

History and Biography. William Manchester combines lively writing and indefatigable research in *American Caesar,* the life of Douglas MacArthur. Arthur M. Schlesinger's *Robert Ken-*

nedy and His Times was criticized for its partiality but praised for its insights into national politics.

A. Scott Berg's *Max Perkins: Editor of Genius* recounts Perkins' relationship with writers from Hemingway to James Jones. Dorothy Commins sheds new light on O'Neill and Faulkner in *What Is an Editor? Saxe Commins at Work.* Richard Lebeaux' *Young Man Thoreau* is a fresh look at his metamorphosis from timid youth to social prophet.

Theodore H. White, who has chronicled several presidential campaigns, discusses his own life and work in *In Search of History.* Richard Nixon speaks of his achievements and failures in *RN.* H. R. Haldeman offers his own recollections of the Nixon presidency in *The Ends of Power.*

In *A Distant Mirror,* the historian Barbara Tuchman vividly describes the tumultuous changes in 14th century Europe and suggests that the people's inability to adjust politically or philosophically parallels the modern position.

Inventing America, Garry Wills' fresh examination of the thought of Thomas Jefferson, argues persuasively that Jefferson was heavily influenced by Scottish rationalism and intended such phrases as, "the pursuit of happiness" and "all men are created equal" to be taken literally.

A major inquiry into American jurisprudence is begun in A. Leon Higginbotham, Jr.'s *In the Matter of Color: Race and the American Legal Process: The Colonial Period.* David Stannard's *The Puritan Way of Death* is an important study of religious and social change.

Leslie Fiedler's *Freaks* is a penetrating analysis of society's fears and desires as revealed by its attitudes toward deformed people. Richard D. Altick's *The Shows of London* deals with a similar theme but focuses on the interaction of science and entertainment in the 18th and 19th centuries.

Edward O. Wilson continued his controversial inquiry into the genetic component of human behavior in *On Human Nature.*

When she died in late 1975, Hannah Arendt was working on her major philosophical inquiry, *The Life of the Mind.* The two completed volumes published in 1978, *Thinking* and *Willing,* testify to her acumen.

William Barrett discusses the relevance of philosophy in a technological age in *The Illusion Technique.* Susan Sontag's *Illness as Metaphor* is a penetrating essay showing how, before diseases were understood, they were often assumed to be the fault of the victim.

The Snow Leopard, Peter Matthiessen's account of his quest for mystical experiences in Tibet, and *The Starship and the Canoe,* Kenneth Brower's story of an astrophysicist whose son has moved to the wilderness, portray the confusion of modern culture.

JEROME H. STERN
Department of English
Florida State University

Children's Literature

There were about 1,700 children's books published in the United States in 1978, an increase of about 200 over the 1977 total. However, many of the products counted by official publishing sources were "nonbooks." Publishers flooded the mass market with coloring books, games, activity kits, calendars, riddle and joke books, and a new species of book-magazine. Noticeable in the nonbook category were cutouts, pop-ups, and stories spawned by the movie *Star Wars.*

Publishers of juvenile books were especially concerned with diminishing profits. Higher prices failed to halt the steady decline in profits. Library budgets, which publishers depend on for about 80% of their sales, were severely cut throughout the United States. Discussion at the American Library Association's (ALA) summer meeting in Chicago focused on the lack of taxpayer support for libraries and on proposals for charging library patrons.

Publishers were optimistic about paperbacks for children. They continued to produce better quality picture books and more original novels in paperback form, while engaging in more aggressive marketing techniques. They also placed renewed emphasis on bookstore sales of hardcover books.

Awards. The ALA's John Newbery Medal for the most distinguished contribution to American children's literature went to Katherine Paterson for *Bridge to Terabithia,* the story of a country boy, a city-bred girl, and their secret hideaway in the woods. The ALA's Randolph Caldecott Medal for the most distinguished picture book was awarded to Peter Spier for *Noah's Ark.* The National Book Award for children's books went to Judith and Herbert Kohl for *The View From the Oak,* an imaginative exploration of how a variety of living creatures experience time, space, and communication. Betsy Byars won the Child Study Children's Book Committee Award for *The Pinballs,* about three neglected children who meet in a foster home and gain confidence in themselves and the future.

The year saw the 50th anniversary of the first Mickey Mouse cartoon ("Steamboat Willie"), and many publishers took due notice of this observance by issuing dozens of titles featuring Disney creations. The year also saw the centennial observation of early works by the Victorian illustrator Randolph Caldecott; several publishers issued treasuries of his vintage works.

For Young Readers. For the picture book audience (ages 3 to 7), the most noteworthy books were Alice and Martin Provensen's *A Peaceable Kingdom,* a handsomely illustrated Shaker alphabet book; Raymond Briggs' *The Snowman,* a wordless picture book; Beni Montresor's *Bedtime!,* an extravagantly colorful fantasy; Mitsumasa Anno's *Anno's Journey,* a pen-and-watercolor presentation of a European trip with real and fanciful details; *Ed Emberley's A B C,* brilliantly colored and ingenious; Peter Spier's *Bored, Nothing to Do!,* about two boys who build an airplane; and Tomie de Paola's *The Clown of God,* about a juggler offering his gift to the Christ child.

For children between 6 to 10, the best books were Arnold Lobel's *Grasshopper on the Road,* six charming stories about insects; Richard Kennedy's *The Dark Princess,* an original fairytale illustrated by Donna Diamond; and Florence Parry Heide's and Sylvia Worth Van Clief's *Fables You Shouldn't Pay Any Attention To,* illustrated by Victoria Chess.

In the 9-to-12 category, the most outstanding works were Daniel M. Pinkwater's *The Last Guru,* the story of a 12-year-old boy who becomes a billionaire; Robbie Branscum's *To the Tune of a Hickory Stick,* about two children escaping from a mean guardian; Paula Fox's *The*

© 1977 BY KATHERINE PATERSON. BY PERMISSION OF THOMAS Y. CROWELL. ILLUSTRATION BY DONNA DIAMOND.

KATHERINE PATERSON

BRIDGE TO TERABITHIA

Illustrated by Donna Diamond

The 1978 John Newbery Medal was awarded to Katherine Paterson for *Bridge to Terabithia,* above. Peter Spier won the Randolph Caldecott Medal for *Noah's Ark.*

Little Swineherd and Other Tales; Sid Fleischman's *Humbug Mountain,* a comic western yarn; and Felice Holman's *The Murderer,* the story of a Jewish boy growing up in an anti-Semitic Pennsylvania mining community in 1932.

Teen-Age Literature. In novels for teen-agers and young adults there was a continuing emphasis on themes of lesbianism, homosexuality, pregnancy, runaways, retardation, alcoholism, and senility. The topics were handled with delicacy and restraint. Noteworthy in that regard is the account of the love between two young girls in Sandra Scoppettone's *Happy Endings Are All Alike.*

The most outstanding book of the year for readers 12 years old and up was *The Book of the Dun Cow,* by Walter Wangerin, Jr. In this Christian allegory, animal characters become involved in the eternal struggle between good and evil.

Other outstanding novels for the 12-and-over category are M. E. Kerr's *Gentlehands,* about a boy's urbane grandfather on Long Island who turns out to have been the commandant of a Nazi concentration camp; *Ned,* by Paxton Davis, a fictionalized biography of Lawrence of Arabia; Piri Thomas' *Stories From El Barrio,* about growing up Puerto Rican in New York City; Paul Zindel's *The Undertaker's Gone Bananas,* a slightly madcap murder mystery; Richard Peck's *Father Figure,* about a boy coming to terms with his long-absent father after his mother's death; and Lois Duncan's *Killing Mr. Griffin,* about a group of teen-agers responsible for the death of their English teacher.

Quality biographies of Mary Harris ("Mother") Jones, Edgar Cayce, R. Buckminster Fuller, Tutankhamen, Tom Seaver, and countless sports figures, appeared in 1978. Outstanding among the sports biographies was Robert Lipsyte's *Free to Be Muhammad Ali.*

GEORGE A. WOODS
Children's Book Editor, "The New York Times"

© 1977 BY PETER SPIER. REPRINTED BY PERMISSION OF DOUBLEDAY & COMPANY, INC.

NOAH'S ARK

Illustrated by Peter Spier

Canadian Literature: English

In 1978, Canadian authors writing in English dealt frequently with their country's past.

Nonfiction. Pierre Berton's *The Wild Frontier* describes the exciting lives of seven figures in Canadian history, and George Woodcock's *Faces from History* is remarkable for its photographs of 120 celebrated countrymen. Historian A. R. M. Lower examines the sweep of western civilization in his authoritative *A Pattern for History.* Ivan Avacumovic, an expert on Canadian left wing politics, traces the socialist movement from J. S. Woodsworth to Ed Broadbent in his scholarly *Socialism in Canada.*

Alex I. Inglis' *Northern Vagabond,* a biography of J. B. Tyrrell, convinces the reader that Tyrrell, a scientist, miner, and adventurer who helped open up the Canadian north at the turn of the 20th century, deserves wider recognition.

Silver Donald Cameron's *Seasons in the Rain* is a perceptive look at the province of British Columbia through word pictures of selected residents. Poet Sid Marty writes eloquent prose in *Man for the Mountains,* a chronicle of his adventures in the Canadian Rockies. With colorful text and breathtaking photography, Randy Morse's *The Mountains of Canada* describes some well-known Canadian peaks.

Peter C. Newman tells the story of a fabulously wealthy family in *Bronfman Dynasty. E. P. Taylor—The Biography of Edward Plunket Taylor,* by Richard Rohmer, is about Canada's legendary man of wealth and horse racing.

Henry Milner's *Politics in the New Quebec* is an informed view of the workings of the Parti Québécois government. Douglas H. Fullerton, a former adviser to Quebec Premier René Lévesque, provides an anti-separatist view of Quebec and its people in *The Dangerous Delusion.* Former federal cabinet minister Walter L. Gordon gives a nationalist view of the Quebec crisis and Canada's economic problems in *What's Happening in Canada. The Canadian Ethnic Mosaic,* edited by Leo Driedger of the University of Manitoba, examines immigration policy and ethnic groups in Canada.

Probably the handsomest Canadian book of 1978 was Roloff Beny's *Iran—Elements of Destiny,* with magnificent photographs and drawings. *Modern Painting in Canda,* by Terry Fenton and Karen Wilkin, is comprehensive and well illustrated. Bernard Ostry's *The Cultural Connection* looks at art in Canada and at government support of it.

In *Spellcraft,* poet Robin Skelton claims that "spell-making is a skill and can be learned by anyone with sufficient psychic energy and powers of concentration." *The Hidden Hugh MacLennan* is a selection of that leading author's letters, essays, and speeches.

In *Vineland 1000—A Canadian View of Wine,* Andrew Sharp provides witty, well informed answers to many questions about wine.

REPRINTED BY PERMISSION OF THE CANADIAN PUBLISHERS, McCLELLAND AND STEWART LIMITED, TORONTO

Aritha van Herk's award-winning first novel is *Judith*, a tale of a city woman who manages a farm.

Canada's national game is examined by humorist Eric Nicol and illustrator Dave More in *The Joy of Hockey.* Iris Nowell, in *The Dog Crisis,* points out the dangers of an unlimited dog population.

Poetry. *The Classic Shade* is a revised and updated edition of A. J. M. Smith's *Selected Poems* that reaffirms Smith's position as a leading figure in Canadian poetry.

New West Coast, edited by Fred Candelaria, is an anthology of current West Coast Canadian poetry, an impressive testimony to the number and talent of the region's poets. *The Poets of Canada,* edited by John Robert Colombo, gives samples of work by 200 Canadian poets.

Margaret Atwood, one of Canada's best known poets and novelists, illustrated and hand lettered her attractive poem for children, *Up in the Tree.* Earle Birney's *Fall by Fury,* his first volume of new poems in five years, shows him to be a master of many forms. Irving Layton, one of Canada's leading poets, had two volumes published in 1978: *The Tightrope Dancer* and *The Love Poems of Irving Layton.*

David McFadden's new volume, *On the Road Again,* is a humorous and readable poetic view of people and places across Canada. Peter Trower writes about the life of the working man in *Ragged Horizons.* The latter is Trower's fourth volume. Al Purdy's *Being Alive* is a selection of poems from 1958 to 1978.

Fiction. Canadian historian Donald Creighton turned to the novel in 1978 with *Takeover*, the story of a family distillery.

In *A Casual Affair: A Modern Fairytale*, novelist Sylvia Fraser, author of *The Candy Factory*, treats the themes of love and sex. The story of an affair between a woman artist and her diplomat lover is punctuated by the author's original fairytales.

George Bowering, a well-known Canadian poet, novelist, and short story writer, displays all three talents in *Protective Footwear: Stories and Fables*. *Skevington's Daughter*, by John Mills, is an example of a genre now rare in contemporary letters, the epistolary novel. It is also a very entertaining one. Robert Harlow's *Making Arrangements* is about some racetrack characters involved in a kidnapping.

Alice Munro, one of Canada's best short story writers, presented twelve fine tales in *Who Do You Think You Are?* Aritha van Herk won the Seal Books First Novels Award with *Judith*, the engrossing story of how a woman changes her life by leaving the city to manage a farm.

A young girl grows to womanhood in Gail Henley's *Where the Cherries End Up*. Marian Engel, in *The Glassy Sea*, describes a woman's journey on the sea of life. Selwyn Dewdney's *Christopher Breton* is about the conflicts in the life and mind of an artist.

DAVID SAVAGE
Simon Fraser University

Canadian Literature: Quebec

The literary prizes awarded to French Canadian authors in 1977–78 revealed that Quebec literature has reached a state of maturity hardly imaginable 35 years ago.

France's coveted Prix Goncourt was almost won by the Acadian writer Antonine Maillet for her novel *Les Cordes-de-bois*, a chronicle of life in a New Brunswick fishing village. In Quebec, the Prix Belgique-Canada went to Jacques Godbout, whose stature as a novelist and spokesman for the literary community is well known. The Governor General's prize for fiction went to Gabrielle Roy for her new novel, *Les Enfants de ma vie*, about her experiences as a schoolteacher in Manitoba; in the area of drama the prize went to Michel Garneau for his work in achieving a balance between personal authorship and collective creation; and in the field of nonfiction the prize went to Denis Monière for a most important book entitled *Le Développement des idéologies au Québec*, a comprehensive analysis of the major currents of thought in Quebec.

The Prix David went to Anne Hébert for the totality of her work; this includes such haunting novels of repressed passion as *Kamouraska*, as well as poetry and drama. Victor Barbeau, the founder of the Académie canadienne-française, received the Prix France-Québec at the same time that he published his memoirs, *La Tentation du passé*.

The most important novel of the year was Gérard Bessette's seventh work, *Les Anthropoïdes*. This adventure story, about an adolescent coming into maturity, takes place in the prehistoric period of Asiatic migration to North America. Other important novels include *Les Nuits de L'Underground*, a feminist perspective of lesbianism by the already familiar Marie-Claire Blais; a novel of love and loneliness by the poet Fernand Ouellette entitled *Tu regardais intensément Geneviève;* and two first novels by young authors: a tale of lost paradise called *Eldorado dans les glaces*, by Denys Chabot, and *L'Emmitouflé*, by Louis Caron, the story of a young Franco-American who deserts the army in Vietnam and takes refuge in Quebec.

The major event of the year in poetry was the long awaited publication of the *Oeuvres créatrices complètes* of the late Claude Gauvreau. This monumental work shows the hallucinatory imagination of one of Quebec's most gifted poets and dramatists. The well-known poet Paul Chamberland published *Extrême survivance, extrême poésie*, a book which takes him even further away from his previous political ideals. Mention also should be made of *Le Cercle de justice*, by Michel Beaulieu, which attempts to express the collective *québécois* self; and *Forges froides*, by Paul Chanel Malenfant, whose work shows the influences of Saint-John Perse and Alain Grandbois.

A great number of plays were produced during the year, the most successful being a theatrical version of Roch Carrier's *Il n'y a pas de pays sans grand-père, Ah, Ah!* by the enigmatic Réjean Ducharme; and a new version of Michel Tremblay's pseudo-classical tragedy *Sainte-Carmen de la Main*. The most notable plays published were Jean-Claude Germain's paraphrase of Felix-Gabriel Marchand's 19th century comedy, *Les Faux brillants*, and a new play by Robert Gurik called *Le Champion*, a reference to Muhammad Ali.

A number of studies on the historian, novelist, and priest Lionel Groulx appeared on the occasion of the 100th anniversary of his birth. The most important were a biography of his controversial nationalist by Georges-Emile Giguère, and a study of the man and his work, *Lionel Groux tel qu'en lui-même*, by the late Guy Frégault. A number of excellent literary studies also appeared. André-G. Bourrassa (*Surréalisme et littérature québécoise*) and Jean Fisette (*Le Texte automatiste*) analyzed the important surrealist period of Quebec literature; Françoise Iqbal wrote a penetrating study of the late Hubert Aquin (*Hubert Aquin romancier*), and Jacques Allard published a highly original interpretation of the French novelist Emile Zola. Finally, some important reeditions appeared: Laurent Mailhot's *Anthologie d'Arthur Buies* and Rene Dionne's edition of Antoine Gérin-Lajoie's Jean Rivard novels.

JONATHAN WEISS, *Colby College*

English Literature

A notable aspect of British letters in 1978 was the emphasis given to verse. This was evidenced by the publication of both new collections of poetry and books about poetry of the past. Numerous memoirs also appeared, and fiction continued to thrive.

Nonfiction. Thomas Hardy's significance as a poet and novelist was reviewed in 1978, the 50th anniversary of his death. Richard Little Purdy and Michael Millgate edited his *Collected Letters;* Richard H. Taylor compiled his *Personal Notebooks;* and Lance St. John Butler edited a collection of essays, *Thomas Hardy After Fifty Years.* Robert Gittings published *The Older Hardy,* the second volume of his biography; and John Bayley wrote *An Essay on Hardy,* about his literary style and insight.

Other Victorian poets are examined by Philip Henderson in *Tennyson: Poet and Prophet,* Paddy Kitchen in *Gerard Manley Hopkins,* James Milroy in *The Language of Gerard Manley Hopkins,* and Brian and Judy Dobbs in *Dante Gabriel Rossetti: An Alien Victorian.*

Poets of the 20th century are discussed in G. S. Fraser's *Essays on Twentieth-Century Poets,* John Wain's *Professing Poetry,* René Hague's *A Commentary on the Anathemata of David Jones,* and Michael Hurd's *The Ordeal of Richard Gurney.* Two modern poets, David Gascoyne and Stephen Spender, speak for themselves in *Journal, 1937–39* and *The Thirties and After,* respectively.

Novelists, painters, and thinkers of the late 19th and early 20th centuries are the subjects of other major works. Full editions of *Sir Leslie Stephen's Mausoleum Book* and *The Diary of George Gissing* were published for the first time in 1978. Lord Birkenhead's biography of Rudyard Kipling, which had been suppressed by Kipling's sister for 30 years, finally appeared. The first three volumes of *The Letters of Sidney and Beatrice Webb* also were published. Duncan

Wilson wrote *A Political Biography,* about the socialist thinker, Leonard Woolf. In *Lives and Letters,* John Carswell writes about the friends of his parents, including Katherine Mansfield, Middleton Murry, and D. H. and Frieda Lawrence. In *The Inklings,* Humphrey Carpenter gives an account of an informal club at Oxford where C. S. Lewis, J. R. R. Tolkien, Charles Williams, John Wain, and Kingsley Amis read their poems and stories. Raleigh Trevelyan's *A Pre-Raphaelite Circle* describes the group of artists that surrounded Pauline and Walter Trevelyan. In *The Case of Walter Pater,* Michael Levey considers Pater's character, milieu, and work. Richard Carline writes about his brother-in-law in *Stanley Spencer at War.* Robin Maugham records memories of his uncle in *Conversations with Willie: Recollections of W. Somerset Maugham.* In *Arnold Bennett,* Frank Swinnerton, at the age of 93, gives his impressions of an old friend. C. P. Snow considers eight realist writers in *The Realists.* And in *The Modes of Modern Writing,* David Lodge attempts to define and classify the major types of literature.

Books about the theater included Michael Baker's *The Rise of the Victorian Actor,* Alan Bird's *The Plays of Oscar Wilde,* John Lahr's *Prick Up Your Ears: The Biography of Joe Orton,* and John Arden's *To Present the Pretence: Essays on the Theatre and Its Public.* Harold Pinter published his *Poems and Prose, 1949–1977* and *The Proust Screenplay.* The latter is a film script based on Proust's *In Remembrance of Things Past.*

Piers Paul Read continued his series of books about famous events with *The Train Robbers,* an account of the British train robbery of 1963. Books surveying broader segments of social history are David Philips' *Crime and Authority in Victorian England,* Sylvia Pankhurst's *The Suffragette Movement,* David Mitchell's *Queen Christabel: A Biography of Christabel Pankhurst,* Jonathan Garnier Ruffer's *The Big Shots: Edwardian Shooting Parties,* and Duff Hart-Davis'

© 1978, SIMON AND SCHUSTER
REPRINTED BY PERMISSION

CONVERSATIONS
WITH WILLIE

Recollections of
W. Somerset Maugham
by Robin Maugham

Robin Maugham wrote of his famous uncle in *Conversations with Willie.* The *Oxford Book of Oxford,* chosen and edited by Jan Morris, traces the history of the renowned university from its founding to 1945.

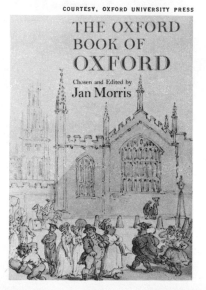

COURTESY, OXFORD UNIVERSITY PRESS

THE OXFORD
BOOK OF
OXFORD

Chosen and Edited by
Jan Morris

Monarchs of the Glen: A History of Deer-Stalking in the Scottish Highlands.

Several books published in 1978 demonstrate that the work of scientists, members of the European resistance groups, and the intelligence service was well coordinated in Britain during World War II. Brian Johnson's *The Secret War* surveys this collaboration. Jozef Garlinski's *Hitler's Last Weapons* describes major contributions of underground groups. R. V. Jones' *Most Secret War: British Scientific Intelligence, 1939–1945* and Solly Zuckerman's *From Apes to Warlords* consider the work of scientists during the war. Ronald Lewin's *Ultra Goes to War* examines the uses of information obtained from the decoding of enemy dispatches. Ewen Montagu's *Beyond Top Secret U* tells how British counter-intelligence agents misled the Nazis by including false information in messages from spies in Britain.

Another interesting view of World War II is given by Frances Partridge in her autobiographical *A Pacifist's War.* Partridge spent the war in rural Wiltshire with her husband, Ralph Partridge, and was visited by members of the Bloomsbury group. Other interesting autobiographies are Monica Dickens' lively *An Open Book;* Philip Mason's *A Shaft of Sunlight;* E. R. Dodds' *Missing Persons,* an account of his life as an Oxford don; and David Higham's *Literary Gent,* the story of his life in publishing and as literary agent for such writers as Graham Greene, John Braine, and the Sitwells.

Fiction. Two eminent writers, Graham Greene and Iris Murdoch, published major novels during the year. Typically, both produced books that are thrillers at one level and moral examinations of the human condition at another. Greene's book, *The Human Factor,* is about a British intelligence officer who, directed by his superiors to cooperate with the South African intelligence service, instead sends information to Russia because of his hatred of *apartheid.* He is finally obliged to flee to Moscow, where he leads a lonely life, separated from his black wife and adopted son. Murdoch's *The Sea, The Sea* is about Charles Arrowby, a producer and playwright in his sixties who withdraws to a remote house by the sea, intending to lead a secluded life of self-examination. Instead, past lovers, their friends and families, and a cousin come to visit him. The jealous ex-husband of a former lover tries to drown him, but he is saved by his cousin. After a brief glimpse of the spiritual power in his cousin, Arrowby returns to his worldly life.

John Wain, Kingsley Amis, Anthony Burgess, and Lawrence Durrell all produced new novels. Wain's *The Pardoner's Tale* is, like Chaucer's tale, a story within a story. Wain writes about Giles Hermitage, a middle-aged novelist whose lover has left him. Hermitage finds a more youthful lover, but she leaves him, too. During these adventures, Giles writes a novel about a middle-aged man whose spirits are revived by an actress whom he rescues from drowning. The protagonist of Amis' *Jake's Thing* is a womanizer who, at the age of 60, loses his sex drive. He consults a sex specialist, joins an encounter group, and finds himself speaking adamantly against the admission of women to his Oxford college. Burgess' book, *1985,* is a novel, and a summary and critique of Orwell's *1984,* and other essays and appendices. Included is a note on the official language of England in 1985, "Worker's English." In the novel, England's economy is controlled by Arab investors and trade unions. It is known as "Tucland," from the initials of the Trade Union Council. Bev Jones, Winston Smith's successor, resists domination until he is put in a mental hospital. Durrell's *Livia* is the second of a projected series of five novels. It, too, contains a novel within a novel, and the two narrators confer by telephone. Avignon, France, is as convincingly recreated as Alexandria was in Durrell's earlier series.

Poetry. Three major poets, R. S. Thomas, John Heath-Stubbs, and Gavin Ewart, published new collections of poems. In *Frequencies,* Thomas continues his attempt to have a dialogue with God or to seek "ultimate reality." He uses modern images—from broadcasting, photography, and space exploration—in this ancient search. John Heath-Stubbs also has a strong religious sense, but his poems, in *The Watchman's Flute,* are more urbane, humorous, and incidental. Gavin Ewart is the most secular and irreverent of the three poets. In *Or Where a Young Penguin Lies Screaming* he ridicules pomposity, humorously records some of his own observations, and assails brutality by presenting it in realistic terms.

Four other poets long familiar to readers of contemporary English verse published new books. In *The Fiesta and Other Poems,* Geoffrey Grigson displays a surer handling of language and rhythm than in some of his earlier works. Donald Davie also shows new control and purpose in *In the Stopping Train.* George Barker's *Villa Stellar* and Basil Bunting's *Collected Poems* add to the stature of these two poets. Barker's work is characterized by its witty, affectionate treatment of people and places, and Bunting's by virtuosity, strong rhythms, and a happy sensuality.

Other notable collections in a fruitful year were A. Alvarez' *Autumn to Autumn,* D. J. Enright's *Paradise Illustrated,* W. S. Graham's *Implements in Their Places,* Peter Jones' *The Garden End,* Andrew Motion's *The Pleasure Steamers,* Craig Raine's *The Onion, Memory,* Michael Schmidt's *A Change of Affairs,* E. J. Thribb's *So. Farewell Then . . . ,* Geoffrey Hill's *Tenebrae,* Peter Dale's *One Another,* Paul Mills' *Third Person,* and Gerald Dawe's *Sheltering Places.*

J. K. JOHNSTONE
University of Saskatchewan

French Literature

Even though works of nonfiction dominated French best-seller lists for most of 1978, the novel remained the most popular literary form.

Fiction. Among the most notable works by recognized authors were Hervé Bazin's *Un Feu dévore un autre feu,* a tale of love and passion against a background of history and revolution; Pierre Bourgeade's *Une Ville grise,* a mixture of political satire and eroticism; Dominique Fernandez's *L'Etoile Rose,* the confessions of a man on the way to sexual liberation; Patrick Modiano's *Rue des Boutiques Obscures,* the story of an amnesia victim in search of his memory; Henri Troyat's *Le Prisonnier Numéro 1,* a novel about Catherine the Great's Russia; Robert Merle's *Fortune de France,* an historical novel about wealthy families during the Renaissance; and Roger Peyrefitte's *L'Enfant de Coeur,* an autobiographical novel about the author's protégé, a boy whom he loved but who also ruined him.

Among the best of many novels written by women in 1978 were Marie Cardinal's *Une Vie pour deut,* a view of love after 20 years of marriage; Françoise Parturier's *Calamité mon amour,* a pitiless satire of love, lovers, and marriage; and Hélène Cixous's *Préparatifs de noces au dela de l'abîme.*

A lesser known novelist who attracted much attention in 1978 was Catherine Rihoit, a 28-year-old assistant professor at the Sorbonne. Her *Bal des Débutantes* is a rich, biting satire on men and academia, the portrayal of an absurd universe where everything proceeds through puns and word transformations.

Nonfiction. The three best-selling works in France in 1978 were nonfiction. *La Billebaude,* by Henri Vincenot, is a most pleasant picture of life, wine growing, and hunting in a small village in Burgundy. It is the heart-felt work of a man who loves his life and his land but disdains progress.

Le Tunnel, by André Lacaze, is a tale of heroism about a little known exploit achieved at the end of World War II—the building of a tunnel between Austria and Yugoslavia by French survivors of Mauthausen, a Nazi concentration camp.

Les Enfants de l'Eté, by Robert Sabatier, is a love song to the land of Provence and a series of childhood memories in the vein of the famous *Allumettes suédoises,* by the same author.

In the area of history and biography, *Moi Zénobie,* by Bernard Simiot, was an outstanding work of 1978. It is a romanticized biography of Zenobia, the famous queen of Palmyra.

Poetry. Perhaps the most important publication of 1978 in poetry was René Char's *Commune Présence,* a selection of poems which summarizes the life and work of a man whom many consider France's greatest living poet.

Samuel Beckett had published *Poèmes,* his complete works in poetry since 1937.

Marc Cholodenko (winner of the Médicis Prize in 1976) brought out a collection of excellent poems. The collection is entitled *Voyages en bordée.*

Other notable collections of poetry published in 1978 are *Vie et Mort d'une Parole,* by Jean-Pierre Colas; *Les Rues sont vides,* by Jacques Parent; and *Centaure, Poèmes à la nuit,* by Paul Marque.

PIERRE E. BRODIN
Lycée Français de New York

German Literature

West German literature developed healthily in 1978, while the expatriation of prominent East German authors again limited that nation's literary output.

West German Fiction. The original of Edgar H. Hilsenrath's *Der Nazi und der Friseur,* an impressive denunciation of Nazi inhumanities, made its long-awaited appearance in 1978. The postwar roamings of displaced Germans were treated realistically and humorously in Christine Brückner's *Nirgendwo ist Poenichen.*

The dangerous tendencies in contemporary Germany were pointed out in Ernst Jünger's *Eumeswil* and Gisela Elsner's *Der Punktsieg,* while Wolfgang Hädecke's *Die Leute von Gomorrha* visualized future ecological disasters. *Der Besiegte,* by Sigrid Brunke, and *Ein fliehendes Pferd,* by Martin Walser, received mixed reviews. Adolf Frisé published the definitive collection of Robert Musil's works, and an edition of Thomas Mann's private journals was also begun.

Nonfiction. Herbert Marcuse, in *Die Permanenz der Kunst,* dismayed his fellow revolutionaries by disavowing the claims of "socialistic realism" and reestablishing the independence of art. Less enlightening was Karl Heinz Bohrer's study of literary trends at the turn of the century, *Die Aesthetik des Schreckens.*

Gudrun Cyprian's study, *Sozialisation in Wohngemeinschaften,* exposed the depressing reality of modern utopian communes, while the Swiss Willy Zeller, in *Die unvollendete Union,* wondered about the European Customs Union. Ursula Erler wrote unevenly on feminine emancipation in *Zerstörung und Selbstzerstörung der Frau.*

General history was enriched by Gerhard Prause's courageous reinterpretation of the biblical King Herod, a knowledgeable discussion of Mao Tse-tung's successors by Klaus Mehnert, and the autobiography of Gen. Hans Speidel. Wolfram Köhler, with *Der Chef-Redakteur—Theodor Wolff,* and Margret Boveri, with *Verzweigungen,* contributed significantly to the rocky history of German liberal journalism. Valentin Senger's *Kaiserhofstrasse 12* is the autobiography of a Jewish escapee from the holocaust.

Poetry. The resigned tone of Rolf Haufs' *Die Geschwindigkeit eines einzigen Tages* and the Rilkean diction of Rainer Malkowski's *Einla-*

dung ins Freie were well accepted by critics. A number of poets formerly living in East Germany, notably Peter Huchel, Karl Krolow, Günter Kunert, and Sarah Kirsch, published new volumes.

Drama. Herbert Achternbusch's monological *Ella,* Thomas Brasch's skeptical *Rotter,* and Gerhard Roth's searching *Sehnsucht* were the outstanding serious dramas of 1978. Among Germany's best comedies of the year were Hartmut Lange's *Frau von Kauenhoven* and Martin Sperr's portrait of a confidence woman, *Die Spitzeder.* Max Frisch's treatment of death in *Triptychon* was so abstract that he felt unwilling to authorize an actual performance.

East Germany. The suppression or expatriation of politically dissident authors continued to limit the quantity of fine East German literature. Franz Fühmann, with *Bagatelle, ringsum positiv,* kept a leading role, while Christa Wolf and Stefan Heym remained under a cloud. Jurek Becker's *Schlaflose Tage* and Hans Joachim Schädlich's *Versuchte Nähe* reached only Western audiences.

ERNST ROSE
Author, "A History of German Literature"

Italian Literature

Italian literary production in 1978 reflected, in its uneasiness and evasiveness rather than in any radical, imaginative critique, the atmosphere of stifling conformism and hypocrisy which today characterize public life in Italy. Creative writers were faced with a political regime that has finally done away with any real cultural dissent. As a result, literary debates were dominated by pamphlets which were not *strictu sensu* literary but which displayed enough anticonformism to be eagerly welcomed by a readership definitely tired of official pomposity and banal left-wing jargon.

The widely sold *Giovanni Leone: La carriera di un presidente,* by Camilla Cederna, is little more than a collection of newspaper clippings. *L'affaire Moro,* by Leonardo Sciascia, is a more serious discussion of the kidnapping and assasination of former Italian Prime Minister Aldo Moro. Large portions of the book were previewed in newspapers and weekly magazines.

In the field of fiction, other than the maudlin winner of the Strega Prize, *Un altare alla madre,* by Ferdinando Camon, novels deserving attention were Giuseppe Pontiggia's *Il giocatore invisibile,* a sort of cultivated psychological thriller on the background of a large university; and Antonio Porta's *Il re del magazzino,* built on a hypothetical scenario of the end of civilization. Two debuts in novel writing were *Fratelli,* a psychological novella by Carmelo Samonà; and *L'ospedale di Manhattan,* an existential narration by Paolo Valesio.

In the field of poetry, specific titles by such well known authors as Fortini, Luzi, Sanguineti, the appearance of new poets writing in the traditional mold, and even the recent experiments in concrete and visual poetry (some of which were shown at the Biennale d'Arte in Venice), seemed to matter less than a new trend, indeed an interesting sociological phenomenon. Large groups of nonprofessional poets, especially young people, have taken to writing their own poems, reading them at public gatherings, and publishing them in newspapers, which used to be strictly political.

PAOLO VALESIO
Yale University

Japanese Literature

The young writers who were prominent on the Japanese literary scene in 1976 and 1977 were still active in 1978, but with the exception of Michitsuna Takahashi, who was awarded an Akutagawa Prize for his short story "Kugatsu no Sora" (The Sky of September), the outstanding works of the year 1978 were by the older generation of writers.

Fiction. The tone was set by Toshio Shinao's *Shi no Toge* (The Thorn of Death) which recounts the nightmares of a marriage streaked with insanity. Published in late 1977, it won the 1978 Yomiuri Literature Prize. Shinichirō Nakamura's *Natsu* (Summer), a novel about a man's search for spiritual and sexual rebirth after the suicide of his wife, captured the Tanizaki Prize. Kiichirō Takahashi also won an Akutagawa Prize for his subtle depiction of a middle-aged widow's love for her former high school student in the short story "Nobuyo." Other notable works were Yasushi Inoue's saga about Japanese immigrants in California, *Wadatsumi* (The Ocean); Junnosuke Yoshiyuki's *Yūgure made* (Until the Twilight); Kyōko Hayashi's short story sequence about Nagasaki atom bomb survivors, *Gyaman Bīdoro;* and Sawako Ariyoshi's historical novel about a switched identity, *Kazunomiya Otome* (Princess Kazu Detained). The latter was the year's best seller.

Nonfiction. An interesting aspect of Japanese nonfiction during 1978 was the increase in amateur writers, whose sundry efforts swelled the publication lists. The major accolades, however, went to established critics and biographers. Among the year's many fine critical biographies of writers and poets, the most outstanding was Shōichi Saeki's *Hyōden Mishima Yukio* (Yukio Mishima: A Critical Biography). Tōru Terada's reading of Dostoevski's work, *Dostoevski o Yomu,* was also notable.

Poetry. Poetry was as prosperous as ever in 1978, with vigorous publishing activity and a marked increase in the number of poets and readers. Especially remarkable was the wider acceptance of modern verse, which had alienated readers with its complexity and length. Among the year's collections and reissues, the selected works of the Meiji poets Mokichi Saito and Takuboku Ishikawa were the most noteworthy.

EMIKO SAKURAI, *University of Hawaii*

Soviet Literature

As has been customary in the Soviet Union for several decades, literary debates in 1978 focused on the duties and artistic goals of the Soviet writer. Although the limits of socialist realism can be stretched in this or that direction by a writer searching for the proper "epos for the revolutionary rebuilding of the world," the basic principles of the doctrine are not to be tampered with. While it is all very well for the artist to strive for freedom from dogmatism, it would be a fatal mistake for him to treat socialist realism as an open system, free to accommodate ideas from other schools. This was the tenor of leading articles in 1978 Soviet literary journals and of speeches by leading members of the powerful Association of Soviet Writers at a conference entitled "Heroes of the Great Tasks of Our Time and Soviet Literature," held in January 1978, in Tiumen.

It is difficult to single out any one of the Soviet novels published in 1978 as particularly outstanding. Once again, many of the more important works depicted Soviet heroism during World War II. These included *Tanki idut rombom* (The Tanks Go in a Romboid Formation), by A. A. Ananev, and the novel by Georgii Markov, *Orly nad Khinganom* (Eagles over Khingan). Georgii Markov and Yurii Bondarev have become the leading figures in Soviet letters. After the death of Fadeev, Bondarev occupies the influential post of the First Secretary of the policymaking Association of Soviet Writers. Markov, as shown in a recent biography by Semen Smolanski, is now considered a classic Soviet writer. Both Bondarev and Markov are having published editions of their *Selected Works*.

A picture of contemporary Soviet letters would be incomplete if one were to ignore the phenomenon of mass produced, inexpensive fiction in a form called the "Novel-Gazette." Each week, a different novel is serialized in this tabloid form. One-and-a-half to two million copies of each issue are sold at a price of 50–60 kopeks (60–70 cents). The gazette thereby fulfills the need for appropriate reading for the Soviet masses. The literature is geared to popular tastes and has wide popular appeal, although it is not necessarily of highest artistic quality. On the other hand, the gazette is obviously an attempt to propagate the officially approved interpretations of various socially and politically sensitive issues. The 1978 series began with a large work in three installments entitled *Vechnyi Zov* (Eternal Call), by Anatolii Ivanov. This edition, which was actually the second part of a novel published earlier, is a particularly crude interpretation of some troubling problems in the Soviet Union's recent past (for example, the Stalinist purges and the collaboration with Nazi Germany). Other issues of the gazette, however, are works of a less primitive character. Petr Proskurin's novel, *Imia tvoe* (Your Name), a continuation of the earlier volume, *Sud'ba* (Fate), depicts, quite suggestively at times, the problems of those who fought in the war and later had to find a place for themselves and their children in society. The tendency to glorify the Soviet system is present, but it is quite skillfully blended into a well constructed plot and interspersed with sensible philosophical reflections. Valentin

TASS FROM SOVFOTO

Yasnaya Polyana, the Museum-estate of Leo Tolstoy, south of Moscow. The 150th anniversary of the writer's birth was marked in 1978.

Rasputin's new story, *Zhivi i pomni* (Live and Remember) belongs with the best of Soviet narrative prose.

In poetry, welcome developments were the reappearances of Bella Akhmadulina and Iunna Moritz, two rare lyrical talents. Akhmadulina had published a new volume of verse, *Svecha* (The Candle), while Moritz, after a prolonged period of obscurity, came out with *Pri svete zhizni* (By the Light of Life). A volume by veteran poet V. S. Zhukov, *Ivolga*, was awarded the Gorkii Prize, while in the field of drama, the Stanislavskii Prize was awarded to S. V. Mikkalkov for his satirical play, *Pena* (Foam).

ZBIGNIEW FOLEJEWSKI
Dept. of Slavic Studies and Modern Languages
University of Ottawa

Spanish and Spanish-American Literature

The second annual Cervantes Prize, the major literary award in the Hispanic world, was granted in 1978 to the Cuban novelist Alejo Carpentier, an early and significant contributor to the contemporary prestige of the Spanish-American narrative.

Fiction. Well-known Spanish-language novelists who published during the year included the Mexican Carlos Fuentes, whose *La cabeza de la hidra* fictionalized a major international conflict over recently discovered Mexican petroleum reserves; and the Spaniard Juan Benet, whose *Del pozo y de Numa* combines both novel and essay in an innovative literary form.

Other interesting novels appearing in 1978 were the Argentinian Abel Posse's *Daimon*, and the work of such established Iberian novelists as Carmen Martín Gaite (*El cuarto de atrás*), Antonio Ferres (*Los años triunfales*), Aquilino Duque (*Los agujeros negros*), Jorge Semprún (*La segunda muerte de Ramón Mercader*), and Luis Martín Delgado (*Lobos, perros y corderos*).

Some significant prizes for fiction were awarded in 1978 as follows: the Nadal Prize to the Spaniard José Asenjo Sedano for *Conversaciones sobre la guerra*, the Ateneo de Sevilla Prize to the Spaniard José Salas Guiror for his *Un viento que pasa*, the Blasco Ibáñez Prize to the Peruvian novelist José Manuel Gutiérrez Sousa for *Así me dijo Arturo*, the Casa de las Américas Prize to the Uruguayan Eduardo Galeano for his *Días y noches de amor y guerra*, and the Gabriel Miró Prize to the Spaniard Luis Marañon for *Doce hombres grises*.

Important publications in the area of short fiction included Arturo del Hoyo's story *Las señas*, which received the important Hucha de Oro Prize: José María Alvárez Ruiz' *Grecia*, awarded the Gabriel Miró Prize for short fiction; and, the great Cuban narrator Severo Sarduy's collection of stories *Para la voz*.

Nonfiction. Major essays published included Fernando Savater's *Panfleto contra todo*, which won the Mundo Prize; Julián Marías' timely *España en nuestras manos;* Juan Goytisolo's collected political articles *Libertad, libertad, libertad;* Carmen Llorca's *Las mujeres de los dictadores;* and José María Gironella's *Carta a mi padre muerto.*

Some significant scholarly publications were Pelayo Hipólito Fernández' *Estudios sobre Ramón Pérez de Ayala;* Guillermo Díaz-Plaja's *Literatura y contorno vital;* and Luis Antonio de Villena's *Dados, amor y clérigos,* which penetrates the medieval world of student poets.

Poetry. Major prizes in this area were awarded as follows: the Adonais Prize went to the Spanish poet Eloy Sánchez Rosillo for *Maneras de estar solo*, with honorable mention for this most coveted prize going to the Argentine poet Luis de Paola for his *Música para películas mudas;* the Spaniard Manuel Caballero Bonald received the Crítica Prize for *Desacrédito del héroe;* the Leopoldo Panero Prize went to the Argentine poet Gustavo García Saravi for his *Salón para familias;* and the Boscán Prize was awarded to the Spanish poet Francisco Toledano for his *Allí estuvo el espejismo.*

A renewed interest in the protest poetry of the 1950's was reflected by the publication of two separate anthologies: Antonio Hernández' *La poética del 50* and Juan García Hortelano's *El Grupo poético de los años 50.* Further evidence of this renewed interest was the expanded re-edition of Angel González' *Palabra sobre palabra*, and the publication of a young José Antonio Gabriel y Galán's *Un pais como éste no es el mío.*

Major poets who published during the year included Angel Crespo, whose *Claro: oscuro* reflects the maturing of an excellent poet; Luis Rosales, whose *Pintura escrita* reveals a new dimension of the outstanding poet of an earlier generation; and Manuel Ríos Ruiz, whose *Razón, vigilia y elegía de Manuel Torre* reflects a new approach to popular poetry.

Significant publications by younger and promising poets included the Argentine Mercedes Roffe's *Poemas*, the Venezuelan Ramón Ordaz' *Esta ciudad mi sangre*, the exiled Cuban Roberto Cazorla's *Alas de la sombra;* and the Spaniards Ana María Fagundo's *Invención de la luz*, Miguel Pérez Riviriego's *Poemas de ausencia*, Juan María Jaen Avila's *Solitarios andenes del recuerdo*, and José María Prieto's *Lector de Fausto.*

Drama. The most significant event of the year was the performance of two unpublished plays of Federico Garcia Lorca, *El público* and *Comedia sin título*, which reveal the Andalusian playwright's innovative powers in 1936, the year of his death.

Among the major awards for drama, the Lope de Vega Prize went to Fernando Fernán Gómez for *Las bicicletas son para el verano*, and the Rómulo y Remo Prize to Julio Martínez de Velasco for *La primera aventura de don Juan.*

ALFRED RODRIGUEZ
The University of New Mexico

LONDON

In 1978, the City of London was again preoccupied with the question of financial stability rather than with the prospect of financial growth. However, with the inflation rate beginning to fall late in the year, there were the first signs of a real prospect of growth.

The slackening of controls over the money supply led to a general lack of investment confidence, and the government gave a limited stimulus to consumption in the spring budget. This was followed by near-crisis level increases in interest rates to damp down the money supply increase. Lax control of the money supply resulted in such nervousness from the investment institutions that they could not be persuaded to buy gilt-edged stocks, and in June the government had to raise interest rates and reintroduce controls on bank lending.

The *Financial Times* Ordinary Shares Index exceeded the 500 mark, then slipped back in the face of an apparently imminent election and the renewal of dividend controls as part of a further, imprecise, deflationary package. During the year, speculation against a weak pound gave way to speculation against the U. S. dollar. Because of substantial gold and dollar reserves, the marked—and expected—reduction in the value of the pound did not lead to any serious run on the pound.

But in 1978 there were the first signs that some of the City's traditional economic strengths —including such businesses as insurance and ship-brokering—were failing to meet the demands of change in international needs. The City, a source of invisible exports for the nation, is about to face much more direct international competition in these fields.

Industrial investment remained low, depressed by the country's low level of production. This was the first year of considerable revenue from North Sea Oil, and the City showed unease over possible government uses of the money. The investment confidence that the oil revenue was expected to create did not materialize. However, with the state-owned British National Oil Corporation now joined with the oil companies involved in North Sea oil production, this climate may improve.

SIMON HOGGART, *The Guardian*

LOS ANGELES

School desegregation and the effects of Proposition 13 on local budgets were the major concerns in Los Angeles during 1978.

Schools. The effort to desegregate schools in Los Angeles created much controversy throughout 1978. A plan for ordered integration was conditionally accepted by the Superior Court in February 1978. This complex plan involved lengthy busing for many students, and thus evoked great parental concern.

Finance. Proposition 13 was at first expected to have a drastically negative effect on local budgets, but subsequent state "bailout" funds prevented this. Only minor cuts were made in city and county operations, but prospects for severe retrenchment in 1979 remained. The city adopted a $1,178 million budget, prior to passage of Proposition 13.

Administrative Matters. Several members of the harbor commission were accused by the city comptroller of extravagant spending. Continuing disagreements between the two top administrators of the Port of Los Angeles led to requests for their resignations.

The director of the Department of Health Services of Los Angeles County resigned in April, criticizing the organization for being cumbersome and outdated. That same month, the city withdrew from the Greater Los Angeles Community Action Agency, a controversial antipoverty "umbrella" organization. Daryl Gates was appointed Los Angeles Police Chief in March, replacing the retired Edward M. Davis.

The Arts. Carlo Maria Giulini assumed the post of music director of the Los Angeles Philharmonic, replacing Zubin Mehta. The J. Paul Getty Art Museum in Santa Monica, which will have the largest endowment of any American museum, spent much of 1978 planning outlays.

Sports. Mayor Tom Bradley and the city council endorsed a special financial arrangement which will bring the 1984 Summer Olympics to Los Angeles. A partnership between the U. S. Olympic Committee and Los Angeles guarantees the city against any losses from the games.

CHARLES R. ADRIAN
University of California, Riverside

Eight Los Angeles taxpayers rented a billboard to thank Howard Jarvis, cosponsor of Proposition 13.

UPI

LOUISIANA

There were some bright spots in Louisiana's economy in 1978. The political front was relatively quiet.

Economy. Of vast potential significance was the legislature's passage of a first use tax on natural gas produced in federally-controlled offshore waters. At year's end, the measure was under litigation and being watched closely by other states with offshore resources. Under the legislation, Louisiana would collect 7 cents per 1,000 cubic feet (28 m³) of all gas sold, processed, treated, measured, or stored in the state. This would add some $170 million to the state treasury every year. A companion state constitutional amendment would allocate the revenues to paying off the state debt and protecting the state's eroding coastline.

Louisiana's tourist industry continued to grow rapidly. In New Orleans it was second only to the shipping industry in contributing to the city's economy. New Orleans had 20,000 hotel rooms, with another 1,500 foreseen in the next few years. The latest available figures showed that tourists spent some $1.8 billion (U. S.) in the state, with $1 billion being spent in New Orleans alone. The tourist industry supported 71,000 jobs, with an annual payroll of $415 million. New Orleans voters approved an additional 1% tax on the city's hotel and motel rooms to finance the construction of a new exhibition and convention center.

The state's industrial investment more than doubled in 1978, from $1.1 to $2.33 billion. Much of the money was used for expanding Louisiana's oil refineries and utility generating plants. Although the labor force grew from 1,496,000 to 1,621,000, the unemployment rate rose from 6.8% to 7.2%. Per capita personal income grew by 10.1%, from $5,405 to $5,950.

Politics. Seven of the state's eight U. S. Representatives were reelected in November. The sole newcomer was State Rep. Claude "Buddy" Leach, a Democrat who received a last minute endorsement from retiring Rep. Joe Waggonner. U. S. Sen. J. Bennett Johnston turned back a challenge from State Rep. Louis "Woody" Jenkins. There was no gubernatorial election.

Late in the year, New Orleans Mayor Ernest Morial proposed a series of city tax increases which would cost the average homeowner between $600 and $700 annually. Included in his proposal was a metropolitan earnings tax, which received sharp opposition from surrounding parishes (counties).

Former U. S. Rep. Otto Passman was indicted for allegedly accepting bribes from the Korean influence buyer, Tongsun Park.

Oil. In September, 42,000 barrels of oil were lost when a salt dome near Hackberry exploded and caught fire. The supply was part of the national Strategic Petroleum Reserve Program. Under this program, the government hopes to have stored some one billion barrels by 1985. At the time of the explosion, there were some 44 million barrels of oil in Louisiana salt domes.

JOSEPH W. DARBY III
"The New Orleans Times-Picayune"

LUXEMBOURG

Politics. The coalition formed by Prime Minister Gaston Thorn between his Democratic Party and the Socialists remained in control despite a plurality of only three seats in the Chamber of Deputies; the 28 seats held by the opposition were divided among the relatively conservative Christian Socialists, the Social Democratic Party, and the Communists. While all parties shared a concern for the future of the economy, differences did arise over abortion and divorce. There was debate over plans to construct a large facility for the expanded European Parliament.

Economy. The gross national product for 1977 (U. S.$2.5 billion) reflected a disappointing 1.3% increase at constant (1970) prices. Unemployment was less than 1%, and the inflation rate fell to 6.7%. The steel industry suffered sharp losses, but ARBED, the duchy's major steel group, planned to invest 18 billion (U. S.) francs from 1978 to 1982 to modernize its plants to meet foreign competition.

Losses in the steel sector were partially compensated for by the growth of new industries. One result of a labor-government-industry conference in April 1977 was the formation of

──── LOUISIANA · Information Highlights ────

Area: 48,523 square miles (125,675 km²).
Population (Jan. 1978 est.): 3,947,000.
Chief Cities (1970 census): Baton Rouge, the capital, 165,963; New Orleans, 593,471; Shreveport, 182,064.
Government (1978): *Chief Officers*—governor, Edwin W. Edwards (D); lt. gov., James E. Fitzmorris, Jr. (D). *Legislature*—Senate, 39 members; House of Representatives, 105 members.
Education (1977–78): *Enrollment*—public elementary schools, 577,452 pupils; public secondary, 261,548; colleges and universities, 153,982 students. *Public school expenditures,* $1,242,251,000 ($1,366 per pupil).
State Finances (fiscal year 1977): *Revenues,* $3,685,114,000; *expenditures,* $3,646,738,000.
Personal Income (1977): $23,187,000,000; per capita, $5,950.
Labor Force (July 1978): *Nonagricultural wage and salary earners,* 1,357,800; *unemployed,* 116,700 (7.2% of total force).

──── LUXEMBOURG · Information Highlights ────

Official Name: Grand Duchy of Luxembourg.
Area: 999 square miles (2,586 km²).
Population (1978 est.): 400,000.
Chief Cities (1976 est.): Luxembourg, the capital, 80,000; (1975 est.): Esch-sur-Alzette, 27,700; Differdange, 18,300.
Government: *Head of state,* Jean, grand duke (acceded 1964). *Head of government,* Gaston Thorn, prime minister (took office June 18, 1974). *Legislature* (unicameral)—Chamber of Deputies.
Monetary Unit: Franc (30.55 francs equal U. S.$1, Sept. 1978).
Manufactures (major products): Steel, rubber, synthetic fibers.
Agriculture (major products): Livestock, dairy products, wine.

the National Society for Credit and Investment (SNCI). SNCI, which began operating in January 1978, will assist the government in attracting foreign investments.

The banking sector has shown the most rapid growth. There were some 94 banks located in the duchy by the end of the year. The $150 million they paid in taxes in 1977 was 10% of the national budget. The increasing revenue from the banking sector has enabled the Thorn ministry to avoid austerity measures.

JONATHAN E. HELMREICH, *Allegheny College*

MAINE

Elections. On March 31, James B. Longley, the only Independent governor in the United States, announced he would not seek reelection. This opened the race to three aspirants: Republican Linwood Palmer, a leader in the state legislature; Joseph Brennan, the Democratic attorney general; and Herman "Buddy" Frankland, a Baptist minister from Bangor who sought to continue the Independent administration. In November, voters put Brennan in Blaine House as Maine's 68th governor. He took 48% of the vote. Palmer received 34% and Frankland 18%.

The U. S. Senate race between incumbent William Hathaway (D) and Congressman William Cohen (R) received national attention. The popular Cohen won an easy victory, garnering 57% of the vote. Congressman David Emery (R) and newcomer Olympia Snow (R) were elected to Congress, leaving Sen. Edmund Muskie as the only Democratic member of Maine's Congressional delegation. Several state legislative races were extremely close. Following recounts, Republicans have control of the Senate and Democrats control the House.

Indian Land Claim. A claim by Maine Indians to 12 million acres (4,860,000 ha) of land made news throughout the year. In February, a three-man government task force recommended an out-of-court settlement, which included a provision requiring 14 major land owners to sell 300,000 acres (121,500 ha) to the Passamaquoddy and Penobscot Indians for $5 an acre. The proposal was roundly denounced as confiscatory by Attorney General Brennan, Governor Longley, and congressmen Cohen and Emery, but it received sympathetic reception from senators Hathaway and Muskie. The stage was set for a war of nerves between the federal government, which supported the Indians, and state officials, who argued for either a court test on the merits or total assumption of responsibility by the federal government for any settlement. In October, in a surprise move, President Carter announced a federal resolution of the two-and-a-half-year-old case along lines suggested by Brennan, Longley, and Cohen. Many observers believed that this volatile issue was largely responsible for Brennan's election as governor and that it contributed to the defeat of Senator

UPI

Maine's newly elected senator, Rep. William Cohen (R) and his family pose for a victory photograph.

Hathaway. By December, only the Indians appeared reluctant to accept the Carter solution which, ironically, Senator Hathaway was credited with formulating.

Economy. Maine enjoyed a good year economically, especially in the manufacturing and tourist industries. However, a drought caused widespread loss in the Aroostook potato crops and was responsible for an extremely low blueberry yield.

The state tax base produced a surplus of nearly $30 million, two thirds of which the governor and legislature voted to rebate to taxpayers.

Environment. Governor Longley finally declared his opposition to the controversial Dickey-Lincoln hydroelectric plant in northern Maine. The project appeared doomed.

RONALD F. BANKS
Department of History
University of Maine, Orono

――――――― **MAINE** · Information Highlights ―――――――

Area: 33,215 square miles (86,027 km²).
Population (Jan. 1978 est.): 1,092,000.
Chief Cities (1970 census): Augusta, the capital, 21,945; Portland, 65,116; Lewiston, 41,779; Bangor, 33,168.
Government (1978): *Chief Officers*—governor, James B. Longley (I). *Legislature*—Senate, 33; House of Representatives, 151 members.
Education (1977–78): *Enrollment*—public elementary schools, 166,704 pupils; public secondary, 79,064; colleges and universities, 40,172 students. *Public school expenditures,* $355,000,000 ($1,427 per pupil).
State Finances (fiscal year 1977): *Revenues,* $1,024,-998,000; *expenditures,* $981,474,000.
Personal Income (1977): $6,221,000,000; per capita, $5,734.
Labor Force (July 1978): *Nonagricultural wage and salary earners,* 410,600; *unemployed,* 32,700 (6.6% of total force).

MALAYSIA

The "boat people" presented major problems for Malaysia's ruling coalition, which was returned to power in federal and state elections.

Elections. On July 8 the ruling National Front Coalition, led by Prime Minister Hussein bin Dato Onn, won a resounding victory at the polls in state and federal elections. The Front captured 132 of the 154 seats in the federal Parliament and retained control of the 10 states which held elections at that time. The primary opposition group, the ethnic-Chinese-based Democratic Action party, increased its number of seats in Parliament from 8 to 16. The Pan-Malaysian Islamic party won 6 seats.

On July 27 Hussein formed a new 23-member cabinet, retaining most members of the previous cabinet, but increasing the number of ethnic Chinese representatives from 5 to 6.

Earlier in the year, the state of Kelantan held elections one month after the federal government ended direct rule of the state on February 12. The United Malays Organization and 2 of its supporting parties won 34 of the 36 seats in the Kelantan State Legislative Assembly.

"Boat People." The number of Vietnamese refugees in makeshift camps on Malaysian shores continued to grow, surpassing 40,000. In the past, the refugees arrived in small groups, but in 1978 they began to arrive en masse. They were turned away by Malay officials, who called upon nations which had played a role in the Indochina war to accept the refugees.

In November more than 2,500 refugees aboard a freighter in the South China Sea off the Malay coast sought permission to land in Malaysia. The government, vowing to tow the ship out to sea, refused. Two hundred of those aboard the freighter crowded onto a smaller vessel hoping to reach shore, in defiance of the government. The boat capsized and 197 drowned. Two days earlier a fishing boat carrying some 250 refugees in the port of Kuala Trengganu was turned around by police and towed toward the sea. The fishing vessel ran aground and capsized. Most of those aboard were lost.

KARL J. PELZER
Professor Emeritus, Yale University

——— **MALAYSIA · Information Highlights** ———
Official Name: Malaysia.
Location: Southeast Asia.
Area: 127,315 square miles (329,744 km²).
Population (1978 est.): 13,000,000.
Chief Cities (1975 est.): Kuala Lumpur, the capital, 500,000; Pinang, 280,000; Ipoh, 255,000.
Government: *Head of state,* Sultan Yahya Putra (took office Sept. 1975). *Head of government,* Hussein bin Dato Onn, prime minister (took office Jan. 1976). *Legislature*—Parliament: Dewan Negara (Senate) and Dewan Ra'ayat (House of Representatives).
Monetary Unit: Ringgit (Malaysian dollar) (2.28 ringgits equal U.S.$1, Sept. 1978).
Manufactures (major products): Steel, automobiles, electronics.
Agriculture (major products): Rubber, palm oil, pepper, timber, cocoa, rice, pine.

MANITOBA

Politics. During its first year in office, Manitoba's Progressive Conservative government proved itself to be one of the most fiscally responsible governments in Canada. On October 24, Premier Sterling Lyon expressed pride in his ministry's prudence and restraint. The annual deficit had been lowered by more than 43%, and government spending had increased by only 3%. The civil service had been reduced by some 1,800 persons, and provincial tax cuts totaled $83 million. Manitoba, he said, is one of the few places in North America where government spending was reduced in real terms without a measurable decrease in the quality or availability of essential government services.

The legislature sat from March 16 to July 21, its longest session ever. The budget, presented by Finance Minister Donald Craik on April 10, predicted revenues of (c.) $1.54 billion (up by 4%), expenditures of $1.65 billion (up by 2.9%), and a deficit of $114 million.

Labor. A record number of strikes plagued Manitoba in 1978. By the end of September, the provincial labor department recorded 275,952 days lost through strikes. Particularly hard hit were the construction, food retailing, and meatpacking industries.

"Mincome Manitoba." The first Canadian experiment in a guaranteed annual income, "Mincome Manitoba," ended on Jan. 1, 1978. A family of four received an annual income of between $5,000 and $7,000 and was permitted to retain a certain percentage of income earned outside the plan. Some 1,300 families were involved. The project had a budget of $17.5 million, 75% paid by the federal government and 25% by the provincial government.

Garrison Dam. The controversial Garrison Project, which could have diverted polluted water from North Dakota into Manitoba, was at last resolved. In August, the U. S. Senate approved a resolution stating that all waters diverted by the project would be kept in the United States.

JOHN A. BOVEY
Provincial Archivist of Manitoba

——— **MANITOBA · Information Highlights** ———
Area: 251,000 square miles (650,090 km²).
Population (1978 est.): 1,036,000.
Chief City (1976 census): Winnipeg, the capital, 560,874.
Government (1978): *Chief Officers*—lt. gov., Francis L. Jobin; premier, Sterling R. Lyon (Progressive Conservative party); chief justice, Court of Appeal, Samuel Freedman; Court of Queen's Bench, A. S. Dewar. *Legislature*—Legislative Assembly, 57 members.
Education (1976–77): *Enrollment:* public elementary and secondary schools, 216,050; private schools, 1,480; Indian (federal) schools, 5,910; post-secondary, 22,-230 students. *Total expenditures,* $409,215,000.
Public Finance (1978–79): *Revenues,* $1,536,000,000; *expenditures,* $1,650,000,000.
Personal Income (average weekly salary, May 1978): $235.89.
Unemployment Rate (July 1978, seasonally adjusted): 6.7%.
(All monetary figures given in Canadian dollars.)

The U. S. Coast Guard cutter *Cuyahoga* is returned to shore following a collision with an Argentine freighter in Chesapeake Bay. Eleven Coast Guardsmen drowned in the October accident.

UPI

MARYLAND

Elections. Harry R. Hughes's victory over Acting Gov. Blair Lee in the state's Democratic primary demonstrated a strong public rejection of the party's Maryland machine, associated with suspended Gov. Marvin Mandel. Lee, as lieutenant governor, had succeeded Mandel when he was convicted of political corruption.

Hughes had resigned in 1977 as secretary of transportation in the Mandel administration, complaining of undue influence over selection of a firm to manage construction of the multimillion-dollar Baltimore subway project. Campaigning heavily with "integrity" as his theme, Hughes easily defeated former Sen. J. Glenn Beall in the general election. Voters also sent four women to Congress.

Amid much controversy over loss of open space, Baltimore voters approved a plan to build a cluster of shops and restaurants, similar to Boston's Quincy Market complex, in a park beside Baltimore harbor, the heart of the city's revitalization area.

Legislation. Laws enacted by the 1978 legislative session provided for capital punishment, some $70 million in property tax relief for homeowners hurt by inflation-induced assessment increases, limited state financial aid for poor women seeking abortions, fair distribution of property in divorces, sweeping penalties against anyone selling or distributing pornographic material, and an increase in the governor's salary from $25,000 to $60,000 a year.

Strikes. The early 1978 coal miners' strike, causing a shortage of local coal, and an abnormally harsh winter combined to precipitate an emergency in western Maryland. Most businesses and industries curtailed operations or closed under a governor's order to conserve energy. Homeowners were hit with electric bills as high as $250 a month when utilities purchased expensive fuel or bought power from out-of-state firms.

After months of fruitless negotiations with the Norfolk & Western railroad, striking railroad clerks set up picket lines in September at the N&W–Chessie System interchange in western Maryland. When other railroad employees honored their strike, the shutdown quickly spread, crippling two thirds of the nation's rail service for several days.

Scandals. An investigation of the General Services Administration, including allegations that federal employees demanded bribes from contractors, grew from a tip given federal prosecutors in Baltimore in 1977 into a nationwide, $100 million scandal in 1978.

Federal charges of bribery and corruption in office against former Maryland congressman Edward A. Garmatz were dismissed.

Disaster. A collision between the Argentine freighter *Santa Cruz* and the U. S. Coast Guard training vessel *Cuyahoga* in Chesapeake Bay sank the *Cuyahoga* and drowned 11 Coast Guardsmen. An inquiry board's investigation pointed toward the need for important changes in the training of U. S. seamen.

Literature. William W. Warner's *Beautiful Swimmers*, the Pulitzer Prize–winning nonfiction study of watermen and crabs of the Chesapeake Bay, was joined on bookshelves by James A. Michener's bestselling *Chesapeake*, a fiction work exploring the history of life along the bay. Michener has become a resident of Maryland's Eastern Shore, where the influence of the Chesapeake on everyday life is profound.

PEGGY CUNNINGHAM
"The News American," Baltimore

MARYLAND • Information Highlights

Area: 10,577 square miles (27,394 km²).

Population (Jan. 1978 est.): 4,149,000.

Chief Cities (1970 census): Annapolis, the capital, 30,095; Baltimore, 905,759; Rockville, 41,821; Hagerstown, 35,862; Bowie, 35,028.

Government (1978): *Chief Officers*—Acting governor, Blair Lee III (D). *General Assembly*—Senate, 47 members; House of Delegates, 141 members.

Education (1977–78): *Enrollment*—public elementary schools, 421,488 pupils; public secondary, 415,464; colleges and universities, 216,583 students. *Public school expenditures,* $1,764,992,000 ($1,912 per pupil).

State Finances (fiscal year 1977): *Revenues,* $3,933,699,000; *expenditures,* $3,918,843,000.

Personal Income (1977): $31,337,000,000; per capita, $7,572.

Labor Force (July 1978): *Nonagricultural wage and salary earners,* 1,586,900; *unemployed,* 98,400 (4.8% of total force).

UPI

Robert Bonin and his wife, Angela, enter a superior court. The Massachusetts Superior Court Chief Justice resigned following a court censure for misconduct.

MASSACHUSETTS

Election upsets highlighted events in Massachusetts in 1978.

Elections. Gov. Michael S. Dukakis, seeking election to a second four-year term, was defeated in the September 19 primary by Edward J. King, a conservative Democrat. King was formerly head of the New England Council, an organization which promotes business development in the region, and of the Massachusetts Port Authority. Dukakis' loss stunned many; his renomination had been regarded as a certainty. The governor's popularity had soared earlier in the year when he led the cleanup operations following a snowstorm which paralyzed the state for one week in early February. In the general election, King went on to defeat Republican Francis W. Hatch, Jr., an eight-term state legislator and the minority leader of the Massachusetts House of Representatives. King's campaign was marked by an emphasis on such issues as abortion, the restoration of capital punishment, and the reduction of state expenditures to cut property taxes.

The November 7 general election also saw the defeat of incumbent Republican Sen. Edward Brooke. Brooke, elected to the Senate in 1966 and the only black to hold that office in the 20th century, was beaten by Paul E. Tsongas, a two-term congressman from the state's fifth district. The year had not been a happy one for Brooke.

A stormy and protracted divorce trial flared up anew in the months preceeding the election. An investigation into Brooke's financial holdings by the U. S. Senate Committee on Ethics did little to help his campaign. Tsongas, running for his first statewide office, had decided to seek the Senate seat after Lt. Gov. Thomas P. O'Neill, III, son of the speaker of the U. S. House of Representatives, declined to run against Brooke. O'Neill went on to win reelection as King's running mate.

In other important electoral contests, Francis X. Bellotti easily won reelection as attorney general. The Democrats also triumphed in races for secretary of state, treasurer, and auditor. In Congressional contests, James M. Shannon, a Democrat, was elected to Tsongas' seat in the fifth district. Democrat Nicholas Mavroulas, mayor of the city of Peabody, won the sixth district seat after incumbent Michael J. Harrington chose not to run again. In the eleventh district, a vacancy created by the retirement of James A. Burke was filled by Democrat Brian Donnelly. Incumbents won in all the remaining congressional races, keeping the Massachusetts delegation at ten Democrats and two Republicans. A proposed amendment to the state constitution, allowing residential and business properties to be taxed at different rates, became a highly controversial issue in the elections. Voters overwhelmingly approved the proposal, which was seen as a victory for Boston Mayor Kevin H. White (*see* BOSTON).

Improprieties. State Superior Court Chief Justice Robert M. Bonin resigned in the wake of misconduct charges, including an allegation that he had attended a "gay rights" rally at which pending court cases were discussed. Bonin's resignation came after censure by the Supreme Judicial Court.

The continuing investigation into alleged payoffs to state legislators by a consulting firm led to the resignation of state Senate President Kevin Harrington, who had been implicated in the scandal.

HARVEY BOULAY
Boston University

MASSACHUSETTS · Information Highlights

Area: 8,257 square miles (21,386 km²).
Population (Jan. 1978 est.): 5,781,000.
Chief Cities (1970 census): Boston, the capial, 641,071; Worcester, 176,572; Springfield, 163,905.
Government (1978): *Chief Officers*—governor, Michael S. Dukakis (D); lt. gov., Thomas P. O'Neill III (D). *General Court*—Senate, 40 members; House of Representatives, 240 members.
Education (1977–78): *Enrollment*—public elementary schools, 603,204 pupils; public secondary, 561,330; colleges and universities, 375,380 students. *Public school expenditures,* $2,467,658 ($1,923 per pupil).
State Finances (fiscal year 1977): *Revenues,* $5,669,-948,000; *expenditures,* $5,520,145,000.
Personal Income (1977): $41,964,000,000; per capita, $7,258.
Labor Force (June 1978): *Nonagricultural wage and salary earners,* 2,516,500; *unemployed,* 203,900 (6.9% of total force).

MEDICINE AND HEALTH

Environmental, political, and scientific issues influenced the field of medicine and health in 1978. The year's biggest news was reproductive and genetic: the birth of a baby fertilized outside its mother's womb and the successful application of recombinant deoxyribonucleic acid (DNA) research. To some, these developments represented the fulfillment of the worst science fiction prophecies: test-tube babies and genetic engineering. To others, these advances augured well for humanity, demonstrating an increasing ability to collaborate with natural forces.

Obstetrics. A healthy baby girl, whose commencement had taken place in a laboratory, was born in England to parents who were unable to have a child by ordinary means. This was the first successful *in vitro* growth of a human embryo. The embryo was made with egg and sperm cells carefully collected from the parents and implanted in the mother's body. This method of fertilization, developed chiefly by a British obstetrician and a physiologist, is now being attempted by several teams of U. S. investigators. The technique has widespread implications for childless couples all over the world.

Investigators in California proved, for the first time in history, that each of a pair of dizygotic twins was the child of a different father. Although reports of this "super-fecundation" phenomenon have circulated for centuries, it was now possible to test the babies and their parents for histocompatibility (HLA) antigens. These tissue markers identify a body's cells as belonging to a particular individual. In this case, differing HLA antigens in the infants reduced the possibility that they had the same father to less than 1 in 140,000.

The "alternative birthing" movement continued to spread in 1978. More women declined to have their babies under sterile, technologically sophisticated hospital conditions. A California midwife was indicted for second degree murder when an infant she delivered died because of a rare abnormality—a "true knot" in the umbilical cord. But highly mechanized obstetrical procedures, it was found, may not always produce the desired improvements in maternal and infant health. One study showed that if high-risk mothers were selected by common sense methods (e.g., on the basis of age and previous obstetric history) and their babies were routinely delivered by cesarean section, the results would be better for both mothers and babies than if the decision to perform the cesarean depended on monitoring the mother during labor. Monitoring techniques not only produce a higher number of infections, but often indicate trouble only when the infant is already injured.

Medical Costs. U. S. health care expenditures continued to climb in 1978. Nearly 12% of federal tax revenues went to health costs; and hospital costs rose by more than 13.5%, nearly 3% more than the general rise in the consumer price index. At the same time, government officials criticized the medical profession, saying that the nation suffers from a maldistribution, rather than a shortage, of physicians. Medical school enrollment continued to decline for the second straight year; in 1978 it decreased by 10%.

New Drug Developments. Just a few years after a fierce national debate over whether to permit experimentation with recombinant, self-replicating DNA, California scientists used the substance to make human insulin. By splicing genetic material, they programmed the *E. coli* bacterium to produce the hormone that millions of diabetics require every day to regulate their carbohydrate metabolism. Results of this work should make high quality insulin cheaper and more available. Representatives of the pharmaceutical industry said, however, that the laboratory-made hormone was still years away from commercial distribution.

Major news in the drug therapy field centered on agents for preventing or ameliorating circulatory disease, especially heart attacks. The kinases, a group of proenzymes that helps dissolve blood clots, were made available for investigation. Preliminary studies showed them to be effective in preventing second heart attacks.

UPI

Large-type London newspaper headlines announce the birth of the first test-tube baby.

Meanwhile, research on several groups of drugs to prevent the clumping of blood components called "platelets" yielded significant results. Investigators believe that long-term use of these so-called antiplatelet drugs, including aspirin and the antigout drug, dipyridamole, could protect people against several types of heart disease.

Other newsworthy drugs for treating, preventing, or reversing heart disease included anti-arrhythmic agents, which act to regulate severe quickening (tachycardia) or slowing (bradycardia) of heartbeat. One study showed that the steady decline in deaths from heart disease in the United States may be related to fluoridation of municipal water supplies. Although deaths from cardiac disease between 1950 and 1970 declined by 15 to 20% in the country as a whole, the decrease was 2.5 to 3 times greater in cities with fluoridated water.

Cardiology. Other developments in cardiology included continuing debate over the results of a Veterans' Administration (VA) study of cardiac bypass surgery for coronary artery disease. The study seemed to show that the operation, in which vein grafts, usually from the saphenous vein in the leg, are used to bypass blocked segments of the coronary arteries, did not significantly increase health and survival. Critics maintained that these results were due to flaws in the study's design. Another new study showed that deterioration in the grafted vessels was due to progression of the original disease, not to the operation.

In an effort to find an alternative to bypass surgery, a team of New York investigators tried compressing the fatty plaque in patients' arteries by means of a balloon-tipped catheter. Bypass is often recommended for patients whose heart vessels have become severely narrowed by the accumulation of plaque. The mechanical compression, performed on patients under anesthesia, costs only one-tenth as much as bypass surgery. Although the technique may help 10% to 15% of surgical candidates, the technique is too new to permit any conclusions about its long-term effectiveness. In another study, investigators proved that passive cigarette smoking is harmful to people with angina pectoris, a painful heart ailment often due to narrowed coronary arteries. Staying in a room with heavy smokers for several hours increased heart rates and lowered exercise capacity in patients with angina.

Medicine and the Law. In New York State, several hospitals were charged with allowing surgical supply salesmen to assist in operations. In several cases, salesmen anonymously admitted to having used surgical equipment, such as staple guns and bone saws, on patients undergoing surgery.

As more electric light and power companies applied for licenses to construct new plants using nuclear fuels, radiation biologists became more concerned about the risks involved. Geneticists and radiologists joined other scientists in warn-

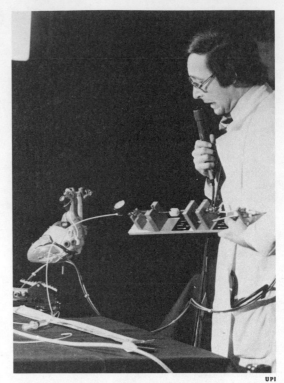

UPI

A doctor demonstrates a small balloon-tipped catheter used to clear nearly clogged heart arteries.

ing against the possible deleterious effects of increasing background radiation, as well as the hazards of long-term storage of nuclear wastes. Among possible ill effects mentioned were genetic mutation and an increase in cancers of all kind, including leukemias.

The Office of Management and Budget (OMB) questioned the usefulness of Professional Standards Review Organizations (PSROs), panels of physicians federally mandated to survey patterns of practice in a given area and to investigate individual practitioners whose patterns deviate widely. If the PSROs do not succeed in at least slowing the increase in health care costs, said the government agency, the program will not continue.

In March 1977, the U. S. Congress agreed to delay for 18 months its proposed ban on saccharin, the artificial sweetener suspected of causing cancer. As the deadline approached, proponents of the ban received new support. Defendants of the noncaloric sweetener argued that its risks were offset by its benefits to diabetics and the obese, but one study showed that use of saccharin may not deter people from using sugar also. For the first time, salt was mentioned as a candidate for the list of food additives that must be specified on package labels. Because salt demonstrably raises blood pressure, Food and Drug Administration (FDA) regulations may soon require food companies to state the salt content of prepared foods. This would allow people with hypertension to avoid unknown sources of dietary salt.

Obesity. In recent years, obesity has emerged as a national health problem. In 1978, The Metropolitan Life Insurance Company released figures showing that since 1961 the average weights of adult American men and women had increased by 0.5 to 1.5%, regardless of height. Many investigators believe the national trend toward obesity is due to overfeeding in infancy. This produces an excess of fat cells which may predispose an individual to continue overeating. Others maintained, however, that obesity has many causes and that overfeeding in infancy must share the blame with other chemical, genetic, and environmental factors.

Genetics. In 1978, for the first time, investigators were able to see a genetic defect. Using a technique called electrophoresis (observation of the movement of charged particles suspended in liquid under the influence of an applied electric field) scientists were able to observe and photograph fragments of DNA in members of a Turkish family with an inherited metabolic defect. Good news for women over 35 was the discovery that the genetic anomaly trisomy 21, the most frequent cause of Down's syndrome, or mongolism, is not associated only with increasing maternal age but with many other factors.

A study in Sweden gave the first plausible support to the hypothesis that chemical dependency may have at least a partial genetic component. In a group of more than 2,300 adopted individuals, investigators found that rates of drug abuse (including alcoholism) were significantly elevated for adopted men whose biological fathers had been chemically dependent. No correlation was found for adopted women or biological mothers.

Cancer. Substances called tumor cell markers assumed even greater importance in cancer research in 1978, as investigators pursued clues to the developmental sequence of neoplasia. High molecular weight proteins called carcino-embryonic antigens (CEA) are the best known of this group of substances. Studies have dealt with the appearance of tumor cell markers in the body fluids of cancer patients in amounts that fluctuate according to the time of day, type of therapy the patient is receiving, patient's response to the therapy, and cycle of administration of therapy. Investigators believe that if they knew what factors govern the release of these markers, called isoenzymes and isohormones, from the cancerous tissues, they would gain further insight into the natural history of cancer.

Preliminary studies of patients with prostate cancer showed that acid phosphatase, an enzyme measured by radioimmunoassay (the technique developed by Solomon Berson and 1977 Nobel laureate Rosalyn Yalow), may be a reliable indicator of the disease. Although measurable quantities of the enzyme were found most often in the serum of men with advanced stages of the disease, investigators hoped that technical refinements might permit mass screenings for prostate cancer.

Cancer epidemiologists from the National Cancer Institute (NCI) and the Center for Disease Control (CDC) found an explanation for the extremely high rate of deaths from lung cancer in men living on the southeastern coast of the United States. During World War II, the major industry in the area was shipbuilding. Occupational exposures to asbestos and other shipyard substances resulted in what epidemiologists call "excess mortality." NCI and CDC believe that these exposures were synergistic with cigarette smoking: they induced lung cancer by themselves but were even more harmful in men who smoked.

Bone Healing. Electromagnetic therapy for slow healing fractures was still in the experimental stage in 1978, but investigators reported good results. Some patients had electrodes implanted at the fracture site and others received charges from sources outside their bodies. Mending of broken bones can be hastened and improved by beaming electromagnetic impulses directly to the bone ends, and batteries can be carried inside the plaster cast. Some orthopedists remained skeptical, but others were convinced that electromagnetic enhancement of healing may soon become commonplace for many bone breaks.

Infectious Diseases. The annual influenza epidemic involved several viral strains, one of them called the Soviet flu. Coming from central Asia, the Soviet flu afflicted President Leonid Brezhnev at the end of 1977. Scientists determined this was the same strain that had been so prevalent throughout the world between 1947 and 1957. Thus, when the virus arrived in the United States in February 1978, young people were hardest hit. Older Americans may have had immunity from previous encounters. Epidemics swept the U. S. Air Force and Naval academies. The worst flu of the season, however, was caused by a native strain of virus, A/Texas. Fortunately, many Americans had cross-immunity from previous vaccinations.

Legionnaires' disease, the bronchial pneumonia that first appeared in Philadelphia in 1976, reappeared in 1978 with its characteristic symptom complex of high fever, diarrhea, cough, and bronchospasm. Outbreaks occurred in Bloomington, Ind., and New York City's garment district. The most unusual cases of legionnaires' disease occurred in five kidney transplant recipients. All of these patients were receiving corticosteroids to suppress their immunity to the transplanted organs. Investigators theorized that the immunosuppressive effect of the steroid therapy may have contributed to the patients' vulnerability to the legionnaire bacillus.

Venereal disease continued in epidemic proportions, the most common being nonspecific or nongonorrheal urethritis (NGU).

MARTHA ROTH, *Medical Writer and Editor*

Mental Health

In 1978 mental health professionals studied and debated the pressing institutional and technical issues of recent years. Alcoholism, the effects of medication for various disorders, child and geriatric mental health, and biofeedback were major areas of research, while community facilities and patients' rights remained popular areas of debate.

Alcoholism. Alcoholism continued to be one of the most devastating health problems in the United States in 1978. Clinical research indicated that even moderate amounts of alcohol significantly affect brain function, that maternal alcohol consumption contributes to fetal malformations, and that alcoholism may be related to genetic factors. A controversial Rand Corporation study reported that a small percentage of alcoholics can return to "normal drinking," but most people involved in the treatment and rehabilitation of alcoholics feel strongly that abstinence is essential to successful treatment.

Psychopharmacology. This area of psychiatry continues to show major progress. Lithium carbonate, perhaps the most specific medication in psychiatry, is effective in treating most patients with severe cyclic mood disorders. Several studies point to a correlation between blood levels of antidepressant medication and clinical response in patients suffering from depression. Specific medications, hopefully with fewer disturbing side effects, have also been developed to treat schizophrenia.

Psychiatrists continue to be concerned about the long-term effects of potent medications, as well as the interaction of these agents with medications for other conditions. The physician and his patient together must weigh the benefits and risks of these potent medications.

Carefully controlled research has tended to support the clinical observation that in the treatment of very serious emotional illnesses, the combination of medication and psychotherapy gives the best results.

Other Research. Research in pharmacology and neurophysiology suggests that naturally occurring morphinelike chemical compounds (endorphins) in the central nervous system are involved in both normal and abnormal behavior. Although this finding may represent a significant advance in the understanding of emotional illness, investigators cannot agree as to whether an excess, deficiency, or abnormal form of endorphin results in mental illness.

Biofeedback is fulfilling its earlier promise of providing relief from certain psycho-physiological symptoms. Responsible authorities in the field, however, warn against inordinate enthusiasm, as expectations of magic may keep the patient from facing basic personal and interpersonal issues that may produce or contribute to the symptom.

Physiological states during sleep are the focus of much research. Electroencephalograms (EEGs) taken during sleep are being studied for clues to which depressed patients will respond to medication. Another area of exploration is the antidepressant effect of sleep deprivation.

Child Mental Health. The clearer identification of specific factors involved in child abuse has led to more sophisticated and useful treatments. An effective treatment approach most often involves both parents and children. Another area that is receiving deserved attention is childhood depression. In contrast to adults, many children express their depression through behavior rather than mood.

Geriatric Mental Health. The need to analyze and suggest solutions to the problems and opportunities of the elderly continued to attract attention in 1978. Poverty, isolation, and illness pose severe problems for the aged, with poverty being the most common and pressing.

Professionals in the field of geriatric medicine have found that a significant percentage of patients thought to be suffering from senility in fact have treatable conditions, such as depression, over-medication, or some physical illness. The over-medication of the aged deserves particular emphasis, as it is not uncommon and clearly represents a preventable condition.

Community Centers and Halfway Facilities. Community mental health services have increased markedly in recent years. Legislation in 1975 created specialized programs for youth, the elderly, alcoholics, and drug abusers, as well as after-care services, screening services, and alternatives to state hospital treatment. In 1977, the National Institute of Mental Health signed $3.5 million in contracts with 16 states for community support experiments. That same year the President's Commission on Mental Health was established by executive order.

Yet a lack of adequate follow-up facilities is evidenced by a continued high rate of psychiatric rehospitalization. A need exists for part-time facilities to provide graduated support and guidance to encourage patient self-sufficiency.

Patients' Rights. The issue of patients' rights has been brought to the fore by a series of important legal decisions. The current emphasis is on "dangerousness" as the criterion for mandatory institutionalization. Mental health professionals worry about severely ill, psychotic patients (most of whom are not dangerous), who barely subsist and are in great emotional turmoil, but who might improve with adequate treatment. The nature of their illness could well interfere with their decision about accepting or rejecting treatment. Although the rights of the individual are central to therapy and the rehabilitation process, there is growing concern that many patients, without the presence of mind to make a reasoned and careful judgment, would exclude themselves from treatment.

CHARLES W. BOREN
Institute of Living, Hartford, Conn.

The Businessman and Stress

The damaging effects of workaday stress on American business and industry have long been recognized. Death of executives due to stress has been estimated to cost U. S. companies between $20 and $30 billion a year. Even more detrimental, however, are the day-to-day consequences of stress and anxiety in the average worker—absenteeism, low productivity, and industrial sabotage. Although businesses have recognized these problems for some 40 years, solutions are elusive and there has been little promise of success. Recently, however, major corporations have begun to invest large sums of money in a variety of stress-management programs, and many smaller companies are enlisting their employees in outside seminars and activities. The consequences of work-related stress, if not eliminated, may at least be minimized through these efforts.

Stress is a natural response of the body to stimulation. The autonomic or vegetative nervous system prepares the body for emergency situations. A series of complicated hormonal reactions causes mobilization of the organ systems to prepare for a "flight or fight" response to the emergency. The problems caused by stress begin when the emergency reaction is prolonged. If the body's machinery is driven too fast for too long, it begins to break down. Which organ system breaks down first varies from person to person because of hereditary and physical characteristics. Heart attacks, high blood pressure, ulcers, alcoholism, drug addiction, and other problems are possible consequences of excessive stress. Since individuals differ so greatly in their response to stress, stress management for large numbers of people in the business setting remains difficult.

Many companies have responded to the stress-induced problems of their employees by attempting to improve working conditions, by providing vacation and sick leave, and by adding medical and counseling staff. Personnel departments are becoming human resource departments, providing information and facilities to promote healthy work and home adjustment. Educational programs have been increased and now include courses in management, psychology, and specific job skills. Yet, although such measures have had a generally positive effect, they are not enough. Thousands of employees still report to their company health service each year with stress problems. Some of the more formal and effective stress-management techniques promoted by large corporations include meditation, relaxation-response training, progressive relaxation, cardiovascular fitness or prevention programs, biofeedback training, and individual stress-management programs.

Meditation or relaxation-response training is a popular approach. The subject learns to develop a passive state of mind, breathe deeply, and repeat a single sound or word, such as "one." Regular practice helps many individuals relax and reduce their blood pressure. However, it is not effective for everyone.

According to the American Association of Fitness Directors in Business and Industry, more than 750 corporations and businesses have instituted cardiovascular fitness programs. Employees who are prone to cardiovascular disease are identified by company health staff or consultant screening services and enter a carefully designed physical fitness program, usually under the guidance of a professional, to increase their resistance to stress.

Progressive relaxation and instant relaxation techniques are also popular among businessmen. These exercises are easy to learn and involve the tensing and relaxing of muscle groups while saying the word "relax." After a little practice, just saying the word "relax," coupled with deep breathing, can bring about a state of complete relaxation.

Some industries have established biofeedback workshops for their employees. Biofeedback is a procedure by which the body's physiological responses are measured by an electronic device. These biosignals are then changed into messages which can be seen or heard. Individuals can then identify the internal cues which signify tension or relaxation and control the physiological responses underlying the stress response. Biofeedback is helpful also in treating such problems as high blood pressure, and migraine and tension headaches.

Because of the uniqueness of stress patterns and the diversity of the stimuli that elicit them, one approach that is gaining support from businessmen is the individual stress-management program. This is a comprehensive program which allows the individual to identify the specific sources of his own stress, formulate an appropriate schedule of relaxation exercises, and arrive at new stress avoidance and coping responses. The individual stress-management approach is particularly appropriate for the business setting. Large numbers of employees can easily develop their own programs with limited professional help or investment in supportive resources.

Thus, the business community is beginning to engage in a whole range of stress-control methods rather than relying on alcohol or tranquilizers to cope with problems. In short, businessmen are learning to manage stress instead of letting stress manage them.

VICTOR P. PEASE

Water completely inundates a church cemetery in Perley, Minn., as severe spring flooding occurs in eastern North Dakota and western Minnesota.

UPI

METEOROLOGY

Global Weather Research. Various phases of the international Global Atmospheric Research Program (GARP) got under way in 1978. The main experiment will start in 1979, using 9,200 land observation posts, 1,000 upper air stations, 7,400 merchant vessels, 3,000 commercial and reconnaissance aircraft, 5 geostationary satellites, and 300 drifting buoys in southern oceans. Intensive study periods of 60 days each will begin in January and May 1979. In addition to extending the validity of weather forecasts, GARP is expected to furnish data on the feasibility of towing Antarctic icebergs to Australia and other dry countries farther north.

In an experiment going on in the Pacific since November 1977, scientists have studied changes in the warm oceanic areas between 20° S and 20° N latitude to 150° W longitude. A flying laboratory of the National Oceanic and Atmospheric Administration collects precise weather data every three days between Hawaii and Papeete. Bathythermographs are also dropped to measure oceanic conditions. Another part of GARP, devoted to the study of monsoon conditions in Asia, found that the intensity of rainfall during the summer is related to low-level winds of high speed in Kenya.

Forecasting. The U. S. National Weather Service has extended weather outlooks from 5 to 10 days. Ten-day forecasts are obtained by computer calculations of winds and temperatures to a height of 10 kilometers (6 mi).

Accurate weather forecasting by computer is handicapped by the coarse grid system which present day computers require for numerical prediction. A new mathematical model using three sizes of nested grid data is capable of providing detailed forecasts. However, they cannot be handled by available computers for timely forecasting.

Severe Storms. Studies on severe storms have shown that high winds in the upper troposphere have prognostic value. If a strong, diverging wind occurs at the 10 kilometer (6 mi) level in combination with a high moisture content below, severe thunderstorms and tornadoes may occur.

Research in Australia suggests that the occurrence of tropical storms requires high humidity and temperatures above 25.5° C (78° F). Rotational motion and turbulent stirring are also needed for storm initiation.

Water spouts, small tornadolike vortices over warm seas, were observed near Florida with lasers from aircraft at distances of only 200 to 500 meters (650 to 1,650 ft). Doppler analysis of the return energy from funnels 4 to 30 meters in diameter (13–100 ft) indicated wind speeds of maximally 90 kilometers per hour (56 mi/h).

Scientists studying lightning at the Kennedy Space Flight Center near Cape Canaveral, Fla., noted a super stroke 10 kilometers (6 mi) long during a summer storm. The leader stroke traveled at a speed of 2,000 kilometers per second (1,240 mi/sec) and the first return stroke at about 200,000 kilometers per second (12,400 mi/sec). Peak currents were estimated at 150–640 kiloamperes. Meanwhile, on the Honshu coast of Japan near Hokuriku, winter thunderstorms showed electrical discharges different from those of summer storms. Lightning to the ground was positive in 78% of the cases, in contrast to the negative discharges usually found. Moreover, the electrical fields were higher than those found in normal thunderstorms, reaching 20 kilovolts per meter.

Solar Influences. The energy output of the sun was measured by precise astronomical observations and from satellites. Both techniques indicated a decrease in solar temperature of about 6° C (11° F) and a corresponding drop of 6 watts per square meter, or about 0.4% of the average solar energy received by the earth. A change of this magnitude could lead to tropospheric pressure changes of half a millibar, negligible as far as general weather changes go. But another sun-weather link, advanced by Ralph Markson of MIT, suggests that the earth-atmosphere system is an electric unit akin to a

UPI

South Boston begins to dig out after the New England area is hit by a series of major snowstorms in 1978.

condenser, the ionosphere at a height of 60 kilometers (40 mi) being the outer shell. Increased ionizing radiation from the sun could change the conductivity of the system and thereby lead to more thunderstorms.

It has also been suggested that a weakening of solar wind might initiate an ice age. Such an event can happen when the solar system moves through one of the spiral bands of the galaxy. The mass density of such a band is estimated to be 1,000 hydrogen molecules per cubic centimeter. The hydrogen molecules could interact at high atmospheric levels with oxygen radicals to form water vapor and clouds. These would reflect solar radiation and thereby reduce surface temperatures on earth.

During the last ice age, the ratio of deuterium to hydrogen in the cellulose of tree rings was low, indicating cold conditions at the time of formation. Old trees dated by carbon-14 indicated maximal glaciation 12,000 to 14,000 years ago. Trees growing 10,000 to 12,000 years ago showed, by a higher deuterium-hydrogen ratio, the transition to warmer conditions; the transition period appeared to be about 2 millennia. The tree rings also indicated that cool summers were the immediate main cause of glaciation.

Weather Modification. In cloud physics, some ice nuclei, acting to freeze subcooled cloud droplets already at —4 to —5° C (23–25° F), have been traced to organic material in sea water. Effluents from paper mills in the state of Washington have been shown to increase the number of cloud droplets more than 30 micrometers in size, compared to similar clouds not affected by smoke from the mills' plume. Such large drops facilitate the formation of rain. Microphysical models of the initiation of precipitation indicate that if cloud base temperatures are warmer than 0° C (32° F), seeding with large water drops is more efficient in causing precipitation than silver-iodide, the usual seeding agent. The time required to produce precipitation decreases as the size of the seed drops increases.

Data from the National Hail Research Experiment, a series of randomized seedings in Colorado and Nebraska, were analyzed in 1978. The hypothesis of Soviet scientists that seeding can decrease the size of hail stones was not supported.

The Weather Modification Advisory Board, created by the U. S. Congress in 1976, submitted its report on June 30, 1978, to the secretary of commerce. Among other things, the group recommended a 20-year program, coordinated by the National Oceanic and Atmospheric Agency (NOAA), for weather resource management. Potential increases of 20–30% in mountain snow pack and rain in the Great Plains are envisaged. Over the long haul, a 10 to 50% reduction in gales accompanying hurricanes is deemed feasible, as is a 50% reduction in damaging hail. The recommended level of federal research funding for 1980 was $37 million, rising to $90 million by 1985.

See also OCEANOGRAPHY.

H. E. LANDSBERG
Institute for Physical Science and Technology
University of Maryland

An elaborate computer system at the National Meteorological Center makes 10-day forecasts possible.

NOAA

METEOROLOGY—
SPECIAL REPORT:

The Weather Year

UPI

Banaras, India, September 1978.

In the annals of weather, 1978 will go down as a year of floods.

December 1977–February 1978. Winter in the United States started early. In the first week of December, the Rockies were already snow-clad. The central and eastern areas of the country were overrun by outbreaks of Arctic air, especially from the middle of January on. The coldest areas were Montana, the Great Plains, Indiana, Ohio, and West Virginia, where temperatures were 5 degrees Celsius (9 degrees Fahrenheit) below average.

The winter of 1978 was wet and snowy compared with 1977. Major snowstorms hit both the plains and eastern states. During the last week in January, blizzards raged through the Midwest, causing more than 100 weather-related deaths. Boston had its worst snowstorm in 100 years. The second major storm of the season hit the Northeast in early February, crippling traffic in Maryland, Pennsylvania, New York, and New England. The snow cover north of the 35th parallel in North America was the heaviest in more than a decade. At the same time, California experienced devastating gales and rains. Inundations and mud slides caused considerable damage in the southern part of the state.

Elsewhere in the world, there were floods in Athens, Venice, and much of Spain. Severe gales and snowstorms afflicted Ireland, England, Wales, and Scotland, where snow drifts reached 50 feet (15 m) in height. Avalanches derailed a train in Switzerland and killed 11 persons in France and Italy. A blizzard on February 19 left 20-foot (6-m) drifts in Devon, England, deposited 2 feet (61 cm) of snow in Stockholm, and sank many fishing vessels off the Norwegian coast.

March–May. Spring in the United States was relatively mild west of the Great Plains and cool in the East. While early March was still wintry from the Rockies to the Atlantic, a warm April made up for this. Precipitation was close to average in the East and Great Plains, but much of the Southwest had twice the average amount. Only central and southeast Texas were dry.

The main feature of the spring was widespread flooding. The Santa Clara River in California overflowed, causing severe damage in Riverside, Malibu, and Santa Monica. Flooding of the Platte River in Nebraska forced the evacuation of 5,000 residents, and the Red River flooded farmlands in North Dakota and Minnesota. The Maumee River rose 10 feet (3 m) above the flood level in Ft. Wayne, Ind. Late in the season, the snow melt and torrential rains caused record floods in the Bighorn, Little Bighorn, and Tongue rivers in Wyoming and Montana. Floods in the panhandle areas of Texas and Oklahoma resulted in several deaths.

Tornadoes hit Mississippi, Alabama, Louisiana, Arkansas, and Florida; 6 persons died and 164 were injured. Severe thunderstorms grounded a freighter on Lake Michigan, toppled a radio tower in Milwaukee, and brought 9 inches (23 cm) of rain to New Orleans.

A tornado disaster in southeastern India killed an estimated 600 persons, and a cyclone leveled the seaport of Kyaukpyu, Burma, with winds in excess of 100 miles (160 km) per hour. Drought prevailed in Laos, Ethiopia, and the Brazilian states of Goias and Parana, where the driest weather in 50 years caused an estimated loss in crops of (U. S.) $1.2 billion.

June–August. Summer temperatures in the United States were about average, but a heat wave in July brought temperatures exceeding 38° C (100° F) to Dallas–Ft. Worth for two weeks. Precipitation varied, but conditions were generally drier than average. However, parts of Minnesota were hit by flash floods, requiring the evacuation of 5,000 persons; more than 30 inches (76 cm) of rain from tropical storm "Amelia" fell on western and central Texas; and the Guadelupe, Media, and Brazon rivers overflowed, killing 26 people.

The number of tropical storms in the North Atlantic and Caribbean rose to five, twice the average, by the end of August. Southern California was struck by a tropical storm for the second summer in a row. In the western Pacific, tropical storm "Agnes" pounded Hong Kong with gales and torrential rains, while rains from storm "Della" caused landslides in the Philippines, burying at least 30 persons.

The monsoon season brought exceptionally heavy rains to India, Pakistan, Bangladesh, and Thailand. The flooding of many rivers, including the Ganges, caused enormous damage, especially to crops, and led to thousands of casualties.

In contrast, drought prevailed in parts of the Sahel, Cape Verde Islands, and Gambia. In the Sudan and Ethiopia, early drought was followed by heavy rain, which did more harm than good.

September–November. The western United States remained warm until late October, but cooled rapidly in November. In the East, temperatures were close to average, but lengthy periods of sunshine gave an extended Indian Summer. At the same time, there was a deficiency in rainfall, especially in the South Atlantic states and parts of the Great Plains. Western Europe also got very little rain, about 40% of the average. A serious drought, threatening 2 million people with famine, developed in Ethiopia.

In contrast, flash floods in mid-September brought death and destruction to Arkansas, Texas, Louisiana, Missouri, Illinois, Indiana, and lower Michigan. Hurricane "Oliva" brought floods to Mexico; some 50,000 persons were left homeless in the states of Oaxaca and Chiapas. But the worst flood of the season occurred in northern India in early September. The rampaging Ganges and Yannona rivers inundated the cities of New Delhi, Benares, and Allahabad. More than 1,000 persons died, and some 600,000 homes were destroyed.

Monsoon floods in the Indochina peninsula in mid-October left thousands of residents facing starvation and millions in need of emergency relief as the rice crops in Thailand and Cambodia were seriously damaged; 20% of the cattle in Vietnam were destroyed, and 500,000 Laotians were threatened with starvation. A tropical storm at the end of November left 500 dead in Sri Lanka and devastated numerous villages in southern India.

In the United States, winter made an early reappearance in the Rocky Mountains and northern Great Plains. During the second week of November, 35 inches (90 cm) of snow fell in the northern Rockies, killing 17 persons in 8 states. A week later, a second major snowstorm hit the same area. Montana reported temperatures of −22° C (−8° F).

H. E. LANDSBERG

UPI

Mexico is rapidly becoming one of the world's leading energy producers. Above, a pipeline is repaired.

MEXICO

Confirmation of the nation's huge petroleum reserves marked a year in which the government tightened controls and raised oil prices to promote economic recovery. New political and social laws were instituted to increase popular support of the regime.

Energy. Petróleos Mexicano (Pemex), the government oil monopoly, announced December 20 that it would be raising the export price of crude oil by 10.7% in 1979. In September, President José López Portillo had reported that the nation's proven reserves of oil equaled about 20 billion (U. S.) barrels, its probable reserves about 37 billion barrels, and its potential reserves about 200 billion barrels. These figures put Mexico in a class with Saudi Arabia. Then on November 13 the government confirmed the discovery of a new oil basin on the Gulf of Mexico with potential reserves of about 100 million barrels. At year's end Pemex reported that proven reserves had climbed to 26 billion barrels. López Portillo set a production target of 2.25 million barrels per day by the end of 1980 (compared with 1.5 million per day in December 1978). The new gas pipeline, financed in part by U. S. capital, continued to make its way toward Monterrey and other northern sites short of the border. The petrochemical industry also was expanded in 1978.

Politics. López Portillo issued a call for an end to negativism. To signal his efforts to liberalize the nation's restrictive politics, the president supported an amnesty law that would free some 300 political prisoners; this came as a surprise because the son of the Mexican ambassador to the United States had been kidnapped and murdered shortly before the bill was proposed. Some observers thought that the law was an effort to forestall defections from the ruling Institutional Revolutionary Party by leftists dissatisfied with the president's conservative policies. The president also sent bills to congress to limit the Senate's power to remove governors and name permanent replacements and to create a constitutional right to information.

The indictment of several former cabinet ministers and high-level officials for fraud and embezzlement gave credence to the anti-corruption campaign. López Portillo asserted that the prosecutions were not an attack on his predecessor but were based on factual evidence.

Several political groups obtained the right to participate in the 1979 congressional elections. The Communist and Socialist Workers parties were to be recognized if they won 1.5% of the national vote in 1979. The rightist Democratic party received permanent status. Fifteen groups requested recognition as national political associations. One was the Leandro Valle association, claiming 130,000 members; the group was led by army officers, suggesting that the military might again overtly enter the political arena.

Several minor civil disturbances occurred in 1978. In January, the tiny, pro-government Authentic Party of the Mexican Revolution seized nine town halls in northern states, claiming victory in local elections; the army dislodged one group. In June, the army retook one town hall in Puebla state from irate citizens who claimed that the National Action party had again won local elections; citizens in Matamoros rioted after a youth was shot by police; and prisoners in Tijuana rioted, protesting living conditions.

Economic Performance. Mexico's economic recovery continued slowly in 1978. Gross domestic production rose by 5%, as compared with 2.8% in 1977. The inflation rate dropped to 14% from a rate of 21% the previous year. Exports increased significantly, with chemicals (20%), petroleum (15%), and mining (11%) leading the way. The fish catch, an important new source of foreign exchange, rose by 25% in the first eight months of 1978; exports earned 11 billion pesos. Tourism increased by 18% in the first five months and was expected to increase an average of 12% for the year; earnings from foreign visitors rose by 33%, and the number of domestic tourists reached 18 million. Industrial production recovered more slowly, however. Electricity and construction rose by 8%. Agricultural production and exports increased, but much food was imported. The year saw a record sugar harvest.

Conservative fiscal policies held the total public debt to (U. S.) $25 billion and the federal domestic debt to 330 billion pesos at mid-year. The rate of increase slowed, and domestic savings increased fourfold in the first half of 1978, compared with the same period in 1977. The larger balance of payments deficit resulted from short-term loans, expected to be paid shortly.

To offset the impact of inflation, minimum wages and pensions were raised. In January, minimum wages advanced between 9.8% and 22%, with the higher rates going to the lowest paid. Federal employees and pensioners, including military pensioners, received increases of up to 12%. The traditional year-end bonus was increased to forty days' pay, half of it payable in December and the other half in January, so as to reduce its inflationary impact.

Economic Policy. To foster a balanced recovery, careful planning, program budgeting, and extensive controls were employed. President López Portillo used strict monetary and fiscal policies to stem inflation, improve the balance of payments, stimulate private investment, and make tax collection more efficient. The National Plan calls for annual increases in key industries and hydrocarbon self-sufficiency by 1982. More sophisticated data collection and analysis, better cost accounting, coordination between Mexico's federal and state governments, and cooperation between public and private enterprise were seen as the means to these economic ends.

Citizens in lower income groups benefited from income tax reduction, new laws against price gouging, rural credit from private banks, title security for agricultural landholdings, and the conversion of social security centers into worker training institutes. State governments began to use newly-delegated powers to reduce their backlogs of land claims. López Portillo publicly admitted that the giant Las Truchas-Lazaro Cardenas steel plant lagged behind its construction and production schedules because of mismanagement. To encourage the industrialization of rural areas, the government offered a 30% discount in the cost of energy in selected regions.

The 1978 budget of 912.5 billion pesos was for the first time organized according to program goals. Almost 32% of this amount would be borrowed; 27% was channeled to industry; 10% to health and social security; 8.4% to education, culture, science and technology; 6% to agriculture; and 26% to debt service. Direct federal government expenditure was only 47.6% of the total; the remainder was spent by decentralized agencies and the states.

Social Policy. New national plans for settlement, family nutrition, and higher education were instituted. The government created a national vaccination card and a new preventive medicine program; a national registry of prisoners; a pedagogical university; and the Medical Center of the West. The president promised to decentralize labor arbitration boards and constitutionally to affirm the right to work.

Foreign Policy. Energy policy, the problem of illegal aliens, and closer U. S.-Mexican cooperation were the topics of discussion when U. S. Vice President Walter Mondale visited Mexico in January and when Secretary of State Cyrus Vance went in May. Mexico publicly stated its refusal to participate in the U. S. energy debate. The presidents of Hungary, Israel, Costa Rica, Brazil, and West Germany visited Mexico to promote friendship and trade relations. Mexican President López Portillo went to Bulgaria and the USSR on state visits.

DONALD J. MABRY
Mississippi State University

───────── **MEXICO · Information Highlights** ─────────

Official Name: The United Mexican States.
Location: Southern North America.
Area: 761,602 square miles (1,972,549 km²).
Population (1978 est.): 66,900,000.
Chief Cities (1976 est.): Mexico City, the capital, 8,-630,000; Guadalajara, 1,640,000; Monterrey, 1,090,000.
Government: *Head of state and government, José López Portillo, president (took office Dec. 1976). Legislature*—Congress:. Senate and Chamber of Deputies.
Monetary Unit: Peso (22.72 pesos equal U. S. $1, Dec. 27, 1978).
Manufactures (major products): Food processing, chemicals, basic metals and metal products, petroleum products.
Agriculture (major products): Corn, cotton, sugarcane, wheat, coffee.

UPI

Michigan Gov. William G. Milliken addresses a crowd of angry protesters near a PBB-contaminated animal burial site.

MICHIGAN

Major events in Michigan during 1978 included reelection of Gov. William G. Milliken, the defeat of Sen. Robert P. Griffin by Carl Levin, voter approval of a tax limitation proposal, and continuing controversy about a toxic chemical accidentally mixed in animal feed five years earlier.

Elections. Governor Milliken, 56, won reelection in the November 7 voting by the largest margin of his three races for the office. He defeated Democrat William B. Fitzgerald. The voters also adopted a constitutional amendment, placed on the ballot by pctition, to limit state spending to 9.5% of the state's total personal income. The amendment also prohibits property taxes from rising faster than the inflation rate, requires voter approval of all general obligation bonds, and requires the state to pay for any services it requires local governments to provide. Two other tax proposals were rejected by voters. One would have cut property taxes in half; the other would have permitted parents to send their children to the public or private school of their choice, using state "vouchers" to pay tuition. Voters also approved a motion raising the state's minimum legal age for drinking alcoholic beverages to 21. Drinking at age 18 had been legal since 1972.

Democrat Carl Levin, 44, a former Detroit City Council president, defeated incumbent U. S. Senator Robert P. Griffin. Griffin apparently was hurt by deciding to run for reelection after formally announcing his retirement from Congress. He had represented Michigan in Congress, as a representative and a senator, for 22 years. U. S. Rep. Charles C. Diggs, Jr., a Detroit Democrat, was reelected despite his conviction for padding his Congressional payroll and mail fraud.

PBB Controversy. Strife continued over PBB—polybrominated biphenyl—accidentally mixed in animal feed in 1973. In the first court decision since the incident, County Circuit Judge William Peterson decided after a 14-month trial that low levels of PBB are harmless, denied all relief to Roy Tacoma, the Falmouth farmer who filed the suit against Michigan Chemical Co. and Michigan Farm Bureau Services, and chided the two companies for paying $40 million in claims to 670 other farmers. But dozens of other suits remained to be decided, and Judge Peterson's ruling—rendered only 10 days before an election in which the Democratic gubernatorial candidate had campaigned on the PBB issue—sparked new controversy. In unrelated court suits, Michigan officials were ordered not to bury cattle contaminated by the chemical, to preclude possible pollution of the state's public water supplies. Several lawsuits remained to be settled as the year drew to a close.

Economy. Sales, production and employment were high in the auto industry throughout the year, contributing to a generally good economic performance for the state. Lee A. Iacocca, unexpectedly fired as president of the Ford Motor Co. in July, became president of Chrysler Corp. in November. Financially-troubled Chrysler, which twice reported record quarterly losses, sought new public financing through a preferred stock issue, and began selling some overseas assets.

Construction started in July on the Joe Louis Arena in Detroit's riverfront Civic Center. The $36 million sports structure will be the new home of the Detroit Red Wings professional hockey team.

CHARLES THEISEN
The Detroit News

——— MICHIGAN • Information Highlights ———

Area: 58,216 square miles (150,779 km²).
Population (Jan. 1978 est.): 9,141,000.
Chief Cities (1970 census): Lansing, the capital, 131,-546; Detroit, 1,513,601.
Government (1978): *Chief Officers*—governor, William G. Milliken (R); lt. gov., James J. Damman (R). *Legislature*—Senate, 38 members; House of Representatives, 110 members.
Education (1977–78): *Enrollment*—public elementary schools, 1,065,004 pupils; public secondary, 971,-072; colleges and universities, 481,767 students. *Public school expenditures*, $4,263,166,000.
State Finances (fiscal year 1977): *Revenues*, $9,689,212,-000; *expenditures*, $9,070,835,000.
Personal Income (1977): $69,554,000,000; per capita, $7,619.
Labor Force (June 1978): *Nonagricultural wage and salary earners*, 3,552,300; *unemployed*, 298,700 (7.0% of total force).

MICROBIOLOGY

Numerous discoveries of major scientific importance and practical application were made in the field of microbiology in 1978.

Ancient Microorganisms. A controversy developed over a group of bacteria which, it was said, are the oldest form of life and represent a new, third primary kingdom. The so-called methanogenic bacteria produce methane by oxidizing gaseous hydrogen and reducing carbon dioxide. It was postulated that they existed some 3.4 (U. S.) billion years ago when the earth's atmosphere consisted largely of hydrogen and carbon dioxide. Several scientists questioned this theory, however, and presented evidence of a high degree of functional relation between the nucleic acid sequences in methanogenic and other bacteria.

Nitrogen Fixation by Bacteria. Various methods of research conducted in 1978 provided insight into the mechanism of nitrogen fixation by the association (symbiosis) of plants and root-nodule bacteria. Legumes are selective with regard to the bacteria they live with; the bacterium *Rhizobium trifolii* is able to enter the root hairs and symbiotically fix nitrogen with clover, although it cannot do so with alfalfa and soybeans. Research indicates that lectin (plant protein) on the surface of clover cells specifically binds the bacteria to the root-hairs and in doing so allows the bacteria to penetrate the clover and form nodules.

Hormone Synthesis by Bacteria. While rumors were spreading throughout 1978 about the cloning of a human being, more realistic and modest scientific research was actually being carried out. Realizing that genetic material could be introduced in bacteria (causing them to form the hormones insulin and somatostatin), a group of scientists was able to clone the gene for ovalbumin, a major egg glycoprotein whose synthesis is controlled by steroid hormones in the hen oviduct.

By inserting the ovalbumin gene into the bacterium *Escherichia coli* on a lambda phage "vector" (a bacterial virus that serves as a gene carrying device), the mass of gene material synthesized can be greatly increased. This technique will enable scientists to conduct more in-depth research concerning the hormone's mechanism of action.

Microbial Resistance to Antibiotics and Drugs. With various bacteria increasing their resistance to antibiotic therapy, efforts were and are being made to determine the source of the resistance (R) factor. The source may be a group of bacteria (species *Bacteroides*) that is a normal inhabitant of the intestine and oral cavities of human beings and animals. These bacteria grow only in the absence of oxygen and are not routinely cultivated in the laboratory. Thus, they may provide an extensive pool of R-factors that are capable of infecting more commonly recognized pathogens, such as those causing gastroenteritis and dysentery.

Chloroquine-resistant strains of the malarial parasite, *Plasmodium falciparum,* have occurred thus far only in Asia and Latin America. In 1978, however, microbiologists learned that the African strain of the parasite can also become chloroquine-resistant.

Microbial Gene Transfer to Plants. The bacterium *Agrobacterium tumefaciens* infects a variety of plants. Once in the plant, the foreign genetic material (DNA) integrates itself into the plant's own DNA. Through genetic engineering, it may now be possible to have plants synthesize proteins that are deficient in certain amino acids required in animal and human diets.

Microbial Diseases. A virus called non A-non B was found to cause posttransfusion hepatitis in human beings. Also, Legionnaire's Disease was discovered to be more widespread than previously expected.

A serious outbreak of venereal disease known as "contagious equine metritis" occurred in thoroughbred race horses in the United States for the first time in 1978. The transmitting agent appeared to be a bacterium resembling the human gonococcus, but one that grows only in the absence of oxygen.

The possibility that viruses might be one of the causes of juvenile diabetes by infecting and destroying pancreatic β-cells was supported in 1978 by research employing reovirus and young mice. Experimental infection of the mice resulted in the destruction of pancreatic β-cells, a reduction in the insulin content of the pancreas, and an alteration in glucose metabolism.

Microbial DNA Research. Strict federal guidelines on the conduct of recombinant DNA experiments continued to be debated in the U. S. Congress in 1978. Although scientists have in recent years pointed out the danger that unforeseen transformations of the bacteria might occur, the need for sweeping new legislation was seen by many to have diminished in 1978.

Patent Ruling on Microorganisms. An international convention dealing with patents for new microbiological processes, metabolic products, and genetically engineered microorganisms was up for ratification in 1978. The U. S. Supreme Court, however, ruled that living organisms cannot be patented and that the issue will have to be resolved in Congress.

International Conferences. Two major international conferences on microbiology were held in 1978. The Fifth International Conference on the Global Impacts of Applied Microbiology was held in Bangkok, Thailand; and the 12th International Congress of Microbiology was conducted in Munich, West Germany. Scientists from some 45 countries participated in these meetings, and important research findings were presented.

J. R. PORTER, *Department of Microbiology*
University of Iowa

UPI

The leaders of Israel and Egypt enter Aspen Lodge, Camp David. Although the negotiations at the presidential retreat ended successfully, 1978 closed without a peace treaty.

MIDDLE EAST

The Middle East in 1978 continued to be unique in its degree of volatility and importance to world affairs. Its importance was both strategic and economic, since Arab and Iranian oil production was essential to the functioning of the whole industrialized world. At the same time, the political volatility of the region increased rather than diminished.

Israeli-Egyptian Negotiations. The series of events that had the lion's share of attention for most of the year was the old story of Arab-Israeli relations. Negotiations between Egypt and Israel, mediated by the United States, formed a long, drawn-out, and ultimately inconclusive pas de trois. The pursuit of peace was carried out before the generally hostile scrutiny of the other Arab states, who adamantly remained on the sidelines.

Policies of Begin and Sadat. The climax of Egyptian-Israeli relations in 1978 was the Camp David summit, September 5–17. All other dealings between the two nations could be regarded as either preliminaries to or consequences of that meeting. The effects of Camp David on the other countries of the Middle East made it the most important development of the entire region. Its significance was not erased by the uncertain nature of its consequences.

Not since World War II, perhaps, had international politics focused so closely on the personalities of a few men. Both Egyptian President Anwar el-Sadat and Israeli Prime Minister Menahem Begin are strong men and hard bargainers. But if they had not demonstrated great self-confidence and determination they would not have progressed so far on the road to peace as in fact they had. Peace would be an incomparably valuable achievement for both of them. Both lead countries whose physical and psychological resources have been strained almost beyond endurance by three decades of hostility and by the four wars that punctuated them. The economies of both Egypt and Israel are nonviable without massive external assistance—from Saudi Arabia and other Arab oil producers in the case of Egypt, and from the United States in the case of Israel.

The difficulties of accommodating both parties are intrinsic and very real. What is at stake for Israel is the normalization of its international status and the termination of its 30-year-long state of war with its neighbors. But Israel is very little inclined to make territorial concessions that might result in a threat to its very existence. Such caution is virtually mandatory in light of Israel's miniscule size and population compared with its Arab neighbors.

For Sadat, normalizing relations with Israel —implying the establishment of regular diplomatic relations, with resident ambassadors and embassies, normal trade relations, and open borders—is so great a gift that he also is very little inclined to make territorial concessions. Basically, Sadat remains attached to the proposition that Israel should give up all its territorial gains of 1967. This attitude surfaced in a remark during the negotiation deadlock of January 1978. Assailing the Israelis as "stiff-necked" and "clever merchants," Sadat claimed that "Begin gave me nothing. It was I who gave him everything. I gave him security and legitimacy and got nothing in return." This was hardly a conciliatory remark from the Israeli point of view. The lack of a sanction from Sadat would hardly have caused Begin to regard the Jewish state as illegitimate.

Neither man, of course, is exactly a free agent. Each has a constituency to worry about. Begin is obliged to bear in mind how security-conscious Israelis (not only right-wing extremists and his own Likud party) might react to any concessions he might make. Sadat, meanwhile, is constrained not only by possible opposition within Egypt but also by fear of alienating the other Arab nations.

Before Camp David. In the first weeks of the year, there was a flurry of state visits intended either to generate support for Sadat's November 1977 peace initiative or organize opposition to it. In the last phase of a seven-nation tour, President Jimmy Carter visited the Middle East January 1–4 and held meetings with King Hussein of Jordan, King Khalid of Saudi Arabia, and President Sadat. The shah of Iran met Sadat at Aswan, Egypt, on January 9 and endorsed his policies; the shah then went on to Saudi Arabia. On the opposite track was Algerian President Houari Boumedienne, who visited Malta, ten Arab countries, the Soviet Union, and Yugoslavia, and conferred with PLO leader Yasir Arafat in Damascus. The tour was aimed at rallying support for a united Arab front opposed to Sadat and at closing the breach between Syria and Iraq.

The Arab "rejectionist" states, except for Iraq, met at Tripoli in December 1977 to state their opposition to President Sadat. They held a second meeting at Algiers, February 2–4. Their efforts to woo Iraq into their camp failed, not because Iraq was more moderate but indeed because it was more implacable in its hostility to Israel than it was to Sadat.

Egypt's isolation within the Arab world was increased by the terrorist incidents at Cyprus, February 18–19. Egypt's attempt to storm an aircraft hijacked by Palestinian terrorists resulted in an embarrassing and bloody confrontation with the Cypriot National Guard. The terrorists had murdered a prominent Egyptian newspaper editor and friend of President Sadat, Yousef Sebai, and commandeered the plane to Larnaca Airport, Cyprus. Egyptian politicians and press accused the PLO and hard-line Arab states of complicity in the murder, and there was an unprecedented wave of anti-Palestinian sentiment in Egypt. This doubtless had its influence on Egyptian attitudes later on.

The cool and even hostile attitudes of most Arab states toward Egypt remained fairly constant throughout the year. No amount of coaxing by the United States could drum up significant support for the Egyptian president. Nor did the landmark U.S. decision, announced in February and endorsed by the Senate in May, to sell sophisticated F-15 warplanes to Saudi Arabia produce any concessions from the Saudis on the price of oil or support of Sadat. Earlier in the year, only Morocco and the sultanate of Oman were genuinely supportive, and even their attitudes became more reserved after the Camp David accords were announced. The moderate states of Jordan and Saudi Arabia, from whom much had been hoped in the way of support, avoided commitment. Jordan would not join in the peace negotiations either when it was first invited to do so in January or at any later time.

The Israeli-Egyptian negotiations of 1978 be-

UPI

An Israeli soldier keeps watch over the Gush Emunim settlement, Shiloh, Israeli-occupied West Bank. Both Israel and Egypt are little inclined to make territorial concessions in peace talks.

gan inauspiciously, with a meeting of the joint Political Committee in Jerusalem, January 17–18, and a meeting of the joint Military Committee in Cairo, January 17–18. The former was abruptly broken off by Sadat. The burning issue of Israel's continuing policy of establishing new settlements in occupied territory arose again and again. Egypt denounced this policy, and the United States deplored it, but Israel continued to build new settlements, though on a small scale. Time and again the flickering flame of negotiation was fanned into life by the efforts of U. S. Secretary of State Cyrus Vance, Under Secretary of State Alfred Atherton, Jr., or President Carter himself. A divided Israeli cabinet decided February 26 that "no new decision was necessary" on the issue of the settlements—meaning that they would continue to be built. And they were.

As irritation with Begin grew, the United States' traditional support of Israel began to show a slow shift toward partisanship with Egypt. Begin's talks with President Carter at the White House, March 21–22, left differences totally unresolved. Israeli Defense Minister Ezer Weizman, who differed with Prime Minister Begin on the settlement question by favoring a moratorium during negotiations, and who seemed at times to be conducting his own foreign policy, held talks with Sadat in Cairo on March 30 and 31, and again at Salzburg, Austria, July 13. The most important talks of the year prior to Camp David were held between Israeli Foreign Minister Moshe Dayan and Egyptian Foreign Minister Mohammed Ibrahim Kamel under conditions of maximum security at Leeds Castle, England, July 18–19. But President Sadat's sense of how little was being achieved in the negotiations became clear on July 26 when he summarily expelled from Cairo the Israeli military mission. On June 6, and again the next day, he had warned publicly that Egypt might be forced to resort to war against Israel. As Prime Minister Begin pointed out on June 8, these threats were hardly compatible with the "no more war" pledges of Sadat's speech before the Knesset in November 1977. On June 30 President Sadat announced he would not allow resumption of the foreign ministers' talks until Israel committed itself to total withdrawal from all occupied Arab territories.

Camp David. The situation was rescued from these diplomatic doldrums by President Carter, who invited Begin and Sadat, with a minimum of advisers, to meet with him at Camp David, Md., on September 5. The invitations were conveyed in letters delivered by Vance when he met with Begin in Jerusalem, August 6–7, and with Sadat in Alexandria, August 7–8. Both heads of state accepted the invitations, and the meetings were held behind impenetrable security barriers until September 17. Although daily briefings were given during the proceedings, they provided no information as to any progress or lack thereof. The

day before convening the Camp David meetings, Carter explained that the "intimate" atmosphere "would promote a degree of personal interchange, without the necessity for political posturing or defense of transient stand or belief." The purpose was not to solve all problems, he said, but "to seek a framework for peace in the Middle East."

President Carter played a major role in the discussions, which several times were on the verge of breaking down. The ceremonial signing of the accords at the White House on September 17, was indeed a triumph for him. The conference had achieved a great deal more than outside observers and the parties themselves ever hoped for.

The Camp David accords were some 3,000 words in length and were divided into two sections: "The Framework of Peace in the Middle East" and the shorter "Framework for the Conclusion of a Peace Treaty Between Egypt and Israel." There were, in addition, nine clarifying letters exchanged among the three men and released by the White House on September 22.

That the accords were achieved at all was the result of certain modifications of attitude by the United States, Egypt, and Israel. Carter gave up the U. S. insistence on a "comprehensive" peace and settled for a narrow Egyptian-Israeli peace. Sadat, contrary to his earlier rejections of a separate peace, agreed to leave the other Arab states and the PLO out in the cold; the Camp David accords merely expressed the *hope* that the other states bordering Israel would follow the Egyptian lead and conclude similar peace treaties with Israel.

The great concession made by Israel was the relinquishing of its military control of and settlements in the Sinai. What made everything possible was the fact that of the five disputed territories occupied by Israel—Sinai, Gaza, the West Bank, East Jerusalem, and the Golan Heights—the one that mattered most to Egypt mattered least to Israel. Sinai alone had been an integral part of Egyptian territory prior to the 1967 war. As for Israel, the Sinai was the least strategic territory in terms of national defense.

The Framework—Egypt and Israel. The future of Sinai is dealt with in the "Framework for the Conclusion of a Peace Treaty Between Egypt and Israel," which opens:

"In order to achieve peace between them, Israel and Egypt agree to negotiate in good faith with a goal of concluding within three months of the signing of this framework a peace treaty between them."

The document states that Egyptian sovereignty is to be restored up to the old border between Egypt and mandated Palestine; that Israeli forces are to be withdrawn, partially to the line from El Arish to Ras Muhammad "between three and nine months after the signing of the peace treaty," fully by "between two and three years after the peace treaty is signed"; and that this timetable applies also to the other provisions regarding the Sinai, outlined below:

—airfields left by the Israelis in the Sinai to be used for civilian purposes only

—unimpeded passage between Egypt and Jordan on a new highway to be constructed near Eilat

—right of passage for Israeli ships through the Suez Canal, in accordance with the Constantinople Convention of 1889

—definition of areas in and near the Sinai where only limited forces would be permitted to the respective parties

—a UN presence on the Mediterranean coast and at the Sharm el-Sheikh area "to ensure freedom of passage through the Strait of Tiran"

In addition, Begin stated in one of the nine supplementary letters that he would put to the Knesset the question of withdrawing from the Israeli settlements in Sinai. The decision to withdraw from Sinai, as well as the Camp David accords themselves, were endorsed by the Knesset on September 28 after a difficult 17-hour debate.

The Framework—General. The more general "Framework of Peace in the Middle East" deals primarily with the future of the West Bank and Gaza. Unlike Sinai, no clear commitment was made either on future sovereignty over these areas or on complete evacuation by Israel. Transitional arrangements "for a period not exceeding five years" are envisaged in the document. A "self-governing authority," to be known as the Administrative Council, is to be "freely elected" by the inhabitants of the West Bank and Gaza.

"A withdrawal of Israeli armed forces will take place and there will be a redeployment of the remaining Israeli forces into specified security locations."

Within three years, Israel, Egypt, Jordan, and an "elected representative of the inhabitants" are to begin negotiations on the final status of the West Bank and Gaza. That status is to be determined within five years. The document also calls for the creation of "a strong local police force" as well as Israeli and Jordanian "joint patrols."

The last part of this general Framework of Peace in the Middle East deals with Egypt and Israel and looks forward to mutual full recognition, normal diplomatic relations, an end to economic boycotts, and possible plans for joint economic development.

By way of commentary on the Camp David accords, it must be said that some of the most noteworthy aspects are silences and omissions. The PLO is nowhere mentioned by name, although there are some phrases that might refer to it (e.g., "The delegations of Egypt and Jordan may include Palestinians from the West Bank and Gaza or other Palestinians as mutually agreed.") More broadly, there is no real acceptance of the possibility of a "Palestinian nation."

This was perhaps the one point that the Arab nations not accepting the Camp David accords found most objectionable.

Of the five disputed territories, only three are dealt with in the accords. The frameworks deal decisively with Sinai and more vaguely with Gaza and the West Bank. The Golan Heights are nowhere mentioned. The question of Jerusalem is dealt with in the supplementary letters, which do no more than record an agreement to differ. Sadat's letter to Carter on that subject read: "Arab Jerusalem is an integral part of the West Bank. . . . Arab Jerusalem should be under Arab sovereignty." Begin, in his letter to Carter, said: "Jerusalem is one city indivisible, the capital of the State of Israel."

Aftermath. Summit conferences have their special advantages and disadvantages. But as many historians and diplomatic experts believe, the latter often outweigh the former. Camp David may in the long run prove an historic milestone on the way to peace. It may also provide a classic warning against rash optimism. Apart from the special conditions of wartime, national leaders in the isolated hothouse atmosphere of a summit conference, away from their advisers and constituents, are under temptation to make concessions that they realize afterward are excessive—promises on which they cannot deliver. They also are subject to temptation, so as to produce tangible results, to agree to vague formulas and ambiguous meanings. "Diplomacy should be precise and disagreeable," said the late British diplomat Sir Harold Nicolson. To the contrary, Camp David was euphoric and vague. The accords are repetitive, vague, and frequently ambiguous. Decisions on many of the issues were postponed.

These defects became all too clear in the remaining months of the year. The three-month "deadline" (a word not used anywhere in the accords) for the signing of a final peace treaty was not met. December 17 passed with a final treaty nowhere in sight. The announcement on October 27 that Begin and Sadat would share the 1978 Nobel Peace Prize was a rather sad irony. The afterglow of Camp David had already begun to fade.

None of the other Arab states gave unequivocal support to Sadat on the Camp David agreements. Many leaders bitterly accused him of deserting the Arab cause. Jordan cautiously refused to participate in the plans for the West Bank, and that area seemed to be lining up more and more behind the PLO. The leaders of Syria, Libya, South Yemen, and the PLO, meeting at Damascus September 21–24, denounced Sadat and decided to break all ties with Egypt. More far-reaching in its implications was Iraq's change in disposition from isolation from the Arab world to cooperation with it. On October 27, Syria and Iraq, longtime enemies, signed a document that envisaged a "full military union." Iraq hosted an Arab summit conference

PHOTOS UPI

In Iran; Shahpur Bakhtiar was asked to form a new civilian government as 1978 ended. Massive anti-shah demonstrations led to the change.

at Baghdad November 2–5 at which 20 Arab states (all except Egypt) and the PLO were represented. It is true that the moderates won the day and that the hostility expressed toward Egypt was restrained, but the decision to withdraw the seat of the Arab League from Cairo underscored the isolation of Sadat.

In the three months after Camp David, both Begin and Sadat gradually fell out of the high spirit of peaceful cooperation. Begin proclaimed with unnecessary harshness that Israel would continue its settlement policy in the West Bank. After Egyptian and Israeli negotiators met in Washington October 12 and 22 and produced a draft treaty that neither Begin nor Sadat found acceptable, the latter began to articulate the theory of "linkage"—that there could be no peace treaty or normalized relations until considerable progress had been made in the West Bank and Gaza. Sadat also launched the idea of Egyptian sovereignty over Gaza.

The idea of linkage finds no justification in the texts of the Camp David accords. The framework for an Egyptian-Israeli peace treaty and the arrangements for the West Bank and Gaza are contained in two separate documents. The timetables given in the accords clearly imply that the peace treaty will come first (within three months) and that the Gaza–West Bank plan involves years of negotiations. Thus, it was difficult to understand why the whole thrust of U. S. policy toward the end of the year was to blame Israel for the lack of a treaty and to exert maximum pressure on it to make concessions.

President Sadat's idea of linkage was an afterthought. It emerged after the Baghdad summit and in all probability was a response to it. By taking a tougher line in the negotiations the Egyptian leader was defending himself against the charge of being too soft on Israel. The year ended with Egyptian-Israeli talks at an impasse.

Political Instability and its Implications. If Egyptian-Israeli negotiations and the rift in the Arab world were the predominant themes of the year, perhaps even more fundamental and ominous was the epidemic tendency in the Middle East toward civil disorder and the disintegration of existing political structures. This coincided with an extensive and highly successful outreach of Soviet power in a vast arc from Afghanistan to Ethiopia.

The prime example of this trend was, of course, the crumbling of authority in Iran. The overthrow of the shah or any serious shift toward the left in Iranian policy might have serious consequences for the West.

The enhancement of Soviet power and the paralysis of the West in Middle Eastern affairs grew more serious throughout the year. In April, Afghanistan underwent a leftist coup, and in November it made a treaty of alliance with the Soviet Union. While Pakistan unsuccessfully appealed to the United States for arms to face this new situation, Soviet arms supplies to its allies in the region were at an all-time high. Lebanon was reverting to civil war, and Turkey was in the throes of turmoil which in December became serious enough to lead to the imposition of martial law in 13 major cities.

The mood of every conservative, moderate, or pro-Western regime in the Middle East in 1978 was one of dread. In December, the Saudi Arabian ambassador in Washington hosted a dinner in honor of the departing Pakistani ambassador. In his speech, he expressed his own view on developments in the Middle East: "Our friends do not seem to realize that a crisis of historic magnitude is close at hand for the Western world and for those who share its values in our entire area." The guest of honor agreed: "I fear," he said, "that historians will look back at 1978 as a watershed year when the balance of power shifted against the Western world."

See also articles on individual countries.

ARTHUR CAMPBELL TURNER
University of California, Riverside

MILITARY AFFAIRS

As has been the case for more than 25 years, worldwide military developments were dominated by the activities of the two superpowers, the United States and the Soviet Union. While the giants maintained an awesome military capability, their primary challenger, the People's Republic of China, and lesser states continued to acquire larger arsenals of increasingly sophisticated equipment.

American strategists, in and out of government, were divided over the significance of Soviet arming activity and over the appropriate U. S. responses. The debate concerning the dimensions of the Soviet military threat and the necessary responses by the United States was unusually intense in 1978.

The Hardline Perspective. Those taking the hardline perspective, i.e., persons advocating greater military preparedness vis-à-vis the Soviet Union, believed that matters had reached a critical stage and required immediate recognition of the threat and subsequent initiation of remedial efforts. The hardliners also seemed to sense what they claimed was a changing public attitude in the United States—one they hoped would support greater defense spending. With this in mind hardliners worked individually and collectively to awaken the public to the Soviet threat, and their suggested responses. Some hardliners even compared their efforts to arouse the nation to the Soviet danger to the ride of Paul Revere, two centuries ago, to warn the countryside of the coming British danger.

Prominent individuals who were active in the warning activity, and who also worked to send hardliners to the Congress, were the retired Air Force intelligence chief, Maj. Gen. George Keegan; retired Army Maj. Gen. John K. Singlaub; and retired Adm. Thomas H. Moorer, who had served as chairman of the Joint Chiefs of Staff. General Singlaub had made news in 1977 when he was removed from his command in Korea after airing his differences with President Carter over the question of the reduction of U. S. forces in Korea. General Singlaub had opposed the troop reduction proposal on the grounds it might induce an attack on South Korea from North Korea.

General Keegan traveled the nation claiming that the Soviet Union could probably kill at least 160 million Americans in a surprise attack. Admiral Moorer wrote to many across the land, "I am not trying to be an alarmist, but the simple fact is the Soviet Union may have already achieved nuclear and military superiority over the United States of America." General Singlaub urged voters in the November national elections to participate in a "massive dove shoot at the polls." His reference was to the need felt by hardliners to turn out of office members of Congress who had rejected a rearming strategy in

Gen. David C. Jones, 56, U. S. Air Force chief of Staff, became chairman of the Joint Chiefs of Staff.

favor of the official policy of détente with the Soviet Union.

The effort to awaken the public to the Soviet military threat, and to send hardliners to the Congress, went far beyond individual activity. Three national groups solicited funds, engaged in mailings of literature to voters, and provided information on their views to the media. These groups were the American Security Council, the Committee on the Present Danger, and the Coalition for Peace Through Strength, formed in August. The strength of the Coalition for Peace Through Strength is suggested by the fact that its membership included five former ambassadors, three former cabinet secretaries, two former chairmen of the Joint Chiefs of Staff. Senators who cochaired the Coalition were J. Bennett Johnson (D-La.); Paul Laxalt (R-Nev.); and Robert Dole (R-Kans.). Cochairmen from the House of Representatives were Walter Flowers (D-Ala.); Richard Ichord (D-Mo.); Ted Risenhoover (D-Okla.); Richard C. White (D-Tex.); Robin Beard (R-Tenn.); Jack Kemp (R-N. Y.); and Robert H. Michel (R-Ill.). The stated purpose of the Coalition for Peace Through Strength was "to reverse the unilateral disarmament trend which has made the United States militarily inferior to the Soviet Union and to work for the adoption of an affirmative strategy of peace through strength."

What triggered the outpouring of effort to upgrade the U. S. military capacity were activities in which the Soviets engaged, or were alleged to have engaged, which were interpreted by hardliners to mean that the United States had fallen behind the USSR militarily. Those worried about the Soviet military buildup cited five general areas of concern.

The first was the fear that the American nuclear retaliatory systems were losing their pre- and post-launch invulnerability as the Soviets built weapons either to strike the U. S. weapons before they could be launched, or to destroy them after being launched. Specifically it was believed that the 1,054 U. S. ICBM's housed underground in steel and concrete shelters could be destroyed before launching by the new ICBM's with which the Soviets are replacing older models. It was feared that those U. S. ICBM's that escaped a Soviet first strike would be destroyed by the Soviet antimissile defenses. While such antiballistic missiles (ABM) are limited to two hundred each by the ABM treaty between the United States and the Soviet Union, hardliners claim the Soviets have cheated and have developed what is termed the surface-to-air missile (SAM) up-grade weapons system. If such a system exists it would be a SAM missile initially designed to intercept and destroy aircraft, which had been upgraded to provide a capability against missile warheads. It was also thought that the SAM-up-grade weapons could be used against U. S. submarine-launched ballistic missile (SLBM) warheads as well.

Concern was expressed about the prelaunch invulnerability of the U. S. submarines which carry 656 SLBM's. The hardline contention was that the Soviets were developing means to detect the craft, a prelude to the possible development of means to destroy submarines.

Concern was also voiced that the 400 plus strategic bombers, mostly 20-year-old B-52's were also becoming vulnerable to destruction. It was suggested that the old planes could not be gotten off their runways in time, should the Soviets launch an SLBM attack from their submarines a few miles off the U. S. coasts. Even if the B-52's could survive such an attack, it was feared they would be destroyed over the Soviet Union by advanced jet interceptors, such as the MIG-25, and by the thousands of SAM's deployed by the Soviets.

The hardline allegation was that the current and past administrations had engaged in willful unilateral disarmament because new systems to replace the contemporary ICBM's, SLBM's, and the B-52's have not been deployed.

Another area of worry for hardliners was the difference in quantity of general purpose forces between the United States and the Soviet Union. Congressman Beard noted that the Soviets possess 42,000 tanks and the United States 6,400; that the Soviets have 38,750 armored personnel carriers, compared with the 11,715 of the United States; that the Soviets operate 9,400 combat aircraft and the United States 7,272; and that the 19,000 Soviet artillery pieces are nearly four times the number of U. S. guns. The Coalition

for Peace Through Strength estimated that the Soviets have 4.8 million men under arms while the United States has 2.1 million.

A third concern was the increasing size and modernization of the Soviet Navy. J. William Middendorf, Secretary of the Navy in the Ford administration, stated, "Though many U. S. ships are superior in quality and our sailors are more experienced, the Soviet navy is more than twice the size of our fleet. In every category except aircraft carriers the Soviet fleet far exceeds ours."

A fourth concern of the hardline group was the lack of American civil defense preparations. The paucity of U. S. civil defense was held to be particularly alarming in view of what was thought to be significant Soviet civil defense efforts.

Lastly, hardliners voiced alarm that the Carter administration might sign a SALT II pact with the Soviet Union which would "legalize and perpetuate Soviet military superiority." (See Arms Control and Disarmament.)

The ominous conclusion drawn by hardline observers of Soviet actions was that the USSR had developed a war-fighting and war-surviving strategy, while the U. S. continued to follow a war avoidance policy. Thus the hardliners feared that in any future confrontation between the two nations the Soviet Union would either bluff its way to achievement of its objectives, or win any war that might actually start.

Carter Administration Perspectives. Administration officials, particularly Secretary of Defense Harold Brown, were aware of the Soviet arming activity, and they were acquainted with the hardline views. However, their perspective was less pessimistic regarding U. S. security. Basically the Carter policy was that if the Soviet threat grew to proportions which were considered endangering to U. S. security, compensatory actions would be taken. The planned response to a Soviet threat to the U. S. nuclear retaliatory systems would be the deployment of follow-on systems. These included the B-1 bomber as a replacement for the B-52's, the Trident submarine and associated SLBM's as a replacement for the currently deployed SLBM's carried on Polaris submarines; and the mobile MX ICBM as a replacement for the Minuteman and Titan ICBM's in fixed locations. Each of the follow-on systems is designed to provide pre- and post-launch invulnerability should these characteristics in the present systems be eroded by Soviet developments. As a short-term means of bolstering the effectiveness of the B-52's, the administration moved ahead with the development of air launched cruise missiles (ALCM's) to be carried aboard the bombers. Thus equipped, the B-52's would not be subject to Soviet air defenses around target areas because they would release the ALCM's hundreds of miles away from the targets.

Regarding general purpose weapons, and especially those involved in the defense of NATO Europe, President Carter announced in October

UPI

The *U. S. S. Saipan*, the Navy's newest amphibious assault ship, arrives in New York Harbor for public view.

his decision to order production of the components of enhanced radiation weapons for the Lance battlefield missile and the eight-inch howitzers. Proponents of the enhanced radiation weapons, which are often termed neutron bombs, claimed the new weapons could effectively neutralize the Soviet superiority in tanks should a war in Europe erupt. As an alternative to enhanced radiation weapons some administration officials preferred what have been called "smart weapons," or as the Pentagon officially terms them, Precision Guided Munitions (PGM's). Such weapons have been made possible by combining advances in microelectronic computation and sensor/guidance systems with new developments in non-nuclear explosives. Proponents claim the resulting weapons, small enough to be carried by infantry, will be capable of destroying the heaviest tanks, and even low-flying aircraft. As Defense Secretary Brown put it, "We need not match the enemy tank for tank, we retain a qualitative edge."

Another new weapon possibility, much further from final development than PGM's, is described as a laser beam device. In time, this weapon might approximate the death ray of the old Buck Rogers comic strip or the zap guns in

the movie *Star Wars*. Pentagon representatives say only that such a weapon is in the feasibility study phase.

A New Perspective. While the hardliners were arguing that the United States possessed too little in the way of military equipment, and the Carter administration was stating the United States was secure with currently deployed weapons, others were suggesting the United States had more than enough military strength vis-à-vis the Soviet Union. The most prominent advocates of this perspective were two academics, Philip Morrison, an MIT professor of physics, and Paul F. Walker, a research fellow at Harvard University. Their 1978 book, *The Price of Our Defense: A New Strategy for Military Spending,* represented a substantial contradiction of many of the views expressed by the hardline groups. It also contained numerous suggestions as to how the Carter administration might reduce defense expenditures by 40%, approximately $50 billion, while providing a more secure defense posture.

The core of the Morrison-Walker thesis was that threat analyses of the USSR should be shifted from counting overall numbers of men and equipment to a determination of the effectiveness of forces which could actually be put into combat. Following this logic Morrison and Walker concluded that several million of the men under arms in the Soviet Union did not comprise an effective fighting force in regard to a confrontation between the superpowers in Europe. For example, the authors calculated that some 700,-000 Soviet soldiers are used in agriculture, transportation, and other jobs normally handled by civilians in other nations. Further, 600,000 soldiers are tied down on the Chinese border, and 550,000 more are involved with strategic defense tasks within the Soviet Union. In another area the two professors noted that the Soviet submarine missile force is not really so effective as it appears to be when the submarines are simply counted. Their point was that the Soviet craft spend much more time out of service in port than do U. S. submarines, thus they constitute a less effective fighting force even though their numbers are greater.

Late in the year, it became clear that the forthcoming Carter budget would increase U. S. military spending by 3% above the inflation rate. In addition, the Pentagon was planning to seek supplemental funds to push development of the mobile M-X missile.

As 1978 ended, it appeared that the task of correctly assessing the Soviet threat would become a matter of even greater debate in the near future. In addition, the U. S. decision to grant full diplomatic recognition to the People's Republic of China and cut its ties with Taiwan would have a profound effect on the general U. S. military scheme.

ROBERT M. LAWRENCE
Colorado State University

MINING

The world's mining and mineral processing industry in 1978 continued its recovery from the 1975 slump.

Value of World Output. Value of total world crude mineral output (including fuels) in 1978 was an estimated (U. S.) $215 billion (constant 1973 dollars), compared with $208.4 billion for 1977; $201.7 billion for 1976; $191.6 billion for 1975; $195.0 billion for 1974; and $191.6 billion for 1973 (all figures revised from those published previously). Estimates for individual countries are not available for 1974–78, but for each of these years, the United States and the USSR were in close contention for first rank, with each accounting for slightly under 20% of the total, far ahead of next-ranked Venezuela and China (each about 6%) and Iran and Canada (each about 5%).

Ferrous Ores and Metals. Preliminary information suggests that 1978 world iron ore output totaled about 870 million tons, slightly greater than in 1977, but below 1974's record high of 913 million tons.

Manganese ore output apparently advanced only slightly, if at all, over the 1977 level. Market economy countries have restrained output owing to reduced steel industry requirements. Cutbacks in Brazilian operations represented the largest single element in reduced production, but lower production levels were noted for South Africa, Australia, and Gabon, and higher output in the USSR and India only partly compensated. Production of chromium and tungsten ores apparently continued to increase in 1978. Continued strife in Rhodesia undoubtedly adversely affected that nation's chromite shipments, but lower shipments to the United States were compensated for by increases elsewhere. There was less Chinese tungsten available on world markets in 1977 and 1978.

Molybdenum ore output in 1978 was expected to be ahead of that of 1977.

World steel output apparently increased by about 3% in 1978, with respect to 1977; principal producers and their estimated production (in million metric tons) were: USSR, 150; United States, 121; Japan, 99; West Germany, 43; China, 29; Italy, 25; France, 24; and United Kingdom, 21.

Nonferrous Ores and Metals. Complete 1978 returns on aluminum, bauxite, copper, lead, magnesium, and zinc probably will show higher output levels than in 1977. Tin production was about even with that of 1977, and nickel and mercury output were declining. Regarding mercury, it is significant that two major producing nations, Italy and Yugoslavia, both with substantial resources, produced no mercury in 1977 and in 1978, totally halting production rather than adding to appreciable world inventories.

Cobalt contributes little to world mineral production value, but this commodity, chiefly a byproduct of copper and nickel, achieved press notoriety in the spring when the Shaba region of Zaire was invaded. This area, the source of much of the world's cobalt, suddenly became a questionable source of supply. Cobalt prices soared, and Russian purchases prior to the outbreak of fighting suggested advanced Soviet knowledge. However, East European cobalt purchases in the West have been increasing since 1973, and production was rapidly restored following European military intervention.

Precious Metals. Despite soaring gold prices, world output in 1978 barely exceeded 1977's 39.4 million ounces, far below the record 50.6 million ounces of 1969. In contrast, 1978 silver output was expected to top 1977's 325 million ounce figure. Recently, total world silver output has been adjusted upward because of increased estimates of Polish output. Poland now ranks as a major world silver source, largely because of byproduct output from deep copper mines which have increased output recently.

The world platinum supply situation is speculative. Neither leading producer, the USSR nor South Africa, reports output, but together they are believed to account for over 90% of the total. A production level of 6 million ounces, not substantially different from recent years, seems indicated for 1978.

Fertilizer Materials. Preliminary reports indicate that output of phosphate rock, potash, and nitrogen fertilizer compounds all topped the historical record highs set in 1977, and that with each, stock buildups of the mid 1970's were drawn down as world consumption advanced.

Nitrogen fertilizer output totaled 45.4 million metric tons in the year ending June 30, 1977, up 4% over the preceding year, and this growth apparently continued into 1978. Leading 1976–77 producers (output in million tons) were: United States, 9.1; USSR, 8.6; China, 4.0 (estimated); India, 1.8; Poland, 1.5; France, 1.4; Japan, 1.4; West Germany, 1.3; the Netherlands 1.3; Rumania, 1.2; United Kingdom, 1.1; and Italy, 1.0. Among these nations, all but China and India met their own domestic requirements.

Other Trends. World asbestos production advanced slightly in 1978 with output increases in the USSR compensating for shortfalls elsewhere. Indications of possible health hazards led to restraint in output.

World 1978 cement output apparently totaled nearly 790 million tons, and gypsum production may have topped 70 million tons.

World sulfur output in 1978 was tentatively estimated at 55 million tons, up about 3% from 1977. This includes elemental sulfur mined and recovered in the elemental form as a byproduct, as well as sulfur recovered as sulfuric acid, H_2S or SO_2 from pyrites, oil, gas, and metallurgical processing operations.

See also Production Tables, pages 576–577.

CHARLES L. KIMBELL
U. S. Bureau of Mines

UPI

Muriel Humphrey, who was appointed to her late husband's Senate seat, declined to seek election.

MINNESOTA

Two events of consequence left their mark on Minnesota politics throughout 1978.

The year opened on a sad note when Sen. Hubert H. Humphrey lost his final bout with cancer on January 13. (*See* Obituary, page 375.) One of the most thoroughly creative and widely beloved political leaders of his time, Humphrey had been the major architect and unchallenged leader of the dominant Democrat-Farmer Labor party (DFL) for over a generation. On Election Day, just 10 months after Humphrey's death, the citizens of the North Star State dealt the DFL the most devastating defeat in its history.

The Year in Politics. On January 25, Gov. Rudy Perpich appointed Muriel Humphrey, the late senator's wife, to fill the seat until the November elections. Her appointment was widely approved, and it saved the DFL from a fight at a time when Minnesota and the nation so deeply missed their "Happy Warrior."

But by the summer, the battle in the DFL over Humphrey's seat was being waged by Robert Short, a self-made millionaire who had served earlier as treasurer of the National Democratic Party, and by Donald Fraser, a U. S. Congressman. Short labeled Fraser too liberal for the times and spent much of his personal fortune sharpening his anti-Fraser campaign. Although he won the September 12 primary, Short's vituperative campaign led to bitterness in the party.

In the November elections, independents and disenchanted DFLers supported David Durenberger, the newest member of Minnesota's Independent-Republican (IR) "team." Reputedly a man of high personal integrity, moderate leanings, and political balance, Durenberger swamped his opponent with 61% of the vote.

Meanwhile, DFL Sen. Wendell Anderson, a former governor, also found himself on the political defensive. Rudy Boschwitz, a highly successful business executive from Plywood, proved to be a genuinely charming and attractive candidate. By August, the Independent-Republican challenger led the DFL incumbent by some 20 points in public opinion polls. Boschwitz flooded the media with an attack on Anderson's record and won the election with a 57% majority.

The third major defeat suffered by the DFL came in the gubernatorial race. DFL Gov. Perpich was opposed by Al Quie, a longtime U. S. Congressman from southeastern Minnesota. Quie's leadership in promoting educational legislation had earned him national respect and recognition. Quie's campaign focused on Perpich's expenditures and accounting practices while in office, and he won the election with 53% of the vote.

These IR gains, coupled with a most remarkable gain of 32 seats in the state House of Representatives (the Senate was not up for election), indicated that Minnesota was ready to turn out the DFL "rascals" and return to a more efficacious two-party system. What seemed clear in post-Humphrey Minnesota was that the state expected certain fundamental changes: greater fiscal restraint; improvements in state management; lowered taxes, or at least the indexing of taxes so as to avoid unwarranted windfalls due to inflated incomes; and fewer costly legislative initiatives. The new IR leadership was expected to gain from Minnesota's resources a rate of economic growth that could support necessary services, maintain an educational system of quality, and expand agribusiness—without raising taxes.

G. THEODORE MITAU
Minnesota State University

—— **MINNESOTA · Information Highlights** ——

Area: 84,068 square miles (217,736 km²).
Population (Jan. 1978 est.): 3,987,000.
Chief Cities (1970 census): St. Paul, the capital, 309,-828; Minneapolis, 434,400.
Government (1978): *Chief Officers*—governor, Rudy Perpich (DFL); lt. gov., Alec G. Olson (DFL). *Legislature*—Senate, 67 members; House of Representatives, 134 members.
Education (1977–78): *Enrollment*—public elementary schools, 402,279 pupils; public secondary, 434,141; colleges and universities, 188,688 students. *Public school expenditures,* $1,898,393,000 ($1,859 per pupil).
State Finances (fiscal year 1977): *Revenues,* $4,385,-035,000; *expenditures,* $4,157,681,000.
Personal Income (1977): $28,337,000,000; per capita, $7,129.
Labor Force (July 1978): *Nonagricultural wage and salary earners,* 1,692,200; *unemployed,* 76,100 (3.8% of total force).

MISSISSIPPI

Politics was the major theme in Mississippi in 1978. The state's first open race for the United States Senate in more than 30 years resulted in a Republican victory, marking the party's initial win in a statewide contest and its first claim to a Senate seat since Reconstruction.

Elections. Forty-year-old Republican Congressman Thad Cochran of Jackson emerged from the November 7 general election as the winner of the seat being vacated by six-term U. S. Sen. James O. Eastland. Cochran who was an easy victor over state Sen. Charles Pickering in the June primary election, captured 45% of the nearly 584,000 votes cast by only slightly more than one half of the state's registered voters.

District attorney and former Laurel mayor Maurice Dantin, the Democratic nominee who had shown considerable strength in leading a field of major contenders in the first primary and then defeating Gov. Cliff Finch in a runoff election, received only 32% of the vote. Independent Charles Evers, long-time civil rights activist and now the black mayor of Fayette, received 23% of the vote and carried 12 counties.

In Congressional races, Mississippi's three incumbent Democrats won reelection, and a Republican, Jon C. Hinson of Tylertown, won the seat vacated by Representative Cochran. Trent Lott (R) was unopposed. Other contests involved two supreme court seats, state circuit and chancery judgeships, and numerous school board posts. Six constitutional amendments, most of which removed obsolete provisions, gained overwhelming approval.

Legislative Actions. In a session that was extended from 90 days to 95 days in order to meet requirements for handling appropriations bills, lawmakers achieved long-sought reforms of the management of 16th section school lands, enacted measures to revitalize the state highway construction program, and effected limited state government reorganization by combining a number of existing agencies into new departments of natural resources and wildlife conservation. Other accomplishments by the legislators included the adoption of a balanced budget for 1978–79 and the removal of the tax on electricity and natural gas sales to residential customers.

The perennial issue of property tax reform was left unsettled when reappraisal and assessment equalization bills were defeated. Gubernatorial succession failed to gain approval, and a restricted "sunset" enactment was vetoed after the legislature had adjourned.

Other Highlights. In November parties to a 12-year-old suit to redistrict the Mississippi legislature failed to reach agreement on a compromise seating plan as ordered by a three-judge federal panel. A separate plan which was en-

WIDE WORLD

Rep. Thad Cochrane (D-Miss.) embraces his wife, Rose, after winning the GOP nomination for the U. S. Senate in June. Cochrane went on to win the November election.

acted by the state legislature but rejected by the U. S. Justice Department under the Voting Rights Act of 1965, was pending before the federal court for the District of Columbia at year's end.

A landmark property assessment equalization suit which had been filed against the State Tax Commission by a coalition of business and civic leaders from across the state was heard by the Hinds County Chancery Court in October and November, but the year ended without a ruling on the issue.

Demanding more jobs and other improvements, blacks in Lexington, Tupelo, and several other cities in North Mississippi throughout the year organized marches, demonstrations, and boycotts against white merchants.

DANA B. BRAMMER
University of Mississippi

—— **MISSISSIPPI · Information Highlights** ——

Area: 47,716 square miles (123,584 km²).
Population (Jan. 1978 est.): 2,404,000.
Chief Cities (1970 census): Jackson, the capital, 153,-968; Biloxi, 48,486; Meridian, 45,083.
Government (1978): *Chief Officers*—governor, Cliff Finch (D); lt. gov., Evelyn Gandy (D). *Legislature*—Senate, 52 members; House of Representatives, 122 members.
Education (1977–78): *Enrollment*—public elementary schools 277,132 pupils; public secondary, 224,893; colleges and universities, 98,420 students. *Public school expenditures*, $618,299,000 ($1,159 per pupil).
State Finances (fiscal year 1977): *Revenues*, $2,030,-629,000; *expenditures*, $1,922,027,000.
Personal Income (1977): $12,019,000,000; per capita, $5,030.
Labor Force (July 1978): *Nonagricultural wage and salary earners*, 795,600; *unemployed*, 80,900 (8.2% of total force).

MISSOURI

Politics occupied the Missouri scene in 1978. "Right-to-work" forces were successful in their efforts to put before the voters a constitutional amendment prohibiting union membership as a condition for employment. When a petition drive was launched early in the year, opponents countered with pleas to citizens not to sign the petitions. Failing in that, labor and its friends instituted a series of court challenges intended to keep the proposal off the ballot. After the courts upheld the legality of the petitions, opponents endeavored to convince voters that the proposal would be detrimental to Missouri's economy. Charges and countercharges, accompanied by heavy expenditures for media advertising, marked the fight. The outcome was a decisive defeat for the amendment. To the surprise of many observers it was defeated in most rural areas as well as in St. Louis and Kansas City.

There was only one state race. Veteran Warren Hearnes (D), governor from 1965 to 1973, was pitted against a newcomer, James Antonio, for the auditor's office. Antonio, a CPA, capitalized on his expertise and his record as deputy auditor to overcome a lack of voter recognition. He also outspent Hearnes by 2–1. The defeat shattered Hearnes' hope for a comeback. All of Missouri's ten congressmen, eight Democrats and two Republicans, were reelected.

The Administration. Gov. Joseph P. Teasdale's stormy administration continued its tumultuous course with more high level dismissals. Some of those removed from office, including Social Services Director James F. Walsh and Public Safety Director William K. Carnes, were vocal in their criticism of the governor, whom they characterized as lacking in administrative skills. Such charges were aired previously by other officials who were unable to work with Teasdale. Of the nine department directors appointed by Teasdale when he assumed office in January 1977, six had left by year-end. Five top-level assistants have also come and gone. The governor defended his actions with the analogy of the coach who must change players to improve the team.

Legislation. Highlights of the 1978 legislative session included a new campaign finance law, a measure to prevent foreigners from buying Missouri farm land, laws enlarging the powers of the state Insurance Division over rates and practices, and a limitation on suits against state and local governmental agencies.

On November 7, the last train left St. Louis' Union Station, which for many years was jammed with travelers departing and arriving on some 400 trains daily. AMTRAK moved its limited operation to other quarters, and Union Station was closed. The future of the 84-year-old National Landmark remained uncertain as 1978 drew to a close.

RUTH W. TOWNE
Northeast Missouri State University

MONTANA

After going into receivership in December 1977, the Milwaukee railroad opened negotiations with the Union Pacific for the sale of its lines west of Butte. This development and the announcement of a possible future curtailment of operations in Montana brought consternation to many towns along the railroad's route. Also of enormous potential significance was the December 1977 announcement by the Decker Coal Company that it would challenge the constitutionality of the state's coal severance tax. In April the four largest coal companies in the state, under prodding from utility customers in Texas and the midwest, paid their first quarter's taxes under protest. This was followed in June by a suit by the coal companies and utilities, filed in Helena's district court, and an August request that the court stop the state from spending coal tax revenues pending the outcome of the suit.

The Environment. The state Board of Natural Resources and Conservation continued to hold hearings to determine allocations of Yellowstone River Basin waters. The board has worked out reservations for municipal use, irrigation, water storage, and instream flow. Instream flow requests included annual reservation of millions of acre-feet by the state Department of Health and Environmental Sciences and Fish and Game

---

MISSOURI • Information Highlights

Area: 69,686 square miles (180,487 km²).
Population (Jan. 1978 est.): 4,815,000.
Chief Cities (1970 census): Jefferson City, the capital, 32,407; St. Louis, 622,236; Kansas City, 507,087.
Government (1978): *Chief Officers*—governor, Joseph P. Teasdale (D); lt. gov., William C. Phelps (R). *General Assembly*—Senate, 34 members; House of Representatives, 163 members.
Education (1977–78): *Enrollment*—public elementary schools, 614,938 pupils; public secondary, 316,294; colleges and universities, 222,264 students. *Public school expenditures,* $1,323,088,000.
State Finances (fiscal year 1977): *Revenues,* $3,099,-660,000; *expenditures,* $2,790,077,000.
Personal Income (1977): $31,943,000,000; per capita, $6,654.
Labor Force (July 1978): *Nonagricultural wage and salary earners,* 1,886,100; *unemployed,* 115,500 (5.1% of total force).

MONTANA • Information Highlights

Area: 147,138 square miles (381,087 km²).
Population (Jan. 1978 est.): 764,000.
Chief Cities (1970 census): Helena, the capital, 22,557; Billings, 61,581; Great Falls, 60,091.
Government (1978): *Chief Officers*—governor, Thomas L. Judge (D); lt. gov., Ted Schwinden (D). *Legislature*—Senate, 50 members; House of Representatives, 100 members.
Education (1977–78): *Enrollment*—public elementary schools, 111,843 pupils; public secondary, 56,889; colleges and universities, 31,646 students. *Public school expenditures,* $331,600,000 ($1,801 per pupil).
State Finances (fiscal year 1977): *Revenues,* $850,823,-000; *expenditures,* $783,421,000.
Personal Income (1977): $4,661,000,000; per capita, $6,125.
Labor Force (July 1978): *Nonagricultural wage salary earners,* 279,000; *unemployed,* 22,400 (5.8% of total force).

Commission, to protect water purity and fish and wildlife.

Politics. In the June primaries, Rep. Max Baucus won the Democratic nomination for a U. S. Senate seat by defeating Paul Hatfield. Gov. Thomas L. Judge had earlier appointed Hatfield to fill the seat vacated by the death of Lee Metcalf. Following a sometimes bitter general campaign, Baucus defeated Republican opponent Larry Williams. Republican Ron Marlenee won reelection in the eastern congressional district, and in the west Democrat Pat Williams won a first term by defeating Jim Waltermire. In state legislative races, Democrats clung to control of the House, but for the first time in more than 20 years Republicans gained control of the Senate by a narrow margin. Voters faced a complicated ballot which included 11 initiatives, referenda, and constitutional amendments. Among those which passed were measures allowing local governments to adopt obscenity ordinances, imposing stringent requirements for locating nuclear plants in the state, and continuing a property tax levy for the support of higher education.

Other Major Events. Proposed construction of two 800-megawatt power plants at Colstrip remained under consideration by the U. S. Environmental Protection Agency and state and federal courts. A three-and-a-half month strike by pilots of Northwest Airlines ended August 15. Overall, agricultural production and prices rose.

RICHARD B. ROEDER, *Montana State University*

MONTREAL

Jean Drapeau, the mayor of Montreal for 21 years, easily defeated two opponents in municipal elections on November 12 to win a seventh term in office. The 62-year-old mayor, Canada's most durable and perhaps most popular politician, gained more than 60% of the vote to defeat Serge Joyal, head of the new Groupe d'Action Municipal (GAM), and Guy Duquette, of the Rassemblement des Citoyens de Montréal (RCM).

Drapeau's reelection came in the face of accusations of administrative errors by the Malouf Commission and acute public reaction to the 1976 Olympics extravaganza (whose cost jumped from C. $120,000,000 in 1970 to a real cost of $1,277,000,000 by 1977). Drapeau's Parti Civique also won 52 of the 54 seats on the city council.

Economically, 1978 was another year of stagnation for Montreal. Unemployment neared 10%; there were few new jobs; and the recovery of the tourist industry was slow. High taxes remained a serious handicap to economic growth. The number of houses for sale in Montreal increased by 33.7%, but prices rose slightly. Companies and head offices continued their long-term trend of moving to Toronto. Only the Sun Life Insurance firm chose to make it a political

gesture. Their move purportedly was prompted by Law 101. The company's business in Quebec subsequently fell by some 25 to 33%.

Despite the turmoil over Law 101 in 1977, most companies in 1978 found the rules to be flexible. However, the Protestant School Board and the Catholic School Board of greater Montreal decided to end classes in English for ineligible children. That practice had cost them millions of dollars in provincial grants.

On the labor front 1978 was more quiet than 1977, despite some harsh conflicts. *La Presse* and *Montréal-Matin,* two major daily newspapers, went on strike for four months over the issue of control of information.

M. Pierre Desmarais II, the mayor of nearby Outremont and the head of the Communauté urbaine de Montréal (CUM), led the struggle against a fiscal reform plan by the provincial government which, in his view, would slash the revenues of Quebec's municipalities.

Montreal was honored for achievements in sports: the Montreal Canadiens won their third consecutive National Hockey League (NHL) Stanley Cup; in October, Île Notre-Dame was the site of the Formula One, Canadian Grand Prix automobile race; the Montreal Alouettes again participated in the Grey Cup. The Alouettes, winners of the cup in 1977, were defeated by Edmonton.

In the arts, the eight new stations in Montreal's subway system gathered numerous prizes for their integration of engineering, art, and architecture. Two international film festivals held in Montreal also were praised.

JEAN-PIERRE WALLOT, *University of Montreal*

MOROCCO

The war in the phosphate-rich former Spanish Sahara territory continued to be the most important event in Morocco in 1978. After a coup toppled the Mauritanian leader in July and effectively ended Mauritania's partnership in the war against the Polisario Front, Morocco's 40,-000-man contingent fought alone, draining the country's resources. Diplomatic efforts to end the war failed.

Sahara War. Morocco's total defense spending almost doubled in 1978 to about (U. S.) $1.9 billion from roughly $1 billion in 1977. Rabat bought 50 Mirage jet fighters from France at a cost of $650 million and negotiated with Westinghouse for an air defense system costing some $200 million. Morocco sought unsuccessfully to buy $100 million in counter-insurgency equipment from the United States.

In three years of war, Polisario insurgents have successfully tied down about half of the Moroccan army in the territory and in Mauritania to the south, by means of lightning strikes on outposts. The phosphate mines at Bu Craa and the conveyor belt which transports ore to El Aaiún port on the Atlantic remained at a

JEAN DECOSSE, GAMMA-LIAISON

The fourth Congress of the Polisario Front, an insurgent group, was held somewhere near Tindouf, Algeria. Since 1975, Polisario insurgents have successfully tied down about half of the Moroccan army.

standstill because of Polisario attacks. Although most of the fighting took place in the Sahara territory, in late 1978 Polisario penetrated into southern Morocco, ambushing army convoys. Morocco blamed the raids on the regular army of Algeria, which arms Polisario and provides bases as well.

Peace Efforts. After a July coup brought down the Mauritanian government because of the war's heavy toll, Polisario declared a unilateral ceasefire with Mauritania. Attempts to negotiate a settlement immediately intensified but then broke down later in 1978 over Morocco's insistence on keeping the territory, and Algeria's continued support of self-determination for the Saharan people. Polisario, too, remained adamant about making a political solution through military force.

Libya, which provides arms to Polisario, was reported pushing the separatists to reach a compromise settlement which could involve a Polisario "mini-state" in the third of the territory annexed by Mauritania. Ivory Coast President Félix Houphouët-Boigny tried to persuade France to halt its limited military intervention on the side of Morocco. Spain, which ceded the territory to Morocco and Mauritania in 1976, as well as Saudi Arabia and Sudan's President Jaafar al-Nemery, attempted to mediate the dispute.

Economy. Defense costs, estimated at $2 million a day for the Saharan war, took a heavy toll on resources in 1978. Another costly international venture was King Hassan's second airlifting within a year of 1,200 Moroccan troops to help shore up the government of Zaire following the invasion of Zaire's Shaba province in May.

Earnings from phosphates stayed low because of depressed world prices, but the Soviet Union announced it would invest some $2 billion in developing a new phosphate mine in southern Morocco and buy up to ten million tons of phosphate a year.

Morocco had more good news in October, when it was announced that substantial oil reserves had been discovered. The oil is expected to cover the country's own needs—now supplied by Iraq and the Soviet Union—and might enable Morocco to become an exporter.

See also AFRICA.

JOSEPH MARGOLIS, *"African Update"*
African-American Institute

───── **MOROCCO · Information Highlights** ─────

Official Name: Kingdom of Morocco.
Location: Northwest Africa.
Area: 180,602 square miles (467,759 km^2).
Population (1978 est.): 18,900,000.
Chief Cities (1973 est.): Rabat, the capital, 385,000; Casablanca, 2,000,000; Marrakesh, 330,000; Fez, 322,000.
Government: *Head of state,* Hassan II, king (acceded 1961). *Head of government,* Ahmed Osman, prime minister (took office 1972).
Monetary Unit: Dirham (3.99 dirhams equal U.S.$1, Sept. 1978).
Manufactures (major products): Coal, electric power, phosphates, iron ore, lead, zinc.
Agriculture (major products): Barley, wheat, citrus, sugar beets, grapes.

ORLANDO, TRANSWORLD FEATURE SYNDICATE

The Wiz, a $23 million adaptation of the Broadway show, starring Diana Ross as Dorothy, was seen to represent the comeback of the musical motion picture.

MOTION PICTURES

Musicals, once the pride of Hollywood, but more recently virtually extinct, showed signs of making a comeback in one of the year's most interesting motion picture developments. Sidney Lumet, who said he spent $23 million making *The Wiz*, predicted a further new wave of musicals. His reasoning: the burgeoning worldwide recording sales make an alliance with them a natural packaging formula.

Events supported this view. The first pressing of *Wiz* albums was sold out before the release of the film. Motown structured the film around Diana Ross, even though it meant making Dorothy a 24-year-old schoolteacher. Michael Jackson, who became a star with the Jackson Five rock group, was cast as the Scarecrow.

The Stigwood Organization, profiting from the success of *Saturday Night Fever* with its Bee Gees score, heavily promoted albums for *Grease*, based on the Broadway show, and *Sgt. Pepper's Lonely Hearts Club Band*, based on the Beatles album. Although critics were cool to both films, record sales were lucrative, and in the case of *Grease*, audiences flocked to the film.

The Buddy Holly Story, with its nostalgic array of rock songs written by the composer-performer who was killed at 22 in a 1955 air crash, demonstrated further public interest. Although less successful, *American Hot Wax* also recalled the days of rock, and *I Wanna Hold Your Hand* tried to cash in on Beatle-worship.

Musicals are the one type of film which other countries have been unable to develop convincingly. (Westerns have been imitated, albeit poorly.) But rising costs and a few gigantic flops (*Hello Dolly, Star*) soured the industry on the risks. With big budgets in vogue again, musicals are more feasible, although style changes are indicated by some of the year's crop. Song-and-dance films like *The Wiz* are closer to old forms; films that integrate the work of a new generation of pop stars, groups, and composers point to another avenue.

Popularity. Hopes of film producers, distributors, and theater operators were considerably buoyed by a sharp upturn in business. After a period of audience decline and the conversion of large theaters into smaller houses, the public streamed back to the movies. Summer business was the best in years. Analysts attempted to learn why. Television no longer appeared to be an automatic competitor. The long-promised boom in video discs had not yet arrived, although more people were buying available recorded films and equipment. That development still posed the greatest long-range challenge to theaters, but meanwhile signs pointed to continuing prosperity for theaters showing the type of films that audiences wanted to see.

With audience numbers in mind, many operators have been increasingly reluctant to book films lacking the magnetism of blockbusters.

Pretty Baby centers on the lives of various women living in the red-light district of New Orleans in 1917. Keith Carradine, Susan Sarandon, and Brooke Shields are the stars.

MAUREEN LAMBRAY, COPYRIGHT © 1978 PARAMOUNT PICTURES CORPORATION. ALL RIGHTS RESERVED.

THE MUSEUM OF MODERN ART, FILM STILLS ARCHIVE

Heaven Can Wait, a new version of Here Comes Mr. Jordan, featured Warren Beatty in the main role.

This reluctance has worked against those film-makers who aim for smaller, special audiences. An exception was *Girl Friends,* an independent drama that Claudia Weill, formerly a documentary maker, filmed on a budget of $500,000 obtained from foundations and friends. It was a hit at the Cannes Film Festival, and Warner Bros. bought it, then signed Weill to make two more films. Her experience gave hope to those wishing to keep "independent cinema" alive.

Works by Neil Simon have enjoyed tremendous success both on the stage and as movies. The film version of *California Suite,* with Alan Alda, Michael Caine, Bill Cosby, Jane Fonda, Walter Matthau, and Elaine May, was released.

Artistic Growth. If any one event could be singled out as the most important for the serious growth of American cinema, it might be Woody Allen's first drama, *Interiors.* The film represented more than a humorist deciding to get a drama out of his system. Those who extolled *Interiors* noted the similarity to the style of Ingmar Bergman and saw Allen, whose comedies have had serious undertones, emerging as an artist of versatility. Allen did not appear in the film. Coincidentally, it was also the year in which Charlie Chaplin's 1923 film *Woman of Paris,* withdrawn after the public reacted coolly to a romantic film in which Chaplin did not star, was rediscovered and hailed by leading critics as a lost masterpiece. Even Chaplin, noted for his efforts to grow as an artist, never did a somber drama. Allen thus moved into a singular position as both a foremost director of comedic films and a new dramatic force in the motion picture business. (*See also* BIOGRAPHY.)

Another surprise was Ingrid Bergman in Ingmar Bergman's *Autumn Sonata.* For years Miss Bergman was appreciated as a luminous Hollywood star, but her wide range of films never established her as an actress of great depth. In *Autumn Sonata,* acting in her native Swedish under Bergman's masterly direction, she gave an astonishingly profound and complex performance as a famed concert pianist who has a night of harrowing emotional confrontation with her estranged daughter (Liv Ullmann). This triumph of Bergman at the age of 63 catapulted her into awards competition. Director Bergman, whose *The Serpent's Egg* (1978) was less well-received than most of his films, earned new acclaim with *Autumn Sonata.*

In some cases artistic growth appeared stunted. Lena Wertmüller, lionized after a series of films culminating with *Seven Beauties,* failed in the eyes of critics and public with *The End of the World in Our Usual Bed in a Night Full of Rain,* her first in English. Subsequently her picture deal with Warner Bros. was scrapped, and she decided to work independently again. John Avildsen, who directed the extraordinarily popular *Rocky,* stumbled with *Slow Dancing in the Big City,* a turgid romantic drama teaming Ann Ditchburn of the National Ballet of Canada as an aspiring ballerina and Paul Sorvino as a Jimmy Breslin-type columnist.

Stars. Jill Clayburgh had earlier commanded attention for her performances in such pictures as *Gable and Lombard* and *Semi-Tough,* but her breakthrough to stardom came as the divorcée in Paul Mazursky's *An Unmarried Woman,* which although not notably realistic, dealt seriously and entertainingly with the problems of a woman trying to reestablish her sense of identity and self-worth. Clayburgh's tour de force put her in contention for awards and earned her a part as an opera singer in Bernardo Bertolucci's *La Luna.*

Rising charismatic actor Richard Gere was recognized for his previous skillful performance in *Looking for Mr. Goodbar.* In both *Days of Heaven* and *Bloodbrothers,* he gave additional signs of dramatic power and appeared destined for star status.

Other new film performers included model Brooke Shields, who caused a stir in her film debut as a child prostitute in Louis Malle's *Pretty Baby.* Also, several performers known for their work on television were making rapid headway. Chevy Chase appeared opposite Goldie Hawn in *Foul Play* and John Belushi won plaudits in the fraternity travesty *National Lampoon's Animal House.* Two performances by television personalities which proved less electrifying to the film world were Farrah Fawcett-Majors in her first film, *Somebody Killed Her Husband* and Henry Winkler in *The One and Only.*

Among the veterans, Warren Beatty was back with good looks and charm in *Heaven Can Wait* (the remake of *Here Comes Mr. Jordan*). Laurence Olivier was busier than ever making the most of a variety of parts beneath his reputation as the world's most distinguished English-speaking actor. He appeared as an auto tycoon in the screen version of Harold Robbin's *The Betsy,* and as a Nazi-hunter in *The Boys from Brazil.* Marlon Brando returned in *Superman.* Even as Peter Seller's new Inspector Clouseau comedy *Revenge of the Pink Panther* was proving to be popular, Sellers announced that he did not want to do any more in the series, but was planning a new series based on the old *Chandu the Magician* radio show.

Vietnam. Slowly, a body of films relating to the Vietnam war began to emerge. The most publicized of all, Francis Ford Coppola's *Apocalypse,* was still in the editing stage and scheduled for spring 1979. The cost had reportedly mounted to $30 million. *Who'll Stop the Rain* was linked to drug traffic and disillusionment in Vietnam, although it turned out to be pri-

COPYRIGHT © 1978, UNITED ARTISTS CORPORATION. ALL RIGHTS RESERVED.

Jon Voight and Jane Fonda star in *Coming Home,* one of the first films involving the Vietnam war.

marily an action vehicle for Nick Nolte, Michael Moriarty and Tuesday Weld. *Coming Home,* with Jon Voight and Jane Fonda, in addition to being concerned with anguish over Vietnam, explored callousness toward crippled veterans. War conditions were depicted in *The Boys In Company C.* Many critics felt that the most effective film thus far about Vietnam was the taut *Go Tell the Spartans,* with Burt Lancaster as a weary officer trying to carry out his duty during the early days of America's military commitment.

Animation and Family Films. The problems of convincing the public to see ambitious animated films not of the Disney genre have militated against animation becoming a lucrative field for theatrical features. In 1978, however, there were two major works. Richard Adams' bestselling novel *Watership Down,* about rabbits who leave their endangered warren to search for peace and freedom, was adapted for the screen and directed by Martin Rosen. Ralph Bakshi, who has earned a reputation for innovation and controversial, socially-conscious animated films, adapted J. R. R. Tolkien's *Lord of the Rings.* Both films were conceived for adults as well as children. In the general area of live action family films, the most lavish was *International Velvet,* starring Tatum O'Neal in a sequel to the film that made Elizabeth Taylor a star. *The Magic of Lassie* played at the famed Radio City Music Hall in New York. (*See* Special Report, page 369.)

International. Simone Signoret, heavy-set and aged, gave an appealing performance in *Madame Rosa,* about a Jewish woman who cares for children of prostitutes in Paris. Franco Brusati, until now best known as a screenwriter, novelist, and playwright, directed *Bread and*

COPYRIGHT © 1978, UNITED ARTISTS CORPORATION. ALL RIGHTS RESERVED.

MOTION PICTURES | 1978

Labor leader Johnny Kovak (Sylvester Stallone) delivers a pep talk to union truckers in *F. I. S. T.* It was Stallone's second starring film role.

JOSEPH ANDREWS. Director, Tony Richardson; screenplay by Allan Scott and Chris Bryant; screenstory by Mr. Richardson; based on the novel by Henry Fielding. With Peter Firth, Ann-Margret, and John Gielgud.

AUTUMN SONATA. Director and writer, Ingmar Bergman. With Ingrid Bergman and Liv Ullmann.

THE BIG FIX. Director, Jeremy Paul Kagan; screenplay by Roger L. Simon, based on his novel. With Richard Dreyfuss, Susan Anspach, and Fritz Weaver.

BLUE COLLAR. Director, Paul Schrader; screenplay by Paul Schrader and Leonard Schrader; suggested by source material by Sydney A. Glass. With Richard Pryor, Harvey Keitel, and Yaphet Kotto.

THE BOYS FROM BRAZIL. Director, Franklin J. Schaffner; screenplay by Heywood Gould; from the novel by Ira Levin. With Gregory Peck and Laurence Olivier.

BREAD AND CHOCOLATE. Director, Franco Brusati; screenplay by Mr. Brusati, Iaia Fiastri and Nino Manfredi, based on a story by Mr. Brusati. With Anna Karina and Nino Manfredi

THE BUDDY HOLLY STORY. Director, Steve Rash; screenplay by Robert Gittlen; story by Mr. Rash and Fred Bauer. With Gary Busey.

CAPRICORN ONE. Director and writer, Peter Hyams. With Elliott Gould, James Brolin, Brenda Vaccaro; Karen Black and Telly Savalas.

CASEY'S SHADOW. Director, Martin Ritt; screenplay by Carol Sobleski; based on a short story by John McPhee. With Walter Matthau and Alexis Smith.

THE CHEAP DETECTIVE. Director, Robert Moore; screenplay by Neil Simon. With Peter Falk, Ann-Margret, Marsha Mason, and Sid Caesar.

COMING HOME. Director, Hal Ashby; screenplay by Waldo Salt and Robert C. Jones; based on a story by Nancy Dowd. With Jane Fonda, Jon Voight, and Bruce Dern.

CROSSED SWORDS. Director, Richard Fleischer; original screenplay by Berta Dominguez D. and Pierre Spengler; final screenplay by George MacDonald Fraser; based on Mark Twain's *The Prince and the Pauper*. With Oliver Reed, Raquel Welch, and Mark Lester.

DAYS OF HEAVEN. Director and writer, Terrence Malick. With Sam Shepard, Linda Manz, Brooke Adams, and Richard Gere.

DEATH ON THE NILE. Director, John Guillermin; screenplay by Anthony Shaffer. With David Niven, Angela Lansbury, Peter Ustinov, and Bette Davis.

DESPAIR. Director, Rainer Werner Fassbinder; screenplay by Tom Stoppard; from the novel by Vladimir Nabokov. With Dirk Bogarde.

A DREAM OF PASSION. Director and writer, Jules Dassin. With Melina Mercouri and Ellen Burstyn.

THE END. Director, Burt Reynolds; screenplay by Jerry Belson. With Burt Reynolds, Dom DeLuise, Sally Field, David Steinberg, and Joanne Woodward.

THE END OF THE WORLD IN OUR USUAL BED IN A NIGHT FULL OF RAIN. Director and writer, Lina Wertmuller. With Giancarlo Giannini and Candice Bergen.

F. I. S. T. Director, Norman Jewison; screenplay by Joe Eszterhas and Sylvester Stallone, based on a story by Mr. Eszterhas. With Sylvester Stallone, Peter Boyle, and Rod Steiger.

FOUL PLAY. Director and writer, Colin Higgins. With Goldie Hawn and Chevy Chase.

GIRL FRIENDS. Director, Claudia Weill; screenplay by Vickie Polon. With Anita Skinner and Bob Balaban.

GO TELL THE SPARTANS. Director, Ted Post; screenplay by Wendell Mayes. With Burt Lancaster.

GREASE. Director, Randal Kleiser; screenplay by Bronte Woodward; adapted by Allan Carr from the Broadway musical. With John Travolta and Olivia Newton-John.

HEAVEN CAN WAIT. Directors, Warren Beatty and Buck Henry; screenplay by Elaine May and Mr. Beatty; based on a Harry Segall play. With Warren Beatty, Julie Christie, and James Mason.

HOOPER. Director, Hal Needham; screenplay by Thomas Rickman and Bill Kerby; story by Walt Green and Walter S. Herndon. With Burt Reynolds and Sally Field.

HOUSE CALLS. Director, Howard Zieff; screenplay by Max Shulman, Julius J. Epstein, Alan Mandel, and Charles Shyer; story by Mr. Shulman and Mr. Epstein. With Walter Matthau, Glenda Jackson, and Art Carney.

INTERIORS. Director and writer, Woody Allen. With E. G. Marshall, Geraldine Page, Maureen Stapleton, and Diane Keaton.

INTERNATIONAL VELVET. Director and writer, Bryan Forbes; suggested by the novel, *National Velvet*. With Tatum O'Neal, Anthony Hopkins, and Christopher Plummer.

COPYRIGHT © 1978 PARAMOUNT PICTURES CORPORATION. ALL RIGHTS RESERVED.

The movie version of *Grease*, the musical of the 1950's era, enjoyed extreme popularity.

A LITTLE NIGHT MUSIC. Director, Harold Prince; screenplay by Hugh Wheeler, based on his book for the musical play suggested by Ingmar Bergman's *Smiles of a Summer Night;* music and lyrics by Stephen Sondheim, based on Mr. Sondheim's Broadway musical. With Elizabeth Taylor, Diana Rigg, and Len Cariou.

LORD OF THE RINGS. Director, Ralph Bakshi; adapted from J. R. R. Tolkien's novel *The Lord of the Rings.* (animated film)

MADAME ROSA. Director and writer, Moshe Mizrahi; based on the book by Emile Ajar. With Simone Signoret and Sammy Ben Youb.

MIDNIGHT EXPRESS. Director, Alan Parker; screenplay by Oliver Stone; based on the book *Midnight Express* by Billy Hayes and William Hoffer. With Brad Davis.

MOMENT BY MOMENT. Director and writer, Jane Wagner; produced by Robert Stigwood. With John Travolta and Lily Tomlin.

MOVIE, MOVIE. Director, Stanley Donen; screenplay by Larry Gelbart and Sheldon Keller. With George C. Scott, Trish Van Devere, and Eli Wallach.

NATIONAL LAMPOON'S ANIMAL HOUSE. Director, John Landis; screenplay by Harold Ramis, Douglas Kenney, and Chris Miller. With John Belushi, Thomas Hulce, Tim Matheson, Stephen Furst, and Donald Sutherland.

OLIVER'S STORY. Director, John Korty; screenplay by Erich Segal and Mr. Korty, based on the book by Mr. Segal. With Ryan O'Neal and Candice Bergen.

PARADISE ALLEY. Director and writer, Sylvester Stallone. With Mr. Stallone, Kevin Conway, Anne Archer, and Joe Spinell.

PRETTY BABY. Director, Louis Malle; screenplay by Polly Platt, from a story by Polly Platt and Louis Malle. With Keith Carradine, Brooke Shields, and Susan Sarandon.

REVENGE OF THE PINK PANTHER. Director, Blake Edwards; screenplay by Frank Waldman, Ron Clark, and Mr. Edwards. With Peter Sellers.

SEPTEMBER 30, 1955. Director and writer, James Bridges. With Richard Thomas and Susan Tyrrell.

THE SERPENT'S EGG. Director and writer, Ingmar Bergman. With Liv Ullmann and David Carradine.

SGT. PEPPER'S LONELY HEARTS CLUB BAND. Director, Michael Schultz; screenplay by Henry Edwards. With Peter Frampton, the Bee Gees, and Donald Pleasence.

A SLAVE OF LOVE. Director, Nikita Mikhalkov; screenplay by Friedrich Gorenstein and Andrei Mikhalkov-Konchalovsky. With Yelena Solovei and Rodion Nakhapetov.

SOMEBODY KILLED HER HUSBAND. Director, Lamont Johnson; screenplay by Reginald Rose. With Farrah Fawcett-Majors, Jeff Bridges, John Wood, and John Glover.

STRAIGHT TIME. Director, Ulu Grosbard; screenplay by Alvin Sargent, Edward Bunker, and Jeffrey Boam; based on Mr. Bunker's novel *No Beast So Fierce.* With Dustin Hoffman and Theresa Russell.

SUPERMAN. Director, Richard Dunner; screenplay by Mario Puzo, David and Leslie Newman, and Robert Benton, from a story by Mr. Puzo. With Christopher Reeves, Marlon Brando, and Gene Hackman.

AN UNMARRIED WOMAN. Director and writer, Paul Mazursky. With Jill Clayburgh, Alan Bates, Michael Murphy, and Cliff Gorman.

VIOLETTE. Director, Claude Chabrol; screenplay by Odile Barski, Herué Bromberger and Frédéric Grendel; from the book by Jean-Marie Fitère. With Isabelle Huppert.

WATERSHIP DOWN. Director and writer, Martin Rosen; from the book by Richard Adams. (animated film)

A WEDDING. Director, Robert Altman; screenplay by Mr. Altman, John Considine, Patricia Resnick, and Allan Nicholls. With Desi Arnaz, Jr., Carol Burnett, Geraldine Chaplin, Howard Duff, and Lillian Gish.

THE WILD GEESE. Director, Andrew V. McLaglen; screenplay by Reginald Rose. With Richard Burton, Roger Moore, Richard Harris, Hardy Kruger, and Stewart Granger.

WHO IS KILLING THE GREAT CHEFS OF EUROPE? Director, Ted Kotcheff; screenplay by Peter Stone; from the novel by Nan and Ivan Lyons. With Robert Morley, George Segal, and Jacqueline Bisset.

WHO'LL STOP THE RAIN. Director, Karel Reisz; screenplay by Judith Rascoe and Robert Stone, adapted from the novel, *Dog Soldiers,* by Robert Stone. With Michael Moriarty, Nick Nolte, and Tuesday Weld.

THE WIZ. Director, Sidney Lumet; screenplay by Joel Schumacher, from the Broadway musical of the same name. With Diana Ross, Michael Jackson, Nipsey Russell, Ted Ross, Lena Horne, and Richard Pryor.

Chocolate, a seriocomedy starring Nino Manfredi. Another Italian language film, *Viva Italia,* featured Alberto Sordi, Vittorio Gassman, and Ugo Tognazzi in satiric comedy vignettes. At the New York Film Festival François Truffaut unveiled his latest, *The Green Room,* in which he also starred as a man consumed by a desire to honor the dead. Also at the festival was Rainer Werner Fassbinder's *Despair,* starring Dirk Bogarde in a story based on Vladimir Nabokov's novel and scripted by Tom Stoppard. There has been an upsurge in Australian filmmaking; one example, *Newsfront,* about newsreel cameramen, was at the New York Film Festival. *The Chant of Jimmy Blacksmith,* about an oppressed aborigine who wages a vendetta, figured prominently in the Toronto Festival of Festivals. The Russian *A Slave of Love,* a compendium of nostalgia and tense drama involving silent film actors caught in the aftermath of the Russian revolution, earned attention. Jules Dassin, the American film director who lives in Greece, teamed his wife, Melina Mercouri, and Ellen Burstyn in an unusual drama, *A Dream of Passion,* about an actress (Mercouri) who is rehearsing a production of *Medea* and her relationship with a modern Medea (Burstyn). From Brazil came the satirical *Dona Flor and Her Two Husbands,* by Bruno Barreto.

Awards. The major news at the Academy Awards presentations was *Annie Hall.* Of all Woody Allen's films, it was the most popular with the public, a feat reflected in its being chosen best picture, with Diane Keaton, star of the film, winning as best actress and Allen named best director. The Oscar for best performance by an actor went to Richard Dreyfuss for *The Goodbye Girl.* The best foreign-language film Oscar went to *Madame Rosa.* The New York Film Critics Circle honored *Annie Hall* for best film, best director, best screenplay, and best actress. The choice of the Film Society of Lincoln Center for its annual award was director George Cukor for his lifetime achievements.

Birthday. Mickey Mouse, Walt Disney's most famous character, was 50 years old, and the Museum of Modern Art in New York honored him with a retrospective of his films, beginning with *Steamboat Willie.*

Inquiry. Accusations of abusive practices have long been rife in the film industry; many directors and performers have complained but have been reluctant to press charges. Cliff Robertson was amazed to discover that a check had been made out to him, bore his endorsement, but in fact had never been sent to him. This led him to launch an inquiry into what had happened to the money. It was learned that a producer had cashed it, and the investigation touched off a prosecution that made the Hollywood community take notice. A further inquiry was planned into motion picture business practices.

WILLIAM WOLF, *Film Critic*
"Cue New York"

MOZAMBIQUE

The plight of the economy and Rhodesian incursions against guerrillas operating from Mozambique worried Mozambique's citizens in 1978, but they had, as well, the satisfaction of having elected a National Assembly.

Politics. Late in 1977 the process of erecting a tiered-system of people's assemblies at local, district, provincial, and national levels was completed under direction of the *Frente de Libertação de Moçambique* (FRELIMO), the only legal party. In March the government passed a military draft for men and women over eighteen.

Economy. Defense against raids from Rhodesia on rebel guerrilla bases was, at 29% or $113 million, the number one priority in the 1978 budget. The worst floods in memory along the Zambezi Valley hurt economic recovery. To overcome the lack of economic data, FRELIMO announced an "offensive for planning" in 1978. Planners in search of models visited China, North Korea, the German Democratic Republic, and the USSR. Officials and representatives of large enterprises met in March to establish the National Planning Commission. Economic crisis prompted a reshuffling of the council of ministers to emphasize financing and development. Private banks, coal mines, and the only oil refinery were nationalized as "strategic."

Foreign Affairs. Cooperation with Tanzania, which began during FRELIMO's independence struggle, deepened in 1978. Both countries agreed jointly to train diplomats in Dar es Salaam. Cuban friendship was solidified beyond the signing of a 20-year Friendship and Cooperation Treaty in October 1977. Havana sent instructors to conventionalize FRELIMO's guerrilla army, and technicians to modernize sugar production. North Korea signed a 20-year friendship treaty. Sweden and Britain contributed greatly to development projects.

Despite its openly expressed hostility to South Africa's racial policies, Mozambique remains forced to rely on its neighbor for 15% of imports, and Pretoria exports 18% of its goods through Maputo's docks, providing valuable revenue to Mozambique.

THOMAS H. HENRIKSEN
State University of New York, Plattsburgh

—— MOZAMBIQUE • Information Highlights ——

Official Name: People's Republic of Mozambique.
Location: Southeastern coast of Africa.
Area: 302,328 square miles (783,029 km²).
Population (1978 est.): 9,900,000.
Chief City (1973 est.): Maputo, the capital, 383,775.
Government: *Head of state and government,* Samora Machel (took office June 1975). *Legislature* (unicameral)—People's Assembly.
Monetary Unit: Escudo (45 escudos equal U.S.$1, Oct. 1978).
Manufactures (major products): Cement, processed food, textiles, beverages, refined oil, chemicals, tobacco, glass.
Agriculture (major products): Cashews, cotton, sugar, copra, sisal, tea, subsistence crops.

MUSIC

Judging from the total number of performances in 1978, classical music appeared to play a larger part in U. S. cultural life than ever before. However, close scrutiny showed that the increased music activity may have had more to do with entertainment than with art.

New Works and Premieres. No new work received more than local recognition; none was significantly acknowledged as a signal work of art or accepted into the regular performance repertory of the highly visible world of public music. The performance exposure and testing of most new music, or at least most advanced music, remained concentrated in a comparatively private world. Many skilled contemporary music ensembles played for special interest audiences in widely dispersed centers, notably universities. Consequently most composers wrote for small forces, which would perform their music, rather than for large orchestras which would not.

Among the few major premieres by symphony orchestras was the first U. S. performance of Krzysztov Penderecki's violin concerto, a conservative work, eclectic in style. It was played by Isaac Stern, soloist, and the Minnesota Orchestra on January 4. A new tuba concerto by William Kraft was introduced by Roger Bobo and the Los Angeles Philharmonic on January 26. On October 12, under Zubin Mehta, the New York Philharmonic played the U. S. premiere of Pierre Boulez' *Notations.*

Typifying the specialized performance circumstances for new music, there was a Karlheinz Stockhausen festival held in mid-January on the University of Houston campus, with seven American premieres of his music, including *Sirius,* for four soloists and electronic tape. At a festival jointly sponsored by the California School for the Arts and the University of California, San Diego, Morton Subotnik's *Game Room and Wild Beasts,* Stockhausen's *Mantra,* and Lou Harrison's *Fugue for Percussion* were offered.

Symphony orchestras, striving to meet ever-increasing financial demands, wooed larger audiences with recycled standard repertories, featuring name soloists and, where possible, star conductors. Two major symphonies changed music leadership in 1978, the New York Philharmonic beginning its season under Zubin Mehta on September 14 and the Los Angeles Philharmonic under Carlo Maria Giulini on October 26. The appointments of Neville Marriner as music director of the Minnesota Orchestra (succeeding Stanislaw Skrowaczewski) and Leonard Slatkin as music director of the St. Louis Symphony were to take effect at the end of the 1978–79 season.

Opera. The opera companies presented a still more limited and traditional repertory than the symphonies, but a few new works were offered. There were U. S. premieres of Thea Musgrave's *Mary, Queen of Scots* (March 29, Virginia Opera) and Stephen Oliver's *The Duchess of Malfi* (August 5, Santa Fe Opera). There were world premieres of John Eaton's *Danton and Robespierre* (April 8, Indiana University), Robert Ward's *Claudia Legare* (April 14, Minnesota Opera) and Krzysztof Penderecki's *Paradise Lost* (November 29, Chicago Lyric Opera). *Paradise Lost,* with a libretto by Christopher Frye based on John Milton's poem, was the only premiere by a major U. S. company. It had been commissioned for the 1976–77 bicentennial season and, when finally completed by Penderecki and mounted in 1978, it drew wide international attention.

COURTESY, GURTMAN AND MURTHA ASSOCIATES

The Performing Arts Company of the People's Republic of China perform the *Peacock Dance.* The group of 150 musicians, singers, dancers, and actors from all parts of China began a tour of the United States in the summer.

Otherwise, what was new in the opera scene were old works never before produced in America: Handel's *Poro* (January, Kennedy Center), Verdi's *Stiffelio* (February 15, Opera Company of Boston), Mercadante's *Virginia* (March, Opera Orchestra of New York), Vivaldi's *Il Farnace* (November 1, Clarion Concerts, New York). The general nostalgia trend in the culture was noted operatically in revivals of operettas, among them Lehar's *The Merry Widow* (April 12, New York City Opera).

Finances. The federal government's support through grants from the National Endowment for the Arts continued strong but became even more crucial as inflation and events on the political and labor scenes affected music adversely. The passage in California of the property tax-cutting Proposition 13 had a restrictive and depressant impact on arts education and performance. Still harder, long-range consequences were anticipated in California and other states where the taxpayer revolt threatened to spread. The newspaper strike which on August 9 shut down *The New York Times, Daily News,* and (until October 5) the New York *Post,* blacked out the center of the country's music commerce for much of the second half of the year. With a serious effect on publicity, attendance, and reviews, the strike was a special hardship on recitalists making New York debuts.

Competitions. Music competitions, which play upon the American love of contests, continued to outweigh New York debut recitals as the most productive way to launch a career. The outstanding victors were Nathaniel Rosen, 30, cellist with the Pittsburgh Symphony, and Elmar Oliveira, 28, violinist from Binghamton, N. Y. On July 3 they became the first Americans in the Tchaikowsky Competition to win the gold medal awards for their instruments, and the first Americans to win in any instrumental category at Moscow since Van Cliburn won the piano award in 1958.

The Van Cliburn International Quadrennial Piano Competition, on the other hand, was won not by an American but by a South African pianist, Steven De Groote. For the first year of the Rockefeller Foundation-Kennedy Center Pianists' Competition, stressing contemporary music performance, Bradford Cowen, 32, of Bethesda, Md., was winner of the first prize—$10,000 and a national concert tour. The biggest vocal competition, the Metropolitan Opera National Council Auditions on April 9 divided first prize honors between Winifred Brown, soprano, and Wendy White, mezzo soprano, who earlier had won the WGN-Illinois Opera Guild Auditions. The Walter W. Naumberg Solo Competition for flutists was won in 1978 by Carol Wincenc in May, and its chamber music award was won by the Emerson String Quartet and Aulos Wind Quintet.

Among the composition competitions, the Pulitzer Prize in Music was awarded to Michael Colgrass' *Déja Vu* for percussion and orchestra (originally commissioned and introduced by the New York Philharmonic). Vincent Persichetti's English Horn Concerto won the first annual Kennedy Center-Friedheim Award. The cosponsoring Music Critics' Association subsequently withdrew from future participation in the Kennedy-Friedheim because of differing views on procedure, the efficacy of such competition, and the appropriateness of its role.

Commemorations. Among the major events were performances commemorating key anniversaries of individual artists. Vladimir Horowitz celebrated the 50th anniversary of his U. S. debut with a performance of Rachmaninoff's *Third Piano Concerto,* with Eugene Ormandy conducting the New York Philharmonic in Carnegie Hall, and again in February in a White House recital for President Jimmy Carter and guests. Andrés Segovia observed the 50th year since his New York debut with a recital in Avery Fisher Hall on February 12.

On August 25, a gala concert honoring Leonard Bernstein's 60th birthday was produced at the Wolf Trap Farm Park for the Performing Arts, by the National Symphony, Mstislav Rostropovich conducting. A large number of musical celebrities attended. Aaron Copland characterized the gala as an unprecedented recognition of an American musician. Upon turning 60, Bernstein announced that his primary occupation would be composition. Copland, on the other hand, who at 78 conducts exclusively, gave no indication that he would once more compose. He was given the American Symphony Orchestra League's Gold Baton Award.

Books containing 50,000 signatures and greetings were presented to Arthur Fiedler when he conducted his 50th Fourth of July concert with the Boston Pops at the Esplanade series he founded. On November 19, more than 60 illustrious opera artists traveled to San Francisco to honor Kurt Herbert Adler in a "Gold and Silver" gala benefit. The occasion was his 25th year as the San Francisco Opera's general director (the longest such tenure since Gatti-Casazza's at the Met, 1908–35) and his 50th year in opera.

The 150th anniversary of Schubert's death was observed in a national tour of Schubert recitals by Andre Watts, pianist, in company with Charles Treger, violinist, and other artists.

There were some 159 music festivals in the 50 states, District of Columbia, and Puerto Rico. Of these, the second annual Spoleto Festival USA (Charleston, S. C.) was the widest-ranging. In 18 days, May 25–June 11, it offered more than 100 events in all the performing arts. Two days were devoted to works of Leoš Janáček, the only important U. S. commemoration of the 50th anniversary of that composer's death. Five operas were also presented at Spoleto USA, including Samuel Barber's *Vanessa,* and *Martin's Lie* and *The Egg,* two one-acters by the festival's founding director, Gian Carlo Menotti.

ROBERT COMMANDAY
"San Francisco Chronicle"

DENVER CENTER FOR THE PERFORMING ARTS

Boettcher Concert Hall, Denver Center for the Performing Arts, opened in 1978. Pianist Vladimir Horowitz, celebrating the 50th anniversary of his U. S. debut, appeared with Zubin Mehta in New York.

UPI

TASS FROM SOVFOTO

Winners of the 1978 quadrennial Tchaikovsky Competition included (*left* to *right*): Elma Oliveira, U. S. violinist; Lyudmila Shemchuk, Soviet singer; Nathaniel Rosen, U. S. cellist; and Mikhail Pletnyov, Soviet pianist.

MICHAEL PUTLAND, RETNA

O. FRANKEN, SYGMA

Popular country music singer Willie Nelson, *above,* recorded *Stardust,* an album of hits from the 1930's and 1940's.

Dolly Parton was named entertainer of the year by the Country Music Association. Her hit disc was *Heartbreaker.*

MUSIC, POPULAR

Popular music did not have a quality year in 1978. The music, under the circumstances, was not so bad as it could have been. The problem was that it did not seem to matter much whether it was good *or* bad—popular music simply could not find many people who would take it seriously. Some would say the music brought this upon itself, by containing little worth attention; others would say popular music, as always, was in the "effect" rather than the "cause" realm, that it reflected trends and fads arising elsewhere, or at least arising generally.

There was diversity, of a sort, but the diversity that was *readily* available (on the radio, the record-sales charts, or coming to town for a concert) was fairly uniform in its lack of depth. On the one hand were entrenched purveyors of satin-shirt slickness, typified by Debbie Boone ("You Light Up My Life") and Barry Manilow, former commercial jingle writer, and on the other hand was much ado from another recycling of the "proletarian rebellion" gambit, called "punk rock" or "new wave," depending on the pretentiousness of the caller. The former offered gloss and an occasional pretty melody, as it took an attitude about lyrics being strictly filler material. (Indeed, the time was right for Willie Nelson, one of the most respected people in country music—which still puts the premium on lyrics—to record *Stardust,* an album of Tin Pan Alley of the 1930's and 1940's.) The latter, Punk Rock, was able to stir some emotions in England, but in America, wave after wave of punks seemed to be rebelling mostly as a lark—

at least from the audience's vantage point—and the only thing that most were clearly rebelling against was competence in playing instruments.

This is not to say all musicians in these two camps were either glib or incompetent, and it is not to say that these were the only camps. Disco music, which had been given a boost in quality by such former rock stars as the Bee Gees, was still going strong, having become as much a factor in rejuvenating the clothing industry as in getting America dancing again. Patti Smith and Bruce Springsteen, still nominally identified with punk rock, continued to try to say something beyond "Hey Baby, let's boogie," and Lou Reed, one of the founders of the term punk, had in *Street Hassle* one of his least compromising albums in years. There was a realm of music somewhere in between the slick and the attempted-profane, music carefully and competently produced but aspiring to a surface relationship with the listener; pleasant, easy, and nontaxing, it tacitly invoked the hamburger advertising slogan, "We do it all for you." If a single album led in this realm it was Eric Clapton's *Slowhand,* with such catchy, easy-going hits as "Lay Down Sally" and "Wonderful Tonight." Bob Seger was another notable practitioner here, his hits led by "Still the Same." Elvis Costello, even though he tried to put more into the words, was making roughly the same kind of music, basically a simplification of the "golden era" rock of the late 1960's. Others working here, at varying levels, included Foreigner, Tom Petty, Eddie Money, and Meat Loaf.

Meat Loaf, a rotund rocker who did nothing particularly new, became popular after his ap-

STEVE SCHAPIRO, SYGMA

The Bee Gees appear in the movie musical *Sgt. Pepper's Lonely Hearts Club Band.*

pearance in the spoof movie *The Rocky Horror Picture.* Movies, for better or worse, snuggled up to pop music in 1978 as they had not done in years. *Thank God It's Friday,* a sort of cheap imitation of *Saturday Night Fever's* lucrative association with disco, was said to lead a parade of pictures planned around pop music and its fashions. Critics generally detested *Sgt. Pepper's Lonely Hearts Club Band* (using Beatles music and starring Peter Frampton and the Bee Gees), but it did sell some sound-track albums. *Grease,* with John Travolta, Olivia Newton-John, Frankie Valli, and others, drew better reviews and was enormously popular with a very young audience. It had been tested on Broadway, of course; yet its music sounded oddly up to date for a 1950's period piece. The most powerful music movie —and, to those looking to take the music seriously, the saddest—was *The Last Waltz,* Martin Scorsese's straightforward treatment of The Band's farewell concert. Numerous Golden Era figures—Joni Mitchell, Neil Young, Van Morrison—helped The Band shut the era down. So did the once-reclusive Bob Dylan.

Dylan spent the year quite visible, in fact. He and the Rolling Stones were major among the Old Guard making U. S. tours, and Dylan's, covering 66 dates, was the longest of his career.

Before that he played in Japan and Australia and made his first European tour in 12 years. Along the way, he wrote some biting new songs, released in the album *Street Legal* that, as usual, set critics at one another's throats. The album had hard words and a soft sound—softened mainly by a ubiquitous chorus—and it attracted friends and enemies and little neutrality. People took *that* seriously. (The Rolling Stones, on the other hand, put the mindless "Miss You" on the radio all summer.) Other old hands given to making the listener think or feel who managed to attract some attention included Billy Joel, Carly Simon, Warren Zevon, and John Prine. Not many newcomers of their sort came forward, but Karla Bonoff (who had written "Home" for Bonnie Raitt) and Jack Tempchin (who had written "Peaceful, Easy Feeling" for the Eagles) made particularly strong impressions.

Popular music has a cyclical nature and its cycle relates to that of other social fashions. The one thing to expect with certainty of popular music is that it will change. It changed in 1978. People took it with a grain of salt, but that provided useful and probably necessary contrast from how seriously they once had taken it—and will again.

NOEL COPPAGE, *"Stereo Review"*

CHRISTOPHER HARRIS, PHOTO TRENDS

The Olympia Brass Band delights the crowd at the New Orleans Jazz Festival.

MUSIC—SPECIAL REPORT:

The Resurgence of Jazz

The America of the 1970's is fostering a beautiful jazz revival. The number of jazz clubs has grown from 10 to 80 in New York City and from 1 to 21 in Boston. The same success story is also unfolding in other major U. S. cities. The attendance at jazz festivals and concerts, as well as the sale of recorded jazz albums, are breaking all past records. Great jazz artists, including Slide Hampton, Art Farmer, and the legendary saxophonist Dexter Gordon, have left their adopted European countries to return home to the United States where they are experiencing a new climate of acceptance, understanding, and appreciation.

This resurgence of the only art form native to the United States is actually the second such comeback for jazz since 1929. During the depression years, jazz lay dormant waiting for the economic turbulence to calm and for a more favorable atmosphere for its creative growth and influence. In the late 1930's and 1940's, jazz music fostered its first major revival.

To understand the 1970's jazz phenomenon more clearly we should consider two important concepts. One, jazz is a musical language of communication and, as in most oral languages, speaks through many different dialects. With this thought in mind it is easy to see how Dixieland, swing, bebop, cool, and rock music are all part of the total musical language of jazz. This variety of dialects gives the public a broad spectrum of jazz styles with which to relate. Interestingly enough, its 1970's success story has included all of the important dialects of jazz. For example, the New Orleans-based Preservation Hall Traditional Jazz Band was widely successful; Benny Goodman returned to Carnegie Hall in January 1978; swing trumpeter Roy Eldridge packed them in at Rick's in Chicago; Charlie (Bird) Parker be-bop record reissues sold well; a musical revue featuring the compositions of 95-year-old Eubie Blake opened on Broadway in September; Alberta Hunter, 81-year-old singer and songwriter, was enjoying a major comeback after several years in retirement; and Herbie Hancock's jazz-rock hit album *Headhunters* exceeded the 2 million sales mark. Consideration number two: U. S. society and jazz have traveled and will continue to move and grow hand-in-hand. Each in its own way influences, molds, and affects the other, neither one leading or following.

In the 1970's we find black and white Americans moving closer together, with a greater sense of tolerance and understanding. Because of this sharing and appreciation of life-styles, the United States is experiencing the positive results of the nonviolent perseverance practiced by the

© 1978 DAN BALIOTTI

Trumpeter Dizzy Gillespie, *above*, vocalist Sarah Vaughan, *above right*, and xylophonist Lionel Hampton, *right*, are among the great jazz musicians who have enjoyed long careers.

CHARLES STEWART, PHOTO TRENDS

black equality movement of the 1950's and 1960's. The sociological and legislative changes brought about by the movement's activity nurtured a cultural integration process. At a concert-lecture at Indiana University, tenor sax star Dexter Gordon was asked if he felt he could function successfully as a black jazz artist in today's American society. His answer was "Yes, the climate is right, much hippier than when I left the country fourteen years ago." He went on to give credit for the change to the equality movement of the 1950's and 1960's and to the antiwar demonstrations.

The 1970's cultural integration experience has helped many Americans accept jazz for what it is, a high quality art form. Jazz, with its newfound respect and appreciation, is now arousing a great interest in our public schools and colleges, where programs are now offered that introduce young people to jazz. There are jazz ensembles in some 29,000 public schools and 500 colleges in the United States. Most of these groups participate in jazz festivals, hold solo and ensemble contests, run clinics, and stage yearly concert performances. Though many are restricted to the big band, commercial jazz-rock level, the public school jazz movement is producing a great number of loyal, knowledgeable, and discriminating jazz enthusiasts who are helping to break attendance records at jazz clubs, festivals, and concerts. Because of this success, other jazz-related activities are being added to a number of school and college music curricula. Jazz-black history courses, classes in jazz improvisation, theory, and arranging, as well as accredited combo units are slowly but steadily finding their way into total music programs. After many years of utter neglect, the U. S. educational system is at last acknowledging this native American art form.

Seeking identity, thousands of musicians outside the United States—in Australia, Japan, Europe, Canada—have turned to jazz-improvisation as a means of communicating a more personal musical language. When a musician improvises a jazz solo, he or she is not only the instrumental soloist but also the composer. This is what improvisation is all about—instant composition. The wonderful ability of jazz to shape itself into a vast variety of moods, colors, shapes, and sounds has drawn to it a new, young (18–30) audience. Many from this fresh jazz audience refuse to join in the proliferation of commercial rock music. At its highest artistic level, in any given dialect, jazz offers the listener the chance to share with the player a very personal, intellectual, and emotional experience.

DOMINIC SPERA

PHOTOS, ADAM SCULL, BLACK STAR

MUSIC—SPECIAL REPORT:

The Disco

Although the discotheque—a small intimate nightclub offering dancing to live or recorded music and frequently featuring movie or slide shows, special lighting and kinetic sound—has been popular since the 1960's, larger and more elaborate discos, such as New York City's Studio 54, *above*, have become the "in" places to see and be seen. The movie *Saturday Night Fever* has contributed to their success. Showy dancing and "far out" costumes add to the disco scene.

NEBRASKA

Record-breaking crops, an exciting election, and controversy over taxation characterized Nebraska in 1978.

Agriculture. Nebraska grain crops were excellent in 1978. Wheat (83,200,000 bu.) fell below 1977 production as did grain sorghum (140,600,-000 bu.). However, both corn (705,600,000 bu.) and soybeans (43,180,000 bu.) had record yields. Contributing to production were increased rain and irrigation, and a fall perfect for crop maturation. Limited storage and lack of transportation to central warehouses were problems.

Elections. Popular Governor J. James Exon (D) was elected to the U. S. Senate by a 2 to 1 margin over Republican Don Shasteen. For the first time in its history Nebraska will have two Democrats in the Senate. Incumbents John Cavanaugh (D) and Virginia Smith (R), and newcomer Douglas Bereuter (R) were elected to the House. Republicans, headed by Congressman Charles Thone who was elected governor, will dominate state offices. Nebraskans defeated a 5% local government spending-lid bill, a bottle bill, and a state school aid bill. Likewise, they defeated proposed constitutional amendments that would have expanded the list of industries to benefit from revenue bonds, provided tax valuation relief on alternate energy systems, and allowed legislators to add per diem and other expenses to their $4,800 annual salaries. Among constitutional amendments approved were those to allow cities to use tax increment financing to redevelop blighted areas, to permit judges to deny bail in sexual assault cases, and to adjust unequal valuations in tax districts which overlap two or more counties.

Legislation and Taxes. The 60-day session of the 85th Legislature spent much of its time debating tax legislation, but it failed to pass any major tax-revision bills. One of the most controversial bills, eventually passed over Exon's veto, allowed Omaha to levy a 1½ cent sales tax for 18 months. Important legislation provided for products liability, decriminalization of public drunkenness, a tightening of gambling regulations, a resolution favoring a national constitutional convention to prohibit abortion, and implementation of the criminal code.

Exon was successful in achieving his announced aim of holding down state taxes. Spending was limited, in part, by his vetoes (13 of 31 vetoes were overridden). In late 1977 the State Board of Equalization lowered the income tax from 18% of federal liability to 16% and the sales tax from 3½% to 3%. Those rates were maintained throughout 1978.

After the Legislature adjourned it was discovered that, while completing legislation on the new criminal code, no provision had been made for a code during the last 6 months of 1978. Therefore, in June a special legislative session met to correct the flaw in the law. Most of the session, however, was devoted to discussion of tax legislation. In the face of a petition drive to put on the November ballot a constitutional amendment limiting local spending to a 5% annual increase, the Legislature passed a 7%-limit bill. Complicating the local tax situation in 1978 was a mandated county revaluation and equalization of assessed real property values.

Miscellaneous. Serious flooding occurred on the lower Elkhorn and Platte rivers in the spring. Creighton University, located in the city of Omaha, inaugurated a new president, Matthew E. Creighton, S. J.

ORVILLE H. ZABEL
Creighton University

NEBRASKA • Information Highlights

Area: 77,227 square miles (200,018 km²).
Population (Jan. 1978 est.): 1,566,000.
Chief Cities (1970 census): Lincoln, the capital, 149,-518; Omaha, 346,929; Grand Island, 31,269; Hastings, 23,580.
Government (1978): *Chief Officers*—governor, J. James Exon (D); lt. gov., Gerald T. Whelan (D). *Legislature* (unicameral)—49 members (nonpartisan).
Education (1977–78): *Enrollment*—public elementary schools, 161,165 pupils; public secondary, 145,042; colleges and universities, 81,316 students. *Public school expenditures*, $456,935,000 ($1,450 per pupil).
State Finances (fiscal year 1977): *Revenues*, $1,119,368,-000; *expenditures*, 1,042,162,000.
Personal Income (1977): $10,491,000,000; per capita, $6,720.
Labor Force (July 1978): *Nonagricultural wage and salary earners*, 601,200; *unemployed*, 22,200 (2.8% of total force).

Gov. J. James Exon (D) and his wife talk with reporters after his election to the U. S. Senate in November. He defeated Republican Don Shasteen by a 2–1 margin.

JOURNAL STAR PRINTING COMPANY

UPI

Andreas van Agt, a Christian Democrat, accepts appointment as prime minister of the Netherlands. He succeeded Socialist Joop den Uyl, *right*.

NETHERLANDS

Politics, terrorism, and the economy headed the news in the Netherlands in 1978.

Politics. A new cabinet, consisting of 6 Liberals and 10 Christian Democrats, had assumed office on Dec. 19, 1977. This ended a record 208-day cabinet formation period. In his opening address, Prime Minister Andreas van Agt stressed the continuity of his government's policies with those of the previous cabinet.

At first the new cabinet was extremely fragile. Liberals and Christian Democrats held only 76 of the 150 Second Chamber seats, and 7 members of the Christian Democratic parliamentary group had pledged only conditional support to the new government. Nevertheless, the cabinet gradually consolidated its position. In February, parliament opposed the introduction and deploy-

---

―――― **NETHERLANDS · Information Highlights** ――――

Official Name: Kingdom of the Netherlands.
Location: Northwestern Europe.
Area: 13,054 square miles (33,811 km²).
Population (1978 est.): 13,900,000.
Chief Cities (1977): Amsterdam, the capital, 738,441; Rotterdam, 601,012; The Hague, 471,137.
Government: *Head of state,* Juliana, queen (acceded Sept. 1948). *Head of government,* Andreas van Agt, prime minister (took office Dec. 1977). *Legislature*— States General: First Chamber and Second Chamber.
Monetary Unit: Guilder (2.16 guilders equal U.S.$1, Sept. 1978).
Manufactures (major products): Metal fabrication, textiles, chemicals, electronics, food stuffs.
Agriculture (major products): Sugar beets, wheat, barley, fruits, potatoes, oats, flax, bulbs, flowers, meat and dairy products.

---

ment of the neutron bomb, while the cabinet preferred to make the Dutch position contingent on arms limitation talks. The cabinet prevailed, but not before Minister of Defense Kruisinga resigned in protest. In March, the cabinet and parliament collided over the sale of enriched uranium to Brazil. Because Brazil had not signed treaties avowing the peaceful use of atomic energy, the parliament demanded special guarantees. A decision to proceed without additional guarantees aroused the ire of parliament, although it did not cause a political crisis.

In November, Christian Democratic parliamentary leader Willem Aantjes was forced to resign when it was revealed that he had been a member of the Nazi SS organization during World War II. Pieter Menten, an art dealer who in 1977 had been sentenced to 15 years in prison for war crimes, was granted a new trial in May and acquitted in December. Menten claimed that he was granted immunity in 1952 in return for keeping silent about the collaboration of Dutch law officials with the Nazis. His acquittal caused a storm of protest.

Terrorism. South Moluccan terrorists continued to plague Dutch authorities. In March, 13 South Moluccans took control of the provincial government building in Assen, killing one man and seizing 71 hostages. The terrorists demanded the release of 21 South Moluccans imprisoned for previous train hijackings. The incident came to an end two days later when police entered the building and caught the terrorists by surprise. Six hostages were injured, one of them fatally. Despite the incident, the Dutch government announced plans to recognize South Moluccans as a cultural minority and to improve housing and education for them. There was no sign that this would placate younger South Moluccans, who continued to demand Dutch support for South Moluccan independence from Indonesia.

Dutch courts debated the extradition of three men wanted in conjunction with the kidnapping of West German businessman Hanns-Martin Schleyer. The three men (including Knut Folkerts, sentenced to 20 years for the murder of a Dutch policeman) appealed the extradition requests and demanded political asylum.

Economy. The economy continued to be a problem in 1978. Unemployment (200,000) and inflation (6.75%) remained unacceptably high. The cabinet continued to emphasize the need to restrict public sector growth in order to allow more room for private investment. In June, the government indicated that further cuts in the public sector would be necessary to stimulate economic growth. The proposed cuts provoked a series of one day strikes and demonstrations by government employees.

See also feature article on international terrorism, pages 44–51.

STEVEN B. WOLINETZ
Memorial University of Newfoundland

NEVADA

Expansion of resorts and casinos, and the election highlighted Nevada events in 1978.

Economy. Nevada's economy, fueled by the opening of several large hotel-casinos in the Reno area, continued to prosper during 1978. The construction of the MGM Grand Hotel in Reno, which opened in May, had set off the building boom and only the lack of sewer plant capacity provided a check on growth. A severe housing crisis afflicted the Reno area and the unemployment rate dropped to 2.4% in August as the new casinos scrambled for workers. (The state's unemployment rate hit a low of 4% in the same month.) By the year's end, 16 airlines were seeking permission to serve the newly discovered Reno tourist attractions. Las Vegas hotel-casinos continued to thrive and expand, despite the competition of legalized casino gambling in Atlantic City.

Elections. After eight years of leadership by popular Democrat Mike O'Callaghan, Nevadans in 1978 elected Republican Robert List, the two-term attorney general, governor. List defeated Lt. Gov. Robert Rose by a comfortable margin in a hard-fought campaign which focused more on personalities than issues. List became the first Republican gubernatorial candidate in this century to carry Clark county (Las Vegas), in which the Democrats have 70% of the two-party registration. Democrat James Santini, Nevada's lone congressman, was reelected in a landslide, and Richard Bryan won the attorney general's office with better than a four-to-one margin over his Republican opponent. The Nevada voters apparently sounded the death knell for the possible legislative ratification of the federal Equal Rights Amendment in Nevada by defeating it by a 2–1 margin in an advisory referendum.

Tax Revenues. Gambling and sales tax revenues for the 1977–78 fiscal year increased by 21.4 and 24%, respectively, over the previous year, with the full impact of the Reno hotel-casinos still to be felt. With a healthy surplus in the state treasury, voters followed the lead of California and approved a constitutional amendment drastically reducing property taxes. How-ever, the amendment must be passed a second time in order to become effective.

Education. Both the Reno and Las Vegas campuses of the University of Nevada suffered enrollment drops of about 4%, while the community college system continued to grow. UNR President Max Milam was fired in a controversial action by the Board of Regents in February and was replaced by political science professor Joseph N. Crowley.

DON W. DRIGGS
University of Nevada, Reno

NEW BRUNSWICK

Political developments made the news in 1978. The Progressive Conservatives were returned to office in a provincial general election, and the Liberal party got a new leader.

Politics. The Conservative government of Richard Hatfield squeaked back into office in the provincial election of October 23. The Tories won 30 of 58 seats in the legislature, the Liberals 28. After providing a Speaker, the Conservatives were left with a majority of just one. They came out of the election with three fewer seats than when the legislature was dissolved, while the Liberals under their new leader, Joseph Daigle, member of the Legislative Assembly (MLA) for Kent North since 1974, gained four seats. At the end, the campaign degenerated into a mudslinging match, in which French-English bigotry played a part.

Robert Higgins, Liberal opposition leader in the legislature, resigned January 25 after his allegations of government interference in a 1973 police investigation were dismissed by the provincial chief justice. Justice Charles Hughes said the New Brunswick justice department did not attempt to thwart an RCMP investigation into charges of illegal kickbacks to the Conservative party.

Fiscal. Finance Minister Fernand Dubé brought down the provincial budget April 4. It called for a $31.5 million tax increase, directly affecting home buyers, rural residents, smokers

——— NEVADA • Information Highlights ———

Area: 110,540 square miles (286,299 km²).
Population (Jan. 1978 est.): 642,000.
Chief Cities (1970 census): Carson City, the capital, 15,468; Las Vegas, 125,787; Reno, 72,863.
Government (1978): *Chief Officers*—governor, Michael O'Callaghan (D); lt. gov., Robert E. Rose (D). *Legislature*—Senate, 20 members; Assembly, 40 members.
Education (1977–78): *Enrollment*—public elementary school, 72,651 pupils; public secondary, 70,793; colleges and universities, 31,412 students. *Public school expenditures*, $229,200,000 ($1,404 per pupil).
State Finances (fiscal year 1977): *Revenues,* $762,457,000; *expenditures,* $632,780,000.
Personal Income (1977): $5,059,000,000; per capita, $7,988.
Labor Force (June 1978): *Nonagricultural wage and salary earners,* 341,200; *unemployed,* 14,500 (4.2% of total force).

——— NEW BRUNSWICK • Information Highlights ———

Area: 28,354 square miles (72,019 km²).
Population (1978 est.): 693,200.
Chief Cities (1976 census): Fredericton, the capital, 45,248; St. John, 85,956; Moncton, 55,934.
Government (1978): *Chief Officers*—lt. gov., Hedard Robichaud; premier, Richard B. Hatfield (Progressive Conservative); chief justice, Supreme Court, Appeal Div., Charles J. A. Hughes; Queen's Bench Div., A. J. Cormier. *Legislature*—Legislative Assembly, 58 members.
Education (1976–77): *Enrollment*—public elementary and secondary schools, 162,700 pupils; private schools, 270; Indian (federal) schools, 860; post-secondary, 12,580 students. *Total expenditures,* $217,081,000.
Public Finance (1978–79): *Revenues,* $1,254,000,000; *expenditures,* $1,216,000,000.
Personal Income (average weekly salary, May 1978): $231.97.
Unemployment Rate (July 1978, seasonally adjusted): 12.9%.
(All monetary figures are in Canadian dollars.)

and drinkers. The budget projected a $38 million surplus on spending of (c) $1.216 billion.

Legislative. The House was prorogued July 25 after a session that witnessed passage of conflict-of-interest legislation. Henceforth it will be forbidden for provincial officials, including cabinet ministers, to hold any office "which may interfere in any way" with their public responsibilities.

Forestry. The federal and provincial governments signed an agreement in Fredericton on July 21 calling for a four-year, $12.6 million program to boost the province's forest industry.

JOHN BEST, Chief, *Canada World News*

NEWFOUNDLAND

The governing Progressive Conservative (PC) party experienced a difficult year. Tight budgets grew even tighter and scandal plagued an increasingly shaky government.

Politics. Allegations of bribery and wrongdoing held the headlines for most of the year. In April, a cabinet minister was alleged to have paid $10,000 to the manager of a large construction project in St. John's in order to keep the man quiet about improprieties during the provincial election of September 1975. In May, discussions on this matter in the Legislative Assembly rose to such a pitch that the speaker was forced to "name" the leader of the opposition party, William Rowe. Rowe and 11 other Liberal Party members accused Premier Frank Moores of misleading the house, and all 12 were expelled by the time the session was adjourned. The charges of wrongdoing did not go away, however, and Moores eventually was forced to accept the resignations of two of his ministers.

In September, PC members of the Public Accounts Committee attempted to oust the opposition chairman. The committee was split into two parts, and the auditor-general was forced to answer to two committees in their investigations of mismanagement in the Department of Public Works.

Economy. Perhaps the only good news had to do with the fishing industry. The 200-mile (370-km) offshore limit brought investors from West Germany and Japan seeking to benefit from an increasingly valuable resource.

── NEWFOUNDLAND · Information Highlights ──

Area: 156,185 square miles (404,520 km²).
Population (1978 est.): 565,200.
Chief Cities (1976 census): St. John's, the capital, 86,576; Corner Brook, 25,198.
Government (1978): *Chief Officers*—lt. gov., Gordon Winter; premier, F. D. Moores (Progressive Conservative); Chief Justice, Robert S. Furlong. *Legislature* —Legislative Assembly, 51 members.
Education (1976–77): *Enrollment*—public elementary and secondary schools, 156,540; private schools, 340; post-secondary, 8,350 students.
Public Finance (1978–79): *Revenues*, $1,057,000,000; *expenditures*, $1,045,000,000.
Personal Income (average weekly salary, May 1978): $236.74.
(All monetary figures are in Canadian dollars.)

After a two-year moratorium on offshore oil exploration near Newfoundland, the oil companies finally agreed to regulations protecting the province's social and economic interests, and exploration began again.

Two mining operations, at St. Lawrence and Baie Verte, shut down, and the oil refinery at Come-by-Chance and papermill at Stephenville remained closed. These contributed to a 16.7% unemployment rate at midyear. The 1978–79 budget increased the provincial sales tax from 10 to 11% and reduced the small business tax from 14 to 12%.

SUSAN MCCORQUODALE
Memorial University of Newfoundland

NEW HAMPSHIRE

Election upsets and continued demonstrations against the Seabrook nuclear power plant focused national attention on New Hampshire in 1978.

Elections. On November 7 Hugh Gallen (D) upset Governor Meldrim Thomson (R) by 10,000 votes and conservative Gordon Humphrey (R) defeated incumbent Senator Thomas McIntyre (D). Thomson, nationally known for his arch-conservatism, appeared to have made a fatal error by supporting the so-called construction work in progress (CWIP) electric rates that would help pay the costs of building the Seabrook nuclear power plant. Gallen pronounced that CWIP was in fact a disguised tax. Never had candidates advertised so extensively on Boston television and Gallen's ads seem to have been quite effective in southern New Hampshire. On February 18 President Carter appeared at a town meeting in Nashua, and campaigned for McIntyre, but McIntyre did not seem to fathom the mood of the voters nor the appeal of newcomer Humphrey. The contests for the House of Representatives saw both incumbents win easily, and Republicans retained control of the legislature and the Executive Council.

Seabrook. Although not itself a political issue, the multi-billion dollar Seabrook plant has been interjected into many parts of New Hampshire life and has caused considerable polarization of opinion. Unlike the 1977 demonstration,

── NEW HAMPSHIRE · Information Highlights ──

Area: 9,304 square miles (24,097 km²).
Population (Jan. 1978 est.): 861,000.
Chief Cities (1970 census): Concord, the capital, 30,022; Manchester, 87,754; Nashua, 55,820; Portsmouth, 25,717.
Government (1978): *Chief Officers*—governor, Meldrim Thomson, Jr. (R). *General Court*—Senate, 24 members; House of Representatives, 400 members.
Education (1977–78): *Enrollment*—public elementary schools, 119,413 pupils; public secondary, 55,205; colleges and universities, 41,270 students. *Public school expenditures*, $236,827,000 ($1,278 per pupil).
State Finances (fiscal year 1977): *Revenues*, $636,339,000; *expenditures*, $677,139,000.
Personal Income (1977): $5,547,000,000; per capita, $6,536.
Labor Force (July 1978): *Nonagricultural wage and salary earners*, 371,200; *unemployed*, 25,000 (5.5% of total force).

Demonstrators, protesting the construction of the Sea-brook Nuclear Power Plant, chain themselves to a sign.

the June 24, 1978, demonstration organized by the Clamshell Alliance was not only peaceful and orderly, but brought some measure of cooperation between the state and the Alliance. Construction continues, but the Public Service Company is still beset by potential court action, continued opposition by the Clamshell Alliance, the pledge of Gallen to seek the repeal of CWIP, and a corporate financial situation that some feel is unsound.

Economy. The state's economy remained healthy, with new companies arriving every month and unemployment hovering in the 3 to 3.5% range. However, a distinctive trend developed in 1978 throughout much of the southern half of the state in the form of anti-growth sentiment. At the March town meetings scores of towns attempted to slow growth through limitations on construction or by subdivision restrictions.

Two items deserving brief mention are the final determination regarding the road through Franconia Notch and the great February snowstorm. A compromise agreed to by all will allow a two-lane parkway to be built through the Notch. The great February snowstorm did not paralyze the state as it had other states in New England, although it caused extensive damage along Hampton Beach.

WILLIAM L. TAYLOR, *Plymouth State College*

NEW JERSEY

A brightening economic picture, the campaign for the United States Senate, casino gambling, and the murder trial of Dr. Mario Jascalevich were prominent events in New Jersey in 1978.

Economic Developments. In his State of the State message in January 1978 Gov. Brendan Byrne called for the annual creation of 70,000 new jobs and urged the New York–New Jersey Port Authority to promote industrial development projects. Four months later the governors of New York and New Jersey and the mayors of New York City, Jersey City, and Newark gave their approval to a Port Authority program that would allow $400 million over a ten-year period to be spent for construction of industrial parks in the three cities.

The Senate Race. Four-term incumbent Republican Clifford Case was upset in the June 8 primary by Jeffrey Bell, a relative unknown who was able to capitalize on his youth and support of the Kemp-Roth tax reduction plan. The Democratic primary was won easily by former New York Knicks basketball star Bill Bradley over state Treasurer Richard Leone. In the campaign itself Bradley assumed the role of moderate, in opposition to Bell's outspoken stand in favor of a massive cut in income taxes and substantial reductions in government spending. On the eve of the election, polls showed Bradley with a commanding lead, but he had been forced to come out for a tax reduction of his own which was smaller than Bell's and which he considered less inflationary. In the final analysis, Bradley's high identification factor and moderate stand on taxes contributed to a substantial victory. (*See* also BIOGRAPHY.)

Casino Gambling. Casino gambling began in Atlantic City over the Memorial Day weekend, after Resorts International had obtained a temporary license from the state. Figures for the month of June revealed that more than $500,000 was taken in each day and the monthly gross was over $16 million. In the meantime Bally Manufacturing, Playboy Enterprises, Penthouse International, and a number of other corporations were moving ahead with plans for multimillion dollar hotel-casino complexes. In the wake of Atlantic City's success, officials in other cities in New Jersey began pushing for legalized jai alai games, and a referendum to that effect was placed on the November ballot. It was defeated, however.

In many quarters there was concern about such side effects of casino gambling as the

---

——— NEW JERSEY · Information Highlights ———

Area: 7,836 square miles (20,295 km²).
Population (Jan. 1978 est.): 7,327,000.
Chief Cities (1970 census): Trenton, the capital, 104,-638; Newark, 382,288; Jersey City, 260,545.
Government (1978): *Chief Officers*—governor, Brendan T. Byrne (D). *Legislature*—Senate, 40 members; General Assembly, 80 members.
Education (1977–78): *Enrollment*—public elementary schools, 890,092 pupils; public secondary, 531,256; colleges and universities, 301,091 students. *Public school expenditures,* $3,102,000,000 ($2,115 per pupil).
State Finances (fiscal year 1977): *Revenues,* $7,038,-175,000; *expenditures,* $6,827,632,000.
Personal Income (1977): $58,589,000,000; per capita, $7,994.
Labor Force (July 1978): *Nonagricultural wage and salary earners,* 2,988,400; *unemployed,* 275,900 (7.9% of total force).

Gambling comes to Atlantic City, N.J. Gov. Brendan Byrne tours the new Resorts International Casino.

involvement of organized crime, the increase of prostitution in Atlantic City, the fact that the proposed casino complexes would uproot the urban poor, or that the actual gambling would be limited to the relatively well-to-do.

The Jascalevich Murder Trial. The trial of Dr. Mario Jascalevich in Bergen County for allegedly poisoning several of his patients at Riverdell Hospital with injections of curare attracted national attention. Issues involving freedom of the press and rights of the accused were raised when a *New York Times* reporter, Myron Farber, refused, in spite of being served with a court subpoena, to turn over his notes on an interview with Jascalevich and some of his colleagues. Farber appealed to the United States Supreme Court, but his case was denied and, rather than obey the subpoena, he served a term in jail. Late in October Jascalevich was acquitted.

HERMANN K. PLATT
Saint Peters College

NEW MEXICO

In 1978 New Mexicans mourned the death, on June 5, of former Senator Joseph Montoya (D) who gained national attention as a member of the Senate Select Committee on Presidential Campaign Activities (Watergate). Voters in November elected rancher Bruce King (D) to the governorship and reelected Sen. Pete Dominici (R). Three residents of Albuquerque, Ben Abruzzo, Maxie Anderson and Larry Newman, created a worldwide stir when, in August, they became the first men to complete a transatlantic flight in a balloon.

Indian Affairs. During the summer 300 delegates from the state's Pueblo, Navajo, and Apache tribes gathered in Albuquerque to attend the first New Mexico Indian caucus, to highlight native American political power.

A bill introduced in the 1978 session of the New Mexico legislature proposed a state constitutional amendment denying Indians voting rights in local elections unless they gave up claims to sovereignty on their reservations.

Native leaders saw the measure as part of a broad national backlash against Indian activism. Their strong opposition contributed to the defeat of the bill.

Health. In late spring more than 30 people were stricken with botulism at a restaurant in Clovis. It was one of the worst outbreaks of food poisoning in recent U. S. history. On the other hand, the incidence of bubonic plague was the lowest in several years, only five cases being reported for 1978.

Scientists at the University of New Mexico's College of Pharmacy announced that they had developed a means of detecting 90% of all types of human cancer through a technique known as nuclear, or radio, pharmacy. Testing of the new procedure is expected to extend over the next two years, with the first tests on patients scheduled to begin in 1980.

Energy. The first National Conference on Hot, Dry Rock Geothermal Energy met in Santa Fe with more than 200 representatives from 18 states and 8 foreign countries participating. A spokesman estimated that known geothermal resources could supply U. S. energy needs for 3,625 years. Solar energy was the focus of interest at northern New Mexico's Nambe Indian Pueblo. There, solar collectors, monitored by Los Alamos scientists, provided more than 60% of the heat required in a new community center.

Debate continued among New Mexicans over the proposed Waste Isolation Pilot Plant, a facility which will allow nuclear waste to be buried in salt beds near Carlsbad. Environmentalists charged that serious hydrological problems were associated with the site and that valuable natural resources in the area would be threatened by the waste disposal.

MARC SIMMONS
Author, "New Mexico, A History"

——— **NEW MEXICO · Information Highlights** ———

Area: 121,666 square miles (315,115 km²).
Population (Jan. 1978 est.): 1,200,000.
Chief Cities (1970 census): Santa Fe, the capital, 41,-167; Albuquerque, 243,751; Las Cruces, 37,857; Roswell, 33,908.
Government (1978): *Chief Officers*—governor, Jerry Apodaca (D); lt. gov., Robert E. Ferguson (D). *Legislature*—Senate, 42 members; House of Representatives, 70 members.
Education (1977–78): *Enrollment*—public elementary schools, 142,872 pupils; public secondary, 139,024; colleges and universities, 55,264 students. *Public school expenditures,* $463,743,000 ($1,403 per pupil).
State Finances (fiscal year 1977): *Revenues,* $1,349,-306,000; *expenditures,* $1,137,043,000.
Personal Income (1977): $6,970,000,000; per capita, $5,857.
Labor Force (July 1978): *Nonagricultural wage and salary earners,* 451,600; *unemployed,* 29,500 (5.5% of total force).

NEW YORK

The Democratic Party strengthened its hold on state government in 1978, as incumbent Gov. Hugh Carey won reelection to a second term and Democratic candidates swept all but one of the other statewide races.

Elections. Carey defeated Republican Assembly Minority Leader Perry B. Duryea, leaving the Republicans with their most severe leadership crisis in two decades. Joining Carey was the state's new lieutenant governor, Mario M. Cuomo. Cuomo was secretary of state when Lt. Gov. Mary Anne Krupsak bolted Carey and challenged him in the party primary in September. The other statewide Democratic winner was Robert Abrams, who defeated Republican Michael Roth to become attorney general.

The Republicans did win a key post, however, with an upset win in the race for state comptroller. Erie county executive Edward V. Regan outpolled New York City Comptroller Harrison J. Goldin. His victory continued a longstanding pattern in which a minority party candidate is elected as either comptroller or attorney general. For most of the last quarter century, however, it was a Democrat—Comptroller Arthur Levitt, who retired in 1978—who was the minority member. Governor Carey's election in 1974 reversed the Republican domination.

Governor Carey trailed in the polls through most of the campaign. But with the aid of media specialist David Garth and with contributions from labor unions and bankers, Carey campaigned as a fiscal conservative and boasted that he had cut taxes by more than $1 billion. Duryea, a Long Island lobster wholesaler who was Assembly Majority Leader under Gov. Nelson Rockefeller, tried to parlay the death penalty into a winning issue. Governor Carey opposed capital punishment. Although most voters favored it, an Election Day poll showed that many of them supported the governor, nevertheless.

State politics and programs appeared headed for major change. In January 1979, two new men would be taking over the key posts of comptroller and attorney general, which were vacated by longtime incumbents Levitt and Republican Louis J. Lefkowitz, respectively. In the legislature, the Democrats retained control of the Assembly, while the Senate remained in Republican hands. But the leadership changed, as Duryea's post of minority leader became vacant and as Assembly Speaker Stanley Steingut was defeated in his Brooklyn district by a comparative unknown.

Governor Carey, the day after his reelection victory, promised tax cuts for the elderly and for businesses. Other, more basic changes were expected.

A new party also emerged on the political scene. The Right to Life Party won enough votes to assure a future spot on the ballot. Its intensive opposition to abortion conflicted with Governor Carey's position that abortions for poor women should be paid for by Medicaid.

Education. The funding of education, especially in city school districts, loomed as a critical issue in 1979. In 1978, the state Court of Appeals struck down a law allowing districts to circumvent constitutional limits on school taxes. While the legislature approved assessment increases to bail out individual districts, a permanent solution was sought—one that may alter the role of property taxes in supporting education.

Environment. As the state continued its Hudson River cleanup, there was a chemical pollution disaster in western New York. The so-called "Love Canal" of Niagara Falls was declared a health hazard, and the state initiated plans to help 239 families relocate, at a cost of $9 million. High incidences of miscarriage, birth defects, liver and bladder disease, and cancer were discovered among residents who lived over what was once a toxic chemical dump. Lawsuit claims by residents of the area may exceed $1 billion.

Tourism. Amid glowing reports of its success in increasing the state's tourist trade, the "I Love New York" campaign, sponsored by the state Department of Commerce, was expanded to selected areas in the United States. Another expected tourist stimulant, the 1980 Winter Olympics at Lake Placid, ran into problems. Organizers discovered that costs were much greater than expected and asked the federal government to increase its contribution from $53 million to $67 million. A general manager was hired to guide future efforts.

Energy. The crisis of the 1976–77 winter was not a problem in 1977–78, as natural gas supplies were adequate. But the state's energy future remained cloudy. Power companies claimed that electrical "brownouts" would occur in the 1980's unless new nuclear plants were built soon. Governor Carey added uncertainty to the issue by reiterating his opposition to new nuclear plants. A brighter note was sounded by the state Energy Office when it announced plans to spend at least $100 million, much of it fed-

—— **NEW YORK** · Information Highlights ——

Area: 49,576 square miles (128,402 km²).
Population (Jan. 1978 est.): 17,860,000.
Chief Cities (1970 census): Albany, the capital, 115,-781; New York, 7,895,563; Buffalo, 462,768; Rochester, 296,233.
Government (1978): *Chief Officer*—governor, Hugh L. Carey (D). *Legislature*—Senate, 60 members; Assembly, 150 members.
Education (1977–78): *Enrollment*—public elementary schools, 1,598,667 pupils; public secondary, 1,630,-881; colleges and universities, 950,857 students. *Public school expenditures,* $8,018,000,000 ($2,282 per pupil).
State Finances (fiscal year 1977): *Revenues,* $22,667,-068,000; *expenditures,* $21,252,546,000.
Personal Income (1977): $135,089,000,000; per capita, $7,357.
Labor Force (June 1978): *Nonagricultural wage and salary earners,* 7,016,500; *unemployed* 579,600.

eral funds, on energy conservation for schools and health facilities.

JOHN H. FAIRHALL
"Albany Times-Union"

NEW YORK CITY

During his first year in office, Mayor Edward I. Koch faced a major fiscal crisis, a rash of labor disputes, and all the problems of a major metropolis. But under his guidance, New York City made great strides toward maintaining its role, in the words of President Carter, of "the cultural, artistic, financial, and diplomatic capital" of the United States.

Finances. With the federal seasonal loan program due to expire on June 30, Mayor Koch revealed January 20 a new, four-year fiscal recovery plan that would require special federal assistance through 1982. But on February 9, the U. S. Senate Banking Committee criticized the plan and concluded that the city "should be able to meet its financial needs and avoid bankruptcy" without the billions in short-term federal loans it had been receiving.

However, on August 8 President Carter signed into law a bill providing the city with $1.65 billion in long-term loan guarantees. The money would be made available in four annual installments: $500 million in 1979, $500 million in 1980, $325 million in 1981, and $325 million in 1982. The city was to achieve a balanced budget by the beginning of fiscal 1983.

The Carter administration had proposed March 2 that the federal government guarantee long-term loans instead of continuing the seasonal loan program. It was this alternative solution that eventually won the support of Congress. The bill was seen as the cornerstone of the city's financial recovery.

On February 6, Gov. Hugh L. Carey and Mayor Koch announced that the city would be receiving $200 million in new state aid. The funds were intended to reduce the estimated $457 million budget deficit for fiscal 1979. Carey signed a bill June 2 extending the life of New York City's Emergency Financial Control Board (EFCB) and increasing the borrowing power of the Municipal Assistance Corporation (MAC). On June 28, the EFCB approved the city's $13.5 billion budget for fiscal 1979.

On April 20, the Carter administration announced that it would spend $55.6 million by September 30 to help rehabilitate the South Bronx.

Labor. In what was considered a prerequisite to receiving federal loan guarantees, the Koch administration on June 5 reached a two-year contract agreement with the 200,000-member municipal labor coalition. The agreement was expected to cost the city about $757 million over the two years and grant its nonuniformed workers a 5.5% pay increase.

The city's three major daily newspapers, *The New York Times, New York Daily News,* and *New York Post* were shut down August 9 by striking pressmen. Rupert Murdoch's *Post* resumed publishing October 5, while the *Times* and *Daily News* did not return to the stands until November 6. During the strike, several interim papers made their appearance. Theaters, retail trade, hotels, and restaurants were hurt surprisingly little by the strike.

Politics. In a relatively quiet election year, State Assembly Speaker Stanley Steingut lost the Brooklyn seat he held for 26 years to Murray Weinstein. State Sen. Roy Goodman (R) defeated William Woodward in Manhattan's East Side "Silk Stocking" district. Earlier in the year, William Green (R) defeated Bella Abzug for the state congressional seat vacated by Koch; Green retained the seat in November by defeating S. Carter Burden.

Other. American Airlines and the Singer Company announced they would be moving from New York City, but the American Stock Exchange, Ebasco Services, and others decided to stay. A full-scale promotional campaign to encourage New Yorkers to remain New Yorkers and to urge outsiders to visit the city was stepped up. Generally, the city enjoyed a good tourist season.

A new law passed during the year called for substantial fines if a dog owner did not sweep off the streets the wastes of his or her pet.

In its worst blizzard since 1947, the city received 18 inches (46 cm.) of snow February 5–7. On January 20, it had had 14 inches (36 cm.) in the worst storm since 1969.

Radio City Music Hall was temporarily saved by a financial plan announced in April (*see* special report, page 369). In June, the U. S. Supreme Court ruled that the owners of Grand Central Terminal could not build an office complex atop the station because it would alter the face of an historic landmark.

William B. Macomber, Jr., became the Metropolitan Museum of Art's first full-time, salaried president; Douglas Dillon, whom he replaced, became chairman of the board. The "Treasures of Tutankhamen" exhibit opened at the museum December 20. The exhibit was sold out for the entirety of its stay in New York weeks before the opening. The cultural scene had been enhanced in April, when Soviet expatriate ballet star Mikhail Baryshnikov announced that he would leave the American Ballet Theater to join the New York City Ballet. Opera star Beverly Sills announced that she would retire from singing and become co-director of the New York City Opera Company in 1980.

The New York Yankees engineered one of the most dramatic comebacks in baseball history by beating out the Boston Red Sox for the American League pennant and defeating the Los Angeles Dodgers in six games to capture their second consecutive World Series victory.

JEFF HACKER

UPI

Radio City Music Hall

It is big, reverberant, and splendid, this monument to art deco. It started out as a vaudeville house and soon came to represent the good life, 1930's style. In 1978, after 46 years of the high kicking Rockettes and vivid extravaganzas, New York City Radio City Music Hall threatened to close down. But the thought of it closing was repugnant to a city that was finally beginning to climb out of fiscal misery, and a rescue plan as elaborate as the hall's Easter show was worked out. "If it survived the depression and wartime," insisted New York Lt. Gov. Mary Anne Krupsak, who helped organize the resuscitation effort, "it can survive now."

It all started in January, when Alton G. Marshall, the president of Rockefeller Center, Inc., announced that diminishing attendance and a massive operating loss would force the hall to close its doors on April 12.

Radio City's balance sheets painted a dismal financial picture. In 1977, the music hall lost $2.3 million. The projected deficit for 1978 was about $3.5 million. Box office revenues plummeted from about $10 million to just over $7 million. In 1967, five million people paid for the privilege of seeing a show in what once had been the country's most prestigious movie house. A decade later, the number was down to 1.8 million.

Efforts to save Radio City began immediately. Politicians, especially those facing elections, rushed to do their part. Ideas ranged from sending the Rockettes on a tour of the country to generate new income, to turning the hall into a new home for the American Stock Exchange.

Those trying to save the hall were motivated by two sets of concerns. One was architectural. The building was a masterpiece of the art deco style, a reaction to the reproduced decor of the past and the modern tendency to avoid ornamentation altogether. Instead, art deco tried to create a new style appropriate for the machine age. The 6,000-plus-seat theater, with its 60-foot (18-m) high entrance hall, 144-foot (44-m) wide stage, broad main staircase, rugs, mirrors, and chandeliers captured this spirit. In an effort to preserve the building, the New York City Landmarks Preservation Commission declared the building's interior a landmark. In the complex maneuvering over the hall's future, however, the Radio City management resisted the move.

The other concern had to do with the type of entertainment offered at the Music Hall. The floor shows attracted families from Paducah, Ky. to Pocatello, Idaho. In their romantic and extravagant style, they stood in sharp contrast to the sleazy entertainment offered only a few blocks away in Times Square. "It's more a family type entertainment," said State Sen. William T. Conklin. "It lends itself to great extravaganzas at holiday seasons." Beyond the family issue stood the crazy, larger-than-life nature of the shows; and, of course, the Rockettes.

It took until the eve of the theater's planned closing on April 12 to work out the complicated salvation plan. The plan called for up to $2 million in public funds—$1.8 million to cover operating deficits and $200,000 for a feasibility study of long-term financial arrangements. The agreement left Rockefeller Center, Inc., responsible for over $2 million in taxes, rent, maintenance, and other costs.

The plan by no means guaranteed Radio City's long-term future. For example, one idea that the feasibility study was designed to explore was the construction of a 20-story office tower over the music hall. Part of the revenues from the office block would go to the operation of Radio City. If this measure were to fall through, so might the entire plan.

But for the time being the hall was saved from the final curtain. The Rockettes were allowed to kick again, and Radio City's popular Easter show would be resurrected for at least one more year.

E. J. DIONNE

NEW ZEALAND

Although beset by rising unemployment and prickly industrial relations, the National Party under Prime Minister Robert Muldoon retained control of the government in the November 25 general elections. Economic prospects remained generally gloomy.

Elections. The legislature was adjourned in October to campaign for the election. Five new parliamentary seats were contested for the first time, raising the total from 87 to 92. The campaign emphasized the economy, unemployment, and government credibility. Public opinion polls consistently gave the National Party a margin of some 10% over the Labour opposition.

In the election, however, there was a swing of 4.5% in favor of Labour. The National Party lost four seats but were returned to power with a majority of seven. The final count showed the conservative National Party with 49 seats and the Labour Party with 42. The new cabinet was quite startling: six backbenchers were promoted, and Muldoon, while retaining his Treasury portfolio, surrendered leadership of the House.

The Economy. The 1977 inflation rate of 15.3% represented a marginal improvement over 1976, and for the year ending June 1978, it was lowered to 12.2%. However, unemployment continued to climb. By September, it had reached 49,229, the highest figure since the great depression of the 1930's. The balance of trade continued to be adverse.

The budget, announced in June, was "liberally sprinkled with election-year largess." Singled out for special benefits were lower-income workers, who received a 10% tax cut, and livestock farmers, who received nearly (N. Z.) $100 million in cash grants. Even though a deficit of $1,050,000,000 was anticipated, taxation accounted for 33.3% of the GNP. The budget was mildly reflationary and was cast in a positive mold of rewards, incentives, and expansion.

Foreign Affairs. Prime Minister Muldoon took two major overseas trips, one to the capitals of the EC (European Community) countries and the other to the conference of Commonwealth finance ministers in Canada. During the latter visit he delivered his first address to the UN General Assembly as prime minister and met with U. S. President Jimmy Carter. In May, Vice President Walter Mondale briefly visited New Zealand, where he reaffirmed a strong U. S. commitment to the ANZUS Treaty.

Domestic Affairs. On April 1, legislation enacting the 200-mile (370-km) restricted coastal zone, the merger of the nation's two state-owned airlines, and a restrictive abortion policy went into effect. A royal commission of inquiry concluded that New Zealand would not need nuclear energy resources until the year 2000. On May 25, in the largest police operation in New Zealand's history, 600 policemen removed Maori protesters from disputed territory at Bastion Point, Auckland; about 230 Maoris were arrested, and another 100 left voluntarily. Sweeping changes in the judicial system were recommended by a royal commission of inquiry into the courts.

G. W. A. BUSH, *University of Auckland*

—— NEW ZEALAND · Information Highlights ——

Official Name: Dominion of New Zealand.
Location: Southwest Pacific Ocean.
Area: 103,736 square miles (268,676 km²).
Population (1978 est.): 3,200,000.
Chief Cities (Mar. 1977): Wellington, the capital, 350,900; Auckland, 801,200; Christchurch, 327,200.
Government: *Head of state,* Elizabeth II, queen, represented by Sir Keith Holyoake, governor general (took office Oct. 1977). *Head of government,* Robert Muldoon, prime minister (took office Dec. 1975). *Legislature* (unicameral)—House of Representatives.
Monetary Unit: New Zealand dollar (0.9433 N. Z. dollar equals U. S.$1, Nov. 1978).
Manufactures (major products): Processed foods, wood products, cement, fertilizers, beverages.
Agriculture (major products): Wheat, potatoes, dairy products, sheep wool, forest products, barley, corn.

NIGERIA

Economic problems sharpened political differences as Nigeria prepared for a return to civil government in 1979.

Economics. The world's oversupply of petroleum caused the Federal Military Government (FMG) to restrict production to an average of less than 2 million barrels a day. The fall in the value of the dollar to which petroleum prices are tied cost Nigeria more than $150 million. Oil revenues for the fiscal year were only $5.2 billion, as compared with $6.4 billion the previous year. Since other exports earn very little, this decline in earnings, which reached approximately $300 million per month in August, was devastating when combined with a domestic inflation rate of approximately 30%. However, such major projects as the Lagos-Ibadan freeway, a refinery, new dams and power projects, improvements of harbor facilities at Warri and Lagos, and the opening of 7 new universities were completed. Cocoa and oil palm industries remained depressed, and Nigeria has not exported peanut products since 1976. The FMG recognized that there was no alternative to austerity and adopted a budget which cut recurrent expenditure by 10% and restricted development plans and aid to the states. Spending by the individual states was also cut by 50%. Consumer goods became more difficult to obtain and the cost of living in the overcrowded cities rose faster than the inflation rate. There were labor disturbances, nurses and doctors went on strike, and the students at all universities demonstrated against the FMG's decision to increase tuition.

Nigeria's economic future was buoyed by a (U. S.) $1 billion loan, repayable over 7 years, which was syndicated in January by a group of major international banks. In December Nigeria received an additional loan of $750 million, repayable over 8 years.

Following enactment of new legislation, North Carolina's counties and towns had the option of permitting the sale of liquor-by-the-drink.

UPI

Politics. Despite economic dislocations, the FMG continued to develop plans to return the government to civilian control in 1979. A Constituent Assembly convening in October 1977 presented its report in May calling for a federal system with an elected president, governors for the states, and a directly elected central legislative body of 450 members. The major difference of opinion over the recommendations concerned the Muslim demand for a Sharia High Court of Appeal. On April 6 a majority of the Assembly voted against such a court. A six-week period of registration of voters for the 1979 elections began on January 14. A total of 47.7 million persons were subsequently registered, some 8 million more than the experts predicted. In July General Obasanjo made an important move toward a transitional government when he separated many senior officers from their political duties. All military governors and some important central government officials were ordered to assume only military duties. Those senior officers who choose to remain as political officers will resign from the army when Nigeria returns to civil rule.

Foreign Affairs. Nigeria continued as one of the leading spokesmen for ousting the white-dominated governments of southern Africa. The External Affairs Commissioner saw the "internal settlement" in Rhodesia as an invitation to civil war and also demanded definite United Nations' action in Namibia. Nigeria defended Angola's right to use Cuban troops, although it deplored foreign intervention in African affairs. The improvement in Nigeria's relations with the West was underscored by President Carter's state visit to Lagos in April.

HARRY A. GAILEY
San Jose State University

NORTH CAROLINA

Typically, politics provided the main topic of conversation during the year.

Election. In a race that attracted national attention because of his conservatism and his record campaign budget of more than $7 million, Republican Jesse Helms was reelected to the U. S. Senate over Insurance Commissioner John Ingram, the surprise victor in the Democratic primary. Democrats retained a 9 to 2 margin in the House and maintained a commanding majority in the state legislature.

Liquor. Shrewd parliamentary tactics in the General Assembly led to the passage of a local option liquor-by-the-drink bill that previously had been rejected. Before year's end several counties and towns had approved the sale of mixed drinks for the first time in 70 years.

The Economy. Unemployment remained relatively low and the state's tax collections high. Governor Hunt even talked of a tax rebate. In

─────── NIGERIA • Information Highlights ───────

Official Name: Federal Republic of Nigeria.
Location: West Africa.
Area: 356,669 square miles (923,772 km²).
Population (1978 est.): 68,400,000.
Chief Cities (1976 est.): Lagos, the capital, 1,100,000; Ibadan, 850,000; Ogbomosho, 435,000; Kano, 400,-000.
Government: *Head of state and government,* Lt. Gen. Olusegun Obasanjo (assumed power Feb. 1976).
Monetary Unit: Naira (0.641 naira equals U. S.$1, Sept. 1978).
Manufactures (major products): Cotton, rubber, petroleum, textiles, cement, food products, footwear, metal products, lumber.
Agriculture (major products): Cocoa, rubber, palm oil, yams, cassava, sorghum, millet, corn, rice, livestock, ground nuts, cotton.

── NORTH CAROLINA • Information Highlights ──

Area: 52,586 square miles (136,198 km²).
Population (Jan. 1978 est.): 5,560,000.
Chief Cities (1970 census): Raleigh, the capital, 123,-793; Charlotte, 241,178; Greensboro, 144,076.
Government (1978): *Chief Officers*—governor, James B. Hunt, Jr. (D); lt. gov., James C. Green (D). *General Assembly*—Senate, 50 members; House of Representatives, 120 members.
Education (1977–78): *Enrollment*—public elementary schools, 816,645 pupils; public secondary, 365,186; colleges and universities, 257,198 students. *Public school expenditures,* $1,849,080,000 ($1,251 per pupil).
State Finances (fiscal year 1977): *Revenues,* $4,574,-592,000; *expenditures,* $4,357,782,000.
Personal Income (1977): $32,791,000,000; per capita, $5,935.
Labor Force (July 1978): *Nonagricultural wage and salary earners,* 2,177,100; *unemployed,* 124,800 (4.5% of total force).

the face of anti-smoking campaigns, Philip Morris USA announced plans for a $250 million cigarette producing center in Cabarrus County. Southern Railway built a $45 million freight classification and forwarding facility at Linwood and gave the old one at Spencer to the state for development as a transportation museum. The announcement by Miller Brewing Company of a new labor contract that will pay a minimum of $9.25 per hour caused anxiety.

Prisons. Courts of appeal found no error in the convictions of the "Wilmington Ten" for fire-bombing and the "Charlotte Three" for burning a stable. Despite international pressure, Gov. Hunt refused to pardon the Wilmington group, but he did reduce the sentences. Central Prison, a century-old architectural landmark in Raleigh, fell to the wrecker's ball, to be replaced by a new structure.

PCB Spill. The state's most shocking story pertained to the deliberate contamination of many miles of North Carolina roadside. A New York man and his two sons were charged with discharging toxic PCB oils from a tank truck along secondary roads at night.

Education. Competency testing was instituted in the public schools in an effort to curb "social promotions." The head of the state teachers' lobby agreed that the tests were biased; in fact, he said, "They are biased against ignorance and poor attitudes." After years of controversy, the University of North Carolina and the Department of Health, Education, and Welfare reached agreement on a plan to desegregate further the university's sixteen branches. State officials tried to assure a restless public that the plan would not lessen the academic standards of the institutions. The National Humanities Center in the Research Triangle Park accepted its first class of fellows.

Culture. The North Carolina Symphony was well received in Washington and in Chicago. Construction continued on the new State Art Museum, and America's Four Hundredth Anniversary Committee was appointed to plan the commemoration of the Roanoke voyages of 1584–87.

Names in the News. Longtime state treasurer and art patron Edwin Gill died. Shearon Harris, utilities head, became chairman of the Chamber of Commerce of the United States. Paul Green, Pultizer prize-winning playwright, received the first North Caroliniana Society Award.

H. G. JONES, *University of North Carolina*

NORTH DAKOTA

Elections, an irrigation and water supply project, and the weather topped the news in 1978 in North Dakota.

Elections. Voters rejected an initiative to place control of health-care costs and health insurance in the hands of the state, and passed an initiative to cut income taxes 37%. Rep. Mark Andrews (R) was reelected, as was Public Service Commissioner Richard Elkin.

Weather. The worst flood in 100 years inundated a 24-county, 70-square-mile (180-km²) area of the Red River Valley, causing the evacuation of 155 families and damage exceeding $18 million. An 8-day February snowstorm paralyzed 9 counties and left 4 persons dead. Five persons were killed and 35 injured in a July tornado which left 71 homeless.

Agriculture. Farmers and ranchers picketed Canadian border ports of entry and turned back incoming cattle trucks. Record harvests of sugarbeets and sunflowers and excellent crops of grain and hay, plus a rise in beef prices, partly dissipated winter's discontent. By November, reserves of wheat, the state's major crop, reached a record 368.8 million bushels. Taiwan bought 5.5 million bushels of wheat and 2.4 million bushels of barley from state farmers. Despite this farmers had little to cheer about: farm product prices remained low; cost of land, machinery and materials spiraled; and shortages of storage facilities and boxcars for transport were critical.

Judiciary. The state Supreme Court, drawing the first new judicial district boundaries since 1919, created seven districts (instead of six), but retained the number of judges, 19. The court also ruled that public school students were entitled to free textbooks, and upheld the right of the governor to bypass a not-yet-named nominating board to appoint a judge.

Garrison. Work on the giant Garrison Diversion irrigation and water supply project, suspended under terms of an Audubon Society lawsuit, resumed after Congress ordered the Carter administration to spend $17.7 million previously appropriated. In November an Audubon restraining order again halted construction. Interior Secretary Cecil Andrus recommended a reduction of 40% in size, to 96,000 acres (39,-000 ha) but Congress allocated funds to continue work on the original size, 247,000 acres (100,000 ha). The money was included in the Public Works bill vetoed by President Carter. The president subsequently signed a compromise measure which contained $747,000 for the Garrison project.

STAN CANN, *The Fargo Forum*

—— NORTH DAKOTA • Information Highlights ——

Area: 70,665 square miles (183,022 km²).
Population (Jan. 1978 est.): 658,000.
Chief Cities (1970 census): Bismarck, the capital, 34,703; Fargo, 53,365; Grand Forks, 39,008.
Government (1978): *Chief Officers*—governor, Arthur A. Link (D); lt. gov., Wayne G. Sanstead (D). *Legislative Assembly*—Senate, 50 members; House of Representatives, 100 members.
Education (1977–78): *Enrollment*—public elementary schools, 58,105 pupils; public secondary, 66,980; colleges and universities, 32,199 students. *Public school expenditures*, $201,500,000 ($1,458 per pupil).
State Finances (fiscal year 1977): *Revenues*, $736,073,-000; *expenditures*, $678,657,000.
Personal Income (1977): $4,044,000,000; per capita, $6,190.
Labor Force (July 1978): *Nonagricultural wage and salary earners*, 230,700; *unemployed*, 12,900 (4% of total force).

NORTHWEST TERRITORIES

A major event in 1978 was the crash in January of a Soviet satellite, Cosmos 954, in the barrens near the Thelon Game Preserve. The search and clean-up operation by the Canadian Armed Forces cost about $13 million.

Satellite Crash. Discussions continued throughout the year as to the extent of the financial responsibility of the Soviet government. Heavy pieces of the satellite landed in an uninhabited area where native people hunt and trap. Some pieces were found to be highly radioactive and very dangerous if contacted directly or within very close range. Attention was also given to monitoring the degree of fallout along the descent path. Small particles were found in an area of 25,000 square miles (65,000 km²) occupied by about 8,000 people.

Land Claims. In October the government of Canada and the Committee for Original Peoples' Entitlement (COPE) signed an agreement in principle on the elements to be included in a land claim. The agreement affects approximately 2,500 Inuit (Eskimo) of the western Arctic. Included are special Inuit wildlife harvesting and management rights, Inuit ownership of 37,000 square miles (95,830 km²) of land, 5,000 square miles (12,950 km²) of which would include subsurface rights, financial compensation of $45 million, and economic and social development programs.

Political Development. Charles M. (Bud) Drury, the prime minister's special representative reviewing constitutional reform in the Northwest Territories, presented a progress report to the council of the NWT in October. He concluded that there is a need for devolution of more responsibility from the federal to the territorial government and from the territorial government to the community.

The Economy. There was a general slow-down of economic activity in the Mackenzie Valley following the decision not to proceed with a gas pipeline through the region.

Legislation. The Territorial Council passed a new wildlife ordinance and voted a budget of more than $268 million.

Ross M. Harvey
*Assistant Director of Information
Government of the Northwest Territories*

─── NORTHWEST TERRITORIES · Information ───
Highlights

Area: 1,304,903 square miles (3,379,699 km²).
Population (1978 est.): 43,700.
Chief City (1976 census): Yellowknife, the capital, 8,256.
Government (1978): *Chief Officer*—commissioner, Stuart M. Hodgson; Chief Justice, Court of Appeal, William A. McGillivray; Judge of the Supreme Court, C. F. Tallis. *Legislature*—Territorial Council, 15 elected members.
Education (Sept. 1978): Enrollment—elementary and secondary schools, 12,766 pupils. Public school expenditures (1977–78): $43,472,000.
Mining (1977 est.): Production value, $218,000,000.
(All monetary figures are in Canadian dollars.)

NORWAY

The effects of the prolonged world recession began to be strongly felt in Norway during 1978. Prime Minister Odvar Nordli's Labor government, worried by rising costs and a growing foreign debt, took steps to curb consumption and inflation. Industrial production fell by 2%, and the gross national product rose by only 3.1%. By the third quarter of the year, unemployment had risen to 43,000 (2.3%).

The year was marked by a series of restrictive economic measures. These included curbs on credit-financed buying, increased interest rates, a relatively moderate spring wages settlement (obtained by compulsory mediation), and the introduction or increase of special taxes on certain consumer goods.

These moves were followed by the introduction of a 15-month wage and price freeze and an austere state budget. For the first time since World War II, most Norwegians faced a decline in the standard of living.

The new austere economic policy had its intended effect. Imports dropped sharply and car sales decreased by almost 50% from the record 1977 level. However, the change came as a shock to many Norwegians. The new program represented a complete reversal of the Labor government's strategy in the preceding four years. They had assumed that the world slump would be relatively short and aimed to sustain the domestic economy by allowing real incomes to rise. The resulting payments deficit was to be covered by borrowing against future offshore petroleum earnings.

Several factors forced the turnaround. The international recession showed no signs of ending. The country's foreign debt grew alarmingly; by the end of 1977, it had reached nearly (U. S.) 85 billion kroner. Meanwhile, the domestic boom had pushed costs so high that Norwegian goods were losing ground on foreign markets. Currency fluctuations strengthened this trend. The krone was devalued several times in relation to the currencies of the European Joint Float (EJF), twice in 1977 and in February and

─── NORWAY · Information Highlights ───

Official Name: Kingdom of Norway.
Location: Northern Europe.
Area: 125,181 square miles (324,219 km²).
Population (1978 est.): 4,100,000.
Chief Cities (Jan. 1977): Oslo, the capital, 462,497; Bergen, 212,755; Trondheim, 135,558.
Government: *Head of state,* Olav V, king (acceded Sept. 1957). *Head of government,* Odvar Nordli, prime minister (took office Jan. 1976). *Legislature* —Storting: Lagting and Odelsting.
Monetary Unit: Krone (5.0176 kroner equal U. S.$1, Dec. 1978).
Manufactures (major products): Pulp and paper, ships, fish, oil and gas, food products, aluminum, ferroalloys, iron and steel, nickel, zinc, nitrogen fertilizers, transport equipment, hydroelectric power, refinery products, petrochemicals, electronics.
Agriculture (major products): Potatoes, barley, apples, pears, dairy products, livestock, oats, wheat, vegetables, berries, furs, wool.

October of 1978. The effect of these devaluations was repeatedly eroded, however, by the steady fall in the value of currencies outside EJF—particularly the U. S. dollar and British pound sterling. Since Norway's incomes from merchant freight and offshore oil are calculated in dollars, and because Britain is one of the country's main export markets, the continued decline of the dollar and pound sterling strongly affected Norwegian export earnings.

Income from North Sea oil and gas, which was to have been Norway's cushion against the world slump, was delayed and reduced by accidents and the slow pace of development. Moreover, oil prices did not rise at the expected rate; in real terms, they fell.

In its new budget, the government announced that it would no longer subsidize industries endangered by the recession. Instead, it would try to encourage labor to move into more profitable industries, thereby promoting a restructuring of Norwegian business and industry.

Key industries which did slightly better in 1978 than the year before were light metals and forest products. Shipping had another difficult year. In the first nine months of 1978, 135 ships, totaling 4.8 million tons dead-weight (t.d.w.) were sold to foreign owners; this cut the merchant fleet to 44 million t.d.w.

THOR GJESTER
Editor, "Okonomisk Revy," Oslo

CANADIAN PRESS

John and Mavis Buchanan thank Nova Scotians for electing the Progressive Conservative leader premier.

NOVA SCOTIA

The year 1978 brought Nova Scotians a moderate improvement in real income, further hike in energy prices, and a change of government.

Legislature and Government. In the September provincial election, the Progressive Conservatives, led by John Buchanan, scored an impressive victory over the Liberals. The final count gave Progressive Conservatives 31 legislative seats, Liberals 17, and New Democrats 4. The number of legislative seats had increased from 46 to 52 since the 1974 election.

The Liberal government, before its defeat at the polls, had promulgated laws to ensure that property belonging to married couples is equally divided between the two spouses upon termination of a marriage. Additional steps were taken for protecting children of unmarried parents, providing a home for children and a center for the treatment and rehabilitation of disabled Nova Scotians. In addition, the government earmarked all future second Sundays in April as Senior Citizens' Day.

Energy. The province continued to make progess in the direction of generating power from sources other than oil. The Nova Scotia Power Corporation (N.S.P.C.) brought on line a 200 Mw hydro power generating plant at Wreck Cove. The construction of two coal fired power generating plants at Lingal made further headway. However, these developments were not expected to provide any relief from escalating power prices. The Public Utility Board granted the N.S.P.C. an increase in power rates averaging 17%.

Economy. Against the backdrop of moderate real growth in the Canadian economy, the provincial economy showed signs of improvement. Capital spending in the manufacturing, primary, and construction sectors was up. Reduction in provincial sales tax kept retail trade brisk, while export trade achieved 9% growth in the first quarter of 1978. The production of goods by the primary and the manufacturing sectors steadily increased.

R. P. SETH
Economics Department
Mount St. Vincent University, Halifax

--- NOVA SCOTIA • Information Highlights ---

Area: 21,425 square miles (55,490 km²).
Population (1978 est.): 840,700.
Chief Cities (1976 census): Halifax, the capital, 117,-882; Dartmouth, 65,341; Sydney, 30,645.
Government (1978): *Chief Officers*—lt. gov., Clarence Gosse; premier, John Buchanan (Progressive Conservative); atty. gen., Harry How; chief justice, Supreme Court, Appeal Div., Ian M. McKeigan; Trial Div., Gordon S. Cowan. *Legislature*—Legislative Assembly, 52 members.
Public Finance (1978–79): Revenues, $1,380,000,000; expenditures, $1,350,000,000.
Personal Income (average weekly salary, May 1978): $221.62.
Unemployment Rate (July 1978, seasonally adjusted): 10.9%.
(All monetary figures are in Canadian dollars.)

HUMPHREY, Hubert Horatio

U. S. senator and vice president: b. Wallace, S. D., May 27, 1911; d. Waverly, Minn., Jan. 13, 1978.

When Hubert Horatio Humphrey died on Jan. 13, 1978, the United States lost one of its most dedicated public servants. We will miss his easy smile, his boundless enthusiasm, his courage, his honesty, and his warmth.

Hubert Humphrey saw government as society's most powerful tool for fashioning the public good. He treated everyone equally. He thought not of social needs, but of human needs. In part, that distinction made Hubert great.

It was his ambition to be president. Although he lived in a time when ambition in politics was regarded by many as unseemly, he was proud of his ambition because he was driven by an intense desire to make things better.

It is difficult to remember how frustrating, discouraging, and depressing a challenge Hubert faced when he came out of the Democratic convention in September 1968. I cannot think of another man who would have responded to that situation with the optimism, the energy, the determination, and the conviction that Hubert did. It was a mark of his optimism and personal courage that his defeat, which must have been devastating, left him neither bitter nor disillusioned. After a year of teaching and writing, in 1970 he ran for the Senate. And he won.

And as a senator, there has never been a more creative, imaginative, persuasive, and effective visionary. It was once said of Hubert, with a sense of ridicule, that he had more answers than there were problems. He did. Hubert was able to perceive problems that others had not yet seen and to begin to think of dealing with them.

He was a social leader in the best sense of the word—from his battle for a civil rights plank in the 1948 Democratic Party platform to his attempt to legislate guaranteed employment in the Humphrey-Hawkins bill 30 years later.

Hubert was boundless in his ability to be optimistic about the future and his determination to make it better. I never knew him to be pessimistic—in private or in public. I never knew him to be discouraged—to mope over a defeat—to give way. I never heard him speak ill of anybody. He always saw the best in people and the good things in his prospects or his circumstances.

Beyond his legislative accomplishments, it was his refusal to accept the results of adversity that most affected us. Despite the pain and the certainty of his death, he never succumbed to self-pity. He never lost his courage or his eagerness for tomorrow. He never stopped thinking, planning, working, or talking. He always had hopes and dreams for the less fortunate.

SEN. EDMUND S. MUSKIE

UPI

HUBERT HORATIO HUMPHREY (1911–1978)

"He taught us how to hope and how to love, how to win and how to lose; he taught us how to live, and finally, he taught us how to die."

Vice President Walter Mondale

--- CAREER HIGHLIGHTS ---

1933: Graduated from the Denver College of Pharmacy.

1936: Married Muriel Buck.

1939: Graduated Phi Beta Kappa from the University of Minnesota.

1940: Took a master's degree in political science from Louisiana State University.

1940–41: Taught at University of Minnesota.

1941–42: Served in and became head of the Minnesota Branch, War Production Administration.

1943: Assistant regional director, War Manpower Progress Commission.

1943–44: Professor, Army Air Force Training program, Macalester College.

1945: Elected mayor of Minneapolis. (Reelected 1947.)

1947: Cofounder of Americans for Democratic Action.

1948: Elected senator from Minnesota. (Reelected 1954 and 1960; elected again 1970.)

1956–57: U. S. delegate to the United Nations.

1958: U. S. delegate to UNESCO Conference in Paris and the Nuclear Test Suspension Conference in Geneva.

1960: Defeated in bid for the Democratic presidential nomination.

1961–64: Assistant majority leader, U. S. Senate.

1965–69: Vice president of the United States.

1968: Defeated for the presidency by Richard M. Nixon.

1969–70: College professor; newspaper columnist.

1970–72: Chairman, Board of Trustees, Woodrow Wilson International Center for Scholars.

1972: Lost Democratic presidential nomination.

1972–74: Chairman, Vice Presidential Selection Commission, Democratic Party.

1977: Unanimously selected by Senate Democrats to a new position, deputy president pro tempore of the Senate.

[1] Arranged chronologically by death date

MENZIES, Sir Robert Gordon

Australian statesman: b. Jeparit, Victoria, Dec. 20, 1894; d. Melbourne, May 14, 1978.

Sir Robert Gordon Menzies, a dominant figure in Australian politics for over four decades, gave political expression to his nation's great post-World War II exuberance for reshaping the economy and invigorating the national outlook. During a period of rapid development and change, Menzies gave Australia a sense of stability and purpose. He sought not active social reform but administrative proficiency, with the overriding aim of fashioning a modern nation in which the individual's opportunity for initiative, enterprise, and reward would remain.

When his father, a storekeeper, was elected to the state parliament, the family moved to Melbourne; there Menzies won scholarships that carried him through the university. He became an attorney and in 1928 was elected to the Victorian parliament, where he gained cabinet posts. In 1934 he stood for national parliament and following election victory became attorney general. He was elected leader of the United Australia Party and consequently prime minister in 1939. Lack of decisiveness in gearing the nation for war, however, resulted in the Labor Party gaining office in 1941.

Menzies became leader of the Opposition and in 1945 established the new Liberal Party. He became prime minister again by leading a Liberal-Country Party coalition to victory in 1949, and was reelected over the next 16 years.

The 1951 ANZUS treaty, aligning Australia and New Zealand with the United States, expressed Menzies' ideal of a regional defense pact. To further the nation's long-range security, he initiated a "national development" program which encouraged large-scale immigration, a nationwide minerals search, and major water conservation/hydroelectric undertakings. Import controls as well as tariffs were used to buttress manufacturing, while rural industries gained generous tax provisions.

Menzies' status as a world figure was enhanced largely through his role in the annual conferences of Commonwealth prime ministers. He was also an advocate of U. S. involvement in the Pacific, and he strongly supported U. S. policy in Vietnam, committing Australian combat troops to the area in 1965. He signed the agreement for the U. S. Navy's communications base at North West Cape, and various U. S. space installations were approved as Australia became America's "reserve platform off Asia."

In 1963 Queen Elizabeth conferred the Order of the Thistle on him, and later he was appointed to the centuries-old English post of Lord Warden of the Cinque Ports.

R. M. YOUNGER

ROCKEFELLER, John D. 3d

American philanthropist, cultural enthusiast, population planning expert: b. New York City, March 21, 1906; d. Mount Pleasant, N. Y., July 10, 1978.

A Lincolnesque man who enjoyed woodchopping, John D. Rockefeller 3d, the eldest grandson of John D. Rockefeller, was described as shy, formal, and generous. He was also a man whose passions centered on Asian and American art, population planning, cultural interaction between the United States and Asia, and philanthropy.

Like his father before him, he showed more interest in using the family fortune than in accumulating more money. To this end, he handled the numerous philanthropic projects of the family. In 1931 he became trustee of the General Education Board of the Rockefeller Foundation which was established by his father to finance projects too large to be handled by other agencies. One such early project was the establishment of the Peking Union Medical College. Rockefeller served the foundation until 1971.

He also served as trustee, chairman, or director of Rockefeller Center, the American Museum of Natural History, his alma mater Princeton University, Lincoln Center, and Colonial Williamsburg.

In 1951 he journeyed to Japan as a consultant with the John Foster Dulles peace mission and later in the year was a member of the U. S. delegation that signed the peace treaty with Japan in San Francisco. While in Japan, he developed an avid interest in art collecting. At the time of his death, his Asian collection represented four main cultures—Chinese, Khmer, Indian, and Japanese—and was considered outstanding. He also collected almost 200 American works of various centuries.

As a result of extensive travels he became a strong advocate of cultural interaction between Asia and the United States and of population planning. In 1956 he established the Asia Society, and eight years later through the John D. Rockefeller 3d Fund, he set up an Asian cultural program which by 1978 had given almost $6 million in grants and fellowships. President Nixon appointed him (1970) chairman of the United States Commission on Population Growth and the American Future.

In 1973 he wrote his first book, *The Second American Revolution* which pondered America's lost humanism and individual initiative.

On July 10, 1978, while traveling to his home in Westchester County, N. Y., he was killed in a head-on auto crash. He is survived by his widow, Blanchette Ferry Hooker Rockefeller; a son, three daughters, and three brothers.

SAUNDRA FRANCE

POPE PAUL VI (1897–1978)
262nd Supreme Pontiff of the Roman Catholic Church

UPI

PAUL VI, Pope (Giovanni Battista Montini)

Churchman, world leader of the Roman Catholic Church from June 21, 1963, to Aug. 6, 1978: b. in Concesio, Italy, Sept. 26, 1897; d. Castel Gandolfo, Italy, Aug. 6, 1978.

Pope Paul VI's 15-year reign as head of some 700 million Roman Catholics was one of the most controversial pontificates in modern Catholic Church history, encompassing the completion and implementation of the Second Vatican Council, steps toward major Church reform, cautious moves toward liberalization, and yet stern approaches to discipline, theological innovation, and morality.

Criticized by Church progressives and traditionalists alike, Paul VI was surprising in his bold efforts to carry out Vatican II directives. His tenure was marked by new initiatives to achieve social justice, the broadening of diplomatic activity by the Vatican, the adoption of détente with Eastern European Communist nations despite opposition from some Church leaders, and the encouragement of shared responsibility, nationally and internationally, in the operation of the Church by the world's bishops.

Paul VI's most controversial and divisive action occurred in 1968 when he issued the encyclical, *Humanae Vitae* (Of Human Life), which upheld traditional Church views against the use of artificial contraception. Later, under his auspices, the Vatican issued statements reiterating Church condemnations of premarital sex and homosexual activity; refused to amend Church laws allowing optional celibacy for priests; and ruled that women cannot be ordained priests.

The most traveled of popes, Paul VI visited almost every continent in quest of world peace— a highlight being his 1965 address to the United Nations. A career diplomat, the pope was convinced of the power of diplomacy in ensuring Church rights internationally and in working for peace and social justice globally. He established ties with more than 40 nations, including the United States, and trebled the number of world conferences at which the Vatican was represented. He met with some 80 world leaders of all political strains.

During his pontificate, Paul VI reestablished the Church's presence in several Communist lands and instituted sweeping changes in the Roman Curia, the Church's central administration, internationalizing it and setting up new commissions to implement Vatican II initiatives on ecumenism and dialogue with non-Christians and nonbelievers. He set up special departments to stimulate lay activity and theological investigation and to enhance social action and social thought in the Church.

In 1967, he issued his major social encyclical, *Populorum Progressio* (On Progress of Peoples), putting in motion a revolutionary outreach in Church social doctrine. In general, it gave local Church leaders free rein to address questions of social justice and spurred such events as the historic Latin American bishops' 1968 conference at Medellin, Colombia.

Paul VI nurtured the growth of missionary Churches and indigenous clergy and hierarchy, particularly in Africa and other Third World areas. He urged national bishops' conferences to assume more responsibility and established a World Synod of Bishops to share policy and decision-making with him in the Church.

Despite strong opposition from the Curia, Paul VI defended ecumenical initiatives by the Church, and himself made daring gestures that included a meeting in Jerusalem with the Orthodox Ecumenical Patriarch, an address to the World Council of Churches in Geneva, and the sanctioning of dialogues with almost every major Protestant denomination.

Background. Born in a farm town outside the northern Italian city of Brescia, Giovanni Battista Montini was the son of a lawyer and editor of the Catholic newspaper in Brescia. Ordained in 1920, Montini entered the Vatican diplomatic service two years later. In 1937, after serving in various diplomatic posts, he was appointed undersecretary of the Vatican Secretariat of State, becoming a close associate of Pope Pius XII. In 1954, he was named Archbishop of Milan and in 1958 raised to the College of Cardinals. In 1963, following the death of Pope John XXIII, he was elected 261st successor to St. Peter. Paul VI died at the papal summer residence.

ROBERT L. JOHNSTON

KENYATTA, Jomo

President of Kenya: b. Ichaweri, Kiambu district, Kenya, early 1890's; d. Mombasa, Aug. 22, 1978.

Jomo Kenyatta, a member of the Kikuyu tribe and Kenya's first president, was educated in Presbyterian mission schools, and in 1914 he was baptized. After involvement with some early nationalist organizations, Kenyatta became spokesman for the Kikuyu who were seeking to reclaim their land in the "White Highlands" of Kenya that had been alienated to Europeans.

After a brief visit to England in 1929, Kenyatta returned there in 1931, and spent the next 15 years in Europe, visiting Moscow and Paris, and completing a master's degree at the London School of Economics. His return to Kenya in 1946 coincided with a growth of nationalist agitation over land and voting rights. Kenyatta organized the Kenya African Union, and this led to accusations that he was the force behind the "Mau Mau" uprising that began in October 1952. Though he forever denied any part in the terrorism that accompanied Mau Mau, Kenyatta was tried and jailed as the leader of the movement.

Freed in 1961, Kenyatta organized the Kenya African National Union (KANU). Elections to the new Parliament in January 1962 gave KANU a huge majority. Kenyatta became prime minister and led the country to independence on Dec. 12, 1963. A year later, Kenya became a republic and Kenyatta was chosen the first president. Under his leadership, Kenyatta proclaimed and enforced a policy of nonracialism regarding blacks and whites alike. Kenya under Kenyatta became a voice for moderation and for a nonsocialistic economic development.

ROBERT GARFIELD

JOHN PAUL I, Pope (Albino Luciani)

Churchman, former Patriarch of Venice, elected to papacy Aug. 26, 1978: b. Forno di Canale (now Canale d' Agordo), Italy, Oct. 17, 1912; d. Vatican City, Sept. 28, 1978.

Pope John Paul I, whose election as successor to Pope Paul VI surprised the world, left that same world in shock when he died suddenly of a heart attack only 33 days after he became "supreme pastor" of the Roman Catholic Church. It was one of the shortest reigns in modern Church history.

Although little known outside Italy, John Paul I—who took the names of his two predecessors—quickly gained wide acceptance as a gentle and pastorally oriented pontiff. He captured the imagination of his audience through folksy and informal talk and a charming smile.

The son of a Socialist glassworker, Albino Luciani was born in the Dolomite Alps of northern Italy on Oct. 17, 1912. Ordained at 22 in 1935 for the Belluno diocese, he did pastoral work and then became vice rector of the local seminary and a theology professor. Later, the future pontiff was named vicar general of the diocese.

Appointed bishop of Vittorio Veneto in 1958 by Pope John XXIII, he was elevated to the Patriarchate of Venice by Pope Paul in 1969. One of his first actions in Venice was to encourage parishes to sell jewels and precious stones to raise money for the poor. Four years later he was made a cardinal. Unlike recent popes, he had no curial or diplomatic experience.

He wrote two books, *Catechism Crumbs,* on teaching, and *Illustrissimi,* on illustrious men, which is a bestseller.

ROBERT L. JOHNSTON

MIKOYAN, Anastas Ivanovich

Soviet statesman: b. Tiflis, Georgian SSR, Nov. 25, 1895; d. Moscow, USSR, Oct. 21, 1978.

Anastas Mikoyan served in high positions of Soviet government longer than any other figure in the history of that nation. He was a vice-premier from 1937 to 1964 and president from 1964 to 1965. He worked in the central government for 48 years and held full membership in the Communist party's Politburo for 31. He was a top government leader in the regimes of Stalin, Khrushchev, and Brezhnev.

Mikoyan's ability to survive was attributed to his expertise in the field of foreign trade. His knowledge of an economic field of which other Soviet leaders were ignorant enabled him to avoid Kremlin infighting.

Born of Armenian parents in the Caucasus, Mikoyan received his higher education at a theological seminary. He joined the Bolshevik (later Communist) party in 1915, fought in the 1917 Bolshevik Revolution, and became a province party chief after the Russian Civil War. Mikoyan became minister of trade in 1926 and at various other times in his career was minister of supplies, food industry, foreign trade, and internal trade. During World War II, he was a member of the State Defense Committee. His visit to Cuba in 1960 marked the beginning of close cooperation between the USSR and the Castro regime. As president, he helped oust Khrushchev from power in 1964.

Because of his advancing age, Mikoyan was honorably retired from the presidency in 1965 and from the Politburo in 1966. He served thereafter as a largely honorary member of the Supreme Soviet Presidium.

ELLSWORTH RAYMOND

ROCKWELL, Norman

Artist and illustrator: b. New York City, Feb. 3, 1894; d. Stockbridge, Mass., Nov. 8, 1978.

For more than 50 years, almost from the time he illustrated his first cover for *The Saturday Evening Post* magazine at age 22, Norman Rockwell reigned supreme as America's most popular artist. His work reportedly was reproduced more often than that of Michelangelo, Rembrandt, and Picasso combined.

Rockwell's reign spanned the decades from America's entry into World War I through the student disorders, civil rights demonstrations, and antiwar protests of the 1960's. During that time he illustrated 317 *Post* covers, almost one of every seven, and even after almost a half-century a Rockwell cover was good for as many as 75,000 extra newsstand sales.

Rockwell's mass appeal and financial success—his income reportedly never fell below $40,000 a year even during the depression—were owed to his unique ability to tug at the viewer's heartstrings, to reawaken nostalgia, sentiment, reverence, and similar emotions.

A typical Rockwell cover depicted a family gathered in thanksgiving around a holiday table; ample Pickwickian gentlemen singing Christmas carols; barefoot lads in tattered overalls, carrying makeshift fishing poles; a runaway boy at a lunch counter confiding in an understanding policeman; and shy young couples bathed in the warmth and innocence of new love.

Rockwell was not without detractors. Social critics accused him of ignoring important public concerns and of perpetuating a vision of an imaginary America. Art critics, while conceding his painstaking craftsmanship and sharp eye for the smallest detail, disparaged him as lacking in subtlety, nuance, and depth.

But the tall, thin, pipe-smoking Mr. Rockwell did not appear to be disturbed by criticism. Indeed, he modestly titled his autobiography *My Adventures as an Illustrator* (1960). And he said of the virtues that he celebrated on canvas: "I unconsciously decided that if it wasn't an ideal world, it should be, and so painted only the ideal aspects of it. . . ." Even his famous wartime covers of the "Four Freedoms," "Rosie the Riveter," and "imaginary G. I., Willie Gillis" tapped a familiar vein.

Rockwell's positive vision of America persisted almost until he became seriously ill about two years before his death, and that vision was perhaps reinforced by the serenity that surrounded him at his home and studio in Stockbridge, Mass. Rockwell was awarded the Presidential Medal of Freedom in January 1977. He is survived by his third wife and three sons from his second marriage.

EDWIN MCDOWELL

MEAD, Margaret

Anthropologist, author, social critic: b. Philadelphia, Pa., Dec. 16, 1901; d. New York City, Nov. 15, 1978.

A friend once said that Margaret Mead "wanted to be a mother to the world." Considering her life-long desire to improve human understanding, her far-ranging work in anthropology and ethnology, and her contributions to a variety of causes, the comment seems well-founded. In fact, she was considered one of the world's most influential women. After a year-long struggle with cancer, during much of which time she continued to work, Margaret Mead died at the age of 76.

Background. Dr. Mead studied psychology at Barnard College (B. A., 1923). While there, she met Dr. Franz Boas of Columbia University who brought her into anthropology, but she never lost her interest in psychology. Defying Dr. Boas, who wanted her to study the North American Indians, she went instead to Polynesia. Upon her return she wrote *Coming of Age in Samoa* (1928) which was an instant best-seller. She received her Ph. D. in 1929 from Columbia.

In 1926 she became curator of ethnology at the American Museum of Natural History, and in 1954 joined Columbia as adjunct professor of anthropology. She served in both posts until her death.

Mead's work in the Pacific, described in her books, *Coming of Age in Samoa, Growing Up in New Guinea* (1930), and *Sex and Temperament in Three Primitive Societies* (1935), brought her to the conclusion that it was the culture of the society rather than the nature of adolescence that caused the problems of adolescence. Her work led her to generalize that each culture had its own psychological profile.

Mead's first book made her a celebrity and she used her position to become a social critic as well as a supporter of numerous causes, including improved race relations, good family life, mental health, scientific freedom, better environment, and the women's movement.

Beginning in the late 1930's, she worked in Bali and New Guinea with her third husband, Gregory Bateson, and their research greatly influenced modern developing anthropology and psychology. She also wrote *And Keep Your Powder Dry* (1942), and *Male and Female* (1949).

Mead was a pioneer in personality and culture studies, in broadening the data base upon which anthropologists develop their conclusions. Although never prolific in theoretical contributions, she brought the anthropological perspective to the public. She was elected president of the American Anthropological Association (1960) and at age 72, president of the American Association for the Advancement of Science.

HERMAN J. JAFFE

UPI

GOLDA MEIR (1898–1978)
a symbol of Israel's courage and idealism

MEIR, Golda

Israeli statesman, diplomat, and prime minister; b. Kiev, Ukraine, May 3, 1898; d. Jerusalem, Israel, Dec. 8, 1978.

When she died of leukemia at the age of 80, Golda Meir was hailed as a giant of world affairs, a symbol of the strength and determination of the state of Israel, and the personification of gentleness and compassion. Her career was the metamorphosis of a persecuted Eastern European Jew into a struggling Palestinian settler and eventual prime minister of the sovereign Jewish state.

During her five years as prime minister, 1969–74, her goal was to see Israel live in peace with its Arab neighbors. "We don't want wars even when we win," she once said. But in October 1973, Egypt and Syria made a surprise attack during the Jewish holiday of Yom Kippur. Despite Israel's victory in that war, Meir lamented: "We do not rejoice in victories. We rejoice when a new kind of cotton is grown and when strawberries bloom in Israel."

Life and Career. Golda Mabovitch was eight years old when her family fled the poverty and pogroms of Kiev to settle in Milwaukee, Wisc. After graduating from high school, she entered Milwaukee Teachers' Training College and became active in the Socialist-oriented Labor Zionist movement. In 1917 she became a teacher in a Jewish Labor school and married Morris Meyerson, an immigrant sign painter.

In 1921, Golda persuaded her husband to travel to Palestine, where they joined Kibbutz Merhavia, a collective farm in the Jezreel Valley. Golda soon emerged as the kibbutz's representative in the Histadrut, the general labor federation. But Morris was unable to adjust to kibbutz living and the couple moved to Jerusalem, where Golda's two children were born and where she began her public career.

Her first appointment was secretary of the Women's Labor Council of the Histadrut. In 1929 she was sent by the precursor of the Israel Labor party to the World Zionist Congress in Zurich. During the 1930's, she traveled extensively in Europe and the United States to bolster support for the Palestinian Jewish community. As her commitment to public service became total, her marriage gradually dissolved. Golda served on the executive committee of the National Council, the chief organ of Jewish self-government under the British mandate. In 1940 she became head of the Histadrut's political department, and during World War II she served on the British War Economic Advisory Council.

By the time Israel won its independence in 1948, Golda Meir was a leading national figure. She was a member of the Provisional Council of State and a signer of the Israeli Declaration of Independence. Meir went to Moscow as Israel's first ambassador to the Soviet Union but was elected to the Knesset (parliament) *in absentia*. In 1949, she became minister of labor in Israel's first cabinet. In that capacity, she was responsible for the absorption of thousands of immigrants—housing programs, vocational training, health facilities, and a national insurance plan. In 1953, as chairman of the Israeli delegation to the UN General Assembly, Meir's dynamic personality and simple eloquence brought her the reputation of a forceful spokesman for her country. In 1956, as foreign minister, she gave staunch support to Prime Minister David Ben-Gurion's policy of retaliating swiftly and powerfully against Arab attacks; this prompted Ben-Gurion to call her "the only man in my cabinet." She served as foreign minister until waning health forced her to resign in 1966.

In February 1969, the sudden death of Prime Minister Levi Eshkol catapulted Golda Meir, a friend and confidant, back into the spotlight. The 70-year-old grandmother was called upon to lead a nation threatened by Egypt's "war of attrition," increased Arab terrorism, and almost total isolation in the world. Her unique personal diplomacy established closer ties with the United States, brought a Sinai disengagement treaty with Egypt in 1974, and established the foundation for future peace negotiations. Although she won reelection after the Yom Kippur war, controversy over the military's lack of preparedness prompted her to resign in June 1974. Her role as adviser, matriarch, and living legend continued to the end.

LIVIA BITTON JACKSON

The following is a selected list of prominent persons who died in 1978.

Alikhanyan, Artemi I. (69), Soviet nuclear physicist; he and his brother, Abram I. Alikhanov, did early work in identifying atomic particles and in studying cosmic rays: d. Yerevan, Feb. 25.

Allen, Clifford R. (66), Democratic congressman from Tennessee; he was elected in 1975 to fill the vacancy of Richard Fulton; he won a full term in 1976. As a congressman he backed measures to reduce energy costs: d. Nashville, Tenn., June 18.

Allen, James B. (65), a conservative Democratic senator from Alabama; he served from 1969–1978; was known as a master parliamentarian who was an expert of the filibuster; most recently he used his talents to block the Panama Canal treaties fight: d. Foley, Ala., June 1.

Andrianov (73), Soviet chemist; pioneered in the synthesis of organic polymers used in heat-resistant insulating resins and varnishes: d. Russia, March 1978.

Ascoli, Max (79), editor-publisher of *The Reporter* magazine from 1949 to 1968; battled Sen. Joseph McCarthy in the 1950's but upset liberals by backing U.S. intervention in Cuba and Vietnam: d. New York City, Jan. 1.

Baldwin, Faith (84), author who specialized in light fiction; published 85 books as well as numerous short stories and articles: d. Norwalk, Conn., March 18.

Barrie, Wendy (65), actress; appeared in movies of the 30's and 40's, was best known for doing the Revlon television ads for *The $64,000 Question*: d. Englewood, N. J., Feb. 2.

Begle, Edward G. (63), professor of education and mathematics at Stanford University; he helped develop the "New Math" curriculum for the elementary and secondary schools: d. Palo Alto, Calif., March 2.

Bergen, Edgar (75), ventriloquist; creator of Charlie McCarthy; he was performing his last engagement at Caesar's Palace in Las Vegas prior to retirement when he collapsed. Mr. Bergen was a vaudevillian who later became well known in radio, the movies, and television. In 1937 he was awarded a special Academy Award for his film shorts and appearances in movie musicals: d. Las Vegas, Sept. 30.

Bernstein, Felicia Montealegre Cohn (56), actress and wife of composer-conductor, Leonard Bernstein; she made her Broadway debut in 1946 in *Swan Song*. She also appeared frequently in television dramas of the 1950's. In 1961 she began narrating concerts with the New York Philharmonic, and in 1973 made her opera debut in *Les Troyens*. She was also politically active: d. East Hampton, L. I., June 16.

Best, Charles Herbert (79), physician who co-discovered the use of insulin in the treatment of diabetes; in the summer of 1921, as an undergraduate student at the University of Toronto, he was invited by Dr. Frederick Banting to work in a laboratory in search of the hormone which turns sugar into energy in the human body. Through this research they discovered insulin. Dr. Banting won the 1923 Nobel Prize for his discovery along with the head of the physiology department at the university. Dr. Best was overlooked for the award. This slight angered Dr. Banting who split his prize money with Dr. Best: d. Toronto, March 31.

Betz, Carl (56), actor; best known for his television roles, first as Dr. Alex Stone, husband on *The Donna Reed Show*, and later as Judd in *Judd for the Defense*, for which he won an Emmy: d. Los Angeles, Jan. 18.

Bilko, Steve (49), baseball player, 1st baseman; played with the St. Louis Cardinals in 1953, then for the Cincinnati Reds, Chicago Cubs, Los Angeles Dodgers, Detroit Tigers, and the Los Angeles Angels. He retired in 1962 after 600 games over 10 seasons, with a career batting average of .249 and 76 home runs: d. Wilkes-Barre, Pa., March 7.

Bleibtrey, Ethelda (76), winner in the 1920's Olympic Games of three gold medals for swimming; she first took up the sport to help overcome curvature of the spine: d. West Palm Beach, Fla., May 6.

Bolin, Wesley (68), governor of Arizona; he was appointed to the post in late 1977 after it was vacated by Raul Castro: d. Phoenix, Ariz., Mar. 4.

Bonnet, Henri (90), French ambassador to Washington from 1944 to 1955; Mr. Bonnet had been a member of the League of Nations Secretariat. He left France in 1940 to work in New York for the Free French. He became France's first post World War II ambassador to the United States: d. Paris, Oct. 25.

Borland, Harold Glen (Hal) (77), writer and naturalist; known for his New York *Times* editorials that chronicled the seasons. He worked for six years for the *Times* and then began to free lance, but he continued for 35 years to produce the seasons' chronicles. In 1968 he won the John Burroughs Medal, considered the country's highest award for nature writing: d. Sharon, Conn., Feb. 22.

EDGAR BERGEN

UPI

Boumedienne Houari (51?), president of Algeria (1965–78); also a leader of the Arab and Third Worlds: d. Algiers, Dec. 27.

Boyer, Charles (79), French-born actor; best known for his role as Pepe LeMoko in the film *Algiers*. He was the epitome of the gallant man—well-dressed, polished, sophisticated—in the numerous film roles that he played: d. Phoenix, Ariz., August 26.

Bradshaw, Robert (61), prime minister of St. Kitts-Nevis-Anguilla in the West Indies; he had served in that office since 1967 when the Islands became a British Associated State: d. Basseterre, St. Kitts, May 24.

Bray, John R. (99), credited with the 1910 invention of the animated cartoon process: d. Bridgeport, Conn., Oct. 10.

Brel, Jacques (49), Belgian singer and song writer; his songs became well known in the United States following the New York musical *Jacques Brel is Alive and Well and Living in Paris:* d. Bobigny, France, Oct. 9.

Brown, George S. (60), USAF general; appointed in 1974 by President Nixon as chairman of the Joint Chiefs of Staff; reappointed by Presidents Ford and Carter, Gen. Brown was forced to retire in June 1978 due to cancer. He was a decorated soldier of World War II and served in Vietnam as commander of the United States air war: d. Washington, D. C., Dec. 5.

Brown, Zara Culley (86), actress; best remembered as the mother of George Jefferson in the CBS television show *The Jeffersons:* d. Los Angeles, Feb. 28.

Byran, Frederick Van Pelt (73), federal judge; best known for his 1959 decision against the ban on the D. H. Lawrence novel, *Lady Chatterley's Lover;* in a decision often compared to a similar case involving James Joyce's *Ulysses* he declared that "the book had significant literary merit, that the Postmaster General (who banned the book from going through the mails on grounds that it was obscene) had no special competence to judge obscenity, and that in a free society the severest restrictions had to be placed on barriers to the flow of ideas": d. New York City, April 17.

Butler, John M. (80), senator from Maryland (1951–1963); he was a political bedfellow of Sen. Joseph McCarthy, and following his election, after an extremely shady campaign, he quickly became an enthusiastic purger of so-called security risks from the government: d. North Carolina, March 16.

CHARLES HERBERT BEST   **CHARLES BOYER**

UPI   UPI

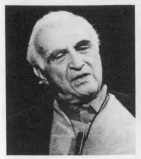

ALL PHOTOS, UPI

CARLOS CHAVEZ   **LUCIUS CLAY**   **JAMES B. CONANT**   **JAMES DALY**

Byron, Goodloe E. (49), Democratic congressman from Maryland since 1971; died of a heart attack while jogging: d. near Hagerstown, Md., Oct. 18.

Busia, Kofi (65), prime minister of Ghana from 1969 until his overthrow by a military coup in 1972; Dr. Busia was a scholar, democrat, and a devout Christian who left Oxford University for Ghana after the overthrow of President Nkrumah in 1966. He became prime minister in 1969 following a general election, but after, a conflict with the military he went into exile in Britain in 1972: d. Oxford, England, August 28.

Catton, Bruce (78), former newsman and editor of *American Heritage* magazine: probably best known for his *A Stillness at Appomattox,* one book from his two-trilogy set on the American Civil War. He won the Pulitzer Prize for this volume: d. Frankfort, Mich., August 28.

Chapman, Richard D. (67), former golf champion; won many national championships in his 30 years of play, including the United States Amateur championship in 1940 and the British Amateur in 1951. Through his affluence he was able to maintain amateur status; he qualified in 19 Masters tournaments and was a member of five U. S. Walker Cup teams: d. Rancho Santa Fe, Calif., Nov. 15.

Chase, Ilka (72), actress and author; best known for the role of Sally Fowler in Clare Boothe Luce's *The Women* and for her memoir *Past Imperfect* in which she took her friends, other writers, and socialites to task: d. Mexico City, Feb. 15.

Chavez, Carlos (79), Mexican composer and conductor; he was also an educator through his work with the National Conservatory and as director of Mexico's Department of Fine Arts. His best known works are Symphony No. 1 ("Antigona"), Symphony No. 2 ("Sinfonia India"), and Symphony No. 4 ("Sinfonia Romantica"). He was renowned as a conductor and led many of the world's best-known orchestras: d. Mexico City, August 2.

Church, Thomas (76), landscape architect; his major works included the University of California campus at Santa Cruz and the Exposition Garden at the 1940 Golden Gate International Exposition: d. San Francisco, August 30.

Clay, Lucius D. (80), American army general; he graduated from West Point in 1915, 27th in a class of 137, and was probably most widely known for his part in the Berlin airlift. Gen. Clay was one of the few professional servicemen ever to reach four-star rank without holding a combat command. His strengths were administrative ability and leadership. He advised Presidents Eisenhower (whom he had encouraged to seek the presidency), Kennedy, and Johnson. In 1961, Kennedy made him his personal representative to Berlin, giving him the rank of ambassador: d. Cape Cod, Mass., Apr. 17.

Colombo, Joseph A., Sr. (54), founder of the Italian-American Civil Rights League; alleged Mafia leader; in 1971 he was shot three times while attending a rally for the above-mentioned league. His injuries left him almost totally paralyzed. At the time he was shot he was under two indictments: d. Newburgh, N. Y., May 22.

Compton, Fay (84), British actress; her career covered 70 years; she first appeared in the title role of Sir James Barrie's *Peter Pan* and proceeded to appear with the most illustrious names in British theater. She performed on Broadway twice and made some American films, among them—Orson Welles' *Othello* in 1955: d. Britain, Dec. 12.

Conant, James B. (84), president of Harvard University for 20 years, scientist, diplomat, educator; he earned a B. A. (1910) and Ph. D. (1916) from Harvard. After a brief tenure with the Chemical Warfare Service he returned to Harvard and in 1929 became professor of organic chemistry and later chairman of the chemistry department. In 1933 at the age of 40 he became president of Harvard. During his 20-year service, he instituted national scholarships for high school graduates throughout the country,

introduced professorships for the purpose of pure research and introduced the Master of Arts in Teaching Program (MAT) to discourage the domination of teacher education by professional teacher colleges. In 1953, upon his withdrawal from the presidency of Harvard, he returned to government service, taking a position as high commissioner to the West German government at Bonn. Later he served as ambassador to the Federal Republic of West Germany. In 1957 he began extensive studies of the public educational system. He received honorary degrees from many of the world's leading universities, in addition to honors from scientific and educational groups. In 1970 President Nixon presented him with an Atomic Pioneer Award for his contributions during World War II: d. Hanover, N. H., Feb. 11.

Cozzens, James Gould (74), novelist; his book *Guard of Honor,* won the 1949 Pulitzer Prize; others of his novels include *The Last Adam* (1933), *Men and Brethren* (1936), *The Just and the Unjust* (1942), and *By Love Possessed* (1957): d. Stuart, Fla., August 9.

Crane, Bob (49), actor; played the role of Col. Hogan in the television series *Hogan's Heroes.* Mr. Crane also appeared in a second television show, *The Bob Crane Show,* which ran for one season: d. Scottsdale, Ariz., June 29.

Crawford, Ralston (71), painter, photographer, and lithographer; he was well known for his abstract paintings where he arranged various shapes into designs suggesting urban life. Mr. Crawford's work is in many galleries: d. Houston, Tex., April 28.

Dailey, Dan (62), Hollywood actor and dancer; he gained fame in the 1940's in movie musicals; he earned an Academy Award nomination in 1948 for his role in *When My Baby Smiles at Me:* d. Hollywood, Calif., Oct. 16.

Daly, James (59), stage and screen actor; best known for his leading role in the popular television series *Medical Center.* He won an Emmy award for his television performance in "The Eagle and the Cage"; d. Nyack, New York, July 3.

Dauphin, Claude (75), French actor; Mr. Dauphin appeared most recently with Simone Signoret in *Madame Rosa.* Other high points for a long stage and film career include Sarte's *No Exit* in 1946, *The Happy Time,* a long-running Broadway hit in 1950, and in 1953, *Little Boy Lost* with Bing Crosby: d. Paris, Nov. 16.

de Chirico, Giorgio (90), modernist painter; his paintings influenced the development of surrealism, but de Chirico later disavowed the work, shifting to neoclassicism and then to realism. In his early work (1910–1920) which, along with the futurist painter Carlo Carrà, he referred to as of the *scuola metafisica* (metaphysical school), he attempted the creation of artistic reality founded on reverie. From this period came such masterpieces as "The Great Metaphysician." By 1920 he had broken with modernism, calling it "horrible bestiality," and influenced by Titian, he began painting romantic subjects. In the 1950's and 1960's his work had become conventional realism: d. Rome, Nov. 21.

de Madariaga, Salvador (92), Spanish author and diplomat; he exiled himself from Spain during the reign of Franco. During those years he produced novels, plays, essays, studies in history, and poetry; his better known works are *Guide for the Reading of Don Quixote* and *Anarchy or Hierarchy.* In addition to his writing, he served in 1931 as ambassador to Washington and later served in Paris as minister of education and of justice: d. Locarno, Switzerland, Dec. 14.

Downs, Bill (63), Washington correspondent for ABC News; he was a CBS reporter to Moscow in 1942, moved to ABC in 1963: d. Bethesda, Md., May 3.

Dudley, William Henry III (47), Olympic gold medal winner; he was a member of the U.S. 800-meter swimming relays in the 1948 London games: d. New Orleans, Jan. 20.

Dupont, Clifford W. (72), elected the Rhodesian Republic's first president in 1970; he held the position for over five years. He thought there should be no lowering of white-minority standards in Rhodesia: d. Salisbury, Rhodesia, June 28.

du Vigneaud, Vincent (77), biochemist; awarded the Nobel Prize in Chemistry in 1955 for his work in the isolation and synthesis of the hormones oxytocin and vasopressin; he was also one of the scientists responsible for the synthesis of penicillin: d. White Plains, N. Y., Dec. 11.

Eliot, Martha May (86), former chief of the U. S. Children's Bureau (1951–1956) who was responsible for the great decline in maternal and infant death rates; along with Dr. Edward Park of Yale, she discovered the preventive value of sunshine and cod liver oil in curing rickets. In 1947 she became the first woman to be president of the American Public Health Association: d. Cambridge, Mass., February 1978.

Etting, Ruth (80), singer and actress; began singing on the radio in Chicago in 1922; her first movie break came when she appeared in *Ziegfeld Follies* in 1927. A movie of her life, *Love Me or Leave Me,* was filmed during the 1950's. Her stormy first marriage ended shortly after her husband tried to shoot Myrl Alderman, Miss Etting's pianist at the time, who eventually became her second husband: d. Los Angeles, Sept. 24.

Fabian, Robert (77), Scotland Yard detective; joined the police department in 1921 and retired in 1949; wrote *Fabian of the Yard:* d. Epsom, Surrey, June 14.

Fields, Totie (48), nightclub entertainer; became well known for poking fun at her considerable bulk. Later, when phlebitis had cost her the loss of her leg, she made an admirable comeback: d. Las Vegas, August 2.

Fine, John S. (85), former governor of Pennsylvania; gained national prominence in 1952 when he threw his support behind Gen. D. Eisenhower in his bid for the Republican nomination. As governor from 1951–1955, he extended the Pennsylvania Turnpike into the hard coal section of Pennsylvania: d. Wilkes-Barre, Pa., May 21.

Flanner, Janet (86), writer for *The New Yorker* magazine; for 50 years she wrote a semi-monthly "Letter from Paris" under the pseudonym Genêt. She settled in Paris in 1922 and for the next 18 years mingled with the writers and artists of the Left Bank community. During World War II she was in New York City, but returned to Paris in 1944 where she continued to write for 30 more years: d. New York City, Nov. 7.

Fontaine, Frank (58), entertainer; best known for the television role of "Crazy Googenheim" opposite Jackie Gleason's "Joe the Bartender": d. Spokane, Wash., August 4.

Forman, Harrison (74), aviator, explorer, photographer, and war correspondent; covered the Sino-Japanese conflict of the late 1930's for the "March of Time" newsreel service. After World War II he wrote books on China, Africa, and photography, and ran a travel agency known for unusual destinations: d. New York City, Jan. 31.

Fosburgh, James W. (67), painter, art adviser, and collector; he gained prominence when he was appointed by President and Mrs. John Kennedy to a committee whose aim was to find American paintings of excellence for the White House. Perhaps his most famous painting was the posthumous portrait of President Kennedy which appeared on the Nov. 5, 1965, cover of *Time:* d. New York City, April 23.

François-Poncet, André (90), diplomat and writer; served as French ambassador to Berlin during Hitler's rise to power and warned repeatedly and futilely of German rearmament; later wrote books on German literature and politics as well as several volumes of memoirs: d. Paris, Jan. 8.

Frick, Ford (83), baseball commissioner from 1951 to 1965; he served for 17 years as National League president before becoming baseball commissioner and was instrumental in establishing the Baseball Hall of Fame in 1938: d. Bronxville, N. Y., April 8.

Galiffa, Arnold (51), former All-American quarterback; played on the 1949 championship football team of West Point: d. Glenview, Ill., Sept. 5.

Geer, Will (76), actor; most recently seen as Grandpa in the television series, *The Waltons,* a role for which he won an "Emmy" in 1975. He appeared in numerous Shakespearian roles and in the stage play *Tobacco Road* in his 60-year career. During the 1950's he was blacklisted for alleged leftist leanings: d. Los Angeles, April 22.

Genn, Leo (72), British lawyer turned actor; appeared in numerous stage roles, among his most famous was in Lillian Hellman's *Another Part of the Forest.* Important films in which he was cast were *Mourning Becomes Electra, The Miniver Story, The Snake Pit,* and *Henry V:* d. London, Jan. 26.

Gilliam, Jim (Junior) (49), baseball player and coach for the Brooklyn and Los Angeles Dodgers; his career spanned

UPI UPI

RUTH ETTING   **TOTIE FIELDS**

26 years beginning in 1953 when he started with the Brooklyn ballclub, replacing Jackie Robinson at second base: d. Inglewood, Calif., Oct. 8.

Gillis, Don (65), composer and former producer of the NBC Symphony radio broadcasts under Arturo Toscanini; best known for his composition, *Symphony 5½,* presented under Toscanini in 1947: d. Columbia, S.C., Jan. 10.

Gordon, Joe (Flash) (63), baseball player; played second base for the New York Yankees from 1938 to 1946 and for the Cleveland Indians from 1947 through 1950. His lifetime batting average is .268, and he hit 253 home runs. He was the league's Most Valuable Player in 1942. After his retirement as a player, he became a manager: d. Sacramento, April 14.

Gordon, John F. (77), president of General Motors (1958–1965): d. Royal Oak, Mich., Jan. 6.

Gordon, Robert Aaron (69), economist, professor emeritus of the University of California; served under Presidents Eisenhower, Kennedy, and Johnson as consultant to the President's Council of Economic Advisers. He was the patriarch of a family devoted to economics: d. Berkeley, Calif., April 7.

Goudsmit, Samuel (76), physicist; was scientific director of a World War II team (Alsos) that spied on the Nazis to determine the status of their development of the atom bomb. While a graduate student in his native Netherlands he co-discovered the spin of electrons in the hydrogen atom. He was an editor of various scientific publications and also taught physics at the University of Michigan, Northwestern University, and the University of Nevada: d. Reno, Dec. 4.

Grant, Duncan (93), painter, decorator, and founding member of the famed Bloomsbury Group; his work was cited for its combination of Post-Impressionist influence and a kind of agreeable paganism. His influence on English art continued for many years until the 1940's and 1950's when it fell into decline, but Grant's star again ascended and on the occasion of his 90th birthday in 1975, he had a show at the Tate Gallery, the first of several: d. Aldermaston, England, May 10.

Greenwood, Charlotte (87), stage and film comedienne from the 1920's through the 1950's. Appeared in the film version of *Oklahoma:* d. Los Angeles, Jan. 18.

Gronchi, Giovanni (91), former president of Italy; served from 1955 until 1962. As president he was an early advocate of efforts to bring socialists and other left-of-center parties into an alliance with the Christian Democrats: d. Rome, Oct. 17.

WILL GEER   **JOE "FLASH" GORDON**

UPI UPI

UPI

UPI

DANIEL JAMES, JR.   **ARAM KHACHATURIAN**

Haddad, Wadi (49), leader of the Popular Front for the Liberation of Palestine; he became a refugee after the creation of the state of Israel in 1948, and was the terrorist behind the first hijacking by the Palestinians in July 1968: d. East Germany, March 28.

Haines, Jesse (85), baseball pitcher; was a member of the famed "Gashouse Gang" and pitched for the St. Louis Cardinals from 1920 to 1937: d. Columbus, Ohio, August 5.

Hasselblad, Victor (72), Swedish inventor of the Hasselblad camera; used in the United States space flights: d. Gothenburg, Sweden, August 5.

Hays, George (85), retired Army lt. general; won a Medal of Honor during World War I for helping to maintain contact with American and French units during the second Battle of the Marne in 1918. During World War II he was with the 2nd Infantry Division, landing at Omaha Beach in Normandy the day following D-day, and later commanded the 10th Mountain Division: d. Pinehurst, N. C., Sept. 7.

Highet, Gilbert (71), classicist, scholar, critic, poet, author, and educator; Dr. Highet of Columbia University early earned a reputation as a popularizer of the classics and established himself as a classicist who was readable. He was admired as a master teacher; one former student declared exposure to a Dr. Highet class a religious as well as an intellectual experience: d. New York City, Jan. 20.

Homolka, Oscar (79), actor; he went to work for Max Reinhardt, then fled Germany because of the Nazis; he settled in England and later America. He is best remembered for his portrayal of the uncle in the Broadway production of *I Remember Mama:* d. Sussex, England, Jan. 27.

James, Daniel ("Chappie") Jr. (58), the first black general in United States history; he took part in an early sit-in demonstration in 1945, flew 101 combat missions in Korea and 78 more in Vietnam: d. Colorado Springs, Colo., Feb.

Kappler, Herbert (70), convicted Nazi war criminal; colonel in Hitler's SS police force; he had served 30 years of a life term imposed by an Italian military tribunal in 1948 for the reprisal shooting of 335 World War II hostages. With the aid of his wife, he escaped from an Italian military hospital Aug. 15 to West Germany, causing a political furor: d. Soltau, West Germany, Feb. 9.

Karsavina, Tamara (93), Russian ballerina; she trained with the Maryinsky (now Kirov) Ballet, but it was as a ballerina with Serge Diaghilev's Ballets Russes that she achieved her greatest fame: d. London, May 26.

Kath, Terry (31), lead guitarist and singer with the jazz-rock band Chicago; he shot himself in the head while toying with a pistol: d. Woodland Hills, Calif., Jan. 23.

Ketchum, William M. (56), U. S. representative (R-Calif., 1973–78): d. Bakersfield, Calif., June 24.

Khachaturian, Aram (74), Russian composer; most famous for his musical composition, "Saber Dance," which was written as part of his ballet, *Gayne:* d. Russia, May 1.

Kipnis, Alexander (87), opera singer and teacher; Mr. Kipnis made a late debut (in 1940) with the Metropolitan Opera in New York: d. Westport, Conn., May 14.

Krag, Jens Otto (63), prime minister of Denmark (1962–68 and 1971–72); in 1972 he astonished his people by resigning as prime minister the day after the bitterly fought vote which brought Denmark into the European Common Market. He later became the chief representative of the Common Market in the United States: d. Jutland, Denmark, June 22.

Kuleshov, Arkady A. (63), Byelorussian poet; he won two Stalin Prizes, an Order of Lenin, an Order of the Red Banner, and several campaign medals. He served as head of the republic's Union of Writers: d. Russia, Feb. 10.

Lear, William Power (75), inventor; was the inventor of the autopilot, the automobile radio, and the small corporate jet: d. Reno, May 14.

Leavis, Frank Raymond (82), critic; perhaps best known for his fiery attack on the novelist C. P. Snow and particularly on Snow's essay *The Two Cultures.* Mr. Leavis was also well known and respected for his literary magazine, *Scrutiny:* d. Cambridge, England, April 14.

Leibowitz, Samuel S. (84), jurist and criminal lawyer for the "Scottsboro Boys" case of the early 1930's. As a judge, he supported conjugal visits to prisons: d. Brooklyn, N. Y., Jan. 11.

Lindner, Richard (76), painter; gained great popularity in the 1960's with what was mistakenly thought "Pop Art," with his paintings of huge predatory femme fatale types, and their often seamy or criminal-type escorts: d. New York City, April 16.

Lowell, Ralph (87), banker, scholar, and philanthropist; Mr. Lowell came from one of Boston's most prominent families and numbered among his forebears James Russell Lowell and Amy Lowell. He was instrumental in establishing the first educational television station in 1954, WGBH-TV: d. Westwood, Mass., May 15.

Lubin, Isador (82), economist; member of Franklin Roosevelt's "Brain Trust," and U. S. Commissioner of Labor Statistics from 1933 to 1946. Later he was the U. S. representative in the Economic and Social Council of the UN and in the General Assembly and the International Labor Organization: d. Annapolis, Md., July 6.

McGrath, Paul (74), actor; was well known as the host of the radio series *Inner Sanctum* and also appeared in numerous daytime soap operas and in many Broadway productions: d. London, April 13.

Macarthur, John D. (80), billionaire real estate and insurance executive; his large holdings included the Bankers Life and Casualty Co., which he built from scratch, and real estate holdings in New York and Florida: d. Florida, Jan. 6.

McCarthy, Joseph V. (90), New York Yankees' manager who led the club to victory in seven World Series in the 1930's and 1940's: d. Buffalo, N. Y., Jan. 13.

McCoy, Tim (86), actor; famed as a cowboy hero, he first appeared in the 1924 movie, *The Thundering Herd;* approximately 80 films were to follow: d. Nogales, Ariz., Jan. 21.

McGinley, Phyllis (72), Pulitzer prize-winning poet, essayist, and author of children's stories; her writings spoke of the mundane, often witty pleasures of life in the suburbs: d. New York, Feb. 22.

Martinson, Harry (73), Swedish Nobel prize-winning poet and novelist, best known for the poem, "Aniara." He shared the 1974 Nobel Prize for Literature with Eyvind Johnson, the late Swedish novelist: d. Stockholm, Feb. 11.

Meehan, Danny (47), dancer, singer, and composer; won outstanding reviews in 1964 while appearing in *Funny Girl* on Broadway; also appeared in the 1974 Broadway show, *Ulysses in Nighttown;* was a nightclub entertainer and wrote the lyrics for the soundtrack of the film, *Joe:* d. New York City, March 29.

Mercader, Ramon (54), assassin of Leon Trotsky in 1940: d. Havana, Oct. 18.

Messerschmitt, Wilhelm (80), German aircraft designer; designed the world's first operational jet fighter and his most famous design, the Model 109, was used by the Germans during the Battle of Britain: d. Munich, Sept. 15.

Metcalf, Lee (66), U. S. senator from Montana (1961–78); he was a liberal Democrat involved in energy conservation, consumer interests, and aid to education: d. Helena, Mont., Jan. 12.

Metcalfe, Ralph H. (68), congressman from Illinois (1970–78) and former Olympic star; founding member of the Congressional Black Caucus and a strong spokesman for black interests: d. Chicago, Oct. 10.

M'Liammoir, Micheal (78), Irish actor and playwright; established Dublin's Gate Theater in 1928 and acted in 300 productions there; played New York in 1961 in a production in which he read Oscar Wilde's plays: d. Dublin, March 6.

Montoya, Joseph M. (62), U. S. senator from New Mexico (1965–77). A Democrat, he came out against U.S. involvement in Vietnam, was interested in consumer protection, aid to the poor, the Indians, and the elderly; served on the Senate Watergate committee in 1973: d. Washington, D. C., June 5.

Moon, Keith (31), drummer for the British rock group The Who; helped create the rock opera spectacular *Tommy:* d. London, Sept. 7.

Moore, Henry (91), British admiral; pursued the German's last major battleship and succeeded in knocking it out of action in April 1944, at Alta Fjord in northern Norway. He also had seen action in World War I, serving as a navigator at the Battle of Jutland: d. Kent, England, March 12.

Moro, Aldo (61), Italian politician; prime minister of Italy (1963–68, 1974–76): d. Rome, May 9.

Morrison, Bret (66), radio star; portrayed "The Shadow" in the radio show of that name: d. Hollywood, Sept. 25.

Moscone, George Richard (49), mayor of San Francisco (1976–78). He was a liberal Democrat who supported welfare, mental health, and the cause of the United Farm Workers: d. San Francisco, Nov. 27.

Moureu, Henri (79), French scientist; helped save Paris from Nazi bombings by helping to find rocket launching sites aimed at Paris: d. Pau, France, July 1978.

Murphy, Robert D. (83), career diplomat; U. S. ambassador to Belgium in 1949 and first post-World War II ambassador to Japan; served as under secretary of state during the Suez crisis of 1956: d. New York City, Jan. 9.

Namgyal, Tenzing (26), crown prince of Sikkim: d. Gangtok, Sikkim, March 11.

Nikodim (48), Russian Orthodox Archbishop of the Metropolitan of Leningrad, and a World Council of Churches' president: d. Vatican City, Sept. 5.

Nobile, Umberto (93), Italian aviator and explorer; In a dirigible and accompanied by fellow explorer, Roald Amundsen, he made one of the first flights over the North Pole, May 12, 1926: d. Rome, July 29.

Oakie, Jack (74), comedian of the 1930's and 1940's; he appeared in more than 100 films; was best known for his caricature of Mussolini to Charlie Chaplin's Hitler in *The Great Dictator* and as the "legs" of *Million Dollar Legs*: d. Northridge, Calif., Jan. 23.

Obolensky, Serge (87), Russian emigre, member of one of the oldest noble families in Czarist Russia; was a distant relative of Czar Nicholas II, and his first wife was Princess Catherine, daughter of Alexander II: d. Grosse Pointe, Mich., Sept. 29.

Ó Dálaigh, Cearbhall (67), president of Ireland from Dec. 1974 to Oct. 1976; resigned after a rift with Defense Minister Patrick Donegan over Ó Dálaigh's use of presidential power to delay legislation giving Irish security forces greater power to detain suspected guerrillas without charges: d. Sneem, Ireland, March 21.

Paley, Barbara Cushing (63), socialite, fashion pace-setter, and wife of William S. Paley, CBS board chairman: d. New York City, July 6.

Pin, Paul Yu (77), China's only Roman Catholic Cardinal: d. Vatican City, August 1978.

Prima, Louis (65), bandleader who played jazz trumpet and sang in a rasping baritone; died of pneumonia after three years in a coma following brain surgery: d. New Orleans, Aug. 24.

Quick, Armand J. (83), known as one of the ten great hematologists of the 20th century; in 1932 he developed the prothrombin time test used in the regulation of the dosage of blood-thinning drugs: d. Milwaukee, Jan. 26.

Rockwell, George (88), comedian, writer and cartoonist; he performed in vaudeville acts and on radio as "Dr. Rockwell." In 1932 he shared the bill that opened the Radio City Music Hall; later he wrote cartoons and started a journal called "Doc Rockwell's Mustard Plaster": d. Brunswick, Me., March 3.

Rubicam, Raymond (85), advertising executive and cofounder of the largest U. S. ad agency; was principally a writer, and copy he wrote is still being used today: d. Scottsdale, Ariz., May 8.

Rueff, Jacques (81), French economist; was noted for his support of the gold standard as the current of exchange in the international monetary system and for his economic

austerity program of 1958 implemented under President Charles de Gaulle. He was also a professor, jurist, adviser to the French and foreign governments, author, and poet. In 1964 he became the first economist ever elected to the French Academy: d. Paris, April 23.

Ryan, Leo Joseph (53), California congressman (1973–78); in his years of public service, Ryan had gained a reputation as a reformer and personal investigator of possible trouble spots. He was on such a mission, investigating constituents' complaints about a religious cult, the Peoples Temple in Guyana, when he was shot and killed by a member of that group. Congressman Ryan was a member of the House International Relations Committee and chairman of the House Subcommittee on the Environment, Energy and Natural Resources: d. Port Kaituma, Guyana, Nov. 18.

Scott, Paul (57), novelist; best known for the novels that make up *The Raj Quartet*. In 1977 he won England's Booker Prize for his novel *Staying On:* d. London, March 1.

Seach, William (101), until his death, oldest living recipient of the Medal of Honor; he was given the award for personal bravery under enemy fire during the 1900 Boxer Rebellion in China: d. Brockton, Mass., Oct. 24.

Seligman, Charles (85), art dealer; he inherited his father's firm, Jacques Seligman and Company, and specialized in bringing modern French art into U. S. collections. Later, he turned his attention to French art of the 17th, 18th, and early 19th centuries: d. New York City, March 27.

Selwyn-Lloyd, Baron (né John Selwyn Brooke Selwyn-Lloyd) (73), member of the House of Commons in Great Britain from 1945 to 1976 when he accepted a barony; as Foreign Secretary was instrumental in the British invasion of the Suez Canal in 1956. In 1960 he became Chancellor of the Exchequer. He spent his last five years in the House of Commons as Speaker: d. Oxfordshire, Eng., May 17.

Serly, Tibor (76), Hungarian-born composer and conductor; probably best known for his completion of Bela Bartok's last compositions, "Third Piano Concerto" and "Viola Concerto": d. London, Oct. 8.

Shaw, Robert (51), novelist, playwright, and actor; became well known to a mass audience when he portrayed "Quint" in the film *Jaws*. He also appeared in *The Sting* and *The Deep*. His novel *The Hiding Place* and his play *The Man in the Glass Booth* were well received: d. near Tourmakeady, Ireland, August 28.

Sheekman, Arthur (76), screenwriter and adapter; a friend of Groucho Marx, he collaborated on such Marx Brothers' classics as *Monkey Business* and *Duck Soup*. In the 1930's despite threats of black listing he helped found the Screen Writers Guild: d. Santa Monica, Calif., Jan. 12.

Siegbahn, Manne (91), Swedish physicist; 1924 winner of the Nobel Prize in physics for his discoveries in X-ray spectroscopics. In 1937 he was appointed head of the Royal Academy of Sciences Research Institute which helped initiate Sweden's nuclear research program. From 1947 to 1957 Siegbahn was the chairman of the Nobel Prize physics committee: d. Stockholm, Sept. 25.

Silone, Ignazio (78), Italian novelist and a founding member of the Italian Communist Party in 1921; he was forced into exile by Mussolini's regime. He wrote two strongly anti-Fascist novels, *Fontamara* (1930) and *Bread and Wine* (1936). He returned to Italy in 1944: d. Geneva, August 22.

Smith, W. Eugene (60), photojournalist; was a combat photographer during World War II; worked for both *Life* and *Newsweek* during a career that spanned 40 years: d. Tucson, Ariz., Oct. 15.

RALPH METCALFE   **JOSEPH M. MONTOYA**   **CEARBHALL Ó DÁLAIGH**   **JACK OAKIE**

ALL PHOTOS, UPI

Sobukwe, Robert Mangalisco (53), black South African nationalist leader of the Pan-African Congress. He was arrested in 1960 after the Sharpeville demonstrations and was given a three year sentence, but then under a special law which camo to be known as the Sobukwe clause, he was held for an additional six years because the government claimed his release would further the cause of Communism: d. Kimberly, South Africa, Feb. 27.

Steiger, William A. (40), Wisconsin congressman (1967–78); a member of the House Ways and Means Committee who gained national attention in 1977 when he sponsored an amendment to cut maximum capital gains tax: d. Washington, D. C., Dec. 4.

Steinberg, William (né Hans Wilhelm) (78), orchestra conductor; served as director of the Pittsburgh Symphony (1952–76); was musical director and conductor of the Boston Symphony (1968–72). He also was the main guest conductor for two seasons with the New York Philharmonic: d. New York City, May 16.

Still, William Grant (83), black classical composer; wrote "Afro-American Symphony" (1931); became the first black musician to conduct a major American orchestra, the Los Angeles Philharmonic, in 1936, and along with poet Langston Hughes he wrote the opera, *Troubled Island*, produced by the New York City Opera in 1949: d. Los Angeles, Dec. 3.

Stone, Edward Durell (76), architect; he followed severe modernistic design until the early 1950's when his work became more personal and ornate. He designed the John F. Kennedy Center in Washington, D. C., the General Motors Building in New York City, the New York Cultural Center, and the U. S. Embassy in New Delhi: d. New York City, August 6.

Student, Kurt (88), German general; one of Germany's first fighter pilots in World War I. In World War II he was awarded the Knight's Cross. In 1949 he was one of two men selected by British and American forces to set up a West German Air Force: d. Demgo, West Germany, July 1.

Trujillo, Flor de Ora (62), daughter of former Dominican Republic President Rafael L. Trujillo; in 1943 she was appointed by her father as first secretary of the Dominican Republic's embassy in Washington: d. New York City, Feb. 15.

Tsiranana, Filibert (66), president of Madagascar (1959–72), elected the first president of the republic in 1959 and declared complete independence from France in 1960: d. Tananarive, Madagascar, April 16.

Tunney, Gene (80), former heavyweight boxing champion; took the heavyweight championship from Jack Dempsey in a ten-round decision in 1926. He defended his title twice (once in a rematch with Dempsey) before retiring undefeated as champion in 1928. Tunney managed his fight earnings well and also became a successful executive and officer of several corporations and banks. He was a literate man who was well versed in Shakespeare and while he was the heavyweight champion, he was invited to lecture on Shakespeare before 200 Yale students; while at Yale he was made an honorary member of Pundits, a society of wits and scholars: d. Greenwich, Conn., Nov. 7.

Tweedsmuir, Baroness (formerly Priscilla Jean Fortescue) (63), member of the British Parliament; she served in the House of Commons representing South Aberdeen, Scotland from 1946 to 1966; later she served in the House of Lords: d. London, March 11.

Venuti, Joe (82?), jazz violinist; trained in the classics, played with dance band leaders Jean Goldkette and Paul Whiteman; also played with guitarist Eddie Lang and made hundreds of jazz recordings: d. Seattle, Wash., Aug. 14.

Von Manteuffel, Hasso (81), German general and former member of the West German parliament; drove a 50-mile (80 km) wedge with his tanks into Allied lines during the 1944 Battle of the Bulge. He also served three years in the West German parliament during the 1950's: d. Reith, Austria, Sept. 24.

Wallenda, Karl (73); aerialist; founder of the "Great Wallendas"; his career spanned more than 50 years. His death resulted from a high wire fall: d. San Juan, P. R., March 22.

Warner, Jack (86), motion picture tycoon, founder along with three elder brothers of Warner Bros. Studios. His company released one of the earliest talking films *The Jazz Singer* in 1927: d. Los Angeles, Sept. 9.

Warner, Sylvia Townsend (85), novelist and short story writer; her first novel, *Lolly Willowes* (1926), was the first choice for the just-established Book of the Month Club. Her great avocation was music and prior to her debut as a novelist she did research on music of the 14th and 15th centuries and was one of the editors of *Tudor Church Music*, a 10-volume study. She published 7 novels, 13 collections of short stories, 5 books of poetry, and a biography of Jane Austen. Many of her short stories appeared in *The New Yorker*: d. Maiden Newton, Dorset, Eng., May 1.

Wengenroth, Stow (71), artist; one of America's leading lithographers; his art is part of the permanent collections of more than two dozen major American museums: d. Gloucester, Mass., Jan. 22.

Wheelock, John Hall (91), poet and editor; his career as a poet began in 1911 with his first book of poetry, *The Human Fantasy;* while a Scribner's editor he worked with Thomas Wolfe, Marjorie Rawlings, Charles Lindbergh, and others: d. New York City, March 22.

Whitehead, Edward (69), commander (retired) of the British Navy and chairman (retired) of Schweppes (USA) Ltd.; for his success in exporting he was awarded the Order of the British Empire by Queen Elizabeth II in 1961: d. Petersfield, Eng., April 16.

Whitehill, Walter Muir (72), director and librarian of the Boston Athenaeum from 1946 to 1973: d. Boston, March 5.

Wills, Chill (76), actor; excelled in character roles; was famous as the voice in the *Francis the Talking Mule* films. In addition he played featured roles in hundreds of movies, including *The Yearling, Giant,* and *Meet Me in St. Louis:* d. Encino, Calif., Dec. 15.

Wilson, Michael (63), screenwriter; produced such scripts as *A Place in the Sun,* for which he received an Academy Award, and *Bridge on the River Kwai*. He was blacklisted for his refusal to testify concerning his alleged Communist Party membership: d. Beverly Hills, Calif., April 9.

Wood, Peggy (86), actress of stage, films, and television; is perhaps best known for her role as the mother in the CBS-TV show *Mama* which ran from 1949 to 1957. In 1966 she was nominated for an Academy Award for best supporting actress for her role as the Mother Superior in *The Sound of Music:* d. Stamford, Conn., March 18.

Wragge, Sydney (70), fashion designer; introduced the idea of modern separates, the sheath dress, and the jumper: d. Boca Raton, Fla., March 10.

Wrathall, John (65), president of Rhodesia (1976–78); was finance minister (1964–76) before being appointed president by Prime Minister Ian Smith: d. Salisbury, Rhodesia, August 30.

Wright, Lloyd (né Frank Lloyd Wright, Jr.) (88), architect; designed private homes, movie sets (for Paramount Studios from 1916–1918), and his most famous design, the Wayfarer's Chapel in Palos Verdes, Calif: d. Santa Monica, Calif., May 31.

Young, Gig (60), actor; best known for his Academy Award-winning performance in *They Shoot Horses, Don't They?* of an apparent self-inflicted gunshot wound: d. New York City, Oct. 9.

Zellerbach, Harold Lionel (83), industrialist and patron of the arts; had been a top executive for the Crown Zellerbach Corporation for 50 years. He contributed considerable funds to the arts and once arranged a $1 million gift to the University of California at Berkeley to help finance a campus theater. In 1957 he was named to head a commission on the refugee problem: d. Hawaiian Islands, Jan. 29.

Zukofsky, Louis (74), poet and teacher; was considered by critics to be one of the most accomplished American poets; he wrote "A-24"; maintained a correspondence with Ezra Pound and a friendship with William Carlos Williams; along with his wife, he did a major translation of the Latin poet Catullus, published in 1971: d. Port Jefferson, N. Y., May 12.

EDWARD WHITEHEAD

PEGGY WOOD

UPI UPI

OCEANIA

In a year of subdued economic activity, political stirrings highlighted events in Oceania in 1978. Recently autonomous nations took a more forceful stance in international discussions, two mininations became independent, and one premier was dismissed following disclosures of election improprieties. Unresolved questions arose concerning the effects of 200-mile (370-km) offshore fishing zones, and there was a drop in tourism attributed in part to the "overfly" policy of the major airlines.

Conferences. In February, a regional meeting of Commonwealth heads of government in Sydney, Australia, brought together South Pacific and southern Asian leaders. The participants supported earlier plans by the South Pacific Forum (SPF) for 200-mile offshore zones.

At the SPF held in Niue in September, a firmer sense of regionalism emerged among island nations and territories. Questions relating to economic development and foreign trade were the focuses of attention. The only real prospect for trade development, it was determined, was special access to both Australian and New Zealand markets. This would lead to a reduction of trade imbalance, while maintaining employment.

In the SPF discussions, a dispute arose over moves to control fish resources in the South Pacific. The United States, France, and Japan opposed any control of the tuna catch. It was proposed that the United States be accepted as a member of the regional fisheries body, but the suggestion proved divisive, with Fiji and Papua New Guinea expressing adamant opposition.

In October, a meeting of labor ministers in Port Moresby, New Guinea, aired the "complex and serious" problem of unemployment. The labor ministers sought the help of the International Labor Organization (ILO) and the South Pacific Commission to carry out a study of labor imbalances and the likely effects of any "guest worker" arrangement to provide labor mobility among the scattered nations of the area.

Politics. The ouster of Sir Albert Henry from his long-held premiership of the Cook Islands was ordered by Chief Justice Gaven Donne (appointed by New Zealand, the sovereign power) when serious irregularities were found in the April general elections which returned Henry's Cook Islands Party to power. The new premier, Dr. Tom Davis, said his aim was economic self-reliance, not political independence. The Cook Islands depend heavily on aid from New Zealand.

There was continuing tension between Papua New Guinea (PNG) and Indonesia over the border between PNG and Irian Jaya. At various times PNG was caring for 1,400 Irian refugees who crossed the border. With the help of a UN negotiator, many of the refugees agreed to return, but the situation remained dangerous and PNG and Indonesia considered joint insurgency measures.

UNITED NATIONS/PHOTO BY M. TZOVARAS

The flag of the newly independent Solomon Islands is raised at UN headquarters for the first time.

In the Anglo-French condominium of New Hebrides, the largest political party, Vanuaaku Pati, pressured the government to hold new elections on the question of independence. In April, the two sides agreed to work together.

Independence. Two former British territories attained independence in 1978: the Solomon Islands, in July; and Tuvalu, in October. (See Solomon Islands; Tuvalu.) When the first Solomon Islands parliamentary session began, Governor General Baddeley Dovesi promised "moderate and prudent policies." The new nation faced prickly questions concerning the orderly transfer of authority from local government to provincial assemblies.

Micronesia's constitution was ratified by four districts, and the vote led to calls for the formation of the Federated States of Micronesia. Some observers felt that the federation might later seek statehood in a joint bid with Guam, American Samoa, and three breakaway districts of Northern Marianas, Palau, and Marshall Islands.

PNG and Australia signed a pact concerning the Torres Strait. All inhabited islands will remain Australian, and that nation will also retain the uninhabited islands to which it has long laid claim. With respect to seabed resources, the pact established a boundary running through the whole area. Another line defined fishery resources, with fishermen of both nations free to operate on either side of the boundary.

Fiji began plywood exports to China, and in October technical experts were sent by Peking to assist on rice- and vegetable-growing projects. Oil searches also were initiated, and early reports strengthened hopes of commercial finds.

R. M. YOUNGER, *Australian Author*

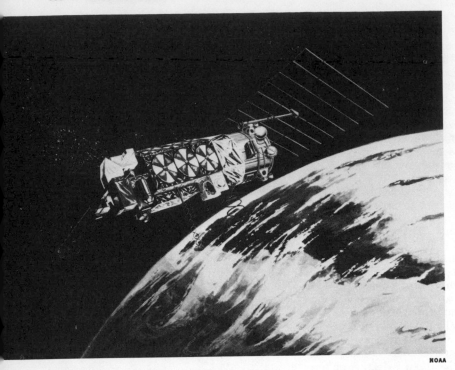

The Tiros-N satellite, launched in September 1978, was scheduled to play a major part in the First Global Geophysical Experiment, the operational phase of which was scheduled to begin late in 1978.

NOAA

OCEANOGRAPHY

Field work and sampling were completed in 1978 for Project GEOSECS (Geochemical Ocean Sections Study). Since 1972 research vessels have covered the Atlantic, Pacific, and Indian Oceans, occupying 300 stations and collecting samples from as many as 44 depths. With the Indian Ocean sampling now completed, about two years of laboratory work remain.

GEOSECS represents the most comprehensive chemical sampling of ocean waters ever undertaken. Information on nearly 40 sea water constituents will be employed in computer models for estimating dispersal rates of waste products. Physical oceanography of major water masses has benefited from studies of stable and radioactive isotopes, nutrients, and chemical components. Geochemical tracers employed for studies of ocean circulation and mixing should prove useful in biological oceanography.

The Deep Sea Drilling Project (DSDP) has most recently been involved in an expanded International Phase of Ocean Drilling (IPOD) with the vessel *Glomar Challenger* in the Pacific Ocean. Coring results have shown that the main Japanese island of Honshu is but a small part of a former land mass that once extended 300 kilometers (186 mi) beyond the present Pacific shore of Honshu to an area now occupied by the Japan Trench. The sequence of sediments uncovered in coring operations demonstrates the rapid subsidence of the land mass from above sea level about 25 million years ago to over two kilometers below the ocean surface today. The landward wall of the Japan Trench was also studied for evidence of the compressional forces between conflicting crustal plates.

Recent cruises have examined the Philippine Sea and the region of the Mariana Trench for details of destruction of the western edge of the Pacific crustal plate where it is being subducted by the overriding Mariana Islands arc. The plate collision builds stresses which result in earthquakes and in tension around the island arc itself, causing new marginal ocean basins behind the island arc in a way similar to the sea-floor spreading seen at mid-ocean ridges. Drilling by DSDP was designed to test the theories for island arc activity by a series of seven holes starting in the east in the Mariana Basin and running across the island arc ridge and the Mariana Trench behind it. Such drilling may provide results that can then be applied to other subduction zones. The cruise is the result of three years of planning by the Joint Oceanographic Institutions for Deep Earth Sampling (JOIDES) which includes several American laboratories and scientists from Japan, West Germany, the USSR, France, and the United Kingdom.

Ocean core samples have been useful in reconstructing ancient climatic patterns, since animal remains reflect the temperature conditions under which they were alive. Project CLIMAP (Climate—Long-Range Investigation, Mapping and Prediction) has thus determined several examples of periodicity or climatic cycles, which are believed related to characteristics of the earth's orbital path. In a review of deep sea cores representing 450,000 years, climate variations with periods of 23,000, 42,000, and 100,000 years can be seen. These cycles are generally in step with the appropriate orbital cycles for the last 350,000 years, beyond which point correlation became very difficult due to restriction of the dating technique. Using different measurements of three different climatic indicators, the pattern is consistent and shows a dominant cycle of 100,000 years corresponding closely to the Milankovitch theory for orbital variations due to eccentricity, obliquity, and precession. Work continues on such questions as how these cycles might affect or control ice ages. Clear-cut confirmation requires better dating, better statistics, and a better understanding of the underlying mechanisms.

Interactions between ocean and atmosphere in the Equatorial Pacific, which produce weather systems that eventually sweep over North America, may also be keys to important shifts in global climate. These interactions were studied in the NORPAX (North Pacific Experiment) Equatorial Shuttle, focused on observations at 150° West longitude for 20° north and south of the Equator. Instrumented aircraft flying between Hawaii and Tahiti collected data relating to the heat storage within water evaporated from the sea, while buoys monitored conditions from the ocean surface to the sea floor. This new data provided the first set of systematic, simultaneous observations on exchanges of matter and energy between ocean and atmosphere for this area. Participating scientists consider the experiment to be a prelude to a similar but more extensive study planned as part of the World Meteorological Organization's global weather experiment.

After long planning, the operational phase of the First Global Geophysical Experiment (FGGE) began in December 1978. The first of two special observational periods sponsored by GARP (Global Atmospheric Research Program) was scheduled for January–February 1979 and would be related to the TIROS-N satellite launched in September 1978. Meteorologists and geophysicists of the United States, France, and Canada have been much involved in the preparation and testing of special systems for FGGE, such as a network of drifting buoys planned as part of the southern hemisphere survey. The first buoy records obtained were compared with satellite information for establishing reference ground-truth values. More tests will be conducted after the TIROS-N satellite is launched to validate data processing programs and the position-fixing accuracy of the system before the field observation period begins.

Infrared images from NOAA-4 and NOAA-5 satellites have been used by physical oceanographers to detect sea surface temperature contrasts in order to identify features of a current system. When this technology was applied to the Agulhas Current system which enters the South Atlantic from the eastern side of South Africa, the sources of the current, its deflection, major bends in the current path and other wave-like features of its passage could be shown. The result was an integration of the large-scale features of the current system beyond the capabilities of conventional shipboard oceanography.

Similar applications may be expected in regions such as the Gulf Stream of the northwest Atlantic where eddies and "rings" result from the interplay of the current system. Satellite coverage of the area shows that a dominant role in the variability of the offshore water is due to the eddies or rings which are introduced by unstable meanders of the Gulf Stream. American and Soviet studies of the phenomenon have been merged into a large-scale mid-ocean dynamics experiment called POLYMODE in which satellites are used as tracking stations for signals broadcast from buoys that may remain in the center of rings for many months after emplacement by a ship or an aircraft. The Kuroshio Current off Japan produces rings which are essentially the same as Gulf Stream rings, as does the Antarctic Circumpolar Current around Antarctica. Such systems may produce effects on fisheries, biological distributions, and chemical mixing rates which remain to be investigated further.

The first orbital satellite dedicated entirely to ocean monitoring went into service with the launch of SEASAT-A on June 26, 1978. The satellite is armed with three types of radar and two kinds of radiometers. SEASAT-A circles the earth 14 times daily in a near-polar orbit at an altitude of 800 kilometers (430 nautical miles) and covers 95% of the global ocean area every 36 hours. It transmits information on surface winds and temperatures, currents, wave heights, ice conditions, ocean topography and coastal storm activity. Such satellite information will not eliminate the use of ships and airplanes, which can make a number of measurements with more precision. Rather it will provide broad scale pictures that surface craft cannot possibly encompass.

At an international conference on Antarctic living marine resources, held in Buenos Aires in July, conservation principles first formulated at a meeting in Canberra in March were agreed to by 13 countries as members of the Antarctic Treaty. The proposed treaty considers the whole marine ecosystem for the area inside the Antarctic Convergence (a meeting of water masses from Antarctica and the southern ocean) where whales, seals, penguins, squid, fish, and other animals all depend on the huge stocks of crustaceans known as "krill." For managing this and related resources, a commission would be established and it would be opened to treaty members and other countries involved in biological research or harvesting operations in the area. A final and formal agreement is expected in 1979. The nations involved are Argentina, Australia, Belgium, Britain, Chile, France, Japan, New Zealand, Norway, Poland, South Africa, the Soviet Union, and the United States.

DAVID A. McGILL
U. S. Coast Guard Academy

UPI

Dennis Kucinich (*left*), the 31-year-old mayor of Cleveland, suspended Police Chief Richard D. Hongisto on March 24.

OHIO

The recall of Cleveland's mayor, and school financing problems were leading Ohio events in 1978.

Election. Ohio voters reelected Columbus Republican Gov. James A. Rhodes to a record-breaking fourth four-year term. Rhodes defeated Democratic Lt. Gov. Richard F. Celeste by about 50,000 votes. Major issues were methods of dealing with school crises, primarily in metropolitan areas, whether either candidate might raise state tax levels, and Rhodes' age (he was born Sept. 13, 1909). Rhodes promised to push for greater state aid for such public school systems as Cleveland's, and to do it without material increases in taxation.

Under Ohio's new party-team ballot arrangement, George V. Voinovich, a Cuyahoga county (Greater Cleveland) commissioner, was elected lieutenant governor. Secretary of State Ted W. Brown (R) was displaced after 18 years in office by Anthony J. Celebrezze, Jr., a Cleveland lawyer.

Two state constitutional changes were approved, modifying procedures for adopting or repealing local charter forms of government, and allowing the legislature to change rules for the labor of prisoners and sale of their products.

Schools. State education officials found no less than 156 of 617 public school districts short of funds and faced with early closings, due primarily to inflation. In June the Legislature

allotted about $100 million for bankrupt or nearly bankrupt school boards. Strikes among teachers and other employees were numerous.

Cleveland's problems illustrated the school crises. September opening of schools was delayed a month as teachers demanded higher wages. A further complication was a 1976 federal court order that large numbers of the 100,-000-plus students had to be bused to achieve better education for minority children. But the school system, often skirting bankruptcy, failed to get any private company to rent buses, dooming the program to an inauspicious start in 1978. School Superintendent Paul Briggs and School Board President Arnold Pinkney resigned. When teachers agreed to a strike settlement, many other employees were laid off and specialized classes were eliminated.

In Brunswick, Medina County, 34 teachers were jailed for a week in April for contempt of court when they would not sign an agreement to return to work.

Novel Election. When Cleveland Mayor Dennis J. Kucinich and top aides antagonized many councilmen and voters through their speeches and the firing of Police Chief Richard Hongisto, a recall petition gained required signatures. In a special balloting Sunday, August 13, Kucinich retained his position by fewer than 300 votes. His term extends to November 1979.

Cleveland Defaults. A gathering financial deficit situation for Ohio's largest city exploded into a default on $14 million debt owed December 15 to six banks. The banks did not take action in 1978 to foreclose for their money, so the city did not face bankruptcy proceedings. A solution was hoped for in an election set for Feb. 27, 1979, when Clevelanders were to decide two issues: whether to increase their city income tax to 1.5% from 1%, and whether to order sale of the city's municipal light plant, presumably to the area's privately owned utility, Cleveland Electric Illuminating Co.

Other. C. William O'Neill, Ohio Supreme Court chief justice for eight years, died August 20.

JOHN F. HUTH JR., *Plain Dealer*, Cleveland

--- **OHIO · Information Highlights** ---

Area: 41,222 square miles (106,765 km²).
Population (Jan. 1978 est.): 10,711,000.
Chief Cities (1970 census): Columbus, the capital, 540,-025; Cleveland, 750,879; Cincinnati, 452,524.
Government (1978): *Chief Officers*—governor, James A. Rhodes (R); lt. gov., Richard F. Celeste (D). *General Assembly*—Senate, 33 members; House of Representatives, 99 members.
Education (1977–78): *Enrollment*—public elementary schools, 1,283,428 pupils; public secondary, 898,551; colleges and universities, 452,754 students. *Public school expenditures*, $3,446,200,000 ($1,469 per pupil).
State Finances (fiscal year 1977): *Revenues*, $8,975,-675,000; *expenditures*, $8,168,648,000.
Personal Income (1977): $75,809,000,000; per capita, $7,084.
Labor Force (July 1978): *Nonagricultural wage and salary earners*, 4,364,400; *unemployed*, 266,700 (5.3% of total force).

OKLAHOMA

The Democrats reclaimed the U.S. Senate seat held by retiring Dewey Bartlett. Gov. David Boren defeated Republican Robert Kamm, former president of Oklahoma State University, and became the first Oklahoman to be directly elected to the Senate while serving as governor. In the gubernatorial race, George Nigh, lieutenant governor for 16 years, defeated Republican Ron Shotts, a former State Representative and Oklahoma University football star.

Elections. Neither Governor Boren nor Lieutenant Governor Nigh won clear majorities in the August party primaries, but both scored easy victories in runoff elections a month later. In November, Boren scored a landslide victory, polling 65.5% of the vote and losing to Kamm in only three counties. Nigh, with a 52% majority, ran strong in rural southern and eastern counties but lost to Shotts in metropolitan Oklahoma and Tulsa counties.

Mike Synar, a 28-year-old Muskogee attorney, upset incumbent Ted Risenhoover in the second Congressional district primary and won the elections in November. Among the four Democratic incumbents reelected to Congress was Tom Steed, from the fourth district, who was sent to Washington for an unprecedented 16th term. Conservative Mickey Edwards, representing most of Oklahoma County, remained the state's sole Republican member in the U.S. House of Representatives.

Legislation. The legislature met from January 3 to April 28 (68 legislative days), the shortest regular session in six years. It appropriated a record general fund budget of $855 million, $103.5 million more than in 1977. Common schools, higher education, highways, and corrections were areas receiving major appropriation increases.

Other legislation passed in 1978 called for financial disclosure statements from lobby groups; provided for an alcoholic treatment program; permitted advertising of eyeglasses; allowed 16-year-old felons to be certified as adults; permitted dismissal of teachers for public homosexual conduct; required licensing of hospitals

COPYRIGHT 1978, THE OKLAHOMA PUBLISHING CO., "THE DAILY OKLAHOMAN," NOV. 12

In Oklahoma's Senate race, Gov. David Boren (D) scored a landslide victory over Republican Robert Kamm.

performing abortions; raised the salaries of the governor and other state officials; increased the state minimum wage; and granted $5 monthly increases to public assistance recipients.

A major defeat for Governor Boren's program was the failure of the state House of Representatives to act on a comprehensive water development plan.

Natural Disasters. Severe winter weather led to unexpected deterioration of roads and highways. Following a prolonged summer drought, 57 of Oklahoma's 77 counties were declared federal disaster areas, making individuals and businesses eligible for government assistance.

Prisons. On August 15, U.S. District Judge Luther Bohanon ruled that "intolerable conditions" exist at McAlester prison, which was burned during riots in 1973, and Granite reformatory. Judge Bohanon ordered that immediate steps be taken to correct "overcrowding," or the prison facilities would be closed. The decision in this suit by the American Civil Liberties Union (ACLU) was politically controversial, since an estimated $30–$50 million had to be expended within one year to bring prison facilities up to acceptable standards.

Higher Education. William Slater Banowsky, former president of Pepperdine University (Calif.), was inaugurated as the president of The University of Oklahoma on November 18.

JOHN W. WOOD
The University of Oklahoma

OKLAHOMA • Information Highlights

Area: 69,919 square miles (181,090 km²).
Population (Jan. 1978 est.): 2,834,000.
Chief Cities (1970 census): Oklahoma City, the capital, 368,856; Tulsa, 330,350; Lawton, 74,470; Norman, 52,-117.
Government (1978): *Chief Officers*—governor, David L. Boren (D); lt. gov., George Nigh (D). *Legislature*—Senate, 48 members; House of Representatives, 101 members.
Education (1977–78): *Enrollment*—public elementary schools, 320,427 pupils; public secondary, 274,041; colleges and universities, 149,051 students. *Public school expenditures,* $990,500,000 ($1,381 per pupil).
State Finances (fiscal year 1977): *Revenues,* $2,283,-116,000; *expenditures,* $2,138,132,000.
Personal Income (1977): $17,839,000,000; per capita, $6,346.
Labor Force (July 1978): *Nonagricultural wage and salary earners,* 1,026,400; *unemployed,* 48,900 (3.9% of total force).

OLDER POPULATION

Demographic trends in 1978 revealed that the number of Americans over 65 is now 10% of the total population, and that there are increasing numbers of persons in advanced old age. In 1973 the median age of the population over 65 was 75; in 1978, it was 82. By the year 2000, it is projected that the population over 75 will increase by 60%, or comprise 44% of the population over 65.

Public Interest. Increasing public support to economic, health, housing and social needs of older Americans was shown in 1978. On Oct. 18, 1978, President Jimmy Carter signed HR 12255, the Comprehensive Older Americans Bill Amendments. As a result, the Older Americans Act, the major government effort on behalf of the nation's elderly, was extended through 1981. The new legislation aims at a more coordinated approach in providing services for the elderly, and eliminates fragmented and duplicated programs. Its highlights include: creation of a new Title III to incorporate what were formerly social services, senior centers, and nutritional programs under Titles III, V, and VII, respectively; a new National Home Delivered Meals program; strengthened programs for legal service and a nursing home ombudsman; expansion of the federal role in long-term care of the aging; an increased funding authorization for the Title V employment program; and provision for a White House Conference on the Aging in 1981. Indeed, the new legislation reflected both awareness of and concern about the needs of older Americans. The awareness and concern was voiced by government officials and by the public.

Crime and the Elderly. Crimes against the elderly continued to receive national attention. According to the latest studies of the FBI's Uniform Crime Reports, victimization rates are very low for the older population in the three most serious crimes—homicide, rape, and aggravated assault—but very high in the crimes of purse snatching and strong-arm robbery. The crime of burglary shows high victimization rates for all age groups.

Research shows generally that the elderly are no more likely than other groups to be victimized. However, adults 65 and over appear to incur heavier economic losses relative to their low income. One view suggests that we need to provide assistance to all people who suffer economically and physically from crime, rather than focus on a particular age group. This approach is used in West Germany where a law was passed in 1976 for "recompensing Victims of Acts of Violence." Compensation to victims of crime is made with funds provided by the German federal government (40%) and by state government (60%).

Better utilization of law enforcement agencies and improving communications between law officers and the elderly continue to be the direction that many states are now taking in programs for the prevention of crimes against the elderly.

Mandatory Retirement. In March 1978, the 1967 Age Discrimination Act was amended by Congress to raise the upper age limit for mandatory retirement from 65 to 70 for nonfederal workers, effective Jan. 1, 1979. A highly controversial piece of legislation, its antagonists argued that this would create unemployment for the young. Its proponents asserted that those who wanted to continue to work needed government protection. Some took the position that mandatory retirement should be eliminated completely, since the option to work should be an individual choice. The provisions of the amendments eliminate age ceilings for most federal employees; allow for forced retirement of tenured college or university faculty between 65 and 70 until July 1982; require a report from the secretary of labor by Jan. 1, 1982 as to the consequences of raising the age ceiling, and to the feasibility of eliminating mandatory retirement. The age eligibility for Social Security payments is not affected by this bill.

Health of Older Americans. There is recognition that delivery of health services must address a range of needs for the comparatively healthy elderly, for those who need alternatives to prevent premature institutionalization, and for those whose needs require institutional care. Major attention in 1978 was toward developing social and community health resources as alternatives to institutionalization.

Education. As the number of public and private continuing education programs increased without interruption, more than 450,000 older Americans were enrolled in classes ranging in complexity from eighth grade level through graduate school.

Future Trends. The new goal in services to the older population seems to be to deal with the total person. This implies concern not only for treatment of disease and survival, but a more humane system of comprehensive care which encompasses the dignity of life itself. Services that affect the quality of life and alternatives to institutionalization are being sought.

International Developments. Israel has opened the first day center and hospital in the Middle East, at Petach Tikva, for the treatment of geriatric disease. The objective is to treat as many older persons as possible as day patients and to prevent the need for hospitalization.

"Service" houses which combine residential domiciliary and day care service are taking hold in Sweden which is moving away from constructing old age homes. Apartments for the well elderly have an alarm connection to a central location in case of emergency. Apartments for the more frail offer additional support so that daily living is facilitated.

See also SOCIAL WELFARE.

CELIA B. WEISMAN, *Director*
Gerontological Institute, Yeshiva University

ONTARIO

During 1978, Canada's most populous province was increasingly concerned with the state of the economy. Restraint was the theme of Treasurer Darcy McKeough's March 7 budget. The budget projected expenditures of (C.) $14.55 billion (an increase of 7%), revenues of $13.5 billion, and a deficit of $1.05 billion. With health care as the largest budget item, Ontario Health Insurance premiums were to be raised by 37.5%. Upset by this measure, the opposition parties threatened to bring down the government and thereby forced McKeough to limit the increase to 18.75%. The loss in revenue was offset by an increase in corporate income tax, cuts in highway and capital spending, and a civil service hiring freeze. Alcohol and tobacco taxes also were raised. To stimulate the economy, Ontario agreed in April to a federal request to cut temporarily the provincial sales tax from 7% to 4%. The reduction encouraged consumer spending, but losses to the treasury precluded extension of the plan beyond October, even though the federal government paid back two thirds of the deficit.

There was good news in August when the Ford Motor Company announced plans to build a $535 million engine plant in Ontario. The plant, expected to provide over 5,000 jobs, was made feasible by $68 million in grants from the provincial and federal governments.

With its plans for new nuclear power stations under attack, Ontario Hydro's proposal to buy some 200 million pounds (91 million kg) of uranium over the next 40 years (at a cost of $7 billion) caused a political storm. The New Democratic Party (NDP) charged that the plan would cause rates to go up and give the mining companies excessive profits. Although rejected by a select committee of the Ontario Legislature, the contract was nevertheless approved by the cabinet.

Politics. In the autumn of 1978, Premier William G. Davis lost several senior ministers. Treasurer Darcy McKeough resigned to take a position in private business, and Solicitor General George Kerr was forced to resign because he had spoken with an assistant Crown attorney on behalf of a constituent. Premier Davis immediately introduced rules prohibiting cabinet ministers from talking about pending cases with officers of the Crown. In September, Industry and Tourism Minister John Rhodes died of a heart attack while accompanying the premier on an official tour of the Middle East.

The increasing attention given to the rights of Franco-Ontarians continued in 1978. Although the government refused to accept a bill to entrench French language rights, $1.9 million were earmarked for the translation of 150 of the province's statutes into French. A confrontation looms with Quebec, where new laws controlling the construction industry effectively bar Ontario

DAN SCHAFFNER, COURTESY, OFFICE OF THE PREMIER, ONTARIO

During a Mideast tour, Ontario's Premier William G. Davis and his wife, Kathy, attended the dedication of Ontario Place, a park in Jerusalem forest.

construction workers from working in the province. Although a bill has been introduced to ban Quebec construction workers from Ontario, and despite calls for its speedy passage by NDP leader Michael Cassidy, the cabinet moved slowly. They preferred to see the Quebec law tested in the Canadian Supreme Court, or else some negotiated solution, before taking any action that might harm national unity.

The growing unpopularity of Pierre Trudeau's Liberal government was demonstrated in Ontario when that party failed to win any of the seven federal by-elections held on October 16. The Liberals lost 5 seats to the Progressive Conservatives and took only about 25% of the popular vote.

PETER J. KING, *Carleton University*

─────── **ONTARIO · Information Highlights** ───────

Area: 412,582 square miles (1,068,587 km²).
Population (1978 est.): 8,460,900.
Chief Cities (1976 census): Toronto, the provincial capital, 633,318; Ottawa, the federal capital, 304,462.
Government (1978): *Chief Officers*—lt. gov., Pauline McGibbon; premier, William G. Davis (Progressive Conservative); chief justice, Supreme Court, High Court of Justice, Gregory T. Evans. *Legislature*—Legislative Assembly, 125 members.
Education (1976–77): *Enrollment*—public elementary and secondary schools, 1,979,700 pupils; private schools, 55,420; Indian (federal) schools, 7,380; post-secondary, 231,800 students. *Total expenditures,* $3,565,253,000.
Public Finance (1978–79 est.): *Revenues,* $13,500,000,-000; *expenditures,* $14,550,000,000.
Personal Income (average weekly salary, May 1978): $263.44.
Unemployment Rate (July 1978 seasonally adjusted): 7.3%.
(All monetary figures given in Canadian dollars.)

OREGON

Drought, property tax relief, and elections occupied the interest of Oregonians during 1978.

Drought. Heavy winter and late summer precipitation in 1978 ameliorated conditions which resulted from the previous year's drought, the severest since the 1930's. But autumn precipitation was, once again, extremely below normal levels.

Tax Relief. A constitutional amendment fashioned after California's Proposition 13 was placed before the voters by initiative petition. In addition, special session of the legislature referred an alternative plan to the voters. The latter, if enacted, would have required the state to refund 50% of the property tax paid by homeowners and renters, with the funds to come from the state's general fund. After a spirited campaign, both measures were rejected by the voters in November. Legislators have assigned the tax issue an extremely high priority for the 1979 session.

Elections. Oregon primary elections, particularly during nonpresidential years, do not command widespread voter attention. The 1978 primary was no exception, drawing approximately 45% of Oregon's voters to the polls. Interest was heightened over the summer, however, with the submission of the tax relief proposals. The general election enjoyed a near-record turnout of approximately 70%. In the primary, special interest focused upon the Republican race for the nomination for governor. Tom McCall, former two-term governor attempting a political comeback, State Sen. Vic Atiyeh, and State Representative Roger Martin sought the nomination. Vic Atiyeh was selected by a significant margin.

The general election exhibited a modest movement toward conservatism in Oregon issues. Senator Atiyeh defeated incumbent governor Bob Straub. Two-term incumbent Republican Senator Mark O. Hatfield, gaining 62% of the votes, easily beat his Democratic opponent, state Sen. Vernon Cook. All five congressional incumbents were reelected. Republicans made significant gains in the state House of Representatives, and Democrats maintained a strong majority in the Senate.

In other action, voters reinstated the death penalty, rejected an increase in both vehicle registration fees and gasoline taxes, approved state-funded abortions, reaffirmed the planning prerogative of the Land Conservation and Development Commission, and made provision for the fitting and sale of dentures by denturists, activity formerly the exclusive domain of licensed dentists.

Education. Voters in local elections passed most operating budgets but rejected most bonding issues for capital construction. Several teacher strikes were held as a number of school districts had difficulty reaching contract agreements with teacher associations.

Other Events. The embattled Trojan nuclear power plant in Rainier was again the subject of numerous strenuous protests during 1978. Its operating license was suspended because of construction deficiencies. The latter defects were being repaired, but the plant stood idle for most of the year.

On May 4 President Jimmy Carter held a regional news conference in Portland. Among the issues discussed were forest policy, Indian land claims, and nuclear waste disposal.

L. CARL BRANDHORST
Oregon College of Education

————OREGON · Information Highlights————

Area: 96,981 square miles (251,181 km²).
Population (Jan. 1978 est.): 2,402,000.
Chief Cities (1970 census): Salem, the capital, 68,856; Portland, 380,555; Eugene, 78,389.
Government (1978): *Chief Officers*—governor, Robert W. Straub (D); secy. of state, Norma Paulus (R). *Legislative Assembly*—Senate, 30 members; House of Representatives, 60 members.
Education (1977–78): *Enrollment*—public elementary schools, 274,570 pupils; public secondary, 198,709; colleges and universities, 141,186 students. *Public school expenditures,* $948,200,000 ($1,809 per pupil).
State Finances (fiscal year 1977): *Revenues,* $2,638,-018,000; *expenditures,* $2,272,393,000.
Personal Income (1977): $16,651,000,000; per capita, $7,007.
Labor Force (July 1977): *Nonagricultural wage and salary earners,* 986,400; *unemployed,* 65,200 (5.5% of total force).

OTTAWA

Relations between the city of Ottawa, Canada's capital, and the federal government became increasingly strained in 1978. Federal civil service appeared to endanger the city's financial structure. The transfer of 20,000 public servants across the Ottawa River to Hull, Que., the nationwide decentralization of government departments, a drive to restrain public service growth, and a determination to build and own office space, as opposed to renting, threatened to create an office vacancy rate of 25%, an (C.) $8 million annual tax revenue loss, and the ruin of many small businesses dependent upon the office towers.

Matters were further exacerbated by the city's contention that federal grants in lieu of taxes on its property were too small. Mayor Lorry Greenberg estimated a shortfall in excess of $33 million. The city threatened to cut off essential services to government buildings unless the grants were increased. The city tried to attract corporate offices to Ottawa so as to lessen its dependence on the Canadian federal government.

Many local politicians called for restrictions on the employment of workers from Quebec in the Ottawa area, but Mayor Greenberg opposed the move as dangerous to national unity.

The province of Ontario decided to ignore most of the recommendations of the controversial Mayo Report. While the report proposed the amalgamation of the village of Rockliffe and

Ottawa and create a "western city" out of rural municipalities, the province disagreed with Dr. Mayo and the city by opting to retain the Ottawa Board of Control. The school boards were left unchanged.

Following a heart attack, Mayor Greenberg announced in August that he would not stand for reelection in 1978. After a spirited campaign, Deputy Mayor Marion Dewar defeated controller Patricia Nichol in the November election.

The daily tabloid *Ottawa Today,* begun in 1977, went bankrupt and ceased publication in April. A new Sunday paper, the *Ottawa Post,* aimed at a more reflective audience, reached the stands in August.

PETER J. KING, *Carleton University*

PAKISTAN

Pakistan was mesmerized and paralyzed throughout the year by the uncertain fate of its former prime minister, Zulfikar Ali Bhutto. Concurrently his successor, General Mohammed Zia ul-Haq, found himself scarcely competent to deal with what a *New York Times* reporter termed "a bewildering array of problems."

Domestic Affairs. On March 18 former Prime Minister Bhutto was convicted and sentenced to death for allegedly ordering the murder of a political opponent. The popular former prime minister appealed the case to the Pakistan Supreme Court, charging that his trial was unfair and politically biased. Several countries, including the United States, the United Arab Emirates, Turkey, and Libya, asked Pakistan to reverse the death sentence of Bhutto. Following the announcement of Bhutto's conviction, many of his supporters demonstrated and clashed with police in many of the nation's cities. Gen. Tikka Kahn, acting head of Bhutto's Pakistan People's Party, was arrested in Lahore on March 20 following his address to several hundred supporters, in defiance of a government ban on such political activity.

General Zia ul-Haq, head of the military government which toppled Bhutto's regime in 1977, continued to strengthen military rule despite his assurance at the time of the coup that he would restore civilian rule in a short time. On October 17 the Zia government imposed press curbs that prompted several leading newspapers to suspend publication. When the newspapers reappeared their pages presented several blank columns to indicate where text or photos had been censored by the government. The government offered justification of the censorship by declaring that "While the press in general has displayed a sense of responsibility, a small section of the press has been taking undue advantage of the liberal policy of the government and betrays a deplorable lack of a sense of responsibility."

The day before the press curbs were imposed the government banned all political parties that were "un-Islamic," prejudiced the country's security or integrity, accepted foreign assistance, or subverted public order.

Thirteen members of the former advisory council were retained as part of a new 17 member cabinet formed by Gen. Zia on July 5. Earlier in the year it was announced that 4 senior officials and 1,746 provincial officials had been dismissed, including Communications Secretary Shah Nawaz Khan and Government Secretary Amirzada Khan.

In July General Zia was quoted as saying "I am fully aware of the fact that I have not been able to achieve fully what I intended to do for the welfare of the people." He also confessed that he had had "no idea" how difficult it was to govern Pakistan. The country, with 75 million people, is overpopulated, rent by language-based separatism, and run by an army junta which is uncertain of its goals.

On July 9 it was reported that more than 122 persons had died in severe flooding in the area of the Afghanistan-Pakistan border. It was reported also that malaria was severely rising, with one in five Pakistanis suffering from the disease.

Foreign Affairs. The United States announced October 24 the resumption of foreign aid to Pakistan following the cancellation of a proposed sale of a nuclear power facility to Pakistan from France. The assistance, which the United States suspended in 1977, was expected to reach $122.4 million for the fiscal year ending September 1979.

On January 12 British Prime Minister James Callaghan met with General Zia during a 2-day stay in Pakistan. The leaders discussed the possible compensation for British insurance companies nationalized by Pakistan in 1972. Later in the year, Britain announced the cancellation of more than $1.74 billion in debts from 17 developing nations, one of which was Pakistan.

Although Pakistan has been a supporter of the Arab cause in the Middle East conflict, Arab gunmen, thought to be Iraqis, attacked a PLO office in Islamabad in August, killing four persons.

CARL LEIDEN
University of Texas, Austin

------- **PAKISTAN · Information Highlights** -------

Official Name: Islamic Republic of Pakistan.
Location: South Asia.
Area: 310,403 square miles (803,943 km²).
Population (1978 est.): 76,800,000.
Chief Cities (1974): Islamabad, the capital, 250,000; Karachi, 3,500,000; Lahore, 2,100,000.
Government: *Head of state,* Fazal Elahi Chaudhri, president (took office Aug. 1973). *Head of government,* Mohammed Zia ul-Haq (took office July 1977). *Legislature*—Parliament: Senate and National Assembly (dissolved July 1977).
Monetary Unit: Rupee (9.931 rupees equal U. S.$1, Sept. 1978).
Manufactures (major products): Cotton textiles, food processing, tobacco, engineering, chemicals, natural gas.
Agriculture (major products): Wheat, cotton, rice.

PARAGUAY

Elections, a modest relaxation of political control, a strain in relations with the United States, and a growing prosperity occurred in Paraguay in 1978.

Domestic Politics. President Alfredo Stroessner won a sixth consecutive five-year term on February 12. Of the more than 1.1 million voters (who by law must vote), more than 280,000 either spoiled their ballots or cast blank ones. Stroessner and his Colorado party claimed the support of 89% of the votes. The opposition termed the elections fraudulent. Because of its victory, the Colorado party was entitled legally to 60% of the seats of both houses of the legislature. Leaders of the opposition refused to attend the president's inauguration on August 15.

Former President Federico Chaves, unseated by Stroessner in 1954, died at the age of 97.

The Political Environment. In January the government agreed to allow a study by the Organization of American States (OAS) of the status of human rights in Paraguay. In February the International League for Human Rights asserted that individual rights in Paraguay were "in crisis." Also in February the government lifted a ten-year-old state of siege in three departments, leaving only Asunción, the capital, still under the decree. By inauguration time the government claimed to have freed all but 24 of the more than 2,000 political prisoners who had been detained since 1976. In June, the OAS General Assembly heard the delegate from Jamaica denounce continued violations of rights in Paraguay. In July the leader of the Liberal party was abducted and detained by the police for several weeks. He was released on August 10, following U. S. protests.

The Economy. The on-going construction and future potential of a giant hydroelectric project jointly undertaken by Brazil and Paraguay on the Parana River contributed to an economic boom. About 15,000 Paraguayans are employed there. The growth rate for the construction sector has been 31.7% and 25.4% in 1977 and 1978, respectively. The agricultural sector grew by 9% in 1977 and by 7% in 1978. Soybeans and cotton have surpassed timber and processed meats as leading exports.

Paraguay received loans of $81 million from Brazil for a new steel mill, and $33 million from the World Bank for highway development.

LEO B. LOTT, *University of Montana*

PENNSYLVANIA

Republican Richard Thornburgh, capitalizing on division within Democratic ranks, scored a come-from-behind victory in the gubernatorial race in November.

Election. Thornburgh, 46, and his Democratic opponent, Peter Flaherty, were Pittsburgh residents, and both campaigned early against corruption in the scandal-plagued administration of Democratic Gov. Milton Shapp. Thornburgh pointed to his record as a federal prosecutor and Flaherty to his seven years as mayor of Pittsburgh, where he acquired the reputation of a party maverick.

In the end, Thornburgh and his running mate, William Scranton III, son of the former governor and former ambassador to the United Nations, overcame a 700,000 deficit in party registration and won by more than 200,000 votes.

The GOP picked up three seats in the state Senate to cut the Democratic margin there to five, and gained an additional 16 seats in the House. That left each party with 101 House members, while the candidates in the one remaining district remained locked in a tie vote. A recount gave the Democratic incumbent the victory. However, the Republicans picked up their 102nd seat and won control of the House on the basis of a recount in another district.

Philadelphia Mayor Frank Rizzo and his supporters asked Philadelphia voters to strike a city charter provision limiting the city's mayors to two terms. In the aftermath of a campaign in which each side accused the other of inciting fear and encouraging bloc voting by race, the Rizzo amendment lost by a wide margin.

In races to decide the state's 25-member congressional delegation, the gain of two seats brought GOP representation to 10. Democrat Joshua Eilberg of Philadelphia, indicted two weeks before the election for an alleged conflict

──── PARAGUAY · Information Highlights ────

Official Name: Republic of Paraguay.
Location: Central South America.
Area: 157,047 square miles (406,752 km²).
Population (1978 est.): 2,900,000.
Chief City (1976 est.): Asunción, the capital, 442,000.
Government: *Head of state and government,* Gen. Alfredo Stroessner, president (took office Aug. 1954). *Legislature*—Congress: Senate and Chamber of Deputies.
Monetary Unit: Guarani (126 guaranies equal U. S.$1, Sept. 1978).
Manufactures (major products): Agricultural processing, wood products, consumer goods, cement, refined oil products, hydroelectric power.
Agriculture (major products): Wheat, corn, manioc, sweet potatoes, beans, rice, sugarcane, fruits.

──── PENNSYLVANIA · Information Highlights ────

Area: 45,333 square miles (117,412 km²).
Population (Jan. 1978 est.): 11,783,000.
Chief Cities (1970 census): Harrisburg, the capital, 68,061; Philadelphia, 1,950,098; Pittsburgh, 520,117.
Government (1978): *Chief Officers*—governor, Milton J. Shapp (D); lt. gov., Ernest P. Kline (D). *General Assembly*—Senate, 50 members; House of Representatives, 203 members.
Education (1977–78): *Enrollment*—public elementary schools, 1,054,040 pupils; public secondary, 1,074,833; colleges and universities, 475,659 students. *Public school expenditures,* $4,858,800,000 ($1,928 per pupil).
State Finances (fiscal year 1977): *Revenues,* $11,091,470,000; *expenditures,* $11,207,936,000.
Personal Income (1977): $82,630,000,000; per capita, $7,011.
Labor Force (July 1978): *Nonagricultural wage and salary earners,* 4,707,000; *unemployed,* 390,200 (7.3% of total force).

of interest, was unseated by Charles Dougherty, who becomes the city's first Republican congressman since 1956. Democratic Rep. Daniel Flood of Wilkes-Barre had been indicted on charges of bribery, conspiracy, and perjury, but won re-election to a 16th term by fewer than 10,000 votes—roughly one eighth of the margin he enjoyed two years earlier.

In other political developments, former Democratic Congressman Frank Clark, 62, who represented southwestern Pennsylvania for 20 years, was indicted on 13 counts of mail fraud, perjury, and income tax evasion; former Pennsylvania House Speaker Herbert Fineman began serving a two-year prison term for obstructing justice. His fellow Philadelphia Democrat, former Senate Majority Leader Henry Cianfrani, received a five-year sentence after pleading guilty to mail fraud, racketeering and obstruction of justice.

U. S. Attorney General Griffin Bell touched off a squabble in January when he attempted to fire U. S. Attorney David Marston of Philadelphia and replace him with a Democrat. Marston countered that he was in the midst of an investigation of Flood and Eilberg, and charged that Eilberg had been in touch with President Carter in an attempt to hurry Marston's ouster. Marston, following his replacement, made an unsuccessful bid for his party's gubernatorial nomination.

Confrontation. A Philadelphia police officer was killed and several members of the radical group MOVE were injured in a shootout in early August after the group reneged on an agreement to comply with a court order to vacate its commune in a residential area.

RICHARD ELGIN
State Desk, *"The Patriot-News," Harrisburg*

PERU

Peru's major political event in 1978 was the convocation of a Constituent Assembly in Lima July 28. Economic measures, which helped postpone payment of a massive foreign debt, provoked severe internal unrest.

Constituent Assembly. Over 3.5 million Peruvians voted June 18 for the first time in ten years for an Assembly of 100 members which would draft a new constitution in preparation for the restoration of civilian rule in 1980. Presiding was Victor Raúl Haya de la Torre, the 83-year-old president of the center-left American Popular Revolutionary Alliance (APRA) which won 1,-241,174 votes and 37 seats. Next came the right-wing Popular Christian Party with 835,294 votes and 25 seats, followed by the extreme-left Workers, Peasants, Students and Peoples' Front (FOCEP) with 433,413 votes and 12 seats. Seven other parties split the remaining 26 seats. Former President Fernando Belaúnde Terry's Popular Action Party refused to participate in the election. Six leftist assemblymen were allowed to return from exile under a July 14 amnesty.

Austerity Measures. On September 15, after lengthy negotiations, the International Monetary Fund (IMF) approved $220 million in standby credits for Peru to meet interest and principal payments on (U. S.) $8.2 billion debts. In July, Peru renegotiated repayment of $185 million in loans with 170 foreign banks. Peru assured the IMF and the international banks that the funds would not be used to repay some $60 million owed the USSR for military aircraft, missiles, tanks, and artillery.

In September, Finance Minister Javier Silva Ruete estimated the 1978 inflation rate would be about 70% compared with 32% in 1977.

Riots plus lengthy strikes by teachers, bankworkers, miners, and public employees followed May 15 price increases for gasoline, public transportation, and basic foodstuffs such as milk and bread. Other measures designed to meet IMF and foreign bank demands included higher taxes, reduced public spending, a 13% devaluation of the currency, reduced imports, and proposed cuts of 35,000 public employees.

Mineral and Fish Meal Production Up. The austerity measures plus increased mineral exports led to a July prediction of the first trade surplus in several years. Copper production in 1977 was a record 341,000 tons, compared with 220,000 tons in 1976, with the main boost coming from the new Cuajone mine opened in 1975. Prospects for further increases were dashed by a July–August strike.

Offshore anchovy stocks recovered to 4.5 million tons from 2 million in 1976, still low, however, compared with the 20 million tons found offshore in the 1960's before overfishing occurred.

Foreign Relations. On Jan. 12, 1978, the Peruvian government announced that Ecuadorian troops attacked a garrison near the border in Peru's Amazon region. Ecuadorian officials denied the charge, but Vice Admiral Alfredo Poveda Burbano, Ecuador's military leader, subsequently telephoned Peruvian President Francisco Morales Bermúdez to discuss the dispute. Officials of the two countries met in Quito, Ecuador's capital, on January 20, and issued mutual declarations of friendship. The border dispute dates from an undeclared war between the two nations in 1941 and an international protocol, not recognized by Ecuador, signed the following year.

NEALE J. PEARSON, *Texas Tech University*

--- **PERU · Information Highlights** ---

Official Name: Republic of Peru.
Location: West coast of South America.
Area: 496,223 square miles (1,285,216 km²).
Population (1978 est.): 17,100,000.
Chief City (1972 census): Lima, the capital, 3,350,000 (met. area).
Government: *Head of state,* Gen. Francisco Morales Bermúdez (took office August 1975). *Head of government,* Gen. Oscar Molina Pallochia, prime minister (took office Jan. 1978).
Monetary Unit: Sol (169.61 soles equal U. S.$1, Aug. 1978).
Manufactures (major products): Mineral processing, fish meal, oil refining, textiles, light engineering.
Agriculture (major products): Cotton, sugar, coffee.

Philippine President Ferdinand E. Marcos' New Society Movement won all the seats in balloting for a National Assembly. But the election, in which there was blatant fraud, failed to convince Filipinos that the Marcos' regime was a democratic one. The voting, in fact, underscored the tightly controlled character of Philippine politics under Marcos.

Politics. The April 7 balloting for an "interim" assembly was designed to convince critics of Marcos in the United States, particularly the Congress, that the Philippine government was a popular and nonrepressive one. Filipino-American military base negotiations were in progress, and Marcos feared that Congress would not support military and economic aid to his country or make substantial payment for continued use of facilities in the islands.

The opposition Laban (People's Force) party, led by jailed former Sen. Benigno Aquino, Jr., contested only 21 seats in Manila of the 200 seats nationwide. Eyewitness accounts indicated that, in some cases, results were recorded without votes being counted.

Three "no-choice" referenda had been held by Marcos following his 1972 takeover, but the April balloting was the first "election" of any kind under martial law. Local elections, earlier promised for later in the year, were postponed.

The assembly took office June 12, when Marcos became premier as well as president in a would-be transition to parliamentary-type government. Marcos said the body would sit for a full six-year term, indicating that an end to martial law was at least six years away.

In May Marcos retired 44 of 77 generals in the first major military shake-up since he seized power. Some 50,000 government troops remained in action against 20,000 Muslim rebels in Mindanao and Sulu in the southern Philippines, while 2,500–3,000 "New People's Army" Communist insurgents operated, somewhat ineffectively, in central Luzon island.

Economy. Government statistics indicated that the overwhelming majority of the country's largely poor people were worse off than they had been at the institution of martial law in 1972. In particular, the real wages of most Filipinos

had declined during the six years of Marcos' "constitutional authoritarianism".

Official figures also indicated a government debt of (U. S.) $6.5 billion to foreign banks at the year's start—a figure that was predicted to increase $2 billion a year in both 1978 and 1979. Nearly 17% of the country's foreign exchange earnings were being employed to repay these loans.

The cost of the war against the Mindanao-Sulu Muslims was especially high, reaching $27.4 million a month for military expenditures.

U. S.-Philippine Relations. Negotiations continued between Manila and Washington over extending U. S. use of Clark Air Base and the Subic Bay naval facility continued, with the chief issue being the matter of American payment for access to these military properties. The United States agreed to accept Philippine sovereignty over both bases and was willing to discuss Filipino jurisdiction over crimes committed by U. S. servicemen on the facilities. But Marcos wanted $1 billion for "rent" of the bases, for a five year period, to avoid annual criticism of his government's alleged human rights violations in the U. S. Congress.

The bases were second only to the Philippine government in the number of Filipinos employed, at a cost to the United States of $200 million. In addition to $100 million in U. S. economic assistance and $39 million in military aid, American private investment in the country reached $850 million in 1978.

Foreign Relations. The government's image abroad was clearly tarnished by the ballot fraud, post-election arrests, and general crackdown on opposition and dissent after the April voting. United States criticism of financial irregularities between American firms and persons close to President Marcos also irked the government. Imelda Marcos, the Philippine president's wife and number one political associate, responded by announcing a Soviet offer to replace a planned American nuclear reactor which figured in such criticism.

Chinese Deputy Prime Minister Li Hsien-nien visited the Philippines in February as part of a worldwide effort by Peking to win friends in its continuing rivalry with the USSR. China was also a rival of Manila, however, in laying claim to the purportedly oilrich Spratly Islands 250 miles (400 km) west of the Philippines—and claimed by Vietnam and Taiwan, as well. Given Filipino dependence on foreign oil supplies, the Marcos government was not expected to relinquish its claim to the islands—a seventh one of which it occupied on the eve of Li Hsien-nien's visit.

Indonesia and Malaysia, both Muslim countries, were unsuccessful in their attempts to mediate differences between Marcos and the Islamic separatists of Mindanao-Sulu.

RICHARD BUTWELL
Murray State University

PHILIPPINES · Information Highlights

Official Name: Republic of the Philippines.
Location: Southeast Asia.
Area: 115,830 square miles (300,000 km²).
Population (1978 est.): 46,300,000.
Chief Cities (May 1975): Manila, the capital, 1,479,116; Quezon City, 956,864; Cebu, 413,025.
Government: *Head of state and government,* Ferdinand E. Marcos, president and prime minister. *Legislature* (unicameral)—National Assembly.
Monetary Unit: Peso (7.3585 pesos equal U. S.$1, Nov. 1978).
Manufactures (major products): Processed foods, tobacco, beverages, rubber products, cement, glass, textiles.
Agriculture (major products): Rice, corn, sugar, copra, coconut oil.

PHOTOGRAPHY

As the electronics revolution in the hardware continued, and as more fast films emerged to permit photographic shooting under virtually any lighting conditions, Americans produced more than 8 (U. S.) billion still images in 1978. On walls, in magazines, in the streets, and even in the courts, photography had taken its place, and the issuance of the first U. S. commemorative postage stamp sanctioned photography as "the official language."

New Equipment. Manufacturers of single-lens reflex (SLR) 35mm cameras were directing the trend summarized in a *New York Times* story, "The Automatics Are Really Taking Over." A compact body, automatic exposure with multi-mode options, digital light-emitting-diode (LED) readouts, and an accessory package including a motorwinder and electronic flash were the keys to success, resulting in more and more features packed into less and less space. The use of electronics lowered the cost of manufacture and also simplified camera operations.

At the annual Photo Marketing Association (PMA) trade show in Chicago, Canon introduced its A-1 with *six* exposure modes—five automatic, including a programmed mode responsible for setting both aperture and shutter speed. Nikon's FE compact automatic was the other show stopper. It featured interchangeable focusing screens usually found only in professional model SLR's. And Chinon brought out two models with integral autowinders, and the industry's first with a built-in intervalometer.

Long before the 1978 *photokina,* the international show held every other year in Cologne, West Germany, three different cameras sported the year's newest feature, autofocusing. To monitor the rangefinder focusing system, Konica's compact still camera, the C35AF, uses two hinged mirrors that key on whatever is in the center of the viewfinder, as does Sankyo's ES-44XL VAF silent model, the first 8mm movie camera with autofocusing. Both cameras utilize the Visitronic Auto/Focus module designed by Honeywell, Inc., a device based on optical contrast measurement that other manufacturers have acquired via licensing agreements. Polaroid's new instant color model uses sonar; when the shutter of the SX-70 Sonar OneStep camera (and the Pronto Sonar OneStep, a second model that followed on its heels) is pressed, a little sonar station above the lens sends out ultrasonic signals which bounce off the subject, return to the camera, and automatically focus the lens.

In another part of the instant camera arena—indeed, the fastest growing segment of the photo market—Eastman Kodak introduced a new line, the Colorburst, and reduced the price of its crank-operated $39.95 Handle by $5.00 to undercut Polaroid's similarly priced OneStep.

In 110/SLR photography that combines the 110-size negative with SLR viewing—a segment previously occupied solely by Minolta's 110 Zoom SLR—Pentax introduced its own auto-exposure contender, the first with interchangeable lenses and an autowinder. Among the traditional (non-SLR) "pocket-sized" 110's, a new wave of even more sophisticated models emerged —with ASA 400 film-speed capability, as well as built-in flash, faster and higher quality lenses, and two focal-length lenses. The Kalimar Tri-Lens was the first 110 to sport a 21mm wide-angle, 34mm normal, and 42mm tele single-element lenses. Kodak introduced a new line of pockets called the Ektra.

The fantasy of one lens for everything came closer to reality in the plethora of new zoom lenses introduced, including the hottest categories: ultra-wide to wide and wide-angle to medium-tele varieties with macro focusing. Canon's new wide-angle FD 24-35mm f/3.5 was the first zoom to use an aspheric element. Many small, lightweight single focal-length lenses became available, as the trend to match the compactness of lenses with the camera bodies continued.

"Tiny" also summarized the trend for many new electronic flash units. The advent of 400-speed color films made smaller guide-numbered units in pocket sizes much more useful. Increasing automation of the darkroom also saw many products go digital, such as Vivitar's three programmable devices to control printing and processing steps. E. Leitz, of 35mm camera fame, moved to the forefront in enlarger engineering with its first all-new enlarger design in 30 years, the Focomat V35 Autofocus. Home darkroom work continued to grow slowly but steadily. New chemicals and materials helped make color processing and printing almost as easy as black-and-white.

Colorburst 100 is a new line in the instant camera field.

COURTESY, EASTMAN KODAK COMPANY

COURTESY, HARRY CULLUIN

"Jerry Dantzic and the Cirkut camera," an exhibition of color panoramic photographs, opened at New York City's Museum of Modern Art in May 1978.

ASA 400 color photography became firmly entrenched in 1978 with the introduction of Agfa CNS 400, the world's fifth high-speed color negative film, and Kodak's daylight 35mm Ektachrome 400 slide film that is capable of being push-processed to 800. Representing a breakthrough in emulsion technology, 3M Company's 400-speed color film was not only balanced for daylight and electronic flash but capable of producing acceptable results under tungsten and fluorescent light without the use of color correcting filters. In short, the development was the first universally balanced slide film. In the black-and-white slot, Fuji brought out its 35mm and 120-size Neopan 400 film as a contender against the other same-speed competitors—Ilford's HP-5 and the universally popular Tri-X. Kodak increased the number of exposures in color film from 20 to 24 in 110, 126, and 35mm formats. GAF—which discontinued its line of film, paper, and cameras for the amateur market in 1977—announced its intention to sell its 9-year-old photo processing business.

Exhibitions and Collections. Industry took a more active role in the creation of photo exhibitions and collections. Spring Mills, a textile manufacturer, committed itself to the presentation of a long-term series conceived and mounted by the Museum of Modern Art (MOMA) in New York City. The first series presented 12 color panoramic views of American landscapes made by Jerry Dantzic with a Cirkut Camera.

Support from Philip Morris, Inc., the National Endowment for the Arts, and N. Y. State Council on the Arts resulted in a major exhibition at the MOMA, "Mirrors and Windows:

American Photography Since 1960." Through more than 200 works by 100 photographers, John Szarkowski, director of the department of photography, sought to provide a new critical framework for the last 20 years of American photo imagery. The thesis touted the basic dichotomy between those who regard the medium as a means of self-expression—a "mirror" of the photographer's sensibility—and those who use it as a method of exploration—a "window" through which the outside world is investigated in a nominally objective manner. A book, a seven-museum nationwide tour, and extensive press coverage helped spread the word about "The Szarkowski Generation" of photography.

Another MOMA exhibition, "New Standpoints: Photography 1940–1955," reviewed the documentary work from that era, and MOMA's "Steichen: The Master Prints, 1895–1914" was one of a handful of shows in the New York City area that covered the photographic contributions of Alfred Stieglitz, Edward Steichen, and those who participated in the Photo-Secessionist movement of the first two decades of the 20th century. At the Metropolitan Museum of Art, some 214 prints from the Stieglitz collection constituted a major show and the entire collection of 580 became a book. Guest curator Helen Gee assembled "Stieglitz and the Photo-Secession: Pictorialism to Modernism, 1902–17" at the New Jersey State Museum in Trenton, then brought part of that installation to the prestigious National Arts Club in New York, the gallery in which the Photo-Secession had first exhibited 76 years earlier. A nationwide tour of "Photographic Crossroads: The Photo League (1936–51)" began at the International Center of Photography in New York City.

"The History of Fashion Photography" was the subject matter covered at an exhibit at the Brooklyn Museum in an entertaining and historically important manner, while the modern tendency to meld fashion photography with "show biz" was apparent in the film *The Eyes of Laura Mars*. And fashion photographer Richard Avedon had a three-decade retrospective at the Metropolitan.

Place was the theme in a number of other shows, including "New York, New York—An Exhibition of 20th Century Photographs Made in New York," with opening night TV coverage; Peter Beard's 20-year study of Africa in a multimedia presentation that included jungle sounds and images displayed on the floor; two shows of photographs of China until 1915 that traveled nationwide; and René Gelpi's portraits of Cuba.

Color photography was appreciated as art in Joel Meyerowitz's multiple light-source views of Cape Cod and Stephen Shore's coverage of "The New York Yankees' Spring Training, 1978." Some of the exhibitions by old favorites who work in black-and-white included a 1928–47 retrospective for Walker Evans, a celebration of the work of humorist "Elliot Erwitt at 50," and

THE METROPOLITAN MUSEUM OF ART, GIFT OF ALFRED STIEGLITZ, 1933

"The Flatiron Building" was part of an exhibit of the works of Edward J. Steichen at the Metropolitan Museum of Art, New York City.

the "Recent and Unseen Work" of André Kertész. Harry Callahan had a 250-print show covering his 30-year career at the Venice Biennale.

New Publications. Documentary photography was a heavy favorite among 1978's new books. Bill Owens gave a crash course in the free-lance facts of life in *Documentary Photography.* Jill Freedman's *Firehouse* quickly went into a second printing. Eugene Richard's *Dorchester Days* covered life in that working-class Boston-area community. *Photography in America: The Formative Years, 1839–1900* provided a comprehensive historical overview, while *American Showcase* made its first annual appearance as a picture-packed sourcebook of the work of 163 of America's top commercial photographers.

After a six-year hiatus, the announcement of the reemergence of the "big picture books" was the major story in the general periodical world. After 23 years in the photographic press as *Camera35,* the magazine (under new ownership) hitched its name to that of *Photo World,* a recently deceased publication. A new magazine, *American Photographer,* made its debut.

Court Suits and General Trends. In the civil antitrust suit brought by Berkey Photo Inc. against Kodak, the court found the defendant guilty of federal antitrust violations in the amateur photographic industry. Kodak was ordered to pay $87.1 million in damages, provide information about its plans to competing photofinishing operations, and sell its photo papers without the company name and logo. The company planned to appeal the decision, a process expected to take several years. In the suit brought by Polaroid against Berkey regarding instant camera infringements, Berkey agreed to discontinue the manufacture of its instant cameras after its current inventory was sold.

According to the latest *Wolfman Report of the Photographic Industry in the United States,* not only had the industry fully recovered from the 1973–75 recession, but it was growing at a "moderately brisk rate." For 1978, the biggest problem was that of the dollar exchange rate. The drop in value of the U. S. dollar against the Japanese yen resulted in an increase in the consumer prices of Japanese-made photo products (practically all high-grade SLR cameras are made in Japan).

Nikon celebrated its 25th anniversary and Minolta its 50th. The latter introduced the Electrographic 301 photocopier, the world's first to utilize fiber optics technology.

BARBARA LOBRON
Writer and Photographer

401

PHYSICS

During 1978, striking new results were obtained in particle physics, and substantial progress was made in such diverse fields as controlled thermonuclear fusion, synchrotron radiation sources, and radioisotope dating.

Particle Physics. Over a decade ago the proliferation of the subatomic particles discovered by high energy physicists started a debate about the definition of an elementary particle. The urge to simplify and unite led to the idea of quarks—a limited number of substructures which combined to form most of the known particles, just as protons and neutrons combine to form nuclei. At first, the positing of three quarks was sufficient to explain the class of particles called hadrons. The discovery a few years ago of the J/psi particle required a fourth. Predictions made assuming this fourth (charmed) quark were quite successful.

However, a new discovery at Fermilab (Batavia, Ill.) seems to require an additional quark. A series of massive resonances (named upsilon particles) near 10 GeV (10 thousand million electron volts) seems unexplainable except by postulating another quark. These findings have now been confirmed at DESY (West Germany). The quarks were introduced to simplify matters, but now their number are growing rapidly.

The other major class of particles (the leptons) seemed to consist of a small fixed number: the electron, the muon, and the electron and muon neutrinos. Now it appears that workers at the storage ring at SLAC (Stanford) have discovered another, much heavier lepton, named the tau particle. There should also be a neutrino associated with the tau particle. The known number of "elementary" particles continues to increase.

Controlled Thermonuclear Fusion. One favored long-term solution to the energy problem is controlled thermonuclear fusion. The raw materials available for this process which fuels the stars are virtually unlimited, but the technical problems related to controlling fusion are also very large. Ultra high temperatures are required to initiate the fusion reaction (10 to 100 million degrees Kelvin) and the materials must be contained.

Most methods of containment have utilized magnetic fields, and the most popular magnetic confinement device has been the tokamak (a Russian acronym) scheme. Four new tokamaks will try to pass the breakeven point. These facilities are being built in England by a European consortium, Japan, the USSR, and the United States. The Tokamak Fusion Test Reactor is being built in Princeton, N. J., at a cost in excess of $200 million and should be operational in 1982. The reactions between deuterium and tritium should produce a number of neutrons and begin to simulate realistically a future operating fusion environment.

The ignition of pellets imploded by beams of light or particles is a later entry into the controlled fusion process. Although pellet fusion with heavy ion beams has aroused some recent enthusiasm, the laser fusion devices are the most advanced. Neutrons from thermonuclear reactions produced by laser pellet implosion have been observed. At Lawrence Livermore Laboratory (California) a new high power laser fusion device began operating in 1978. This facility, called Shiva after the Hindu god of destruction and creation, has 20 laser beams and operates in the 20 million million watt region. If Shiva is successful, the breakeven point is expected to be reached by the next generation laser fusion facility—already called Nova.

Synchrotron Radiation. The electromagnetic spectrum ranges over a wide band of frequencies from radio waves to gamma rays. Excellent sources are available at most wave-lengths, except in the ultraviolet and X-ray region. Since wave-lengths in the X-ray region are about the same size as atoms and molecules, strong sources in this wavelength region are particularly sought after. In recent years synchrotron radiation (emitted from accelerated charged particles) has begun to fill this gap.

Initially, users of synchrotron radiation were secondary users at particle physics accelerators, especially at electron storage rings such as SPEAR (Stanford) and DESY. There has been remarkable success with such procedures as X-ray absorption fine structure in determining the structure of crystal surfaces and of complex and disordered systems which were previously not available for study. These successes cover not only many areas of pure and applied physics, but also many branches of biology and chemistry.

The advent of dedicated synchrotron radiation facilities will provide manifold increases in intensity and in numbers of beam lines. In the preparation of integrated circuitry, the X-ray lithographic techniques could permit one hundred times more information per chip. Applications in biology include the study of the geometry of complex chemical compounds such as hemoglobin. There is even a proposal to build an electron storage ring privately, and to enter joint venture agreements with private manufacturing and development companies. The boom in applications of synchrotron radiation seems permanent.

Radioisotope Dating. The famous radiocarbon dating method received a boost in 1978 from nuclear physics. Radiocarbon dating methods rely on the radioactive decay of carbon-14. The amount of carbon-14 present in the atmosphere, and thus in living tissues, is a constant. Once an organism dies, new carbon-14 ceases to enter it and the carbon-14 present begins to decrease with a half-life of nearly 6,000 years. By measuring the amount of carbon-14 present in objects (by counting the beta particles emitted in radioactive decay), it is possible to date the objects. Although the method works very well, there are some limitations. The problem is to reduce the amount of material needed, shorten the time required to perform the experiment, and extend the dating age limits. Mass spectrometers seem attractive, but there is a crucial problem with nitrogen-14 contamination.

The solution is to use a particle accelerator, as demonstrated by physicists at the University of Rochester (N. Y.) and elsewhere. The material in question was placed in the ion source of a tandem Van de Graaff accelerator and carbon-14 accelerated to high energies. Samples that were two orders of magnitude smaller than standard were used. Since negative ions are formed at one stage in the acceleration process (and negative nitrogen-14 ions are quite unstable), the contamination problem was minimized.

One approach for the future is to build a new dedicated facility, eliminating many of the remaining background problems. Probably more important in the long run is that direct detection techniques with particle accelerators opens a whole new set of radioisotope dating possibilities. With these new techniques, radioactive elements that occur in low concentrations or whose half-lives are too long, could be utilized. Applications ranging from better archeological techniques to testing for leakage near nuclear waste disposal sites are envisioned.

GARY MITCHELL, *Department of Physics*
North Carolina State University

POLAND

Domestic Affairs. The year began with a national conference of the ruling Polish United Workers' Party in Warsaw on January 10. In a letter addressed to the conference, 15 prominent party members demanded more freedoms for the people and a multiparty system of government. Party chief Edward Gierek announced a 10% boost in the minimum wage, promised higher investments in agriculture, called for increased labor productivity, but sidestepped the issue of basic political and economic reform. Vice Premier Jozef Tejchma resigned as minister of culture January 26. In late February, government officials admitted that censorship policies in Poland often had been "excessive." In March, 27 dissident students at Warsaw University were arrested, and in mid-April came reports that prisoners were receiving brutal treatment by the security police. In September, the Roman Catholic Church formally supported the campaign for extension of human and political rights in Poland. An open letter by the Polish bishops on September 17 condemned censorship and repression by the Communist regime as "totalitarian."

The October 16 election of Karol Cardinal Wojtyla, 58, as pope was an unprecedented event in the 1,000-year history of the Polish Roman Catholic Church. It was encouraging to millions of faithful Catholics in Poland struggling against regime censorship and repression.

Economy. In 1978, the Polish economy continued to suffer from foreign trade deficits and shortages of consumer goods. Many Poles traveled to Czechoslovakia to buy products unavailable at home. According to official figures released in July, industrial production rose by 8.6% in 1977, but agricultural output by less than 1%. In late March, the price of gasoline was officially raised about 20% in an effort to cut consumption. On May 28, the government announced a price increase of between 25 and 30% on a variety of alcoholic beverages, claiming that alcoholism had become a major cause of low labor productivity, accidents, and crime.

Official reports in early 1978 placed the rate of inflation at about 4%. It was believed that nearly one third of the government budget was being spent on basic food subsidies. Reports reaching the West indicated, however, that Polish farmers were dissatisfied with the low prices paid to them for government-ordered food. Rural unrest and demonstrations were reported in the Lublin area at midyear.

While government sources claimed that the unfavorable gap between imports and exports was at last being narrowed, nearly 30% of Poland's foreign currency earnings in the first quarter were spent to pay interest on foreign debts. In April, the government attempted to secure increased foreign investment and improve its overall trade prospects by adopting a more realistic floating rate of exchange between the zloty and the U. S. dollar. The Polish trading position was rendered more difficult, however, by a Common Market decision in January to impose "anti-dumping fees" on Polish steel sold in the EEC countries.

Foreign Affairs. In 1978, Poland continued its close relationship with the Soviet Union. In January, Polish Foreign Minister Emil Wojtaszek visited Moscow to report on the visit by President Jimmy Carter. In February, representatives of Poland, East Germany, and Czechoslovakia together monitored Soviet military maneuvers in Byelorussia. In a departure from its previous anti-Israeli policies, the Polish government invited a number of Israeli parliamentarians to the opening of a Jewish museum at Auschwitz on April 19.

ALEXANDER J. GROTH
University of California, Davis

─────── **POLAND · Information Highlights** ───────

Official Name: Polish People's Republic.
Location: Eastern Europe.
Area: 120,724 square miles (312,677 km²).
Population (1978 est.): 35,100,000.
Chief Cities (1976 census): Warsaw, the capital, 1,463,-400; Łodz, 810,000; Cracow, 700,700.
Government: *Head of state,* Henryk Jabłonski, chairman of the Council of State (took office 1972). *Head of government,* Piotr Jaroszewicz, chairman of the Council of Ministers (1970). *First secretary of the United Polish Workers' party,* Edward Gierek (1970). *Legislature* (unicameral)—Sejm.
Monetary Unit: Zloty (19.92 zlotys equal U. S.$1, 1978).
Manufactures (major products): Iron and steel, chemicals, textiles, processed foods, ships, transport equipment.
Agriculture (major products): Grains, sugar beets, potatoes, hogs and other livestock.

POLAR RESEARCH

Antarctic. More than 300 U. S. researchers traveled to Antarctica in 1977–78 to conduct over 90 research projects.

Scientists used a flame-jet drill to pierce the 1,378-foot (420-m) thick Ross Ice Shelf for the first time. The hole enabled researchers to lower television cameras, baited traps, sphincter samplers, and other devices into the water column beneath the ice to search for life and to bring up sediment samples from the bottom of the sea. Scientists found 8.7 to 12 million microorganisms per liter of water recovered at the drill site. This seemed to indicate a metabolically active plankton population in the ice-covered, lightless waters 300 miles (483 km) away from the edge of the ice shelf. Continuing research is designed to show whether these microorganisms flow in from the open sea or are part of an operational food web under the shelf.

More than 300 meteorites were recovered from Antarctica by U. S. and Japanese scientists. Researchers now know to concentrate their searches where glaciers have flowed into obstructing mountains and have undergone ablation. In these "blue ice" areas, wind erosion exposes meteorites which have been buried in the moving glaciers. One of the meteorites discovered was a rare carbonaceous chondrite—having a high carbon content and tiny, bead-like globules called chondrules. Another was the first of an entirely new class of achondritic meteorites. It combines features of the two familiar achondrites—chassignites, which are composed mostly of olivine and diogenites—in proportions not seen before. The sterile environment keeps the meteorites pristine.

Oceanic researchers continued to examine the southern Weddell Sea. The U. S. Coast Guard icebreaker *Glacier* took 118 hydrographic stations over a measured grid to help scientists investigate the mixing of waters in Antarctica.

Scientists expanded and intensified their investigations into the life cycle of krill by maintaining them in sea water aquaria. Researchers also probed the crucial role that krill play in the antarctic marine food web and examined the ways in which other species depend on krill to survive. Additional biological research examined the ways penguins, seals, and marine birds adapt to antarctic conditions and the way human immunity to disease is affected by long stays in Antarctica.

Arctic. U. S. federally sponsored researchers continued to examine the high productivity of the Bering Sea, an area particularly rich in Alaskan pollock. Observations from April to June 1978 indicated that the area is influenced by two different water masses originating over the Bering Sea shelf and the open southern Bering Sea. Each water mass is associated with different plant and animal communities and each participates in a different way in the transfer of organic matter that makes the Bering Sea so productive.

At Svalbard, U. S. geologists explored the history of Precambrian rock outcrops. They examined the stratigraphy of the outcrops, as well as their seismological and geophysical properties. Scientists from the United States, Greenland, Denmark, and England cooperated in a detailed geologic survey of the world's oldest known sedimentary rocks at Isua, Greenland. The rocks are approximately 3.8 billion (U. S.) years old. Scientists investigated the history of the region and searched for evidence of organic molecules that could have been precursors of life.

Environmental assessment of the outer continental shelf area of the Beaufort and Chukchi seas continued in 1978. Researchers investigated currents and circulation patterns, sea ice dynamics, coastal erosion, and the behavior of marine birds and marine mammals in the outer continental shelf environment. Information gained will be used to guide the recovery of oil and natural gas in the region.

In August 1977, the Soviet nuclear icebreaker *Arktika* became the first surface ship ever to sail to the North Pole and back. The voyage demonstrated the possibility of year-round navigation in the Arctic Ocean.

RICHARD P. MULDOON
Polar Programs, National Science Foundation

PORTUGAL

Disenchantment with politics mounted in 1978 as Portugal's leaders unsuccessfully sought to devise a formula for national unity amid grave economic conditions.

Government and Politics. A crisis was narrowly averted in January when the Socialist Party and the Social Democratic Center (CDS) hammered out a coalition. The Socialists, with 102 seats in the 263-member National Assembly, dominated the partnership. Their president, Mário Soares, continued as prime minister. He was appointed to the post in mid-1976 by Antonio Ramalho Eanes, who earlier that year had become the nation's first democratically elected president in a half-century.

Differences over national health insurance and agricultural policy shattered the fragile alliance. The right-of-center CDS urged that lands expropriated by radicals after the 1974 overthrow of dictator Marcelo Caetano be restored to their owners. The party also accused the Socialist agriculture secretary of caving in to the Communists on this explosive issue.

The Social Democratic Center feared a loss of followers if it remained in the government. This fear sharpened in mid-year when Francisco Sa Carneiro returned as president of the Social Democratic Party. An unrelenting critic of the president and prime minister, Sa Carneiro appealed to hundreds of thousands of citizens who were disaffected because of food shortages, poor housing, soaring inflation, high unemployment, and the deadlock and drift of parliamentary politics. Thus, the three CDS cabinet members resigned on July 24, lest the more aggressive Social Democrats siphon off their party's conservative support.

President Eanes, a hard-working, taciturn general, had theretofore remained aloof from the day-to-day maneuvering of the parties. As a result, fellow officers criticized him for being too indulgent toward the Socialists. But the breakup of the coalition exhausted his patience. He dismissed Soares and gave the politicians an ultimatum: forge a new party cabinet or accept a presidentially-backed government composed of highly competent independents and technicians.

When the partisan squabbling continued, the chief executive named as prime minister Alfredo Nobre da Costa, a tough-minded industrialist who had been a director of the Champalimaud steel and cement empire under the dictatorship. Soares, apparently convinced that only he and the Socialists could run the country, condemned the appointment as "an anti-democratic coup." Nobre da Costra's failure to obtain a parliamentary vote of confidence forced him to resign in October.

President Eanes next asked Carlos da Mota Pinto, a 42-year-old law professor, to form a cabinet. Legislators appeared more favorably disposed toward the new appointee, fearing that opposition might provoke the president to call elections before the expiration of their terms in 1980.

Elections. In the next two years voters will choose municipal authorities, regional governments for the Azores and Madeira, a new chief executive, and members of parliament. The prospect of so much balloting prompted Eanes to declare that the "people will say we are spending more time discovering the will of the people than implementing it."

Any election must await the updating of the voting rolls. As many as one tenth of Portugal's adults were not registered because they had arrived from the country's former African territories after the existing electoral list was compiled in early 1975. Enfranchising the *retornados* should benefit, respectively, the Social Democrats, the CDS, and the new right-wing Movement for National Reconstruction.

Economy. Political discord has impeded a resolution of the nation's critical economic problems. These problems spring from an inefficient industrial sector inherited from the dictatorship, the woolly-headed policies of post-Caetano cabinets, low food output in the turmoil-ridden countryside, the massive influx of soldiers and civilians from Angola, Mozambique, and Guinea-Bissau, and the high cost of imports exacerbated by the quintupling of oil prices in recent years.

A series of deflationary measures—devaluation of the escudo, an increase in the bank rate, controls on the budget deficit, restrictions on imports—helped diminish Portugal's balance of payments deficit which totaled (U.S.) $1.4 billion in 1977. These deflationary steps were necessary for the Portuguese government to secure $800 million in credits from the International Monetary Fund and a consortium of 14 western countries.

Long-term economic relief lies with integration into the European Community. On October 16, Portugal formally began negotiating the terms of its membership, which will be achieved, in stages, over a ten-year transitional period provided democracy is preserved.

GEORGE W. GRAYSON
College of William and Mary

Portugal's President António Ramalho Eanes (*left*) meets with UN General Secretary Kurt Waldheim in New York.

UPI

─── **PORTUGAL • Information Highlights** ───

Official Name: Republic of Portugal.
Location: Southwestern Europe.
Area: 35,553 square miles (92,082 km²).
Population (1978 est.): 9,700,000.
Chief Cities (1974 est.): Lisbon, the capital, 775,000; Oporto, 312,000.
Government: *Head of state,* António Ramalho Eanes, president (took office July 1976). *Head of government,* Carlos da Mota Pinto, prime minister (took office October 1978). *Legislature* (unicameral)—Assembly of the Republic.
Monetary Unit: Escudo (45.75 escudos equal U.S.$1, Dec. 28, 1978).
Manufactures (major products): Textiles, clothing, cork products, electronic goods, transport equipment.
Agriculture (major products): Wine, grapes, tomatoes, wheat, olives, fruit, rice, cereals.

UPI

New U. S. Postmaster General William Bolger announces plans to develop a new mail system, INTELPOST.

POSTAL SERVICE

The U. S. Postal Service (USPS) remained a subject of controversy during 1978. Finances, rising mail rates, legislative policy, union-management relations, and experiments with new methods of electronic communications provided the main issues.

Finances. Though still reflecting a loss, the USPS's fiscal situation continued to improve. By November 1978 it seemed likely that the deficit for fiscal year (FY) 1978, ending September 30, would be less than that of $688 million for FY 1977. This compares with a $1.2 billion deficit for FY 1976 and one of more than (U. S.) $2 billion in 1970, the year before the USPS replaced the old Post Office Department. Several factors underlie this financial improvement. The total volume of U. S. mail of all kinds continued to increase to a projected 95 billion items in FY 1978, compared with 92 billion in 1977.

General rate increases for all classes of mail became effective on May 29, 1978. Of special significance was the rise in the first class letter rate from 13 to 15 cents for the first ounce. The first class letter has long been the most profitable category. Productivity has continued to improve as a result of mechanization, supervisory and management development, and better procedures and morale, none of which characterized the last years of the old department. During 1977 pro-

ductivity went up 5.2%, compared with 2.3% for the private sector in general.

By the end of 1978 a businesslike, no deficit postal system seemed almost within reach.

Legislative Proposals. Nevertheless, 1978 saw a concerted attack on the Postal Act of 1970. This was spearheaded by publishers, those who want to end parts of the postal monopoly, and others bearing the burden of a rising rate structure, the form of which was mandated by the 1970 legislation creating the USPS.

The 1970 law directs USPS to work to break even by apportioning "the costs of all postal operations to all users of the mail on a fair and equitable basis." That is, each type of user—general public, publisher, advertiser, bulk mailer, etc.—must pay his own share and no segment of the public can be required to subsidize any other user segment.

The principal proposals would abolish both the "fair share" and "no deficit" concepts and frankly subsidize postal operations from general tax revenues as a public and business service. Other schemes would open up segments of the postal monopoly to private enterprise, or return the entire service to a less independent and more politically controlled status. Initial strong support for a new postal act early in 1978 dwindled by autumn because of growing public opposition to any form of deficit financing and low priorities by the administration. But debate over postal communications cost allocations was expected to continue.

Collective Bargaining. By July 1978 law revision was overshadowed by postal labor negotiations. Main issues included pay and layoff protection. With personnel about 86% of total costs, USPS management fought pay increases more strongly than usual. Public anti-bureaucratic attitudes and legislative proposals to dismantle the postal system led the postal unions' leadership to accept an August proposal for a relatively small 19.5% pay increase over the three year life of the pact, balanced by continuance of a no layoff clause.

The rank and file of the three major postal unions turned down this offer. Negotiations stalemated except for an agreement to refer the pay and layoff provisions to binding arbitration. On Sept. 15, 1978, arbitrator James J. Healy ordered the August proposal into effect, but with two changes. He increased the pay award; and, for new employees, management gained revision of the no layoff clause.

The settlement was viewed as more favorable to USPS than prior agreements, but whether volume and productivity increases would balance added personnel costs was uncertain.

Electronic Communications. Of more long-run importance was evidence that the USPS was preparing to face the challenge of electronic communications. Already, 80% of U. S. messages go by telephonic means. In March USPS signed a contract with the Communications Satellite

Corp. to develop a system of facsimile mail called INTELPOST (International Electronic Post), aimed at business users who must transmit many long reports and action documents overseas.

Domestic organizations with large volumes of correspondence, bills, and invoices should benefit from a new ECOM (Electronic Computer Originated Mail) system developed through contract with Western Union. A new and cheaper system should permit large volumes of electronic messages to go easily from Western Union into the nationwide USPS delivery system.

World Postal Scene. Rising personnel costs and antiquated technology and procedures are plaguing postal systems worldwide. Though often criticized, the USPS leads the world in new postal technology and in productivity per employee, and is second only to Canada in low first class rates. However, Canadians' complaints about service and costs have been escalating; Canada's recent deficits have been proportionately much greater, and public subsidies much higher than in the United States.

On September 27 the Letter Carriers Union of Canada signed a tentative contract with the federal government, ending a four-day postal strike. Earlier in the year Prime Minister Pierre Elliott Trudeau announced plans to replace the Canadian Post Office with a semi-independent crown corporation.

PAUL P. VAN RIPER
Texas A&M University

J. P. LAFFONT, SYGMA

Alexander B. Campbell, premier of Prince Edward Island since 1966, retired from politics in September.

PRINCE EDWARD ISLAND

The province almost got a change of government in 1978—but not quite. It did get a new premier, and said goodbye to the old one, Alex Campbell.

Politics. In the provincial general election on April 24, the ruling Liberals won 17 legislative seats and the Conservatives 15. After providing a Speaker, the Liberals were left with a razor-thin majority of one. The election campaign never generated any commanding issues, although the Tories complained that the government was not devoting enough attention to primary industries.

Bennett Campbell, a 35-year-old teacher from Cardigan, a Member of the Legislative Assembly (MLA) since 1970, and a member of the provincial cabinet since 1972, was sworn in September 18 as the island's 25th premier. He replaced Alex Campbell, premier since 1966, who retired from politics.

Fiscal. The government presented a budget June 15. A $12 million deficit was projected on expenditures of $265 million and revenues of $253 million but the government dipped into an investment account to reduce the deficit to $3.2 million. At least 15 departments and agencies underwent budget cuts.

Legislative. The legislature was prorogued July 12 after a five-week session. Lt. Gov. Gordon Bennett gave royal assent to 25 pieces of legislation, among them a family law reform bill based on the concept of the equality of partners to a marriage. Another bill extended rent controls indefinitely, but provided an annual review. The salaries of MLAs were increased to $10,000 from $7,000 and expense allowances to $5,000 a year from $3,000.

Road to the Isles. The Atlantic Provinces Chamber of Commerce in its annual policy statement issued October 10 recommended that the federal government take a new look at a Prince Edward Island-New Brunswick causeway. The chamber suggested that a fixed crossing between P. E. I. and the mainland—promised by Ottawa in 1958—"becomes more imperative each year."

JOHN BEST, *Chief, Canada World News*

PRINCE EDWARD ISLAND • Information Highlights

Area: 2,184 square miles (5,656 km²).
Population (1978 est.): 122,200.
Chief Cities (1976 census): Charlottetown, the capital, 17,063; Summerside, 8,592.
Government (1978): *Chief Officers*—lt. gov., Gordon L. Bennett; premier, Bennett Campbell (Liberal); chief justice, Supreme Court, John Paton Nicholson. *Legislature*—Legislative Assembly, 32 members.
Education (1976–77): Enrollment—public elementary and secondary schools, 27,480 pupils; Indian (federal) schools, 50; post-secondary, 2,210. Total expenditures, $47,891,000.
Personal Income (average weekly salary, May 1978): $194.56.
Unemployment Rate (July 1978, seasonally adjusted): 9.1%.
(All monetary figures given in Canadian dollars.)

PRISONS

The number of inmates in U. S. prisons continued to rise and the length of terms being served increased. Severe overcrowding, with accompanying tensions, has prompted almost every state to initiate plans for the construction of additional prisons. The Justice Department issued a set of detailed standards aimed at improving, and making more uniform, conditions in the nation's prisons, which contained more than 500,000 persons late in 1978. A Supreme Court decision cast doubts on the legality of capital punishment statutes in approximately 25 states. A statement by United Nations Ambassador Andrew Young that the United States had its own "political prisoners" caused a stir in some circles, but prisons remained, with respect to public awareness and budgetary commitments, the most remote part of the criminal justice system, containing disproportionately large numbers of minorities and the poor.

Crowding. For the past several years 200 to 400 more persons have entered the nation's prisons each week than have been discharged. The United States has the highest imprisonment rate in the Western world, more than double that found in any other NATO country. On any day in 1978 there were more than 500,000 persons behind bars, an increase of more than 30% since 1973. Severe overcrowding was cited by officials as an important factor in two prison uprisings in July. At the Pontiac Correctional Center in Illinois, built in 1871 to hold 600 prisoners, nearly 2,000 inmates staged a riot in which three guards were killed. In the Georgia State Prison in Reidsville, built to house 1,100 prisoners and currently containing almost 2,500, a riot broke out on July 23 in which a guard and two inmates were stabbed to death. Although there had been repeated racial violence in the prison, and admitted overcrowding, Georgia officials blamed the riot on television press coverage of the Pontiac incident the previous day.

With prison officials in more than a dozen states under court orders to reduce overcrowding and improve conditions, plans for the construction of new prisons continued in almost every state. Costs for a single new prison cell can be as much as $30,000, and one expert estimates that if all prisons now being planned were built, the cost would exceed (U. S.) $3 billion. In California, after voters approved property tax cutback Proposition 13, prison construction funds were dropped from the state budget.

National Standards. The buildings currently used as prisons in the United States were built over a long period of time, a few before the Civil War. Jurisdiction over the inmates rests with officials at many different levels of government—federal, state, and local. Consequently, conditions vary greatly among the country's 200 long-term institutions, approximately 1,000 minimum and medium security facilities, and more than 4,000 locally administered jails. Many of these facilities are not required to report to a central authority, and few keep strictly accurate and adequate records. In August, the U. S. Department of Justice and the American Correctional Association, a group of professionals and scholars in the corrections field, drafted a set of uniform and specific standards designed to improve conditions in the nation's prisons. Seven manuals, containing more than 1,500 standards, were issued for adult male, female, and juvenile correctional facilities and programs. Areas covered include forms of discipline, rights of inmates, living and working conditions, recreation activities, and administrative principles. Federal facilities would be required to meet the standards while other prisons would be urged to comply on a voluntary basis through a system of accreditation. To be accredited, local officials would allow their facilities to be regularly monitored and inspected according to the national standards. If the facility did not pass the inspections, the features could be used to justify more appropriations from state and federal governments by citing specific needs which prevent the facility from complying with national standards.

Death Penalty. In 1972 the Supreme Court decided that capital punishment could stand but struck down existing laws on the ground that they were "freakishly" imposed, often with discrimination against minorities. In the ensuing years many states enacted new laws in an effort to comply with the court's decisions. Except for the execution of Gary Gilmore by a Utah firing squad in January 1977, there has been a *de facto* moratorium on capital punishment in the United States since 1966. But by mid-1978 there were almost 500 men and women in 24 states awaiting execution. A 7–1 Supreme Court decision in July 1978 ruled against an Ohio law, judging that it excessively limited the consideration of "mitigating circumstances," and therewith removed 101 prisoners from that state's death row and raised serious questions about the legality of capital punishment statutes in 25 other states. The decision virtually ensured several more years of litigation before a constitutionally acceptable death-penalty law could be devised.

Political Prisoners. Ambassador Andrew Young's statement, made just before judgment was announced in the trials of Soviet dissidents Aleksandr Ginzburg and Anatoly Shcharansky, that the United States had "hundreds, maybe thousands of people I would categorize as political prisoners," provoked a storm of controversy. Although Young, who had been arrested in the 1960's as a civil rights activist, stated he was not equating the political freedom of the two countries, his statement provoked numerous responses and denials.

See also CRIME; LAW.

DONALD GOODMAN
John Jay College of Criminal Justice
City University of New York

PRIZES AND AWARDS

NOBEL PRIZES ($165,000 each)

Chemistry: Peter Mitchell, British biochemist, director of Glynn Research Laboratories in England, for his explanation of how plants and animals convert nutrition into energy.

Economics: Herbert A. Simon, professor at Carnegie-Mellon University, Pittsburgh, for pioneering research in the "decision-making process within economic organizations."

Literature: Isaac Bashevis Singer, Polish-born U. S. short-story writer and novelist in Yiddish, "for his impassioned narrative art which, with roots in Polish-Jewish cultural tradition, brings universal human conditions to life."

Medicine or Physiology: Daniel Nathans and Hamilton C. Smith, microbiologists at Johns Hopkins University, and Werner Arber of the University of Basel in Switzerland for their research with restrictive enzymes which "should help in the prevention and treatment of malformations, hereditary disease and cancer."

Peace Prize: Menahem Begin, prime minister of Israel, and Anwar el-Sadat, president of Egypt, "to honor past actions" and to "encourage further efforts to work out practical solutions" toward a Mideast peace.

Physics: Arno A. Penzias and Robert W. Wilson ($82,500 shared), Bell Telephone Laboratories, for their discovery of cosmic microwave background radiation which has "made it possible to obtain information about cosmic processes that took place a very long time ago, at the time of the creation of the universe"; and to Pyotr Leontevitch Kapitsa ($82,500), Russian scientist, whose "discoveries, ideas and new techniques—such as a device to produce liquid helium—have been basic to the modern expansion of the science of low-temperature physics."

ART

American Academy and Institute of Arts and Letters Awards
 Academy-Institute Awards ($3,000): art—William Dole, Daniel Maloney, Herman Maril, Richard McDermott Miller, Sara Roszak, Reuben Tam, Ulfert Wilke; music—Wallace Berry, Curtis O. B. Curtis-Smith, Elie Siegmeister, Richard Swift
 Arnold W. Brunner Prize in Architecture: Cesar Pelli
 Distinguished Service to the Arts: Rep. John Brademas
 Charles E. Ives Scholarships in Music ($4,000): Daniel Brew-Baker, Justin Dello Joio, Lee Scott Goldstein, Arthur W. Gottschalk, Thomas Mountain, David Olan
 Award of Merit Medal for Sculpture: Tony Smith
 Rosenthal Award in Art ($4,000): Clifford Ross
 Marjorie Peabody Waite Award ($1,500): Dane Rudhyar

American Institute of Architects Awards
 Gold Medal Award: Philip Johnson
 AIA 25-Year Award: Charles Eames Home in Pacific Palisades, California

"Dance" Magazine Awards: Raoul Gelabert; Bella Lewitzky; Mikhail Baryshnikov

Kennedy Center Honors: Marian Anderson, contralto; George Balanchine, choreographer; Richard Rodgers, composer; Arthur Rubinstein, pianist; Fred Astaire, singer-dancer-actor

National Academy of Recording Arts and Sciences Grammy Awards for excellence in phonograph records
 Album of the year: *Rumours,* Fleetwood Mac
 Classical album of the year: *Concert of the Century,* recorded live from Carnegie Hall, May 18, 1976, various artists, Thomas Frost, producer
 Country music song: *Don't It Make My Brown Eyes Blue,* Richard Leigh, songwriter
 Jazz vocal performance: *Look to the Rainbow,* Al Jarreau
 New artist: Debby Boone
 Record of the year: *Hotel California,* The Eagles
 Song of the year: *Evergreen,* Barbra Streisand and Paul Williams; *You Light Up My Life,* Joe Brooks (tied)

Pulitzer Prize for Music: Michael Colgrass, *Déja Vu for Percussion Quartet and Orchestra*

UPI

Debby Boone won a Grammy as 1978's best new artist.

JOURNALISM

Sidney Hillman Awards: Bill Moyers for his CBS-TV documentary "The Fire Next Door"; Philip Caputo for his book *A Rumor of War;* Eliot Marshall, *The New Republic,* for a series on health care; Stan Swofford, *The Greensboro* (N. C.) *Daily News,* for a series on the Wilmington 10 defendants

Overseas Press Club Awards
 Book on foreign affairs: David McCullough, *The Path Between the Seas*
 Business news reporting from abroad: Cary Reich, *Institutional Investor*
 Cartoon on foreign affairs: Ed Fischer, *Omaha World-Herald*
 Daily newspaper or wire service reporting from abroad: Robert C. Toth, *Los Angeles Times,* for his coverage of the Soviet Union
 Magazine interpretation of foreign affairs: Joseph B. Treaster, *Atlantic Monthly*
 Magazine reporting from abroad: *Newsweek*
 Photographic reporting from abroad: James P. Blair, *National Geographic*
 Radio interpretation of foreign news: NBC news, "Euro-Communism: A Quiet Revolution"
 Radio spot news from abroad: CBS news coverage of Egypt's Premier Sadat in Israel
 Television interpretation of foreign affairs: ABC news, the Barbara Walters Sadat-Begin interviews
 Bob Considine Memorial Award: Jim Hoagland, *The Washington Post*
 Robert Capa Gold Medal: Eddie Adams, The Associated Press
 Madeline Dane Ross Award: Reza Baraheni, "The Shah's Torture Chambers," *Penthouse Magazine*

George Polk Memorial Awards
 Commentary: Red Smith, *The New York Times*
 Criticism: Peter S. Prescott, *Newsweek*
 Editorial cartoons: Jeff MacNelly, *The Richmond News Leader*
 Foreign reporting: Robert C. Toth, *Los Angeles Times*
 Local radio and television: John Stossel, WCBS-TV News
 Local reporting: Len Ackland, *The Des Moines Register*
 Magazine reporting: Daniel Lang, *The New Yorker*
 National reporting: Walter Pincus, *The Washington Post*
 News photography: Eddie Adams, The Associated Press
 Radio and television reporting: Barry Lando, "60 Minutes"
 Science: *The New England Journal of Medicine*
 Special award for professional "integrity": Carey McWilliams, *The Nation*

Pulitzer Prizes

Commentary: William Safire, *The New York Times*

Criticism: Walter Kerr, *The New York Times*

Editorial cartooning: Jeffrey K. MacNelly, *The Richmond News Leader*

Editorial writing: Meg Greenfield, *The Washington Post*

Feature photography: J. Ross Baughman, The Associated Press

General local reporting: Richard Whitt, Louisville *Courier-Journal*

International reporting: Henry Kamm, *The New York Times*

National reporting: Gaylord Shaw, *Los Angeles Times*

Public service: Jonathan Neumann and William K. Marimow, *The Philadelphia Inquirer*

Special award: Richard L. Strout, for Washington coverage, *The Christian Science Monitor* and the *New Republic*

Special local reporting: Anthony R. Dolan, *Stamford* (Conn.) *Advocate*

Spot news photography: John Blair, United Press International

LITERATURE

Academy of American Poets Walt Whitman Award ($1,000): Karen Snow, *Wonders*

American Academy and Institute of Arts and Letters Awards

Academy-Institute Awards ($3,000): Renata Adler, William Arrowsmith, Lerone Bennett, Jr., Terrence Des Prés, Leslie Epstein, Michael Herr, Murray Kempton, Alison Lurie, Toni Morrison, Page Smith

Gold Medal for history: Barbara W. Tuchman

Gold Medal for the short story: Peter Taylor

Rosenthal Award ($4,000): Douglas Day

Zabel Award ($2,500): Joan Didion

Bancroft Prizes for best books in American history or diplomacy ($4,000 each): Alfred D. Chandler, Jr., *The Visible Hand: The Managerial Revolution in American Business;* Morton J. Horwitz, *The Transformation of American Law: 1780–1860*

Canada's Governor General's Literary Awards

English fiction: Timothy Findley, *The Wars*

French fiction: Gabrielle Roy, *Ces enfants de ma vie*

English nonfiction: Frank Scott, *Essays on the Constitution*

French nonfiction: Denis Monière, *Le développement des idéologies au Québec*

English poetry and drama: Douglas Gordon Jones, *Under the Thunder the Flowers Light Up the Earth*

French poetry and drama: Michel Garneau, *Les célébrations* and *Adidou Adidouce* (declined award)

National Book Awards ($1,000)

Biography: W. Jackson Bate, *Samuel Johnson*

Children's literature: Judith and Herbert Kohl, *The View from the Oak: The Private Worlds of Other Creatures*

Contemporary thought: Gloria Emerson, *Winners and Losers: Battles, Retreats, Gains, Losses and Ruins From a Long War*

Fiction: Mary Lee Settle, *Blood Tie*

History: David McCullough, *The Path Between the Seas: The Creation of the Panama Canal 1870–1914*

Poetry: Howard Nemerov, *Collected Poems*

Translation: Richard and Clara Winston, Uwe George's *In the Deserts of This Earth*

Special achievement medal: S. J. Perelman

Pulitzer Prizes

Biography: Walter Jackson Bate, *Samuel Johnson*

Fiction: James Alan McPherson, *Elbow Room*

General nonfiction: Carl Sagan, *The Dragons of Eden: Speculations on the Evolution of Human Intelligence*

History: Alfred D. Chandler, Jr., *The Visible Hand: The Managerial Revolution in American Business*

Poetry: Howard Nemerov, *Collected Poems*

Special award: E. B. White, for the full body of his work

MOTION PICTURES

Academy of Motion Picture Arts and Sciences ("Oscar") Awards

Actor: Richard Dreyfuss, *The Goodbye Girl*

Actress: Diane Keaton, *Annie Hall*

Cinematography: Vilmos Zsigmond, *Close Encounters of the Third Kind*

Costumes: John Mollo, *Star Wars*

Director: Woody Allen, *Annie Hall*

Documentary feature: *Who Are the Debolts? And Where Did They Get Nineteen Kids?*

Film: *Annie Hall*

Foreign language film: *Madame Rosa* (France)

Original score: John Williams, *Star Wars*

Original screenplay: Woody Allen and Marshall Brickman, *Annie Hall*

Original song score and adaptation: Jonathan Tunick, *A Little Night Music*

Screenplay based on material from another medium: Alvin Sargent, *Julia*

Song: Joseph Brooks, *You Light Up My Life*

Supporting actor: Jason Robards, *Julia*

Supporting actress: Vanessa Redgrave, *Julia*

Jean Hersholt Humanitarian Award: Charleton Heston

Irving G. Thalberg Award: Walter Mirisch

Honorary Award: Margaret Booth

Cannes Film Festival Awards

Best actor: Jon Voight, *Coming Home*

Best actress (shared): Jill Clayburgh, *An Unmarried Woman;* Isabelle Uppert, *Violette Nozoiere*

Best director: Nagisa Oshima, *Empire of Passion* (Japan)

Best film: *The Tree of Clogs* (Italy)

Special jury prize (shared): *The Shout* (Britain); *Ciao Mascio* (Italy)

PUBLIC SERVICE

B'nai B'rith Anti-Defamation League's Hubert H. Humphrey Freedom Prize ($10,000 shared): John Chancellor, NBC News; Walter Cronkite, CBS News; Barbara Walters, ABC News; "for their initial interviews with Prime Minister Begin and President Sadat which gave impetus and thrust to the peace process between Israel and Egypt"

Louis Dembitz Brandeis Medal for distinguished legal services: Edward H. Levi, Law School, Stanford University, California

National Aeronautics and Space Administration's Distinguished Public Service Medal: Rep. Olin E. Teague (D.-Tex.), retiring chairman, House Science and Technology Committee

Roger E. Joseph Memorial Award ($10,000): Victor Kugler, Toronto, Canada, who hid the Anne Frank family from the Nazis for 25 months for "encouraging the values and ideals which derive from religious teachings"

Rockefeller Public Service Awards ($10,000 each): Benny Ray Bailey, Warren Grady Stumbo, East Kentucky Health Services Center, for "outstanding work in the area of promoting the improvement of health and health services and controlling health costs"; Margaret C. Snyder, UN Economic Commission for Africa, for "outstanding work in the area of strengthening international cooperation in dealing with key issues of interdependence"; Stanley Sporkin, Securities and Exchange Commission, Charles R. Work, attorney, and William A. Hamilton, Institute for Law and Social Research, for "outstanding contribution

Jason Robards received a second consecutive Oscar.

UPI

in the area of administering justice and reducing crime"; Rev. Jesse Jackson, civil-rights leader, for public service

U. S. Presidential Medal of Freedom (presented by President Jimmy Carter, July 26, 1978): Arthur J. Goldberg

SCIENCE

Bristol-Myers Award for distinguished achievement in cancer research ($25,000): James and Elizabeth Miller, biochemists

Columbia University's Louisa Gross Horwitz Prize for research in biology and biochemistry ($25,000): David H. Hubel, Harvard University; Vernon B. Mountcastle, Johns Hopkins University; Torsten N. Wiesel, Harvard University

Congressional Space Medals of Honor (presented by President Jimmy Carter, Oct. 1, 1978): Neil A. Armstrong; Frank Borman; Charles Conrad, Jr.; John H. Glenn, Jr.; Virgil I. (Gus) Grissom (posthumously); Alan B. Shepard, Jr.

Albert Lasker Awards ($15,0000)

Basic medical research (shared): John Hughes, Imperial College of Science and Technology, London; Hans W. Kosterlitz, University of Aberdeen; Solomon H. Snyder, Johns Hopkins University

Clinical medical research (shared): Robert Austrian, University of Pennsylvania School of Medicine; Emil C. Gotslich, Rockefeller University; Michael Heidelberger, New York University School of Medicine

Special public service (shared): Theodore Cooper, former director of the National Heart, Lung, and Blood Institute; Elliot L. Richardson, former Secretary of Health, Education, and Welfare

Pahlevi Environment Prize ($50,000): Thor Heyerdahl, Norwegian explorer and ethnologist; Mohamed El-Kassas, Egyptian plant ecologist

Theodore Weicker Memorial Award ($10,000): Ernest Bueding, Johns Hopkins University Medical School

Wolf Foundation Awards ($100,000)

Agricultural science (shared): George F. Sprague, University of Illinois; John C. Walker, University of Wisconsin

Chemistry: Carl Djerassi, Stanford University, California

Mathematics (shared): Izrail M. Gelfand, Moscow State University; Carl L. Siegel, University of Göttingen, West Germany

Medicine (shared): Jean Dausset, Paris; George D. Snell, Jackson Laboratories, Bar Harbor, Maine; J. Van Rood, University of Leiden, Netherlands

Physics: Chien Shiung Wu, Columbia University

TELEVISION AND RADIO

Academy of Television Arts and Sciences ("Emmy") Awards

Actor—comedy series: Carroll O'Connor, *All in the Family* (CBS)

Actor—drama series: Edward Asner, *Lou Grant* (CBS)

Actor—drama or comedy special: Fred Astaire, *A Family Upside Down* (NBC)

Actor—limited series: Michael Moriarty, *Holocaust* (NBC)

Actor—single performance in a drama or comedy series: Barnard Hughes, "Judge," *Lou Grant* (CBS)

Actress—comedy series: Jean Stapleton, *All in the Family* (CBS)

Actress—drama series: Sada Thompson, *Family* (ABC)

Actress—drama or comedy special: Joanne Woodward, "See How She Runs," *G. E. Theater* (CBS)

Actress—limited series: Meryl Streep, *Holocaust* (NBC)

Actress—single performance in a drama or comedy series: Rita Moreno, "The Paper Palace," *The Rockford Files* (NBC)

Children's special: *Halloween is Grinch Night* (ABC)

Classical program in the performing arts: American Ballet Theater, "Giselle," *Live from Lincoln Center* (PBS)

Comedy series: *All in the Family* (CBS)

Comedy-variety or music series: *The Muppet Show* (SYN)

Drama series: *The Rockford Files* (NBC)

Informational series: *The Body Human* (CBS)

Limited series: *Holocaust* (NBC)

Program achievement: *The Tonight Show Starring Johnny Carson* (NBC)

Special—drama or comedy: *The Gathering* (ABC)

Supporting actor—comedy series: Rob Reiner, *All in the Family* (CBS)

Supporting actor—drama series: Robert Vaughn, *Washington: Behind Closed Doors* (ABC)

Supporting actress—comedy series: Julie Kavner, *Rhoda* (CBS)

Supporting actress—dramatic series: Nancy Marchand, *Lou Grant* (CBS)

The Humanitas Prizes

$25,000 award for 90-minute category: John Sacret Young for *Special Olympics*

$15,000 award for one-hour category: Carol Evan McKeany and David Jacobs for "Annie Laurie" presented on *Family*

$10,000 award for the 30-minute category: Larry Rhine and Mel Tolkin for "The Brother" presented on *All in the Family*

Special nonmonetary award for a news/documentary: "The Aliens," *CBS Reports*

George Foster Peabody Awards

Radio: KXYZ, Detroit, *Winter's Fear: The Children, the Killer, the Search;* Paul Hume, WGMS, Rockville, Md., *A Variable Feast;* WHA, Madison, Wisc., *Earplay;* KSJN, Saint Paul, *The Prairie was Quiet;* KPFA, Berkeley, Calif., *Science Story;* National Public Radio, Washington, *Crossroads: Sea Island Sketches;* WHLN, Harlan, Ky., for coverage of the April 1977 floods in Harlan

Television: NBC, *Tut: The Boy King* and, with Arthur Rankin and Jules Bass, *The Hobbit;* ABC, David Wolper, *Roots* and Lorimar Productions and *Green Eyes;* WNET and WETA, Arlington, Va., *The McNeil/Lehrer Report;* WNET, *A Good Dissonance Like a Man;* WNET, *Police Tapes;* WNBC, *F. I. N. D. Investigative Reports,* part of *NewsCenter 4;* WNBC, *Buyline: Betty Furness;* WPIX, *The Lifer's Group—I Am My Brother's Keeper,* part of WPIX *Editorial Report;* WCBS, *Camera Three;* The Metropolitan Opera Association, *Live From the Met,* as exemplified by performances of *La Bohème* and *Rigoletto;* Norman Lear, *All in the Family;* KABC, Los Angeles, *Police Accountability,* part of *Eyewitness News;* KCMO, Kansas City, Mo., *Where Have All the Flood Cars Gone?,* part of *Eyewitness News;* WBTV, Charlotte, N. C., *The Rowe String Quartet Plays on Your Imagination;* London Weekend Television of London, *Upstairs, Downstairs;* MTM Productions, *The Mary Tyler Moore Show;* Steve Allen, KCET, Los Angeles, *Meeting of the Minds;* Multimedia Program Productions, Cincinnati, *Joshua's Confusion*

THEATER

Antoinette Perry ("Tony") Awards

Actor (drama): Barnard Hughes, *Da*

Actor (musical): John Cullum, *On the Twentieth Century*

Actress (drama): Jessica Tandy, *The Gin Game*

Actress (musical): Liza Minnelli, *The Act*

Choreography: Bob Fosse, *Dancin'*

Costume design: Edward Gorey, *Dracula*

Director (drama): Melvin Bernhardt, *Da*

Director (musical): Richard Maltby, Jr., *Ain't Misbehavin'*

Featured actor (drama): Lester Rawlins, *Da*

Featured actor (musical): Kevin Klein, *On the Twentieth Century*

Featured actress (drama): Ann Wedgeworth, *Chapter Two*

Featured actress (musical): Nell Carter, *Ain't Misbehavin'*

Most innovative production of a revival: *Dracula*

Musical: *Ain't Misbehavin'*

Play: *Da*

Score: Cy Coleman, Betty Comden, Adolph Green, *On the Twentieth Century*

Special awards: Charles Moss; Stan Dragoti; The Long Wharf Theater, New Haven, Conn.

Lawrence Langer Award for distinguished lifetime achievement in the theater: Irving Berlin

The New York Drama Critics' Circle Theater Awards

American play: no award

Musical: *Ain't Misbehavin'*

Play: *Da*

Pulitzer Prize for Drama: Donald L. Coburn, *The Gin Game*

PUBLISHING

Although publishers recorded record profits from higher circulation and advertising revenues, some dark spots remained. Higher costs for labor and paper, along with problems with the U. S. Postal Service, resulted in some caution.

New Yorkers were without their three major dailies for three months after pressmen went out on strike. And the controversial court case involving *The New York Times* reporter M. A. Farber reached the U. S. Supreme Court. At issue were the notes Farber used in a series of stories involving three New Jersey murders in the mid-1960's. Farber was jailed briefly, and both he and his paper were heavily fined by New Jersey courts. The Supreme Court refused to review contempt of court convictions against Farber and the *Times*.

Another free press challenge came in the Supreme Court's decision in the *Stanford Daily* case which upheld the authority of the police to obtain a search warrant and without warning conduct a search of the newspaper offices.

Books. Record sales, higher prices, and worry over mergers highlighted the book world in 1978. *Publishers Weekly,* the authority for the industry, reported industry sales of (U. S.) $4.6 billion in 1977 and $5 billion for 1978. It also estimated that there were 478,000 book titles in print, with 27,413 added in 1977.

Paperback rights brought millions, with Mario Puzo's *Fools Die* selling for $2.2 million; Colleen McCullough's *The Thorn Birds* for $1.9 million; and William Safire's *Full Disclosure* for $1.4 million.

Authors were concerned that mergers might limit their markets. Among firms involved were Charles Scribner's Sons and Atheneum, CBS and Fawcett Publications, Prentice-Hall and Arco, J. B. Lippincott and Harper & Row.

The American Booksellers Association was concerned that only 5 to 6% of the population were regular book buyers. Although revenues were up, the numbers of volumes sold hardly changed.

Television and movie tie-ins aided sales of such titles as *Star Wars, Close Encounters, Jaws 2, Holocaust, I, Claudius,* and others. Books on exercising were high among bestsellers, topped by James Fixx' *The Complete Book on Running.* Erma Bombeck answered the nation's search for humor with her bestseller, *If Life Is a Bowl of Cherries—What Am I Doing in the Pits?*

Newsweek reported on "a lusty tale of power, money, and ambition" in an account of a few authors who dominate the market. Mario Puzo's *Fools Die* quickly hit the top list, earned a premium price from Book-of-the-Month Club and $25,000 for a portion in the new *Life* magazine. James A. Michener's *Chesapeake* likewise jumped out in front.

Libraries feared budget cuts in taxpayers' revolts. Legal problems involved former agents of the Central Intelligence Agency (CIA), their publishers, and the U. S. Justice Department. The American Library Association complained of increasing pressures to censor material while state obscenity laws were tested in courts.

Echoes of Watergate were heard. Richard Nixon's publisher, Warner Books, "delighted with the success" of *RN: The Memoirs of Richard Nixon,* signed him for another book. Others urged: "Don't buy books by crooks or unindicted coconspirators."

Religious books were strong again, with new volumes expected from Billy Graham, Roy Rogers, Dale Evans, and others. *The Living Bible*'s cumulated sales passed 23 million; the *Good News Bible* sold more than 10 million and Graham's books more than 12 million copies.

Book clubs and mail order firms reported record sales of $750 million, while both imports and exports increased. Harlequin Books, with 12 new titles monthly, were selling very well.

James Herriot's *All Things Wise and Wonderful* led *Publishers Weekly*'s nonfiction list at the start of 1978. Later leaders included *The Complete Book of Running; If Life Is a Bowl of Cherries . . .;* Carlos Castaneda's *The Second Ring of Power;* Nancy Friday's *My Mother, My Self;* H. R. Haldeman's *The Ends of Power;* and Theodore H. White's *In Search of History: A Personal Adventure.*

In fiction, J. R. R. Tolkien's *The Silmarillion* and Colleen McCullough's *The Thorn Birds* were early leaders, followed by Sidney Sheldon's *Bloodline,* Graham Greene's *The Human Factor,* Robert Ludlum's *The Holcroft Covenant,* Judith Krantz' *Scruples,* James A. Michener's *Chesapeake,* and Puzo's *Fools Die.*

Hardcover successes moved to paperback leadership, including Dr. Wayne Dyer's *Your Erroneous Zones;* Steven Spielberg's *Close Encounters of the Third Kind;* Robin Cook's *Coma: A Novel;* John Jakes' *The Lawless;* Hank Searls' *Jaws 2;* McCullough's *The Thorn Birds;* Harold Robbins' *Dreams Die First;* and Jay Anson's *The Amityville Horror.*

Magazines. The magazine business was "hot" in 1978. *Life* was back and *Look* was scheduled for 1979. Record incomes were reported from advertising, while per-copy price hikes aided circulation income.

Life was "less newsy, higher quality, more pictorial" than when halted in 1972. Circulation, started at 700,000, was not projected to reach its record 8.5 million of the 1960's. *Look* was resurrected by Daniel Filipacchi, French publisher of *Nouveau Paris Match.*

With advertising revenues of (U. S.) $1.4 billion for the first eight months of 1978, the industry was headed for another record year. In Canada, similar optimism prevailed, with locally produced magazines likewise reporting gains.

TV Guide broke advertising records with $176 million in 1977; more was expected in 1978. It continued its circulation lead, some 20 million copies weekly. Time, Inc., reported record revenues of (U. S.)$1.25 billion in 1977 and profits of $90.5 million.

Leaders at mid-1978 included 48 magazines with a million or more circulation. *TV Guide* averaged 19.8 million per issue, according to Audit Bureau of Circulation, followed by *Reader's Digest,* 18.5; *National Geographic,* 9.9; *Family Circle,* 8.2; *Better Homes & Gardens* 8; *McCall's,* 6.5; *Ladies' Home Journal,* 6; *National Enquirer,* 5.7; and *Good Housekeeping,* 5.2. In advertising revenue, *TV Guide* reported $90 million for the first half of 1978, slightly ahead of *Time,* with $89.7 million.

Tony Schwartz, an associate editor of *Newsweek,* said people "want to read about themselves and how to make their lives better." Such feelings resulted in more consumer and service articles, with more help in handling money. Less news was desired about societal trends, while specialization continued with such newcomers as: *Executive Female Digest, Elected Public Officials, Geo, Human Nature, Male Chauvinist, Omni, Professional Woman, Self, Sport Style, Texas Woman, Your Place, Vital,* and others. Some 270 magazines were started in 1977.

Success was indicated by increased frequency of editions. *Family Circle* was to become a "new kind of marketing tool" as a triweekly in 1979; *Woman's Day* went to 14 issues; *Esquire, Forbes,* and *Fortune* were among those that went fortnightly. *Restaurant Business* added three issues for 1979, reflecting the boom in this business.

Reader's Digest revived its Arabic edition, dead since 1967. *Family Circle* added a Japanese edition; *Better Homes & Gardens* went to Australia, *Fortune* to Asia, and *Newsweek* to Latin America. *Parents' Magazine* was sold to a West German publisher, Gruner & Jahr.

The merger between W. R. Simmons & Associates and Axiom Market Research Bureau into Simmons Market Research Bureau is expected to quiet controversies over readership studies that have marked the industry in recent years.

With potential paper shortage and higher postage costs some publishers switched to gravure printing to use lighter-weight coated stock. Others published in more areas to cut zone costs. Private carriers expanded efforts in major cities to offset postal hikes ahead.

Black-oriented magazines such as *Ebony* continued to lose qualified staffers. Owner John Johnson noted a "definite shortage of black salespeople." The Internal Revenue Service and associations with scientific journals debated tax charges on their ad pages. Meanwhile, consumer groups sought to make publishers more responsible for the contents of advertisements.

The *Christian Herald* reached its 100th year, *Sunset* its 80th, and *Forbes* its 60th.

Newspapers. Record-breaking deals were made in the newspaper world in 1978, led by the $370 million merger of Gannett and Combined Communications Corp. which Gannett chairman Paul Miller termed a "logical media mix."

Among many other changes were Gannett's purchase of the Wilmington, Del., *News-Journal* for $60 million; the Time, Inc., acquisition of *The Washington Star* for $20 million; and Capital Cities' purchase of the Wilkes-Barre papers for $9 million.

The trend to group ownership continued. By late 1978, *Editor & Publisher* reported "half of the circulation of the 1,753 daily newspapers roll off the presses owned by 20 publishing groups." For the 668 Sunday papers the percentage reached 56. There are 167 groups owning 1,095 dailies. Knight-Ridder leads in combined circulation, while Gannett, with 79 units, controls the largest number of titles.

The top ten groups accounted for 22.6 million of the 61,495,140 total daily circulation in the United States. Groups in order of circulation were Knight-Ridder, Gannett, Tribune (Chicago), Newhouse, Dow Jones, Scripps-Howard, Times Mirror, Hearst, Cox, and Thomson.

Knight-Ridder planned a $20 million plant for the Lexington, Ky., *Herald-Leader. The Baltimore Sun* set aside $24 million for pressroom equipment, *The Detroit Free Press* designed a completely computer-controlled mailroom in its new $45 million facility, and the Pittsburgh *Press* and Cincinnati *Enquirer* also planned extensive expansion.

Publishers added to their commitments. The *Los Angeles Times* upped its San Diego operations, while the Orlando, Fla., *Sentinel Star* added 11 "little sentinel" editions for its trade area. *The Wall Street Journal* added its 11th domestic printing plant, near Seattle.

Circulation leaders in 1978, according to the Audit Bureau of Circulation, included the New York *Daily News,* 1,824,836; *Los Angeles Times,* 1,020,208; *The New York Times,* 878,714; followed by the *Chicago Tribune,* Detroit *News,* New York *Post, Chicago Sun Times, The Detroit Free Press, The Washington Post,* and Philadelphia *Bulletin.* Sunday leaders were the New York *Daily News, The New York Times, Los Angeles Times,* and *Chicago Tribune,* all over a million.

The 102-year-old *Chicago Daily News* died, suffering from declining circulation, an ailment affecting afternoon dailies. In New York the new *Trib* survived three months, losing probably $4 million. Labor problems and the failure of merchants to provide ads were blamed.

Newsprint consumption, estimated at 10.5 million tons in 1978, was predicted to reach 12.5 by 1985. Experiments continued with kenaf, a fibrous plant that might replace woodpulp in newsprint.

See THE POWER OF THE MEDIA (page 38).

WILLIAM H. TAFT, *University of Missouri*

Oxford University Press, 1478–1978

In 1478—14 years before Columbus discovered America and only some 25 years after Gutenberg developed the art of printing from movable type—an itinerant German printer, Theodoric, surnamed Rood ("The Red" in Low German), printed his first book, *Exposito Sancti Hieronymi in Symbolum Apostolorum,* in Oxford, England. From that small beginning exactly 500 years ago, the Oxford University Press eventually grew into the oldest and most influential publishing house in the English-speaking world.

For the first 150 years, printing in Oxford was generally undistinguished, reflecting in quality and substance the shifting trends of royal politics and censorship. There were, however, a number of important volumes: Capt. John Smith's *A Map of Virginia,* 1612, the first description of that colony; Robert Burton's celebrated *Anatomy of Melancholy,* 1621; and Heylin's *Microcosmos,* 1621, the first modern work on geography printed in England.

The Oxford University Press, as it exists today, was established in the mid-17th century at the initiative of two eminent men, Archbishop Laud and Bishop Fell. From the beginning, the intent was to publish learned and educational books, as well as the Bible. The tremendous success of Clarendon's *History of the Rebellion* at the end of the century brought both prestige and profit to the university. Hoping for continued profits, the university sought to expand and develop the Press, but its output during the first half of the 18th century was disappointing; only 14 new titles were published. In 1755, William Blackstone became a director of the Press and put forward strong recommendations for its reorganization. These measures coincided with a rising demand for Bibles, which during the middle of the 19th century became the commercial mainstay of the Press.

The most important figure in the Oxford University Press during the 19th century was Bartholomew Price. At his urging, the Press entered the field of text book publishing, which to this day remains one of its central and most rewarding concerns. Price is especially remembered for his support of Sir James Murray's *New English Dictionary* (now known as the *Oxford English Dictionary*), which set the standard for modern lexicography.

The remarkable expansion of the university's publishing program led to the establishment of 23 overseas branches. The first and most important of these incorporated in New York in 1896. Originally, this corporation only distributed Bibles printed in England. In 1909, however, it published its first American book, *The Scofield Reference Bible.* This was followed by medical and scientific works, and, more recently, historical studies by such scholars as Samuel Eliot Morison and Henry Steele Commager, as well as such best sellers as Rachel Carson's *The Sea Around Us* and Edmund Wilson's *The Dead Sea Scrolls.* For the past half century, the highest standards of printing and design have been the pride of the Oxford University Press.

In 1978, The Pierpont Morgan Library in New York City and the Oxford University Press organized and mounted an extensive exhibition to celebrate the 500th anniversary of printing in Oxford. This traveling exhibition included such items as the first book printed in Oxford, proof sheets and drawings, autograph letters, and paintings. It presented a view of English publishing history and a record of the achievements of the Oxford University Press.

THOMAS V. LANGE

OXFORD UNIVERSITY PRESS

John Smith's *Map of Virginia*, with a description of the country, its people, government, commodities, and religion, was printed at Oxford by Joseph Barnes in 1612.

Puerto Rico's Senate Majority Leader Miguel Hernandez-Agosto addresses UN Decolonization Committee in August.

PUERTO RICO

A slightly improved economy and constant debate over the political status of the island were the most important features of Puerto Rican affairs in 1978.

Economy. The tourism, manufacturing, and construction sectors registered improvements; only agriculture continued to be a burden on the island's economy. With the opening of a new convention center, tourism increased by about 20%. Some 6,000 new jobs were added to the industrial sector; 59 factories were closed down, but 79 new ones were opened. More impressive was the 15.6% increase of the overall payroll in the manufacturing sector. The construction industry spent about (U. S.) $1.2 billion, an increase of 14.8% over 1977. More encouraging yet was the fact that about one half of those expenditures came from the private

------ **PUERTO RICO** · Information Highlights ------

Area: 3,421 square miles (8,860 km²).
Population (1978 est.): 3,400,000.
Chief Cities (1978 est.): San Juan, the capital, 544,-596; Bayamon, 231,456; Ponce, 206,282.
Government (1978): *Chief Officers*—governor, Carlos Romero Barceló (New Progressive Party); secretary of state, Reinaldo Paniagua Diez. *Legislature*—Senate, 27 members; House of Representatives, 51 members.
Manufactures (major products): Rum, distilled spirits, beer, cement, electricity.
Agriculture (major products): Sugarcane, coffee, tobacco, pineapples, molasses.

sector (an increase of 37% over 1977), thus easing federal and insular expenditures.

In 1978, more than $3 billion in federal funds was pumped into the island economy. The food stamp program alone accounted for more than $600 million. Education, highway construction, housing, and various emergency employment programs also received sizable U. S. subsidies. The overall economic growth of the island was estimated to be 5%, but the unemployment rate, while declining from a high of 22% in 1977, still hovered around 17%.

Politics. Although the elections were still two years away, the question of Puerto Rico's relationship with the United States kept political debate at a high pitch. Gov. Carlos Romero Barceló indicated that he would schedule a plebiscite if he were to be elected for a second term in 1980. The opposition party maintained that a plebiscite was unnecessary because Puerto Rico had endorsed the present Commonwealth status by a 60% majority in 1967.

The debate was continued in the Decolonization Committee of the United Nations. All factions of insular political opinion went before the UN committee to argue that the current status was unsatisfactory. The supporters of Commonwealth status argued for greater autonomy; those in favor of statehood argued for permanent incorporation into the United States; and those favoring independence also argued their cause. By a vote of 10 to 0, with 12 abstentions, the committee approved a Cuban resolution holding that Puerto Rico's status should be freely determined by its people.

THOMAS G. MATHEWS
University of Puerto Rico

QUEBEC

Political headlines underlined new and old conflicts between the Canadian federal government and the Quebec provincial government. Matters of dispute included federal grants to municipalities, the 2 or 3% rebate on provincial sales tax (with a net loss of Canadian $184 million to the Quebec government), alleged illegal activities of the Royal Canadian Mounted Police (RCMP) in Quebec, federal proposals for constitutional reform, federal versus provincial economic policies and the lack of new investment in Quebec, and the advantages and disadvantages of federalism. Regarding the latter issue, the federal government estimated that Quebec had gained $5.2 billion since 1960 by being a member of the Canadian nation; the province said that such membership had cost the province $731 million.

Independence Referendum and Legislation. Throughout the year, Quebec prepared to hold a referendum on the question of independence for the province. Commenting on the forthcoming referendum, Premier René Lévesque said that "for the first time in their history," Quebeckers have been given "an instrument to decide their future." The goal of the Lévesque government is a sovereignty-association arrangement between Quebec and Canada. Lévesque stated that for Quebec "sovereignty and association will have to come without a break and concurrently, once Quebeckers have given us such a mandate in a referendum." Sovereignty means that Quebec would alone make laws applying to that part of North America and it alone would have the power to tax within its boundaries. To Lévesque, association means that no customs barriers would exist between Canada and Quebec. The two countries would share a common currency and a joint central bank. Campaign propaganda by Lévesque's Parti Québécois was expected to be aimed at the undecided who want strong constitutional change (70% of Quebeckers) and who, with the estimated 30% favoring a sovereignty-association arrangement, could become the majority.

The Liberal party and the hardcore federalists are major forces opposing Quebec's independence. During 1978, the Liberals elected Claude Ryan, former publisher of the Montreal newspaper, *Le Devoir*, as their new leader. Ryan promised that as party leader his major objectives would be party and national unity. The provincial Social Credit party, another force against separatism, changed its name to Les Democrates. Pierre Sevigny became the party's new leader.

In June the National Assembly passed bills giving the government a greater voice in major civil service appointments, implementing parts of the James Bay agreement with the Cree and Inuit peoples of northern Quebec and establishing the framework for the independence referendum. In accord with the new legislation, the ballots of the independence referendum are to be written in French and English, as well as in an Indian or Eskimo language in areas of large native population. Special committees will monitor campaign spending by all sides throughout the referendum. On September 15, Premier Lévesque announced that the referendum would be postponed until the fall of 1979 "at the earliest," following the federal elections.

In November the National Assembly approved legislation giving the province power to establish its own selection rules for immigrants while adhering to general federal guidelines.

Economy. Although the creation of more than 60,000 new jobs in the first ten months of the year helped the economy to bounce back somewhat from a recent downturn, unemployment remained high at 10–11%, and the inflation rate stood at between 9 and 10%. On the positive side, retail sales scored measurable gains during the first months of the year. The increase was due in part to a lowering of the provincial income tax by an average of 7.5% and of the sales tax in such areas as clothing, shoes, textiles, and furniture by 8% for a 50-week period.

A few large corporations, including Cadbury and Sun Life, moved their operations or head-offices from Quebec to Ontario. As a result, Sun Life, which blamed law 101 (Frenchifying the province's public life, business, and education) for the move, lost 20–25% of its business in Quebec. In general, most corporations seemed to accept the flexible regulations edicted by law 101. In fact, a few big plants even moved to Quebec. The province's decision to acquire or expropriate American-owned Asbestos Corp. had not been implemented as the year ended. John Rhodes, Ontario's minister of industry and tourism, charged in September that Quebec was offering up to $17 million in interest-free loans for five years to encourage a Timmins, Ont., company to expand in Quebec rather than in Ontario. A grant of $40 million by the federal government to the Ford Motor Company for its new $500 million plant at Windsor, Ont., a high employment area, drew sharp criticism from the Quebec government.

Provincial Finance Minister Jacques Parizeau presented Quebec's budget, which he said was aimed at assisting the "average guy," to the National Assembly on April 18. The document included increases in personal income tax exemptions for married couples, the handicapped, the elderly, and dependent children over age 18. The budget also raised taxes for single persons earning more than $22,000 and married taxpayers with incomes above $30,000. Total spending and revenue for 1978–79 were estimated at $13.3 billion and $12.3 billion respectively.

New Agreements With Ottawa. During the year, the federal government and the province of Quebec signed agreements on a five-year, $200 million project to improve water purification systems in the area of Montreal, to continue construction of the autoroute system linking the Mirabel International Airport and the Montreal area, and a five-year cost-sharing arrangement on 80 different tourism projects.

Lieutenant Governor. Sen. Jean-Pierre Coté, a former Liberal party cabinet minister, succeeded Hughes Lapointe as lieutenant governor.

JEAN-PIERRE WALLOT, *University of Montreal*

QUEBEC · Information Highlights

Area: 594,860 square miles (1,540,687 km²).

Population (1978 est.): 6,290,000.

Chief Cities (1976 census): Quebec, the capital, 177,082; Montreal, 1,080,546; Laval, 246,243.

Government (1978): *Chief Officers*—lt. gov., Jean-Pierre Coté; premier, René Lévesque (Parti Québécois). *Legislature*—Legislative Assembly, 110 members.

Education (1976–77): *Enrollment*—public elementary and secondary schools, 1,318,800 pupils; private schools, 105,170; Indian (federal) schools, 4,700; post-secondary, 201,600 students. *Total school expenditures,* $2,824,519,000.

Public Finance (1978–79): *Expenditures,* $13,300,000,000; *revenues,* $12,300,000,000.

Personal Income (average weekly salary, May 1978): $261.79.

Unemployment Rate (July 1978, adjusted): 10.5%.

(All monetary figures are in Canadian dollars.)

RECORDINGS

During 1978, the pop music recording industry discovered that its audience had grown up. In the field of classical recordings, the year's outstanding discovery was the 75-year-old Hungarian pianist Ervin Nyiregyházi, who had disappeared after a brilliant success in the early 1920's. Desmar released material taped at a recital, and the Ford Foundation backed the International Piano Archives in recording him anew for Columbia. The results hit the top of the classical charts.

The tricentenary of the birth of Italian composer Antonio Vivaldi was celebrated, and recordings of his works multiplied. Among the more exotic repertoire brought to records were Haydn's *Orlando Paladino* and *L'Isola Disabitata,* Mozart's *Mitridate,* and Nielsen's *Maskarade.*

On the technical front, the advent of digital recording (pulse code modulation), with its dynamic range and freedom from distortion, began to overtake direct-to-disc recording, and threatened to become an advance that, like stereo, required recording everything over again. Despite disagreement on a standard format, prerecorded video cassettes became commercially viable and video discs seemed certain to follow.

POPULAR

The Audience and Market. Warner Communications issued a report revealing that buyers aged 25 to 49 accounted for the lion's share of record sales. The post World War II baby boom kids who bought rock'n'roll had come of age and were continuing to buy records.

Pop discs of *all* kinds garnered sales of over $3.5 billion in the United States alone. The Warner report disclosed the following breakdown of records purchased: rock—36%; easy listening and country—14% each; soul, rhythm and blues (R & B), and disco—13% in total; classical—5%; jazz—4%. Small percentages of miscellaneous accounted for the remainder.

The Bee Gees. Disco madness reached new heights. Although Donna Summer and Carol Douglas were among the established royalty of disco, the Bee Gees held sway. Saturday Night Fever, the high-stepping soundtrack of the popular film, contained seven Bee Gees hits and had unprecedented sales of 30 million copies worldwide. The Bee Gees were not limited to disco, though; their reign over a broad selection of pop was remarkable. With four singles simultaneously topping the charts, they duplicated the Beatles' feat of 1964. They also starred in the film *Sgt. Pepper's Lonely Hearts Club Band.*

Soundtracks, Punk Rock, Reggae. Film soundtracks became popular, and many were integral to the success of the films they supported. *Grease, The Buddy Holly Story, FM,* and *The Last Waltz* gave birth to discs that were much in demand. *Saturday Night Fever* and its weaker

COURTESY, CAPITOL RECORDS

COURTESY, COLUMBIA RECORDS

COURTESY, ARISTA RECORDS INC. 1978

COURTESY, WARNER BROTHERS RECORDS INC.

sister, *Thank God It's Friday,* appealed to the disco crowd, and *The Wiz* tapped R & B fans.

Punk rock, or New Wave, died as a movement, although several of its artists moved into the mainstream. Blondie and Elvis Costello achieved sales highs. Patti Smith broke the top forty with a single from her album, *Easter.*

Reggae, the fascinating pop music of the Caribbean, failed to sustain its hold on the American record-buying public.

Country, Jazz, Rhythm and Blues. Healthier than ever, though, were the fusion movements in country and jazz. Although artist crossovers harvested complaints from some critics, their commercial success was undeniable. Weather Report was representative of jazz fusion, while John Denver continued to straddle the border between country and rock. Country music queen Dolly Parton enjoyed enormous success with two crossover discs, *Here You Come Again* and *Heartbreaker.*

Country stalwarts like Tammy Wynette and Mel Tillis continued to hover at the top of the country charts, as did the real individualists— Waylon Jennings and Willie Nelson. Nelson even came up with an album of straight pop standards. Called *Stardust,* the album launched a *country* single—Irving Berlin's "Blue Skies."

R & B pumped up its commercial success by continuing to expand into the discos. Established R & B artists were welcomed on the dance floor.

PAULETTE WEISS, *"Stereo Review"*

POPULAR RECORDINGS OF 1978

CLASSICAL

BEETHOVEN: *Symphonies* (complete). Von Karajan, Berlin Philharmonic (Deutsche Grammophon).
BIZET: *The Pearlfishers.* Cotrubas, Prêtre, Paris Opera (Angel).
Cilea: *Adriana Lecouvreur.* Scotto, Domingo, Levine, Philharmonia Orchestra (Columbia).
HOLST: *Band Suites 1 & 2.* Fennell, Cleveland Symphonic Winds (digital recordings) (Telarc).
LISZT: *Piano Music.* Nyiregyházi (Columbia).
MAHLER: *Symphony No. 1.* Ozawa, Boston Symphony (Deutsche Grammophon).
MAHLER: *Symphony No. 4.* Von Stade, Abbado, Vienna Philharmonic (Deutsche Grammophon).
MAHLER: *Symphony No. 9.* Giulini, Chicago Symphony (Deutsche Grammophon).
MOZART: *La Clemenza di Tito.* Baker, Leppard, English Chamber Orchestra (Philips).
Prokofiev: *Peter and the Wolf.* Bowie, Ormandy, Philadelphia Orchestra (RCA).
RACHMANINOFF: *Piano Concerto No. 3.* Horowitz, Ormandy, New York Philharmonic (RCA).
VERDI: *Il Trovatore.* Price, Obraztsova, Von Karajan, Berlin Philharmonic (Angel).
VIVALDI: *Gloria.* Berganza, Muti, Philharmonia Orchestra (Angel).
WAGNER: *Orchestral Excerpts.* Solti, Chicago Symphony (London).
WILLIAMS: *Star Wars.* Mehta, Los Angeles Philharmonic (London).

CLASSICAL RECITAL ALBUMS

VLADIMIR HOROWITZ: *Golden Jubilee Recital* (RCA).
RICHARD KAPP AND PHILHARMONIA VIRTUOSI OF NEW YORK. Greatest Hits of 1720 (Columbia).
LUCIANO PAVAROTTI: Bravo Pavarotti! (London).
JOAN SUTHERLAND AND LUCIANO PAVAROTTI: Operatic Duets (London).

POPULAR

ABBA: *The Album* (Atlantic)
ABBA: *Greatest Hits* (Atlantic)
ATLANTA RHYTHM SECTION: *Champagne Jam* (Polydor)
BLUE OYSTER CULT: *Agents of Fortune* (Columbia)
BOSTON: *Don't Look Back* (Epic)
BROTHERS JOHNSON: *Blam!* (A & M)
JACKSON BROWNE: *Running on Empty* (Asylum)
JIMMY BUFFETT: *Son of a Son of a Sailor* (ABC)
ERIC CLAPTON: *Slowhand* (RSO)
THE COMMODORES: *Natural High* (Motown)
JOHN DENVER: *I Want to Live* (RCA)
DOOBIE BROTHERS: *Taking It to the Streets* (Warner Bros.)
BOB DYLAN: *Street Legal* (Columbia)
FOREIGNER: *Double Vision* (Atlantic)
CRYSTAL GAYLE: *We Must Believe in Magic* (United Artists)
GENESIS: *And Then There Were Three* (Atlantic)
ANDY GIBB: *Shadow Dancing* (RSO)
HEART: *Dog and Butterfly* (Portrait)
HEATWAVE: *Central Heating* (Epic)
ISLEY BROTHERS: *Showdown* (T-Neck)

JEFFERSON STARSHIP: *Earth* (Grunt)
WAYLON JENNINGS & WILLIE NELSON: *Waylon and Willie* (RCA)
JETHRO TULL: *Best of* (Chrysalis)
BILLY JOEL: *The Stranger* (Columbia)
KISS: *Double Platinum* (Casablanca)
KENNY LOGGINS: *Nightwatch* (Columbia)
LYNYRD SKYNYRD: *Lynyrd Skynyrd's First and . . . Last* (MCA)
BARRY MANILOW: *Even Now* (Arista)
JOHNNY MATHIS: *You Light Up My Life* (Columbia)
MARSHALL TUCKER BANK: *Carolina Dreams* (Capricorn)
PAUL McCARTNEY & WINGS: *London Town* (Capitol)
MEAT LOAF: *Bat Out of Hell* (Cleveland International)
JONI MITCHELL: *Don Juan's Reckless Daughter* (Asylum)
MOODY BLUES: *Octave* (London)
WILLIE NELSON: *Stardust* (Columbia)
RANDY NEWMAN: *Little Criminals* (Warner Bros.)
TED NUGENT: *Double Live Gonzo* (Epic)
O'JAYS: *So Full of Love* (Philadelphia Int'l)
PABLO CRUISE: *Worlds Away* (A & M)
DOLLY PARTON: *Heartbreaker* (RCA)
DOLLY PARTON: *Here You Come Again* (RCA)
TEDDY PENDERGRASS: *Life Is a Song Worth Singing* (Philadelphia Int'l)
TOM PETTY AND THE HEARTBREAKERS: *You're Gonna Get It* (ABC)
GERRY RAFFERTY: *City to City* (United Artists)
KENNY ROGERS: *Ten Years of Gold* (United Artists)
ROLLING STONES: *Some Girls* (Rolling Stones)
LINDA RONSTADT: *Living in the USA* (Asylum)
BOB SEGER AND THE SILVER BULLET BAND: *Stranger in Town* (Capitol)
CARLY SIMON: *Boys in the Trees* (Elektra)
PAUL SIMON: *Greatest Hits* (Columbia)
BRUCE SPRINGSTEEN: *Darkness on the Edge of Town* (Columbia)
BARBRA STREISAND: *Songbird* (Columbia)
DONNA SUMMER: *Live and More* (Casablanca)
JOE WALSH: *But Seriously, Folks* (Asylum)
THE WHO: *Who Are You* (MCA)

JAZZ

GEORGE BENSON: *Weekend in L. A.* (Warner Bros.)
STANLEY CLARKE: *Modern Man* (Nemperor)
THE CRUSADERS: *Images* (ABC)
DEXTER GORDON: *Sophisticated Giant* (Columbia)
HERBIE HANCOCK: *Sunlight* (Columbia)
QUINCY JONES: *Sounds* (A & M)
CHUCK MANGIONE: *Feels So Good* (A & M)
NOEL POINTER: *Hold On* (United Artists)
JEAN-LUC PONTY: *Cosmic Messenger* (Atlantic)
JOE SAMPLE: *Rainbow Seeker* (ABC)
GROVER WASHINGTON, JR.: *Live at the Bijou* (Kudu)
WEATHER REPORT: *Mr. Gone* (Columbia)

MUSICALS, MOVIES, TELEVISION

AIN'T MISBEHAVIN': original cast (RCA)
GREASE: soundtrack (RSO)
SATURDAY NIGHT FEVER: soundtrack (RSO)
THE LAST WALTZ: soundtrack (Warner Bros)
THE WIZ: soundtrack (MCA)

REFUGEES

The international refugee problem is massive, seemingly perpetual, and global in scope. It accelerates in waves following natural catastrophes, warfare, and extremist revolutions. It is multifaceted: who are the refugees; who will care for them; where can they find temporary asylum and permanent settlement?

During the past generation the refugee and displaced persons problem has involved millions of individuals and cost the international community billions of dollars. Immediately after World War II there were East Europeans and East Asians uprooted by hostilities and peace arrangements. They were followed by enormous numbers of displaced or fleeing Palestinians, Africans, and South and Southeast Asians, as well as lesser numbers of South Americans, Cubans, and Cypriots. In late 1978, refugees totaled more than 5 million.

In recent years the largest blocs of refugees have included 1.5 to 2 million Palestinian Arabs, more than 2 million exiles and expellees in Africa (particularly in the Horn and southern regions), some 200,000 displaced Turkish and Greek Cypriots, and between 150,000 and 200,000 Burmese who fled to Bangladesh. In the three years following the Vietnam war an estimated 330,000 to 500,000 Indochinese escaped from Cambodia (Kampuchea), Laos, and Vietnam, and the flow continues. The vast majority of today's refugees, therefore, originate in Africa and Asia (including the Middle East).

The Communist takeover in Indochina in 1975 produced several pressing difficulties. Thousands of refugees escaped overland from Laos and Cambodia into Thailand, where approximately 115,000 are held in temporary camps, or by small water craft (the "boat people") seeking asylum in East Asian countries. The United States, followed by Australia, Canada, and France, has led the world in providing new homes for them.

In Cambodia, several hundred thousand Chinese have been displaced and trapped in remote rural areas as a result of the government's relocation efforts. In Vietnam, Chinese are forced to renounce their Chinese citizenship or leave the country. In addition, the ranks of Chinese refugees continue to increase annually as thousands escape from the mainland.

As a consequence of such developments, the international community is burdened with critical tasks of providing machinery to administer common policies and programs, immediate sanctuary, eventual homelands, and funds to pay the costs of national and combined programs.

Limited, "temporary" assistance is supplied by several international agencies. Under a statute approved by the UN General Assembly (1950) and a Convention Relating to the Status of Refugees (1951, amended in 1967), subscribed to by about 70 countries, general refugee

UPI

Escaping political turmoil in Burma, a young girl and a child take refuge in an eastern Bangladesh camp.

assistance was assumed by the UN Office of the High Commissioner for Refugees (UNHCR). This includes emergency relief, repatriation, and resettlement. For three decades the Palestinian refugees have been dealt with separately, originally by the UN Relief for Palestinian Refugees, created by the General Assembly in 1948. This was converted into the UN Relief and Works Agency for Palestine Refugees (UNWRA).

Excluding the financial agencies (such as the World Bank and the International Monetary Fund), both the UNHCR and UNWRA are among the 10 most costly of some 60 UN agencies. In recent years they have expended approximately $175 million annually—or more than 10% of the (U. S.) $1.6 billion UN expenditures. The United States contributes between 40% and 45% of these costs, and more than 50% for Indochinese refugees.

Since 1945 the United States has accepted about 2 million refugees, plus an estimated quarter of a million regular immigrants. The refugees include some 675,000 Cubans, 600,000 East Europeans, 165,000 Indochinese (with another 30,000 expected within a year), and lesser numbers of Chinese, Asian residents of Uganda following their expulsion in 1972, and a steady stream from other Communist countries and the Middle East. In 1978 the United States reaffirmed its support for joint UN programs and provided a home for many refugees.

ELMER PLISCHKE, *University of Maryland*

RELIGION

General Survey

Perhaps the most significant events of 1978 were connected with the papacy of the Roman Catholic Church. The year witnessed the death on Aug. 6, 1978, of Paul VI, and the brief pontificate of John Paul I, formerly Albino Cardinal Luciani, Archbishop of Venice. The supreme pontiff of the world's Roman Catholics, selected by the College of Cardinals on Oct. 16, 1978, is Pope John Paul II, formerly Karol Cardinal Wojtyla, Archbishop of Cracow, Poland. He is the first non-Italian pope since 1523.

Soviet Georgia arrested a government official, Viktor Rtskhiladze, who led a campaign to save an ancient cave monastery from gradual destruction by a Soviet Army artillery range. Severe damage has already been done to 6th century frescoes found in the cave.

Dissension within the Episcopal Church has led to the first major schism in that communion in more than a hundred years. The Church's decision to ordain women, to revise the Book of Common Prayer, and to relax traditional stands on such matters as abortion and homosexuality, has led to the formation of the Anglican Church in North America.

The policy of the Church of Jesus Christ of Latter Day Saints (Mormons) of excluding blacks from the church's priesthood was revoked by the denomination's president, Spencer Kimball. This is probably the most dramatic shift in Mormon policy since the renunciation of polygamy in 1890. The change bodes well for the church as it expands far beyond its regional and national bounds. A 1977 attempt to impugn the Book of Mormon had ended in discord.

Israel approved a new law in December 1977 making it illegal to offer material benefits for religious conversion. Although Christianity was not specified, remarks during the Knesset debate showed that the increase in evangelical Christian activity was a primary cause of the action.

A trend toward conservatism and fundamentalism is apparent in the Islamic world. At a conference in Cairo prior to the hadj (pilgrimage to Mecca), leading scholars urged Muslims to give up Western style legal codes and return to the Sharia, the true way of Islam. In Iran, Islamic conservatism led to violence in opposition to the modernizing policies of the shah.

U. S. CHURCH AND RELIGIOUS ASSOCIATION MEMBERSHIP

Religious Body	Members	Religious Body	Members
Advent Christian Church	30,997	Independent Fundamental Churches of America	87,582[1]
American Baptist Association	1,071,000[1]	International Church of the Foursquare	
American Baptist Churches in the U. S. A.	1,593,574	Gospel	89,215[6]
American Carpatho-Russian Orthodox		Jehovah's Witnesses	577,362
Greek Catholic Church	100,000	Jewish Congregations	6,115,000[3]
American Lutheran Church	2,402,261	Lutheran Church in America	2,974,749
Antiochian Orthodox Christian Archdiocese		Lutheran Church-Missouri Synod	2,757,271
of North America	152,000	Mennonite Church	96,092
Armenian Apostolic Church of America	125,000[3]	Moravian Church in America	
Armenian Church of America	372,000[3]	Northern Province	32,765
Assemblies of God	1,302,318	National Baptist Convention, U. S. A., Inc.	5,500,000[10]
Associate Reformed Presbyterian Church	31,854	National Baptist Convention of America	2,668,799[11]
Baptist General Conference	117,973	National Primitive Baptist Conventon, Inc.	250,000
Baptist Missionary Association of America	216,471	New Apostolic Church of North America	24,361
Buddhist Churches of America	60,000[1]	North American Old Roman Catholic Church	60,124[1]
Bulgarian Eastern Orthodox Church	86,000[4]	Old Order Amish Church	14,720[3]
Christian and Missionary Alliance	150,492	Orthodox Church in America	1,000,000[1]
Christian Church (Disciples of Christ)	1,278,734	Pentecostal Church of God of America, Inc.	135,000[1]
Christian Churches and Churches of Christ	1,040,856	Pentecostal Holiness Church	74,108[3]
The Christian Congregation, Inc.	79,230	Plymouth Brethren	74,000
Christian Methodist Episcopal Church	466,718[7]	Polish National Catholic Church of America	282,411[9]
Christian Reformed Church	211,061	Presbyterian Church of America	68,993
Church of Christ, Scientist		Presbyterian Church in the United States	877,664
Church of God (Anderson, Ind.)	170,285	Progressive National Baptist Convention, Inc.	521,692[5]
Church of God (Cleveland, Tenn.)	365,124	Reformed Church in America	350,734
Church of God in Christ	425,000[7]	Reorganized Church of Jesus Christ of	
Church of God in Christ, International	501,000[4]	Latter-day Saints	185,839
Church of Jesus Christ of Latter-day Saints	2,391,892	Roman Catholic Church	49,325,752
Church of the Brethren	178,157	Romanian Orthodox Episcopate of America	40,000
Church of the Nazarene	449,205	Russian Orthodox Church in the U. S. A.,	
Churches of Christ	2,500,000	Patriarchal Parishes of the	51,500[1]
Community Churches, National Council of	125,000	The Salvation Army	380,618
Congregational Christian Churches, National		Serbian Eastern Orthodox Church for the U. S. A.	
Association of	90,000	and Canada	65,000[5]
Conservative Baptist Association of America	300,000	Seventh-Day Adventist	509,792
Cumberland Presbyterian Church	92,995	Southern Baptist Convention	12,917,992
Episcopal Church	2,882,064	Triumph the Church and Kingdom of	
Evangelical Covenant Church of America	73,458	God in Christ (International)	54,307[3]
Evangelical Free Church of America	70,490[4]	Ukrainian Orthodox Church in the U. S. A.	87,745[6]
Evangelical Lutheran Churches, The		Unitarian Universalist Association	184,522
Association of	95,186	United Church of Christ	1,801,241
Free Methodist Church of North America	68,180	United Free Will Baptist Church	100,000[12]
Free Will Baptists	229,498	The United Methodist Church	9,861,028
Friends United Meeting	65,585	United Pentecostal Church, International	405,000
General Association of Regular Baptist Churches	240,000	The United Presbyterian Church in the U. S. A.	2,607,321
General Baptists (General Association of)	70,000[2]	The Wesleyan Church	96,337
Greek Orthodox Archdiocese of North		Wisconsin Evangelical Lutheran Synod	399,114
and South America	1,950,000		

Figures are mainly for the years 1976 and 1977. [1]1975. [2]1974. [3]1972. [4]1971. [5]1967. [6]1966. [7]1965. [8]1963. [9]1960. [10]1958. [11]1956. [12]1952. (Source: National Council of Churches of Christ in the U. S. A., *Yearbook of American and Canadian Churches 1978*.)

The New York State Board of Regents on Feb. 22, 1978, denied an application from Rev. Sun Myung Moon's Unification Church requesting degree-granting status for the cult's Unification Theological Seminary in Barrytown, N. Y.

Professor James M. Charlesworth of Duke University has been collecting, translating, and analyzing the Pseudepigrapha, a number of non-canonical books of the intertestamental period. Scholars are looking with increased interest to this Hebraic material which may establish a much closer relationship than is frequently assumed between Jewish and Christian thought at the time of Christ.

A District Court in New Jersey ruled that Transcendental Meditation must be considered a religious system in spite of disclaimers from leaders of the Meditation movement. Thus considered, instruction of TM in federally funded schools is accounted illegal. The decision results from the suit filed by parents, conservative Christian clergy, and religious libertarians who charged that TM was a form of Hinduism.

In June 1978 the Princeton Research Center issued its first major survey. The center, formed in 1977 by George Gallup, Jr., with the purpose of gaining a better understanding of the "nature and depth of religious commitment," is evidence of a growing trend among religious leaders to use social scientific data in their ministries. By analyzing and interpreting the results of surveys and polls religious leaders hope to gain an awareness of prevailing attitudes among the faithful in order to promote spiritual growth.

RICHARD E. WENTZ
Arizona State University

Far Eastern

The People's Republic of China reported renewed religious activity among Christians during 1978. It was reported that, for the first time since the Cultural Revolution, Chinese Roman Catholics attended Mass at Peking Cathedral and Protestant Chinese attended regular service in Nanking. Relaxation of religious policy was demonstrated further by the visit to a Buddhist pagoda in Peking by a diplomat from a Buddhist nation.

Student interest in the study of Far Eastern religions seems to have tapered off in recent years. During the late 1960's and early 1970's this interest was partly associated with the private search for alternate realities and altered consciousness. The study of Oriental traditions appears to have stabilized, along with the quest for religious experience. This means that the academic study of Far Eastern religions has entered a maturation stage in which faddism and novelty no longer impede serious scholarship.

An alert Buddhist layman from Thailand was responsible for the recovery of a missing statue of Buddha worth $500,000. The artifact had been stolen en route from Thailand to a temple in Denver, Colo. The 500-year-old statue was discovered at Chicago's Maxwell Street flea market.

Brahman priests in Pushkar, one of India's most sacred sites, protested the influx of priests who were charging fees to conduct blessing rituals for pilgrims who bathed in the sacred lake and worshiped the god Brahma. The protests called attention to the fact that true Brahman priests take no money unless it is offered voluntarily.

The sacred 1500-mile (2,400-km) Ganges River flows into the Bay of Bengal in eastern India, near the present state of Bangladesh. The pilgrimage centers on its course are especially sacred at Rishikesh and the holy city of Hardwar in northern Uttar Pradesh. The number of Hindus making pilgrimage to the holy sites reached almost unprecedented heights in 1978.

RICHARD E. WENTZ

Islam

Currents of both conservatism and dynamism swept the Islamic world in 1978. Increasing demands for a return to traditional values reflected efforts by religious leaders to impede the penetration of Communism, which they regard as dangerous and atheistic. The conviction of many Muslims, that westernization has often been synonymous with secularization and the denigration of Islamic concepts, reinforced the attraction of traditionalism. In several countries, government opponents resorted to religious issues as vehicles for social, economic, and political protest.

The periodic eruption of public disturbances in Iran during 1978 illustrated this problem. Demonstrations encouraged by anti-shah political forces and the country's religious leaders forced the government to reassess policies and practices these groups found objectionable. Similar agitation occurred in Egypt and Turkey, and Saudi Arabia enforced traditional Koranic laws to emphasize its commitment to Islamic values.

At the same time, Saudi Arabia also promoted the spread of Islamic culture in the non-Muslim world. The Saudi government helped build a mosque and Islamic center in Switzerland and announced plans to invest millions of dollars in urban renewal projects in several U. S. cities. The latter scheme was aimed at enhancing the appeal of Islam to black Americans and creating a positive image of Islam in the United States.

Muslim insistence on religious freedom also stimulated political controversies. Many Burmese Muslims, charging the Buddhist government with persecution, sought refuge in neighboring, predominantly Muslim, Bangladesh. Similar fears of mistreatment kept Muslims in the southern Philippines armed as guerrillas. Dissidents in the Comoro Islands overthrew a regime denounced by local Muslims for its religious suppression.

KENNETH J. PERKINS
University of South Carolina

WIDE WORLD

Israel's Menahem Begin mingles with the audience after addressing Jewish leaders in New York City.

Judaism

The year 1978 marked the 30th anniversary of the State of Israel. It was a year of mounting hopes for peace, soaring fears of national betrayal, increased bloodshed by Arab terrorists, worldwide upsurge of neo-Nazi activity, and escalation of Soviet anti-Semitism.

The momentous Camp David peace plan set in motion conflicting waves of response among Jews. Popular sentiment swelled in celebration of peace prospects, but there was also a surge in opposition to territorial concessions. Many Jews regarded the territories in question as biblically established and nonnegotiable. In Israel, while jubilant crowds greeted the promise of peace, Jewish settlers from Sinai, Judea, Samaria, and the Golan Heights staged demonstrations to denounce the betrayal of religious Zionist doctrine and the return of the territories. The religious "Gush Emunim" occupied new sites in Judea and Samaria until the army forcibly removed them. In the United States and elsewhere, Jewish leaders praised the peace efforts, while rabbinical scholars warned against infringement of "halacha" (Jewish law) in giving away parts of the Holy Land. Representatives of various Christian denominations also expressed their belief in Israel's scriptural right to all lands now held.

Increased Arab terrorist attacks against Israeli civilians added to the mood of ambivalence. Memories of the holocaust were revived also by an alarming proliferation of neo-Nazi activity in the United States, West Germany, Austria, France, Brazil, Chile, and Argentina. West German President Walter Scheel cautioned his people that the phenomenon was not a passing fad. His warning was echoed by the president of the World Jewish Congress and by data on American Nazis compiled by the Trends Analysis Division of the American Jewish Committee.

The Soviet Union stepped up its anti-Semitic propaganda in the media, literature, and the courts. The Brussels Conference on Soviet Jewry found that Moscow has become an international center for the dissemination of anti-Semitic literature. Continued harassment of Jews wishing to emigrate to Israel spurred worldwide solidarity, manifested in rallies, marches, petitions, and hunger strikes. The trials and harsh prison sentences of Jewish dissidents Anatoly Shcharansky, Vladimir Slepak, and Ida Nudel prompted mass demonstrations by Jews and non-Jews in the United States, Canada, Europe, and Israel.

In the American Jewish community, women gained increasing recognition. In Reform and Reconstructionist seminaries, 75 women studied for the rabbinate; and in two Orthodox synagogues women were elected to the executive board. In Israel a bill exempting women from army service solely on statement of religious objection stirred nationwide protest.

LIVIA E. BITTON JACKSON
Herbert H. Lehman College, CUNY

The American Jew: Is There a Dilemma?

One of the most familiar themes of American journalism during much of 1978 was the "dilemma" of the American Jew with regard to conflicting U. S. and Israeli policies in the Middle East. On one hand, Jews in the United States remained deeply committed to the security of Israel, while on the other, they confronted a president and administration increasingly at odds with the policies of the Israeli government. As widely reported by the media, American Jews were substantively more in agreement with the position of the Carter administration but emotionally committed to Israel. The dilemma was said to have reached its peak in May, when Congress approved the administration's decision to sell advanced military aircraft to Saudi Arabia and Egypt. However, the results of the Camp David meetings in September seemingly laid this dilemma to rest. The framework for peace with Israel and the prospective settlement of the Arab-Israeli conflict were greeted with expressions of boundless pleasure and mutual esteem by all parties.

The history of this ostensible dilemma is itself of some importance. The first real pressure on the American Jewish community came in March 1975, when the Israeli government, under Prime Minister Yitzhak Rabin, rejected proposals by U. S. Secretary of State Henry Kissinger for a second interim agreement with Egypt. A substantial and not very subtle campaign was orchestrated by Washington to place the blame on Israel for not reaching an agreement. The rather blatant character of U. S. pressure, coupled with an obvious Israeli willingness to agree on a *fair* settlement, led most American Jews to remain steadfastly on the side of Israel during this period.

It was not until Jimmy Carter took office in January 1977 that the problem resurfaced in any serious form. It first became an issue after the Carter-Rabin meeting in March 1977. Carter apparently discovered for the first time that the so-called Allon Plan was not merely Israel's opening proposal but its final position—the bottom line. It is well to recall that Menahem Begin was not the first Israeli prime minister to be termed intransigent by President Carter. After the Carter-Rabin meeting, the White House let it be known that the president thought Rabin was being stubborn.

The Israeli elections in May 1977, which led to the toppling of the Labor coalition and the installation of a new government led by Menahem Begin and the Likud party, briefly interrupted U. S. pressure on Israel but at the same time opened new doubts among certain segments of American Jewry. The Labor party had dominated the Israeli political scene for so long that

the Likud opposition, from Begin on down, were unknown to most American Jews. Although Begin's own personal charm and grace helped dissipate the image of the Likud party as a gang of right-wing extremists, his firm stance with regard to the administered territories of Judea, Samaria, and Gaza sharply increased the suspicions of many American Jews. World opinion seemed to be that Israel should evacuate most, if not all, of the West Bank as an accommodation to the Palestinian Arabs.

Thus, by the end of the summer of 1977, the stage was set for the first real wrenching away of the American Jewish community from its unqualified support of Israel.

The catalyst was Egyptian President Anwar el-Sadat's visit to Jerusalem in November 1977. Sadat's very effective personal approach, a certain ineptness on the part of Begin, strong U. S. support for the Sadat initiative, and even stronger media bias against the Israeli position led to a badly distorted, although not entirely dishonest perception of subsequent events. Whatever interests all but the tiniest minority of Israelis perceived as vital were rejected in the United States as manifestations of Israeli intransigence, while Sadat's very firm and uncompromising position was hailed as flexible and moderate.

Despite formal denials, President Carter seemed to begin a more direct campaign to weaken the unwavering American Jewish support for Israel. This was part of an overall plan to isolate the Jewish state so that it would have to accept the U. S. terms for peace. The administration attempted to woo American Jewish leaders outside the recognized "Israel lobby," with intimations that American Jews might be accused of having dual loyalty. In an effort to bypass the Conference of Presidents of Major Jewish Organizations, the traditional spokesman for the American Jewish Community in matters relating to Israel, Carter invited leaders of the major local Jewish federations to the White House. When he found that the locally-based leaders were not any more open to his designs than their representatives in the Conference of Presidents had been, Carter and his administration intensified their campaign in expectation of success.

The Jewish leaders who did reject what they saw as Begin's extreme position faced a difficult problem. On one hand, they were not about to abandon Israel, especially in the face of American pressure. On the other hand, they wanted to avoid being forced into Begin's camp. That, indeed, became the real dilemma of American Jewry. American Jews were not afraid of opposing the U. S. administration. It was the fact that Begin's policies were less than acceptable to some of their leaders that created the problem. But the pressure exerted by the Carter administration proved counterproductive. The recognized leaders of the community resolved their dilemma by continuing to back Israel. Carter's campaign had reawakened latent fears of anti-semitism and revived their fundamentalist attitude toward Israel. It had not caused any worry about their position in American life.

Thus, on the eve of Camp David, the major dilemma facing the American Jewish leadership was how best to proceed with the defense of Israel's interests without completely supporting Begin's policies. But the unexpected results of the Camp David talks brought matters into line once again. Begin's willingness to support the relinquishment of Israeli settlements in the Sinai in order to achieve a separate peace with Egypt squared perfectly with the views of the American Jewish leadership.

As for Judea, Samaria, and the Gaza district, American Jewish leaders had never properly understood the autonomy plan, in part because the U. S. media had paid little attention to it and in part because the Israelis were notably lax in explaining it. Once the plan seemed to become the basis for a tripartite agreement, they accepted it completely. For those advocating Israeli withdrawal from the administered territories, the plan seemed suitable; for those wanting Israel to retain control of the territories (without inheriting their Arab majorities), the plan also held promise. The Knesset's decision to support the Camp David agreement made matters even easier for the American Jewish community. Thus, as the peace talks with Egypt convened in October, Israel was able to count on the full support of American Jews.

In many respects, then, the presumed dilemma of the American Jew was a creation of the U. S. mass media. Following their own sense of what American Jewish views and Israeli policy should be, the media emphasized the position of the small number of American Jews who were willing to come out against Israel at critical moments; they then projected this posture onto the American Jewish community as a whole.

Although a majority of American Jews probably were in some disagreement with Begin's initial policies in the administered territories, they were not pleased with the policy of the new U. S. administration vis-à-vis Israel. In the aftermath of Vietnam, no group of Americans is so convinced of the rightness of official policy that it would feel threatened if it disagreed. As shown by the decline in Jewish support for President Carter and the drop in Jewish contributions to the Democratic party, American Jewry is no exception. Thus, the real dilemma of the American Jew was not how to reconcile their U. S. and Israeli sympathies, but how to continue support for Israel without seeming to endorse all of Begin's positions on certain key issues.

DANIEL J. ELAZAR

Orthodox Eastern Church

Four of the fifteen autocephalous (self-governing) churches which comprise world Orthodoxy received new primates between late 1977 and 1978. The Orthodox Church in Rumania is now headed by Patriarch Justin, formerly bishop of Moldavia. In the USSR the provincial council of the Catholicate of Georgia (Iberia) elected Elias, former Metropolitan of Sukhumi as its head. On the island of Cyprus, Metropolitan Chrysostomos of Paphos was chosen in a November 1977 popular election to succeed the late Archbishop Makarios as head of the church. In October of 1977 in Montreal, Canada, the Orthodox Church in America, the youngest of the autocephalous churches, held a council of clergy and laity which elected Bishop Theodosius of Pittsburgh as its primate. The forty-four-year-old American-born bishop assumed the leadership of the church as archbishop of the metropolitan see of New York. During his first year of service he led the restructuring of ecclesiastical departments in the OCA, and continued efforts toward the unification of all Orthodox dioceses in America.

Major Orthodox gatherings were held in Sofia for the 30th anniversary of the restoration of the patriarchate in Bulgaria, and in Moscow on the occasion of the celebration of the 60th anniversary of the reestablishment of the patriarchate in Russia. Conferences, such as that at Holy Cross Theological School in Brookline, Mass., in August 1978, sponsored by the Orthodox Theological Society in America, prepared for the Great and Holy Council of the Orthodox Churches.

The Patriarchate of Constantinople provided a new "charter" for its dependent Greek Orthodox Archdiocese in America led by Archbishop Iakovos which called for the restructuring of dioceses at the same time that it retained control over the election of bishops and ecclesiastical policy. The new "charter" was greeted as a step toward the unification of the Orthodox of various national backgrounds in America by the Greek Archdiocese, while others viewed it as a symbolic act without substance.

The Russian Orthodox Church lost one of its most influential hierarchs, Metropolitan Nikodim of Leningrad, leader of the church's foreign affairs activity, who died at an audience in Rome with Pope John Paul I. Metropolitan Antony of Minsk succeeded Nikodim as Metropolitan of Leningrad, while the direction of the church's external affairs remained unsettled.

At the Lambeth Conference in England and at the Faith and Order Meeting of the World Council of Churches in Bangalore, India, Orthodox spokesmen continued to call for Church unity based on biblical and traditional doctrines and practices, and continued to voice opposition to the ordination of women to the priesthood.

THOMAS HOPKO
St. Vladimir's Orthodox Theological Seminary

Protestantism

In the early 1960's, American religious leaders were given some of the credit for passing major civil rights legislation. But by the late 1960's, the war in Vietnam precipitated a break between succeeding Democratic and Republican administrations and official Protestant church leadership. President Gerald Ford began the reversal of this pattern with invitations to religious leaders to meet with him in the White House. But it remained for a "born-again" Southern Baptist from Georgia, President Jimmy Carter, to open wide the White House doors to American church leaders.

Long ignored by official Washington, church officials found themselves on invitation lists for receptions, special briefings, and official delegations, including two separate trips to Rome to represent the United States at papal inaugurations. The Panama Canal treaties were ratified by the U. S. Senate in 1978, and among the groups who went to the White House to listen to the president's case for the treaties were influential church leaders who presumably returned home to add their weight to public pressure on wavering senators.

But by late in the year, some activist-oriented church leaders were having second thoughts about White House hospitality. A day-long session to discuss the administration's urban program drew some complaints that the president wanted church groups to serve a lobbying function, an activity forbidden nonprofit organizations.

Drawing a distinction between lobbying and "moral influence" troubled religious leaders who wanted some voice in the shaping of official policies, but who feared the co-option of their religious strength by government leaders. Many clergy persons apparently decided that the need for moral influence was vital enough to risk the appearance of co-option, so they continued to participate in briefings and receptions, including, in mid-November, an all-day session presenting the administration's rationale for strategic arms limitation talks with the Soviet Union.

The distinction between church life and legal structures came under discussion when the United Presbyterian Church grappled with the issue of whether or not to ordain persons to the ministry regardless of sexual preference. In an annual session meeting in San Diego, delegates determined that "our present understanding of God's will" precludes practicing homosexuals from being ordained to the ministry.

In a compromise agreement the Presbyterians declared that they reached their decision on the basis of current understanding, and not on doctrinal grounds. Since the Assembly had supported protection of the civil rights of homosexuals at the same time it disapproved of the ordination of homosexuals, some delegates filed an "affirmation of conscience" charging that the Presbyterians had asked society to be more "gracious and free" than the church.

Conflict of another sort divided domestic church opinion when the World Council of Churches (WCC) approved a grant of $85,000 to one side of the internal struggle being waged in Rhodesia. Bishop Abel Muzorewa, a black church leader who has participated in the "settlement" with Prime Minister Ian Smith, traveled through the United States to rally his fellow churchmen against the Patriotic Front opposition groups that received the WCC grant. He found support from many Protestants, including some of his fellow United Methodist bishops who felt the WCC grant, though designated for humanitarian purposes, still represented identification with one "side" in an internal political struggle. Representatives from U. S. churches met in a WCC conference in October and reaffirmed the program of the world body to provide financial and spiritual support for the Program to Combat Racism, the WCC unit that made the Rhodesian grant.

Within U. S. denominations, participants in the Consultation on Church Union (COCU) scheduled a 1979 plenary meeting, the first since 1976, and announced that ordination would be a major agenda item. Although momentum toward Protestant church union has slowed since the formation of COCU in the early 1960's, COCU President Rachel Henderlite reports that a deadline of 1983 has been set for churches of the participating denominations to receive a proposal to create a united COCU denomination.

The legal responsibilities of a national church body were argued in a California superior court in late 1978. The case grew out of a class-action suit filed on behalf of residents of a retirement home complex in southern California, Arizona, and Hawaii. The suit charges that Pacific Homes Inc., which filed for bankruptcy in 1977, had defaulted on long-term-care contracts which had been sold to residents of seven retirement homes and long-term care facilities. At issue was whether the responsibility for the financial failure of the facilities was limited to the bankrupt corporation, or whether it included the larger United Methodist Church and all of its connectional agencies. The advertisers who originally promoted this sale of homes were identified as agencies of the United Methodist Church. The court must decide whether or not that identification extends to financial liability. Implications are far-reaching, not only for the United Methodist Church, but for all national church bodies. If a national church is found to be financially responsible for local church liabilities, the definition of the United Methodist Church, which considers itself connectional and not a single corporate body, would be changed by court decree. The case is expected to reach the Supreme Court of the United States.

JAMES M. WALL
Editor, The Christian Century

Organ pipes are an important design element of the new St. Peter's Lutheran Church in New York City.

UPI

The Year

in Religion

William P. Lytle, newly elected moderator of the United Presbyterian Church USA, addresses its 190th General Assembly, held in San Diego in May.

Also in May, the 245th Clergy-Laity Congress of the Greek Orthodox Church in North and South America approved a new chapter permitting the clergy and laity more participation in the church's administration.

UNITED PRESBYTERIAN CHURCH USA

COURTESY, GREEK ORTHODOX ARCHDIOCESE OF NORTH AND SOUTH AMERICA

UPI

Pope Paul VI, who died August 6, lies in state in St. Peter's Basilica, Vatican City.

FABIAN, SYGMA

Only after much public urging did Pope John Paul I permit himself to be borne in a papal chair. His pontificate lasted 33 days. Karol Cardinal Wojtyla, *below*, addresses the crowd following his election as pope. He chose the name John Paul II.

UPI

Roman Catholicism

The world's Catholics were shaken in 1978 by the deaths of two popes, and "surprised by the Holy Spirit" in the election of two others. At the same time, Church leaders continued to wrestle with human rights questions, terrorism and violence, new challenges to Church authority, issues affecting women's roles, family life, youth, and emerging lay ministries.

After Paul VI and his successor of only 34 days, Pope John Paul I, formerly Albino Cardinal Luciani of Venice, died, the Church was stunned by the election of the first Polish pope who is also the first non-Italian pope in 455 years and the first pope from a Communist nation. The death of 80-year-old Paul VI was expected, but the demise of his 65-year-old successor was not. The subsequent election of Karol Cardinal Wojtyla of Cracow astounded the entire world.

The Church that the new pope, John Paul II, inherited was confronted during the year with a wide variety of problems, in both the secular and religious spheres.

Generally, the Church voiced renewed pleas for a deepening spirituality among its members as a sign to the poor and oppressed of the world. Evangelization and efforts promoting Christian social justice were also emphasized.

Specifically, the year witnessed more intense criticism by Church leaders of repressive regimes, especially in Africa and Latin America; growing concern over dissident French traditionalist Archbishop Marcel Lefebvre, who continued to defy pope and Vatican by ordaining priests and setting up rival institutions; condemnation of political terrorism and violence that culminated in the kidnapping and death of former Italian Premier Aldo Moro and the brutal slaying of missionaries in Africa and Latin America.

The Church responded to the birth of the first test tube baby by urging development of strict moral guidelines. It supported the controversial return by the United States to Hungary of the Crown of St. Stephen, urged an end to civil strife, and deplored the increase of divorce, abortion, and immorality in Christian nations.

Members of Episcopal-Catholic and Lutheran-Catholic commissions reached "points of convergence" on such questions as authority, ministry, Eucharist, and infallibility after years of dialogue. For the first time in decades, the Shroud of Turin was displayed and scientifically tested.

Pope Paul, before his death, used the 10th anniversary of his controversial encyclical, *Humanae Vitae,* to reaffirm the Church's stand against artificial birth control. He also spoke against the indiscriminate use of general absolution and extraordinary ministers of the eucharist, particularly in the United States.

His successor, John Paul I, made a strong plea for prayers in behalf of Egyptian-Israeli peace talks at Camp David. It was in that pope's arms that Russian Orthodox Metropolitan Nikodim died of a heart attack.

In the United States, the Church saw the defeat of a major legislative proposal it favored—tuition tax credits. In some parts of the country, bishops fought against the passage of laws favoring homosexuals. Elsewhere, bishops endorsed a labor boycott against a major textile firm, and urged government aid for an ecumenical effort to save an Ohio steel mill. Catholic leaders also condemned anti-Jewish rallies by Nazi groups.

After a long investigation, a fundraiser for a religious order, Pallottine Fr. Guido Carcich, pleaded guilty in Baltimore to a charge of misappropriating over $2 million in funds raised for the missions. Several dioceses began to examine their ties to United Way campaigns because of the membership of such alleged "proabortion" groups as Planned Parenthood.

The first national meeting of lay leaders was held in Annapolis, Md., to chart a future course for lay involvement in the Church. In addition, the bishops launched a five-year plan aimed at ministry to the family. The Knights of Columbus, who paid for the telecasts via satellite of events surrounding the deaths and elections of popes, launched a sociological study of the religious behavior of youth.

Among those who died were Fr. Leonard Feeney, central figure in the famed Boston heresy case, and philosopher Etienne Gilson.

See also Biography; Obituaries.

ROBERT L. JOHNSTON
Editor, The Catholic Review

The Shroud of Turin, venerated as the cloth that wrapped Christ's body, was tested and displayed.

ROBERT WILCOX

Boston's historic Faneuil Hall area was redeveloped in three stages. Completed in 1978, the marketplace contains 13 restaurants and 137 stores.

PAT ZIMMERMAN

RETAILING

During 1978 retailing trends in the more than 1 million American stores of all kinds included mergers, marketing strategies aimed mainly at building a greater market share in existing trading areas rather than in new ones, and a strict hold on inventories as a means of coping with a queasy consumer shopper.

Urban socioeconomic changes brought some major developments in downtown retail centers. This resulted not from the increasing cost of operating old stores but from the removal of some downtown blight and from the return of many middle-income residents to the cities. Because of this, retail managements decided to close a number of long-established but archaic stores and replace them with smaller, more productive versions nearby. The most notable such move was the decision to demolish the 90-year-old, 25-story J. L. Hudson Company store in downtown Detroit, the country's tallest and one of its three-largest department stores, and eventually to replace it with a more compact, contemporary store. A similar move was taken by Gimbel Brothers in Philadelphia, and plans for such action were also announced elsewhere.

Mergers. Two well-known retail chains, which had been involved in abortive takeover moves, acquired several smaller but also well-known independents. After failing to acquire Marshall Field & Company in Chicago, Carter Hawley Hale Stores, Inc., of Los Angeles, bought control of both John Wanamaker, Inc., Philadelphia, and Thalhimer Brothers Company, Richmond, Va. Marshall Field acquired five Liberty House stores on the West Coast and the John Breuner furniture chain in California. But the year's largest retail merger was the $275 million purchase of Mervyn's, Inc., a highly-successful apparel store chain, by the Dayton-Hudson Corporation, Minneapolis, the same company which had decided to close the Hudson store in Detroit.

Expansion. Retailing's most dramatic growth company, the K-Mart Corporation of Troy, Mich., continued in 1978 to carry out the nation's largest retail expansion program, opening 170 stores during the year. In the previous two years, K-Mart had added a total of 432 stores, many of them vacant units of the W. T. Grant Company, the large retailer that had gone bankrupt in 1976 and had been closed. The aggressive K-Mart expansion had enabled the company in 1977 to pass the JCPenney Company as the nation's second-largest retailer in sales after Sears Roebuck & Company, Chicago. One of K-Mart's successful tactics was in taking the industry's lead in opening new stores in smaller cities and towns.

But JCPenney, spurning sheer volume growth, achieved strong profit gains in 1978 by stressing fashion merchandise, first in women's apparel, then in men's and children's clothing, and finally in home furnishings. With annual sales of more than $19 billion in 1978, Sears appeared to have a safe margin over the hard-running K-Mart, with its $11 billion in sales. Penney's was close by, with a shade less in sales. Although Sears suffered some profit and volume erosion in 1978, a recovery in 1979 was forecast as the year ended. Revitalized management skills were expected to contribute to the turnaround.

Specialty Chains. Impressive strides were made in 1978 by regional specialty store chains, such as Mervyn's, Limited Stores, the Gap, and others. Double-digit advances in sales and earnings came from such management policies as inventory assortments limited to most-wanted items, speedy expansion into suburban malls, and skillful pricing competition on a regional basis.

The year's inflation rate most hurt the department stores which cater largely to middle-income shoppers. Yet those stores, while hewing to strong controls on inventory accumulation, opened additional stores in existing market areas in order to capitalize on their ongoing promotional programs there, and the middle-class department stores also continued to emulate the most successful specialty stores by pruning their departments to only the most popular merchandise.

Isadore Barmash, *The New York Times*

Shopping Malls

Shopping malls—sprawling concrete retail centers surrounded by acres of cars and usually located at major urban and suburban intersections—may seem as indigenously American as apple pie, country music, and baseball. In 1948, retailers followed the flow of people to the suburbs and began building ever larger shopping centers. The suburban mall has since emerged as the community center of many a town. City halls, office buildings, libraries, and even schools and hospitals have relocated within or adjacent to the shopping mall.

In addition to the thousands employed there and the many thousands who shop within it, the typical suburban mall is also a magnet for youths and senior citizens. The latter two groups are attracted by the bright lights, recreational centers, and nighttime activities.

At the beginning of 1978, there were 19,400 shopping centers in the United States, compared to fewer than 100 in 1950, according to the International Council of Shopping Centers. *Shopping Center World,* a trade publication, reported that between its January 1975 and January 1977 industry censuses, the malls' share of total U.S. retail sales jumped from 28% to 36.3%. A year later, the malls' share of the retail pie had increased to about 37.7%, or about $242 billion of the country's $642.5 billion of sales.

Not all shopping malls rose in the suburbs. Although the suburban centers at least in part represented retailers' efforts to cope with downtown sales erosion by "going where the people were," the return in the 1970's of middle- and upper-income consumers to the city gradually brought about the establishment of several major urban shopping malls. Successful in-town centers were built in Los Angeles, New York, Chicago, Detroit, and Philadelphia. Some centers also included hotels and apartments.

Oddly enough, the first American shopping center proved to be 25 years ahead of its time. The Country Club Plaza was opened in 1922, 5 miles (8 km) south of Kansas City, Mo. But it was not until the immediate post-World War II period, when the massive population growth in the suburbs created the term, "fertile acres," that developers ventured outside the cities to introduce new centers. The first of these were simple, square "anchor" stores with a series of smaller shops clustered around them or on either side. Most were "strip" centers, so called because of their linear arrangement. But, as the centers' popularity grew, more complex and aesthetic structures were built, largely without the extensive windows that the downtown stores needed to attract passersby. The regional center, the next step after the "strips," had two anchor stores and from 50 to 75 stores. This was followed by the "super-regional," in which as many as four major department or specialty stores and as many as 150 shops now draw an estimated 200,000 shoppers daily and many more on weekends.

Two factors rendered suburban malls even more attractive. Climate-controlled and fully enclosed malls were built, and existing centers were altered to allow convenient shopping during either fair or foul weather. Sunday blue laws were gradually relaxed, allowing centers to operate seven days a week.

The big shopping malls, however, became a subject of controversy. Critics claimed that their huge traffic attraction created highway congestion and polluted the atmosphere. But center-developers countered the criticism by insisting that highway networks were being improved and that automobile pollution-control devices would ease the problem of foul air.

The environmentalists' charges were not, however, the only problems that confronted the shopping malls. Soaring construction costs and the need to conserve energy led to a slowing in the rate of new centers. At their peak in the 1960's, 1,200 new malls yearly appeared across the United States, but by 1975 the annual rate had dropped to about 750. Rising rental costs caused a fallout of many small tenants as well as some anchor stores. But most of these empty stores, including hundreds of shuttered branches of the bankrupt W.T. Grant Company, were taken over by more viable retail concerns.

In the 1970's, more pragmatic and better-financed urban renewal programs began to include shopping centers. The success of the suburban shopping mall had demonstrated the wisdom of that move. Where people shop, they also tend to relax—in movie houses, theaters, recreation centers, restaurants, night clubs, and discotheques. Nothing underscored the concept more firmly than the range of activities offered in suburban shopping malls—symphony concerts, arts-and-crafts shows, self-improvement seminars, boat and fashion shows, etc.

While the annual construction rate of new centers will continue below the peak, an expected population increase of 27 million by 1990 should boost yearly retail sales in the United States to some $833 billion. Shopping malls should account for about half, according to Albert Sussman, executive vice president of the International Council of Shopping Centers. Under the pressures of construction costs, the energy shortage, and the likelihood that the American car will get smaller, however, malls will likely undergo vast changes. Their acreage will be reduced, and smaller stores and smaller parking lots will become more common.

ISADORE BARMASH

THE EDWARD J. DEBARTOLO CORPORATION

Randall Park Mall, outside Cleveland, contains a convention center, hotel, office buildings, and a theater.

Shoppers at the Columbia (Md.) Mall can enjoy not only the flowers—Japanese gardens are featured in the spring—but also a fine art collection from the Baltimore Museum.

PHOTOS DAVID CUBBAGE—TRC

DAVID CUBBAGE—TRC

ARTHUR SHAY

The Gallery at Market East in Philadelphia saw 1 million visitors during its first week of operation.

A fantastic, seven-story glass elevator is a major feature of the Water Tower in Chicago.

DAVID CUBBAGE—TRC

The performance of a local string quartet is an additional attraction at the Hulen Mall in Fort Worth, Tex.

RHODE ISLAND

The great February blizzard was the most memorable event in 1978.

Blizzard. Beginning around noon on Monday, February 6th, a savage storm dumped three to four feet of snow on the state. Homeward bound traffic found the highways impassable, and hundreds of abandoned cars hopelessly clogged the major arteries. It took nearly a week, and massive assistance from flown-in heavy army equipment, to dig the state out. The President declared Rhode Island a major federal disaster area.

The Economy. The state's economy continued to improve during the year. Employment figures for June, August and September were each hailed as the highest in Rhode Island's history, with the total for September reaching 405,600. Manufacturing jobs were the highest since 1953. The unemployment rate dropped to 5.9% in August. On the other hand, a study showed that hourly manufacturing wages, the lowest in the Northeast, remained well below the U. S. average. The long awaited release of surplus Navy land for sale to private interests was obtained.

Government. The 1978 General Assembly session was a quiet but modestly productive one. Budget increases were kept well within the 8% limit mandated the year before. Among the many bills passed was one requiring fire drills in college dormitories. Its passage was prompted by the fatal fire at Providence College in 1977 which took 7 lives.

Also enacted was a major overhaul of the state's election laws. This included a revamped "closed" primary to replace provisions previously invalidated by the courts. Other changes were designated to liberalize and streamline the election process.

Superior Court Presiding Justice Joseph Weisberger was elected to the Supreme Court by the General Assembly.

Politics. The November election brought few major surprises. Reelected Democrats included Governor J. Joseph Garrahy and the other state officers. A new Democratic attorney general also was elected. The legislature remained overwhelmingly Democratic. Sen. Claiborne Pell and first district Congressman Fernand St. Germain won reelection easily; in the second district Edward Beard was reelected, though in a surprisingly close race. The only Republican victor was Mayor Vincent Cianci of Providence, who won a second term handily in a traditionally Democratic city. An unprecedented ten out of eleven bond referenda were defeated. The single exception was for mental health facilities.

ELMER E. CORNWELL, JR.
Brown University

RHODE ISLAND · Information Highlights

Area: 1,214 square miles (3,144 km²).
Population (Jan. 1978 est.): 935,000.
Chief Cities (1970 census): Providence, the capital, 179,116; Warwick, 83,694; Pawtucket, 76,984.
Government (1978): *Chief Officers*—governor, J. Joseph Garrahy (D); lt. gov., Thomas R. DiLuglio (D). *Assembly*—Senate, 50 members; House of Representatives, 100 members.
Education (1977–78): Enrollment—public elementary schools, 93,579 pupils; public secondary, 73,050; colleges and universities, 63,691 students. *Public school expenditures*, $320,245,000 ($1,763 per pupil).
State Finances (fiscal year 1977): *Revenues,* $1,037,637,000; *expenditures,* $972,252,000.
Personal Income (1977): $6,332,000,000; per capita, $6,775.
Labor Force (July 1978): *Nonagricultural wage and salary earners* 398,200; *unemployed* 30,500 (6.9% of total force).

RHODESIA

For Rhodesia 1978 was a traumatic year. After the tension, insecurity, and bloody guerrilla warfare of the previous year, Prime Minister Ian Smith's negotiation in March of an internal agreement without the guerrilla leaders seemed to many in the country to hold out new hope for the future. Whites looked above all for an end, first, to the war, and then to sanctions. Blacks looked for an end to white supremacy, the dismantling of racial discrimination, a new constitution, and a general election based on universal suffrage by December 31. In view of the widespread international condemnation of the agreement, the refusal to recognize, let alone encourage, the pact, and the commitment of the United Nations, the Organization of African States, the United States, and Britain to the leaders of the external Patriotic Front—Joshua Nkomo and Robert Mugabe—such expectations were probably always unrealistic.

At the end of the year none of the hopes had been realized, and the general situation had deteriorated seriously. The new constitutional proposals had not yet been presented to the white electorate. The elections were postponed until April 1979. Although the biracial Executive Council of the transition government moved positively, it moved exceedingly slowly to scrap discriminatory legislation. Emigration among the whites reached a new high. The Patriotic Front stepped up its guerrilla activities and the casualties on both sides and among civilians—like the financial and social burdens of the war—continued to escalate. Disillusionment concerning the ability of the transition government to achieve a cease-fire mounted steadily. And to add to the trouble Rhodesia experienced the worst atrocities of its six-year history. An end to the slaughter seemed no nearer in December than it had a year earlier. Meanwhile the joint Anglo-American diplomatic initiative continued to concentrate on bringing about an all-parties conference which would include the leaders of the Patriotic Front.

Internal Affairs. On March 3, after three months of negotiations, Prime Minister Smith signed an agreement with the three internal black leaders, Bishop Muzorewa, the Rev. Sithole and Chief Chirau, which looked toward

Rhodesian leaders sign agreement calling for black majority rule.

black majority rule by December 31. The agreement provided for an interim government comprising an executive council of the four signatories and a ministerial council of equal numbers of blacks and whites. The government's primary tasks were to draw up a constitution and arrange for elections—on the basis of adult suffrage—to a 100-seat parliament, 28 of the seats to be reserved to whites for 10 years. A wide range of protections for the minority white population was agreed to, as was the stipulation that 78 votes in the new chamber would be necessary to pass legislation changing any of the constitution. The completed constitution was to be submitted to the present electorate for approval. The UN's Security Council responded to the agreement on March 14 by declaring it illegal and unacceptable and calling on member states not to recognize it. Britain, Canada, France, the United States and West Germany abstained from the 10–0–5 vote.

On March 21 the three leaders were sworn in and met with Prime Minister Smith for the first meeting of the Executive Council. There it was agreed that the Ministerial Council would number 18 members in 9 posts, each post to be held jointly by a black and white co-minister. The black cabinet posts were distributed equally among the three leaders' organizations. On April 10 the interim government rejected Anglo-American proposals for a new conference involving the externally based Patriotic Front leaders who reiterated their determination to continue the guerrilla war. Attempts by Washington and London to bridge the gap between the interim government's position and that of the Patriotic Front leaders, preparatory to an all-parties conference, failed. Smith's October visit to the United States did not change the position.

The interim government was not without its strains. The dismissal on April 28 of the black co-Minister of Justice, Byron Hove, for remarks critical of civil service discrimination, produced a major crisis and the threat of a walkout by Bishop Muzorewa and his party. There were serious differences over the pace of change, over Smith's secret effort in mid-August to detach Nkomo from the United Front with a new settlement, over the principle of a new all-party conference, over tribal representation, and over the October 27 decision to register all blacks, aged 18–25 years, for national service by December. White emigration rose in October to the highest monthly figure yet—a net loss of 1,582—and estimates for the year put the figure as high as 12,000. The cost of the war was said to exceed $1.2 million a day.

The War. The year was marked by the escalation and mounting ferocity of the guerrilla war. On December 11, in a daring raid, the first of its kind, guerrillas set fire to Rhodesia's largest oil storage complex, in Salisbury. On June 23 guerrillas entered the Elim Pentecostal Mission, 5 miles (8 km) west of the Mozambique border, and brutally murdered 12 missionaries, wives, and children. On September 3 an Air Rhodesia Viscount leaving Kariba was shot down by a SAM 7 missile, killing 38. Ten survivors, including 7 women and 2 children, who stayed by the plane, were shortly after murdered by guerrillas. The Rhodesian security forces conducted a number of large-scale air strikes and raids on guerrilla bases in Mozambique. But the largest military operation of the war was mounted October 21 against Nkomo's bases in Zambia as far north as Lusaka.

RONALD B. BALLINGER
Rhode Island College

RHODESIA · Information Highlights

Official Name: Rhodesia.
Area: 150,673 square miles (390,245 km²).
Population (1978 est.): 7,000,000.
Chief Cities (1976 est.): Salisbury, the capital, 568,000; Bulawayo, 340,000.
Government: *Head of government,* Ian Smith, prime minister (took office 1964).
Monetary Unit: Rhodesian dollar (1.46 R. dollars equal U. S.$1, April 1978).
Agriculture (major products): Tobacco, sugar, tea, groundnuts, cotton, corn, millet, sorghum, wheat.

RUMANIA

Domestic Affairs. On Jan. 26, 1978, Rumanians celebrated President Nicolae Ceauşescu's 60th birthday with nationwide festivities. When the Central Committee of the Communist party met in March, there were a reported 2,747,000 party members, or about 27% of the active adult population. Resolutions adopted at the meeting called for larger representation of women and workers in the party hierarchy; more active youth organizations; and better training of party members. Ceauşescu recommended a new profit-sharing system for industrial workers. In April, Ceauşescu publicly criticized "excessive centralism" in national policies and called for increased worker participation in the management of industrial enterprises.

In June, in a speech to the Conference of Rumanian Fine Arts, he emphasized that artists in all fields must be "active detachments" of the Communist party. In July and again in September, he reported to the Central Committee that the "net production" of the national economy fell below the "planned level." In July, Ion Pacepa, a senior intelligence adviser, sought asylum in the West. Soon after, Minister of Interior Teodor Colman and other high officials were removed from office. On August 28, Amnesty International accused Rumanian authorities of violating human rights by abusing psychiatric patients.

Foreign Affairs and Trade. After Stefan Andrei replaced George Macovescu as foreign minister in March, Rumania's participation in international affairs increased markedly. Government, political, and business leaders of Japan, the United States, West Germany, France, and other nations visited Bucharest. Rumanian state and party leaders paid official visits to some 15 nations. President Ceauşescu was accorded warm and ceremonious receptions in the United States in April and in Great Britain in June.

Rumania's relations with China were openly friendly. In August, Chinese Premier Hua kuofeng visited Bucharest amid strong criticism from the Soviet Union, Albania, and Bulgaria.

Trade between Rumania and the United States reached $493 million, still well under the $1 billion (U. S.) target set for 1980. To improve the situation, the United States accorded Rumania a line of credit for $110 million to purchase American feed grain. This supplemented an existing credit of $23 million for the purchase of soybeans. In exchange, Rumania deposited $53 million in the United States for high grade American coal. In June, representatives of some 60 U. S. corporations attended a session of the Rumanian-American Economic Council in Bucharest.

In 1977, Rumanian exports to the European Community (EC) grew to $1.3 billion. Imports amounted to $1.2 million. A group of 28 international banks gave Rumania a loan of 300 million Eurodollars, payable in eight years.

In 1977, 17% of Rumania's total foreign trade was with the Soviet Union. In 1960, it was about 40%.

JAN KARSKI
Georgetown University

RUMANIA • Information Highlights

Official Name: Socialist Republic of Rumania.
Location: Southeastern Europe.
Area: 91,700 square miles (237,500 km²).
Population (1978 est.): 21,900,000.
Chief Cities (Jan. 1977): Bucharest, the capital, 1,934,-025; Constanta, 290,226; Ploieşti, 254,592.
Government: *Head of state,* Nicolae Ceauşescu, president and secretary general of the Communist Party (took office 1965). *Head of government,* Manea Manescu, premier (took office March 1974). *Legislature* (unicameral)—Grand National Assembly.
Monetary Unit: Leu (4.97 lei equal U. S.$1, 1977).
Manufactures (major products): Power; mining, forestry, and construction materials; metal products; chemicals; machines; processed foods; textiles.
Agriculture (major products): Corn, potatoes, wheat, oil seeds.

SAN FRANCISCO

Late in 1978 San Francisco was stunned by the murders of its mayor and a city supervisor.

City Hall Murders. On November 27 Mayor George Moscone and city supervisor Harvey Milk were shot and killed in City Hall. Later that day former supervisor Daniel White surrendered to police. White, recently resigned from the Board of Supervisors, had asked Mayor Moscone to reappoint him. The mayor's decision was to be announced on November 27. Dianne Feinstein, President of the Board of Supervisors, became acting mayor.

Peoples Temple. In November members of the San Francisco-based Peoples Temple community in Guyana killed Representative Leo Ryan of San Francisco and three newsmen before engaging in a bizarre mass murder/suicide of more than 900 people. (See Feature Article, page 34.)

Art. John D. Rockefeller, 3rd, left his 200-work, $10-million American art collection to the Fine Arts Museum of San Francisco.

EDWARD M. KURDYLA, JR.

SASKATCHEWAN

Premier Allan Blakeney led the New Democratic Party (NDP) back into office in the October 18 legislative election. The NDP took 44 seats, and the Progressive Conservatives gained the remaining 17. For the first time in Saskatchewan history, the Liberal Party failed to hold a single seat. The NDP victory was attributed to effective management of a burgeoning resource industry. The party's 27-point election program included reduced income tax, lower property tax for the elderly, and property improvement grants to renters.

The Economy. Unprecedented programs for resource development had far-reaching effects on the economy. One such program was a $99 million, eight-year agreement to develop heavy oil reserves at Lloydminster. Signed by the Saskatchewan government, Petro-Canada, Gulf Oil Limited, and Saskoil, the agreement calls for the exploration of 500,000 acres (202,500 ha.) of land, plus development of at least two tertiary recovery systems.

The province's economic future was also brightened by an $80 million expansion of the Inter-Provincial Steel and Pipe Corporation (IPSCO) Plant near Regina. This was considered necessary to win a major share of the pipe contracts for the proposed Alaska Highway gas pipeline.

Eighty-seven companies, spending some $60 million, explored for uranium in 1978, placing Saskatchewan among the top uranium-producing areas in the world.

The Legislature. C. Irwin McIntosh, a North Battleford publisher, was sworn in as Saskatchewan's fifteenth lieutenant-governor, following the death of George Porteous in February.

A quiet legislative session yielded sweeping changes in education and statutory approval for the Saskatchewan Heritage Fund. Ownership of Saskatchewan farm land was limited to 160 acres (65 ha.) for persons living outside the province.

Regina's 75th Anniversary. A yearlong calendar of events marked the 75th year of Regina's city status. The observances culminated in a visit by Queen Elizabeth II and Prince Philip.

DOROTHY HAYDEN, *Regina Public Library*

SAUDI ARABIA

Caution was the byword of the Saudi Arabian government as it continued military and economic growth while maintaining a close relationship with the United States.

Military. In 1978, Saudi Arabia became the world's largest purchaser of U. S. armaments and other military facilities, spending an estimated (U. S.) $4.9 billion. After a long debate, the U. S. Senate voted, May 15, to sell 60 F-15 warplanes to Saudi Arabia. The Saudis had assured the United States that the planes would be used for defense purposes only and would not be

stationed close to the Israeli border. Fear of Soviet expansion in the Red Sea area, a desire to protect their oil fields better, and a growing suspicion of Iran led Saudi Arabia to increase expenditures on its 45,000-man Army and 35,000-man National Guard.

Finance and Economy. Although Saudi Arabia continued its phenomenal economic growth in 1977–78, the world surplus of oil and the decline in value of the U. S. dollar created unexpected financial problems. By May, oil production had decreased to about 7,000,000 barrels per day from the 9,000,000 it had averaged in 1977. As a result, the government ordered a 33% reduction in the budget and began to sell foreign securities to ease the cash-flow problem. The purchase of the 40% of the Arabian-American Oil Company still held by private concerns was delayed.

However, internal economic development continued with such large-scale contracts as $3 billion for the expansion of the telephone system. Saudi foreign reserves were estimated at $51 billion and the rate of inflation was reduced from 30% to 10%. In 1977, over 27 billion tons of goods were imported. The import bonanza began to transform the cities and general life style in Saudi Arabia.

Foreign Affairs. The Mideast peace initiative by Egyptian President Anwar el-Sadat was cautiously welcomed by Saudi Arabia, which continued its massive financial support of that country. Although the Saudis repeatedly stressed the importance of self-determination for Palestinians, they refused to criticize Sadat publicly for making a separate peace with Israel. For the first time, Israeli Arabs were allowed to make the pilgrimage to Mecca.

Saudi foreign policy was closely coordinated with that of the United States. President Carter visited Riyadh in January and King Khalid met with him again in Washington in October.

On December 17, Oil Minister Ahmed Zaki Yamani joined with the other representatives of the Organization of Petroleum Exporting Countries (OPEC) in announcing a 14.49% increase in the price of crude oil for 1979. OPEC representatives said that the increases were imposed because of the decreasing value of the U. S. dollar, still the OPEC pricing currency, and because of the slowdown in production of Iranian oil. Still, Yamani was "not happy" with the

—— SASKATCHEWAN • Information Highlights ——

Area: 251,700 square miles (651,900 km²).
Population (1978 est.): 945,600.
Chief Cities (1976 census): Regina, the capital, 149,593; Saskatoon, 133,750; Moose Jaw, 32,581.
Government (1978): *Chief Officers*—lt. gov., C. Irwin McIntosh; premier, Allan Blakeney; chief justice, Court of Appeal, E. M. Culliton; Queen's Bench, F. W. Johnson. *Legislature*—Legislative Assembly, 60 members.
Education (1976–77): *Enrollment*—public elementary and secondary schools, 216,050 pupils; private schools, 1,480; Indian (federal) schools, 5,910 students; post-secondary, 16,960 students. *Total expenditures,* $343,770,000.
Personal Income (average weekly salary, May 1978): $249.04.
Unemployment Rate (July 1978, seasonally adjusted): 3.9%.
(All monetary figures are in Canadian dollars.)

—— SAUDI ARABIA • Information Highlights ——

Official Name: Kingdom of Saudi Arabia.
Location: Arabian Peninsula in southwest Asia.
Area: 830,000 square miles (2,149,690 km²).
Population (1978 est.): 7,800,000.
Chief Cities (1976 est.): Riyadh, the capital, 667,000; Jidda, 561,000; Mecca, 367,000.
Government: *Head of state and government,* Khalid ibn Abd al-Aziz al-Saud, king (acceded March 1975).
Monetary Unit: Riyal (3.305 riyals equal U. S.$1, Nov. 1978).
Manufactures (major products): Petroleum products, cement, fertilizers.
Agriculture (major products): Dates, vegetables, grains.

Saudi Arabia's King Khalid and Crown Prince Fahd await the departure of President Carter at Riyadh's International Airport. The crown prince assumed greater responsibility in 1978 as a result of the king's failing health.

UPI

size of the increase and hoped that there would be a price freeze for 1980. "I tried my best to make it a little bit lower," he said, "but the market is in a unique situation, especially with the Iran crisis."

King Khalid gave substantial monetary support to the anti-Soviet governments of Zaire, Somalia, and North Yemen and to Eritrean secessionists in Ethiopia. Saudi Arabia tried but failed to secure a settlement to the civil war in Lebanon. Saudi troops took a more active role in the Arab peacekeeping force in October, as they replaced some Syrian units in Beirut.

Government. The conflict between rapid modernization and Islamic moral standards was revealed in three separate incidents during the year—the execution of a Saudi princess on charges of adultery; the punishment of foreigners who sold alcohol in the country; and the minister of labor's reiteration that women would not be allowed to work.

Although King Khalid continued to rule, his failing health left greater responsibility in the hands of Crown Prince Fahd. In September, the king went to the Cleveland (Ohio) Clinic to undergo open heart surgery and remained there for a month. Despite hints of a split in the royal family over foreign policy issues, there were no basic changes in the cabinet, army, or administration.

WILLIAM L. OCHSENWALD
Virginia Polytechnic Institute

SINGAPORE

A massive airline expansion and a soaring Asiadollar highlighted Singapore activities.

Singapore Airlines. On May 9 Singapore Airlines announced an agreement with The Boeing Company to purchase nearly $900 million worth of jets, the first of which would be delivered in 1982. Singapore Airlines agreed to buy 10 long-range 747 jumbo jets and 4 medium-range 727 trijets. The airline also took an option on 3 additional 747's and 2 additional 727's. Fifty percent of the deal was to be financed through foreign banks.

Cabinet Change. In July the government announced a restructuring of the cabinet, dividing the Ministry of National Development and Communications into separate ministries. Lim Kim San retained responsibility for national development, while Ong Teng Cheong became the new minister of communication. Ong, acting minister of culture, was senior minister of state for communications.

International Banking. Singapore was the center of intense international banking activity in 1978 as trading of Singapore bank certificates of deposit (CD's) began on January 4. The Singapore CD's were yielding substantially higher rates than those in Europe and the United States, placing the Asiadollar in competition with the Eurodollar for investors' funds.

Foreign Affairs. Richard Kneip resigned as governor of South Dakota after being named U. S. ambassador to Singapore.

KARL J. PELZER
Professor Emeritus, *Yale University*

────── SINGAPORE • Information Highlights ──────

Official Name: Republic of Singapore.
Location: Southeast Asia.
Area: 224 square miles (580 km²).
Population (1978 est.): 2,300,000.
Chief City (1974 est.): Singapore, the capital, 1,327,500.
Government: *Head of state,* Benjamin H. Sheares, president (took office Jan. 1971). *Head of government,* Lee Kuan Yew, prime minister (took office 1959). *Legislature* (unicameral)—Parliament.
Monetary Unit: Singapore dollar (2.161 S. dollars equal U. S.$1, Nov. 1978).
Manufactures (major products): Refined petroleum, processed rubber.
Agriculture (major products): Tobacco, vegetables, fruits, some rubber and coconut palms.

UPI

Secretary of Health, Education, and Welfare, Joseph Califano, unveils the Carter administration's national health insurance program.

SOCIAL WELFARE

A worldwide rise in the inflation rate in 1978 forced most industrial countries of Western Europe to scrutinize their welfare programs, leading to general reductions in many cases. Political unrest and terrorism, especially in Spain and Italy, were attributed to bleak employment prospects for educated youth, generating much discussion but little action as the governments of those nations wrestled with inflation. Great Britain's Labour government maintained a firm commitment to its three-year-old anti-inflation policies that improved the balance of payments position but diluted further the welfare programs and the standard of living of many groups in that society. In France, the Giscard d'Estaing government responded to political pressures from the left and the right by undertaking implementation of Premier Raymond Barre's economic plan, which overturned a half-century of welfare history (in the case of removal of bread subsidies, almost two centuries). Wage subsidies and some forms of family allotments were abolished in the interest of reducing government spending. Similar measures in West Germany kept wages frozen and reduced almost all types of social welfare spending. In the Soviet Union, Poland, and other Marxist economies, the major innovations were the adoption of new rules for workers in factories, with more input from the workers themselves, more frequent "relaxation periods" for workers in the Ukraine's heavy industries, and improved old-age pensions for farmers in Poland's private sector.

In the United States, the year began with the mild shock of the Social Security Act reforms going into effect. The shock lay in workers finding much of their previous year's salary increases wiped out by the higher deductions from their pay checks, since the changes were paid for by higher definition of the taxable wage base and raising the tax rate for the roughly 100 million participants in Social Security programs. The reaction was strong enough to make several Congressional leaders call for reconsideration of the reforms. The furor died down within a few months, but the need for an income tax reduction that would offset future increases in Social Security taxes took on greater urgency with the realization that larger increases in the taxable wage base, from $17,700 to $22,900, and of the tax rate, from 6.05% to 6.13%, would go into effect automatically on Jan. 1, 1979.

Meanwhile, the Carter administration began the year still pressing for its welfare reform bill, including a Program for Better Jobs and Income based in part on experiments with the negative income tax idea, providing direct payments to low-income groups. A national health program was in the works, and a presidential Commission on Mental Health was recommending bold new efforts at keeping patients out of state mental hospitals or welfare hotels by improving home treatment and preventive medicine, at an estimated cost of $600 million over five years. A White House Conference on Handicapped Individuals also recommended steps on behalf of its constituents. In addition, a White House Conference on Families, which would generate further ideas in the welfare field, was called for 1979.

Most of these new proposals, or beefed-up old ones, were gradually pushed aside during the summer and autumn, as the great "tax revolt" in California brought a sweeping victory for Proposition 13 (the Jarvis-Gann state constitutional amendment, cutting property taxes and limiting their growth in the future). Primarily a revolt by owners of small homes which had rapidly risen in value and consequently in tax vulnerability over the past decade, making the property tax, on which state governments relied for the bulk of their revenues, increasingly regressive, the California vote in June sparked a rash of similar efforts and campaign debates across the United States and reversed the political context of discussion and action about social welfare.

Congress and the Carter administration had both shown greater sensitivity to the problems of burgeoning costs, ineffective or duplicative administration of programs, and the need to consolidate and rationalize national welfare institutions. Secretary of Health, Education, and Welfare (HEW) Joseph A. Califano, Jr., stepped up his efforts in that direction in the first half of the year. His department was running 350 different programs, had a budget for 1978 of (U. S.) $182 billion (36% of total federal outlays), and had 150,000 employees. With a talent for generating disputes, Califano became perhaps the most controversial member of the Carter cabinet. He made blunt comments on smoking as a danger to health (having quit only recently himself) that offended tobacco interests; on rising hospital costs that offended medical lobbyists; and on drug hazards that offended doctors and pharmaceutical companies. But he did reorganize several older programs, reclassified the jobs of 20,000 of the department's civil servants, and recruited several assistants with outstanding reputations for effective handling of large bureaucracies. One achievement was the revitalization of the VISTA program, all but moribund when Carter was elected, into a major force in alleviating some of the problems of the urban ghettos.

The problems of big cities and the hard-core unemployed were particular targets of HEW efforts. CETA, created with the Comprehensive Employment and Training Act of 1973, was revised so as to give more aid to structurally unemployed under a new Title II of the Act, and to cyclically unemployed under a new Title VI. Of the $10 billion allocated to this effort in 1977, more than $8 billion went for salaries of municipal employees who were part of the program. In May, an amendment to Title XX of the Social Security Act included a special urban aid plan. The National Health Service Corps, which had 80% of its doctors providing medical services to rural areas which had suffered acute shortages of doctors, came under pressure to shift some of its personnel to the underserved inner-city neighborhoods.

Early in the year, Congress had been slowly responding to administration efforts to extend welfare by passing the Comprehensive Rehabilitation Services Amendments of 1978, which authorized spending more than $7 billion over the next five years, and which started a number of new programs on behalf of the handicapped. The Comprehensive Older Americans Act Amendments of 1978 authorized more than $4 billion and initiated measures that reinforced the decision outlawing compulsory retirement at 65 years of age.

In these areas, Congress had been establishing executive-branch advisory committees to oversee the administration of these programs. About 400 advisory committees were attached to HEW by mid-1978, and efforts to consolidate them met with resistance. On the other hand, it was the Congressional Budget Office that helped kick off a tax revolt within the federal government.

A Budget Office study on the impact of the President's Program for Better Jobs and Income claimed that it would increase the number of Americans receiving some form of welfare from 44 to 66 million, and that little of the increases

in benefits (costing $20 billion) would actually reach people with incomes below the poverty line. Other studies, particularly one by Stanford University economist Martin Anderson, lent credence to the growing chorus of complaints from conservative economists, welfare experts, and political critics, who claimed that the War on Poverty was over and that the major task was to consolidate the welfare system without extending it. Congressional leaders informed the president on June 22 that this thesis had gained enough support to make the passage of the welfare reform bill, even in compromised forms, impossible. By then it was also clear that the proposed national health insurance plan, to which President Carter had pledged his backing, also had no chance of enactment. Estimates that it would cost between $40 and $60 billion threw the plan into direct conflict with the previously announced goal of reducing federal expenditures from 22.6% to 21% of GNP by 1981. Complaints about operations reached a new crescendo at every level of government. Charges concerning the misuse of CETA funds by municipalities, the organization of health care, and the failure of the Occupational Safety and Health Act to inspect more than 10% of the nation's work places annually, were but the main features of a wide-spread disenchantment with bureaucracy in welfare.

In the administration of welfare benefits, however, the hottest issue remained the question of public funding for abortions on demand. The passage of the Hyde amendment to the HEW budget in December 1977 allowed the use of federal funds for medicaid abortions only under special conditions. A group of women's rights and welfare rights organizations joined in filing a class action suit challenging the constitutionality of the Hyde amendment on the grounds that it was the result of undue religious influence, but the prospects for success along that line seemed dim. Meanwhile, the National Right to Life

Protests and a White House conference drew increasing attention to the problems of the handicapped.

UPI

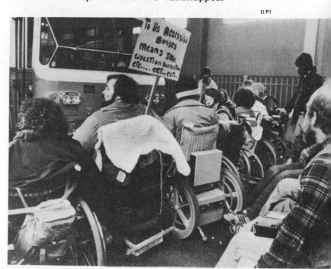

Committee, claiming a membership of 11 million, and the Friends for Life, along with similar opponents of abortion, often with the support of the Roman Catholic and other churches, mounted greater public attacks on abortion than at any time since the Supreme Court held it to be legal in 1973. No longer focusing on the question of abortion for welfare recipients, they sought instead a full reversal of the court's decision, and apparently helped inspire activities reminiscent of the civil disobedience tactics used by anti-Vietnam War activists. There were widespread incidents of harassment of women who patronized abortion clinics, of vandalism that destroyed much equipment in the clinics, several attempts at arson, and some harassment of doctors who performed abortions.

The number of welfare-associated abortions declined dramatically during the year, partly because of the Hyde amendment and partly because of anti-abortion pressures at the state level. Sixteen states continued to provide funding for abortions on demand for poor women, accounting for 65% of the 275,000 welfare-funded operations in 1977, but the elimination of federal Medicaid funding and additional restrictions in the other 34 states reduced state funded operations. In New Jersey, for example, which once funded 10,000 abortions a year, there were only 240 publicly-funded cases.

Although increasingly confined to those women who could afford to pay for them, abortions continued to augment and reached an estimated 1.5 million in 1978. A study of two-year-old data revealed that of the women who had abortions, 75% were unmarried, 67% were white, and 66% were under 25 years of age. Family planning experts called the phenomenon an "epidemic of pregnancies," and blamed much of it on still inadequate birth control education and restrictions on sale of contraceptives.

Some of the reduction of public funding for abortions was offset by help in meeting costs from the Planned Parenthood associations. But they, and many other old and new organizations, began lining up in defense of abortions and in defense of the 1973 Supreme Court decision. Initially, opposing forces seemed to have gained the initiative, persuading 13 states by mid-year to pass resolutions calling for a constitutional convention to draft an amendment that would ban abortions altogether. On the other hand, the American Civil Liberties Union joined with the pro-abortion groups, making a woman's right to choose an abortion its top priority issue of the year and challenging restrictive state and local legislation on this issue wherever they could. The National Abortion Rights Action League attributed its rapid growth of members, representing a four-fold increase in 1977 and no apparent diminution in that rate, to the publicity generated by cutting off funds for the poor who wanted abortions. But toward the end of the year, what had been a welfare rights issue was transformed into a struggle over women's rights, civil rights, and the right to life, with the same passions aroused on all sides. The campaigns continued to mount in the elections, embracing many questions about national values, religious and other kinds of ethics, family life, and individual rights, but the welfare component, consigned at least for the time being to state government, was no longer significant. In this area, too, retreat was the order of the day.

See also OLDER POPULATION.

MORTON ROTHSTEIN
University of Wisconsin-Madison

SOLOMON ISLANDS

The South Pacific's third largest ministate was launched at Honiara, on Guadalcanal, on July 7, 1978, when the Union Jack was lowered after 85 years and colonial status was ended. The Duke and Duchess of Gloucester represented Queen Elizabeth at the ceremonies during which a new green, yellow and blue Solomon Islands flag was raised for the first time.

At the inauguration, oaths of allegiance were administered by Chief Justice Renn Davis to the 37-year-old governor-general, Baddeley Devesi, and the 35-year-old prime minister, Peter Kenilorea. The constitutional arrangements for the new nation of some 250,000 Melanesian people were framed by the Solomons legislature, which decided to remain under the British Crown, with provision for a native-born governor-general and a single-house parliament. Provincial administrations have considerable authority—a concession to the strong current of regional autonomy evident in the western outliers.

First visited by the Spanish in the mid-16th century, the Solomons were named in the belief that they were the long-lost source of King Solomon's gold. After this initial contact, the islands were seldom visited until the 19th century, when islanders were taken for plantation work. In World War II the islands marked the limit of Japan's southward drive and were the scene of heavy fighting before the invaders were overwhelmed by U. S. forces in 1943.

Palm oil remains the dominant export. The new nation joined the United Nations but will not maintain permanent representation anywhere abroad, relying instead on roving missions. Poor communications, a shortage of professional skills, and scanty resources limit Solomons prospects. Britain and Australia have pledged foreign aid.

R. M. YOUNGER, *Australian Author*

— SOLOMON ISLANDS · Information Highlights —

Location: South Pacific.
Area: 11,500 square miles (29,210 km²).
Population (1978 est.): 250,000.
Chief City (1976 census): Honiara (capital) 14,993.
Government (1978): Head of State Elizabeth II, queen; Baddeley Devesi, governor-general. Head of government, Peter Kenilorea, prime minister.
Agriculture (major products): coconuts, cocoa, rice.

LIAISON

Defense Minister P. W. Botha is inaugurated as the eighth prime minister of South Africa.

SOUTH AFRICA

After the internal disturbances of 1976–77, South Africa during 1978 presented a political situation clearly dominated by the ruling National party government and its determination to maintain the apartheid state.

The general election at the end of 1977 had given the government the largest electoral victory in the 17 elections since 1910. The three opposition parties won only 30 of the 165 seats. The Progressive Federal party became the new official opposition with 17 seats in the House of Assembly. The New Republic party won 10 and the South African party 3. Prime Minister B. Johannes Vorster said "the results exceeded my wildest expectations."

Nevertheless, 1978 was marked by uncertainty, tension, and mounting international pressures both with regard to internal policies and external relations. The deteriorating Rhodesian situation, the crisis in negotiations over the future of Namibia (South West Africa), rising unemployment, the simmering realities of Soweto and acute black housing shortages, the Crossroads "squatters camp" affair, the shortage of investment capital, and the confirmation of a vast political and financial scandal—and attempted cover-up—in the ministry of information, were matters of great concern. And to these could be added the unknown effect of the crisis in Iran upon the supply of oil to South Africa. On February 26, Robert Sobukwe, founder of the banned Pan African Congress, died in Kimberley of lung cancer. His last 18 years had been spent in prison or under government restrictions.

The most immediately significant events took place in the last three months of the year. These events included the resignation of the prime minister; the election of his successor; the resignation of C. Mulder, the second ranking cabinet minister and former minister of information—that department was disbanded in June; the decision to proceed unilaterally with elections in Namibia; the struggle over the leadership of the powerful Transvaal wing of the National party; and the recall of Parliament to consider the report of a special judicial committee on the budgeting and use of secret funds channeled to the ministry of information.

Internal Affairs. On September 20 Prime Minister Vorster announced his retirement from the office he had held for 12 years. He was subsequently elected state president and inaugurated on October 12. He succeeded Nicolaas D. Diederichs who died in August. For the first time since 1958 the party caucus was forced to vote. It chose the 62 year-old Defense Minister, P. W. Botha, leader of the Cape Wing and a member of Parliament since 1948, by 98 votes to 74 over Mulder, the leader in the Transvaal.

Faced with the continuing revelation of abuses in the use of public funds uncovered after months of mounting controversy by Supreme Court Justice Anton Mostert in his capacity as a one-man commission concerned with foreign exchange violations, and by the opposition press, Botha asked for Mulder's resignation. He then dismissed Judge Mostert from his commission and appointed a three-man judicial commission of inquiry. As successor to Mulder, he appointed P. Koornhof to handle the government's relations with blacks. Koornhof is regarded as "verligte" (enlightened) as opposed to Deputy Minister A. Treurnicht, who was passed over. Eleven days later, November 25, by a vote of 63 to 45, Treurnicht defeated Botha's choice, Labour Minister S. P. Botha, for the leadership of the Transvaal wing of the National party. This post, which Mulder also resigned, is generally regarded as the second most important one in the party hierarchy. In National party terms the election was seen as a defeat for the "verligtes," and a problem for the new prime minister. Treurnicht, 57-year-old former minister of the Dutch Reformed Church and leader of the conservatives, was opposed both to the concessions over "petty apartheid" and Vorster's constitutional proposals which the new prime minister was expected to implement. But in his first speech in his new post, Treurnicht stressed the unity and solidarity of the party.

The second anniversary of the Soweto riots was observed June 16 without violence but with considerable police activity. Some 5,000 blacks were arrested at road blocks and raids, most of them just prior to the commemoration services. Many were charged with past offenses. Earlier in the month it was announced that the new Soweto Community Council elected in February and April—only 5% of those eligible voted—was to be given the same civic powers as white municipalities. This followed the release in March of N. Motlana, the Soweto Committee of Ten leader, P. Qoboza, the prominent black editor, and 11 others among those detained without trial since October 1977. The school boycott going on since September 1977 was virtually over by the end of March, but enrollment in the Soweto schools was reportedly only half the 1976–77 figure. That same month, after a General Bar Council deputation approached the ministry of justice, James Kruger, the justice minister, announced that he would appoint jurists to visit detainees and arrange regular examinations by district surgeons.

On May 17 Kruger announced that he was closing the file on the death of black consciousness leader Steven Biko. The department report showed that while the security police had made "errors of judgment," no disciplinary action was required. On the eve of the first anniversary of Biko's death, September 12, the security police arrested all of his close friends and relatives, including his sister and brother-in-law, under the Internal Security Act. Spokesmen for the Biko family said no formal memorial gatherings had been planned, but a number of black consciousness leaders were arrested in various parts of the country. Four days later, September 14, hundreds of armed police raided Crossroads, the crowded squatter camp on the outskirts of Cape Town, where some 20,000 men, women, and children live as families in defiance of the law. But as a result of strong protest, Koornhof announced November 20 that government plans to demolish the camp had been postponed indefinitely.

Namibia (South West Africa). In his resignation speech, Vorster announced the rejection of the UN-backed five Western powers' plan for Namibia's independence. He said that instead the government would proceed unilaterally with elections before the end of the year. The threat of UN economic sanctions notwithstanding, the elections were held December 4–8. As expected, the government-favored Democratic Turnhalle Alliance (DTA) won; SWAPO (South West African People's Organization) boycotted them; and the UN condemned them in advance.

See also AFRICA; BIOGRAPHY: Botha, P. W.
RONALD BALLINGER, *Rhode Island College*

SOUTH CAROLINA

A successful legislative session and the November elections highlighted the events of South Carolina in 1978.

Election. Democrat Richard W. Riley was elected governor with 61% of the vote, carrying every county but one. Sen. J. Strom Thurmond was elected to his 5th U. S. Senate term, overcoming strong opposition from Democrat Charles D. Ravenel. Democrat Nancy Stevenson, elected lieutenant governor with 64% of the vote, became the first woman to be elected to a statewide office. With Carrol A. Campbell, Jr., winning in the 4th district, the Republicans gained one seat in Congress. Voters approved constitutional amendments establishing a 5% reserve fund of state revenues and reducing the separation period for divorce from 3 years to one.

Government. The state had a large surplus which was placed in the reserve fund. The general assembly held a long but very fruitful session. Among the major laws enacted were: a school equalization finance act to equalize per pupil expenditure throughout the state and to fund additional programs; reorganization of the higher education commission, giving it more authority and removing the institutional members; revision of the aid to dependent children program; the increase of medicaid benefits; a plan to control federal expenditures granted to departments; extension of the homestead exemption to municipal property taxes; the revision of insurance laws; and passage of sunset legislation.

─── **SOUTH AFRICA · Information Highlights** ───

Official Name: Republic of South Africa.
Location: Southern tip of Africa.
Area: 471,445 square miles (1,221,037 km²).
Population (1978 est.): 27,500,000.
Chief Cities (1970 census): Pretoria, the administrative capital, 543,950; Cape Town, the legislative capital, 691,296; Johannesburg, 642,967; Durban, 495,458.
Government: *Head of state,* B. Johannes Vorster, president (took office Oct. 1978). *Head of government,* P. W. Botha, prime minister (took office Sept. 1978). *Legislature*—Parliament: Senate and House of Assembly.
Monetary Unit: Rand (0.8696 rand equals U. S.$1, Dec. 28, 1978).
Manufactures (major products): Textiles, chemicals, fertilizers, automobiles, fabricated metals, fish.
Agriculture (major products): Sugarcane, tobacco, corn, citrus fruits, wheat, dairy products, wool.

The ERA amendment was defeated. Two new office buildings for state legislators were completed.

Economy and Development. Unemployment dropped to 4% and tax collections exceeded revenue predictions. Industrial expansion receded. A $56 million port terminal expansion began in Charleston and $162 million was approved for state capital improvements. Prolonged dry weather cut yields in major state crops. Cotton acreage dropped sharply, with most of the land now being planted in soybeans. Revenues from tobacco and peaches were good. Environmentalists continued to attack the Russell Dam, the Barnwell nuclear facility, and changes in the river system.

Education. Adult and vocational education expanded, the public school drop-out rate was reduced to the national level, performance on the SAT tests increased to within 4 points of the U. S. average, and kindergartens were available to all five-year-olds. Short courses were given to parents, instructing them how to aid their children in schools. A Mental Competency Testing Program in the public schools was authorized.

Social and Cultural. The state started a subsidized housing program for medium income families through a bond issue. The Babcock Center of Columbia received a $3.5 million grant from HUD to erect private homes for the mentally retarded. Work began on modern housing additions for prisoners, and the first cottage complex for the mentally ill opened in the state.

ROBERT H. STOUDEMIRE
University of South Carolina

SOUTH DAKOTA

Economic gain, legislative action, and general elections were in the news in South Dakota in 1978.

Election. Three-term Governor Richard Kneip, ineligible for another term, resigned in 1978 to become the U. S. ambassador to Singapore. In the November election Republican Attorney General William Janklow defeated Democrat Roger McKellips for Kneip's seat. Rep. Larry Pressler (R) defeated former Rapid City Mayor Don Barnett (D) in the race to replace retiring U. S. Sen. James Abourezk. Republicans won two thirds of the seats in both houses of the state legislature and won the offices of secretary of state, auditor, treasurer, and attorney general.

In an important regional election of officers to the Oahe Conservancy Subdistrict Board, voters reelected three advocates of pipelines to transport water from the Missouri River to arid counties and urban communities in the northeastern part of the state. The vote was thought to assure the replacement of a federal canal-reservoir plan with one more in keeping with public opinion about the preservation of land surface and ecology.

In voting on referenda, South Dakotans supported a constitutional amendment to prevent increases in sales and property taxes without support by two thirds of the members of each house in the legislature or the approval of the electorate. They also repealed the Dairy Marketing Act to reduce the cost of milk, defeated a measure to raise rates charged to consumers of large amounts of energy, and rejected a proposal to tighten controls on obscenity.

Legislation. In a "house-keeping" session typical of recent years, the legislature's most dramatic action was the increase of state allocations to $194.5 million for the purpose of giving greater support to educational and social needs. At the same time they reduced annual revenue by $40 million through the repeal of an unpopular property tax, without supplying means to raise funds from another source. They also rejected appeals to reconsider South Dakota's ratification of the Equal Rights Amendment, increased the minimum wage to $2.30 an hour, and denied the use of state funds to pay costs of abortions for indigent women.

Economy. Unemployment dropped to 3.2%, tourism boomed, and agriculture flourished under favorable conditions. After several years of drought and sagging prices, farmers expressed cautious optimism with the return of ample rainfall and higher prices.

HERBERT T. HOOVER
University of South Dakota

— **SOUTH CAROLINA · Information Highlights** —

Area: 31,055 square miles (80,432 km²).
Population (Jan. 1978 est.): 2,894,000.
Chief Cities (1970 census): Columbia, the capital, 113,-542; Charleston, 66,945; Greenville, 61,436.
Government (1978): *Chief Officers*—governor, James B. Edwards (R); lt. gov., W. Brantley Harvey, Jr. (D). *General Assembly*—Senate, 46 members; House of Representatives, 124 members.
Education (1977–78): *Enrollment*—public elementary schools, 373,796 pupils; public secondary, 246,927; colleges and universities, 125,245 students. *Public school expenditures,* $906,100,000 ($1,293 per pupil).
State Finances (fiscal year 1977): *Revenues,* $2,414,-949,000; *expenditures,* $2,334,336,000.
Personal Income (1977): $16,186,000,000; per capita, $5,628.
Labor Force (July 1978): *Nonagricultural wage and salary earners,* 1,114,100; *unemployed,* 84,200 (6.3% of total force).

— **SOUTH DAKOTA · Information Highlights** —

Area: 77,047 square miles (199,552 km²).
Population (Jan. 1978 est.): 691,000.
Chief Cities (1970 census): Pierre, the capital, 9,699; Sioux Falls, 74,488; Rapid City, 43,836.
Government (1978): *Chief Officers*—governor, Richard F. Kneip (D); lt. gov., Harvey Wollman (D). *Legislature*—Senate, 35 members; House of Representatives, 70 members.
Education (1977–78): *Enrollment*—public elementary schools, 93,987 pupils; public secondary, 49,643; colleges and universities, 31,110 students. *Public school expenditures,* $221,260,000 ($1,322 per pupil).
State Finances (fiscal year 1977): *Revenues,* $543,702,-000; *expenditures,* $528,910,000.
Personal Income (1977): $4,104,000,000; per capita, $5,957.
Labor Force (July 1978): *Nonagricultural wage and salary earners,* 240,000; *unemployed,* 11,600 (3.3% of total force).

UPI

An experimental Japanese communications satellite, BSE, was launched from the Kennedy Space Center in April.

SPACE EXPLORATION

The year 1978 marked the 20th anniversary of the National Aeronautics and Space Administration (NASA), which was created on Oct. 1, 1958. The civilian space agency was mandated to develop and utilize space technology for practical applications and to expand our knowledge of the earth, its environment, the solar system, and the universe. The first two NASA decades witnessed the manned exploration of the moon, the unmanned exploration of Mars, astronomical observations of the universe from space, and the use of space communications and space remote-sensing for improved global communications, environmental monitoring, and earth resource management.

It was also a record year for manned endurance in space, with Soyuz 29 cosmonauts Vladimir Kovalenok and Alexander Ivanchenkov orbiting the earth in the Salyut 6 space station for a record 140 days.

The planet Venus was orbited and probed by the U. S. Pioneer Venus and the USSR Venera

11 and 12, launched in mid-1978. Earth application satellites expanded into many new areas.

MANNED SPACE FLIGHT

The USSR continued to work toward the development of a permanent space station orbiting the earth. The Salyut 6 space station, launched on Sept. 29, 1977 and maneuvered into a 219 × 209 mile (352 × 336 km) orbit, was used extensively in 1978.

Soyuz 26, 27, 28. The crew of Soyuz 26, cosmonauts Yuri Romanenko and Georgi Grechko, began their mission in the Salyut 6 on Dec. 11, 1977, and remained aboard the space station for 96 days, departing on March 17. Their mission broke the previous space record of 84 days established in 1974 by U. S. astronauts Gerald Carr, William Pogue, and Edward Gibson. Two manned flights, Soyuz 27 and 28, and one unmanned tanker/transport satellite, Progress 1, were employed in resupply missions during the 96-day record-breaking stay. All missions were launched from Baikonur Cosmodrome. Soyuz 27 crew, cosmonauts Vladimir Dzhanibekov and Oleg Makarov of the USSR, began their mission January 10, docked with Salyut 6, and returned on January 16.

Soyuz 28, manned by cosmonauts Alexei Gubarev of the USSR and Vladimir Remek of Czechoslovakia, was launched on March 2, docked with Salyut 6, and returned March 10.

Soyuz 29, 30, 31. Salyut 6 was inactive for about three months, from March 27 to June 15, when Soyuz 29 was launched. Cosmonauts Vladimir Kovalenok and Alexander Ivanchenkov reactivated Salyut 6 and remained aboard for a record-breaking stay of 140 days. When they returned to earth on November 2, they were made "Heroes of the Soviet Union." During their mission aboard Salyut 6 the cosmonauts performed zero-gravity processing experiments on more than 30 materials, including triple material semiconductors. They also took thousands of earth photographs for earth resources surveys and studied the earth's ozone layer. Resupply was provided by Soyuz 30 and 31 and three unmanned tanker/transport satellites, Progress 2, 3 and 4. Soyuz 30 was launched June 27, docked with Salyut 6, and returned on July 5. A Polish cosmonaut, Miroslaw Hermaszewski, joined Pyotr Klimuk of the USSR for the resupply mission. Meanwhile, the crew of Soyuz 29 remained aboard Salyut 6 to break the U. S. record of 936 total man-days in space on August 2.

In the second manned resupply mission, Sigmund Jaehn, a German cosmonaut, joined Valery Bykovsky of the Soviet Union aboard Soyuz 31, which was launched August 26, docked with Salyut 6, and returned September 3. The previous record of 71 persons sent into space, held by the United States, was broken by the USSR when the launch of Soyuz 31 took their 72nd cosmonaut into space.

PLANETARY PROBES

Pioneer Venus. The U. S. Pioneer Venus 1 and 2 were launched May 20 and August 7 to conduct a detailed scientific study of the planet Venus. Pioneer Venus 1 was scheduled to orbit the planet on December 4 and Pioneer Venus 2 on December 9. Venus 2 was to split into a bus and four atmospheric probes. Venus has been explored previously by 3 U. S. spacecraft (flybys) and 10 USSR spacecraft (8 landers and 2 flybys).

The Pioneer Venus flights are the first to study the atmosphere and weather of another planet on a global scale. Pioneer Venus 1, the first US spacecraft to orbit the planet, was programmed to orbit the planet for at least eight months, providing the longest observations to date.

The Pioneer Venus flights will help to determine why the planet Earth and the planet Venus have atmospheres that evolved so differently in spite of such total similarities as size, mass, material composition, and distance from the sun. Also of interest is understanding why the surface of Venus is so much warmer than the earth (approximately 900° F or 480° C) in spite of the fact that Venus absorbs about the same amount of energy as the earth. The similarities in energy absorption are a result of the more reflective cloud cover on Venus, which compensates for it being closer to the sun than the earth is.

Venus presents an excellent opportunity to study the mechanics of atmospheres because it rotates more slowly than Earth and has no oceans. Understanding the atmosphere of Venus can help us learn more about the complex forces that determine the weather and climate of the earth. Also, understanding the greenhouse effect of the atmosphere of Venus, which is composed of 97% carbon dioxide that is essentially opaque to outgoing heat radiation, may provide a characterization of the modest greenhouse effect on the earth's atmosphere of the carbon dioxide concentration that has been increasing. Large scale burning of fuels since 1850, increasing the carbon dioxide source, and deforestation, reducing the sink, are felt to be two of the causes that could conceivably lead to an increase in the earth's surface temperature.

The bus and four probes on Pioneer Venus 2 will obtain data on the composition of the upper atmosphere from various geographical locations on the planet on both the day and night sides. The probes were not designed to survive impact, yet one of the probes continued to transmit data one hour after landing.

The USSR launched Venera 11 and 12 spacecraft in the direction of Venus on September 9 and 14. These craft successfully orbited and probed Venus in December.

EARTH-ORBITING SATELLITES

The USSR launching of the 1,000th satellite in the Cosmos series on March 31, 1978 highlighted a year of great activity for earth-orbiting application satellites, scientific satellites and communication satellites.

The use of radioactively-fueled generators to produce electric power in earth-orbiting satellites came into serious question as Cosmos 954, an ocean surveillance satellite, fell on northern Canada on January 24. Its nuclear reactor, containing approximately 100 pounds (45 kg) of enriched U-235, essentially intact, presented a health safety hazard. Heretofore, the use of such generators has been confined to deep space probes where solar energy use is not feasible.

Earth Application Satellites. Landsat 3, launched on March 5 into a 570-mile (917-km) sun synchronous orbit, headed the list of seven U. S. earth applications satellite launches. Landsat 3 is very similar to Landsat 1 and 2, carrying both the multispectral scanner (MSS) and the Return Beam Vidicon cameras (RBV) to provide synoptic remote-sensing coverage of the earth's resources. On Landsat 3, however, the MSS contained an additional fifth channel in the thermal region. Moreover, the spatial resolution of the black and white RBV was increased to 40 meters versus 80 meters on Landsat 1 and 2. The five and one-half year old Landsat 1, operating in a seriously degraded mode, was deactivated following successful operation of Landsat 3. Thus, Landsat 2 and 3 are continuing to supply nine-day repeat space remote-sensing coverage of principal areas of interest on the earth's land mass. Landsat data are being used in a wide variety of earth resource applications such as agriculture, range, forestry, water resources, land cover inventory, and non-renewable resources.

The Large Area Crop Inventory Experiment

Ronald E. McNair, *left*, Frederick D. Gregory, and Guy Bluford were named among new astronaut candidates.

UPI

UPI

The Soyuz 29 crew, Vladimir Kovalenok and Alexander Ivanchenkov, set a record for time in space, 140 days.

(LACIE), a three-year experiment involving the use of Landsat data to assist in global wheat production forecasting, was completed.

The Heat Capacity Mapping Mission (HCMM), designated Applications Explorer Mission 1 and launched April 26, was the first in a new Scout-sized series of earth application payloads. HCMM was launched into a 385-mile (620-km) sun synchronous orbit with mid-latitude crossing times selected to measure the minimum and maximum earth surface temperatures. HCMM contains a two-channel Heat Capacity Mapping Radiometer operating in the visible and near infrared spectrum during the day and in the thermal infrared spectrum both day and night. The day-night thermal infrared data will be tested to determine their usefulness in such applications as rock-type discrimination, soil moisture monitoring, inferring plant stress from canopy temperature, measuring and mapping urban heat islands and mapping surface temperature changes on land and water bodies.

Seasat-A, the first U. S. ocean monitoring satellite, was launched June 26 from the Western Test Range (WTR), Lompoc, California, with an Atlas Agena launch vehicle into a 500-mile (800-km) circular polar orbit. Orbiting the earth 14 times a day, Seasat covers 95% of the ocean's surface every 36 hours, providing the first synoptic, world-wide observation of the ocean. The objective of Seasat-A is to prove the feasibility of employing a multiple-satellite network to provide continuous, near real-time world ocean monitoring. Ultimately, an operational ocean monitoring system could provide ships at sea with improved route charting, including weather conditions, sea state and hazards. Seasat 1 experienced a power failure on October 10 and terminated data transmission. Fortunately, 99 days of operation provided data which presently are being analyzed by a team of investigators to determine the utility of the instruments. These instruments include all-weather active and passive microwave sensors, plus a visible and infrared radiometer for support. The information obtained from these sensors is expected to provide a better understanding of sea surface and atmospheric interaction

Nimbus-G, the first U. S. satellite dedicated to the monitoring of environmental pollutants in the earth's atmosphere, was launched on October 24 from WTR into a 593-mile (955-km) near-polar orbit. Nimbus-G is the last in a series of seven environmental research satellites, the first of which was launched in August 1964. The data from Nimbus-G's eight scientific instruments will help determine the physical characterization of the global atmosphere, the dynamic atmosphere-ocean interface, and earth's heat balance. This information is vital to our understanding of climate, oceanography, atmospheric pollution and regional and global weather patterns. Areas of specific interest addressed by these sensors include the status of the ozone in the stratosphere, the earth's temperature, and ocean pollution.

Weather Satellites. Tiros-N, the first of eight satellites in the third generation of environmental satellites, was launched Oct. 13, 1978, into a 540-mile (865-km) near-circular polar orbit from WTR. Tiros-N's Advanced Very High Resolution Radiometer (AVHRR), Automatic Picture Transmission (APT) system, and High Resolution Picture Transmission (HRPT) system will provide local area weather coverage on a global basis.

Five geosynchronous meteorological satellites, three from the United States (GOES-1, -2, -3), one from Japan (GMS-1), and one from the European Space Agency (Meteosat-1) will operate as a continuous global weather observation system in support of the Global Atmospheric Research Project (GARP) in 1978. GOES-3, launched June 16 by the United States, was used as a substitute for the USSR geosynchronous meteorological satellite which failed to achieve orbit stationing over the Indian Ocean. The First Global GARP Experiment (FGGE), initiated on December 1, will utilize meteorological and oceanographic satellite, aircraft, ship, and ground data in an international experiment to study worldwide atmospheric processes.

Scientific Satellites. The United States launched International Ultraviolet Explorer (IUE) on January 26, the International Sun Earth Explorer-C (ISEE) on August 12, and the High Energy Astronomical Observatory-2 (HEAO) on November 13. IUE will complement and extend the astronomical observations made by the NASA OAO-2 and the ESA TD-1 craft.

An international team of astronomers will conduct star observations with IUE in the 1,150° to 3,200° angstrom range in the ultraviolet portion of the spectrum. The mission is being conducted in cooperation with ESA and the British Science Research Council.

ISEE-3 joins ISEE-1 and 2 to measure the solar wind and other solar phenomena unperturbed by the earth's influence. The information from the ISEE satellites should provide a better understanding of solar-terrestrial weather and climate phenomena.

HEAO-2 joined HEAO-1 to continue high energy astrophysical measurements. A new black hole candidate in the constellation Ara was discovered in 1978, bringing the total number of candidates to four. Black holes are extremely dense collapsed stars with gravitational fields so strong that they prevent the emission of light energy, thus making the stars invisible to direct observation.

ESA launched GEOS-II on July 14 to conduct scientific investigations of waves and particles in the magnetosphere.

The USSR launched Prognoz 7 on October 31. It carried both Soviet and French instruments to study solar activity, electromagnetic radiation, and gamma rays for comparison with measurements from Venus-bound Venera 11 and 12.

Japan launched three scientific satellites; International Sounding Satellite (ISS-2) on February 16, and two International Magnetospheric Satellites (EXOS-1 and 2) on February 4 and September 16.

Communication Satellites. A total of 16 communication satellites were launched in 1978. These included five from the United States in the Intelsat-IVA, Fleetsatcom and Comstar series, six from the USSR in the Molniya-I and Raduga series, two from Japan in the BSE series, and one each from NATO and Canada, in the NATO-III and Telsat series, respectively. Fleetsatcom-A and B, in support of U. S. Navy Fleet communications, were launched in February and December. Intelsat IV A (F5 and F6), with the capacity to relay more than 6,000 simultaneous telephone messages and two television programs, were launched January 6 and March 31. A Communication Satellite Corporation (COMSAT) COMSTAR-C was launched June 29.

An experimental Japanese broadcast satellite, BSE-A was launched April 7. A Canadian domestic communications satellite, Anik-B was launched December 15. A third satellite in support of NATO communications, NATO III-C was launched November 18. Meanwhile, the USSR launched Molniya-I series communication satellites on January 24, March 3, June 2, July 14, and August 22 and a Raduga series communication satellite on July 19.

SPACE TRANSPORTATION DEVELOPMENTS

Space Shuttle. The U. S. Space Shuttle development continued with the first orbiter test flight scheduled for 1979. Ground vibration testing of the Space Shuttle as a complete vehicle was conducted at the George C. Marshall Space Flight Center in Huntsville, Alabama. The Space Shuttle orbiter, external tank, and solid rocket boosters were mated and vibration tested in the vertical launch position in the facilities originally constructed for the testing of the Saturn V moon rocket.

In preparation for Shuttle operations in the 1980's, NASA selected 35 new astronaut candidates to undergo two years of training. The group included six women and four minorities, selected from more than 8,000 applicants. Also, four crews were named for the early Shuttle flights. They were John Young, Robert Crippen, Joe Engle, Richard Truly, Fred Haise, Jack Lousma, Vance Brand, and Charles Fullerton. Five scientists were selected to serve as payload specialists during the first Spacelab mission scheduled for the latter part of 1980. The Spacelab, a manned laboratory for use in the Space Shuttle, continued development in Europe under sponsorship by the European Space Agency (ESA).

A plan to utilize the Space Shuttle to save the Skylab Space Station (launched in 1973) was abandoned because of a slip in the shuttle launch schedule. Skylab will enter the earth's atmosphere and disintegrate in 1979.

MICHAEL A. CALABRESE

The crescent-shaped earth and moon, photographed by the Voyager I spacecraft.

UPI

Communication with Extraterrestrial Life

Arecibo Observatory, scene of searches for extraterrestrial life.

CORNELL UNIVERSITY PHOTO

Nothing in science is so tantalizing as the prospect of communicating with alien civilizations. Contact with new and different worlds would enrich our lives, practically and aesthetically, in unimaginable ways. The success of the films *Star Wars* and *Close Encounters of the Third Kind* evidences a growing fascination with the idea of life on other planets. Indeed, there is growing optimism that contact with extraterrestrial life is within our technological grasp. New and expanded programs aimed at the discovery of life on other planets hold promise for success in the 20th century.

The first modern attempts to detect life on other planets were made in 1960 with a small radio telescope at the National Radio Astronomy Observatory in Green Bank, W. Va. In the years following, experts debated the question of how best to detect potential alien civilizations. It was agreed that scanning for radio signals with large radio telescopes was indeed the most promising approach. All serious searches for extraterrestrial life are therefore being carried out in this manner.

The present procedure, in most cases, is to search for signals in the direction of nearby stars, monitoring as many frequency channels as possible. Usually, frequencies near the basic 21-cm wavelength spectral line of atomic hydrogen are used. This is because it is the basic line of the most abundant element in the universe, and because it is the line with the greatest number of photons. This would be the most natural and obvious "meeting place" for civilizations trying to solve the problem of which frequency to use.

A telescope such as the one at Arecibo, Puerto Rico, can detect signals of a strength equal to its own transmissions, from anywhere in the Milky Way galaxy. Despite the use of such large radio telescopes, however, the search for life on other planets remains extremely difficult and time-consuming, with little chance of immediate success. This is because signals from an estimate of only one in ten million stars would be strong enough for us to detect; moreover, the exact wavelength of any transmission would be unknown to us. Yet, on the basis of that estimation and the size of our galaxy, there should still be ten thousand detectable civilizations in the Milky Way alone.

Among the most powerful searches yet conducted were those by Patrick Palmer and Benjamin Zuckerman at the National Radio Astronomy Observatory; nearly 1,000 nearby stars were examined, with a 256-channel receiver system. At Arecibo, scientists examined five galaxies, as well as nearby stars, with a system that monitors 3,024 channels simultaneously. The most sensitive search, employing the Arecibo 304.8-meter (1,000-ft) telescope and a very narrow frequency band, was conducted in 1978 by Dr. Paul Horowitz of Harvard University. Horowitz looked at some 200 nearby stars with a system monitoring more than 65,000 channels simultaneously. Powerful searches are also being conducted at the Ohio State University Radio Observatory, the Hat Creek Observatory of the University of California, and the Algonquin Radio Observatory of the National Research Council of Canada. A large, long-term program has been organized in the Soviet Union, where a new 600-meter (1,-968.5-ft) radio telescope at the Academy of Sciences will be used.

The National Aeronautics and Space Administration (NASA) has proposed the construction of radio receivers that can monitor billions of frequencies simultaneously. This appears to be the most promising and economical next step in the search for extraterrestrial life. NASA has asked Congress for several million dollars a year to support this project. Plans for a series of extremely large radio telescopes, known as Project Cyclops, have also been made. The project would cost billions of dollars, however, and it is therefore unlikely that the system will be built in the near future.

FRANK D. DRAKE

SPAIN

Spain continued to emerge from the long shadows of fascism as King Juan Carlos I and Prime Minister Adolfo Súarez showed themselves to be adroit leaders. The year's most important political event was the drafting of a new national constitution, to which the Chamber of Deputies and the Senate gave 97% approval in late October.

Constitution. This fundamental law, which was ratified by the people in December, establishes a "parliamentary monarchy." It empowers the king, who would also be supreme commander of the armed forces, to nominate the prime minister, convene and dissolve the Cortes (parliament), give royal approval to laws, and grant pardons.

The document promises religious freedom, but, without designating an official faith, stipulates a close relationship between the state and the Roman Catholic Church. Other provisions outlaw torture, ban capital punishment for civilians, permit the formation of trade unions, and guarantee the right to private property. The government may, when the national interest dictates, intervene in the economy and reserve resources to the public sector.

In an effort to mollify the Basques, Catalans, and other groups, the constitution assures the "right of autonomy of the various nationalities and regions," which can use their own flags and languages.

The new charter enjoys support from the Communists and Socialists on the left, Súarez's Union of the Democratic Center in the middle, and the Popular Alliance on the right.

Political Violence. Fervently opposed to a new legal order are such guerrilla bands as the First of October Anti-Fascist Resistance Group (GRAPO) and the Basque separatist organization ETA. These terrorists specialize in indiscriminate bombings and the assassination of police and military officers. In the three years after Generalissimo Francisco Franco's death in late-1975, there were 115 political deaths—63 by terrorists and 47 by the police. Much of the bloodshed occurred in the northern Basque country.

Such political violence, a Spanish phenomenon that predates the bloody civil war of the 1930's, has raised hackles in the 200,000-man army. But Juan Carlos, a personable young monarch with diplomas from several military colleges, thus far has persuaded his generals to back the fledgling experiment in democracy.

The officer corps, with deep roots in the 40-year Francoist dictatorship, is reluctant to challenge the growing power of the civilian politicians who have vigorously promoted national cohesion. Nowhere is their reluctance greater than in the matter of economic policy.

Economy. Since the sharp rise in oil prices in late-1973, Spain, the world's tenth industrial power, has been afflicted by a declining growth rate, falling investment, rising unemployment, and a brisk rate of inflation, which reached 26.4% in 1977.

Immediately after the June 1977 parliamentary elections, the government, in consultation with the political parties, fashioned a series of austerity measures, including restrictive wage and monetary policies designed to promote internal and external stability. This program, which proved highly unpopular with businessmen, reduced price increases to 7.2% during the first half of 1978. During the same period, the balance of payments recorded a surplus of $2.5 million compared with a deficit of $1 million from January to July of 1977.

Despite the creation of 130,000 public service jobs, unemployment still beset 7% of the workforce at the end of the year—a situation that contributed to labor unrest. Moreover, the levels of both investment and industrial output remained low.

Spain views integration into the European Community as the long-term solution to its economic problems. In April the country received a favorable response to its application for membership, which will be achieved, in stages, over a ten-year transitional period. The United States would also like to see Spain join the North Atlantic Treaty Organization.

Foreign Affairs. Spain's major military concern has been North Africa where Algeria has championed independence for the Spanish-held Canary Islands, an archipelago off the Moroccan coast. Súarez has tried to convince Morocco's king and France's president of the "Spanishness" of these islands. Meanwhile, Juan Carlos visited China, Iran, and Iraq in mid-1978 to advance the case for Spanish sovereignty, negotiate trade agreements, and put his country on the diplomatic map.

Signs of a relaxation of social conventions appeared in April when the Chamber of Deputies lifted a 40-year ban on the marketing of contraceptives. Polls reveal that 70% of Spanish women now use a birth control device and 74% favor family planning.

GEORGE DE GREGORIO
College of William and Mary

SPAIN · Information Highlights

Official Name: Spanish State.
Location: Iberian Peninsula in southwestern Europe.
Area: 195,270 square miles (505,750 km²).
Population (1978 est.): 36,800,000.
Chief Cities (1975): Madrid, the capital, 3,500,000; Barcelona, 2,000,000; Valencia, 700,000.
Government: *Head of state,* Juan Carlos I, king (took office Nov. 1975). *Head of government,* Adolfo Súarez González, prime minister (took office July 1976). *Legislature*—Cortes: Senate and Chamber of Deputies.
Monetary Unit: Peseta (70.7 pesetas equal U. S.$1, Dec. 28, 1978).
Manufactures (major products): Processed foods, textiles, footwear, petrochemicals, steel, automobiles, ships, consumer goods.
Agriculture (major products): Cereals, vegetables, citrus fruits, feedgrains, wine, olives and olive oil, livestock.

SPORTS

An Overall View

Professional sports in America, like the economy, took a ride on an inflationary rollercoaster in 1978 but managed to maintain a state of relatively good health. Superstars continued to demand and receive astronomical salaries. The major team sports—pro football, baseball, basketball, and hockey—enjoyed large profits and attracted fans in droves, despite increases in ticket prices. Television continued to be the most influential factor in the financial underpinning.

Stronger than ever, the women's sports movement developed new followers and stars almost overnight and blossomed with a new pro league in basketball, the fastest growing of women's sports. There was a great deal of litigation among men's teams and players. Some unusual franchise and player shifts gained headlines. FANS (Fight to Advance the Nation's Sports), a consumer advocacy group, took up the banner for consumer protection. The public had much at stake—70% of the arenas used by professional teams had been built with public funds, incurring indebtedness that would last into the next century.

Television awarded the National Football League (NFL) almost a 300% increase in contract revenue to televise its games. Pete Rozelle, the NFL commissioner, negotiated a $656 million contract with the three major networks and the NFL raised the number of regular-season games scheduled for each team from 14 to 16. At the other extreme, the National Hockey League (NHL), which had taken only $180,000 in TV revenues in 1977, was still without a network contract to show its games.

The scramble for free agents abated somewhat, but took some unusual twists. Many players were signed to multimillion-dollar pacts, indicating that the phenomenon would not soon pass. The New York Yankees, who almost single-handedly had cornered the free-agent market in 1977 and thereby won a World Series championship, still felt insecure. They spent several more millions to acquire Andy Messersmith, a pitcher who had been one of the original free agents; Rich Gossage, a star relief hurler; and Rawly Eastwick, a top-rated young pitcher who did not last the season with the Yankees.

Player shifts plagued the National Basketball Association (NBA). The New York Knicks, hoping to restore fan confidence, signed free agent Marvin Webster to a multimillion dollar pact after he had led Seattle to the play-offs. An unusual shift involved the Boston Celtics and the Buffalo Braves. The Celtics, the most successful team in pro basketball history, traded ownership and six players with the Braves, whose franchise in turn was transferred to San Diego. The New

Jersey Nets of the NBA, who had moved from Long Island, N. Y., in 1977, and their owner, Roy Boe, suffered heavy financial losses and a debt of $19 million. Boe, who also held ownership in the New York Islanders, a contending team in the NHL, ran into trouble when he was sued for $10 million by a limited partner in the Islanders for allegedly diverting funds from the Islanders to the Nets. Boe was divested of the presidency of the Islanders, and the team was put in the hands of a manager. Ultimately, the Nets were purchased by a group approved by the NBA, which had given Boe an ultimatum to get his finances in order or have the franchise taken from him by the league.

Björn Borg of Sweden, the Wimbledon champion, was the biggest moneymaker in tennis. Including ancillary benefits (worldwide commercials, endorsement contracts, etc.) his annual earnings zoomed to more than $1.5 million. Football's O. J. Simpson was not only the highest salaried athlete in sports, but also perhaps the most pampered. He asked to be traded from Buffalo to San Francisco because he did not like Buffalo's cold climate. When he went, the star running back took with him a salary of $733,358 a year—a rate of $45,835 per game. Baseball's top-paid man was Reggie Jackson of the Yankees, a controversial athlete who lent his name to a candy bar manufactured by a large food distributing conglomerate. Jackson's annual paycheck from the Yankees is $580,000—or almost $1,000 each time he goes to bat. Following the 1978 season, Pete Rose of the Cincinnati Reds became a free-agent. He later signed a contract with the Philadelphia Phillies, with an annual salary estimated at $800,000.

Martina Navratilova, a 22-year-old defector to the United States from Czechoslovakia, rocketed to popularity and high six-figure income by excelling on the American tennis tour. She set a record by winning six straight tournaments and 30 consecutive matches. Her crowning achievement came when she defeated Chris Evert of the United States for the Wimbledon championship. Nancy Lopez, 20, stirred new interest in women's golf by virtually taking over the Ladies Professional Golf Association (LPGA) tour. She gave new life to the LPGA, which for years played for low purses and struggled to find sponsor credibility.

Amid all this, FANS was critical of price increases for tickets to major events. The group's inquiries were directed at improving conditions at ball parks and arenas, claiming that fans were "ignored, duped, and exploited." It went so far as to question the price of hot dogs, cold drinks, and the like, sold to spectators in the nation's stadiums and arenas.

GEORGE DE GREGORIO
Sports Department, "The New York Times"

The Year in Sports

PHOTOS UPI

Highlights of the 1978 sports season included: Martina Navratolova winning the women's singles title at Wimbledon; Nancy Lopez establishing an earnings' record on the women's pro golf tour; and Affirmed, Steve Cauthen up, capturing horse racing's Triple Crown.

DOUBLE EAGLE II

On August 17, Ben Abruzzo, Max Anderson, and Larry Newman, three businessmen from Albuquerque, N. M., landed their mammoth, helium-inflated balloon, *Double Eagle II*, in the fields of Miserey, France. Still 60 miles (97 km) from their destination of Le Bourget airport, site of Charles Lindbergh's triumphant landing 51 years before, the trio had nonetheless completed the first crossing of the Atlantic in a balloon. The 3,100-mile (4,989-km) journey from Presque Isle, Me., had taken a total of 5 days, 17 hours, and 6 minutes. Since the first attempt in 1873, the Atlantic had been tried 17 times before. On the 18th attempt, the first for Abruzzo, Anderson, and Newman, history was made. Their next goal? Around the world in 30 days!

PHOTOS UPI

"Unless frontiers are challenged from time to time—whether they be flying a balloon, breaking an altitude record in a plane, or writing a fine piece of literature—we don't move forward as a society."

Ben Abruzzo

"There are no books or music up there, but there is the whole world to see. It's completely silent, and you move with the clouds. When you come over land you are standing on a balcony, and the world going by underneath you is . . . a magnificent sight."

Max Anderson

PHOTOS, HEINZ KLUETMEIER/SPORTS ILLUSTRATED

XI COMMONWEALTH GAMES

The 48 nations invited to Edmonton, Alberta, Canada, to participate in the 1978 Commonwealth Games celebrated the 50th anniversary of that event with an intimacy and sentimentality unknown to other international competitions. At opening day ceremonies on August 3, Queen Elizabeth II and Prince Philip welcomed some 1,800 athletes from many parts of the Commonwealth. In addition to existing facilities, the city of Edmonton built a new stadium and facilities for several of the ten different sports. When competition ended on August 12, Canada was in first place with 45 gold medals, England finished second with 27, and Australia third with 24.

FINAL MEDAL STANDINGS

	Gold	Silver	Bronze		Gold	Silver	Bronze
Canada	45	31	33	Malaysia	1	2	1
England	27	28	33	Ghana	1	1	1
Australia	24	33	27	Guyana	1	1	1
Kenya	7	6	5	Tanzania	1	1	0
New Zealand	5	7	9	Trinidad	0	2	2
India	5	4	6	Zambia	0	2	2
Scotland	3	5	5	Bahamas	0	1	0
Jamaica	2	2	3	Papua–New Guinea	0	1	0
Wales	2	1	5	Western Samoa	0	0	3
N. Ireland	2	1	1	Isle of Man	0	0	1
Hong Kong	2	0	0				

COURTESY OF THE U.S. OLYMPIC COMMITTEE

NATIONAL SPORTS FESTIVAL

The first National Sports Festival, sponsored by the U. S. Olympic Committee, attracted some 2,100 athletes in 26 amateur sports to the mountains of Colorado, July 27–30. This "national Olympics," fashioned after similar events in other countries, was established to foster U. S. athletic talent and to arouse public interest in the U. S. Olympic endeavor.

Soccer superstar Pelé demonstrates basic techniques to a group of boys. Camps specializing in the teaching of soccer have become increasingly popular.

ROBERT HOLLIDAY

SPORTS—
SPECIAL REPORT:

The Rising Popularity of American Soccer

Joining the footballs, basketballs, and baseballs as favorite items on America's playgrounds these days is the soccer ball.

Although there is no way to gauge the exact number of young men, women, and children playing the sport today, the United States Soccer Federation (USSF), which conducts soccer programs at all age levels across the country, estimates that there are some 350,000 youths (under 19 years old) registered for organized competition. This represents an increase of nearly 100% since 1974–75. In addition, there are some 70,000 participants aged 19 and over, compared with 62,000 in 1974–75.

The growth of competition at the high school level has been phenomenal. In 1974, the National Federation of High School Athletics reported 3,356 boys' soccer teams and 98,482 male participants. Girls' totals during the same period were 409 teams and 10,717 participants. Two years later, the number of boys' teams and participants had gone up to 4,195 and 112,743, respectively; for girls, 599 and 11,534. The 1978 figures were estimated at 5,000 boys' teams and 125,000 male players, and 700 girls' teams and over 12,000 female players.

Interest in soccer at the intercollegiate level has also risen dramatically in the last few years. In 1973, the National Collegiate Athletic Association had two soccer divisions. Division I had 118 member schools and Division II had 253. Now there are three divisions, with 139 schools playing in Division I, 75 in Division II, and 223 in Division III. In addition, hundreds of schools field teams in the National Association of Intercollegiate Athletics.

The rising popularity of soccer in the United States is evidenced also by the success of the North American Soccer League (NASL), now a full-fledged major league organization. In 1978, the NASL fielded 24 teams from Fort Lauderdale to Vancouver and experienced its best year in terms of attendance (*see table*). Similarly, media coverage has gone from almost nothing to the 572 credentials issued for the 1978 Soccer Bowl.

As attendance and media coverage of NASL competition increased, so, too, did a desire to Americanize the game. Two North Americans were required to start every match in 1978, and no less than 16 active players on each team's 30-man roster had to be North American. By 1980 the number of starting North Americans will increase to three; four will have to start by 1982; and five by 1984.

The NASL already boasts such native American stars as Kyle Rote, Jr., of the Dallas Tornado; Gary Etherington (the 1978 Rookie of the Year) and Werner Roth, both of the Cosmos; Jim McAlister of the Seattle Sounders; goalkeeper Alan Meyer of the San Diego Sockers. As America's youths begin to learn and play soccer at an earlier age, the number of native stars will grow even larger.

The major focuses of attention these days, however, are the 1980 Olympic Games in Mos-

North American Soccer League Attendance			
Year	Total	Year	Total
1972	395,000	1976	2,755,000
1973	648,000	1977	3,675,000
1974	1,182,000	1978	5,300,000
1975	1,809,000		

cow and the 1982 World Cup finals in Spain. The U. S. National team went on a seven nation tour of Europe in the fall of 1978 to prepare for the qualifying rounds of the World Cup, which begin in 1980. The Americans hope to reach the final 16 teams and proceed to the championship matches in Spain. Meanwhile, qualifying rounds for the 1980 Olympics begin in the sum-

mer of 1979. The U. S. National "B" team (composed mainly of amateurs) played in the President's Cup tournament in Seoul, Korea, in the fall of 1978 as a final tune-up.

As more and more youngsters discover the sport, its popularity will grow. The playgrounds should be filled with soccer balls for a long time.

JIM HENDERSON

AUTO RACING

Al Unser, Mario Andretti, Cale Yarborough, and Bobby Allison, four of the greatest drivers in auto racing history, wrote their names even larger in the record books during the 1978 season.

Unser became the first man to capture the United States Auto Club (USAC) Triple Crown, by winning the 500-mile (800-km) races at Indianapolis, Pocono, and Ontario, Calif. Unser, now a three-time winner at Indianapolis, also took the Ontario race in 1977 for a string of four straight "500" victories. He ran his career total of "500" triumphs to seven, matching the legendary A. J. Foyt.

Andretti, the Italian-born American star who forsook the oval tracks of the United States to pursue the World Championship, achieved his

dream by winning six of 14 Grand Prix races. Andretti became only the second American to win the Formula One title. Phil Hill took the crown in 1961.

Yarborough won 10 events and sped to an unprecedented third straight National Association for Stock Car Racing (NASCAR) championship.

Allison, winner of just about everything else the NASCAR could offer, finally grabbed the one prize that had eluded him—the Daytona "500."

Janet Guthrie, who in 1977 became the first woman to drive at Indianapolis, returned to that event and delighted her fans by finishing ninth.

Death claimed another Grand Prix star, Sweden's Ronnie Peterson. He died as a result of injuries received in a first-lap accident at Monza.

BOB COLLINS
The Indianapolis Star

AUTO RACING

World Champion: Mario Andretti, U. S.
USAC: Tom Sneva, U. S.
NASCAR: Cale Yarborough, U. S.
Can-Am: Alan Jones, Australia

Major Race Winners

Indianapolis 500: Al Unser, U. S.
Pocono 500: Al Unser
California 500: Al Unser
Daytona 500: Bobby Allison, U. S.

Grand Prix for Formula One Cars, 1978

Argentinian: Mario Andretti
Brazilian: Carlos Reutemann, Switzerland
South African: Ronnie Peterson, Sweden
Long Beach: Carlos Reutemann
Monaco: Patrick Depaillier, France
Belgian: Mario Andretti
Spanish: Mario Andretti
Swedish: Niki Lauda, Austria
French: Mario Andretti
British: Carlos Reutemann
West German: Mario Andretti
Austrian: Ronnie Peterson
Dutch: Mario Andretti
Italian: Niki Lauda
United States: Carlos Reutemann
Canadian: Giles Villeneuve, Canada

Driving a Ferrari 312 T3, Carlos Reutemann wins the 1978 British Grand Prix.

UPI

BASEBALL

On July 17, 1978, the defending world champion New York Yankees were in a mess. That day they lagged 14 games behind the Boston Red Sox in the American League Eastern Division and manager Billy Martin suspended star slugger Reggie Jackson for bunting against orders.

A few days after suspending Jackson, Martin made a cutting remark about the suspended outfielder and team owner George Steinbrenner, calling them liars. The next day, July 24, Martin was forced to resign. The world champions seemingly were headed for a fall. It would take a miracle to recover the Yankees' former standing.

In the finest storybook tradition, however, the miracle happened. Incredibly, the Yankees emerged as world champions for the 22nd time in their history.

Bob Lemon, recently fired as manager of the Chicago White Sox, took over the Yankee post from Martin. Under the calm direction of Lemon, the Yankees made the greatest comeback in American League history. They erased the 14-game deficit and pulled even with the Red Sox at season's end.

A one game play-off for the Eastern Division title was held October 2 in Boston's Fenway Park. The Yankees won, 5–4, sparked by shortstop Bucky Dent's three-run homer. The winning pitcher was Ron Guidry, who had one of the most remarkable seasons ever recorded by a major league hurler. He finished the regular season with a 25–3 record, nine shutouts, 248 strike-outs and a 1.74 earned-run average. He was unanimously voted the American League Cy Young Award.

Then, for the third consecutive year, the Yankees met the Kansas City Royals in the American League championship series. For the third consecutive year, the Yankees defeated the Royals, this time three games to one, with Guidry pitching the pennant-winning victory.

The Yankees faced the Los Angeles Dodgers in the World Series for the second successive year. In the National League championship series the Dodgers had defeated the Philadelphia Phillies in four games. The series ended dramatically when Phillies center fielder Garry Maddox dropped a line drive, giving the Dodgers a chance to score the winning run.

The World Series opened in Los Angeles, and the Dodgers won the first two games. All they had to do to win the world championship was win two of the five possible remaining games. They could not win even one.

The Yankees became the first team in the 75-year history of the World Series to win four straight games after losing the first two. The momentum changed in game 3 in New York, when Yankee third basemen Graig Nettles made four spectacular plays, preventing the Dodgers from scoring five, or perhaps six, runs. The Yankees won, 5–1, with Guidry pitching his 27th victory of the year. He did not have to pitch again. The Yankees went on to sweep all three games in New York, and then wrapped up

Rod Carew, *left*, the American League batting champion, slides into third during the 1978 All-Star Game, as Pete Rose awaits the throw. Yankee lefthander Ron Guidry won the league's Cy Young Award with a record of 25–3.

PHOTOS UPI

FOCUS ON SPORTS

Sparkling infield play helped the New York Yankees defeat the Los Angeles Dodgers in the 75th World Series.

the world championship in game 6 with a 7–2 victory in Los Angeles. The finale produced two unlikely heroes—Brian Doyle and Dent, the last two batters in the lineup. Each had three hits, and they combined to knock in five runs. Dent, with 10 hits, seven RBIs, and a .417 average, was named the most valuable player in the series.

Including postseason play, the Yankees had a 55–23 record under Lemon, the first American League manager to win a pennant after taking over in the middle of a season.

Guidry's phenomenal pitching statistics were rivaled by the slugging figures of Jim Rice, the Red Sox outfielder. Rice pounded 46 homers, 213 hits, and batted in 139 runs—all major league highs—while batting .315. He was later named the league's most valuable player.

Rod Carew, after hitting .388 in 1977, slipped to .333 but still won his seventh American League batting title for the Minnesota Twins.

In the National League, the Pittsburgh Pirates' Dave Parker overcame a shattered cheekbone to repeat as batting champion, with a .334 average and won the league's MVP award. George Foster of the Cincinnati Reds again led the league in homers (40) and RBIs (120).

At age 40, Gaylord Perry of the San Diego Padres won 21 games and the league's Cy Young Award. Teammate Rollie Fingers posted a remarkable 37 saves in relief, and the Houston Astros' J. R. Richard notched 303 strikeouts.

For all the glossy individual feats, one man captivated baseball fans more than any other for a substantial part of the season. Pete Rose, the

scrappy, 37-year-old third baseman of the Cincinnati Reds, stole the hearts of baseball fans with one of the longest hitting streaks in baseball history—44 games.

In May, Rose became only the 13th player in baseball history to collect 3,000 hits. But that was only a prelude of what was to come. Rose hit safely on June 14 and just kept going. On July 24, in New York, he tied the modern National League record of 38 consecutive games set by Tommy Holmes of the Boston Braves in 1945. The next night, Rose broke that mark and, on August 1 in Atlanta, he matched the all-time league mark of 44 games set by Wee Willie Keeler of the old Baltimore Orioles in 1897. Only one longer streak remained—56 games by Joe DiMaggio of the Yankees in 1941.

But Rose's binge ended at 44. On August 2, Atlanta pitchers Larry McWilliams and Gene Garber held Rose hitless. "He pitched me," said Rose referring to Garber, "like it was the seventh game of the World Series." During the 44 games, Rose batted .385 (70 for 182).

Ironically, Rose ended his 16-year career with Cincinnati after the season. Unhappy with the Reds' contract offer, he became the biggest name in the baseball's third re-entry draft. He eventually signed a lucrative, long-term contract with the Phillies.

There was also tragedy in the playing ranks in 1978. On September 23, Lyman Bostock, just reaching stardom with the California Angels, was killed by a shotgun blast in Gary, Ind. Bostock was riding in the rear seat of an automobile when he was shot, apparently by mistake. Police said the intended victim was the assailant's estranged wife, who was seated next to Bostock.

Bostock, 27, had left the Minnesota club after the 1977 season and signed with California for a reported $2.7 million for five years. At the time of his death, he was batting .296 for the Angels; in his last two seasons with the Twins, he had batted .323 and .336.

Other deaths included: Ford C. Frick, 83, baseball commissioner (1951–65) and National League president (1934–51); Jesse "Pop" Haines, 85, Hall of Fame pitcher who starred for the St. Louis Cardinals; Joe McCarthy, 90, former Yankee manager; and Jim Gilliam, 49, Los Angeles coach whose death saddened the Dodgers.

Joining the Hall of Fame at Cooperstown, N. Y., were Eddie Mathews, slugging third baseman for the Milwaukee and Atlanta Braves; Larry MacPhail, the executive who introduced night baseball to the majors; and Addie Joss, a star pitcher for Cleveland early in the century.

BOB BROEG
Sports Editor, "St. Louis Post-Dispatch"

Davey Lopes of the Dodgers completes a double play against the Phillies in the National League play-offs.
UPI

BASEBALL

Professional—Major Leagues

AMERICAN LEAGUE
(Final Standings, 1978)

Eastern Division	W	L	Pct.	Western Division	W	L	Pct.
New York....	100	63	.613	Kansas City....	92	70	.568
Boston........	99	64	.607	California......	87	75	.537
Milwaukee....	93	69	.574	Texas........	87	75	.537
Baltimore......	90	71	.559	Minnesota....	73	89	.451
Detroit........	86	76	.531	Chicago......	71	90	.441
Cleveland......	69	90	.434	Oakland........	69	93	.426
Toronto........	59	102	.366	Seattle........	56	104	.350

NATIONAL LEAGUE
(Final Standings, 1978)

Eastern Division	W	L	Pct.	Western Division	W	L	Pct.
Philadelphia...	90	72	.556	Los Angeles....	95	67	.586
Pittsburgh.....	88	73	.547	Cincinnati.....	92	69	.571
Chicago.......	79	83	.488	San Francisco..	89	73	.549
Montreal......	76	86	.469	San Diego.....	84	78	.519
St. Louis......	69	93	.426	Houston......	74	88	.457
New York.....	66	96	.407	Atlanta........	69	93	.426

Play-offs—American League: New York defeated Kansas City, 3 games to 1; National League: Los Angeles defeated Philadelphia, 3 games to 1.

World Series—New York defeated Los Angeles, 4 games to 2. First Game (Dodger Stadium, Los Angeles, Oct. 10): Los Angeles 11, New York 5; Second Game (Dodger Stadium, Oct. 11): Los Angeles 4, New York 3; Third Game (Yankee Stadium, New York, Oct. 13): New York 5, Los Angeles 1; Fourth Game (Yankee Stadium, Oct. 14): New York 4, Los Angeles 3; Fifth Game (Yankee Stadium, Oct. 15): New York 12, Los Angeles 2; Sixth Game (Dodger Stadium, Oct. 17): New York 7, Los Angeles 2.

All-Star Game (San Diego Stadium, July 11): National League 7, American League 3.

Most Valuable Players—American League: Jim Rice, Boston; National League: Dave Parker, Pittsburgh.

Cy Young Memorial Awards (outstanding pitchers)—American League: Ron Guidry, New York; National League: Gaylord Perry, San Diego.

Managers of the Year—American League: Bob Lemon, New York; National League: Joe Altobelli, San Francisco.

Rookies of the Year—American League: Lou Whitaker, Detroit; National League: Bob Horner, Atlanta.

Leading Hitters—(Percentage) American League: Rod Carew, Minnesota, .333; National League: Dave Parker, Pittsburgh, .334. (Runs Batted In) American League: Jim Rice, Boston, 139; National League: George Foster, Cincinnati, 120. (Home Runs) American League: Jim Rice, 46; National League: George Foster, 40. (Runs) American League: Ron LeFlore, Detroit, 126; National League: Ivan DeJesus, Chicago, 104.

Leading Pitchers—(Earned run average) American League: Ron Guidry, New York, 1.74; National League: Craig Swan, New York, 2.43. (Victories) American League: Ron Guidry, 25; National League: Gaylord Perry, San Diego, 21. (Strikeouts) American League: Nolan Ryan, California, 260; National League: J. R. Richard, Houston, 303.

No-Hit Games Pitched—Bob Forsch, St. Louis Cardinals v. Philadelphia Phillies; Tom Seaver, Cincinnati Reds v. St. Louis.

Professional—Minor Leagues, Class AAA

American Association (play-offs): Omaha Royals
International League (Governor's Cup): Richmond Braves
Pacific Coast League: tie—Tacoma Yankees, Albuquerque Dodgers

Amateur

NCAA Class I: University of Southern California
NAIA: Emporia (Kan.) State
Little League World Series: Taiwan

BASKETBALL

For the second year in a row, a second-place team finished on top in the National Basketball Association. The Washington Bullets, under coach Dick Motta, captured the league championship by defeating the Seattle Supersonics, four games to two, in the final round of the play-offs. In college competition, Kentucky gained its fifth NCAA championship, and UCLA, long a power in the men's ranks, won its first women's title.

THE PROFESSIONAL SEASON

It would be unfair to claim that the Bullets did not deserve the NBA championship, their first since the franchise was founded in 1961. In the play-offs, they swept past the Atlanta Hawks, the San Antonio Spurs, the Philadelphia '76ers, and the Supersonics to earn an honor that almost nobody gave them a chance of winning.

Still, not even the most enthusiastic Washington supporters could deny that the Portland Trail Blazers had the most powerful team in the league until injuries to center Bill Walton and others wiped out their chances of repeating as champions. Despite injuries to five key players, coach Jack Ramsay's team posted the

RON KOCH, NBA

Washington's Elvin Hayes (11) takes a rebound as the Bullets defeat Seattle for the NBA crown.

best regular season record in the NBA—58–24. (After the season, Walton demanded to be traded to another team because of the Trail Blazers' allegedly indiscriminate use of pain killers for his injury.)

When it became obvious that the Trail Blazers' makeshift lineup would be overmatched in the play-offs, the '76ers, champions of the Atlantic Division, were seen as the "on paper" favorites. Their emphasis on individual play, however, again proved their undoing. With inferior manpower but superior teamwork, the Bullets defeated the '76ers, four games to two, in the Eastern Conference semifinal series. In the Western Conference, the Supersonics eliminated the crippled Trail Blazers, 4–2, in the quarterfinals, and knocked out the Denver Nuggets, 4–2, in the semifinals.

The title round thus presented a rarity—second and third place clubs squaring off for the big prize. The well-played, tension-filled

PROFESSIONAL BASKETBALL

National Basketball Association
(Final Standings, 1977–78)

Eastern Conference

Atlantic Division

	W	L	Pct.
*Philadelphia '76ers	55	27	.671
*New York Knickerbockers	43	39	.524
Boston Celtics	32	50	.390
Buffalo Braves	27	55	.329
New Jersey Nets	24	58	.293

Central Division

	W	L	Pct.
*San Antonio Spurs	52	30	.634
*Washington Bullets	44	38	.537
*Cleveland Cavaliers	43	39	.524
*Atlanta Hawks	41	41	.500
New Orleans Jazz	39	43	.476
Houston Rockets	28	54	.341

Western Conference

Midwest Division

	W	L	Pct.
*Denver Nuggets	48	34	.585
*Milwaukee Bucks	44	38	.537
Chicago Bulls	40	42	.488
Detroit Pistons	38	44	.463
Indiana Pacers	31	51	.378
Kansas City Kings	31	51	.378

Pacific Division

	W	L	Pct.
*Portland Trail Blazers	58	24	.707
*Phoenix Suns	49	33	.598
*Seattle Supersonics	47	35	.573
*Los Angeles Lakers	45	37	.549
Golden State Warriors	43	39	.524

*Qualified for play-offs

NBA Champion: Washington Bullets
All Star Game: East 133, West 125

Individual Honors

Most Valuable Player: Bill Walton, Portland
Most Valuable Player (play-offs): Wes Unseld, Washington
Rookie of the Year: Walter Davis, Phoenix
Coach of the Year: Hubie Brown, Atlanta
Leading Scorer: George Gervin, San Antonio; 2,232 points; 27.21 per game
Leading Rebounder: Leonard Robinson, New Orleans; 15.7 per game

series culminated in a 105–99 seventh game victory for the Bullets. Game 4, played in the Seattle Kingdome, was seen by the largest crowd in NBA play-off history—39,457. Wes Unseld, veteran center for the Bullets, was voted the most valuable player in the play-offs.

Bill Walton of the Trail Blazers won the most valuable player award for the regular season, and George Gervin of San Antonio edged out David Thompson of Denver for the scoring title. On the final afternoon of the season, Thompson scored 73 points against the Detroit Pistons, but Gervin came back with 63 against the New Orleans Jazz to win the scoring title, 27.21 points per game to 27.15.

Kevin Porter of the New Jersey Nets led the league in assists, with an average of 10.2 per game. Porter also set an NBA record for most assists in one game when he "dished off" 29 times against New Orleans February 24. Leonard "Truck" Robinson of New Orleans led the league in rebounding, Walter Davis of the Phoenix Suns was voted rookie of the year, and Hubie Brown of Atlanta was honored as coach of the year.

The 1977–78 NBA season was darkened by an unprecedented number of fights. Kareem Abdul-Jabbar and Kermit Washington, both of the Los Angeles Lakers, threw devastating punches at opposing players and were given stiff penalties by league commissioner Lawrence O'Brien.

The season also marked the farewell of John Havlicek, one of the NBA's all-time leading scorers, who retired after 16 years with the Boston Celtics.

In an historic postseason transaction, the owners of the Boston Celtics and Buffalo Braves swapped franchises, with the latter team moving to San Diego for the 1978–79 season.

THE COLLEGE SEASON

The Kentucky Wildcats defeated the stubborn Duke Blue Devils, 94–88, in the NCAA finals at the St. Louis Checkerdome. The victory gave Kentucky its first championship under coach Joe B. Hall and its first since 1958 when the team was coached by the late Adolph Rupp.

Kentucky led the game from the beginning and appeared to be headed for a romp as it built a 64–50 lead with 12 minutes to play. The Wildcats became anxious, however, and began taking wild shots. The Blue Devils capitalized and shaved the deficit to 92–86 with 22 seconds left. Coach Hall was forced to return his regulars to the court to ensure the victory.

The hero of the game was Jack Givens, later to be a first round draft choice of the Atlanta Hawks. Givens, a springy 6-foot, 4-inch (1.93 m) forward, scored 41 points for Kentucky and was a runaway choice as the most valuable player. His point total fell just three shy of the title game record set by Bill Walton of UCLA in 1973.

Kentucky, it was said, actually received stiffer competition earlier in the tournament than it did in the finals. The Wildcats defeated Michigan State, 52–49, in the Mideast Regional finals, and won over Arkansas in the NCAA semifinals, 64–59. Despite such competition, Kentucky was clearly the class of the field, and their success vindicated the pollsters who had voted them Number 1 in the regular season.

Duke reached the championship game by defeating Rhode Island (63–62), Pennsylvania (84–80), Villanova (90–72), and Notre Dame (90–86).

Arkansas earned third place in the tournament by nosing out Notre Dame, 71–69. UCLA, rated second in the polls for the regular season, was beaten by Arkansas, 74–70, in the West Regional semifinals.

The irony of the tournament was that Marquette, which won the 1976–77 tournament in the last hurrah of Al McGuire, one of basketball's most colorful coaches, was one of the first of the 32 qualifying teams to be eliminated.

In the National Invitational Tournament at Madison Square Garden in New York City, The University of Texas defeated North Carolina State, 101–93, in the championship game.

Butch Lee, the outstanding guard from Marquette, was awarded the Rupp Trophy as the top college basketball player of 1977–78.

Women's Competition. UCLA defeated Maryland, 90–74, for the championship of the Association of Intercollegiate Athletics for Women. All-American Ann Meyers led the way with 20 points and 10 rebounds. The victory of UCLA ended the three-year reign of Delta State of Cleveland, Miss. Montclair (N. J.) State took third place with a 90–88 decision over Wayland (Tex.) Baptist.

BOB WOLF, *"The Milwaukee Journal"*

COLLEGE BASKETBALL

Conference Champions

Atlantic Coast: Duke
Big Eight: Missouri
Big Sky: Weber State
Big Ten: Michigan State
East Coast: Temple
Eastern Eight: Villanova
Ivy League: Pennsylvania
Metro-7: Louisville
Mid-American: Miami (O.)
Mid-Eastern: North Carolina A&T
Missouri Valley: Creighton
Ohio Valley: Western Kentucky
Pacific-8: UCLA
Southeastern: Kentucky
Southern: Furman
Southland: (tie) McNeese State and Lamar
Southwest: Houston
Southwestern: (tie) Southern U. and Jackson State
Sun Belt: New Orleans
West Coast Athletic: San Francisco
Western Athletic: New Mexico

Tournaments

NCAA: Kentucky
NIT: Texas
NCAA Div. II: Cheyney State
NCAA Div. III: North Park
AIAW (Women): UCLA

BOXING

With Muhammad Ali again leading the way, boxing in 1978 produced surprises, much controversy and drama, and record attendance and gate receipts.

The biggest surprise came on February 15 when a 24-year-old former Olympic champion and former United States Marine, Leon Spinks, dethroned Ali as heavyweight champion. Spinks, who had fought only seven previous pro bouts, won a split decision at Las Vegas, Nev., and sent the heavyweight division into turmoil almost immediately.

Ali had taken the bout lightly and did not train sufficiently. At 224 pounds (101.6 kg), he was overweight, as well as overconfident. Spinks piled up points in the early rounds as Ali chose to toy with him. Ali rallied in the 11th and 12th rounds, but Spinks would not let his chance to become the champion slip away, swarming all over Ali in the 14th. The 15th round was a donnybrook, with Ali opening up his entire arsenal in a desperate attempt to score a knockout. Spinks withstood Ali's best shots, retaliating strongly to assure victory.

Shortly after his triumph, Spinks backed off from an agreement to defend his title against Ken Norton, another former Marine, who had fought Ali three times. Spinks chose instead to give Ali a rematch. The World Boxing Council (WBC), one of two governing bodies in boxing, stripped Spinks of its version of the title and declared Norton its champion. This left Spinks

UPI

Leon Spinks and Mohammed Ali met twice in the ring during 1978. Spinks won in February; Ali regained the heavyweight boxing crown six months later.

BOXING
World Professional Champions
(Year of achieving title in parentheses)

Junior Flyweight—Yoko Gushiken, Japan (1976), World Boxing Association (WBA); Kim Sung-Jun, South Korea (1978), World Boxing Council (WBC).
Flyweight—Betulio Gonzalez, Venezuela (1978) ,WBA; Miguel Canto, Mexico (1975), WBC.
Bantamweight—Jorge Lujan, Panama (1977), WBA; Carlos Zarate, Mexico (1976), WBC.
Junior Featherweight—Ricardo Cardona, Colombia (1978), WBA; Wilfredo Gomez, Puerto Rico (1977), WBC.
Featherweight—Eusebio Pedroza, Panama (1978), WBA; Danny Lopez (1976), WBC.
Junior Lightweight—Sammy Serrano, Puerto Rico (1976), WBA; Alexis Arguello, Nicaragua (1978), WBC.
Lightweight—Roberto Duran, Panama (1972, 1978), knocked out Esteban de Jesus, Puerto Rico (1976, WBC) to win undisputed title.
Junior Welterweight—Antonio Cervantes, Colombia (1977), WBA; Saensak Muangsurin, Thailand (1976), WBC.
Welterweight—José Cuevas, Mexico (1976), WBA; Carlos Palomino, Westminster, Calif. (1976), WBC.
Middleweight—Hugo Corro, Argentina (1978). Title undisputed.
Junior Middleweight—Masashi Kudo, Japan (1978), WBA; Rocky Mattioli, Italy (1977), WBC.
Light Heavyweight—Mike Rossman, Turnersville, N.J. (1978), WBA; Marvin Johnson, Indianapolis, Ind. (1978), WBC.
Heavyweight—Muhammad Ali, Chicago (1964, 1974, 1978), WBA; Larry Holmes, Easton, Pa. (1978), WBC.

National AAU Champions
(Biloxi, Miss., April 19–22)

106 Pounds—James Cullins, Bladensburg, Md.
112 Pounds—Mike Felde, Missoula, Mont.
119 Pounds—Jackie Beard, Jackson, Tenn.
125 Pounds—Eichi Jumawan, Wahiawa, Hawaii
132 Pounds—Melvin Paul, New Orleans, La.
139 Pounds—Donald Curry, Fort Worth, Tex.
147 Pounds—Roger Leonard, U.S. Air Force
156 Pounds—J. B. Williamson, U.S. Marines
165 Pounds—Jeff McCracken, U.S. Marines
178 Pounds—Elmer Martin, U.S. Navy
Heavyweight—Greg Page, Louisville, Ky.

with only the World Boxing Association (WBA) version of the title. The WBC ordered Norton to defend against Larry Holmes, a strong contender. Norton was a heavy favorite to beat Holmes in his first defense at Las Vegas. Holmes, who had been a sparring mate for Ali, scored an upset and became the WBC champion on a split decision.

The 36-year-old Ali regained the WBA title from Spinks on September 15 at the Superdome in New Orleans in a spectacular show that broke gate and attendance marks. A crowd of 70,000 paid $7 million, the biggest gate in boxing history, to see if Ali could become the first man to regain the heavyweight title three times. Ali called on all his ring experience to frustrate Spinks. Ali handled younger Spinks with clinching tactics that made Spinks seem like an amateur. Ali won easily on a unanimous decision.

On the same card, Victor Galindez of Argentina defended his WBA light heavyweight title for the 11th time, against Mike Rossman of Turnersville, N. J. Rossman scored a 13th-round knockout when the referee stopped the fight because of cuts over Galindez' eyes.

Roberto Duran of Panama, the WBA's lightweight champion who had lost only once in 61 fights, knocked out the WBC champion, Esteban de Jesus in the 12th round and took undisputed possession of the lightweight crown on January 21. In 1972, de Jesus had won a decision in a nontitle bout in New York. In 1974, in defense of his WBA crown, Duran had stopped de Jesus in the 11th round.

GEORGE DE GREGORIO

FOOTBALL

Following the defeat of Joe Paterno's Penn State team in the Sugar Bowl, the Crimson Tide of Alabama was rated No. 1 in the Associated Press poll and Southern California was ranked as the nation's best in the final United Press International ratings. Professionally, the Dallas Cowboys and the Pittsburgh Steelers met again in the Super Bowl game.

THE COLLEGE SEASON

From all the bowl bids offered, Joe Paterno chose the Sugar Bowl on the expectation that his No. 1-ranked Nittany Lions would face the No. 2-ranked team and that a victory would erase any doubt that Penn State was deserving to be named the national champion. His hope was realized—2nd-rated Alabama became Penn State's opponent at New Orleans.

But Paterno's best-laid plans went awry. The Lions, called by Paterno the best he ever coached at Penn State, made inexplicable errors. They failed to anticipate Alabama's blitzing tactics in the first half, gaining a mere 21 yards. Only 1 yard away from the goal line, they failed to score the tying touchdown. (This series of plays helped linebacker Barry Krauss gain the game's MVP award.) They had a 12th man on the field in the closing minutes, nullifying a bad Alabama punt that would have given them possession on the Tide 20. And so Penn State lost, 14–7, and Paterno admitted he had been "outcoached" by Bear Bryant.

As a result, Alabama was voted the No. 1 team in the Associated Press poll and also received the MacArthur Bowl, awarded by the National Football Foundation and Hall of Fame to the team they consider the national champion.

However, in the final United Press International poll, Southern California, which had beaten Alabama earlier in the season and downed Michigan in the Rose Bowl, narrowly edged the Tide for the top position.

Penn State. Paterno had achieved his long-sought goal of a No. 1 ranking at midseason after the Nittany Lions were left as the only major undefeated eleven in the nation. Penn State kept its unbeaten distinction and the top spot for the rest of the regular campaign. It was frequently the defenders that proved to be the decisive factor for Penn State. On offense the Nittany Lions featured the passing arm and play-calling of Chuck Fusina and the reliable place-kicking of Matt Bahr. He established a National Collegiate Athletic Association record by booting 22 field goals and was perfect on 31 points-after-touchdown attempts.

What is remarkable is that this recognition had not arrived sooner for the mild-mannered Paterno, whose personality and perspective about football are in marked contrast to the many leading coaches with their life-or-death approach to the sport. In his previous 13 years at Penn State, he had enjoyed a higher winning percentage (.833) than any of his peers. He also had had three undefeated teams (1968, 1969, and 1973) that had gone on to victory in major bowl games. Paterno, who has described football as just another extra-curricular activity, notes with pride that 94% of his players have received their degrees in the standard four years. His players are given no special consideration in such areas as curriculum, housing, and off-the-field privileges.

The Bowl Games. USC earned its Rose Bowl berth as it usually does, by beating the University of California, Los Angeles. The score was 17–10. Charles White, the latest in a long

---

COLLEGE FOOTBALL

Conference Champions

Atlantic Coast—Clemson
Big Eight—Nebraska, Oklahoma (tied)
Big Ten—Michigan, Michigan State (tied)
Ivy League—Dartmouth
Mid-American—Ball State
Missouri Valley—New Mexico State
Pacific Ten—Southern California
Southeastern—Alabama
Southern—Furman, Tennessee-Chattanooga (tied)
Southwest—Houston
Southwestern—Grambling
Western Athletic—Brigham Young
Yankee—Massachusetts

Heisman Trophy—Billy Sims, Oklahoma

NCAA Champions

Division I—Florida A&M
Division II—Eastern Illinois
Division III—Baldwin-Wallace

NAIA Champions

Division I—Angelo State
Division II—Concordia

Major Bowl Games

Holiday Bowl (San Diego, Dec. 22)—Navy 23, Brigham Young 16
Liberty Bowl (Memphis, Dec. 23)—Missouri 20, Louisiana State 15
Sun Bowl (El Paso, Tex., Dec. 23)—Texas 42, Maryland 0
Tangerine Bowl (Orlando, Fla., Dec. 24)—North Carolina State 30, Pittsburgh 17
Fiesta Bowl (Tempe, Ariz., Dec. 25)—Arkansas 10, UCLA 10
Peach Bowl (Atlanta, Dec. 25)—Purdue 41, Georgia Tech 21
Gator Bowl (Jacksonville, Fla., Dec. 29)—Clemson 17, Ohio State 15
Cotton Bowl (Dallas, Jan. 1)—Notre Dame 35, Houston 34
Orange Bowl (Miami, Jan. 1)—Oklahoma 31, Nebraska 24
Rose Bowl (Pasadena, Jan. 1)—Southern California 17, Michigan 10
Sugar Bowl (New Orleans, Jan. 1)—Alabama 14, Penn State 7

Final College Rankings

Team	AP Writers	UPI Coaches	Team	AP Writers	UPI Coaches
Alabama	1	2	Clemson	6	6 (tie)
USC	2	1	Notre Dame	7	6 (tie)
Oklahoma	3	3	Nebraska	8	8
Penn State	4	4	Texas	9	9
Michigan	5	5	Houston	10	11

PHOTO, RON MEREDEITH

The University of Oklahoma defeats the University of Texas, 31–10, in a regular season contest. At the time, the Oklahoma Sooners were ranked No. 1.

line of all-American USC tailbacks, was the hero. In the process he became the leading rusher in Trojan and conference record books.

Michigan went to the Rose Bowl again primarily because of its resourceful quarterback, Rick Leach. The Wolverines defeated Ohio State, 14–3, for a share of the Big Ten title with Michigan State. The Trojans' 17–10 Rose Bowl was marred by a controversy over whether White, crossing the goal line for the deciding score, had fumbled before or after plunging into the end zone.

Nebraska, despite having edged Oklahoma, 17–14, earlier in the season, was a decided underdog in their Orange Bowl meeting. It was the first time that the two Big Eight rivals were the opponents in the annual Miami extravaganza. With Thomas Lott directing the Sooners' devastating wishbone offense, Oklahoma made up, in part, for their previous defeat, winning by 31–24 after building a 31–10 lead.

Notre Dame put on a dramatic 23-point rally in the fourth quarter to overtake Houston, 35–34, in the Cotton Bowl. The Irish's Joe Montana passed 8 yards to Chris Haines as time ran out and Joe Unis kicked the vital extra point.

In the Gator Bowl, the reign of 65-year-old Woody Hayes as Ohio State's head coach ended after he had compiled a 205–61–10 record at Ohio State and had twice led the Buckeyes to the national championship (1954 and 1968). He was dismissed for punching a Clemson player, Charlie Bauman, on the sideline late in the game. Bauman had just made an interception that sealed Clemson's 17–15 triumph. The volatile Hayes apparently could not contain his frustration.

THE PROFESSIONAL SEASON

The Pittsburgh Steelers became the first team to win three Super Bowls. The Steelers earned the honor by defeating the Cowboys 35–31 in Super Bowl XIII at Miami, Jan. 21, 1979.

Pittsburgh had been a slight favorite, primarily because of its defense. The Steelers grudgingly had given up 195 points, the league low, in the 16-game schedule and only 15 points in two play-off triumphs. Led by linebackers Jack Ham and Jack Lambert, the Steel Curtain defense had been so resistant to the rush in the previous seven games that the opposition was held to fewer than 100 yards each time.

The Steelers had been no slouch on offense either as they locked up their division title with the league's best won–lost record (14–2). Terry Bradshaw had his best season and deservedly garnered most of the all-pro quarterback awards. Two fleet and acrobatic receivers, Lynn Swann and John Stallworth, helped immensely, and Franco Harris and Rocky Bleier supplied the necessary punch on the ground. The Cowboys, on the other hand, had not shown much consistency despite their depth of talent. After ten games they were 6–4, and fans began to doubt that the defending Super Bowl champions would reach the title contest. Nevertheless, the Cowboys ended up with the most points (384) in the league as Roger Staubach directed their explosive if erratic attack. And on defense they yielded only 208 points. Tackle Randy White and ends Ed "Too Tall" Jones and Harvey Martin were outstanding up front, and in Cliff Harris and Charley Waters, Dallas boasted two safetymen of all-pro stature.

UPI

Dallas' Tony Dorsett became the third NFL player to gain more than 1,000 yards in his first two seasons.

NFC. In both of their play-off triumphs, the Cowboys demonstrated how uneven their performances could be. The Los Angeles Rams held the Cowboys scoreless for the first half of the National Conference title game, but Waters broke open the contest in the third period. He twice intercepted Pat Haden passes to pave the way for touchdowns. The Cowboys' offense finally got rolling for an 89-yard scoring drive, sparked by Tony Dorsett's 53-yard scamper, and Dallas won convincingly 28–0.

The loss was the Rams' fourth in five years in the conference finale, and Los Angeles has yet to make the Super Bowl. The Rams, whose running corps was depleted by injuries during the campaign were further handicapped when John Cappelletti, their best remaining back, was sidelined in the first quarter and Haden left with a fractured thumb in the third.

The Cowboys played poorly in the first half of their play-off opener, and the Atlanta Falcons led, 20–13. To make matters worse, Staubach was knocked out of the game late in the second period with a concussion. But Danny White, the team's punter and No. 2 quarterback, rallied the Cowboys to a 27–20 victory.

AFC. In the American Conference, the Steelers ended the Houston Oilers' dream of becoming only the third wild-card team to get to the Super Bowl, by defeating them 34–5. A heavy and chilling Pittsburgh rain caused the teams to fumble the icy pigskin. Houston's Earl Campbell had the finest rookie season of any running back since Jim Brown broke in with the Cleveland Browns in 1957. The Oilers' No. 1 draft choice was the first pro freshman since Brown to lead the league in rushing (1,450 yards). He and the superb passing of Dan Pastorini enabled Houston to gain the play-offs. But in the final, Campbell fumbled three times and finished with only 62 yards on 22 carries. In their play-off opener, the Steelers trounced the Denver Broncos, 33–10.

Grey Cup. The Edmonton Eskimos defeated the Montreal Alouettes, 20–13, to capture the Canadian Football League's Grey Cup.

LUD DUROSKA
"The New York Times"

PROFESSIONAL FOOTBALL

National Football League
Final Standings

AMERICAN CONFERENCE
Eastern Division

	W	L	T	Pct.	Points For	Agst.
New England	11	5	0	.688	358	286
Miami*	11	5	0	.688	372	254
Jets	8	8	0	.500	359	364
Buffalo	5	11	0	.313	302	354
Baltimore	5	11	0	.313	239	421

Central Division

	W	L	T	Pct.	Points For	Agst.
Pittsburgh	14	2	0	.875	356	195
Houston*	10	6	0	.625	283	298
Cleveland	8	8	0	.500	334	356
Cincinnati	4	12	0	.250	252	284

Western Division

	W	L	T	Pct.	Points For	Agst.
Denver	10	6	0	.625	282	198
Oakland	9	7	0	.563	311	283
San Diego	9	7	0	.563	355	309
Seattle	9	7	0	.563	345	358
Kansas City	4	12	0	.250	243	327

* Clinched play-off berth

Play-offs
Houston 17, Miami 9
Pittsburgh 33, Denver 10
Houston 31, New England 14
Pittsburgh 34, Houston 5

NATIONAL CONFERENCE
Eastern Division

	W	L	T	Pct.	Points For	Agst.
Dallas	12	4	0	.750	384	208
Philadelphia*	9	7	0	.563	270	250
Washington	8	8	0	.500	273	283
St. Louis	6	10	0	.375	248	296
Giants	6	10	0	.375	264	298

Central Division

	W	L	T	Pct.	Points For	Agst.
Minnesota	8	7	1	.531	294	306
Green Bay	8	7	1	.531	249	269
Detroit	7	9	0	.438	290	300
Chicago	7	9	0	.438	253	274
Tampa Bay	5	11	0	.313	241	259

Western Division

	W	L	T	Pct.	Points For	Agst.
Los Angeles	12	4	0	.750	316	245
Atlanta*	9	7	0	.563	240	290
New Orleans	7	9	0	.438	281	298
San Francisco	2	14	0	.125	219	350

* Clinched play-off berth

Play-offs
Atlanta 14, Philadelphia 13
Los Angeles 34, Minnesota 10
Dallas 27, Atlanta 20
Dallas 28, Los Angeles 0

Super Bowl: Pittsburgh 35, Dallas 31

GOLF

Tom Watson again was the leading player on the United States professional golf tour in 1978, but he by no means dominated the news during an exciting season.

The 29-year-old Watson swept the key statistical categories. He led the PGA Tour in money winnings for the second straight year, this time with a record total of $362,429 that boosted his career earnings to $1,201,391. Although he failed to capture a major championship, he won five tournaments, the Vardon Trophy for low stroke average of 70.16, and top spot on *Golf Digest's* performance average list at .758.

Veteran Gary Player produced some early season excitement when he shot a final-round 64 to win the Masters, then followed with victories the next two weeks at the Tournament of Champions and the Houston Open. The Masters title was Player's third and his ninth major championship. It was his first U. S. victory since 1974 and propelled him to money winnings of $177,336, the best U. S. year ever for the 42-year-old Hall of Famer from South Africa.

Jack Nicklaus gave no sign of faltering. Although he played a limited schedule, he won three tournaments on the U. S. tour, including the Tournament Players Championship and the British Open, his first major title since 1975. The only other player with three victories on the men's tour was Andy Bean. He finished third on the money list with $267,241.

Dr. Gil Morgan, a licensed optometrist who won the Glen Campbell-Los Angeles Open, early in the year, and the $100,000 first prize in the World Series of Golf, earned *Golf Digest's* Most Improved Player Award.

John Mahaffey, a consistent money-winner who twice had U. S. Open titles within his reach, only to lose, incurred a succession of injuries that forced him off the tour in late 1976 and 1977. He was improving only gradually in 1978 until he shot a 66 at fabled Oakmont Country Club to win the PGA Championship. He followed that with victory the next week at the American Optical Classic in Sutton, Mass., to earn *Golf Digest's* Comeback of the Year Trophy.

The other major championship went to Andy North, who survived at difficult Cherry Hills in Denver, Colo., to win the U. S. Open. It was the 28-year-old North's first major title and only his second victory on tour.

The Ladies Tour. Nancy Lopez, with nine victories and a record $189,814 in earnings, dominated the Ladies Professional Golfers Association tour. Her five victories in a row in mid-season included the LPGA Championship and, after just half a previous season on tour, earned her LPGA Rookie and Player of the Year awards.

Almost lost in the brilliance of Miss Lopez' performance was a four-victory season by Jane Blalock, who finished second on the money list with $117,768.

Hollis Stacy won her second consecutive U. S. Women's Open, holding off JoAnne Carner and Sally Little in a dramatic last-round battle.

Sandra Post captured the Colgate-Dinah Shore Classic and the year's richest prize of $36,000.

Two other players went over $100,000 as the LPGA purse total grew to $3.6 million. Pat Bradley won three tournaments and $110,287 and Mrs. Carner, who won two events plus the unofficial Colgate Triple Crown, earned $108,092.

LARRY DENNIS, *Golf Digest*

GOLF
Winners—1978 PGA Tour
Joe Garagiola-Tucson Open—Tom Watson (276)
Phoenix Open—Miller Barber (272)
Bing Crosby National Pro-Am—Tom Watson (280)
Andy Williams-San Diego Open—Jay Haas (278)
Hawaiian Open—Hubert Green (274)
Bob Hope Desert Classic—Bill Rogers (339)
The Glen Campbell-Los Angeles Open—Gil Morgan (278)
Jackie Gleason Inverrary Classic—Jack Nicklaus (276)
Tournament Players Championshp—Jack Nicklaus (289)
Masters Tournament—Gary Player (277)
Mony Tournament of Champions—Gary Player (281)
First NBC New Orleans Open—Lon Hinkle (271)
Byron Nelson Golf Classic—Tom Watson (272)
Kemper Open—Andy Bean (273)
Danny Thomas-Memphis Classic—Andy Bean (277)
United States Open—Andy North (285)
Canadian Open—Bruce Lietzke (283)
Western Open—Andy Bean (282)
PGA Championship—John Mahaffey (276)
World Series of Golf—Gil Morgan (278)

Other Tournaments
British Open—Jack Nicklaus (281)
U.S. Amateur—John Cook
British Amateur—Peter McEvoy
U.S. Public Links—Dean Prince
World Amateur—Team: United States (873); Individual: Bobby Clampett (United States) (287)

Winners—1978 LPGA Tour
Orange Blossom Classic—Jane Blalock (212)
Bent Tree Classic—Nancy Lopez (289)
Sunstar Classic—Nancy Lopez (285)
Baltimore Classic—Nancy Lopez (212)
Coca-Cola Classic—Nancy Lopez (210)
Golden Lights—Nancy Lopez (277)
LPGA Championship—Nancy Lopez (275)
Bankers Trust—Nancy Lopez (214)
Mayflower Classic—Jane Blalock (209)
Wheeling Classic—Jane Blalock (207)
Colgate-European Open—Nancy Lopez (289)
Colgate-Far East Open—Nancy Lopez (216)
Golden Lights—Jane Blalock (276)

Other Women's Tournaments
U.S. Amateur—Cathy Sherk
World Amateur—Team: Australia (596); Individual Cathy Sherk (Canada) (294)

HOCKEY

The Montreal Canadiens were the toast of the National Hockey League (NHL) in 1977–78 as they compiled a regular season record of 59-10-11 and won the Stanley Cup for the third year in a row. The Winnipeg Jets captured the Avco Cup, symbolic of World Hockey League (WHL) supremacy, and the Soviet Union won the World Cup tournament in Prague, Czechoslovakia.

NHL. The Montreal Canadiens have often been called the "New York Yankees of ice hockey." When they defeated the Boston Bruins four games to two in their best-of-seven championship series, the Canadiens won the Stanley Cup for the 21st time in the team's history. This matched the total number of World Series triumphs by the baseball Yankees.

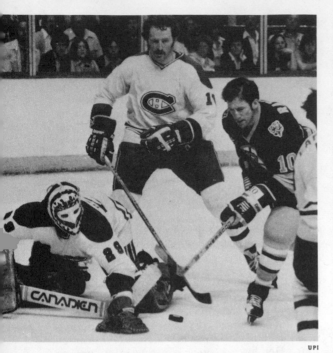

UPI

For the third consecutive year, the Montreal Canadiens captured the Stanley Cup. The Canadiens defeated the Boston Bruins, four games to two.

The Canadiens reached the finals by defeating the Detroit Red Wings four games to one in the quarterfinal series and the Toronto Maple Leafs four games to none in the semifinals.

In the championship series, the Canadiens outclassed the Bruins 4–1 in the opening game and won the second game 3–2 in overtime. Both matches were played in the Montreal Forum. Back on home ice, the Bruins were sparked by the goaltending of Gerry Cheevers and tied the series at two games apiece with surprising victories of 4–0 and 4–3 in Games 3 and 4. Veteran Canadien defenseman Larry Robinson made life difficult for the Bruins in Games 5 and 6, however, as he led his team to back-to-back 4–1 victories. Robinson, with 21 points in the 15 games, wound up in a tie with Guy Lafleur (*see also* BIOGRAPHY) for individual scoring honors in the play-offs. Robinson also won the Conn Smythe Trophy as the most valuable player in the play-offs.

Lafleur repeated as the league's regular season scoring champion with 132 points (60 goals and 72 assists), well ahead of runners-up Bryan Trottier of the New York Islanders (123 points) and Darryl Sittler of the Toronto Maple Leafs (117 points). For the second straight year Lafleur also won the Hart Trophy as the league's most valuable player. Ken Dryden and Michel (Bunny) Larocque, both of the Canadiens, shared the Vezina Trophy for goaltending.

The Canadiens, Bruins, Chicago Black Hawks, and New York Islanders captured their

HOCKEY

National Hockey League
(Final Standings, 1977–78)

Campbell Conference

Patrick Division

	W	L	T	Pts.	Goals For	Goals Against
N. Y. Islanders	48	17	15	111	334	210
Philadelphia	45	20	15	105	296	200
Atlanta	34	27	19	87	274	252
N. Y. Rangers	30	37	13	73	279	280

Smythe Division

	W	L	T	Pts.	Goals For	Goals Against
Chicago	32	29	19	83	230	220
Colorado	19	40	21	59	257	305
Vancouver	20	43	17	57	239	320
St. Louis	20	47	13	53	195	304
Minnesota	18	63	9	45	218	325

Wales Conference

Norris Division

	W	L	T	Pts.	Goals For	Goals Against
Montreal	59	10	11	129	359	183
Detroit	32	34	14	78	252	266
Los Angeles	31	34	15	77	243	245
Pittsburgh	25	37	18	68	254	321
Washington	17	49	14	48	195	321

Adams Division

	W	L	T	Pts.	Goals For	Goals Against
Boston	51	18	11	113	333	218
Buffalo	44	19	17	105	288	215
Toronto	41	29	10	92	271	237
Cleveland	22	45	13	57	230	325

Stanley Cup: Montreal Canadiens

All-Star Game: Wales Conference 3, Campbell Conference 2

Individual Honors

Hart Trophy (most valuable player): Guy Lafleur, Montreal Canadiens
Ross Trophy (leading scorer): Guy Lafleur
Norris Trophy (best defenseman): Denis Potvin, N. Y. Islanders
Lady Byng Trophy (sportsmanship): Butch Goring, Los Angeles Kings
Vezina Trophy (top goaltender, shared): Ken Dryden and Michel Larocque, Montreal Canadiens
Calder Trophy (rookie of the year): Mike Bossy, N. Y. Islanders
Conn Smythe Trophy (most valuable in play-offs): Larry Robinson, Montreal Canadiens
Coach of the Year: Bobby Kromm, Detroit Red Wings

World Hockey Association
(Final Standings, 1977–78)

	W	L	T	Pts.	Goals For	Goals Against
Winnipeg	50	28	2	102	381	270
New England	44	31	5	93	335	269
Houston	42	34	4	88	296	302
Quebec	40	37	3	83	349	347
Edmonton	38	39	3	79	309	307
Birmingham	36	41	3	75	287	314
Cincinnati	35	42	3	73	298	332
Indianapolis	24	51	5	53	267	353

Avco Cup: Winnipeg Jets

All-Star Game: Quebec Nordiques 5, All-Stars 4

Individual Honors

Leading Scorer: Marc Tardif, Québec Nordiques
Most Valuable Player: Marc Tardif
Most Valuable Player in Play-offs: Bob Guindon, Winnipeg Jets
Most Sportsmanlike: Dave Keon, New England Whalers
Rookie of the Year: Kent Nilsson, Winnipeg Jets
Defenseman of the Year: Lars-Erik Sjoberg, Winnipeg Jets
Top goalie: Al Smith, New England Whalers
Coach of the Year: Bill Dineen, Houston Aeros

Intercollegiate Champions

NCAA: Boston University

respective divisional championships. The Islanders were sparked by Mike Bossy's 53 goals (91 total points), the first rookie ever to score more than 50 goals in a season. Other play-off entrants were the New York Rangers, Buffalo Sabres, Los Angeles Kings, Atlanta Flames, and Colorado Sabres.

In an interesting post-season development, the coach of the Philadelphia Flyers, Fred

Shero, tendered his resignation and was named coach-general manager of the Rangers.

WHA. The Winnipeg Jets dominated league play from start to finish in 1977–78. They captured the regular season title with a record of 50-28-2, and swept the New England Whalers in four straight games (4–1, 5–2, 10–2, and 5–3) in the championship series. The Whalers, with grandfather Gordie Howe and his sons Mark and Marty in the lineup, were stymied offensively throughout the series.

Winnipeg reached the finals by eliminating the Birmingham Bulls four games to one, while New England qualified by defeating the defending champion Québec Nordiques.

Former NHL star Bobby Hull and Swedish-born teammates Anders Hedberg and Ulf Nilsson sparked Winnipeg's season-long effort. Mike Antonovich of New England, however, won the play-off scoring title with 17 points. Just after the playoffs, Hedberg and Nilsson, who had become free agents, announced they would join the New York Rangers of the NHL for the 1978–79 season.

World Cup. The Soviet Union ended a two-year drought by winning its 13th world championship in 16 years. The Soviets defeated Czechoslovakia 3–1 in the final game of the World Cup tournament held in Prague, Czechoslovakia, in April and May 1978.

Although Czechoslovakia had won the previous encounter between the two teams by an identical score, the Soviets were awarded the gold medal because they had scored more goals (36 to 35) during the whole tournament.

The Soviet Union was led by 20-year-old Vjatsheslav Fetison and veterans Boris Michailov, Helmut Balderis, Valeri Kharlamov, Alexander Maltsev, Alexander Golikov, and goaltender Vladislav Tretiak.

Canada earned its first World Cup Medal by defeating Sweden 3–2 for third place. Other teams competing in the tournament were East Germany, Finland, the United States, and West Germany.

ED CONRAD
Editor-in-chief, "Sunday Express," Montreal

HORSE RACING

The Triple Crown rivalry between Affirmed and Alydar highlighted the 1978 horse racing season in the United States. Affirmed, owned by the Harbor View Farm of Louis Wolfson, became the 11th horse in history to capture the Kentucky Derby, Preakness, and Belmont Stakes, the three races that make up the Triple Crown. Alydar, representing the famed Calumet Farm, became the first horse in history to finish second in all three races.

Affirmed, with Steve Cauthen up, won the Derby by one-and-a-half lengths and, in a stirring stretch run, edged Alydar by a neck in the Preakness. The two rivals then staged an epic battle in the Belmont, Affirmed winning by a head. The duel was considered by many to be the greatest horse race of all time.

Affirmed triumphed in 8 of his 11 starts in 1978 and set a record for annual earnings with $901,541. He was voted Horse of the Year, beating out Seattle Slew, who won the award in 1977, and Exceller. But in the Marlboro Cup, the first time two Triple Crown winners ever competed against each other, Seattle Slew was the victor by three lengths. The two horses met again in the Jockey Club Gold Cup, but this race was won by Exceller.

Seattle Slew won five of seven races in 1978 and was retired with a record of 14 victories in 17 starts and earnings of $1,208,726. Forego, the Horse of the Year in 1974, 1975, and 1976, was forced to retire because of physical problems. A winner in 34 of 57 lifetime starts, Forego earned $1,938,957 during his career, to rank second behind Kelso on the all-time list.

Jockey Darrel McHargue established a record for purse money won by a rider's mounts in a single season. His mounts earned $6.2 million.

Harness Racing. Abercrombie won a total of $703,260 in purse money, a record for harness horses in one year.

Quarter Horses. With a time of 21.84 seconds, Moon Lark won the $1.2 million All American Futurity at Ruidoso Downs, taking $437,500.

JIM BOLUS, *Sports Department*
"The Courier-Journal," Louisville, Ky.

HORSE RACING

Major U. S. Thoroughbred Races

Belmont Stakes: Affirmed, $184,300 (value of race)
Californian: J. O. Tobin, $214,550
Champagne Stakes: Spectacular Bid, $133,750
Flamingo: Alydar, $159,000
Florida Derby: Alydar, $150,000
Hollywood Derby: Affirmed, $284,750
Hollywood Gold Cup: Exceller, $350,000
Hollywood Invitational: Exceller, $200,000
Jockey Club Gold Cup: Exceller, $321,800
Kentucky Derby: Affirmed, $239,400
Laurel Futurity: Spectacular Bid, $142,280
Man O' War Stakes: Waya, $132,875
Marlboro Cup: Seattle Slew, $300,000
Preakness Stakes: Affirmed, $188,700
San Juan Capistrano: Exceller, $200,000
Santa Anita Derby: Affirmed, $195,300
Santa Anita Handicap: Vigors, $300,000
Travers: Alydar, $104,800
Turf Classic: Waya, $200,000
Washington, D.C. International: Mac Diarmida, $200,000
Woodward Stakes: Seattle Slew, $163,000

Major U. S. Harness Races

Cane Pace: Armbro Tiger, $307,594
Hambletonian: Speedy Somolli, $241,280
Kentucky Futurity: Doublemint, $100,000
Kentucky Pacing Derby: Scarlet Skipper, $183,755
Little Brown Jug: Happy Escort, $186,760
Meadowlands Pace: Falcon Almahurst, $560,000
Messenger Stake: Abercrombie, $167,862
Roosevelt International: Cold Comfort, $200,000
Woodrow Wilson: Scarlet Skipper, $481,250
Yonkers Trot: Speedy Somolli, $233,594

Argentina wins soccer's World Cup finals, defeating Holland, 3–1, in overtime.

UPI

SKIING

World Cup skiing continued to be dominated by Europeans in 1978, but American skiers for the first time won three Cup events in a row. Ingemar Stenmark of Sweden won his third consecutive overall individual title, and Hanni Wenzel of Liechtenstein garnered her first women's overall crown. In the team standings, Austria finished first with 905 points, followed by Switzerland with 517, and the United States with 411. It was the highest finish of a U. S. team since 1970.

Stenmark skied to the overall, slalom, and giant slalom titles by getting off to a big, early lead. He swept the first six races in the slalom and giant slalom, and, as early as January 9, had scored the maximum number of points for those two events. Stenmark clinched the overall crown March 4 at Stratton, Vt., despite a loss in the slalom to Steve Mahre of White Pass, Wash., by a mere .062 seconds.

Franz Klammer of Austria, with 96 points, won the downhill title for the fourth straight time.

Steve Mahre's slalom victory marked the first time American skiers had won three successive World Cup events. His twin brother, Phil, earlier won the giant slalom at Stratton and the slalom in France. Phil Mahre was runner-up to Stenmark in the overall standings, 150 points to 116, and was third in the slalom and giant slalom for the season. It was one of the best showings ever by an American.

Miss Wenzel totaled 154 points for the women's overall crown, giving Liechtenstein its first Cup title. Miss Wenzel also captured the slalom title, and Miss Morerod gained the giant slalom crown. The women's downhill title went to Mrs. Moser with 125 points. Cindy Nelson of the United States was the runner-up in the downhill event with 91 points.

GEORGE DE GREGORIO

SOCCER

The year 1978 was a big one for soccer, both in the United States and at the international level. The New York Cosmos proved they did not need the legendary Pélé to win a North American Soccer League (NASL) championship, as they captured their second straight crown. Argentina laid claim to being the best team in the world, however, with a 3–1 victory over Holland in the finals of the World Cup.

NASL. Without the retired Pelé, the Cosmos rolled to a 24–6 regular season record and won the NASL's National Conference Eastern Division championship in a breeze. They then captured the league title in a grueling six-game playoff series that culminated August 27 with a 3–1 Soccer Bowl win over Tampa Bay before 74,901 fans at Giants Stadium in East Rutherford, N. J.

The year started out as a risk for the NASL but ended with an all-time record five million-plus fans going through the gates. The league increased its membership from 18 to 24 teams and accepted ten new franchises all together. Teams from Philadelphia, New England, San Diego, and Colorado were revived, and Memphis, Houston, Detroit, California, Oakland, and Tulsa were brought in. The league realigned itself into American and National conferences, with three divisions in each. The schedule was increased from 26 to 30 regular season games.

World Cup. Buoyed by the brilliant play of Mario Kempes (six goals in the tournament), Argentina captured its first World Cup since 1930. It took a 30-minute overtime for the host country to defeat Holland, 3–1, for the championship. Brazil beat Italy, 2–1, for third place.

Argentina had not been favored to win the tournament and actually lost a match in the first round, 1–0, to Italy; they advanced to the next round as only the second team from Group I. Poland and defending champion West Germany survived Group II; Austria and Brazil came through Group III; and Peru and Holland emerged from Group IV.

In Group B, Argentina came into its semifinal match with Peru needing to win by at least four goals in order to beat out Brazil for a berth in the finals. The Argentinians won, 6–0. In Group A, Holland's 2–1 come-from-behind win over Italy earned them a spot in the finals for the second straight time.

Argentina led the championship match, 1–0, until Holland tied it up with only nine minutes left to play. A goal by Kempes in the 14th minute of overtime broke the tie, and Daniel Bertoni sealed the victory for Argentina with another goal six minutes later.

JIM HENDERSON, *Tampa Tribune*

SOCCER

North American Soccer League
(Final Standings, 1978)

National Conference

East

	W	L	G.F.	G.A.	Pts.
New York	24	6	88	39	212
Washington	16	14	55	47	145
Toronto	16	14	58	47	144
Rochester	13	17	47	52	125

Central

	W	L	G.F.	G.A.	Pts.
Minnesota	17	13	58	43	156
Tulsa	16	14	49	46	141
Dallas	14	16	51	53	131
Colorado	8	22	34	66	81

West

	W	L	G.F.	G.A.	Pts.
Vancouver	24	6	68	29	199
Portland	20	10	50	36	167
Seattle	15	15	50	45	138
Los Angeles	9	21	36	69	88

American Conference

East

	W	L	G.F.	G.A.	Pts.
New England	19	11	62	29	165
Tampa Bay	18	12	63	48	165
Fort Lauderdale	16	14	50	59	143
Philadelphia	12	18	40	58	111

Central

	W	L	G.F.	G.A.	Pts.
Detroit	20	10	68	36	176
Chicago	12	18	57	64	123
Memphis	10	20	43	58	101
Houston	10	20	37	61	96

West

	W	L	G.F.	G.A.	Pts.
San Diego	18	12	63	56	164
California	13	17	43	49	115
Oakland	12	18	34	59	103
San Jose	8	22	36	81	83

NASL Champion: New York Cosmos
NASL MVP: Mike Flanagan, New England Tea Men
ASL Champion: New York Apollos
World Cup: Argentina
European Cup: Liverpool
Copa Libertadores (South America): Boca Juniors
NCAA Champion: University of San Francisco

SWIMMING

Tracy Caulkins, a 15-year-old ninth-grader from Nashville, Tenn., established a firm beachhead for American women swimmers who hope to end the supremacy of the East Germans in the 1980 Olympics.

Her assault began in April when she won 5 gold medals in the National Amateur Athletic Union (AAU) Short Course championships at Austin, Tex., setting 5 U. S. records. In June,

she won 6 events and shattered one U. S. mark in the Women's Meet of Champions at Mission Viejo, Calif. In mid-August, at the National AAU Long Course meet in The Woodlands, Tex., Miss Caulkins swam to 1 world record, 4 U. S. marks, and 5 more gold medals. She bettered the world mark in the 200-meter individual medley (2:15.09) and erased U. S. records in the 100- and 200-meter breaststrokes, 200-meter butterfly, and 400-meter individual medley.

Two weeks later in the World Aquatic Championships at West Berlin, Tracy Caulkins set 2 world marks, tied 1, and again won 5 gold medals. Her world marks came in the 200- and 400-meter individual medleys, with times of 2:14.07 and 4:40.83, and she equaled the 200-meter butterfly standard at 2:09.87.

Three other U. S. women also set world records in 1978—Linda Jezek of Los Altos, Calif., in the 200-meter backstroke (2:11.93); Cynthia Woodhead of Los Angeles in the 200-meter freestyle (1:58.53); and Kim Linehan of Sarasota, Fla., in the 400-meter freestyle (4:07.66).

Among American men, Jesse Vassallo of Mission Viejo, Calif., lowered his world mark in the 400-meter individual medley to 4:20.05, and Steve Lundquist of Jonesboro, Ga., set a world record in the 200-meter individual medley with a time of 2:04.39.

GEORGE DE GREGORIO

SWIMMING

Men's U. S. Long-Course Champions

100-Meter Freestyle: David McCagg, Fort Myers, Fla.
200-Meter Freestyle: Bill Forrester, Auburn University
400-Meter Freestyle: Jeff Float, Sacramento, Calif.
1,500-Meter Freestyle: Ed Ryder, Mission Viejo, Calif.
100-Meter Backstroke: Bob Jackson, San Jose, Calif.
200-Meter Backstroke: Jesse Vassallo, Mission Viejo, Calif.
100-Meter Breaststroke: Steve Lundquist, Jonesboro, Ga.
200-Meter Breaststroke: Jeff Freeman, Santa Clara Swim Club
100-Meter Butterfly: Joe Bottom, San Ramon, Calif.
200-Meter Butterfly: Steve Gregg, Huntington Beach, Calif.
200-Meter Individual Medley: Jesse Vassallo
400-Meter Individual Medley: Jesse Vassallo
400-Meter Freestyle Relay: Florida Aquatics (Rowdy Gaines, David McCagg, Keith Dickson, David Larson)
400-Meter Medley Relay: Cummins Engine Swim Club (Ind.) (Mark Kerry, Rick Hofstetter, Jim Halliburton, Jim Montgomery)
800-Meter Freestyle Relay: Florida Aquatics (Bill Forrester, Keith Dickson, David Larson, Rowdy Gaines)
Team: Florida Aquatics

Women's U. S. Long-Course Champions

100-Meter Freestyle: Cynthia Woodhead, Riverside, Calif.
200-Meter Freestyle: Cynthia Woodhead
400-Meter Freestyle: Kim Linehan, Sarasota, Fla.
800-Meter Freestyle: Kim Linehan
100-Meter Backstroke: Linda Jezek, Los Altos, Calif.
200-Meter Backstroke: Linda Jezek
100-Meter Breaststroke: Tracy Caulkins, Nashville, Tenn.
200-Meter Breaststroke: Tracy Caulkins
100-Meter Butterfly: Joan Pennington, Nashville, Tenn.
200-Meter Butterfly: Tracy Caulkins
200-Meter Individual Medley: Tracy Caulkins
400-Meter Individual Medley: Tracy Caulkins
400-Meter Freestyle Relay: Nashville Aquatic Club (Tracy Caulkins, Mary Ann Dempster, Macie Phillips, Joan Pennington)
400-Meter Medley Relay: Nashville Aquatic Club (Joan Pennington, Tracy Caulkins, Karline Miller, Jann Gerard)
800-Meter Freestyle Relay: Mission Viejo (Calif.) Nadadores (Diane Griebel, Kim Black, Sharyl Barnicoat, Jennifer Hooker)
Team: Nashville Aquatic Club

TENNIS

The spectacular growth of tennis during the previous ten years began to level off in 1978. Its growth rate was not likely again to approach that of the decade beginning in May 1968 with the birth of Open competition.

As in the businesses of equipment manufacturing and indoor clubs, where marginal concerns disappeared in a financial mire, the world of professional tennis partially reflected a financial "softness." After five years of sputtering, it looked like World Team Tennis (WTT) would die quietly. The irony of WTT's failure was that the league's greatest strength, its women stars (including Chris Evert, Martina Navratilova, and Billie Jean King) turned on their owners and refused to sign contracts for 1979. Team tennis suffered a loss of $30 million over the five years. The only ones who profited were such players as King, Evert, Navratilova, Virginia Wade, Ilie Nastase, and Vitas Gerulaitis, who each pocketed more than $120,000 a year for only 14 weeks of work.

There also were some high notes in 1978. The opening of the National Tennis Center at Flushing Meadows, N. Y., new home of the U. S. Open, was a fabulous event. Despite the distraction of airplanes flying directly overhead, the spacious stadium provides dramatic viewing from every one of its 20,000 seats. The opening of the center in time for the 1978 U. S. Open in September was miraculous, considering that it was built in less than one year.

Performances by the world's superstars were more erratic than usual, but their individual achievements were still extraordinary. Chris Evert still did not lose a match on clay, a string that goes back to 1973. But she did lose to Martina Navratilova at Wimbledon, putting a small crack in her claim to be the best woman player in the world. Navratilova had for several years been the most physically gifted and most powerful of all the women players but had had difficulty harnessing that strength—until the 1978 Wimbledon.

Evert came back, however, playing with the rhythm of a metronome. She cruised through the

TENNIS

Major Team Competitions

Davis Cup: United States.
Federation Cup: United States.
Wightman Cup: Great Britain.
World Team Tennis: Los Angeles Strings.

Major Tournaments

U.S. Open—Men's Singles: Jimmy Connors; women's singles: Chris Evert; men's doubles: Stan Smith and Bob Lutz; women's doubles: Billie Jean King and Martina Navratilova; men's 35 singles: Marty Riessen; junior men's singles: Per Hjertquist (Sweden); junior women's singles: Linda Siegel; Hall of Fame Doubles: Richard Savitt and Fred Stolle.

U.S. Clay Court Championships—Men's Singles: Jimmy Connors; women's singles: Dana Gilbert; men's doubles: Gene Mayer and Hank Pfister; women's doubles: Helena Anliot (Sweden) and Helle Sparre-Viragh (Denmark).

U.S. National Indoors—Men's Singles: Jimmy Connors; men's doubles: Brian Gottfried and Raul Ramirez (Mexico).

National Men's 35 Clay Court Championship—Men's Singles: Bob Carmichael; men's doubles: Gene Scott and Bob Carmichael (South Africa).

U.S.T.A. Women's Clay Court Championship—Women's Senior Singles: Judy Alvarez; 35 doubles: Judy Alvarez and Norma Veal; 45 singles: Nancy Reed; 45 doubles: Evelyn Houseman and Nancy Neeld; 55 singles: Dodo Cheney; 55 doubles: Dodo Cheney and Amy Yee.

National Junior—Singles: David Dowlen; doubles: Bonderant-Willenborg.

National Girl's 18's—Singles: Tracy Austin; doubles: Tracy Austin and Maria Fernandez.

Colgate Grand Prix Masters—Men's Singles: Jimmy Connors; men's doubles: Bob Hewitt, South Africa and Frew McMillan, South Africa.

Other U. S. Championships

NCAA (Division 1)—Singles: John McEnroe; doubles: John Austin and Bruce Nichols; team: Stanford.

NAIA—Singles: Francois Synaeghel; doubles: Jeff and Bruce Gibson; team: East Texas State.

Women's Intercollegiate Championship—(USTA) Singles: Stacy Margolin (USC); doubles: Sherry Acker and Judy Acker; team: USC.

AIAW—Singles: Jeanne DuVall (UCLA); doubles: Kathy Jordan and Barbara Jordan; team: Stanford.

Professional Championships

U.S. Pro Championships—Men's Singles: Manuel Orantes, Spain; men's doubles: Balazs Taroczy, Hungary, and Victor Pecci, Paraguay.

World Championship Tennis Tour—Men's Singles: Vitas Gerulaitis; men's doubles: Wojtek Fibak, Poland, and Tom Okker, Netherlands.

Virginia Slims Tour—Final: Martina Navratilova.

Other Countries

Wimbledon—Men's Singles: Björn Borg, Sweden; women's singles: Martina Navratilova; men's doubles: Bob Hewitt, South Africa and Frew McMillan, South Africa; women's doubles: Wendy Turnbull, Australia and Kerry Reid, Australia; junior boy's: Ivan Lendl, Czechoslovakia; junior girl's: Tracy Austin.

Australian Open—Men's Singles: Vitas Gerulaitis; men's doubles: Ray Ruffels, Australia and Alan Stone, Australia; women's singles: Evonne Goolagong Cawley, Australia; women's doubles: cancelled by rain.

French Open—Men's Singles: Björn Borg, Sweden; men's doubles: Hank Pfister and Gene Mayer; women's singles: Virginia Ruzici, Rumania; women's doubles: Mima Jausovec, Yugoslavia and Virginia Ruzici, Rumania.

Italian Open—Men's Singles: Björn Borg, Sweden; men's doubles: Victor Pecci, Paraguay and Belus Prajoux, Chile; women's singles: Regina Marsikova; women's doubles: Mima Jausovec, Yugoslavia and Virginia Ruzici, Rumania.

Canadian Open—Men's Singles: Eddie Dibbs; men's doubles: Wojtek Fibak, Poland and Tom Okker, Netherlands; women's singles: Regina Marsikova, Czechoslovakia; women's doubles: Regina Marsikova, Czechoslovakia and Pam Teeguarden.

LEADING MONEY WINNERS IN 1978

Virginia Slims

Martina Navratilova	$214,350	Virginia Wade	$ 58,900
Evonne Goolagong	111,450	Rosemary Casals	52,300
Billie Jean King	68,025	Kerry Reid	36,700
Betty Stove	67,000	Chris Evert	30,500
Wendy Turnbull	63,300	Dianne Fromholtz	22,450

World Championship Tennis

Vitas Gerulaitis	$284,786	Raul Ramirez	$ 74,407
Wojtek Fibak	98,429	Jimmy Connors	65,000
Ilie Nastase	92,811	Sandy Mayer	59,205
Björn Borg	85,800	Brian Gottfried	56,182
Eddie Dibbs	80,904	Dick Stockton	54,324

Men's Overall Season Earnings
(as of Jan. 15, 1979)

Björn Borg	$691,886	Vitas Gerulaitis	$425,845
Eddie Dibbs	582,872	Ilie Nastase	402,422
Jimmy Connors	543,307	Wojtek Fibak	383,843
Raul Ramirez	450,110	Harold Solomon	354,732
John McEnroe	445,024	Brian Gottfried	300,539

Women's Overall Season Earnings

Martina Navratilova	$500,757	Evonne Goolagong	$180,844
Chris Evert	454,486	Betty Stove	177,243
Virginia Wade	297,527	Virginia Ruzici	151,379
Kerry Reid	208,766	Billie Jean King	149,492
Wendy Turnbull	187,758	Regina Marsikova	87,706

UPI

Chris Evert, *left*, displays her trophy after defeating Pam Shriver in the women's finals of the U. S. Open. The tournament was held at the new National Tennis Center in the Flushing Meadow section of Queens, N. Y.

U. S. Open without losing a set, while Navratilova was tripped in the semifinals by teenager, Pam Shriver. If this was not enough to reestablish Evert's supremacy, surely her thrashing of the field (including Navratilova) in the Colgate Series in November was.

While the number one men's player of 1977, Guillermo Vilas, did not entirely disappear from the scene, he certainly did not come close to challenging Björn Borg or Jimmy Connors for top honors. Borg won Wimbledon and the French Open with devastating, one-sided performances against Vilas and Connors. Through August, the 22-year-old Swede clearly was the best in the field. However, just before the finals of the U. S. Open, Borg suffered a nagging thumb injury. He courageously took the court against Connors but gave only a perfunctory performance.

In the Davis Cup competition, the United States defeated Britain for its first Challenge Round victory in six years. In the Wightman Cup, the U. S. women lost to Britain for the first time since 1958.

In 1978, four youngsters served notice to Evert, Borg, and Connors that their crowns would not fit so comfortably in a few years. The 16-year-old U. S. Open finalist, Pam Shriver, and the 19-year-old Argentine, José Luis Clerc, won Rolex's Rookie of the Year Honors. The 1977 winners, Tracy Austin and John McEnroe, continued to surprise the tennis community.

EUGENE L. SCOTT, *Publisher, "Tennis Week"*

TRACK AND FIELD

Henry Rono of Kenya, a student at Washington State University, dominated the track scene in 1978 as few other long-distance runners have in the past. The smooth-striding Rono, who seems tireless in competition, shattered four world records and numerous meet standards during the outdoor season. He reduced the 5,000 meter world record by 4.5 seconds at Berkeley, Calif. in April. His time was 13:08.04.

A month later he lopped 3.4 seconds off the 3,000-meter steeplechase record with an 8:05.4

clocking in Seattle, Wash., erasing the 1967 effort by Anders Garderud of Sweden. In June, in Vienna, Austria, he broke by 8 seconds the 1977 mark of Samson Kimobwa, also a Kenyan, in the 10,000-meter run, with a time of 27:22.5.

Rono continued his revision of the record book later in June at Oslo, Norway, by breaking the 4-year-old record (7:35.2) in the 3,000 meters.

For only the third time in 16 meets and for the first time since 1969, the United States defeated the USSR in a dual meet in July at Berkeley, Calif. In combined men's and women's scoring, the United States won, 190–177. U. S. men triumphed, 119–102, but the women lost, 75–71.

Vladimir Yashchenko of the Soviet Union raised his world record in the high jump to 7 ft.-8 in. (2.3 m) in June at Tbilisi. Wolfgang Schmidt of East Germany broke the world record in the discus in August at East Berlin with a throw of 233 ft.-5 in. (71.1 m).

GEORGE DE GREGORIO

TRACK AND FIELD
Men's U. S. Outdoor Champions

100-Meter Dash: Clancy Edwards, Santa Ana, Calif.
200-Meter Dash: Clancy Edwards
400-Meter Dash: Maxie Parks, Athletes in Action
800-Meter Run: James Robinson, Inner City Athletic Club
1,500-Meter Run: Steve Scott, Irvine, Calif.
5,000-Meter Run: Marty Liquori, Florida A.A.
10,000-Meter Run: Craig Virgin, Athletes West
3,000-Meter Steeplechase: Henry Marsh, Athletes West
110-Meter Hurdles: Renaldo Nehemiah, Scotch Plains, N.J.
400-Meter Hurdles: James Walker, Athletes in Action
Pole Vault: Dan Ripley, unattached
High Jump: Dwight Stones, Desert Oasis T.C.
Long Jump: Arnie Robinson, Los Angeles
Triple Jump: James Butts, Athletes in Action
Hammer Throw: Boris Djerassi, New York A.C.
Javelin: Bill Schmidt, Knoxville, Tenn.
Discus: Mac Wilkins, Portland, Ore.
Shotput: Al Feuerbach, Santa Cruz, Calif.

Women's U. S. Outdoor Champions

100-Meter Dash: Leleith Hodges, Texas Women's University
200-Meter Dash: Evelyn Ashford, Los Angeles
400-Meter Dash: Lorna Forde, Brooklyn, N.Y.
800-Meter Run: Ruth Caldwell, Citrus Track Club
1,500-Meter Run: Jan Merrill, Waterford, Conn.
3,000-Meter Run: Jan Merrill
10,000-Meter Run: Ellison Goodall, Duke University
100-Meter Hurdles: Debby LaPlante, Englewood, N.J.
400-Meter Hurdles: Debby Esser, Iowa State University
Javelin: Sherry Calvert, Lakewood International
Shotput: Maren Seidler, San Jose State College
Discus: Lynne Winbigler, Oregon T.C.
Long Jump: Jodi Anderson, Los Angeles
High Jump: Louise Ritter, Texas Women's University

SPORTS SUMMARIES

ARCHERY—Freestyle: Men: Darrell Pace, Cincinnati; women: Anna Marie Lehmann, West Germany. Barebow: men: Anders Rosenberg, Sweden; women: Suizuko Kobuchi, Japan. **National Archery Association:** target: men: Darrell Pace, Cincinnati; women: Luann Ryon, Riverside, Calif. Field: freestyle: men: Darrell Pace; women: Winnie Eicher, Duncansville, Pa.; barebow: men: Rick Krause, Pine Grove, Pa.; women: Rebecca Wallace, Palmyra, Pa.

BADMINTON—World: singles: men: Liem Swie King, Indonesia; women: S. Ng, Malaysia; doubles: men: Tjun-Tjun and Johan Wahjudi, Indonesia; women: Regina Masli and T. Widiastuti, Indonesia; mixed: Regina Masli-Christian, Indonesia; team: women: Japan.

BOWLING—American Bowling Congress: Regular Division: singles: Rich Mersek, Cleveland (739): doubles: Bob Kulaszewicz and Don Gazzana, Milwaukee (1,352); all-events: Chris Cobus, Milwaukee (1,994); team: Berlin's Pro Shop, Muscatine, Iowa (3,077). Classic Division: Bill Beach, Sharon, Pa. (701); doubles: Steve Fehr and Dave Newrath, Cincinnati (1,300); all-events: Bill Beach (1,941). Booster Division: team: Bush Pest Control, Austin, Tex. (2,741). **Women's International Bowling Congress:** Open Division: singles: Mae Bolt, Berwyn, Ill. (709): doubles: Barbara Shelton, Jamaica, N. Y. and Annese Kelly, Brooklyn, N. Y. (1,211); all-events: Annese Kelly (1,896); team: Cook County Vending, Chicago (2,956).

BRIDGE—World: pairs: Open: Gabino Cintro and Marcelo Branco, Brazil; women: Kathie Wie and Judi Radin, New York; mixed: Barry Crane, Studio City, Calif., and Mrs. Kerri Shuman, Los Angeles.

CANOEING—Flatwater: kayak: men: 500 and 1,000 meters: Steve Kelly, New York; 10,000 meters: Brent Turner, St. Charles, Ill.; women: 500: Leslie Klein, Hadley, Mass.; 5,000: Ann Turner, St. Charles, Ill. Canoe: men: 500 meters: Roland Muhlen, St. Charles, Ill.; 1,000: Jay Kearney, Lexington, Ky.; 10,000: Kurt Doberstein, St. Charles, Ill. **Whitewater:** kayak: men: Eric Evans, Belchertown, Mass.; women: Linda Harrison, Newark, Del.; canoe: Angus Morrison, Wayzata, Minn.

CROSS-COUNTRY—AAU (10,000 meters): Greg Meyer, Boston (29:36.3); team: Mason-Dixon A. C., Washington. **NCAA** Division I (10,000 meters): Alberto Salazar, Oregon (29:30); team: Texas-El Paso; Division II (10,000 meters): James Schankel, California Tech, San Luis Obispo (30:34); team: San Luis Obispo; Division III (8,000 meters): Dan Henderson, Wheaton; team: North Central (Ill.). **NAIA** (5 miles): Kelly Jensen, Southern Oregon (25:07); team: Pembroke State. **IC4A** (5 miles): Sydney Maree, Villanova (24:04); team: Villanova. Women: **AAU** (5,000 meters): Julie Brown, Northridge, Calif. (16:32:6.5); team: Liberty A. C., Cambridge, Mass. **AIAW** (5,000 meters): Mary Decker, Colorado (16:59.4); team: Iowa State. **World** (men (12,300 meters): John Treacy, Ireland (39:25); women (4,728 meters): Grete Waitz, Norway (16:19).

CURLING—World: United States: men: Superior, Wis.; women: Wausau, Wis. (Sandy Robarge, skip); Canada: Alberta (Mike Chernoff, skip).

CYCLING—World: Road: men: Amateur: Gilbert Glaus, Switzerland; pro: Gerrie Knetemann, Netherlands; women: Beate Habetz, West Germany. Track: sprint: men: Anton Tkac, Czechoslovakia; women: Galina Zareva, USSR; pursuit: men: Detleff Macha, East Germany. **United States:** Road: men (114 miles): Dale Stetina, Indianapolis; women (40 miles): Barbara Hintzen, Grosse Pointe Farms, Mich. Track: sprint: men: Leigh Barczewski, West Allis, Wis.; women: Sue Novarra, Flint, Mich.; pursuit: men: Dave Grylls, Grosse Pointe, Mich.; women: Mary Jane Roech, Philadelphia; time trial: Jerry Ash, Burbank, Calif.

DOG SHOWS—Westminster (New York): Best: Ch. Cede Higgens, Yorkshire terrier, owned by Barbara and Charles Switzer, Seattle (3,072 dogs entered). **International** (Chicago): Best: Ch. Kishniga's Desert Song, borzoi, owned by Dr. Richard Meen, Campbellville, Ontario (3,602 entries).

FENCING—World: Foil: Didier Flament, France; épée: Alexander Pusch, West Germany; saber: Victor Krovopuskov, USSR; women's foil: Valentina Siderova, USSR. **United States:** foil: Marty Lang, New York Athletic Club; épée: Brooke Makler, Philadelphia; saber: Stanley Lekach, New York Athletic Club; women's foil: Gay Dasaro, San Jose, Calif. **Collegiate:** NCAA: foil: Ernest Simon, Wayne State; épée: Bjorne Vaggo, Notre Dame; saber: Michael Sullivan, Notre Dame; team: Notre Dame; **Intercollegiate Women's Fencing Assn.:** Individual: Stacey Johnson, San Jose State; team: San Jose State.

GYMNASTICS—World: Men: all-around: Nikolai Andrianov, USSR; floor exercise: Kurt Thomas, Terre Haute, Ind.; rings: Andrianov; vault: Junichi Shimizu, Japan; pommel horse: Zoltan Magyar, Hungary; high bar: Shigeru Kasamatsu, Japan; parallel bars: Eizo Kenmotsu, Japan. Women: all-around: Elena Mukhina, USSR; floor exercise: Elena Mukhina; balance beam: Nadia Comaneci, Rumania; uneven bars: Marcia Frederick, Milford, Conn.; vault: Nelli Kim, USSR; team: USSR. **United States:** AAU: Elite: all-around: Men: Phil Cahoy, Nebraska Gym Club; women: Karen Lemond, Reno, Nev. Advanced: all-around: men: Jim Mikus, Reading, Pa.; women: Mary Kay Brown, Buffalo, N. Y. **U. S. Gym Federation:** all-around: men: Kurt Thomas, Indiana State; women: Kathy Johnson, Belcher, La. **NCAA:** all-around: Division I: Bart Conner, Oklahoma; Division II: Casey Edwards, Wisconsin-Oshkosh; team:

Division I: Oklahoma; Division II: Illinois, Chicago Circle; **NAIA:** all-around: Casey Edwards, Wisconsin-Oshkosh; team: Wisconsin-Oshkosh. **AIAW:** all-around: Ann Carr, Penn State; team: Penn State.

HANDBALL—United States Handball Association: 4-wall: singles: open: Fred Lewis, Miami, Fla.; masters: Rene Zamorano, Tucson, Ariz.; golden masters: Jack Briscoe, St. Louis; doubles: open: Stuffy Singer, Los Angeles, and Marty Decatur, New York; masters doubles: Pete Tyson and Dick Roberson, Austin, Tex.; golden masters doubles: Ken Schneider and Bud Perelman, Chicago.

HORSE SHOWS—World: Three-Day: overall: Bruce Davidson, Unionville, Pa.; team overall: Canada. Dressage: J. Michael Plumb, Chesapeake, Md.; team: United States; cross-country: Bruce Davidson; jumping: Bruce Davidson. Stadium Jumping: Gerd Wilfang, West Germany; team: Britain. **American Horse Shows Assn.:** Equitation Medals: Hunter Seat: Hugh Mutch, Weston, Conn.; Stock Seat: Lisa Graybehl, Moraga, Calif. Dressage Champions: First Level: Royal Rival, owned by Lendon Gary, Dixmont, Me.; 2d level: Masada, Nancy Harris, Metamora, Mich.; 3d level: Fanfar, Janice Kieler, Santa Maria, Calif.; 4th level: J. Ashton Moore, San Juan Bautista, Calif.; junior: Electra Ganas, Carnegie, Pa.

ICE SKATING, FIGURE—World: singles: men: Charles Tickner, Littleton, Colo.; women: Anett Poetzsch, East Germany; pairs: Irina Rodnina and Aleksandr Zaitsev, USSR; dance: Nataliy Linichuk and Gennadij Karponosov, USSR. **United States:** singles: men: Charles Tickner, Littleton, Colo.; women: Linda Fratianne, Northridge, Calif.; pairs: Tai Babalonia, Mission Hills, Calif., and Randy Gardner, Los Angeles; gold dance: Stacey Smith and John Summers, Wilmington, Del.

ICE SKATING, SPEED—World: men's all-around: Eric Heiden, Madison, Wis.; women's all-around: Tatiana Averina, USSR. Sprints: men's all-around: Eric Heiden; women's all-around: Liubov Sadchikova, USSR. **United States:** National Outdoor: men's all-around: Bill Heinkel, Racine, Wis.; women's all-around: Paula Class, St. Paul, and Betsy Davis, Montclair, N. J.; sprints: men's all-around: Eric Heiden; women's all-around: Beth Heiden, Madison, Wis. National Indoor: men's all-around: Stan Wisniewski, Sierra Madre, Calif.; women's all-around: Debbie Carlstrom, Des Plaines, Ia.

LACROSSE—NCAA: Division I: Johns Hopkins; Division II: Roanoke. **U. S. Women's Lacrosse Association:** Penn State.

MOTORBOAT RACING—United States: offshore: Betty Cook, Newport Beach, Calif.; unlimited hydroplanes: champion: Atlas Van Lines, owned and driven by Bill Muncey, La Mesa, Calif.; APBA Gold Cup: Atlas Van Lines. Distance races: Isle of Wight: Betty Cook; Lombardo Gold Cup: Betty Cook; Bacardi Trophy: Joey Ippolito, Hallandale, Fla.; Benihana Grand Prix: Billy Martin, Clark, N. J.

MOTORCYCLE RACING—Grand National Championship: Jay Springsteen, Lapeer, Mich. Motocross champions: 125 cc: Broc Glover, El Cajon, Calif.; 250 cc: Bob Hannah, Whittier, Calif.; 500 cc: Rick Burgett, Sandy, Ore.; Supercross Bob Hannah; Trans AMA: Bob Hannah.

PARACHUTING—World: overall: men: Nicolai Usmayev, USSR; women: Cheryl Stearns, U. S. Army, Fort Bragg, N. C. **United States:** men: master overall: Bob Van Duren, U. S. Army, Fort Bragg, N. C.; senior overall: Matt O'Gwynn, Fort Bragg, N. C.; women: overall: Cheryl Stearns, Fort Bragg, N. C.

POLO—National Champions: open: Abercrombie & Kent, Oak Brook, Ill.; Gold Cup: Abercrombie & Kent; collegiate: California-Davis.

RACQUETBALL—singles: men: open: Jeff Bowman, San Diego, Calif.; senior: Bill Schmidtke, Minneapolis; professional: Marty Hogan, St. Louis; women: open: Alicia Moore, Soquel, Calif.; senior: Judy Thompson, Davenport, Iowa; professional: Shannon Wright, San Diego. Doubles: men's open: Mark Malowitz and Jeff Kwartler, Houston, Tex.; women's open: Barb Tennesson and Ev Dillon, Minneapolis.

RODEO—Professional Rodeo Cowboys Association: all-around: Tom Ferguson, Miami, Okla.; steer wrestling: Tom Ferguson; calf roping: Dave Brock, Pueblo, Colo.; saddle bronc riding: Joe Marvel, Battle Mountain, Nev.; bull riding: Butch Kirby, Alba, Tex.; bareback bronc riding: Jack Ward, Springdale, Ark.; team roping: Brad Smith, Prescott, Ariz., and George Richards, Humboldt, Ariz.; barrel racing: Lynn McKenzie, Shreveport, La.

ROLLER SKATING—World Artistic: singles: men: Thomas Nieder, West Germany; women: Natalie Dunn, Bakersfield, Calif.; dance: Fleurette Arnesault, Cambridge, Mass., and Dan Little, Farmingdale, N. Y.; pairs: Robbie Coleman and Pat Jones, Memphis, Tenn. **United States:** singles: men: Paul Jones, Flint, Mich.; women: Robbie Coleman, Memphis, Tenn. **International Singles:** men: Lex Kane, Toledo, Ohio; women: Natalie Dunn, Bakersfield, Calif. Figures: men: Curt Craton, Fountain Valley, Calif.; women: Patti Marshalewski, Concord Ville, Pa.; Pairs: Paul Price and Tina Kneisley, Brighton, Mich.; dance: John LaBriola and Debra Coyne, Fountain Valley, Calif.

ROWING—World: men: singles: Peter Michael Koble, West Germany; doubles: Alf and Frank Hansen, Norway; pairs: Bernd and Jorg Landvoight, East Germany; eights: East Germany; women: singles: Christine Hahn, East Germany;

Johns Hopkins University captures the 8th annual NCAA lacrosse championship. Brazil's Djalma Castro (*left*) and Panama's Eduardo Lowe Harbin compete in the Pan American karate championships in Montreal.

PHOTOS UPI

doubles: Bulgaria; pairs: East Germany; eights: USSR. **United States:** men: singles: Jim Dietz, New York A. C.; dash: Dietz; doubles: Tiff Wood and Greg Stone, Harvard; eights: U. of Penn-Penn A. C.; women: singles: Lisa Hanson, Long Beach, Calif.; lightweight: Jean Lennox, Seattle; dash: Lisa Hanson; eights: lightweight: College B. C., Philadelphia. **Intercollegiate Champions:** I. R. A.: varsity: Syracuse; second varsity: Pennsylvania; freshmen: Syracuse, Dad Vail Regatta: eights and overall: Coast Guard Academy. Eastern sprints: heavyweight: varsity: Yale; second varsity: Harvard; freshmen: Northeastern; Rowe Cup: Harvard; lightweights: varsity and second varsity: Harvard; freshmen: Dartmouth; Jope Cup: Harvard. Western sprints: heavyweight: varsity: British Columbia; junior varsity: California-Irvine; freshmen: Orange Coast; lightweights: varsity: British Columbia. **British Royal Henley:** Diamond sculls: Tim Crooks, England; double sculls: Chris Baillieu and Mike Hart, England; Silver Goblets (pairs): Jim Clark and John Roberts, England; Wyfold Cup (fours): Molesey Boat Club, England; Prince Philip Cup (fours): Trakia Club, Bulgaria; Ladies Plate (eights): Imperial College, London; Princess Elizabeth Cup (schoolboy eights): Eton College, England; Thames Cup (eights): London R. C.; Grand Challenge Cup (eights) —Trakia Club, Bulgaria.

SHOOTING—Trapshooting: Grand American Vandalia, Ohio, Handicap, men: Reg Jachimowski, Antioch, Ill. (27 yds.) 100; women: Freida Summer, Washington, Ind. (21) 98; junior: tie between Dave Durant, Waukesha, Wis. (22) and Gary Guydosh, Bloomingdale, Ohio (19) 98; veteran: Carl Fritz, Cincinnati (20½) 98; Overall: men: Dan Bonillas, Los Banos, Calif., 979; women: Loral I. Delaney, Anoka, Minn. 942. **National Skeet Shooting Association champions:** men: Walter Badorek, Klamath Falls, Ore. (550); women: Ila Hill, Birmingham, Mich. (543); senior: Tom Hanzel, San Antonio, Tex. (535); veteran: Tom Sanfilipo, Fairfield, Calif. (532); junior: John R. Dail, Anderson, S. C. (546).

SOFTBALL—World: women: United States. **United States:** fast pitch: men: Billard Barbell, Reading, Pa.; women: Class A: S & K Rigging, Arcola, Ill.; slow pitch: Campbell's Carpets, Concord, Calif.; industrial slow pitch: GE-Wacos, Louisville, Ky. 16-inch: Chicago Bobcats; Class A: Peabody Coal Co., Rockport, Ky.; Church: Grace Methodist Blacks, Oklahoma City. Women: fast pitch: Raybestos Brakettes, Stratford, Conn.; slow pitch: Bob Hoffman's Dots, Miami, Fla. Class A: Stillwater (Okla.) A's; **Collegiate:** UCLA.

SQUASH RACQUETS—U. S. Squash Racquets Association: singles: Mike Desaulniers, Montreal; 35's: Roger Alcaly, New York; 40's: George Morfitt, Vancouver; 45's: Les Harding, Seattle; 50's: Henri Salaun, Boston; doubles: Tom Page, Princeton, N. J., and Gil Mateer, Bethlehem, Pa.; veterans: Ted Simmons, St. Louis, and Mel Sokolow, New York. **U. S. Women's Squash Racquets Association:** singles: Gretchen Spruance, Wilmington, Del.; senior singles: Goldie Edwards, Pittsburgh; doubles: Jane Stauffer and Barbara Maltby, Philadelphia; mixed: Joyce Davenport, Philadelphia and Ralph Howe, New York. **Collegiate:** singles: men: Mike Desaulniers, Harvard; women: Gail Ramsay, Penn State.

TABLE TENNIS—United States: singles: men: Norio Takashima, Japan; women: Hong Ja Park, South Korea; doubles: men: Masami Ohshima and Norio Takashima, Japan; women: Seong Heui Kim and Hon Ja Park, South Korea; mixed: Errol Caetane and Mariann Domonkos, Canada; seniors: men: Jack Howard, Hermosa Beach, Calif.; women: Yvonne Kronlaga, Elliott City, Md.

VOLLEYBALL—World: men: USSR; women: Cuba; **U. S. Volleyball Association:** men: open: Chucks Steak House, Los Angeles; senior: Balboa Bay Club, Newport Beach, Calif.; women: open: Nick's Fish Market, Beverly Hills, Calif.; senior: Nick's Fish Market. **AAU:** Chucks Steak House; men: **Collegiate:** NCAA: Pepperdine; NAIA: George Williams; AIAW: Southern California.

WATER SKIING—United States: men: open: Ricky McCormick, Winter Haven, Fla.; senior: Ken White, Bynum, Tex.; veteran: Dr. Harry Price, Libertyville, Ill.; women: open: Deena Brush, West Sacramento, Calif.; senior: Vicki Johndrow, Odessa, Fla.

WEIGHT LIFTING—World: 114 pounds: Kanybok Osmanaliev, USSR; 123. Daniel Nunez, Cuba; 132: Nikolai Kolesnikov, USSR; 148: Yanko Rusev, Bulgaria; 165: Roberto Urrutia, Cuba; 181: Yurik Vardanyan, USSR; 198: Rolf Milser, West Germany; 220: David Rigert, USSR; 242: Yuriy Zaitsev, USSR; super heavyweight: Jurgen Heuser, East Germany. **United States: AAU:** 114: Ronald Crawley, Washington, D. C.; 123: Stewart Thornburgh, Charleston, Ill.; 132: Don Warner, York, Pa.; 148: Don Abrahamson, Maitland, Fla.; 165: David Jones, Eastman, Ga.; 181: Michael Archut, Chicago; 198: Lee James, York, Pa.; 220: Kurt Setterberg, Warren, Ohio; 242: Mark Cameron, York, Pa.; super heavyweight: Tom Stock, Belleville, Ill.

WRESTLING—Freestyle: World: 105.5 pounds: Serge Kornilaev, USSR; 114.5: Anatol Belogazo, USSR; 125.5: Tomiyama Hideari, Japan; 132.5: Vladimir Junine, USSR; 149: Pavel Pinguin, USSR; 163: Leroy Kemp, Madison, Wis.; 180.5: Magomedkhan Arazilov, USSR; 198: Une Neipert, East Germany; 220: Harald Buttner, East Germany; over 220: Sosian Andiev, USSR. **United States: AAU:** 105.5: Bob Weaver, New York A. C.; 114.5: Jim Haines, Madison, Wis.; 125.5: Tomiyama Hideaki, Japan; 136.5: Tim Cysewski, Iowa City; 149.5: Jim Humphrey, Oklahoma; 163: Chuck Yagla, Iowa City; 180.5: John Peterson, Athletes in Action; 198: Ben Peterson, Madison, Wis.; 220: Larry Bielenberg, Sunkist Kids, Arizona; heavyweight: Greg Wojciechowski, Toledo, Ohio; team: New York A. C. **NCAA:** Division I: 118 pounds: Andy Daniels, Ohio University; 126: Mike Land, Iowa State; 134: Ken Mallory, Montclair State; 142: Dan Hicks, Oregon State; 150: Mark Churella, Michigan; 158: Leroy Kemp, Wisconsin; 167: Keith Stearns, Oklahoma; 177: Mark Lieberman, Lehigh; 190: Ron Jeidy, Wisconsin; heavyweight: Jimmy Jackson, Oklahoma State; Team: Iowa.

YACHTING—U. S. Yacht Racing Union Champions: Mallory Cup (men): Glenn Darden, Fort Worth, Tex.; Adams Trophy (women): Bonnie Shore, Newport, R. I.; Mertz Trophy (women's single-handed): Meredith O'Dowd, Riverside, R. I.; Adams Memorial (women's double-handed): Sandy Ray, Westport, Conn., and Carol Hayes, West Haven, Conn.; Sears Cup (junior): Mark Thompson, Jamestown, Pa.; Smythe (junior single-handed): Richard Merriman, St. Petersburg, Fla.; Champion of Champions (men): Tom Lindley, Newport Beach, Calif.; Prince of Wales (club): Galveston Bay Cruising Assn.; National Sea Exploring: Grant Hill and Tom Herrschaft, North Hollywood, Calif. **Other Championships:** Congressional Cup: Dick Deaver, Los Angeles; Bacardi Cup: Peter Wright, Elmhurst, Ill. Ocean racing: Newport, R. I., to Bermuda (635 miles; 162 boats) overall winners: Bermuda Trophy (measurement Handicap System ratings): Babe, Class F, Arnie Gay, Annapolis, Md.; Tamerlane Trophy (International Offshore Rule ratings): Acadia, Class B, Burt Keenan, New Orleans, Little America's Cup (International catamarans): Patient Lady IV (Duncan McLane, Norton, Conn., skipper).

Compiled by BILL BRADDOCK

SRI LANKA

The 30th anniversary of Sri Lanka's independence was marked by the change from a parliamentary to a presidential system of government, the adoption of a new constitution, continuing economic difficulties, a considerable "liberalization" of the economy, and an increase in crime and subversive activities.

Politics. On February 4, Junius R. Jayewardene, head of the United National Party (UNP) and prime minister since July 1977, was sworn in as the first president of Sri Lanka under the new system of presidential government. On February 5, Ranasinghe Premadasa was sworn in as prime minister.

On September 7, at a special session of the National State Assembly, a new constitution was proclaimed. It gave the president such extraordinary power that many critics called it "a blueprint for dictatorship." It provided for direct election of the president, the use of a national referendum by the president when important measures are blocked by parliament, and the election of assembly members by proportional representation. Important concessions were made to the Tamil-speaking minority: the granting of national language status to Tamil, the removal of a distinction between nationality by descent and by registration, and the application of fundamental rights provisions in the constitution to stateless persons of Indian origin for a period of 10 years.

In late July, a three-man presidential commission began public hearings on "the misuse and abuse of power" by the previous government of Mrs. Sirimavo Bandaranaike (May 1970 to July 1977). The UNP government sponsored legislation to deprive certain individuals of their rights to vote and hold public office, and it prepared to take legal action against them.

Law and order in the country deteriorated visibly, with a marked increase in crimes and subversive activity. In May, President Jayewardene called on the armed forces to help maintain public order in 22 districts.

Economy. With an unemployment rate of about 20%, a foreign debt so large that repayments in late 1978 were equal to export earnings, the need to import 40% of its food, industrial plants operating at about 50% capacity, and heavy subsidies for social welfare programs, the state of the economy continued to be unsatisfactory. In 1978, the government continued its "liberalization" policy, highlighted by the removal of controls on prices, imports, and foreign investments. Positive developments were the expansion of irrigation facilities, an increase in foreign exchange earnings, and a favorable balance of trade.

A controversial decision by the government was to establish a large free-trade zone north of Colombo. The government claimed that this would boost the country's exports and create thousands of new jobs.

NORMAN D. PALMER
University of Pennsylvania

STAMP COLLECTING

For the United States, 1978 may well be called a year of postal confusion. On January 11, a new miniature-size experimental definitive was issued with hopes that smaller stamps could save Washington millions of dollars in production costs. The public generally liked the miniatures, but, oddly, the Postal Service continued to produce king- and jumbo-size stamps for the rest of the year.

On January 20, two stamps recalling Capt. James Cook's 1778 voyages to Hawaii and Alaska were so printed that half a pane has a blue portrait design attached to a green design of his ship sailing prow down. Other special stamps include units of four different designs for "Quilting in America," "American Dance," "American Owls," and "American Trees." For the 1978 international stamp show, the Postal Service printed sheetlets of eight different 13¢ stamps. These were sold exclusively in Toronto from June 10 to 18. In the United States they did not become available to collectors until August 28, and only for orders placed before July 30.

The biggest confusion, however, came as a result of rate hikes. The Postal Service hoped that the rate would go to 16¢ for letters and 11¢ for postal cards. It already had supplies of three different stamps inscribed, simply, "A/US Postage." These were put on sale when the 15¢ rate was begun. Because they have no specific value

SELECTED U. S. COMMEMORATIVE STAMPS, 1978

Subject	Denomination	Date
Carl Sandburg	13¢	Jan. 6
Indian (miniature)	13¢	Jan. 11
Capt. Cook	2x13¢	Jan. 20
Harriet Tubman	13¢	Feb. 1
American Dance	4x13¢	April 26
French Alliance	13¢	May 4
Cancer Detection	13¢	May 18
Jimmy Rodgers	13¢	May 24
Photography	15¢	June 26
George M. Cohan	15¢	July 3
Mars Mission	15¢	July 20
American Owls	4x15¢	Aug. 26
Molly Pitcher (card)	10¢	Sept. 8
Wright Brothers	2x31¢	Sept. 23
American Trees	4x15¢	Oct. 9
Christmas	2x15¢	Oct. 18

designation, they are invalid on international mail. Also issued was an innovational postal card marked "Domestic Rate," with no value designation but sold at 10¢. When many foreign governments announced stamps to honor the 75th anniversary of the Kitty Hawk flight, Washington belatedly added two 31¢ commemoratives to their original schedules.

The deaths of Paul VI and John Paul I brought "interregnum" issues from the Vatican, "memorial" sets from other countries, and "coronation" stamps after the elections of John Paul I and John Paul II.

ERNEST A. KEHR
Stamp News Bureau

STOCKS AND BONDS

Resurgent inflation, high interest rates, and a slumping dollar set the mood for a tumultuous year in the U. S. securities markets.

After a sharp decline in January and February, the stock market staged powerful rallies in April and again in midsummer. But then prices collapsed, losing more than (U. S.) $100 billion in total market value in a two-week sell-off that came to be known as the October Massacre.

This violent activity was accompanied by unprecedented trading volume. On August 3, a record 66.37 million shares changed hands on the New York Stock Exchange. And for the year as a whole, NYSE volume of 7.2 billion shares far surpassed the previous high of 5.36 billion recorded in 1976.

For all their ups and downs, the popular market averages showed only modest net changes at the end of the year. The Dow Jones average of 30 industrials declined 26.16 points, or 3.15%, finishing at 805.01.

Standard & Poor's 500-stock composite index, by contrast, rose 1.62%. But for the second consecutive year the strongest performer among the indicators at the major exchanges was the American Stock Exchange market value index, which gained 17.7% after a rise of better than 16% the year before.

This signaled a revival of interest in the so-called secondary stocks—smaller companies without the widespread public recognition of NYSE-listed blue chips like General Motors or American Telephone & Telegraph.

By far the "hottest" of all the secondary issues in 1978 were the gambling stocks. Speculation in shares of companies with links to the casino gambling business began to build up well before Resorts International, a company listed on the Amex, opened a casino in Atlantic City, N. J., in late May. As the casino, the first of its kind in the United States outside Nevada, issued impressive initial reports on its business, the gambling-stock craze on Wall Street reached a fever pitch. Resorts International's class B shares doubled in a single week in late summer.

By then numerous analysts were issuing warnings that the speculative activity had gotten out of hand, and that the risks of a shakeout were high. As it turned out, they were right.

From a peak of 69½ (adjusted for a stock split), Resorts' class A shares fell to the low 20's in December. Resorts' class B nosedived from an adjusted high of 108 to the mid-30's.

Another source of concern about over-speculation was spiraling margin debt—the use of money borrowed from brokers to pay part of the cost of buying stock. Total margin debt outstanding, as reported by the NYSE, reached a record level of more than $12 billion early in the autumn.

When the market started down in October, it touched off a wave of margin calls—requests from brokers for additional collateral from borrowers—that led to forced selling of more stock. The revival of speculative interest also breathed life into the depressed market for new issues—companies making their initial sales of stock to the public.

Issues like Federal Express and Floating Point Systems soared in their initial days of trading in the over-the-counter market. But by the end of the year most of these new high-flyers, like the rest of the market, had fallen considerably from their peaks.

The background for all this volatile activity was a complex pattern of economic problems and uncertainties. The inflation rate, after two years of relative calm, climbed back toward the two-digit levels of 1974. That, in turn, helped send the dollar into a protracted slide in foreign exchange markets. And credit-tightening by the Federal Reserve, aimed at curbing inflation and supporting the dollar, drove interest rates steadily higher.

COMMON STOCK PRICES
New York Stock Exchange Indexes[1]

	Composite	Industrial	Transportation	Utility	Finance	Dow-Jones industrial average[2]
1972	60.29	65.73	50.17	38.48	78.35	950.71
1973	57.42	63.08	37.74	37.69	70.12	923.88
1974	43.84	48.08	31.89	29.79	49.67	759.37
1975	45.73	50.52	31.10	31.50	47.14	802.49
1976	54.46	60.44	39.57	36.97	52.94	974.92
1977	53.69	57.86	41.09	40.92	55.25	831.17
1978	53.62	58.87	41.58	37.69	55.01	805.01

[1]Dec. 31, 1965 = 50; [2]includes 30 stocks;

The prime lending rate charged by banks rose from 7.75% to 11.75% in 1978.

That added up to a difficult environment not only for stocks, but also for the bond market, since rising rates on interest-bearing securities translate directly into lower prices for those securities.

Yields on high-grade bonds, which stood at less than 8% at the end of 1977, were approaching 9% by the close of 1978.

The decline of the dollar brought home to Wall Street as never before the growing importance of foreign investors in the U. S. stock market. A falling dollar, analysts pointed out, means losses for a Swiss or West German or Japanese investor in an American stock even if the stock's nominal price, stated in dollars, holds steady.

Studies by the Securities Industry Association showed that foreign investors, a negligible factor in the market until the late 1960's, had become by the mid-1970's net buyers of several billion dollars' worth of U. S. stocks a year.

World Markets. Investors who turned away from Wall Street to other market centers in Europe and the Orient found their chances a bit better than in New York. An early December compilation of the performance of 15 world stock markets by the firm of Granger & Co. showed only one—the Swiss market, which was off about 6% —ranking behind the U. S. Even after sharp declines late in the year, the Hong Kong and Singapore markets were ahead by better than 20%.

France's market was up more than 40%; South Africa and Italy, 25%, and Australia 8%. Markets in England and West Germany registered only narrow gains, but they were still in the plus column. Canada, with its strong position in natural resources, posted a 20% rise. In Japan, a notable bastion of industrial strength, the market also climbed 20% and hit an all-time high.

Also reaching a new high during the year was the price of gold, the mystical metal with its following of ardent advocates who regard it as a haven from inflation and currency turmoil.

Gold bullion reached prices of better than $240 per troy ounce in the London and Zurich markets as of early fall. But then it, like other investments, took a spill late in the year, and dropped into the $200's in December.

CHET CURRIER, *The Associated Press*

SUDAN

Nearly bankrupt because of heavy foreign financing of its long-range development plans, Sudan was ruffled in 1978 by a series of economic crises. Politically, President Jaafar al-Nemery scored successes with his policy of reconciliation with the opposition.

Economy. Behind in its loan payments on outstanding foreign debts of up to (U. S.) $4 billion, Sudan bowed to pressure from international lenders in June, devaluing its currency 20%, and curbing development spending. Nemery admitted that Sudan's development schemes had "exhausted our national economy," but said they would not be abandoned. However, he said the emphasis in 1978 would be on removing economic bottlenecks, cutting spending, imposing financial discipline, and fighting inflation, running at about 25%.

There were continuing difficulties in importing key items such as fertilizers for the cash crops, cotton and groundnuts. Much of these crops were destroyed when heavy rains flooded cultivable land in the fertile Nile valley of the north and central regions in July. Half a million people were left homeless and 100 villages were swept away.

A new influx of war refugees from neighboring Ethiopia's Eritrea province also strained resources. As many as 250,000 refugees from Eritrea and elsewhere were said to be living in make-shift camps in the eastern region of the country.

Exacerbating these problems were severe countrywide fuel shortages which disrupted relief efforts and forced the government to call in foreign aid to help distribute foodstuffs. In the capital, Khartoum, chronic fuel shortages closed down many businesses and brought about serious shortages of essential commodities.

Offsetting the bleak economic outlook were reports, dismissed by Nemery as premature, that a Standard Oil of California subsidiary, prospecting in the southern region, had discovered vast deposits of oil.

Politics. Nemery's bold program of reconciliation with political enemies paid dividends in 1978. His policy of granting amnesty to jailed dissidents and luring back political exiles by offering them a part in national development began in 1977 with the return of former Prime Minister Sadik al-Mahdi. In 1978, the Sudanese leader appointed Mahdi and other prominent opposition leaders to the central committee of the ruling party. Mahdi apparently won a concession from Nemery for freer elections to the national assembly in February. Some 140 of the 304 seats were filled by opposition politicians. Mahdi's group in exile later agreed to disband, as did another antigovernment party which had staged a coup attempt in January 1977.

JOSEPH MARGOLIS *"African Update"*
African-American Institute

────── SUDAN • Information Highlights ──────

Official Name: Democratic Republic of Sudan.
Location: Northeast Africa.
Area: 967,500 square miles (2,505,825 km²).
Population (1978 est.): 17,100,000.
Chief Cities (April 1973): Khartoum, the capital, 333,906; Omdurman, 299,399.
Government: *Head of state,* Gen. Jaafar Mohammed al-Nemery, president (took office Oct. 1971). *Legislature* (unicameral)—People's Assembly.
Monetary Unit: Pound (0.4 pound equals U. S.$1, Sept. 1978).
Manufactures (major products): Cement, textiles, pharmaceuticals, shoes, processed foods.
Agriculture (major products): Cotton, sesame seeds, peanuts, gum arabic, sorghum, wheat, sugarcane.

SWEDEN

Politics. On Oct. 5, 1978, Premier Thorbjörn Fälldin resigned over the issue of nuclear power. Fälldin, a strong opponent of nuclear energy, had intended to resign earlier in the year when his Center (Agrarian) Party failed to agree with its coalition Liberal and Conservative parties over the fueling of new nuclear power stations. Sweden had eight operating stations; a dispute over whether to build a ninth and tenth led to the cabinet's downfall.

On October 13, Liberal Party leader Ola Ullsten was elected prime minister by parliament. Ullsten, 46, had been voted the new leader of the Liberal Party on March 4 upon the resignation of Per Ahlmark. As head of the caretaker government, Ullsten will serve an 11-month term until a general election in September 1979. On October 18 he announced his cabinet, which included several women; all members were from the Liberal Party. Hans Blix was named minister of foreign affairs.

Economy. Despite a slight increase in exports, Sweden's economic crisis continued in 1978. Industrial employment continued to drop, and more than 140,000 Swedes were expected to be unemployed in January 1979. Only one shipyard continued to build ships, the other three publicly owned yards being kept open for repairs only. The average hourly wage in industry at midyear was (U. S.) $6.23, up by $6.7% over mid-1977. The inflation rate was brought down to 5–6% from two-digit inflation the year before.

Foreign Relations. In a speech at the UN General Assembly on September 26, then Foreign Minister Karin Söder emphasized the principal thrusts of Sweden's foreign policy: disarmament, redistribution of resources, human rights, and equal rights for women.

Domestic Affairs. Sweden's birth rate, 11.6 per 1,000 inhabitants, continued to be the lowest on record. The 1978 population was estimated to be 8,300,000.

A giant underground oil storage complex, with a total capacity of 2.6 million cubic meters, is being built on the west coast of Sweden. It is claimed to be the largest in the world.

An international symposium entitled "Research on Linnaeus Today—Progress and Prospects" was held in Uppsala and Stockholm May 26–28 to celebrate the bicentennial of the death of the Swedish botanist Carolus Linnaeus. A similar meeting was arranged simultaneously by the Linnaean Society of London.

Harry E. Martinson, poet, novelist, and co-winner of the 1974 Nobel Prize for Literature (with Swedish novelist Eyvind Johnson) died on Feb. 11, 1978 at the age of 73.

Royal Family. King Carl Gustav and Queen Silvia made official visits to the Soviet Union and Yugoslavia in 1978. Carl Gustav became the first Swedish king to visit the Soviet Union since his great-grandfather, Gustav V, visited the czar in 1908.

MAC LINDAHL
Harvard University

SWITZERLAND

Terrorist activities and the economy dominated Swiss affairs during 1978.

Terrorism. In December 1977, Swiss border guards were involved in a gunfight with two East German political terrorists seeking to transport ransom money through Switzerland. The deaths of two Swiss policemen in October 1977 and March 1978 also were attributed to West German terrorist activity. Bomb explosions in the Bernese Jura region on Jan. 24, 1978, were seen as protests against the trial of 13 Jura separatists charged with damaging military and communications installations. In an effort to coordinate antiterrorist surveillance, the interior ministers of Switzerland, Italy, Austria, and West Germany agreed on April 9 to establish an informational "hotline" among the four countries.

On Nov. 9, 1977, the Swiss government lifted the 20-year statute of limitations on war crimes, crimes against humanity, and terrorist activity. On Feb. 9, 1978, it passed a bill requiring licenses for all rifles.

Referenda. On February 27, Swiss voters approved a law giving the federal government power to act directly to control inflation and unemployment, and to enact legislation on matters of public finance, banking, and foreign trade. On May 28, voters rejected a proposal that would have allowed abortions for nonmedical reasons.

——— SWEDEN • Information Highlights ———

Official Name: Kingdom of Sweden.
Location: Northern Europe.
Area: 173,000 square miles (448,068 km²).
Population (1978 est.): 8,300,000.
Chief Cities (1976): Stockholm, the capital, 661,258; Göteborg, 442,410; Malmö, 240,220.
Government: *Head of state,* Carl XVI Gustaf, king (acceded Sept. 1973). *Head of government,* Ola Ullsten, prime minister (took office Oct. 1978). *Legislature* (unicameral)—Riksdag.
Monetary Unit: Krona (4.337 kronor equal U. S.$1, Nov. 1978).
Manufactures (major products): Machinery, instruments, metal products, automobiles, aircraft.
Agriculture (major products): Dairy, grains, sugar beets, potatoes, wood.

——— SWITZERLAND • Information Highlights ———

Official Name: Swiss Confederation.
Location: Central Europe.
Area: 15,943.4 square miles (41,293.2 km²).
Population (1978 est.): 6,200,000.
Chief Cities (1977 est.): Bern, the capital, 146,800; Zurich, 383,000; Basel, 188,800.
Government: *Head of state,* Willi Ritschard, president. *Legislature*—Federal Assembly: Council of States and National Council.
Monetary Unit: Franc (1.6295 francs equal U. S.$1, Nov. 1978).
Manufactures (major products): Watches, clocks, precision instruments, machinery, chemicals, pharmaceuticals, textiles, generators, and turbines.
Agriculture (major products): High-quality cheese and other dairy products, livestock, fruits, grains, potatoes, and wine.

The Economy. Statistics released during 1978 indicated that Switzerland ranked second in the world in 1977 in both per capita income ($8,870) and per capita GNP ($10,000). Exports in the first half of 1978 increased by 34.9% over the first half of 1977, while imports increased by 35%.

Swiss financial circles were rocked by the news on April 14 that the U. S. brokerage firm of Merrill Lynch and Co., through its purchase of White Weld Holding, had acquired a 30% interest in Crédit Suisse, one of Switzerland's "big four" banks. Of even greater concern was the steady appreciation of the Swiss franc in relation to the U. S. dollar and the German mark. In October, this reached such alarming proportions that Swiss banks announced their intention to purchase sizeable quantities of U. S. dollars.

PAUL C. HELMREICH, *Wheaton College, Mass.*

SYRIA

When Syrian President Hafez al-Assad began his second term on March 8, he emphasized his commitment to consolidating national unity and decentralizing the government. However, Assad's main concerns in 1978 were neither popularizing his regime nor revamping a stagnant domestic economy. Instead, Assad concentrated on Syria's role in Lebanon and the fragmentation of inter-Arab politics caused by Egyptian President Anwar el-Sadat's controversial peace initiative with Israel.

Arab Affairs. Syrian opposition to Sadat's peace initiative and the results of the Camp David summit in September were based less on strategy than on Assad's dissatisfaction with the tactics of his former ally. Assad also sought a negotiated peace with Israel based on UN Resolution 242 but, unlike Sadat, gave first priority to a united Arab front. Assad spent much of 1978 violently criticizing Sadat and attempting to persuade moderate and radical Arab regimes to join together and isolate the Egyptian president.

On January 9, Assad accused Sadat of seeking a separate peace with Israel and destroying unified Arab peace efforts which were just beginning to show signs of progress. Declaring that Sadat had virtually capitulated to the Israelis, Assad stated categorically that peace in the Middle East could not be achieved without Arab unity.

In February, Assad and Foreign Minister Abdel Halim Khaddam announced the formation of the "Steadfastness and Confrontation Front," composed of Syria, Libya, Algeria, South Yemen, and the Palestine Liberation Organization (PLO). Since none of the members except Syria had a common border with Israel and since none of them formally recognized Israel's existence, the radical alliance was ineffectual from the outset.

After the Egyptian peace initiative it appeared that the Arab ability to wage war against Israel had disappeared. Assad therefore sought to strengthen Syria's military capabilities. In mid-January, reports that the Soviet Union was increasing its military aid to Syria were confirmed. Assad, seeking to expand his supply of sophisticated Soviet weapons, visited Moscow in late February and again in October.

Assad's efforts to isolate Sadat were tempered by Syria's heavy reliance on foreign aid, especially from the oil-producing, politically moderate bloc led by Saudi Arabia. It was estimated that Saudi Arabia alone provides Syria with $500 million a year for economic security and the purchase of weapons. Despite clamoring by the radical Arab states for a Soviet-backed military pact and a cooling of relations with the United States (which will provide Syria with some $90 million in 1978–79), Assad resisted because of his ties with the ardently anticommunist Saudis.

However, Assad did not retreat from his anti-Egyptian offensive. Throughout the summer, and especially after the Camp David accords were announced in September, he traveled to almost every Arab capital seeking support and dissuading other heads of state from joining Sadat. After a successful reconciliation with Iraqi leaders, longtime rivals of Syria, Assad pushed for an anti-Egyptian Arab summit conference. The summit convened on November 2 in Baghdad. At the conference, Assad scored a political triumph when the moderate Arab states accepted a proposal to offer Sadat (U. S.) $5 billion every year for a decade in exchange for not signing a separate peace with Israel. On November 4, Sadat rejected the offer. Assad, with the support of the radical states, sought to strengthen his own position in the Arab world.

Role in Lebanon. Although most of the cost of keeping 28,000 Syrian troops in Lebanon was borne by the Arab League, Syria paid a heavy price in frustration. Assad's goals in Lebanon were to restore stability, assure the Muslims a greater role in national politics, and secure his southern flank against Israel. None of these was accomplished. Syrian troops were forced to avoid armed conflict with Israel after its invasion and three-month occupation of southern Lebanon.

F. NICHOLAS WILLARD

SYRIA · Information Highlights

Official Name: Syrian Arab Republic.
Location: Southwest Asia.
Area: 71,500 square miles (185,184 km²).
Population (1978 est.): 8,100,000.
Chief Cities (1975 est.): Damascus, the capital, 1,042,-245; Aleppo, 778,523; Homs, 267,132.
Government: *Head of state,* Lt. Gen. Hafez al-Assad, president (took office March 1971). *Head of government,* Abdul Rahman Khulayfawi, prime minister (took office Aug. 1976). *Legislature* (unicameral)—People's Council.
Monetary Unit: Pound (3.95 pounds equal U. S.$1, Sept. 1978).
Manufactures (major products): Petroleum, textiles, cement, glass, soap, food processing, phosphates.
Agriculture (major products): Wheat, barley, sugar beets, tobacco, sheep and goats, grapes, tomatoes.

TANZANIA

Internal affairs, especially economic development, dominated Tanzanian politics during 1978. The stagnation of the economy led to the major internal disturbance of the year.

Student Riots. Students at Dar es Salaam University rioted in March protesting the rise in government salaries at a time when most Tanzanians were in severe economic stress. The government responded by expelling 360 students, including President Nyerere's son, Emmy, and ordering them back to their home villages and banning them from state jobs or organizations.

Economy. With a stagnant economy, the government tried to continue the development of a rural-based socialist society. Helped by more than $300 million in aid from Western nations the government began a program of compensation to peasants displaced by the "ujamaa village" movement of the past. Nearly $36 million was committed to the construction of the new capital in the inland city of Dodoma. To provide labor for this, and for sisal plantations, Nyerere ordered unemployed youths in Dar and other major cities sent to the villages for agricultural work. Most were recent arrivals, or school-leavers hoping for a white-collar job with the government, and were seen as potential social and political problems.

Tanzania was also hurt economically by the feud with Kenya which severed air and road service between the two countries and led to a $2.5 million loss to the key tourist industry. On the positive side, Belgium offered funds for the Kagera River hydroelectric project, and a possible return of the U. S. Peace Corps (barred since 1969) was suggested.

Internal Affairs. To mark the first anniversary of the new ruling party, Nyerere granted amnesty to more than 7,000 prisoners, including 26 of some 1,500 political prisoners. The nation was rocked by a cholera outbreak in the winter of 1977–78 which took nearly 1,000 lives and led to the closure of all schools in Dar.

Foreign Affairs. Tanzania played a key but low-profiled role in 1978. Nyerere continued to support the Rhodesian guerrilla movement of Joshua Nkomo and Robert Mugabe, providing them with training camps in Tanzania. Nyerere attacked the U. S. "obsession" with Cubans in

Africa, but relations with the United States remained friendly, especially after a March visit by Ambassador Andrew Young. Both sides agreed to restraint over the issues that mixed African and big-power politics. Reports of border fighting with Uganda persisted throughout the year.

See also AFRICA.

ROBERT GARFIELD, *DePaul University*

TANZANIA • Information Highlights

Official Name: United Republic of Tanzania.
Location: East Africa.
Area: 364,900 square miles (945,087 km²).
Population (1978 est.): 16,500,000.
Chief City (1975 est.): Dar es Salaam, the capital, 517,000.
Government: *Head of state,* Julius K. Nyerere, president (took office 1964). *Chief Minister,* Edward Moringe Sokoine, prime minister (took office Feb. 1977). *Legislature* (unicameral)—National Assembly.
Monetary Unit: Shilling (7.676 shillings equal U. S.$1, Aug. 1978).
Manufactures (major products): Textiles, agricultural processing, light manufacturing, refined oil, cement.
Agriculture (major products): Sugar, maize, rice, wheat, cotton, coffee, sisal, cashew nuts, tea, tobacco, pyrethrum, cloves.

TAXATION

Tax revision throughout most industrial nations for 1978 reflected the dual goals of easing tax burdens on families facing higher living costs and encouraging capital investment needed to speed economic growth. While tax reductions were prevalent, they were designed cautiously in an effort to ease existing problems without setting off another round of inflation.

THE UNITED STATES

Congressional Action. In the closing hours of its 95th session, Congress approved a tax bill meeting most of the objections of the Carter administration to earlier drafts of the measure. The Revenue Act of 1978 cut individual income taxes by $12.8 billion in 1979, business taxes by $3.7 billion, and capital gains taxes by $2.2 billion. Dealing mainly with tax cuts, the law called for a few tax increases, including repeal of the deduction for state and local gasoline taxes. For individuals, the law increased personal exemptions from $750 to $1,000 and raised the standard deduction (now called the zero-bracket amount) from $2,200 to $2,300 for single taxpayers, from $3,200 to $3,400 for joint returns, and from $1,600 to $1,700 for married people filing separate returns. It also provided for fewer and wider tax brackets to mitigate the effects of inflation moving taxpayers into higher brackets; extended indefinitely the earned-income credit for the working poor; and increased the credit to 10% of earned income up to a maximum of $500, instead of $400. Reversing the pattern of recent tax changes, the law provided the largest share of tax relief for those in middle and upper incomes. The average tax reduction for all income levels was 7%, but two-thirds of the reductions will benefit taxpayers with incomes above $20,000.

For business, the law provided a cut in the top corporate rate from 48% to 46% and a graduated rate structure for corporations with taxable income of less than $100,000. The new rates range from 17% on income up to $25,000 to 40% on income between $75,000 and $100,000. The top rate, previously effective on income above $50,000, now applies to income above $100,000. The law liberalized the investment tax credit to enable companies to use it to offset 90% of their taxes, rather than 50%, and extended permanently the 10% rate.

For investors the law reduced the maximum rate on capital gains from 49% to 28%, primarily by raising the capital gains exclusion from 50% to 60%. As a result of the law, homeowners aged 55 or over will be allowed to avoid tax, once-in-a-lifetime, on up to $100,000 of gains from the sale of homes.

Congress also approved several other tax changes. The Energy Act of 1978 provided tax credits for residential energy-conserving expenditures and a "gas-guzzler" tax beginning on 1980 car models not meeting prescribed mileage standards. In the Foreign Earned Income Act of 1978, Congress modified provisions for the tax treatment of Americans working abroad, mainly by providing a new deduction for excess costs of living in foreign countries above those in the highest cost U. S. metropolitan area (excluding Alaska).

State and Local Revenue. State and local governments in 1978 continued to experience surpluses on their general operations; revenue receipts in fiscal year 1978 exceeded expenditures by almost $11 billion. Tax collections were $192 billion, an increase of $18 billion or 10% over 1977. The previous year's rise had been somewhat higher, $19 billion or 12%. Federal grants to states and localities totaled $80 billion in fiscal 1978, a rise of $12 billion or 17% over 1977. Gains in each of the two preceding years had been 19%.

For the first time in four years, state legislation on major taxes resulted in more reductions than increases. Under the measures approved, taxpayers in 21 states will pay about $2.5 billion less each year, primarily through lower sales and income taxes. Partly offsetting were increases in taxes in eight states, estimated to add more than $200 million annually to tax payments, mainly through higher levies on motor fuels.

The "Tax Revolt." The growing dissatisfaction of citizens with inflation's effect on their living standards and tax burdens was reflected in tax movements, sometimes characterized as a "tax revolt," at both the national and state levels. The most dramatic result occurred in California, where rapidly rising real estate values were automatically raising property taxes by more than the rise in real incomes, and where high taxes had left the state government with a surplus of almost $6 billion. In a June election, California voters approved a citizen's initiative, Proposition 13, amending the state constitution to lower local property taxes by more than $7 billion annually. Alternately labeled the Jarvis-Gann amendment for its sponsors, Proposition 13 reduced property tax assessments to 1% of their market value in 1976, limited future assessment increases to 2% annually, and placed restraints on the ability of local governments to raise non-property taxes. The assessment limitation will apply except when property changes hands. While the long-term effect of Proposition 13 remains in doubt, the California state government quickly channeled $5 billion of its surplus funds to local governments, thus mitigating for

one year the impact of the property tax reduction on local government services.

The California initiative apparently gave a substantial boost to tax and/or expenditure limitation drives across the country. Voters in Idaho and Nevada approved Proposition 13-type measures, limiting property assessments to 1% of market or full cash value. Nevada's action must be approved again in 1980 to become effective. Voters in Oregon and Michigan, however, defeated similar property-tax cutting measures.

The majority of states searching for fiscal restraint chose more moderate plans than California's and generally aimed at expenditure control rather than immediate tax reduction. Arizona voters approved a constitutional amendment to limit state appropriations to 7% of state personal income, except when over-ridden by a two-thirds vote of the legislature. In Michigan, one of three tax relief initiatives on the ballot was approved; it limits the increase in state spending to the rise in the state's personal income. Voters in Illinois approved an advisory measure, asking the legislature to establish a ceiling on spending by both state and local government. Spending limitations were approved also by voters in Hawaii and Texas. Earlier in the year Tennessee became the first state to place constitutional limits on state spending; future increases will be limited to the percentage growth in the state's economy. In five other states, voters in November authorized a variety of constitutional measures to impose moderate restraints on taxes or spending.

The tax-slashing mood evidenced in California and other states carried over to the national level to some extent. The Kemp-Roth bill, a proposal to reduce federal income taxes by one-third over the next three years, attracted some support but failed to receive approval of the tax-writing congressional committees. At the same time, an influential group of private citizens was organized to spearhead a campaign to place constitutional limits on federal spending.

Supreme Court Decisions. The major tax decisions of the Supreme Court dealt with state, rather than federal, taxation. In a case with significant implications for corporate taxpayers, the court ruled on the validity of an interstate agreement concerning state taxation of the income of multistate businesses. Initiated in 1967, and with a current membership of 19 states, the Multistate Compact had not been acted upon by Congress, even though 12 bills proposing its approval had been introduced. In *U. S. Steel* v. *Multistate Tax Commission* the court upheld the constitutionality of the compact and the commission that administers it. U. S. Steel and other large companies suing the commission held, among other claims, that the compact violated the provision of the constitution that requires congressional approval of any agreement among the various 50 states.

Falling back on previous decisions, the court said the prohibition against such agreements applied only to combinations enhancing the power of the member states against the federal government, and that the compact did not encroach upon federal supremacy. The court also struck down the companies' claims that the compact unreasonably burdens interstate commerce and that actions by the commission violate the rights of taxpayers under the 14th Amendment to the constitution.

In another decision involving multistate taxation, *Moorman Manufacturing Company* v. *G. D. Bair,* the court approved Iowa's single factor sales formula as the basis for apportioning business' taxable income among different states. The case was of special interest because Iowa alone uses a single factor formula; all but one of the other states taxing corporate income consider sales, payroll, and property in allocating taxable income among the states. The appellant was an Illinois corporation engaged in the manufacture and sale of animal feeds, selling 20% of its output in Iowa. The Supreme Court agreed with a lower court's finding that an apportionment formula is not subject to constitutional attack unless the taxpayer proves that the formula has produced an income attribution out of all proportion to the business transacted within the state, and that the appellant had not made such a showing.

Forty-one years after striking down Washington state's tax on stevedoring, the court pronounced the same tax constitutional. In *Washington Department of Revenue* v. *Association of Washington Stevedoring Companies,* the appellants challenged the state's second attempt to apply its business and occupation tax to stevedoring. In its turnaround, the court fell back on a 1977 decision, *Complete Auto Transit, Inc.* v. *Brady,* holding that a state may properly tax the privilege of engaging in interstate commerce. The court also struck down the companies' claim that the tax violated the export-import clause of the constitution.

In *First Federal Savings and Loan Association of Boston* v. *State Tax Commission,* the court upheld the Massachusetts state excise tax on federal savings and loan associations, as measured by net income. The association had argued that the tax violated the Home Owners' Loan Act of 1933, which holds that no tax on a federal savings and loan association can be greater than that imposed by the state on similar local thrift and home financing institutions.

In a case involving federal taxation, the court ruled on an issue in the growing controversy over fringe benefits taxation. In *Central Illinois Public Service Co.* v. *U. S.,* the court held that employer reimbursements for lunch expenses to employees on non-overnight company trips are not wages subject to withholding. The government had argued that the reimbursements, made by the employer in 1963, were subject to withholding because they were a part of the employees' gross income.

OTHER COUNTRIES

Canada. The Canadian government introduced tax reductions designed to increase consumer spending power, reduce pressures on prices, and stimulate business investment. The largest cut was in the federal manufacturers' sales tax, from 12% to 9%, for a reduction of $280 million in 1978–79 and $1 billion in the following year. Various measures were introduced to encourage corporate investment, including new accelerated depreciation for research and development expenditures, an increase from 5% to 7% in a three-year-old temporary investment tax credit, and an indefinite extension of the credit.

Europe. Britain reduced income taxes by the equivalent of $4.7 billion, largely through creating a new tax "band" of 25% on the first $1,048 of taxable income; the lowest rate on income above that level remains at 34%. There were also increases in personal allowances and reductions in some taxes for middle-income earners. In an opposite move, Britain increased from 45% to 60% the basic tax on North Sea oil reserves. West Germany approved a $6.4 billion tax cut measure.

As a part of its inflation control plan, the French government announced a freeze on all major tax rates for 1978 and 1979. Other changes in France included postponement for another year of a scheduled capital gains tax on security sales and income tax reductions through the automatic adjustment of the tax structure for inflation. Spain approved a tax cut of between 15% and 50% for companies that stimulate capital investment in 1979. Portugal levied temporary surcharges on income, real estate, and sales taxes for 1978, but reduced taxes on individual and business incomes and capital gains for 1979.

Belgium raised the top marginal rate on individual income from 60 to 67.5% and increased rates on certain other income which is taxed separately. Provisions allowing depreciation at will were repealed; but a 15% investment deduction will be allowed on qualifying additional investments made in Belgium in 1979–80. Tax changes in Ireland included repealing the wealth tax, adjusting capital gains for inflation, increasing personal allowances under the income tax, and making permanent the provision for depreciation at will for plant, machinery, and industrial buildings. Greece repealed the luxury consumption tax on most items except motorcars.

Japan. Japan enacted a one-year investment tax credit of 10% of the cost of qualifying machinery and equipment. The credit is limited to 20% of the tax due, but excesses may be carried over to one of the next three years. Japan also adopted measures to counteract tax evasion on the income of foreign subsidiaries of Japanese firms.

ELSIE M. WATTERS, *Tax Foundation*

COURTESY OF NATIONAL BROADCASTING COMPANY, INC.

Greer Garson starred as the wealthy Aunt March in the four-hour miniseries *Little Women*.

TELEVISION AND RADIO

Three events were of special interest and concern in the 1978 broadcasting year: the networks' ratings race, ever more feverish; the appointment of Fred Silverman to the presidency of the National Broadcasting Company (NBC); and the unveiling of the House Communications Subcommittee's proposed revision of the 1934 Communications Act. In addition, public television celebrated its 25th anniversary.

Ratings Race. The networks' drive for audience numbers has gone on unrelentingly ever since the American Broadcasting Company (ABC) jumped into the lead in the fall of 1976. The two other networks had some hope that they might cut into ABC's lead with the advent of the new season in September and, in fact, NBC enjoyed a temporary success with the World Series. But the high ratings of the *Roots* rerun and of ABC's mix of girls-girls-girls shows (for example, *Charlie's Angels, Three's Company*), low comedy (*Happy Days, Laverne & Shirley*), and sports kept ABC on average a solid point or more ahead.

Programs. In the nine months from September of 1977 to the following June, the networks offered the astonishing total of 102 shows, not counting movie nights. Some two dozen of these were new programs, presented in three-to-six week runs as hopefuls for the fall. With the new season in September, thirteen long-run series were missing—including *Kojak, Carol*

Burnett, Maude, Bob Newhart, Baretta—either because of falling ratings or because their stars had tired of the series grind. Forty established shows returned; twenty new ones were offered. Of these last, *Taxi* (ABC) and *Mork & Mindy* (ABC), looked like contenders for long runs. Four new shows were canceled after three episodes, one of them, Mary Tyler Moore's *Mary*, for restructuring and later return. Otherwise the catchup networks elected to go pretty much with what they had until new product was ready for introduction in January.

NBC's New President. The jockeying for ratings has led to many changes of high-level personnel at NBC and CBS. None was more surprising than the announcement that Fred Silverman, the dominant figure in ABC's programming ascendancy, would become president and chief executive officer of NBC when his contract with ABC expired at the end of May. Silverman's formidable talents have been directed entirely to programming; he compensated for his limited managerial experience by naming Jane Cahill Pfeiffer, a former IBM vice president, to be chairman of NBC, leaving him free to concentrate on programming. Ms. Pfeiffer thus becomes broadcasting's highest-ranked woman. Silverman assumed his new post too late in the year to have more than a passing effect on NBC's immediate program schedule, but he made it clear that he planned to continue NBC's emphasis on "quality" programs.

Communications Act Proposal. In June, the U. S. House Communications Subcommittee and its chairman Lionel Van Deerlin (D.-Calif.) unveiled a revision of the 1934 Communications Act. Nearly two years in preparation, the proposal was a far cry from the old act. Its principal feature was a license fee based on the size of a station's market ("the value of the spectrum space"). The resulting funds would be split four ways. They would supply all the funding for a new regulatory commission, of limited powers, replacing the present Federal Communications Commission (FCC); the funds would provide the only source of government support for public broadcasting, to be put under a new governing structure; they would provide new support for the encouragement of minority ownership, and for an increase in telecommunications services to rural areas. As an acknowledged "trade-off," the bill promised far less regulation of electronic media. Radio would be almost totally deregulated, its licenses granted for an indefinite term, revocable only on technical grounds. The term for television licenses would be five years for the present and become indefinite after ten years.

The new legislation would do away with the requirement that stations operate "in the public interest, convenience, and necessity." It would reduce the number of stations that could be owned by a single entity from the present 21 (7 TV, 7 AM, 7 FM) to 10 (5 TVs and 5 radio, in any mix of AM and FM). And it would permit the ownership of only one kind of station in one market. Existing combinations of ownership would, of course, be, "grandfathered." Cable would be freed of federal regulations, leaving it to state and local jurisdictions.

Although cable and radio interests were in general pleased with the revision, opposition to most of its features was widespread, coming from the industry, the FCC, and public interest groups. Representative Van Deerlin and his committee promised to rewrite the revision, to be presented for consideration by both houses of Congress sometime in 1979.

Meantime, Ernest Hollings (D-S. C.), chairman of the Senate Communications Subcommittee, promised still another study to amend rather than rewrite the old 1934 Communications Act.

The attempt to open Congress to radio and TV coverage made a small gain. For the first time in its history, the Senate, on February 8, allowed radio, tapping into the Senate's own microphone system, to carry live the Panama Canal debate. National Public Radio (NPR) gave the debate three full days of coverage, thereby increasing its listeners five-fold in the polled cities of Washington, New York, and Los Angeles. Early in June, the House of Representatives gave permission for a similar tap of its microphones, but barred any broadcasting from the galleries. There was less industry interest evidenced this time, in part because the networks and Congress were feuding over who should control television coverage of Congressional sessions, planned to begin in 1979.

Federal Communications Commission. Proper standards on which to base license renewal decisions in the face of challenges has been a major problem for the FCC, the courts, and Congress for 13 years. The latest instance revolves around WESH-TV, Daytona Beach, Fla. In 1976 the FCC granted license renewal to the incumbent licensee, Cowles Broadcasting, largely on the ground of "superior performance"; the challenger appealed the FCC's decision. In September 1978 a three-judge panel of the U. S. Court of Appeals in Washington, D. C., reversed the FCC's renewal to the incumbent and ordered the Commission to take another look. The panel faulted the FCC for "the tacit presumption that the incumbent is to be preferred over competing applicants," pointing to diversification of ownership, the integration of ownership and management, and the possibility of minority ownership as equally important criteria in license awards. In the case of WESH-TV the incumbent is a group owner; the challenger has no broadcast holdings.

To the industry at large, the decision seemed

ED FISCHER/OMAHA WORLD HERALD—THE MCNAUGHT SYNDICATE

"AND YOU, CONGRESSMAN— HOW DO YOU FEEL ABOUT THE CONGRESS BEING TELEVISED?"

Holocaust, a four-part drama about the Nazi persecution of Jews, was seen in part or in full by 120 million viewers, the second largest audience in the history of "entertainment" programming. The miniseries aired April 16–19.

NBC

to mean that "superior performance" on the part of any incumbent would no longer be enough to dam a flood of competing applicants at renewal time. The FCC planned to ask for a full nine-member court rehearing of the case, and Cowles Broadcasting planned an appeal to the U. S. Supreme Court.

Cable. What early proponents of cable television hoped the medium might become seems to be coming to pass in Columbus, Ohio. There, Warner Cable, the nation's fourth largest, is offering an innovative two-way cable system called Qube. At the heart of Qube's 30 channels of entertainment, information, and education are

Fred Astaire and Helen Hayes star in *A Family Upside Down*, the story of an elderly couple separated by illness.

NBC

individual push-button consoles, roughly book-size, linking 20,000 homes to a central computer and thus providing virtually instant subscriber response to programs. Some of Qube's channels carry pay television programs; the linkage makes it possible to bill the subscriber only for what he watches. As well, Qube produces as much as six hours daily of live programming. Qube does not yet pay its own way, but Warner Cable thinks it's the way of the future and will install it in other towns where it has cable systems.

MISCELLANEOUS DEVELOPMENTS

"7 Dirty Words." In July the U. S. Supreme Court by a 5–4 vote upheld the FCC in its censure of WBAI (FM) New York for broadcasting, in 1973, the George Carlin "Filthy Words" recorded monologue. The narrowly-argued majority opinion was widely considered a major blow against broadcasting's rights under the First Amendment.

"Gone With The Wind." CBS paid $35 million for exclusive television rights to *Gone With The Wind*, giving the network 20 showings over the next 20 years. In its television premiere in 1976 *GWTW* obtained the then-highest rating ever for a TV entertainment program.

Football. The cost for network and local rights, radio and TV, to broadcast college and professional football games during the fall of 1978 zoomed to over $200 million. In 1977 the figure was $82.5 million.

ABC Evening News. Long a poor third in this competition, ABC revamped its evening news format in June. It now has three anchormen, based in London, Washington, and Chicago, with Barbara Walters doing special reports and interviews and Howard K. Smith doing commentary. The changes led to an increase of a rating point or so, mostly at the expense of CBS's *Walter Cronkite and the Evening News*.

JOHN M. GUNN
Formerly, Professor of Radio-TV-Film
State University of New York at Albany

THE 1978 TELEVISION SEASON
— Some Sample Programs

ABC News Special—A special news report on the year 1968 with clips from the presidential campaigns, the assassinations of Martin Luther King, Robert Kennedy, and others. ABC, June 11.

AFI Salute to Henry Fonda—Salute by the American Film Institute to Henry Fonda, its recipient of the Life Achievement Award. CBS, March 15.

Anna Karenina—Ten-part adaptation of Tolstoy's novel; hosted by Alistair Cook; starring Nicola Pagett, Stuart Wilson, Eric Porter. PBS, Feb. 5.

Black Beauty—Five-part adaptation of the 1877 novel by Anna Sewell, with the setting changed to late 19th century Maryland. Narration by David Wayne; NBC, Jan. 31.

CBS Turns 50—CBS celebrated its 50 years in broadcasting with a nine-and-one-half hour special shown over seven nights. Each night had highlights of famous CBS shows that aired on that particular night. CBS, March 26 through Apr. 1.

CBS Reports: The Politics of Abortion—One-hour special examining the abortion issue. CBS, April 22.

Centennial—A 26-hour adaptation of the James Michener novel; starring Raymond Burr, Richard Chamberlain, Sally Kellerman. NBC, Oct. 1 (debut).

The Collection—Harold Pinter's 1961 play; with Laurence Olivier, Malcolm McDowell, Alan Bates, and Helen Mirren. PBS, Oct. 25.

Coppélia—A telecast Live from Lincoln Center; the ballet was choreographed by George Balanchine and Alexandra Danilova; with Patricia McBride and Helgi Tomasson. PBS, Jan. 31.

Count Dracula—A Great Performances three-part adaptation of Bram Stoker's 1897 novel; with Louis Jourdan. PBS, March 1.

Duchess of Duke Street—A BBC 15-part series about a kitchen maid who used her cooking abilities to gain her way to the upper classes in Edwardian England; with Gemma Jones. PBS, Oct. 22.

Fame—A Hallmark Hall of Fame presentation of Arthur Miller's comedy; with Richard Benjamin, José Ferrer, Robert Alda. NBC, Nov. 30.

A Family Upside Down—A made-for-television movie about an elderly couple who must face separation when the husband, a heart attack victim, is confined to a nursing home; with Helen Hayes and Fred Astaire. NBC, April 9.

Fifty Years of Country Music—From the Grand Ole Opry, a three-hour salute to country music; hosted by Glen Campbell, Dolly Parton, and Roy Clark. NBC, Jan. 22.

First You Cry—A made-for-television movie based on the book by Betty Rollin, recounting her experience with breast cancer; with Mary Tyler Moore, Richard Crenna, Anthony Perkins. CBS, Nov. 8.

The Great Whales—National Geographic documentary that reviewed the history of *Cetaces* and photographed a variety of species. PBS, Feb. 16.

Happy Birthday, Bob—A 75th birthday celebration for Bob Hope from the John F. Kennedy Center for the Performing Arts in Washington, D. C. NBC, May 29.

Holocaust—A nine-and-one-half hour miniseries focusing on the Nazi slaughter of European Jews during World War II. The play centered on the Weiss family, who were a symbol of the Jewish people; with Fritz Weaver, Michael Moriarty, and Rosemary Harris. NBC, April 16.

Home to Stay—A made-for-television movie about an aging and rather infirm farmer who is fighting off going to a nursing home; with Henry Fonda, Michael McGuire, Kristen Vigard. CBS, May 2.

Horowitz at the White House—Pianist Vladimir Horowitz marked the 50th anniversary of his American debut with a White House concert. PBS, Feb. 26.

King—Three-part miniseries on the life of Martin Luther King, Jr. NBC, Feb. 12.

The Last Tenant—An ABC Theatre award-winning drama about an aged father who wants to remain independent; with Lee Strasberg. ABC, June 25.

The Legacy of L. S. B. Leakey—A National Geographic documentary on the anthropologist-archaeologist and his discoveries in the Olduvai Gorge of Tanzania. PBS, Jan. 9.

Leningrad Ice Show—Soviet ice skaters performed in Leningrad; hosts were Sally Struthers and Harry Morgan. CBS, Aug. 29.

Leontyne Price at the White House—Recital from the East Room of the White House; David Garvey accompanied Miss Price on the piano. PBS, Oct. 8.

Les Miserables—1978 made-for-television movie based on the Victor Hugo novel; with Richard Jordan, Anthony Perkins, John Gielgud. CBS, Dec. 27.

Live from the Met—Three-hour presentation from the Metropolitan Opera House of Placido Domingo in Mascagni's *Cavalleria Rusticana* and Leoncavallo's *Pagliacci;* hosted by Tony Randall. PBS, April 5.

Marie Curie—Five-part dramatization on the life of Marie Curie; hosted by Dr. Rosalyn Yalow, 1977 Nobel Prize winner in Medicine. PBS, Dec. 17.

The Martha Graham Dance Company—In Performance at Wolf Trap. PBS, April 4.

Mickey Mouse is 50—A salute from The Wonderful World of Disney to Mickey Mouse. NBC, Nov. 19.

Mourning Becomes Electra—Five-part adaptation of Eugene O'Neill's play; with Joan Haskett, Bruce Davison, Roberta Maxwell. PBS, Dec. 6.

Nashville Remembers Elvis on his Birthday—Ninety-minute tribute to Elvis Presley. NBC, Jan. 8.

Pearl—A three-part miniseries about military life in Hawaii at around the time of the bombing of Pearl Harbor; with Angie Dickinson, Dennis Weaver, Robert Wagner, Lesley Ann Warren. ABC, Nov. 16.

Person to Person—Selected Interviews—A 13-part series rebroadcasting the most famous interviews of Edward R. Murrow's series of the 1950's. PBS, July 6.

Priceless Treasures of Dresden—Exhibition of works of art from the East German city of Dresden dating back to the 15th century. PBS, June 27.

Professional Foul—A Great Performance 90-minute production by British playwright Tom Stoppard in which a philosophy professor faces a moral problem; with Peter Barkworth. PBS, April 26.

A Recital by Luciano Pavarotti—A special presentation by Luciano Pavarotti live from the Metropolitan Opera House. PBS, Feb. 12.

The Red River—A special which examined the human heart and circulatory system. CBS, Mar. 6.

Rostropovich at the White House—'Cellist Mstislav Rostropovich accompanied on the piano by his daughter Elena performed at the White House. PBS, Sept. 17.

Ruby and Oswald—Three-hour made-for-television movie on the assassination of President Kennedy and the murder of Lee Harvey Oswald; with Frederic Forrest and Michael Lerner. CBS, Feb. 8.

The Saint of Bleecker St.—A Live from Lincoln Center telecast of Gian-Carlo Menotti's opera; with Catherine Malfitano and Enrico Di Giuseppe. Menotti appeared between the acts to discuss the work. PBS, April 19.

A Salute to Irving Berlin—A 90-minute special in which hosts Steve Lawrence and Eydie Gorme and guests Sammy Davis, Jr., and Carol Burnett paid a musical tribute to the composer. NBC, Aug. 22.

See How She Runs—G. E. Theater drama about a 40-year-old divorced and dowdy woman who takes up jogging and discovers that it becomes a way of self-expression; with Joanne Woodward. CBS, Feb. 1.

Solzhenitsyn at Harvard: A View and an Evaluation—Russian author Aleksandr Solzhenitsyn's address to the graduating class of Harvard University; with Harrison Salisbury. PBS, June 8.

Stars Salute Israel at 30—An all-star cast celebrated the 30th anniversary of the independence of Israel. With Vice President Mondale, Henry Fonda, Paul Newman, Barbra Streisand. ABC, May 8.

Terrorism/The World at Bay—A two-hour special report on terrorists, their identity, methods, motives, and the ability of governments to deal with them. PBS, March 21.

The Turk in Italy—A Live from Lincoln Center telecast of Rossini's comic opera; with Beverly Sills and the New York City Opera company. PBS, Oct. 4.

Vietnam: 30 Months After the 30-Year War—A documentary on Vietnam three years after the war. The program focused on Hanoi, in the north, where food rationing continues and Saigon (renamed Ho Chi Minh City), in the south, where the black market continues to prosper. PBS, April 20.

Public Television at 25

The year 1978 marked the 25th anniversary of public broadcasting. During its quarter century, public television has grown from an experiment in televised education to a major network offering a wide range of programming, including the highly praised *Sesame Street* for the youngsters, award-winning news programs, live performances from the Metropolitan Opera House and other cultural centers, live telecasts of major soccer matches, and serializations of literary classics. While several study groups pondered possible improvements in public broadcasting's structure and financing, Congress passed a bill providing for it through 1983. The bill lowered from $2.50 to $2 the amount the Corporation for Public Broadcasting must raise to match each federal dollar. It set federal allocations at $180 million for 1981, $200 million for 1982, and $220 million for 1983, requiring that a "substantial amount" of the funds for building and expanding public broadcasting facilities go to radio, that a "significant proportion" be spent on program production and that a "substantial amount" go to independent producers. The bill continued the ban on editorializing by public stations. While "grandfathering" existing salaries of public television officials, it provided that henceforth no officer would be paid more than the U. S. cabinet-level figure of $66,000.

In June, Newton Minow, a former FCC chairman, became president of the Public Broadcasting Service. And in September, Robben W. Fleming was named president of the Corporation for Public Broadcasting. Minow, who in the early 1960's had characterized television as "a vast wasteland," assumed his new position with the belief that "in time public television will become a major, major force in American life." As PBS chairman, Minow hopes to reduce the public television bureaucracy, increase the amount of live broadcasting, do more programs in the areas of news and public affairs, and also institute new programs of special interest for the older population.

In an interview for *TV-Guide,* the 52-year-old Minow pointed out that "America has always been a very optimistic country: people getting up in the morning and thinking they can change the world a little, make a better life for the kids. A lot of people don't feel that way any more. So what I'm searching for—and I don't know if we can do it—is some way for public television to make a difference in this."

JOHN M. GUNN

PBS

Marc Singer is Petruchio. Fredi Olster is Katherina.

Leontyne Price

Ned Sherrin, host, We Interrupt This Week

PHOTOS COURTESY, WNET/THIRTEEN

PBS offerings of 1978 included: The American Conservatory Theatre's production of *The Taming of the Shrew,* Verdi's *Requiem* with Leontyne Price, and a current-affairs quiz show.

TENNESSEE

Constitutional reform and the November elections dominated events in Tennessee in 1978. It was a difficult year for the city of Memphis, which experienced several serious strikes.

Constitutional Reform. The first major constitutional reform in a quarter of a century was accomplished when voters approved 12 of 13 proposed changes in the fundamental law. The most controversial change was the repeal of a provision establishing at 10% the maximum rate of interest banks and lending agencies can charge for borrowed money. The legislature was given the right to fix rates. Other provisions allow an incumbent governor to serve a second four-year term, changed the structure of county government, deleted a provision prohibiting intermarriage between the races, and reduced the voting age to eighteen.

Politics. In the most expensive gubernatorial campaign in the state's history, Nashville lawyer and former Nixon associate Lamar Alexander defeated wealthy Knoxville banker Jake Butcher. In the race for U. S. Senator, incumbent Howard Baker easily defeated Democratic nominee Jane Eskind of Nashville, winning a third term. The Democratic campaign was highlighted by a visit to Nashville by President Carter and by taped television endorsements by Sen. Edward Kennedy of Massachusetts.

Education. Enrollments in grades K–12 declined slightly, while institutions of higher learning continued to grow. Nearly 90,000 students were registered in the state's colleges and universities, and Tennessee State University, the state's traditionally black school, experienced a 9% increase. Arthur DeRosier, nationally recognized authority on Choctaw Indians, was inaugurated as president of East Tennessee State University. Commissioner of Education Sam Ingram was appointed president of Middle Tennessee State University to replace M. G. Scarlett, who resigned at the end of the year to accept a regents' professorship at Memphis State University.

A new school of medicine was opened at East Tennessee State University with 24 students, which represented the culmination of a 17-year

UPI

A Memphis store owner appraises the damage after looting broke out during a three-hour blackout on March 16.

effort to establish a medical school in the state's Appalachian region. At the same time, officials there announced the establishment of a Center for Appalachian Studies at Johnson City. Meharry Medical College, the state's traditional Negro school of medicine, announced the receipt of $4 million in federal distress grants to improve its program.

Economy. Late in the year an improved economy brought about a decline in the state's unemployment from nearly 7 to 5%. Among the cities, Nashville and Knoxville had the lowest rate, at about 4%. On the farms, vastly improved cattle and hog prices helped push farm income to 213% of farm income a decade ago. With a record crop of nearly 30 million bushels, soybeans continued to lead as the chief money-maker for Tennessee farmers. Tobacco was second.

People in the News. Dead were Congressman Clifford Allen; Dr. Matthew Walker, thirty-year chairman of Meharry Medical College's department of surgery; Maybelle Carter, matriarch of the Grand Old Opry and mother-in-law of entertainer Johnny Cash; and United States District Judge Frank Gray.

State Senator William Boner was elected to Allen's seat in Congress, and Thomas Wiseman, lawyer and former state treasurer and gubernatorial candidate, was appointed to the court to replace Gray.

ROBERT E. CORLEW
Middle Tennessee State University

----- **TENNESSEE · Information Highlights** -----

Area: 42,244 square miles (109,412 km²).

Population (Jan. 1978 est.): 4,344,000.

Chief Cities (1970 census): Nashville, the capital, 447,877; Memphis, 623,530; Knoxville, 174,587.

Government (1978): *Chief Officers*—governor, Ray Blanton (D). *General Assembly*—Senate, 33 members; House of Representatives, 99 members.

Education (1977–78): *Enrollment*—public elementary schools, 541,869 pupils; public secondary, 336,555; colleges and universities, 188,344 students. *Public school expenditures,* $1,149,539,000 ($1,136 per pupil).

State Finances (fiscal year 1977): *Revenues,* $2,933,-213,000; *expenditures,* $2,854,020,000.

Personal Income (1977): $24,869,000,000; per capita, $5,785.

Labor Force (July 1978): *Nonagricultural wage and salary earners,* 1,673,800; *unemployed,* 132,600 (6.8% of total force).

UPI

Sen. John Tower, *left*, congratulates William Clements, Jr., the first Republican to be elected governor of Texas in 105 years.

TEXAS

Texas continued to rank among the fastest growing states in the nation. Politics, the economy, and energy policy were the focuses of attention in 1978.

Politics. In a close and hotly-contested primary election, state Attorney General John Hill defeated the incumbent governor, Dolph Briscoe, for the Democratic gubernatorial nomination. William Clements, Jr., a conservative, won the Republican nomination unopposed. Clements was considered the underdog on the eve of the election, despite endorsements by Gerald Ford and John Connally. On Election Day, however, Clements scored a razor-thin victory, to become the first Republican governor of Texas in 105 years.

Robert Kreuger, a Democratic U. S. Representative from central Texas, mounted a challenge for the U. S. Senate seat held by John Tower. Although somewhat vulnerable because of his extreme conservatism, Tower was supported by the powerful oil and gas interests in the state and narrowly defeated his opponent on November 8.

Economy. Spurred by the example of Proposition 13 in California, Gov. Dolph Briscoe convened a special session of the Texas legislature to consider the problem of tax relief. A small reduction in the state utility tax was effected, but property tax reductions were minimal. An attempt by state Rep. Wayne Peveto to overhaul the entire tax code failed, but several pending legal cases were expected to resolve the issue.

Leading spokesmen for the oil and gas industries, the backbone of Texas economy, called for a national energy policy which would encourage domestic exploration and reduce U. S. dependence on imported fuel. An oil strike by Texaco in Atlantic coastal waters near Baltimore, Md., lent support to their position.

Mexican Aliens. Attracted by Texas' high wages for agricultural labor, many Mexicans illegally crossed the border at various points along the Rio Grande. The U. S. Border Patrol and Mexican police appeared unable to stop the traffic. The problem was compounded when Mexican-American civil rights groups insisted that the state must bear the cost of educating children of illegal aliens, even though the parents pay no taxes.

Throughout Texas, black and Mexican-American civil rights groups demanded federal protection of their rights. However, the same organizations expressed their disappointment at the U. S. Supreme Court's ambiguous finding in the Bakke case. They continued to insist on affirmative action programs to protect minority education and employment rights.

Weather. In 1978, Texans suffered through an unusually hot summer. In Dallas there were a number of deaths, particularly among the elderly, attributed to heat stroke. By the end of the summer, many parts of the state were reporting near-drought conditions. Galveston, Houston, and smaller communities along the Gulf coast weathered heavy rains during the hurricane and tropical storm season.

Sports. Texas sports fans had a banner year. In January, the Dallas Cowboys defeated the Denver Broncos to win the Super Bowl but lost a most exciting contest to Pittsburgh in Super Bowl XIII, Jan. 21, 1979. The Houston Oilers drafted Heisman Trophy winner Earl Campbell and made it to the AFC championship game. In basketball, the University of Texas captured the National Invitation Tournament (NIT) in New York.

STANLEY E. SIEGEL, *University of Houston*

TEXAS • Information Highlights

Area: 267,338 square miles (692,405 km²).
Population (Jan. 1978 est.): 12,954,000.
Chief Cities (1970 census): Austin, the capital, 251,808; Houston, 1,232,802; Dallas, 844,401.
Government (1978): *Chief Officers*—governor, Dolph Briscoe (D); lt. gov., William P. Hobby (D). *Legislature*—Senate, 31 members; House of Representatives, 150 members.
Education (1977–78): *Enrollment*—public elementary schools, 1,516,676 pupils; public secondary, 1,326,166; colleges and universities, 647,593 students. *Public school expenditures,* $4,038,834,000 ($1,257 per pupil).
State Finances (fiscal year 1977): *Revenues,* $8,847,332,000; *expenditures,* $7,829,437,000.
Personal Income (1977): $87,280,000,000; per capita, $6,803.
Labor Force (July 1978): *Nonagricultural wage and salary earners,* 5,125,500; *unemployed,* 317,200 (5.2% of total force).

In preparation for Bangkok's 200th anniversary, 1982, city officials have ordered the weekend market, a major retail, socializing, and tourist area, closed.

UPI

THAILAND

In its continuing search for peace and security, Thailand in 1978 moved to end border fighting with Cambodia and to improve relations with Laos, Cambodia, and China. A largely quiet domestic scene was highlighted by a cabinet shift in August and the adoption of a new constitution in December.

Foreign Affairs. The beginning of the year saw a continuation of bloody border clashes with Cambodia. Cambodian and rebel forces raided villages along the border, killing and kidnapping hundreds of Thais. Foreign Minister Upadit Pachariyangkun visited Cambodia in early February, and the two countries agreed to normalize relations and work toward resolving their long-standing differences. Although border fighting persisted, an agreement was reached in July when the Cambodian deputy premier visited Bangkok.

The lessening of tension on the Cambodian border intensified another problem of Thailand—the influx of refugees. In addition to the Cambodians entering Thailand, Laotians and Vietnamese also poured into the country. Thailand was neither happy to have them nor willing to retain them. It appeared, in fact, that anti-Communist factions given sanctuary in Thailand may have been responsible for raids into Cambodia and the flaring up of that dispute. On February 16, a Thai official disclosed that his country was forcing Laotian refugees back across the border. However, those regarded as having escaped for political reasons were taken in by refugee camps supervised by the United Nations High Commissioner for Refugees.

The refugee problem and the dispute with Cambodia affected Thailand's relations with the rest of Indochina, and it was the goal of Prime Minister Kriangsak Chamanan to "mend fences." In addition to the agreement with Cambodia, Kriangsak welcomed Laotian diplomats to Bangkok March 25; the result was an optimistic joint communiqué. On January 10, Thailand and Vietnam signed a trade agreement covering civil aviation, and economic and technical cooperation; between September 6 and 10 the two

nations reached agreements on a variety of issues. Another major step in the search for security was a one-week visit to China by Prime Minister Kriangsak, beginning March 29.

U. S. Vice President Walter Mondale visited Bangkok May 4–5 and announced that the United States would give financial help for resettling refugees and would extend military aid.

Domestic Affairs. On August 13 it was announced that Prime Minister Kriangsak had appointed two of his military rivals—Gen. Yos Thephasdin and Adm. Adorn Sirikaya—deputy defense ministers. He also appointed himself defense minister and turned over his previously held position of interior minister to former defense minister Lek Neaomali.

After months of debate the National Legislative Assembly approved a new permanent national constitution. It was signed on December 21 and promulgated the following day.

Rapidly rising population continues to beset almost every country in Asia. Thailand's new family program, however, has been most successful. The success of the campaign was largely the accomplishment of Mechai Viravaidya, who calls himself a "guerrilla fighter of family planning." Mechai combined aggressive and flamboyant methods of advertising to make birth control popular. He personally handed out contraceptive devices, along with T-shirts, stickers, and other promotional items.

CARL LEIDEN
The University of Texas, Austin

--- **THAILAND · Information Highlights** ---

Official Name: Kingdom of Thailand.
Location: Southeast Asia.
Area: 209,411 square miles (542,373 km²).
Population (1978 est.): 45,000,000.
Chief Cities (1975 est.): Bangkok, the capital, 4,000,-000; Chiang Mai, 100,000.
Government: *Head of state,* Bhumibol Adulyadej, king (acceded June 1946). *Head of government,* Kriangsak Chamanan, prime minister; President of the National Policy Council, Sangad Chaloryoo; *Legislature*—National Assembly: Senate and House of Representatives.
Monetary Unit: Baht (20.20 baht equal U. S.$1, Sept. 1978).
Manufactures (major products): Processed foods, textiles, wood, cement.
Agriculture (major products): Rice, rubber, tapioca, corn, sugar, pineapple.

MARTHA SWOPE

THEATER

Imogene Coca, John Cullum, and Madeline Kahn are featured in *On the Twentieth Century*. The music is by Cy Coleman; books and lyrics are by Betty Comden and Adolph Green.

For the American theater 1978 was a prosperous year. Not even New York City's long newspaper strike did serious damage to show business. In fact, successful Broadway shows abounded, creating a shortage of available theaters for new productions. By the end of the year, however, plans were afoot to restore several playhouses long lost to legitimate theater.

Yet no one was likely to argue that 1978 was a year to be long remembered for its contribution to theatrical art. Surely the year's most notable innovation was the sudden rise to prominence of a new genre, the bookless musical, an entertainment that combined song, dance, and some kind of unifying theme but strictly avoided anything resembling a plot. Dramatists continued to be preoccupied with the behavior of old people, whether they were represented as flirtatious, as in *The Kingfisher,* contemplative, as in *On Golden Pond,* or merely rambunctious, as in *Da.* No doubt this emphasis catered to a presumed rise in the average age of Broadway audiences, although the long-running *Grease* and *The Wiz,* undaunted by competition with their cinematic incarnations, continued to beckon to youth.

In the long run, a commercial breakthrough may have provided the most important event of the year—the discovery that bringing plays from the tiny showcases of Off-Off-Broadway's neighborhood theaters to the vast palaces of Broadway

was good business. In the past such transfers usually failed. The new experiences of 1978 demonstrated that the successful transfer to Broadway of *A Chorus Line* in 1975 was not a fluke and that it clearly showed the way for other shows. Within the year, such Off-Off-Broadway houses as the Manhattan Theater Club, the Circle Repertory, and the Hudson Guild were frequented by Broadway producers looking for new vehicles, especially since new vehicles were not coming from the old familiar places or even the old familiar people.

New York saw virtually no new Broadway plays of English or continental origin. If there were a new foreign presence on the American theatrical scene, it was, astonishingly, Russian. The most dynamic figure in the American musical theater, Harold Prince, confined himself in 1978 to directing *On the Twentieth Century* for another management and to directing a musical in London. The most acclaimed of the older American dramatists, Tennessee Williams, Arthur Miller, and Edward Albee, were relatively silent. (Williams' new play *Crève Coeur,* at the Spoleto, U. S. A. Festival of Charleston, S. C., with Shirley Knight in the cast, seemed no more than an amalgam of the veteran dramatist's old themes. A musical play by Miller and Stanley Silverman was scheduled and then cancelled at the Goodspeed Theater in Connecticut. Albee directed programs of his older plays for a nationwide tour.) Several of the younger dramatists, including David Mamet, Sam Shepard, and Lanford Wilson, contributed new plays, but only one, Bernard Slade, hitherto regarded primarily as a commercial dramatist, notably enhanced his reputation.

Little was heard from the ebullient impresario Joseph Papp. Profits from the continuing Broadway run of *A Chorus Line* provided the margin that kept his Public Theater going, but he effected only one successful transfer to Broadway and was unable to maintain long runs for most of the Public plays that the critics praised. The Vivian Beaumont Theater in Lincoln Center, which Papp abandoned in 1977, remained closed, and so, for "classical" revivals of Broadway quality the New York public had to depend solely on the Circle in the Square.

As the year ended, it was announced that the Beaumont would be run by a committee that included a house dramatist, Edward Albee, and five directors—Woody Allen, Sarah Caldwell (artistic director of the Opera Company of Boston), Liviu Ciulei (a frequent visitor from Rumania), Robin Phillips (director of the theater at Stratford, Ontario), and Ellis Rabb (founder of the long-lived APA Repertory Company).

Musicals. Two of the bookless musicals celebrated the music of black composers of jazz. The first to arrive, the vivacious *Ain't Misbehavin',* based on the songs of the late "Fats" Waller, opened Off-Off-Broadway at the Manhattan Theater Club but moved downtown to become one of the principal hits of the Broadway season. The comparably sprightly *Eubie!,* which started its life at an obscure Off-Off-Broadway theater, was eminently aided by the energetic dancing of the Hines Brothers. The show made good use of the tunes of Eubie Blake, who, at the age of 95, was present on opening night. Later in the year, the Manhattan Theater Club tried to repeat its success by presenting *A Lady Needs a Change,* a show based on the songs of the late Dorothy Fields, but this show seemed not destined for rebirth on Broadway.

Without the slightest trace of a book or a plot, the sixteen featured players of *Dancin'* vigorously performed dance numbers choreographed by Bob Fosse in his characteristic style. Only Ann Reinking's name was likely to be recognized by the general public, but the general public came nevertheless. Capitalizing on the surprising popular interest in dance, the American Dance Machine, which is dedicated to reconstructing dance numbers from old Broadway musicals, offered a program of dance sequences which it had saved from oblivion.

Two of the non-book musicals managed, even in the absence of anything resembling a plot, to convey certain themes. *Runaways*—written, composed, and directed by Elizabeth Swados—dealt, as one might expect, with children who run away from home. Combining rehearsals with research, Ms. Swados set out to convey "the profound effects of our deteriorating families" and the new environments which rebellious children substituted for them. Only three members of the company were professionals. *Runaways* owed its long rehearsal period—and, indeed, its existence—to the sponsorship of its original home, Joseph Papp's Public Theater.

With considerable skill, *Working,* based on the documentary book of the same name by Studs Terkel, showed a great number of typical Americans at work, but it never found its audience and it did not stay long on Broadway.

Broadway also had its share of conventional musicals based on plots. Prominent among them was *On the Twentieth Century,* based on the Hecht-MacArthur comedy, *Twentieth Century.* As the eccentric Broadway producer bent on signing up the film star whose talent he regards as his own creation, John Cullum gave a plausible imitation of John Barrymore in the movie version. As the lunatic philanthropist (a man in the original) Imogene Coca gave great pleasure to nostalgic fans. But it was possible to argue that the real star of the evening was the set, with its witty variations on the theme of a train speeding across the country.

The Best Little Whorehouse in Texas, a bawdy celebration of an actual brothel that was closed, we are told, by petty-minded officials, began at a small theater before moving to Broadway. But something else in its curious history may be of more significance, especially for Broadway's future. Originally a project at the Actors Studio, it was taken over at an early stage of its life by Universal Pictures. No previous Broadway production has been so completely guided and owned by a film studio. Theater circles wondered if it was a portent future activity.

Henry Fonda and Jane Alexander are jurists of different viewpoints in *First Monday in October.*

RICHARD BRAATEN

MARTHA SWOPE

The Tony Award for Best Musical went to *Ain't Misbehavin'*, based on the music of the late "Fats" Waller. The show opened originally at the Manhattan Theater Club.

Ballroom, too, had a curious history. It is based on Jerome Kass' television play, *Queen of the Stardust Ballroom,* about a widow who shocks her over-protective family by going dancing every night and finding an admirer. This project began under Michael Bennett's direction in the workshop of the Public Theater, where Bennett had directed *A Chorus Line.* Joseph Papp was reluctant to move it to Broadway, and so his associate of many years, Bernard Gersten, left Papp's organization to become one of the show's Broadway producers. Finally on Broadway, the dancing was expert and evoked nostalgia, and Dorothy Loudon and Vincent Gardenia were extremely winning in the leads, but the book is mawkish and all too reminiscent of television's high-minded but sentimental domestic dramas.

Hello, Dolly! was a revival of the classic musical, with Carol Channing shining in the role she created. *Timbuktu!* came close to being a revival of *Kismet,* with the same plot and much of the same music but with a change of locale to an ancient African capital; overproduction here overpowered even the insistent charm of Eartha Kitt. *A History of the American Film* was a loving, nostalgic burlesque of old film motifs. Alexis Smith supplied the only interesting elements of *Platinum* in her portrayal of a singing star of films trying to become a rock

singer; along with *Ballroom,* it testified to Broadway's continuing concern with the vitality of age. *King of Hearts,* drawn from a popular "cult" movie about a soldier in World War I who finds a lunatic asylum to be a happy refuge from war, dissipated its energies and even failed to make sufficient use of the considerable talents of Millicent Martin.

Plays. The most striking American play on Broadway was surely *Tribute,* by Bernard Slade (a native of Canada), a comedy drama in which Jack Lemmon movingly and resourcefully played a lovable failure of great charm; facing death and buoyed up by the love of his many friends, he still has to win the loyalty of his estranged son. The other most admired play of the year was Hugh Leonard's *Da,* an Irish work which came to Broadway by way of the Hudson Guild Theater. In this drama, a son's memory focused on the difficult, exasperating father of the title, played with great spirit by Barnard Hughes.

Not all transfers to Broadway succeeded. David Mamet's *The Water Engine,* a pleasant, modest entertainment, was a simulation of a 1930's radio drama about the mysterious disappearance of a man who has invented a machine that will run on water. Its success at the Public inspired inordinate expectations. A dramatic monologue, *Mr. Happiness,* was added to fill the evening, and *The Water Engine* set out on its ill-considered, brief journey to Broadway. Richard Wesley's *The Mighty Gents* originated in 1977 at the Manhattan Theater Club, where it was called *The Last Street Play.* On Broadway, this serious play about Harlem street gangs did not last a week. Another play of black life, Phillip Hayes Dean's *Paul Robeson,* came under fire from black groups for its alleged failure to deal frankly with all the controversial aspects of the late singer's life. After closing, *Paul Robeson* had a brief second life, playing in alternation with one of Joseph Papp's Broadway successes.

Other plays on Broadway were aimed more frankly at popular audiences. One which certainly achieved its aim was Ira Levin's *Deathtrap,* a comedy thriller which had its audience gasping as John Wood applied his energetic style to a portrait of a writer of mystery plays. Another was a new play about Sherlock Holmes, Paul Giovanni's *The Crucifer of Blood,* a free adaptation of Arthur Conan Doyle's *The Sign of Four.* Paxton Whitehead's Sherlock Holmes was suitably dedicated, even though Giovanni introduced elements that put Conan Doyle's values in question. But what was most distinctive about this play was its use of spectacular visual effects, including a dimly lit scene in which the audience was persuaded that boats were moving around the stage. *First Monday in October,* by Jerome Lawrence and Robert E. Lee, was a vehicle de-

signed to permit Henry Fonda to be seen to customarily good effect playing a Supreme Court justice who resembled William O. Douglas and to be paired with Jane Alexander as an ingratiating young reactionary colleague.

Broadway's three importations, in addition to *Da,* included David Williamson's *Players,* an Australian exposé of the cruel machinations that contribute to the operation of a football team. The two other plays about the romantic life of old people had charm but not much substance. They were: from England, *The Kingfisher,* by William Douglas Home, with Claudette Colbert, Rex Harrison, and George Rose, and, from Russia, Alexei Arbuzov's *Do You Turn Somersaults?,* with Mary Martin and Anthony Quayle.

As the year began, the English director Frank Dunlop started a new season with his company at the Brooklyn Academy of Music (BAM). He achieved a certain success with his productions of Shaw's *The Devil's Disciple* and Molnar's *The Play's the Thing* but ran into trouble when he deserted comedy and directed *Julius Caesar* with everyone cast against type. The BAM company staged Samuel Beckett's classic West Berlin production of his *Waiting for Godot;* the results were dubious. The Circle in the Square pursued a safer policy and presented four comedy classics—*13 Rue de l'amour,* by Feydeau; *Once in a Lifetime,* by Kaufman and Hart; Gogol's *The Inspector General;* and Shaw's *Man and Superman.*

Lester Rawlings, Brian Murray, and Barnard Hughes (*right*) star in the Tony Award-winning *Da,* the story of a son's desire to come to terms with his father and himself.

MARTHA SWOPE

BROADWAY OPENINGS OF 1978

PLAYS

Cheaters, by Michael Jacobs, directed by Robert Drivas; with Jack Weston, Lou Jacobi, Rosemary Murphy, and Doris Roberts; January 15–February 11.

The Crucifer of Blood, written and directed by Paul Giovanni, based on Conan Doyle's *The Sign of Four;* with Paxton Whitehead; September 28–.

Da by Hugh Leonard; directed by Melvin Bernhardt; with Barnard Hughes and Brian Murray; May 1–.

Deathtrap, by Ira Levin; directed by Robert Moore; with John Wood and Marian Seldes; February 26–.

Diversions and Delights, by John Gay, based on the works of Oscar Wilde; directed by Joseph Hardy; with Vincent Price; April 12–22.

Do You Turn Somersaults?, by Aleksei Arbuzov, translated from the Russian by Ariadne Nicolaeff; directed by Edwin Sherin; with Mary Martin and Anthony Quayle; January 9–21.

The Effects of Gamma Rays on Man-in-the-Moon Marigolds, by Paul Zindel; directed by A. J. Antoon; with Shelley Winters and Carol Kane; March 14–26.

First Monday in October, by Jerome Lawrence and Robert E. Lee; directed by Edwin Sherin; with Henry Fonda and Jane Alexander; October 3–December 9.

Gorey Stories, adapted by Stephen Currens; October 30.

The Inspector General, by Nikolai Gogol, translated from the Russian by Betsy Hulick; directed by Liviu Ciulei; with Max Wright, Theodore Bikel, and Helen Burns; September 21–November 19.

The Kingfisher, by William Douglas Home; directed by Lindsay Anderson; with Claudette Colbert, Rex Harrison, and George Rose; December 6–.

Man and Superman, by George Bernard Shaw; directed by Stephen Porter; with George Grizzard; December 14–.

The Mighty Gents, by Richard Wesley; directed by Harold Scott; with Dorian Harewood; April 16–23.

The November People, by Gus Weill; directed by Arthur Sherman; with Cameron Mitchell and Jan Sterling; January 10–16.

Once in a Lifetime, by Moss Hart and George S. Kaufman; directed by Tom Moore; with John Lithgow, Jayne Meadows Allen, George S. Irving, and Max Wright; June 15–August 27.

Patio/Porch, by Jack Heifner; directed by Garland Wright; with Fannie Flagg and Ronnie Claire Edwards; April 13–30.

Paul Robeson, by Phillip Hayes Dean; directed by Lloyd Richards; with James Earl Jones; January 19–February 26; reopened, March 9–April 30.

Players, by David Williamson; directed by Michael Blakemore; with Fred Gwynne and Rex Robbins; September 6–24.

Stages, by Stuart Ostrow; March 19.

Taxi, Taxi, by Leonard Melfi; directed by Edward Berkeley; with Julie De Laurier, Al Corley, Paula Christopher, and Dolly Jonah; December 28–31.

13 Rue de l'amour, by Georges Feydeau, translated and adapted from the French by Mawby Green and Ed Feilbert; directed by Basil Langton; with Louis Jourdan and Patricia Elliott; March 16–May 21.

Tribute, by Bernard Slade; directed by Arthur Storch; with Jack Lemmon; June 1–December 2.

The Water Engine and Mr. Happiness, by David Mamet; directed by Steven Schachter; March 6–19.

MUSICALS

Ain't Misbehavin', revue with music by "Fats" Waller; conceived and directed by Richard Maltby, Jr.; with Nell Carter, Andre De Shields, Armelia McQueen, Ken Page, Charlene Woodward; May 9–.

Angel, book by Ketti Frings and Peter Udell, from Ketti Frings' play *Look Homeward, Angel;* music by Gary Geld, lyrics by Peter Udell; directed by Philip Rose; with Don Scardino, Frances Sternhagen, and Fred Gwynne; May 10–14.

Ballroom, book by Jerome Kass, music by Billy Goldenberg, lyrics by Alan and Marilyn Bergman; directed and choreographed by Michael Bennett; with Dorothy Loudon and Vincent Gardenia; December 14–.

The Best Little Whorehouse in Texas, book by Larry L. King and Peter Masterson; music and lyrics by Carol Hall; directed by Peter Masterson and Tommy Tune; with Henderson Forsythe; June 19–.

A Broadway Musical, by Charles Strouse and Lee Adams; directed and choreographed by Gower Champion; with Warren Berlinger; December 21.

Dancin', directed and choreographed by Bob Fosse; with Ann Reinking; March 27–.

Eubie!, music by Eubie Blake, musical supervision by Danny Holgate; choreographed by Henry LeTang and Billy Wilson; conceived and directed by Julianne Boyd; with Gregory and Maurice Hines; September 20–.

Hello, Dolly!, based on Thornton Wilder's play *The Matchmaker;* music and lyrics by Jerry Herman; directed by Lucia Victor; with Carol Channing and Eddie Bracken; March 5–July 9.

A History of the American Film, revue by Christopher Durang; music by Mel Marvin; with April Shawhan and Swoosie Kurtz; March 30–April 16.

King of Hearts, book by Joseph Stein; based on the film directed by Philippe de Broca; music by Peter Link, lyrics by Jacob Brackman; directed and choreographed by Ron Field; with Millicent Martin and Don Scardino; October 22–December 3.

On the Twentieth Century, based on plays by Ben Hecht, Charles MacArthur, and Bruce Millholland; book and lyrics by Betty Comden and Adolph Green, music by Cy Coleman; directed by Harold Prince; with John Cullum, Madeline Kahn, and Imogene Coca; February 19–.

Platinum, book by Will Holt and Bruce Vilanch; music by Gary William Friedman, lyrics by Will Holt; directed and choreographed by Joe Layton; with Alexis Smith; November 12–December 10.

Runaways, written, composed, and directed by Elizabeth Swados; May 13–December 31.

Stop the World I Want to Get Off, book, music, and lyrics by Leslie Bricusse and Anthony Newley; with Sammy Davis, Jr., and Marian Mercer; August 3–27.

Timbuktu!, book by Luther Davis based on the musical *Kismet;* music and lyrics by Robert Wright and George Forrest from Alexander Borodin and African folk music; directed and choreographed by Geoffrey Holder; with Eartha Kitt, Melba Moore, Gilbert Price, and Ira Hawkins; March 1–September 10.

Working, adapted by Stephen Schwartz from the book by Studs Terkel; songs by Craig Carnelia, Micki Grant, Mary Rodgers, Susan Birkenhead, Stephen Schwartz, and James Taylor; directed by Stephen Schwartz; May 14–June 6.

Russian Plays. It was an unusual year for Russian impact on the American stage. Two Russian directors presented Russian plays at American regional theaters. At Houston's Alley Theater, Galina Volchek's production of Mikhail Roshchin's *Echelon,* a play about an evacuation in World War II, won more praise for its director than for its author. At the Guthrie Theater of Minneapolis, Anatoli Efros' playful rendering of Nikolai Gogol's comedy classic *The Marriage* was an unqualified success. At the Circle in the Square in New York, the Rumanian Liviu Ciulei directed an elaborate production of Gogol's *The Inspector General.* Michael Lessac won favorable attention at the Off-Off-Broadway Colonnades Theater by staging his own adaptation of Mikhail Bulgakov's early Soviet play *Molière in Spite of Himself.* Across the street at the Public Theater another Rumanian, Andrei Serban, directed a workshop version of his own dramatization of Bulgakov's novel *The Master and Margarita.* Meanwhile, the Arena Stage of Washington, which was the first American theater to show a consistent interest in the Soviet theater, offered *Duck Hunting,* a thoughtful comedy by one of the most admired of recent Soviet dramatists, Alexander Vampilov.

Off-Broadway. As usual, most of the new and interesting American plays made their appearance Off-Broadway. They included Sam Shepard's *The Curse of the Starving Class* and *Buried Child,* two studies of rustic grotesques, and at the Trinity Square Theater of Providence, *Seduced,* about Howard Hughes; Thomas Babe's *Fathers and Sons,* an antiheroic version of the legend of Wild Bill; Lanford Wilson's *The 5th of July,* depicting the problems of some surviving rebels of the 1960's; Dick Goldberg's *Family Business,* about four brothers in conflict; Arthur Kopit's *Wings* (first seen at the Yale Theater in New Haven, then at the Public, presumably scheduled for Broadway in 1979), about a woman who has had a stroke; Marsha Norman's *Getting Out,* about a young woman released from jail and trying to go straight; and Ernest Thompson's *On Golden Pond,* about an old couple who become reconciled to life and death. Luis Valdez' *Zoot Suit,* about Chicanos in 1942, was staged at the Mark Taper Forum in Los Angeles. The play was scheduled to open on Broadway in March 1979.

At the end of the year Eli Wallach and Anne Jackson (Mrs. Wallach) opened in a revival of the 1955 Pulitzer Prize winning play *The Diary of Anne Frank.* The title role was played by their daughter Roberta, and the role of Anne Frank's sister Margot was played by the Wallach's other daughter, Katherine.

The Stratford Theater of Connecticut returned to life with a coolly received production of *Twelfth Night.* At Stratford, Ontario, artistic director Robin Phillips was taken ill and cancelled some late openings in what was going to be the busiest season in the festival's history (a

COURTESY, GUTHRIE THEATER

The Guthrie Theater in Minneapolis offered Henrik Ibsen's *The Pretenders,* staged by Alvin Epstein.

season that included Maggie Smith in *As You Like It* and *Macbeth*). Subsequently Phillips resigned but was persuaded to confine his absence to a year's leave.

England. In England, the principal dramatists continued to write—Harold Pinter, *Betrayal,* about another romantic triangle; Tom Stoppard, *Every Good Boy Deserves Favor,* about an East European dissident, intended to be performed with a symphony orchestra, and *Night and Day,* about journalists in an African revolution; Edward Bond, *The Woman,* a novel view of the Trojan War; and David Hare, *Plenty,* a study of postwar disillusionment. And yet, at the end of the year a critics' prize went to a new writer, Brian Clark, for *Whose Life Is It, Anyway?,* a moving portrait of an invalid who asks to die. The biggest event in the popular theater was *Evita,* by Tim Rice and Andrew Lloyd Webber, directed by Harold Prince, a politically ambiguous musical about Juan Peron's first wife. The ambition of the National (which presented the new plays by Pinter, Bond, and Hare) continued to be enormous, and yet the Royal Shakespeare Company still rendered splendid service, easily surpassing the National's Albert Finney in *Macbeth* with its own Alan Howard in *Coriolanus.* Late in the year, Peter Brook returned to the Royal Shakespeare to direct Howard and Glenda Jackson in an uncut *Antony and Cleopatra* that offered few of the innovations expected by Brook's public.

HENRY POPKIN
State University of New York at Buffalo

TOKYO

Economic Woes. Despite an inflation rate of only 4% in 1978, Tokyo remains the world's most expensive city. While it is especially so for Americans and other foreign visitors, the residents of Tokyo pay more for their daily necessities than any other urban population in the world.

Moreover, this bustling city teeters on the brink of bankruptcy, and the fiscal year ending in March 1979 seems the worst ever. The annual shortfall is estimated to be about (U. S.) $1.4 billion. The money-strapped Metropolitan Government even started selling 4,058 plots of its land, worth $451 million. But the measure has been largely unsuccessful; by late 1978, only $58 million worth of land had been sold.

Governor. The year 1978 was not rosy for Gov. Ryokichi Minobe, who served his 12th year in office. Besides Tokyo's ailing economy, the socialist- and communist-backed governor had other worries. His ruling parties in the assembly lost their majority, and opinion polls showed that his popularity was down. The gubernatorial election is scheduled for April 1979, but Minobe announced long before that he would not run.

Crime. Despite all its problems, Tokyo is a safe place to live. A woman can walk alone at night without fear of being mugged. In 1977, there were only 229 murders and 337 rapes in a city of 8.5 million inhabitants.

Miscellaneous. A 787-ft (240-m) building, "Sunshine 60," was opened in downtown Tokyo in 1978. Equipped with the world's fastest elevators, this 60-story office tower rises higher than any other building in Asia. In July, the Sumida River fireworks festival was revived after 17 years of suspension. With the help of 4,900 firemen and policemen, 15,000 fireworks of various designs and colors were launched into the skies of Tokyo.

HIROTAKA YOSHIZAKI
"The New York Times," Tokyo

TORONTO

One of the most significant events for Toronto in 1978 took place on July 1, when the Ontario Municipal Board approved a controversial plan to allow the city government to control high-rise development in the downtown area. This plan, the only one of its kind to be approved in a North American city, also forces a mixture of offices, apartments, and stores in the city's core. Approval came just before Mayor David Crombie resigned to enter federal politics and was the capstone to his five-and-one-half years in office. Fred Beavis, his interim successor, became the first Roman Catholic mayor in the city's history.

Transportation. In January 1978, the new (C.) $220 million Spadina Subway was opened, but because of a series of delays and breakdowns the number of riders in the first few months was lower than hoped. In March, the commuter "GO" trains were upgraded by the addition of two-level passenger cars, increasing the capacity of each car by 68 seats. Two months later, the first northbound commuter line was established.

Education. It was another bleak year for the Toronto public school system. Declining enrollment brought about continued cutbacks in teaching staffs. Similar problems plagued education at the university level. The University of Toronto was forced to lower its entrance requirements for the Faculty of Arts and Sciences to make up for decreased admissions. In March there was a major student rally in front of the Provincial Legislature in Toronto to protest cuts in government aid to colleges and universities.

Miscellaneous. In April 1978, the Sun Life Assurance Company decided to move its head office from Montreal to Toronto because of restrictive language legislation in the Province of Quebec.

The crash of an Air Canada DC-9 at the Toronto airport in June killed two people.

ERIC JARVIS, *University of Western Ontario*

COURTESY, ROY MITCHELL PHOTOGRAPHY

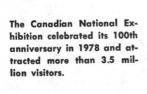

The Canadian National Exhibition celebrated its 100th anniversary in 1978 and attracted more than 3.5 million visitors.

TRANSPORTATION

The overall economic setting for transportation in the United States was good in 1978. The nation enjoyed relative prosperity and a decreasing rate of unemployment. Evidencing the prosperity the stock market enjoyed the most vigorous days of trading in history. Such robust economic activity is a good sign for a derived-demand industry such as transportation. Because no one ships anything and few travel except for some good purpose, the greater the level of prosperity the greater the movement of goods and people by the transportation industry of the nation. Most of the modes of transportation had their resources strained by heavy traffic.

For years the United States has muddled along without a clear and definite statement of transportation policy. Instead, the nation has continued its traditional method of meeting transportation ills by providing given cures for given problems. Still very much needed is the marriage of a coherent and rational transportation policy, with clearly stated goals and objectives.

If the economy was buoyant, the weather struck terrible blows to the transportation system of the nation. The winter of 1977–78 was in many ways even more devastating than the one that preceded it. Not only were there interruptions in service, particularly of the passenger railroads in the Northeast, but there was severe damage to rail equipment, with great delays in the movement of freight. The highways were also battered by the winter weather, and the spring thaw tore apart highways which, in many cases, had been only indifferently patched after the ravages of the winter of 1976–77.

Ships and Shipping. The water carriers continued to enjoy the advantage of publicly provided facilities for which they need not pay any user charge. In 1978 Congress, supported by the Carter administration, enacted a controversial tax on the fuel used by the inland waterways. As finally approved, the bill combined creation of a waterway trust fund, supported by a barge fuel tax, with the construction of a new dam and lock on the Mississippi River at Alton, Ill.

The water carriers enjoyed a tremendous upsurge in the movement of grain as shippers sought to move two years' crops which had been stored, due to low prices. The lack of regulation of most inland water carrier rates permitted the carriers to move that commodity at higher prices.

British shipping industries continued to founder as British Shipbuilders, Ltd., reported a loss of $85 million for the period July 1, 1977, to March 31, 1978, the first nine months as a nationalized company.

The USSR nuclear-powered icebreaker *Sibir* successfully opened a new Arctic Ocean shipping route when it led a cargo ship from the western Soviet Arctic port of Murmansk to Magadan on the Sea of Okhotsk, May 5–June 12, 1978. The 3,360-nautical-mile (6,223-km) trip, aided by tracking and weather satellites, extended the regular Arctic shipping season of July–August by two months.

A West German dock workers' strike, January 25–30, virtually halted all traffic at West Germany's major ports. In Australia, dock workers staged job actions from mid-April until June 5, seriously disrupting traffic in Sydney and Melbourne harbors. Protest stoppages also occurred at Brisbane, Fremantle, and Adelaide.

Pipelines. Interest in coal slurry pipelines—slurry is a mixture of half water and half ground coal—was high in 1977 and continued in 1978. But a General Accounting Office study showed that while slurry pipelines were, indeed, quite feasible as a means of moving large quantities of coal, the railroads would have little trouble in moving that commodity, and the additional coal movements would be a valuable contribution to the revenues of the financially malnourished rail carriers.

The Alaska pipeline continued to operate with few problems through 1978. The trouble with moving the Alaska oil was not the Alaska pipeline but the absence of means of moving the oil from the west coast of the United States to inland points.

Highway Transportation. The trucking business experienced a boom because of the strong demand for consumer goods. Most motor carriers enjoyed record demands for their services. Yet, while the revenues of most trucking carriers rose to high levels, higher costs cut seriously into those revenues. All segments of the industry were not so prosperous as the amount of business handled might have seemed to indicate.

Truckers continued to fight a Carter administration proposal to deregulate much of the motor carrier industry. They made much of the point that smaller cities and towns would be likely to lose good trucking service if the carriers were not obliged to serve them as regulated carriers. The specters of rate cutting like that of the days before the Motor Carrier Act of 1935, and of the devastation that would be worked on the large firms by the rate cutting practices of marginal operators in the industry hovered over the motor carrier discussions.

Trucking company management made a determined effort to increase the fuel efficiency of their equipment. Cab-mounted air deflectors, more efficient engines, and more efficient trailer designs were adopted. The results of the effort and investment were mixed because of the difficulty of getting truck drivers to observe the 55-mile (88-km) per hour speed limit.

The intercity motor bus companies, dominated by Greyhound and Trailways, did not have a good year. The actual number of passengers carried by the intercity bus lines, even though larger than the number moved by all the rest of the intercity for-hire passenger carriers put together, continued to decline. To help make up for the loss in traffic, the operators raised fares. This drove prospective customers, particularly from the lower-income segment of the market, away from the intercity bus system. The Interstate Commerce Commission recognized this and refused to allow the bus companies to raise fares as high as they proposed.

Low-price bus fare schemes worked well in generating additional passengers in some markets, but these promotional efforts failed when fare cuts produced revenue far below expectations. Meanwhile, the fare cuts introduced by the airlines included some air fares that were highly competitive with bus fares.

Greyhound believed that only 18% of its route miles were profitable from passenger operations. Package freight and the charter business continue to be the profitable side of the intercity bus business. Despite the rise in demand for both services in 1978, other burdens on the intercity bus industry made it difficult to afford new equipment as the average age of intercity buses continued to advance.

The intercity bus industry kept up its campaign against subsidies to AMTRAK, the federally supported railroad corporation, at the same time calling for subsidies for itself from both state and federal levels of government.

U. S. highways continued to deteriorate at an alarming pace, especially the heavily traveled Interstate System. Much of the blame was placed on heavily loaded trucks, which in many states reached a gross weight of 80,000 pounds (36,-287 kg). The states found they had insufficient funds to do the necessary maintenance and repairs. The problems were especially severe in the Northeast and Midwest where the winter weather had taken its toll. Federal legislation was proposed that would provide funds for maintenance, and many states considered raising taxes to pay for highway repair.

Air. Booming is the word that best describes the airline business in 1978. Much of this was due to the policy of the Civil Aeronautics Board (CAB), under chairman Alfred E. Kahn, permitting airlines to experiment with discount fares without the prior permission of the CAB. The year 1978 began with a noteworthy lowering of some transatlantic fares, an action that was soon followed by U. S. domestic airlines seeking to fill seats. They succeeded beyond all expectation. (In October Kahn resigned to become chairman of the Council on Wage and Price Stability.)

As the discount fare plans bloomed in the spring of 1978 airlines were concerned that fare reductions would not be profitable. However, by midsummer it was obvious that revenues were climbing far faster than costs, and more and more seats were filled on existing flights. Some airline stocks rose in response to the profits.

Prior to adjourning in October, Congress passed an airline deregulation bill. Major provisions of the legislation included: the elimination of CAB control over airline routes by the end of 1981, allowing the airlines themselves to decide on routes; the end (Jan. 1, 1983) of CAB's authority to set fares; and the simplification of merger procedures. By Jan. 1, 1984, the CAB is to recommend whether the regulatory agency should be continued beyond Jan, 1, 1985. If it is discontinued, its functions are to be assumed by the departments of justice and transportation and the U. S. Postal Service. President Carter signed the bill into law on October 23.

An on-going worry for the airlines is the need to replace equipment. Federal environmental law demands that airlines reduce airplane engine noise and particle pollutants at the same time that they increase the fuel efficiency. Although buying new planes or retrofitting old ones is a lengthy and costly endeavor, the industry took

COURTESY, GMC

General Motors delivered advance-design buses to the Public Transit Corporation in Long Beach, Calif.

COURTESY, MCDONNELL DOUGLAS

In the debate over the best design for 1980's aircraft, the McDonnell Douglas DC-9 Super 80 and the Lockheed L-1011 had their supporters.

COURTESY, LOCKHEED

some major steps designed, in part, to meet federal requirements.

In July United Airlines announced plans to purchase 30 Boeing 767 jetliners at a cost of $1.2 billion. The 767 was described by Boeing as the first of a new generation of airliners—twin-engine 757 and 767, and tri-engine 777—which would match the airlines' short-, medium-, and long-haul and varying capacity needs for the next decade. By contrast, both Lockheed and Mc-Donnell Douglas seemed to believe that their already operative trijets—the L-1011 and the DC-10—would prove to be correctly sized for the coming decade. But whatever their projections, the airframe manufacturers were moved by the 1978 traffic surge to put new emphasis on schemes to modify, by expansion or contraction, both the range and the capacity of their transports, whether extant or still on the drawing boards. For their part, the airline operators were rethinking their long-term equipment needs.

U. S. plane manufacturers met strong competition from Airbus Industries—a German, French, British, and Spanish combination—which managed to win a contract to supply 30 planes for Eastern Airlines. The Airbus, which was already in production, was the first major foreign competition for the U. S. airframe industry in many years. American manufacturers were somewhat cheered by large orders for their equipment from Japan and other eastern countries, but the worry persisted that competition from foreign planes would grow.

In September, Pan Am and National Airlines announced a merger agreement, subject to CAB approval. Observers felt that National's domestic routes—mainly along the east coast—would nicely complement the international routes of Pan Am. A merger agreement in principle was announced by Continental and Western airlines. If approved by the CAB, the new company would become the nation's seventh largest airline.

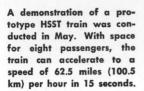

A demonstration of a prototype HSST train was conducted in May. With space for eight passengers, the train can accelerate to a speed of 62.5 miles (100.5 km) per hour in 15 seconds.

UPI

On August 15, Northwest Airlines, the 7th largest commercial airline in the United States, announced the end of a 109 day strike by its pilots.

On September 25, a Pacific Southwest Airlines Boeing 727 and a Cessna 172 collided in midair. The collision, occurring above a residential neighborhood 5 miles (8 km) from San Diego's Lindbergh Field, took 144 lives. It also raised serious questions about the safety of small private craft flying in airspace heavily congested with large commercial planes.

Rail. Earnings figures for 1977 showed that U. S. railroads as a whole earned only 1.2% return on investment. Nineteen seventy-eight proved to be no better; the hard winter was a severe blow to railroads operating throughout the Northeast and Midwest. Operating costs increased and lines were closed by heavy snow. A lengthy coal strike substantially cut coal loadings, affecting the principal commodity that the railroads move. The hard winter and the coal strike combined to produce high costs and low revenues, resulting in severe deficits during the first quarter of 1978. U. S. railroads lost $274,000,-000, the largest quarterly deficit in history. Even the usually prosperous Chessie System (The Chesapeake & Ohio and the Baltimore & Ohio) and Norfolk and Western suffered as the coal strike greatly diminished their overall traffic. At the end of September a strike of the Brotherhood of Railway and Airline Clerks against the Norfolk and Western spread across the nation. President Carter took action under the Railway Labor Act and ordered the strikers back to work after appointing an emergency board to investigate the matter and report back in 30 days. An additional 30-day cooling off period delayed any return to the picket lines until after Thanksgiving.

The end of winter and the coal strike produced a substantial rise in traffic. But as the demand to ship both coal and grain increased, it became evident that there were not enough grain cars to move what amounted to two years' harvest at once. Shippers, unhappy, were forced to use truck and water transportation. Shipper complaints brought an Interstate Commerce Commission (ICC) investigation and fines on railroads for failing to provide enough cars. Some coal mines were forced to shut down and coal mines in eastern Kentucky lost contracts because of inability to deliver.

CONRAIL—the Consolidated Rail Corporation—experienced equipment shortage due to the poor condition of cars and locomotives that it had obtained from bankrupt rail companies. This, in combination with the severe winter and the coal strike, caused CONRAIL's deficit to increase beyond expectation, postponing its projected break-even point from 1979 to 1980. To bolster CONRAIL, in late 1978 Congress authorized $1.2 billion in subsidies over the next five years. The first president of CONRAIL, Richard Spence, resigned unexpectedly in June.

Despite CONRAIL's continuing problems, enormous improvements were made in property. Hundreds of miles of all-welded rail were laid during 1977 and 1978, and millions of crossties were replaced. Massive rebuilding of cars and locomotives took place and large quantities of new cars and locomotives were ordered. Projections for 75,000 new railway car orders in 1978 buoyed the industry.

When the Milwaukee Road entered bankruptcy in December 1977, the bankruptcy trustee sought to reduce the physical plant that was too big for the company's traffic. In late summer the Milwaukee proposed the abandonment of most of its line to the Pacific coast west of Butte, Mont. The line was completed in 1916.

AMTRAK's operating deficit increased to new highs while Congress and the administration seemed reluctant to supply the bail-out funds. In the spring, Secretary of Transportation Brock Adams issued a report on AMTRAK that called for a reduction in route structure and schedules. If adopted, route mileage would be cut from 27,000 to 18,900 miles (43,452 to 30,416 km). The move would reduce AMTRAK's deficit from $665 million to $547 million. Congress agreed to freeze AMTRAK's routes until the fall of 1979 and to provide the lion's share of AMTRAK's needed support. AMTRAK President Paul Reistrup resigned and was replaced by Alan Boyd, the first secretary of transportation and former president of the Illinois Central Gulf Railroad.

In the USSR work continued on the BAM (Baikal-Amur Railway). The line, covering a 1,965-mile (3,162-km) expanse of wilderness in Siberia, runs from the town of Ust-Kut near Lake Baikal to Komsomolsk in the east, 565 miles (995 km) north of Vladivostok. BAM, north of the Trans-Siberian Railway, is expected to be completed in 1983 at a cost of $15 billion.

In France, the French National Railways moved to extend its electrification and was pressing to export its expertise and technology.

In Canada, VIA Rail Canada started operations. The new rail passenger carrier, similar to the U. S. AMTRAK, will operate a service combining the trains of the Canadian Pacific and Canadian National railroads.

Mass Transit. Transit ridership, continuing the trend started in 1973–74, increased. Many cities enjoyed large increases in patronage. New York City, however, lost many riders as a reflection of the falling number of jobs in the city. The size of the New York City transit market is so great that its softness held down the total nationwide increases to modest proportions.

Streetcars were delivered to both Boston and San Francisco in 1978. Great interest will be attracted by the operation of these light rail vehicles, because it appears that between now and the end of the century many of the major capital improvements in mass transportation will be by means of light rapid transit rather than through the construction of heavy, completely grade-separated rapid transit systems.

Manufacturers of transit equipment did not have a good year. The uncertainty about federal

Construction of Atlanta's major new rapid transit system advances.
COURTESY, METROPOLITAN ATLANTA RAPID TRANSIT AUTHORITY

rules and regulations mandating low floor buses was to blame. AM General Corporation and Mercedes Benz left the North American bus business. The AM General Corporation may return to bus building; in only five years in the bus business it had managed to capture a third of the market. Mercedes Benz was marketing a small bus that had proven attractive to small city transit operations and in special uses. Mercedes did not feel that it was worthwhile to re-engineer its vehicles in order to meet federal rules and regulations.

New types of advance-design buses were being delivered, however. The first of these was delivered to Public Transit Corporation in Long Beach, Calif., by General Motors. Flxible-Grumman delivered its first order of new-design buses to Atlanta.

Construction of heavy rapid transit systems continued in Washington and Atlanta. In late August, Secretary Adams took a position favoring construction of the entire 100-mile (160-km) Washington system. The airport line, linking Washington National Airport with downtown Washington, is so far the most successful in attracting riders. Indeed, the whole Washington rapid transit system now open to the public is carrying far more than the expected number of patrons.

Construction of the Atlanta rapid transit system continued. The first part of the system was scheduled to open on Christmas Day 1978. Atlanta has managed to keep on schedule and within cost estimates, truly a noteworthy achievement.

The San Francisco Bay Area Rapid Transit District extended subway service to seven days a week and added evening service.

The 1978 Congressional session also passed "the first total surface transportation bill." Approximately $51 billion was authorized for federal highway–mass transit aid programs for the next two to four years. In addition, the Highway Trust Fund was extended for five years.

In Great Britain the continued operation of the High Speed Trains attracted more patrons to British rail intercity service in 1978. The east coast route from London to Edinburgh recorded a 10% traffic increase after the addition of the new trains. The new higher speed Advanced Passenger Train was unveiled prior to testing.

Toronto added six new streetcars designed by Ontario's Urban Transportation Development Corporation. The cars, built in Switzerland, will act as prototypes for 190 new streetcars to be produced by Hawker-Siddeley at Thunder Bay, Ontario. Meanwhile, Edmonton, Alberta, opened a new 4.5 mi (7.2 km) light rapid transit line using cars built in Germany. The Edmonton opening marks the first new electric railway service in Canada in many years.

GEORGE M. SMERK
Professor of Transportation
Indiana University

TRAVEL

There has never been a year for travel quite like 1978. Travelers fanned out across the world in record numbers, the travel industry showed historic profits, and rules that have governed travel for decades crumbled.

Air Travel. The increase in air travel was phenomenal, thanks mainly to the proliferation of somewhat confusing but economical discount fares on both domestic and international routes. U. S. domestic air traffic increased approximately 20%, with the pace picking up early. Major airlines earned substantial profits—approximately $73 million—during the first quarter of the year, normally a poor one. This was the first really profitable first quarter for U. S. airlines in a decade. A severe winter over much of the country was credited for the heavy traffic, particularly to Florida and the Caribbean.

But travel was heavy during the summer, too. An estimated 3 million people flew domestic carriers during the fourth of July weekend, making it the biggest weekend in U. S. civil aviation history. Most U. S. scheduled airlines set traffic records. As a whole they earned an estimated record of (U. S.) $19.9 billion. International air travel rose, too, particularly on transatlantic routes where the multiplication of discount and excursion fares created a virtual price war. Summer saw very heavy air traffic, with passenger increases of nearly 20% common.

Bargain and promotional fares on the Atlantic run, particularly between New York and London, contributed to passenger volume and added to the widespread public confusion about airfares. The most intricate rate structure was on the New York-London route, which also had the most bargains. By mid-June, passengers had no less than 18 different fares to choose from. The lowest fare was the $149 round trip between Boston and Amsterdam offered by Pan American. The fare was introduced June 15 and withdrawn a month later, following chaotic scenes which saw angry passengers storming ticket counters after being stranded for days at Holland's Schiphol Airport.

A more orderly situation prevailed in London in early summer as hundreds of would-be passengers, mostly young backpackers, camped out in improvised "Lakervilles" for days until they could get aboard the Laker Airways "Skytrain" to New York. Freddie Laker, the ebullient British charter airline operator, whose no-frills, one-way, first-come, first-served Skytrain service sparked the price war in the airways, was awarded a knighthood by Queen Elizabeth. On September 26, Sir Freddie inaugurated similar service between London and Los Angeles at fares of $162 westbound and $220 eastbound.

So many passengers were flying with discount tickets that full fare passengers, mostly businessmen, were grumbling. In response, several airlines, notably British Airways and Trans World

PHOTOS U.S. TRAVEL SERVICE

U. S. Travel Service posters encourage foreigners to visit the United States. Camping and backpacking in such areas as California's Sierra National Forest (*below*) remain popular.

WAYNE WOODRUFF

Air travel booms. Long lines at airports throughout the world were quite common during 1978.

PAT ZIMMERMAN

Airways (TWA), introduced a three-tiered price system, separating full fare economy/coach passengers from those holding discount tickets and offering them a few extras such as choice of meals and speedier luggage handling.

Icelandic Airlines, not a member of the International Air Transport Association (IATA), had traditionally offered the lowest fares across the Atlantic. To meet the discount fare competition, Icelandic introduced a simplified budget fare of $149.50, one-way New York-Luxembourg, with no advance reservations, maximum or minimum stay, or other restrictions.

And, in a move to revive the supplemental carrier industry, the Civil Aeronautics Board (CAB) eliminated virtually all restrictions on charters, creating a new entity called a "public charter." Despite their simplicity and flexibility —one way or round trip, no advance purchase or minimum or maximum stay requirement—the public seemed to prefer discount fares to public charters. In a further move to aid charter operators, the CAB indicated that it would relax its ban on supplemental carrier operators owning tour companies.

The most significant action of the year was the congressional decision to "de-regulate" the civil aviation industry. The board will continue to set a ceiling on airfares, but carriers can raise them by as much as 10% without board approval and can reduce them up to 70%.

Reflecting President Carter's belief that competition would result in lower fares and improved efficiency, the CAB let a number of domestic carriers, such as Delta and Braniff, fly the Atlantic, and encouraged competition on domestic routes. Pan Am and National sought permission to merge, a $350 million transaction.

International Travel. The state of the U. S. and Canadian dollars was a major factor affecting travel in 1978. Western Europe's currencies generally remained solid, and Europeans found travel abroad increasingly cheaper. As a result, 26 million Germans vacationed outside their country in 1978. More than 20 million international travelers visited the United States, an increase of 7% over 1977.

Cruises. Cruise ships continued to be popular, particularly in the Caribbean. An attempt by Venture Cruise Lines to offer budget cruises to "nowhere" on the *America* ended abruptly when passenger complaints of overcrowding and unsanitary conditions forced the ship to turn back to New York on its initial voyage. The Italian Line's *Marconi* returned to New York after an absence of many years. The line began a cruise program to the Caribbean in mid-December.

The U. S. government increased traveler's duty free allowances from $100 to $300 for goods bought in foreign destinations, and from $300 to $600 for items purchased in U. S. insular possessions, such as the Virgin Islands.

WILLIAM DAVIS, *The Boston Globe*

China now welcomes visitors. *Below:* Western tourists try on fur coats in a friendship store in Peking.

ALEX LANGLEY, DPI

TUNISIA

Simmering discontent of organized labor over the stagnating economy and the Tunisian government's authoritarian rule, starting with widespread strikes in late 1977, culminated in the first nationwide general strike on Jan. 26, 1978. A bloody confrontation, in which more than a hundred people were killed and over a thousand arrested, it plunged the country into its worst political crisis. But after government repression of militants in the trade union movement, Prime Minister Hedi Nouira, constitutional successor to ailing President-for-life Habib Bourguiba, apparently emerged with his power consolidated.

General Strike. Tunisia's only trade union confederation, the 650,000-member General Union of Tunisian Workers (UGTT), called the January strike ostensibly in protest over attacks on union offices, allegedly by progovernment goon squads, and arrests of trade unionists. But the strike turned into an explosion of anger over the rule of Bourguiba's one-party regime, the Destourian Socialist Party (PSD). A month before the strike, Interior Minister Tahar Belkhodja, who had urged conciliation toward the unions and greater freedom of expression, was dismissed from the cabinet. Five other government ministers resigned in sympathy.

In the strike's aftermath, the government arrested more than 1,000 people, including UGTT general secretary Habib Achour and other union leaders, accusing them of plotting the violent overthrow of the government with the help of outside forces.

Achour had been a member of the PSD political bureau and of its central committee, but in late 1977 rank and file activism forced the union to break with the PSD and the UGTT developed into the de facto opposition to the government. The Bourguiba regime then launched a campaign against the UGTT, charging it had been infiltrated by "leftists and crypto-fascists," and proposed a purge of the union executive. Following the detentions of union leaders in early 1978, the entire dozen-member UGTT executive was replaced and the trade union movement was purged of militants.

Trials. Several hundred people were tried and sentenced to prison terms of up to ten years

--------- **TUNISIA • Information Highlights** ---------

Official Name: Republic of Tunisia.
Location: North Africa.
Area: 63,170 square miles (163,610 km²).
Population (1978 est.): 6,000,000.
Chief City (1975 census): Tunis, the capital, 550,404.
Government: *Head of state,* Habib Bourguiba, president-for-life (took office 1957). *Chief minister,* Hedi Nouira, prime minister (took office Nov. 1970). *Legislature* (unicameral)—National Assembly.
Monetary Unit: Dinar (0.413 dinar equals U. S.$1, Sept. 1978).
Manufactures (major products): Crude oil, phosphates, olive oil, textiles, construction.
Agriculture (major products): Wheat, olives, grapes, citrus fruits, truck crops, and fish.

after the general strike. The length of the pretrial detentions provoked international concern. Amnesty International, the human rights organization, charged that some detainees were tortured, and the death in prison of one union leader was attributed to maltreatment.

The major trial of Achour and 29 colleagues did not take place until October. Although the government, which alleged that arms caches had been found at UGTT offices, sought to hold the trial in criminal court, the court referred the case to the State Security Court, which judges political cases. The defense had maintained that the trials were political.

After an eight-day trial, the court found Achour and 23 others guilty of plotting to overthrow the government. The state asked for the death penalty, but the court meted out sentences ranging from six months to ten years, with Achour getting ten years at hard labor.

Succession. President-for-life Bourguiba, 75, spent most of 1978 in Paris, seeking medical treatment. Prime Minister Nouira's crushing of the opposition apparently gave him, as leader of the hardline group, the clear edge in the jockeying for succession.

JOSEPH MARGOLIS, *"African Update"*
African-American Institute

TURKEY

After Prime Minister Süleyman Demirel resigned on Dec. 31, 1977, President Fahri Kuruturk called on former Prime Minister Bülent Ecevit of the Republican People's Party to head the governing coalition. The coalition also included representatives of the Republican Reliance Party and the Democrat Party. The new government announced on January 4 that it would protect and strengthen the republic as a "national, democratic, secular and social state based on human rights," as stipulated in the Turkish Constitution. A dynamic foreign policy would promote Turkey's national rights in the Aegean Sea and seek to ensure the "continued freedom and security of Turkish Cypriots." The government would spare no effort, as announced on January 17, to assist in the creation in Cyprus of a bizonal, bicommunal, independent, non-aligned federated state. Internal security and public order continued to plague both Demirel and Ecevit. A total of 159 persons were killed between January and May 1978. Colleges and universities, especially in Istanbul and Ankara, were closed for varying lengths of time.

On December 26 the Ecevit government declared martial law in Istanbul and other cities to end three days of street fighting. Dozens of people were killed in the political-religious clashes.

Economy. The economic situation in Turkey deteriorated further during 1977–78. By March 1978, prices had increased by 56.2% over the 1976 level. Unemployment reached 3,200,000 (20%) at the beginning of 1978. The trade

Bülent Ecevit, who became prime minister of Turkey as 1978 began, addresses the UN General Assembly.

deficit stood at about (U. S.) $4 billion and the Turkish lira (TL) had to be devalued. During the first few months of his administration, Prime Minister Ecevit introduced several measures to stabilize the economy, including limitations on foreign travel by Turkish citizens; foreign currency allowances were reduced by 50%. The budget was limited to TL 264 billion and planners envisaged an economic growth rate of 6.1% in 1978. This compared with the 5% rate of 1977 and the 10% demanded by some Turkish leaders. Exports were to be expanded by 45.5%, to reach (U. S.) $2.55 billion in 1978, while imports were to be fixed at $5 billion. Maximum interest rates on medium- and long-term loans were raised on Feb. 28, 1978, to 16%.

Foreign Relations. As Prime Minister Ecevit indicated upon taking office in January 1978, Turkey pursued a dynamic foreign policy, looking toward peace with its Balkan and Arab neighbors and the solution of the Aegean and Cyprus problems with Greece. In May 1978, Ecevit visited Washington, D. C., to discuss Turkish-American relations, which had been strained since the landing of some 40,000 Turk-

ish troops on the island of Cyprus in July 1974 and the American embargo of arms shipments to Turkey. Following favorable action by the U. S. Congress in July and August, President Carter lifted the arms embargo, and on October 4 Turkey agreed to reopen four bases which the United States had used for electronic intelligence monitoring.

Prime Minister Ecevit also visited West Germany May 10–13 to discuss economic relations. Among other things, a loan of 130 million Deutsche Marks (DM) was negotiated.

The fact that Turkey expressed its intention to play a fully integrated role in NATO did not militate against a visit of the Chinese foreign minister (June 12–15). Moreover, several agreements were signed as a result of Ecevit's visit (June 21–25) to the USSR. The final joint communiqué stressed a peaceful note. The USSR endorsed intercommunal talks on Cyprus in the hope of promoting a political settlement of that dispute. A Black Sea agreement on fishing and mineral rights, it was thought, might serve as a model for solution of similar problems in the Aegean. Under a new trade agreement, the USSR will supply Turkey 3 million tons of crude oil annually in exchange for wheat, processed minerals, and other raw materials. A declaration of friendship, reaffirming the principles of a similar 1972 agreement, also was signed. However, the declaration does not have the force of a treaty and does not affect Turkey's commitments under NATO.

HARRY N. HOWARD, *Middle East Institute*

TUVALU

Tuvalu, the world's second smallest nation, celebrated its independence on Oct. 1, 1978. The official ceremonies in Funafuti, with Lord Napier representing Queen Elizabeth, brought to an end 86 years of British colonial rule.

The eight islands of Tuvalu, formerly known as the Ellice Islands, have a population of fewer than 10,000. Because of limited resources—mainly sea harvest and coconut palms—independence required financial backing. The British government provided (U. S.) $12.5 million as a farewell gift, about $2 million of it as budgetary funds and the remainder as development aid to be spent over three years. Australia also provided funds and pledged further support.

Independent Tuvalu will continue to be part of the British Commonwealth, with a governor general (Penitala Teo) possessing reserve powers and a Westminster-style parliamentary system. The latter faces the task of absorbing the strong

---

TURKEY · Information Highlights

Official Name: Republic of Turkey.
Location: Southeastern Europe and southwestern Asia.
Area: 306,870 square miles (794,793 km²).
Population (1978 est.): 42,200,000.
Chief Cities (1975 census): Ankara, the capital, 1,704,-004; Istanbul, 2,547,364; Izmir, 636,834.
Government: *Head of state,* Fahri Korutürk, president (took office April 1973). *Head of government,* Bülent Ecevit, prime minister (took office January 1978). *Legislature*—Grand National Assembly: Senate and National Assembly.
Monetary Unit: Lira (25.25 liras equal U. S.$1, Sept. 1978).
Manufactures (major products): Textiles, processed foods, mining.
Agriculture (major products): Cotton, tobacco, cereals, sugar beets, fruit, nuts.

TUVALU · Information Highlights

Location: Southwest Pacific.
Area: 9.5 square miles (24.6 km²).
Population (1978 est.): c. 10,000.
Chief City: Funafuti, the capital.
Government: *Head of state,* Elizabeth II, queen; represented by Penitala Teo, governor general. *Head of government,* Toalipi Lauti, prime minister.

traditions of island-village councils. Another task of the new government will be to maintain unity within the scattered island group.

Prime Minister Toalipi Lauti, who during the final colonial phase showed less trepidation about independence than others around him, quickly opened exploratory discussions with U. S. officials in the hope of entering a treaty covering the defense and economic development of the islands. Soon after Tuvalu's independence, Lauti confidently joined the Niue meeting of the South Pacific Forum.

R. M. YOUNGER, *Australian Author*

UGANDA

The bloody and erratic rule of President Idi Amin continued in 1978, largely because of the record-high price of coffee, Uganda's major export.

Internal Affairs. Despite predictions of his overthrow and at least 13 assassination attempts, Amin tightened his hold on Uganda. His power was buttressed by some 15,000 Nubian troops on loan from the Sudan. The Ugandan army itself was still being purged of soldiers and officers whom Amin felt to be potentially disloyal. The murders and expulsions extended even to the dreaded State Research Bureau, the secret police who have been running Amin's internment and mass-murder camps for years. Reports on the camps and prisons describe conditions and practices nearly identical with those of Nazi Germany.

Among the more prominent victims were Robert Scanlon, an Englishman thought to be one of Amin's closest advisors, who was beaten to death in prison; and Vice President and Defense Minister Gen. Mustafa Adrisi. Adrisi, a close ally of Amin for all eight years of his rule, was badly injured in a suspicious car crash in April and reportedly flown to Cairo for treatment, but he was not heard of thereafter.

Religion. Although only 6% of Ugandans are Muslim, Amin continued his campaign to Islamize the country "at any price." He continued to remove Christians from government posts, made Friday the major weekly holiday, and announced a ban on all Christian churches save the Roman Catholic, Anglican, and Ortho-

dox. Although Amin himself barely practices the Muslim faith, he has made it a test of loyalty to his regime. Most civilians killed or arrested in Uganda are Christian; whatever their involvement in anti-Amin activities, Christians are always the first to be taken in any crackdown.

Economy. The boom in world coffee prices sustained Amin's regime in 1978; coffee represents 93% of Uganda's total exports. Terror and looting by the army, secret police, and high government officials, however, virtually destroyed the internal economy, and basic consumer goods often were unobtainable. Over $500 million worth of coffee was exported in 1978, but much of the income was lost through theft and smuggling.

Foreign Affairs. Uganda continued to be shunned by most African leaders, who find Amin an embarrassment to the continent. Attempts to censure or investigate the Amin regime were defeated or sidetracked in the UN and the Organization of African Unity (OAU).

Late in the year, fighting along the Uganda-Tanzania border was reported. On November 1, Uganda reported that its forces captured 710 square miles (1,839 km²) of Tanzanian territory. The villainous Amin captured headlines when he challenged Tanzanian President Julius Nyerere to a boxing match to resolve the dispute.

In the U. S. Congress, there were calls for a ban on all private trade with Uganda, a ban on the importation of Ugandan coffee, and the expulsion of the Ugandan *chargé d'affaires* (on grounds of spying).

ROBERT GARFIELD, *De Paul University*

————**UGANDA** • Information Highlights ————

Official Name: Republic of Uganda.
Location: East Africa.
Area: 91,134 square miles (236,037 km²).
Population (1978 est.): 12,700,000.
Chief City (1976 est.): Kampala, the capital, 410,000.
Government: *Head of state and government,* Gen. Idi Amin, president-for-life (assumed power Feb. 1971). *Legislature* (unicameral)—National Assembly (dissolved Feb. 1971).
Monetary Unit: Shilling (7.669 shillings equal U. S.$1, Aug. 1978).
Manufactures (major products): Processed agricultural products, steel, copper, cement, shoes, fertilizer, beverages.
Agriculture (major products): Coffee, tea, cotton, tobacco.

UPI

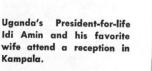

Uganda's President-for-life Idi Amin and his favorite wife attend a reception in Kampala.

TASS FROM SOVFOTO

The Soviet delegation arrives in Bonn; a Soviet-German economic cooperation pact was later signed.

USSR

Cool U. S.-Soviet relations, exemplified by U. S. restrictions on trade and scientific exchange in response to the trials of Soviet political dissidents, prevailed in 1978. Disarmament negotiations continued throughout the year, but no SALT II (Strategic Arms Limitation Talks II) treaty was concluded. Both countries also tried and convicted each other's alleged spies.

Soviet-Chinese relations, bad for 20 years, deteriorated further in 1978, mainly because of the USSR's anxiety over Communist China's hostility toward Vietnam and rapprochement with Japan and the United States.

Within the USSR, the Soviet government imprisoned many dissidents and tried to disrupt groups in several major cities who were monitoring Soviet lack of compliance with the human rights provisions of the 1975 Helsinki Pact of Security and Cooperation in Europe. Meanwhile several spectacular Soviet space flights set new world records, and the USSR reaped the largest grain crop in Russian history.

FOREIGN AFFAIRS

United States. Friction between the United States and USSR began early in 1978 and continued throughout the year. During March, the Soviet government asked the United States for a treaty mutually renouncing the manufacture of neutron bombs—small nuclear weapons which the United States was planning to produce. But in April, when President Jimmy Carter unilaterally decided that the United States would

not produce the neutron bomb, the USSR refused to match his peaceful act by any Soviet concession in the SALT II negotiations.

Relations worsened in May when U. S. officials arrested Vladimir P. Zinyakin, an attaché of the Soviet Mission to the United Nations, and Rudolph P. Chernyayev and Valdik A. Enger, two Soviet employees of the UN Secretariat, for espionage. Because of his diplomatic immunity, Zinyakin was immediately expelled from the United States. During October, a U. S. court sentenced each of the other two Soviet citizens to 50 years in prison.

In May, Soviet electronic listening devices were discovered in the chimney of the U. S. Embassy in Moscow. A protest was lodged with the Soviet government, but the reply was that the devices were American machinery monitoring Soviet radio-telephone transmissions.

During June, the Soviet government expelled two American guides from the U. S. agricultural exhibit touring the USSR. Both were accused of making anti-Soviet statements while the exhibit was on display in the Ukrainian city of Kiev.

Despite his company's sale of $300 million worth of machinery to the USSR during the previous four years, F. Jay Crawford, Moscow representative of the U. S. International Harvester Company, was arrested by Soviet police in June for alleged smuggling and currency speculations. In September, he received a five-year suspended sentence from a Moscow court and was expelled from the USSR.

In July, a bomb planted by unknown persons exploded in the New York office of *Intourist*, the Soviet travel agency. No one was injured.

In July, a Moscow court ruled that Craig R. Whitney and Harold D. Piper, Moscow correspondents for *The New York Times* and *The Baltimore Sun,* respectively, each had to pay $1,647 in court costs and publish retractions of previous articles concerning a convicted Soviet Georgian nationalist, Zviad Gamsakhurdia. Whitney and Piper had reported that Gamsakhurdia did not actually make the confession shown on Soviet television. In August, the reporters finally agreed to pay the court costs but refused to publish the retraction. The court then closed the case, and both reporters were allowed to remain in the country.

Meanwhile, because of the numerous trials of Soviet dissidents seeking human rights, trade and scientific relations with the United States deteriorated. During May, 38 U. S. scientists cancelled their planned visits to the USSR in protest against the Moscow trial of a Soviet dissident scientist. When the trials of Soviet dissidents continued, President Carter, in July, cancelled the planned visits of two U. S. government scientific delegations to the USSR, stopped the $6.8 million sale of a huge U. S. computer to the Soviet news agency TASS, and ordered a U. S. military team not to participate in the world helicopter contests taking place in the USSR. In August, a dozen U. S. geneticists voluntarily refused to attend the International Conference of Genetics in Moscow.

In October, because of the numerous Soviet restrictions hampering operation of its Moscow office, Pan American Airways terminated its ten years of Moscow-New York service, thus ending the only U. S. airline activity in the USSR.

Among the few cases of U. S.-Soviet cooperation during 1978 was the installation of a new Moscow-Washington "hot line." The previous radio-cable system was replaced by a space satellite connection, which would allow faster communication in time of crisis.

In October, at the request of the United States, a Soviet trawler rescued ten U. S. naval aviators from the north Pacific Ocean, where their reconnaissance plane had been downed by engine failure.

In an unusual request, the U. S. government in November asked the Soviet government to restrain Vietnam from invading Cambodia.

Europe. Soviet relations with most European nations were harmonious in 1978. The USSR concluded cultural exchange pacts with Finland and Norway, consular and cultural exchange treaties with Greece, an agreement on Baltic Sea fishing with East Germany, and a 25-year treaty of economic cooperation with West Germany.

In contrast, the Belgrade Conference on European Security and Cooperation concluded in March after eight months of unfruitful debate. None of the major issues dividing East and West were resolved. The United States and

Leonid Brezhnev signs autographs after decorating the six Salyut 6 cosmonauts with hero medals. The Soviet president called the space work "a remarkable new step in unraveling the mysteries of the universe."

UPI

other Western democracies accused the Soviet Union of violating human rights, while the USSR declared that arms limitation was a more important issue which should not be jeopardized by such accusations. At the insistence of the Soviet bloc of European nations, the conference's final communiqué ignored the issue of human rights.

In June, Vladimir Rezun, a Soviet diplomat in the office of the United Nations in Geneva, defected to Great Britain. The next month, Arvids Jurksha, a Soviet scientist, was recalled from Britain by the Soviet government after being arrested for hooliganism on an English train.

As part of the Sino-Soviet dispute, the USSR condemned Communist China's cessation of technical aid to Albania and the anti-Soviet speeches by Chinese Premier Hua Kuo-feng during his visits to Rumania and Yugoslavia in August.

Middle East and Asia. In an effort to increase its influence in the Middle East, the USSR concluded a technical aid pact with Pakistan, a cultural exchange agreement with Cyprus, and treaties with Turkey on trade, nonaggression, cultural exchange, and fishing rights and oil prospecting in the Black Sea.

The USSR welcomed a coup in Afghanistan on April 28, which brought the Communist-led People's Democratic Party of Afghanistan into power. During the spring, new Soviet-Afghan technical aid pacts helped bolster the new Kabul government. A 20-year treaty of friendship and cooperation was signed in December.

Throughout the year, Soviet leaders publicly disapproved of all peace negotiations between Egypt and Israel. The Soviet government took the position that Egypt was betraying other Arab nations. In March, it strongly denounced the brief Israeli invasion of Lebanon. The Soviet Red Cross immediately sent bandages and medication to aid the ravaged Palestinians in that country.

Syrian President Hafez al-Assad visited the USSR during both February and October, and on each occasion was promised more shipments of Soviet arms to strengthen Syrian troops on the Israeli frontier.

Relations between the USSR and Communist China began badly, when in January, the Soviet press condemned what it described as an invasion of Vietnam by Cambodian troops allegedly trained, armed, and advised by Communist Chinese military officers. During February, the USSR proposed to China a joint Sino-Soviet statement of mutual peaceful coexistence. China rejected the proposal unless the Soviet army was withdrawn from Mongolia and the Sino-Soviet frontier, which the USSR refused to do.

On May 11, China protested to the USSR that two days earlier a Soviet helicopter and 18 naval boats allegedly crossed the Ussuri River border between China and Siberia and landed 30 Soviet soldiers on Chinese soil. The soldiers were accused of shooting and wounding several Chinese residents and beating 14 others. China demanded a Soviet apology and punishment of the guilty soldiers. The USSR replied that a Soviet river patrol chasing armed criminals accidentally landed on a Chinese riverbank thinking it was a Soviet river island, and after discovering their error, withdrew without harming anyone.

As hostilities between China and Vietnam increased during the summer, the Soviet press began to criticize the Chinese Communist government for inciting Vietnamese Chinese against the Vietnam regime, for ending its technical aid to Vietnam, and for instigating clashes on the Sino-Vietnam frontier.

The Council of Mutual Economic Assistance (CMEA), which included the USSR, Cuba, the Eastern European bloc, and Mongolia, added Vietnam to its membership. On November 2, as Sino-Vietnamese tension increased, the USSR and Vietnam concluded a 25-year treaty of friendship. The treaty included a clause that the two countries would mutually consult and cooperate if either were attacked or threatened.

In January, the USSR offered to conclude a nonaggression treaty with Japan, but the Japanese refused because the draft pact ignored their request for the return of four islands north of Japan which the USSR seized at the end of World War II. The Soviet Union violently disapproved of a treaty of friendship between Japan and China. The Soviet press described it as a "dangerous alliance."

An unusual accident occurred on April 20, when a South Korean passenger plane en route from Paris to Alaska suffered navigational instrument trouble, turned back from the Arctic Ocean into Soviet air space, and was shot down by a Soviet fighter plane 280 miles (450 km) south of the Arctic seaport of Murmansk. Gunfire from the Soviet fighter killed two passengers, badly injured two others, and hurt 11 more. A U. S. plane was allowed passage to Murmansk to evacuate the survivors. In its description of the incident, the Soviet press did not mention that any passengers were injured or killed.

Africa. The USSR concluded two technical aid treaties with Benin, trade and technical aid pacts with Morocco, and friendship, cultural exchange, trade, and technical aid agreements with Ethiopia. All together, the USSR rendered technical aid to 27 African countries, of which more than 18 were receiving Soviet arms. In addition, the USSR openly admitted that it was arming black guerrillas fighting the white governments of Rhodesia and South Africa.

In May, Soviet President Leonid I. Brezhnev publicly announced his disapproval of French aid to Chad and of the U. S.-French-Belgian aid to Zaire. The aid was to help suppress provincial revolts in those two African countries. The USSR insisted that no Soviet arms were being sent to provincial rebels in Zaire.

Latin America. In an effort to woo Latin American governments, the USSR in 1978 signed

PHOTOS UPI

Weddings in the headlines: Olympic gymnast Olga Korbut, *above*, married rock singer Leonid Bortkevich; Christina Onassis, Greek shipping heiress, took Sergei Kausov, former Soviet Merchant Marine official, as her husband.

a trade pact with Jamaica, a technical aid pact with Mexico, and cultural exchange, fishing and trade agreements with Guyana. In all, ten Latin American nations received technical aid from the Soviet Union. The principal recipient continued to be Cuba, where the USSR was building or rebuilding 93 industrial projects.

In the autumn, the Soviet government expressed its sympathy with the rebel cause in the Nicaraguan civil war.

Canada. Although Soviet-Canadian trade was satisfactory, political relations worsened in February when Canada expelled 12 Soviet diplomatic, consular, and trading personnel on grounds of espionage. In June, a Moscow court sentenced Asta Sokov, a Canadian citizen, to eight years in a prison camp for allegedly trying to smuggle $43,000 worth of jewelry out of the USSR.

SPACE AND DEFENSE

Space Program. In January, the Soviet space program suffered a setback when an unmanned reconnaissance satellite, with 100 pounds (45 kg) of uranium fuel in its nuclear motor, crashed in northwest Canada, disintegrating in the atmosphere as it fell. A search team of U. S. and Canadian scientists found several highly radioactive fragments in the crash area. In the autumn, the USSR launched two other unmanned rockets which eventually landed on the planet Venus.

A series of successful manned flights began on Dec. 10, 1977, when Soyuz 26, with Georgi Grechko and Yuri Romanenko aboard, was lofted into space. Soyuz 26 docked with the Salyut 6 space station on December 11. Next, on Jan. 10, 1978, Soyuz 27 was launched with Vladimir Dzhanibekov and Oleg Makarov aboard. Dzhanibekov and Makarov docked their craft with Salyut 6 on January 11 and returned to earth on January 16. Progress I, an un-

manned supply rocket, went aloft on January 20, docked with Salyut 6 on January 22, refueled the space station, and then disconnected to disintegrate in the atmosphere. On March 2, Soyuz 28, staffed by Aleksei Gubarev, a Soviet, and Vladimir Remek, a Czech, was launched. Soyuz 28 docked with Salyut 6 on March 3 and returned to earth on March 10. The original Soyuz 26 crew finally returned to earth on March 16.

A string of similar feats began on June 15 with the launching of Soyuz 29. The crew of Vladimir Kovalenok and Alexander Ivanchenkov, who docked their craft with Salyut 6 on June 17 and did not return to earth until November 2, set a world record of 140 days in space. While in the space station they were visited from June 28 to July 5 by the crew of Soyuz 30, Pyotr Klimuk and Miroslaw Hermaszewski (a Pole), who then returned to earth. A similar visit from August 27 to September 3 was made by the crew of Soyuz 31, Valery Bykovsky and East German Sigmund Jaehn. Three more unmanned supply rockets refueled the space station during the summer and fall.

In addition to the world record for longevity in space, these flights marked the first successful use of supply rockets, the first time two rockets were simultaneously attached to a space station, and the first flights into space by astronauts who were not U. S. or Soviet citizens.

Armed Forces. In 1978, the Soviet armed forces comprised about 4,400,000 men. In terms of equipment, the USSR ranked first in the world in number of tanks, intercontinental ballistic missiles, submarine-based and medium-range missiles, medium-range bombers, and submarines. But Soviet armament lagged behind the United States in number of aircraft carriers, long-range bombers, tactical nuclear weapons, and total nuclear warheads. In the autumn, President Brezhnev publicly admitted that the Soviet

UPI

American newsmen Hal Piper (*left*) and Craig Whitney
were questioned and subjected to court costs by the
USSR for articles on a Georgian nationalist.

Union had once produced an experimental
neutron bomb.

In February, Soviet paratroops carried out
maneuvers near the Polish border, with military
observers from Belgium, France, Great Britain,
Holland, Switzerland, West Germany, and the
United States permitted to observe.

Government and Politics. Death claimed several prominent Soviet personalities during 1978:
68-year-old Mstislav V. Keldysh, the head of
Soviet space research, on June 24; Fyodor D.
Kulakov, 60, one of the youngest members of
the Soviet party Politburo, on July 17; and 83-
year-old Anastas Mikoyan, former Soviet president, vice-premier, and Politburo member, on
October 21 (*see* Obituary, page 379).

Although obviously in poor health, 72-year-
old Leonid Brezhnev remained the top Soviet
leader in 1978. He held simultaneously the positions of president, secretary-general of the Soviet
Communist party, and chairman of the Soviet
Defense Council. During the year, he received
special decorations from Bulgaria, Peru, and the
USSR, published two additional volumes of his
selected works, and had his portrait printed on
a new Soviet postage stamp.

Dissidents. During 1978, Soviet courts took
strong measures to break up dissident groups,
which in several regions were collecting data on
the government's lack of compliance with the
human rights provisions of the 1975 Helsinki
Pact. Among the dissidents punished in 1978
were Miroslav Marinovich and Mikola Matuse-
vich, both of the Ukraine, each sentenced to 7
years in prison; Yuri F. Orlov, of Moscow,
7 years in prison; Aleksandr Ginzburg, Moscow,
8 years; Viktoras Petkus, Lithuania, 10 years;
and Anatoly B. Shcharansky, Moscow, 13 years.
Meanwhile, untold numbers of Soviet Jews desir-
ing to leave the Soviet Union were imprisoned
or sent into internal exile.

In March, retired Gen. Pyotr G. Grigorenko,
world famous cellist Mstislav Rostropovich, and
the latter's wife, opera star Galina Vishnevskaya,
were all deprived of their Soviet citizenship while
temporarily living abroad and forbidden to return
to the USSR. Whereas the general was a severe
critic of the Soviet regime, neither of the two musicians was a dissident, although both of them
did express their sympathy with the human rights
campaign.

The most startling defection by a Soviet
citizen in 1978 was by Arkady N. Shevchenko,
a UN undersecretary-general heading the Department of Political and Security Affairs. In
April he refused to return to the USSR and was
forced to resign from his post at the UN. The
Soviet government claimed that he had become
a prisoner of U. S. intelligence agencies.

The request in December of Kirill Kondrashin for asylum in the Netherlands was a blow to
Soviet cultural prestige. As the conductor of the
Moscow Philharmonic, Kondrashin had, over
two decades, established a world reputation for
the Soviet showcase orchestra.

Minorities. In 1978, the individual Soviet republics comprising the USSR adopted new constitutions to conform with the national constitution
adopted in late 1977. In April, mass demonstrations in Tbilisi, the capital of Georgia, forced
the local government to insert a paragraph in its
new constitution ensuring that Georgian would
remain the official language of the republic.

Religion. When Pope Paul VI died in August,
the Russian Orthodox Church delegation attending his funeral was led by Metropolitan Nikodim
of Leningrad, who died on September 5 while
conversing with Paul's newly-elected successor,
John Paul I. Official harassment of organized
religion continued in the USSR, with the Bud-
dhists, Seventh Day Adventists, Pentecostalists,
and Jews being the main targets.

Culture and Education. The USSR boasted
that it had one third of the world's newspaper
circulation, one fourth of the world's scientists,
and one third of its doctors.

In January, a new law doubled the number of
hours spent on manual job training in Soviet

───── **USSR · Information Highlights** ─────

Official Name: Union of Soviet Socialist Republics.
Area: 8,649,540 square miles (22,402,308 km²).
Population (1978 est.): 261,000,000.
Chief Cities (Jan. 1977): Moscow, the capital, 7,819,-
000; Leningrad, 4,425,000 Kiev, 2,079,000.
Government: *Head of state,* Leonid I. Brezhnev, presi-
dent (took office June 1977). *Head of government,*
Aleksei N. Kosygin, premier (took office Oct. 1964).
Secretary general of the Communist party, Leonid
I. Brezhnev (took office 1964). *Legislature*—Supreme
Soviet: Soviet of the Union, Soviet of Nationalities.
Monetary Unit: Ruble (0.75 ruble equals U. S.$1, 1977;
0.66 ruble equals U. S.$1, 1978 tourist rate).
Manufactures (major products): Minerals, ferrous and
nonferrous metallurgy, fuels and power, building
materials, chemicals, machine building.
Agriculture (major products): Wheat, rye, corn, oats,
linseed, sugar beets, sunflower seeds, potatoes,
cotton and flax, cattle, pigs, sheep.

high schools, increased the number of school workshops, and required students to perform more manual labor during summer vacations and the regular school year.

ECONOMY

Industry. Soviet industrial production increased by about 5% in 1978, compared with 5.7% in 1977. The slowdown admittedly was due to such industrial problems as under-utilized machinery, inefficient management, and a shortage of labor, especially in Siberia. Yet the USSR still ranked first in the world in output of coal, oil, iron, steel, cement, locomotives, and machine tools.

Agriculture. Despite adverse weather conditions, the USSR reaped a grain harvest of about 235 million metric tons, the largest in Russian history and about 15 million tons above the expected amount. The Soviet Union ranked first in the world in output of cotton, flax, wheat, and milk.

To improve crops further, a new law in the summer of 1978 cancelled (U. S.) 7.3 billion rubles of collective and state farm debts to the Soviet government, exempted from income tax all collective farms whose annual profits were below 25%, and, as of Jan. 1, 1979, raised the government purchase price of milk, wool, mutton, potatoes, and vegetables produced on collective farms. Also, collective and state farms would henceforth pay as much as 50% of the cost of building private homes for their peasant workers.

Transportation. In 1978, Soviet railways controlled 11% of all the railroad track in the world but transported 25% of the world's railway passengers and 53% of world rail freight. The Soviet merchant marine was the eighth largest in the world and competed vigorously with Western shipping companies, which complained that Soviet ships underpriced their capitalist competitors.

In November, a Soviet railway car ferry began operating across the Black Sea between the USSR and Bulgaria.

Aeroflot, the Soviet government-controlled airline, claimed to be the largest in the world. It operated regular flights to 3,600 cities in the Soviet Union and 100 cities in 81 foreign countries. An admitted problem of domestic flights was that only 40% of Soviet airports were equipped with paved runways.

Trade. In April, the Soviet government adopted new customs regulations forbidding the importation of gold; rubles; and any books, magazines, newspapers, films, photographs, manuscripts, phonograph records, pictures, or sound tapes "detrimental to the USSR politically and economically."

In 1978, the USSR was the world's largest exporter of raw materials and gave technical assistance to 40 foreign countries.

Standard of Living. Despite continual economic growth, the standard of living in the Soviet Union remained mediocre. There were store shortages of meat, eggs, milk, fruit, vegetables, shoes, clothing, and furniture. Housing was cramped, and there were not enough telephones. In March, the Soviet press estimated that the annual per capita income was only $1,973, compared with $2,670 in France, $3,270 in West Germany, and $4,345 in the United States.

See also AFRICA; ARMS CONTROL; MILITARY AFFAIRS; SPACE EXPLORATION.

ELLSWORTH RAYMOND
Professor of Politics
New York University

TASS FROM SOVFOTO

President Brezhnev enjoys a laugh with a group of railroad workers. Soviet industrial production increased by about 5% in 1978.

UPI

The UN Security Council votes to retain the UN peacekeeping force in Lebanon for an additional month.

UNITED NATIONS

For the United Nations, 1978 was a year of building. In most major areas of the UN's political and economic involvement, diplomatic frameworks were constructed or sustained against the threat of collapse. The mechanisms that emerged from this painstaking multilateral process were significant in themselves. But in each case the tests of their ultimate utility were postponed until the future.

The General Assembly staged a spectacular and star-studded Special Session on Disarmament in May and June, but its principal achievement—beyond returning the arms race to the spotlight of world public opinion—was a restructuring of the permanent negotiating machinery on disarmament.

Five Western nations (the United States, Britain, Canada, France, and West Germany), acting through the Security Council, put forth a detailed plan for granting independence to the territory of Namibia through UN-supervised elections. As the year ended, the future of Namibia hung in the balance and with it the credibility of Western policy toward Africa.

In the Cyprus dispute and in the economic dialogue between the industrialized nations and the Third World, the UN pumped new life into negotiating mechanisms that had been threatened by stalemate.

The organization's traditional preoccupation with the Middle East continued throughout 1978, but its impact was diminished by the emphasis on negotiations between Egypt and Israel outside the sphere of the UN. On March 19, the Security Council created its third Middle East buffer force, this one in southern Lebanon.

General Assembly. The major event in the 33rd year of the UN was the General Assembly's Special Session on Disarmament (May 23–June 30), the first global conference on arms limitations in four decades. It attracted high-ranking speakers from 126 nations, including U. S. Vice President Walter Mondale and the prime ministers of Britain, Canada, West Germany, France, and India. What emerged from the conference was an agreement to revive the UN Disarmament Commission—composed of all UN members—and to broaden the Geneva negotiating forum, renamed the Committee on Disarmament. The chairmanship of the Geneva committee, which had been held jointly by the United States and Soviet Union, would now rotate among all 40 members. This led France to reenter the forum, leaving China as the only nuclear power unrepresented.

The regular Assembly session opened on September 19. It elected Colombian Foreign Minister Indalecio Lievano as its president, admitted the Solomon Islands as its 150th member (later, Dominica became the 151st), and settled down to an agenda of 129 familiar items.

In 1977, the assembly had established the Committee of the Whole on Global Economic Issues as the major forum for dialogue between rich and poor nations. But on Sept. 8, 1978, the committee suspended its first session because of a procedural stalemate over the extent of the body's power to reach substantive decisions. A compromise finally was reached on October 19. It defined the committee's mandate to hold negotiations on fundamental economic issues which "shall be expressed in agreed conclusions of practical content."

During the assembly debates on the Middle East and the related question of Palestine, numerous attacks were leveled by the Arab nations and their supporters on the accords reached by Egypt and Israel at Camp David. On December 7, the assembly adopted a resolution stating that any Middle East agreement must include the Palestine Liberation Organization (PLO) and affirm the Palestinian right to sovereignty. The vote was 97 to 19, with 25 abstentions. On the same day, an omnibus resolution on the Middle East was adopted by a vote of 100 to 4, with 33 abstentions. This measure called for the reconvening of the Geneva peace conference, a comprehensive settlement, total Israeli withdrawal from occupied territories, and recognition of Palestinian rights. One week later, an Iraqi proposal calling for a total arms embargo against Israel was adopted, 72 to 30, with 37 abstentions.

Among the other decisions taken by the assembly were a measure censuring Nicaragua for the repression of its civilian population, and an agreement to reconvene the 33rd session in 1979 if the Security Council proved unable to take effective action to secure the independence of Namibia. Resolutions were adopted on Rhodesia, apartheid, Cyprus, Belize, Western Sahara, East Timor, and a "new world information order."

Security Council. The council spent most of its efforts in 1978—both in public meetings and behind-the-scenes consultations—on the question of Namibia. The Western plan for independence, presented in March, was accepted by South Africa on April 25 and by SWAPO, the Namibian liberation movement recognized by the UN, on July 12. A 50-man UN team toured the territory in August, and Secretary General Kurt Waldheim submitted his detailed proposal for implementation of the Western plan on August 31.

The plan called for a 7,500-man UN Transition Assistance Group (UNTAG), 360 policemen, and 1,200 civilians to supervise the elections, at a cost of about $300 million. The timetable called for a cessation of hostilities, withdrawal of most South African occupation troops, the release of political prisoners and the return of exiles, elections under UN supervision, the adoption of a constitution, and, finally, independence —all within seven months.

What seemed like a diplomatic triumph for the West quickly turned sour. On September 20, South Africa rejected the Waldheim report and scheduled internal elections for December that would exclude SWAPO. Nevertheless, on September 29, the Security Council endorsed the Waldheim proposals. On November 13, the council called upon South Africa to cancel the elections under the threat of economic sanctions. The five Western nations abstained from voting on this measure.

The elections produced an expected victory for the coalition backed by Pretoria. South Africa, carefully maintaining ambiguity about its ultimate intentions, promised to press the victors to cooperate with the United Nations. This allowed the West to delay consideration of sanctions until 1979.

Earlier in the year, the council took action on the Rhodesia question after the announcement of an "internal settlement" between black leaders and the white minority regime of Ian Smith. On March 14, the council adopted a resolution, with the five Western nations again abstaining, that condemned the internal settlement as a maneuver to allow the "racist minority" to retain power.

On the following day, members of the Arab League sent a message to Waldheim urging the UN to halt the Israeli invasion of southern Lebanon. On March 19, the Security Council adopted an American resolution establishing the UN Interim Force in Lebanon (UNIFIL). Its first objective was achieved with the final Israeli pullback on June 13. An uneasy peace was restored in early October, after the council unanimously called for an end to the violence so that "national reconciliation" could take place "on the basis of unity, territorial integrity, and independence." At year's end, the final objective of UNIFIL—the restoration of Lebanese authority in the south—had not been achieved in areas controlled by the Christian militia of Lt. Col. Saad Haddad. Waldheim publicly laid the blame on Israel for thwarting this goal and encouraging Haddad's intransigence.

The council also helped lay the groundwork for a new round of negotiations between feuding Greek and Turkish Cypriots. On November 15, it established a six-month time limit for intercommunal talks on Cyprus under the aegis of Secretary General Waldheim.

Secretariat. To promote the UN's role in the development of Third World nations and to enhance the power of those nations in the UN, Kenneth Dadzie of Ghana was named on March 14 to the newly created post of director general for development and international economic cooperation.

On April 14, citing "differences with his government," the top-ranking Soviet member of the Secretariat, Undersecretary for Political and Security Council Affairs Arkady Shevchenko, took a leave of absence. He later resigned his post and took asylum in the United States.

UPI

In February, Dinh Ba Thi, Vietnam's ambassador to the UN, was expelled from the United States.

On October 31, Cambodia invited the secretary general for a visit, in the hope that his presence might head off the escalating border conflict with Vietnam. Two days later, the United States formally brought the fighting to the attention of the Security Council. At year's end, Secretary General Waldheim indicated that he intended to make the trip.

The growing politization of the Secretariat became an issue when Israel and a number of Western countries protested the activities of a unit set up to promote Palestinian rights. A film on that topic prepared by the UN Office of Public Information was withheld after both Israel and the PLO complained that it was unbalanced. The film was to have been the centerpiece of the UN's first "International Day of Solidarity with the Palestinian People," which was celebrated on November 29. Demonstrations supporting and opposing the PLO were staged outside UN headquarters.

The politization issue again arose when the General Assembly decided to create a governmental committee to oversee the output of the Office of Public Information. Also, staff members of the Secretariat staged a slowdown on December 15 to protest a new limitation on the promotion of career employees. They charged that the restriction was designed to reserve high Secretariat positions for outsiders sponsored by foreign governments.

Economic and Social Council. The council held three sessions in 1978 under the chairmanship of Donald Mills of Jamaica. It called for more aid to 15 African nations facing severe hardship and to various national liberation movements.

The Commission on Human Rights, a subsidiary body, revealed nine countries that had been named for "gross" violations of human rights—Bolivia, Equatorial Guinea, Ethiopia, Indonesia, Malawi, Paraguay, South Korea, Uganda, and Uruguay. At the request of Great Britain, the commission also discussed allegations of massive human rights violations by the government of Cambodia.

A UN committee that had been investigating the violation of rights in Chile was allowed to visit that country for the first time on July 13. In November it reported to the General Assembly that the situation in Chile had improved but that violations continued.

Trusteeship and Decolonization. The Trusteeship Council, meeting in May, continued to press for a unitary government in the last territory under its jurisdiction—the Trust Territory of the Pacific Islands (Micronesia), which is administered by the United States. The council agreed to send observers to the July 12 referendum in the territory, in which voters in the Marshall Islands and the Palau district opted for separate status.

The special committee on decolonization considered the situations in Namibia, Rhodesia, Puerto Rico, and a number of smaller states. The debate on Puerto Rico in September attracted speakers from virtually every political faction in that commonwealth, despite continued opposition by the United States to UN involvement. A resolution by Cuba finally was adopted by a vote of 10 to 0, with 12 abstentions. It called for the complete sovereignty of the Puerto Rican people and charged the United States with obstructing the quest for independence.

Legal Activities. The UN Conference on the Law of the Sea held two sessions in 1978. It met for a total of 12 weeks to consider six "hard-core issues" ranging from mineral rights to curbs on pollution. No breakthroughs were reported.

A special committee established to draft a convention outlawing the taking of hostages held its first meeting in 1978. But the talks quickly were stalemated over the issue of whether national liberation movements should be exempted from such a ban. The General Assembly called for a renewed effort regarding international terrorism in 1979.

UNESCO. On November 22, the UN Educational, Scientific, and Cultural Organization unanimously approved a compromise declaration on worldwide press information. The declaration eliminated from an earlier document a controversial passage calling for state control of the media. The final text endorsed the principle of freedom of information and called on developed nations to help improve the world news organizations of the Third World.

See also Feature Article on Terrorism, pages 44–51; LAW: INTERNATIONAL.

MICHAEL J. BERLIN, *"New York Post"*

ORGANIZATION OF THE UNITED NATIONS

THE SECRETARIAT

Secretary General: Kurt Waldheim (until Dec. 31, 1981)

THE GENERAL ASSEMBLY (1978)

President: Indalecio Liévano Aguirre (Colombia). The 151 member nations were as follows:

Afghanistan	German Democratic	Norway
Albania	Republic	Oman
Algeria	Germany, Federal	Pakistan
Angola	Republic of	Panama
Argentina	Ghana	Papua-New Guinea
Australia	Greece	Paraguay
Austria	Grenada	Peru
Bahamas	Guatemala	Philippines
Bahrain	Guinea	Poland
Bangladesh	Guinea-Bissau	Portugal
Barbados	Guyana	Qatar
Belgium	Haiti	Rumania
Belorussian SSR	Honduras	Rwanda
Benin	Hungary	São Tomé and
Bhutan	Iceland	Príncipe
Bolivia	India	Saudi Arabia
Botswana	Indonesia	Senegal
Brazil	Iran	Seychelles
Bulgaria	Iraq	Sierra Leone
Burma	Ireland	Singapore
Burundi	Israel	Solomon Islands
Cambodia	Italy	Somalia
Cameroon	Ivory Coast	South Africa
Canada	Jamaica	Spain
Cape Verde	Japan	Sri Lanka (Ceylon)
Central African	Jordan	Sudan
Empire	Kenya	Surinam
Chad	Kuwait	Swaziland
Chile	Laos	Sweden
China, People's	Lebanon	Syria
Republic of	Lesotho	Tanzania
Colombia	Liberia	Thailand
Comoros	Libya	Togo
Congo	Luxembourg	Trinidad and Tobago
Costa Rica	Madagascar	Tunisia
Cuba	Malawi	Turkey
Cyprus	Malaysia	Uganda
Czechoslovakia	Maldives	Ukrainian SSR
Denmark	Mali	USSR
Djibouti	Malta	United Arab Emirates
Dominica	Mauritania	United Kingdom
Dominican Republic	Mauritius	United States
Ecuador	Mexico	Upper Volta
Egypt	Mongolia	Uruguay
El Salvador	Morocco	Venezuela
Equatorial Guinea	Mozambique	Vietnam
Ethiopia	Nepal	Western Samoa
Fiji	Netherlands	Yemen
Finland	New Zealand	Yemen, Democratic
France	Nicaragua	Yugoslavia
Gabon	Niger	Zaire
Gambia	Nigeria	Zambia

COMMITTEES

General: Composed of 25 members as follows: The General Assembly president; the 17 General Assembly vice presidents (heads of delegations or their deputies of China, Cyprus, Democratic Yemen, Denmark, Ecuador, France, Gabon, Guatemala, Indonesia, Lesotho, Madagascar, Netherlands, Peru, Sierra Leone, USSR, United Kingdom, United States); and the chairmen of the following main committees, which are composed of all 151 member countries:

First (Political and Security): Frank E. Boaten (Ghana)

Special Political: Bernhard Neugebauer (German Democratic Republic)

Second (Economic and Financial): Peter Jankowitsch (Austria)

Third (Social, Humanitarian and Cultural): Lucille Mair (Jamaica)

Fourth (Trust and Non-Self-Governing Territories): Mowaffak Allaf (Syria)

Fifth (Administrative and Budgetary): Morteza Talieh (Iran)

Sixth (Legal): Enrique Gaviria (Colombia)

THE SECURITY COUNCIL

Membership ends on December 31 of the year noted; asterisks indicate permanent membership.

Bangladesh (1980)	Gabon (1979)	Portugal (1980)
Bolivia (1979)	Jamaica (1980)	USSR*
China*	Kuwait (1979)	United Kingdom*
Czechoslovakia (1979)	Nigeria (1979)	United States*
France*	Norway (1980)	Zambia (1980)

Military Staff Committee: Representatives of chief of staffs of permanent members.

Disarmament Commission: Representatives of all UN members.

THE ECONOMIC AND SOCIAL COUNCIL

President: Donald O. Mills (Jamaica). Membership ends on December 31 of the year noted.

Algeria (1981)	Iran (1979)	Spain (1981)
Argentina (1980)	Iraq (1979)	Sudan (1979)
Barbados (1981)	Ireland (1981)	Sweden (1980)
Brazil (1981)	Italy (1979)	Syria (1979)
Cameroon (1980)	Jamaica (1979)	Tanzania (1980)
Central African	Japan (1980)	Trinidad and
Empire (1980)	Lesotho (1980)	Tobago (1980)
China (1980)	Malta (1980)	Turkey (1981)
Colombia (1979)	Mauritania (1979)	Ukrainian SSR
Cyprus (1981)	Mexico (1979)	(1979)
Ecuador (1981)	Morocco (1981)	USSR (1979)
Finland (1980)	Netherlands (1979)	United Arab
France (1981)	New Zealand (1979)	Emirates (1980)
German Democratic	Pakistan (1981)	United Kingdom
Republic (1981)	Philippines (1979)	(1980)
Germany, Federal	Poland (1979)	United States
Republic of (1981)	Rumania (1979)	(1979)
Ghana (1981)	Rwanda (1979)	Upper Volta (1979)
Hungary (1980)	Senegal (1981)	Venezuela (1981)
India (1980)	Somalia (1979)	Zambia (1981)
Indonesia (1981)		

THE TRUSTEESHIP COUNCIL

Acting President: Shiela Harden (United Kingdom)

China[2]	France[2]	United Kingdom[2]
	USSR[2]	United States[1]

[1] Administers Trust Territory. [2] Permanent member of Security Council not administering Trust Territory.

THE INTERNATIONAL COURT OF JUSTICE

Membership ends on February 5 of the year noted.

President: Eduardo Jiménez de Aréchaga (Uruguay, 1979)
Vice President: Nagendra Singh (India, 1982)

Isaac Forster (Senegal, 1982)	Manfred Lachs (Poland, 1985)
André Gros (France, 1982)	Sir Humphrey Waldock
Taslim Olawale Elias (Nigeria, 1985)	(United Kingdom, 1982)
Herman Mosler (Federal Republic of Germany, 1985)	José Maria Ruda (Argentina, 1982)
Shigeru Oda (Japan, 1985)	Richard Baxter (United States, 1988)
Salah El Dine Tarazi (Syria, 1985)	Abdullah Ali El-Erian (Egypt, 1988)
Robert Ago (Italy, 1988)	José Sette Camara (Brazil, 1988)
Platon Morozov (USSR, 1988)	

SPECIALIZED AGENCIES

Food and Agriculture Organization (FAO); Intergovernmental Maritime Consultative Organization (IMCO); International Atomic Energy Agency (IAEA); International Bank for Reconstruction and Development (World Bank, IBRD); International Civil Aviation Organization (ICAO); International Development Association (IDA); International Finance Corporation (IFC); International Labor Organization (ILO); International Monetary Fund (IMF); International Telecommunication Union (ITU); United Nations Educational, Scientific and Cultural Organization (UNESCO); Universal Postal Union (UPU); United Nations International Children's Emergency Fund (UNICEF); World Health Organization (WHO); World Meteorological Organization (WMO).

UNITED STATES

As 1978 began the United States was at peace abroad and seemed to have entered a period of social and political stability at home. But the wars, riots, scandals, assassinations, and other traumas that marked the mid-1960's and early 1970's had left their mark on the national consciousness and altered the country's role in the world.

DOMESTIC AFFAIRS

In the wake of Watergate, a sense of cynicism and alienation lingered on. Many Americans distrusted their government and seriously questioned the relevance of the political system to their own lives.

President Jimmy Carter seemed to reflect this mood in his State of the Union address on January 19. "Government cannot solve our problems," Carter declared. "It can't set our goals; it cannot define our vision." And events during the year underlined the seemingly unyielding nature of the major problems that government and the president had to address. The most vexing difficulties were in the economic area, where shifts in the world's balance of power and conflicting domestic pressures combined to threaten the prosperity of giant corporations and individual wage earners alike.

The Economy. The percentage of total employment continued the rise begun in 1977. In January the jobless rate fell to 6.3%, the lowest since October 1974. And the number of workers holding jobs increased to a record 92.9 million. With minor fluctuations the trend continued. In October unemployment dropped to 5.8%, though unemployment among black teenagers was high.

But the news from the other front of the economic struggle, the fight against inflation, was bleak. The consumer price index, which had registered a 6.8% increase during 1977, climbed at an even faster rate, close to 10%. Food prices, medical care, housing, and transportation all contributed to the escalation. The dollar declined in value overseas as buying power dropped at home.

On April 11 the president announced he would limit pay increases for federal employees to 5.5% and freeze the pay of White House staffers and high level federal officials. Carter said he intended these limits to set an example for private employees. Robert S. Strauss, the president's special trade representative, was selected to coordinate the campaign of voluntary restraint; the president disavowed, as he had done before, any intention of instituting mandatory wage and price controls.

On May 12 the president announced that he would reduce his earlier tax-cut proposal from (U. S.) $25 billion to $19.4 billion and also postpone its effective date by three months, until Jan. 1, 1979.

With Carter's hopes of holding down living costs frustrated, the Federal Reserve Board pressed its own efforts to curb inflation by raising interest rates. On August 18 the discount rate, the charge on loans to commercial banks, was increased from 7.25% to 7.75%, near the record high of 8% established in April 1974. But on September 27 Carter declared that interest rates were "too high" and warned that further boosts could damage the economy. If Congress would cooperate with him in controlling inflation, he said, "That would be an inducement for the Federal Reserve to start bringing the interest rate down."

On October 24 the president announced a new anti-inflation program in a nationally televised address. Declaring that "it is time for all of us to make a greater and more coordinated effort" he called for workers to limit wage increases to 7%, asked companies to hold price increases to .5% below increases in 1976 and 1977, and proposed a tax rebate for employees who complied with his wage standard, if consumer prices rose more than 7% in 1979. The president also promised to reduce the budget deficit to less than $40 billion in the next fiscal year. The president then named Alfred E. Kahn, a 61-year-old economist who, as chairman of the Civil Aeronautics Board, had spearheaded deregulation of the airline industry, to succeed Robert S. Strauss as chairman of the Council of Wage and Price Stability.

Carter called his program "a good opportunity for the government and the private sector to work together in harmony." But the first reaction from the currency markets in Europe and Asia was a further decline in the dollar, reflecting the belief that the action was not strong enough. Some union leaders balked at complying with the recommended 7% wage increase limit. And the labor department reported that the cost of living had climbed .8% in September.

Alarmed by the continuing decline in the dollar, which he said was "clearly not warranted" by basic economic conditions, the president on November 1 announced a series of broad actions, including a pledge of massive U. S. inter-

—— **UNITED STATES** • Information Highlights ——

Official Name: United States of America.
Area: 3,615,123 square miles (9,363,169 km²).
Population (1978 est.): 218,400,000.
Chief Cities (1975 est.): Washington, D. C., the capital, 711,518; New York, 7,481,613; Chicago, 3,099,391; Los Angeles, 2,727,399; Philadelphia, 1,815,808.
Government: *Head of state and government,* Jimmy Carter, president (took office Jan. 1977). *Legislature* —Congress: Senate and House of Representatives.
Monetary Unit: Dollar.
Manufactures (major products): Motor vehicles, aircraft, ships and railroad equipment, industrial machinery, processed foods, chemicals, electrical equipment and supplies, fabricated metals.
Agriculture (major products): Wheat, rye, corn, barley, oats, soybeans, tobacco, cotton, sorghum, fruits.

"ON THE WAY HOME, WE CAN READ SOME OF THIS STUFF WE'VE BEEN VOTING ON"

COPYRIGHT 1978 BY HERBLOCK IN "THE WASHINGTON POST"

vention to bolster the dollar in foreign markets and a boost in the Federal Reserve Board's discount rate to 9.5%. The immediate reaction was favorable. The dollar increased in value and stock prices soared. But some economists and labor leaders warned that the stern measures could bring on a recession.

The Administration. Though the economy was the most serious problem confronting the Carter administration it was only one of many difficulties besetting the president and his advisers. Underlying the troubles was the president's difficulty in gaining the confidence of the nation in his leadership, a weakness attested to by the public opinion polls. The steady decline of the approval of the president, as measured by various surveys, had begun in 1977 during the controversy over Bert Lance, Carter's close friend, who was forced to resign as director of the Office of Management and Budget, and the negative trend continued during much of 1978. Adding to Carter's embarrassment were surveys which showed that most Democrats preferred Sen. Edward M. Kennedy of Massachusetts as their party's candidate for the presidential nomination in 1980. The polls seemed to reflect a widespread perception of the president as uncertain and ineffective and of his administration as lacking focus and direction. Carter's image also was damaged by his acknowledgment that he had pressed the Justice Department to replace David Marston, a Republican-appointed U. S. attorney in Philadelphia, who had been active in prosecuting allegations of corruption involving Democrats, including two Congressmen.

Carter took cognizance of his predicament early in April when he summoned his cabinet and senior White House staff members to the presidential retreat at Camp David for a weekend series of intensive meetings. White House Press Secretary Jody Powell later reported that "the president pointed out some mistakes he thinks he has made but he made it damn clear that we've had 15 months now and the shakedown cruise is over." And Carter himself predicted: "We'll do things better."

Gradually, events began to move in the president's favor. Following ratification of the Panama Canal treaties by the Senate in March and April, the administration's time and resources were freed to focus on domestic policy programs. A number of changes in White House personnel—particularly the appointments of Anne Wexler, formerly a Commerce Department official and liberal political organizer, as a political coordinator, and of Gerald Rafshoon, who had handled Carter's advertising during the 1976 campaign, as communications director, had positive effects.

On August 17, in a demonstration of what his aides said was his strengthened resolve, the president vetoed a $36.9 billion Pentagon authorization bill because of his objection to a $2 billion nuclear carrier. On September 17, an effort to override the veto in the House, which required a two-thirds vote, failed even to get a majority. The president won another test of strength with the Congress in September when he vetoed a $10.2 billion public works bill that ignored his proposals for tighter economic monitoring of dams and other federal water projects. Despite the exertions of Congressional leaders in his own party, the effort to override failed, 223 to 190, 53 votes short of the 276 needed for an override.

The sustaining of these vetoes and the passage of modified versions of his energy and civil service reform proposals enhanced President Carter's prestige with both branches of Congress and the public and gave his administration additional confidence.

But by far the president's biggest achievement of 1978, and the most beneficial to him politically, was the successful conclusion of the Middle East Summit meeting at Camp David in September, during which Egypt and Israel agreed to negotiate a peace treaty. That dramatic event produced a big jump in the president's poll ratings; the Gallup Poll showed his positive score climbing 17 points, to 56%. But the next survey recorded a six point drop in his standings to 50%, which indicated that if Carter was to hold and increase the respect he had won for his leadership in foreign affairs, he would have to demonstrate similar success in the domestic arena.

The Congress. The top-heavy Democratic majorities in the 95th Congress did not assure smooth sailing for President Carter's legislative programs. The Congress spent most of its second session haggling and wrangling over politically sensitive issues. And the lawmakers had to endure a nonstop 34-hour weekend session before they adjourned on October 15. Though the final hours of the session saw action on several important measures and a flock of lesser items, many were substantially altered from the president's original request and a number of other significant items died on the floor or in committee.

Part of the problem was Congressional resentment, shared to an extent by Democratic leaders, of the president as an outsider, unfamiliar and at times seemingly unconcerned with traditional Capitol Hill prerogatives. Another cause of friction was that Carter forced the legislators into consideration of several particularly complex and controversial issues.

Probably the most emotional controversy centered on the Panama Canal treaties which resulted from negotiations that began in 1964 between the United States and Panama. President Carter made the treaties a mainstay of his foreign policy, putting the full prestige of his office behind the drive for ratification. After months of intense national debate, the basic treaty, providing for the turnover of the canal to Panama by the year 2000, was approved on March 16 by the Senate by a vote of 68 to 32, one more than required for ratification. On April 18 the neutrality treaty, guaranteeing the United States right to defend the canal after the year 2000, was approved by an identical vote.

The president's energy proposals, originally heralded as "the moral equivalent of war," and submitted to the Congress on April 20, 1977, were just as vital to his domestic policy as the canal treaties were to his conduct of foreign policy, and they aroused almost as much controversy. The president hailed the proposal that finally emerged from the Congress as a victory. "We have declared to ourselves and the world our intent to control our use of energy and thereby to control our own destiny as a nation," the president said.

But the five-part package that he signed into law was considerably narrower in scope than his original goals. Stripped from the final version was the proposed tax on domestic crude oil, to raise prices to the world level, which had been the heart of the president's original plan. Also eliminated were Carter's proposals for a tax on use of natural gas by industry and utilities and for a boost in the federal gasoline tax.

Moreover, the president's plan for extension of natural gas price controls was watered down by a House-Senate compromise which phased in higher prices until 1985, when controls on newly discovered gas would be removed. The measure was intended to end price differences between gas sold intrastate and interstate, which had re- sulted in surpluses in some states and shortages in others. Besides the natural gas revisions, Congress also voted for tax credits for home insulation, penalties for gas guzzling autos, reform of utility rate-making, and authority to force industries to convert from oil and gas to coal.

An $18.7 billion tax reduction, to take effect in 1979, resulted from another lengthy legislative battle. The final version represented a compromise between the $16.3 billion tax cut voted by the House and the $29.1 billion reduction approved by the Senate. The debate was complicated by the president's scaling down of his own original $25 billion proposed reduction because of inflation. And it was heavily politicized by Republican support for a three-year, one-third cut in tax rates cosponsored by Rep. Jack Kemp of New York and Sen. William Roth of Delaware.

Many legislators felt that a tax cut of some sort was justified if only to offset a rise in social security rates scheduled for 1979 and the continued pressure of inflation on most taxpayers. In fact, not many taxpayers will enjoy a net tax reduction in 1979 because of the Social Security rate climb and inflation. The bill increased personal exemptions from $750 to $1,000, a change that would benefit upper-middle income groups more than the poor. Critics complained that the bill was overly regressive, giving too much to investors and businessmen and too little to those on the lower end of the economic scale.

Carter signed the bill, though it contained hardly any of the basic reforms he had called for in the tax code and though Congress, against his wishes, cut the tax on capital gains by raising the amount of gains excluded from taxation from 50% to 60%. This change was designed to spur investment and economic growth.

But the president could claim some clear legislative victories. In foreign affairs, in addition to ratifying the canal treaties, the Senate approved Carter's plan to sell $4.8 billion worth of jet fighters to Saudi Arabia, Israel, and Egypt, over the objections of many Jewish leaders. Congress also gave the president authority to remove the three-year-old partial embargo on arms sales to Turkey. The embargo had been imposed in 1975 because of Turkey's use of U. S. military equipment to invade Cyprus in 1974.

Congress paved the way for fulfillment of Carter's oft-repeated campaign pledge to overhaul the federal bureaucracy by passing the civil service reform act. The new legislation reorganized the civil service commission and established a new grade for top level federal employees who would no longer get automatic pay raises but could be rewarded with merit raises and bonuses.

Another Carter campaign plank, the Humphrey-Hawkins full employment bill, was also passed in modified form. But observers felt that the law's goal of reducing unemployment to 4%

UPI

With the cherry blossoms in bloom, the First Family enjoy a stroll to the Jefferson Memorial.

by 1983 was weakened by inclusion of a provision that established as a goal the reduction of the inflation rate to 3% by the same year.

In other actions supporting administration proposals, the Congress extended the deadline for ratification of the Equal Rights Amendment by 39 months, passed and sent to the states another Constitutional amendment giving full representation in Congress to the District of Columbia, and agreed to provide long term federal guarantees of up to $1.65 billion for bonds issued by financially troubled New York City. But several measures endorsed by the administration were defeated, including labor law reform and proposed ceilings on hospital revenues and

spending. Major proposals for welfare reform and national health insurance were deferred until 1979.

In a statement issued following the adjournment of Congress, the president pointed out that "the American people can be justly proud of the work the Congress has done in solving some of the nation's most pressing problems." (*See also* page 563.)

Scandals. An unusual number of allegations of unethical or illegal behavior distracted the attention of some lawmakers and added to public suspicions about the political process. The most widespread scandal continued to be the so-called Koreagate affair, having to do with Congressmen

A memorial service for the late Sen. Hubert Humphrey is held in the Rotunda of the capitol.

UPI

taking gifts from South Korean lobbyists. Congress and the Justice Department had begun investigating the affair in 1977. On March 31 former Rep. Otto Passman (D-La.) was indicted on charges of accepting bribes from South Korean businessman Tongsun Park, the central figure in the influence peddling charges. And on April 24, another former Democratic Congressman, Richard T. Hanna of California, pleaded guilty on one count of conspiracy to defraud the government in connection with the Koreagate case.

But progress of the probe was impeded by the inability of U. S. investigators to question Kim Dong Jo, former South Korean ambassador to the United States, who was suspected of having made payments to some Congressmen. And on August 2, Leon Jaworski resigned as special counsel to the House Ethics Committee, because he contended there was little more that could be done without Kim Dong Jo's testimony.

The House investigation reached its conclusion on October 13, when the House voted to reprimand three California Democratic Congressmen—Reps. Edward Royball, Charles H. Wilson, and former Majority Whip John McFall—for failing to report cash contributions from Tongsun Park.

The personal finances of two U. S. senators, Edward Brooke (R-Mass.) and Herman Talmadge (D-Ga.), were subjected to the scrutiny of the Senate Ethics Committee as a result of disclosures made during divorce proceedings. Brooke admitted on May 26 that he had given false information about a $49,000 loan in a sworn deposition taken in 1977 in connection with his divorce. In the deposition, he said the money had come from a Massachusetts liquor dealer, but later he said all but $2,000 had been given him by his late mother-in-law. The Senate inquiry into the matter was interrupted when the ethics committee counsel resigned, charging that Brooke's representatives had withheld information. The senator lost his bid for reelection in November.

Talmadge's divorce proceedings brought to light the fact that from 1970 to 1976 the senator had written only one check, for $300, for cash. Talmadge, a millionaire, said he had used "small gifts of cash" from friends and supporters to pay his out-of-pocket expenses. He subsequently paid the Senate $37,125.90 to cover improper expense claims that had been made on his behalf.

On the House side, Rep. Charles C. Diggs, Jr., (D-Mich.) was convicted October 7 on charges of taking more than $101,000 in kickbacks from Congressional office staff members. He said he would appeal. Rep. Daniel Flood (D-Pa.) was indicted twice—for allegedly lying about payoffs made to him and to a former aide and also for bribery and conspiracy. Rep. Joshua Eilberg (D-Pa.) was indicted October 24 for allegedly receiving illegal compensation for helping a Philadelphia hospital get a $14.5 million federal grant. And Rep. J. Herbert Burke (R-Fla.) pleaded guilty September 26 to charges of being disorderly and resisting arrest in a Florida bar featuring nude dancers. It is interesting to note that Diggs and Flood were reelected in November.

Assassinations. The House Assassinations Committee delved into two tragic and still somewhat mysterious episodes from the past, the 1963 slaying of President John Kennedy and the 1968 killing of civil rights leader Martin Luther King, Jr. The Kennedy hearings, which opened September 6, lasted three weeks. Much of the early testimony focused on the controversial conclusion of the Warren Commission that only three shots had been fired during the assassination. The so-called three bullet theory was central to the commission's finding that Lee Harvey Oswald was the sole assassin of the president. Afer hearing testimony from acoustical experts who asserted the probability of gunfire from two locations, the committee concluded that President Kennedy "was probably assassinated as a result of a conspiracy." The committee "was unable to identify the other gunman or the extent of the conspiracy," and recommended that the Justice Department determine the need for further investigations. Other witnesses included Oswald's widow, Marina, who said she believed her husband had slain Kennedy, and former President Gerald Ford, a member of the Warren Commission, who said that new evidence about CIA plots against Cuban President Fidel Castro did not alter his belief that the Warren Commission's findings were correct. And in a tape-recorded interview, Castro himself said it would have been "insane" for him to participate in a conspiracy to kill Kennedy. The committee said that it "believes, on the basis of circumstantial evidence available to it, that there is a likelihood that James Earl Ray assassinated Dr. Martin Luther King as a result of a conspiracy."

The King hearings began August 14. The committee heard from the Rev. Ralph David Abernathy, a former chief aide to King, who said he believed King's death had been part of a conspiracy, but admittedly could not offer any hard facts to support his contention. James Earl Ray, King's convicted killer, told the committee that he was innocent of the crime. He said he had been persuaded by his lawyer, Percy Foreman, to plead guilty at his 1969 trial to help the sales of a book which had been written about him. Ray said he had been framed by a man named Raoul whom he did not otherwise identify and whose existence law enforcement offices have never been able to establish. The committee resumed its hearings into the case on November 10, and in December concluded that Ray's motive for the slaying was $50,000 offered by a right-wing St. Louis businessman who wanted King killed. But Ray apparently never collected the money.

ROBERT SHOGAN, *Los Angeles Times*

MARVIN LICHTNER, FROM LEE GROSS, INC.

Californians demonstrate their support for Proposition 13, reducing the state's property tax by 57%. The measure received wide public attention and caused a general revolt by taxpayers across the country.

THE ECONOMY

The U. S. economy during 1978 continued to ride the crest of a basically stimulative environment characterized by heavy consumer expenditures, particularly for durable goods, large-scale demands for money and credit, and a rapidly expanding money supply. While some success in reducing unemployment was achieved, other problems re-emerged and intensified considerably. The relatively high rate of price inflation, already a nagging concern, accelerated to an even more unacceptable level. Persistently high trade deficits, combined with deteriorating confidence in U. S. authorities to deal successfully with existing problems, sent the dollar reeling in many key international markets.

As the year wore on, inflationary pressures, concern over the consumer's ability and willingness to continue spending and adding to his large debt burdens, and ominous dollar pressures abroad increasingly threatened to abort the business advance. In response to such pressures, the authorities began to implement some corrective measures. These included passage by Congress of an energy program, a significant firming of money and credit policy by the Federal Reserve, which sent interest rates skyrocketing, and joint action by the Federal Reserve and Treasury to try to reduce inflationary pressures and prop up the dollar abroad. A program of voluntary wage-price guidelines was also instituted by the White House.

Output. Total output continued to move ahead in 1978, but followed an irregular pattern. In the first quarter the modest rise in the gross national product (GNP) was insufficient to match the pace of inflation, so that growth in real terms came to a temporary standstill. This was primarily caused by disruptions that resulted from severe winter conditions. The economy bounced back in the second quarter as the GNP passed the $2 trillion mark, rising at an annual rate of over 8%. After adjusting for higher prices, output increased by nearly 8% during that period. In the third quarter the GNP rose by about 11%, and although the rate of advance was cut to about 4% in real terms, this was still a respectable showing. In the first three quarters of 1978, therefore, total output measured in constant 1972 dollars was 3.8% higher than in the comparable period of 1977, and prices had risen by over 7%.

During the first three quarters, most major sectors contributed to the advance, with the exception of foreign trade. Consumer spending, buoyed by increasing employment and rising after-tax income, pushed ahead by nearly 11%, to over $1.3 trillion. Outlays for nondurables and services were well maintained, while expenditures for durables, such as household goods and automobiles, were particularly strong.

To a great extent, however, individual's spending patterns were maintained at some expense to households' liquidity, as personal savings were reduced relative to income and consumers continued to assume heavy debt burdens. By the third quarter nearly 25% of consumption was debt-financed, compared with previous cyclical peaks of around 21%. The amassing of large debt by individuals, including mortgages and installment credit, began to bring into question the consumers' willingness and ability to continue along this path. The chief worries concerned the influence of a potential relaxation of consumer debt expansion on overall spending.

Gross private domestic investment increased by 16% in the first three quarters of the year versus the 1977 period to $339 billion. Of this, $16.5 billion represented net inventory accumulations, about the same as a year earlier. Capital investment by both households and business showed adequate and similar gains ranging in the 16–18% area. While household capital additions were generally considered to have been more than adequate during this period, those of business were somewhat disappointing in view of earlier expectations. New plant and equipment spending by business in 1978 was estimated to rise by a shade over 12%, about in line with the year before. But allowing for a rate of price inflation of nearly 8%, real net additions to productive capacity were largely held to be insufficient under the circumstances.

U. S. international trade continued to be a drag on the GNP during this period in spite of the spectacular decline of the dollar which, theoretically at least, tended to make U. S. goods relatively cheaper and more competitive in certain foreign markets. The United States was a net importer of some $13.6 billion on average in the first three quarters of the year, considerably above the 1977 level. Heavy dependence on energy imports and the inability to offset such imports by sufficiently large exports of agricultural products and heavy machinery, traditional mainstays of U. S. export trade, were largely responsible for this problem. As the year matured, however, a mild improvement in exports began to be noticed.

The government's fiscal involvement in the economy was, as has been usual lately, stimulative in spite of a considerable reduction in the federal deficit, when compared with the original estimates. Total federal spending approached $441 billion on average during the three-quarter time span and at this level was more than 6% higher than a year earlier. State and local government outlays increased much more rapidly than did those of the federal government. However, the state and local budget for the 50 states as a whole remained in surplus.

Monetary Policy and the Capital Markets. In response to a rapidly expanding money supply, which was to an important extent responsible for adverse price developments during the year, the Federal Reserve showed adamant determination to pursue a tightening money and credit

GROSS NATIONAL PRODUCT

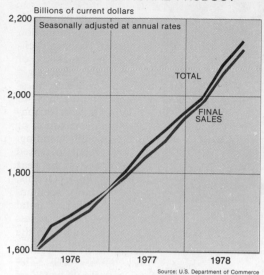

Billions of current dollars

Seasonally adjusted at annual rates

TOTAL

FINAL SALES

Source: U.S. Department of Commerce

UNEMPLOYMENT RATE

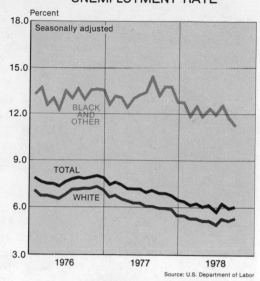

Percent

Seasonally adjusted

BLACK AND OTHER

TOTAL

WHITE

Source: U.S. Department of Labor

CORPORATE PROFITS

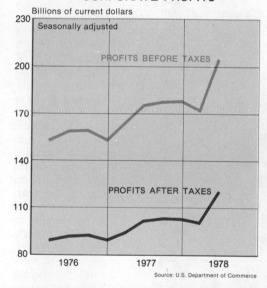

Billions of current dollars

Seasonally adjusted

PROFITS BEFORE TAXES

PROFITS AFTER TAXES

Source: U.S. Department of Commerce

PERSONAL INCOME

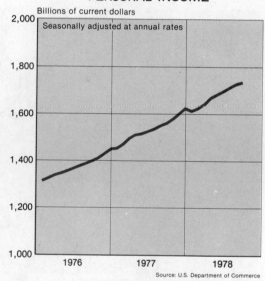

Billions of current dollars

Seasonally adjusted at annual rates

Source: U.S. Department of Commerce

policy. The nation's basic money stock (M_1), currency plus demand deposits, began to increase well in excess of the central bank's long-range upper target limit of 6.5% in March 1978 and this trend generally remained in effect throughout most of the year.

The Federal Reserve responded to the situation by carrying out tightening maneuvers decisively and often. It influenced a persistently rising federal funds rate, which increased from under 7% in mid-April to nearly 10% in early December. The discount rate was raised six times, from 6.5% to 9.5% by December. Other money market rates followed suit and longer-term rates generally rose, but not nearly so much. In all, such conditions were bearish for the money and capital markets on balance and proved detrimental to the equities market as well.

The central bank's policy efforts were characterized by an insistence on promoting higher money costs as the method by which money supply growth could be brought under control and at the same time making sure that sufficient funds were available so as not to stifle the economic expansion. Not a great deal in the way of tangible results had been achieved by the end of November. Although money supply growth did slow in the months of October and November, the evidence was far from conclusive that conditions were finally being reshaped, and price inflation persisted near double-digit levels.

See also Feature Article on Inflation (pages 10–16); Energy; International Trade and Finance; Stocks and Bonds; Taxation.

JACKSON PHILLIPS, *Executive Vice President Moody's Investors Service, Inc.*

EVANS, LIAISON

Democrat Bill Bradley campaigns hard and successfully for the New Jersey Senate seat held by Clifford Case.

Surrounded by supporters and his family, New York's Gov. Hugh Carey (D) delivers victory speech as he is elected to a second term.

UPI

ELECTIONS

The U. S. election result that received the greatest public attention and had the broadest impact in 1978 came not on election day, November 7, but in the California primary on June 6. By an overwhelming majority of 65% the voters in the largest state approved a ballot initiative, Proposition 13, that made a drastic 57% cut in the property tax rate. The measure set a limit of 1% of real value on property tax rates throughout the state, put a ceiling of 2% a year on tax increases and required a two-thirds vote of the legislature for any increase in other taxes.

On the same day, Ohio voters defeated nearly 60% of 198 proposals for additional financing of local schools. And in New Jersey, a conservative Republican, Jeffrey Bell, whose campaign was centered on a proposed 33% cut in federal income tax rates defeated the liberal incumbent, Sen. Clifford Case, for the GOP Senate nomination. The combination of these results, particularly the Proposition 13 vote, led many office holders and political analysts to conclude that a right-wing tide, brought in by a taxpayer's revolt, was washing over the country. The Republican Party made a legislative proposal, co-sponsored by Sen. William Roth (Dela.) and Rep. Jack Kemp (N. Y.), calling for a one-third,

UPI

William Milliken, a GOP moderate, is successful in his bid for another term as governor of Michigan.

EVANS, LIAISON

Former President Gerald Ford spent the fall season campaigning for GOP candidates across the country.

UPI

UPI

In a major win for the Democrats, Carl Levin, a liberal, unseats Sen. Robert B. Griffin of Michigan.

Nancy Landon Kassebaum takes time out from her Senate campaign in Kansas for a family portrait.

three-year cut in federal income tax rates, the centerpiece of its fall campaign. All around the country taxpayer groups pushed drives to put variations of Proposition 13 on the ballot.

But in the rush by politicians to join the tax cut bandwagon, a number of aspects of the California result and the attitude of voters around the country were sometimes overlooked. The Proposition 13 landslide in California had been aided by special circumstances. Property tax rates there had been climbing much faster than in most other states. Moreover, the state government had a healthy (U. S.) $5 billion surplus in the treasury to offset the revenue losses from the property tax reduction. Public opinion

surveys suggested that voters were not opposed to government in general but rather to waste and inefficiency; they wanted taxes cut but were reluctant to give up essential government services. And as the campaign developed, a number of polls showed that voters were almost always more concerned about curbing the threat of inflation than they were about the burden of high taxes.

This attitude limited the effectiveness of the Kemp-Roth bill as a campaign issue. The issue was blurred by the fact that many Democrats announced support for a tax cut.

Apart from the economic issue Republicans had counted on President Carter's low standing in the polls to hurt the Democrats. But Carter's apparent success at Camp David seemed to have erased whatever negative impact his presidency was having on the candidacies of his fellow Democrats. And the announcement of his efforts to combat inflation shortly before election day appeared to enhance his standing and probably boosted some Democratic campaigns.

As a consequence of these offsetting points, the returns on November 7 were decidedly mixed. The Republicans made respectable gains across the board. But their success was on a smaller scale than they had achieved in 1966 when Lyndon Johnson was in the White House, or than the Democrats had registered in 1974 when Republican Gerald Ford was president. The conservative trend and the tax revolt also scored less decisively than many had anticipated.

In the House of Representatives the Republicans made a net gain of 12 seats, cutting the Democratic majority down to 117. The GOP gained eight seats in the 39 districts where Democratic incumbents chose not to run again. But the Republicans lost five seats in the 19 districts where their incumbents did not seek reelection, for a net gain of only three among the "open seats" which had been the chief GOP target. The Republicans scored most of their gains among seats held by Democrats who had been elected in 1974, when the Watergate issue helped elect Democrats in many normally Republican areas. Seven Democrats from this group were defeated.

In the Senate the Republicans made a net gain of three, cutting the Democratic majority to 18. This was a relatively good showing, since Republicans had controlled 17 of the 35 Senate seats at stake in the 1978 voting. Conservatives took special satisfaction in the defeat of five incumbent Democratic senators with liberal voting records. Thomas McIntyre lost to Gordon Humphrey in New Hampshire; Dick Clark was defeated by Roger Jepsen in Iowa; Wendell Anderson was beaten by Rudy Boschwitz in Minnesota; Floyd Haskell lost to William Armstrong in Colorado; and William Hathaway was beaten by William S. Cohen in Maine.

But in Michigan, incumbent conservative Republican Robert Griffin was defeated by liberal Democrat Carl Levin. And in two states liberal Republican senators were replaced by equally liberal Democrats; Paul Tsongas defeated incumbent Edward Brooke in Massachusetts and Bill Bradley beat Bell in New Jersey.

The most impressive GOP gains were scored in Minnesota where Boschwitz's victory over Anderson was matched by David Durenberger's defeat of Robert E. Short, for the Senate seat once held by Hubert Humphrey. In Mississippi, Republican Thad Cochran defeated Democrat Maurice Dantin for the seat held by James Eastland, giving the GOP its first Mississippi senator since Reconstruction. In South Dakota, Republican Larry Pressler beat Democrat Don Barnett for the seat of James Abourezk (D).

But the Democrats won previously Republican Senate seats in Oklahoma where David Boren beat Robert Kamm and in Nebraska where J. J. Exon defeated Donald Shasteen.

The Republicans were expected to make their biggest advance in the governors races, and they did, increasing the number of GOP controlled statehouses from 12 to 8, including Texas, where William Clements, Jr., upset John Hill, and Pennsylvania, where Richard Thornburgh beat Peter Flaherty. Two Republican incumbents lost bids for reelection: Meldrim Thomson, Jr., in New Hampshire, beaten by Hugh Gallen, and Robert Bennett of Kansas, defeated by John Carlin. Three Democratic incumbents were defeated—Rudy Perpich of Minnesota by Albert Quie, Robert Straub of Oregon by Victor Atiyeh, and Martin Schreiber of Wisconsin by Lee Dreyfus.

A significant aspect of the gubernatorial results was the strengthening of the ranks of GOP moderates. Moderate Republicans James Rhodes of Ohio, William Milliken of Michigan, and James Thompson of Illinois held on to control of their big states. Among the new Republican governors Richard Thornburgh and Lee Dreyfus are considered to hold moderate views on national issues.

Although the success of Proposition 13 helped get other tax- and spending-limit proposals on the ballots in a number of states, the results on these measures were also mixed. Charles Crawford, director of the National Taxpayers Union, said the "ripple effect" of Proposition 13 was not so great as expected. In only two states, Idaho and Nevada, did voters approve outright rollbacks of property taxes to 1%, and in Nevada, the proposal must be approved again in 1980 before it takes effect. Most voters followed the pattern in Michigan, where drastic measures to cut property taxes by 43% and remove property tax support from education were defeated and a more moderate proposal to hold state taxes to a fixed percentage of state personal income and link property tax increases to inflation was passed. Arizona adopted an amendment holding state spending to 7% of total personal income, North Dakota voters passed a measure cutting state income taxes for individuals and raising them for corporations, and South Dakota adopted a law requiring a two-thirds instead of majority vote of the legislature to raise sales or property tax rates. Measures to cut or limit taxing or spending lost in Colorado, Nebraska, and Oregon.

In state referenda that drew national attention, a measure to allow casino gambling in Miami Beach and Hollywood, Fla., was defeated; New Jersey and Virginia voters said no to jai alai and horse racing betting, respectively; and California rejected Proposition 5, which would have restricted smoking in public places.

See also articles on the states.

ROBERT SHOGAN

Camp David, the presidential retreat in the Catoctin Mountains in Maryland, was the scene of 1978 Egyptian-Israeli peace negotiations.

President Carter welcomes the Israeli and Egyptian negotiators, Foreign Minister Moshe Dayan and Defense Minister Ali Hassan, to the White House.

PHOTOS UPI

FOREIGN AFFAIRS

The year produced mixed results—the historic Camp David agreements, incomplete negotiations on the SALT II and law of the sea arrangements, anxieties like terrorism and the plunging dollar, and festering problems in subsaharan Africa. The year ended most dramatically—the United States and the People's Republic of China agreed to establish diplomatic relations.

Objectives and Expectations. Together with the permanent goals of peace and security, President Carter and Secretary of State Cyrus Vance reiterated a series of foreign policy objectives. These included maintaining close relations with allies, achieving racial equality in southern Africa, normalizing relations with Communist China, restraining weapons proliferation, stabilizing political and military competition with the USSR, and promoting human rights, economic development, and free trade. Regarding Third World countries, Carter and Vance emphasized the need to support national economic development, to share technology, stabilize commodity prices, and permit no new international cartels.

Specific expectations for the year included ratification of the Panama Canal treaties, securing a new SALT accord, producing a breakthrough in Mideast peace negotiations, and gaining greater trust and credibility abroad. Success in achieving these goals was uneven. In certain respects policies worked at cross-purposes, and in many matters—such as the seabed treaty, Third World development, and southern Africa—serious problems remained as the year ended.

Conduct of Foreign Relations. Three new states gained independence in 1978, increasing the international community of nations to 160. These were Dominica (Caribbean), Solomon Islands (Pacific), and Tuvalu (Ellice Islands, Pacific). The United States maintained diplomatic missions to some 140 countries, plus special missions to Communist China and Cuba, and 112 consular establishments; 133 governments were diplomatically represented in Washington.

President Carter made four summit trips abroad, including two early tours largely to Third World countries, a one-day trip to Panama to exchange Canal Treaty ratifications in June, and an industrial powers' economic summit in Bonn in July. He also participated in a Washington NATO summit in May and the Camp David negotiations in September. Secretary Vance went abroad on many missions, and dozens of foreign leaders went to Washington.

The United States was represented at more than 1,000 international conferences and sessions of international agencies in 1978, including UN conclaves on disarmament, science and technology development, and the law of the sea, as well as meetings on African peacekeeping and the Israeli-Egyptian settlement. On Jan. 1, 1978, the United States was party to 962 treaties and 5,616 executive agreements, and during the year subscribed to approximately 15 new treaties and 425 agreements.

United Nations System. Despite its diminished popular image in the United States, the UN was given renewed support by the U. S. government, and the president stressed the need for resolving problems of global interdependence. Congress mandated a review of the UN and its specialized agencies and of their value to the United States. Specific issues addressed in the president's report include peacekeeping and security functions, decision making processes, financing, human rights, restructuring of economic and social programs, technical assistance, the composition and function of the secretariat, and methods of augmenting U. S. participation. The report made suggestions for change, which dealt less with structural reorganization and ways to enhance U. S. interests than with techniques for increased institutional coordination.

China. In mid-December it was announced that the United States and China would establish full diplomatic relations on Jan. 1, 1979; embassies would open in the two capitals on March 1, 1979; and Chinese Deputy Prime Minister Teng Hsiao-ping, a key figure in the move, would visit Washington early in the new year. In opening relations with Peking, the United States cut its formal ties with the Nationalist government on Taiwan. However, Peking agreed that the U. S. defense treaty with Taiwan would not have to be abrogated until one year after recognition. Although the U. S. action was condemned by American conservatives and the Taiwanese, the Carter administration felt that the United States was finally accepting an international reality. According to one White House staff member, the idea of the United States "not having relations with nearly a billion people is just ridiculous."

Western Hemisphere. On June 21 President Carter addressed the General Assembly of the Organization of American States. He reiterated U. S. dedication to the goals of peace, security, the preservation of human rights and dignity, an end to repression and terrorism, and a more equitable international economic system.

After months of bitter debate, the Senate approved in March and April the Panama Canal treaties, signed in September 1977. Approval was achieved only after a special understanding was appended clarifying U. S. rights to defend the canal after the year 2000, and granting U. S. ships transit priority in time of war.

U. S.-Cuban relations continued relatively unchanged. Cuban military adventuring in Africa still constituted the most serious impediment to normalization. Modest steps were taken, but the United States refused to lift certain trade embargo restraints pending settlement of unsatisfied claims of American nationals and corporations.

Mideast. The most dramatic development in Mideast relations were the Israeli-Egyptian conferences at Camp David and Washington. The Camp David summit talks, hosted personally by President Carter, September 5–17, produced two historic documents. These include a "Framework for Peace in the Middle East," fixing basic principles for a general settlement, and a "Framework for the Conclusion of a Peace Treaty Between Egypt and Israel." They were signed in a televised ceremony at the White House Sunday evening, September 17, and explained more fully to Congress by the president the following day.

Ministerial-level negotiations were initiated at Blair House on October 13, and an Egyptian-Israeli draft treaty provides for a fixed boundary, withdrawal of Israeli forces from the Sinai, free passage of Israeli ships through the Suez, the positioning of military troops, and the establishment of normal relations, including termination of the economic boycott and full recognition of Israel. The year ended without the treaty being signed by Egypt and Israel.

Africa. In Zaire, historic rivalries fueled a serious outburst. When Zaire's Shaba Province was invaded from Angola, the United States cooperated with other nations to rescue those trapped by the fighting, to preserve Zaire's territorial integrity, and to prevent economic collapse.

The Namibian situation reached a critical stage. The United States, together with Britain, Canada, France, and Germany, sought transition to independence in a fair and peaceful way. It induced both South Africa and SWAPO (South West Africa People's Organization) to agree to a number of important principles, but no acceptable solution was found in 1978.

In Rhodesia, the United States joined with the British to produce a plan to fuse the interests of the "external nationalists" ("Patriotic Front") with those of Ian Smith and the moderate black leaders who supported him on an "internal set-

The foreign ministers of South Africa, the United States, and Britain—Pik Botha, Cyrus Vance, and David Owen—meet in Pretoria for the first round of talks on independence for South West Africa.

UPI

tlement." Despite Smith's visit to the United States to solicit support for his proposal for transition to independence, time for a peaceful solution was waning.

Human Rights. Human rights remained a primary and explicit foreign policy theme. Actions taken included reducing military assistance to serious violators of human rights, raising human rights issues in global and regional forums, and bringing the pressure of world opinion to bear on governments to conform with principles they had previously endorsed. Yet, the Human Rights Covenants and the Genocide Convention languished in the Senate.

International Terrorism. The United States participated in an ad hoc UN committee, formed in February, to draft an international convention against the taking of hostages. At the economic summit in Bonn in July, the United States and six other major industrial powers agreed to sever all commercial airline service to countries that provide sanctuary to aircraft hijackers or refuse to return hostages.

Disarmament. The United States and 148 other states participated in the five-week General Assembly Special Session on Disarmament to reverse the arms spiral. It produced a "Final Document" of 129 articles dealing with objectives, a "declaration" of collective policy, a program of action, and implementation machinery. Participants redefined fundamental principles, priorities, and procedures, agreed on the dangers of arms proliferation, but consummated no concrete conventions or commitments. (*See also* ARMS CONTROL.)

Seas and Seabed. Meeting in the seventh session of the Third UN Conference on the Law of the Sea, the United States and more than 150 other countries continued negotiations on a comprehensive convention to govern the use of the ocean and its resources. Substantial progress was made on about 80% of the nearly 400 articles. However, critical problems remained, of which the most crucial is the nature and authority of an international regime for mining the deep seabed.

Disagreement between the Third World and the technologically advanced countries centered on the system of exploiting the seabed, resources policy to control seabed production, and government of international institutions to manage exploitation. The U. S. Congress debated a proposal to empower American interests to commence seabed mining by 1980.

The Dollar, Trade, and Aid. Dollar depreciation was severe. Analysts attributed this to the large and persistent U. S. trade deficit, large American oil imports, and high internal inflation rates. The powers at the Bonn summit agreed to adopt economic stimulus programs. In November the president instituted a number of corrective measures, but the real causes of the exchange problem persisted.

The Carter administration launched a major thrust to invigorate U. S. foreign assistance programs. It proposed a budget of some $4.5 billion—consisting of $1.6 billion in bilateral development aid, $2.7 billion for security assistance, and $282 million for programs of the UN and the Organization of American States. These were supplemented by $3.5 billion to the International Bank and other international financial agencies to help poorer nations with physical development programs, and $1.4 billion for the Food for Peace program. This total of approximately $9.5 billion of assistance represents an increase of nearly 33% over the preceding year.

In addition to supporting developing countries in building their own scientific and technological infrastructure for economic growth, the United States participated in a series of UN conferences on science, technology, and technical cooperation.

See also feature articles on Panama Canal (pages 17–25); terrorism (pages 44–51).

ELMER PLISCHKE, *University of Maryland*

The Civil Service

"Reform the bureaucracy" has been a prominent slogan in recent U. S. political campaigns. Behind this slogan lies considerable citizen feeling that the public services of U. S. federal, state, and local governments are overgrown and unresponsive. In any event, 1978 saw the approval of an unusual number of civil service reform measures of importance.

These new laws mainly affect the civil service of the national government, for most citizens seem to believe that the bureaucracy in Washington, D. C., is the main root of their difficulties. Insofar as the federal civil service represents dominant policies, services, and regulations, this is true. But insofar as sheer size is concerned, it is not.

U. S. Public Employment. By the end of 1977 total civilian public employment in the United States reached 15.4 million persons, or close to 1 out of 6 of the employed civilian labor force. Add 2 million in the uniformed military services and the ratio is more than 1 out of 6.

However, the federal civil service accounts for only a little over 2.8 million persons. Contrary to popular opinion, more than 80% of "the bureaucracy" is much closer to home. That is, 1977 saw nearly 3.5 million persons employed in state government and more than 9 million in local government (county, municipal, township, school district, and special district).

Since 1950 federal employment has indeed grown from 2.1 to 2.8 million, but this growth has been barely proportionate to the growth of the nation's population. Moreover, it is not well understood that only 13% of the federal civil service works in Washington, D. C. There are more federal employees living and working in California or New York than in the District of Columbia and vicinity.

Between 1950 and 1978 the number of state and local government personnel tripled. State employment was only 1.1 million and that of local government 3.2 million in 1950, compared with 1978's combined total of nearly 12.6 million. While the federal service has grown by a third, that of the state and local governments has expanded 300%.

State and Local Personnel Actions. In 1978 the main efforts to curb the expansion of state and local civil services were indirect.

A growing number of localities are aiming at controlling public expenditures through limiting taxation by such means as California's "Proposition 13," which holds property taxes to 1% of assessed valuation and requires two-thirds votes for imposition of new taxes. The full impact of such laws is yet unclear, but they are sure to make the expansion of all governments, and their civil services, difficult. Indeed, there is

some fear that tax relief alone may lead to a decline in quality of such important local functions as police, fire, hospitals, highways, and education. Together these account for about 70% of state and local public employment, with education alone nearly 50%.

Another kind of indirect influence on state and local public employment has come through an increasing number of federal regulations stemming from conditional grants-in-aid or from the implementation of constitutional civil rights guarantees.

Under the Intergovernmental Personnel Act of 1970 the U. S. Civil Service Commission took over from the Department of Health, Education, and Welfare the setting of minimum standards for the employment of state and local employees paid from many federal grant-in-aid funds. On Feb. 14, 1978, the Commission proposed uniform guidelines for all such employment, which involves about a third of state and local civil service workers. On August 25 the federal government's Equal Employment Opportunity Commission, Civil Service Commission, Department of Labor, and Department of Justice jointly issued fairly stringent "Uniform Guidelines on Employee Selection Procedures" stemming from the various civil rights acts passed by Congress since the early 1960's. While eliminating confusion in the application of many federal laws, these steps tended further to limit the initiative available to state and local governments in employing and utilizing their own personnel.

In fact, from these and several earlier federal laws a fundamental constitutional question has arisen: Is such federal intervention gradually destroying the federal system indirectly, something that could not be done directly? Only in the case of *The National League of Cities* v. *Usery,* decided June 24, 1976, has the U. S. Supreme Court indicated there might be a limit to such intervention. Then the court struck down by a 5–4 vote a 1974 federal law extending coverage of the Fair Labor Standards Act (minimum wage) to state and local workers.

Federal Civil Service Reform. The most important direct actions in 1978 to modify a major civil service system came in the federal government. These were through Reorganization Plan No. 2, approved by Congress on August 11, and the Civil Service Reform Act of 1978, signed by President Carter on October 13. Together, these actions abolished the historic U. S. Civil Service Commission (dating back to 1883), created a new Senior Executive Service for the higher levels, introduced a new type of merit pay for these higher levels, and for the first time put into law a framework for federal public employee labor relations. These acts do not change the basic nature of the federal personnel system, but they provide for important modifications and a new administrative structure. Upon signing the bill, the president pointed out: "During my campaign for president, I made reorganization of the government a top priority, and this monumental civil service reform bill takes a long step toward meeting that commitment to the American people. It's a centerpiece of our efforts, joint efforts to bring efficiency and accountability and competence to the federal government that will exceed what we have known in the past.

"This legislation provides a fundamental and, I think, long overdue reform of the federal bureaucracy."

Early in 1979 the Civil Service Commission will be replaced by two agencies. A separate Office of Personnel Management, under a director appointed by the president and confirmed by the Senate, will take over supervision of most of the federal government's civilian personnel system. A three-member, bipartisan Merit Systems Protection Board, appointed by the president and confirmed by the Senate for nonrenewable terms of seven years, will become the new top appeals board for employee grievances. It can also investigate and punish a new list of prohibited personnel practices and is given special authority to protect "whistleblowers" who speak out against improper government actions. The outgoing Commission, which held all these functions, was criticized for being the judge of its own actions.

A new Senior Executive Service (SES) is to be created, consisting of 8,000 persons occupying top level administrative and technical posts at General Schedule levels 16 through 18 (the supergrades) and below level III (subcabinet) of the Executive Pay Schedule. Persons now occupying these posts would have the right to join or not join. SES members could be moved around at the convenience of the government in the manner of the Foreign Service. Career members would have reemployment rights if placed in and removed from one of the non-career (political) posts which may comprise no more than 10% of the total SES.

A new performance appraisal board system would be established for the SES with pay increases tied primarily to merit rather than time in grade. Each year up to 5% of the SES could receive incentive bonuses of $10,000 and up to 1% could be named distinguished executives and receive bonuses of $20,000. Maximum pay for an executive would be that of level I (cabinet) of the Executive Pay Schedule, currently $66,-000. Maximum pay for most potential SES members is now between $47,500 and $52,500.

Labor Relations. The labor relations section of the act essentially includes the provisions of Executive Order 11491, as amended, which now governs federal employee labor relations. But the law does permit some expansion of topics which may be the subject of bargaining and gives a right of appeal to the federal courts.

The system will operate under the guidance of a statutory Federal Labor Relations Authority of three bipartisan members, comparable to the National Labor Relations Board governing the private sector and replacing the present ex officio Federal Labor Relations Council. The Federal Service Impasses Panel, designed to assist management and labor to arrive at agreements, is to be continued as a unit of the FLRA.

Other provisions of the reform act give federal managers slightly more freedom in dealing with incompetent employees. A new combination of automatic and merit pay increases is provided for General Schedule levels 13 through 15; there is no change in the pay system of other federal employees. Total federal civilian employment is limited for three years to the number employed on Sept. 30, 1977, which provides for a small reduction in force easily obtained through attrition. And the Office of Personnel Management is given unusual authority to conduct experiments in personnel management with sizeable groups of federal employees.

Other Federal Acts. April 1978 amendments to the Age Discrimination in Employment Act of 1967 eliminated mandatory retirement for most federal employees after Sept. 30, 1978. In July, Congress approved the President's Reorganization Plan No. 1, placing the Equal Employment Opportunity Commission in a central coordinating role for most affirmative action processes and ending a confused jurisdictional situation involving four different federal agencies. In September the president signed the Federal Employees' Flexible and Compressed Work Schedules Act which permits experiments with flexible work hours (flexitime). Experiments can include work weeks of four 10-hour days and other variations not previously permitted.

October and November saw additional actions in rapid succession. To set an anti-inflationary example, President Carter limited comparability (to the private sector) pay raises in the federal civil service to 5.5%. The Federal Employees Career Part-Time Employment Act of 1978 requires federal agencies to expand opportunities for part-time employment at all levels up to the supergrades, a move of special interest to women. On October 27 the president signed a federal ethics bill which requires public financial disclosures from more than 14,000 top officials, including the president, vice president, members of Congress, and the Supreme Court. A new Office of Government Ethics will handle questions and complaints, and a special prosecutor will investigate charges of misconduct by top officials.

Early in November the president approved the first law banning employee unions of uniformed military personnel. This replaced a Department of Defense administrative directive toward the same end.

PAUL P. VAN RIPER

The FBI in Transition

The Federal Bureau of Investigation, rocked by charges of misconduct and embarrassing disclosures of earlier, secret operations, struggled to chart a new course in 1978.

William H. Webster, a soft-spoken, Republican judge serving on the Eighth U. S. Circuit Court of Appeals in St. Louis, was personally selected by President Carter to replace the outgoing FBI director, Clarence M. Kelley. Webster, only the third director in the 54-year history of the FBI, promised to serve a full 10-year term, the maximum allowed under a recently enacted law.

Since the death in 1972 of J. Edgar Hoover, the bureau's first director, the once-sterling public image of the FBI had become tarnished, and many of its 8,000 agents were demoralized. The news media carried one report after another of clandestine FBI activities, including illegal break-ins, wiretaps, mail openings, misuse of public funds, and attempts to smear the reputations of certain political activists.

Cointelpro, or the Counterintelligence Program, was one of the largest of these secret operations. Conducted under cover by Hoover for 15 years, Cointelpro was first directed against the Communist Party in the United States. Later it was expanded to include left-wing and right-wing groups, such as the Black Panthers, Ku-Klux Klan, and the Fair Play for Cuba Committee, a pro-Castro group. Under the Freedom of Information Act, the bureau was forced to reveal 52,648 pages of documents detailing the operation, which began in 1956. These documents showed, among other things, that the FBI had recruited prostitutes to trap leaders of the Fair Play for Cuba Committee in compromising acts; had conducted operations in Mexico against Communist organizations; and had tried to disrupt the Students for a Democratic Society (SDS) with misleading leaflets distributed on college campuses.

In January 1978, a Justice Department report officially revealed for the first time that Hoover had benefited personally from FBI services and materials. FBI workers, the report said, had built a portico on the former director's house, and also had constructed there a fishpond, complete with lights and a pump. FBI employees painted Hoover's residence every year while he was on vacation and serviced all of his appliances without charge. The report also gave details of a conflict of interest at the bureau in the selection of a supplier of electronic equipment.

Perhaps most unsettling to FBI agents were criminal charges brought in 1977 and 1978 against past and present officials of the bureau. Many thought the charges were unjustified. In April 1977, a federal grand jury brought a five-count indictment against John J. Kearney, a former FBI supervisor in New York City. The indictments charged that under Kearney's direction, from 1970 to 1972 agents had illegally tapped phones and opened mail while hunting for members of the Weather Underground, a radical faction of the SDS. These indictments marked the first time an agent had ever been charged with a felony for actions in the course of FBI duty. In another unprecedented action, 300 FBI agents demonstrated in Kearney's behalf outside the federal courthouse in New York City. A year later, Attorney General Griffin Bell ordered the charges against Kearney dismissed because, Bell explained, Kearney was "only carrying out orders."

That same day, however, Bell announced indictments of higher FBI officials: L. Patrick Gray III, former acting director of the FBI; W. Mark Felt, former acting associate director; and Edward S. Miller, former chief of counterintelligence. These indictments also stemmed from illegal break-ins against the Weathermen.

Further, Bell sought disciplinary action against 68 agents who allegedly had been involved in "black bag" jobs in New York City. J. Wallace LaPrade, former FBI office chief in New York, was moved to Washington as a disciplinary action, and later fired.

These developments were greeted with dismay by FBI agents in the field. Ten days after Gray was indicted, 100 agents in the Indianapolis office presented Bell with a letter which said, in part: "We are of the opinion, in this field office, that the FBI is being systematically destroyed for reasons unknown to us. . . . We feel that, to date, we have not received the support from the attorney general's office that reflects the faith and trust in the FBI, which we believe we have earned through our dedicated efforts over the years."

In a tense meeting at the Indianapolis office, Bell explained that the decision to prosecute had been a tough one. He noted that Hoover had ordered the break-ins to cease in 1966, but that the practice had continued. The 50 agents who met with Attorney General Bell remained grim-faced.

All of this made the new director's job a difficult one. As an attorney, and later a judge, Webster had gained little administrative or law enforcement experience. As FBI chief, he was faced with the task of establishing control over the nationwide FBI system (including 59 field offices) and simultaneously ridding the bureau of cliques held over from the Hoover era.

In one of his first major decisions, Webster shocked many agents by elevating James B.

The FBI was much in the news in 1978. William H. Webster, *above*, became its new director; L. Patrick Gray, *above, right*, former acting director, and Edward S. Miller, former chief of counterintelligence, were indicted on charges stemming from illegal activities against the Weathermen. FBI members generally supported Gray and Miller.

PHOTOS UPI

Adams, a hardcore Hooverite, to the number 2 spot in the bureau. Former Director Kelley had been unable to carry out some of the changes he wanted because of resistance from staunch followers of Hoover. Webster, many agents feared, might not realize the dangers of failing to cut the old Hoover ties.

Nevertheless, Webster announced he would carry out Kelley's philosophy of taking on high quality cases instead of a large quantity of cases. This meant moving away from more easily solved crimes that might produce impressive statistics and focusing on more widespread and difficult problems, such as organized crime, government corruption, and foreign espionage.

In 1978, the FBI investigated more than 500 cases of government corruption. These ranged from simple bribery of patrolmen on the beat all the way to government kickback schemes.

The FBI's role in counterespionage continues to grow, as the number of Communist diplomats, dependents, tourists, trade representatives, students, and seamen entering the country rises.

Webster also announced that the bureau was taking steps to head off the spread of European-style terrorism to the United States. Anti-terrorism training programs at the FBI Academy in Quantico, Va., are being intensified, he said.

In almost all kinds of crime, Webster told an Atlanta audience, the informant remains "the most effective tool in law enforcement." Webster revealed that the FBI was using 42 informants on domestic security and terrorism, 1,060 informants on organized crime, and 1,789 informants who supply criminal information.

To answer yet another criticism of the FBI, Webster ordered a sharp increase in the recruitment of minority and women agents. In mid-1978, out of some 8,000 FBI agents, there were only 150 blacks, 163 of Hispanic origin, 14 American Indians, and 34 Asian-Americans. There were 96 women agents. Within a few months, Webster managed to boost the number of women and minority trainees in an incoming class of 40 special agents, to 20.

JOHN DILLIN

URUGUAY

A thinly disguised military dictatorship continued to govern the Latin American nation of Uruguay throughout 1978.

Politics. On March 2, Lt. Gen. Gregorio Alvarez took over as commander-in-chief of the army and de facto head of the regime. Aparicio Méndez, the titular president, took orders from the military leaders, headed by Alvarez.

General Alvarez, regarded as a moderate, met resistance from more extreme military elements. A new periodical, *El Talero,* appeared in March and began attacking Alvarez for being "soft." In June, Alvarez dismissed hard-line Gen. Amaury Prantl as chief of intelligence and placed him under house arrest. These actions aroused protests from the Fourth Cavalry Regiment and other supporters of Prantl. On July 8, Foreign Minister Alejandro Rovira, another hard-liner, was forced to resign.

Repression. Although the government insisted that it had no political prisoners, it admitted in February that 2,336 persons were being held for crimes of "subversion and sedition." In June, the Military Supreme Court acknowledged that there were 1,900 Uruguayans in jail for "crimes against state security" and that 2,511 others had been released over the previous six years after having served their sentences.

The oppressiveness of the regime brought numerous protests from abroad. In December 1977, the European Community (EC) urged the government to free all political prisoners. In February 1978, the Organization of American States (OAS) refused to hold its annual meeting in Montevideo because of the nature of the Uruguayan regime. On July 1, the OAS General Assembly urged Uruguay to cease its human rights violations. Leading officials of the U. S. Department of Defense and Department of State supported these moves.

On April 3, Amnesty International asked President Méndez to investigate charges that political prisoners were being tortured. He took no action. Late in June, the Inter American Commission on Human Rights accused the Uruguayan government of wholesale violations of human rights—arbitrary arrests, torture, and murder of political prisoners. Although Foreign Minister Rovira rejected these accusations, he said that the government would continue to "cooperate" with the commission.

Foreign Affairs. Uruguay's only allies seemed to be other hard-line military governments in Latin America. It was one of only three nations in the UN Human Rights Commission to vote against a condemnation of the Chilean regime of Gen. Augusto Pinochet.

A visit by Brazilian President Ernesto Geisel early in the year indicated that government's support of the Uruguayan regime. But while in Montevideo, Geisel sought and helped obtain the release of a Brazilian journalist, Flavio Tavares, who had been held in an Uruguayan prison.

Economy. Uruguay's economy continued to be critical. At the end of 1977, unemployment was estimated at 12.8%. It did not change significantly during 1978. By the end of April, the cumulative cost of living increase for the year was 12.3%. Although the government enacted several wage increases, real wages continued to decline. The continuing foreign economic problems were reflected in the frequent devaluations of the Uruguayan peso.

ROBERT J. ALEXANDER
Rutgers University

URUGUAY • Information Highlights

Official Name: Eastern Republic of Uruguay.
Location: Southeastern coast of South America.
Area: 68,536 square miles (177,508 km²).
Population (1978 est.): 2,800,000.
Chief City (1975 census): Montevideo, the capital, 1,-229,748.
Government: *Head of state,* Aparicio Méndez, president (took office Sept. 1976). *Head of government:* Lt. Gen. Gregorio Alvarez, commander-in-chief. *Legislature*—General Assembly (suspended June 1973).
Monetary Unit: Peso (5.93 pesos equal U. S.$1, June 1978).
Manufactures (major products): Processed meat, textiles, wools and hides, shoes, handbags and leather wearing apparel, cement, fish, refined petroleum.
Agriculture (major products): Livestock, grains.

UTAH

Religion, politics, and a bizarre multi "suicide" were major events in Utah in 1978.

Religion. The Church of Jesus Christ of Latter Day Saints (Mormons) has historically banned black males from ordination to the priesthood of the church. Women have never been eligible to join the priesthood. On June 9, 1978, acting on what was declared a revelation from God, following "supplication (to) the Lord for divine guidance," Church officials announced "that the long-promised day has come when every faithful, worthy man in the Church may receive the holy priesthood, with power to exercise its divine authority ... (and) accordingly, all worthy male members of the Church may be ordained ... without regard for race or color." The previous exclusion of blacks had been based on the teachings of the church founder, Joseph Smith, with reference to the Book of Abraham that people of African lineage bore the "Curse of Cain" and could not hold the priesthood until the Lord spoke through revelation. That revelation came in June 1978, and in mid-September, Joseph Freeman, Jr., 26, became the first black to be ordained into the Melchizedek priesthood of the LDS church.

Politics. Republicans dominated the Utah 1978 elections in the most sweeping victory in over a decade. Republican Dan Marriott won a second term in the 2nd Congressional District by more than 62% of the vote. Democratic incumbent Gunn McKay retained his seat in the 1st Congressional District by a very narrow margin.

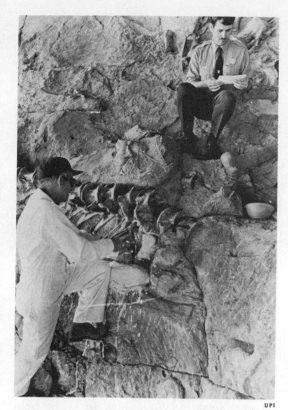

UPI

Paleontologists at the Dinosaur National Monument, near Vernal, Utah, discover the bone of a stegosaurus.

In the Utah Senate, the Democrats lost seven seats to the GOP, turning over control of that body to the Republicans by a margin of 19 to 10, just one short of the required two-thirds vote necessary to override vetoes by the incumbent Democratic governor, who was not up for re-election this year.

In the Utah House of Representatives, Republicans gained 10 new seats, to widen their control to 50 Republicans versus 25 Democrats.

A major issue on the ballot for the most populous area of the state (Salt Lake City–Salt Lake County) was a proposition to offer a single government for the city and the unincorporated

----

UTAH · Information Highlights

Area: 84,916 square miles (219,932 km²).
Population (Jan. 1978 est.): 1,287,000.
Chief Cities (1970 census): Salt Lake City, the capital, 175,885; Ogden, 69,478; Provo, 53,131.
Government (1978): *Chief Officers*—governor, Scott M. Matheson (D); secy. of state, David S. Monson (R). *Legislature*—Senate, 29 members; House of Representatives, 75 members.
Education (1977–78): *Enrollment*—public elementary schools, 173,486 pupils; public secondary 143,846; colleges and universities, 88,461 students. *Public school expenditures,* $530,135,000 ($1,279 per pupil).
State Finances (fiscal year 1977): *Revenues,* $1,237,-698,000; *expenditures,* $1,177,333,000.
Personal Income (1977): $7,510,000,000; per capita, $5,923.
Labor Force (July 1978): *Nonagricultural wage and salary earners,* 518,300; *unemployed,* 19,800 (3.6% of total force).

parts of the county, which would have created an entity of approximately 450,000 persons. The issue was bitterly contested. Proponents—led by former Gov. Calvin L. Rampton and including the current Mayor Ted Wilson (D), Sen. Jake Garn (R), and former Gov. and Mayor J. Bracken Lee (R)—were opposed by a coalition of businessmen and city and county commissioners, who labeled themselves "We the People." This proposal was defeated by a vote of 91,781 to 60,709. Following the vote, city and county commissioners vowed to negotiate for "functional consolidation" in various departments, such as personnel, parks, and some law enforcement activities.

Salt Lake Suicide Plunge. The family of a man who called himself Immanuel David, a self-proclaimed descendant of the biblical House of David, in August committed one of the most bizarre multi-suicides in the nation's history. David had recently been found dead in a nearby canyon. Either in despondency or in the belief that they were intended to join him, his wife and seven children plunged from an 11th floor balcony of a downtown Salt Lake City hotel. The wife and six of the children died immediately. The seventh child survived and remains under professional care.

LORENZO K. KIMBALL
The University of Utah

VENEZUELA

Presidential elections, pride in continued stability of democracy, and progress in economic development highlighted 1978.

Domestic Affairs. On January 23, 1978, Venezuela celebrated the 20th anniversary of the overthrow of its last dictatorship. Since 1958, three democratically elected presidents have completed their terms. The first of these men, Romulo Betancourt, was honored during the year for his 50 years of continuous political activity and service. The government issued warnings on subversion, and teaching institutes were closed as student riots erupted in 1978.

On March 3 a government-owned Venezuelan airliner crashed in the Caribbean Sea moments after takeoff from the Caracas airport, killing all 47 persons aboard.

Renny Ottolina, the popular Venezuelan television personality and presidential candidate was presumed dead after the plane in which he was traveling was lost on March 16 off the coast of Venezuela.

Presidential Elections. Presidential elections took place on December 3, 1978. About 6 million persons participated (voting is obligatory) in choosing from a field of six candidates. Acción Democrática, the majority party, chose Luis Piñerúa Ordaz as its candidate in the first party primary ever held in Venezuela. Luis Herrera Campíns was nominated by the Social Christian party, the other major political force. Both parties used U. S. campaign and polling experts.

UPI

The presidents of the United States and Venezuela discuss international issues at Miraflores Palace, Caracas. The portrait is of liberator Simon Bolivar.

Late summer indications pointed to plurality victory for one of the major parties. Since no party was expected to win a majority of congressional seats, coalition government seemed certain.

Luis Herrera Campíns, whose Social Christian party numbered half the registrants of the Acción Democrática party, won the election. He was to be inaugurated early in 1979.

Economic Development. In his annual message to Congress, President Carlos Andrés Pérez

pointed to a school enrollment of 4.28 million; the addition of 1,830 hospital beds; a reduction in infant mortality of 19.2% over the past four years, and an increase in those covered by Social Security from 977,000 in 1973 to 1.3 million in 1978. The number of private dwellings in the total housing picture rose from 60.6% in 1973 to 62.8% in 1976. The government approved plans for 7 new universities and opened 38 new technical schools in 1977. Since 1976 jobs have been created for 153,000 persons; the average monthly income per family is now about $500, up $100 from 1977. The government has invested (U. S.) $1.9 billion in sanitary facilities, $450 million in telecommunications, $1.2 billion in hydroelectric development and $1.4 billion in transportation and port improvements. The Venezuelan aluminum industry has become self-sufficient with the discovery of 500 million tons of bauxite, the essential ingredient of the metal. Iron ore reserves will last 135 years at the current annual production rate of 15 million tons.

In January of 1978 Venezuela received large foreign bank loans. The first was a $1.2 billion 10-year loan syndicated by Swiss Bank Corp., Manufacturers Hanover Ltd., and Dai-Ichi Kangyo Bank of Japan. The second loan, to be used in financing public works projects in Caracas, totaled $178 million in credit from several Arab banks.

Foreign Affairs. In 1978 Venezuela's President Pérez welcomed President Carter (March), Prince Charles of England (March), the vice president of China, Chi Peng-fei (June), and Portuguese President Antonio Ramaldo Eanes (May). President Pérez visited Washington, D. C. and Jamaica.

The Venezuelan president championed the Panama Canal Treaties and spoke out critically on political repression in Nicaragua. He urged President Somoza to discuss Nicaragua's internal situation in any international forum of his choosing. The Nicaraguan president accused Venezuela of trying to overthrow his government. Venezuela was one of 8 states to sign a treaty pledging its effort in an international plan to make Amazonia "a fertile field of cooperation." The government contributed to a fund for financing development programs in the Caribbean area and was the largest single contributor of foreign aid in Latin America, pledging a sum of $3.2 billion. In July, the city of Caracas was host to the World Theater Festival. Venezuela and the Dutch Antilles resolved their boundary differences in the Gulf of Venezuela in midsummer.

The Venezuelan embassy in El Salvador was occupied by students and peasants in mid-April. The occupation was to protest attacks on peasants by Orden (National Democratic Organization) vigilantes, a paramilitary right-wing group, in the San Pedro Perulapan area in March.

LEO B. LOTT
University of Montana

VENEZUELA • Information Highlights

Official Name: Republic of Venezuela.
Location: Northern coast of South America.
Area: 352,143 square miles (912,050 km²).
Population (1978 est.): 13,100,000.
Chief Cities (1974): Caracas, the capital, 2,400,000; Maracaibo, 900,000; Barquisimeto, 350,000.
Government: *Head of state and government,* Carlos Andrés Pérez, president (took office March 1974). *Legislature*—Congress: Senate and Chamber of Deputies.
Monetary Unit: Bolivar (4.29 bolivares equal U. S.$1, Sept. 1978).
Manufactures (major products): Refined petroleum products, iron and steel, paper products, aluminum, textiles, transport equipment, consumer goods.
Agriculture (major products): Coffee, bananas, sugar, rice, corn, dairy, meat, and poultry products.

VERMONT

Elections. Despite his authoritative style and legislative rebuffs of his reorganization proposals, Republican Gov. Richard A. Snelling was reelected in November by an almost two-to-one margin over Edwin Granai, assistant majority leader of the state House of Representatives. Vermont's only U. S. congressman, Republican James Jeffords, won more than 75% of the vote to secure a third term over Democratic newcomer S. Marie Dietz, an anti-abortion candidate who had narrowly won the September primary. Democrat Madeleine Kunin, chairman of the Vermont House Appropriations Committee, upset Peter Smith to become Vermont's second woman lieutenant governor. Att. Gen. M. Jerome Diamond easily won reelection over Republican Dennis Bradley.

The national tax revolt was reflected in demands to limit the state budget. However, the election produced only minor shifts in legislative strength: the Republicans regained a narrow majority in the state House and retained control of the Senate, 20 to 10.

Legislation and Public Policy. The 1978 legislature responded to a $21 million-surplus from the previous year by cutting taxes and increasing appropriations for welfare and the Vermont State College system beyond the levels recommended by Governor Snelling. Tax cuts included repeal of the poll tax, elimination of an income tax surcharge, and recognition of federal credits. Repeal of the sales tax on clothing was passed in the House but not in the Senate. Other significant legislation included land use valuation for farm credits.

Proposals to modify the state's "Miller Formula" for aid to local schools, to restructure the Public Service Board to include an independent consumer advocate, and to weaken the statutory call for a state land use plan, all died in committee. Vermont's environmental controls law (Act 250) passed a major test when the Pyramid Corporation's proposal for a regional shopping mall in Williston was denied by the District Environmental Commission.

--------- **VERMONT · Information Highlights** ---------

Area: 9,609 square miles (24,887 km²).
Population (Jan. 1978 est.): 486,000.
Chief Cities (1970 census): Montpelier, the capital, 8,609; Burlington, 38,633; Rutland, 19,293; Bennington, 14,586.
Government (1978): *Chief Officers*—governor, Richard A. Snelling (R); lt. gov., T. Garry Buckley (R). *General Assembly*—Senate, 30 members; House of Representatives, 150 members.
Education (1977–78): *Enrollment*—public elementary schools, 61,557 pupils; public secondary, 41,377; colleges and universities, 29,506 students. *Public school expenditures*, $169,586,000 ($1,488 per pupil).
State Finances (fiscal year 1977): *Revenues*, $572,-997,000; *expenditures*, $535,769,000.
Personal Income (1977): $2,814,000,000; per capita, $5,823.
Labor Force (July 1978): *Nonagricultural wage and salary earners*, 184,900; *unemployed*, 11,800 (4.9% of total force).

Economic growth, highlighted by the opening of a multimillion dollar computer and components plant of the Digital Corporation in South Burlington, continued to center in Chittenden County. Long-term electric power supplies were threatened by shutdowns of the state's only nuclear power plant in Vernon and by apprehension over the environmental impact of a wood-burning plant proposed by Burlington's municipal electric department. A state-sponsored plant for reprocessing whey (a by-product of the state's substantial cheese industry) went into production amid great uncertainty about its financial viability and the environmental impact of its effluent.

The whey problem precipitated a test of Vermont's "Right-to-Know" law with respect to meetings of public bodies. The Emergency Board, composed of the governor and legislative leaders with interim financial powers, met to allocate funds for the Whey Pollution Abatement Authority. The meeting was unpublicized and convened under irregular circumstances. The Attorney General initiated a prosecution, but the charges were dismissed by the state Supreme Court.

A skier paralyzed in a fall at a Vermont resort was awarded $1,500,000 by a state court. The decision was upheld by the Vermont Supreme Court, but the legislature, perceiving a threat to the state's principal winter industry, responded by defining and limiting the personal injury liability of ski resorts.

ROBERT V. DANIELS and SAMUEL B. HAND
University of Vermont

VIETNAM

The worst flooding in 35 years struck Vietnam in 1978, compounding the difficulties the country faced as a result of widespread mismanagement, corruption, demoralization, and military mobilization in support of a worsening war with Cambodia (Kampuchea) and mounting border tension with China.

Domestic Affairs. There were no apparent rifts in Vietnam's top political leadership as the country's 17-member Politburo continued to direct the country with an unusual degree of consensus. Some 800,000 persons remained in political re-education camps—from which no one was known to have been released in the three-and-a-half years since the fall of Saigon (now Ho Chi Minh City).

More than one million southerners had been relocated in "New Economic Zones" by the end of 1978 as part of a government plan to resettle 10 million Vietnamese, mostly from the south, in 20 years.

Because of the war with Cambodia, an additional 350,000 men and women were inducted into the armed forces in which there was reportedly widespread corruption, and from which there was considerable desertion.

UPI

Vietnam's Prime Minister Pham Van Dong traveled to Thailand and the Philippines during 1978.

Economy. Faced with worsening problems of food shortages, declining factory worker productivity, and low morale on the part of laborers in the conquered south, Vietnam experienced its worst flooding since World War II. Some 500,-000 homes were washed away, nearly 3 million tons of rice were destroyed, and four-and-a-half million persons were made homeless or otherwise seriously affected—3 million of these requiring emergency relief. A total of 2.3 million acres (932,000 ha) were reported to be under water. The consequences of the unseasonably heavy rains, which destroyed newly built irrigation canals and generally disrupted fulfillment of goals of the 1976–80 five-year plan, will undoubtedly be felt for years.

In addition to the flood damage, another 900,000 acres (365,000 ha) of crops were destroyed by insects because of a short supply of pesticides and insufficient spraying equipment.

The country's economic problems, which also included a severe shortage of building materials, were further compounded by China's dramatic curtailment of all of its aid projects in midyear.

Hanoi introduced new currency, a unified dong, but limited citizens to $50 and peasants to $25.

War With Cambodia. The war with Cambodia which began with forays by the Phnom Penh government across the Vietnamese border in 1977, steadily escalated during the year. Vietnamese-piloted MiG fighters accompanied U. S.-built F-5 and A-37 jet aircraft on bombing runs against Cambodian troop concentrations as the conflict grew. A reported 100,000–120,000 Vietnamese soldiers were poised along the frontier with Cambodia in November, allegedly awaiting the rains' end to mount an offensive.

Hanoi's ally, the Soviet Union, sent weapons, ammunition and military advisers to aid Vietnam, while China pledged its support of Phnom Penh and provided the Cambodians with various types of military assistance. As late as October, Vietnam rejected a Cambodian offer of peace talks, demanding that Phnom Penh first agree to a cease-fire and withdraw troops allegedly occupying Vietnamese territory.

In support of its war effort, Hanoi declared a state of alert and general mobilization and placed the country on a war footing. Reports in October indicated that rail traffic in the country had been disrupted by massive troop movements. These various war activities further stimulated discontent in southern Vietnam with the northerner-dominated government.

Sino-Vietnamese Relations. Vietnam also faced a very precarious situation along its northern border with China. The Sino-Vietnamese controversy began with the strong negative reaction of ethnic Chinese businessmen in Vietnam to the Communist government's nationalization of their activities, particularly in Ho Chi Minh City's adjacent suburb of Cholon. Nearly 160,-000 of them fled to China, setting in motion a chain of events that resulted in the closing of Chinese consulates in June.

In July, Peking terminated its aid program to Vietnam and called back all of its advisers. Such aid was estimated between (U. S.) $10–18 billion in the years 1958–78. Alleged Vietnamese unwillingness to allow additional Chinese to depart the country caused the new tension along the border between the countries—where Hanoi and Peking accused one another of massing troops and building fortifications.

Foreign Relations. If Cambodia and China were Vietnam's main adversaries, the USSR was its chief friend. According to Peking, the Soviets built a guided missile base in central Vietnam (allegedly directed toward China) and were seeking access to the former U. S. naval facility at

───── **VIETNAM · Information Highlights** ─────

Official Name: Socialist Republic of Vietnam.
Location: Southeast Asia.
Area: 127,246 square miles (329,566 km²).
Population (1978 est.): 49,200,000.
Chief Cities (1976 est.): Hanoi, the capital, 1,443,500; Ho Chi Minh City, 3,460,500; Haiphong, 1,191,000; Da Nang, 500,000.
Government: *Head of state,* Ton Duc Thang, president (took office 1969). *Head of government,* Pham Van Dong, premier (took office 1954). *First secretary of Communist Party,* Le Duan. *Legislature* (unicameral)—National Assembly.
Monetary Unit: Dong (2.50 dongs equal U. S.$1, May 1978).
Manufactures (major products): Phosphate fertilizer, cement, electric energy, processed foods.
Agriculture (major products): Rice, sugarcane, tea, sweet potatoes, cassava, rubber, corn, fruits.

UPI

In Paris, Vo Van Sung, Hanoi's ambassador to France, outlines his nation's view of hostilities with Cambodia.

Cam Ranh Bay. In late July, surprisingly but perhaps as part of the price for Soviet support, Hanoi became the tenth member of the Moscow-directed and largely Communist East European-composed Council of Mutual Economic Assistance.

On November 3 Vietnam and the USSR signed a 25-year treaty of friendship and cooperation to provide "economic, scientific and technical cooperation with the purpose of accelerating socialist and communist construction."

RICHARD BUTWELL, *Murray State University*

VIRGINIA

Former Secretary of the Navy John Warner (R) defeated former Attorney General Andrew Miller (D) in an extremely tight senatorial race. Warner had lost the nomination at his party's June convention, but when the original nominee, Richard Obenshain, died in an August plane crash, Warner was tapped by the Republican State Committee.

The Democratic party, hoping to minimize the chronic divisiveness which had denied it significant statewide victories for a decade, held a convention instead of the customary primary to select its nominee. Miller, elected attorney general in 1969 and 1973 but defeated in the Democratic primary for governor in 1977, easily won the nomination.

Considering Warner's lack of elective experience and his late start, his victory demonstrated the growing potency of the Republican party in the state. In the races for Virginia's ten Congressional seats, Republicans returned six Congressmen by easy margins or without opposition, while two liberal Democratic Congressmen from the Washington suburbs barely won reelection.

The electorate defeated a proposal to permit parimutuel horse race gambling on a local option basis.

Legislative Session. The General Assembly also reflected a conservative temperament when it once again declined to ratify the Equal Rights Amendment. Further, it supported Gov. John Dalton's ruling that Medicaid money should not be used to fund abortions, and it defeated a resolution aimed at validating collective bargaining agreements between local school boards and teacher organizations.

Democratic legislative leaders attempted to change the composition of local electoral boards to reflect the dominant party in the legislature rather than the party of the governor, as required by current law. But public criticism prodded some Democratic legislators to turn against the proposal, which was therefore defeated in committee. The Assembly also approved a constitutional amendment to provide a special extended Legislative session to consider gubernatorial vetoes made after adjournment. A legal technicality kept the proposal off the November ballot. Governor Dalton vetoed a bill requiring party identification on state ballots.

Dalton proved to be more racially moderate than his predecessor, Mills Godwin. He honored

UPI

John Warner and his wife Elizabeth Taylor meet the press on election night. The former secretary of the Navy was later declared Virginia's new senator.

campaign pledges by appointing recent alumni, including blacks, to college governing boards. He also appointed a black woman to his cabinet. And unlike Godwin, he signed a bill that designated January 1 as a state holiday in honor of Martin Luther King. More important, Dalton abandoned Godwin's opposition to federal government pressures for minority enrollment quotas in Virginia's colleges. He worked out an agreement with the U. S. Office of Civil Rights (OCR) that featured scholarships designed to encourage blacks to attend previously all-white institutions. But late in the year a snag developed when OCR insisted that two previously segregated institutions in Norfolk eliminate duplicating programs.

Economy. Labor unrest dampened Virginia's economy during 1978. The nationwide coal strike paralyzed the far southwest counties early in the year. In midyear, an extended strike by the clerks of the Norfolk and Western Railway likewise halted coal production.

Miss America. Kylene Barker of Galax became the first Miss Virginia to win the Miss America title at Atlantic City.

WILLIAM LARSEN, *Radford College*

─────── **VIRGINIA · Information Highlights** ───────

Area: 40,817 square miles (105,716 km²).
Population (Jan. 1978 est.): 5,177,000.
Chief Cities (1970 census): Richmond, the capital, 249,-430; Norfolk, 307,951; Virginia Beach, 172,106.
Government (1978): *Chief Officers*—governor, John Dalton (R); lt. gov., Charles Robb (D). *General Assembly*—Senate, 40 members; House of Delegates, 100 members.
Education (1977–78): *Enrollment*—public elementary schools, 640,927 pupils; public secondary, 441,257; colleges and universities, 257,529 students. *Public school expenditures,* $1,812,509,000 ($1,464 per pupil).
State Finances (fiscal year 1977): *Revenues,* $4,098,-080,000; *expenditures,* $3,926,729,000.
Personal Income (1977): $35,246,000,000; per capita, $6,865.
Labor Force (July 1978): *Nonagricultural wage and salary earners,* 2,011,700; *unemployed,* 129,800 (5.2% of total force).

VIRGIN ISLANDS

On Jan. 2, 1978, the governor of the Virgin Islands, Cyril King, died of stomach cancer at the age of 56. King, the second elected governor of the Virgin Islands, had served three stormy years of his four-year term. He and his successor, Lt. Gov. Juan Francisco Luis, had been elected as independents, unaffiliated with either the local Democratic or Republican parties. But the island legislature was solidly in the hands of the Democratic Party, and the nonvoting resident commissioner in Congress, Ron De Lugo, is also a Democrat. Such strong party loyalties did not produce a smoothly run government, although they did promote honesty and inhibit political favoritism. The new governor was born on the neighboring Puerto Rican island of Vieques but spent practically all of his life on St. Croix of the Virgin Islands.

Constitution. The early part of 1978 was taken up with the preparation of a constitution. Although two draft constitutions had been prepared in previous years, this was the first undertaking to be authorized by the U. S. Congress. At the end of April, the final draft was almost unanimously approved by the Virgin Islands' 60-member constitutional assembly. Important changes from the original act included an increase of the unicameral legislature from 15 to 17 members, the setting up of three municipal governments on each of the three major islands, and the establishment of a Virgin Islands Supreme Court. The document first went to President Jimmy Carter, who approved it, and then to Congress. A public referendum on the constitution was not scheduled until after the November elections, so as to separate the referendum process from any electoral campaign.

Elections. The November 7 elections were carried out in an orderly fashion, despite hotly contested races at all levels. Of the almost 28,000 eligible voters in the Virgin Islands, 77.3% participated in the elections. The two candidates for governor were Ron De Lugo, the Democratic Resident Commissioner, and Juan Luis, the independent incumbent governor. The two candidates for De Lugo's vacated post were Melvin Evans, the first elected governor of the Virgin Islands, and Janet Watlington, De Lugo's administrative assistant. Watlington had won the Democratic nomination in a closely contested primary election; Evans ran as an independent Republican. While they elected a legislature controlled by the Democrats, voters rejected that party's candidates for the other top offices. Luis, the independent, defeated De Lugo, the Democrat, by a vote of 10,978 to 7,568. The independent Republican Melvin Evans narrowly defeated Janet Watlington, by a vote of 10,458 to 9,588.

THOMAS G. MATHEWS
*Institute of Caribbean Studies
University of Puerto Rico*

WASHINGTON

Initiatives and propositions dominated the November general elections in 1978. Washington officials continued to debate Indian fishing rights.

Elections. King county (Seattle) voters narrowly defeated a $35 million farmlands-preservation bond issue. Many cities and counties across the nation, beset by problems of housing and industrial development of agricultural land, watched the proposition closely. If enacted, the county would have been authorized to purchase development rights to agricultural land in the county to prevent its use for other than farmland. The value of the development rights would have been the difference between the value of the land as farmland and its value in an alternative use. County officials vowed to propose the proposition again.

Washington voters, by an almost two-to-one margin, followed a national trend and passed an initiative to prohibit busing of school children to a school more distant than the second school nearest to the place of residence. Immediately after passage, the Seattle School District, which was operating under the nation's first voluntary or non-court-ordered desegregation plan, announced it would sue to test the constitutionality of the results.

Seattle voters, by a 63% vote, rejected an initiative that would have repealed those parts of a Seattle nondiscrimination ordinance guaranteeing nondiscrimination on the basis of sexual orientation. Seattle thus became the first city or county in the nation to declare by popular vote that sexual preference could not be a lawful basis for discrimination in hiring or housing.

In the congressional races, voters of the solidly Democratic seventh Congressional district, after electing Republican Jack Cunningham in a run-off election in 1977 to complete the term of Rep. Brock Adams when he was named Secretary of transportation, returned to form and elected Mike Lowry (D), former member of the King County Council. Incumbents won

in all other congressional districts except the second, where Al Swift (D) won the seat being vacated by Lloyd Meeds (D). This resulted in a congressional delegation of six Democrats and one Republican.

Indian Fishing Rights. After more than four years of controversy between Indians and non-Indian commercial fishermen, the U. S. Supreme Court in October agreed to review the 1974 decision of U. S. District Court Judge George Boldt to grant treaty Indians the right to catch half the annual salmon run returning to traditional off-reservation Indian fishing grounds. The Supreme Court had declined to hear an appeal in 1974 shortly after Judge Boldt's decision. The court's decision to review the original decision was prompted by questions of jurisdiction raised in 1977 when Washington State Supreme Court Justice Charles T. Wright ruled that the State Department of Fisheries could not distinguish between Indians and non-Indians when establishing regulations regarding allowable catch.

In the years since Judge Boldt's decision, there have been dozens of protests by non-Indians, some of which erupted into shootings and boat rammings. The issue of fishing rights has figured prominently in congressional elections during the past several years.

WARREN W. ETCHESON
University of Washington

WASHINGTON, D. C.

A proposed amendment to the U. S. Constitution granting the District of Columbia voting representation in the Senate and House of Representatives was passed by Congress on August 22 and sent to the individual state legislatures for ratification. The proposal requires the approval of 38 states within seven years if it is to become an amendment to the constitution. New Jersey ratified the amendment on September 11, and Ohio did so on November 30, but efforts failed in California, Delaware, and Pennsylvania. If the amendment is adopted, Washington would send two senators and one or two representatives (depending on its population) to Congress. Since 1970, the District of Columbia has sent one nonvoting representative to the House of Representatives. Walter E. Fauntroy has been elected to that post five times.

Proponents argue that the city's 750,000 residents who pay taxes without representation must have full participation in the federal decision-making process. Opponents argue that Washington, D. C., is a city and not a state; that the majority of its residents are liberal, black, and Democratic; and that its delegates would dilute the representation of the states.

The amendment also would grant Washington electoral votes equal to the number of its senators and representatives (repealing the 23rd Amendment, which gave it three electoral votes).

—— WASHINGTON • Information Highlights ——

Area: 68,192 square miles (176,617 km²).

Population (Jan. 1978 est.): 3,684,000.

Chief Cities (1970 census): Olympia, the capital, 23,111; Seattle, 530,831; Spokane, 170,516; Tacoma, 154,581.

Government (1978): *Chief Officers*—governor, Dixy Lee Ray (D); lt. gov., John A. Cherberg (D). *Legislature* —Senate, 49 members; House of Representatives, 98 members.

Education (1977–78): *Enrollment*—public elementary schools, 395,237 pupils; public secondary, 381,226; colleges and universities, 262,961 students. *Public school expenditures,* $1,527,425,000 ($1,825 per pupil).

State Finances (fiscal year 1977): *Revenues,* $4,478,-273,000; *expenditures,* $4,092,803,000.

Personal Income (1977): $27,534,000,000; per capita, $7,528.

Labor Force (June 1978): *Nonagricultural wage and salary earners,* 1,471,300; *unemployed,* 109,700 (6.2% of total force).

WIDE WORLD

Congress debated authorizing additional funds for the unfinished Philip Hart Senate Office Building.

Moreover, the District would be able to participate in proposing and ratifying future constitutional amendments.

Government. Marion Barry, a former community activist, president of the Washington

An amendment, granting D. C. voting representation in Congress, was sent to the states for ratification.

H. J. Res. 554

Ninety-fifth Congress of the United States of America

AT THE SECOND SESSION

Begun and held at the City of Washington on Thursday, the nineteenth day of January, one thousand nine hundred and seventy-eight

Joint Resolution

Proposing an amendment to the Constitution to provide for representation of the District of Columbia in the Congress.

Resolved by the Senate and House of Representatives of the United States of America in Congress assembled (*two-thirds of each House concurring therein*), That the following article is proposed as an amendment to the Constitution of the United States, which shall be valid to all intents and purposes as part of the Constitution when ratified by the legislatures of three-fourths of the several States within seven years from the date of its submission by the Congress:

"ARTICLE —

"SECTION 1. For purposes of representation in the Congress, election of the President and Vice President, and article V of this Constitution, the District constituting the seat of government of the United States shall be treated as though it were a State.

"SEC. 2. The exercise of the rights and powers conferred under this article shall be by the people of the District constituting the seat of government, and as shall be provided by the Congress.

"SEC. 3. The twenty-third article of amendment to the Constitution of the United States is hereby repealed.

"SEC. 4. This article shall be inoperative, unless it shall have been ratified as an amendment to the Constitution by the legislatures of three-fourths of the several States within seven years from the date of its submission.".

THOMAS P. O'NEILL, JR.,
Speaker of the House of Representatives.

QUENTIN BURDICK,
Acting President of the Senate-pro Tempore.

I certify that this Joint Resolution originated in the House of Representatives.

EDMUND L. HENSHAW, JR.,
Clerk.

BY W. RAYMOND COLLEY,
Deputy Clerk.

[Received by the Office of the Federal Register, National Archives and Records Service, General Services Administration, August 28, 1978]

school board, and at-large member of the city council, was elected the city's second mayor under home rule, on November 7. Barry narrowly won the Democratic Party primary on September 12 against incumbent Mayor Walter Washington (initially appointed by President Johnson in 1967 and elected in 1974) and city council chairman, Sterling Tucker. Arrington Dixon, a lawyer, former computer science instructor, and ward council member since 1974, was elected council chairman. The only new member elected to the council was Betty Anne Kane, formerly on the Board of Education. Kane was the first white person to be elected to city-wide office since the beginning of home rule. Nearly half the new council membership is female. No other big city is governed by a legislative body with such a high proportion of women. In 1979, Democrats will occupy the mayor's office and 11 of the 13 city council seats.

Transportation. The Metro subway system was extended into Maryland during the year. Four new stations and 5.5 miles (8.9 km) were added to the Red Line, connecting it to Silver Spring (Montgomery county), Md., on February 6. The new Orange Line, with five stations and 7.6 miles (12.2 km) in length, was joined with the existing Blue Line at Stadium-Armory Station. A total of 31 miles (50 km) and 33 stations of the Metro system was operating, and approximately one third of the projected system was completed. The construction cost exceeded $1.8 billion by the end of 1978. Hours were expanded to offer late night and Saturday service.

New Attraction. The new East Building of the National Gallery of Art, a modern structure designed by I. M. Pei, was opened on June 1. It is situated on the Mall near the original gallery and is linked to it by an underground tunnel with moving sidewalks. (*See also* ART.)

MORRIS J. LEVITT, *Howard University*

WEST VIRGINIA

Familiar themes dominated much of West Virginia's news during 1978—flooding, following a severe winter, industrial accidents, an economy largely shaped by developments in the bituminous coal industry, and a hot political race.

Accidents. The worst non-coal mine construction accident in the state's history—and one of the worst in the nation's—claimed 51 lives April 27 when scaffolding collapsed inside a power company's cooling tower near St. Mary's on the Ohio River. Investigation of possible causes, including faulty concrete, insufficient setting-up time for earlier pourings, and persistent charges of safety violations, continued at year's end.

Coal Strike. When the 110-day strike by the United Mine Workers ended in late March, it had cost the state's 60,000 union miners more than $280 million in wages, and had left total personal income estimates almost $750 million below predicted levels. More than $40 million was lost to the state in tax revenues as a result of the stoppage, and 25% of the year's normal production was not mined.

The contract's terms did not provide the recovery hoped for, since many customers had switched to other suppliers during the strike. Within a few weeks of the resumption of production hundreds of empty coal cars were left standing on railway sidings near newly-closed mines.

Government. The West Virginia legislature, facing certain revenue losses during the coal strike, provided Gov. John D. (Jay) Rockefeller IV with substantial new tax production, mainly earmarked for road improvement. Described as a session that would have a long-term impact on the pocketbook, it produced 5¢ more on each pack of cigarettes, 2¢ more on each gallon of gasoline, and a 25% increase in vehicle license plate costs.

An election reform measure was passed in the closing hours of the 60-day session, shortening the time between primary and general elections, stiffening penalties for vote fraud, and giving corporations the right to have political funds similar to those of unions.

Politics. From the pre-primary period, political interest centered on the race for the U.S. Senate between incumbent Jennings Randolph and Republican challenger Arch Moore, two-time governor and former Congressman. Randolph, who holds the distinction of being the only active member of either house who was in Congress during the "100 days" of Franklin D. Roosevelt in 1933, defeated Moore by about 1% of the half million votes cast. Incumbent congressmen Harley Staggers, John Slack, and Robert Mollohan defeated Republican challengers; Democrat Nick Rahall was unopposed. The state legislature remained in Democratic hands.

Weather. Along with much of the rest of the nation, the Mountain State recorded its second

UPI

Near St. Mary's, W. Va., April 27, 51 men died as a scaffolding at a partially completed cooling tower collapsed.

record-breaking winter in a row, with heavy snow, rain and flash floods all coming before the end of January. Federal, state and private relief efforts were still under way in the southern valleys as another winter approached. Severe flooding returned in December.

Economy. The state's economy suffered with employment, overall industrial production, electric power generation, contract construction, and freight car loadings all down. Only lumber and farm income were up, among the conventional economic indicators, as the state still reflected the effects of the coal strike which had marred the year's beginning.

DONOVAN H. BOND
West Virginia University

── WEST VIRGINIA · Information Highlights ──

Area: 24,181 square miles (62,629 km²).
Population (Jan. 1978 est.): 1,873,000.
Chief Cities (1970 census): Charleston, the capital, 71,-505; Huntington, 74,315; Wheeling, 48,188.
Government (1978): *Chief Officers*—governor, John D. Rockefeller, IV (D); secy. of state, A. James Manchin (D). *Legislature*—Senate, 34 members; House of Delegates, 100 members.
Education (1977–78): *Enrollment*—public elementary schools, 234,174 pupils; public secondary, 167,195; colleges and universities, 81,121 students. *Public school expenditures*, $593,460,000.
State Finances (fiscal year 1977): *Revenues*, $1,875,-742,000; *expenditures*, $1,832,035,000.
Personal Income (1977): $11,129,000,000; per capita, $5,986.
Labor Force (July 1978): *Nonagricultural wage and salary earners*, 629,100; *unemployed*, 41,200 (5.7% of total force).

WISCONSIN

A dramatic victory sent a Republican to the governor's chair in Wisconsin, ending eight years of Democratic control and strengthening the two party system in the state.

Dreyfus Election. Lee S. Dreyfus was an "outsider," having no legislative experience and having played no role in the Republican party. His career had been that of a communications specialist and educator; for 11 years he was chancellor of the University of Wisconsin, Stevens Point. He declared that he was a "Republicat," and took on the Republican party leadership in running against the endorsed GOP candidate, Congressman Robert Kasten, in the September 12 primary. Dreyfus easily beat Kasten, 197,279 to 143,361.

Meanwhile, in the Democratic party, there was a similar battle going on. Lt. Gov. Martin J. Schreiber had been acting governor since July 1977 when Patrick Lucey was named ambassador to Mexico. It had been assumed that Schreiber, a former state senator, could be nominated without opposition. But David Carley, a wealthy businessman and long-time power in the party, also ran. It was an expensive campaign, with Carley spending $417,000 and Schreiber $386,-000 (Dreyfus spent $108,000 to Kasten's $513,-000). Schreiber won, 217,573 to 132,901.

Dreyfus' momentum continued. He aroused audiences with his populist speeches and used his trademark red vest as a campaign symbol. Democrats called him a flim-flam man, but he defeated Schreiber, 816,056 to 673,813.

In a post-election interview, Schreiber acknowledged that he could not defend what should have been a Democratic asset—the state is expected to have a $280 million budget surplus at the end of the 1977–79 biennium. Dreyfus declared that the money had been unfairly collected from the people and urged a change in the income tax system. Schreiber proposed property tax relief. The 1979 Legislature, prompted by Dreyfus, will have to decide which action to adopt.

Republicans made other gains in November, though not so many as might have been expected considering Dreyfus' victory. Democrats lost their two-thirds margin in the Assembly, but still control it, 60–39. They also lost a seat in the Senate, but have a 21–12 majority. Republicans picked up their third of the state's eight congressional districts when Tobias Roth, a state legislator from Appleton, defeated Robert Cornell, a Roman Catholic priest who was seeking his third term.

Russell Olson, a Republican legislator from Bassett, was elected lieutenant governor, but other state offices remained in Democratic hands: Vel Phillips as secretary of state, Bronson La Follette as attorney general, and Charles Smith as treasurer.

Legislature. Two public accountability bills were passed in a brief legislative session. One places further controls on lobbyists, including restrictions on campaign contributions. The other revises the ethics code, barring state officials from taking immediate employment with a firm with which their agencies were connected. The legislature also approved a revision of the court system, merging county and circuit courts.

Economy. Most sectors of the Wisconsin economy prospered with the state recording gains in population and employment. Unemployment was lower than the U. S. average. Farm receipts were up as milk prices continued strong.

PAUL SALSINI, *The Milwaukee Journal*

WISCONSIN • Information Highlights

Area: 56,154 square miles (145,439 km²).

Population (Jan. 1978 est.): 4,673,000.

Chief Cities (1970 census): Madison, the capital, 172,-007; Milwaukee, 717,372; Racine, 95,162.

Government (1978): *Chief Officers*—acting governor, Martin J. Schreiber (D). *Legislature*—Senate, 33 members; Assembly, 99 members.

Education (1976–77): *Enrollment*—public elementary schools, 522,600 pupils; public secondary, 422,737; nonpublic, 189,400; colleges and universities, 179,-444 students. *Public school expenditures,* $1,601,-287,000 ($1,635 per pupil).

State Finances (fiscal year 1977): *Revenues,* $4,931,-994,000; *expenditures,* $4,555,535,000.

Personal Income (1977): $32,047,000,000; per capita, $6,890.

Labor Force (July 1978): *Nonagricultural wage and salary earners,* 1,892,500; *unemployed,* 116,700 (5.0% of total force).

WIDE WORLD

Republican Lee S. Dreyfus, *right,* won 55% of the vote in the November 7 gubernatorial election, to defeat acting governor, Democrat Martin J. Schreiber.

UPI

Former Congresswoman Bella Abzug (*front row, center*) joins a group of Hollywood celebrities in "one of the last of the red-hot fund raising rallies for the Equal Rights Amendment."

WOMEN

Undoubtedly, the biggest women's issue in 1978 was the continuing struggle for the federal Equal Rights Amendment (ERA) and the extension of the time limit for its ratification.

Setbacks. Ever since 1975, when it was ratified by the 34th of the necessary 38 states, ERA was in trouble. During this time only one state—Indiana—approved it, while three—Idaho, Nebraska, and Tennessee—rescinded their earlier yes votes. And though opinions differed on the legality of such measures, they were, at least to some extent, indicative of the heated controversy surrounding the amendment.

In 1978 all efforts to add more states to the supportive roster failed. The South Carolina Senate not only voted against ratification on February 7, but the day after crushed a proposal for a statewide advisory referendum on the issue. On March 16 Kentucky became the fourth state to vote rescission, although Lt. Gov. Thelma Stovall, in the absence of Gov. Julian M. Carroll, vetoed that action four days later. The Illinois House of Representatives rejected ERA on June 7; it was the seventh straight year that the state legislature had done so. Illinois remained the only Northern industrialized state to hold out against the amendment.

To put more pressure on such recalcitrants the National Organization for Women (NOW), beginning in February 1977, asked its supporters among national organizations to hold their conventions or business meetings only in those states that had ratified ERA. But the boycott, to which numerous groups consented, did not sway any of the hold-outs to change their votes, and there

was some evidence that the move might have been counter-productive. Two of the states—Missouri and Nevada—moreover, challenged the boycott in court on the grounds that it violated antitrust laws as an illegal restraint of trade. It was estimated in April that the boycott had, up to that time, cost the nonratifying states about $100 million in lost convention business.

Extending the Deadline. Early in the year it became fairly clear to all involved that ERA was not moving. As the March 22, 1979, deadline for national ratification drew closer, the hopes of the amendment's supporters of achieving their goal grew dimmer. Consequently, the tactics in the protracted struggle were shifted. No longer was the main emphasis on quick ratification by the three more states needed, but rather on the extension by Congress of the time in which this might be achieved.

Typically, the proposal to extend the deadline for ratification for seven years became as hotly contested as the amendment itself, though not quite along the same lines. *The New York Times,* for example, declared itself "ardently . . . for its ratification," but argued against extension, asking "What would the E.R.A. supporters think of such a procedure if, for more than six years, they had successfully resisted an amendment, say, to outlaw abortions?" To such arguments NOW President Eleanor Smeal answered: "There can be no time limits on equality."

Proponents of the extension pointed out that the issue of women's suffrage had been debated for 70 years before the 19th Amendment was finally passed. The female members of Congress, headed by Sen. Hubert Humphrey's widow, Muriel, came out in force against the paper's arguments, correcting it on points of history as well as legalities. "E.R.A.," they stated, "was born in 1923, not in 1972, as *The Times* says. It took Congress 50 years to decide that women were constitutionally entitled to equal treatment and equal opportunity." AFL-CIO President George Meany castigated *The Times* for "abandoning the fight for justice."

Action in Congress. Resolutions for extension of the ratification deadline were introduced in both houses of Congress in May. The following month some 1,200 individuals and organizations signed a petition, published as an advertisement in *The New York Times,* urging immediate passage. In July a crowd of nearly 100,000 people, including a good number of men, marched in Washington in demonstration of support, both for the deadline extension and the amendment itself. President Jimmy Carter urged Congress to approve the extension, and both former President Gerald Ford and his wife, Betty, were also said to have lobbied for it. Opposition, however, was considerable. When the House resolution was reported out of the Judiciary Committee, the time limit had been scaled down to 39 months, instead of the seven years originally sought. So amended, the resolution passed the full House of Representatives on August 15 by a vote of 233–189—not exactly a landslide. The Senate resolution, on the other hand, faced a threat of filibuster, and Majority Leader Robert Byrd refused to call it up unless there appeared to be enough votes to ensure cloture. A concentrated effort by NOW and other sympathetic organizations was launched on September 26, with a rally in Washington. The endeavors were not in vain. On October 6, the Senate voted in favor of extending the time period for ratification to June 30, 1982, thereby giving the Equal Rights Amendment a major new lease on life. The outcome pleased President Carter who expressed the hope that "states which have not yet ratified the amendment will now take speedy advantage of this additional opportunity to do so." ERA opponents vowed to challenge the extension in the courts.

Wives Fighting Back. While ERA was battered considerably in 1978, some battered wives drew a great deal of attention during the year by their successful legal battles. The focus was on those who, tested beyond endurance, had killed their husbands and, rather than plead guilty and go to prison as such defendants usually have done, contested the charges on the grounds of self-defense or temporary insanity. Some of these cases ended in acquittal or a guilty verdict on a greatly reduced charge, while others drew only light sentences in recognition of ameliorating circumstances.

Perhaps the most publicized case was that of Francine Hughes, a Michigan housewife who had endured years of beatings by her husband before getting a divorce. When the estranged husband moved back into her home and again began to abuse her, she soaked his bedroom with gasoline when he was asleep and set a match to it. He died; Mrs. Hughes was acquitted.

Evelyn Ware's case was similar. A battered Oklahoma wife, she had fled to California and found a job in order to escape her husband's blows, only to have him follow, move in with her, and resume his physical violence. She shot him five times in the chest and head and, pleading self-defense, was found not guilty. So was Sharon Brown of Florida, who emptied a gun into her husband on their front lawn as he attacked her with a kitchen knife. She was acquitted after two former wives of the man testified to his violent nature. Sharon McNearney of Michigan, fearing what her husband, who had frequently beaten her, might do to her again, admittedly fired a shotgun blast at him. She, too, was acquitted. Even Jennifer Patri of Wisconsin, who shot her husband twice in the back and then went to considerable lengths to conceal the killing, was found guilty only on the reduced charge of manslaughter. She drew a 10-year sentence.

Phyllis Schlafly leads an anti-ERA rally in the rotunda of the Illinois Capitol. Later, the Illinois legislature refused to ratify the amendment.

UPI

The Larger Problem. Though such cases are spectacular and noteworthy for the trend they seem to represent, now that the cause of battered wives has become a prominent feminist issue, it should not be forgotten that the reverse is still much more common: spouse-killers are usually found guilty and sent to prison. But incidents ending in the use of deadly force are just a tiny part of the larger problem of abused wives, which is vastly more common than most people have believed. Thus, one study has indicated that some 28 million U. S. wives have been beaten by their husbands, resulting in 4.7 million serious injuries. Other studies have shown that firm handling of wife-abusers might have averted many later fatalities. For example, half of all the spouse-killings in Kansas City, Mo., occur after the police have been called to the affected homes at least five previous times because of family disturbances.

If the situation is similar elsewhere, there is hope that the new policy of the New York City Police Department of arresting wife-beaters may prevent some violent deaths in the future. The reversal of the department's previous practice, which came into effect in October, grew out of a suit by 12 women, charging the city's police and Family Court with unlawful denial of assistance after repeated beatings by their husbands. Without admitting guilt, the Police Department, in an out-of-court settlement, obligated itself both to arrest men for felonious assaults against their wives (provided there is reason to believe the crime has been committed) and to make mandatory the arrest of husbands who assault or threaten their wives after the women have obtained court orders of protection. It was the hope of those involved in the case that the agreement would act as a precedent and have far-reaching consequences in the rest of the country.

Women Abroad. Physical violence against women has actually become the focal point of the feminist struggle in some other countries. Thus, for example, the movement in Spain, which began in 1975—the year Generalissimo Franco died—has made its greatest inroads by rallying its supporters against the lenient treatment of rapists by the country's system of justice. It is estimated that up to 80% of all rapes in Spain go unreported, and the women's movement asserts that sexual abuse in the country has both social and political content, being used as a weapon by men to defend their macho society.

France is another country where rapes have been treated indifferently by the courts. Consequently, it was a major event in 1978, when two rape victims for the first time in the annals of French justice reached so far as to be heard in the Cours d'Assizes—the criminal court that handles serious felonies. Ironically, the fact that the two women were admitted lesbians helped the prosecution considerably, since it nullified the principal defense of the rapists—that of an implied consent. But the road to success was not

UPI
Six women were named as astronauts early in 1978.

easy. By the time the three culprits were sentenced, the matter had dragged through the courts for four years.

Physical abuse of another kind was the theme of an exhibition in Copenhagen, Denmark, by the Icelandic graphic artist Ragnheidur Jónsdóttir. With striking symbolism, she depicted the drudgery of the woman tied to her home as housewife and child-bearer by presenting her in the form of an empty maternity dress hung out to dry on a clothesline or held down in a chair—uncannily reminiscent of the electric chair—by the weight of pregnancy. Such ideas fall on fertile ground in Scandinavia, where women have actually come a long way toward equality with men—although the road ahead may still be a bit longer. All the Scandinavian countries, except Iceland, for instance, have women serving as cabinet ministers. The ratio is highest in Norway and Sweden, where one out of every four ministers is a woman.

See also CRIME.

MAY NEWMAN HALLMUNDSSON
Pace University

WIDE WORLD

Gov. Ed Herschler testifies on coal slurry pipelines before the House Interior and Insular Affairs committee.

WYOMING

The November elections, investigations into alleged government corruption, and social crimes in Rock Springs dominated 1978 events in the state of Wyoming.

Elections. Democratic incumbent Ed Herschler narrowly edged his Republican opponent to retain the governor's chair. Herschler credited his agricultural and environmental policies and his proposal to reduce property taxes while raising the severance tax as reasons for his narrow victory. Herschler had been hurt by charges of scandal in his administration.

In the U.S. Senate race Republican state legislative leader Alan Simpson, son of former governor and U.S. Sen. Milward Simpson, was elected to retiring Republican Clifford Hansen's seat. Dick Cheney, former White House Chief of Staff for President Gerald Ford, captured the lone congressional seat for the Republicans.

Republicans increased their hold on the state legislature: Senate, 19–11; House 42–20. For the first time women will outnumber men on the state's boards and commissions. The secretary of state, new state treasurer, and new superintendent of public instruction are women.

Scandals Charged. A statewide grand jury investigated charges of corruption in state government and local affairs in Rock Springs. The state attorney general was indicted on common law charges that he had failed to investigate evidence of embezzlement at three state institutions, had warned his brother on a drug investigation, and

misused funds. The charges were subsequently dismissed.

Before a grand jury investigation of Rock Springs prostitution, gambling, and drug trafficking was completed, a subpoenaed undercover agent was killed and the local police chief was charged with first degree murder.

Energy and Water. In September a federal judge in Nebraska ordered construction halted on the Grayrocks Dam and Reservoir which was to supply water for the (U.S.) $1.6 billion Laramie River Power Station project being built near Wheatland, indicating that the project might harm nesting grounds of the whooping crane and that the environmental impact statement did not assess adequately the project's effect on water. Representatives from state governments, power cooperatives, and environmental groups met several times in an attempt to resolve the dispute. A bill to permit construction of coal slurry pipelines by eminent domain was killed by the U.S. House of Representatives. The Wyoming legislature had previously approved the use of Wyoming water for the production of the coal slurry.

The state signed a new agreement with the federal government allowing the state to regulate mining and reclamation on federal land. The federal government retained final jurisdiction over issuance of mining permits but the state will enforce mining and reclamation activities.

Legislature and University. In its regular session the state legislature was unable to agree on the university request to establish a new medical school. In a special session the legislature reconsidered and denied funding for the school. In July the dean of the skeleton medical school and the president of the University of Wyoming resigned.

Other Events. The U.S. Department of Transportation proposed a discontinuation of AMTRAK passenger rail service in Wyoming within a year. Wyoming construction projects suffered from a shortage of cement, and spring rains caused heavy damage in ten northern counties.

JOHN B. RICHARD, *University of Wyoming*

─────── **WYOMING · Information Highlights** ───────

Area: 97,914 square miles (253,597 km²).
Population (Jan. 1978 est.): 414,000.
Chief Cities (1970 census): Cheyenne, the capital, 40,-914; Casper, 39,361; Laramie, 23,143; Rock Springs, 11,657.
Government (1978): *Chief Officers*—governor, Ed Herschler (D); secy. of state, Thyra Thomson (R). *Legislature*—Senate, 30 members; House of Representatives, 62 members.
Education (1977–78): *Enrollment*—public elementary schools, 48,805; public secondary, 43,516; colleges and universities, 19,727 students. *Public school expenditures,* $202,500,000 ($1,872 per pupil).
State Finances (fiscal year 1977): *Revenues,* $563,-376,000; *expenditures,* $448,313,000.
Personal Income (1977): $3,073,000,000; per capita, $7,562.
Labor Force (July 1978): *Nonagricultural wage and salary earners* 187,700; *unemployed,* 5,900 (2.7% of total force).

YOUTH

The pendulum of young people's attitudes and goals has been swinging fast. Gone is the revolutionary fervor of the early 1970's, when a combination of civil rights activism and opposition to the war in Vietnam shaped the outlook of at least the most vocal youth leadership. By contrast with that era's mixture of anger and exuberance, the youth of the late 1970's appears almost somber and detached from broader concerns. A new introspective, if not egocentric, realism has replaced the missionary zeal to reform the world and to remake its institutions.

The Youth Culture, which became a dominant force in the 1950's, when the babies of the post World War II boom were reaching adolescence, has lost some of its acceptability. As the U. S. population ages, designers and merchandisers no longer consider the youth market as dominant.

New Attitudes. Changing economic conditions are in large measure responsible for changes in youth attitudes. In a period of middle-class boom, young people, particularly of college age, found it easy to turn their backs on competitive traditions and standards of behavior. In a headlong rush toward an egalitarianism, students demanded, and often achieved, the abolition of grades and tests, and the replacement of more specific qualitative judgments with a new pass/fail system. Along with the student's war against university administrations, young people attacked large corporations as representatives of the established systems.

Accompanying phenomena of that era were the drug culture and the turn toward communal living, indicating an attempt to find new values and mores outside the system.

As the competition for jobs and concern about careers sharpened in response to the slowdown of growth in the American economy as well as in the population itself, young people increasingly returned to the search for personal security and success within the system they had so recently spurned or tried to change. By 1978, the extreme of anti-competitive fervor had given way to what many educational and social observers view as a new excess in peer competition, at least among the college-going age group. In particular, the race for admission to law and medical schools as well as to graduate schools of business has turned many campuses into sober, achievement-oriented arenas of competitive struggle. The pass/fail innovation in most colleges gave way to a scramble for A's again.

Employment. Even though middle-class youths from relatively affluent homes also feel the impact of inflation, a wide gap remains between them and their disadvantaged contemporaries. While the overall U.S. unemployment rate is about 6%, teen-age unemployment is about 17%. Even worse, 39% of out-of-school nonwhite youths are out-of-work.

In response to this problem, the Labor Department provided in 1978 six cities—Baltimore, Boston, Detroit, Cincinnati, Denver, and Seattle—with special grants of more than $15 million each to test a program that guarantees jobs to all teen-agers who want to work and who, at the same time, agree to stay in or return to high school. Thus, the program tried to address itself simultaneously to two serious problems—youth unemployment and the danger that inadequate education will turn teen-age joblessness into chronic unemployability. The need for such remedies was underscored by the disclosure that approximately 13% of all high school graduates subsequently prove to be functionally illiterate, i.e. lacking the skills needed for such tasks as reading labels or filling out job applications.

The harsh effects of chronic youth unemployment on society as a whole were dramatically presented in the American Broadcasting documentary, *Youth Terror: The View from Behind the Gun.* The program showed that, having grown up without the expectation of jobs, many of these young people of the urban slums eventually find the excitement and profitability of crime to be an easier and more appealing existence that makes the idea of work, even if jobs were available, pale by comparison.

Youth unemployment has become a matter of international concern. According to a report from the International Labor Office in Geneva, university degrees are in many parts of the world (in contrast to the United States) "becoming tickets to nowhere." Unemployment among youths between the ages of 15 and 24 in 23 industrial member nations of the Organization for Economic Cooperation and Development exceeds 10%. Sweden's Dr. Ulf Otto warned that mass unemployment may be causing an increasing number of suicides among young people.

Statistics provided by the International Labor Office indicate that by 1981 France will have a surplus of 16,000 engineers, architects, and scientists; in Japan almost one third of all 1976 university graduates were unable to find jobs by the end of that year; in the United States it is projected that over a ten-year period beginning in 1974 there may be a surplus of 950,000 graduates. Some European countries are experimenting with the concept of paid educational leaves for older workers who may wish to return to school or college, as a means of opening up more job opportunities for young people. In the United States there is some concern that Congress, by eliminating 65 as the mandatory retirement age, may have initiated a policy that has the opposite effect—making it more difficult for young people to enter the job market.

Torsten Husén, director of the Institute for the Study of International Problems in Education at the University of Stockholm, points to changing youth attitudes toward education as a consequence of the difficulty of obtaining employment. Young people, says Professor Husén, "are opposed to curricula centered on specific occupational skills because they feel they are being locked into occupations from which it will be difficult to escape." Particularly young people from more affluent homes give more importance "to personal fulfillment, security, and the chance to devote time to rewarding leisure activities."

Although jobs in academic areas continue to be scarce, earlier fears that the college diploma would lose its value in the United States, as it has in a number of European countries, have not been borne out. While youth unemployment among the uneducated is high—second only to Italy—the American Council on Education reports that job offers to college graduates in the 1977–78 period finished at a pace that equaled or exceeded the boom years of the 1960's. According to the College Placement Council, jobs offered to bachelor's degree recipients were up 35% over the previous year and 90% over 1975–76. Offers to holders of master's degrees were up only 3%, but offers at the doctoral level rose 20%, and almost 60% above 1975. The most substantial gains were registered in engineering and in business related disciplines, followed by the sciences and, at a slightly lower rate, the humanities and social sciences. The percentage increase in job offers to women with bachelor's degrees was considerably higher than in offers to men.

Educational Skills. Less encouraging were recurring complaints that young people's skills, particularly in writing, had been declining. The Educational Testing Service reported that verbal scores on the Scholastic Aptitude Tests declined 49 points (on a 600-point scale) between 1963 and 1977. The National Assessment of Educational Progress reported that 17 year olds' command of the mechanics of writing declined between 1970 and 1974, and that only half of them could organize their ideas on paper.

A pamphlet prepared by the Association of American Publishers to help college freshmen get the most out of their textbooks had to be rewritten on a ninth-grade level. At the University of California at Berkeley, which admits only students from the top 12% of the state's high school graduates, nearly half of the freshmen are so deficient in writing ability that they need a remedial course popularly known as "bonehead English." Observers believe that lack of sufficient writing practice in school and the amount of time spent watching television have contributed to these problems. At the same time, the National Assessment also found many teenagers are ignorant of American government, with fewer than half able to name even one of their senators or representatives in Congress. In the first half of the 1970's, the ability of 17 year-olds to explain the basic concepts of democracy declined from 86% to 74%.

Running counter to these trends, a sizable minority of young people are taking an active part in government. In 1978, some 450 students from 24 states met in Washington for the sixth annual National Student Lobbying conference, cosponsored by the National Student Association and the National Student Lobby. To increase their power, the two organizations merged.

FRED M. HECHINGER
President, The New York Times Co. Foundation

FRANÇOIS BOTA, LIAISON

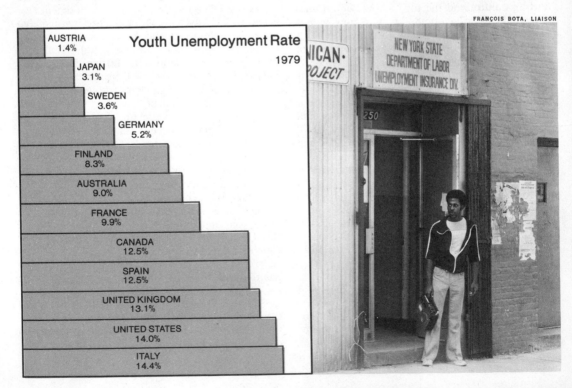

YUGOSLAVIA

Despite ample evidence that the tightened one-party rule and a system of self-management were incompatible, 1978 was a year of political stability.

The Communist Party. The League of Communists of Yugoslavia (LCY) held its 11th Congress in Belgrade, June 20–23, in the presence of nearly 2,300 party delegates and some 130 representatives of foreign Communist and left-wing parties. Among the most prominent visitors were Fyodor Kulakov, member of the politburo of the Soviet Communist Party, and Enrico Berlinguer, Italian Communist Party leader. Chinese Communists sent a warm message of greeting. The Congress itself brought no surprises and confirmed Tito's preeminence at the helm of the LCY. A new 166-member Central Committee, with 96 newcomers, was elected. That body in turn elected the new Presidium of the Central Committee, consisting of 24 members (instead of the previous 39). Stane Dolanc was elected the Presidium's secretary. Personnel changes and streamlining of the LCY leadership were intended to enhance its effectiveness and control.

Politics. The new Yugoslav Federal Assembly met on May 15. Its convocation ended a five-month process of designating and electing delegates to the communal, intermunicipal, provincial, and republican assemblies. This process is a unique feature of the Tito regime since the abolition of previous parliamentary procedures. The Federal Assembly, with 220 delegates, and the Chamber of Republics and Autonomous Provinces, with 88 delegates, topped the hierarchy of indirectly elected delegations. The Federal Assembly reelected Veselin Djuranović as prime minister and approved the new 29-member Federal Council. Among the council's many new members was Josip Vrhovec, the new foreign minister. Army generals Nikola Ljubičić and Franjo Herljević kept their respective positions as ministers of national defense and internal affairs.

Economy. As in previous years, the economy continued to be uneven. Industrial production for the first eight months of 1978 increased by 8.3% in comparison with the same period in 1977. Wheat and corn harvests were only slightly below the high figures for 1977. A record tourist season and a high level of remittances by workers employed abroad were other economic assets.

Conversely, the economy suffered from a 14–15% annual inflation rate, a low (3%) level of labor productivity, the indebtedness of numerous business enterprises, and a large trade imbalance. In the first nine months of 1978, exports equaled $4,100,000,000 and imports $7,250,-000,000. The greatest obstacle to Yugoslavia's foreign trade was the European Community (EC). The Joint Venture Act, approved on April 15 by the Federal Assembly, was intended to attract more foreign capital.

Foreign Relations. An official visit to Yugo-

Yugoslav President Tito joins the Carters in waving to crowd from a White House balcony.

UPI

slavia by Chinese chairman Hua Kuo-feng, August 21–29, was the most important diplomatic event of the year. It followed Tito's 1977 visit to China and signified a full reconciliation, on both state and party levels, between the two countries. Hua met Tito twice, traveled extensively, and was enthusiastically greeted everywhere. He was lavish in his praise for Yugoslavia's system of self-management, its armed forces, and its policy of nonalignment. Hua stressed that Yugoslav-Chinese relations were based on Marxism-Leninism and that "we are linked by a similar past and united in a joint struggle."

Hua's visit to Yugoslavia evoked an unfavorable reaction in the Soviet Union. The official Soviet news agency, TASS, denounced it on August 22 as "undermining the unity of socialist countries." In a speech on September 7, Tito complained about criticism from the Soviet government and "fabrications" by the Soviet press. He declared that "we have done nothing directed against the Soviet Union."

Enrico Berlinguer, of the Italian Communist party, visited Yugoslavia, October 10–11, and met with Tito. Berlinguer noted "a broad identity of views" between the Italian and Yugoslav Communist parties. However, Edvard Kardelj, the most prominent Yugoslav political theorist, maintained that Eurocommunism could not be expected to take hold in any communist-ruled country.

Yugoslav-Bulgarian relations continued to be strained, despite a continual exchange of delegations. A resolution adopted by the 11th LCY Congress denounced Bulgaria's denial of the rights of the Macedonian national minority. The Bulgarian delegation to the congress rejected this accusation.

Relations between Yugoslavia and the United States, which have improved significantly under the Carter administration, were further enhanced by Tito's visit to Washington, March 6–10 and one by a high-level Yugoslav military delegation, headed by Nikola Ljubičić, at the end of September. Ljubičić held talks with U. S. Secretary of Defense Harold Brown and visited a number of U. S. military installations.

MILORAD M. DRACHKOVITCH
Stanford University

────── **YUGOSLAVIA • Information Highlights** ──────
Official Name: Socialist Federal Republic of Yugoslavia.
Location: Southeastern Europe.
Area: 98,650 square miles (255,504 km²).
Population (1978 est.): 22,000,000.
Chief Cities (1974 est.): Belgrade, the capital, 845,000; Zagreb, 602,000; Skopje, 389,000.
Government: *Head of state,* Tito (Josip Broz), president (took office 1953). *Head of government,* Veselin Djuranović, prime minister (took office March 1977), *Legislature*—Federal Assembly: Federal Chamber and Chamber of Republics and Provinces.
Monetary Unit: Dinar (18.9 dinars equal U. S.$1, Aug. 1978).
Manufactures (major products): Processed food, machinery, textiles, nonferrous metals, wood.
Agriculture (major products): Corn, wheat, sugar beets, tobacco.

YUKON

Economic development, the appointment of a new chief executive officer, and news regarding land claims were major 1978 events in the Yukon Territory.

Economy. The mining industry experienced no strikes in 1978, and the five operating mines had a total mineral production valued at (C.) $210,215,000 for 1977. The Clinton Creek Asbestos Mine officially shut down in August because of a lack of mineral deposits. The tourism industry enjoyed its most productive year since 1975, hosting over 250,000 visitors and adding about $30 million to the Yukon economy. Passage of a U. S. energy bill in September cleared the way for construction of the $10 billion (U. S.) Alaska Highway natural gas pipeline to be built through the southern Yukon beginning in 1981. Two major highway projects were completed in 1978. The Dempster Highway, a 417-mile (671-km) link between Dawson City, Yukon and Inuvik, Northwest Territories, was completed in the autumn but remains impassable until mid-1979 due to the lack of a ferry crossing on the Peel River. The Skagway/Carcross Road, linking Skagway, Alas., with the Yukon highway system, was completed in October.

Politics. Yukon Commissioner Dr. Arthur M. Pearson left his federally appointed position as chief executive officer of the Yukon government, Oct. 18, 1978, in the face of criminal charges by the Royal Canadian Mounted Police of illegal transfer of mining claims.

A public inquiry into the possibility of judicial wrongdoing by senior government officials, including the commissioner and deputy commissioner, concluded that only "errors in judgment" had been made.

The November 1978 territorial election marked the first time in the 80-year history of Yukon politics that a party system was adopted by the electorate. The number of elected members was increased from 12 to 16 in 1978.

Land Claims. The federal government set aside 15,000 square miles (38,850 km²) of land in northern Yukon as part of a land claims settlement with the Inuvialuit natives of the Northwest Territories. There was no major progress toward a final settlement of the land claim by the 6,000 Yukon Indians.

ANDREW HUME
Whitehorse, Yukon

────── **YUKON • Information Highlights** ──────
Area: 207,076 square miles (536,327 km²).
Population (1978 est.): 22,100.
Chief City (1976 census): Whitehorse, the capital, 13,-311.
Government (1978): *Chief Officers*—commissioner, James Smith; deputy commissioner, Douglas Bell; Chief Justice, Court of Appeal, H. C. B. Maddison; Judge of the Supreme Court, John L. Farris. *Legislature*—Territorial Council, 16 members.
Education (1977–78): *Enrollment*—public elementary and secondary schools, 4,990 pupils.

ZAIRE

The armed invasion of southern Zaire by Katangan rebels in May 1978 and the subsequent intervention of French and Belgian troops brought Zaire to the front pages of the world's newspapers. It added to tensions between the United States and its European allies and the Soviet Union, Cuba, and East Germany.

Although the year ended with Zaire still near bankruptcy, the crisis did not pull the nation apart. Instead, it sparked what Western diplomats regarded as one of the most important efforts in recent years to reduce military tension in Africa.

At the same time, Zaire's President Mobutu Sese Seko dodged Western pressure to share internal political power, and he emerged from the invasion with his regime strengthened. It was expected that there would be at least a temporary end to the flareups of violence in the southern province of Shaba (formerly Katanga), the location of some of Africa's richest mineral deposits.

The diplomatic move which helped stabilize the situation, and for which Western diplomats claimed a large part of the credit, was the renewal of diplomatic relations between Zaire and its Marxist neighbor to the south, Angola. It was in Angola that the rebel FNLC (National Front for the Liberation of the Congo) was based.

At the time of the May invasion, U. S. President Jimmy Carter charged that the invaders had been trained and incited by Cuban advisers in Angola. Angola charged that Mobutu's government was supplying arms and support to the UNITA (National Union for the Total Independence of Angola) guerrillas resisting the government.

Western policymakers, who had once encouraged Mobutu to support UNITA in the hope of keeping pressure on Angola's Marxist government, had begun to reevaluate that strategy even before the invasion. The invasion itself convinced them to concentrate on improving relations with Angolan President Agostinho Neto.

In August, Neto visited Kinshasa, the capital of Zaire, and in October, Mobutu went to Luanda, Angola. For the first time since the Marxist MPLA (Popular Movement for the Liberation of Angola) took power in 1975, embassies were opened and ambassadors named.

Mobutu apparently dropped his support for UNITA, and Neto apparently succeeded in moving the most heavily armed Zairian refugees in his country away from the border. He promised to enforce tighter controls and repeatedly denied that he had encouraged the FNLC to invade.

Guerrilla Invasion. In mid-May, a motley band of about 4,500 irregulars, supported by armed and unarmed civilians in the Shaba region, moved into southern Zaire through Angola and Zambia. More successful than in their aborted 1977 invasion, the rebels pushed into the mining town of Kolwezi, the center of Zaire's thriving copper and cobalt industries.

Initially well disciplined, the rebels soon began drinking and demanding booty from white mining technicians, mainly Belgians, some French, and about 100 Americans. Many of the 2,000 Europeans managed to flee in the early stages of the invasion.

But the rebels then went on a rampage against the remaining whites in Kolwezi, with small firearms mowing down men, women, and children. The bodies of at least 90 Europeans were recovered, and as many as 130 may have been killed. Several thousand black residents of Shaba also were killed.

Shocked by increasingly strident reports from its embassy in Kinshasa, France decided to act a few days after Kolwezi fell to the rebels. Using airplanes and parachutes supplied by the United States, the 2nd parachute regiment of the French Foreign Legion was dispatched from Corsica and dropped on Kolwezi.

Within four days, Kolwezi and the surrounding area were cleared of invaders, order was established, and the evacuation of the remaining whites had begun. Meanwhile, Belgian troops had landed at a nearby airport, but they stayed out of most of the fighting. The invaders fled back to Angola through Zambia.

The incident was an embarrassment to the 30,000-man Zairian army, whose forces in the area had exacted tribute from the Shaba citizens but had been powerless in the face of the invasion. President Mobutu, who had repeatedly shifted command of the army so as to avoid a coup against him, promised after the invasion to clean up corruption in the army and to improve its effectiveness with the help of French and Moroccan advisers.

A pan-African peace-keeping force was put together to maintain quiet in the region. The force was comprised of troops from Morocco, Senegal, Togo, and Gabon, and a medical team from the Ivory Coast. In addition, a four-nation monitoring group was formed under the Organization of African States (OAS) in an effort to protect the border from further invasions.

Mining and the Economy. Despite the restoration of peace, most European technicians refused to return to the region. However, Zaire managed

---

ZAIRE · Information Highlights

Official Name: Republic of Zaire.
Location: Central equatorial Africa.
Area: 905,365 square miles (2,344,895 km²).
Population (1978 est.): 26,700,000.
Chief Cities (July 1, 1974): Kinshasa, the capital, 2,008,352; Kananga, 601,239.
Government: *Head of state and government,* Mobutu Sese Seko, president (took office Nov. 1965). *Legislature* (unicameral)—National Legislative Council.
Monetary Unit: Zaire (0.78 zaire equals U. S.$1, Sept. 1978).
Manufactures (major products): Processed and unprocessed minerals, consumer products, metal and chemical products, construction materials, steel.
Agriculture (major products): Palm oil, coffee, rubber, tea, bananas, cotton, cocoa (cash crop), manioc, plantains, corn, rice, vegetables, fruits, sugar (cash crop).

PATRICK CHAUVEL, SYGMA

A French soldier guards a captured Katangan rebel during the guerrilla invasion of southern Zaire.

to resume nearly full copper production within three months of the invasion, using Zairian and a few European technicians.

The national copper mining company, Gecamines, which is closely supervised by Belgian interests, predicted that total production for 1978 would be as much as 90% of original projections. However, Western experts felt that it would be difficult to maintain steady production without the help of more foreign engineers.

The two major economic problems remaining for Zaire were its enormous foreign debt (to Western banks and governments and to the International Monetary Fund) and its difficulties in internal economic management.

At (U. S.) $3 billion, the debt was equal to the nation's gross national product. With international copper prices still low after a sharp decline in 1975, the government found it impossible to keep up with loan payments. Despite repeated meetings with Western diplomats and bank representatives, no satisfactory payment schedule was worked out after the Shaba invasion, whose turmoil further curtailed the inflow of foreign exchange.

Nevertheless, an international consortium headed by Citibank announced that it would make a new loan of $215 million to help straighten out Zaire's economy. The banks were seeking to avoid a default or rescheduling of the loan, which would damage the nation's credit rating. However, Western experts expected that Zaire would have to borrow several hundred million dollars more in 1979.

In exchange for its continued support, the International Monetary Fund effectively took control of the national bank. A retired official of West Germany's Bundesbank, Irwin Blumenthal, was named principal director of the Zaire central bank, effectively putting him in control of the nation's foreign currency transactions. And at President Mobutu's request, the UN named a British expert to control the Finance Ministry.

Nevertheless, these moves provoked criticism among many financial experts. About 20% of the national budget, for example, continued to be funneled through the presidency. In 1977, Mobutu himself singled out corruption as the "mal Zairois" (Zairian illness), and many observers doubted that the system could be changed.

In fact, it was widely believed that discontent with administrative inefficiency and corruption was at the root of the Shaba invasion. Inflation, at about 80%, was completely out of control. Wage increases in the previous two years were estimated to have been 40% less than price increases. According to one report, a sack of cassava, the basic food, cost about 20 zaires, twice the legal minimum monthly wage. Soldiers, government employees, policemen, and businessmen felt obliged to demand from the people what Mobutu has called the "invisible tax" (bribes) in order to make their own incomes meet their needs.

Domestic Affairs. Although Mobutu impressed foreign diplomats with his openings toward Angola, he disappointed his Western allies with his domestic policies. On the positive side, he released a large number of political prisoners after the invasion, including former Foreign Minister Karl-i-Bond, who had been sentenced to death for his alleged role in the 1977 Shaba invasion. Mobutu also announced an amnesty, which brought back thousands of refugees from Angola. After the executions of 27 military leaders and civilians on charges of treason early in 1978, the new policy was viewed as a liberalization.

But Mobutu continued to keep control of the government in his own hands, leaving his cabinet responsible only for bureaucratic decisions. He was widely accused of favoring people from his native region of Equateur in the north and of persecuting tribespeople from such southern regions as Shaba.

Under Zaire's constitution, the president of the nation's only political party, the Popular Movement of the Revolution, is automatically named president of the country. In late 1977, an unopposed Mobutu was overwhelmingly reelected for a third seven-year term, despite a constitutional provision limiting presidents to two terms.

JIM BROWNING, *Paris-based Journalist*

ZOOLOGY

Two contrasting aspects of zoology received extensive coverage by the popular press in 1978. One may prove to be highly important, and the other was merely a publicity stunt to sell a book. These topics were animal rights and human clones.

The expanding legal, social, and moral awareness of human rights precipitated a gingerly inspection of animal rights by the United States National Institutes of Health. Supporters of animal rights variously argued against hunting, fishing, the use of animals in laboratory experiments, and in extreme cases, even against the use of pesticides to kill crop-destroying insects. "Dolphin rights" was used unsuccessfully as a defense in a Hawaiian courtroom by a university graduate student who was brought to trial for releasing two experimental dolphins. In England, supporters of animal rights entered a "guerrilla phase." The "animal liberation front" conducted a campaign of sabotage and violence against animal breeding organizations and research laboratories using animals in experiments.

In contrast, the report of a human clone was clearly nothing other than a hoax. "Cloning" in various invertebrates and certain lower vertebrates is a normal mode of reproduction. Professor Robert Vrijenhock of Rutgers University reported the existence of cloning in several groups (including insects and other invertebrates) and reported in detail on clonal populations of small minnows in a desert stream in northwest Mexico (*Science,* Feb. 3, 1978). Few zoologists doubt that human clones are possible since, in one sense, identical twins are clones, but the case reported in 1978 was inconsistent with known embryological processes and current technology.

Another development, which went unnoticed by the popular press, may prove to be the most important of 1978. This was the use of a tiny free-living nematode (*Caenorhabditis elegans*)

PHOTOS UPI

Right: A scientist at the National Marine Fisheries Service examines near-extinct Atlantic Ridley turtles. The U. S. National Park Service and Mexican government are attempting to save the Kemp's Ridley turtle, *above and below.*

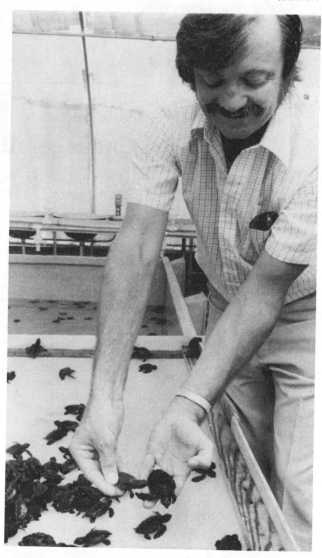

as a replacement for the fruit fly, *Drosophila,* and the bacterium, *Escherichia coli,* in genetic and other intensive biological studies.

Paleozoology. John E. Repetski of the U. S. Geological Survey reported the discovery of a fish fossil in Wyoming about 40 million years older than any previously reported vertebrate (*Science,* May 5, 1978).

Professor Thor A. Hansen of Yale University showed that ancient (Lower Territory) marine gastropods with planktonic (free swimming) larvae were more widely distributed and survived much longer before extinction (average, 4.4 million years) than relatives with nonplanktonic larvae (average, 2.2 million years).

Professors Robert Bakker (Johns Hopkins University) and John Ostrum (Yale University) presented a reinterpretation of data concerning dinosaurs. They and others contended that dinosaurs were not cold-blooded, like modern reptiles, but warm-blooded like most modern birds and mammals. Although not accepted by most paleozoologists, their arguments are causing wide reconsideration of old "truisms" about dinosaurs.

Another fossil discovery brought into question basic assumptions concerning the origin and evolution of modern birds. James Jenson of Brigham Young University reported fragments from the Late Jurassic period in eastern Colorado that may prove to be the remains of a bird at least as old as, and even more advanced than, *Archaeopteryx,* previously thought to be the oldest.

Evolution. Just as the fossil record provides glimpses of evolutionary changes in animals, so do intensive evaluations of living animals. Professor John A. Endler of Princeton University has used this method to promote a theory of macroevolution (that speciation occurs over a relatively short period of time as a result of internally controlled changes in the animal). His views are presented in the book *Geographic Variation, Speciation, and Clines* (Princeton University Press).

Still another approach to interpreting evolution was provided by Professor Dorothy A. Miller of Columbia University. Utilizing modern cytological techniques, Professor Miller showed that, contrary to the conclusions of other researchers, modern man is probably more closely related to the gorilla than he is to the chimpanzee.

Drs. Robert W. Sussman (Washington University, St. Louis) and Peter H. Raven (Missouri Botanical Garden) summarized data concerning the co-evolution of nectar-producing traits in certain flowering plants and nectar-feeding adaptations in bats, nonflying mammals, and birds, which insured pollination in plants.

ZOOLOGY—SPECIAL REPORT:

The Endangered Species

The year 1978 was the most eventful one for wildlife supporters since the U. S. Congress passed the Endangered Species Act of 1973, the most comprehensive and important bill ever enacted to guard against the threat of wildlife extinction. By encouraging state and public participation in the protection of ecosystems and habitats, this legislation provided a mechanism whereby to balance industrial development with adequate concern and responsibility for its consequences. With continued public support, the bill's purpose may be realized—the preservation of endangered species for their "esthetic, ecological, educational, historical, recreational, and scientific values."

The authors and supporters of the Endangered Species Act recognized that extinction was not a new phenomenon. Historically, it has occurred as a consequence of natural environmental changes. Because this was a slow process, other species were able to adapt, and a balance of species and habitats was maintained. Human activities, however, have altered the evolutionary process to such a degree that there has been an alarming increase in the number of vanishing species. In the United States and Puerto Rico, only two mammals and three birds became extinct between 1600 and 1850; between 1850 and 1973, however, more than 50 species were lost. Since the law was passed in 1973, 109 species have been added to the endangered or threatened (likely to become endangered in the foreseeable future) list. All told, there are some 200 species so listed.

In 1978, the first species, the Tecopa pupfish, was removed from the endangered list. It was not removed because its numbers increased, however, but because it was presumed to be extinct. Stream channelization, pollution, and the introduction of competing, nonnative species into its only known habitat (in California) were considered the probable causes of its extinction. Officials of the U. S. Fish and Wildlife Service (USFWS), responsible for administering the Endangered Species Act, announced that if certain man-engineered projects had been carefully planned, the loss of this unique life form could have been avoided.

Provisions in the Endangered Species Act to promote environmental considerations in planning dams and other projects were made mandatory in January 1978. Since 1973, there have been more than 8,000 consultations between USFWS officials and various federal agencies

Behavior. Numerous studies of animal behavior were published in 1978. W. G. Eberhard of the Universidad del Valle in Cali, Colombia, reported "aggressive chemical mimicry" in a spider (*Science,* Dec. 16, 1977). Most relatives of this spider expend much energy spinning and maintaining complex orb webs to capture insects. This particular species, however, spins a web consisting only of a sticky ball at the end of a short vertical thread. It then secretes a pheromone which attracts male moths to the area. The spider then swings the ball at the moth and traps it. The spider descends the thread, paralyzes its prey, and feeds on it.

Older, woolly aphids, like various others of the species, have a commensal relation with certain types of ants. The ants protect the aphids and feed on a sweet honeydew secreted by them. Thomas Eisner and his colleagues at Cornell University reported on a predatory, larval lacewing that successfully lives in these colonies, feeding on the aphids and avoiding the ants (*Science,* Feb. 17, 1978). Avoidance is accomplished by a "wolf in sheep's clothing" technique. The lacewings coat themselves in a waxy wool removed from the backs of the aphids. Thus adorned, they are able to feed on the aphids without being recognized by the protective ants. S. Lustick, B. Battersby, and M. Kelty of Ohio State University reported that herring gulls orient themselves toward the sun during the breeding season to minimize heat absorption. As the sun moves across the sky, the gull gradually changes its position to reduce exposed body area.

Desert scorpions utilize compressional and surface waves in the sand to locate burrowing prey from distances of over 50 centimeters (19 inches). This behavior was described by P. H. Brownell of the University of California at Riverside.

Environmental Extremes. The existence of specialized life forms in hot springs, glacial waters, high elevations, and the deep sea has long been recognized. Until recently, the recovery of living multicellular deep sea organisms, at least, has not been performed. As the result of decompression, otherwise uninjured deep sea forms die en route to the surface. A. A. Yayanos of Scripps Institution of Oceanography at San Diego reported capturing live crustacean amphipods from a depth of 5,700 meters (18,700 ft) in the Pacific Ocean (*Science,* June 2, 1978). These amphipods, up to 9 cm (3.54 inches) in length, were successfully transferred to the surface in a specially designed pressure retaining trap.

E. LENDELL COCKRUM
University of Arizona

P. CAULFIELD, BRUCE COLEMAN AGENCY

U. S. FISH AND WILDLIFE SERVICE

NEW YORK ZOOLOGICAL SOCIETY PHOTO

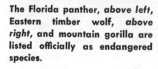
The Florida panther, *above left,* Eastern timber wolf, *above right,* and mountain gorilla are listed officially as endangered species.

U. S. FISH AND WILDLIFE SERVICE

BALD EAGLE

U. S. FISH AND WILDLIFE SERVICE

"There is no way to restore the dodo bird or any other extinct species. But it's not too late to rescue some of those that still cling to life." National Wildlife Federation.

WHOOPING CRANE

NEW YORK ZOOLOGICAL SOCIETY PHOTO

BLACK-TAILED PRAIRIE DOG

BLACK-FOOTED FERRET

NEW YORK ZOOLOGICAL SOCIETY PHOTO

whose activities might jeopardize the continued existence of a listed species. Only three cases were not resolved administratively and these were taken to court.

The most important court case involved the endangered snail darter—a small fish that requires fast-flowing, shallow fresh water to live and spawn—and the Tellico Dam, a portion of the Tennessee Valley Authority (TVA) multipurpose project on the Little Tennessee River. Court injunctions against further construction of the project, and a 1978 U. S. Supreme Court decision supporting them, were based on the language and intent of the Endangered Species Act.

The snail darter controversy and the prospect of similar conflicts in the future led Congress to hold oversight hearings on the Endangered Species Act. Environmentalists expressed strong support for leaving its procedures intact, while development-oriented interests wanted projects more easily exempted. The result was a revised act that would avoid conflicts with public works projects. It established a cabinet-level committee that could exempt specific projects from the act's provisions, but only if rigorous criteria were met. Further support for endangered species conservation came with an announcement from the TVA's newly appointed board chairman, S. David Freeman, that he would review alternatives to the Tellico Dam.

Other examples of species brought back from near extinction furnish hope. Although there are fewer than 4,000 bald eagles left in the continental United States, growing concern by the general population and efforts by the National Wildlife Federation give cause for optimism for this magnificent bird.

The American alligator, once on the brink of extinction because of its valuable hide, was put under total protection and has also made an amazing recovery in certain regions.

Despite an oil project in their migration route from the Bering Strait to calving areas in Mexico, California gray whales, once believed to be completely wiped out by commercial whalers, now number approximately 11,000.

Loss of marshes, unregulated shooting, predation, and egg predation once brought the U. S. population of whooping cranes to fewer than 25. Efforts by the National Audubon Society and the USFWS, however, have increased the number to more than 110. Greater sandhill cranes now act as foster parents for whooper eggs taken from captive and wild flocks.

Efforts to save endangered species often involve emergency actions that only buy time, and they must not overshadow the need to control the ultimate causes of extinction. Continuing public commitment is needed to stop the accelerating pace of habitat destruction. The delicate relationships among all living things must be more fully understood and appreciated.

THOMAS L. KIMBALL

STATISTICAL AND TABULAR DATA

TABLE OF CONTENTS

THE U. S. GOVERNMENT

THE EXECUTIVE BRANCH

President: Jimmy Carter   Vice President: Walter Mondale

THE CABINET

Secretary of Agriculture	Bob Bergland
Secretary of Commerce	Juanita M. Kreps
Secretary of Defense	Harold Brown
Secretary of Energy	James P. Schlesinger
Secretary of Health, Education, and Welfare	Joseph A. Califano, Jr.
Secretary of Housing and Urban Development	Patricia Roberts Harris
Secretary of the Interior	Cecil D. Andrus
Department of Justice—Attorney General	Griffin B. Bell
Secretary of Labor	Ray Marshall
Secretary of State	Cyrus R. Vance
Secretary of Transportation	Brock Adams
Secretary of the Treasury	W. Michael Blumenthal

THE SUPREME COURT

Chief Justice   Warren E. Burger (1969)[1]

Associate Justices

William J. Brennan, Jr. (1956)
Potter Stewart (1958)
Byron R. White (1962)
Thurgood Marshall (1967)

Harry A. Blackmun (1970)
Lewis F. Powell, Jr. (1971)
William H. Rehnquist (1971)
John Paul Stevens (1975)

[1] date of appointment

UNITED STATES: 96TH CONGRESS

SENATE MEMBERSHIP

(As of January 1979: 59 Democrats, 41 Republicans)

Letters after senators' names refer to party affiliation—D for Democrat, R for Republican. Single asterisk (*) denotes term expiring in January 1981; double asterisk (**), term expiring in January 1983; triple asterisk (***), term expiring in January 1985; (1) ran as independent.

ALABAMA
***H. Heflin, D
*D. Stewart, D

ALASKA
***T. Stevens, R
*M. Gravel, D

ARIZONA
*B. Goldwater, R
**D. DeConcini, D

ARKANSAS
*D. Bumpers, D
***D. Pryor, D

CALIFORNIA
*A. Cranston, D
**S. I. Hayakawa, R

COLORADO
***W. Armstrong, R
*G. Hart, D

CONNECTICUT
*A. A. Ribicoff, D
**L. P. Weicker, Jr., R

DELAWARE
**W. V. Roth, Jr., R
***J. R. Biden, Jr., D

FLORIDA
**L. M. Chiles, Jr., D
*R. B. Stone, R

GEORGIA
*H. E. Talmadge, D
***S. Nunn, D

HAWAII
*D. K. Inouye, D
**S. M. Matsunaga, D

IDAHO
*F. Church, D
***J. A. McClure, R

ILLINOIS
***C. H. Percy, R
*A. E. Stevenson, D

INDIANA
*B. Bayh, D
**R. G. Lugar, R

IOWA
***R. Jepsen, R
*J. C. Culver, D

KANSAS
***N. Kassebaum, R
*R. J. Dole, R

KENTUCKY
***W. Huddleston, D
*W. H. Ford, D

LOUISIANA
*R. B. Long, D
***J. B. Johnston, D

MAINE
**E. S. Muskie, D
***W. Cohen, R

MARYLAND
*C. M. Mathias, Jr., R
**P. S. Sarbanes, D

MASSACHUSETTS
**E. M. Kennedy, D
***P. Tsongas, D

MICHIGAN
***C. Levin, D
**D. W. Riegle, Jr., D

MINNESOTA
**D. Durenberger, R
***R. Boschwitz, R

MISSISSIPPI
***T. Cochran, R
*J. C. Stennis, D

MISSOURI
*T. F. Eagleton, D
**J. C. Danforth, R

MONTANA
***M. Baucus, D
**J. Melcher, D

NEBRASKA
***J. Exon, D
**E. Zorinsky, D

NEVADA
**H. W. Cannon, D
*P. Laxalt, R

NEW HAMPSHIRE
***G. Humphrey, R
*J. A. Durkin, D

NEW JERSEY
***W. Bradley, D
**H. A. Williams, Jr., D

NEW MEXICO
***P. V. Domenici, R
**H. Schmitt, R

NEW YORK
*J. K. Javits, R
**D. P. Moynihan, D

NORTH CAROLINA
***J. Helms, R
*R. B. Morgan, D

NORTH DAKOTA
*M. R. Young, R
**Q. N. Burdick, D

OHIO
*J. H. Glenn, Jr., D
**H. M. Metzenbaum, D

OKLAHOMA
*H. L. Bellmon, R
***D. Boren, D

OREGON
***M. O. Hatfield, R
*B. Packwood, R

PENNSYLVANIA
*R. S. Schweiker, R
**H. J. Heinz, III, R

RHODE ISLAND
***C. Pell, D
**J. H. Chafee, R

SOUTH CAROLINA
***S. Thurmond, R
*E. F. Hollings, D

SOUTH DAKOTA
*G. S. McGovern, D
***L. Pressler, R

TENNESSEE
***H. H. Baker, Jr., R
**J. Sasser, D

TEXAS
***J. G. Tower, R
**L. M. Bentsen, D

UTAH
*J. Garn, R
**O. Hatch, R

VERMONT
*R. T. Stafford, R
*P. J. Leahy, D

VIRGINIA
**H. F. Byrd, Jr., D (1)
***J. Warner, R

WASHINGTON
*W. G. Magnuson, D
**H. M. Jackson, D

WEST VIRGINIA
***J. Randolph, D
**R. C. Byrd, D

WISCONSIN
**W. Proxmire, D
*G. Nelson, D

WYOMING
***A. Simpson, R
**M. Wallop, R

HOUSE MEMBERSHIP

(As of January 1979: 276 Democrats, 157 Republicans, 2 vacant)

"At-L." In place of Congressional district number means "representative at large." *Indicates elected Nov. 7, 1978; all others were reelected in 1978.

ALABAMA
1. J. Edwards, R
2. W. L. Dickinson, R
3. W. Nichols, D
4. T. Bevill, D
5. R. Flippo, D
6. J. H. Buchanan, Jr., R
7. *R. Shelby, D

ALASKA
At-L. D. Young, R

ARIZONA
1. J. J. Rhodes, R
2. M. K. Udall, D
3. B. Stump, D
4. E. Rudd, R

ARKANSAS
1. W. V. Alexander, Jr., D
2. *E. Bethune, Jr., R
3. J. P. Hammerschmidt, R
4. *B. Anthony, Jr., D

CALIFORNIA
1. H. T. Johnson, D
2. D. H. Clausen, R
3. *R. Matsui, D
4. *V. Fazio, D
5. J. L. Burton, D
6. P. Burton, D
7. G. Miller, D
8. R. V. Dellums, D
9. F. H. Stark, Jr., D
10. D. Edwards, D
11. Vacant
12. P. N. McCloskey, Jr., R
13. N. Y. Mineta, D
14. *N. Shumway, R
15. *T. Coelho, D
16. L. E. Panetta, D
17. *C. Pashayan, R
18. *W. Thomas, R
19. R. J. Lagomarsino, R
20. B. M. Goldwater, Jr., R
21. J. C. Corman, D
22. C. J. Moorhead, R
23. A. C. Beilenson, D
24. H. A. Waxman, D
25. E. R. Roybal, D
26. J. H. Rousselot, R
27. R. K. Dornan, R
28. *J. Dixon, D
29. A. F. Hawkins, D
30. G. E. Danielson, D
31. C. H. Wilson, D
32. G. M. Anderson, D
33. *W. Grisham, R
34. *D. Lungren, R
35. J. Lloyd, D
36. G. E. Brown, Jr., D
37. *J. Lewis, R
38. J. M. Patterson, D
39. *W. Dannemeyer, R
40. R. E. Badham, R
41. B. Wilson, R
42. L. Van Deerlin, D
43. C. W. Burgener, R

COLORADO
1. P. Schroeder, D
2. T. E. Wirth, D
3. *R. Kogovsek, D
4. J. P. Johnson, R
5. *K. Kramer, R

CONNECTICUT
1. W. R. Cotter, D
2. C. J. Dodd, D
3. R. N. Giaimo, D
4. S. B. McKinney, R
5. *W. Ratchford, D
6. T. Moffett, D

DELAWARE
At-L. T. B. Evans, Jr., R

FLORIDA
1. *E. Hutto, D
2. D. Fuqua, D
3. C. E. Bennett, D
4. W. V. Chappell, Jr., D
5. R. Kelly, R
6. C. W. Young, R
7. S. M. Gibbons, D
8. A. P. Ireland, D
9. *B. Nelson, D
10. L. A. Bafalis, R
11. *D. Mica, D
12. *E. Stack, D
13. W. Lehman, D
14. C. D. Pepper, D
15. D. B. Fascell, D

GEORGIA
1. R. B. Ginn, D
2. M. D. Mathis, D
3. J. Brinkley, D
4. E. H. Levitas, D
5. W. F. Fowler, Jr., D
6. *N. Gingrich, R
7. L. P. McDonald, D
8. B. L. Evans, D
9. E. L. Jenkins, D
10. D. D. Barnard, Jr., D

HAWAII
1. C. Heftel, D
2. D. K. Akaka, D

IDAHO
1. S. D. Symms, R
2. G. V. Hansen, R

ILLINOIS
1. *B. Stewart, D
2. M. F. Murphy, D
3. M. A. Russo, D
4. E. J. Derwinski, R
5. J. G. Fary, D
6. H. J. Hyde, R
7. C. Collins, D
8. D. Rostenkowski, D
9. S. R. Yates, D
10. A. J. Mikva, D
11. F. Annunzio, D
12. P. M. Crane, R
13. R. McClory, R
14. J. N. Erlenbom, R
15. T. J. Corcoran, R
16. J. B. Anderson, R
17. G. M. O'Brien, R
18. R. H. Michel, R
19. T. Railsback, R
20. P. Findley, R
21. E. R. Madigan, R
22. *D. Crane, R
23. C. M. Price, D
24. P. Simon, D

INDIANA
1. A. Benjamin, Jr., D
2. F. J. Fithian, D
3. J. Brademas, D
4. D. Quayle, R
5. E. H. Hillis, R
6. D. W. Evans, D
7. J. T. Myers, R
8. *H. Deckard, R
9. L. H. Hamilton, D
10. P. R. Sharp, D
11. A. Jacobs, Jr., D

IOWA
1. J. A. S. Leach, R
2. *T. Tauke, R
3. C. E. Grassley, R
4. N. Smith, D
5. T. R. Harkin, D
6. B. W. Bedell, D

KANSAS
1. K. G. Sebelius, R
2. *J. Jeffries, R
3. L. Winn, Jr., R
4. D. Glickman, D
5. *R. Whittaker, R

KENTUCKY
1. C. Hubbard, Jr., D
2. W. H. Natcher, D
3. R. L. Mazzoli, D
4. G. Snyder, R
5. T. L. Carter, R
6. *L. Hopkins, R
7. C. D. Perkins, D

LOUISIANA
1. R. L. Livingston, Jr., R
2. C. C. Boggs, D
3. D. C. Treen, R
4. *C. Leach, D
5. J. Huckaby, D
6. W. H. Moore, R
7. J. B. Breaux, D
8. G. W. Long, D

MAINE
1. D. F. Emery, R
2. *O. Snowe, R

MARYLAND
1. R. E. Bauman, R
2. C. D. Long, D
3. B. A. Mikulski, D
4. M. S. Holt, R
5. G. N. Spellman, D
6. *Beverly Byron, D
7. P. J. Mitchell, D
8. *M. Barnes, D

MASSACHUSETTS
1. S. O. Conte, R
2. E. P. Boland, D
3. J. D. Early, D
4. R. F. Drinan, D
5. *J. Shannon, D
6. *N. Mavroules, D
7. E. J. Markey, D
8. T. P. O'Neill, Jr., D
9. J. J. Moakley, D
10. M. M. Heckler, R
11. *B. Donnelly, D
12. G. E. Studds, D

MICHIGAN
1. J. Conyers, Jr., D
2. C. D. Pursell, R
3. *H. Wolpe, D
4. D. A. Stockman, R
5. H. S. Sawyer, R
6. M. R. Carr, D
7. D. E. Kildee, D
8. B. Traxler, D
9. G. A. Vander Jagt, R
10. *D. Albosta, D
11. *R. Davis, R.
12. D. E. Bonior, D
13. C. C. Diggs, Jr., D
14. L. N. Nedzi, D
15. W. D. Ford, D
16. J. D. Dingell, D
17. W. M. Brodhead, D
18. J. J. Blanchard, D
19. W. S. Broomfield, R

MINNESOTA
1. *A. Erdahl, R
2. T. M. Hagedorn, R
3. B. Frenzel, R
4. B. F. Vento, D
5. *M. Sabo, D
6. R. M. Nolan, D
7. A. Stangeland, R
8. J. L. Oberstar, D

MISSISSIPPI
1. J. L. Whitten, D
2. D. R. Bowen, D
3. G. V. Montgomery, D
4. *J. Hinson, R
5. T. Lott, R.

MISSOURI
1. W. L. Clay, D
2. R. A. Young, D
3. R. A. Gephardt, D
4. I. Skelton, D
5. R. Bolling, D
6. E. T. Coleman, R
7. G. Taylor, D
8. R. H. Ichord, D
9. H. L. Volkmer, D
10. B. D. Burlison, D

MONTANA
1. *P. Williams, D
2. R. Marlenee, R

NEBRASKA
1. *D. Bereuter, R
2. J. J. Cavanaugh, D
3. V. Smith, R

NEVADA
At-L. J. D. Santini, D

NEW HAMPSHIRE
1. N. E. D'Amours, D
2. J. C. Cleveland, R

NEW JERSEY
1. J. J. Florio, D
2. W. J. Hughes, D
3. J. J. Howard, D
4. F. Thompson, Jr., D
5. M. Fenwick, R
6. E. B. Forsythe, R
7. A. Maguire, D
8. R. A. Roe, D
9. H. C. Hollenbeck, R
10. P. W. Rodino, Jr., D
11. J. G. Minish, D
12. M. J. Rinaldo, R
13. *J. Courter, R
14. *F. Guarini, D
15. E. J. Patten, D

NEW MEXICO
1. M. Lujan, Jr., R
2. H. Runnels, D

NEW YORK
1. *W. Carney, R
2. T. J. Downey, D
3. J. A. Ambro, D
4. N. F. Lent, R
5. J. W. Wydler, R
6. L. L. Wolff, D
7. J. P. Addabbo, D.
8. B. S. Rosenthal, D
9. *G. Ferraro, D
10. M. Biaggi, D
11. J. H. Scheuer, D
12. S. A. Chisholm, D
13. S. J. Solarz, D
14. F. W. Richmond, D
15. L. C. Zeferetti, D
16. E. Holtzman, D
17. J. M. Murphy, D
18. S. W. Green, R
19. C. B. Rangel, D
20. T. Weiss, D
21. *R. Garcia, D
22. J. B. Bingham, D
23. *P. Peyser, D
24. R. L. Ottinger, D
25. H. Fish, Jr., R
26. B. A. Gilman, R
27. M. F. McHugh, D
28. S. S. Stratton, D
29. *G. Solomon, R
30. R. C. McEwen, R
31. D. J. Mitchell, R
32. J. M. Hanley, D
33. *G. Lee, R
34. F. Horton, R
35. B. B. Conable, Jr., R
36. J. J. LaFalce, D
37. H. J. Nowak, D
38. J. Kemp, R
39. S. N. Lundine, D

NORTH CAROLINA
1. W. B. Jones, D
2. L. H. Fountain, D
3. C. O. Whitley, Sr., D
4. I. F. Andrews, D
5. S. L. Neal, D
6. L. R. Preyer, D
7. C. Rose, D
8. W. G. Hefner, D
9. J. G. Martin, R
10. J. T. Broyhill, R
11. L. Gudger, D

NORTH DAKOTA
At-L. M. Andrews, R

OHIO
1. W. D. Gradison, Jr., R
2. T. A. Luken, D
3. *T. Hall, D
4. T. Guyer, R
5. D. L. Latta, R
6. W. H. Harsha, R
7. C. J. Brown, R
8. T. N. Kindness, R
9. T. L. Ashley, D
10. C. E. Miller, R
11. J. W. Stanton, R
12. S. L. Devine, R
13. D. J. Pease, D
14. J. F. Seiberling, D
15. C. P. Wylie, R
16. R. Regula, R
17. J. M. Ashbrook, R
18. D. Applegate, D
19. L. Williams, R
20. M. R. Oakar, D
21. L. Stokes, D
22. C. A. Vanik, D
23. R. M. Mottl, D

OKLAHOMA
1. J. R. Jones, D
2. *M. Synar, D
3. W. W. Watkins, D
4. T. Steed, D
5. M. Edwards, R
6. G. English, D

OREGON
1. L. AuCoin, D
2. A. Ullman, D
3. R. B. Duncan, D
4. J. Weaver, D

PENNSYLVANIA
1. M. Myers, D
2. *W. Gray, D
3. R. F. Lederer, D
4. *C. Dougherty, R
5. R. T. Schulze, R
6. G. Yatron, D
7. R. W. Edgar, D
8. P. H. Kostmayer, D
9. B. Shuster, R
10. J. M. McDade, R
11. D. J. Flood, D
12. J. P. Murtha, D
13. L. Coughlin, R
14. W. S. Moorhead, D
15. *D. Ritter, R
16. R. S. Walker, R
17. A. E. Ertel, D
18. D. Walgren, D
19. W. F. Goodling, R
20. J. M. Gaydos, D
21. *D. Bailey, D
22. A. J. Murphy, D
23. *W. Clinger, Jr., R
24. M. L. Marks, R
25. *E. Atkinson, D

RHODE ISLAND
1. F. J. St Germain, D
2. E. P. Beard, D

SOUTH CAROLINA
1. M. J. Davis, D
2. F. D. Spence, R
3. B. C. Derrick, Jr., D
4. *C. Campbell, Jr., R
5. K. Holland, D
6. J. W. Jenrette, Jr., D

SOUTH DAKOTA
1. Tom Daschle, D
2. J. Abdnor, R

TENNESSEE
1. J. H. Quillen, R
2. J. J. Duncan, R
3. M. L. Lloyd, D
4. A. Gore, Jr., D
5. *W. H. Boner, D
6. R. L. Beard, Jr., R
7. E. Jones, D
8. H. Ford, D

TEXAS
1. S. B. Hall, Jr., D
2. C. Wilson, D
3. J. M. Collins, R
4. R. Roberts, D
5. *W. H. Boner, D
6. *P. Gramm, D
7. B. Archer, R
8. B. Eckhardt, D
9. J. Brooks, D
10. J. J. Pickle, D
11. *J. Marvin Leach, D
12. J. C. Wright, Jr., D
13. J. E. Hightower, D
14. *Joe Wyatt, D
15. E. de la Garza, D
16. R. C. White, D
17. *C. Stenholm, D
18. *M. Leland, D
19. *K. Hance, D
20. H. B. Gonzalez, D
21. *T. Loeffler, R
22. *R. Paul, R
23. A. Kazen, Jr., D
24. *M. Frost, D

UTAH
1. G. McKay, D
2. D. D. Marriott, R

VERMONT
At-L. J. M. Jeffords, R

VIRGINIA
1. P. S. Trible, Jr., R
2. G. W. Whitehurst, R
3. D. E. Satterfield, III, D
4. R. W. Daniel, Jr., R
5. D. Daniel, D
6. M. C. Butler, R
7. J. K. Robinson, R
8. H. E. Harris, II, D
9. W. C. Wampler, R
10. J. L. Fisher, D

WASHINGTON
1. J. M. Pritchard, R
2. *A. Swift, D
3. D. L. Bonker, D
4. M. McCormack, D
5. T. S. Foley, D
6. N. D. Dicks, D
7. *M. Lowry, D

WEST VIRGINIA
1. R. H. Mollohan, D
2. H. O. Staggers, D
3. J. Slack, D
4. N. J. Rahall, D

WISCONSIN
1. L. Aspin, D
2. R. W. Kastenmeier, D
3. A. J. Baldus, D
4. C. J. Zablocki, D
5. H. S. Reuss, D
6. Vacant
7. D. R. Obey, D
8. *T. Roth, R
9. *F. J. Sensenbrenner, Jr., R

WYOMING
At-L. *R. Cheney, R

PUERTO RICO
Resident Commissioner
B. Corrada

DISTRICT OF COLUMBIA
Delegate
W. E. Fauntroy, D

UNITED STATES

Major Legislation Enacted in 1978

SUBJECT	PURPOSE
Mandatory Retirement	Raises mandatory retirement to age 70 for federal government employees and many other employees. Signed April 6. Public Law 95-256.
Arts & Humanities	Authorizes a White House Conference on the Arts and a White House Conference on the Humanities. Signed May 3. Public Law 95-272.
Energy Conservation	Provides federal loans and loan guarantees to small businesses for energy research and conservation. Signed July 4. Public Law 95-315.
New York City	Provides long term loan guarantees to New York City. Signed August 8. Public Law 95-339.
Climate	Establishes a national program to improve understanding of climatic changes, both natural and man-induced. Signed September 17. Public Law 95-367.
Coinage	Replaces current dollar coin with a smaller "Anthony dollar" coin in memory of suffragette Susan B. Anthony. Signed October 10. Public Law 95-447.
Civil Service Reform	Signed October 13. Public Law 95-454. *See* UNITED STATES: *Civil Service.*
Jefferson Davis	Posthumously restores full rights of citizenship to Jefferson Davis, president of the Confederacy. Signed October 17. Public Law 95-466.
Water Research	Authorizes the Office of Water Research and Technology within the Department of the Interior to support basic water research and practical ways to solve the problem of water quality. Signed October 17. Public Law 95-467.
Federal Judiciary	Creates 35 new judgeships on the court of appeals and 117 on the district courts. Signed October 20. Public Law 95-486.
Agricultural Trade Policy	Provides for the establishment of international agriculture trade offices; provides three- to ten-year loans to establish grain reserves; increases the authority of the Agriculture Department's representatives in the U. S. consulates, and provides short-term loans to Communist China to enable it to buy U. S. farm products. Signed October 21. Public Law 95-501.
Waterway User Tax	Imposes a user tax on the nation's inland waterway system. Signed October 21. Public Law 95-502.
Airline Deregulation	Signed October 24. Public Law 95-504. *See* TRANSPORTATION.
Foreign Intelligence	Requires a judicial warrant for all electronic surveillance for foreign intelligence or counterintelligence purposes in the United States in which communications of U. S. persons might be intercepted. Signed October 25. Public Law 95-511.
Off-Track Betting	Allows interstate off-track betting on horse racing under certain circumstances. Signed October 25. Public Law 95-515.
Government Ethics	Makes personal financial disclosure by members of all branches of government mandatory; establishes a special office of government ethics, and allows for the appointment of a special prosecutor for investigative purposes. Signed October 26. Public Law 95-521.
Full Employment (Humphrey-Hawkins)	Sets national goals of 4% unemployment and 3% inflation by 1983. Signed October 27. Public Law 95-523.
Rape Victims	Protects the privacy of rape victims in federal trials. Signed October 30. Public Law 95-540.
Sex Discrimination	Protects American women from occupational discrimination on the basis of pregnancy. Signed October 31. Public Law 95-555.
American Samoa	Provides the territory of American Samoa with a nonvoting delegate to the U. S. House of Representatives. Signed October 31. Public Law 95-556.
Education	Provides more generous education grants to low and middle income students; expands the Guaranteed Student Loan program. Signed November 1. Public Law 95-566.
Public Television	Reorganizes the nation's public broadcasting system; authorizes $40 million for each fiscal year, 1979–81. Signed November 2. Public Law 95-567.
Cigarette Bootlegging	Seeks to control illegal interstate traffic in cigarettes. Signed November 2. Public Law 95-575.
Presidential Papers	Ensures that the papers of a U. S. president remain public property after the expiration of a president's term. Signed November 6. Public Law 95-591.
Taxation	Signed November 6. Public Law 95-600. *See* TAXATION.
Amateur Sports	Designates the U. S. Olympic Committee as the coordinating body for amateur sports, restructures the Olympic Committee and many of its constituent organizations. Signed November 8. Public Law 95-606.
Energy	Signed November 9. Public Laws 95-617, 618, 619, 620, 621. *See* ENERGY.
Endangered Species	Signed November 10. Public Law 95-632. *See* ZOOLOGY: *A New Look at the Endangered Species.*

POPULATION
Vital Statistics of Selected Countries

	Estimated population mid-1978	Birthrate per 1,000 population[1]	Deathrate per 1,000 population[1]	Infant mortality per 1,000[1]	Life expectancy at birth[2]	Urban population (%)	Population projection to yr. 2000
World	4,219,000,000	29	12	99	60	39	6,233,000,000
Afghanistan	17,800,000	48	22	190	40	15	31,200,000
Albania	2,600,000	32	8	87	68	34	4,100,000
Algeria	18,400,000	48	14	145	53	52	36,400,000
Angola	6,400,000	47	23	203	38	18	11,700,000
Argentina	26,400,000	23	9	59	68	80	32,900,000
Australia	14,300,000	17	8	14	72	86	19,900,000
Austria	7,500,000	12	13	18	71	52	8,000,000
Bangladesh	85,000,000	47	20	153	46	9	153,500,000
Belgium	9,900,000	12	12	14	71	87	10,700,000
Bolivia	4,900,000	47	18	157	48	34	8,700,000
Brazil	115,400,000	36	8	109	61	60	205,200,000
Burma	32,200,000	38	15	140	50	22	52,700,000
Cambodia	8,200,000	47	18	150	45	12	14,700,000
Cameroon	8,000,000	41	21	137	41	29	13,700,000
Canada	23,600,000	16	7	14	73	76	31,300,000
Cen. Afr. Empire	1,900,000	43	21	190	41	36	3,400,000
Chile	10,800,000	25	7	56	63	79	15,400,000
China, mainland	930,000,000	22	8	65	65	24	1,213,000,000
China, Taiwan	16,900,000	26	5	25	70	63	22,100,000
Colombia	25,800,000	33	9	90	61	64	46,700,000
Cuba	9,700,000	21	5	27	70	60	14,700,000
Cyprus	600,000	20	10	27	71	42	800,000
Czechoslovakia	15,200,000	19	11	21	70	67	17,000,000
Denmark	5,100,000	13	11	10	74	67	5,400,000
Dominican Republic	5,100,000	39	9	96	58	47	10,600,000
Ecuador	7,800,000	40	9	66	60	41	14,800,000
Egypt	39,600,000	38	12	108	53	44	63,500,000
Ethiopia	30,200,000	49	25	162	42	12	53,900,000
Finland	4,800,000	14	9	10	71	59	4,800,000
France	53,400,000	14	10	13	73	70	61,200,000
Germany, East	16,700,000	12	14	14	72	76	17,400,000
Germany, West	61,300,000	10	12	17	71	92	65,600,000
Ghana	10,900,000	49	20	115	49	31	21,400,000
Greece	9,300,000	16	8	23	72	65	9,900,000
Guatemala	6,600,000	43	12	75	53	36	12,200,000
Haiti	4,800,000	39	17	115	50	23	7,100,000
Hungary	10,700,000	18	12	30	69	50	11,100,000
India	634,700,000	34	14	129	49	21	1,017,700,000
Indonesia	140,200,000	38	14	137	48	18	226,400,000
Iran	35,500,000	45	14	104	57	47	65,400,000
Iraq	12,200,000	48	14	104	53	65	24,200,000
Ireland	3,200,000	22	10	15	71	52	4,000,000
Israel	3,700,000	28	7	20	73	86	5,600,000
Italy	56,700,000	14	10	19	72	53	61,800,000
Japan	114,400,000	16	6	9	74	76	132,100,000
Jordan	2,900,000	48	13	97	53	42	5,800,000
Kenya	14,800,000	48	15	119	50	10	31,300,000
Korea, North	17,100,000	34	9	70	61	43	27,400,000
Korea, South	37,100,000	24	7	47	65	48	53,500,000
Laos	3,600,000	44	21	175	40	15	5,800,000
Lebanon	2,900,000	40	9	59	64	60	5,600,000
Liberia	1,700,000	50	21	159	45	28	3,000,000
Libya	2,800,000	48	9	130	53	30	5,300,000
Malaysia	13,000,000	31	6	41	68	27	21,700,000
Mexico	66,900,000	42	8	66	65	64	135,200,000
Morocco	18,900,000	45	14	133	53	38	35,400,000
Netherlands	13,900,000	13	8	11	74	76	16,000,000
New Zealand	3,200,000	18	8	16	72	81	4,300,000
Niger	5,000,000	52	24	200	39	9	9,600,000
Nigeria	68,400,000	49	21	157	41	18	134,800,000
Norway	4,100,000	13	10	10	75	45	4,500,000
Pakistan	76,800,000	44	14	139	51	26	145,100,000
Panama	1,800,000	32	7	47	66	50	3,200,000
Paraguay	2,900,000	39	8	65	62	37	5,300,000
Peru	17,100,000	40	11	80	56	55	31,200,000
Philippines	46,300,000	35	10	80	58	32	84,700,000
Poland	35,100,000	20	9	24	71	55	40,200,000
Portugal	9,700,000	19	10	39	69	26	10,800,000
Rhodesia	7,000,000	48	13	122	52	19	15,200,000
Rumania	21,900,000	20	10	31	70	48	26,000,000
Saudi Arabia	7,800,000	49	19	152	45	21	14,900,000
Solomon Islands	200,000	36	13	52	—	9	400,000
South Africa	27,500,000	40	15	117	52	48	51,000,000
Spain	36,800,000	18	8	11	72	61	45,300,000
Sudan	17,100,000	48	16	141	49	20	33,300,000
Sweden	8,300,000	12	11	9	75	83	9,200,000
Switzerland	6,200,000	12	9	11	73	55	6,900,000
Syria	8,100,000	45	14	114	57	47	16,000,000
Tanzania	16,500,000	47	22	167	44	7	33,100,000
Thailand	45,100,000	33	10	89	61	13	83,300,000
Tunisia	6,000,000	36	13	135	55	50	10,500,000
Turkey	42,200,000	34	11	119	57	45	71,100,000
Uganda	12,700,000	45	15	160	50	7	24,800,000
USSR	261,000,000	18	9	28	69	62	313,000,000
United Kingdom	56,000,000	12	12	14	72	76	61,600,000
United States	218,400,000	15	9	15	73	74	260,400,000
Uruguay	2,800,000	21	10	49	69	83	3,400,000
Venezuela	13,100,000	36	7	49	65	75	23,200,000
Vietnam	49,200,000	41	19	115	48	22	80,300,000
Yemen	5,800,000	49	19	155	45	9	10,900,000
Yugoslavia	22,000,000	18	8	36	68	39	25,600,000
Zaire	26,700,000	45	18	160	44	29	49,900,000

[1] 1975–1976 data   [2] per 1,000 live births   Source: 1978 World Population Data Sheet, Population Reference Bureau, Inc.

NATIONS OF THE WORLD

A PROFILE AND A SYNOPSIS OF MAJOR 1978 DEVELOPMENTS*

Region	Population in millions[1]	Capital	Area Sq mi (km²)	Head of Government[2]
Bahamas, Caribbean	0.2	Nassau	5,380 (13,935)	Lynden O. Pindling, prime min.

The government, trying to reduce a 23% unemployment rate, ordered all illegal aliens out of the country by the end of June. Chiefly affected were Haitian immigrants, estimated to have made up as much as 17.6% of the islands' population.

| Bahrain, W. Asia | 0.3 | Manama | 240 (622) | Isa ibn Salman, emir Khalifa ibn Salman, prime min. |

The Financial Times of London rated Manama as the world's 7th costliest city.

| Barbados, Caribbean | 0.3 | Bridgetown | 166 (431) | John M. G. Adams, prime min. |

Reports in February and March indicated that Barbados' balance of payments deficit in 1977 had been only about $10 million ($19.5 million in 1976), while the island's gross national product had grown by 3% (5% in 1976). Inflation reached 8% during the year (5% in 1976).

| Benin, W. Africa | 3.4 | Porto-Novo | 43,483 (112,622) | Mathieu Kerekou, pres. |

Following bloody street battles in July between natives of Libreville, Gabon, and immigrant workers from Benin, all 10,000 Benin laborers in that country were expelled. Relations with Gabon have been cool since Benin accused it of aiding an attempted coup in 1977.

| Bhutan, S. Asia | 1.3 | Punakha | 18,147 (47,000) | Jigme Singhye Wangchuk, king |
| Botswana, S. Africa | 0.7 | Gaborone | 231,804 (600,372) | Sir Seretse Khama, pres. |

Fifteen Botswana soldiers and two civilians were killed in February, when Rhodesian troops, claiming to be chasing Zimbabwe terrorists, raided a border area. Botswana subsequently closed a post on the border and required visas for travelers entering the country from Rhodesia.

| Burundi, E. Africa | 4.0 | Bujumbura | 10,747 (27,834) | Jean-Baptiste Bagaza, pres. |

A United Nations refugee official reported in February that 11,000 Burundians had fled to neighboring Zaire as a result of tribal warfare in their country.

| Cameroon, Cen. Africa | 8.0 | Yaoundé | 183,568 (475,442) | Ahmadou Ahidjo, pres. |

The government announced that Zimmer Plastic of West Germany had agreed to build a synthetic leather factory in the country. The cost was estimated at $4.9 million.

| Cape Verde, W. Africa | 0.3 | Praia | 1,557 (4,033) | Aristides Pereira, pres. |

Cape Verde received $6.6 million from Sweden during the year as aid to development and for drought relief. The African Development Fund granted $4.1 million to create a television network.

| Cen. Afr. Empire, Cen. Africa | 1.9 | Bangui | 240,534 (622,984) | Bokassa I, emperor |

Emperor Bokassa in July appointed Education Minister Henri Maldou to the prime minister's post, replacing Ange Patasse who had headed the cabinet since December 1976.

| Chad, Cen. Africa | 4.3 | N'Djamena | 495,752 (1,284,000) | Félix Malloum, pres. |

Accusing Libya of occupying large tracts of its territory and supporting antigovernment rebels, Chad severed relations with its northern neighbor in February. Relations were resumed later in the month, following a cease-fire with the rebels. When fighting broke out again in April, President Malloum invoked French assistance. He charged Libya with invasion and called on the Organization of African Unity to demand withdrawal.

| Comoros, E. Africa | 0.3 | Moroni | 838 (2,171) | Ahmed Abdallah, pres. |

President Ali Soilih was ousted on May 13. An executive body, led by former President Ahmed Abdallah, assumed power. On May 29 Soilih was fatally shot, allegedly while trying to escape. After the draft of a new constitution was approved overwhelming in an October 1 referendum, Mohammed Ahmed resigned as co-president. Diplomatic relations with France were established.

| Congo, Cen. Africa | 1.5 | Brazzaville | 132,046 (342,000) | Joachim Yombi Opango, pres. |

Ten people were executed on February 7 for their part in the assassination of President Marien Ngouabi on March 18, 1977. Four others received life sentences at hard labor. In August a plot to overthrow President Opango was foiled.

| Djibouti, E. Africa | 0.1 | Djibouti | 8,494 (22,000) | Hassan Gouled, pres. B. G. Hamadou, prime min. |

Foreign Minister Abdallah Mohammed Kamil on February 5 formed a new government designed to maintain ethnic balance. The government was dismissed in September, and Barkat Gourad Hamadou was named to form a cabinet. Aerial spraying to control the worst plague of locusts in the Horn of Africa in more than a decade was begun in June.

* Independent nations not covered separately (pages 70–560) or under Central America. [1] 1978 estimates. [2] As of Dec. 31, 1978.

Nation, Region	Population in millions	Capital	Area Sq mi (km²)	Head of Government
Dominican Republic, Caribbean	5.1	Santo Domingo	18,818 (48,734)	Antonio Guzman, pres.

(see Caribbean)

Nation, Region	Population in millions	Capital	Area Sq mi (km²)	Head of Government
Equatorial Guinea, Cen. Africa	0.3	Malabo	10,831 (28,051)	Francisco Macías Nguema, pres.

The Roman Catholic Church was banned in June, although more than 80% of the population of Equatorial Guinea adhere to it. The official Vatican newspaper charged that some 50,000 people had been murdered during President Macías Nguema's ten-year reign of terror.

Fiji, Oceania	0.6	Suva	7,055 (18,272)	Ratu Sir Kamisese Mara, prime min.

Five hundred Fijian soldiers, representing half of the country's military establishment, took up duty in Lebanon in June as part of the United Nation's peacekeeping force there.

Gabon, Cen. Africa	0.5	Libreville	103,346 (267,667)	Albert-Bernard Bongo, pres.

The University of Libreville was closed in February after students rioted over the distribution of government grants. The students were ordered to join the security forces to learn discipline and respect for public property. See also Benin.

Gambia, W. Africa	0.6	Banjul	4,361 (11,295)	Sir Dawda K. Jawara, pres.

Gambia signed a treaty of nonaggression and mutual assistance with Guinea, the Ivory Coast, Liberia, Senegal, and Togo at a March 17–18 meeting in Monrovia, Liberia.

Grenada Caribbean	0.1	St. George's	133 (344)	Eric M. Gairy, prime min.

Grenada in July became the 11th country of the Western Hemisphere to ratify the 1969 American Convention on Human Rights, thereby bringing it into force.

Guinea, W. Africa	4.8	Conakry	94,925 (245,857)	Ahmed Sékou Touré, pres.

Guinea in March agreed to reestablish full diplomatic relations and to strengthen commercial and cultural ties with neighboring Senegal and Ivory Coast, thereby ending years of discord. The conciliation meeting in Monrovia was arranged by Liberian President William Tolbert.

Guinea-Bissau, W. Africa	0.6	Bissau	13,948 (36,125)	Luíz de Almeida Cabral, pres.

Guinea-Bissau granted the Soviet Union fishing rights off its coast in exchange for the building of a fish-processing plant and the modernization of the country's fishing port. Francisco Mendes, prime minister since 1974, was killed in an auto accident in Lisbon, Portugal, July 7.

Haiti, Caribbean	4.8	Port-au-Prince	10,714 (27,750)	Jean-Claude Duvalier, pres.

President Jean-Claude Duvalier somewhat eased his rule. The press was allowed to criticize the government, and workers were given permission to elect new representatives. Haiti ratified the American Convention on Human Rights. See also Bahamas.

Ivory Coast, W. Africa	7.2	Abidjan	124,502 (322,462)	Félix Houphouët-Bolgny, pres.

The minimum wage was raised by 25% in the private and 10% in the public sector in 1978.

Jamaica, Caribbean	2.1	Kingston	4,244 (10,991)	Michael Manley, prime min.

The island continued to be bedeviled by economic woes. The Jamaican dollar was devalued by 10%, and a strike paralyzed the sugar industry at the height of the harvest. While the workers won a 20% pay increase, the harvest was much reduced. On the brighter side, Hungary agreed to build a $500-million alumina refinery, and tourism revived after a two-year decline.

Kuwait, W. Asia	1.1	Kuwait	6,880 (17,818)	Jabir al-Ahmad al-Sabah, emir and prime min.

Like other oil-producing nations of the Middle East, Kuwait cut back its economic development program during the year. The country, however, remained the first in the world in terms of gross national product per capita in 1977. See also Bahrain.

Lesotho, S. Africa	1.3	Maseru	11,720 (30,355)	Moshoeshoe II, king Chief Lebua Jonathan, prime min.

Two alleged agents of South Africa's Bureau of State Security (BOSS), were arrested in Maseru in March, when they reportedly tried to buy state secrets from a senior Lesotho government official.

Liberia, W. Africa	1.7	Monrovia	43,000 (111,369)	William R. Tolbert, pres.

The iron and rubber industries, which are partly owned by U.S. interests and together earn the country 75% of its foreign exchange, were hit by strikes at the beginning of the year. Violence broke out when the Ministry of Labor ordered a return to work.

Liechtenstein	0.024	Vaduz	62 (160)	Francis Joseph II, prince Hans Brunhart, premier

Liechtenstein became the 22d member of the Council of Europe in September. In February parliamentary elections, the Fatherland Union won 8 of 15 seats. Hans Brunhart became premier.

Region	Population in millions	Capital	Area Sq mi (km²)	Head of Government
Madagascar, E. Africa	8.0	Antananarivo	226,656 (587,041)	Didier Ratsiraka, pres.

Three people were killed during two days of riots in Antananarivo in late May. The rioters, said to have been armed unemployed men and disenchanted students, set fire to buildings and looted shops. The police responded with firearms and tear gas.

Malawi, E. Africa	5.4	Lilongwe	45,747 (118,484)	Hastings Kamuzu Banda, pres.

The first contested elections in 17 years took place on June 29, resulting in the rejection of 31 out of 47 incumbent members of parliament. Malawi is a one-party state, but voters could choose between two or three candidates in each constituency. All candidates were previously approved by President Banda and screened for "good English" by a university staff. President Banda announced August 14 that foreign journalists would once again be prohibited from entering Malawi. Banda charged that the foreign press had misrepresented conditions in his country during the election campaign.

Maldives, S. Asia	0.1	Male	115 (298)	Ibrahim Nasir, pres.
Mali, W. Africa	6.3	Bamako	478,764 (1,240,000)	Moussa Traoré, pres.

Three members of the ruling military committee (all planners of the 1968 coup that brought President Traoré to power), and the minister of foreign affairs, were arrested early in 1978, charged with high treason. Three senior executives of state firms were also detained. All allegedly conspired to overthrow the president and prevent the scheduled return to civilian rule in 1979.

Malta, Mediterranean	0.3	Valletta	112 (316)	Dom Mintoff, prime min.

The island experienced widespread political violence. Numerous bombings—mostly directed at Prime Minister Mintoff's opposition—were linked by the Manchester Guardian to a government program of intimidation. Mintoff was accused of harassing the press, the legal profession, and law enforcement officials in order to stay in power. The ruling Labor Party—merged with the General Workers' Union in May—was also charged with using thugs to hound opponents of the regime.

Mauritania, W. Africa	1.5	Nouakchott	397,953 (1,030,700)	Mustapha Ould Salek, pres. of military committee

President Mokhtar Ould Daddah, head of state since independence in 1960, was ousted in a bloodless coup on July 10. A Military Committee for National Redress, led by the army chief of staff, Col. Mustapha Ould Salek, took over. The Polisario Front, Western Sahara's liberation movement, which has been fighting Mauritania and Morocco since 1975, declared a moratorium of hostilities to allow the new regime to review the country's foreign policy. The Salek government, however—considered pro-Western—reaffirmed all previous foreign-policy commitments.

Mauritius, E. Africa	0.9	Port Louis	790 (2,045)	Sir Seewoosagur Ramgoolam, prime min.

Mauritius had an economic crisis as the demand for, and the price of, sugar decreased. Sugar is planted on more than 90% of all cultivable land. The island's tourism also declined.

Mongolia, E. Asia	1.6	Ulan Bator	604,247 (1,565,000)	Yumjaagin Tsedenbal, pres Jambyn Batmönh, prime min

Col. Gen. Jarantayn Avhia was appointed minister of defense.

Nauru, Oceania	0.007	Nauru	8 (21)	Hammer de Roburt, pres.

The island experienced great governmental instability. Hammer de Roburt became president on May 15 succeeding Lagumot Harris, who resigned. Roburt was the third president in less than a month.

Nepal, S. Asia	13.4	Katmandu	54,362 (140,797)	Birendra Bir Bikram, king Kirtinidhi Bista, prime min.

King Birendra relaxed the strong control he has held over the country. A ban on several newspapers was lifted—though they may still not criticize the king—and some public meetings were allowed.

Niger, W. Africa	5.0	Niamey	489,189 (1,267,000)	Seyni Kountché, pres.

Owing to its successful exploitation of uranium, Niger in mid-April raised its minimum wage by 20% and abolished income taxes for the majority of citizens. President Seyni Kountché reorganized the cabinet.

Oman, W. Asia	0.8	Muscat	82,029 (212,457)	Qabus ibn Said, sultan

Following a coup in neighboring Democratic Yemen, Oman in July sent a delegation to China for assistance. Rebels, aided by Democratic Yemen, had tried to seize power in Oman in 1976.

Papua New Guinea, Oceania	3.0	Port Moresby	178,259 (461,691)	Michael Somare, prime min.

Papua New Guinea proclaimed a national economic zone of 200 miles in adjacent waters in 1978.

Qatar, W. Asia	0.1	Doha	4,247 (11,000)	Khalifa bin Hamad al-Thani, emir

On March 14 Qatar and France signed an agreement on arms production and technical assistance.

Rwanda, E. Africa	4.5	Kigali	10,169 (26,338)	Juvénal Habyalimana, pres.

Rwanda began an ambitious development plan with a budget of $600 million.

Nation, Region	Population in millions	Capital	Area Sq mi (km²)	Head of Government
Sao Tomé and Principe, W. Africa	0.09	São Tomé	372 (964)	Mañuel Pinto da Costa, pres.
Senegal, W. Africa	5.4	Dakar	75,750 (196,192)	Léopold S. Senghor, pres.

President Senghor won reelection and his Socialist Party captured 80 out of 100 seats in the National Assembly in February elections. Three parties competed for the votes, and permission for a fourth to operate was later announced. A ban on political activities had been lifted in 1977.

Seychelles, E. Africa	0.1	Victoria	108 (280)	F. Albert René, pres.

A coup against President René was said to have been thwarted in May, while he was abroad.

Sierra Leone, W. Africa	3.3	Freetown	27,699 (71,740)	Siaka P. Stevens, pres.

Voters in a June referendum overwhelmingly approved a bill passed by parliament, making Sierra Leone a one-party state. President Stevens was subsequently sworn in for a seven-year term.

Somalia, E. Africa	3.4	Mogadishu	246,200 (637,657)	Mohammed Siad Barre, pres.

(see Africa).

Surinam, S. America	0.5	Paramaribo	63,037 (163,265)	Johan H. E. Ferrier, pres. Henck A. E. Arron, prime min.

Surinam extended its territorial waters to 12 miles and established a 200-mile economic zone.

Swaziland, S. Africa	0.5	Mbabane	6,704 (17,363)	Sobhuza II, king

Swaziland has a new constitution, more in harmony with the country's traditional laws than the British-style charter suspended by King Sobhuza in 1973. Secret ballot is abolished.

Togo, W. Africa	2.4	Lomé	21,622 (56,000)	Gnassingbe Eyadéma, pres.

Togo was granted a $7-million loan from the European Investment Bank for building a palm-oil factory and storage plant.

Tonga, Oceania	0.1	Nuku'alofa	270 (699)	Taufa'ahau Tupou IV, king Prince Tu'ipelehake, prime min.
Trinidad and Tobago, Caribbean	1.1	Port-of-Spain	1,980 (5,128)	Eric E. Williams, prime min.

The government announced plans to build a $334-million aluminum smelter with a capacity of 150,000 tons; operation is scheduled to begin in 1982.

United Arab Emirates, W. Asia	0.8	Abu Dhabi	32,278 (83,600)	Zaid ibn al-Nuhayan, pres. Maktum ibn al-Maktum, prime min.

Dubai placed troops on alert in a dispute with Abu Dhabi over the appointment of a new UAE commander in chief. It was the most serious crisis within the union since its establishment in 1971.

Upper Volta, W. Africa	6.5	Ouagadougou	105,869 (274,200)	Sangoulé Lamizana, pres.

Upper Volta returned to civilian rule in 1978. Legislative elections under a new constitution, permitting the existence of three parties took place on April 30. Four weeks later President Lamizana, who has ruled the country since 1966, was elected president.

Western Samoa, Oceania	0.2	Apia	1,097 (2,841)	Malietoa Tanumafili II, head of state Tupuola Efi, prime min.

The British government disclosed in July that it would convert Western Samoa's debts to the United Kingdom into aid grants.

Yemen, W. Asia	5.8	Sana	75,290 (195,000)	Ali Abdullah Saleh, pres.

President Ghashmi was assassinated on June 24, when a bomb hidden in a Democratic Yemeni envoy's bag exploded. Suspicion, however, eventually fell on northern Yemeni rebels. A coup against the new president was thwarted in October; some 20 people were subsequently executed as plotters.

Yemen, Democratic, W. Asia	1.9	Madinet al-Shaab	128,559 (332,968)	Abdul Fattah Ismail, pres.

President Salim Rubayi Ali was overthrown and put to death on June 26, accused of planning to seize total power. The coup came two days after the assassination of President Ghashmi of Yemen, in which Ali was at first implicated. General elections, the first in the country since independence in 1967, were held in December. Abdul Fattah Ismail, secretary general of the Yemeni Socialist party which was formed in October, was elected president.

Zambia, E. Africa	5.5	Lusaka	290,585 (752,614)	Kenneth D. Kaunda, pres.

Zambia paid the price for allowing Zimbabwe rebels under Joshua Nkomo to use its soil as a base for raids into Rhodesia. Repeated "hot-pursuit" forays and air attacks by Rhodesian government forces resulted in numerous deaths, considerable destruction, and grumblings among the populace. Although the only candidate, President Kaunda won reelection on December 12.

WORLD ECONOMIC INDEXES

World economic recovery "has been one of the major problems in the world economy during the last few years. We have passed through different phases of world disequilibrium. In 1974, the increase in oil prices and resulting BOP (balance of payments) disequilibria pushed the world into a serious recession and the major concerns were clear: reduce inflation and bring about satisfactory recovery in the world economy. We have learned since, I think, that these two things are related: that one has to reduce inflation if one wishes to achieve a healthy recovery of the world economy. In addition, economic recovery is related to BOP adjustments. So long as there are large BOP deficits, one cannot really expect economies to recover."

H. JOHANNES WITTEVEEN
Outgoing Managing Director, International Monetary Fund

Name & Region	Consumer Price Index—1977 1970 = 100 All items	Food	Wholesale Price Index—1977 1970 = 100	Industrial Production Index—1977 1970 = 100	Unemployment Rate %—1977	Foreign Trade 1977—Million U.S. Dollars Imports	Exports	Estimated GNP 1977—Million U.S. Dollars	GNP Per Capita—1976 U.S. Dollars
AFGHANISTAN	133.2					349[2]	223[2]	2,300	160
ALBANIA									540
ALGERIA	140.1	162.3[1]				6,664	5,233	10,100	990
ANGOLA									330
ANTIGUA	236.0	277.8							
ARGENTINA	6,539.0	6,632.4[1]	19,412.0	128.0	2.3[2]	4,162	5,651	76,400	1,550
AUSTRALIA	207.6	193.0	189.9	112.0	5.6	12,175	13,002	92,000	6,100
AUSTRIA	161.0	153.5	143.4	130.0	1.8	12,248	9,808	47,700	5,330
BAHAMAS	141.1	146.1				3,560[1]	2,879[1]		3,310
BAHRAIN						2,029	1,822	1,700	2,410
BANGLADESH	278.2	266.1				764[1]	414[1]	6,900	110
BARBADOS	267.0	297.0				273	95		1,550
BELGIUM	174.8	169.3	150.7	117.0	9.9	40,142[6]	37,457[6]	73,400	6,780
BENIN						150[1]	46[1]	650[8]	130
BHUTAN									70
BOLIVIA	288.4	316.5			3.2[1]	582	713	2,500	390
BOTSWANA	141.7	137.8							410
BRAZIL	357.3	371.6	538.1			12,204[1]	12,054	177,000	1,140
BRUNEI						269[2]	1,023[2]	382	
BULGARIA				175.0		6,329	6,329	18,600	2,310
BURMA	274.5	290.7				185	223	4,200	120
BURUNDI	163.6	171.2				74	95	405	120
CAMEROON	181.8	191.3[1]				900	671	1,700[1]	290
CANADA	165.4	182.1	195.0	132.0	8.1	39,561	41,452	197,900	7,510
CAPE VERDE	303.4	342.0							260
CEN. AFR. EMP.	188.4	193.0	151.9			63	82	300[1]	230
CHAD	134.3	145.3				116	63	5,200	120
CHILE	166,166.0	208,672.0	481,255.0		13.9	2,189	2,190	9,800	1,050
CHINA								350,000	410
CHINA (TAIWAN)								20,100	1,070
COLOMBIA	365.1	447.9	448.2			1,563	2,302	12,900	630
CONGO	156.9	158.0[1]				156	182[1]	610	520
COSTA RICA	204.4	201.1	260.6			1,006	798		1,040
CUBA						4,066[1]	3,573[1]	4,500	860
CYPRUS	148.5	163.5		154.0	3.0	620	318	154	1,480
CZECHOSLOVAKIA						11,149	10,818	49,600	3,840
DENMARK	188.7	202.0	189.1		7.7	13,239	10,117	43,800	7,450
DOMINICA	235.9	228.1							
DOM. REP.	195.6	184.8	187.3			848	794	4,300	780
ECUADOR	235.2	283.0				1,440	1,192	5,900	640
EGYPT	147.3	174.0	155.7	140.0[1]	2.5[2]	4,808[7]	1,726	13,300	280
EL SALVADOR	180.8	179.1	306.7			950	959	2,550	490
EQ. GUINEA									330
ETHIOPIA	178.4	186.4				349	330		100
FIJI	199.3	211.0				306	173		1,150
FINLAND	227.1	247.7	232.7	127.0	6.1	7,603	7,670	31,700	5,620
FRANCE	183.2	196.5	169.2	126.0		70,498	63,560	374,800	6,550
FRENCH GUIANA	194.3	197.8				150	8		

Name & Region	Consumer Price Index—1977 1970 = 100 All items	Food	Wholesale Price Index—1977 1970 = 100	Industrial Production Index—1977 1970 = 100	Unemployment Rate %—1977	Foreign Trade 1977—Million U.S. Dollars Imports	Exports	Estimated GNP 1977—Million U.S. Dollars	GNP Per Capita—1976 U.S. Dollars
GABON						498	1,017	1,810	2,590
GAMBIA	216.9	245.1	164.4[2]	164.0[2]		78	48		180
GERMANY, E.				152.0		14,334	12,024	54,600	4,220
GERMANY, W.	146.3	143.7	144.5	116.0	4.6[1]	100,672	117,895	508,600	7,380
GHANA	351.5	414.1[1]	234.4[2]			805[2]	760[2]	4,100	580
GIBRALTAR	245.9	299.4				38[1]	3[1]		
GREECE	226.9	245.5	249.8	170.0		6,778	2,724	26,300	2,590
GUADELOUPE	197.5	206.7				376	79		1,500
GUATEMALA	124.4	121.7	176.4[2]			839[1]	760[1]	4,600	630
GUINEA									150
GUINEA-BISSAU									140
GUYANA	170.5	208.7				364[1]	269[1]	498	540
HAITI	213.9	229.9				207[1]	127[1]	1,234	200
HONDURAS	154.3	170.8				580	504	1,300	390
HONG KONG	118.0	114.0				10,457	9,626		2,110
HUNGARY	125.0	127.5	127.0[1]	150.0		6,522	5,832	658	2,280
ICELAND	527.0	609.5			0.5[1]	607	513		6,100
INDIA	174.5	171.5	184.9	138.0		6,592	6,222	101,000	150
INDONESIA	324.4	373.4	323.0			6,230	10,853	43,100	240
IRAN	222.4	204.5	172.4[1]			13,750	24,245	72,600	1,930
IRAQ	161.0	168.8	147.5[1]			3,470[1]	9,664	16,300	1,390
IRELAND	250.0	264.2	140.1	137.0	11.8	5,378	4,396	9,200	2,560
ISRAEL	521.7	569.8	561.0	154.0	3.9	4,663	2,959	14,200	3,920
ITALY	236.6	240.5	277.5	123.0	7.2	47,580	45,063	193,700	3,050
IVORY COAST	206.4	223.7				1,752	2,155	5,980[8]	610
JAMAICA	238.0	252.3			22.4[1]	861	856	2,970[1]	1,070
JAPAN	203.6	209.0	167.8	127.0	2.0	70,660	80,470	677,000	4,910
JORDAN	127.7	131.0				1,381	249	1,300	610
KENYA	177.7	178.8				1,284	1,213	3,700	240
KOREA, N.								9,800	470
KOREA, S.	258.7	305.8	290.8	407.0	3.8	10,810	10,046	31,500	670
KUWAIT	153.1	179.0				3,327[1]	9,804	12,000	15,480
LAOS	457.3	544.9[2]						256	90
LEBANON								2,900	
LESOTHO	171.2	188.7							170
LIBERIA	189.7	188.3				464	447	910	450
LIBYA	137.6	107.4				3,212[1]	10,113	18,500	6,310
LUXEMBOURG	166.0	167.4		99.0		40,142[6]	37,457[6]	2,490	6,460
MADAGASCAR	168.9	178.8				285[1]	275[1]	1,795	200
MALAWI	170.7	178.7				235	195	925	140
MALAYSIA	152.8	170.9		178.0		4,024	4,565	12,300	860
MALI		245.2				145	67	615	100
MALTA	147.0	162.5				513	289		1,390
MARTINIQUE	202.8	199.6				428	128		2,350
MAURITANIA	133.6	136.0				207	157	210[1]	340
MAURITIUS	220.2	218.2				442	312		680
MEXICO	263.8	267.3	288.9	147.0		5,489	4,063	83,800	1,090
MONGOLIA								2,800	860
MOROCCO	131.8	135.0	191.5	142.0[1]		3,194	1,300	9,500	540
MOZAMBIQUE	171.6	187.9[1]		83.0[2]		417[2]	202[2]		170
NEPAL	163.0	171.3						1,600[1]	120
NETHERLANDS	175.6	162.8		127.0	5.3	45,616	43,703	104,100	6,200
NETH. ANTILLES	172.4	232.6				3,661[1]	2,524[1]		1,680
NEW ZEALAND	217.4	217.2	230.5			3,363	3,142	13,600	4,250
NICARAGUA	123.2	125.1				755	633	2,020	750
NIGER	219.7	255.1				127[1]	134[1]	825[1]	160
NIGERIA	274.6	358.2			1.4	11,306	11,823	34,200	380
NORWAY	178.0	181.0	172.0	138.0	1.8[1]	12,877	8,717	36,200	7,420
OMAN								2,500	2,680

Name & Region	Consumer Price Index—1977 1970 = 100 All items	Food	Wholesale Price Index—1977 1970 = 100	Industrial Production Index—1977 1970 = 100	Unemployment Rate %—1977	Foreign Trade 1977—Million U.S. Dollars Imports	Exports	Estimated GNP 1977—Million U.S. Dollars	GNP Per Capita—1976 U.S. Dollars
PAKISTAN	233.9	246.6[3]	255.3			2,454	1,152	17,600	170
PANAMA	109.1	104.5[4]	217.0		6.5[1]	861	237[1]		1,310
PAPUA N.G.	176.0	181.3				567	723		490
PARAGUAY	197.4	222.2				308	279	2,000	640
PERU	333.9	369.2			5.2[1]	1,780[1]	536	13,000	800
PHILIPPINES	182.3	178.5[5]	270.4	141.0[1]	3.9[2]	4,270	3,151	20,000	410
POLAND	118.1	117.8[1]		204.0		14,674	12,336	86,100	2,860
PORTUGAL	302.5	345.4	268.0	155.0		4,963	2,023	16,400	1,690
PUERTO RICO	160.0	182.9	180.1		19.9				2,430
QATAR									11,400
RÉUNION	197.3	217.9				502	114		1,920
RHODESIA	160.1	159.9	195.8	121.0			105[1]	3,100	550
RUMANIA								51,400	1,450
RWANDA						114	92	515	110
SAMOA, W.	163.8	166.8				41	13		350
SAUDI ARABIA						8,694[1]	41,527	55,400	4,480
SENEGAL	211.5	239.9		174.0		576[2]	461[2]	1,700	390
SEYCHELLES	320.4	162.2							580
SIERRA LEONE	191.0	209.7				153[1]	127	720	200
SINGAPORE	127.0	125.1	109.8			10,471	8,241	6,500	2,700
SOMALIA	182.9	207.0				162[2]		425	110
SOUTH AFRICA	193.8	202.6	230.4			5,893	6,158	43,800	1,340
SPAIN	258.8	260.2	223.4	170.0	2.8[1]	17,846	10,230	123,600	2,920
SRI LANKA	147.0	148.9				695	714	4,000	200
SUDAN	210.8	201.2				1,060	661	4,400	290
SURINAM	178.8	186.6				266[1]	330[1]		1,370
SWAZILAND	200.7	201.7							470
SWEDEN	180.1	193.4	188.0	111.0	1.8	19,566	18,823	83,000	8,670
SWITZERLAND	149.2	141.2	132.5	103.0		17,979	17,682	60,100	8,880
SYRIA	195.1	197.7[1]	191.4[1]		6.2[1]	2,672	1,063	6,500	780
TANZANIA	223.9	257.9				704	501	2,900	180
THAILAND	173.1	192.7	194.5			4,613	3,493	18,100	380
TOGO	215.0	251.5				201[1]	105[1]	565	260
TONGA	177.6	187.6							
TRIN. & TOB.	228.7	241.6			15.0[1]	1,772	2,174		2,240
TUNISIA	144.9	148.2	161.7	150.0		1,825	921	5,000	840
TURKEY	323.3	362.0	272.5[1]			5,694	1,753	46,600	990
UGANDA	434.2	490.4				80[1]	359[1]	3,200[8]	240
USSR	99.7	100.9[1]	97.0[1]	159.0		40,817	45,161	645,000	
UN. ARAB EM.								7,700	13,990
UN. KINGDOM	249.0	294.3	340.2	106.0	6.2	63,677	57,547	263,600	4,020
USA	156.1	167.3	175.9	129.0	7.0	156,758	119,042	1,890,000	7,890
UPPER VOLTA						145[1]	53[1]	795	110
URUGUAY	3,299.2	3,490.6	2,281.0[1]		12.7[1]	669	599	3,600	1,390
VENEZUELA	153.0	184.7	180.2	98.0[1]	11.4[1]	6,023[1]	9,299[1]	36,100	2,570
YEMEN						1,040	8[1]	1,200	250
YEMEN, S.						414[1]	249[1]	224	280
YUGOSLAVIA	311.6	329.5	265.0	167.0	12.0	9,634	5,254	37,800	1,680
ZAIRE	722.6	873.0				610	981	3,500	140
ZAMBIA	201.7	209.4	184.5	110.0		670	897	2,200	440

[1] 1976. [2] 1975. [3] 1971 = 100. [4] 1975 = 100. [5] 1972 = 100. [6] Includes Belgium and Luxembourg. [7] Excludes petroleum. [8] Gross domestic product.

Sources of Information: "Monthly Bulletin of Statistics;" "Statistical Yearbook," United Nations. "The Military Balance 1978–1979," The International Institute for Strategic Studies. "1978 World Population Data Sheet," Population Reference Bureau, Inc.

AGRICULTURAL PRODUCTION: SELECTED COUNTRIES (1976)

(in thousand metric tons)

	Coffee	Cotton	Eggs	Maize	Milk[1]	Potatoes	Rice	Soybeans	Wheat
AFGHANISTAN	...	54	16	800	604	23	448	...	2,930
ALBANIA	...	7	4	280	287	122	18	...	390
ALGERIA	...	...	17	...	651	580	2	...	2,060
ANGOLA	72	13	3	450	140	35	25	...	13
ARGENTINA	...	140	213	5,855	5,747	1,528	309	695	11,200
AUSTRALIA	...	25	183	131	6,442	697	417	45	11,713
AUSTRIA	...	...	88	936	3,210	1,746	...	...	1,234
BANGLADESH	...	1	25	...	1,420	903	17,627	...	218
BELGIUM[2]	...	...	210	30	3,900	879	...	...	932
BOLIVIA	16	12	15	342	93	824	113	15	69
BRAZIL	389	397	522	17,845	10,767	1,816	9,560	11,227	3,226
BULGARIA	...	1	102	3,031	1,817	350	41	99	3,152
BURMA	...	16	72	64	402	50	9,307	10	60
CAMEROON	80	18	7	355	56	40	19	...	...
CANADA	...	...	297	3,771	7,693	2,350	...	250	23,587
CHAD	...	55	3	10	184	...	50	...	2
CHILE	...	...	54	248	1,018	539	95	...	866
CHINA	5	2,373	3,761	33,114	5,629	41,244	129,054	12,053	43,001
COLOMBIA	510	145	104	810	2,200	1,126	1,560	111	59
COSTA RICA	87	...	16	89	267	25	150	...	...
CUBA	25	...	85	125	637	119	420	...	...
CZECHOSLOVAKIA	...	...	225	514	5,648	4,214	...	...	4,807
DENMARK	...	...	71	...	5,045	575	...	...	592
DOM. REP.	42	...	22	35	293	29	258	...	...
ECUADOR	83	8	20	216	830	533	368	15	39
EGYPT	...	396	76	3,047	1,820	893	2,300	11	1,960
EL SALVADOR	159	62	28	342	294	16	36	...	...
ETHIOPIA	170	20	70	1,200	698	174	...	...	694
FINLAND	...	...	86	...	3,278	948	...	...	654
FRANCE	...	...	755	5,544	31,060	4,673	35	...	16,150
GERMANY, E.	...	...	287	...	8,118	6,816	...	...	2,715
GERMANY, W.	...	...	883	480	22,189	9,808	...	...	6,702
GREECE	...	113	139	501	1,704	991	82	...	2,351
GUATEMALA	149	99	33	686	320	30	24	...	48
HONDURAS	45	7	19	289	187	5	26	...	1
HUNGARY	...	...	222	5,141	2,142	1,396	32	42	5,148
INDIA	84	1,019	82	6,257	25,446	7,306	64,363	120	28,846
INDONESIA	179	5	67	2,572	57	127	23,300	482	...
IRAN	...	160	130	80	2,125	550	1,566	102	6,044
IRAQ	...	12	17	51	469	46	163	1	1,312
IRELAND	...	...	40	...	4,550	1,179	...	...	200
ISRAEL	...	54	96	14	705	175	...	...	206
ITALY	...	1	775	5,321	10,021	2,989	907	...	9,516
IVORY COAST	305	26	5	117	...	...	420	...	...
JAPAN	...	...	1,815	11	5,265	3,200	15,292	110	222
KENYA	80	5	18	1,550	750	370	39	...	200
KOREA, N.	...	3	72	2,100	...	1,300	3,800	300	145
KOREA, S.	...	2	168	84	128	591	7,243	290	82
MADAGASCAR	93	13	10	123	29	123	1,814	...	...
MALAWI	...	6	10	1,100	29	98	33	...	1
MALAYSIA	5	...	109	26	...	...	1,853	...	...
MALI	...	41	6	81	114	...	237	...	2
MEXICO	242	211	422	8,393	4,164	695	460	319	3,363
MOROCCO	...	7	66	493	537	170	18	1	2,135
MOZAMBIQUE	...	28	9	450	72	42	45	...	3
NEPAL	...	...	13	787	695	314	2,385	...	387
NETHERLANDS	...	...	334	5	10,538	4,783	...	...	710
NEW ZEALAND	...	...	53	232	6,538	250	...	...	427
NICARAGUA	59	99	28	201	263	...	61	2	...
NIGERIA	3	61	113	1,050	316	30	405	70	20
NORWAY	...	...	37	...	1,894	484	...	...	65
PAKISTAN	...	412	66	764	9,780	321	4,106	...	8,691
PANAMA	5	...	14	64	74	11	144	...	...
PARAGUAY	9	34	18	351	128	4	57	284	29
PERU	60	65	51	670	846	1,930	570	3	148
PHILIPPINES	80	...	170	2,767	...	20	6,455	9	...
POLAND	...	...	449	231	16,573	49,951	...	...	5,745
PORTUGAL	...	...	45	429	819	1,003	97	...	694
RHODESIA	...	39	8	1,400	255	23	5	...	90
RUMANIA	...	...	270	11,583	4,621	4,788	37	213	6,724
SENEGAL	...	15	6	47	110	5	112	...	...
SOUTH AFRICA	...	19	162	7,312	2,560	672	3	19	2,239
SPAIN	...	39	617	1,545	5,904	5,659	406	6	4,436
SRI LANKA	9	...	16	27	196	28	1,253	1	...
SUDAN	...	124	21	50	1,377	25	12	...	264
SWEDEN	...	...	105	...	3,247	1,058	...	...	1,763
SWITZERLAND	...	...	41	114	3,473	769	...	...	408
SYRIA	...	155	35	51	665	126	1	...	1,790
TANZANIA	55	69	20	1,619	700	84	380	1	60
THAILAND	...	27	140	2,675	...	10	15,800	114	...
TURKEY	...	475	155	1,310	5,006	2,850	251	9	16,578
UGANDA	192	41	15	629	351	366	16	5	17
USSR	...	2,590	3,059	10,138	89,058	85,102	2,001	480	96,900
UN. KINGDOM	...	...	805	...	14,420	4,789	...	...	4,740
USA	1	2,304	3,826	159,173	54,592	16,228	5,246	34,425	58,307
URUGUAY	...	...	17	210	750	166	213	23	505
VENEZUELA	50	23	98	532	1,193	135	277	...	1
VIETNAM	5	2	111	320	...	14	10,800	33	...
YEMEN	5	10	3	72	240	76	...	...	52
YUGOSLAVIA	...	2	184	9,106	3,991	2,928	23	48	5,979
ZAIRE	86	13	17	410	27	47	190	1	2

Source: UN Statistical Yearbook 1977. Note. Some of the figures are provisional or estimates.
[1] Total production from all sources, including cows, buffaloes, sheep, and goats. [2] Includes Luxembourg.

INDUSTRIAL PRODUCTION: SELECTED COUNTRIES (1976)

	Beer	Cotton yarn	Crude steel	Cement	Gasoline	Motor vehicles	Newsprint	Nitrogen fertilizer[6]	Sugar
	in thousand hectoliters	in thousand metric tons	in thousand metric tons	in thousand metric tons	in thousand metric tons	in thousands	in thousand metric tons	in thousand metric tons	in thousand metric tons
AFGHANISTAN	...	1	...	125	...	...	...	26	10
ALBANIA	...	...	...	800	160	...	...	45	21
ALGERIA	415[1]	9[1]	206	1,329	816	...	...	33	20
ANGOLA	650	...	...	650	51	...	...	...	50
ARGENTINA	2,839	92	2,244	5,717	4,022	180[4]	...	18	1,551
AUSTRALIA	19,158	26	7,937	5,040	9,479	457[4]	206	220	3,395
AUSTRIA	7,783	21	4,376	5,880	1,597	3	154	239	426
BANGLADESH	...	40	90	141	...	...	...	130	110
BELGIUM	14,544	54	12,145	7,504	3,935	1,117[3]	88[5]	652[5]	721
BOLIVIA	...	.3[1]	...	232	400	...	...	...	240
BRAZIL	13,980	70	9,092	19,147	10,287	973[4]	127	195	7,236
BULGARIA	4,695	79	2,460	4,362	1,680	22	...	663	230
BURMA	30[1]	8[1]	...	233	194	...	...	56	80
CANADA	20,511	62[1]	13,137	9,898	26,564	1,640	7,895	960	156
CHILE	1,069	...	456	964	950	7[3]	133	100	240
CHINA	1,750	...	27,000	35,000	...	...	1,100	3,827	4,000
COLOMBIA	8,194[2]	28[2]	252	3,612	2,299	36[3]	...	66	935
COSTA RICA	270[1]	...	...	362	48	...	...	31	200
CUBA	2,200	22	250	2,501	985	...	...	68	6,151
CZECHOSLOVAKIA	22,629	125	14,693	9,552	1,585	218	79	563	620
DENMARK	8,328	2	723	2,355	1,397	1[3]	...	109	432
DOM. REP.	445[1]	1[1]	...	582	321	...	...	...	1,287
ECUADOR	1,060[1]	1[1]	...	616	715	...	...	2	309
EGYPT	286[1]	193	457	3,290	1,976	...	...	200	576
EL SALVADOR	484	5	...	322	133	...	...	5	261
ETHIOPIA	422[1]	11[1]	...	117[1]	79	...	...	...	136
FINLAND	2,659	12	1,644	1,825	1,692	28[4]	991	190	77
FRANCE	24,585	253	23,221	29,517	17,840	3,843	258	1,462	2,721
GERMANY, E.	21,202	138	6,740	11,344	2,982	202	96	776	609
GERMANY, W.	91,391	208	42,415	34,152	18,228	3,876	501	1,290	2,844
GHANA	500[1]	...	...	700	224	...	...	...	12
GREECE	1,440	79[1]	800	8,760	991	...	...	273	386
GUATEMALA	572	...	...	341[1]	136	...	...	5[1]	517
HONDURAS	248	...	...	234	85	...	...	...	81
HUNGARY	6,765	59	3,652	4,298	1,157	13	...	492	395
ICELAND	29	...	...	144	...	...	...	11	...
INDIA	941	1,006	9,310	18,684	1,314	80	57	1,857	5,033
INDONESIA	470	...	...	1,810	1,561	79[3]	...	250	1,380
IRAN	...	...	...	5,500	4,202	168[3]	...	156	650
IRAQ	193[1]	1[1]	...	2,385	520	...	...	25	11
IRELAND	4,492[2]	5	58	1,569	415	47[3]	...	91	150[2]
ISRAEL	351	22	70	1,999	941	7[3]	...	48	40
ITALY	7,377	164	23,446	36,327	14,492	1,590	264	985	1,758
IVORY COAST	815	6[1]	...	757	270	5[3]	...	4	22
JAMAICA	606	...	...	365	225	...	...	3[1]	368
JAPAN	37,236	33	107,399	68,712	22,244	7,847	2,341	1,149	506
KENYA	1,642	...	...	983	363	...	...	...	182
KOREA, S.	1,896	175	2,698	11,873	627	50[3]	155	510	...
LEBANON	30	...	...	1,700	180	...	...	1	10
LUXEMBOURG	789	...	4,566	299	...	...	...	...	...
MADAGASCAR	257	...	...	70	93	...	...	...	114
MALAYSIA	...	18	...	1,739	30	44[3]	...	39	50
MEXICO	19,357	158[1]	5,243	12,691	8,036	319[4]	56	650	2,710
MOROCCO	316	...	1[1]	2,140	356	31[3]	...	13	250
MOZAMBIQUE	655	3	...	258[1]	80	...	...	5	220
NETHERLANDS	13,862	33	5,190	3,481	7,231	108[4]	122	1,253	947
NEW ZEALAND	4,096	...	...	999	1,414	82[3]	275	...	...
NIGERIA	3,161	5[1]	...	1,274	632	6[3]	...	...	30
NORWAY	1,875[1]	2	898	2,680	1,050	...	466	337	...
PAKISTAN	35	350	...	3,196	310	...	...	309	677
PANAMA	433	...	...	311	281	...	...	...	161
PARAGUAY	...	34	...	155	60	...	...	...	62
PERU	5,041	...	349	1,966	1,451	51[3]	...	57	930
PHILIPPINES	6,000	33	...	4,229	1,810	...	83	48	2,984
POLAND	12,347	219	15,231	19,804	2,348	312	...	1,548	1,774
PORTUGAL	3,054	112	389	3,713	767	69[3]	1	176	12
RHODESIA	900	...	300	541	...	...	...	65	220
RUMANIA	7,625	165	10,733	13,088	3,880	109	44	1,331	561
SAUDI ARABIA	...	...	...	1,104	1,480	...	...	84	...
SENEGAL	224	.2[1]	...	380	115	...	...	9	...
SOUTH AFRICA	5,389	48	6,926	7,048	3,504	252[3]	212	332	2,113
SPAIN	17,130	49	11,085	25,296	5,166	864	105	883	1,162
SRI LANKA	30	6	...	426	94	...	...	...	24
SUDAN	...	...	...	182[1]	120	...	...	...	140
SWEDEN	4,562[1]	6	5,168	2,798	2,458	307	1,136	151	301
TANZANIA	...	...	...	244	117	...	...	6	110
THAILAND	750	67[1]	163	4,422	1,408	...	...	6	1,757
TRIN. & TOB.	302	...	...	242	1,272	12[3]	...	46	205
TUNISIA	278	7[1]	103	478	130	4[3]	...	5	5
TURKEY	1,709	127	1,457	13,154	1,950	110[3]	80	212	1,090
UGANDA	389[1]	...	12	88	...	...	...	...	20
USSR	59,152	1,583	144,805	124,246	...	2,027	1,390	8,531	8,500
UN. KINGDOM	65,635	133	22,274	15,780	15,284	1,706	326	1,071	657
USA	185,257[1]	1,230	116,121	68,311	297,538	11,477	3,104	9,790[7]	6,163
VENEZUELA	...	...	754	3,838	5,742	163[3]	...	75	510
YUGOSLAVIA	8,685	117	2,751	7,621	1,923	244[3]	90	389	580
ZAIRE	4,762[1]	...	...	770[1]	68	...	...	...	65
ZAMBIA	...	...	...	452[1]	180	...	...	7	80

[1] 1975. [2] 1974. [3] Assembly only. [4] Production and assembly. [5] Includes Luxembourg. [6] 1976–77. [7] Excludes sodium nitrate; includes data for Puerto Rico.
Source: UN Statistical Yearbook 1977.

ENERGY: PRODUCTION AND CONSUMPTION

	Coal Reserves (in million metric tons)	Coal Production (in thousand metric tons)	Electricity[1] (in million kilowatt hours)	Natural Gas (in teracalories[2])	Petroleum Reserves (in million metric tons)	Petroleum Production (in thousand metric tons)	Total Energy Production*	Total Energy Consumption*
AFGHANISTAN	...	160	696	23,678	...	...	3.62	.81
ALBANIA	...	...	2,000	1,500	19	2,500	4.55	2.2
ALGERIA	9	...	4,615	93,867	1,231	50,423	91.62	12.61
ANGOLA	...	...	1,300	200	179	4,494	6.75	1.08
ARGENTINA	155	615	30,328	63,995	362	20,800	41.82	46.4
AUSTRALIA	25,540	67,820	76,598	52,759	307	20,515	119.86	90.83
AUSTRIA	1	...	35,331	20,950	23	1,931	9.96	30.15
BANGLADESH	760	...	1,710	7,513	...	...	1.14	2.63
BELGIUM	253	7,662	47,349	282	...	...	8.81	59.82
BOLIVIA	...	...	1,130	14,681	19	1,890	5.04	1.84
BOTSWANA	506	224	332	...	...	...	...	...
BRAZIL	3,256	3,256	88,383	6,787	110	8,121	26.47	79.84
BULGARIA	29	295	27,742	312	2	117	14.08	41.26
BURMA	13	13	968	1	9	1,163	1.78	1.51
CAMBODIA	...	...	150	...	...	...	...	.13
CAMEROON	...	...	1,336	...	...	...	.16	.64
CANADA	8,463	20,798	293,367	673,111	842	62,152	258.80	230.28
CHILE	97	1,245	9,276	...	51	938	5.73	10.32
CHINA	300,000	480,000	...	11,090	2,461	85,000	614.78	590.06
COLOMBIA	150	3,620	15,292	36,530	129	7,553	18.73	16.66
CONGO	...	...	117	16,645	64	2,002	3	.2
COSTA RICA	...	...	1,646	149	...	...	.18	1.02
CUBA	...	...	7,198	196	...	144	.25	11.6
CZECHOSLOVAKIA	5,540	28562	62,746	7,287	2	131	83.84	110.34
DENMARK	...	...	19,645	...	7	195	.29	26.99
DOM. REP.	...	...	2,690	...	...	...	.02	3.3
ECUADOR	...	...	1,885	326	183	9,488	14.1	3.33
EGYPT	25	...	11,000	11,000	218	16,756	27.26	18.00
EL SALVADOR	...	...	1,199	...	...	...	.09	1.07
ETHIOPIA	...	...	674	...	...	...	.04	.76
FINLAND	...	...	27,804	...	...	...	1.41	24.47
FRANCE	1,380	23,300	194,600	66,524	7	1,057	45.10	231.92
GABON	...	...	230	466	76	11,305	16.69	.68
GERMANY, E.	200	458	89,150	26,904	3	60	79.25	113.96
GERMANY, W.	44,001	95,902	333,651	161,473	44	5,524	165.88	364.28
GHANA	...	...	4,226	...	...	...	.51	1.62
GREECE	...	...	16,661	...	19	...	7.68	20.62
GUATEMALA	...	...	1,250	...	3	7	.05	1.61
GUINEA	...	...	500	...	...	...	.01	.42
HONDURAS	...	...	590	...	...	...	.06	.75
HUNGARY	450	2,934	22,050	48,457	30	2,142	22.21	37.66
ICELAND	...	...	2,426	...	...	...	.29	1.00
INDIA	21,365	100,870	95,335	10,625	396	8,659	121.09	132.92
INDONESIA	163	193	3,790	82,379	1,547	74,195	113.84	30.43
IRAN	385	900	17,311	211,284	6,596	295,084	467.36	49.77
IRAQ	...	...	4,645	18,497	4,735	112,284	167.70	8.36
IRELAND	22	49	8,609	...	...	...	2.41	10.02
ISRAEL	...	...	10,357	535	...	36	.13	9.01
ITALY	1	2	163,550	143,318	48	1,102	28.43	184.46
JAPAN	7,443	18,396	511,776	26,525	4	580	38.21	414.87
JORDAN	...	...	501	...	...	...	...	1.46
KUWAIT	...	...	5,202	51,978	10,029	108,046	169.10	9.47
LEBANON	...	...	1,250	...	...	...	.1	1.58
LIBERIA	...	...	887	...	...	...	.04	.72
LIBYA	...	...	1,485	35,488	3,244	93,452	145.58	4.04
MADAGASCAR	60	...	343	...	...	...	.02	.55
MALAWI	...	...	318	...	...	...	.04	.29
MALAYSIA	...	...	6,441	836	196	8,026	12.06	7.63
MEXICO	5,316	5,650	46,612	120,286	1,127	41,336	91.44	76.40
MOROCCO	15	702	3,329	798	...	9	.95	4.86
NETHERLANDS	3,705	...	58,138	806,711	13	1,371	118.06	85.70
NEW ZEALAND	297	2,315	20,910	8,903	75	477	6	11.35
NICARAGUA	...	...	1,040	...	...	...	.05	1.07
NIGERIA	359	310	3,400	5,890	1,662	103,479	153.58	6.09
NORWAY	2	519	82,199	3,234	785	13,828	31.41	21.19
PAKISTAN	24	1,349	10,876	43,783	12	305	8.33	13.11
PANAMA	...	...	1,508	...	...	...	.01	1.52
PARAGUAY	...	...	700	...	...	...	.08	.52
PERU	211	...	8,650	4,240	98	3,775	7.06	10.34
PHILIPPINES	...	158	14,736	...	...	...	.76	14.38
POLAND	32,425	179,303	104,101	57,981	5	455	200.35	180.51
PORTUGAL	15	193	10,146	...	...	...	.79	10.13
RUMANIA	70	7,111	58,266	330,499	160	14,700	83.90	86.56
SAUDI ARABIA	...	...	2,250	55,000	15,455	425,804	643.99	17.56
SIERRA LEONE	...	...	200	...	...	...	...	.32
SOUTH AFRICA	24,224	75,730	79,087	...	...	...	76.32	87.40
SPAIN	1,272	10,696	90,821	12	33	1,772	19.4	86.31
SRI LANKA	...	...	1,202	...	...	...	.13	1.45
SWEDEN	60	12	86,416	...	...	...	8.7	49.71
SYRIA	...	...	1,785	1,081	382	10,041	14.94	5.65
TANZANIA	309	1	685	...	...	...	.06	1.07
THAILAND	...	...	10,295	...	...	...	.68	13.22
TUNISIA	...	...	1,525	2,401	299	3,710	5.8	2.61
TURKEY	191	4,632	18,231	...	12	2,595	12.2	29.83
UGANDA	...	...	729	...	...	...	.11	.58
USSR	165,802	494,377	1,111,420	2,668,307	8,152	519,677	1,674.10	1,349.86
UN. KINGDOM	98,877	123,822	276,976	362,347	1,373	11,630	198.18	295.28
UNITED STATES	317,451	585,684	2,123,406	4,996,843	4,181	401,211	2,049.70	2,485.45
URUGUAY	...	...	2,800	...	...	...	.15	3.10
VENEZUELA	14	89	23,276	118,270	2,608	120,153	199.00	35.08
YUGOSLAVIA	82	587	43,573	17,124	47	3,880	29.42	43.46
ZAIRE	720	109	3,502	...	19	1,251	2.37	1.58
ZAMBIA	74	784	7,034	...	...	...	1.62	2.81

* In million metric tons of coal equivalent.

[1] Total gross generation of electricity both from enterprises generating primarily for public use and industrial establishments generating primarily for their own use.

[2] Teracalories = U.S. trillions of calories.

WORLD MINERAL PRODUCTION

Aluminum, smelter (thousand metric tons)

	1976	1977
United States	3,857	4,117
USSR[e]	1,600	1,640
Japan	919	1,188
Canada	633	983
West Germany	697	742
Norway	597	628
France	385	389
United Kingdom	335	349
Italy	206	260
China[e]	200	250
Australia	232	248
Netherlands	256	241
Spain	211	211
Rumania	207	209
Yugoslavia	198	197
India	212	184
Other countries[a]	1,752	1,825
Total	12,497	13,661

Antimony, mine[b] (metric tons)

	1976	1977
Bolivia	15,307	15,156
China[e]	12,000	12,000
South Africa	10,736	11,730
USSR[e]	7,700	7,900
Turkey	4,328	e4,500
Mexico	2,546	e2,700
Thailand	3,671	e2,500
Canada	2,300	2,120
Yugoslavia	2,021	e2,100
Morocco	1,415	1,409
Australia	1,708	e1,400
Guatemala	1,120	e1,130
Italy	1,009	825
Czechoslovakia[e]	700	750
Other countries[a]	3,053	3,315
Total	69,614	69,535

Asbestos[c] (thousand metric tons)

	1976	1977
USSR[e]	2,290	2,460
Canada	1,536	1,543
South Africa	370	380
China[e]	175	200
Rhodesia[e]	165	200
Italy	165	e153
Brazil	93	e95
United States	104	92
Other countries[a]	211	212
Total	5,109	5,335

Barite[c] (thousand metric tons)

	1976	1977
United States	1,120	1,355
USSR[e]	400	450
India	195	315
China[e]	270	300
Ireland	323	e300
West Germany	262	e290
Mexico	270	280
Peru	331	280
Iran	170	170
France	150	e150
Morocco	137	140
Italy	179	136
Other countries	1,330	1,181
Total	5,137	5,347

Bauxite[c] (thousand metric tons)

	1976	1977
Australia	24,084	26,070
Jamaica	10,312	11,433
Guinea	11,316	11,320
USSR[e]	6,620	6,780
Surinam	4,613	4,924
Greece	2,551	2,983
Hungary	2,918	2,948
Guyana	2,686	2,731
Yugoslavia	2,033	2,044
France	2,330	2,028
United States	1,989	2,013
India	1,448	1,511
Indonesia	940	1,301
China[e]	990	1,200
Brazil	998	e1,000
Other countries	4,161	4,583
Total	79,989	84,869

Cement[c] (million metric tons)

	1976	1977
USSR	124.2	127.0
Japan	68.7	73.1
United States	67.6	72.6
China[e]	30.0	40.0
Italy	36.3	38.2
West Germany	34.2	32.2
France	29.4	28.7
Spain	25.2	28.0
Poland	19.8	21.3
India	18.7	19.1
Brazil	19.1	18.5
United Kingdom	15.8	15.5
South Korea	11.9	14.2
Rumania	12.5	13.9
Turkey	12.4	13.8
Mexico	12.6	13.2
East Germany	11.3	12.1
Other countries[a]	185.7	196.0
Total	735.4	777.4

Chromite[c] (thousand metric tons)

	1976	1977
South Africa	2,409	3,317
USSR	2,100	2,180
Albania	830	880
Turkey[e]	710	630
Rhodesia[e]	610	600
Finland	414	594
Philippines	428	537
India	402	351
Brazil	186	190
Madagascar	221	180
Iran	150	165
Other countries[a]	160	176
Total	8,630	9,800

Coal, all grades[f] (million metric tons)

	1976	1977
USSR	712	722
United States	621	630
China[e]	480	500
East Germany	247	254
Poland	219	227
West Germany	224	208
United Kingdom	124	e122
Czechoslovakia	118	121
Australia	106	110
India	105	104
South Africa	77	85
North Korea	41	41
Yugoslavia	37	39
Canada	25	28
Rumania	25	e27
Bulgaria	25	25
France	25	25
Hungary	25	25
Greece	22	24
Other countries[a]	111	91
Total	3,369	3,408

Copper, mine[b] (thousand metric tons)

	1976	1977
United States	1,457	1,364
Chile	1,005	1,056
USSR[e]	800	830
Canada	731	781
Zambia	709	658
Zaire	444	482
Peru	220	350
Philippines	233	269
Poland	267	e268
Australia	218	220
South Africa	197	208
Papua New Guinea	176	182
Yugoslavia	120	116
China[e]	100	100
Mexico	89	90
Japan	82	81
Indonesia	76	64
Other countries[a]	571	574
Total	7,495	7,693

Diamond (thousand carats)

	1976	1977
Zaire	11,821	11,213
USSR[e]	9,900	10,300
South Africa	7,023	8,033
Botswana	2,384	2,691
Ghana	2,283	e2,300
South West Africa	1,694	2,001
Venezuela	833	700
Sierra Leone	481	450
Tanzania	438	e375
Angola[e]	340	353
Other countries	876	1,054
Total	38,073	39,470

Fluorspar[g] (thousand metric tons)

	1976	1977
Mexico	1,004	955
USSR[e]	490	500
Spain	285	399
France	354	370
South Africa	291	351
China[e]	350	350
Mongolia[e]	302	320
Thailand	174	223
United Kingdom	217	200
Italy	210	186
United States	171	154
Other countries[a]	624	672
Total	4,472	4,680

Gas, natural, marketed production[h] (billion cubic feet)

	1976	1977
United States	19,952	19,925
USSR	11,336	12,219
Netherlands	3,436	3,447
Canada	3,067	3,160
China[e]	1,600	1,900
United Kingdom	1,316	1,358
Rumania	1,054	e1,115
Iran	794	1,080
West Germany	658	678
Mexico	578	e537
Italy	552	485
Libya	506	e410
Other countries[a]	4,610	4,818
Total	49,459	51,132

Gold, mine[b] (thousand troy ounces)

	1976	1977
South Africa	22,936	22,502
USSR	7,700	7,850
Canada	1,692	1,717
Papua New Guinea	1,228	e1,200
United States	1,048	1,100
Rhodesia[e]	600	600
Philippines	501	558
Ghana	532	481
Australia	495	e475
Dominican Republic	414	348
Spain[e]	270	270
Colombia	298	e263
Mexico	163	213
Brazil	158	e170
Yugoslavia	157	e160
Other countries[a]	1,450	1,478
Total	39,642	39,385

Graphite[c] (thousand metric tons)

	1976	1977
USSR[e]	95	95
North Korea[e]	75	75
Mexico	60	e60
China[e]	50	50
South Korea	42	e45
Austria	33	e35
India	33	e33
Madagascar	14	e15
West Germany	14	e14
Other countries[a]	33	32
Total	449	454

Gypsum[c] (thousand metric tons)

	1976	1977
United States	10,368	12,147
Canada	6,002	7,039
Iran	6,500	e6,700
France[e]	5,900	5,800
USSR[e]	5,000	5,200
Spain[e]	4,200	4,300
Italy	e4,200	4,180
United Kingdom	3,350	e3,300
West Germany	2,100	e2,100
Mexico	1,414	1,496
Poland[e]	1,250	1,250
Australia	926	900
Austria	770	809
India	727	768
Other countries[a]	10,040	9,522
Total	62,747	65,511

Iron Ore[c] (million metric tons)

	1976	1977
USSR	239.1	237.7
Australia	93.3	96.1
Brazil	94.1	e87.0
China[e]	65.0	65.0
United States	81.3	56.6
Canada	58.6	56.3
India	43.4	42.3
France	45.2	36.6
South Africa	15.7	26.5
Sweden	29.9	25.4
Liberia	18.8	18.1
Venezuela	18.7	14.4
Mauritania	9.7	9.8
North Korea[e]	9.5	9.5
Other countries[a]	78.1	75.8
Total	900.4	857.1

Iron, steel ingots (million metric tons)

	1976	1977
USSR	144.8	147.0
United States	116.3	113.7
Japan	107.4	102.4
West Germany	42.4	39.0
China[e]	25.0	27.0
Italy	23.4	23.3
France	23.2	22.1
United Kingdom	22.3	21.2
Poland	15.6	17.8
Czechoslovakia	14.7	15.1
Canada	13.3	13.6
Rumania	10.7	11.6
Belgium	12.1	11.3
Brazil	9.2	11.1
India	9.4	9.9
Australia	7.7	7.3
South Africa	7.1	7.3
East Germany	6.7	6.8
Mexico	5.3	5.5
Netherlands	5.2	4.9
Luxembourg	4.6	4.3
Austria	4.5	4.1
Sweden	5.1	3.8
Yugoslavia	2.8	3.8
Other countries[a]	38.6	39.8
Total	677.4	673.7

Lead, primary smelter (thousand metric tons)

	1976	1977
United States	592	549
USSR[e]	500	510
Australia	343	335
Japan	219	218
Canada	175	187
France	159	173
Mexico	190	138
Yugoslavia	111	130

Lead, primary smelter (cont'd) (thousand metric tons)

	1976	1977
Belgium	104	117
Bulgaria	112	112
West Germany	101	105
China[e]	100	100
Spain	76	89
Peru	74	79
Poland	75	75
North Korea[e]	70	70
Italy	45	e45
Other countries[a]	380	387
Total	3,426	3,419

Magnesium (thousand metric tons)

	1976	1977
United States[e]	115.0	120.0
USSR[e]	63.0	65.0
Norway	38.8	38.2
Japan	11.2	9.4
France	8.0	8.7
Canada	6.1	7.6
Italy	7.0	7.3
China[e]	1.0	1.0
Total	250.1	257.2

Manganese Ore[c] (thousand metric tons)

	1976	1977
USSR	8,636	8,500
South Africa	5,452	5,048
Gabon	2,277	1,851
India	1,760	1,774
Australia	2,154	1,387
China[e]	1,000	1,000
Brazil	1,696	e900
Mexico	453	486
Ghana	312	267
Hungary	165	161
Other countries[a]	824	691
Total	24,729	22,065

Mercury[b] (76-pound flasks)

	1976	1977
USSR[e]	56,000	58,000
Spain	40,134	37,700
United States	23,133	28,244
Algeria	31,000	e26,000
China[e]	26,000	20,000
Mexico	15,026	e15,230
Czechoslovakia[e]	5,800	5,800
Turkey	4,529	e4,300
Italy	22,278	....
Yugoslavia	12,503	....
Other countries[a]	3,591	3,605
Total	239,994	198,879

Molybdenum, mine[b] (metric tons)

	1976	1977
United States	51,362	55,523
Canada	14,619	16,431
Chile	10,899	e11,000
USSR[e]	9,350	9,700
China[e]	1,500	1,500
Other countries[a]	886	893
Total	88,616	95,047

Nickel, mine[b] (thousand metric tons)

	1976	1977
Canada	240.8	235.4
USSR[e]	160.0	168.0
New Caledonia	118.9	109.1
Australia	83.1	85.8
Cuba	36.8	37.0
Dominican Republic	24.4	24.2
South Africa	22.4	23.0
Greece	27.6	e19.0
Rhodesia[e]	16.0	16.0
Philippines	18.8	15.0
Indonesia	19.9	14.0
United States	14.9	13.0
Botswana	12.6	12.1
Other countries[a]	24.8	24.7
Total	821.0	796.3

Petroleum, crude (million barrels)

	1976	1977
USSR	3,822	3,991
Saudi Arabia	3,140	3,358
United States	2,976	2,985
Iran	2,168	2,080
Iraq	884	827
Venezuela	840	817
Nigeria	756	765
Libya	704	759
United Arab Emirates	713	733
Kuwait	786	719
China[e]	646	653
Indonesia	550	615
Canada	489	482
Algeria	384	410
Mexico	327	358
United Kingdom	89	272
Qatar	182	162
Australia	153	157
Argentina	146	157

Petroleum, crude (cont'd) (million barrels)

	1976	1977
Egypt	120	151
Other countries[a]	1,317	1,375
Total	21,192	21,826

Phosphate Rock (thousand metric tons)

	1976	1977
United States	44,662	47,256
USSR	24,200	24,200
Morocco	15,656	17,027
China[e]	3,750	4,100
Tunisia	3,294	3,614
Togo	2,009	2,857
South Africa	1,702	2,403
Senegal	1,799	1,869
Jordan	1,717	1,781
Vietnam[e]	1,500	1,500
Israel	639	1,232
Christmas Island	1,033	1,186
Nauru	755	1,146
Other countries[a]	4,924	5,801
Total	107,640	115,972

Potash (thousand metric tons of K_2O equivalent)

	1976	1977
USSR	8,310	8,500
Canada	4,996	6,089
East Germany	3,161	e3,244
West Germany	2,036	2,341
United States	2,177	2,229
France	1,600	1,580
Other countries[a]	1,979	1,789
Total	24,259	25,772

Pyrite[c] (thousand metric tons)

	1976	1977
USSR[e]	8,100	9,700
Spain	2,349	2,404
China[e]	2,000	2,000
Rumania[e]	870	880
Italy	850	863
South Africa	845	808
Japan	958	798
North Korea[e]	700	700
West Germany	523	531
Finland	674	484
United States	762	442
Yugoslavia	440	e440
Sweden	404	402
Norway	368	369
Portugal	416	362
Other countries[e]	2,036	2,127
Total	22,295	23,310

Salt[c] (million metric tons)

	1976	1977
United States	40.11	39.41
China[e]	30.00	30.00
USSR	14.00	15.50
West Germany	11.82	e12.41
United Kingdom	8.01	e8.00
France	6.42	e6.50
Canada	5.99	5.93
Australia[e]	4.70	4.80
Mexico	4.59	e4.50
Rumania	4.21	e4.50
Italy	4.01	e4.20
Poland	3.82	e3.90
Spain	3.15	e3.20
Netherlands	3.03	3.11
India	3.07	e3.00
East Germany	2.56	e2.60
Other countries[a]	18.68	19.64
Total	168.17	171.20

Silver[b], mine (million troy ounces)

	1976	1977
Mexico	42.64	47.03
USSR[e]	44.00	45.00
Canada	41.20	42.76
United States	34.33	38.17
Peru	35.58	30.10
Australia	25.07	27.42
Poland[e]	16.10	17.70
Japan	9.30	9.65
Chile	7.29	e7.65
Bolivia	5.09	5.89
Sweden	4.62	e4.82
Yugoslavia	4.63	4.69
Spain	3.11	e3.54
Honduras	2.96	3.21
South Africa	2.82	3.13
Other countries[a]	33.41	34.72
Total	312.15	325.48

Sulfur, all forms[i] (thousand metric tons)

	1976	1977
United States	11,877	11,443
USSR[e]	9,920	10,370
Canada	7,339	7,296
Poland	5,210	5,150
Japan	2,647	2,825

Sulfur, all forms[i] (cont'd) (thousand metric tons)

	1976	1977
France	1,996	2,185
Mexico	2,230	1,976
West Germany	1,390	1,627
China[e]	1,200	1,360
Spain	1,347	1,200
Iraq	670	675
Italy	629	634
Iran	399	530
Finland	487	427
Other countries[a]	4,773	5,517
Total	52,114	53,215

Tin, mine[b] (thousand metric tons)

	1976	1977
Malaysia	63.4	58.7
USSR[e]	31.0	33.0
Bolivia	29.8	32.6
Indonesia	23.4	24.0
Thailand	20.5	e23.1
China[e]	20.0	20.0
Australia	10.1	10.0
Brazil	5.9	6.4
Zaire	4.0	3.6
Other countries[a]	19.9	18.9
Total	228.0	230.3

Titanium Materials[c,j] (thousand metric tons)

	1976	1977
Ilmenite		
Australia	995	1,081
Norway	767	828
United States	592	579
USSR[e]	380	400
Malaysia	180	154
Finland	123	125
Other countries[a]	160	215
Total ilmenite	3,197	3,382
Rutile		
Australia	395	324
Other countries[a]	33	35
Total rutile	428	359
Titaniferous slag		
Canada	823	711
Japan	3	1
Total titaniferous slag	826	712

Tungsten, mine[b] (metric tons)

	1976	1977
China[e]	9,000	9,000
USSR[e]	8,000	8,200
Bolivia	3,039	2,981
United States	2,644	2,732
South Korea	2,565	2,528
Australia	2,450	2,333
North Korea[e]	2,150	2,150
Thailand	1,896	2,035
Canada	1,720	1,800
Turkey	928	1,200
Austria	541	1,116
Portugal	1,276	1,010
Brazil	980	e1,000
Other countries[a]	4,472	4,395
Total	41,661	42,480

Uranium Oxide (U_3O_8)[b,j] (metric tons)

	1976	1977
United States	11,521	13,426
Canada	6,636	7,020
South Africa	3,254	3,962
South West Africa	909	3,587
France	2,138	2,473
Niger	1,722	1,887
Gabon	1,085	1,068
Other countries[a]	969	1,193
Total	28,234	34,616

Zinc, smelter (thousand metric tons)

	1976	1977
Japan	742	778
USSR[e]	720	735
Canada	473	495
United States	453	408
West Germany	305	342
Belgium	235	274
Australia	243	249
France	233	238
Poland	240	228
Mexico	171	171
Italy	191	169
Spain	161	159
Finland	111	138
North Korea[e]	138	135
Netherlands	123	109
China[e]	100	100
Yugoslavia	105	99
Bulgaria	90	90
South Africa	66	76
Other countries[a]	565	573
Total	5,465	5,566

a Estimated in part. b Content of ore. c Gross weight. d Includes calculated bauxite equivalent of estimated output of aluminum ores other than bauxite (nepheline concentrates and alunite ores). e Estimate. f Includes anthracitic, bituminous, and lignitic coal (including that coal classified in Europe as "brown coal"). g Marketable gross weight. h Marketed production (includes gas sold or used by producers; excludes gas reinjected to reservoirs and gas flared or vented to atmosphere which has no economic value and which does not represent a part of world energy consumption). i Includes: (1) Frasch-process sulfur, (2) elemental sulfur mined by conventional methods, (3) by-product recovered elemental sulfur, and (4) recovered sulfur content of pyrite and other sulfide ores. j Excludes output (if any) by Albania, Bulgaria, China, Czechoslovakia, East Germany, Hungary, North Korea, Mongolia, Poland, Rumania, the USSR, and Vietnam. Compiled by Charles L. Kimbell, U.S. Bureau of Mines.

EDUCATION: SELECTED COUNTRIES

		Primary (in thousands)		Secondary (in thousands)		Higher (in thousands)		Expenditures	
	Year	Teachers	Students	Teachers	Students	Teachers	Students	% of GNP	% of total publ. exp.
ALGERIA	1975	65	2,663	20	512	...	42	4[3]	11[1]
ARGENTINA	1975	196	3,579	170[1]	1,283[1]	45	597	6.3	18.8[3]
AUSTRALIA	1975	78	1,790	74	1,096	20	275	5.7	14.4
AUSTRIA	1975	...	502	...	756	...	97		8.5
BAHRAIN	1974	...	44	...	18	.08	.7		8.8[2]
BOTSWANA	1976	4	126	.9	16	.05[2]	.5[2]		14.6[2]
BULGARIA	1975	48	980	27	344	12	128	5.5	8.5
BURUNDI	1975	4	129	...	14	.2	1	2.4	22.1
CANADA	1975	...	2,555	...	2,640	...	818	7.9	
CEN. AFR. EMP.	1975	3	221	...	24	...	.3[3]	3[4]	17[4]
CHAD	1974	3	208	...	14	...	.5[2]	2.2[2]	11.9[2]
CHILE	1976	...	2,243	...	466	11[2]	150[2]	3.8[3]	12.5[3]
COLOMBIA	1974	115	3,792	66	1,284	18	149	3.3[4]	21.2[4]
CONGO	1975	5	319	...	...	.2	3		18.2
CUBA	1975	77	1,796	42	554	6[3]	68[3]		
CYPRUS	1975	2	57	2	49	.07	.6	4.3	14.3
CZECHOSLOVAKIA	1975	96	1,881	25	321	21	155	4.7	7
ECUADOR	1975	32	1,266	24	380	...	58[5]	3.2[6]	19.8[6]
EGYPT	1975	118	4,121	79	2,108	19[3]	408[3]	5.8	
EL SALVADOR	1976	...	796	...	59	2[3]	26	3.6[4]	28.4[4]
FINLAND	1974	23	406	...	...	4	72	6.7[2]	16.7[2]
FRANCE	1975	257	4,602	...	...	...	772[3]	4.7[3]	17.3[3]
GAMBIA	1975	.9	25	.3	7	...	...	3.5[3]	
GERMANY, E.	1975	159	2,579	...	461	34[3]	307[3]	5.6[3]	7.6[3]
GERMANY, W.	1975	...	6,425	...	3,815	104	836	4.5[3]	14.4[3]
GHANA	1975	38	1,157	22	549	1	9		19.7[3]
GUINEA-BISSAU	1975	3	68	.2	2	...	...	1.2[5]	10[5]
HONDURAS	1976	...	483	3[2]	52[2]	.8[2]	13[3]	3.3[3]	21.7[3]
HUNGARY	1975	67	1,051	23	372	12	108	4.8	6.1
ICELAND	1974	1	27	2	25	.6[2]	3[2]	4.2[2]	13.3[2]
INDIA	1975	1,559	64,708	...	...	...	2,230[3]	3.1	26.1
INDONESIA	1975	603	18,233	219	3,361	...	278		12.5
IRAN	1975	152	4,468	82	2,183	12[3]	135[3]		12.2[3]
IRAQ	1975	69	1,765	...	...	3[3]	79[3]	6.5	10.8
IRELAND	1975	13	405	19	271	4	40	7.3[3]	8.3[3]
ISRAEL	1975	...	535	...	...	14[3]	75[3]	5	11.7
ITALY	1975	253	4,835	...	4,840	42	977	5.9[3]	29.6[3]
IVORY COAST	1975	15	673	...	119	...	9[1]		
JAMAICA	1975	12	370	6	214	.6[4]	8[4]	7.1[3]	20.2[3]
JAPAN	1975	417	10,365	512	9,125	192	2,249	5.5	22.6
JORDAN	1975	11	386	8	164	.6[3]	9[3]	4.4	
KENYA	1976	89	2,895	12	289	...	11[3]	5.9[3]	20.5[3]
KOREA, S.	1976	110	5,504	88	3,397	14	325	4.1[4]	22.8[4]
KUWAIT	1975	6	112	9	109	.6	8		13.6
LESOTHO	1976	4	221	.8	18	.07[3]	.6[3]	4.4[6]	
LIBYA	1975	24	556	12	166	.8[3]	12[3]		
MALAWI	1975	11	642	1	17	.2	1	2.4[3]	13.4[3]
MALI	1975	9	253	...	...	.3[3]	2[3]	4.7	26.9
MAURITIUS	1975	6	151	2	67	.2	1	3.1[3]	9.9[3]
MEXICO	1975	256	11,461	170	2,939	45	520		13.1[3]
MONGOLIA	1975	...	130	...	185	.8	10		18.1[5]
MOROCCO	1975	37	1,548	...	...	2	45	5.3[4]	20.5[4]
NEPAL	1976	21	644	11	263	2[2]	24[2]		12[2]
NETHERLANDS	1975	53	1,453	...	1,284	...	288	7.9[4]	25.1[4]
NEW ZEALAND	1975	21	393	12	352	4[3]	67[3]	5.6[3]	17[3]
NIGER	1975	4	142	.6	14	.07	.5		19.5[3]
NORWAY	1974	45	387	...	331	...	65	7.1[2]	14.7[2]
OMAN	1975	2	55	.2	1	...	...		1.7
PAKISTAN	1975	131	5,294	109	2,032	5[4]	112[4]	2.3	5.2
PANAMA	1976	13	343	6	128	1[3]	24[3]	5.9[3]	21.7[3]
PAPUA, N.G.	1975	8	238	2	41	...	6[3]	6.8[6]	15.3[6]
PERU	1976	74	2,961	35	890	12	191	3.4	8.5
POLAND	1975	208	4,310	...	1,441	...	575	2.4	
PORTUGAL	1974	35	933	49	668	4[4]	604[4]		
RUMANIA	1975	145	3,020	43[3]	802[3]	14	165		26.6[3]
RWANDA	1975	8	402	.8	12	.1[3]	1[3]	11.5	11.7
SAUDI ARABIA	1975	35	686	16	223	2	26	3.3[3]	18.9[3]
SIERRA LEONE	1975	6	206	3	50	.3	2	2.9	8.6
SINGAPORE	1975	11	328	8	183	1	23	1.7	11
SPAIN	1974	...	3,624[1]	...	2,918	28	453	2.7[3]	10[3]
SRI LANKA	1976	...	1,385	...	1,088	23	15[3]	8[3]	14[3]
SUDAN	1975	32	1,169	13	282	1	21	5[2]	10[2]
SWAZILAND	1976	...	93	1	18	.1	1	7.5[3]	
SWEDEN	1975	34	699	55[3]	532[3]	...	163		19.9[3]
TANZANIA	1975	30	1,592	3	63	.4	3		11.9
THAILAND	1975	...	6,686	...	...	...	78		20.7
TOGO	1975	6	363	2	65	.2	2	5.3[2]	15[2]
TUNISIA	1976	24	968	9[2]	202	3	23		26.4[3]
TURKEY	1974	159	5,355	57[4]	1,517[4]	14	219	5.6[5]	20.6[5]
UGANDA	1975	29	974	3	55	.6	5		17
USSR	1975	2,399	35,961	...	10,738	317	4,854	7.6	12.9
UN. KINGDOM	1973	242	5,386	312	4,230	...	547	6.2	18.1
USA	1975	1,354	26,846	1,109	20,546	670	11,185		17.4[1]
UPPER VOLTA	1975	3	141	.8	16	.2	1		
URUGUAY	1974	14	331	...	194[4]	2[2]	33[2]	5.3[4]	21.8[4]
VENEZUELA	1974	63	1,990	36	631	16[2]	214[2]	.7[3]	6.1[3]
YEMEN	1975	7	255	1	24	...	2		
YEMEN, SOUTH	1974	6	196	...	40	.09	.9	3.5[6]	10.9[6]
YUGOSLAVIA	1974	128	2,867	23	828	...	395[2]	5[2]	

Source: UN Statistical Yearbook 1977.
Note: [1] 1976. [2] 1975. [3] 1974. [4] 1973. [5] 1972. [6] 1971.

HEALTH: SELECTED COUNTRIES

	Year	Hospitals	Total beds	Population per bed	Year	Physicians	Population per physician	Dentists	Nursing personnel
AUSTRIA	1975	...	85,461	88	1975	15,702	479	1,464	27,343
BAHRAIN	1975	10	1,012	257	1975	177	1,469	21	915
BANGLADESH	1975	281	13,610	5,644	1975	5,103	15,054	...	1,214
BARBADOS	1975	13	2,161	111	1975	166	1,446	17	668
BELGIUM	1974	479	87,164	112	1975	18,506	530	2,273	...
BENIN	1975	57	3,984	781	1975	95	32,737	10	1,055
BOTSWANA	1975	21	2,074	332	1974	63	10,476	5	460
BRAZIL	1973	4,431	382,952	266	1972	48,726	2,025	27,553	24,315
BULGARIA	1975	...	75,037	116	1975	18,770	465	3,701	34,683
BURMA	1975	436	25,567	1,180	1975	5,550	5,436	596	4,816
BURUNDI	1972	136	4,221	806	1974	81	45,432	6	590
CANADA	1974	1,368	206,763	109	1975	39,104	584	8,922	172,000
CEN. AFR. EMP.	1972	52	3,161	522	1975	96	20,833	3	293
CHAD	1974	45	3,464	1,140	1975	84	...	3	786
CHILE	1975	304	38,319	362	1975	4,414	...	1,345	22,276
COLOMBIA	1975	825	44,642	530	1973	10,625	2,184	3,150	12,114
CONGO	1975	121	6,912	195	1975	213	6,338	...	2,061
COSTA RICA	1975	43	7,549	261	1975	1,293	1,524	360	3,438
CUBA	1975	365	39,863	234	1974	8,200	1,121	2,800	...
CYPRUS[1]	1975	115	3,286	195	1975	547	...	175	1,022
CZECHOSLOVAKIA	1975	422	149,976	99	1975	35,383	418	6,440	88,488
DOM. REP.	1973	339	12,618	351	1973	2,374	1,866	516	3,332
EGYPT	1975	1,454	79,399	469	1975	8,037	...	2,447	12,460
EL SALVADOR	1975	75	7,127	563	1974	1,083	3,592	391	3,824
FINLAND	1975	379	71,115	66	1975	6,701	703	3,254	38,555
FRANCE	1973	...	534,023	98	1975	77,882	678	25,272	266,642
GERMANY, E.	1974	584	184,214	92	1975	31,300	538	7,720	...
GERMANY, W.	1975	3,481	729,791	85	1974	120,260	516	31,613	222,932
GHANA	1975	252	16,486	599	1975	939	10,511	47	6,882
GREECE	1975	722	58,501	155	1975	18,421	491	5,930	14,750
GUYANA	1975	42	3,969	199	1974	237	3,249	22	...
HAITI	1975	62	3,917	1,169	1975	394	...	41	823
HONDURAS	1975	44	4,602	598	1975	919	2,992	197	2,141
HUNGARY	1974	...	90,104	116	1975	21,127	499	2,461	49,927
INDONESIA	1975	1,115	83,696	1,625	1974	7,027	18,863	1,900	14,784
IRAN	1974	535	49,194	650	1973	11,373	2,752	1,846	14,973
IRAQ	1975	187	22,942	485	1975	4,500	2,471	698	3,535
IRELAND	1975	215	33,772	93	1975	3,772	830	905	15,600
ISRAEL	1975	86	19,501	174	1973	9,143	351	1,789	...
ITALY	1972	2,189	575,162	95	1973	109,166	502	...	2,666
JAMAICA	1974	34	7,780	257	1974	570	3,509	107	3,674
JAPAN	1975	8,294	1,163,726	...	1974	126,822	...	40,630	346,756
JORDAN	1974	27	1,986	937	1975	744	3,629	145	331
KOREA, S.	1974	175	22,089	1,515	1974	15,722	2,206	2,422	19,842
LAOS	1975	38	3,232	401	1976	156	21,667	15	1,028
LESOTHO	1974	107	2,114	482	1975	49	21,224	2	275
LIBYA	1975	53	10,080	242	1975	2,586	944	207	990
LUXEMBOURG	1975	26	3,848	94	1974	368	978	113	...
MADAGASCAR	1975	886	19,781	405	1975	752	10,665	84	2,256
MALAYSIA	1975[2]	310	40,171	668	1975	2,003	18,443	342	9,190
MAURITIUS	1975	34	3,230	266	1975	346	...	40	1,183
MONGOLIA	1974	396	13,648	103	1974	2,604	538	116	5,052
MOROCCO	1975	133	23,140	748	1975	1,238	13,982	128	8,936
NEPAL	1974	55	1,858	6,630	1974	338	36,450	8	335
NETHERLANDS	1973	600	136,216	99	1975	21,825	625	4,350	44,000
NEW ZEALAND	1973	...	31,959	93	1975	4,110	747	1,046	18,779
NICARAGUA	1975	65	4,675	462	1975	1,400	1,543	350	...
NIGER	1974	56	3,734	1,200	1975	83	55,422	4	626
NIGERIA	1975	...	53,889	1,168	1975	4,248	14,814	168	19,607
NORWAY	1975	866	56,636	71	1975	6,886	582	...	29,500
PAKISTAN	1975	1,345	33,948	2,070	1975	17,929	...	703	6,010
PANAMA	1975	61	5,880	284	1975	1,251	1,335	222	...
PARAGUAY	1975	143	3,816	694	1975	2,229	1,189	679	1,174
POLAND	1975	1,265	264,103	129	1975	58,226	584	15,949	129,690
PORTUGAL	1975	548	52,268	181	1975	11,101	851	489	18,178
QATAR	1973	...	661	130	1974	96	938	7	247
RHODESIA	1974	253	19,285	316	1974	904	6,748	147	4,534
RUMANIA	1974	...	191,910	110	1973	25,870	805	5,289	36,419
RWANDA	1975	250	7,201	583	1975	104	40,385	4	251
SENEGAL	1975	43	5,635	735	1975	307	13,485	38	3,064
SINGAPORE	1975	14	8,005	281	1975	1,622	1,387	419	5,767
SOUTH AFRICA	1973	788	156,245	152	1973	12,060	2,016	1,767	53,835
SPAIN	1974	1,261	185,218	190	1975	55,000	647	3,446	...
SRI LANKA	1973	456	39,732	333	1972	3,251	4,007	280	6,458
SUDAN	1975	147	16,020	982	1975	1,400	11,236	159	11,957
SURINAM	1975	16	2,288	184	1974	202	2,030	15	476
SWAZILAND	1975	33	1,717	285	1975	65	7,538	5	2,885
SWEDEN	1974	725	124,350	66	1974	13,260	615	7,180	58,030
SYRIA	1975	93	6,865	1,071	1975	2,400	3,063	765	1,267
THAILAND	1974	314	51,215	796	1975	5,000	8,374	652	21,432
TOGO	1972	26	3,075	680	1974	106	20,472	6	854
TRIN. & TOB.	1975	25	4,815	224	1975	550	1,964	58	1,873
TURKEY	1975	807	85,872	456	1975	21,714	1,804	5,046	24,411
UGANDA	1975	420	18,156	636	1975	426	27,113	38	2,432
USSR	1975	...	3,009,200	85	1975	733,700	347	101,500	1,232,000
UN. KINGDOM	1975[3]	...	499,581	...	1975[3]	75,609	...	15,924	218,137
USA	1975	7,336	1,401,624	152	1973	338,111	622	107,320	1,349,000
UPPER VOLTA	1971	148	4,675	1,174	1976	108	57,130	7	1,193
VENEZUELA	1975	380	35,867	334	1975	13,108	915	3,497	28,853
YEMEN	1972	37	4,200	1,443	1974	245	26,449	11	568
YUGOSLAVIA	1975	490	127,646	167	1974	24,920	849	4,793	46,860
ZAIRE	1973	...	72,090	327	1973	818	28,802	22	9,285

Source: UN Statistical Yearbook 1977.
[1] Data refer to Greek population only.   [2] Partly based on 1973 figures.   [3] Partly based on 1974 figures.

MILITARY STRENGTH: COMPARISONS OF DEFENSE EXPENDITURES 1975–1978

Country	$ Million 1975	1978	$ Per Head 1975	1978	% of Government Spending[1] 1975	1978	% of GNP[2] 1974	1977
WARSAW PACT[3]								
Bulgaria	457	438	52	49	6.0	5.1	2.7	2.5
Czechoslovakia	1,706	1,818	116	121	7.3	7.1	3.8	3.8
Germany, East	2,550	n.a.	148	n.a.	7.9	n.a.	5.4	5.9
Hungary	506	658	48	62	3.5	3.7	2.4	2.6
Poland	2,011	2,545	59	73	7.0	8.6	3.0	3.0
Rumania	707	923	33	43	3.7	3.8	1.7	1.7
Soviet Union[4]	124,000	n.a.	490	n.a.	n.a.	n.a.	11–13	11–13
NATO[5]								
Belgium	1,971	n.a.	200	n.a.	10.0	n.a.	2.8	3.4
Canada	2,965	3,635	130	153	11.9	8.9	2.1	1.8
Denmark	939	1,320	185	259	7.3	6.5	2.2	2.5
France	13,984	17,518	264	325	20.2	20.3	3.6	3.6
Germany	16,142	21,355	259	337	24.4	22.9	3.6	3.4
Incl. aid to W. Berlin	19,540	26,731	313	422	29.2	28.7	4.3	4.2
Greece	1,435	1,523	159	164	25.5	18.3	4.0	5.0
Italy	4,700	5,610	84	98	9.7	7.9	2.9	2.4
Luxembourg	22	37	65	100	3.0	2.9	0.9	1.1
Netherlands	2,978	4,208	218	301	11.0	9.5	3.4	3.6
Norway	929	1,291	232	316	8.2	9.6	3.1	3.1
Portugal	1,088	568	124	62	35.2	10.6	6.6	3.3
Turkey	2,200	2,286	55	54	26.6	22.0	3.7	5.7
United Kingdom	11,118	13,579	198	239	11.6	11.2	5.1	5.0
United States	88,983	113,000	417	517	23.8	23.0	6.1	6.0
OTHER EUROPE								
Austria	410	718	54	91	3.7	3.9	0.9	1.1
Finland	388	454	83	95	5.0	6.1	1.4	1.3
Ireland	128	193	41	59	4.3	3.5	1.4	1.6
Spain	1,701	2,363	48	64	14.5	13.2	1.9	1.7
Sweden	2,483	2,946	303	355	10.5	11.7	3.4	3.4
Switzerland	1,047	1,547	160	240	19.3	18.0	1.8	1.9
Yugoslavia[3]	1,705	2,332	80	106	49.9	52.9	5.1[6]	5.2
MIDDLE EAST								
Algeria	285	456	17	25	4.7	5.7	1.8[6]	3.9
Egypt	6,103	n.a.	163	n.a.	42.0	n.a.	22.8	n.a.
Iran	8,800	9,942	268	273	24.9	23.8	14.0[6]	10.9
Iraq	1,191[7]	n.a.	107	n.a.	43.7	n.a.	18.7	10.2
Israel	3,552	3,310	1,045	887	50.1	30.4	31.8	29.9
Jordan	155	304	57	103	22.0	25.6	12.1	15.5
Libya	203	448	83	162	13.7	19.5	1.4	1.8
Morocco	224	681	13	37	4.5	11.6	3.0	3.6
Saudi Arabia	6,771	13,170	1,153	1,704	20.0	35.1	7.3	13.6
Sudan	120	n.a.	7	n.a.	15.1	n.a.	4.3	5.4
Syria	706	1,121	96	138	25.3	24.1	11.0[6]	16.4
AFRICA								
Ethiopia	84	165	3	6	19.4	21.6	3.3	n.a.
Nigeria	1,786	n.a.	28	n.a.	11.8	n.a.	2.9	7.8
Rhodesia	102	242	16	35	12.3	17.1	2.6	7.7
South Africa	1,332	2,622	53	95	18.5	19.7	3.2	5.1
ASIA								
Australia	2,492	n.a.	184	n.a.	8.6	n.a.	3.6	2.9
China[3]	n.a.	34,380	n.a.	36	n.a.	n.a.	n.a.	8.5
China (Taiwan)	1,007	n.a.	61	n.a.	n.a.	n.a.	7.2	8.3
India	2,660	3,571	4	6	21.1	16.0	2.7	3.1
Indonesia	1,108	1,691	9	12	16.7	14.5	2.6	3.5
Japan	4,620	8,567	42	74	6.6	n.a.	0.9	0.9
Korea, North[3]	n.a.	1,030	n.a.	60	n.a.	n.a.	n.a.	10.5
Korea, South	943	2,600	28	72	29.2	35.4	4.3	6.5
Malaysia	385	699	31	54	17.3	13.4	3.8	4.4
New Zealand	243	n.a.	79	n.a.	4.3	n.a.	1.8	1.8
Pakistan	725	938	10	12	12.3	42.7	8.4	4.6
Philippines	407	793	10	17	19.3	17.2	2.1	3.4
Singapore	344	n.a.	152	n.a.	18.1	n.a.	5.1	6.3
Thailand	542	n.a.	13	n.a.	25.7	n.a.	3.2	4.1
LATIN AMERICA								
Argentina	1,031	1,659	41	63	9.7	14.9	1.9	n.a.
Brazil	1,283	2,039	12	18	9.3	8.6	1.3	1.1
Colombia	106	173	n.a.	6	n.a.	7.6	0.8	1.1
Cuba[3]	n.a.	784	n.a.	80	n.a.	8.6	n.a.	n.a.
Mexico	586	557	10	8	2.4	2.9	0.7[6]	0.6
Peru	383	n.a.	24	n.a.	15.3	n.a.	2.4	3.1
Venezuela	494	615	41	47	5.4	5.9	1.6	1.4

n.a. Not available.
[1] This series is designed to show national trends only; differences in the scope of the government sector invalidate international comparisons.
[2] Based on local currency. GNP estimated where official figures unavailable.
[3] The difficulty of calculating suitable exchange rates makes conversion to dollars imprecise.
[4] Estimated in rubles.
[5] Defense expenditures based on NATO definition, but some 1978 figures estimated from nationally-defined data. Figures from 1977 are provisional.
[6] Gross domestic product at market prices, not GNP.
[7] Nine-month figure only.

Source: "The Military Balance 1978–1979," The International Institute for Strategic Studies.

SOCIETIES AND ORGANIZATIONS

This article lists some of the most noteworthy associations, societies, foundations, and trusts of the United States and Canada. The information has been verified by the organization concerned.

Academy of Motion Picture Arts & Sciences. Membership: 4,100. Executive director, James M. Roberts. Headquarters: 8949 Wilshire Blvd., Beverly Hills, Calif. 90211.

Alcoholics Anonymous (The General Service Board of A. A., Inc.). Membership: over 1,000,000 in more than 30,000 affiliated groups. Chairman, John L. Norris, M. D. Headquarters: 468 Park Ave. S., New York, N. Y. Mailing Address: Box 459, Grand Central Station, New York, N. Y. 10017.

American Academy and Institute of Arts and Letters. Membership: 250. Executive director, Margaret M. Mills. Headquarters: 633 West 155th St., New York, N. Y. 10032.

American Academy of Political and Social Science. Membership: 14,500, including 6,000 libraries. Annual meeting: Philadelphia, April 1979. President, Marvin E. Wolfgang. Headquarters: 3937 Chestnut St., Philadelphia, Pa. 19104.

American Anthropological Association. Membership: 10,-268. President, Francis L. K. Hsu; executive director, Edward J. Lehman. Headquarters: 1703 New Hampshire Ave. NW, Washington, D. C. 20009.

American Association for the Advancement of Science. Membership: 129,000 and 291 affiliated groups. Meeting: Houston, Jan. 3–8, 1979. President, Edward E. David, Jr.; executive officer, William D. Carey. Headquarters: 1515 Massachusetts Ave. NW, Washington, D. C. 20005.

American Association of Museums. Membership: 6,000. Annual meeting: Cleveland, June 1979. Director, Lawrence L. Reger. Headquarters: 1055 Thomas Jefferson St., Suite 428, Washington, D. C. 20007.

American Association of University Professors. Membership: 77,680. President, Martha Friedman. Headquarters: One Dupont Circle NW, Washington, D. C. 20036.

American Association of University Women. Membership: 190,000. President, Dr. Marjorie Bell Chambers; general director, Dr. Helen B. Wolfe. Headquarters: 2401 Virginia Ave. NW, Washington, D. C. 20037.

American Astronomical Society. Membership: 3,500. Meetings, 1979: Mexico City, Jan. 7–10; Wellesley, Mass., June 10–13. President, I. R. King; executive officer, H. M. Gurin. Address: 211 FitzRandolph Rd., Princeton, N. J. 08540.

American Automobile Association. Membership: 19,000,-000 in 210 affiliated clubs. President, James B. Creal. Headquarters: 8111 Gatehouse Rd., Falls Church, Va. 22042.

American Bankers Association. Membership: 13,844. President, A. A. Milligan. Headquarters: 1120 Connecticut Ave. NW, Washington, D. C. 20036.

American Bar Association. Membership: 225,964. President, S. Shepherd Tate; executive director, Bert H. Early. Headquarters: 1155 East 60th St., Chicago, Ill. 60637.

American Bible Society. 1977 Scripture distribution: 213,-563,569 copies. Annual meeting: New York City, May 10, 1979. President, Edmund F. Wagner. Headquarters: 1865 Broadway, New York, N. Y. 10023.

American Booksellers Association, Inc. Membership: 5,500. National convention: Los Angeles, May 26–30, 1979. President, Charles S. Haslam; executive director, G. Roysce Smith. Headquarters: 122 East 42nd St., New York, N. Y. 10017.

American Cancer Society, Inc. Membership: 194 voting members; 58 charter divisions. Executive vice president, Lane Adams. Headquarters: 777 Third Ave., New York, N. Y. 10017.

American Chemical Society. Membership: 112,000. National meetings, 1979: Honolulu, April 1–6; Washington, D. C., Sept. 9–14. President, Gardner W. Stacy; executive director, Raymond P. Mariella. Headquarters: 1155 16th St. NW, Washington, D. C. 20036.

American Civil Liberties Union. Membership: 200,000. Board chairman, Norman Dorsen. Headquarters: 22 East 40th St., New York, N. Y. 10016.

American Council of Learned Societies. Membership: 42 professional societies concerned with the humanities and the humanistic aspects of the social sciences. President, R. M. Lumiansky; vice president, Gordon B. Turner. Headquarters: 345 East 46th St., New York, N. Y. 10017.

American Council on Education. Membership: 1,294 colleges and universities, 110 associated organizations, 57 affiliates, 61 constituent organizations, and 5 international affiliates. Annual meeting: Washington, D. C., Oct. 10–12, 1979. President, Jack W. Peltason. Headquarters: One Dupont Circle NW, Washington, D. C. 20036.

American Dental Association. Membership: 131,000. President, Frank P. Bowyer, D. D. S.; president-elect, Joseph P. Cappuccio, D. D. S.; executive director, C. Gordon Watson, D. D. S. Headquarters: 211 E. Chicago Ave., Chicago, Ill. 60611.

American Economic Association. Membership: 17,900 and 6,600 subscribers. Annual meeting: Atlanta, Dec. 28–30, 1979. President, Tjalling C. Koopmans. Headquarters: 1313 21st Ave. S., Nashville, Tenn. 37212.

American Farm Bureau Federation. Membership: 2,895,-257 families. Annual meeting: January. President, Allan Grant. Headquarters: 225 Touhy Ave., Park Ridge, Ill. 60068.

American Geographical Society. Fellows and subscribers: 2,000. President, Richard H. Nolte; director, Sarah K. Myers. Headquarters: Broadway at 156th St., New York, N. Y. 10032.

American Geophysical Union. Membership: 12,000 individuals and 32 organizations. Meetings, 1979: Washington, D. C., May 28–June 1 and San Francisco, Dec. 3–7. President, Allan V. Cox; executive director, A. F. Spilhaus, Jr. Headquarters: 1909 K St. NW, Washington, D. C. 20006.

American Heart Association. Membership: 140,000 in 55 affiliates, 125 chapters and about 1,000 local subdivisions. President, W. Gerald Austen, M. D. Headquarters: 7320 Greenville Ave., Dallas, Tex. 75231.

American Historical Association. Membership: 15,000. President, William J. Bouwsma; executive director, Mack Thompson. Headquarters: 400 A St. SE, Washington, D. C. 20003.

American Horticultural Society. Membership: 35,000 individuals, 400 organizations, institutions and commercial establishments. National congress: Portland, Oreg., September, 1979. President, Dr. Gilbert S. Daniels. Headquarters: Mt. Vernon, Va. 22121.

American Hospital Association. Membership: 29,133 persons; 6,276 institutions. Annual meeting: Washington, D. C., February 4–7, 1979; convention: Chicago, Aug. 27–30, 1979. Chairman of the board of trustees, W. Daniel Barker; president, John Alexander McMahon. Headquarters: 840 North Lake Shore Dr., Chicago, Ill. 60611.

American Hotel & Motel Association. Membership: 7,000. Annual convention, Houston, Dec. 4–6, 1979. Executive vice president, Robert L. Richards. Headquarters: 888 Seventh Ave., New York, N. Y. 10019.

American Institute of Aeronautics and Astronautics. Membership: 22,500 plus 4,000 student members. Executive secretary, James J. Hartford. Headquarters: 1290 Avenue of the Americas, New York, N. Y. 10019.

American Institute of Architects. Membership: 26,000. President, Ehrman B. Mitchell, Jr., FAIA. Headquarters: 1735 New York Ave. NW, Washington, D. C. 20006.

American Institute of Biological Sciences. Membership: 9,000 with 41 adherent societies and 12 affiliate organizations. Annual meeting: Stillwater, Okla., Aug. 12–17, 1979. President, Paul Pearson; executive director, Richard Trumbull. Headquarters: 1401 Wilson Boulevard, Arlington, Va. 22209.

American Institute of Certified Public Accountants. Membership: 135,000. Annual meeting: New Orleans, Oct. 14–16, 1979. Chairman of the board, Joseph P. Cummings; president, Wallace E. Olson. Headquarters: 1211 Avenue of the Americas, New York, N. Y. 10036.

American Institute of Chemical Engineers. Membership: 40,517. President, J. Y. Oldshue; executive director, J. C. Forman. Headquarters: 345 E. 47th St., New York, N. Y. 10017.

American Institute of Graphic Arts. Membership: 2,000. President, Richard Danne; executive director, Caroline Hightower. Headquarters: 1059 Third Ave., New York, N. Y. 10021.

American Institute of Mining, Metallurgical and Petroleum Engineers, Inc. Membership: 64,810. Annual meeting: New Orleans, Feb. 18–22, 1979. President, Wayne L. Dowdey. Headquarters: 345 East 47th St., New York, N. Y. 10017.

American Legion, The. Membership: 2,700,000. Headquarters: 700 N. Pennsylvania St., Indianapolis, Ind. 46206.

American Library Association. Membership: 33,767. Semiannual conventions, 1979: Chicago, Jan. 21–27; Dallas, June 24–30. Executive director, Robert Wedgeworth. Headquarters: 50 E. Huron St., Chicago, Ill. 60611.

American Lung Association. Membership: 175 affiliated groups. Annual meeting: Las Vegas, May 1979. President, Ethelene J. Crockett. Headquarters: 1740 Broadway, New York, N. Y. 10019.

American Management Associations. Membership: 65,000. Chairman of the board, Lee S. Bickmore; president and chief executive officer, James L. Hayes. Headquarters: 135 West 50th St., New York, N. Y. 10020.

American Mathematical Society. Membership: 16,403. President, Peter D. Lax; secretary, Everett Pitcher. Headquarters: P. O. Box 6248, Providence, R. I. 02940.

American Medical Association. Membership: 202,000. President, Tom E. Nesbitt, M. D.; executive vice president, James H. Sammons, M. D. Headquarters: 535 N. Dearborn St., Chicago, Ill. 60610.

American Meteorological Society. Membership: 9,000 including 120 corporate members. President, Dr. George C. Cressman; executive director, Dr. Kenneth C. Spengler. Headquarters: 45 Beacon St., Boston, Mass. 02108.

American Newspaper Publishers Association. Membership: 1,286. Annual convention: New York City, April 23–25, 1979. Chairman and president, Allen H. Neuharth. Headquarters: 11600 Sunrise Valley Drive, Reston, Va. 22091. Mail Address: P. O. Box 17407, Dulles International Airport, Washington, D. C. 20041.

American Nurses' Association. Membership: 200,000 in 53 state and territorial associations. National convention: Houston, June 8–13, 1980. President, Barbara Nichols; executive director, Myrtle K. Aydelotte, Ph. D. Headquarters: 2420 Pershing Road, Kansas City, Mo. 64108.

American Physical Society. Membership: 29,988 American and foreign. Annual meeting: New York City, Jan. 29–Feb. 1, 1979. President, Norman F. Ramsay; executive secretary, W. W. Havens, Jr. Headquarters: 335 East 45th St., New York, N. Y. 10017.

American Psychiatric Association. Membership: 24,406; 72 district branches. Annual meeting: Chicago, May 14–18, 1979. President, Jules Masserman, M. D. Headquarters: 1700 18th St. NW, Washington, D. C. 20009.

American Psychological Association. Membership: 46,000. Annual meeting: New York City, Sept. 1–5, 1979. President, M. Brewster Smith. Headquarters: 1200 17th St. NW, Washington, D. C. 20036.

American Red Cross. Divisions: 67; Chapters: 3,128. National convention: Kansas City, Mo., May 13–16, 1979. Chairman, Frank Stanton; president, George M. Elsey. Headquarters: 17th and D Sts. NW, Washington, D. C. 20006.

American Society of Civil Engineers. Membership: 76,000. President, Walter E. Blessey. Headquarters: 345 East 47th St., New York, N. Y. 10017.

American Society of Composers, Authors, and Publishers. Membership: 16,500 composers and authors; 6,500 publishers. President, Stanley Adams; secretary, Morton Gould. Headquarters: One Lincoln Plaza, New York, N. Y. 10023.

American Society of Mechanical Engineers. Membership: 84,000. President, Orval L. Lewis. Headquarters: 345 East 47th St., New York, N. Y. 10017.

American Society of Newspaper Editors. Membership: 800. National convention: Washington, D. C., April 1979. President, John Hughes. Headquarters: Box 551, 1350 Sullivan Trail, Easton, Pa. 18042.

American Sociological Association. Membership: 14,000. Annual meeting: Boston, Aug. 27–30, 1979. President, Amos H. Hawley. Headquarters: 1722 N St. NW, Washington, D. C. 20036.

American Statistical Association. Membership: 13,000. President, H. O. Hartley; secretary, Fred C. Leone. Headquarters: 806 15th St. NW, Washington, D. C. 20005.

American Youth Hostels, Inc. Membership: 70,000; 28 councils in the United States. President, Dick Leary. Headquarters: National Campus, Delaplane, Va. 22025.

Archaeological Institute of America. Membership: 6,500; subscribers, 24,000. President, Robert H. Dyson, Jr. Headquarters: 53 Park Place, New York, N. Y. 10017.

Arthritis Foundation. Membership: 73 chapters. Annual meeting: Denver, May 31–June 1, 1979. Chairman, H. M. Poole, Jr.; president, Clifford M. Clarke. Headquarters: 3400 Peachtree Rd. NE, Atlanta, Ga. 30326.

Association of American Publishers. Membership: approx. 340. Annual meeting: May 1979. Chairman of the board, Winthrop Knowlton; president, Townsend W. Hoopes; vice president, Thomas D. McKee. Addresses: One Park Ave., New York, N. Y. 10016 and 1707 L St. NW, Washington, D. C. 20036.

Association of Junior Leagues, Inc. Membership: 235 member Leagues in U. S., Canada, and Mexico. Annual conference: Atlanta, May 6–10, 1979. President, Mrs. Alice H. Weber. Headquarters: 825 Third Ave., New York, N. Y. 10022.

Association of Operating Room Nurses, Inc. Membership: 25,500 with 250 local chapters. Convention: March 4–9, 1979. President, Jean Davis. Headquarters: 10170 E. Mississippi Ave., Denver, Colo. 80231.

Benevolent and Protective Order of Elks. Membership: 1,634,488 in 2,230 Lodges. Grand exalted ruler, Homer Huhn, Jr.; grand secretary, S. F. Kocur. Headquarters: 2750 Lake View Ave., Chicago, Ill. 60614.

Big Brothers/Big Sisters of America. Membership: 370+ local affiliated agencies. Annual convention: San Francisco, June 26–30, 1979. Executive vice president, L. P. Reade. Headquarters: 220 Suburban Station Bldg., Philadelphia, Pa. 19103.

B'nai B'rith. Membership: 500,000 in about 3,000 men's, women's, and youth units. President, David M. Blumberg; executive vice president, Dr. Daniel Thursz. Headquarters: 1640 Rhode Island Ave. NW, Washington, D. C. 20036.

Boys' Clubs of America. Membership: 1,071,000 in 1,100 clubs. National conference: St. Louis, May 27–31, 1979. President, John L. Burns; national director, William R. Bricker. Headquarters: 771 First Ave., New York, N. Y. 10017.

Boy Scouts of America. Membership: total youth members and leaders—4,718,138 in 417 Scouting councils. Biennial meeting: New Orleans, May 21–23, 1980. President, Downing B. Jenks; chief scout executive, Harvey L. Price. National Office: North Brunswick, N. J. 08902.

Camp Fire Girls, Inc. Membership: 750,000 in over 35,000 communities. President, Dr. Faith LaVelle; national executive director, Dr. Hester Turner. Headquarters: 4601 Madison Ave., Kansas City, Mo. 64112.

Canadian Library Association. Membership: 3,688 personal, 1,032 institutional, 4,720 total. Annual conference, 1979: Ottawa. Executive director, Paul Kitchen. Headquarters: 151 Sparks St., Ottawa, Ont. K1P 5E3.

Canadian Medical Association. Membership: 30,000. Annual meeting: Toronto, June 18–21, 1979. President, K. O. Wylie, M. D. Headquarters: 1867 Alta Vista Dr., Ottawa, Ont. K1G 0G8.

Chamber of Commerce of the United States of America. Membership about 4,000 trade associations and local and state chambers, more than 72,000 business members. President, Richard L. Lesher; chairman of the board, Shearon Harris. Headquarters: 1615 H St. NW, Washington, D. C. 20062.

Common Cause. Membership: 250,000. Chairwoman: Nan Waterman. Headquarters: 2030 M St. NW, Washington, D. C. 20036.

Consumers Union of United States, Inc. Executive director: Rhoda H. Karpatkin. Headquarters: 256 Washington St., Mount Vernon, N. Y. 10550.

Council of Better Business Bureaus. Membership: 1,000. Headquarters: 1150 17th St. NW, Washington, D. C. 20036.

Council on Foreign Relations, Inc. Membership: 1,800. Annual meeting: New York City, fall, 1979. President, Winston Lord. Headquarters: 58 East 68th St., New York, N. Y. 10021.

Daughters of the American Revolution (National Society). Membership: 207,202 in 3,093 chapters. Continental congress: Washington, D. C., April 16–20, 1979. President general, Mrs. George Upham Baylies. Headquarters: 1776 D St. NW, Washington, D. C. 20006.

Esperanto League for North America. Membership: 1,000. Congress: July 1979. President, William R. Harmon. Headquarters: P. O. Box 1129, El Cerrito, Calif. 94530.

Foreign Policy Association. Chairman, Carter L. Burgess. Headquarters: 345 E. 46th St., New York, N. Y. 10017.

Freemasonry, Ancient Accepted Scottish Rite of (Northern Masonic Jurisdiction): Supreme Council, 33°. Membership: 511,687 in 113 valleys. Sovereign grand commander, Stanley F. Maxwell. Headquarters: 33 Marrett Rd., Lexington, Mass. 02173.

Freemasonry, Ancient and Accepted Scottish Rite of (Southern Jurisdiction): Supreme Council, 33°. Membership: 650,000 in 217 affiliated groups. Sovereign grand commander, Henry C. Clausen. Headquarters: 1733 16th St. NW, Washington, D. C. 20009.

Future Farmers of America. Membership: 507,356 in 50 state associations. Executive secretary, Coleman Harris. Headquarters: Box 15160, Alexandria, Va. 22309.

Gamblers Anonymous. Membership: 6,500. National executive secretary, James J. Zeysing. Headquarters: 2705¼ W. Eighth St., Los Angeles, Calif. 90005.

Garden Club of America, The. Membership over 13,500 in 182 member clubs. Annual meeting: Milwaukee, June 4–6, 1979. President, Mrs. Benjamin M. Belcher. Headquarters: 598 Madison Ave., New York, N. Y. 10022.

General Federation of Women's Clubs. Membership: 10,000,000 in 14,000 U. S. organizations and 36 abroad. National convention: New Orleans, June 4–8, 1979. President, Mrs. Oscar C. Sowards. Headquarters: 1734 N St. NW, Washington, D. C. 20036.

Geological Society of America. Membership: 13,000. Annual meeting: San Diego, Nov. 5–8, 1979. President, Leon T. Silver; executive director, John C. Frye. Headquarters: 3300 Penrose Place, Boulder, Colo. 80301.

Girl Scouts of the U. S. A. Membership: 3,140,000. National president, Dr. Gloria D. Scott; national executive director, Frances R. Hesselbein. Headquarters: 830 Third Ave., New York, N. Y. 10022.

Humane Society of the United States. Annual convention: Orlando, Fla., November 7–10, 1979. President, John A. Hoyt. Headquarters: 2100 L St. NW, Washington, D. C. 20037.

Institute of Electrical and Electronics Engineers, Inc. Membership: 180,000. President, Ivan A. Getting. Headquarters: 345 East 47th St., New York, N. Y. 10017.

Jewish War Veterans of the U. S. A. Membership: 100,000 in 750 units. National commander, Herman Moses; national executive director, Col. Irwin R. Ziff. Headquarters: 1712 New Hampshire Ave. NW, Washington, D. C. 20009.

Kiwanis International. Membership: 292,000 in 7,300 clubs in U. S. and abroad. President, Hilmar L. Solberg. Headquarters: 101 East Erie St., Chicago, Ill. 60611.

Knights of Columbus. Membership: 1,280,000. Supreme knight, Virgil C. Dechant. Headquarters: Columbus Plaza, New Haven, Conn. 06507.

Knights of Pythias, Supreme Lodge. Membership: 151,065 in 1,406 subordinate lodges. Supreme chancellor, Victor C. Jorgensen. Office: 47 N. Grant St., Stockton, Calif. 95202.

League of Women Voters of the U. S. Membership: 137,-000. President, Ruth J. Hinerfeld. Headquarters: 1730 M St. NW, Washington, D. C. 20036.

Lions International. Membership: 1,250,000 in 32,000 clubs in 150 countries and areas. Annual convention: Montreal, June 1979. President, Ralph A. Lynam. Headquarters: 300 22nd St., Oak Brook, Ill. 60570.

Mental Health Association. Membership: 1,000 state and local organizations. Executive director, Brian O'Connell. National Headquarters: 1800 North Kent St., Arlington, Va. 22209.

Modern Language Association of America. Membership: 30,000. President, Walter J. Ong, S. J.; executive director, William D. Schaefer. Headquarters: 62 Fifth Ave., New York, N. Y. 10011.

National Academy of Sciences. Membership: approx. 1,200. Annual meeting: Washington, D. C., April 1979. President, Philip Handler. Headquarters: 2101 Constitution Ave. NW, Washington, D. C. 20418.

National Association for the Advancement of Colored People. Membership: 450,000 in 1,700 units. National convention: Louisville, June 24–29, 1979. President, W. Montague Cobb, M. D.; board chairman, Margaret Bush Wilson; executive director, Benjamin L. Hooks. Headquarters: 1790 Broadway, New York, N. Y. 10019.

National Association of Manufacturers. Membership: 13,-000. President, Heath Larry. Headquarters: 1776 F St. NW, Washington, D. C. 20006.

National Audubon Society. Membership: 400,000. President, Elvis J. Stahr; senior vice president, Paul M. Howard, Jr. Headquarters: 950 Third Ave., New York, N. Y. 10022.

National Conference of Christians and Jews, Inc. Membership: 70 regional offices. President, David Hyatt. Headquarters: 43 West 57th St., New York, N. Y. 10019.

National Council of the Churches of Christ in the U. S. A. Membership: 31 Protestant, Anglican, and Orthodox denominations. President, Dr. William P. Thompson; general secretary, Dr. Claire Randall. Headquarters: 475 Riverside Dr., New York, N. Y. 10027.

National Council on the Aging. Membership: 3,200. Executive director, Jack Ossofsky. Headquarters: 1828 L St. NW, Washington, D. C. 20036.

National Easter Seal Society for Crippled Children and Adults. Membership: 50 state and territorial societies. President, Charles C. Campbell. Headquarters: 2023 W. Ogden Ave., Chicago, Ill. 60612.

National Education Association of the U. S. Membership: 1,800,000 with units in every state, and 12,000 local affiliates. Annual meeting: Detroit, Mich., July 1979. President, John Ryor. Headquarters: 1201 16th St. NW, Washington, D. C. 20036.

National Federation of Business and Professional Women's Clubs, Inc. Membership: 170,000 in 3,800 clubs. President, Geraldine Eidson. Headquarters: 2012 Massachusetts Ave. NW, Washington, D. C. 20036.

National Federation of Independent Business, Inc. Membership: 542,000. President, Wilson S. Johnson. Headquarters: 150 West 20th Ave., San Mateo, Calif. 94403.

National Federation of Music Clubs. Membership: 500,000 in 4,300 clubs and 12 national affiliates. Biennial convention: Portland, Oreg., April 1979. President, Mrs. Frank A. Vought. Headquarters: 310 S. Michigan Ave., Chicago, Ill. 60604.

National Foundation—March of Dimes, The. Membership: 1,375 chapters. President, Charles L. Massey. Headquarters: 1275 Mamaroneck Ave., White Plains, N. Y. 10605.

National Organization for Women (NOW). Membership: 99,000 members, 700 local groups. President, Eleanor Smeal. Headquarters: 425 13th St., Suite 1001, Washington, D. C. 20004.

National PTA (National Parent-Teacher Association). Membership: 6,328,348 in 29,480 local units. National convention: Milwaukee, June 10–13, 1979. President, Mrs. Grace Baisinger. Headquarters: 700 North Rush St., Chicago, Ill. 60611.

National Safety Council. Membership: 15,000. National Safety Congress and Exposition: Chicago, Oct. 15–18, 1979. President, Vincent L. Tofany. Headquarters: 444 N. Michigan Ave., Chicago, Ill. 60611.

National Urban League, Inc. President, Vernon E. Jordan, Jr. Headquarters: 500 East 62nd St., New York, N. Y. 10021.

National Woman's Christian Temperance Union. Membership: about 250,000 in 6,000 local unions. National convention: Oakland, Calif., Aug. 21–27, 1979. President, Mrs. Herman Stanley. Headquarters: 1730 Chicago Ave., Evanston, Ill. 60201.

Parents Without Partners. Membership: 170,000. International convention, Atlanta, July 11–15, 1979. Executive director, Virginia L. Martin. International office: 7910 Woodmont Ave., No. 1000, Washington, D. C. 20014.

Phi Beta Kappa. Membership: 275,000. Secretary, Kenneth Greene. Headquarters: 1811 Q St. NW, Washington, D. C. 20009.

Photographic Society of America. Membership: 18,700. Executive secretary, Philip Katcher. Headquarters: 2005 Walnut St., Philadelphia, Pa. 19103.

Planned Parenthood Federation of America, Inc. (Planned Parenthood—World Population). Chairperson of the Federation, Henrietta H. Marshall. Headquarters: 810 Seventh Ave., New York, N. Y. 10019.

Rotary International. Membership: 823,000 in 17,700 clubs functioning in 153 countries. International convention: Rome, June 10–14, 1979. General secretary, Harry A. Stewart. Headquarters: 1600 Ridge Ave., Evanston, Ill. 60201.

Salvation Army. Membership: 380,618. National commander: Paul S. Kaiser. Headquarters: 120 W. 14th St., New York, N. Y. 10011.

Special Libraries Association. Membership: 11,000. Annual conference: Honolulu, June 1979. President, Vivian D. Hewitt; executive director, F. E. McKenna. Headquarters: 235 Park Ave. S., New York, N. Y. 10003.

United Dairy Industry Association (including American Dairy Association, Dairy Research Inc., National Dairy Council). Annual convention: Houston, March 25–28, 1979. Executive vice president, John W. Sliter. Headquarters: 6300 N. River Rd., Rosemont, Ill. 60018.

United States Jaycees, The. Membership: 375,617 in 8,803 affiliated groups. Annual meeting: Nashville, June 1979. President, Barry Kennedy. Headquarters: P. O. Box 7, Tulsa, Okla. 74102.

United Way of America. Chairman of the board of governors, Clifton C. Garvin, Jr. Headquarters: 801 N. Fairfax St., Alexandria, Va. 22314.

Veterans of Foreign Wars of the United States. Membership: V. F. W. and Auxiliary: 2,445,000. Commander-in-chief: Eric Sandstrom. Headquarters: V. F. W. Building, Broadway at 34th St., Kansas City, Mo. 64111.

World Council of Churches (U. S. Conference). Membership: 28 churches or denominations in U. S. Moderator, Robert J. Marshall. Headquarters: 475 Riverside Dr., New York, N. Y. 10027.

Young Men's Christian Associations (National Council). Membership: 9,000,000 in 1,836 organizations. National board chairman, Elija M. Hicks, Jr. Headquarters: 291 Broadway, New York, N. Y. 10007.

Young Women's Christian Association of the U. S. A. Members and participants: approx. 2,400,000. President, Elizabeth Steel Genné; executive director, Sara-Alyce P. Wright. Headquarters: 600 Lexington Ave., New York, N. Y. 10022.

Zionist Organization of America. Membership: 120,000 in 600 districts. President, Dr. Joseph P. Sternstein; national executive director, Leon Ilutovich. Headquarters: ZOA House, 4 East 34th St., New York, N. Y. 10016.

MAJOR UNIVERSITIES AND COLLEGES, U.S. AND CANADA

Note: Symbols and abbreviations that follow the name of each school listed are as follows: Level of Instruction—(1) senior college granting bachelor's and/or first professional degree; (2) senior college granting master's and/or second professional degree; (3) college or university offering a doctoral program. Student Body—All colleges and universities are co-educational unless indicated: (M) men only; (W) women only; (S) separate colleges for men and women. Control—(Pub.) district, municipal, state, or federal; (Pvt.) proprietary, corporation, or church. Enrollment statistics for U.S. universities and colleges are for the 1977–78 academic year; Canadian statistics are for the 1976–77 academic year.

Name and Location	Level	Control	Enrollment
Abilene Christian University, Abilene, Tex...	2	Pvt.	4,928
Acadia University, Wolfville, Nova Scotia....	2	Pvt.	3,323
Adams State College, Alamosa, Colo.........	2	Pub.	2,400
Adelphi University, Garden City, N.Y........	3	Pvt.	11,243
Adrian College, Adrian, Mich..............	1	Pvt.	912
Akron, The University of, Akron, Ohio......	3	Pub.	23,121
Alabama, University of, in Birmingham, Ala..	3	Pub.	12,540
Alabama, University of, in Huntsville, Ala...	3	Pub.	4,011
Alabama, University of, in University, Ala....	3	Pub.	16,821
Alabama Agricultural and Mechanical University, Normal, Ala..............	2	Pub.	4,613
Alabama State University, Montgomery, Ala.	2	Pub.	4,754
Alaska, University of, Northern Region, Fairbanks, Alaska....................	3	Pub.	10,752
Alaska, University of, South Central Region, Anchorage, Alaska..................	2	Pub.	4,961
Albany State College, Albany, Ga..........	1	Pub.	2,167
Alberta, The University of, Edmonton......	3	Pub.	23,698
Albion College, Albion, Mich..............	1	Pvt.	1,705
Albright College, Reading, Pa.............	1	Pvt.	1,541
Albuquerque, University of, Albuquerque, N. Mex.................................	1	Pvt.	2,394
Alcorn State University, Lorman, Miss......	2	Pub.	2,776
Alderson-Broaddus College, Philippi, W. Va..	1	Pvt.	971
Alfred University, Alfred, N.Y.............	3	Pvt.	1,470
Allegheny College, Meadville, Pa..........	2	Pvt.	1,912
Alma College, Alma, Mich.................	1	Pvt.	1,170
Alverno College, Milwaukee, Wis..........	1	Pvt.	1,101
American International College, Springfield, Mass.................................	2	Pvt.	2,076
American University, Washington, D.C......	3	Pvt.	12,373
Amherst College, Amherst, Mass..........	2	Pvt.	1,502
Ana G. Méndez Educational Foundation, Rio Piedras, P.R...........................	1	Pvt.	747
Anderson College, Anderson, Ind..........	1	Pvt.	2,030
Andrews University, Berrien Springs, Mich...	3	Pvt.	2,837
Angelo State University, San Angelo, Tex....	2	Pub.	5,245
Antioch University, Yellow Springs, Ohio....	2	Pvt.	4,670
Appalachian State University, Boone, N.C....	2	Pub.	9,687
Aquinas College, Grand Rapids, Mich.......	2	Pvt.	1,684
Arizona, University of, Tucson, Ariz........	3	Pub.	28,658
Arizona State University, Tempe, Ariz......	3	Pub.	35,278
Arkansas College, Batesville, Ark..........	1	Pvt.	471
Arkansas, University of, Fayetteville, Ark....	3	Pub.	14,752
Arkansas, University of, Little Rock.........	2	Pub.	9,238
Arkansas, University of, Pine Bluff, Ark......	1	Pub.	3,171
Arkansas Technical University, Russellville..	2	Pub.	2,669
Arkansas State University, State University..	2	Pub.	7,303
Armstrong State College, Savannah, Ga......	2	Pub.	3,159
Art Center College of Design, Pasadena, Calif.................................	2	Pvt.	1,396
Art Institute of Chicago, Schools of the, Chicago, Ill............................	2	Pvt.	1,688
Asbury College, Wilmore, Ky..............	1	Pvt.	1,272
Ashland College, Ashland, Ohio............	3	Pvt.	2,208
Assumption College, Worcester, Mass.......	2	Pvt.	1,836
Athens State College, Athens, Ala..........	1	Pvt.	1,321
Atlanta University, Atlanta, Ga............	3	Pvt.	1,117
Atlantic Christian College, Wilson, N.C......	1	Pvt.	1,647
Auburn University, Auburn, Ala...........	3	Pub.	17,977
Auburn University at Montgomery, Ala......	2	Pub.	4,164
Augsburg College, Minneapolis, Minn.......	1	Pvt.	1,751
Augusta College, Augusta, Ga.............	2	Pub.	3,887
Augustana College, Rock Island, Ill.........	2	Pvt.	2,342
Augustana College, Sioux Falls, S. Dak......	2	Pvt.	2,228
Aurora College, Aurora, Ill................	1	Pvt.	910

Name and Location	Level	Control	Enrollment
Austin College, Sherman, Tex.............	2	Pvt.	1,192
Austin Peay State University, Clarksville, Tenn.................................	2	Pub.	4,519
Averett College, Danville, Va..............	1	Pvt.	1,058
Avila College, Kansas City, Mo............	1	Pvt.	1,961
Azusa Pacific College, Azusa, Calif.........	2	Pvt.	2,113
Babson College, Babson Park, Mass........	2	Pvt.	2,791
Baker University, Baldwin City, Kans.......	1	Pvt.	950
Baldwin-Wallace College, Berea, Ohio......	2	Pvt.	3,053
Ball State University, Muncie, Ind..........	3	Pub.	18,241
Baltimore, University of, Baltimore, Md.....	2	Pub.	5,474
Bank Street College of Education, N.Y.C.....	2	Pvt.	621
Baptist College at Charleston, S.C..........	1	Pvt.	2,310
Bard College, Annandale-on-Hudson, N.Y...	1	Pvt.	697
Barry College, Miami, Fla.................	2	Pvt.	1,845
Bates College, Lewiston, Me..............	1	Pvt.	1,366
Bayamón Central University, Bayamón, P.R..	1	Pvt.	2,614
Baylor University, Waco, Tex..............	3	Pvt.	9,453
Beaver College, Glenside, Pa..............	2	Pvt.	1,566
Bellarmine College, Louisville, Ky..........	1	Pvt.	1,782
Belmont College, Nashville, Tenn..........	1	Pvt.	1,267
Beloit College, Beloit, Wis................	2	Pvt.	1,044
Bemidji State University, Bemidji, Minn.....	2	Pub.	5,226
Benedict College, Columbia, S.C...........	1	Pvt.	2,031
Benedictine College, Atchison, Kans........	1	Pvt.	905
Bentley College, Waltham, Mass...........	2	Pvt.	5,942
Berea College, Berea, Ky.................	1	Pvt.	1,458
Berklee College of Music, Boston, Mass.....	1	Pvt.	2,534
Berry College, Mount Berry, Ga............	2	Pvt.	1,628
Bethany College, Bethany, W. Va..........	1	Pvt.	993
Bethany Nazarene College, Bethany, Okla...	2	Pvt.	1,297
Bethel College, St. Paul, Minn............	1	Pvt.	1,853
Bethune-Cookman College, Daytona Beach..	1	Pvt.	1,678
Biola College, La Mirada, Calif............	3	Pvt.	3,098
Birmingham-Southern College, Birmingham, Ala.................................	1	Pvt.	1,202
Biscayne College, Miami, Fla..............	2	Pvt.	2,329
Bishop College, Dallas, Tex...............	1	Pvt.	1,782
Black Hills State College, Spearfish, S. Dak..	2	Pub.	2,566
Bloomfield College, Bloomfield, N.J........	1	Pvt.	2,341
Bloomsburg State College, Bloomsburg, Pa...	2	Pub.	6,400
Bluefield State College, Bluefield, W. Va.....	1	Pub.	2,417
Boise State University, Boise, Idaho........	2	Pub.	10,288
Boston College, Chestnut Hill, Mass........	3	Pvt.	13,946
Boston State College, Boston, Mass........	2	Pub.	11,417
Boston University, Boston, Mass...........	3	Pvt.	24,414
Bowdoin College, Brunswick, Me...........	2	Pvt.	1,347
Bowie State College, Bowie, Md...........	2	Pub.	2,875
Bowling Green State University, Bowling Green, Ohio..........................	3	Pub.	17,724
Bradley University, Peoria, Ill..............	2	Pvt.	5,050
Brandeis University, Waltham, Mass........	3	Pvt.	3,624
Brandon University Brandon Manitoba.....	1	Pvt.	2,418
Brescia College, Owensboro, Ky...........	1	Pvt.	893
Briar Cliff College, Sioux City Iowa........	1	Pvt.	1,040
Bridgeport, University of, Bridgeport, Conn..	2	Pvt.	7,263
Bridgewater College, Bridgewater, Va.......	1	Pvt.	823
Bridgewater State College, Bridgewater, Mass.................................	2	Pub.	8,050
Brigham Young University, Provo, Utah.....	3	Pvt.	28,580
Hawaii Campus, Laie, Oahu............	1	Pvt.	1,686
British Columbia, University of, Vancouver ..	3	Pub.	24,914
Brock University, St. Catharines, Ont.......	2	Pub.	5,009
Brown University, Providence, R.I..........	3	Pvt.	6,711
Bryant College, Smithfield, R.I............	2	Pvt.	4,945

Name and Location	Level	Control	Enrollment
Bryn Mawr College, Bryn Mawr, Pa.........	3	Pvt.	1,589
Bucknell University, Lewisburg, Pa.........	2	Pvt.	3,240
Buena Vista College, Storm Lake, Iowa......	1	Pvt.	1,068
Butler University, Indianapolis, Ind........	2	Pvt.	4,025
Caldwell College, Caldwell, N.J. (W)........	1	Pvt.	792
Calgary, University of, Calgary, Alberta.....	3	Pub.	13,478
California, University of:			
Berkeley.............................	3	Pub.	34,528
Davis...............................	3	Pub.	19,568
Irvine...............................	3	Pub.	9,515
Los Angeles..........................	3	Pub.	48,577
Riverside............................	3	Pub.	6,380
San Diego............................	3	Pub.	14,272
San Francisco........................	3	Pub.	3,684
Santa Barbara........................	3	Pub.	18,075
Santa Cruz...........................	3	Pub.	10,864
California College of Arts & Crafts, Oakland..	2	Pvt.	1,115
California Institute of Technology, Pasadena.	3	Pvt.	1,667
California Institute of the Arts, Valencia.....	2	Pvt.	651
California Lutheran College, Thousand Oaks	2	Pvt.	2,489
California Polytechnic State University, San Luis Obispo, Calif.....................	2	Pub.	15,899
California State College, Bakersfield, Calif...	2	Pub.	3,868
California State College, San Bernardino....	2	Pub.	5,391
California State College, Stanislaus, Calif....	2	Pub.	3,703
California State College, California, Pa......	2	Pub.	4,653
California State Polytechnic University, Pomona, Calif.........................	2	Pub.	14,322
California State University, Chico, Calif......	2	Pub.	13,751
California State University, Dominguez Hills...............................	2	Pub.	7,865
California State University, Fresno, Calif.....	2	Pub.	15,490
California State University, Fullerton, Calif...	2	Pub.	22,969
California State University, Hayward, Calif...	2	Pub.	12,584
California State University, Long Beach.....	2	Pub.	36,895
California State University, Los Angeles.....	2	Pub.	26,411
California State University, Northridge, Calif.	2	Pub.	30,241
California State University, Sacramento.....	2	Pub.	21,876
Calumet College, East Chicago, Ind........	1	Pvt.	1,736
Calvin College, Grand Rapids, Mich........	2	Pvt.	4,075
Cameron University, Lawton, Okla..........	1	Pub.	5,076
Campbell College, Buies Creek, N.C........	1	Pvt.	2,217
Campbellsville College, Campbellsville, Ky...	1	Pvt.	691
Canisius College, Buffalo, N.Y..............	2	Pvt.	3,924
Capital University, Columbus, Ohio.........	2	Pvt.	2,688
Cardinal Stritch College, Milwaukee, Wis....	2	Pvt.	1,173
Carleton College, Northfield, Minn..........	1	Pvt.	1,696
Carleton University Ottawa, Ont...........	3	Pub.	16,131
Carlow College, Pittsburgh, Pa.............	1	Pvt.	871
Carnegie-Mellon University, Pittsburgh, Pa..	3	Pvt.	5,315
Carroll College, Helena, Mont.............	1	Pvt.	1,362
Carroll College, Waukesha, Wis............	1	Pvt.	1,288
Carson-Newman College, Jefferson City, Tenn................................	1	Pvt.	1,562
Carthage College, Kenosha, Wis............	2	Pvt.	1,615
Case Western Reserve University, Cleveland	3	Pvt.	8,108
Castleton State College, Castleton, Vt.......	2	Pub.	2,088
Catawba College, Salisbury, N.C............	1	Pvt.	914
Catholic University of America, Washington .	3	Pvt.	7,237
Catholic University of Puerto Rico, Ponce..	2	Pvt.	11,762
Cedar Crest College, Allentown, Pa. (W)....	1	Pvt.	893
Centenary College of Louisiana, Shreveport..	1	Pvt.	912
Central Arkansas, University of, Conway, Ark.................................	2	Pub.	5,190
Central Connecticut State College, New Britain, Conn.........................	2	Pub.	12,251
Central Methodist College, Fayette, Mo.....	1	Pvt.	592
Central Michigan University, Mt. Pleasant, Mich................................	3	Pub.	17,973
Central Missouri State University, Warrensburg, Mo.....................	2	Pub.	9,789
Central State University, Wilberforce, Ohio..	1	Pub.	2,230
Central State University, Edmond, Okla.....	2	Pub.	12,846
Central University of Iowa, Pella, Iowa......	1	Pvt.	1,393
Central Washington University, Ellensburg, Wash................................	2	Pub.	7,900

Name and Location	Level	Control	Enrollment
Chadron State College, Chadron, Nebr.......	2	Pub.	2,069
Chaminade College of Honolulu, Hawaii.....	2	Pvt.	2,581
Chapman College, Orange, Calif............	2	Pvt.	5,686
Charleston, College of, Charleston, S.C......	2	Pub.	5,193
Chestnut Hill College, Philadelphia, Pa. (W) .	1	Pvt.	893
Cheyney State College, Cheyney, Pa........	2	Pub.	2,914
Chicago, University of, Chicago, Ill..........	3	Pvt.	9,425
Chicago State University, Chicago, Ill........	2	Pub.	7,025
Christian Brothers College, Memphis, Tenn..	1	Pvt.	1,002
Christopher Newport College, Newport News, Va..................................	1	Pub.	3,619
Cincinnati, University of, Cincinnati, Ohio. . .	3	Pub.	33,687
Citadel, The, Charleston, S.C..............	2	Pub.	3,358
Claflin College, Orangeburg, S.C............	1	Pvt.	911
Claremont Men's College, Claremont, Calif. (M)................................	1	Pvt.	867
Clarion State College, Clarion, Pa...........	2	Pub.	4,791
Clark College, Atlanta, Ga.................	1	Pvt.	1,792
Clark University, Worcester, Mass..........	3	Pvt.	3,060
Clarkson College of Technology, Potsdam, N.Y.................................	3	Pvt.	3,445
Clemson University, Clemson, S.C..........	3	Pub.	11,115
Cleveland Institute of Art, Cleveland, Ohio...	1	Pvt.	759
Cleveland State University, Cleveland, Ohio.	3	Pub.	17,915
Coe College, Cedar Rapids, Iowa...........	1	Pvt.	1,139
Colby College, Waterville, Me..............	2	Pvt.	1,658
Colgate University, Hamilton, N.Y..........	2	Pvt.	2,455
Colorado, University of, Boulder, Colo......	3	Pub.	21,767
Colorado Springs.....................	2	Pub.	4,127
Denver..............................	2	Pub.	8,832
Colorado College, Colorado Springs, Colo....	2	Pvt.	1,927
Colorado School of Mines, Golden, Colo.....	3	Pub.	2,584
Colorado State University, Fort Collins, Colo.	3	Pub.	17,812
Colorado Women's College, Denver (W).....	1	Pvt.	416
Columbia College, Columbia, Mo...........	1	Pvt.	2,829
Columbia College, Columbia, S.C...........	1	Pvt.	910
Columbia Union College, Takoma Park, Md..	1	Pvt.	814
Columbia University, New York, N.Y.	3	Pvt.	16,561
Barnard College, New York (W)..........	1	Pvt.	2,122
Teachers College, New York............	3	Pvt.	4,973
Columbus College, Columbus, Ga..........	1	Pub.	4,936
Concord College, Athens, W. Va............	1	Pub.	1,730
Concordia College, Moorhead, Minn........	1	Pvt.	2,647
Concordia Teachers College, River Forest, Ill.	2	Pvt.	1,118
Concordia Teachers College, Seward, Nebr...	2	Pvt.	1,129
Concordia University, Montreal............	3	Pvt.	24,147
Connecticut, University of, Storrs, Conn.....	3	Pub.	21,686
Connecticut College, New London, Conn.....	2	Pvt.	1,983
Converse College, Spartanburg, S.C.........	2	Pvt.	934
Cooper Union, New York, N.Y..............	2	Pvt.	930
Coppin State College, Baltimore, Md........	2	Pub.	3,104
Cornell College, Mount Vernon, Iowa.......	1	Pvt.	851
Cornell University, Ithaca, N.Y.............	3	Pvt.	17,081
Creighton University, Omaha, Nebr.........	3	Pvt.	4,979
Cumberland College, Williamsburg, Ky......	1	Pvt.	1,947
Curry College, Milton, Mass...............	1	Pvt.	978
Daemen College, Buffalo, N.Y..............	1	Pvt.	1,395
Dakota State College, Madison, S. Dak......	1	Pub.	902
Dalhousie University, Halifax, Nova Scotia ..	3	Pvt.	8,238
Dallas, University of, Irving, Tex............	3	Pvt.	1,909
Dallas Baptist College, Dallas, Tex..........	1	Pvt.	1,068
Dartmouth College, Hanover, N.H..........	3	Pvt.	4,195
David Lipscomb College, Nashville, Tenn....	1	Pvt.	2,172
Davidson College, Davidson, N.C...........	1	Pvt.	1,331
Davis and Elkins College, Elkins, W. Va.....	1	Pvt.	970
Dayton, University of, Dayton, Ohio........	3	Pvt.	9,620
Defiance College, Defiance, Ohio...........	1	Pvt.	829
Delaware, University of, Newark, Del........	3	Pub.	19,018
Delaware State College, Dover, Del.........	1	Pub.	2,130
Delaware Valley College of Science & Agriculture, Doylestown, Pa.............	1	Pvt.	1,597
Delta State College, Cleveland, Miss........	2	Pub.	2,819
Denison University, Granville, Ohio.........	1	Pvt.	2,116
Denver, University of, Denver, Colo.........	3	Pvt.	7,753
DePaul University, Chicago, Ill.............	3	Pvt.	11,366
DePauw University, Greencastle, Ind.......	2	Pvt.	2,416

Name and Location	Level	Control	Enrollment
Detroit, University of, Detroit, Mich.........	3	Pvt.	8,094
Detroit Institute of Technology, Detroit......	1	Pvt.	1,412
Dickinson College, Carlisle, Pa.............	1	Pvt.	1,743
Dickinson State College, Dickinson, N. Dak..	1	Pub.	1,044
Dillard University, New Orleans, La.........	1	Pvt.	1,158
District of Columbia, University of, Washington, D.C......................	2	Pub.	1,124
Dominican College of San Rafael, San Rafael, Calif.......................	2	Pvt.	688
Dordt College, Sioux Center, Iowa..........	1	Pvt.	1,112
Dowling College, Oakdale, N.Y.............	2	Pvt.	2,377
Drake University, Des Moines, Iowa........	3	Pvt.	6,732
Drew University, Madison, N.J.............	3	Pvt.	2,155
Drexel University, Philadelphia, Pa.........	3	Pvt.	9,825
Drury College, Springfield, Mo.............	2	Pvt.	2,254
Dubuque, University of, Dubuque, Iowa.....	1	Pvt.	1,090
Duke University, Durham, N.C. (incl. Trinity College & Women's College) (S)........	3	Pvt.	9,402
Duquesne University, Pittsburgh, Pa........	3	Pvt.	7,124
D'Youville College, Buffalo, N.Y...........	1	Pvt.	1,517
Earlham College, Richmond, Ind...........	2	Pvt.	1,146
East Carolina University, Greenville, N.C....	2	Pub.	13,899
East Central Oklahoma State University, Ada, Okla.........................	2	Pub.	3,793
East Stroudsburg State College, East Stroudsburg, Pa.....................	2	Pub.	4,054
East Tennessee State University, Johnson City, Tenn........................	3	Pub.	10,037
East Texas Baptist College, Marshall, Tex....	1	Pvt.	844
East Texas State University, Commerce, Tex.	3	Pub.	9,594
Eastern Connecticut State College, Willimantic, Conn....................	2	Pub.	2,945
Eastern Illinois University, Charleston, Ill....	2	Pub.	10,102
Eastern Kentucky University, Richmond, Ky.	2	Pub.	13,679
Eastern Mennonite College, Harrisonburg, Va.............................	1	Pvt.	1,139
Eastern Michigan University, Ypsilanti......	2	Pub.	19,104
Eastern Montana College, Billings, Mont....	2	Pub.	3,453
Eastern Nazarene College, Wollaston, Mass.	2	Pvt.	810
Eastern New Mexico University, Portales....	2	Pub.	4,041
Eastern Oregon State College, La Grande....	2	Pub.	1,476
Eastern Washington University, Cheney, Wash.............................	2	Pub.	6,837
Eckerd College, St. Petersburg, Fla.........	1	Pvt.	881
Edgecliff College, Edgecliff, Ohio...........	1	Pvt.	921
Edinboro State College, Edinboro, Pa......	2	Pub.	6,382
Elizabeth City State University, Elizabeth City, N.C........................	1	Pub.	1,620
Elizabethtown College, Elizabethtown, Pa....	1	Pvt.	1,950
Elmhurst College, Elmhurst, Ill.............	1	Pvt.	2,769
Elmira College, Elmira, N.Y...............	2	Pvt.	2,882
Elon College, Elon College, N.C...........	1	Pvt.	2,225
Embry-Riddle Aeronautical University, Daytona Beach, Fla...................	1	Pvt.	4,261
Emerson College, Boston, Mass.............	2	Pvt.	1,570
Emmanuel College, Boston, Mass...........	2	Pvt.	1,110
Emory and Henry College, Emory, Va.......	1	Pvt.	856
Emory University, Atlanta, Ga..............	3	Pvt.	7,572
Emporia State University, Emporia, Kans....	2	Pub.	6,386
Evangel College, Springfield, Mo...........	1	Pvt.	1,291
Evansville, University of, Evansville, Ind.....	2	Pvt.	4,906
Fairfield University, Fairfield, Conn.........	2	Pvt.	4,791
Fairleigh Dickinson University, Rutherford, Teaneck, Madison, N.J...............	3	Pvt.	19,569
Fairmont State College, Fairmont, W. Va.....	1	Pub.	4,724
Fayetteville State University, Fayetteville, N.C..............................	1	Pub.	2,930
Ferris State College, Big Rapids, Mich.......	1	Pub.	9,965
Findlay College, Findlay, Ohio.............	1	Pvt.	988
Fisk University, Nashville, Tenn............	2	Pvt.	1,124
Fitchburg State College, Fitchburg, Mass....	2	Pub.	5,827
Florida, University of, Gainesville, Fla.......	3	Pub.	29,894
Florida Agricultural & Mechanical University, Tallahassee, Fla.............	2	Pub.	5,982
Florida Atlantic University, Boca Raton, Fla..	3	Pub.	6,968
Florida Institute of Technology, Melbourne..	3	Pvt.	3,758
Florida Memorial College, Opa Locka, Fla....	1	Pvt.	641
Florida Southern College, Lakeland, Fla.....	1	Pvt.	2,236
Florida State University, Tallahassee, Fla....	3	Pub.	20,676
Florida Technological University, Orlando..	2	Pub.	10,893
Fordham University, New York, N.Y........	3	Pvt.	15,413
Fort Hays State University, Hays, Kans......	2	Pub.	5,678
Fort Lewis College, Durango, Colo.........	1	Pub.	2,760
Fort Valley State College, Fort Valley, Ga....	2	Pub.	1,963
Framingham State College, Framingham, Mass.............................	2	Pub.	5,320
Francis Marion College, Florence, S.C.......	1	Pub.	2,659
Franklin & Marshall College, Lancaster, Pa..	1	Pvt.	2,793
Franklin Pierce College, Rindge, N.H.......	1	Pvt.	1,096
Friends University, Wichita, Kans..........	1	Pvt.	907
Frostburg State College, Frostburg, Md......	2	Pub.	3,503
Furman University, Greenville, S.C.........	2	Pvt.	2,749
Gallaudet College, Washington, D.C........	3	Pvt.	1,129
Gannon College, Erie, Pa..................	2	Pvt.	3,580
Gardner-Webb College, Boiling Springs, N.C.	1	Pvt.	1,312
General Motors Institute, Flint, Mich.......	1	Pvt.	2,354
Geneva College, Beaver Falls, Pa...........	1	Pvt.	1,395
George Mason University, Fairfax, Va.......	2	Pub.	9,610
George Peabody College for Teachers, Nashville, Tenn......................	3	Pvt.	1,934
George Washington University, Washington .	3	Pvt.	23,188
George Williams College, Downers Grove, Ill.	2	Pvt.	1,405
Georgetown College, Georgetown, Ky.......	2	Pvt.	989
Georgetown University, Washington, D.C....	3	Pvt.	11,623
Georgia, University of, Athens, Ga..........	3	Pub.	22,974
Georgia College, Milledgeville, Ga..........	2	Pub.	3,599
Georgia Institute of Technology, Atlanta, Ga.	3	Pub.	10,068
Southern Technical Institute, Marietta...	1	Pub.	2,188
Georgia Southern College, Statesboro, Ga...	2	Pub.	6,439
Georgia Southwestern College, Americus....	1	Pub.	2,324
Georgia State University, Atlanta, Ga........	3	Pub.	20,686
Gettysburg College, Gettysburg, Pa.........	1	Pvt.	1,938
Glassboro State College, Glassboro, N.J.....	2	Pub.	10,887
Glenville State College, Glenville, W. Va.....	1	Pub.	1,527
Goddard College, Plainfield, Vt.............	2	Pvt.	1,722
Golden Gate University, San Francisco, Calif.	2	Pvt.	9,093
Gonzaga University, Spokane, Wash........	2	Pvt.	2,966
Gordon College, Wenham, Mass............	1	Pvt.	985
Goshen College, Goshen, Ind..............	1	Pvt.	1,210
Goucher College, Baltimore, Md............	2	Pvt.	944
Graceland College, Lamoni, Iowa...........	1	Pvt.	1,343
Grambling State University, Grambling, La..	1	Pub.	3,895
Grand Canyon College, Phoenix, Ariz........	1	Pvt.	1,198
Grand Valley State College, Allendale, Mich.	2	Pub.	7,469
Great Falls, College of, Great Falls, Mont....	1	Pvt.	1,247
Greenville College, Greenville, Ill..........	1	Pvt.	895
Grinnell College, Grinnell, Iowa............	1	Pvt.	1,205
Grove City College, Grove City, Pa.........	1	Pvt.	2,244
Guam, University of, Agana, Guam.........	2	Pub.	4,343
Guelph, University of, Guelph, Ont..........	3	Pub.	10,539
Guilford College, Greensboro, N.C..........	1	Pvt.	1,684
Gustavus Adolphus College, St. Peter, Minn.	1	Pvt.	2,198
Gwynedd-Mercy College, Gwynedd Valley, Pa...............................	1	Pvt.	1,189
Hamilton College, Clinton, N.Y. (M)........	1	Pvt.	980
Hamline University, St. Paul, Minn.........	1	Pvt.	1,852
Hampden-Sydney College, Hampden-Sydney, Va. (M)..............	1	Pvt.	723
Hampton Institute, Hampton, Va...........	2	Pvt.	2,734
Hanover College, Hanover, Ind.............	1	Pvt.	894
Hardin-Simmons University, Abilene, Tex...	2	Pvt.	1,649
Harding College, Searcy, Ark..............	2	Pvt.	2,841
Harris Teachers College, St. Louis, Mo......	1	Pub.	1,905
Hartford, University of, West Hartford, Conn.............................	3	Pvt.	9,420
Hartwick College, Oneonta, N.Y............	1	Pvt.	1,515
Harvard University, Cambridge, Mass.......	3	Pvt.	21,095
Hastings College, Hastings, Nebr..........	1	Pvt.	736
Hawaii, University of, at Hilo.............	1	Pub.	3,232
at Manoa........................	3	Pub.	20,937

Name and Location	Level	Control	Enrollment
Heidelberg College, Tiffin, Ohio............	1	Pvt.	933
Henderson State College, Arkadelphia, Ark..	2	Pub.	2,979
Hendrix College, Conway, Ark..............	1	Pvt.	959
High Point College, High Point, N.C........	1	Pvt.	1,004
Hillsdale College, Hillsdale, Mich...........	1	Pvt.	1,048
Hiram College, Hiram, Ohio..............	1	Pvt.	1,193
Hobart & William Smith Colleges, Geneva, N.Y. (S)...........................	1	Pvt.	1,821
Hofstra University, Hempstead, L.I., N.Y....	3	Pvt.	10,089
Hollins College, Hollins College, Va.......	2	Pvt.	1,012
Holy Cross, College of the, Worcester, Mass.	2	Pvt.	2,691
Holy Family College, Philadelphia, Pa.......	1	Pvt.	1,204
Holy Names College, Oakland, Calif.........	2	Pvt.	612
Hope College, Holland, Mich..............	1	Pvt.	2,330
Houghton College, Houghton, N.Y.........	1	Pvt.	1,253
Houston, University of, Houston, Tex.......	3	Pub.	29,297
Houston Baptist University, Houston, Tex...	1	Pvt.	1,764
Howard Payne College, Brownwood, Tex....	1	Pvt.	1,406
Howard University, Washington, D.C.......	3	Pvt.	9,891
Humboldt State University, Arcata, Calif.....	2	Pub.	7,944
Idaho, College of, Caldwell, Idaho.........	2	Pvt.	891
Idaho, University of, Moscow, Idaho.......	3	Pub.	7,678
Idaho State University, Pocatello, Idaho.....	2	Pub.	8,152
Illinois, University of, Urbana & Chicago, Ill..	3	Pub.	56,615
Illinois at the Medical Center, University of, Chicago, Ill.......................	3	Pub.	4,141
Illinois Benedictine College, Lisle, Ill.......	2	Pvt.	1,870
Illinois College, Jacksonville Ill...........	1	Pvt.	740
Illinois Institute of Technology, Chicago, Ill...	3	Pvt.	6,853
Illinois State University, Normal, Ill........	3	Pub.	20,111
Illinois Wesleyan University, Bloomington...	2	Pvt.	1,703
Immaculata College, Immaculata, Pa. (W)...	1	Pvt.	1,171
Incarnate Word College, San Antonio, Tex...	2	Pvt.	1,479
Indiana Central University, Indianapolis, Ind.	2	Pvt.	3,249
Indiana State University, Terre Haute, Ind...	3	Pub.	11,916
Indiana University, Bloomington, Ind.......	3	Pub.	31,884
Indiana University Regional Campuses Fort Wayne......................	2	Pub.	6,270
Kokomo......................	1	Pub.	2,481
Northwest at Gary................	2	Pub.	4,736
Purdue at Indianapolis.............	2	Pub.	21,700
South Bend.....................	2	Pub.	6,167
Southeast at New Albany...........	2	Pub.	4,008
Indiana University of Pennsylvania, Indiana, Pa..............................	3	Pub.	11,727
Insurance, College of, New York, N.Y.......	2	Pvt.	1,679
Inter American University of Puerto Rico, San Germán, P.R....................	2	Pvt.	6,597
Iona College, New Rochelle, N.Y...........	2	Pvt.	5,127
Iowa, University of, Iowa City, Iowa........	3	Pub.	23,644
Iowa State University, Ames, Iowa.........	3	Pub.	23,138
Iowa Wesleyan College, Mount Pleasant...	1	Pvt.	798
Ithaca College, Ithaca, N.Y...............	2	Pvt.	4,712
Jackson State University, Jackson, Miss.....	2	Pub.	7,844
Jacksonville State University, Jacksonville, Ala..............................	2	Pub.	7,011
Jacksonville University, Jacksonville, Fla....	2	Pvt.	2,162
James Madison University, Harrisonburg, Va..............................	2	Pub.	8,402
Jersey City State College, Jersey City, N.J...	2	Pub.	9,720
John Carroll University, Cleveland, Ohio....	2	Pvt.	3,637
Johns Hopkins University, Baltimore, Md....	3	Pvt.	9,856
Johnson C. Smith University, Charlotte, N.C.	1	Pvt.	1,545
Johnson State College, Johnson, Vt.........	1	Pub.	1,152
Juilliard School, The, New York, N.Y.......	3	Pvt.	1,218
Juniata College, Huntingdon, Pa...........	1	Pvt.	1,123
Kalamazoo College, Kalamazoo, Mich.......	1	Pvt.	1,534
Kansas, University of, Lawrence, Kans......	3	Pub.	23,862
Kansas State University, Manhattan, Kans...	3	Pub.	19,045
Kean College of New Jersey, Union, N.J.....	2	Pub.	13,117
Kearney State College, Kearney, Nebr.......	2	Pub.	6,047
Keene State College, Keene, N.H...........	2	Pub.	3,314
Kent State University, Kent, Ohio..........	3	Pub.	19,731
Kentucky, University of, Lexington, Ky......	3	Pub.	22,362
Kentucky State University, Frankfort, Ky....	2	Pub.	2,252
Kentucky Wesleyan College, Owensboro, Ky.	1	Pvt.	765
Kenyon College, Gambier, Ohio............	1	Pvt.	1,467
King's College, Wilkes-Barre, Pa...........	1	Pvt.	2,210
Knox College, Galesburg, Ill..............	1	Pvt.	1,003
Knoxville College, Knoxville, Tenn.........	1	Pvt.	735
Kutztown State College, Kutztown, Pa.......	2	Pub.	5,187
Lafayette College, Easton, Pa..............	1	Pvt.	2,291
Lake Erie College, Painesville, Ohio........	2	Pvt.	987
Lake Forest College, Lake Forest, Ill........	2	Pvt.	1,104
Lake Superior State College, Sault Ste. Marie, Mich.........................	1	Pub.	2,261
Lakehead University, Thunder Bay, Ont.....	2	Pvt.	3,752
Lamar University, Beaumont, Tex..........	3	Pub.	12,826
Lambuth College, Jackson, Tenn..........	1	Pvt.	773
Lander College, Greenwood, S.C...........	1	Pvt.	1,698
Langston University, Langston, Okla.......	1	Pub.	1,045
La Salle College, Philadelphia, Pa..........	2	Pvt.	6,227
Laurentian University of Sudbury, Sudbury, Ont.............................	2	Pub.	5,038
Laval University, Quebec, Que.............	3	Pvt.	20,698
La Verne, University of, La Verne, Calif......	3	Pvt.	3,464
Lawrence Institute of Technology, Southfield, Mich.............................	1	Pvt.	4,714
Lawrence University, Appleton, Wis.........	1	Pvt.	1,082
Lebanon Valley College, Annville, Pa........	1	Pvt.	1,290
Lee College, Cleveland, Tenn.............	1	Pvt.	1,287
Lehigh University, Bethlehem, Pa..........	3	Pvt.	6,187
Le Moyne College, Syracuse, N.Y...........	1	Pvt.	1,874
Lenoir Rhyne College, Hickory, N.C........	1	Pvt.	1,268
Lesley College, Cambridge, Mass..........	2	Pvt.	2,129
Lethbridge, The University of, Lethbridge, Alberta...........................	1	Pub.	1,984
Lewis & Clark College, Portland, Oreg......	2	Pvt.	3,150
Lewis-Clark State College, Lewiston, Idaho..	1	Pub.	1,446
Lewis University, Lockport, Ill.............	2	Pvt.	4,074
Lincoln University, Jefferson City, Mo.......	2	Pub.	2,386
Lincoln University, Lincoln University, Pa....	1	Pvt.	1,176
Linfield College, McMinnville, Oreg........	2	Pvt.	1,019
Livingston University, Livingston, Ala......	2	Pub.	1,384
Livingstone College, Salisbury, N.C........	1	Pvt.	983
Lock Haven State College, Lock Haven, Pa...	1	Pub.	2,375
Loma Linda University, Loma Linda, Calif....	3	Pvt.	5,014
Long Island University, Greenvale, N.Y. (incl. Brooklyn Center; Brooklyn College of Pharmacy; C.W. Post & Southampton campuses, Long Island, N.Y.)..........	3	Pvt.	22,325
Longwood College, Farmville, Va...........	2	Pub.	2,305
Loras College, Dubuque, Iowa............	2	Pvt.	1,638
Loretto Heights College, Denver, Colo......	1	Pvt.	912
Louisiana College, Pineville, La............	1	Pvt.	1,352
Louisiana State University at Shreveport, Shreveport, La......................	3	Pub.	3,111
Louisiana State University & Agricultural Mechanical College System, Baton Rouge and New Orleans, La..................	3	Pub.	25,493
Louisiana Tech University, Ruston, La.......	3	Pub.	8,971
Louisville, University of, Louisville, Ky......	3	Pub.	17,398
Lowell, University of, Lowell, Mass.........	3	Pub.	14,042
Loyola College, Baltimore, Md.............	2	Pvt.	4,570
Loyola Marymount University, Los Angeles..	2	Pvt.	6,027
Loyola University, Chicago, Ill.............	3	Pvt.	13,068
Loyola University, New Orleans, La.........	2	Pvt.	4,332
Lubbock Christian College, Lubbock, Tex....	1	Pvt.	1,094
Luther College, Decorah, Iowa............	1	Pvt.	1,952
Lycoming College, Williamsport, Pa........	1	Pvt.	1,298
Lynchburg College, Lynchburg, Va.........	2	Pvt.	2,283
Lyndon State College, Lyndonville, Vt.......	1	Pub.	1,158
Macalester College, St. Paul, Minn........	2	Pvt.	1,744
Madonna College, Livonia, Mich...........	1	Pvt.	2,521
McGill University, Montreal, Que..........	3	Pvt.	19,222
McMaster University, Hamilton, Ont........	3	Pvt.	13,976
MacMurray College, Jacksonville, Ill........	1	Pvt.	743
McMurry College, Abilene, Tex............	1	Pvt.	1,225
McNeese State University, Lake Charles, La.	2	Pub.	5,490

Name and Location	Level	Control	Enrollment
Maine, University of, at Farmington	1	Pub.	1,936
Maine, University of, at Orono	3	Pub.	10,970
Maine, University of, at Presque Isle	1	Pub.	1,365
Manchester College, North Manchester, Ind.	2	Pvt.	1,097
Manhattan College, Bronx, N.Y.	2	Pvt.	4,507
Manhattan School of Music, New York, N.Y.	3	Pvt.	822
Manhattanville College, Purchase, N.Y.	2	Pvt.	1,415
Manitoba, University of, Winnipeg, Man.	3	Pub.	20,710
Mankato State University, Mankato, Minn.	2	Pub.	11,268
Mansfield State College, Mansfield, Pa.	2	Pub.	2,940
Marian College, Indianapolis, Ind.	1	Pvt.	787
Marietta College, Marietta, Ohio	2	Pvt.	1,666
Marion College, Marion, Ind.	1	Pvt.	896
Marist College, Poughkeepsie, N.Y.	2	Pvt.	2,045
Marquette University, Milwaukee, Wis.	3	Pvt.	10,855
Mars Hill College, Mars Hill, N.C.	1	Pvt.	1,756
Marshall University, Huntington, W. Va.	2	Pub.	11,221
Mary Hardin-Baylor College, Belton, Tex.	1	Pvt.	1,103
Marycrest College, Davenport, Iowa	2	Pvt.	986
Marygrove College, Detroit, Mich.	2	Pvt.	811
Maryland, University of, at Baltimore	3	Pub.	4,674
Baltimore County, Catonsville	3	Pub.	5,346
at College Park	3	Pub.	37,866
Eastern Shore, Princess Anne	1	Pub.	1,016
University College, College Park	1	Pub.	12,410
Maryland Institute, College of Art, Baltimore	2	Pvt.	925
Marymount College, Tarrytown, N.Y.	1	Pvt.	682
Marymount Manhattan College, N.Y.C.	1	Pvt.	2,068
Mary Washington College, Fredericksburg, Va.	1	Pub.	2,369
Marywood College, Scranton, Pa.	2	Pvt.	2,923
Massachusetts, University of, Amherst	3	Pub.	23,616
Massachusetts, University of, Boston, Mass.	2	Pub.	8,362
Massachusetts College of Art, Boston, Mass.	2	Pub.	1,721
Massachusetts Institute of Technology, Cambridge, Mass.	3	Pvt.	9,104
Memorial University of Newfoundland, St. John's, Nfld.	3	Pub.	9,860
Memphis State University, Memphis, Tenn.	3	Pub.	21,275
Mercer University, Macon, Ga.	2	Pvt.	2,150
Mercy College, Dobbs Ferry, N.Y.	1	Pvt.	7,054
Mercy College of Detroit, Detroit, Mich.	1	Pvt.	2,226
Mercyhurst College, Erie, Pa.	1	Pvt.	1,343
Meredith College, Raleigh, N.C. (W)	1	Pvt.	1,537
Merrimack College, North Andover, Mass.	1	Pvt.	3,250
Messiah College, Grantham, Pa.	1	Pvt.	1,051
Metropolitan State College, Denver, Colo.	1	Pub.	13,500
Miami, University of, Coral Gables, Fla.	3	Pvt.	14,165
Miami University, Oxford, Ohio	3	Pub.	14,727
Michigan, University of, Ann Arbor, Mich.	3	Pub.	36,740
Dearborn Campus	1	Pub.	5,480
Flint	1	Pub.	3,801
Michigan State University, East Lansing	3	Pub.	47,383
Michigan Technological University, Houghton, Mich.	3	Pub.	6,807
Middle Tennessee State University, Murfreesboro, Tenn.	3	Pub.	10,223
Middlebury College, Middlebury, Vt.	3	Pvt.	1,914
Midwestern State University, Wichita Falls, Tex.	2	Pub.	4,651
Miles College, Birmingham, Ala.	1	Pvt.	1,430
Millersville State College, Millersville, Pa.	2	Pub.	6,182
Millikin University, Decatur, Ill.	1	Pvt.	1,346
Mills College, Oakland, Calif.	2	Pvt.	980
Millsaps College, Jackson, Miss.	1	Pvt.	866
Milwaukee School of Engineering, Milwaukee, Wis.	2	Pvt.	2,513
Minnesota, University of, Minneapolis	3	Pub.	64,629
Duluth	2	Pub.	8,996
Morris	1	Pub.	1,713
Minot State College, Minot, N. Dak.	2	Pub.	2,444
Mississippi, University of, University, Miss.	3	Pub.	9,570
Mississippi College, Clinton, Miss.	2	Pvt.	2,976
Mississippi State University, Mississippi State, Miss.	3	Pub.	12,379
Mississippi University for Women, Columbus, Miss. (W)	2	Pub.	2,862
Mississippi Valley State University, Itta Bena, Miss.	1	Pub.	2,945
Missouri, University of:			
Columbia	3	Pub.	23,983
Kansas City	3	Pub.	10,995
Rolla	3	Pub.	5,403
St. Louis	3	Pub.	11,700
Missouri Southern State College, Joplin, Mo.	1	Pub.	3,774
Missouri Western State College, St. Joseph	1	Pub.	3,769
Molloy College, Rockville Center, N.Y.	1	Pvt.	1,343
Moncton, University of, Moncton, N.B.	2	Pub.	5,102
Monmouth College, Monmouth, Ill.	1	Pvt.	700
Monmouth College, West Long Branch, N.J.	2	Pvt.	3,896
Montana, University of, Missoula, Mont.	3	Pub.	8,262
Montana College of Mineral Science and Technology, Butte, Mont.	2	Pub.	1,182
Montana State University, Bozeman, Mont.	3	Pub.	9,802
Montclair State College, Upper Montclair, N.J.	2	Pub.	15,801
Montevallo, University of, Montevallo, Ala.	2	Pub.	3,004
Montreal, University of, Montreal, Que.	3	Pvt.	22,686
Loyola College, Montreal, Que.	1	Pvt.	4,000
Moorhead State University, Moorhead, Minn.	2	Pub.	6,029
Moravian College, Bethlehem, Pa.	1	Pvt.	1,657
Morehead State University, Morehead, Ky.	2	Pub.	7,041
Morehouse College, Atlanta, Ga. (M)	1	Pvt.	1,532
Morgan State University, Baltimore, Md.	2	Pub.	6,091
Morningside College, Sioux City, Iowa	2	Pvt.	1,521
Morris Brown College, Atlanta, Ga.	1	Pvt.	1,640
Morris Harvey College, Charleston, W. Va.	1	Pvt.	1,997
Mount Allison University, Sackville, N.B.	2	Pvt.	1,417
Mount Holyoke College, South Hadley, Mass. (W)	2	Pvt.	1,927
Mount Mary College, Milwaukee, Wis. (W)	1	Pvt.	1,102
Mount St. Joseph-on-the-Ohio, College of, Mt. St. Joseph, Ohio	1	Pvt.	1,098
Mount St. Mary's College, Los Angeles, Calif.	2	Pvt.	1,038
Mount St. Mary's College, Emmitsburg, Md.	2	Pvt.	1,586
Mount St. Vincent, College of, Bronx, N.Y.	1	Pvt.	1,465
Mount St. Vincent University, Halifax, Nova Scotia	2	Pvt.	2,225
Mount Union College, Alliance, Ohio	1	Pvt.	1,086
Muhlenberg College, Allentown, Pa.	1	Pvt.	1,894
Mundelein College, Chicago, Ill.	2	Pvt.	1,519
Murray State University, Murray, Ky.	2	Pub.	7,740
Muskingum College, New Concord, Ohio	1	Pvt.	984
National College of Education, Evanston, Ill.	2	Pvt.	3,639
Naval Postgraduate School, Monterey, Calif.	3	Pub.	1,018
Nazareth College of Rochester, N.Y.	2	Pvt.	2,658
Nebraska, University of, Lincoln, Nebr.	3	Pub.	22,256
Nebraska, University of, at Omaha, Nebr.	2	Pub.	14,696
Nebraska Wesleyan University, Lincoln	1	Pvt.	1,108
Nevada, University of, Las Vegas	2	Pub.	8,760
Reno	3	Pub.	8,266
New Brunswick, University of, Fredericton	3	Pub.	7,789
New England College, Henniker, N.H.	1	Pvt.	1,178
New Hampshire, University of, Durham	3	Pub.	10,522
New Haven, University of, West Haven, Conn.	2	Pvt.	6,889
New Jersey Institute of Technology, Newark.	3	Pub.	5,774
New Mexico, University of, Albuquerque	3	Pub.	22,028
New Mexico Highlands University, Las Vegas, N. Mex.	2	Pub.	2,182
New Mexico Institute of Mining & Technology, Socorro, N. Mex.	3	Pub.	1,021
New Mexico State University, Las Cruces	3	Pub.	12,166
New Rochelle, College of, New Rochelle, N.Y.	2	Pvt.	3,564
New School for Social Research, N.Y.C.	3	Pvt.	4,206
New York, City University of, New York:			
Bernard M. Baruch College, New York	2	Pub.	14,152
Brooklyn College, Brooklyn	2	Pub.	20,812
City College, New York	2	Pub.	15,110
College of Staten Island	2	Pub.	12,086

Name and Location	Level	Control	Enroll-ment
New York, City University of (Con't.)			
Graduate School and University Center, New York	3	Pub.	2,681
Herbert H. Lehman College, Bronx	2	Pub.	9,222
Hunter College, New York	2	Pub.	17,716
John Jay College of Criminal Justice, New York	2	Pub.	6,822
Queens College, Flushing	2	Pub.	20,614
York College, Flushing	1	Pub.	4,055
New York, Polytechnic Institute of, Brooklyn, N.Y.	3	Pvt.	4,624
New York, State University of:			
College of Environmental Science and Forestry, Syracuse	3	Pub.	2,147
Downstate Medical Center, Brooklyn	3	Pub.	1,447
Maritime College, Bronx	2	Pub.	1,085
State University College at Brockport	2	Pub.	10,033
State University College at Buffalo	2	Pub.	11,260
State University College at Cortland	2	Pub.	5,615
State University College at Fredonia	2	Pub.	4,977
State University College at Geneseo	2	Pub.	5,153
State University College at New Paltz	2	Pub.	7,543
State University College at Oneonta	2	Pub.	6,427
State University College at Oswego	2	Pub.	8,332
State University College at Plattsburgh	2	Pub.	6,067
State University College at Potsdam	2	Pub.	4,964
State University at Albany	3	Pub.	14,679
State University at Binghamton	3	Pub.	9,916
State University at Buffalo	3	Pub.	21,111
State University at Stony Brook	3	Pub.	14,994
Upstate Medical Center, Syracuse	3	Pub.	866
New York Institute of Technology, Old Westbury, L.I., N.Y.	2	Pvt.	12,859
New York University, New York, N.Y.	3	Pvt.	31,200
Newberry College, Newberry, S.C.	1	Pvt.	831
Niagara University, Niagara University, N.Y.	2	Pvt.	4,170
Nicholls State University, Thibodaux, La.	2	Pub.	6,190
Norfolk State College, Norfolk, Va.	1	Pub.	7,238
North Adams State College, North Adams, Mass.	2	Pub.	2,751
North Alabama, University of, Florence, Ala.	2	Pub.	5,229
North Carolina, University of:			
Asheville	1	Pub.	1,632
Chapel Hill	3	Pub.	19,954
Charlotte	2	Pub.	8,504
Greensboro	3	Pub.	9,964
Wilmington	1	Pub.	3,616
North Carolina State University at Raleigh	3	Pub.	17,730
North Carolina Agricultural and Technical State University, Greensboro, N.C.	2	Pub.	5,218
North Carolina Central University, Durham	2	Pub.	4,859
North Central College, Naperville, Ill.	1	Pvt.	1,084
North Dakota, University of, Grand Forks	3	Pub.	9,373
North Dakota State University, Fargo	3	Pub.	8,107
North Georgia College, Dahlonega, Ga.	2	Pub.	1,818
North Park College and Theological Seminary, Chicago, Ill.	2	Pvt.	1,359
North Texas State University, Denton, Tex.	3	Pub.	17,151
Northeast Louisiana University, Monroe, La.	3	Pub.	9,098
Northeast Missouri State University, Kirksville, Mo.	2	Pub.	5,737
Northeastern Illinois University, Chicago, Ill.	2	Pub.	10,148
Northeastern Oklahoma State University, Tahlequah, Okla.	2	Pub.	6,131
Northeastern University, Boston, Mass.	3	Pvt.	34,236
Northern Arizona University, Flagstaff, Ariz.	3	Pub.	12,661
Northern Colorado, University of, Greeley, Colo.	3	Pub.	11,048
Northern Illinois University, De Kalb, Ill.	3	Pub.	24,737
Northern Iowa, University of, Cedar Falls, Iowa	2	Pub.	10,634
Northern Michigan University, Marquette, Mich.	2	Pub.	9,306
Northern Montana College, Havre, Mont.	1	Pub.	1,319
Northern State College, Aberdeen, S. Dak.	2	Pub.	2,425
Northrop University, Inglewood, Calif.	2	Pvt.	1,851
Northwest Missouri State College, Maryville, Mo.	2	Pub.	4,390
Northwest Nazarene College, Nampa, Idaho	1	Pvt.	1,242
Northwestern Oklahoma State University, Alva, Okla.	2	Pub.	1,887
Northwestern State University of Louisiana, Natchitoches, La.	3	Pub.	6,216
Northwestern University, Evanston, Ill.	3	Pvt.	15,323
Norwich University, Northfield, Vt.	3	Pvt.	1,490
Notre Dame of Maryland, College of, Baltimore	1	Pvt.	839
Notre Dame, College of, Belmont, Calif.	2	Pvt.	1,131
Notre Dame, University of, Notre Dame, Ind.	3	Pvt.	8,690
Nova University, Fort Lauderdale, Fla.	3	Pvt.	8,147
Oakland University, Rochester, Mich.	3	Pub.	11,051
Oberlin College, Oberlin, Ohio	2	Pvt.	2,830
Occidental College, Los Angeles, Calif.	2	Pvt.	1,784
Oglethorpe University, Atlanta, Ga.	2	Pvt.	860
Ohio Dominican College, Columbus, Ohio	1	Pvt.	910
Ohio Northern University, Ada, Ohio	1	Pvt.	2,729
Ohio State University, Columbus, Ohio	3	Pub.	51,002
Ohio University, Athens, Ohio	3	Pub.	13,467
Ohio Wesleyan University, Delaware, Ohio	1	Pvt.	2,322
Oklahoma, University of, Norman, Okla.	3	Pub.	19,719
Oklahoma Baptist University, Shawnee	1	Pvt.	1,549
Oklahoma Christian College, Oklahoma City	1	Pvt.	1,379
Oklahoma City University, Oklahoma City	2	Pvt.	2,807
Oklahoma Panhandle State College, Goodwell, Okla.	1	Pub.	1,048
Oklahoma State University, Stillwater, Okla.	3	Pub.	21,930
Old Dominion University, Norfolk, Va.	2	Pub.	14,188
Olivet Nazarene College, Kankakee, Ill.	2	Pvt.	1,862
Oral Roberts University, Tulsa, Okla.	2	Pvt.	3,774
Oregon, University of, Eugene, Oreg.	3	Pub.	16,701
Oregon College of Education, Monmouth	2	Pub.	3,828
Oregon Institute of Technology, Klamath Falls, Oreg.	1	Pub.	2,235
Oregon State University, Corvallis, Oreg.	3	Pub.	16,502
Ottawa, University of, Ottawa, Ont.	3	Pvt.	18,080
Otterbein College, Westerville, Ohio	1	Pvt.	1,594
Ouachita Baptist University, Arkadelphia, Ark.	2	Pvt.	1,686
Our Lady of the Lake University, San Antonio, Tex.	2	Pvt.	1,780
Ozarks, School of the, Point Lookout, Mo.	1	Pvt.	1,148
Pace University, New York, N.Y. Pleasantville and White Plains, N.Y.	3	Pvt.	10,461
	3	Pvt.	6,458
Pacific, University of the, Stockton, Calif.	3	Pvt.	6,103
Pacific Lutheran University, Tacoma, Wash.	2	Pvt.	3,228
Pacific Union College, Angwin, Calif.	2	Pvt.	2,204
Pacific University, Forest Grove, Oreg.	2	Pvt.	1,058
Pan American University, Edinburg, Tex.	2	Pub.	9,125
Parks College of Aeronautical Technology, Cahokia, Ill.	1	Pvt.	656
Pembroke State University, Pembroke, N.C.	1	Pub.	2,334
Pennsylvania, University of, Philadelphia	3	Pvt.	21,667
Pennsylvania State University, University Park, Abington, Fogelsville, Altoona, Chester, Dubois, Dunmore, Erie, Hazleton, Hershey, King of Prussia, McKeesport, Media, Middletown, Monaca, Mont Alto, New Kensington, Reading, Schuylkill Haven, Sharon, Uniontown, Wilkes-Barre and York, Pa.	3	Pub.	60,180
Pepperdine University, Malibu and Los Angeles, Calif.	3	Pvt.	8,815
Pfeiffer College, Misenheimer, N.C.	1	Pvt.	994
Philadelphia College of Art, Philadelphia, Pa.	2	Pvt.	1,510
Philadelphia College of Pharmacy & Science, Philadelphia, Pa.	3	Pvt.	1,156
Philadelphia College of Textiles & Science, Philadelphia, Pa.	2	Pvt.	2,477
Phillips University, Enid, Okla.	2	Pvt.	1,439

Name and Location	Level	Control	Enrollment	Name and Location	Level	Control	Enrollment
Pittsburgh State University, Pittsburgh, Kans.	2	Pub.	4,908	St. Benedict, College of, St. Joseph, Minn. (W)	1	Pvt.	1,992
Pittsburgh, University of, Pittsburgh, Bradford, Greensburg, Johnstown, and Titusville, Pa.	3	Pvt.	29,365	St. Bonaventure University, St. Bonaventure, N.Y.	3	Pvt.	2,715
Pitzer College, Claremont, Calif.	1	Pvt.	826	St. Catherine, College of, St. Paul, Minn. (W)	1	Pvt.	2,109
Plymouth State College, Plymouth, N.H.	2	Pub.	3,265	St. Cloud State University, St. Cloud, Minn.	2	Pub.	11,167
Point Loma College, San Diego, Calif.	2	Pvt.	1,905	St. Edward's University, Austin, Tex.	2	Pvt.	1,968
Point Park College, Pittsburgh, Pa.	1	Pvt.	2,018	St. Francis, College of, Joliet, Ill.	1	Pvt.	2,927
Pomona College, Claremont, Calif.	1	Pvt.	1,315	St. Francis College, Fort Wayne, Ind.	2	Pvt.	1,577
Portland, University of, Portland, Oreg.	2	Pvt.	2,540	St. Francis College, Brooklyn, N.Y.	1	Pvt.	3,972
Portland State University, Portland, Oreg.	3	Pub.	15,888	St. Francis College, Loretto, Pa.	2	Pvt.	1,525
Prairie View Agricultural & Mechanical University, Prairie View, Tex.	2	Pub.	5,147	St. Francis Xavier University, Antigonish, Nova Scotia	2	Pvt.	2,773
Pratt Institute, Brooklyn, N.Y.	2	Pvt.	4,211	St. John Fisher College, Rochester, N.Y.	1	Pvt.	1,943
Presbyterian College, Clinton, S.C.	1	Pvt.	822	St. John's University, Collegeville, Minn. (M)	2	Pvt.	1,943
Prince Edward Island, University of, Charlottetown, P.E.I.	1	Pub.	2,332	St. John's University, Jamaica and Staten Island, N.Y.	3	Pvt.	16,714
Princeton University, Princeton, N.J.	3	Pvt.	6,086	St. Joseph College, West Hartford, Conn.	2	Pvt.	1,138
Principia College, Elsah, Ill.	1	Pvt.	886	St. Joseph's College, Rensselaer, Ind.	2	Pvt.	1,034
Providence College, Providence, R.I.	3	Pvt.	5,930	St. Joseph's College, Philadelphia, Pa.	2	Pvt.	5,696
Puerto Rico, University of, P.R.	3	Pub.	41,344	St. Lawrence University, Canton, N.Y.	2	Pvt.	2,484
Puget Sound, University of, Tacoma, Wash.	2	Pvt.	3,914	St. Leo College, St. Leo, Fla.	1	Pvt.	1,039
Purdue University, Lafayette, Ind.	3	Pub.	30,303	St. Louis University, St. Louis, Mo.	3	Pvt.	9,496
Calumet at Hammond	2	Pub.	6,977	St. Mary's College, Moraga, Calif.	2	Pvt.	1,745
Fort Wayne	2	Pub.	6,270	St. Mary's College, Notre Dame, Ind. (W)	1	Pvt.	1,751
				St. Mary's College, Winona, Minn.	2	Pvt.	1,258
Quebec, University of, Quebec, Que.	3	Pub.	33,463	St. Mary's College of Maryland, St. Mary's City, Md.	1	Pub.	1,170
Queen's University at Kingston, Ont.	3	Pvt.	12,954	St. Mary's Dominican College, New Orleans, La.	1	Pvt.	754
Quincy College, Quincy, Ill.	1	Pvt.	981	St. Mary's University, Halifax, N.S.	2	Pub.	2,730
Quinnipiac College, Hamden, Conn.	2	Pvt.	3,585	St. Mary's University, San Antonio, Tex.	2	Pvt.	3,160
				St. Michael's College, Winooski, Vt.	2	Pvt.	1,718
Radford College, Radford, Va.	2	Pub.	5,623	St. Norbert College, De Pere, Wis.	1	Pvt.	1,525
Randolph-Macon College, Ashland, Va.	1	Pvt.	931	St. Olaf College, Northfield, Minn.	1	Pvt.	2,968
Randolph-Macon Woman's College, Lynchburg, Va. (W)	1	Pvt.	763	St. Peter's College, Jersey City, N.J.	1	Pvt.	4,430
Redlands, University of, Redlands, Calif.	2	Pvt.	2,965	St. Rose, College of, Albany, N.Y.	2	Pvt.	2,384
Reed College, Portland, Oreg.	2	Pvt.	1,228	St. Scholastica, College of, Duluth, Minn.	2	Pvt.	1,306
Regina, University of, Regina, Sask.	3	Pub.	5,601	St. Teresa, College of, Winona, Minn.	1	Pvt.	962
Regis College, Denver, Colo.	1	Pvt.	1,076	St. Thomas, College of, St. Paul, Minn.	2	Pvt.	4,139
Regis College, Weston, Mass. (W)	2	Pvt.	1,062	St. Thomas, University of, Houston, Tex.	2	Pvt.	1,769
Rensselaer Polytechnic Institute, Troy, N.Y.	3	Pvt.	5,816	St. Vincent College, Latrobe, Pa. (M)	2	Pvt.	961
Rhode Island, University of, Kingston, R.I.	3	Pub.	14,451	St. Xavier College, Chicago, Ill.	2	Pvt.	1,802
Rhode Island College, Providence, R.I.	2	Pub.	8,812	Salem College, Salem, W. Va.	1	Pvt.	980
Rhode Island School of Design, Providence	2	Pvt.	1,485	Salem State College, Salem, Mass.	2	Pub.	8,038
Rice University, Houston, Tex.	3	Pvt.	3,686	Salisbury State College, Salisbury, Md.	2	Pub.	4,300
Richmond, University of, Richmond, Va.	2	Pvt.	4,220	Salve Regina—The Newport College, R.I.	2	Pvt.	1,550
Rider College, Trenton, N.J.	2	Pvt.	5,871	Sam Houston State University, Huntsville, Tex.	3	Pub.	10,683
Ripon College, Ripon, Wis.	1	Pvt.	942	Samford University, Birmingham, Ala.	2	Pvt.	3,950
Rivier College, Nashua, N.H.	2	Pvt.	1,701	San Diego, University of, San Diego, Calif.	2	Pvt.	3,611
Roanoke College, Salem, Va.	1	Pvt.	1,280	San Diego State University, San Diego, Calif.	3	Pub.	31,873
Robert Morris College, Coraopolis, Pa.	2	Pvt.	4,105	San Francisco, University of, San Francisco	3	Pvt.	6,392
Rochester, University of, Rochester, N.Y.	3	Pvt.	8,005	San Francisco Art Institute, San Francisco	2	Pvt.	882
Rochester Institute of Technology, Rochester, N.Y.	2	Pvt.	11,963	San Francisco State University, San Francisco, Calif.	3	Pub.	27,490
Rockford College, Rockford, Ill.	2	Pvt.	1,189	San Jose State University, San Jose, Calif.	2	Pub.	32,849
Rockhurst College, Kansas City, Mo.	2	Pvt.	3,422	Sanoma State College, Sonoma, Calif.	2	Pub.	6,263
Roger Williams College, Bristol, R.I.	1	Pvt.	3,348	Santa Clara, University of, Santa Clara, Calif.	3	Pvt.	7,295
Rollins College, Winter Park, Fla.	2	Pvt.	4,939	Santa Fe, College of, Santa Fe, N. Mex.	1	Pvt.	1,268
Roosevelt University, Chicago, Ill.	2	Pvt.	6,996	Sarah Lawrence College, Bronxville, N.Y.	2	Pvt.	991
Rosary College, River Forest, Ill.	2	Pvt.	1,395	Saskatchewan, University of, Saskatoon	3	Pub.	13,895
Rose-Hulman Institute of Technology, Terre Haute, Ind. (M)	2	Pvt.	1,149	Savannah State College, Savannah, Ga.	2	Pub.	2,824
Russell Sage College, Troy, N.Y.	2	Pvt.	4,502	Science and Arts of Oklahoma, University of, Chickasha, Okla.	1	Pub.	1,195
Rutgers University, New Brunswick, Newark, Camden, N.J.	3	Pub.	49,045	Scranton, University of, Scranton, Pa.	2	Pvt.	4,460
Ryerson Polytechnical Institute, Toronto	1	Pvt.	10,493	Seattle Pacific University, Seattle, Wash.	2	Pvt.	2,276
				Seattle University, Seattle, Wash.	2	Pvt.	3,616
Sacred Heart, University of the, Santurce, P.R. (W)	1	Pvt.	5,051	Seton Hall University, South Orange, N.J.	3	Pvt.	9,132
Sacred Heart University, Bridgeport, Conn.	1	Pvt.	2,695	Seton Hill College, Greensburg, Pa. (W)	1	Pvt.	936
Saginaw Valley State College, University Center, Mich.	2	Pub.	3,530	Shaw University, Raleigh, N.C.	1	Pvt.	1,356
St. Ambrose College, Davenport, Iowa	1	Pvt.	1,657	Shepherd College, Shepherdstown, W. Va.	1	Pub.	2,827
St. Andrews Presbyterian College, Laurinburg, N.C.	1	Pvt.	563	Sherbrooke, University of, Sherbrooke, Que.	3	Pvt.	8,131
St. Anselm's College, Manchester, N.H.	1	Pvt.	1,884	Shippensburg State College, Shippensburg, Pa.	2	Pub.	6,021
St. Augustine's College, Raleigh, N.C.	1	Pvt.	1,775	Siena College, Loudonville, N.Y.	1	Pvt.	2,755
				Simmons College, Boston, Mass.	3	Pvt.	2,598
				Simon Fraser University, Burnaby, B.C.	3	Pub.	8,282

Name and Location	Level	Control	Enrollment
Simpson College, Indianola, Iowa	1	Pvt.	839
Sioux Falls College, Sioux Falls, S. Dak.	1	Pvt.	720
Skidmore College, Saratoga Springs, N.Y.	1	Pvt.	2,307
Slippery Rock State College, Slippery Rock, Pa.	2	Pub.	6,079
Smith College, Northampton, Mass.	3	Pvt.	2,635
South, University of the, Sewanee, Tenn.	2	Pvt.	1,093
South Alabama, University of, Mobile, Ala.	2	Pub.	6,708
South Carolina, Medical University of, Charleston, S.C.	3	Pub.	2,028
South Carolina, University of, Columbia, S.C.	3	Pub.	23,577
South Carolina State College, Orangeburg	2	Pub.	3,839
South Dakota, University of, Vermillion	3	Pub.	7,042
Springfield, S. Dak.	1	Pub.	814
South Dakota School of Mines & Technology, Rapid City, S. Dak.	3	Pub.	1,812
South Dakota State University, Brookings	3	Pub.	6,846
South Florida, University of, Tampa, Fla.	3	Pub.	22,950
Southeast Missouri State University, Cape Girardeau, Mo.	2	Pub.	8,889
Southeastern Louisiana University, Hammond, La.	2	Pub.	7,073
Southeastern Massachusetts University, North Darmouth, Mass.	2	Pub.	5,198
Southeastern Oklahoma State University, Durant, Okla.	2	Pub.	4,236
Southern Arkansas University, Magnolia, Ark.	2	Pub.	1,891
Southern Baptist Theological Seminary, Louisville, Ky.	3	Pvt.	2,070
Southern California, University of, Los Angeles, Calif.	3	Pvt.	29,497
Southern Colorado, University of, Pueblo	2	Pub.	5,659
Southern Connecticut State College, New Haven, Conn.	2	Pub.	12,163
Southern Illinois University, Carbondale, Ill.	3	Pub.	22,535
Southern Illinois University, Edwardsville, Ill.	3	Pub.	12,060
Southern Maine, University of, Portland-Gorham	3	Pub.	8,000
Southern Methodist University, Dallas, Tex.	3	Pvt.	8,677
Southern Missionary College, Collegedale, Tenn.	1	Pvt.	1,912
Southern Mississippi, University of, Hattiesburg, Miss.	3	Pub.	11,830
Southern Oregon State College, Ashland, Oreg.	2	Pub.	4,275
Southern University and Agricultural and Mechanical College, Baton Rouge, La.	2	Pub.	8,225
Southern Utah State College, Cedar City, Utah	1	Pub.	1,879
Southwest Baptist College, Bolivar, Mo.	1	Pvt.	1,469
Southwest Missouri State University, Springfield, Mo.	2	Pub.	13,207
Southwest Texas State University, San Marcos, Tex.	2	Pub.	14,670
Southwestern at Memphis, Tenn.	1	Pvt.	1,024
Southwestern Baptist Theological Seminary, Fort Worth, Tex.	3	Pvt.	2,892
Southwestern Louisiana, University of, Lafayette, La.	3	Pub.	13,277
Southwestern Oklahoma State University, Weatherford, Okla.	2	Pub.	5,403
Southwestern University, Georgetown, Tex.	1	Pvt.	956
Spalding College, Louisville, Ky.	2	Pvt.	973
Spelman College, Atlanta, Ga. (W)	1	Pvt.	1,273
Spring Hill College, Mobile, Ala.	1	Pvt.	811
Springfield College, Springfield, Mass.	3	Pvt.	2,747
Stanford University, Stanford, Calif.	3	Pvt.	11,823
Steed College, Johnson City, Tenn.	1	Pvt.	1,130
Stephen F. Austin State University, Nacogdoches, Tex.	2	Pub.	10,751
Stephens College, Columbia, Mo.	1	Pvt.	1,797
Stetson University, DeLand, Fla.	2	Pvt.	2,753
Steubenville, College of, Steubenville, Ohio	1	Pvt.	860
Stevens Institute of Technology, Hoboken, N.J.	3	Pvt.	2,300
Stonehill College, North Easton, Mass.	1	Pvt.	2,334
Strayer College, Washington, D.C.	1	Pvt.	1,795
Suffolk University, Boston, Mass.	3	Pvt.	6,373
Sul Ross State College, Alpine, Tex.	2	Pub.	2,284
Susquehanna University, Selinsgrove, Pa.	1	Pvt.	1,592
Swarthmore College, Swarthmore, Pa.	2	Pvt.	1,289
Sweet Briar College, Sweet Briar, Va. (W)	1	Pvt.	666
Syracuse University, Syracuse, N.Y.	3	Pvt.	19,806
Tampa, University of, Tampa, Fla.	2	Pvt.	2,274
Tarleton State College, Stephenville, Tex.	1	Pub.	3,317
Taylor University, Upland, Ind.	1	Pvt.	1,500
Temple University, Philadelphia, Pa.	3	Pvt.	36,339
Tennessee, University of, System:			
Chattanooga	2	Pub.	6,628
Knoxville	3	Pub.	30,311
Martin	2	Pub.	4,957
Health Sciences, Memphis	3	Pub.	2,126
Nashville	2	Pub.	5,551
Tennessee State University, Nashville, Tenn.	2	Pub.	5,362
Tennessee Technological University, Cookeville, Tenn.	2	Pub.	7,270
Texas, University of, System:			
Arlington	3	Pub.	17,201
Austin	3	Pub.	41,660
El Paso	3	Pub.	15,836
Texas Agricultural & Mechanical University, College Station, Tex.	3	Pub.	28,833
Texas Arts and Industries University, Kingsville, Tex.	2	Pub.	6,667
Texas Christian University, Fort Worth, Tex.	3	Pvt.	6,213
Texas Lutheran College, Seguin, Tex.	1	Pvt.	1,361
Texas Southern University, Houston, Tex.	2	Pub.	9,548
Texas Tech University, Lubbock, Tex.	3	Pub.	22,358
Texas Wesleyan College, Fort Worth, Tex.	1	Pvt.	1,588
Texas Woman's University, Denton, Tex.	3	Pub.	9,024
Thiel College, Greenville, Pa.	1	Pvt.	1,048
Thomas Jefferson University, Philadelphia.	3	Pvt.	1,799
Thomas More College, Fort Mitchell, Ky.	1	Pvt.	1,296
Toledo, University of, Toledo, Ohio	3	Pub.	17,498
Toronto, University of, Toronto, Ont.	3	Pub.	43,944
Tougaloo College, Tougaloo, Miss.	1	Pvt.	1,005
Towson State College, Towson, Md.	2	Pub.	15,360
Transylvania University, Lexington, Ky.	1	Pvt.	750
Trent University, Peterborough, Ont.	2	Pvt.	3,538
Trenton State College, Trenton, N.J.	2	Pub.	10,819
Trevecca Nazarene College, Nashville, Tenn.	1	Pvt.	802
Trinity College, Deerfield, Ill.	1	Pvt.	900
Trinity College, Hartford, Conn.	2	Pvt.	2,114
Trinity College, Washington, D.C.	2	Pvt.	899
Trinity University, San Antonio, Tex.	2	Pvt.	3,524
Tri-State University, Angola, Ind.	1	Pvt.	1,377
Troy State University, Troy, Ala.	2	Pub.	4,348
Tufts University, Medford, Mass.	3	Pvt.	6,937
Tulane University, New Orleans, La.	3	Pvt.	9,463
Tulsa, University of, Tulsa, Okla.	3	Pvt.	6,362
Tuskegee Institute, Tuskegee Institute, Ala.	2	Pvt.	3,616
Union College, Barbourville, Ky.	2	Pvt.	1,133
Union College, Lincoln, Nebr.	1	Pvt.	923
Union College, Schenectady, N.Y.	3	Pvt.	3,159
Union University, Jackson, Tenn.	1	Pvt.	1,156
United States Air Force Academy, Colorado Springs, Colo.	1	Pub.	4,572
United States Coast Guard Academy, New London, Conn.	1	Pub.	996
United States International University San Diego, Calif.	3	Pvt.	2,373
United States Merchant Marine Academy, Kings Point, N.Y.	1	Pub.	1,115
United States Military Academy, West Point, N.Y.	1	Pub.	4,474
United States Naval Academy, Annapolis, Md.	1	Pub.	4,354
Upsala College, East Orange, N.J.	2	Pvt.	1,675
Ursinus College, Collegeville, Pa.	1	Pvt.	1,677
Utah, University of, Salt Lake City, Utah	3	Pub.	21,880
Utah State University, Logan, Utah	3	Pub.	9,436

Name and Location	Level	Control	Enrollment
Valdosta State College, Valdosta, Ga.	2	Pub.	5,132
Valley City State College, Valley City, N. Dak.	1	Pub.	1,016
Valparaiso University, Valparaiso, Ind.	2	Pvt.	4,439
Vanderbilt University, Nashville, Tenn.	3	Pvt.	7,199
Vassar College, Poughkeepsie, N.Y.	2	Pvt.	2,338
Vermont, University of, Burlington, Vt.	3	Pub.	10,702
Victoria, University of, Victoria, B.C.	3	Pvt.	7,462
Villanova University, Villanova, Pa.	3	Pvt.	9,212
Virgin Islands, College of the, St. Thomas, V.I.	2	Pub.	2,219
Virginia, University of, Charlottesville, Va.	3	Pub.	22,794
Virginia Commonwealth University, Richmond, Va.	3	Pub.	19,140
Virginia Military Institute, Lexington, Va. (M)	1	Pub.	1,342
Virginia Polytechnic Institute and State University, Blacksburg, Va.	3	Pub.	19,648
Virginia State College, Petersburg, Va.	2	Pub.	5,259
Virginia Union University, Richmond, Va.	2	Pvt.	1,485
Wabash College, Crawfordsville, Ind. (M)	1	Pvt.	825
Wagner College, Staten Island, N.Y.	2	Pvt.	2,715
Wake Forest University, Winston-Salem, N.C.	3	Pvt.	4,619
Walla Walla College, College Place, Wash.	2	Pvt.	1,864
Walsh College, Canton, Ohio	1	Pvt.	611
Wartburg College, Waverly, Iowa	1	Pvt.	1,141
Washburn University of Topeka, Kans.	2	Pub.	5,883
Washington, University of, Seattle, Wash.	3	Pub.	37,120
Washington and Jefferson College, Washington, Pa.	2	Pvt.	1,260
Washington and Lee University, Lexington, Va. (M)	1	Pvt.	1,693
Washington College, Chesterton, Md.	2	Pvt.	830
Washington State University, Pullman, Wash.	3	Pub.	16,665
Washington University, St. Louis, Mo.	3	Pvt.	11,147
Waterloo, University of, Waterloo, Ont.	3	Pvt.	17,895
Wayland Baptist College, Plainview, Tex.	1	Pvt.	1,148
Wayne State College, Wayne, Nebr.	2	Pub.	2,365
Wayne State University, Detroit, Mich.	3	Pub.	34,389
Waynesburg College, Waynesburg, Pa.	1	Pvt.	772
Weber State College, Ogden, Utah	1	Pub.	8,741
Webster College, St. Louis, Mo.	2	Pvt.	3,919
Wellesley College, Wellesley, Mass.	1	Pvt.	2,144
Wesleyan University, Middletown, Conn.	3	Pvt.	2,692
West Chester State College, West Chester, Pa.	2	Pub.	8,545
West Coast University, Los Angeles, Calif.	2	Pvt.	1,450
West Florida, University of, Pensacola, Fla.	2	Pub.	5,051
West Georgia College, Carrollton, Ga.	2	Pub.	5,477
West Liberty State College, West Liberty, W. Va.	1	Pub.	2,734
West Texas State University, Canyon, Tex.	2	Pub.	6,623
West Virginia College of Graduate Studies, Institute, W. Va.	2	Pub.	2,803
West Virginia Institute of Technology, Montgomery, W. Va.	1	Pub.	3,312
West Virginia State College, Institute, W. Va.	1	Pub.	3,884
West Virginia University, Morgantown, W. Va.	3	Pub.	21,565
West Virginia Wesleyan College, Buckhannon, W. Va.	2	Pvt.	1,773
Western Carolina University, Cullowhee, N.C.	2	Pub.	6,529
Western Connecticut State College, Danbury, Conn.	2	Pub.	5,414
Western Illinois University, Macomb, Ill.	2	Pub.	13,865
Western Kentucky University, Bowling Green, Ky.	2	Pub.	13,490
Western Maryland College, Westminster, Md.	2	Pvt.	2,080
Western Michigan University, Kalamazoo, Mich.	3	Pub.	22,496
Western Montana College, Dillon, Mont.	2	Pub.	837
Western New England College, Springfield, Mass.	3	Pvt.	4,519
Western New Mexico University, Silver City, N. Mex.	2	Pub.	1,852
Western Ontario, The University of, London, Ont.	3	Pub.	19,882
Western State College of Colorado, Gunnison, Colo.	2	Pub.	3,152
Western Washington State College, Bellingham, Wash.	2	Pub.	9,360
Westfield State College, Westfield, Mass.	2	Pub.	4,090
Westmar College, Le Mars, Iowa	1	Pvt.	660
Westminster College, Fulton, Mo. (M)	1	Pvt.	651
Westminster College, New Wilmington, Pa.	2	Pvt.	1,829
Westminster College, Salt Lake City, Utah	1	Pvt.	1,464
Westmont College, Santa Barbara, Calif.	1	Pvt.	979
Wheaton College, Wheaton, Ill.	2	Pvt.	2,353
Wheaton College, Norton, Mass. (W)	1	Pvt.	1,332
Wheelock College, Boston, Mass.	2	Pvt.	946
Whitman College, Walla Walla, Wash.	1	Pvt.	1,121
Whittier College, Whittier, Calif.	2	Pvt.	1,837
Whitworth College, Spokane, Wash.	2	Pvt.	1,688
Wichita State University, Wichita, Kans.	3	Pub.	15,723
Widener College, Chester, Pa.	2	Pvt.	3,632
Wilberforce University, Wilberforce, Ohio	1	Pvt.	1,123
Wilfrid Laurier University, Waterloo, Ont.	2	Pvt.	6,353
Wilkes College, Wilkes-Barre, Pa.	2	Pvt.	2,784
Willamette University, Salem, Oreg.	2	Pvt.	1,775
William and Mary, College of, Williamsburg, Va.	3	Pub.	6,129
William Carey College, Hattiesburg, Miss.	2	Pvt.	1,678
William Jewell College, Liberty, Mo.	1	Pvt.	1,730
William Paterson College of New Jersey, Wayne, N.J.	2	Pub.	12,138
William Penn College, Oskaloosa, Iowa	1	Pvt.	616
William Woods College, Fulton, Mo. (W)	1	Pvt.	932
Williams College, Williamstown, Mass.	2	Pvt.	1,956
Wilmington College, Wilmington, Ohio	1	Pvt.	857
Windham College, Putney, Vt.	1	Pvt.	211
Windsor, University of, Windsor, Ont.	3	Pvt.	11,598
Winnipeg, The University of, Winnipeg, Man.	2	Pvt.	5,868
Winona State University, Winona, Minn.	2	Pub.	4,532
Winston-Salem State University, Winston-Salem, N.C.	1	Pub.	2,165
Winthrop College, Rock Hill, S.C.	2	Pub.	4,283
Wisconsin, University of:			
Eau Claire, Wis.	2	Pub.	10,344
Green Bay, Wis.	2	Pub.	3,642
Kenosha, Wis.	2	Pub.	5,182
La Crosse, Wis.	2	Pub.	8,554
Madison, Wis.	3	Pub.	39,022
Menomonie, Wis.	2	Pub.	6,463
Milwaukee, Wis.	3	Pub.	24,281
Oshkosh, Wis.	2	Pub.	9,694
Platteville, Wis.	2	Pub.	4,607
River Falls, Wis.	2	Pub.	5,019
Stevens Point, Wis.	2	Pub.	8,880
Superior, Wis.	2	Pub.	2,418
Whitewater, Wis.	2	Pub.	9,589
Wittenberg University, Springfield, Ohio	2	Pvt.	2,644
Wofford College, Spartanburg, S.C.	1	Pvt.	1,012
Woodbury University, Los Angeles, Calif.	2	Pvt.	1,274
Wooster, College of, Wooster, Ohio	1	Pvt.	1,808
Worcester Polytechnic Institute, Worcester, Mass.	3	Pvt.	3,192
Worcester State College, Worcester, Mass.	2	Pub.	5,698
Wright State University, Dayton, Ohio	2	Pub.	13,682
Wyoming, University of, Laramie, Wyo.	3	Pub.	9,031
Xavier University, Cincinnati, Ohio	2	Pvt.	6,493
Xavier University of Louisiana, New Orleans, La.	2	Pvt.	1,855
Yale University, New Haven, Conn.	3	Pvt.	9,709
Yeshiva University, New York, N.Y.	3	Pvt.	3,985
York College of Pennsylvania, York, Pa.	2	Pvt.	3,382
York University, Downview, Ont.	3	Pub.	14,321
Youngstown State University, Youngstown, Ohio	2	Pub.	15,696

INDEX

INDEX

Main article headings appear in this index as bold-faced capitals; subjects within articles appear as lower-case entries. Both the general references and the subentries should be consulted for maximum usefulness of this index. Illustrations are indexed herein. Cross references are to the entries in this index.

B

C

U

V

Van Agt, Andreas (Du. prime minis.) 362
Vance, Cyrus (Amer. pub. offi.) 76, 529, 530
Israel 266
Illus. 531
Vandalism:
Art 103
Van Deerlin, Lionel (Amer. cong.) 483
Variable Rate Mortgage 238
Vaughan, Sarah (Amer. singer):
Illus. 359
Venera (spacecraft) 445
Venereal Disease 323, 332
VENEZUELA 537, 291
Archaeology 93
Mining 341
Statistical Data 565, 572 fol.
Tunnel 197
United States 292
Venus (planet):
Space Probes 445
Venuti, Joe (It.-Amer. mus.) 386
VERMONT 539
Versailles, Chateau de:
Bombing 204
Illus. 48
Very Large Array Radio Telescope 113
Vesco, Robert (Amer. bsman.) 149
Videla, Jorge (Arg. pres.) 97
VIETNAM 539, 109
China, People's Republic of 158
Laos 289
Malaysia 318
Refugees 419
Statistical Data 565, 573, 577
Thailand 489
USSR 510
Vietnam War:
Motion Pictures 349
Vikings (people) 93
Violence: *see* Crime; Terrorism
VIRGINIA 541
VIRGIN ISLANDS 542
Virus 332
VISTA Program (U.S.) 439
Voight, Jon (Amer. act.):
Illus. 349
Volleyball 473
Vorster, B. Johannes (S.Afr. prime minis.) 78, 441
Vo Van Sung (Viet. ambassador):
Illus. 541

W

Wage-Price Guidelines (econ.) 282
Wages and Salaries 282, 283
Agriculture 83

Black Americans 201
Canada 142
Civil Service 533
Great Britain 227
Hispanic-Americans 202
Sports 450
United States 518
Waldheim, Kurt (Aus. states.) 515, 516
Illus. 405
Wales: *see* Great Britain
Walker, Paul (Amer. writ.) 340
Wallace, George C. (Ala. gov.) 86
Wallenda, Karl (Ger. aerialist) 386
Walton, Bill (Amer. athl.) 459, 460
Warner, Jack (Amer. bsman.) 386
Warner, John (Amer. sen.) 541
Illus. 542
Warner, Sylvia Townsend (Eng. nov.) 386
Warsaw Pact 580
WASHINGTON, state 543
Archaeology 93
WASHINGTON, D.C. 543
Mass Transit 502
Washington Bullets (basketball team) 459, 460
Waste Disposal 151
Nuclear Wastes 366
Toxic Chemicals 199
Watana Dam, Alas. 196
Water 199
Garrison Diversion Project 372
Water Pollution 199
Watership Down (film) 349
Water Skiing 473
Water Spouts (meteorol.) 326
Water Tower, Chicago, Ill.:
Illus. 432
Watson, Tom (Amer. athl.) 465
WCC: *see* World Council of Churches
Weapons 339, 340
Weather: *see* Meteorology
Weather Satellites 446
WEBSTER, William H. (Amer. pub. offi.) 131, 534
Weddell Sea, Antarc. 404
Weight Lifting 473
Weill, Claudia (Amer. film dir.) 348
Weizman, Ezer (Isr. pub. offi.) 265, 266, 335
Illus. 60
Welfare: *see* Social Welfare
Wenzel, Hanni (Liecht. athl.) 468
Wertmüller, Lena (It. dir.) 348
West Berlin, Ger. 225
Western Samoa 569
Statistical Data 572
Western Somali Liberation Front 80, 200
Western Union 407
West Germany: *see* Germany, Federal Republic of
West Indies: *see* Caribbean; and specific islands and political divisions

WEST VIRGINIA 545
Whaling 198
Wheat 82 fol., 211, 573
Kansas 276
Nebraska 261
North Dakota 372
Whey (cheese by-product) 539
Whistle, nov. (Jones) 302
White, Byron (Amer. justice) 293
White, Theodore H. (Amer. writ.):
Illus. 304
White-Collar Crime 170
Whitehead, Edward (Brit. mil. off.) 386
Wholesale Price Index 570 fol.
See also Inflation
Whooping Crane 550, 560
Wilderness Controversy, Alas. 87
Wilderness Protection:
Idaho 241
Wildlife Protection 198, 199, 558, 560
Great Britain 230
Kenya 278
Tennessee 295
Wyoming 550
Wills, Chill (Amer. act.) 386
Wilmington Ten 372
Wilson, Sir Harold (Brit. states.) 230
Wilson, Robert W. (Amer. radio astron.) 409
Windows:
Interior Design 254
Winds 326
WINE INDUSTRY 252
Winnipeg Jets (hockey team) 467
Wiretapping 295
WISCONSIN 546
Wiz, The (film) 351
Illus. 347
Woman of Paris (film) 348
WOMEN 547
Battered Women 170
Civil Liberties and Civil Rights 162, 294
FBI Agents 535
Religion 422, 424
Wood, Peggy (Amer. act.) 386
Woolly Aphids (insects) 559
World According to Garp, The, nov. (Irving) 302
World Bank:
Argentina 98
Caribbean 148
World Council of Churches 425
World Cup (soccer trophy) 468
World Hockey Association 467
World Series (baseball) 456
World Team Tennis 470
World Trade: *see* International Trade and Finance
Wouk, Herman (Amer. writ.) 302
Wrestling 473
Wright, Lloyd (Amer. arch.) 386
WSLF: *see* Western Somali Liberation Front
WYOMING 550

Y

Yachting 473
YALOW, Rosalyn Sussman (Amer. sci.) 131
Yamani, Ahmed Zaki (Saudi Ar. pub. offi.) 436
Yarborough, Cale (Amer. auto racer) 455
Yellowstone River 344
Yemen 569
Saudi Arabia 437
Statistical Data 565, 572, 573, 578, 579
Yemen, Democratic 569
Statistical Data 572, 578
Young, Andrew (Amer. ambassador) 408, 479
YOUTH 551
See also Children
YUGOSLAVIA 553
Automobiles 116
Bulgaria 136
China, People's Republic of 157
Mining 341
Statistical Data 565, 572 fol.
YUKON, terr., Can. 554

Z

ZAIRE 555, 75, 78
Angola 90
Belgium 119
Cuba 173
France 217
Germany, Federal Republic of 224
Mining 341
Mobutu Sese Seko 128
Morocco 346
Saudi Arabia 437
Statistical Data 565, 572 fol., 579
USSR 510
United States 530
Zambia 78, 569
Germany, Federal Republic of 224
Statistical Data 572, 574 fol.
Zaire 555
Zero (Nicar. rev.):
Illus. 150
Zhivkov, Todor (Bulg. pol.) 136
Zia ul-Haq, Mohammed (Pak. gen.) 395
Ziaur Rahman (Bangladesh pres.) 117
Zinc 577
ZOOLOGY 557
Polar Research 404
Wildlife Protection 198, 199, 230, 278, 295, 550, 558, 560
Zukofsky, Louis (Amer. poet, educ.) 386